INTERNATIONAL LAW

International Law

Third Edition

GLEIDER HERNÁNDEZ

OXFORD
UNIVERSITY PRESS

OXFORD
UNIVERSITY PRESS

Great Clarendon Street, Oxford, OX2 6DP,
United Kingdom

Oxford University Press is a department of the University of Oxford.
It furthers the University's objective of excellence in research, scholarship,
and education by publishing worldwide. Oxford is a registered trade mark of
Oxford University Press in the UK and in certain other countries

First Edition 2019
Second Edition 2022

Published in the United States of America by Oxford University Press
198 Madison Avenue, New York, NY 10016, United States of America

British Library Cataloguing in Publication Data
Data available

Library of Congress Control Number: 2025930969

ISBN 978–0–19–891847–9

Printed in the UK by
Bell & Bain Ltd., Glasgow

For my little stars, Luca and Abel. May you never forget how precious you are

Preface to the third edition

With its third edition, *International Law* is becoming part of my life, a triennial cycle of updates, reflection, revision, and at times, frantic final adjustments in the face of rapidly evolving debates. By now the triennial cycle is etched into my routine, even if there never seems to be enough time to recount fully the developments in the immense, diverse field of international law. What is more, the global reach of the textbook, and my encounters with the readership over the years, have made me keenly aware of my responsibility, as an author of a generalist textbook, towards the next generation of students. This textbook, therefore, is not a personal *cri de cœur*; as my students know by now, I do not always agree with what I teach, or what I have written, but I believe that it represents the state of debate in the field. This textbook, in its multiple editions, is my attempt to tell the story of international law as most international lawyers understand it.

Perhaps the best way to explain this is to return to the first edition, in which I confessed to my own hubris, and that the drafting process led me to a decision, that to understand international law one had to find the right balance between new and critical approaches and the orthodox narratives through which the discipline was built. As I wrote in 2019, such 'classic' narrations 'are those that become internalized to the discipline, that serve to reinforce its structural configuration, and that are imparted on to future generations. Understanding that narrative, whether one seeks to capitalize and build upon it, or to shatter it, is a necessary part of one's international legal education.' My experiences since then only seem to reconfirm to me that we must study the toolbox with which international law was built to understand its vocabulary, whatever we might then do with these tools.

I continue to come to terms with my privileged status as a tenured male, Western professor in an elite European university, fluent only in Western languages and legal traditions, at the epicentre of the networks that undergird our discipline. I feel it important to acknowledge my vantage point as a privileged insider, and to quash any sense that I might speak objectively. I am, at best, a narrator: this textbook aims to expose the doctrinal and political debates that have constructed international law. I would invite students to take my perspective as merely one voice amongst many, and to reflect and above all to read broadly.

I wish to convey my gratitude to a few individuals. My thanks go to Brooke James at Oxford University Press and previously, to Olivia Carter and Liana Green, for skilfully nudging me to timely submission of the manuscript, and to the copy editors, indexers and production team, in particular Saranya Subramani, who was instrumental to this edition., I am much obliged to my students, who have provoked me and taught me how to improve my writing continuously. I am indebted to Pauline Janssens, Karel Brackeniers, and Antoine De Spiegeleir, all of whom provided generous substantive and stylistic comments, though all errors are of course mine. I am fortunate to be surrounded by many professional friends who have supported me, sent suggestions and comments, proposed refinements, and occasionally read drafts of new text. You are too numerous to acknowledge, but I am grateful to you all.

Thanks are due to my husband Patrick, for your endless patience and caustic humour, and for reminding me that, despite my penchant for flowery language, this remains a book for students. Finally, to my gentle, inquisitive, and exuberant sons, Luca and Abel, to whom I have once again dedicated this edition. Without the joy and light that they bring to my days, this manuscript would have been completed months sooner.

Structure and method of the book

The textbook remains resolutely focused on students making first contact with international law; it is designed to impart knowledge about core concepts and principles, to highlight doctrinal controversies and theoretical debates, and situate contemporary developments and challenges. So far as possible, a balance between accessibility and detail has been maintained with an eye for the needs of students. I have aimed for students to acquire the techniques and vocabulary necessary to enter the international legal profession, should they so choose, and I hope to invite them to reflect on international law's potential as an instrument for change. Though to newcomers, the complexity of the field is of course daunting, I have tried to present complex issues accessibly whenever possible. The book is accompanied by modest, but hopefully useful online resources for exam revision and further discussion.

The third edition is a general update to account for recent developments, and was shaped in particular by the armed conflict in Ukraine since February 2022, and the violence that has beset Gaza since October 2023. These two conflicts have resonated far beyond the battlefield and their effects may ultimately go much further than this edition can reflect. Naturally, several topics have also undergone refinement, such as the transversal impact of climate change law, the emergence of potentially disruptive new technologies, and exciting new doctrines and judgments relating to classical areas such as the law of treaties, State responsibility, and extraterritorial jurisdiction. So far as is possible, this book is current as at 31 December 2024.

New to this edition

- Treatment of recent events, including: the armed conflict between Ukraine and Russia; the Israel invasion of Gaza after the Hamas attacks of 7 October 2023; the ongoing Yemeni conflict relating to the Houthis; governmental instability in Niger, Mali, and Sudan; and the European Union's anti-coercion instrument.
- Coverage of recent ICJ judgments and opinions of note, including *Policies and Practices of Israel in the Occupied Palestinian Territory* advisory opinion; *Allegations of Violations of the Genocide Convention (Ukraine v Russia)*; *Violations of the Genocide Convention* cases (*Gambia v Myanmar; South Africa v Israel)*; *Violations of the Torture Convention (Canada and the Netherlands v Syria)*; *Alleged Violations of Sovereign Rights (Nicaragua v Colombia)*; *Certain Iranian Assets (Iran v United States)*; and *Embassy of Mexico in Quito (Mexico v Ecuador).*
- Coverage of regional and international courts, including ITLOS (e.g., *Commission of Small Island States in respect of Climate Change* advisory opinion; *Delimitation of the Maritime Boundary (Mauritius v Maldives)*); ICC decisions such as the arrest warrants against President Putin and Prime Minister Netanyahu; ECtHR judgments such as *Verein KlimaSeniorinnen v Switzerland*, *Carême v France*, and *Ukraine and the Netherlands v Russia*; CJEU judgments (e.g., *Venezuela v European Council*; *Commission and Council v Front Polisario*); and the IACtHR (e.g., *Habitantes de la Oroya v Peru).*
- Integration of key proposals of the ILC, including work on general principles and subsidiary sources, immunity of State officials, and the effects of sea-level rise in international law.
- Coverage of selected domestic practice and judgments (e.g., *WZW Klimaatzaak v Belgium (Belgium)*; *Al-Masirir v Saudi Arabia*; *Basfar v Wong*; *Ukraine v Law Debenture Trust (UK)*; *Cengiz v bin Salman (USA)*), and new legislative developments such as reforms to foreign State immunity legislation (China) and modifications of criminal law and procedure (Ukraine).
- Coverage of emerging treaty and other international law developments, including biodiversity beyond national jurisdiction; climate change agreements at multilateral COPs; and new forms of accountability for armed conflicts.
- Ongoing debates and proposals, including the establishment of a potential special tribunal for aggression in Ukraine; the intensification of unilateral coercive measures by Western States against Russia and Venezuela; the outcome of global climate negotiations; and ongoing work on the regulation of multinational enterprises.

Guide to the book

***International Law* is written with the student in mind. Its accessible style will ensure you gain a sound understanding of the subject area and a range of supporting features will enrich your learning and enable you to engage with the debates and developments.**

This guide shows you how to use those features so that you can get the most out of your studies.

Historical background

'Historical background' boxes provide essential context around how the law has developed, enabling you to understand the key principles behind the topics covered.

Theory and debates

'Theory and debates' boxes highlight the key issues and encourage you to think critically and carefully around areas of debate, giving you the confidence to analyse and question the law.

Contemporary developments

'Contemporary developments' boxes encourage you to engage with the latest controversies in international law, inspiring you to go further and consider how they affect the world today.

Case spotlight

'Case spotlight' boxes highlight seminal cases and explore the key issues and principles derived from them, providing useful illustration framing the law in its practical context.

Further reading

At the end of each chapter is a list of annotated recommended further reading, carefully selected to help supplement your knowledge and develop your research skills.

Outline contents

Part IV International disputes and responses to breaches

Part V Specialized regimes

Detailed contents

Part II Subjects of international law

Part III International law in operation

List of abbreviations

AB	Appellate Body (WTO)
AC	Appeal Cases (Law Reports, England and Wales)
ACHR	American Convention on Human Rights
ACnHPR	African Commission on Human and Peoples' Rights
ACtHPR	African Court of Human and Peoples' Rights
AD	Annual Digest and Reports of International Law Cases (16 vols, now ILR)
ADP	ILC Draft Articles on Diplomatic Protection
AFDI	Annuaire français de droit international
African HRLJ	African Human Rights Law Journal
AJCL	American Journal of Comparative Law
AJIL	American Journal of International Law
All ER	All England Law Reports
American University JILP	American University Journal of International Law and Politics
AP	Additional Protocol
ARIO	Articles on the Responsibility of International Organizations (ILC)
ARSIWA	Articles on Responsibility of States for Internationally Wrongful Acts
Art	Article
ASEAN	Association of Southeast Asian Nations
ASIL	American Society of International Law
ASP	Assembly of States Parties
AU	African Union (formerly the OAU)
Australian YBIL	Australian Yearbook of International Law
BFSP	British and Foreign State Papers
BIICL	British Institute of International and Comparative Law
BIT	bilateral investment treaty
BYBIL	British Yearbook of International Law
CA	Court of Appeal (UK)
CAR	Central African Republic
CAT	International Convention against Torture
CBD	Convention on the Conservation of Biological Diversity
CCDCOE	NATO Cooperative Cyber Defence Centre of Excellence
CCS	Convention on the Continental Shelf
CEDAW	Convention on the Elimination of All Forms of Discrimination against Women
CERD	International Convention on the Elimination of Racial Discrimination
CESCR	Committee on Economic, Social and Cultural Rights

Cd, Cmd, or Cmnd	Command Papers (UK)
Cf (Latin *confer*)	compare
CFCs	chlorofluorocarbons
CITES	Convention on International Trade in Endangered Species
CJEU	Court of Justice of the European Union
CJICL	Cambridge Journal of International and Comparative Law
CLCS	Commission on the Limits of the Continental Shelf
CLJ	Cambridge Law Journal
CLR	Commonwealth Law Reports
CMLR	Common Market Law Reports
CMW	International Convention on the Protection of the Rights of All Migrant Workers and Members of Their Families
CoE	Council of Europe
CommMW	Committee on the Protection of the Rights of All Migrant Workers and Members of their Families
COP	Conference of Parties
CPPED	International Convention on the Protection of All Persons from Enforced Disappearance
CRC	Convention on the Rights of the Child
CRPD	Convention on the Rights of Persons with Disabilities
CRRF	Comprehensive Refugee Response Framework
CSM	Convention on Special Missions
CTS	Convention on the Territorial Sea or Consolidated Treaty Series
CUP	Cambridge University Press
CWC	Chemical Weapons Convention
DRC	Democratic Republic of the Congo
DSB	Dispute Settlement Body (of the World Trade Organization)
DSU	Understanding on Dispute Settlement
EAC	Extraordinary African Chambers
EC	European Community
ECCC	Extraordinary Chambers of the Courts of Cambodia
ECHR	European Convention on Human Rights and Fundamental Freedoms
ECHR Ser	Reports of the European Court of Human Rights
ECJ	European Court of Justice
ECOSOC	United Nations Economic and Social Council
ECOWAS	Economic Community of West African States
ECR	European Court Reports
ECSI	European Convention on State Immunities
ECtHR	European Court of Human Rights
EEA	European Economic Area
EEC	Eurasian Economic Community
EEZ	exclusive economic zone
EFTA	European Free Trade Area (beyond the EU)
EHRR	European Human Rights Reports
EIA	environmental impact assessment
EJIL	European Journal of International Law
et seq	and following
ETS	European Treaty Series

EUQD	European Union Directive on the Qualification of Third-Country Nationals or Stateless Persons
EWCA (Civ)	Law Report (England and Wales), Court of Appeal, Civil Division
EWHC (Admin)	Law Report (England and Wales), High Court, Administrative Division
EWHC (Ch)	Law Report (England and Wales), High Court, Chancery Division
EWHC (QB)	Law Report (England and Wales), High Court, Queen's Bench Division
FATCA	Foreign Account Tax Compliance Act (USA)
FBAR	Report of Foreign Bank and Financial Accounts (USA)
FCO	Foreign and Commonwealth Office (UK)
Finnish YBIL	Finnish Yearbook of International Law
FPLC	Force patriotique pour la libération du Congo
FRY	Federal Republic of Yugoslavia (see SFRY)
FSIA	Foreign Sovereign Immunities Act (USA)
FTA	free trade agreement
FYROM	former Yugoslav Republic of Macedonia
F.2d	Federal Reporter (2nd series) (USA)
G20	Group of Twenty
GA	General Assembly of the United Nations
GAOR	Official Records of the General Assembly
GATS	General Agreement on Trade in Services
GATT	General Agreement on Tariffs and Trade
GCR	Global Compact on Refugees
GEF	Global Environmental Facility
German LJ	German Law Journal
GGE	Group of Governmental Experts on Advancing Responsible State Behaviour in Cyberspace (United Nations)
GYBIL	German Yearbook of International Law
Hansard	Official record of UK parliamentary debates (Lords or Commons)
Harvard JIL	Harvard Journal of International Law
HFCs	hydrofluorocarbons
HIPC	heavily indebted poor country
HL	House of Lords (UK)
HMSO	Her Majesty's Stationery Office (UK)
Hong Kong SAR	Hong Kong Special Administrative Region
HRC	Human Rights Committee
HRC	Human Rights Council
HRLJ	Human Rights Law Journal
HRLR	Human Rights Law Review
IAC	international armed conflict
IACnHR	Inter-American Commission on Human Rights
IACtHR	Inter-American Court of Human Rights
IAEA	International Atomic Energy Agency
IATA	International Air Transport Association
IATTC	Inter-American Tropical Tuna Commission
IBRD	International Bank for Reconstruction and Development

ICAO International Civil Aviation Organization
ICC International Criminal Court or International Chamber of Commerce
ICCPR International Covenant on Civil and Political Rights
ICESCR International Covenant on Economic, Social and Cultural Rights
ICISS International Commission on Intervention and State Sovereignty
ICJ International Court of Justice
ICLQ International and Comparative Law Quarterly
ICRC International Committee of the Red Cross
ICRW International Convention for the Regulation of Whaling
ICSFT International Convention for the Suppression of the Financing of Terrorism
ICSID International Centre for Settlement of Investment Disputes
ICSU International Council of Scientific Unions
ICTR International Criminal Tribunal for Rwanda
ICTY International Criminal Tribunal for the Former Yugoslavia
IDA International Development Association
IDP internally displaced person
IFC International Finance Corporation
IHL international humanitarian law
IHRL international human rights law
IJRL International Journal on Refugee Law
ILA International Law Association
ILC International Law Commission
ILC Ybk International Law Commission Yearbook
ILM International Legal Materials
ILO International Labour Organization
ILR International Law Reports (formerly AD)
IMF International Monetary Fund
IMO International Maritime Organization
INLA Irish National Liberation Army
IO international organization
IOTC Indian Ocean Tuna Commission
IPCC Intergovernmental Panel on Climate Change
Iran–US CTR Iran–United States Claims Tribunal Reports
ISDS investor–State dispute settlement
ITC International Tin Council
ITLOS International Tribunal for the Law of the Sea
ITLOS Reports International Tribunal for the Law of the Sea Reports
ITO International Trade Organization
ITU International Telecommunications Union
IUCN International Union for the Conservation of Nature

IUSCT	Iran–United States Claims Tribunal
IUSCTR	Iran–United States Claims Tribunal Reports
IWC	International Whaling Commission
JARPA	Japanese Whale Research Program under Special Permit in the Antarctic
JCE	joint criminal enterprise
JICJ	Journal of International Criminal Justice
JIDS	Journal of International Dispute Settlement
JIEL	Journal of International Economic Law
JIL	journal of international law
JIM	Joint Investigative Mechanism
JLPICT	Journal of the Law and Practice of International Courts and Tribunals
KB	King's Bench Division (Law Reports, England and Wales)
KFOR	Kosovo Force (NATO-led peacekeeping force deployed in Kosovo)
KSC	Kosovo Specialist Chambers
Leiden JIL	Leiden Journal of International Law
LGTBQIA2S+	lesbian, gay, bisexual, transgender, questioning, intersex, asexual, two-spirit
LGDJ	Librairie générale de droit et de jurisprudence
LJ/LJJ	Lord Justice/Lords Justice
LL.R	Lloyd's Law Reports
LMOs	living modified organisms
LNOJ	League of Nations Official Journal
LNTS	League of Nations Treaty Series
LQR	Law Quarterly Review
LRIL	London Review of International Law
Manchester UP	Manchester University Press
MARPOL	International Convention for the Prevention of Pollution from Ships
Mercosur	Mercado Común del Sur
MFN	most-favoured-nation treatment
Michigan JIL	Michigan Journal of International Law
MICT	International Residual Mechanism for Criminal Tribunals
MIGA	Multilateral Investment Guarantee Agency
MLC	Movement for the Liberation of the Congo
MLR	Modern Law Review
MONUC	United Nations Organization Mission in the Democratic Republic of the Congo
MONUSCO	United Nations Organization Stabilization Mission in the Democratic Republic of the Congo
MOU	memorandum of understanding
MPEPIL	Max Planck Encyclopedia of Public International Law (OUP, 2012)
MPUNYB	Max Planck United Nations Year Book of International Law
MPYUNL	Max Planck Yearbook of United Nations Law
NAFO	North Atlantic Fisheries Organization
NAFTA	North American Free Trade Agreement (see USMCA)

NATO	North Atlantic Treaty Organization
NDC	nationally determined contribution
Netherlands YBIL	Netherlands Yearbook of International Law
NGO	non-governmental organization
NIAC	non-international armed conflict
NIEO	New International Economic Order
NILR	Netherlands International Law Review
NPT	Nuclear Non-Proliferation Treaty
NQHR	Netherlands Quarterly for Human Rights
NT	national treatment
NYULR	New York University Law Review
OAS	Organization of American States
OAU	Organization of African Unity
OECD	Organization for Economic Co-operation and Development
OHCHR	Office of the United Nations High Commissioner for Human Rights
OJ	Official Journal of the European Communities
OJLS	Oxford Journal of Legal Studies
ONUC	United Nations Operation in the Congo
OPEC	Organization of the Petroleum Exporting Countries
OPRC	International Convention on Oil Pollution Preparedness
OR	Ontario Reports
OSCE	Organization for Security and Co-operation in Europe
OSPAR	Convention for the Protection of the Marine Environment of the North-East Atlantic
OTP	Office of the Prosecutor (ICC)
OUP	Oxford University Press
PCA	Permanent Court of Arbitration
PCIJ	Permanent Court of International Justice (replaced by the ICJ)
PDVSA	Petroleos de Venezuela S.A.
PLO	Palestinian Liberation Organization
PMSC	private military security company
POP	Persistent Organic Pollutant
POW	prisoner of war
QB	Queen's Bench Division (Law Reports, England and Wales)
R2P	Responsibility to Protect
RCC	Revolutionary Command Council (Iraq)
RECIEL	Review of European, Comparative & International Environmental Law
Recueil des Cours	Recueil des Cours de l'Académie de droit international de La Haye (Collected Courses of the Hague Academy of International Law)
RGDIP	Revue générale de droit international public
RIAA	Reports of International Arbitral Awards
Rio 1992	Conference of the Parties at Rio de Janeiro, 1992

Rio+20	Conference of the Parties at Rio de Janeiro, 2012
SADC	Southern African Development Community
SC	Security Council
SCOR	Official Records of the Security Council
SCSL	Special Court for Sierra Leone
SDR	Special Drawing Right
SFRY	Socialist Federal Republic of Yugoslavia
SIA	State Immunity Act (UK)
SIPR	Stockholm International Peace Research Institute
SPS Agreement	Agreement on the Application of Sanitary and Phytosanitary Measures
SSA	Straddling (Fish) Stocks Agreement
STL	Special Tribunal for Lebanon
SUA	Convention for the Suppression of Unlawful Acts against the Safety of Maritime Navigation
Sydney LR	Sydney Law Review
TAC	total allowable catch
TEU	Treaty on European Union (Lisbon, 2007)
TIAS	Treaties and other International Agreements (USA)
TRIM	Trade-Related Investment Measure
TRIPS	Agreement on Trade-Related Aspects of Intellectual Property
TRNC	Turkish Republic of Northern Cyprus
TWAIL	Third World Approaches to International Law
UAR	United Arab Republic
UC Press	Press of the University of California
UDHR	Universal Declaration of Human Rights
UK	United Kingdom
UKHL	Online law report of the House of Lords (UK)
UKMIL	United Kingdom Materials on International Law (in BYBIL)
UKTS	United Kingdom Treaty Series
UNAMID	African Union/United Nations Hybrid operation in Darfur
UNAMIR	United Nations Assistance Mission for Rwanda
UNAMIS	United Nations Mission in the Sudan
UNAMSIL	United Nations Mission in Sierra Leone
UNCC	United Nations Compensation Commission
UNCnHR	United Nations Commission on Human Rights
UNCIO	United Nations Conference on International Organization
UNCITRAL	United Nations Commission on International Trade Law
UNCLOS	United Nations Convention on the Law of the Sea
UNCTAD	United Nations Conference on Trade and Development
UNDP	United Nations Development Programme
UN Doc	United Nations official document
UNECE	United Nations Economic Commission for Europe

UNESCO	United Nations Educational, Scientific and Cultural Organization
UNEP	United Nations Environment Programme
UNFCCC	United Nations Framework Convention on Climate Change
UNGA	United Nations General Assembly
UNGA Res	United Nations General Assembly Resolution
UNHCR	United Nations High Commissioner for Refugees (now UN Refugee Agency)
UNICEF	United Nations Children's Fund
UNIDO	United Nations Industrial Development Organization
UNIDROIT	International Institute for the Unification of Private Law
UNJY	United Nations Juridical Yearbook
UNMIH	United Nations Mission in Haiti
UNMIK	United Nations Mission in Kosovo
UNMISS	United Nations Mission in South Sudan
UNSC	United Nations Security Council
UNSC Res	United Nations Security Council Resolution
UNTS	United Nations Treaty Series
U Penn Press	University of Pennsylvania Press
UP	University Press
UPC	Union des patriotes congolais
UPR	universal periodic review
US/USA	United States/United States of America
USGPO	US Government Printing Office
USMCA	United States–Mexico–Canada Agreement (to replace NAFTA)
U of Toronto LJ	University of Toronto Law Journal
VCCR	Vienna Convention on Consular Relations
VCDR	Vienna Convention on Diplomatic Relations
VCLT	Vienna Convention on the Law of Treaties
Virginia JIL	Virginia Journal of International Law
WCPFC	Western and Central Pacific Fisheries Commission
WHC	World Heritage Convention
WHO	World Health Organization
WIPO	World Intellectual Property Rights Organization
WMO	World Meteorological Organization
Yale JIL	Yale Journal of International Law
ZACC	Constitutional Court of South Africa
ZaöRV	Zeitschrift für auslandisches und öffentliches Recht und Völkerrecht/Heidelberg Journal of International Law

Glossary of legal terms

a fortiori Indicates that if A is so, then B will equally be so, as the same reasons apply even more strongly to B.

ab initio From the outset.

*accession*Same effect as ratification, but not preceded by signature.

acquiescence To accept tacitly, without protest.

acta jure gestionis A class of acts performed not by right of sovereignty by a State in the territory of another State, such as a commercial activity (*cf acta jure imperii*).

acta jure imperii A class of acts performed by right of sovereignty by a State in the territory of another State (*cf acta jure gestionis*).

acte de gouvernement In French law, an act of government that cannot be challenged before the courts (see 'justiciability').

actio popularis An action brought by a member of a community in the interest of the community as a whole.

actus reus An act or conduct that is a constituent element of a crime.

ad hoc Created or done for a particular purpose.

amicus curiae Literally 'friend of a court', an impartial adviser to a court of law in a particular case.

annexation The incorporation of territory by a State.

Anschluss The annexation of Austria by Germany in 1938.

aut dedere aut judicare The legal obligation either to try an accused or extradite them to another State willing to do so.

comity An exhortation to adhere to rules of courtesy, politeness, or goodwill, usually observed by governments and courts.

compromissory clause A clause found in a treaty providing for the submission of a matter or matters arising thereunder to arbitral or judicial dispute settlement.

contra legem Contrary to law (of equity).

*coup d'état*A sudden, violent seizure of power from a government.

cuius regio eius religio 'Whose realm, their religion', the notion that a ruler could determine the religion of their subjects without outside interference.

culpa Negligence or fault.

debellatio The complete defeat and destruction of a belligerent party.

de facto A state of affairs that is true in fact but not legally sanctioned.

de jure A state of affairs in accordance with law.

delicta juris gentium Crimes against the law of nations itself.

diligentia quam in suis In international law, the standard of vigilance a State is expected to exercise in respect of its own interests or nationals.

dispositif Operative or decisive clause or part of a judgment.

dolus specialis Specific intent to cause harm by committing an act.

domaine reservé Literally 'reserved domain', the areas of State activity that are essentially internal and fall within its domestic jurisdiction or competence.

Dominion Now obsolete, used to refer to the self-governing territories of the British Commonwealth.

embargo An official ban on any activity; in international law, usually a ban on trade, commercial activities, or the passage of vessels.

eo nomine By or under that name.

erga omnes (An obligation) owed to all other subjects of law.

erga omnes partes (An obligation) owed to all other parties to a legal instrument.

estoppel A principle that precludes an actor or person from asserting something contrary to what has been implied by a previous action or statement.

ex aequo et bono In international law, the power of a dispute-settlement body to dispense with consideration of the law and instead decide on the basis that they consider fair or equitable.

ex iniuria ius non oritur Unjust acts cannot create law; a right cannot arise from wrongdoing.

ex post facto (Law) with retrospective action or force.

exceptio inadimpleti contractus An objection that another party has not performed their obligations in an agreement in question.

force majeure Unforeseeable, irresistible circumstances that prevent an actor or person from fulfilling an obligation.

forum prorogatum Literally 'prorogated jurisdiction', the power of a court to take jurisdiction through the consent of parties being given after the initiation of proceedings.

good offices Participation as a friendly intermediary for the purpose of resolving a dispute between parties, but without proposing a settlement.

hors rs de combat Literally 'outside combat', out of action due to injury or damage.

hostis humani generis Enemy of all mankind; beyond legal protection and thus can be dealt with by any State.

immunity Protection or exemption from an obligation or penalty, as well as from legal proceedings.

in absentia While the person involved is not present, usually referring to legal proceedings.

in favorem tertii In favour of a third party.

inadimplenti non est adimplendum The non-respect by one party to an agreement releases the other party from having to perform any further obligations under it.

inchoate Not fully formed or developed, but can be completed by subsequent acts.

infra legem In a manner consistent with accepted law.

inter se Between or among themselves.

intra legem A decision that is consistent with the rules of law.

jurisdiction The power or competence to make legal decisions and judgments.

jus ad bellum Literally 'right to war', the criteria to determine whether entering into war is permissible; the law on the use of force.

jus cogens Peremptory rule of international law from which no derogation is permitted (*cf jus dispositivum*).

jus dispositivum Law adopted by consent; the body of general international law which accommodates opting out, adjustment, or derogation (*cf jus cogens*).

jus gentium The law of nations, or international law.

jus in bello Literally 'law in war', the law of armed conflict.

jus naturale Natural law, or a body of unchanging moral principles regarded as a basis for all human conduct.

jus sanguinis Literally 'right of blood', a principle of nationality law by which citizenship is determined by the citizenship of one's parents.

jus soli Literally 'law of the soil', the right of anyone born on the territory of a State to nationality or citizenship.

jus tractatuum The right to conclude treaties.

justiciability Concerns the limits upon legal issues over which a court can exercise its jurisdiction.

la compétence de la compétence The power (usually by a court or tribunal) to determine one's own jurisdiction.

legation A group of governmental representatives in a foreign country with lower status than an embassy or diplomatic mission.

levée en masse Involuntary mass conscription of individuals.

lex arbitri In an arbitral proceeding, the applicable law.

lex ferenda Norms that are being sought to become established as law.

lex lata Established, valid, or binding law.

lex posterior derogate priori (lex posterior) The principle that a more recent legal rule prevails over an inconsistent, earlier legal rule.

lex specialis A specific legal rule that departs, or is an exception to, a general legal rule.

litispendence The part of a legal proceeding being pending, undetermined; the time during which an action is pending.

locus standi The right of a party to appear and to be heard before a court.

lucrum cessans The compensation awarded for loss of reasonably expected future gain or profit, as distinguished from actual loss.

mala fides Literally 'in bad faith', to deceive or defraud.

mare liberum A navigable body of water that is open to all nations.

mens rea The necessary mental intention to commit a criminal act.

modus operandi Mode of operation, preferred means of performing an action.

nemo judex in sua causa propria No one should be judge in their own case.

no-fly zone An area in which aircraft are forbidden to fly, especially in times of conflict.

non liquet Literally 'the law is not clear', referring to a judicial finding to that effect.

non-refoulement The practice of not forcing refugees or asylum seekers to return to a country in which they are likely to be subjected to persecution.

odious debt A concept to describe illegitimate forms of debt; for example, those incurred by despotic or authoritarian regimes, against the interests of the population.

opinio juris sive necessitatis The view that something is required by considerations of law or of necessity.

pacta sunt servanda What has been agreed to shall be respected.

pacta tertiis nec nocent nec prosunt No benefit may be derived, and no injury suffered, from something agreed between third parties.

par in parem non habet imperium Between equals, neither has dominion over the other.

party An actor that has consented to be bound by an agreement and for which the agreement is in force.

perestroika In the former Soviet Union, the policy or practice of restructuring or reforming the economic and political system.

perfidy In the law of armed conflict, a form of deception in which an actor makes a promise with the intention of breaking that promise.

persona non grata A foreign national prohibited from entering or remaining in the territory of another State.

plenipotentiary A person invested with the full power to act independently on behalf of their government; typically a diplomat.

prima facie True, valid, or sufficient at first impression.

proprio motu (An action taken) on one's own initiative.

raison d'être Reason or justification for being or existence.

ratification Following signature, the expression by a State of its consent to be bound by a treaty, usually through legislative processes.

ratione materiae By reason of the nature of the relevant subject.

ratione personae By reason of the person concerned.

rebus sic stantibus A fundamental change of circumstances.

renunciation The formal rejection of a claim, right, or position.

res communis Land or sea that can be used by any State or is subject to a common regime.

res judicata A matter that has been judicially determined and cannot be further pursued.

res nullius Land or an object that has not yet been claimed by a legal subject.

restitutio in integrum The restoration to an injured party to the situation that existed before a wrongful act had occurred.

retorsion (Act of) retaliation which is not unlawful.

secession Formal withdrawal of a group from a larger entity, usually a political State.

seisin In international law, the power of an international tribunal to deal with a case.

severability The possibility for a clause in a treaty or agreement, if held to be unlawful or unenforceable, to be removed from the remainder of the treaty or agreement.

sovereignty In international law, the right of a State to act independently of other States, subject only to the restrictions imposed by international law.

special agreement (compromis) An agreement between two or more States to submit a dispute to a designated dispute-settlement body, such as an arbitral tribunal or court.

State A subject of international law with an effective government that has jurisdiction over a defined territory and permanent population, and the capacity to enter into legal relations with other States.

status quo ante The state of affairs that existed previously.

terra nullius Territory that has not been claimed by any State.

trace parallèle The low-water mark, paralleling the coasts of the State.

travaux préparatoires The preparatory documents and materials that were used in preparing the final form of an agreement or treaty.

ultra vires Beyond legal competence or authority.

Usus In international law, the usages and practices of States; an alternative term for the practice required to support the existence of a custom.

utres magis valeat quam pereat That the thing may rather have effect than to fail/to be destroyed.

Table of international cases

African Commission on Human and Peoples' Rights (ACnHPR)

African Court of Human and Peoples' Rights

Ethiopia–Eritrea Boundary Commission

Ethiopia–Eritrea Claims Commission

European Court of Human Rights

European Court of Justice

ICSID

Inter-American Court of Human Rights

International Criminal Court

International Criminal Tribunal for the Former Yugoslavia

International Criminal Tribunal for Rwanda

International Tribunal for the Law of the Sea

Iran-US Claims Tribunal

Special Court for Sierra Leone

Special Tribunal for Lebanon

United Nations Human Rights

US-Mexico Mixed Claims

World Trade Organization/GATT

Table of domestic cases by country

Germany

Greece

Hong Kong

Israel

Italy

Japan

Kenya

Kosovo

Netherlands

United States of America

Table of international instruments and other documents

Table of domestic instruments by country

Netherlands, The

New Zealand

Nigeria

Pakistan

Peru

Portugal

Russian Federation

Singapore

Slovenia

South Africa

Spain

Switzerland

Thailand

United Arab Republic

United Kingdom

United States of America

Vietnam

PART I
The structure of international law

1

The history and nature of international law

1.1 Introduction: international law as law

Ubi societas, ubi jus is an ancient Roman maxim, which proclaims that 'where there is society, there is law'. Law has indeed played an important role in human societies, and perhaps one should be unsurprised at its pervasive character. Law lays out both the rules according to which societies can fulfil their values and aspirations, and provides the framework through which that society will be governed. Through law, rules are established regarding what is permissible and what is prohibited; what rights, duties, and obligations exist for participants in those systems; and the place of actors or officials such as legislatures, courts, and the police, with powers to change, interpret, or enforce the rules of the system. Virtually all national legal systems, at least one of which each reader of this book will probably be acquainted with, discharge these very basic functions.

International law is somewhat different. Rather than regulating the behaviour of individuals in their relations with one another, it is usually portrayed as a legal framework to govern the relations between 'States', the organized political entities which are the primary subjects of international law. Strictly speaking, in focusing on 'international law'—a term first used by Jeremy Bentham to describe the law between nations[1]—this book will be dedicated to the study of 'public international law', the distinct legal order regulating relations between States.

'Public international law' is to be distinguished from 'private international law', which describes the principles that determine the applicability of a certain law or set of laws to situations involving individuals with a foreign or transboundary element. These might include international marriages, or business transactions such as the sale of goods, in which there might be a choice between the laws of different countries. Private international law regulates the conflicts between *rules* of different domestic legal orders, rather than relations between States; these are reserved for public international law.

Today, public international law has exceeded its foundations as the law of inter-State relations, and operates as an integral part of the daily lives of individuals. Yet, the inner logic and substrate of international law remain based in an inter-State system.

[1] J Bentham, *Introduction to the Principles of Morals and Legislation* (1780).

International law has always been purposive, structuring relations between States for specific ends. Those purposes have shifted over time, in line with political and social developments; accordingly, the underlying ideas and assumptions about the role of law in international society have also evolved. There is thus some value summarily to trace some international legal history, as that helps to provide the background to its contemporary structure.

For as long as organized human groups or societies have existed, rules have developed to regulate their relations with one another; they have exchanged tributes, signed treaties of alliance or friendship, and even exchanged diplomats. In regions with an abundance of independent communities, such as Mesopotamia (from at least 2100 BC), northern 'Vedic' India (from about 1600 BC), and classical Greece (from 600 BC), a historical record exists of these interactions.[2] At the United Nations Library in Geneva, testimonies exist of a treaty dating back to 2500 BC, signed between the Kingdom of Elba, in what is now northern Syria, and the Kingdom of Abousal (in modern-day Iraq, on the Euphrates). The 'Eternal Treaty' agreed between an Egyptian pharaoh and Hittite king, is another such example; and Roman peace treaties systematically established a framework for future cooperation.[3] By the seventh century AD, the Islamic world had developed a substantial body of law governing relations between Muslim States and with the non-Muslim world.[4]

In mediaeval Western Europe after the fall of the Roman Empire, there existed a patchwork of feudal entities and kingdoms ranging from the self-governing, independent cities of northern Italy to the heterogeneous, decentralized Holy Roman Empire.[5] Over time, feudal arrangements were to fall away in favour of centralized structures, especially in France, England, Portugal, and Spain, which began to take on the characteristics of a 'State': a permanent political unit, supported by institutions and bureaucracies, and independent courts with an authority to give final judgments.[6]

After the Protestant Reformation in central and northern Europe, in which John Calvin and Martin Luther denounced the ecclesiastical structure of the Roman Catholic Church and papal supremacy,[7] a number of religious wars were to plague Europe, culminating in the Thirty Years' War (1618–48). These were to end with the Peace of Westphalia, the name for several treaties signed at Münster and Osnabrück in 1648, and which is very much part of the founding myth in the emergence of 'modern international law'.

[2] These, and other ancient examples, are covered in A Nussbaum, *A Concise History of the Law of Nations* (rev edn, Macmillan, 1954), 1–7; and DJ Bederman, *International Law in Antiquity* (CUP, 2001). See also reference to the 'Eternal Treaty' between the Hittite and Egyptian empires (*c* 1258 BC) in Chapter 7.

[3] See R Lesaffer, 'Peace Treaties and the Formation of International Law' in B Fassbender and A Peters (eds), *Oxford Handbook on the History of International Law* (OUP, 2012), 71.

[4] See S Neff, *Justice among Nations: A History of International Law* (Harvard UP, 2014), 5; H Khadduri, 'Islam and the Modern Law of Nations' (1956) 50 AJIL 358.

[5] Neff, *ibid*, 55–9.

[6] See JR Strayer, *On the Medieval Origins of the Modern State* (Princeton UP, 1979), 9–10.

[7] R Grote, 'Westphalian System' in MPEPIL, vol X, 865, para 4.

HISTORICAL BACKGROUND The Pope and the Holy Roman Emperor before Westphalia

Today, the Pope is the Head of the Roman Catholic Church and is the ruler of the Vatican City, essentially confined to St Peter's Basilica within Rome, Italy. Historically, however, the 'Papal States' ruled over substantial territories in central Italy, including the whole of Rome. Moreover, during the Middle Ages the Pope maintained that, as the head of the Catholic Church, ecclesiastical law would purportedly apply to all Catholic sovereigns: this included the prevention or punishment of violations of natural law, or even the removal of disobedient rulers from power. Thus the Pope claimed both to be a sovereign ruler *and* to extend authority above other sovereigns.

Conversely, the 'Holy Roman Empire', famously mocked by Voltaire as 'neither holy, neither Roman, neither an empire', was an entirely different entity. The Empire had, since the period of the Crusades, also laid claim to universal patronage over all Christianity, though in practice its feudal jurisdiction was centred primarily on German-speaking lands. The Empire was not a unitary State, but an elective monarchy with limited feudal powers over hundreds of princely sub-units that formally owed allegiance to the Emperor, but effectively acted as independent entities.

The historical interest in both the Papacy and the Holy Roman Empire is their claim to supremacy: both advanced claims to lead a universal Christian polity, especially during the period of the Crusades, when West Europeans invaded what is now Israel and Palestine. However, the advent of the sovereign State system as we understand it today, coupled with the Protestant Reformation, meant such claims became increasingly untenable and would be definitively abandoned in 1648 with the Peace of Westphalia.

1.2 The founding myths of modern international law

1.2.1 The Peace of Westphalia (1648)

There are diverging views on the 1648 Peace of Westphalia, often taken as the conceptual starting point for modern international law in the European State system then spread around the world through European colonialism, and its basic foundations remain relevant today. It has been argued, for example, that the 'Westphalia thesis' focuses unduly on the conceptual basis for international law and not on the daily activities governed by international law—such as treaties, embassies, claims to jurisdiction or immunity—which go back far beyond 1648 and have structured international relations for millennia.[8]

For all this, it behoves us to dwell on the Peace of Westphalia and its definitive rejection of the secular power of the Pope over the internal affairs of other States, precisely because of what its profound Eurocentrism reveals about the founding myths

[8] V Lowe, *International Law* (Clarendon Press, 2007), 9; and S Beaulac, 'The Westphalian Legal Orthodoxy—Myth or Reality?' (2000) 2 Journal of the History of International Law 148. An instant classic is M Koskenniemi, *To the Uttermost Parts of the Earth: Legal Imagination and International Power 1300–1870* (CUP, 2021).

surrounding international law.[9] According to the Peace Treaties, Catholic and Protestant States would henceforth be sovereign and equal, under no higher power. Intellectually, this represented a decisive move away from the concept of the Christian universal law of nations.[10] Nevertheless, international law retained certain concepts with theological origins. For example, the Spanish Scholastic Francisco de Vitoria argued that the indigenous peoples of the Americas, not being Christians, could not be sovereign because one of the attributes of sovereignty was the capacity to engage in 'just war', and it was impossible for non-Christians to engage in a just war.[11] In doing so, Vitoria's thoughts on the 'Indians' would serve to facilitate the Spanish conquest, as they could paradoxically only exist as violators of the laws of war, and not subjects of the law.[12]

Under the Peace of Westphalia, each State, and in particular the thousands of small entities which made up the Holy Roman Empire, would henceforth be free to choose for themselves which religion to adopt: *cuius regio eius religio* ('whose realm, their religion'). European States were now considered as equal and sovereign in their relations with one another, without external interference unless consent was expressly given, usually by treaty. The concept of sovereignty was not new: it was borrowed from Jean Bodin's theory of 'absolute sovereignty' in the sixteenth century, according to which a sovereign would not be bound by the laws they personally instituted, but only the laws of God and of nature.[13] The rule on non-interference had, moreover, been embodied in the 1555 Peace of Augsburg.[14] Nevertheless, the characterization of the State as an organized territorial entity capable of guaranteeing its commitments was established in Westphalia, which stands out as more than a peace treaty, but as one of the first modern instances of conscious, multilateral ordering through law—in Europe at least.

1.2.2 **The rise and decline of natural law (1648–1815)**

Within Europe, the 1648 Peace of Westphalia marks an intellectual break with earlier thinking about the law of nations. The most famous international lawyer of the period is the Dutchman Hugo de Groot (or Hugo Grotius), who was instrumental in establishing the freedom of the seas, in that they could not be appropriated by one State (as argued Spain and Portugal and, to an extent, England) but were open to all. This doctrine was particularly beneficial to Dutch commercial interests; in particular, those of

[9] See N Tzouvala, 'The Specter of Eurocentrism in International Legal History' (2021) 31 Yale Journal of Law and the Humanities 413. But *cf* the attempt to suggest a move towards a more global history in B Fassbender and A Peters, 'Introduction: Towards a Global History of International Law' in B Fassbender and A Peters (eds), *The Oxford Handbook of the History of International Law* (OUP, 2012), 1.

[10] Religion's place in the law of nations during the Middle Ages was especially prominent in the law of war: see Nussbaum (n 2) 17–23; Neff (n 4) 94 *et seq*.

[11] See A Anghie, *Imperialism, Sovereignty, and the Making of International Law* (CUP, 2005), 26; *cf* Nussbaum (n 2) 79–84 (Vitoria) and 84–91 (Suárez); and I de la Rasilla y del Moral, 'Francisco de Vitoria's *Unexpected Transformations and Reinterpretations* for International Law' (2013) 15 ICLR 287.

[12] On the 'Spanish Scholastic' tradition, see M Koskenniemi, 'Empire and International Law: The Real Spanish Contribution' (2011) 61 U of Toronto LJ 1.

[13] Jean Bodin, *Six Books of the Commonwealth* (Tooley tr, Basil Blackwell, 1967); and A Gardot, 'Jean Bodin—Sa place parmi les fondateurs du droit international' (1934) 50 Recueil des Cours 549.

[14] See DP O'Connell, 'Territorial Claims in the Grotian Period' in CH Alexandrowicz (ed), *Studies in the History of the Law of Nations* (Springer, 1970), 1–5.

the Dutch East India Company.[15] Grotius would also contribute to the modern understanding of the laws of war, covered in Chapters 14 and 15 of this book. However, his lasting contribution was in his depiction of the nature of international law. In his seminal book *On the Law of War and Peace*, he portrayed international law as a combination of two distinct bodies, *jus gentium* and *jus naturale*.[16]

Grotius' natural law scholarship based in reason, not religion, influenced several writers in the eighteenth century. Samuel Pufendorf (1632–94) attempted to rebut his claims, infusing *jus naturale* with reason and Christian morality, and claiming that it prevailed over practices of *jus gentium*, such as custom or treaties.[17] Christian Wolff (1679–1754) struck a different path, seeking to describe *jus gentium* according to scientific principles and promoting the establishment of an overarching 'supreme state' which would gather all nations in 'following the leadership of nature'.[18] Wolff would inspire Immanuel Kant's concept of a 'world federation' (*civitas gentium*), which would embrace all the peoples of the earth and ensure, in his famous terms, a 'perpetual peace'.[19]

THEORY AND DEBATES Distinguishing *Jus Gentium* from *Jus Naturale*

Vitoria and Suárez's attempts to develop the concept of an international *jus gentium* (law of nations) formed the foundations for Grotius' work. For Vitoria, *jus gentium* did not describe the law between nations, but would describe the laws that applied to a community of all world citizens (F de Vitoria, 'De Indis III' 2 in JB Scott (ed), *The Classics of International Law; De Indis et de Jure Belli Relectiones* by Franciscus de Vitoria (1917)). Suárez would distinguish *jus gentium inter se* (applicable to relations between nations) from *jus gentium intra se* (the laws applicable within nations), suggesting that the former included the law of war and peace, diplomatic relations, and trade agreements (F Suárez, 'De Legibus ac Deo Legislatore II 19' in JB Scott (ed), *The Classics of International Law: Selections from Three Works of Francisco Suárez* (1944), 19, para 8). Suárez's distinction would carve out the international *jus gentium* from national legal orders in which matters such as religion, marriage, property, and contracts were regulated (*ibid*, 20, para 7).

Grotius' greatest contribution was to create a distinction between the international *jus gentium* and *jus naturale*. For Grotius, *jus naturale* described the laws that 'existed within nature'; these were universal, eternal, and could be discovered through the full use of human reasoning. *Jus gentium*, conversely, was distinct, purely a human creation, subject to change from time to time, and variable from place to place. Its source of validity was the consent of States:

> amongst all or most States there might be, and in Fact there are, some Laws agreed on by common Consent, which respect the Advantage not of one Body in particular, but of all in general. And this is what is called the law of Nations [*jus gentium*], when used in Distinction to the Law of Nature [*jus naturale*] (Grotius, *De Iure Belli ac Pacis* (1625, ed Tuck 2005), I. Prelim. §§XVIII, XXVII).

[15] See WSM Knight, *The Life and Works of Hugo Grotius* (Oceana, 1925).

[16] Grotius, *De Iure Belli ac Pacis* (1625, ed Tuck, 2005); Koskenniemi (n 8) 77.

[17] See Nussbaum (n 2) 147–50.

[18] C Wolff, *Ius Gentium Methodo Scientifica Pertractatum* (1749, tr Drake and Hemelt, 1934), §20.

[19] I Kant, *Perpetual Peace* (1795) 105. See further, P Capps, 'The Kantian Project in International Legal Theory' (2001) 12 EJIL 1003; A Perreau-Saussine, 'Immanuel Kant in International Law' in S Besson and J Tasioulas (eds), *The Philosophy of International Law* (OUP, 2010), 53.

Emmerich de Vattel (1714–67) proved to be the most influential in the 'Grotian' tradition. A self-proclaimed adherent of Grotian thought, he wrote *Le droit des gens* (*The Law of Nations*) to prepare a practical and accessible handbook for practising lawyers and statesmen;[20] it has been called the 'first international law textbook'.[21] Rejecting Wolff's exhortation of the supreme State, Vattel's work entrenched the doctrine of the equality of States, irrespective of their relative power, within a collective European State system bound by a common interest.[22] Delineating clearly between 'laws of conscience' (natural law) and 'laws of action' (positive law), Vattel asserted that only the latter were relevant, a seminal argument in the gradual move to positivism within international law (see Section 1.2.3).[23]

The seventeenth and eighteenth centuries were notable for the supplanting of religiosity with a reliance on human reason and the concept of 'natural rights' of individuals, culminating in the American and French Revolutions of 1776 and 1789. The USA represented the first modern instance where a State, as a political entity, was founded through the free choice of people to associate with one another under a common set of laws and government.[24] This idea fuelled the French Revolution of 1789; and though Napoleon Bonaparte overthrew the revolutionaries in 1799, he launched a military offensive to spread revolutionary ideals throughout Europe.[25]

HISTORICAL BACKGROUND The Legacy of the Haitian Revolution, 1791-1804

As with most international law books, regrettably, this textbook focuses on the institutional and structural features of international law from a Eurocentric or Western perspective, from Westphalia to the Congress of Vienna to the League of Nations. Even doctrines such as the concept of self-determination are often depicted as emerging from the American and French Revolutions, and only gaining momentum in the post-World War II decolonization movement.

Yet obviously, this does not capture the whole picture. For example, the 1791–1804 Haitian Revolution was rooted in a long struggle to overthrow slavery on the island of Hispaniola (in the indigenous Taíno language, Ayti), where the native population had been decimated (and dispossessed) by Spanish colonization; and where under the 1697 Treaty of Ryswick, the west of the island became the French colony of Saint-Domingue. Throughout the 1700s, France

[20] E de Vattel, *Le droit des gens* (1758). Some of the best work on de Vattel has been written by E Jouannet, *Emer de Vattel et l'émergence doctrinale du droit international* (Pedone, 1998). For an introductory summary in English, see E Jouannet, 'Emer de Vattel' in B Fassbender and A Peters (eds), *The Oxford Handbook of the History of International Law* (OUP, 2012), 1118–22.

[21] See, e.g., J Crawford, *Brownlie's Principles of Public International Law* (9th edn, OUP, 2019), 8.

[22] De Vattel (n 20) III.iii.§47.

[23] See Nussbaum (n 2) 156–64; Neff (n 4) 194–8; W Grewe, *The Epochs of International Law* (M Byers tr, de Gruyter, 2000), 549–60. See also N Onuf, '*Civitas Maxima*: Wolff, Vattel and the Fate of Republicanism' (1994) 88 AJIL 280.

[24] See G Stourzh, *Alexander Hamilton and the Idea of Republican Government* (Stanford UP, 1970) 45; C Rossiter, *Seedtime of the Republic: The Origin of the American Tradition of Political Liberty* (Harcourt Brace, 1953) 12 *et seq*.

[25] See generally Grewe (n 23) 492 *et seq*; EJ Kolla, *Sovereignty, International Law and the French Revolution* (CUP, 2017).

would implement a racialized system of slavery in Saint-Domingue to promote a lucrative trade in sugar and coffee, forcing 800,000 Africans into its colony.

In 1791, in parallel with the revolutionary uprisings against royalty, tyranny, and oppression in France itself, slave revolts began in Saint-Domingue (see C Fick, *The Making of Haiti: The Saint Domingue Revolution from Below* (University of Tennessee Press, 1991), 154). Although by 1794 the French National Convention abolished slavery across France's colonies, Napoleon would nevertheless seek to restore colonial rule by force. When, in 1804, French forces were expelled from the island, Jean-Jacques Dessalines declared the independence of a new State: Haiti.

Haiti was born of the desire for self-determination of its inhabitants, but it struggled for recognition as an independent State. Its former colonial master, France, actively sought to undermine the freed slaves, *inter alia* by rupturing trade networks, for fear that anti-colonial slave rebellions might spread to other slaving colonies, such as Grenada or Martinique. Though Great Britain and the nascent USA would trade with the Haitians, they refused fully to acknowledge Haiti as a new State, in part due to slavery within their own borders. Belatedly, in 1825 France recognized Haiti's independence while extorting a payment of 150 million francs from it to compensate for the loss of slave property—a tactic that would legitimate the notion of racialized slave property and, as with future occupations by foreign powers such as France and the USA, would undermine the fragile Haitian State and contribute to the trope whereby Haitians were incapable of self-government.

Haiti's history colours its present. Though formally independent for over two centuries and a United Nations member, Haiti has been subject to repeated armed, violent interventions and even occupation by foreign powers; special mention must be made of a lengthy occupation by the USA from 1915 to 1934. Haiti faces humanitarian catastrophe once again: on 21 October 2024, the head of Haiti's Transitional Presidential Council formally requested that a Multinational Security Support Mission already present be converted to a full-fledged UN peacekeeping operation, just five years after their last departure.

For further reflections, see R Knox, 'Valuing Race? Stretched Marxism and the Logic of Imperialism' (2016) 4 London Review of International Law 81; and L Obrégon, 'Haiti and the Cosmopolitan Ambition' in M García-Salmones and P Slotte (eds), *Cosmopolitans in Enlightenment Europe and Beyond* (Peter Lang, 2013), 59.

1.2.3 **The nineteenth century and the rise of positivism (1815–1914)**

1.2.3.1 **The Congress of Vienna and the emergence of the 'Concert of Europe'**

The 1815 Congress of Vienna marked a turning point in European international relations. For the first time, certain 'Great Powers' (Austria, Great Britain, Prussia, Russia, and a rehabilitated France) within the 'Concert of Europe' could intervene collectively, where they deemed it necessary to preserve peace. The notion that certain States carried special responsibilities under international law, premised on a claimed or assumed cultural, material, or legal superiority, has persisted well into the twenty-first century.

Though the Concert of Europe system lacked any formal institutional structure and depended entirely on the goodwill of the Great Powers themselves, the system would entrench the idea that certain values needed safeguarding through international law. Between 1815 and 1870, the Concert of Europe convened more than twenty times to deal with revolutionary uprisings and forestall inter-State conflicts, particularly in the early years of the system: Austria intervened in Naples and Sardinia in the 1820s; Britain, France, and Russia intervened to secure the independence of Greece in 1832; and all the major powers intervened to secure the independence of Belgium in the 1830s. This resulted in the creation of a public law system in Europe through which the balance of power, and thus peace, would be maintained; it would serve Europe and facilitate its global expansion and conquest of much of the rest of the world.[26]

The Concert system would eventually unravel, with the last major interventions being those of the Western powers to defeat Russia in the Crimean War (1856)[27] and to prevent Russia from unduly punishing Turkey at the Congress of Berlin (1878). That said, its legacy that 'some States are more equal than others' persists to some degree: there are still five permanent members of the United Nations Security Council (see later, Section 1.4.2) which alone hold the power of veto in the only international organ capable of authorizing binding enforcement measures on all other States.

1.2.3.2 **The dominance of positivism**

Returning to doctrine, the nineteenth century was marked by key intellectual developments with respect to the law of nations. That movement coincided with the ideas of the Enlightenment taking hold within academic disciplines, including a commitment to scientific rationality and a preference for logical, empirical methods for uncovering knowledge. Within international law, the emergence of *positivism* as a dominant method of thinking would be a decisive blow against natural law reasoning, and laid the foundations for the contested claim that, despite its roots in Europe, the language of international law was in fact universal, rather than merely an instrument for expanding the material power of Europe and its settler offshoots.[28]

HISTORICAL BACKGROUND Auguste Comte and the Concept of Positivism

It was the French philosopher Auguste Comte who first coined the term 'positivism' to describe the move away from theological and metaphysical ways of thinking, looking instead at what has been created by human beings (see A Comte, *The Course in Positive Philosophy* (1830) and A Comte, *A General View of Positivism* (1848)).

Comte sought to apply the term across the natural and social sciences; but given the evolution of international law described earlier, positivism aptly describes the views about international law which became mainstream in the nineteenth century. Foremost among these was a decisive rejection of natural law as a valid source of international law. Positivists contended that only laws which had been consented to by States were valid, as these were the only entities

[26] G Simpson, *Great Powers and Outlaw States* (CUP, 2004), 93–115; and M Jarrett, *The Congress of Vienna and its Legacy: War and Great Power Diplomacy after Napoleon* (IB Tauris, 2013).

[27] The 1856 Paris Peace Treaty is also notable for how it belatedly 'recognized' the admission of Turkey to the 'advantages of public law and the European Concert': see Grewe (n 23) 462–3.

[28] For a rich alternative conception of the place of Eurocentrism in the nineteenth century, see A Becker Lorca, 'Universal International Law: Nineteenth-Century Histories of Imposition and Appropriation' (2010) 52 Harvard ILJ 475; and more generally, A Becker Lorca, *Mestizo International Law: A Global Intellectual History 1842–1933* (CUP, 2014).

empowered to create international law. Such rules could be consented to expressly, through written treaties, or they could emerge from unwritten practice, taking the form of custom. Moral or ethical considerations would henceforth be irrelevant in relation to whether a rule was valid or binding. Thus, rather than reflecting some higher political purpose, law became the instrument with which to achieve political goals and not their source.

The turn to positivism was to have far-reaching consequences for legal reasoning. Within domestic legal orders, law became dependent on the will of the sovereign, and it followed that, '[s]ince the Law of Nations is based on the common consent of individual States, and not of individual human beings, States solely and exclusively are the subjects of International Law'.[29] Within positivism, the centrality of the State would entrench a number of canonical principles which are still vital today, including:

- sovereign equality and the requirement of consent of a State to be bound by an obligation;
- freedom of a State from interference by another State in its internal affairs; and
- the entitlement of a State to ensure its survival or self-preservation, including by acts that might breach international law.[30]

1.2.3.3 Further developments in the nineteenth century

The nineteenth century was marked by unprecedented cooperation between States. The first permanent international organizations were founded, including the International Telegraphic Union (1865) and the Universal Postal Union (1874). Special arrangements were made to ensure freedom of navigation on the Rhine and Danube rivers, as well as the construction of the Suez and Panama canals. States began to engage in multilateral treaty-making on matters of common concern, such as the first Geneva Convention (1864) protecting the wounded during wartime.[31] These efforts would culminate in the 1899 and 1907 Hague Peace Conferences, the thirteen Hague Conventions on the conduct of war, and the Permanent Court of Arbitration, the first permanent institution to offer permanent services in relation to inter-State dispute settlement.[32]

Positivism also wrought changes for the discipline of international law, which began to be studied as a distinct subject within European universities. International law academics began to organize themselves professionally, with the foundation of both the

[29] L Oppenheim, *International Law* (1st edn, Longman, Green, 1905), 18; see also R Ago, 'Positive Law and International Law' (1957) 51 *AJIL* 691.

[30] These are examined later, in Section 1.6; but of course theory moved forward. A key recent work on the consolidation of international legal positivism from the late nineteenth century to the mid-twentieth, through Oppenheim and Kelsen in particular, is the work of M García-Salmones, *The Project of Positivism in International Law* (OUP, 2013).

[31] Convention for the Amelioration of the Condition of the Wounded in Armies in the Field (22 August 1864).

[32] See S Rosenne, *The Hague Peace Conferences of 1899 and 1907 and International Arbitration—Reports and Documents* (TMC Asser Press, 2001).

Institute of International Law and the International Law Association in 1873. Textbooks began to proliferate in several European languages in Europe and the Americas[33] which emphasized the cataloguing and systematizing of the raw materials of State practice to appeal to both the scholar and practitioner of international law.

Moreover, international lawyers recast themselves as neutral observers of political and diplomatic questions, and instead engaged in a technical, expert study of international legal rules. The strategy of depoliticization and professionalization of international lawyers during the nineteenth century was crucial in serving to advance Europe's self-proclaimed 'civilizing mission' during its unparalleled material and intellectual dominance of the world.[34] European States restricted participation in international relations primarily to Christian States; although the USA and the Latin American republics would soon enter the international State system, they were essentially offshoots of Europe, dominated by white, European settlers and replicating their internal structures, including adherence to the same capitalist economic model.

1.3 Colonialism and empire

Though colonialism was to reach its zenith in the nineteenth century, from the late fifteenth century onwards Europeans had engaged in the conquest of new territories in the pursuit of commodities, new trade routes, and political power. The role of international law in this phenomenon was twofold. On the one hand, in principle, international law could be a tool to resist European claims to expansion. As described earlier, Vitoria and Suárez had claimed to set limits on Spanish colonial expansion in the Americas, in particular with respect to the treatment of native populations; and Grotius maintained that certain resources, such as the high seas, could not be appropriated by a single State. Much later in 1807, Great Britain (as it was then known) would legislate to abolish the international slave trade and claim the right to board foreign ships to prevent that trade; and during the 1884–85 Congress of Berlin, European powers were exhorted to adhere to certain minimum standards of treatment of native populations as they proceeded to carve up the continent according to their own strategic preferences.[35]

Yet that rose-tinted, optimistic vision pales before the reality that, in many respects, international law was complicit, providing the legal vocabulary and concepts which

[33] See, e.g., H Wheaton, *Elements of International Law* (1st edn, 1836) (English, US); R Phillimore, *Commentaries upon International Law* (T and JW Johnson, 1854–61) (English, UK); AW Heffter, *Das Europäisches Völkerrecht der Gegenwart* (1st edn, Schröder, 1844) (German); C Calvo, *Derecho internacional teórico y práctico de Europa y América* (D'Amyot, 1868) (Spanish, Argentina); T Funck-Brentano and A Sorel, *Précis du droit des gens* (E Plon, 1877) (French); P Fiore, *Il Diriotto Internazionale Codificato et la Sua Sanzione Giuridica* (Unione Tipografica, 1890) (Italian).

[34] This is a central argument in M Koskenniemi, *The Gentle Civilizer of Nations: The Rise and Fall of International Law 1870–1960* (CUP, 2005), 127–36; see also Anghie (n 11) and Becker Lorca (n 28).

[35] See WN Medlicott, *The Congress of Berlin and After: A Diplomatic History of the Near East Settlement 1878–1880* (Methuen, 1938).

facilitated the conquest of non-European lands by European powers.[36] This can be illustrated by a number of doctrines which emerged during the colonial period, used even during and after the independence of the Latin American republics in the first third of the nineteenth century. Foremost is the *uti possedetis* principle, through which newly independent States' territorial claims would follow existing colonial boundaries—which had often been drawn not out of respect for local populations, but to accommodate imperial interests.[37] As late as the beginning of the twentieth century, indigenous populations were deemed to be perfectly capable of concluding lucrative trading contracts with Europeans conferring exclusive trading rights upon them, but were systematically denied recognition as sovereign States for being insufficiently stable or lacking a sufficient level of civilization to understand and to carry out the commands of international law.[38] Grotius' acclaimed freedom of the high seas facilitated European access to newly colonized lands and the protection of trade monopolies; and, of course, the trafficking of slaves.[39] Under international law, it was justifiable to enslave 'pagan' enemy-subjects at least since the time of Vitoria,[40] and the slave trade was explicitly lawful until the Brussels Conference of 1890.[41] Finally, the 1884 Congress of Berlin would become notorious, not because of its humanitarianism with respect to African populations, but because the European powers used international legal rules to facilitate the 'Scramble for Africa', in which almost all of the continent was divided between them.[42]

HISTORICAL BACKGROUND The 1884 Congress of Berlin

The 1884 Berlin Conference was called by German Chancellor Otto von Bismarck at the request of Portugal, and laid the legal foundation for the partitioning of Africa. There were fourteen European States represented, but no African representatives whatsoever: '[n]ever before, in the history of mankind, had a concert of one continent gathered together to plan how to share out another continent without the knowledge of the latter's leaders' (GN Uzoigwe, 'The Results of the Berlin West Africa Conference: An Assessment' in S Förster, WJ Mommen, and R Robinson (eds), *Bismarck, Europe and Africa: The Berlin Conference 1884–1885 and the Onset of Partition* (OUP, 1988), 541).

[36] Vital arguments on this point include the books by Anghie (n 11) and S Pahuja, *Decolonizing International Law* (CUP, 2013).

[37] V Nesiah, 'Placing International Law: White Spaces on a Map' (2003) 16 Leiden JIL 1; C Storr, 'Denaturalising the Concept of Territory in International Law' in J Dehm and U Natarajan (eds), *Locating Nature: Making and Unmaking International Law* (CUP, 2020).

[38] Vitoria (n 11) first articulated the doctrine in the wake of Spanish colonization of the Americas, but even John Westlake and Lassa Oppenheim still invoked the concept of 'civilization' to justify imperial practices: see M Clark, 'A Conceptual History of Recognition in British International Legal Thought' (2016) 87 BYBIL 18. See also N Tzouvala, *Capitalism as Civilisation* (CUP, 2020), esp ch 2, 'The Standard of Civilisation in the Nineteenth Century', in which racialized and civilizational tropes were invoked to withhold recognition.

[39] See M Craven, 'Colonialism and Domination' in B Fassbender and A Peters (eds), *The Oxford Handbook of the History of International Law* (OUP, 2012), 862 *et seq*.

[40] Anghie (n 11) 27.

[41] See JS Martínez, *The Slave Trade and the Origins of International Human Rights Law* (OUP, 2012).

[42] Anghie (n 11) 91–6; also see T Packenham, *The Scramble for Africa* (Abacus, 1992).

The Berlin Act of 26 February 1885 purported to prohibit slavery and protect freedom of trade and navigation. Instead, it provided the legal basis for European States to acquire territory the inhabitants of which were considered not to have attained 'civilization' and, consequently, could not hold sovereignty. The ancient doctrine of *terra nullius* was resuscitated to facilitate the conquest of vast and populated territories in Africa, with substantial indigenous populations, on the basis that they were 'ownerless'. The various forms of political organization of the African populations were deemed unable to 'own' territory as they were not sufficiently organized politically to be regarded as States in international law (J Fisch, 'Africa as *Terra Nullius*: The Berlin Conference and International Law' in S Förster, W Mommsen, and R Robinson (eds), *Bismarck, Europe and Africa: The Berlin Africa Conference 1884–1885 and the Onset of Partition* (OUP, 1988), 347, 354, *et seq*).

Another extraordinary outcome of the Berlin Conference was the recognition that King Leopold II of the Belgians could exercise sovereignty, through a private association, over an 'independent' Congolese State. In practice, Leopold II would exploit the Congo and extract its natural resources as though it were a personal possession.

For further information, see M Craven, 'Between Law and History: the Berlin Conference of 1884–1885 and the Logic of Free Trade' (2015) 3 LRIL 31; and the multimedia source database archived at 'Africa and the New Imperialism: European Borders on the African Continent, 1870–1914' (www.amdigital.co.uk).

The onslaught of European colonialism was virtually universal: only a few Asian and African States were able to resist European expansion. China and Siam (now Thailand) avoided that fate by signing a series of 'capitulations', unequal treaties giving European powers substantial trading rights and privileges in their territories.[43] Japan embarked on an audacious programme of modernization in the late nineteenth century, culminating in its own emergence as an imperial power.[44] Of the non-European powers, only the Ottoman Empire benefited from a position of formal equality, grudgingly bestowed upon it due to its substantial territories in the Balkans.[45] A few other countries—chiefly Persia (now Iran), Afghanistan, Nepal, and Bhutan—escaped formally being placed under European sovereignty or a protectorate, but were obliged to make far-reaching concessions to European powers.[46] Imperial expansion of Europe would continue well into the twentieth century: Ethiopia, the last independent African State, was conquered violently by Mussolini's Italy in 1936.[47]

[43] These included far-reaching exemptions from the application of domestic law in favour of the 'extraterritorial' application of the law of the European State: see A Peters, 'Unequal Treaties' in MPEPIL (2007), and the more critical approach of Tzouvala (n 38), ch 2.

[44] Japan concluded its first treaties with the USA in 1854 and with Germany in 1896. It would sign an alliance with Great Britain in 1902, and acceded to the Universal Postal Union in 1886. See further, G Le Moli, '"Parity with all Nations": the "Coolie" Trade and the Quest for Recognition by China and Japan' (2021) 34 Leiden JIL 879.

[45] In the modern era, the first treaty between a European State and the Ottoman Empire was the Instrument for the Prolongation of the Peace between the Holy Roman Emperor and the Sultan (1 July 1649) 1 CTS 457.

[46] Grewe (n 23) 443.

[47] The League's inaction in the face of desperate entreaties by Ethiopia is recounted vividly in *ibid*, 601–2.

1.4 The twentieth century

The twentieth century saw the consolidation of the international legal system which is still in place today. The dominant intellectual approach remained rooted in legal positivism, though with an increased awareness of the social foundations of law and, in the last decades of the twentieth century, increased reflection on its normative foundations. The twentieth century was punctuated by the two world wars, unprecedented in their violence and global reach, and the proliferation of international institutions which marked the end of each war. Though we are warned that the story of international law should not only be told through its crises and ruptures, as this serves to justify the status quo,[48] this approach is useful in mapping out how institutions were often created in response to political crises.

1.4.1 World War I and the League of Nations (1919–45)

Much has been written about the root causes and effects of the Great War (or World War I; 1914–18).[49] World War I marks the shift from a European-dominated international order to one in which other parts of the world, particularly the USA, were to gain an enhanced role. World War I ended with the Paris Peace Conference of 1919, in which the Allies (chief among them the UK, France, Italy, Japan, and the USA) were to impose terms on the defeated powers, in particular Germany, in the Treaty of Versailles.[50]

By far the most important development, for international lawyers at least, was the signing of the Covenant of the League of Nations, an ambitious endeavour that aimed at nothing less than, as Article 1 stated, to 'organize the international life of the family of nations'.[51] Headquartered in Geneva, the League was the first inter-State organization that aspired to universal membership, open to 'any fully self-governing State, Dominion or Colony'; it employed the first permanent international civil servants, working independently of all States.[52] Its broad mandate went beyond traditional technical matters, and included the establishment of the 'Mandate system' of governance over former German and Ottoman territories. For the first time, and perhaps in a last gasp of European colonialism, an international institution was tasked with 'creating sovereignty out of the backwards peoples and territories' under mandate.[53]

[48] H Charlesworth, 'International Law: A Discipline of Crisis' (2002) 65 MLR 377, 391.

[49] See, e.g., J Keegan, *The First World War* (Vintage, 2000); M Macmillan, *The War that Ended Peace: How Europe Abandoned Peace for the First World War* (Profile Books, 2014).

[50] A classic history of the League is EH Carr, *The Twenty Years' Crisis 1919–1939* (Perennial, 1939; Palgrave Macmillan reissue, 2001).

[51] See Art 1 of the Covenant of the League of Nations, in Part I of the Treaties of Peace between the Allies and each of the Central Powers in Versailles (Germany), Saint-Germain (Austria), Neuilly (Bulgaria), and Trianon (Hungary) (28 June 1919); for the Treaty of Versailles, see [1919] UKTS 4, 225 CTS 188. For a critical history, see GF Sinclair, *To Reform the World: International Organizations and the Making of Modern States* (OUP, 2017).

[52] A good history of the League is that of G Scott, *The Rise and Fall of the League of Nations* (Macmillan, 1973); see also Nussbaum (n 2) 251–90.

[53] See Anghie (n 11) 133; and generally, S Pedersen, *Guardians: The League of Nations and the Crisis of Empire* (OUP, 2015).

The League convened an Assembly in which all its members were represented. However, it was utterly dominated by its Council, on which permanent seats were held by the UK, France, Italy, and Japan, in a manner redolent of the earlier Concert of Europe, and thus further embedded the idea that powerful States had a special guardianship in the name of the 'international community'. In this respect, the League represents a bridge from the informal system of the Congress of Vienna to the institutional structures of the United Nations today.

HISTORICAL BACKGROUND The Permanent Court of International Justice (PCIJ), 1922

The League era was marked by the establishment of the Permanent Court of International Justice in The Hague. The very first international court, the PCIJ emerged after several earlier efforts at international adjudication had failed to bear fruit, and was tasked with the mandate of applying international law. The enumeration of the sources of international law to be applied by it, in Article 38 of the PCIJ Statute, would be the cornerstone of international legal sources (see Chapter 2).

The PCIJ bench would be dominated by European and American judges, which reflected the fact that only a few African and Asian States were not under colonial rule. Nevertheless, it would deliver thirty-two judgments between States and twenty-seven advisory opinions to organs of the League, and made a number of pronouncements regarded by scholars and practitioners as highly influential in the development of international law.

Regarded as modestly successful, the PCIJ was reborn within the UN system as the International Court of Justice (ICJ), which cites the case law of the PCIJ and with which there is much continuity: see Chapter 12 for further details on the structure of the ICJ.

On the relationship between the PCIJ and the ICJ, see G Hernández, *The International Court of Justice and the Judicial Function* (OUP, 2014), ch II.

Pursuant to Articles 12, 13, and 15 of the League Covenant, member States undertook to avoid recourse to war until a 'cooling-off' period of three months after a judicial or arbitral decision, or a report of the Council of the League. If a League member were to have resort to war in breach of the Covenant, all members were under a duty to sever trade and financial relations, including with nationals of the offending State.[54]

Another important milestone of the interwar (1919–39) period would be the signing of the 1928 'Kellogg–Briand Pact', known after the names of the American and French foreign secretaries who had led its adoption.[55] In the Pact, parties forswore resort to war as a means of national policy. Though weakened by the lack of an enforcement mechanism and a rather robust exception allowing recourse to war in

[54] Covenant of the League, Art 16.

[55] General Treaty for Renunciation of War as an Instrument of National Policy (1928) 94 LNTS 57 (No 2137). For a fascinating history, see O Hathaway and S Shapiro, *The Internationalists: How a Radical Plan to Outlaw War Remade the World* (Simon and Schuster, 2017).

self-defence,[56] the Kellogg–Briand Pact played a crucial role in laying down a prohibition on aggressive war which would later be embodied in the UN Charter.[57]

Although the League period would see several further innovations, including the first multilateral human rights treaties,[58] it was fatally crippled from the start by the non-participation of several crucial powers, and its failure to prevent the start of World War II. Despite the strong support of Woodrow Wilson, the US Senate did not ratify the Covenant of the League, partly due to the strong opposition to 'foreign entanglements' led by Senator Henry Cabot Lodge.[59] The Soviet Union, ostracized for its revolutionary communist government, joined only belatedly in 1934, and would be expelled in 1939 following its invasion of Finland. Germany, a defeated power, would only be granted admission in 1926 and would withdraw in 1933 under Hitler. Japan and Italy, despite being permanent Council members, withdrew in order to pursue territorial ambitions in Manchuria in 1932 and Ethiopia in 1936, respectively.[60]

1.4.2 **The United Nations during the Cold War (1945–89)**

World War II was fought across the world with unprecedented savagery, with more than 60 million killed by its end. It was in response to this that the Charter of the United Nations was signed in San Francisco on 26 June 1945, signifying a new chapter in the international order through the creation of this new organization.[61] The Charter came into force on 24 October 1945, in the shadow of the immense destruction wrought by the dropping of atomic bombs on Hiroshima and Nagasaki in August 1945. The need to prevent further war and strengthen international order had scarcely seemed more pressing.

Like the League of Nations, the United Nations aimed above all to preserve international peace and security; however, as Article 1 of the Charter demonstrates, the UN's purposes went further. The Charter contained lofty aspirations for the UN, especially to promote respect for equal rights and the self-determination of peoples and a 'universal peace' between States. It also called for cooperation on economic, social, cultural, and humanitarian questions, and promoted respect for human rights without discrimination. Article 1 charged the United Nations itself to be a centre for harmonizing the

[56] This exception was interpreted expansively: the USA contended through the 'Monroe Doctrine' that it could intervene in self-defence throughout the Americas, and the UK asserted a right to defend 'certain regions of the world, the welfare and integrity of which constitute a special and vital interest for our peace and security': see A Cassese, *International Law* (2nd edn, OUP, 2003), 37.

[57] See later, Section 1.4.2.

[58] See, e.g., the Convention to Suppress the Slave Trade and Slavery (1926) 60 LNTS 254 (No 1414); and the eight fundamental ILO Conventions which created international labour standards for the first time: see <http://www.ilo.org/global/standards/introduction-to-international-labour-standards/conventions-and-recommendations/lang--en/index.htm>. Nicolas Politis, an influential Greek scholar, commended these tentative acknowledgements of individual human rights as a first 'wobble' in the 'iron cage' of State sovereignty: see N Politis, *Les nouvelles tendances du droit international* (Hachette, 1927), 91–2.

[59] See further, M Macmillan, *Paris 1919: Six Months that Changed the World* (Random House, 2003).

[60] Italy was the only State subjected to sanctions under the League system, but these were only imposed after Ethiopia had been fully conquered.

[61] Charter of the United Nations, 1 UNTS xvi; UKTS 67 (1946), Cmd 7015 (signed 26 June 1945, entry into force 26 October 1945).

actions of States in the attainment of these common ends, and it has fostered a number of specialized agencies and subsidiary organs to help it to attain these purposes.

The United Nations Organization is headquartered in New York, signifying a shift of the centre of power away from Europe, and it has gone much further than the League in creating multilateral institutions to maintain collective security and promote international cooperation. The UN's institutional structure, with six principal organs (see Chapter 6, Section 6.7.1) represented an iterative evolution from the basic structure of the League, with a deliberative General Assembly composed of all States, a powerful Security Council with responsibility (and considerable discretion) over collective security, and the ICJ, the continuation of the PCIJ, as its principal judicial organ. The United Nations figures prominently throughout this book; the following discussion will be limited to its origins and the three pillars of peace and security, international cooperation, and development.

The UN Charter's striking feature is the ambitious prohibition, in Article 2(4), on recourse to war and the use of force in inter-State relations. Chapter VII of the Charter endows the Security Council with the power to order sanctions which bind all States, or even to take forcible measures against a State which is a threat to, or has breached, international peace and security. Article 51 of the Charter recognizes an inherent right to take forcible measures in self-defence—the only exception in the Charter.[62] The Security Council's composition became crucial to the new system of collective security: with permanent seats (and a veto on substantive matters under Article 27(3)) for China,[63] France, the Soviet Union, the UK, and the USA, it again reprises the Great Power-dominated approach which had prevailed after the Congress of Vienna and throughout the League period.

A second pillar of the Charter system is the promotion of international cooperation. The UN and its specialized agencies facilitate collaboration across sectors ranging from human rights to civil aviation, food, agriculture and health standards, and atomic energy. These are supported by the 'Bretton Woods' financial institutions, the World Bank and the International Monetary Fund, which guarantee economic stability and encourage economic development and trade liberalization along a free-market model.[64]

The third pillar, in relation to development, reflects the gaining of independence of dozens of former European colonies across Africa and Asia. By 1960, newly independent States (then known as the 'Third World') had gained a numerical majority in the General Assembly. They challenged the Eurocentric orientation of international law through informal groupings such as the 'Non-Aligned Movement' and the 'Group of 77' (G77), and sought to use international law to address their relative disadvantage in economic, social, and political development.[65] Some of the chief objectives of the newly

[62] These are addressed in Chapter 14. Article 43 of the Charter even envisages the creation of a standing UN peacekeeping force, though this never materialized.

[63] In 1945, it was the 'Nationalist' Government of Chiang Kai-Shek which was represented on the Council; the Communist People's Republic of China would only take up the Chinese seat after the passing of UNGA Res 2758 (25 October 1971).

[64] See Chapter 20 for further discussion.

[65] See RP Anand, 'Attitude of the Afro-Asian States towards Certain Problems of International Law' (1966) 15 ICLQ 35; TO Elias, *New Horizons in International Law* (Hague Academy Publications, 1980); Pahuja (n 36); and J von Bernstorff and P Dann (eds), *The Battle for International Law (I): South-North Perspectives on the Decolonization Era* (OUP, 2019).

independent States were achieving recognition of the right of self-determination of colonized peoples,[66] a commitment to racial equality,[67] and a renewal of the scope of State sovereignty to account for economic development and permanent sovereignty over natural resources.[68] Newly independent States also played a key role in what in the 1980s was heralded as the 'new law of the sea', the balancing of interests that was achieved with the adoption of the United Nations Convention on the Law of the Sea (UNCLOS).[69]

The Charter era also saw a significant change with the subjects of international law themselves: States. Nearly immediately after the inception of the UN, a significant rivalry characterized the relations between the capitalist USA and its allies, on the one hand (the so-called 'First World'), and the communist Soviet Union and its allies, on the other (the so-called 'Second World'). Through the wielding of the veto, the Cold War[70] would paralyse the United Nations, and in particular the Security Council, for several decades after 1945.[71] Deadlock would ensue on a great number of significant geopolitical issues of the period, with important historical episodes including the Berlin Airlift of 1961, the Cuban Missile Crisis of 1962, and the Vietnam War, which ended only in 1975. The Cold War would persist until 1989, when the communist East European States would transition to liberal, free-market economies, culminating with the dissolution of the Soviet Union in 1991.[72]

HISTORICAL BACKGROUND The Legacy of Communist (Soviet) Approaches to International Law

It would seem today that to study 'communist' approaches to international law is largely obsolete, given the collapse of the Soviet Union and the integration of China, Vietnam, and other communist States into the globalized economy. Yet it is instructive to recall some of its legacies, as the classic Marxist–Leninist theory of international law in fact envisaged a post-State paradigm for global governance based on socialist values. It was claimed that as States would undergo communist revolutions and adopt non-capitalist economic systems, they would eventually wither away in favour of 'socialist internationalism'.

[66] See the Declaration on the Granting of Independence to Colonial Countries and Peoples, UNGA Res 1514 (XV) (14 December 1960). The principle of self-determination of peoples would later be enshrined in Art 1 of the two human rights covenants: see further Chapter 16, Section 16.3.2.

[67] See International Convention on the Elimination of All Forms of Racial Discrimination (adopted 21 December 1965, entry into force 4 January 1969), 660 UNTS 165.

[68] See Chapter 20, Section 20.1, for the discussion on the declaration and plan of action for the 'New International Economic Order'.

[69] On the drafting history of UNCLOS, see Chapter 18, Section 18.2; and O Schachter, *International Law in Theory and Practice* (Martinus Nijhoff, 1991), ch XIII ('The New Law of the Sea').

[70] The term 'Cold War', generally understood to reference the indirect and non-military confrontation which had emerged after World War II between the Soviet Union and the Western Allies, was first used by George Orwell in the UK *Observer* newspaper (10 March 1946).

[71] Though there were eighteen peacekeeping missions during the Cold War, there were few military interventions authorized by the Security Council before 1990, the most prominent exception being the intervention in the Korean peninsula: see Chapter 14, Section 14.5.2.2.2.

[72] A vivid history of the impact of that specific period is the edited book by M Craven, S Pahuja and G Simpson (eds), *International Law and the Cold War* (CUP, 2019).

For the Soviet Union, being surrounded by capitalist States, a 'transitional' approach became necessary, whereby other States could be engaged on the basis of international law, but only as a temporary measure before attaining universal socialism. Ultimately, as Grigory Tunkin would describe it in his *Theory of International Law* (WE Butler tr, Harvard UP, 1974), the communist approach to international law would develop three tenets (p 4):

(i) principles of socialist internationalism would govern relations between socialist States;

(ii) principles of equality and self-determination would be invoked in a battle against colonialism; and

(iii) principles of peaceful coexistence would form an overarching framework for international relations.

Because socialist internationalism presupposed justified interventions to preserve socialism, the Soviet Union intervened forcibly in Hungary (1956) and Czechoslovakia (1968) on the basis of the first principle (Tunkin, 431–43). Between socialist and capitalist States, however, 'peaceful coexistence' was interpreted as a strong protection against intervention, so that States with different social systems could coexist (G Tunkin, 'Co-existence and International Law' (1958) 95 Recueil des Cours 1, 51, *et seq*). The People's Republic of China, the other major communist State, would not fully embrace the Soviet vision of international law (see C Kim, 'The People's Republic of China and the Charter-based International Legal Order' (1978) 72 AJIL 317).

The obvious tension between how socialist States could relate to one another and how they were to coexist with capitalist States was never fully resolved. As the onset of *perestroika* (reform of the economic and political system) took hold in the Soviet Union, its foreign policy also shifted. With the end of the Cold War and the 1991 disintegration of the Soviet Union, Russia and its other successor States would abandon claims to a distinctive socialist approach.

Russia does not today advocate for a wholly different theory of international law, despite a distinct tradition of scholarship that stands apart: see further L Malksöo, *Russian Approaches to International Law* (OUP, 2015).

Though the sovereign State has remained the central subject of international law post-1945, great strides were achieved in new sectors such as the oceans (see Chapter 18) and outer space, or the laws of armed conflict (Chapter 15). The first treaties on disarmament, including the Treaty on the Non-Proliferation of Nuclear Weapons,[73] were signed. The 1972 Stockholm Declaration heralded new thinking on protection of the global environment (Chapter 19). The recognition of individual human rights would also advance greatly, beginning with the adoption of the 1948 Universal Declaration of Human Rights, and culminating with the adoption of the two great human rights covenants in 1966.[74] These would be complemented by regional human rights treaty frameworks and courts in the Americas, Europe, and Africa.[75]

[73] 729 UNTS 161 (signed 1 July 1968, entry into force 5 March 1970).

[74] International Covenant on Civil and Political Rights (signed 19 December 1966, entry into force 23 March 1976), 999 UNTS 171; International Covenant on Economic, Social and Cultural Rights (signed 19 December 1966, entry into force 3 January 1976), 993 UNTS 3.

[75] American Convention on Human Rights (signed 22 November 1969, entry into force 18 July 1978) 1144 UNTS 123; European Convention on Human Rights (signed 4 November 1950, entry into force 3 September 1953) 213 UNTS 221; and African Charter on Human and People's Rights (signed 27 June 1981, entry into force 21 October 1986) 1520 UNTS 217.

1.5 International law since 1989

1.5.1 The end of the Cold War

The Cold War came to an abrupt end in 1989, with the collapse of communist governments across Eastern Europe and, in 1991, the disintegration of the Soviet Union into fifteen States. The Russian Federation (or 'Russia') inherited the Soviet Union's permanent seat on the Security Council, albeit with a vastly diminished territory and population. States would no longer be divided into three ideologically divided 'worlds'; and the promise of a revitalized international legal order seemed to beckon. Scholarship relating to new developments, though still filtered through the lens of positivism, began to take on a strongly normative character, guided by liberal ideals of democracy and free-market economics.[76]

1.5.2 The 1990s and 2000s

At first glance, developments in the 1990s seemed to suggest that the international order had been revitalized. The Security Council began to authorize new interventions in Kuwait (1990), Somalia (1992), Bosnia-Herzegovina and other parts of the former Yugoslavia (1992–5), and Haiti (1994).[77] The World Trade Organization, the institutional successor to the General Agreement on Tariffs and Trade (GATT), was established in 1994.[78] The docket of the ICJ sprang to life, with more cases decided in the 1990s and 2000s than in the entire lifespan of the Court and its predecessor.[79] In 1994, Protocol 11 of the European Convention on Human Rights (ECHR) allowed individuals to petition the European Court of Human Rights (ECtHR) directly and endowed that Court with compulsory jurisdiction over all parties to the Convention. Finally, after establishing temporary, 'ad hoc' Tribunals in relation to the international crimes committed in conflicts in the former Yugoslavia and Rwanda, the Rome Statute for the International Criminal Court (ICC) was adopted in 1998, establishing a permanent international court to prosecute individuals having committed international crimes.[80]

The first decades of the 2000s have not kept pace with the rapid institutional changes of the 1990s. There have been ambitious measures, such as the UN Sustainable Development Goals,[81] that have been characterized by renewed concern with issues requiring global collective action, such as over terrorism, damage to the global environment, and inequality in economic development. However, these have usually proven incremental in their scope.

[76] This would arrogantly be called 'the end of history': F Fukuyama, *The End of History and the Last Man* (Free Press, 1992); see also TM Franck, *The Power of Legitimacy among Nations* (OUP, 1990).

[77] These are covered later, in Chapter 14.

[78] The WTO is covered later, in Chapter 20.

[79] The ICJ and its work are covered later, in Chapter 12.

[80] The history leading up to the ICC is covered later, in Chapter 17.

[81] UNGA Res 70/1 (21 October 2015).

1.6 The contemporary international legal system

The historical overview provided in this chapter was intended to provide the reader with a sense that international law did not spring up in a vacuum, but has evolved over time to address new challenges and the needs of States. There have been few revolutions, whether conceptual or institutional; instead, international law has evolved incrementally, with States devising new institutions or methods of lawmaking to suit their needs. The metaphor of *sedimentation* comes to mind, with new features gradually deposited over the system's foundations without disturbing them.

In what follows, we will survey the foundational concepts that underpin the current international legal order.

1.6.1 Sovereign equality of States

The foundational premise upon which international law has always rested is that it purports to regulate relations between States. States, it is true, are not metaphysical entities but political communities ultimately composed of individuals, and represented in their activities by them. Yet, and partly as a consequence of the positivist legal theory that still dominates mainstream thinking, the doctrine persists that States are autonomous entities capable of expressing a will or an interest, characterized by a number of features including an effective governmental apparatus, control over a distinct territory, and authority over a population.[82] International law also regulates the conduct of international and regional organizations (chief among them the United Nations) that have been created by States to fulfil specific functions; these will be addressed in Section 1.6.4 and in Chapter 6. It is also true that international law has grown in complexity and also regulates, in an ancillary way, the conduct of other actors, such as individuals, multinational corporations, and even non-governmental organizations, as will be seen throughout this book. However, these remain secondary characters in a legal order dominated by States and, to a degree international organizations.

A striking feature of States is their 'sovereign equality', a linchpin of international law embodied in Article 2(1) of the UN Charter, and which embraces two distinct notions. 'Equality' is formal: whatever the population, economic weight, or military power of a State, it enjoys equal footing as an international legal subject. As Vattel famously observed, 'a dwarf is as much a man as a giant; a small republic is no less a sovereign State than the most powerful kingdom'.[83] As the General Assembly proclaimed in its Declaration on Friendly Relations in 1970, '[a]ll States enjoy sovereign equality. They have equal rights and duties and are equal members of the international community, notwithstanding differences of an economic, social, political or other nature.'[84]

[82] A Verdross and B Simma, *Universelles Völkerrecht: Theorie und Praxis* (3rd edn, Duncker & Humblot, 1984), para 380 argue that a State is a *civitas perfecta*, binding a nation's people (*Staatsvolk*) permanently together through a 'community of destiny' (*Schicksalsgemeinschaft*).

[83] Vattel, *Le droit des gens* (n 20), i, 47 ('Préliminaires', §18).

[84] UNGA Res 2625 (XXV), 'Declaration on Principles of International Law concerning Friendly Relations and Co-operation among States in accordance with the Charter of the United Nations' (24 October 1970).

Bodin's theory of sovereignty, outlined earlier, has both outward-facing and inward-facing dimensions, referring to both the freedom of a State from the commands of any other State, and its 'original', exclusive power to wield legal authority, by force if necessary, over its subjects.[85] Externally, sovereignty of a State requires that no other State seeks to undermine its sovereignty, for example by overthrowing its government or seeking to influence it through coercion.[86] On the internal plane, sovereignty endows a State with the exclusive power to exercise public functions over the individuals and territory under its jurisdiction. It may pass laws, prescribe regulations, and establish institutions such as courts, administrative bodies, and police to apply and enforce its legislation.[87] Though in a globalized world States are increasingly interconnected and interdependent, sovereignty remains a key concept through which to assess the place of States.

1.6.2 **Decentralized authority**

The decentralized nature of international law is its second characteristic feature. This is unlike most national legal systems, usually called 'domestic' or 'municipal' legal orders by international lawyers, where there is usually a single entity recognized as sovereign. International law recognizes multiple and equal sovereign entities, States, and purports to regulate relations between them. With no legislature that stands supreme over States, it therefore remains a *horizontal* legal order with no superior authority. This means that States must come together to create new legal obligations, such as through treaties or through customary international law. In Chapter 2, the sources through which States create new international law will be examined.

1.6.3 **The basis of obligation of international law**

The external dimension of sovereignty suggests that, subject to respect for the sovereignty of other States, States enjoy considerable freedom of action. They may design their political or economic system as they wish, and pass legislation that reflects the values they wish to enshrine. States' freedom of action was historically quite broad, including recourse to war (see earlier, Sections 1.2.1 and 1.4.1), a perfectly legitimate instrument of a State's foreign policy. Today, the UN Charter and several important multilateral instruments limit States' freedom of action, especially prohibiting force against other States, and enjoining them to respect certain fundamental human rights. What is more, the emergence of peremptory norms (see Chapter 3) have further entrenched non-derogable obligations that all States must respect.

[85] Bodin (n 13) 28. By 'original' is meant that the power in question is inherent in statehood and does not derive from a higher order: see B Fassbender, 'Die Souveränität des Staates also Autonomic Rahmen der völkerrechtlichen Verfassing' in H-P Mansel et al (eds), *Festschrift für Erik Jayme* (Sellier European Law Publishers, 2004), 1089, 1090.

[86] H Kelsen, 'The Principle of Sovereign Equality of States as a Basis for International Organization' (1944) 53 Yale LJ 207, 208.

[87] A classic work on a sovereign's power to enact legislation is John Austin, *The Province of Jurisprudence Determined* (John Murray, 1832), 117.

Under the classical view of international law, the binding nature of such obligations for States seems, above all, based on *consent*. Consent entails that only those obligations to which a State has committed itself will be considered binding.[88] An important consideration in this regard is the principle of *reciprocity*, which means simply that States consent to limit their freedom of action for mutual benefit. Regulated conduct is thus relational, with reciprocity a pragmatic policy to protect a State's interests on the basis of law.[89] Accordingly, a State, several States, or all States may create new legal norms to govern the relations between them, provided that they express their consent to be bound by such rules.

Consent and reciprocity are accompanied by the requirement, now reflected in Article 2(2) of the UN Charter, that obligations assumed by States be performed in good faith.[90] 'Good faith' is an appeal to mutual consideration and cooperation between States, to act without fraud or malice. Though legal disputes will inevitably arise, they will arise due to genuine differences of opinion and not purely strategic interests. Another reflection of the principle of good faith is found in Article 26 of the Vienna Convention on the Law of Treaties, which enjoins States to comply with their agreements in good faith: *pacta sunt servanda*.[91]

A strictly positivist view on the nature of international law would entail that, as a system, it is entirely based on consent, and that no 'objective law' besides those which have been consented to can exist.[92] As Hersch Lauterpacht memorably put it in his 8th edition of *Oppenheim's International Law*, if consent is crucial to international law, '[t]he sources of International Law are therefore twofold, namely: (1) *express* consent, which is given when States conclude a treaty stipulating certain rules for the future international conduct of the parties; (2) *tacit* consent, that is, implied consent or consent by conduct, which is given through States having adopted the custom of submitting to certain rules of international conduct'.[93]

The strictly consent-based vision has come under tentative challenge.[94] To take a notable example, Verdross and Simma, in their German-language textbook *Universelles Völkerrecht*, argued that State consent was insufficient to ground international law as a system. Instead, they contended that a presupposed, overarching notion bound States and other subjects of international law, a *formlosen Konsensus* ('shapeless consensus') through which States recognize one another as equal and sovereign, but also subject to 'original norms' necessary for the creation of further law. Their theory contends that international law, or its fundamental precepts at least, has transcended the 'mere' will of States and stands above their agreements.[95] They argued strongly in favour of

[88] H Lauterpacht, *Oppenheim's International Law* (8th edn, Longman and Sons, 1955), 15.

[89] See J Combacau and S Sur, *Droit international public* (12th edn, LGDJ, 2016), 28.

[90] On good faith more generally, see R Kolb, 'Article 2(2)' in B Simma et al (eds), *Commentary to the Charter of the United Nations* (3rd edn, OUP, 2012), 167–73.

[91] On good faith and *pacta sunt servanda*, see later, Chapter 7, Section 7.4.1.

[92] Combacau and Sur (n 89) 22–3.

[93] Lauterpacht (n 88) 25.

[94] See, e.g., Crawford, *Brownlie's Principles* (n 21) 16.

[95] A Verdross and B Simma, *Universelles Völkerrecht. Theorie und Praxis* (Duncker & Humblot, 1976), in para 21, suggest that Kant's *Völkerbund*, through which a State's security is a matter both for it and to be protected through a global institution, has been transformed into positive law through the adoption of the UN Charter.

imperative norms of law which are absolutely valid,[96] a related concept to the idea of peremptory norms of international law (*jus cogens*). Though in no way suggesting that States are no longer sovereign and equal, their claim is that States are henceforth regulated under and within the international legal system. In a recent work, Anne Peters has taken these ideas even further, suggesting that a process of 'humanization' has taken place such that international law has been restructured into a system where the interests of individuals are paramount.[97] Such a radical account may represent more of a cry for reform than a reflection of existing law, and has not gone without vehement objection;[98] but it gives pause for reflection as to the current trajectory of international law.

1.6.4 **Is international law a 'system'?**

This brings us to the point that has plagued international legal scholars for centuries; namely, whether international law constitutes a functioning system that deserves the name of law. John Austin famously suggested in the nineteenth century that international law was only 'law improperly so-called', as it lacked an overarching sovereign who could issue commands that could be enforced through the application of coercive force or sanction.[99]

THEORY AND DEBATES Hart, Kelsen, and the Nature of the International Legal System

The positivist tradition that thrived in the nineteenth century continues to underpin the foundations of thinking about international law today. How is it, then, that two of the most distinguished positivist scholars in domestic law theory, Hans Kelsen and Herbert Hart, rejected the idea that international law could be viewed as a proper legal system?

Hans Kelsen sought, above all, to distil the essence of law from notions of morality, ethics, and justice, which to him were matters of politics. Law was a system of rules which provided normative guidance for human behaviour, and legal rules depended for their validity on a prior norm. Each norm depended on a higher norm for its validity, with the highest norms dependent on what is termed the basic norm (*Grundnorm*), a foundation for the entire legal system (H Kelsen, 'The Pure Theory of Law' (translated into English in (1934) 50 LQR 474, 477–85)). Such a system could not be said to exist in international law, which he regarded as a primitive legal order resembling a pre-State society, given its lack of legislative, adjudicative, and enforcement organs (see H Kelsen, *Principles of International Law* (2nd edn, Princeton UP, 1966), 563, *et seq*).

[96] *Ibid*, paras 45–51.

[97] A Peters, *Beyond Human Rights: The Legal Status of the Individual in International Law* (J Huston tr, CUP, 2016), 25, 408, 430, 553–4.

[98] See Combacau and Sur (n 89) 75, who deny the objective character of the UN Charter and insist that international law is nothing more than the legal acts of States, with no systematic structure linking these.

[99] Austin, *Province of Jurisprudence* (n 87) 171.

Herbert Hart drew on the work of Kelsen but adopted a 'descriptive sociological' approach, portraying a legal system as encompassing three separate categories of legal rules: (i) primary rules, which set out standards of conduct and interaction; (ii) secondary rules (rules of adjudication, enforcement, and change), which underpinned the primary rules and confirmed their validity; and (iii) a master 'rule of recognition' which enables an observer to identify the components of the system and to treat them as legal. Hart's theory depended on the 'internal point of view' of legal officials, systemic agents who are entrusted with the application of the secondary rules, and their acceptance of the system that could generate primary rules through the process of secondary rules. It was this combination that constituted the essence of law (see HLA Hart, *The Concept of Law* (3rd edn, Clarendon Press, 2012), ch V). Hart regarded international law as lacking in the 'rule of recognition', and also deficient with respect to secondary rules of adjudication, enforcement, and change (ch X).

For further reading, see J von Berstorff, *The Public International Law Theory of Hans Kelsen* (CUP, 2010); the articles collected in 'The European Tradition of International Law' (1998) 9 EJIL 287 *et seq*; and for a more critical perspective, J Beckett, 'The Hartian Tradition in International Law' (2008) 1 Journal of Jurisprudence 57.

It is perhaps too easy to dismiss these arguments by contending that international law's existence as a legal system depends ultimately on one's theoretical conception of a legal system. But if one looks at the daily operation of international law, compliance with international legal obligations is regarded as being very high. Yet there exist few enforcement mechanisms, aside from the limited institutional safeguards States might have created through international organizations. Quoted to the point of cliché, Louis Henkin famously opined that '[a]lmost all nations observe almost all principles of international law and almost all of their obligations almost all of the time'.[100]

It is true that international law arises in the media most often because of its perceived failings: from trade disputes to humanitarian catastrophes to violent armed conflicts, the inability of international law to secure the common good is well known. Less known, however, are the mundane functions that international law facilitates: the delivery of international postage, the stability of the world's telecommunications infrastructure, and the delivery of goods and services across the globe each day demonstrate that compliance with international law remains, in the main, surprisingly high.[101] As James Crawford put it in the most recent edition of *Brownlie's Principles of Public International Law*, '[i]nternational law provides—in significant part—not merely the vocabulary of inter-State relations but its underlying grammar'.[102] The present author agrees: it is too simplistic to adhere to the view that international law is not law because it is institutionally deficient. International law contains many of the seeds of a

[100] L Henkin, *How Nations Behave* (2nd edn, Columbia UP, 1979), 47.

[101] In an important piece published in 1997, Harold Koh took Henkin's point further: see HH Koh, 'Why Do Nations Obey International Law?' (1997) 106 Yale LJ 2599.

[102] Crawford, *Brownlie's Principles* (n 21) 14–15.

recognizable legal system, including recognized legal sources (Chapter 2), international legal persons in the form of States and international organizations (Chapters 5 and 6), rules of interpretation to be applied by impartial third parties (Chapter 7), precepts of responsibility for breach (Chapter 10), and even a hierarchy of norms (Chapter 3). What is more, there is a sophisticated and well-developed community of international lawyers who share a common vocabulary and approach to international law, and are highly influential within foreign ministries, universities, legal practice, and even non-governmental activism: to adopt another cliché, they are the 'invisible college' of international lawyers.[103] Though a system based on the consent of States, its primary legal subjects, it is no less a legal system for it.

1.7 Contemporary debates in international law

Though the key principles of contemporary international law described previously are vital to understanding the subject, it is important briefly to address some persuasive criticisms of international law. The development of international law has been decidedly Eurocentric, not merely in its origins but because the regional law on inter-State relations from Europe has somehow managed, through imperial expansion accompanied by a repeated claim to being a universal language, to remain globally relevant even today.[104] Even within the dominant Western traditions, scholarship has outlined differences between American and European approaches to international law.[105] Cogent concerns have been expressed about the purported universality of public international law.[106] Moreover, there is prominent scholarship on non-Western approaches, including a Chinese approach to international law,[107] an Islamic approach to international law,[108] and the international law tradition in Latin America.[109]

[103] O Schachter, 'The Invisible College of International Lawyers' (1977) 72 Northwestern University LR 217. See also G Hernández, 'The Responsibility of the International Legal Academic: Situating the Grammarian in the "Invisible College"' in J d'Aspremont, T Gazzini, A Nollkaemper, and W Werner (eds), *International Law as a Profession* (CUP, 2017), 160.

[104] Tzouvala (n 9) 430–2 suggests that it is this Eurocentrism that requires scrutiny, as it remains relevant today in the development of the international State system.

[105] E Jouannet, 'French and American Perspectives on International Law: Legal Cultures and International Law' (2006) 58 Melbourne LR 292, 299; A Bradford and EA Posner, 'Universal Exceptionalism in International Law' (2011) 52 Harvard ILJ 1, 35; see also, generally, M Byers and G Nolte (eds), *United States Hegemony and the Foundations of International Law* (CUP, 2013).

[106] A Roberts, *Is International Law Really International?* (OUP, 2017), has undertaken a comparative empirical analysis of international legal education and the influence of national legal cultures.

[107] Xue Hanqin, *Chinese Contemporary Perspectives on International Law* (Brill, 2012), 151–7; H Chiu, 'Communist China's Attitude Toward International Law' (1966) 60 AJIL 245, 260; C Kim, 'The People's Republic of China and the Charter-based International Legal Order' (1978) 72 AJIL 317.

[108] T Roeder, 'Traditional Islamic Approaches to Public International Law—Historic Concepts, Modern Implications' (2012) 72 ZaöRV 521, 522.

[109] Becker Lorca (n 28). See also L Obregón, L Betancur and J Amaya-Castro (eds), *The Oxford Handbook on International Law in the Americas* (OUP, 2023); JP Scarfi, *The Hidden History of International Law in the Americas: Empire and Legal Networks* (OUP, 2017).

Beyond calling attention to various regional traditions, some innovative international legal scholarship has increasingly drawn from a broadly 'critical tradition', calling attention to the negative consequences of international law for those who have been excluded from participating in its development.[110] Most of these critical approaches are not in themselves coherent projects, but rather umbrella terms used to capture a range of challenges in the purported neutrality and universality of international law.

Three such traditions merit particular mention. Postcolonial scholars, in particular those adopting 'Third World Approaches to International Law' (TWAIL), have called attention to Eurocentric colonial legacy in international law, demonstrating how the early distinctions between the European and non-European world, notably through the terms 'civilized' and 'uncivilized', may persist in today's contemporary legal order.[111] Recently, powerful critiques have emerged about the legacy of racism on the international plane.[112] TWAIL has its ambivalences, as it does not necessarily reflect the strategic priorities of developing States that were formerly considered the 'Third World', but focuses rather on the interests of Third World peoples.[113] A feminist critique has powerfully challenged the purported neutrality and objectivity of international law, suggesting that the hierarchies and oppression engendered by international law exist not as a matter of necessity but as a culturally and historically specific development.[114] After the collapse of communism in the Soviet Union and Eastern Europe, there has been a reconsideration of Marxist perspectives in international law which has challenged the capitalist foundations of international law, calling for an understanding and analysis of the material conditions and history that have caused the emergence of the ideas that now structure international law.[115] Together, such challenges would serve to discredit the myth that international law is politically neutral. They have, in turn, fed into scholarship that takes on the critical challenge but

[110] See, e.g., A Orford (ed), *International Law and its Others* (CUP, 2006); F Johns, *Non-Legality in International Law* (CUP, 2013).

[111] See, e.g., B Rajagopal, *International Law from Below: Development, Social Movements, and Third World Resistance* (CUP, 2003); NK Modirzadeh, '"Let Us All Agree to Die a Little": TWAIL's Unfulfilled Promise' (2023) 65 Harvard ILJ 79; *cf* G Abi-Saab, 'The Third World Intellectual in Praxis: Confrontation, Participation, or Operating Behind Enemy Lines?' (2016) 37 Third World Quarterly 1957.

[112] ET Achiume and DW Carbado, 'Critical Race Theory Meets Third World Approaches to International Law' (2021) 67 *UCLA Law Review* 1462; and C Gevers, 'Unwhitening the World: Rethinking Race and International Law' (2021) 67 UCLA Law Review 1652; M Al Attar, 'Must International Legal Pedagogy Remain Eurocentric?' (2021) 11 Asian JIL 176.

[113] A Anghie, *The Third World and International Order: Law, Politics and Globalization* (Martinus Nijhoff, 2003); BS Chimni, 'Third World Approaches to International Law: A Manifesto' (2006) 8 International Community Law Review 3–27; U Baxi, 'What May the "Third World" Expect from International Law?' in R Falk, B Rajagopal, and J Stevens (eds), *International Law and the Third World* (Routledge-Cavendish, 2008).

[114] See H Charlesworth and C Chinkin, *The Boundaries of International Law: A Feminist Analysis* (Manchester UP, 2000); G Heathcote, *Feminist Dialogues on International Law: Successes, Tensions, Futures* (OUP, 2019); S Kouvo and Z Pearson (eds), *Feminist Approaches to International Law: Between Resistance and Compliance* (Hart, 2011).

[115] See, e.g., C Miéville, *Between Equal Rights: A Marxist Theory of International Law* (Pluto Press, 2005); BS Chimni, *International Law and World Order* (2nd edn, CUP, 2017); and the collection of essays in S Marks (ed), *International Law on the Left: Re-examining Marxist Legacies* (CUP, 2008), esp 1–13.

has sought to defend the positivist foundations of international law, even if through different methodological lenses.[116]

Some scholars have tried to describe international law through the cognate discipline of international relations scholarship, drawing from various schools. One of these is 'Realism', which dismisses law as secondary and focuses on the struggle for power between States.[117] Another is 'institutionalism', which would suggest that though law and institutions are often instrumentalized, they offer distinct advantages which induce States to respect law and join institutions they regard as legitimate.[118] One might also consider 'network theories' of transnational communication, rooted in liberalism, which seek to describe how individuals, acting within and between international institutions, are the primary actors in international society.[119] Finally, there is 'constructivism', a theory that regards all reasons for action as socially constructed, and that international law exists primarily as a vocabulary to justify behaviour because it can potentially constrain certain behaviour, but equally facilitate other forms of behaviour.[120] These theories have sought to describe international law not merely by enumerating its rules, but by capturing patterns of behaviour that might apply to the individuals behind States and institutions.

In a banal, descriptive way, international law is universal simply because it encompasses States from all continents which govern the vast majority of the world's population. But that misses the point: 'universalism' in its deeper sense requires one to transcend the particular, and to adopt an international law that can be neutral and impartial in its regulation of all humankind. Perhaps this is an unattainable aspiration in light of the diversity of the world's peoples and their experiences. As such, though this book will focus primarily on the meaning and application of international legal rules and principles, the present author takes seriously the challenges highlighted by these more critical responses to international law, for these may enable understanding of today's international law as the outcome of a political and legal process, and not merely a decontextualized set of rules.

1.8 Conclusion: the place of international law today

The history of international law sketched out summarily here is but an introduction; a core observation remains that, rather than through decisive ruptures, international law has developed through a process of gradual iteration. At present, the global space is undergoing an accelerated period of evolution, often referred to as *globalization*, 'the intensification of worldwide social relations which link distant localities in such a way

[116] See, e.g., J Kammerhofer, *Uncertainty in International Law: A Kelsenian Perspective* (Routledge, 2012); J d'Aspremont, *Formalism and the Sources of International Law* (OUP, 2011).

[117] See A Guzmán, *How International Law Works: A Rational Choice Theory* (OUP, 2008); JL Goldsmith and EO Posner, *The Limits of International Law* (OUP, 2005). These draw on the emblematic H Morgenthau, *Politics among Nations: The Struggle for Power and Peace* (5th edn, Alfred A Knopf, 1978).

[118] See, e.g., RO Keohane, *After Hegemony: Cooperation and Discord in the World Political Economy* (Princeton UP, 1984); SD Krasner (ed), *International Regimes* (Cornell UP, 1983); T Franck, *The Power of Legitimacy among Nations* (n 76); and T Franck, *Fairness in International Law and Institutions* (OUP, 1995), ch 2.

[119] See, e.g., A-M Slaughter, *A New World Order* (Princeton UP, 2004); and the earlier A-M Slaughter Burley, 'International Law and International Relations Theory: A Dual Agenda' (1993) 87 AJIL 205.

[120] See, e.g., J Brunnée and S Toope, *Legitimacy and Legality in International Law: An Interactional Perspective* (CUP, 2010).

that local happenings are shaped by events occurring many miles away and vice versa';[121] and indeed there has been much change to global political and economic structures. Such changes, in turn, have challenged long-standing social and legal structures to the point where new schemes for global governance are constantly being proposed.[122] A further area of enquiry concerns the protection of the global environment. Air and water know no boundaries, of course, and though the most effective regulation of environmental standards is at the local or domestic level, it has become evident that global collective action has become necessary in the face of transboundary and global environmental concerns.[123] Further examples of cross-border issues of global collective concern include responses to terrorist acts, especially as these are generally committed by non-State actors; issues of cyber-security which have emerged due to rapid technological innovation; and of course pandemics such as Covid-19, with deadly global reach. Whether international law can meet the challenges faced by humanity today remains to be seen.

This is not to say that international law is part of some inexorable march towards progress: more international law does not necessarily mean a more just world. International law has been utilized to propagate highly problematic ideas in the past.[124] Yet for all this, because international law provides a framework and vocabulary for the conduct of international relations, one which is used by States and other powerful actors, it remains an indispensable part of international society, and a powerful tool in global governance. International law is purposive, but not in its promotion of ethical values; above all, it is designed to safeguard the stability and coherence of the international State system.[125] In this respect, stability and coherence are privileged over contested notions of justice or political pressures for greater equality among and between States.

Rather than challenge the relevance of international law, the reader is advised to maintain a healthy pragmatism about whether international law is a force for 'good' or 'justice', especially regarding the relevance of law in international society. Whatever one's political or ethical commitments, for the student of international law it is key to understand the inner logic of international law: what arguments are legitimated and considered to be legally valid, what practices are considered to be relevant, and what processes are used. Whatever one's political convictions or methodological preferences, it is undeniable that international law has been profoundly shaped by historical currents and has, in turn, contributed tremendously to the shaping of events and developments around the world. It is in that spirit that this book will proceed to describe the phenomenon that we call international law.

[121] A Giddens, *The Consequences of Modernity* (Polity Press, 1991), 64. See also S Sassen, *A Sociology of Globalization* (WW Norton, 2007).

[122] See, e.g., DD Avant, M Finnemore, and SK Sell (eds), *Who Governs the Globe?* (CUP, 2010); E Benvenisti, *The Law of Global Governance* (Hague Academy Publications, 2014); and J Klabbers and T Piiparen (eds), *Normative Pluralism and International Law: Exploring Global Governance* (CUP, 2013).

[123] See Chapter 19.

[124] For a provocative account of international law and historical methodology, see A Orford, *International Law and the Politics of History* (OUP, 2021).

[125] Though see further Tzouvala (n 38), who argues that international law's structures and preference for order are specific in their facilitation of global capitalism and accumulation, with force being used to maintain that economic structure.

Further reading

A Anghie, *Imperialism, Sovereignty, and the Making of International Law* (CUP, 2004).

An incisive postcolonial narrative which portrays international law as an outgrowth of imperialism, and central to the colonization of the non-European world.

B Chimni, *International Law and World Order: A Critique of Contemporary Approaches* (2nd edn, CUP, 2017).

An avowedly critical analysis that engages with international law's history and various contemporary theories to assess its relevance for global collective problems.

L Ehrlich, 'The Development of International Law as a Science' (1962) 105 Recueil des Cours 173.

Traces an intellectual history of the field of international law through the conceptual move of international lawyers towards a more scientific approach.

B Fassbender and A Peters (eds), *The Oxford Handbook of the History of International Law* (OUP, 2012).

A comprehensive and broad-ranging collection of essays aiming to narrate a 'global history' of international law.

W Grewe, *The Epochs of International Law* (M Byers tr, de Gruyter, 2000).

Originally published in German, this is a monumental tome on the history of international law, told through the prism of 'epochs' dominated by one State or idea.

P Guggenheim, 'Contributions à l'histoire des sources du droit des gens' (1958) 94 Recueil des Cours 1.

A concise French-language narration of the debates concerning the sources of international law as they have evolved through history.

E Jouannet, *The Liberal-Welfarist Law of Nations: A History of International Law* (CUP, 2012).

A fluid, non-linear account of international law which describes its history as an oscillation between liberal and welfarist conceptions of it.

M Koskenniemi, *The Gentle Civilizer of Nations: The Rise and Fall of International Law 1870–1960* (CUP, 2005).

A critique of the civilizing impulses in international legal history, which semi-biographically studies key figures across various legal traditions.

S Neff, *Justice among Nations: A History of International Law* (Harvard UP, 2014).

A practical, historical account of international law's development, and how it has been contested.

A Nussbaum, *A Concise History of the Law of Nations* (rev edn, Macmillan, 1954).

Though somewhat dated, this detailed and comprehensive account of international law's history is a classic reference in the field.

S Pahuja, *Decolonizing International Law* (CUP, 2013).

Focused on the period of decolonization and contemporary discourses on development, this ambitious study situates contemporary discourses through a history of ideas.

N Tzouvala, *Capitalism as Civilisation: A History of International Law* (CUP, 2020).

An innovative Marxian approach to international legal history that, through a close reading of legal texts, argues for an understanding of the concept of 'civilization' as a driving force in the imposition of global capitalist modernity.

2

Sources of international law

2.1 Introduction: sources and the nature of international law

2.1.1 **Sources, States, and consent**

Like all modern legal orders, understanding the inner workings of international law requires reflection on certain basic questions: how do we know what is, and what is not, law? How did a given legal rule come to have that status? Is there a person or a body empowered to make, interpret, or change the law? In most national legal orders, there is a central legislative organ that produces laws and regulations, or perhaps delegates authority to administrative organs; there will additionally be courts or other judicial bodies with the jurisdiction to interpret and apply that law. Because such institutions do not exist in international law, at least not in the form recognizable to a national lawyer, much ink has been spilt regarding the sources of international law. This is, in part, due to the decentralized character of international lawmaking, but also perhaps to reinforce the claim that international law is in fact a proper legal system.

Difficulties in explaining the sources of international law are compounded by the fact that, as described in the previous chapter, the authority to develop international law is generally regarded as deriving from the consent of States. This is not to say that all international law is made by States; States frequently delegate lawmaking authority to specific bodies or organs, and they may acquiesce or consent to a legal rule which originated in a non-State institution. In that light, it should be unsurprising that competing theories have emerged which seek to ground international lawmaking in alternatives to State consent, from 'community interests',[1] to considerations of humanity or democracy,[2] or a wider social process which demands 'fairness'.[3] Moreover, there are those who

[1] C Tomuschat, 'Obligations Arising for States Without or Against their Will' (1993) 241 Recueil des Cours 195; B Simma, 'From Bilateralism to Community Interest in International Law' (1994) 250 Recueil des Cours 219; G Abi-Saab, 'Les sources du droit international—Un essai de déconstruction' in E Jiménez de Aréchaga and M Rama-Montaldo (eds), *Le droit international dans un monde en mutation* (Fundacion de Cultura Universitaria, 1994), 29.

[2] See, e.g., A Peters, L Koechlin, T Förster, and GF Zinkernagel (eds), *Non-State Actors as Standard Setters* (CUP, 2009); A Cassese, *International Law* (2nd edn, OUP, 2004), Part I; S Besson, 'Theorizing the Sources of International Law' in J Tasioulas and S Besson (eds), *The Philosophy of International Law* (OUP, 2010).

[3] See, e.g., T Franck, *Fairness in International Law and Institutions* (Clarendon Press, 1998).

contend that international lawyers use sources inappropriately and that our 'doctrine of sources' is in fact a formalist technique used to serve certain political interests,[4] or those who have pointed out the gendered and Eurocentric bias of how international law has traditionally been made.[5]

2.1.2 **Distinguishing formal and material sources of international law**

It is important to set out a few preliminary concepts which may help to understand the framework through which sources are commonly understood. One key distinction is that between the formal and material sources of international law. *Formal sources* are those methods for law-creation which are legally binding on their addressees and of general application; these are generally regarded as binding due to the consent of the addressee to them. *Material sources* are sources that are not legally binding, but may provide evidence that sheds light on the existence of a legally binding rule. Material sources can be found in a wide variety of instruments, ranging from a judgment of an international court, a study of the International Law Commission (ILC), a resolution of a political organ, or even a textbook on international law. The point is that material sources can gather or compile evidence of a binding legal rule.[6]

Accordingly, after explaining some overarching points, this chapter will first address the 'traditional' formal sources of international law, treaties, custom, and general principles (Sections 2.2.2–2.2.4), before turning to subsidiary or material sources of international law (Section 2.2.5). Section 2.3 will then consider other potential sources, which have not yet been universally recognized as such. These include the resolutions of international organizations, codes of conduct emanating from civil society, final acts at high-level meetings, statements of bodies that monitor treaties, and other forms of so-called 'soft law'.

2.2 Article 38 of the Statute of the International Court of Justice

2.2.1 ***Lex arbitri* or an authoritative general statement?**

In a curious example which demonstrates the complexity of sources doctrine in international law, it is a provision of a treaty, in this case Article 38 of the Statute of the International Court of Justice (ICJ Statute),[7] which is the traditional starting point when speaking about international legal sources. Technically, Article 38 of the ICJ Statute

[4] T Skouteris, 'The Force of a Doctrine: Article 38 of the PCIJ Statute and the Sources of International Law' in F Johns, R Joyce, and S Pahuja (eds), *Events: The Force of International Law* (Routledge, 2011), 68; D Kennedy, 'The Sources of International Law' (1987) 2 American University JILP 1.

[5] See H Charlesworth, 'Law-making and Sources' in J Crawford and M Koskenniemi (eds), *The Cambridge Companion to International Law* (CUP, 2012), 187; A Anghie, BS Chimni, K Mickelson, and O Okafor (eds), *The Third World and International Legal Order: Law, Politics and Globalisation* (Kluwer, 2003).

[6] See R Jennings and A Watts, *Oppenheim's International Law* (9th edn, Longman and Sons, 1992), vol I, 23; and J Crawford, *Brownlie's Principles of Public International Law* (9th edn, OUP, 2019), 21.

[7] Statute of the International Court of Justice, *as annexed to* the Charter of the United Nations (26 June 1945), 892 UNTS 119.

only lays out the categories of sources to be applied by the ICJ: its *lex arbitri* (applicable law). Yet, in practice, Article 38, which was transposed nearly verbatim from the 1922 Statute of the PCIJ,[8] has long been regarded as the authoritative, complete statement of the sources of international law.[9] This is in part due to the incorporation of the ICJ Statute into an annex of the UN Charter, a treaty ratified by virtually all States; but one could also argue that Article 38, even though arguably dated, remains the focal point for international lawyers, a convenient shorthand that furnishes guidance as to what is generally acceptable international legal reasoning.[10]

Article 38(1) lays out a number of key points, foremost being that the ICJ's function 'is to decide in accordance with international law';[11] it enumerates the following sources as being applicable:

a. international treaties (conventions), whether general (multilateral) or particular (between a smaller group of States), so long as they establish recognizable rules;
b. international custom, 'as evidence of a general practice accepted as law';
c. general principles of law 'recognized by civilized nations';
d. 'subsidiary means for the determination of rules of law', naming expressly judicial decisions and the 'teachings of the most highly qualified publicists of the various nations'.

Though treaties come first in the enumeration contained in Article 38, and are discussed in depth in Chapter 7, it is traditional to begin with the category of customary international law, and for good reason: though more complex, understanding custom is a key first step in understanding sources in international law more generally.

THEORY AND DEBATES Is There a Hierarchy of Sources in International Law?

A preliminary question must be asked of sources before turning to their substance: does a hierarchy exist between them? Though Chapter 3 addresses the hierarchy of *norms* in international law, it is worth discussing the hierarchy of *sources* here.

The original design of Article 38 suggests that treaties, customary law, and general principles enjoy equality between them, but prevail over the subsidiary means of determining the law. Article 38 does not distinguish between the three primary sources: they are equally capable of generating legal norms of comparable weight, and they overlap and coexist with one

[8] (16 December 1920) 112 BFSP 317.

[9] See, e.g., M Hudson, *A Tribunal of Nations: The Permanent Court of International Justice 1920–1939* (Columbia UP, 1939), 601–12; *Oppenheim's International Law* (n 6) 24, 44; M Sørensen, *Les sources du droit international* (Munskgaard, 1946), 49; and C Rousseau, *Droit international public* (Sirey, 1980), vol 1.

[10] GI Hernández, *The International Court of Justice and the Judicial Function* (OUP, 2014), 30; see also J d'Aspremont, *Formalism and the Sources of International Law* (OUP, 2011), 149. *Cf* J Kammerhofer, 'Uncertainty in the Formal Sources of International Law: Customary International Law and Some of Its Problems' (2004) 15 EJIL 523.

[11] Article 38(1) is to be distinguished from Art 38(2), which allows for the Court to decide *ex aequo et bono* (in accordance with equity); see Section 2.2.4.3 for further discussion.

another without any hierarchy (*Military and Paramilitary Activities in and against Nicaragua (Nicaragua v United States), Merits, ICJ Reports 1986*, p 14, para 176).

If a conflict emerges between applicable legal rules, it can be resolved on the basis of guiding principles such as general harmonization, or applying conflict-resolution techniques such as *lex specialis derogat legii generali* ('specific rules prevail over rules of general application') or *lex posterior derogat priori* ('more recent law prevails over an inconsistent earlier law'). When compared with customary international law, treaty obligations are *lex specialis*, generating more specific obligations between parties. Thus, a treaty may codify or depart from existing custom; but equally so, new customary rules might emerge which depart from or add to an existing treaty framework. Accordingly, should an inconsistency arise, it is to be presumed that parties to a treaty were aware of the existing customary rule and have decided to exclude its application. This occurred in *Dispute regarding Navigational and Related Rights (Costa Rica v Nicaragua)*, where the ICJ disregarded the possible application of customary law in the presence of a treaty that 'completely define[d] the rules applicable' to the situation at hand (*ICJ Reports 2009*, p 213, para 36).

If there is any hierarchy of sources at all, it would be between 'ordinary' sources and the category of what are called 'peremptory norms' or norms of *jus cogens*. Under Article 64 of the 1969 Vienna Convention on the Law of Treaties (VCLT), any treaty which is in conflict with such norms 'becomes void and terminates'. Chapter 3 addresses these in detail.

For further reading, see the classic M Akehurst, 'The Hierarchy of the Sources of International Law' (1974–5) 47 BYBIL 273; and ILC, 'Conclusions of the Work of the Study Group on the Fragmentation of International Law', ILC Ybk 2006, vol II, pt 2, p 182 *et seq*, especially conclusion 31.

2.2.2 **Customary international law**

2.2.2.1 **Understanding the concept of 'custom'**

People interacting with one another in a group, however small, tend to develop standards of behaviour to govern relations between them. These need not be written down, but can develop through social practices which are gradually accepted as rules by the members of the group. In more organized societies, such rules, embedded in social practices, come to be regarded as a form of 'customary law', a recurring interaction among individuals and groups that is accompanied by the acknowledgement that such a mode of interaction produces certain expectations of conduct that ought to be satisfied.[12] A key feature of custom is that it does not emerge from a deliberative lawmaking process, but rather, through the accretion of social practices of individual actors which crystallize, often over a long period of time.[13]

[12] R Unger, *Law in Modern Society* (Free Press, 1976), 49. See also DJ Bederman, *Custom as a Source of Law* (CUP, 2010), for a comparative study of customary law across legal systems.

[13] Hans Kelsen defined custom as 'unconscious and unintentional lawmaking': see H Kelsen, *Principles of International Law* (Berkeley UP, 1952), 307–8.

To speak of 'customary international law' is to recognize that the international practices of States can create new legal rules.[14] Given the decentralized character of international lawmaking, custom as a source of law gives prominence to the consent of States, even if merely through a sort of tacit agreement, as a means for the creation of new international law.[15] In this respect, the evolution of custom is revelatory both of the history and underlying nature of international law. Though, formally, the concept of custom gives equal value to the practice of all States, it is accepted across the scholarly spectrum that customary law analysis tends to give prominence to certain categories of States, perhaps due to their influence, skill in international legal relations, or power.[16]

Moving beyond such charged ideological debates, practical questions abound as regards how to identify a new rule of custom as a source of law. What exactly constitutes the general practice of States, and how does it evidence customary international law? How does one distinguish a general practice accepted as law from one which is merely motivated by courtesy, tradition, or expediency?[17] Given that a 'State' is not a sentient being but a social construct consisting of governmental ministries, departments, agencies, and, ultimately, individual officials, which evidence is determinative of a State's 'acceptance' of a general practice as law? Finally, can a rule of customary international law bind even those States which objected to it and, if so, how does this play out in practice? These, and other questions, contribute to the enduring debate among international lawyers about the role of custom within the international legal order.

2.2.2.2 **The two elements of custom**

The reference in Article 38 to 'international custom, as evidence of a general practice accepted as law' highlights two necessary elements: a material element relating to the actual practice of States in their relations (traditionally called *usus*, 'usages'); and a subjective belief of States that such behaviour is 'law' (traditionally known as *opinio juris sive necessitatis*, 'an opinion as to law or necessity'). Traditionally, international lawyers follow this inductive approach: in *Libya/Malta Continental Shelf*, the ICJ famously stated that customary international law is to be 'looked for primarily in the actual practice and *opinio juris* of States'.[18] Though such an approach is not

[14] A number of key works on the place of custom in international law are listed in the Further Reading at the end of this chapter. In 2018 the International Law Commission adopted a relevant set of conclusions on the method of identifying custom: see ILC, 'Draft Conclusions on Identification of Customary International Law, with Commentaries', ILC Report 2018, UN Doc A/73/10, 122–56.

[15] As was pointed out by D Anzilotti, *Corso di Diritto Internazionale* (3rd edn, Padova, 1928), vol 1, 71–6.

[16] A point lucidly made by H Thirlway, *The Sources of International Law* (2nd edn, OUP, 2019), 80–1; see also the more radical critique in BS Chimni, 'Customary International Law: A Third World Perspective' (2018) 112 AJIL 1, 24–5.

[17] Crawford (n 6) 23 suggests that the term 'usage' can distinguish custom from non-binding practices. Acts such as ceremonial salutes at sea, or the conferral of certain parking privileges to diplomatic officials, would thus not be characterized as legal requirements but simply as a matter of 'international comity'.

[18] *Continental Shelf (Libyan Arab Jamahiriya/Malta), Judgment, ICJ Reports 1985*, p 13, 29. The Court would quote this passage approvingly in *Jurisdictional Immunities of the State (Germany v Italy), Judgment, ICJ Reports 2012*, p 99, 122–3. See further ILC, 'Draft Conclusions on the Identification of Customary International Law' (n 14), Draft Conclusion 2; and M Lando, 'Identification as the Process to Determine the Content of Customary International Law' (2022) 42 *OJLS* 1040, esp 1045–47.

without problems,[19] particular attention will be paid to the method used in ICJ judgments which, even though formally merely a subsidiary source of law, are emblematic of how, in practice, international lawyers regard the development of customary law.

THEORY AND DEBATES Elements of Custom: What Intensity is Required?

A long-standing debate between international lawyers concerns the duration, consistency, and generality of practice and *opinio juris* required for a new customary rule to crystallize. Historically, the passage of time was controversial, though today it is of lesser importance provided that there exists a 'constant and uniform usage practised by the States in question' (*Asylum* case, 266; interestingly, the Court concluded that practice was so uncertain and contradictory as not to constitute a customary rule). In *Anglo-Norwegian Fisheries* (at 131), the Court added that a small degree of inconsistency does not prevent the emergence of a customary rule when it is outweighed by a large amount of consistent practice. Similar reasoning has been adopted in other cases, including *Icelandic Fisheries Jurisdiction*, pp 23–6; and *Nicaragua (Merits)*, para 186. The ILC's Draft Conclusion 8 on the Identification of Custom suggests that any relevant practice must be general, sufficiently widespread and representative, and consistent; but that 'no duration is required'.

In *North Sea Continental Shelf* (1969), the Court turned to the question of time, or duration, required for a new rule to crystallize:

> the passage of only a short period of time is not necessarily, or of itself, a bar to the formation of a new rule of customary international law on the basis of what was originally a purely conventional rule, an indispensable requirement would be that within the period in question, short though it might be, State practice, including that of States whose interests are specially affected, should have been both extensive and virtually uniform (para 74).

The elastic criterion of 'duration' is vividly illustrated by the emergence of newer technologies which are quickly adopted by a few technologically advanced States. For example, in the 1960s only the USA and Soviet Union were sufficiently capable of exploring outer space. Because of Cold War politics and a fear that outer space could be militarized, virtually all States, through a General Assembly resolution, commended the signing of the Outer Space Treaty by the two superpowers, which bound them to regard outer space as a demilitarized zone. Bin Cheng argued at the time that 'instant custom' would be possible in such situations, as the *opinio juris* is so strong that consistency of practice is not necessary for the creation of a new customary rule (B Cheng, 'United Nations Resolutions on Outer Space: "Instant" International Customary Law?' (1965) 5 Indian JIL 35).

Today, one wonders whether the rapid pace of technological and scientific change in areas such as global health law (especially the Covid-19 pandemic), climate change, or in cyberspace, could also give rise to 'instant custom'.

[19] See, e.g., Chimni (n 16) 27 who cautions that the ICJ, whether engaging in deductive, inductive, or assertion-based analysis in respect of custom, does so 'using western understandings of what is good for the international community'; and for a broader analysis, J d'Aspremont, *The Discourse on Customary International Law* (OUP, 2021).

2.2.2.2.1 *The requirements for a 'general practice'*

Distilled to its essence, the notion of State practice encompasses the action or inaction of States in their relations with each other, or in relation to recognized international actors such as international organizations. 'Practice' is therefore a dynamic phenomenon: the actions of one actor may be accepted, tolerated, or rejected by other actors, which may adopt a similar course of action. When examining State practice in relation to jurisdictional immunities, the ICJ stated that:

> State practice of particular significance is to be found in the judgments of national courts faced with the question whether a foreign State is immune, the legislation of those States which have enacted States dealing with immunity, the claims to immunity advanced by States before foreign courts and the statements made by States.[20]

The actions of any of the State's organs and agents, therefore, may constitute relevant practice if the said action relates to the international field.[21] The State's actions can range from an international act such as signing a treaty, to any number of internal executive or administrative acts, the passing of legislation, and even the decisions of courts.[22] It must be said, though, that an issue arises if, within a State, different organs are engaged in conflicting practices, as sometimes might happen if the judiciary takes a different position to the executive branch.

Because custom is fluid, an intriguing question arises: where is the line drawn between a State disobeying an existing rule and the first indication that such non-compliance indicates the emergence of a new rule? When the ICJ considered the existence of customary rules on the use of force in the merits phase of *Nicaragua*, it considered that 'instances of State conduct inconsistent with a given rule should generally have been treated as breaches of that rule, not as indication of the recognition of a new rule'.[23] The Court here identified the potentially contradictory character of inconsistent conduct, which can be evidence that a new rule is emerging or simply a breach of the existing rule. The key is the manner in which the inconsistent conduct is justified by the acting State, and whether it is accepted or rejected by other States. The paradoxical situation that conduct may be simultaneously unlawful, yet constitutive of a new legal rule, will be further explored in relation to *opinio juris*.

[20] *Jurisdictional Immunities of the State* (n 18) 123.

[21] See *Interhandel Case (Switzerland v United States), Preliminary Objections, ICJ Reports 1959*, p 6, 27; and (1950) ILC Ybk vol II, 368–72.

[22] See also ILC, 'Draft Conclusions on the Identification of Customary International Law' (n 14), Draft Conclusion 5; Draft Conclusion 6 provides an illustrative list of forms of relevant practice. See further *Arrest Warrant (Democratic Republic of the Congo v Belgium), Judgment, ICJ Reports 2002*, p 3, 23–4, involving the issue of an arrest warrant against a serving foreign minister of another State; and *Nottebohm (Liechtenstein v Guatemala), Second Phase, ICJ Reports 1955*, p 4, 22, on the conferral of nationality by decree.

[23] *Military and Paramilitary Activities in and against Nicaragua (Nicaragua v United States), Merits, ICJ Reports 1986*, p 14, para 186.

HISTORICAL BACKGROUND The Concept of a 'Specially Affected State' and the Role of Power in the Making of International Law

The particular relevance of certain States in the formation of a customary rule was recognized by the ICJ in *North Sea Continental Shelf*, where the Court noted that 'State practice, including that of States whose interests are specially affected, should have been both extensive and virtually uniform' (para 74). A classic example of a 'specially affected State' would be that the practice of States with actual coastlines, and not that of landlocked States, would be relevant in the delimitation of maritime boundaries.

Historically, the doctrine of the 'specially affected' State has often reflected the asymmetrical power relations between States, however formally equal they might be. In the nineteenth century, the practice of Great Britain (as it then was) was indispensable in relation to the law of the sea; and in the twentieth, it was the practice of the USA in relation to the law of armed conflict, or that of the USA and the Soviet Union in relation to outer space. What is more, the practice of Western States has regularly prevailed in matters of international economic law; in particular, the law on foreign investment. As has been argued, being 'specially affected' may be used as a 'respectable disguise' by powerful States which ensures that their views are always taken into account (see GM Danilenko, *Law-Making in the International Community* (Nijhoff, 1993), 96; and the more recent, provocative BS Chimni, 'Customary International Law: A Third World Perspective' (2018) 112 AJIL 1, esp 45–46).

A vivid illustration of the place of power may be found in the context of the 1996 *Legality of the Threat or Use of Nuclear Weapons* advisory opinion. Several non-nuclear States argued that the States actually possessing a nuclear arsenal, five of which occupy permanent seats on the Security Council, were not specially affected and could not block the emergence of a new customary rule. The Court did not take a position on this highly contentious point.

More recently, the Marshall Islands tried to challenge several declared nuclear powers for having failed to disarm, but its claims before the ICJ were dismissed in 2016 due to the cases being inadmissible (see, e.g., the ICJ's 2016 decision in *Obligations Concerning Negotiations Relating to Cessation of the Nuclear Arms Race and to Nuclear Disarmament (Marshall Islands v United Kingdom), Preliminary Objections, ICJ Reports 2016*, p 255). It remains to be seen whether other issues of global collective concern to which certain States are disproportionately exposed, such as sea-level rise or human migration flows, will give rise to new interpretations of being 'specially affected'.

2.2.2.2.2 Evidence of 'acceptance as law' *(opinio juris sive necessitatis)*

The second element for custom to crystallize, *opinio juris*, suggests a psychological element on the part of the State as to its opinion on the legal status of a rule. The emphasis on a psychological or mental state reveals the ancient origins of *opinio juris* in municipal law, where an enquiry into the states of mind of individuals is more straightforward.[24] Over time, a form of the concept has been accepted within international law.

[24] See Crawford (n 6) 26. The concept originated as far back as the writings of St Isidore of Seville, *Etymologiae, Liber V: De Legibus et Temporibus*, reproduced in A Barney, WJ Lewis, JA Beach, and O Berghof, *The Etymologies of Isidore of Seville* (CUP, 2010), ch 3, §§ 3–4: Custom is '. . . accepted as law when written law is lacking: it does not make a difference whether it exists in writing or reason, since reason too commits to law . . . Custom is so called also because it is in common usage'.

In the PCIJ's *Lotus* judgment, it held that the act of abstention alone is insufficient: 'only if such abstention were based on [a State] being conscious of a duty to abstain would it be possible to speak of an international custom.'[25]

The question of how exactly to determine what a particular State was thinking in relation to a given action remains problematic. One possible solution is that of Sir Hersch Lauterpacht, who suggested establishing a presumption that all uniform conduct by States was evidence of *opinio juris* unless the contrary was proven.[26] Again, it is probably evident that the very fluidity of the process by which customary rules change and develop raises a paradox: if new rules depend on new practice and new *opinio juris*, what does this suggest for the first State to depart from an existing customary rule? The uncomfortable situation arises that conduct which is inconsistent with an existing customary rule might simultaneously breach the existing rule and serve as evidence that a new rule has emerged. One cannot dismiss the concern that, with respect to customary international law, 'law breaking is an essential method of law making.'[27]

CASE SPOTLIGHT ***North Sea Continental Shelf (Federal Republic of Germany v Denmark; Federal Republic of Germany v the Netherlands), Judgment, ICJ Reports 1969*, p 3**

A tremendously influential judgment of the ICJ concerned competing claims by Denmark, the Netherlands, and then-West Germany over the delimitation of their respective continental shelves. The 1969 judgment came at a time of great evolution in the respective law on maritime delimitation, and the 1982 United Nations Convention on the Law of the Sea was still some years in the making.

All parties had been relying upon customary law. The Netherlands and Denmark argued that the 'equidistance-special circumstances principles' rule in Article 6 of the 1958 Geneva Convention on the Continental Shelf applied, even though West Germany had not ratified the Convention. As the equidistance rule would have given the Netherlands and Denmark a proportionally larger share of the continental shelf, West Germany opposed the claim that this was a rule of customary law.

The Court agreed with West Germany, arguing not only that a treaty could not bind third parties that had not ratified it, but also that Article 6 was not a crystallization of custom. In so

[25] Though in *Case of the SS 'Lotus' (France v Turkey), Judgment, 1927, PCIJ, Ser A, No 10*, p 28, *opinio juris* was not acknowledged explicitly. The PCIJ there referred to the requirement that States refrain from a certain act due to 'recogniz[ing] themselves as being obliged to do so.' See also ILC, 'Draft Conclusions on the Identification of Customary International Law' (n 14), Draft Conclusion 9, which suggests the practice must be undertaken 'with a sense of legal right or obligation.'

[26] See H Lauterpacht, *The Development of International Law by the International Court* (CUP, 1958), 380. See also A D'Amato, *The Concept of Custom in International Law* (Cornell UP, 1971), 74, who suggested *opinio juris* required a claim of legality in advance of, or concurrently with, a given act or practice.

[27] J Crawford and T Viles, 'International Law on a Given Day' in K Ginther et al (eds), *Völkerrecht zwischen normativen Anspruch und politischer Realität. Festschrift für Karl Zemanek zum 65. Geburtstag* (Duncker & Humblot, 1994), 45. See further, on this point, Thirlway, *Sources* (n 16) 94–6.

doing, the Court made some canonical statements with respect to custom, and which acts are relevant in assessing the existence of a customary rule:

> Not only must the acts concerned amount to a settled practice, but they must also be such, or be carried out in such a way, as to be evidence of a belief that this practice is rendered obligatory by the existence of a rule of law requiring it. The need for such a belief, i.e., the existence of a subjective element, is implicit in the very notion of the *opinio juris sive necessitatis* (para 77).

That highly influential statement is often cited by the Court itself (see, e.g., *Nicaragua (Merits)*, pp 108–9; or the more recent *Ahmadou Sadio Diallo (Merits)*, paras 30–1). It also bears emphasizing that the Court regards the two components of custom as closely intertwined: acts of practice can be evidence of the existence of an *opinio juris*, and *opinio juris*—the belief or state of mind that something is required by law—distinguishes the birth of a new rule from a mere breach of an existing rule, even if the same act may be evidence of both.

It is for this reason that *opinio juris* is key in the formation of custom, and why the mere existence (or absence) of practice does not determine what might constitute a customary rule. The better view, perhaps, is to recall the relational manner in which custom develops, and to view *opinio juris* as a discursive, deliberative element which allows for the rationalization of practice into something more coherent, which allows for development to occur.[28]

More prosaically, such a deliberative element, at least between States, was observed by the ICJ in the merits phase of *Nicaragua*, when faced with the question of how to determine whether there existed a customary international law prohibition on the use of force: '[r]eliance by a State on a novel right or an unprecedented exception to the principle might, if shared in principle by other States, tend towards a modification of customary international law'.[29] Put more simply, one State may assert a right, whether through its practice or through its *opinio juris*, and other States affected by that claim may react by objecting to the assertion of the first State, or by refraining from objecting. It is through the combined interactions of all the involved States that the development of a new rule proceeds.[30]

Would it suffice for a State to be regarded as having acted mistakenly, believing a rule to exist where there was none? The Court avoided responding to the question in the 2012 *Jurisdictional Immunities of the State* judgment, in which Italy had asserted that there existed a new exception to the customary law on immunity, based on the practice of its own domestic courts (and, briefly, those of Greece). The ICJ rejected the Italian claim after examining the contrary practice of other States, accompanied by

[28] Chimni (n 16) 38–43, favours a 'post-modern' approach based on 'deliberative reason' to *opinio juris*, representing views beyond those of States, such as those in civil society, minority peoples, and social movements.

[29] For technical reasons, the Court did not have jurisdiction to examine the US conduct in relation to the United Nations Charter prohibition on the use of force: for further details, see Chapter 7, Section 7.3 ('Reservations to treaties').

[30] Thirlway, *Sources* (n 16) 72–3.

opinio juris, but did not take a view as to whether Italy's view was justified or otherwise appropriate.[31] The Court's silence on the matter seemed sensible: it is one thing to reject a State's interpretation of the prevailing *opinio juris*, but quite another to accuse a State of misrepresenting its own *opinio juris* wilfully and deceitfully.

HISTORICAL BACKGROUND Claims to the Continental Shelf

Though the law of the sea will be examined in Chapter 18, a classic example of how custom can be made is how States began to claim sovereignty over the continental shelf after 1945. Historically, States had only laid claim to land above sea level, and to a narrow strip of sea adjoining the land; but, in 1945, US President Truman issued a proclamation to the effect that the USA 'regards the natural resources of the subsoil and sea bed of the continental shelf . . . as appertaining to the United States, subject to its jurisdiction and control' (1945 'Truman Proclamation', in 4 Whiteman Digest of Int L 756).

This novel US claim raised the question as to whether the USA was violating the freedom of the high seas of other States, which provided that no part of the high seas could be subject to a State's jurisdiction. Presumably, had other States objected strongly to the US claim, it would not have been accepted within international law. However, many States quickly formulated similar claims to the adjacent continental shelf and its resources, including the UK (also in respect of several Caribbean dependencies), as well as several States in Latin America and the Persian Gulf. The US position became the first indication of a crystallization of a new customary rule. For a history of these claims, see SV Suárez, *The Outer Limits of the Continental Shelf: Legal Aspects of their Establishment* (Springer, 2008), ch 2.

It was noted already by 1951 that such claims seemed to be 'acquiesced in by the generality of Powers, or at least not actively gains aid by them' (see *Petroleum Development v Sheikh of Abu Dhabi*, awarded by Lord Asquith of Bishopstone (1951) 18 ILR 144, 154). By 1958, the Geneva Convention on the Continental Shelf (499 UNTS 311) was signed, in which it was made clear that States could assert claims over their continental shelves; it would later be recodified in the 1982 UNCLOS, and practice continues to develop the law. One can see, in this illustration, how the novel US claim sparked a dynamic process leading to the emergence of a new rule of customary international law.

A challenge in identifying *opinio juris* is the difficulty in identifying the relevant materials to infer its existence, as these are similar to those for State practice: legislation, treaties, acts of the government, and judicial decisions. This makes sense, as it would be rather odd for a State to act while simultaneously denying the legality of its acts. However, since *opinio juris* is a matter of ascertaining the belief of a State, a broad range of additional materials can also be invoked, ranging from guidance to State officials in the form of military manuals or diplomatic guidelines,[32] pleadings before international

[31] *Jurisdictional Immunities of the State* (n 18) paras 76–8.

[32] ILC, 'Draft Conclusions on Identification of Customary International Law' (n 14), Draft Conclusion 10, para 2, and Commentary, esp para 5.

courts,[33] correspondence from one State to another State or to a private actor,[34] and even the position taken by a State within an international organization.[35] In fact, the ICJ has occasionally referred to certain General Assembly resolutions to confirm the existence of *opinio juris*, focusing on the content of the resolution in question and the conditions for its adoption.[36] Paramount, therefore, is the content of a document or instrument and whether it demonstrates the attitude or belief of States; and not the form it has taken. This is why, though not a formal source of international law, the work of the ILC has been cited approvingly by the Court when assessing the existence of a customary rule.[37] The ILC and its mandate will be discussed later, in Section 2.3.4.

2.2.2.2.3 ***The relativity of custom***

Given that a State cannot possibly be expected to consent or object to every single new instance of relevant practice, silence that is tantamount to acquiescence figures prominently in the emergence of a new rule of customary international law.[38] That said, the threshold is high: 'acquiescence is equivalent to tacit recognition manifested by unilateral conduct which the other party may interpret as consent'; it must be 'compelling'; and it presupposes 'clear and consistent acceptance' on the part of the acquiescing party.[39] If so established, acquiescence contributes to the formation of a new general rule of customary international law and will bind all States. International law allows for three situations where the application of a customary legal rule is not universal. These are: *persistent objection*, in relation to a new rule; *subsequent objection*, in relation to a change in an existing rule; and the possibility of *particular or localized forms of custom*. Though non-universality does not impair the emergence of the rule as custom, it does mean that the rule is not *opposable* (cannot be invoked) in respect of a State that has availed itself of the exception.[40]

[33] *Ibid*, para 4. [34] *Ibid*, para 6; see also Draft Conclusion 12, Commentary, para 6.

[35] *Nicaragua (Merits)* (n 23) 191; see also *Texaco Arbitration (Libya v United States)* (1978) 53 ILR 490 and *Armed Activities in the Territory of the Congo (Democratic Republic of the Congo v Uganda), Judgment, ICJ Reports 2005*, p 169, 251, where the General Assembly's Declaration on Permanent Sovereignty over Natural Resources was considered to be evidence of customary international law.

[36] See, e.g., *Legality of the Threat or Use of Nuclear Weapons, Advisory Opinion, ICJ Reports 1996*, p 226, 254–5; *Western Sahara, Advisory Opinion, ICJ Reports 1975*, p 12, 31–3; *East Timor (Portugal v Australia), Jurisdiction and Admissibility, ICJ Reports 1995*, p 90, 102; *Construction of a Wall in the Occupied Palestinian Territory, Advisory Opinion, ICJ Reports 2004*, p 136, 171–2.

[37] Examples now abound, but the first ever reference to the ILC by the Court was only in the 1997 judgment in *Gabčíkovo-Nagymaros (Hungary/Slovakia), Merits, ICJ Reports 1997*, p 7, 38–42. Two other prominent cases which cite to the Commission's work are *Application of the Convention on the Prevention and Punishment of the Crime of Genocide (Bosnia and Herzegovina v Serbia and Montenegro), Merits, ICJ Reports 2007*, p 43, paras 173, 214, 385, 398, 420, 431, and 460; and *Jurisdictional Immunities of the State* (n 18) paras 58, 93, 137.

[38] D Azaria, 'State Silence as Acceptance: A Presumption and an Exception' (2024) 93 *BYBIL* (unpaginated), who engages with classic works in this area, including by IC MacGilbbon, 'Customary International Law and Acquiescence' (1957) 33 *BYBIL* 15, M Akehurst, 'Custom as a Source of International Law' (1974–5) 47 BYBIL 1, and J Barale, 'L'acquiescement dans la jurisprudence internationale' (1965) 11 *AFDI* 389.

[39] See, e.g., *Gulf of Maine (United States/Canada), Judgment, ICJ Reports 1984*, p 246, 305; and more recently, *Maritime Dispute (Peru v Chile), Judgment, ICJ Reports 2014*, p 3, para 91; and *Maritime Delimitation in the Indian Ocean (Somalia v Kenya), Judgment of 12 October 2021*, para 52. See also *Boundary Dispute (Burkina Faso/Mali), Judgment, ICJ Reports 1986*, p 554, 597.

[40] See E Bjorge, 'Opposability and Non-Opposability in International Law' (2021) 90 *BYBIL* (unpaginated).

Persistent and subsequent objection

The 'persistent objector' rule allows a State to exempt itself from the application of a new customary rule if it can be demonstrated that it had objected persistently, and explicitly, during the period in which that norm was emerging.[41] A 'subsequent objector', conversely, has accepted the original rule but objects to proposed changes to that rule. Accordingly, where a State demonstrably objects to the emergence of a new rule—or to the subsequent modification of an existing rule—and provided other States appear to acquiesce to that protest, the objector will not be bound by the scope of the new rule. Clear examples of persistent objection include the refusal by the USA and Japan in the 1970s to accept territorial sea claims[42] and, more recently, China's refusal to accept the restrictive doctrine of sovereign immunity.[43]

Persistent and subsequent objections are rarely invoked in practice. Though the doctrines adhere faithfully to a consensualist vision of international law, they raise the challenging situation that customary law applies in a non-uniform way between States, binding some but not others, and perhaps invariably in favour of power asymmetries.[44] This asymmetrical arrangement undermines the idea that custom is of general application, binding all States, and can potentially make the identification of legal obligations extremely difficult.

CASE SPOTLIGHT ***Anglo-Norwegian Fisheries (United Kingdom v Norway), Judgment, ICJ Reports 1951*****, p 116**

The persistent objector rule was invoked by both parties in the *Anglo-Norwegian Fisheries* case. Norway had laid claim to a special delimitation regime for its unusual coastline of fjords and bays (called 'straight baselines'); it maintained that throughout history it had always opposed the idea that maritime boundaries could only extend for a few nautical miles off a coastline. By contrast, the UK argued for the existence of a standard regime applicable to all States, allowing the claiming of a fisheries zone of only ten nautical miles from their coast.

The Court sided with Norway, and rejected the UK view that any such rule existed as a matter of law. The Court's reasoning was, in substance, that Norway had departed from established rules, a departure to which other States had acquiesced; in theory it was an instance of subsequent objection. However, the Court was not explicit in this, and instead gave credence to the principle of persistent objection, concluding that even if a general rule existed at that time, it 'would appear to be inapplicable as against Norway inasmuch as she has always opposed any attempt to apply it to the Norwegian coast' (p 131).

[41] See, on this point, Thirlway (n 16) 99–102; JI Charney, 'The Persistent Objector Rule and the Development of Customary International Law' (1986) 56 BYBIL 1; A Green, *The Persistent Objector in International Law* (CUP, 2016); and ILC, 'Draft Conclusions on the Identification of Customary International Law' (n 14), Commentary to Draft Conclusion 15.

[42] See DP O'Connell, *International Law of the Sea* (OUP, 1982), vol I, 156, 163–4.

[43] *Democratic Republic of the Congo v FG Hemisphere Associates LLC* (8 June 2011) FACV No 5 of 2010, Hong Kong Court of Final Appeal. China's objections are further analysed in Chapter 9, Section 9.2.3.2.

[44] See Chimni (n 16) 24–5; P Dumberry, 'Incoherent and Ineffective: The Doctrine of Persistent Objector Revisited' (2010) 59 ICLQ 779.

Though ultimately the Court rejected the British claim that there already existed a new general rule, the *Anglo-Norwegian Fisheries* case was central in laying out the criteria for objection. The judgment also illustrates the challenges in how change in customary rules is managed, and how, especially when there is no overwhelming consensus for a change, you may have different States objecting to different rules, and a complex mesh of legal relations. Though often such a situation proves only to be transitional in character, the transition can stretch out over many decades.

A problematic reality remains that a newly-independent State is deemed to be bound by all existing customary law from the date of its independence: consent is inferred from the aspiration towards statehood and recognition by other States, suggesting that the new State accepts the international legal order as it has already been established.[45] The more radical alternative—that a new State is not bound by existing custom—might be in keeping with a consent-based legal order and the principle of self-determination for newly independent States; however, a *tabula rasa* or 'clean slate' approach regarding custom raises serious issues of incoherence and potential chaos in the identification of legal obligations binding new States, and such an approach has generally been rejected even by newly independent States asserting their statehood.

Particular custom

International law provides for rules of customary law that apply only exceptionally to a subset of States: though known sometimes as 'local' or 'regional' custom, the ILC has preferred the term 'particular' custom, which will be used here.[46] In the ICJ's *Asylum* judgment, Colombia had alleged that specific practices of diplomatic asylum existed which were peculiar to Latin American States, and binding on Peru. Recognizing that local custom could exist in principle, the Court concluded that a 'party which relies on a custom of this kind must prove that this custom is established in such a manner that it has become binding on the other party', and held that Colombia had failed to prove that any such custom was binding on Peru.[47] Other attempts to assert norms of regional custom at the ICJ have been unsuccessful.[48] That said, it has been claimed that certain obligations in the European Convention on Human Rights have become regional customary law.[49]

[45] G Abi-Saab, 'The Newly Independent States and the Rules of International Law: An Outline' (1962) 8 *Howard Law Journal* 95.

[46] See ILC, 'Draft Conclusions on the Identification of Customary International Law' (n 14), Draft Conclusion 15, and Commentary, 154 *et seq*; and Thirlway (n 16) 103–5.

[47] *Asylum (Colombia v Peru), Judgment, ICJ Reports 1950*, p 266, 276. See also *Haya de la Torre (Colombia v Peru), Judgment, ICJ Reports 1951*, p 71.

[48] See *Rights of Nationals of the United States of America in Morocco (France v United States), Judgment, ICJ Reports 1952*, p 176, 199–200; and *Dispute regarding Navigational and Related Rights (Costa Rica v Nicaragua), Judgment, ICJ Reports 2009*, p 213, paras 34–6.

[49] E De Wet, 'The Emergence of International and Regional Value Systems as a Manifestation of the Emerging International Constitutional Order' (2006) 19 Leiden JIL 611, 617; A Pellet, 'Comments in Response to Christine Chinkin and in Defence of *Jus Cogens* as the Best Bastion against the Excesses of Fragmentation' (2006) 17 Finnish YIL 83, 89.

The notion of 'bilateral custom' binding only two States has been more successful. Returning to the *Right of Passage* case, Portugal had contended that there existed a 'right of access' between certain Portuguese enclaves in Indian territory. The ICJ agreed: '[t]he Court sees no reason why long continued practice between two States accepted by them as regulating their relations should not form the basis of mutual rights and obligations between the two States'.[50]

However, though a State may object persistently to the creation of a new rule, it cannot claim unilaterally to be bound by special custom applying only to itself. To give an example, it is untenable that a special custom exists that the USA alone is unbound by the principle against intervention in another State's affairs.[51]

2.2.2.2.4 ***The enduring relevance of custom***

Custom has a number of disadvantages in relation to treaties, given that it is unwritten, shaped through the practice of all States, and there are difficulties in ascertaining whether a new rule has emerged. What is more, decades of substantial treaty-making have led to treaties existing in a great number of new areas, from economic regulation to the environment, armed conflict, and the prosecution of individuals in international criminal law. The making of customary law has therefore been on the wane since the advent of the UN Charter in 1945.

However, custom retains an important structuring role. It allows for a holistic vision of how treaties interrelate with one another, and of how treaties can also contribute to lawmaking. In areas where the need for international regulation might arise more quickly than the negotiation, drafting, and ratification of a new treaty, it is useful to look at practice and how it is received by other States. Finally, in areas where negotiating or modifying a written agreement proves politically impossible, custom can provide guidance as to how to act, and practice and *opinio juris* can shape and develop emergent international customary rules without requiring new written rules.

2.2.3 **Treaties and conventions in force**

Treaties, also known interchangeably as 'conventions', 'pacts', 'agreements', 'charters', and 'covenants', are a formal instrument through which States can agree that certain obligations will be binding between them. A convenient definition is provided in Article 2(1) VCLT: 'an international agreement concluded between States in written form and governed by international law, whether embodied in a single instrument or in two or more related instruments and whatever its particular designation'.[52] Though treaties are studied in detail in Chapter 7, they merit addressing here as they are, by far, the predominant source of rights and obligations in today's international legal order;[53] and

[50] *Right of Passage over Indian Territory (Portugal v India), Merits, Judgment, ICJ Reports 1960*, p 6, 39, 44. See G Cohen-Jonathan, 'La coutume locale' (1961) 7 AFDI 119.

[51] Thirlway, *Sources* (n 16) 104.

[52] Vienna Convention on the Law of Treaties (signed 23 May 1969, entered into force 27 January 1980), 1155 UNTS 331.

[53] Lord McNair wryly referred to treaties as the 'sadly overworked workhorses of the international legal order': see AD McNair, *The Law of Treaties* (Clarendon Press, 1961), 739.

are the embodiment of the basic principle *pacta sunt servanda* ('agreements shall be kept'). That principle, in turn, is embodied in Article 26 VCLT, itself a multilateral treaty which aimed to codify much of pre-existing general international law on the subject. For example, though France has prominently refused to ratify the VCLT, the ICJ has applied many of its provisions in disputes involving France as an expression of customary international law.[54] This has meant that when the ICJ has had to interpret treaties in cases involving France as a party, it will do so only when the relevant provision of the VCLT represents a codification of customary international law which is thus binding on France as a non-party.[55] Chapter 7 of this book is devoted to treaties, so this brief overview will only cover the nature of treaties as a source of international law, and their relation to other sources.

It is a basic principle that 'a treaty only creates law as between the States which are parties to it',[56] and it is true that a treaty is better understood as a source of obligation between parties rather than a rule that binds more generally. Consequently, a treaty should not create obligations for a State which is not a party (a 'third State'), as to do so is to impose obligations on it without its consent. This principle is embodied in the Latin maxim *pacta tertiis nec nocent nec prosunt* ('a treaty binds the parties only, and not a third'). However, that only tells part of the tale; not only do treaties influence the development of other sources of international law, but they are also very much a part of the process through which custom is made. Even a bilateral treaty on a highly specific topic, such as extradition or the levying of customs duties, can be regarded as relevant in the development of international law. For example, if that bilateral treaty follows a standard form adopted widely in similar treaties between other States, the most common provisions or even the treaty as a whole might constitute evidence of a customary international rule.[57]

Perhaps more visible are 'lawmaking treaties', multilateral conventions which create a regime of legal rules of general application, and not merely limited to the conduct of the parties *inter se* ('between each other'). Many examples of such lawmaking treaties are covered in this book: from the Geneva Conventions laying down basic obligations in relation to armed conflicts; human rights instruments such as the Torture Convention and Genocide Convention, which seek to prohibit such conduct universally and without exception; and sector-specific, comprehensive treaties such as UNCLOS or the Antarctic Treaty. Though there is no formal distinction between 'lawmaking' treaties and 'ordinary' treaties, usually a treaty regarded as

[54] Prominent recent examples include *Sovereign Rights and Maritime Spaces (Peru v Chile), Judgment, ICJ Reports 2016 (vol. I)*, p 19, para 15; and *Maritime Delimitation in the Indian Ocean (Somalia v Kenya), Preliminary Objections, ICJ Reports 2018*, p 3, at 22–4.

[55] See, e.g., *Mutual Assistance in Criminal Matters (Djibouti v France), Judgment, ICJ Reports 2008*, p 177, p 219, para 112. See also France's explanation as to why it voted against ratification of the VCLT: UN Conference on the Law of Treaties, 2nd Sess, OR A/CONF.39/11/Add.1, 203–4.

[56] *Certain German Interests in Polish Upper Silesia, Judgment, 1926, PCIJ, Ser A, No 7*, p 5, 29.

[57] See *SS Wimbledon, Judgment, 1923, PCIJ, Ser A, No 1*, p 25; *Panevezys-Saldutiskis Railway, 1939, PCIJ, Ser A/B, No 17*, (Sep Op Erich) 51–2; *Nottebohm* (n 22) 22–3. See also R Baxter, 'Treaties and Custom' (1970) 129 Recueil des Cours 31, 75–91; and Sørensen (n 9) 96–8.

'lawmaking' will benefit from widespread acceptance by States, specific terms in the treaty which go further than merely setting obligations but instead 'create general rules, and which arguably also guide States and other actors that are not parties'.[58] In *North Sea Continental Shelf*, the Court had to consider whether then-West Germany was bound by certain provisions of the 1958 Convention on the Continental Shelf, which it had signed but not ratified, and thus was not a party. The Court accepted that a provision of a treaty can lead to the creation of new customary rules, if the provision was 'of a fundamentally norm-creating character', and thus capable of forming the basis of an emergent or pre-existing customary law binding on a non-party State.[59]

Another interaction between treaties and other sources of international law relates to overlap: what happens if a treaty comes into being which covers the same ground as a customary rule? The ICJ, in the merits phase of *Nicaragua*, rejected the idea that existing custom would be superseded or absorbed into the treaty:

> even if a treaty norm [in that case, the UN Charter] and a customary norm relevant to the present dispute were to have exactly the same content, this would not be a reason for the Court to hold that the incorporation of the customary norm into treaty law must deprive the customary norm as to its applicability as distinct from the treaty norm.[60]

An existing customary rule will thus continue to exist irrespective of the adoption of the treaty rule, which surely makes sense as two rules with the same content may be subject to different principles of interpretation and application. In *Nicaragua*, the distinction was relevant as the Court did not have jurisdiction over the treaty obligations, but did have jurisdiction to look at customary international law.[61] What this points to, above all, is the fact that developments in State practice and *opinio juris* may come to influence or even modify the interpretation of a treaty provision. To illustrate, in its 1996 advisory opinion in *Nuclear Weapons*, the ICJ interpreted the right to self-defence under Article 51 of the UN Charter in light of requirements of necessity and proportionality that are not found in the text of that provision.[62] However, not all treaty rules enter into customary law. In *Nicaragua*, the Article 51 requirement that any exercise of the right to self-defence be reported to the Security Council was not held to have crystallized into custom.[63]

[58] See *Reparation for Injuries suffered in the Service of the United Nations, Advisory Opinion, ICJ Reports 1949*, p 174, 185; *Legal Consequences for States of the Continued Presence of South Africa in Namibia (South West Africa) notwithstanding Security Council Resolution 276 (1970), Advisory Opinion, ICJ Reports 1971*, p 16, 59; and Y Dinstein, 'The Interaction between Customary International Law and Treaties' (2006) 322 Recueil des Cours 247.

[59] *North Sea Continental Shelf (Federal Republic of Germany v Denmark; Federal Republic of Germany v the Netherlands), Judgment, ICJ Reports 1969*, p 3, 41–2.

[60] See *Nicaragua (Merits)* (n 23) 94–5. See also *Mutual Assistance in Criminal Matters* (n 52) 222, where the Court could refer to certain rules of customary law 'reflected in' the VCLT despite the fact that France was not a party to that treaty.

[61] See W Czaplinski, 'Sources of Law in the *Nicaragua* Case' (1989) 39 ICLQ 151.

[62] *Nuclear Weapons* (n 36) 244–5.

[63] *Nicaragua (Merits)* (n 23) 105.

2.2.4 **General principles recognized by 'civilized nations'**

2.2.4.1 **The place of general principles in Article 38**

Article 38(1)(c) of the ICJ and PCIJ Statutes provides that 'general principles of law recognized by civilized nations' also constitute a source of international law. It is from the outset more constructive to clarify the unfortunate use of the term 'civilized nations', meant at the time to exclude representation of municipal legal orders then considered 'uncivilized', as a relic of outdated European chauvinism.[64] Though it is grimly accurate that the notion of 'civilization' has been invoked in international law to facilitate structures of exclusion and domination,[65] within Article 38, at least, the term is probably best reconstrued as a term of art to suggest that a principle should exist across a broad range of legal systems, traditions, and regions. Already the ILC, in its Draft Conclusions on General Principles of Law (adopted on first reading), proposes instead to substitute the term with the notion of 'community of nations', drawing from Article 15(2) of the ICCPR.[66]

The category of 'general principles of law' in Article 38 of the PCIJ Statute arose from a concern by its drafters that the Court might find that there were no treaty or customary rules which could resolve a dispute. It was thought inappropriate in such cases to oblige the Court to declare what is known as a *non liquet* ('the law is not clear')—in essence, a gap in the law.[67] Legally speaking, it was preferable for the Court to deduce a relevant rule from general principles of law, many of which already existed in various municipal legal systems, to close such possible gaps. There was nothing new in this, as already in 1910 an arbitral tribunal had found that if international law did not contain an express rule to resolve a dispute, 'the function of jurisprudence is to resolve the conflict of opposing rights and interests by applying, in default of any specific provisions of law, the corollaries of general principles, and so to find . . . the solution of the problem'.[68]

Draft Conclusion 3 also tentatively suggests that a second category of general principles originates within the international legal system itself.[69] It proposes that such endogenous general principles exist when they are recognized as being intrinsic to the international legal system, in that they are specific to it, and reflect and regulate its basic

[64] H Thirlway, 'The Law and Procedure of the International Court of Justice 1960–1989 (Part II)' (1990) 61 BYBIL 1; B Cheng, *General Principles of Law: As Applied by International Courts and Tribunals* (Stevens & Sons, 1953), 25.

[65] See, e.g., M Koskenniemi, *The Gentle Civilizer of Nations* (CUP, 2001), ch 2; N Tzouvala, *Capitalism as Civilization* (CUP, 2021), chs 1–2.

[66] See Report of the ILC on the Work of its 74th Session, UN Doc A/78/10 (2023), paras 40–1, esp paras 3–4 of the Commentary to Draft Conclusion 2.

[67] *Ibid*, Draft Conclusion 10, and paras 1–3 and 6 of the commentary thereto. See further Hernández (n 10) 259 *et seq* on recourse to general principles as a gap-filling device in the law; and 31–2, recalling the drafting history of what became Art 38(1)(c). See further H Lauterpacht, 'Some Observations on the Prohibition of *Non Liquet* and the Completeness of the Legal Order' in FM van Asbeck et al (eds), *Symbolae Verzijl* (Nijhoff, 1958), 196; and L Siorat, *Le problème des lacunes en droit international. Contribution à l'étude des sources du droit et de la fonction judiciaire* (Pichon and Durant-Auzias, 1958).

[68] See British–US Arbitral Tribunal in *Eastern Extension, Australasia and China Telegraph Co Ltd case* (1923) Nielsen's Report 40, 75–6, cited in Cheng (n 61) xiii.

[69] ILC, Draft Conclusions on General Principles of Law (n 66), Draft Conclusion 3.

features.[70] Though this potential second category is not without controversy, even being disputed within the ILC itself,[71] the ILC suggests that general principles formed in this matter may be discerned by reference to other existing rules in the international legal system such as treaties or custom. The ILC also posits that it provides an illustrative list of general principles specific to the international legal system, such as consent by States to the jurisdiction of courts; the principle of *uti possedetis* under which colonial administrative borders are maintained upon independence to ensure continuity; and certain humanitarian principles related to international humanitarian law.[72]

Unlike with treaties and customary international law, general principles are not derived from the consent of a State to be bound. In Draft Conclusion 4, the ILC endorses a descriptive, two-step analysis: first, the identification of a 'principle common to the various legal systems of the world' and, secondly, whether that principle can be transposed into international law.[73] In Draft Conclusion 5, the ILC proposes that a wide and representative comparative analysis of national legal systems is required. General principles of law seem to be defined by their structural character: to avoid gaps in the international legal system, to aid in the interpretation of other primary sources in novel situations, and to ensure that, even if there is no immediate and obvious rule applicable to a given international situation, international law is coherent and complete—in other words, that 'every international situation is capable of being determined as a matter of law'.[74]

Some examples of general principles recognized by the ICJ include the obligation to make reparation for breach of an obligation;[75] recognition of the principles of estoppel (which precludes a party from asserting, in court, the contrary of what has been implied by their own previous conduct or statements);[76] acquiescence;[77] abuse of rights and the

[70] See *ibid*, Commentary to Draft Conclusion 7 at para 4.

[71] *Ibid*, Commentary to Draft Conclusion 7, paras 11–3. Thirlway, *Sources* (n 16) 109 *et seq* is much more sceptical about the existence of general principles unanchored in domestic law, though at 117, he concedes that certain general principles seemed to find recognition within the specific context of international judicial proceedings. For a more favourable position, see J Ellis, 'General Principles and Comparative Law' (2011) 22 EJIL 949, 970; and I Saunders, *General Principles as a Source of International Law* (Hart, 2021), 147.

[72] *Ibid*, Commentary to Draft Conclusion 7, paras 5–10. See further E Bjorge, 'General Principles of Law Formed within the International Legal System' (2023) 72 *ICLQ* 845.

[73] *Ibid*, Draft Conclusion 4. In Draft Conclusion 6 and its accompanying commentary, the ILC explains that transposition refers to the potential incompatibility of a principle derived from domestic law, and acts as a safeguard against these.

[74] Ibid, Draft Conclusion 10. Oppenheim's *International Law* (n 6) 13; Thirlway, *Sources* (n 16) 111–12. On the law-creative power bestowed by judges through this doctrine, see Hernández (n 10) ch VIII.

[75] See *Factory at Chorzów (Merits) (Germany v Poland), Judgment, 1928, PCIJ, Ser A, No 17*, p 31. For a detailed account of PCIJ and ICJ case law identifying further general principles, see M Dordeska, *General Principles Recognized by Civilized Nations (1922–2018)* (Brill, 2020).

[76] This is especially if the other party has relied to their detriment on such conduct or statements: see, e.g., *Gulf of Maine* (n 38) 309; *Obligation to Negotiate Access to the Pacific Ocean (Bolivia v Chile), Preliminary Objections, ICJ Reports 2018*, p 1, 49–50. See further A Kulick, 'About the Order of Cart and Horse, Among Other Things: Estoppel in the Jurisprudence of International Investment Arbitration Tribunals' (2016) 27 EJIL 107.

[77] See *Legal Status of Eastern Greenland, 1933, PCIJ, Ser A/B, No 53*, p 22, 52–4, 62, 69; *North Sea Continental Shelf* (n 56) 26; and *Elettronica Sicula SpA (United States v Italy), Judgment, ICJ Reports 1989*, p 15, 44.

requirement of good faith;[78] *nemo judex in sua causa propria* ('no one should be judge in their own case');[79] *lis pendens* (another suit is pending before another procedure);[80] and *res judicata* ('the matter has already been judged').[81] Of course, the ICJ is not the only relevant international court, and its decisions are only subsidiary in character; there are many other judicial bodies, such as regional human rights courts and tribunals, specialized international bodies such as ITLOS, and the international criminal tribunals, investment arbitral tribunals, and, of course, the decisions of national courts.[82]

Recently, the Covid-19 pandemic has impelled discussions as to whether due diligence, in particular in relation to the customary law obligation to prevent transboundary harm in another State (the 'no harm' principle as long recognized in the *Corfu Channel* judgment), may also be a general principle requiring certain conduct by States in fulfilling their international legal obligations. For example, has been argued that in early 2020, Chinese officials were under an obligation to take preventive measures to halt the transboundary spread of the Covid-19 virus, such as those foreseen in the 2005 International Health Regulations of the World Health Organization (WHO): these included efforts of monitoring and response, early notification to other States, and promptly to acknowledge the existence of a public health emergency.[83] The point is not that these would have succeeded in containing the virus—they would not—but such efforts might have allowed States to mitigate contagion and put in place further preventive measures.

THEORY AND DEBATES The General Principle of 'Clean Hands'

The general principle *in adimplenti non est adimplendum* is often understood as the 'clean hands' doctrine. Simply put, it prevents a party from complaining of the misconduct of another if it has engaged in similar misconduct. Perhaps because of its roots in equity, the clean hands doctrine has not always enjoyed concrete support under international law. For example, in the PCIJ's judgment in *Diversion of Water from the River Meuse (Belgium v the Netherlands)*, though both parties complained of a breach by the other, only Judges Hudson (at p 77) and Anzilotti (at p 49) mentioned the principle in their individual opinions.

[78] *Nuclear Tests (Australia v France; New Zealand v France), Jurisdiction and Admissibility, ICJ Reports 1974*, p 253, 267; and the earlier *Free Zones of Upper Savoy and the District of Gex, Second Phase, 1930, PCIJ, Ser A, No 24*, p 12; and *1932, PCIJ, Ser A/B, No 46*, p 96, 167.

[79] *Interpretation of Article 3, paragraph 2, of the Treaty of Lausanne, Advisory Opinion, 1925, PCIJ, Ser B, No 12*, p 32.

[80] *Certain German Interests in Polish Upper Silesia, Preliminary Objections, 1925, PCIJ, Ser A, No 6*, p 20.

[81] *Effect of Awards of Compensation made by the United Nations Administrative Tribunal, Advisory Opinion, ICJ Reports 1954*, p 47, 53; *Application of the Genocide Convention* (n 37) paras 113–15; *Delimitation of the Continental Shelf between Nicaragua and Colombia beyond 200 Miles (Nicaragua v Colombia), Preliminary Objections, ICJ Reports 2016*, p 100, paras 58–61.

[82] See ILC, Draft Conclusions on General Principles of Law (n 66), Commentary to Draft Conclusion 8, paras 2–4, 7. Saunders (n 72) develops a 'tetrahedral' model considering the function, type, methodology, and legitimacy of a general principle to survey a range of existing principles.

[83] The 2005 International Health Regulations have been adopted by the World Health Assembly, which under Arts 21 and 22 of the Constitution of the WHO, may enact binding regulations on member States, unless they opt out directly. See further O Hathaway and A Philips-Robins, 'WHO's Pandemic Response and the International Health Regulations' *Just Security* Blog (8 December 2020).

The principle has been invoked by parties before the ICJ in other cases (e.g., the USA in *Nicaragua*, *LaGrand*, and *Oil Platforms*, Israel in *Construction of a Wall*, though admittedly without much success). However, a form of it, the principle *ex iniuria ius non oritur* ('unjust acts cannot create law'), was applied in the ICJ's 1997 judgment in *Gabčíkovo-Nagymaros Project (Hungary/Slovakia), ICJ Reports 1997*, p 7. In that case, neither Hungary nor Slovakia had been complying with a 1977 Treaty between them relating to the construction of a dam on the River Danube; by applying the *ex iniuria ius non oritur* principle, the Court rejected the idea that breaches could void obligations under that Treaty. As such, though the clean hands doctrine may not have found explicit recognition in that judgment, one can see the relevance of equity in concrete cases.

The ICJ has repeatedly declined to apply the 'clean hands' rule in international law and puts into question its validity. In its 2023 judgment in *Certain Iranian Assets ((Iran v United States), Judgment, ICJ Reports 2023*, p 51), the Court dismissed the United States' use of the doctrine, recalling that it had never endorsed the 'clean hands' principle, which had to be treated 'with the utmost caution' (para 81). In 2024, the Court again rejected the invocation of the doctrine as a defence on the merits, arguing that it is inapplicable in a dispute where the Court's jurisdiction is established and the application is admissible: see *Application of the International Convention for the Suppression of the Financing of Terrorism and of the International Convention on the Elimination of All Forms of Racial Discrimination (Ukraine v Russia)*, Judgment of 31 January 2024, paras 36–8, 155.

2.2.4.2 **The challenge in finding and applying general principles in international law**

In the main, if a principle is widely recognized to exist within the national legal orders of a large majority of States, and even when compared across different legal traditions, it may be called a general principle of law by international lawyers.[84] However, such a comparative method has its own methodological problems given the inherent challenge of comparing a wide range of different legal systems and deriving common standards from them.[85] It has certainly never prevailed before the ICJ. In *Right of Passage*, Portugal unsuccessfully adduced a comparative study of sixty-four municipal legal systems to argue for a general principle of law to support its claim to a right of passage.[86] In their recent dispute, both Timor-Leste and Australia sought to identify the existence of a general principle of legal professional privilege by reference to a wide range of legal families and systems, across all regions.[87] Moreover, ascertaining the existence of a general principle in municipal law does not suffice for wholesale borrowing from

[84] See, e.g., P Guggenheim, 'Contribution a l'histoire des sources du droit ds gens' (1958) 94 Recueil des Cours 6, 78, referring to the work of the Committee of Jurists, and specifically, the views of Elihu Root (USA) and Lord Phillimore (UK); and Hernández (n 10) 31–2.

[85] See generally Ellis (n 72); Saunders (n 72) 147.

[86] *Right of Passage* (n 47). See also Malta's unsuccessful claim relying on domestic legal systems in *Continental Shelf (Tunisia/Libyan Arab Jamahiriya), Application by Malta to Intervene, ICJ Reports 1981*, p 3.

[87] *Questions relating to the Seizure and Detention of Certain Documents and Data (Timor-Leste v Australia), Provisional Measures, ICJ Reports 2014*, p 417.

municipal law, but requires a careful transposition of only those norms which are compatible with international law and the obligations contained in it.[88]

In sum, general principles must meet two conditions: to be common within the various municipal legal orders, and to as applicable with, or at least compatible with, the broader framework of international law.[89] As Lord McNair explained,

> The way in which international law borrows from [general principles of law recognized by civilized nations] is not by means of importing private law institutions 'lock, stock and barrel', ready-made and fully equipped with a set of rules . . . the true view of the duty of international tribunals in this matter is to regard any features or terminology which are reminiscent of the rules and institutions of private law as an indication of policy and principles rather than as directly importing these rules and institutions.[90]

Perhaps due to the difficulties in tracing general principles back to the consent of States, the ICJ, and before it the PCIJ, have been sparing in referring to them, and when doing so have tended to use vague terms that could apply interchangeably to customary international law and to general principles.[91] One area, however, in which the Court has relied heavily on municipal law concepts has been with respect to the status of limited liability corporations.[92]

2.2.4.3 **The place of equity as a general principle**

'Equity', a reference to general considerations of fairness and reasonableness, has long existed within common law legal systems. Within international law, it plays a curious role. For example, Article 38(2) of the ICJ Statute offers States the possibility of consenting to a dispute between them being decided *ex aequo et bono*, and thus to depart from settled rules of law. This is equity *contra legem* ('contrary to law'), or at least *ultra legem* ('beyond the law'), which involves a high degree of unpredictability. Perhaps for this reason, Article 38(2) has never been invoked by parties in a dispute before the ICJ.[93]

More relevant for our purposes is the role of equity *infra legem*, as a general principle which provides guidance for the resolution of a dispute.[94] In *North Sea Continental*

[88] C de Visscher, *Theory and Reality in Public International Law* (3rd edn, Bruylant, 1968), 400–2. *Cf* H Thirlway, 'Concepts, Principles, Rules and Analogies: International and Municipal Legal Reasoning' (2002) 294 Recueil des Cours 268, who cautions against such borrowing in general.

[89] See ILC, Draft Conclusions on General Principles of Law (n 66), Draft Conclusions 4 and 6. In the Commentary to Draft Conclusion 6, paras 4–6. In para 7, the ILC suggests that accordingly, a degree of recognition by the community of nations is required.

[90] See *International Status of South West Africa, Advisory Opinion, ICJ Reports 1950*, p 128, Separate Opinion of Lord McNair, 148.

[91] Besides *Right of Passage* (n 47), see also *Reservations to the Convention on the Prevention and the Punishment of the Crime of Genocide, Advisory Opinion, ICJ Reports 1951*, p 15, 23; *North Sea Continental Shelf* (n 56) para 17.

[92] *Barcelona Traction Heat, Light and Power Company (Belgium v Spain), Second Phase, ICJ Reports 1970*, p 3, 37; *Ahmadou Sadio Diallo (Guinea v Congo), Judgment, ICJ Reports 2010*, p 639, para 47.

[93] See Hernández (n 10) 67–8; and generally C Titi, *The Function of Equity in International Law* (OUP, 2021), a refreshing contribution that examines the place of equity as a general principle of international law, especially ch 7 on equity *ex aequo et bono*.

[94] See, e.g., *Diversion of the Meuse, 1937, PCIJ, Ser A/B No 70*, p 4, 73 (Separate Opinion of Judge Hudson). In Titi (n 91), ch 3, the relevant practice of international courts and tribunals is examined.

Shelf, the Court declared that its delimitation of the maritime boundaries between the three States should be effected 'in accordance with equitable principles'.[95] That approach was followed in the later *Maritime Delimitation in the Black Sea*.[96] There are also several cases, primarily in relation to maritime rights but also in respect of boundary disputes, where the Court has considered equity, equitable considerations, or an equitable result to form part of a specific international legal rule.[97] However, in *Barcelona Traction*, the Court dismissed without comment a Belgian submission that considerations of equity should allow it to exercise diplomatic protection over shareholders in a Canadian company.[98] Equity is also found in treaties: Articles 69–70 of the 1982 UNCLOS provide that States should apportion resources in their exclusive economic zone on an 'equitable basis',[99] and the 1997 Watercourses Convention lays great emphasis on equity in relation to certain obligations contained in it.[100] As such, the better view with respect to equity is that, though not itself a source of law, it is one of the guiding principles which can steer the interpretation and application of existing legal rules.[101]

2.2.5 **Subsidiary sources of international law**

Article 38(1)(d) enumerates two further categories, judicial decisions and the 'writings of the most eminent publicists'. Unlike the formal sources (treaties, customary law, and general principles), these two are identified explicitly as 'subsidiary means for the determination of rules of law'. To do so rests on the idea that a judge or 'publicist' (an author writing a scholarly work) will, in fashioning a legal argument, rely on formal sources of law to develop their argument. In this respect, it is useful to refer to these as 'material sources' of international law, relevant because of their content, method, and style of reasoning.[102] Such material sources remain subsidiary, a means to identify the sources that apply; but of course, due to decades of tradition and deference, subsidiary sources are key evidence of the existence of other formal sources of international law.

[95] *North Sea Continental Shelf* (n 56) 53.

[96] *Maritime Delimitation in the Black Sea (Romania/Ukraine), Judgment, ICJ Reports 2009*, p 61, para 111.

[97] See, e.g., *Fisheries Jurisdiction (United Kingdom v Iceland), Jurisdiction and Admissibility, ICJ Reports 1974*, p 3, 30–5 (in relation to fisheries); and *Continental Shelf (Tunisia/Libyan Arab Jamahiriya), Judgment, ICJ Reports 1982*, p 18, 60 (in relation to maritime delimitation); and *Frontier Dispute (Burkina Faso/Mali), Judgment, ICJ Reports 1986*, p 554, 631–3 (in relation to the division of a frontier pool).

[98] *Barcelona Traction* (n 87) para 93.

[99] See Chapter 18, Section 18.5, on this point. UNCLOS is peppered with further references to equitable principles, especially in relation to maritime delimitation (Art 74) and delimitation of the continental shelf (Art 83).

[100] Convention on the Law of the Non-Navigational Uses of International Watercourses (signed 21 May 1997, entered into force 17 August 2014), UNGA Res 51/229 (7 November 1996), Annex, Part I Introduction, esp Art 5.

[101] Though Titi (n 91) contends that across contemporary international law, equity is a normative general principle: see esp 199–203, and ch 8, where she argues that most general principles such as the clean hands doctrine, estoppel, and abuse of rights are 'variations' of equity.

[102] See Thirlway, *Sources* (n 16) 6–8. The ILC's ongoing work on subsidiary sources has already lead to the publication of two reports: see in particular ILC, 'Second Report on Subsidiary Means for the Determination of Rules of International Law' (CC Jalloh, Special Rapporteur), UN Doc A/CN.4/769 (30 January 2024).

Due to the spread of the case-based common law tradition throughout the Anglophone world, many English-speaking lawyers are surprised at first by the fact that judicial decisions are not a formal source of international law. But Article 59 of the Court's own Statute makes clear that its decisions have 'no binding force except as between the parties and in respect of that particular case', and serves to exclude a binding system of precedent as a source of new legal rules.[103] This is consistent with a consent-based view of international law, where a State might find that a judgment in which it had no representation suddenly elucidated a rule of international law to which it was bound.

The formally subsidiary character of judicial decisions significantly understates their actual influence and authority, especially those of the ICJ, references to which are abundant throughout international legal literature.[104] Many significant PCIJ and ICJ judgments have played a decisive role in the development of international law, on topics ranging from the legal personality of international organizations,[105] to rules on the use of force,[106] and customary law on the delimitation of maritime boundaries.[107] Though the Court continues to proclaim publicly that it does not regard its previous judgments as binding, one of the most striking statements was that it would in fact adhere rather faithfully to its previous decisions:

> To the extent that the decisions contain findings of law, the Court will treat them as it treats all previous decisions: that is to say that, while those decisions are in no way binding on the Court, it will not depart from its settled jurisprudence unless it finds very particular reasons to do so.[108]

It is worth adding that the practice of adhering to previous judicial decisions goes further than merely 'determining' the law; certain judicial decisions have been determinative as to the existence of international legal rules.[109] As ILC Special Rapporteur Charles Jalloh has put it, the reasoning and conclusions of previous rulings may not be binding, but they have 'persuasive and practical value in helping to resolve subsequent legal disputes'.[110]

[103] See *Polish Upper Silesia* (n 53) 19; H Waldock, 'General Course on Public International Law' (1962) 106 Recueil des Cours 5, 91; Sørensen (n 9) 161; Hudson (n 9) 207; Thirlway, *Sources* (n 16) 137–9; Hernández (n 10) ch VI.

[104] See ILC, 'Second Report on Subsidiary Means' (n 109), paras 89–96.

[105] See, e.g., *Reparation for Injuries* (n 55).

[106] See, e.g., *Nicaragua (Merits)* (n 23); see also *Oil Platforms (Islamic Republic of Iran v United States), Judgment, ICJ Reports 2003*, p 161.

[107] See, e.g., *Maritime Delimitation in the Black Sea* (n 94); *North Sea Continental Shelf* (n 56); *Continental Shelf (Libya/Malta)* (n 18); *Continental Shelf (Tunisia/Libya)* (n 95).

[108] See *Application of the Convention on the Prevention and Punishment of the Crime of Genocide (Croatia v Serbia), Jurisdiction, ICJ Reports 2008*, pp 412, 428–9.

[109] See Hernández (n 10) 180 *et seq* on the authority of judicial decisions in international law; but *cf* Thirlway, *Sources* (n 16) 137–8.

[110] ILC, 'Second Report on Subsidiary Means' (n 102), para 203. In Annex II, Draft Conclusions 7 and 8 are presented; they respectively confirm the absence of a rule of precedent and the persuasive value of previous decisions.

The ICJ is not alone; the reference in Article 38 to 'judicial decisions' also extends to international arbitral awards, the judgments of other international tribunals such as the International Criminal Court (ICC), the International Criminal Tribunal for the former Yugoslavia (ICTY), and the decisions of the various panels constituted under the World Trade Organization (WTO). Moreover, after decades of caution, the ICJ itself has also begun to cite the decisions of other international bodies, including arbitral tribunals,[111] the ICTY,[112] the European Court of Human Rights,[113] and human rights treaty bodies.[114]

It should be mentioned that the reference to judicial decisions also applies to the decisions of municipal courts. First, the judgments of domestic courts may be a material source of international law, as they might contain a useful interpretation of a given rule which is considered persuasive.[115] More commonly, as municipal courts are State organs, their decisions have been presented as evidence of State practice and have been treated by the Court as such.[116] The question in such cases is not whether the municipal court has correctly stated the law but, rather, the extent to which its decision represents relevant practice which might crystallize into a new customary rule.[117]

Let us summarily address the teachings of eminent publicists.[118] As the history of international law surveyed in Chapter 1 demonstrates, the dominant jurists influencing international law were nearly exclusively European,[119] which has led to charges of

[111] The *Alabama Claims Arbitration* (1872) 1 Moore Intl Arbitrations 495 was cited in *Nottebohm* (n 22) 119 and *Applicability of the Obligation to Arbitrate under Section 21 of the United Nations Headquarters Agreement of 26 June 1947, Advisory Opinion, ICJ Reports 1988*, p 12, 34. *Delimitation of the Continental Shelf between the United Kingdom of Great Britain and Northern Ireland, and the French Republic (UK, France)* (1977) XVIII RIAA 3 was cited in *Continental Shelf (Tunisia/Libya)* (n 95) 57; *Gulf of Maine* (n 38) 293; *Land and Maritime Boundary between Cameroon and Nigeria (Cameroon v Nigeria; Equatorial Guinea Intervening), Merits, ICJ Reports 2002*, p 303, 432; *Maritime Delimitation in the Black Sea* (n 94) 129.

[112] *Application of the Genocide Convention* (n 37) para 223.

[113] *Jurisdictional Immunities of the State* (n 18) para 90.

[114] *Diallo* (n 87) para 66; *Application of the International Convention on the Elimination of All Forms of Racial Discrimination (Qatar v United Arab Emirates), Preliminary Objections, Judgment, ICJ Reports 2021*, p 71, para 101; *Armed Activities on the Territory of the Congo (Democratic Republic of the Congo v Uganda), Reparations, Judgment, ICJ Reports 2022*, p 13, para 188.

[115] In *Accordance with International Law of the Unilateral Declaration of Independence by the Provisional Institutions of Self-Government of Kosovo, Advisory Opinion, ICJ Reports 2010*, p 403, para 55, the Court expressly declined to analyse the *Re Secession of Quebec* reference given by the Supreme Court of Canada, on the basis that it was not relevant for that opinion. See further Thirlway, *Sources* (n 16) 140–2.

[116] See earlier Section 2.2.5. In *Arrest Warrant* (n 22) para 56, the parties had relied upon *R v Bow Street Metropolitan Stipendiary, ex parte Pinochet Ugarte (No 3)* [1999] UKHL 17; [2000] AC 147 (House of Lords (UK)); *SOS Attentat et Castelnau d'Esnault v Qadaffi, Head of State of the State of Libya*, Crim 13 mars 2000, no 1414 (Court of Cassation (France)). In *Jurisdictional Immunities of the State* (n 18), the ICJ relied on judgments of national courts from around the world in assessing the existence of a rule on immunity (see Chapter 9).

[117] See further A Roberts, 'Comparative International Law? The Role of National Courts in Creating and Enforcing International Law' (2011) 60 ICLQ 57.

[118] The ILC's Draft Conclusions, provisionally adopted in 2024, allow for 'any other means', but specifically enumerate decisions of courts and tribunals and teachings as distinct categories of subsidiary means. See Second Report on Subsidiary Means' (n 109) 68, Annex I, Draft Conclusion 2.

[119] A point vividly exemplified in A Anghie, *Imperialism, Sovereignty and the Making of International Law* (CUP, 2005); and M Koskenniemi, *The Gentle Civilizer of Nations: The Rise and Fall of International Law (1870–1960)* (CUP, 2001).

Eurocentrism.[120] Though academic writings by no means constitute a legal source in the formal sense, the role of '*la doctrine*' (in the French sense) can stimulate new directions for policy and practice.[121] This tendency is potentially amplified by the inclination of the many eminent publicists to serve as advisers to governments, officials in international organizations, and international judges, thus increasing their lawmaking influence in another capacity.[122] For this reason, there are comparatively fewer references to writings by international courts, and virtually no examples of the ICJ so doing.

2.3 Beyond Article 38: other possible sources

A century of practice has developed around the enumeration of sources in Article 38; however, the dynamics of international lawmaking are such that many other materials may constitute compelling evidence of the existence of a new rule. Without embarking on a complex discussion as to whether new sources have in fact emerged, a brief mapping exercise should assist in identifying potential additional authorities that might contribute to the formation of an international legal rule.

2.3.1 Unilateral acts of a State

In defined circumstances, the unilateral acts of a State are capable of binding that State. The easiest such cases are those where a State works through traditional channels, such as the ratification of a specific treaty or an objection to an act by another State which might prevent the formation of a new customary rule. Clearly, not every unilateral statement will have a binding effect; however, in very specific situations a unilateral act by a State not directed to a specific addressee may give rise to international legal obligations. The ILC has been studying the topic for some time, and in 2006 adopted ten 'Guiding Principles applicable to unilateral declarations of States capable of creating legal obligations'.[123]

To be binding, the unilateral act must be accepted, recognized, or somehow acknowledged by another State. If it is met with absolutely no reaction, it cannot be legally relevant. In this sense, unilateral acts are a sort of 'inchoate' (incomplete) treaty, which is only completed by subsequent events.[124] Here it is useful to recall the ICJ's reasoning

[120] Amongst several, see Chimni (n 16); A Becker Lorca, *Mestizo International Law* (CUP, 2016); CF Amerasinghe, 'South Asian Antecedents of International Law' in K Wellens (ed), *International Law—Theory and Practice* (Kluwer, 1998), 3; TO Elias, *Africa and the Development of International Law* (Martinus Nijhoff, 1972).

[121] See, e.g., M Lachs, 'Teachings and Teaching of International Law' (1976-III) 151 *Recueil des Cours* 161; GI Hernández, 'The Responsibility of the International Legal Academic: Situating the Grammarian within the "Invisible College"' in A Nollkaemper, W Werner, J d'Aspremont, and T Gazzini (eds), *International Law as a Profession* (CUP, 2017).

[122] A point memorably made by O Schachter, 'The Invisible College of International Lawyers' (1977–8) 72 Northwestern University LR 217.

[123] (2006) ILC Ybk vol II, pt 2, 369–81. See, more generally, E Kassoti, *The Juridical Nature of Unilateral Acts of States in International Law* (Brill, 2015); MI Torres Cazorla, *Los Actos Unilaterales de los Estados* (Tecnos, 2010); and A Rubin, 'The International Legal Effect of Unilateral Declarations' (1977) 71 AJIL 1.

[124] See Thirlway, *Sources* (n 16) 51–9.

in the *Nuclear Tests* dispute. After protests from Australia and New Zealand following atmospheric nuclear testing in French Polynesian territories, a unilateral declaration by the Prime Minister of France that it would no longer conduct such testing in the South Pacific was held to be a unilateral act assuming an international legal obligation:

> It is well recognized that declarations made by way of unilateral acts, concerning legal or factual situations, may have the effect of creating legal obligations . . . When it is the intention of the State making the declaration that it should become bound according to its terms, that intention confers on the declaration the character of a legal undertaking.[125]

Because Australia and New Zealand were entitled to rely on France's promise, it was held that their claims were 'moot', or no longer had any object. The Court's decision is inextricably bound to other controversies as nuclear weapons have always been a delicate issue for the Court;[126] however, following this judgment it has no longer been seriously disputed that a unilateral act of a State is capable, in certain circumstances, of generating a legal obligation.

2.3.2 **Resolutions of the General Assembly**

The General Assembly of the United Nations is composed of all member States of that organization. Unlike the Security Council, however, it has no formal power under the UN Charter to issue resolutions binding on member States.[127] Yet, some resolutions of the General Assembly have proven highly influential in the development of international law, as they have provided an outlet for States to make statements which can constitute evidence of their *opinio juris* as to the existence of a rule. This would depend on several factors, such as the clarity or ambiguity of the terms of the resolution, the voting pattern of States, and whether the terms of the resolution reflect earlier resolutions or form part of a pattern of future resolutions. For example, in *Nicaragua (Merits)*, the Court noted that the relevant '*opinio juris* may, with all due caution, be deduced from, *inter alia*, the attitude of the Parties and the attitude of States towards certain General Assembly resolutions', and referred to General Assembly Resolution 2625, the Declaration on Friendly Relations between States, as evidence to support its conclusions.[128]

General Assembly resolutions may also represent a starting point for the progressive development of international law. In *Nuclear Weapons*, the Court noted the 'normative value' of General Assembly resolutions: '[t]o establish whether this is true . . . it is necessary to look at its content and the conditions of its adoption . . . a series of resolutions may show the gradual evolution of the *opinio juris* required for the establishment of a new rule'.[129] This is particularly so when they are near-unanimous or unanimous.

[125] *Nuclear Tests* (n 72) para 43.

[126] The casting vote of the President, to break a tie, has only been used twice in the modern ICJ era: in the 1996 *Nuclear Weapons* advisory opinion (n 36), and in *Obligations Concerning Negotiations Relating to Cessation of the Nuclear Arms Race and to Nuclear Disarmament (Marshall Islands v United Kingdom), Preliminary Objections, ICJ Reports 2016*, p 833.

[127] See Arts 24–5 of the UN Charter, discussed later in Chapter 6.

[128] *Nicaragua (Merits)* (n 23) 99–100.

[129] See *Nuclear Weapons* (n 36) 254–5.

2.3.3 **Resolutions of the Security Council**

The UN Security Council is composed of only fifteen States elected by the General Assembly, and has primary responsibility under the UN Charter for the maintenance of international peace and security.[130] What sets the Security Council apart is that, under Article 25 of the Charter, UN members have agreed that the 'decisions' (and not merely the resolutions) of the Security Council will be carried out by all its members. Though not formally a lawmaking organ, though, the Council has the power to create international legal obligations binding on all States.[131] What is more, under Article 103 of the Charter, obligations created by the Council will prevail over obligations under any other international agreement in the case of a conflict.

In recent years, the Security Council has begun to pass resolutions, especially in relation to terrorism and disarmament, that have gone beyond a specific threat to international peace and security, and have created rules of a general character that apply to all members. For example, just weeks after the 9/11 attacks in the USA, the Council passed Resolution 1373,[132] which set out general rules on the fight against terrorism directed towards all UN members, rather than just a particular State or situation. Such rules have been characterized as coming close to 'legislating'.[133]

2.3.4 **'Soft' law**

Finally, by way of clarification, a brief excursion into the so-called concept of 'soft law' must be made. Unlike 'hard law', which represents legally binding rules, 'soft law' is the name given to the body of standards, commitments, declarations, policy guidelines, codes of conduct, and other instruments which do not impose legally binding obligations on States, or any other legal actors for that matter.[134] That non-binding quality is the distinguishing feature of 'soft' law, which in this respect is a misleading term.[135]

What is the relevance, then, of soft law? Simply put, because of international law's decentralized structure, soft law instruments have the potential to contribute to the development of new 'hard' law.[136] Soft law instruments are frequently invoked when States have not yet arrived at the consensus necessary to enter into binding obligations, such as the imposition of human rights obligations on multinational corporations,[137] the

[130] UN Charter, Art 24(1). [131] See Chapter 14, Section 14.5, 'Collective Security'.

[132] UNSC Res 1373 (28 September 2001).

[133] See, e.g., S Talmon, 'The Security Council as World Legislature' (2005) 95 AJIL 193; J Álvarez, 'Judging the Security Council' (1996) 90 AJIL 22; D Joyner, 'The Security Council as Legal Hegemon' (2012) 43 Georgetown JIL 225.

[134] See, e.g., AT Guzman, 'The Design of International Agreements' (2005) 16 EJIL 579; A Aust, 'The Theory and Practice of Nonbinding International Agreements' (1984) 35 ICLQ 787; O Schachter, 'The Twilight Existence of Nonbinding International Agreements' (1977) 71 AJIL 296.

[135] See, e.g., J d'Aspremont, 'Softness in International Law: A Self-Serving Quest for New Legal Materials' (2008) 17 EJIL 1090; J Klabbers, 'The Redundancy of Soft Law' (1996) 65 Netherlands JIL 173; and the special *Symposium on Soft Law* of the Leiden Journal of International Law, (2012) 25 Leiden JIL 309.

[136] A leading study in this regard is that of D Shelton (ed), *Commitment and Compliance: The Role of Non-Binding Norms in the International Legal System* (OUP, 2000). Less enthusiastic about the role of soft law are A Boyle and C Chinkin, *The Making of International Law* (CUP, 2007).

[137] See, e.g., OECD Guidelines for Multinational Enterprises (last revised 2011), available at <http://mneguidelines.oecd.org/guidelines>.

protection of the environment,[138] and questions relating to the financing of terrorism.[139] A cynical posture is not unwarranted: soft law can constitute a form of subterfuge, a non-binding instrument that States can point to as a substitute for action. Being constructive for a moment, however, soft law can point to future directions for the law itself, a political intention to take action that can set in motion a process leading to binding legal rules. If adopted, the June 2021 proposal for the legal definition of a new international crime of 'ecocide' might be just such a step, with significant early momentum.[140]

THEORY AND DEBATES The Lawmaking Influence of the International Law Commission

One controversy remains the influence of the ILC, a subsidiary organ of the General Assembly which has the mandate of promoting the 'progressive development of international law and its codification' (ILC Statute, Art 2). Formally, of course, it is not a primary source of international law; it does not produce treaties or generate custom. However, the Commission's thirty-four members are elected by the General Assembly and represent all regions of the world; and over the years they have produced detailed reports and commentaries that have proven substantively influential on State practice and the drafting of treaties. As such, debate remains as to the extent of their influence: are they merely the writings of distinguished publicists or something more?

Much of the Commission's appeal with States has been in its working methods, which consist in a detailed, thorough analysis of State practice and possible instances of *opinio juris*, and how these may evidence the emergence of a new customary legal rule. Moreover, in operation the ILC tends systematically to invite comments and consultations from the General Assembly and States. This State-centric and relatively cautious methodology has proved popular with States and, as described earlier, the Commission's work has long been cited approvingly by the ICJ, on topics ranging from the continental shelf, the use of force, limitations on State immunity, and the scope of compensation to be awarded as reparation. In this respect, the ILC's work is probably best understood as an 'indirect' but influential source of international law.

The Commission's work has been particularly influential in relation to treaties and custom. Regarding treaties, the ILC will study a topic and propose a set of draft articles which can be taken up by the United Nations and trigger a process of treaty negotiation. Indeed, conventions on diplomatic and consular relations, the law of treaties, and the law of the sea, grew out of draft articles originally proposed by the ILC. As regards custom, many draft articles and reports do not make it into the form of a convention but can prove influential as a codification of custom, such as the articles on responsibility of States for internationally wrongful acts responsibility, diplomatic protection, or the prevention of transboundary harm. In fact,

[138] E.g., the 1972 Stockholm Declaration on the Human Environment and the 1992 Rio Declaration on the Environment and Development contained principles that later shaped State practice and *opinio juris*, and influenced environmental treaties. See Chapter 19, Section 19.2.2.

[139] See, e.g., the 2014 Basel Committee on Banking Supervision, 'Sound Management of Risks related to Money Laundering and Financing of Terrorism', available at <http://www.bis.org/publ/bcbs275.pdf>.

[140] See *Report of the Independent Expert Panel for the Legal Definition of Ecocide: Commentary and Core Text* (June 2021), available at <https://www.stopecocide.earth/expert-drafting-panel>. Recent legal developments suggest increased endorsement of the concept, including the EU's 2024 revisions of its Environmental Crimes Directive 2024/1203 (2024), and national legislative proposals, including in Azerbaijan, Belgium, Canada, Finland, Peru, and Sweden. See also the call for international recognition of the crime of ecocide in Report of the Secretary-General, 'Protection of Civilians in Armed Conflict', UN Doc S/2024/385 (14 May 2024), para 45.

much of the Commission's recent work on non-binding instruments, such as its studies of customary law, reservations to treaties, and even peremptory norms, has from the outset been designed to provide a guide to States, rather than a potential source of treaty texts.

For further reading on the development of international law by the ILC, see F Bordin, 'Reflections of Customary International Law: The Authority of Codification Conventions and ILC Draft Articles in International Law' (2014) 63 ICLQ 535; and D Azaria, 'Codification by Interpretation': The International Law Commission as an Interpreter of International Law' (2020) 31 EJIL 171.

2.4 Conclusion: the enduring relevance of sources

International law has traditionally derived the validity of its rules from State consent and, due to its decentralized character, its sources doctrine often appears fiendishly complex to the international law newcomer. However, the relative complexity of international legal thinking on sources should not mask the fact that, as with all legal systems, the classification of legal sources is driven by an enduring quest for relevance. To understand sources theory is to distinguish what law is from what law is not and, in so doing, to preserve the autonomy of international law as a functioning system. Sources theory provides reassurance for international lawyers that our discipline is a legal one; it is an attempt to remove politics, values, and other extra-legal considerations from our craft.

For all this, we should not allow that professional reassurance to shield our eyes from the emergence of relevant, dynamic processes through which the traditional processes of law-creation are changing. Though there is an enduring reliance on Article 38 and, with it, a sources theory reliant on the consent of States, the influence of non-State actors in lawmaking continues to deepen, reflecting shifts in power within the system and making the denial of politics increasingly difficult. With these struggles over politics also come struggles over values, and in the next chapter the key question will be explored as to whether international law has taken in certain values to the extent that they now constitute superior norms, prevailing over all other norms of international law.

Further reading

G Abi-Saab, 'Les sources du droit international—Un essai de déconstruction' in E Jiménez de Aréchaga and M Rama-Montaldo (eds), *Le droit international dans un monde en mutation* (Fundacion de Cultura Universitaria, 1994), 29.

A measured, progressive account of the doctrine of sources in international law.

M Akehurst, 'Custom as a Source of International Law' (1974–5) 47 BYBIL 1.

For decades, perhaps the indispensable study of customary international law.

A D'Amato, *The Concept of Custom in International Law* (Cornell UP, 1971).

A refreshing account of customary law as a pattern of conduct and repetition that generates new legal rules.

J d'Aspremont, *Formalism and the Sources of International Law* (OUP, 2011).

Ambitious resuscitation of a formalist approach to the sources of international law.

A Boyle and C Chinkin, *The Making of International Law* (CUP, 2007).

A broad survey of both sources doctrines as well as emerging lawmaking processes.

G Fitzmaurice, 'Some Problems Regarding the Formal Sources of International Law' in *Symbolae Verzijil: présentées au Professeur JHW Verzijl, Á l'Occasion de son LXXième Anniversaire* (Nijhoff, 1958), 153.

This classic piece remains highly influential in understanding the modern doctrine of sources.

D Kennedy, 'The Sources of International Law' (1987) 2 American University JILP 1.

An incisive and welcome critique on the discourse surrounding the sources of international law.

V Lowe, 'Are the Method and Character of Norm-creation Changing?' in M Byers (ed), *The Role of Law in International Politics* (OUP, 2000), 207–26.

An engaging essay by a leading academic and international law advocate.

A Pellet and D Müller, 'Article 38' in A Zimmermann, C Tomuschat, K Oellers-Frahm, and C Tams (eds), *The Statute of the International Court of Justice* (3rd edn, OUP, 2019), 819.

Often referred to as the 'flagship' chapter in the newly revised commentary, this piece is a magisterial compendium of the Court's treatment of sources.

AE Roberts, 'Traditional and Modern Approaches to Customary International Law: A Reconciliation' (2001) 95 AJIL 757.

Extremely clear, this award-winning article engagingly sets out the modern operation of custom.

M Sørensen, *Les sources du droit international* (Munskgaard, 1946).

A classic French-language treatise written by a prominent Danish academic.

H Thirlway, *The Sources of International Law* (2nd edn, OUP, 2019).

A freshly updated and systematic survey prepared by an expert in sources theory, with decades of practice experience at the ICJ.

3

Hierarchy of norms in international law

3.1 Introduction: why does hierarchy matter?

The traditional narrative is to portray international law as a consent-based, horizontal system of rules, in opposition to municipal legal systems which, at least as a general observation, establish a hierarchy of norms based on the particular source from which a norm derives. Thus, in the case of conflict, rules of a constitutional nature prevail over ordinary legislation, which in turn prevails over administrative decrees. A similar hierarchy would apply in respect of judicial decisions: the judgments of a supreme or constitutional court prevail over those of a mid-ranking appellate court, which in turn would prevail over those of an administrative tribunal. Establishing a hierarchy of norms and sources allows for a community to elevate certain fundamental principles over 'ordinary' norms, and to establish order and clarity in the relations between norms, authoritative institutions, and legal subjects.[1]

As described earlier in Chapter 2, international law is a consent-based system with no centralized law-creating authority. Accordingly, it remains a challenge to discern which norms or rules might have a 'peremptory' character, in that they would prevail in the case of conflict. Formally, each primary source of international law possesses equal rank and status,[2] and Article 38 of the ICJ Statute makes no hierarchical distinction between international conventions, international custom, and general principles of law, though that lack of hierarchy is not as clear-cut in practice.[3] As discussed in Chapter 2, Article 38 remains the only provision of a general nature in which States

[1] See M Koskenniemi, 'Hierarchy in International Law: A Sketch' (1997) 8 EJIL 566; and M Akehurst, 'The Hierarchy of the Sources of International Law' (1974–5) 47 BYBIL 273.

[2] Akehurst (n 1) 274–5; H Thirlway, *The Sources of International Law* (2nd OUP, 2019), 5–8.

[3] See ILC, 'Fragmentation of International Law: Difficulties Arising from the Diversification and Expansion of International Law' (2006) UN Doc A/CN.4/L.682, 47, which suggests that 'treaties generally enjoy priority over custom and particular treaties over general treaties'; and A Pellet and D Müller, 'Article 38' in A Zimmerman, C Tomuschat, K Oellers-Frahm, and C Tams (eds), *The Statute of the International Court of Justice: Article by Article Commentary* (3rd edn, OUP, 2019), 819: while there is no formal hierarchy between the sources, the International Court uses them in successive order and 'to a great extent, custom steps aside in favour of treaty law'.

have acknowledged the sources of the legal rules to which they agree to be bound.[4] The consent-based classical view of international law, moreover, contains few general principles to resolve a conflict that might arise between competing rules contained in a primary source. Two conflict-resolution principles, for example that later norms may supersede earlier norms (*lex posterior derogate priori*) or that a special (specific) rule may prevail over a general rule (*lex specialis derogat legi generali*), only address conflict between equivalent norms of law; they do not recognize that some rules may enjoy a hierarchically superior status than others.[5]

3.2 The emergence of *jus cogens* in international law

In the last half-century, a special class of general rules endowed with peremptory legal force has emerged. Known interchangeably as 'peremptory norms' or 'norms of *jus cogens*', these are regarded as possessing a hierarchically superior status than 'ordinary' rules of international law, and would prevail over the latter in cases of conflict. As such, whether an ordinary rule exists in treaty or customary law, or is a general principle, it is null and void if in conflict with a rule of *jus cogens*. Such a concept was, at first, regarded as revolutionary. Prosper Weil famously coined the term 'relative normativity' to decry the changes *jus cogens* would impose on the very structure of international law, transforming from a system where all norms were equal into a system with certain 'higher' norms, of which the source of validity was uncertain, and possibly putting into question the validity of 'ordinary' norms.[6]

Perhaps Weil's caution is somewhat overstated, in that positive international law has long recognized that certain norms prevail over others. The Covenant of the League of Nations, in declaring that 'war or threat of war [is] a matter of common concern to the whole League',[7] imposed an obligation on all States to suspend trading and diplomatic relations with a State in breach of the Covenant.[8] These would be ordinary treaty obligations, but a supremacy clause abrogated all obligations inconsistent with the Covenant.[9] The UN Charter follows a similar logic embedding a prohibition against the threat or use of force,[10] and giving powers to the Security Council under Chapter VII to take measures that bind all States.[11] But above all, the Charter contains a supremacy clause through which obligations flowing from the Charter (and, in

[4] See G Hernández, *The International Court of Justice and the Judicial Function* (OUP, 2014), chs 2, 29–30, for a fuller exposition on this point.

[5] The *lex posterior* and *lex specialis* rules are further addressed by the ILC in its Fragmentation Report (n 3) para 8.

[6] P Weil, 'Towards Relative Normativity in International Law?' (1983) 77 AJIL 413; originally published as P Weil, 'Vers une normativité relative en droit international' (1982) RGDIP 5.

[7] Covenant of the League of Nations, Art 11.

[8] *Ibid*, Art 14.

[9] *Ibid*, Art 20.

[10] UN Charter, Art 2(4). The prohibition is not absolute, however: see the inherent right to use force in self-defence in Art 51.

[11] *Ibid*, Chapter VII (Arts 39–51). The Security Council is further described in Chapter 6, Section 6.7.1.1.2, and the use of its collective security powers is addressed in Chapter 14, Section 14.5.

particular, Chapter VII resolutions adopted by the Security Council) prevail over any conflicting obligations.[12]

Neither Article 20 of the Covenant nor Article 103 of the Charter are norms of *jus cogens*; they are treaty rules specifying priority in times of conflict of norms.[13] Moreover, other examples of priority clauses exist: for example, Article 311(3) of the UN Convention on the Law of the Sea expressly assigns its provisions priority over earlier conventions on the law of the sea, and enjoins States against concluding subsequent agreements that would derogate from obligations under UNCLOS.[14] The concept of *jus cogens* thus extends the same concept into general international law, specifying priority when no treaty provision exists to do so.

Natural law scholarship had long recognized certain principles as necessary or immutable (*jus necessarium* or *jus naturale*),[15] distinct from *jus dispositivum* ('law adopted by consent') legal rules which normally apply, but which can be superseded through rules of equivalent character, such as conclusion of a treaty or the emergence of a new customary rule.[16] The dominance of positivism from the nineteenth century onwards would reject this view in favour of a system of equal sovereign States whose actions were limited only by binding rules to which they had consented.[17] In other words, only *jus dispositivum* was relevant, and there would be no category of higher legal rules.[18] It was in the twentieth century that the concept of *jus cogens* would be used to describe rules of imperative law which applied regardless of any attempt to depart from them.[19]

HISTORICAL BACKGROUND Norms of *Jus Cogens* at the Vienna Conference on the Law of Treaties

The ILC was one of the first institutions to use the term *jus cogens*, which it introduced in its Draft Articles on the Law of Treaties to be considered by States at the Vienna Conference on the Law of Treaties in 1968.

The proposal was met with much controversy. Certain Western States were resistant to a concept which undermined their conception of international law, with France in particular expressing strong opposition (see *Official Records of the United Nations Conference on the Law*

[12] *Ibid*, Art 103.

[13] ILC, 'First Report on *Jus Cogens*' (Special Rapporteur Dire Tladi), UN Doc CN.4/693 (8 March 2016), 15.

[14] The law of the sea is considered further in Chapter 18.

[15] See, e.g., H Grotius, *De Jure Belli ac Pacis* (1625), 1.1.X.5; E de Vattel, *Le droit des gens* (1758), para 9; C Wolff, *Jus Gentium* (1764), para 5. The natural law origin of *jus cogens* is acknowledged in the ILC's 'First Report on *Jus Cogens*' (n 13) 30–1.

[16] The distinction was well set out by Sir Gerald Fitzmaurice in the ILC's Third Report on the Law of Treaties (1958) ILC Ybk vol II, 40, para 76.

[17] As memorably enshrined in the *Case of the SS 'Lotus' (France v Turkey), Judgment, 1927, PCIJ, Ser A, No 10*, p 18.

[18] See H Kelsen, *Pure Theory of Law* (1943 CH Wilson tr (1934) 50 LQR 474, 483–4).

[19] See, e.g., A Verdross, '*Jus Dispositivum* and *Jus Cogens* in International Law' (1966) 60 AJIL 55, building in particular on A Verdross, 'Forbidden Treaties in International Law' (1937) 31 AJIL 571. See also the Separate Opinion of Judge Schücking in *Oscar Chinn, Judgment, 1934, PCIJ, Ser A/B, No 63*, p 63, 148, which represents the first use of the term in judicial practice, and the arbitral award of the French–Mexican Claims Commission in the *Pablo Najera* case, Decision No 30-A (1928), V RIAA 466, 470. A detailed history of the emergence of the concept is found in Tladi, 'First Report on *Jus Cogens*' (n 13), esp 9–23.

of Treaties, First Session (1968), 309–10, §§26–34). Much of the opposition of Western States stemmed from whether peremptory norms represented a shift from a horizontal legal order based on the consent of States to a value-driven international order.

Nevertheless, the concept proved popular with three groups of States. Foremost were newly independent States which saw the upholding of *jus cogens* as an opportunity to condemn colonial and imperial practices, such as slavery and apartheid (see, e.g., *Official Records*, 300, §9 (Sierra Leone), 327, §§68–70 (Mali)). Socialist States regarded *jus cogens* as a useful category to ensure the peaceful coexistence of States with different social and economic structures (see, e.g., *Official Records*, 312–13 §55–63 (Romania); 322, §6 (Ukraine)). Finally, a number of States were receptive to the humanitarian aspects of *jus cogens* (see *Official Records*, 295, §§68–70 (Scandinavian States and Greece); 305–6, §§66–71 (Cyprus), 315, §§1–5 (Spain), and 323, §§21–4 (Canada)).

The outcome of the Vienna Conference would be the adoption of the VCLT, including Article 53, which recognizes the concept of *jus cogens*.

For further reading on the history of the Vienna Conference debates in relation to norms of *jus cogens*, see Dire Tladi, Special Rapporteur for the ILC in its First Report on *Jus Cogens* (2016), 16–19.

The VCLT is currently ratified by 116 States; as explained in Chapter 2, Section 2.2.3, its provisions are widely regarded as a codification of customary international law. The VCLT contains the following provision in Article 53, which is generally regarded as the first recognition of the concept of *jus cogens* in a treaty provision:

> A treaty is void if, at the time of its conclusion, it conflicts with a peremptory norm of general international law. For the purposes of the present Convention, a peremptory norm of general international law is a norm accepted and recognized by the international community of States as a whole as a norm from which no derogation is permitted and which can be modified only by a subsequent norm of general international law having the same character.[20]

The clearest significance of Article 53 VCLT is the recognition of a category of norms which is hierarchically superior to ordinary rules of international law.[21] Article 53 VCLT specifies several crucial aspects of norms of *jus cogens*: they are non-derogable in all circumstances; they are norms applicable to all States; and they are accepted and recognized as peremptory by the international community of States as a whole.[22] Moreover, only a new rule of *jus cogens* can modify or supersede an existing rule with that same character.[23] These characteristics suggest that law made by consent can, in

[20] See also the Vienna Convention on the Law of Treaties between States and International Organizations, (signed 1986, not yet in force) 25 ILM 543, Art 53, which mirrors the VCLT.

[21] See ILC, 'Draft Conclusions on Identification and Legal Consequences of Peremptory Norms of General International Law (*Jus Cogens*), With Commentaries': see Report of the International Law Commission on the Work of its 73rd Session, UN Doc A/77/10 (2022) GAOR 77th Session Supp 10, Chapter IV, at Draft Conclusion 2.

[22] See *ibid*, Draft Conclusion 4.

[23] VCLT Art 64; see also Art 71.

some cases, be overridden by fundamental or superior values of public order, not unlike in a municipal legal order.[24]

Though the recognition of *jus cogens* in the VCLT was a significant development in its day, it must be said that it codified only a narrow subset of the potential effects of *jus cogens*. As Andrea Bianchi has cautioned, '[t]o hold that *jus cogens* is nothing but a legal technique aimed at preserving the formal integrity of the system by characterising as inderogable some of its procedural norms is tantamount to overlooking what the function performed by *jus cogens* was meant to be'.[25] In some respects, therefore, the VCLT is more a starting point than the final word in respect of peremptory norms in international law.

3.3 The role of *jus cogens* and the challenge of relative normativity

Though Article 53 VCLT explains certain attributes of rules of *jus cogens*, it sheds light neither on their origin nor on how they may be ascertained to exist. Such uncertainty has led to continued debate about whether norms of *jus cogens* are simply another form of positive law based on consent, or the expression of a non-consent-based source of law.[26] Bruno Simma has argued that once recognition by States has been given, the question of the source of *jus cogens* is more or less irrelevant.[27] The ICJ and other international courts have recognized in recent cases that norms of *jus cogens* reflect fundamental or essential values of international law which, to a degree, belies the normative character of *jus cogens*.[28] Others have argued that *jus cogens* rules can evolve from the common values of all nations.[29]

The question arises, then, whether norms of *jus cogens* are logically necessary. Robert Kolb has developed a typology under which various norms of *jus cogens* can be justified by reference to logical necessity, or whether they embody values of international 'public order' or 'public utility'.[30]

It has boldly been argued by Alexander Orakhelashvili that norms of *jus cogens* constitute an autonomous body of superior rules, independent of any source of international law, especially since many peremptory norms might fail to satisfy the requirements for customary law-formation.[31] Antonio Cassese also called for a decidedly naturalist method of ascertaining the existence of norms of *jus cogens*, claiming that the elements

[24] D Shelton, 'Normative Hierarchy in International Law: A Sketch' (2006) 100 AJIL 291, 297 *et seq*; G Gaja, '*Jus Cogens* Beyond the Vienna Conventions' (1981) 172 Recueil des Cours 29.

[25] A Bianchi, 'Human Rights and the Magic of *Jus Cogens*' (2008) 19 EJIL 491, 495.

[26] A Hameed, 'Unravelling the Mystery of *Jus Cogens* in International Law' (2014) 84 BYBIL 52.

[27] B Simma, 'From Bilateralism to Community Interest' (1994-I) 250 Recueil des Cours 229, 292.

[28] *Application of the Convention on the Prevention and Punishment of the Crime of Genocide (Bosnia and Herzegovina v Serbia and Montenegro), Judgment, ICJ Reports 2007*, p 43, 104, para 147; *Prosecutor v Furundžija*, (Appeals Chamber Judgment) Case No IT-95-17/1A, Judgment of 21 July 2000 (2002) ILR 121, 153–4; *Al-Adsani v United Kingdom*, ECHR No 35763/97, ECHR 2001-XI, 34 EHRR 11 (Grand Chamber), para 30; see also ILC, 'Second Report on *Jus Cogens*' (n 21) 10.

[29] C Tomuschat, 'Obligations arising for States Without or Against their Will' (1003) 241 Recueil des Cours 307.

[30] R Kolb, *Peremptory International Law—Jus Cogens: A General Inventory* (Hart, 2015), 45–7.

[31] A Orakhelashvili, *Peremptory Norms in International Law* (OUP, 2006), 109, 113.

of State practice and *opinio juris* used in ascertaining custom were no longer required, given the superior status of norms of *jus cogens*.[32]

There are two aspects of peremptory norms as outlined in Article 53 VCLT, however, that seem to contradict the naturalist position. First, new norms of *jus cogens* can come to modify or supersede existing norms of *jus cogens*, which suggests that they are not immutable—a hallmark of the natural law approach.[33] Secondly, to be regarded as *jus cogens*, a two-step process is required. It must be recognized by the international community of States as a whole, which suggests that it must be recognized by a very large majority of States from all parts of the world.[34] Moreover, under Article 53 VCLT, a possible norm of *jus cogens* must also be recognized by States as non-derogable and thus, in circular fashion, also one of *jus cogens*.[35]

The positivist approach to *jus cogens* evades these contentious points, contending that peremptory norms are most commonly based in a subset of customary international law.[36] Indeed, the ILC's Draft Conclusion 5 points to customary international law as the 'most common basis' for peremptory norms.[37] But this is not uncontested: Hugh Thirlway, hardly a natural lawyer, has argued that given their universal application, norms of *jus cogens* are essentially a *feature* of general customary law. He suggests that while the idea of *jus cogens* reflects an 'ineradicable moral element', this is not the reason for their elevated status. Instead, *jus cogens* status attaches to a rule which has emerged through State practice and *opinio juris*, provided there is sufficient evidence of its recognition as such by States.[38]

[32] A Cassese, 'For an Enhanced Role of *Jus Cogens*' in A Cassese (ed), *Realizing Utopia: The Future of International Law* (OUP, 2012), 158, 164–5. *Cf* 157, who suggests that if *jus cogens* norms exist without following the custom-generative process, they ought not to be classed as custom at all, but as something entirely different.

[33] See R Kolb, *Théorie du* jus cogens (PUF, 2001), 31.

[34] See ILC, Draft Conclusion 7(2) (n 21); and 'Second Report on *Jus Cogens*' (n 21), para 67. The threshold of a 'very large majority' of States had already been suggested in 1968: see Statement by Mr Yasseen, *Official Records of the United Nations Conference on the Law of Treaties*, First Session (1968), 472, §12.

[35] ILC, Draft Conclusion 6, especially 6(2) (n 21). See, e.g., E de Wet, '*Jus Cogens* and Obligations *Erga Omnes*' in D Shelton (ed), *The Oxford Handbook of International Human Rights Law* (OUP, 2013), 542; J Vidmar, 'Norm Conflicts and Hierarchy in International Law: Towards a Vertical International Legal System?' in E de Wet and J Vidmar (eds), *Hierarchy in International Law: The Place of Human Rights* (OUP, 2011), 25; and Hameed (n 26) 62.

[36] See ILC, 'Second Report on *Jus Cogens*' (n 21) para 14; and *cf* R Kolb, 'The Formal Source of *Ius Cogens*' (1998) 53 ZaöRV 77, fn 42, who asks, if *jus cogens* can be created by consensus, why by consensus alone, and not by custom or treaty?

[37] See ILC, Draft Conclusion 5 (n 21), which at 5(2) suggests that treaty provisions and general principles 'may also serve as bases for peremptory norms'. It has been noted in relation to general principles that, despite little practice, nothing seems to exclude the possibility that they serve as a source of *jus cogens*: see 'Second Report on *Jus Cogens*' (n 21) 26–7, Kolb (n 30) 96; and S Knuchel, *Jus Cogens: Identification and Enforcement of Peremptory Norms* (Schulthess, 2015), 52. *Cf* Thirlway (n 2) 162. Finally, at Draft Conclusion 9, *ibid*, judicial decisions, 'in particular those of the International Court of Justice', are regarded as subsidiary means of determining the peremptory character of a norm.

[38] Thirlway (n 2) 160–3. See also V Lowe, *International Law* (Clarendon Press, 2007), 59–60; I Sinclair, *Vienna Convention on the Law of Treaties* (Manchester UP, 1984), 218–24; ILC, 'First Report on *Jus Cogens*' (n 13) 32; ILC, 'Second Report on *Jus Cogens*' (n 21) 36.

CONTEMPORARY DEVELOPMENTS The International Law Commission and the Draft Conclusions on Peremptory Norms (*Jus Cogens*)

The vibrant debate on the nature and scope of peremptory norms of *jus cogens* has been galvanized by the ILC, which in 2015 added the topic to its areas of active consideration. Special Rapporteur Dire Tladi produced substantial reports that addressed the historical development and legal nature of the concept (First Report), possible conditions for how a norm of *jus cogens* can come to be accepted and recognized (Second Report), the legal consequences of *jus cogens* (Third Report), and the potential for regional *jus cogens* and what specific norms might qualify (Fourth Report).

In 2022, after incorporating a range of State comments and observations (see Fifth Report), the Commission adopted its final Draft Conclusions, with commentaries, and recommended them to the General Assembly (see UN Doc A/77/10, 2022, Chapter IV, paras 32–34). It has now concluded its work on the topic.

Though not a formal source of international law, the Draft Conclusions have already established their authority: the ILC's authority as a collective and deliberative organ is much higher than the views of any one individual, and it is particularly influential in the codification and, potentially, the progressive development of international law. Moreover, the ILC's measured, consultative approach is generally respected by States and routinely cited by international courts: though hardly radical it is an indirect, but highly influential, actor.

As with the ILC, the ICJ appears to adopt an approach which conceives of *jus cogens* within a consent-based paradigm. Most prominently, in its 2012 judgment in *Obligation to Extradite or Prosecute*, the Court concluded that the prohibition of torture was both part of customary international law and a peremptory norm, pointing to State practice, domestic implementation, and *opinio juris* to support those conclusions.[39] Though the Court was not explicit, its analysis would suggest that it regarded the same materials as evidence of two distinct propositions: the acceptance of the prohibition as customary international law, as well as evidence of its peremptory status.[40]

The ILC Special Rapporteur also listed the same categories of sources for the identification of *jus cogens* as would be relevant for identifying customary international law: treaties, resolutions adopted by international organizations, public statements on behalf of States, official publications, governmental legal opinions, diplomatic correspondence, and decisions of national courts.[41] However, the judgments of other international courts and tribunals, as well as domestic courts, seem to oscillate between consent and natural law-based solutions.[42]

[39] *Obligation to Prosecute or Extradite (Belgium v Senegal), Judgment, ICJ Reports 2012*, p 449, para 99. See also *Military and Paramilitary Activities in and against Nicaragua (Nicaragua v United States), Merits, ICJ Reports 1986*, p 14, 190, where the *jus cogens* nature of the prohibition on the use of force was evinced primarily by reference to the views of State representatives; and *Legality of the Threat or Use of Nuclear Weapons, Advisory Opinion, ICJ Reports 1996*, p 226, para 79, which suggests that certain rules of humanitarian law are 'intransgressible' principles of customary international law.

[40] Further commentary on this significant judgment is given later, in Section 3.4.

[41] See Draft Conclusion 8 (n 21); see further 'Second Report on *Jus Cogens*' (n 21) 46. But *cf* Kolb (n 30) 97, who suggests that *jus cogens* can be embodied in any source.

[42] These are described in detail in ILC, 'First Report on *Jus Cogens*' (n 13) 34–5.

Neither theory seems fully satisfactory, and arguably, *jus cogens* might only be understood if one can grasp the interaction between natural law and positivist theories.[43] Though neither can provide a comprehensive explanation, each theory 'can unveil and illuminate aspects of international law which remain inaccessible or off-limits to the other'.[44]

3.4 Obligations *erga omnes*

Before further exploring the scope of norms of *jus cogens*, one must consider a related category known as rights or, more commonly, obligations *erga omnes* ('owed to all'). These are also ascribed a special status within international law.[45] Though there is a high degree of overlap between these categories, they are conceptually distinct; though all peremptory norms give rise to obligations *erga omnes*, the reverse is not necessarily true.[46]

The existence of obligations *erga omnes* was acknowledged by the ICJ, albeit rather in passing, in *Barcelona Traction, Light and Power Company*. In a statement which had little to do with the rights of Belgian shareholders at the heart of that dispute, given that Belgium was not allowed to exercise diplomatic protection on behalf of them, the ICJ explained how certain 'obligations of a State towards the international community as a whole . . . are the concern of all States. In view of the importance of the rights involved, all States can be held to have a legal interest in their protection; they are obligations *erga omnes*'.[47] Though obligations *erga omnes* would be further acknowledged in later decisions, such as *East Timor* and *Construction of a Wall* in relation to the right of a people to self-determination,[48] it would not be until 2012, in *Obligation to Prosecute or Extradite*, that the ICJ would apply the concept in a concrete dispute.[49] There, the ICJ concluded that all States parties to the Convention against Torture, including Belgium, had a legal interest in ensuring compliance with obligations contained in the Convention; these were characterized as 'obligations *erga omnes partes*'.[50]

[43] See, on this point, M Koskenniemi, *From Apology to Utopia: The Structure of Legal Argument* (CUP reissue, 2005), 307–8.

[44] Simma (n 27) 34.

[45] Two leading works on obligations *erga omnes* are C Tams, *Enforcing Obligations* Erga Omnes *in International Law* (CUP, 2005); and S Villalpando, *L'émergence de la communauté internationale dans la responsabilité des États* (PUF, 2005).

[46] See Draft Conclusion 17 (n 21), and especially the Commentary thereto, para 3; see further Tams, *ibid*, 149, for a lucid explanation of these distinctions; and see later, Section 3.5.2, for a list of norms of *jus cogens*.

[47] *Barcelona Traction Heat, Light, and Power Co (Belgium v Spain), Second Phase, ICJ Reports 1970*, p 3, para 33.

[48] See *East Timor (Portugal v Australia), Jurisdiction, ICJ Reports 1995*, p 90, paras 28–9; *Construction of a Wall in Occupied Palestinian Territory, Advisory Opinion, ICJ Reports 2004*, p 136. This finding has been strengthened by the Court's 2024 advisory opinion in *Policies and Practices of Israel in the Occupied Palestinian Territory, including East Jerusalem, Advisory Opinion of 19 July 2024*.

[49] Though in the last five years the situation has changed dramatically, the present author has written on the conceptual reasons for the traditional parsimony of the Court to engage with obligations *erga omnes*: see GI Hernández, 'A Reluctant Guardian: The International Court of Justice and the Concept of "International Community"' (2013) 83 BYBIL 13.

[50] *Obligation to Prosecute or Extradite* (n 39) para 68. It is worth mentioning that at para 55, Belgium had presented a claim that the prohibition against torture was also an obligation *erga omnes* under customary law.

CASE SPOTLIGHT ***Obligation to Prosecute or Extradite (Belgium v Senegal), Judgment, ICJ Reports 2012, p 449***

At issue was a request by Belgium to Senegal to extradite the former president of Chad, Mr Hissène Habré, who was accused of engaging in torture, war crimes, and crimes against humanity against thousands of victims during his term in office (1982–90). Mr Habré had been residing in Senegal as a political asylee for nearly two decades. Belgium contended that Senegal had breached its obligations under the Convention against Torture in failing to prosecute or extradite Mr Habré, despite repeated requests from Belgium for his extradition.

Belgium, in asserting its legal right to submit a claim, argued that several Chadian nationals who had been tortured were now Belgian nationals, and that it was therefore a 'specially affected' State (para 65, using wording from Art 41(2) Articles on State Responsibility for Internationally Wrongful Acts (ARSIWA)). Belgium further contended that the nationality of the victims was irrelevant because all States parties to the Convention were entitled to demand that other States parties fulfil their obligations thereunder (para 65).

The Court agreed with Belgium that all States parties had a common interest in the prevention of acts of torture and impunity for those committing such acts. It declared that the Convention created obligations *erga omnes partes* in which all parties had a legal interest to claim for cessation, regardless of whether an applicant had a special interest (para 68). It would represent the first time that the Court had recognized that the *erga omnes* nature of an obligation could entitle an applicant to standing, though this would occur again two years later in *Whaling in the Antarctic (Australia v Japan; New Zealand intervening), ICJ Reports 2014*, p 226. It should be emphasized, however, that the Court in these cases has only recognized obligations *erga omnes partes* limited to obligations flowing from a treaty; it has not as yet recognized any obligations *erga omnes* flowing from customary international law.

The Court has now gone further, reaffirming in its 2019 *Separation of the Chagos Archipelago* that all States have a legal interest in protecting the right to self-determination, an obligation *erga omnes*.[51] In its 2022 judgment on preliminary objections in *Application of the Genocide Convention (The Gambia v Myanmar)*, the *erga omnes* character of the prohibition against genocide in the Convention was successfully invoked by The Gambia to contend that, even as a non-injured State, it had standing to pursue a claim before the Court.[52] The ICJ is not alone: ITLOS has long determined that certain environmental obligations under UNCLOS, relating to preservation of the environment of the high seas and the deep seabed, have an *erga omnes* character.[53]

[51] *Legal Consequences of the Separation of the Chagos Archipelago from Mauritius in 1965, Advisory Opinion, ICJ Reports 2019*, p 95, para 180.

[52] *Application of the Convention on the Prevention and Punishment of the Crime of Genocide (The Gambia v Myanmar), Preliminary Objections, ICJ Reports 2022*, p 477, paras 106–10. The finding on standing was relied upon by the Court in *Application of the Convention on the Prevention and Punishment of the Crime of Genocide in the Gaza Strip (South Africa v Israel), Order on Provisional Measures of 26 January 2024*, para 33.

[53] *Responsibilities and Obligations of States Sponsoring Persons and Entities with Respect to Activities in the Area, Advisory Opinion, ITLOS Reports 2011*, p 59, para 180.

One clarification is important: obligations *erga omnes partes* are based in a treaty and are far easier for a court or tribunal to recognize as binding on the parties than an obligation not contained in a treaty. Dozens of treaties contain such provisions allowing all other parties the right to claim for a breach by one party, thus enabling a multilateralization of enforcement.[54]

THEORY AND DEBATES Distinguishing Norms of *Jus Cogens* from Obligations *Erga Omnes*

It might confuse the newcomer to international law that there are two separate categories of rules benefiting from a higher—or at least differentiated—status vis-à-vis the ordinary rules of international law: norms of *jus cogens* and obligations *erga omnes*. What is more, there is in fact a great overlap between them in substance. For example, the prohibitions against both genocide (in *Application of the Genocide Convention (Bosnia v Serbia)*) and torture (in *Obligation to Prosecute or Extradite (Belgium v Senegal)*) are simultaneously norms of *jus cogens* and obligations *erga omnes*—though the opposite is not true. The ILC explained this distinction in its Commentary to Draft Conclusion 17 on *jus cogens* (para 3), in which it argues that, though all norms of *jus cogens* give rise to obligations *erga omnes*, the reverse is not true, giving as examples obligations *erga omnes* such as those relating to common spaces or common heritage regimes. A further example of an obligation *erga omnes* which is not also a peremptory norm of *jus cogens* could be the obligations in relation to whaling which were the issue in the *Whaling in the Antarctic* dispute between Australia and Japan.

Accordingly, the conceptual distinction matters in practice. To qualify a norm as being one of *jus cogens* is to comment on its substantive nature, and to recognize its higher status than 'ordinary' rules of international law and its non-derogable character. *Jus cogens* is a broad concept that has consequences across much of general international law.

Conversely, to qualify an obligation as *erga omnes* entails a much narrower outcome, relating principally only to its scope of application. Put more simply, who is bound by the obligation and who has standing (a legal interest) to claim in case of breach? These have, of course, procedural implications: an obligation *erga omnes* can potentially be invoked by any member of the international community of States, even if they have sustained no direct injury. For example, a State involved in international litigation might refer to the status of the norm as *jus cogens* to suggest that another norm must yield before it, or as an obligation *erga omnes* to establish its standing to make a claim.

For further reading, see S Villalpando, 'The Legal Dimension of the International Community: How Community Interests are Protected in International Law' (2010) 21 EJIL 387; and C Tams, *Enforcing Obligations* Erga Omnes *in International Law* (CUP, 2005).

[54] OA Hathaway, A Hachem, and J Cole, 'A New Tool for Enforcing Human Rights: *Erga Omnes Partes* Standing' (2023) 62 *Columbia Journal of Transnational Law* 259.

3.5 The scope of rules of *jus cogens*

3.5.1 Legal effects of *jus cogens*

Scant practice exists with respect to the effects of peremptory norms—and for good reason:

> Settled practices of States as regards *jus cogens* are elusive to grasp because most, if not all, rules of *jus cogens* are prohibitive in substance; they are rules of abstention. How does one marshal conclusive evidence of abstentions? Abstentions *per se* mean nothing; they become meaningful only when considered in the light of the intention underlying them.[55]

Though the effects of *jus cogens* are not as clear as one would like,[56] the following section seeks to sketch out the possible effects of norms of *jus cogens* that have been identified in practice and judicial decisions.

3.5.1.1 Non-derogability, and the nullity of a treaty in conflict with *jus cogens*

A fundamental characteristic of elevating a rule to one of *jus cogens* is that it is non-derogable. As Article 53 VCLT provides, if at the time of its conclusion a provision in a treaty is in violation of *jus cogens*, the treaty *as a whole* (and not merely the offending provision) will be void *ab initio* (devoid of all legal effect from the outset).[57] Parties to a treaty voided in this manner are under a legal obligation to wipe out so far as possible, the consequences of any acts performed under that treaty.[58]

In other words, States cannot, through mutual consent, attempt to derogate from a peremptory norm. Article 64 VCLT specifies a further effect: '[i]f a new peremptory norm of general international law emerges, any existing treaty which is in conflict with that norm becomes void and terminates'. If a treaty becomes void in this manner, however, it is not *ab initio*: rights and obligations thereunder may be maintained prior to termination, but only to the extent that their maintenance is not in itself in conflict with the new peremptory norm.[59]

To recap, a rule of *jus cogens* may only be superseded by a new norm which also possesses the same character. Accordingly, no derogation of a rule of a peremptory rule of *jus cogens* is permitted by way of a treaty reservation,[60] the development of a new customary rule,[61] or a unilateral act of a State.[62] Similarly, there are no defences (circumstances precluding wrongfulness) that can be raised to excuse the breach of a peremptory norm.[63]

[55] B Simma and P Alston, 'The Sources of Human Rights Law' (1988–9) 12 Australian YBIL 82, 103–4. In a contrary vein, see MJ Glennon, 'De l'absurdité du droit imperatif (*jus cogens*)' (2006) RGDIP 529, 532.

[56] Kolb (n 30) 110–15 suggests that given this lack of clarity, incremental judicial development might help to clarify the effects of norms of *jus cogens*.

[57] See ILC Draft Conclusion 10(1) (n 21); and Draft Conclusion 11, which further clarifies that offending provisions are not separable: the treaty is void as a whole.

[58] ILC Draft Conclusion 12(1), *ibid.*

[59] ILC Draft Conclusion 12(2), *ibid.*

[60] ILC Draft Conclusion 13, *ibid.*

[61] ILC Draft Conclusion 14, *ibid.*

[62] ILC Draft Conclusion 15, *ibid.*

[63] ILC Draft Conclusion 18, *ibid.*

3.5.1.2 Universal scope of application of norms of *jus cogens*

A second important effect of characterizing a norm as *jus cogens* is, as Article 53 VCLT provides, that it is universally applicable as a rule of 'general international law'; accordingly, all peremptory norms give rise to obligations *erga omnes*.[64] Such universal applicability distinguishes norms of *jus cogens* from treaties, which require the ratification of a State, or from customary international law, which does not apply to States that have persistently objected to them.[65] Universal application is a facet of non-derogability; it would be nonsensical to suggest that a norm from which no derogation is permitted can only apply to some States.[66] Though some scholars have argued for a sort of 'regional *jus cogens*',[67] the concept did not fare well in the ILC: in response to State comments, Special Rapporteur Tladi acknowledged a potential incompatibility between the existence of regional *jus cogens* and their universal, non-derogable character.[68] In their final Draft Conclusions on the topic, the Commission concluded that the universal character and applicability of a peremptory norm precluded the application of regional or bilateral norms of *jus cogens*.[69]

3.5.1.3 Non-recognition of breaches of norms of *jus cogens*

ARSIWA has laid out several particular consequences of a serious breach of a peremptory norm, defined in Article 40(2) as a 'gross or systematic failure' to fulfil the relevant obligation. Under Article 41(1), States must cooperate to bring to an end, through lawful means, a serious breach of *jus cogens*. Further, under Article 41(2), States are under an obligation not to recognize as lawful any serious breach of a peremptory norm, and are prohibited from rendering aid or assistance in maintaining the unlawful situation. Though these may reflect progressive development more than the state of the existing law,[70] the core obligation to abstain from recognizing the consequences of a severe breach of international law has support in State practice. Examples include the collective non-recognition of Japan's invasion of Manchuria in 1934,[71] the rejection of the unilateral declaration of independence of white-dominated Rhodesia,[72] the non-recognition

[64] ILC, Draft Conclusion 17, *ibid*. See also Gaja (n 24) 283; L Hannikainen, *Peremptory Norms (*Jus Cogens*) in International Law: Historical Development, Criteria, Present Status* (Finnish Lawyers Publishing Company, 1988), 5; ILC, 'First Report on *Jus Cogens*' (n 13) 41.

[65] See Chapter 2, Section 2.2.2.2.3.

[66] ILC, 'First Report on *Jus Cogens*' (n 13) 41; and ILC, 'Second Report on *Jus Cogens*' (n 21) 14–15.

[67] The European human rights system has often been used as the potential example: see Kolb (n 30) 97 *et seq*; Gaja (n 24) 284; see also E De Wet, 'The Emergence of International and Regional Value Systems as a Manifestation of the Emerging International Constitutional Order' (2006) 19 Leiden JIL 611, 617.

[68] ILC, 'Fifth Report on Peremptory Norms of General International Law (*Jus Cogens*)', UN Doc CN.4/747 (21 January 2022), paras 45–55. For more detail, see ILC, 'Fourth Report on Peremptory Norms of General International Law (*Jus Cogens*)', UN Doc CN.4/727 (31 January 2019), paras 28–47.

[69] ILC, Draft Conclusions on Peremptory Norms (*Jus Cogens*) (n 21), Commentary to Draft Conclusion 2, paras 12–3.

[70] As conceded by the ILC in the ARSIWA: see Report of the International Law Commission on the Work of its 53rd Session, UN Doc A/56/10 Chapter IV (2001) GAOR 56th Session Supp 10, Commentary to Art 41, p 114, para 3.

[71] The Manchurian episode is recounted in J Crawford, *The Creation of States in International Law* (2nd edn, OUP, 2006), 75–8, 132–3.

[72] UNSC Res 216 (12 November 1965).

of South Africa's administration in Namibia (then South West Africa),[73] and the rejection of the annexation of Kuwait by Iraq.[74]

CASE SPOTLIGHT ***Construction of a Wall in Occupied Palestinian Territory, Advisory Opinion, ICJ Reports 2004, p 136***

The General Assembly had asked the Court to consider what legal consequences attached to Israel's construction of a 'Separation Barrier' within Palestinian territory under its occupation since 1967. Israel refused to participate in the oral proceedings, though it submitted written documents challenging the propriety of the Court responding to the request, and invoked security concerns as a justification for constructing the wall.

The Court first had to determine whether it should respond to the request, and ultimately decided that it would do so despite Israel's objections. After it dismissed Israel's security objectives as a valid justification for constructing the wall in occupied Palestinian territory (pp 192–4), the Court considered whether legal obligations had been breached. It concluded that, in building the wall, Israel was in breach of obligations 'to respect the right of the Palestinian people to self-determination' and 'obligations under international humanitarian law and international human rights law' (p 197).

A key advance made by the Court was in illuminating the effects of a breach of obligations *erga omnes*: 'in view of the character and the importance of the rights and obligations involved', the Court declared that all other States were under an obligation not to recognize the unlawful situation resulting from the construction of the wall, as well as under an obligation not to render aid or assistance in maintaining the resulting situation' (p 200). The Court also concluded that all States parties to the four Geneva Conventions were under an obligation to ensure that Israel complied with its obligations under international humanitarian law. As such, collective obligations of non-recognition have become an important consequence of a breach of an obligation *erga omnes*.

3.5.1.4 **Other possible consequences**

Other possible consequences of peremptory norms find less strong support or are more specific in nature. In the *Kosovo* advisory opinion, the ICJ noted that certain unilateral declarations of independence were condemned by the Security Council for being connected with the unlawful use of force or other serious breaches of a norm of *jus cogens*.[75] The ICTY in *Furundžija* suggested that *jus cogens* norms produce a 'deterrent effect', signalling the absolute values protected by a peremptory norm.[76] It has, moreover, been

[73] See UNSC Res 276 (30 January 1970); and *Legal Consequences for States of the Continued Presence of South Africa in Namibia (South West Africa) notwithstanding Security Council Resolution 276 (1970), Advisory Opinion, ICJ Reports 1971*, p 16, 56, paras 125–6, though the Court did temper this by saying that certain administrative acts, such as the administration of births, deaths, and marriages, should not be invalid as invalidity of such acts would be to the detriment of the inhabitants of Namibia.

[74] See UNSC Res 662 (9 August 1990).

[75] See *Accordance with International Law of the Unilateral Declaration of Independence in respect of Kosovo, Advisory Opinion, ICJ Reports 2010*, p 403, 436–7, para 81. Similarly, in Opinion No 10 of the 'Badinter'-Arbitration Commission on Yugoslavia (4 July 1992), reprinted in (1993) 4 EJIL 90, recognition of an aspiring State could not be extended to an entity which had violated 'imperative' rules of international law.

[76] *Furundžija* (n 28) paras 154–7.

suggested that the entering of a reservation by a State to a multilateral treaty (reservations are covered in Chapter 7) will have no legal effect if in conflict with a peremptory norm.[77] These, and other possible consequences of norms of *jus cogens*, highlight its potentially pervasive aspects on what had heretofore been conceived of as a strictly horizontal international legal order.[78]

Certain possible consequences of characterizing a norm as *jus cogens* have been ruled out. Foremost, a claim of a breach of a rule of *jus cogens* does not go so far as to confer jurisdiction to the ICJ or to any other forum.[79] As was considered in the *Armed Activities in the Territory of the Congo* case, 'the mere fact that rights and obligations *erga omnes* or peremptory norms of general international law (*jus cogens*) are at issue in a dispute cannot in itself constitute an exception to the principle that its jurisdiction always depends on the consent of the parties'.[80] Moreover, in *Jurisdictional Immunities of the State*, the ICJ ruled that international legal rules on immunity do not yield merely because of a claim that a peremptory norm has been breached.[81] The Court concluded that the usual rules of State immunity (see Chapter 9) continue to apply in domestic courts, even in relation to acts that were clearly in breach of a peremptory norm. It added that there was no conflict between rules of *jus cogens* and the customary law on State immunity, taking the view that the former were of a substantive character whereas the latter were of a procedural nature, and as such did not relate to the same question.[82]

CONTEMPORARY DEVELOPMENTS The Effect of a Security Council Resolution in Breach of a Norm of *Jus Cogens*

A fascinating question arose in a 1993 request in *Application of the Convention on the Prevention and Punishment for the Crime of Genocide (Bosnia and Herzegovina v Federal Republic of Yugoslavia), Order on Provisional Measures, ICJ Reports 1993*, p 325. Bosnia had argued that an arms embargo imposed by the Security Council against all parties made it

[77] See UN Human Rights Committee, General Comment No 24 (1994, CCPR/C/21/Rev.1/Add.6), para 8. See also ILC, 'Guide to Practice to Reservations to Treaties' (2011) ILC Ybk vol II, pt 2, para 4.4.3; and ILC, 'Third Report on *Jus Cogens*' (Special Rapporteur Dire Tladi), UN Doc CN.4/714 (12 February 2018), paras 69–76.

[78] For a list of further possible effects, see ILC's Third Report (n 74) 31 *et seq*. These include: (1) the non-applicability of circumstances precluding wrongfulness (paras 80–5; see further Chapter 10, Section 10.3); (2) duties of cooperation arising to bring about an end to a breach of a peremptory norm (paras 90–4); (3) a duty of non-recognition and non-assistance to a breaching party (paras 95–102); (4) individual criminal responsibility (paras 113–20; see further Chapter 17); (5) effects on the jurisdiction of an international court (paras 133–6); and (6) effects of norms of *jus cogens* on other sources of international law (paras 137–59).

[79] *Armed Activities in the Territory of the Congo (Democratic Republic of the Congo v Rwanda), ICJ Reports 2006*, p 6, paras 31–2.

[80] *Ibid*, 52, para 125. However, *cf* Case T-315/01, *Kadi v Council of the European Union* [2005] ECR II-3649, where the Court of First Instance of the European Union based certain powers of judicial review on the legal character of the norms involved.

[81] *Jurisdictional Immunities of the State (Germany v Italy; Greece intervening), ICJ Reports 2012*, p 99, 547, paras 95–6. See also ILC Third Report (n 74) paras 121–32, for a detailed study of judicial practice on immunities and *jus cogens*.

[82] *Ibid*, para 93.

impossible for Bosnia to defend itself against the better equipped Serbs; it argued that to respect the resolution would be tantamount to violating *jus cogens*, in that genocide would be committed against its nationals.

The Court did not respond to the point, though Judge ad hoc Lauterpacht, in his Dissenting Opinion, p 440, pointed out that 'the relief which Article 103 of the Charter may give the Security Council in case of conflict between one of its decisions and an operative treaty obligation cannot—as a matter of simple hierarchy of norms—extend to a conflict between a Security Council resolution and *jus cogens*. Indeed, one only has to state the opposite proposition thus—that a Security Council resolution may even require participation in genocide—for its unacceptability to be apparent.'

What, then, to do in such a situation? Antonios Tzanakopoulos has suggested that States can take 'countermeasures' (discussed later in Chapter 13) in response to a Security Council resolution in breach of *jus cogens* (A Tzanakopoulos, *Disobeying the Security Council* (OUP, 2011)). What is more, in the controversial *Yusuf* and *Kadi* judgments, the European Court of First Instance (CFI) considered that it could review Security Council resolutions for compatibility with rules of *jus cogens*, as the Security Council was also bound by such rules (Case T-306/01, *Yusuf v Council of the European Union* [2005] ECR II-3533; Case T-315/01, *Kadi v Council of the European Union* [2005] ECR II-3649, para 231). However, the Court of Justice of the European Union (ECJ), on appeal, decided that the CFI had no competence to engage in a review of the Council's resolutions as it had (Joined Cases 402/05 and 415/05, *Kadi and Al Barakaat International Foundation v Council* [2008] ECR I-6351). Given the increased activity of the Security Council in recent decades, the consequence of a conflict between its resolutions and a norm of *jus cogens* remains salient.

3.5.2 **Instances of peremptory norms**

At first, the ICJ was sparing with its use of the term *jus cogens*, though in its 1970 *Barcelona Traction* judgment it did suggest that acts of aggression and of genocide, and certain fundamental human rights violations such as slavery and racial discrimination, were breaches of *obligations erga omnes*.[83]

In 1986, in the merits phase of *Nicaragua*, the Court examined the assertion that the prohibition against aggression was of a peremptory character, but only as evidence of its customary law status.[84] In its 1996 advisory opinion in *Nuclear Weapons*, the Court explicitly avoided consideration of the *jus cogens* nature of certain 'fundamental rules of humanitarian rules applicable in armed conflict', instead qualifying these as 'intransgressible principles of customary international law',[85] a deliberately ambiguous term that, three years later, the ILC would interpret as pointing to the peremptory character of these norms.[86] It was only in 2006 that the ICJ belatedly recognized that genocide was

[83] *Barcelona Traction* (n 47) para 34. See Hernández (n 49) for a detailed history of the Court's treatment of *jus cogens* norms.

[84] *Nicaragua (Merits)* (n 39) para 190.

[85] *Nuclear Weapons* (n 39) paras 79, 83.

[86] See ARSIWA (n 67) Commentary to Art 40, para 5: '[i]n the light of the description by the ICJ of the basic rules of international humanitarian law applicable in armed conflict as "intransgressible" in character, it would also seem justified to treat these as peremptory'.

'assuredly' prohibited, as a matter of *jus cogens*, in *Armed Activities in the Congo*.[87] Even then, as discussed earlier (see Section 3.5.1.2), the Court ascribed no specific effect to the *jus cogens* character of the prohibition against genocide.

Though States have rarely, in practice or even in expressing their *opinio juris*, insisted on the character of a rule as *jus cogens*, there exists a degree of international consensus that certain legal rules have taken on that character. Though international courts have generally been circumspect—for example, the UN Tribunal for the Law of the Sea has never directly addressed the concept—there now exists a growing body of international case law and other materials which affirm the *jus cogens* nature of certain norms. During the study of peremptory norms that would lead to its 2022 Draft Conclusions, the ILC had identified certain norms as being *jus cogens*, in particular in its work on the law of treaties, the law of State responsibility, and on the fragmentation of international law.[88]

There are of course dangers in arriving at an exhaustive list of *jus cogens* norms. As the ILC's Commentary to Draft Conclusion 23 indicates, even a non-exhaustive list would require detailed study of many potential norms of *jus cogens*. Accordingly, the Commission chose, in Draft Conclusion 23, to refer to an annex to norms previously recognized by the Commission itself as a 'non-exhaustive list' that is 'without prejudice to the existence or subsequent emergence' of other norms of such status.[89] The annex to Draft Conclusion 23 thus lists the following:

- the prohibition of aggression;
- the prohibition of genocide;
- the prohibition of crimes against humanity;
- the basic rules of international humanitarian law;
- the prohibition of racial discrimination and apartheid;
- the prohibition of slavery;
- the prohibition of torture;
- the right to self-determination.

Here, the caution of the ILC will be heeded; the sections that follow, which depart modestly from the order set out in the ILC's Draft Conclusions, will briefly analyse each substantive rule and the sources which have suggested that they may possess a peremptory status.

3.5.2.1 **Prohibition on aggression or aggressive force**

The prohibition on the aggressive use of force, in violation of Article 2(4) of the UN Charter, was the first peremptory norm to be recognized, albeit implicitly, by the ICJ in the merits phase of its *Nicaragua* judgment.[90] Though the Court noted that both parties

[87] *Armed Activities in the Territory of the Congo* (n 76) p 64.

[88] See ILC, 'Draft Conclusions on Peremptory Norms' (n 21) Commentary to Draft Conclusion 23, paras 4–6.

[89] *Ibid*, para 3.

[90] See *Nicaragua (Merits)* (n 39) 100–1. See further ILC, Commentary to Draft Conclusion 23 (n 21) para 7; and the ARSIWA (n 67), Commentary to Art 40, paras 76–7, which take the view that the ICJ recognized the peremptory status of the prohibition.

(Nicaragua and the USA) had acknowledged the *jus cogens* nature of the prohibition on the use of force, it did not set out its own view.[91] Not all uses of force are violations of a *jus cogens* norm, admittedly, as some small forcible incursions do not cross the threshold of an armed attack;[92] and there is of course the significant exception in Article 51 of the Charter that using force in self-defence is permitted. Only the use of aggressive force, or an 'act of aggression', seems to rise to a breach of *jus cogens*.

A useful definition of an 'act of aggression' was introduced as an amendment to the Rome Statute of the ICC in 2010: 'the use of armed force by a State against the sovereignty, territorial integrity or political independence of another State, or in any other manner inconsistent with the Charter of the United Nations'.[93] The amendment transposes wording used by the General Assembly in its Resolution on the Definition of Aggression. Article 2 of that resolution explains that the use of armed force constitutes prima facie evidence of an act of aggression, unless the acts concerned or their consequences are not of sufficient gravity.[94] There are further illustrative examples listed in the Rome Statute amendment that would constitute acts of aggression, such as the invasion of another State's territory, bombardment or blockade of a State's coasts, allowing State territory to be used for the purpose of attacking another State's territory, or sending armed bands or mercenaries to commit any of the said acts.[95] The amendment to the Rome Statute entered into force in 2017, and is considered further in Chapter 17, Section 17.3.4.

A contemporary illustration, discussed in Chapter 14, is the Russian invasion of Ukraine, which was condemned as an 'act of aggression' by the General Assembly in March 2022.[96]

3.5.2.2 **Prohibition on genocide**

The prohibition on genocide, defined in the Genocide Convention as a category of violent acts committed 'with intent to destroy, in whole or in part, a national, ethnical, racial or religious group',[97] emerged as a concerted international response to the crimes committed by the Nazi regime during World War II. As early as 1951—though not using the language of *jus cogens*—the Court had acknowledged in the *Reservations to the Genocide Convention* advisory opinion that 'the principles underlying the Convention are principles which are recognized by civilized nations as binding on States, even without any

[91] *Ibid*, para 190.

[92] *Ibid*, para 191: 'it will be necessary to distinguish the most grave forms of the use of force (those constituting an armed attack) from other less grave forms'.

[93] The Rome Statute is amended to define the *crime* of aggression in Art 8*bis*(1) Rome Statue: the 'crime of aggression means . . . an act of aggression which, by its character, gravity and scale, constitutes a manifest violation' of the Charter.

[94] See 'Definition of Aggression', UNGA Res 3314 (XXIX) (1974), Arts 2–3. At Art 5, it is laid out that the prohibition on aggressive force is not derogable.

[95] See amendments to Rome Statute for the International Criminal Court, adopted in 2010 and entering into force in 2017, UN Doc C.N.651.2010.TREATIES-8.

[96] GA Resolution ES-11/1 (2 March 2022).

[97] Convention on the Prevention and Punishment of the Crime of Genocide (signed 9 December 1948, entered into force 12 January 1951), 48 UNTS 277, Art 2.

conventional obligation'.[98] That said, it was not until its 2006 *Armed Activities on the Territory of the Congo* judgment that the Court expressly declared that the prohibition of genocide is 'assuredly' a norm of *jus cogens*.[99] In the 2007 *Application of the Genocide Convention (Bosnia v Serbia)* judgment, and again in 2015, the Court reconfirmed the *jus cogens* character of the prohibition against genocide.[100] The prohibition is also found in abundant judicial decisions and treaty practice.[101] As Special Rapporteur Tladi concludes, '[i]t is inconceivable that today anyone would question the peremptory status of the prohibition of genocide'.[102]

It should also be noted that the Court in that case clarified a long-standing doctrinal dispute: though the Genocide Convention did not prohibit the commission of genocide '*expressis verbis*' (explicitly), the Court took the view that the obligations to prevent genocide and to prevent private individuals from committing genocide embodied in Articles I and III of the Convention, respectively, necessarily implied a prohibition on a State committing genocide.[103]

3.5.2.3 **Prohibition on crimes against humanity and war crimes**

The following categories of norms of *jus cogens* consist of 'crimes against humanity' and 'war crimes', recognized as breaches of *jus cogens* norms by the ICJ in 2012.[104] Lists of such acts, that illustrate the scope and content of crimes against humanity and war crimes, were embodied in Articles 7 and 8(2) of the Rome Statute, respectively, and are discussed in depth in Chapter 17, Sections 17.3.2–17.3.3. To give a sense to the reader here as to what type of acts constitute war crimes, they often amount to 'grave breaches' of protections found in treaties such as the Geneva Conventions;[105] the ILC has referred to them as 'basic rules of international humanitarian law' to apply both to international and non-international armed conflicts.[106] Though the ILC pointedly declined to offer an illustrative list,[107] these likely include the use of human shields, enforced conscription

[98] *Reservations to the Convention on Genocide, Advisory Opinion, (1951) ICJ Reports 1951*, 15, 23. See further ILC, Commentary to Draft Conclusion 23 (n 21) para 8.

[99] See *Armed Activities in the Territory of the Congo* (n 76) para 32.

[100] *Application of the Convention on the Prohibition and the Punishment of the Crime of Genocide (Bosnia and Herzegovina v Serbia and Montenegro), Merits, ICJ Reports 2007*, p 43, 111. See also *Application of the Convention on the Prohibition and the Punishment of the Crime of Genocide (Croatia v Serbia), Merits, ICJ Reports 2015*, p 3, at 47–8.

[101] See, e.g., *Jorgić v Germany*, No 74613/01, ECHR 2007 XI, para 68; *Prosecutor v Zoran Kupreškić et al* (Judgment) IT-95-16 (14 January 2000), para 520. Further discussion on genocide as an international crime can be found in Chapter 17, Section 17.3.1.

[102] ILC, 'Fourth Report *on Jus Cogens*' (n 66) para 82.

[103] *Application of the Genocide Convention (Bosnia v Serbia)* (n 97) 113. *Cf* P Gaeta, 'On What Conditions can a State be held Responsible for Genocide?' (2007) 18 EJIL 631.

[104] *Jurisdictional Immunities of the State* (n 78); see also *Construction of a Wall* (n 48); there, the Court did not qualify the prohibition against population transfers as a norm of *jus cogens*, though it did qualify the self-determination of the Palestinian people to be an obligation *erga omnes*.

[105] Considered in further depth in Chapter 15. In *Nuclear Weapons* (n 39) para 83, and *Construction of a Wall* (n 48) para 155, the Court's terminology was not explicitly to call them *jus cogens*, instead calling them 'intransgressible': see earlier, Section 3.5.2, and ILC, 'Fourth Report on *Jus Cogens*' (n 66) paras 117–18.

[106] ILC, Draft Conclusion 23*(d)* (n 21) and Commentary, para 10.

[107] *Ibid*, para 10.

of children, or the taking of hostages, at a scale and intensity so as to be elevated into a war crime. Despite any terminological inconsistency, there is abundant practice and judicial recognition of the notion that some rules of international humanitarian law cannot be breached.[108]

Conversely, crimes against humanity are crimes committed on a widespread and systematic scale against any civilian population, such as ethnic cleansing, rape, sexual slavery, enforced prostitution, or deportation or forced transfer. In the *Nuclear Weapons* advisory opinion, the ICJ had considered these to be violations of 'intransgressible' principles of international humanitarian law.[109] As with war crimes, there is abundant recognition of both the concept of crimes against humanity and of which prohibitions, including torture, might fall within it.[110] There is also recent case law from domestic courts on specific crimes against humanity.[111]

CONTEMPORARY DEVELOPMENTS The ILC Draft Convention on Crimes Against Humanity

There already exist multilateral conventions prohibiting genocide and torture, and the four Geneva Conventions enshrine many obligations relating to war crimes. However, crimes against humanity have been a more nebulous category, enumerated in the Rome Statute but without the support of influential States such as the USA, China, Russia, and India. For this reason, in 2014 the ILC decided to investigate the topic and established a Drafting Committee to propose a Draft Convention on Crimes against Humanity.

After four reports by the Special Rapporteur, Sean Murphy (USA), the Draft Articles on the Prohibition and Punishment of Crimes against Humanity were adopted by the ILC in 2019 (see UN Doc A/74/10 (2019)). Commentaries to each Draft Article, which explain the scope and content of each provision, have also been published. Amongst these Draft Articles, Article 2 adopts virtually the same definition and enumeration of crimes against humanity as appears in the Rome Statute; Article 4 imposes an obligation of prevention on States; and Articles 6 and 7 impose an obligation to criminalize all such acts in domestic law. Other obligations include provisions relating to extradition, cooperation, and mutual assistance between States.

[108] *Ibid*, paras 117–21, referring in particular to *Jurisdictional Immunities of the State* (n 78) para 93 (which admits the principle that certain principles of humanitarian law are of *jus cogens*, but without deciding the matter); *Kupreškić* (n 98) para 520; *Prosecutor v Tadić* (Decision on the Defence Motion for Interlocutory Appeal on Jurisdiction) ICTY-94-1-A (2 October 1995), para 143.

[109] See earlier, Section 3.5.2.

[110] See, e.g., *Obligation to Prosecute or Extradite* (n 39) para 99; *Kupreškić* (n 98) para 520; *Miguel Castro-Castro Prison v Peru, Judgment (Merits, Reparations and Costs)*, IACtHR (25 November 2006) para 402. A full study by the ILC is the Draft Articles on the Prohibition and Punishment of Crimes against Humanity, UN Doc A/74/10 (2019); and ILC, 'Fourth Report on *Jus Cogens*' (n 66) paras 86–90.

[111] In May 2023, the Military Tribunal of Uvira (Democratic Republic of the Congo) convicted Munyololo Mbao, alias Ndarumanga, for 'forced pregnancy' as a crime against humanity; in November 2024, the German Federal Court of Justice upheld a conviction of former Gambian President Yahya Jammeh for several murders as a crime against humanity; and in December 2024, an appellate court in Belgium found the State guilty of crimes against humanity for the forced removal of five mixed-race children from their mothers in colonial Congo.

Since 2019, work continued through the Sixth (Legal) Committee of the General Assembly, and in November 2024, a resolution was adopted by consensus to convene an intergovernmental conference to adopt a binding treaty text on the basis of the Draft Articles (see UN Doc A/C.6/79/L.2/Rev.1, 22 November 2024). Even as Draft Articles, much of ILC's work is already a codification of existing customary international law, and the Articles are already State practice or to be referred to by international courts. For example, a newly-adopted 2024 treaty called The Ljubljana–The Hague Convention, covering international co-operation, mutual legal assistance and extradition in respect of atrocity crimes, has reprised the same definition of crimes against humanity in Article 5(2) and Article 5(3).

For further reading on the Draft Articles, see CC Jalloh, 'The International Law Commission's First Draft Convention on Crimes against Humanity' (2020) 52 Case Western Reserve JIL 331; and LN Sadat, 'A Contextual and Historical Analysis of the International Law Commission's 2017 Draft Articles for a New Global Treaty on Crimes against Humanity' (2018) 16 JICJ 683.

3.5.2.4 **The prohibition against torture**

Article 1 of the Convention against Torture defines torture as the intentional infliction on a person of severe pain or suffering for purposes such as obtaining information or a confession, intimidation, or discrimination. The Convention also requires that the pain or suffering be instigated by, or with the consent of, a public official or an official acting in a public capacity; this excludes purely private acts.[112] In the 2012 *Obligation to Prosecute or Extradite* judgment, the ICJ declared that 'the prohibition of torture is part of customary international law and it has become a peremptory norm (*jus cogens*)'.[113] It has also been recognized as *jus cogens* in the ICTY's *Furundžija* judgment,[114] by the Inter-American Court of Human Rights (IACtHR) in *Espinoza Gonzáles v Peru*,[115] by the African Commission on Human and Peoples' Rights (ACnHPR) in *Saleh al-Asad v Djibouti*,[116] by the ECtHR in the *Al-Adsani v UK* decision,[117] and by the UN Human Rights Committee in *Georgopoulos v Greece*.[118]

3.5.2.5 **The prohibition against slavery and the slave trade**

Throughout the nineteenth century, States progressively banned slavery within their domestic legislation, culminating in the 1926 Slavery Convention. The Slavery Convention sought to prevent and suppress the slave trade (Art 2(a)) and progressively to bring about

[112] Convention against Torture and Other Cruel, Inhuman or Degrading Treatment or Punishment (signed 4 February 1984, entered into force 26 June 1987), 1465 UNTS 85, Art 1.

[113] *Obligation to Prosecute or Extradite* (n 39) para 99. The 'Fourth Report on *Jus Cogens*' (n 66) paras 69–77, lists further examples of case law and practice.

[114] *Furundžija* (n 28) 257–8, 260–2.

[115] *Espinoza Gonzáles v Peru, Judgment (Preliminary Objections, Merits, Reparations and Costs)*, IACtHR Ser C No 289 (20 November 2014), para 141.

[116] *Mohammed Abdullah Saleh al-Asad v Djibouti*, ACnHPR Com 383/10 (Decision of April–May 2014), para 179.

[117] *Al-Adsani v United Kingdom* (n 28).

[118] *Georgopolous v Greece*, HRC Communication, UN Doc CCPR/C/99/D/1799/2008 (14 September 2010), para 5.

the complete abolition of all forms of slavery (Art 2(b)).[119] Though the ICJ has not yet addressed the *jus cogens* status of slavery, it has found widespread recognition elsewhere, including the ILC Commentaries to the Draft Articles on the Law of Treaties[120] and those to the ARSIWA.[121] It has also been recognized as a peremptory norm by the IACtHR[122] and by the Office of the UN High Commissioner for Human Rights.[123]

3.5.2.6 **Systematic racial oppression, in particular apartheid**

The 1973 Apartheid Convention, in Article II, defined apartheid as a crime against humanity which encompassed acts committed with the purpose of domination or systematic oppression of one racial group over another racial group.[124] The very use of the word *apartheid* (from the Dutch/Afrikaans 'apartness') reflects the situation in South Africa which prevailed until 1990, where white settlers sought to reinforce a system of racial segregation in defiance of international condemnation. As with slavery, the ICJ has not pronounced itself on the *jus cogens* nature of the prohibition, though the ILC has done so, affirming its peremptory status in its commentaries to the ARSIWA.[125] However, the UN Security Council has declared apartheid regimes as 'illegal racist régimes'[126] and 'against the conscience and dignity of mankind and incompatible with the rights and dignity of man, the Charter of the United Nations and the Universal Declaration of Human Rights'.[127] Apartheid is also listed as a crime against humanity in Article 7 of the Rome Statute, when it fulfils the other conditions for crimes against humanity.[128] Taken together, these examples would seem to confirm the peremptory character of these prohibitions. It bears noting that in its 2024 advisory opinion, the Court found, though without further elaboration, that Israel's policies of factual and legal separation of Palestinians and Israelis were a breach of Article 3 of the International Convention on the Elimination of All Forms of Racial Discrimination, which calls out both racial segregation and apartheid as 'particularly severe forms of racial discrimination'.[129]

[119] Convention to Suppress the Slave Trade and Slavery (signed 25 September 1926, in force 9 March 1927), 60 LNTS 253. Other treaties which prohibit slavery in absolute terms include the International Covenant on Civil and Political Rights (signed 16 December 1966, entered into force 23 March 1976), 993 UNTS 3, Art 8; and Protocol Additional to the Geneva Conventions of 12 August 1949, and relating to the Protection of Victims of Non-International Armed Conflicts (Protocol II) (signed 8 June 1977, entered into force 7 December 1978), 1125 UNTS 609, Art 4(2).

[120] ILC, Draft Articles on the Law of Treaties with Commentaries, 1966 ILC Ybk vol II 187, 248.

[121] ARSIWA (n 67) 31, 112; ILC, Commentary to Draft Conclusion 23 (n 21) para 12. See further ILC, 'Fourth Report on *Jus Cogens*' (n 66) paras 103–7.

[122] *Aloeboetoe et al v Suriname, Reparations and Costs*, IACHR Series C No 15, IHRL 1396 (10 September 1993), paras 56–7.

[123] D Weissbrodt and M Dottridge, *Abolishing Slavery and its Contemporary Forms*, Office of the United Nations Commissioner for Human Rights, UN Doc HR/PUB/02/4 (2002), para 6.

[124] International Convention on the Suppression and Punishment of the Crime of Apartheid (signed 30 November 1973, in force 18 July 1976), 1015 UNTS 243. See M Jackson, 'The Definition of Apartheid in Customary International Law and the International Convention on the Elimination of All Forms of Racial Discrimination' (2022) 71 *ICLQ* 831.

[125] See ARSIWA (n 67), Commentary to Art 40, 112.

[126] See, e.g., the condemnation of Southern Rhodesia in UNSC Res 448 (30 April 1979).

[127] UNSC Res 473 (13 June 1980).

[128] See Chapter 17, Section 17.3.2.

[129] *Policies and Practices of Israel* (n 48) paras 225, 229.

3.5.2.7 **The right to self-determination**

A frequent candidate for inclusion as a norm of *jus cogens* is the right to self-determination, mentioned in the UN Charter.[130] Certainly, respect for self-determination is an obligation *erga omnes*: in *East Timor* the ICJ declared: '[that] the right of peoples to self-determination, as is evolved from the Charter and from United Nations practice, has an *erga omnes* character, is irreproachable ... it is one of the essential principles of contemporary international law'.[131] In *Construction of a Wall*, the Court emphasized the weight and the character and importance of self-determination as an obligation *erga omnes* that triggered obligations for all States.[132] It is true that there is limited evidence of self-determination as an accepted and recognized norm of *jus cogens*,[133] and there is some uncertainty: most of the evidence of the *jus cogens* status of the right to self-determination is limited to situations of colonial domination and not, for example, in the context of the secession of part of an existing State. In 2024, the ICJ concluded that, in cases of foreign occupation such as that of Palestine, the right to self-determination constituted a peremptory norm.[134] Self-determination will be considered later, in Chapter 5.

3.5.2.8 **Possible further candidates for *jus cogens***

As desirable as it might be to include other norms, the ILC recognized that there is no firm consensus for the characterization as *jus cogens* of other norms. Special Rapporteur Tladi did indicate that three such norms—the prohibition on enforced disappearances,[135] the right to life,[136] and the principle of *non-refoulement* of refugees[137]—enjoy a degree of support. However, he considered support to be markedly less favourable to rules such as the principle of non-discrimination (distinguishing between racial and gender discrimination), the destruction of the natural environment (though in recent years, there have been advanced proposals to criminalize 'ecocide'), the prohibition of human trafficking, the right to due process, and the prohibition of terrorism.[138]

Beyond the ILC's work, two further concepts merit brief mention. The crime of piracy, one of the earliest international crimes (see Chapter 17), indeed attracts universal jurisdiction. By the nineteenth century, the prohibition of piracy was a deeply entrenched and arguably non-derogable rule, in that a treaty to facilitate the commission of piracy

[130] UN Charter, Art 1.

[131] *East Timor* (n 48) paras 28–9. Of special relevance to the Court was the foundational character of the 1960 Declaration on the Granting of Independence to Colonial Countries and Peoples, GA Res 1514 (XV), paras 1–2.

[132] *Construction of a Wall* (n 48) para 156, in application of Art 41(2) of the ASR.

[133] In its Commentary to Draft Conclusion 23 on Peremptory Norms (*Jus Cogens*) (n 21), at para 14, the ILC invokes earlier Commission statements: see, e.g., ARSIWA (n 67) Commentary to Art 16, para 5, and Commentary to Art 40, para 5. More recently, in *Bernard Anbataayela Mornah v Benin, Burkina Faso, Côte d'Ivoire, Ghana, Mali, Malawi, Tanzania and Tunisia, Judgment of 22 September 2022*, ACHPR App No 0289/2018, the African Court of Human and Peoples' Rights acknowledged the 'resonance' and 'deep meaning' of self-determination in Africa (para 290), affirming its peremptory status (para 298).

[134] *Policies and Practices of Israel* (n 48) para 233.

[135] See ILC, 'Fourth Report on *Jus Cogens*' (n 66) paras 125–7.

[136] *Ibid*, paras 128–30.

[137] *Ibid*, paras 131–3.

[138] *Ibid*, paras 123–4, 135–7.

would likely not have been considered valid.[139] However, the peremptory character of piracy is contestable, as piracy refers to the acts of violence committed by an individual or group upon a vessel at sea.[140] If committed by a State, such acts would invariably be subsumed by the prohibition on the use of aggressive force (see earlier, Section 3.5.2.1) or the commission of a war crime (see earlier, Section 3.5.2.3). Furthermore, unlike most established norms of *jus cogens*, there does not appear to exist any treaty obligation or customary rule which imposes on States a positive obligation to suppress piracy. In respect of human rights, most human rights provisions separate out those which may not be derogated from. Since 2020, the Covid-19 outbreak has made clear the extent to which many human rights obligations which seem just as important, including those of assembly and movement, were explicitly suspended, for example by ten mostly Central and East European States which are parties to the ECHR.[141]

Another important structural principle which has been proposed as a peremptory norm is *pacta sunt servanda* ('obligations shall be faithfully observed'), as embodied in Article 26 VCLT.[142] Kolb, for example, considers *pacta sunt servanda* a rule of *jus cogens* by 'logical necessity' rather than a value-based assessment.[143] Certainly, it is a cardinal principle of international law; without it, the absurdity would arise that a State bound by a treaty obligation might be able to object to the rule to which it is bound through its own treaty obligations.[144]

Nonetheless, there are three possible arguments against its unqualified characterization as a peremptory norm.[145] First, there are at least two significant departures from *pacta sunt servanda* under Articles 61–2 VCLT, which provide for supervening impossibility of performance and *rebus sic stantibus* ('fundamental change of circumstances'). Articles 61 and 62 go further than mere exceptions, in that they are justifications for non-compliance: rather than a legal exception, they allow a State to depart lawfully from its existing treaty commitments.[146] Moreover, as considered in Chapter 2, customary international law evolves and shifts over time, and an act could thus simultaneously be a breach of an existing rule and the first instance of a new rule of custom.[147] Finally, the ARSIWA envisage a category of circumstances precluding wrongfulness which excuse a State from responsibility for a breach of international law (see Chapter 10, Section 10.3), such as distress, self-defence, or a plea of necessity.[148] Though such circumstances must have been unforeseen at the time the obligation was contracted, these challenge the view that *pacta sunt servanda* is a peremptory norm, applying to all States, that admits of no derogation.

[139] See ILC, 'First Report on *Jus Cogens*' (n 13) 13, citing Hannikainen (n 62) 48–9.

[140] See United Nations Convention on the Law of the Sea, signed 10 December 1982, in force 16 November 1994, 1833 UNTS 3, Art 101(a), which defines piracy as an action 'committed for private ends', and Art 102, which likens the acts of a governmental ship whose crews have mutinied to acts committed by a private ship.

[141] The Council of Europe maintains an up-to-date list at <https://www.coe.int/en/web/conventions/derogations-covid-19>. For further comment, see A Lebret, 'COVID-19 Pandemic and Derogation to Human Rights' (2020) 7 Journal of Law and the Biosciences 1.

[142] See, e.g., Crawford, *Creation of States* (n 68) 99–100; MW Janis, 'The Nature of *Jus Cogens*' (1978–9) 3 Connecticut JIL 359, 362.

[143] See Kolb (n 30) 56–8.

[144] Lowe (n 38) 58.

[145] For detailed arguments to this effect, see Orakhelashvili (n 31) 45; Thirlway (n 2) 32.

[146] VCLT, Arts 61–2.

[147] See Chapter 2, Section 2.2.2.2.2.

[148] ARSIWA (n 67) Arts 20–5.

3.6 Conclusion: a hierarchy of norms?

The effects of recognizing a hierarchy of norms in international law, through the legal category of norms of *jus cogens*, is potentially profound. Though practice remains somewhat incoherent, renewed attention is being paid to the concept of *jus cogens* by States, judicial institutions, the ILC, and others. However, one should remain wary of the fact that arguments grounded in *jus cogens* have rarely been invoked by States, and still more rarely prevailed before international courts and tribunals. Nevertheless, as an accepted part of the international legal order, peremptory norms will continue to develop over time, and have the potential to reshape the nature and substance of international law. Even if the category remains unsettled and controversial, it is worth recalling Georges Abi-Saab's famous metaphor that the category of *jus cogens* is like an 'empty box', useful because it provides a space that may one day be filled.[149] Perhaps that day has finally come.

Further reading

D COSTELLOE, *Legal Consequences of Peremptory Norms in International Law* (CUP, 2017).

A practical account of *jus cogens* that situates their place in international law through a consequentialist, effects-based approach.

L HANNIKAINEN, *Peremptory Norms* (Jus Cogens) *in International Law* (Lakimiesliiton Kustannus: Finnish Lawyer's Publishing Co, 1988).

A comprehensive work that explores the place of peremptory norms from a historical perspective.

M JANIS, 'The Nature of *Jus Cogens*' in L May and J Brown (eds), *Philosophy of Law: Classical and Contemporary Readings* (Wiley, 2010).

A lucid and thoughtful conceptual account of the origins of *jus cogens*, drawing on natural law theory.

R KOLB, *Peremptory International Law—Jus Cogens: A General Inventory* (Hart, 2015).

A formal, clear, conceptual account of norms of *jus cogens*.

M KOSKENNIEMI, 'Hierarchy in International Law: A Sketch' (1997) 8 EJIL 566.

In his incisive style, the author maps out the role of the concept of hierarchy as part of a continued debate to restructure or reimagine international law.

A ORAKHELASHVILI, *Peremptory Norms in International Law* (OUP, 2006).

A systematic and meticulous examination of practice and case law relating to peremptory norms and their effects within international law.

[149] G Abi-Saab, 'The Uses of Article 19' (1999) 10 EJIL 341.

M Ragazzi, *The Concept of International Obligations* Erga Omnes (OUP, 1997).

An excellent treatment of the relation between obligations *erga omnes* and norms of *jus cogens* within the international legal order.

C Tams, *Enforcing Obligations* Erga Omnes *in International Law* (CUP, 2005).

Primarily focused on the effects of a breach of obligations *erga omnes*, this tightly structured work dispelled any doubts as to their existence.

C Tomuschat, 'Obligations Arising for States Without or Against Their Will' (1993-IV) 241 Recueil des Cours 191.

This contribution focused on the fact that peremptory norms could exist irrespective of the consent of States to be bound by them, and sought to outline a conceptual justification for their existence.

P Weil, 'Towards Relative Normativity in International Law?' (1983) 77 AJIL 413.

A classic cry against the structural shift engendered by the concept of peremptory norms and a robust defence of the horizontality of international law.

4

International law and municipal law

4.1 Introduction: interactions between legal orders

4.1.1 Conceptualizing the relationship

If international law is a distinct legal order, *autonomous* from 'municipal' legal orders (a term used interchangeably with 'national', 'internal', 'local', or 'domestic' by international lawyers), then from the outset one might reasonably ask how these legal orders relate to one another. Though international law deals primarily with inter-State relations, and municipal law addresses relationships between individuals or between individuals and the State, there are many overlapping issues on which both international and national regulation are necessary, such as the environment, trade, and human rights.

Though the international legal order asserts its primacy over municipal legislation, it leaves to domestic constitutions the question of how international legal rules should be applied or enforced in municipal orders. As such, finding ways of resolving possible conflicts between international and municipal legal rules remains an evergreen area of interest. There is great practical significance in the question: a dispute might come before an international court as to whether municipal law has created an obligation binding a party; a municipal court may be called upon to interpret the scope of an international legal norm; and, above all, there might be apparent conflicts between what international law and municipal law prescribe. This chapter therefore focuses on how different municipal legal orders have addressed international law and how international law treats municipal law.

4.1.2 The 'monism' versus 'dualism' debate

Two conflicting doctrines define the relationship between international and municipal legal orders. Termed 'dualism' and 'monism', they have troubled international lawyers for decades. While the controversy between these two has been criticized as 'unreal, artificial and strictly beside the point',[1] it is useful to consider the story they trace for the relationship of international law with other legal orders.

[1] See G Fitzmaurice, 'The General Principles of International Law Considered from the Standpoint of the Rule of Law' (1957) 92-II Recueil des Cours 1, 71. See also JG Starke, 'Monism and Dualism in the Theory of International Law Considered from the Standpoint of the Rule of Law' (1957) 92 Recueil des Cours 5, 70, *et seq.*

Dualism is usually understood as emphasizing the autonomy and distinct nature of municipal legal orders, in which the State is sovereign and supreme. In its most traditional sense, dualism maintains that neither legal order has the power to create or to modify any legal rules from the other.[2] If an international legal rule is to apply within a municipal order, it is only to the extent to which it is accepted or tolerated by the sovereign State. As such, it is municipal law which will determine how a conflict of rules is to be resolved.[3] In short, according to dualist theory, they are legal orders which operate independently from one another. Prominent States considered to be dualist include the UK and the USA, and similar common law jurisdictions, as well as the Scandinavian States. Their purported dualism arises because, though they recognize a place for customary international law and duly ratified treaties within their municipal legal order, they require positive evidence that a treaty obligation has been appropriately 'transformed', usually through judicial recognition or statutory incorporation, into municipal law.[4] The practice of incorporating treaties by these States will be explored later, in Section 4.2.2.2.2; however, it bears noting that the formalism demanded by the dualist perspective can be challenging. It was well suited to a time when international law and national law governed different and non-overlapping topics. However, a significant limitation in dualism's appeal is that it fails to address the increase in international legal rules that overlap with municipal legal rules; for example, in relation to individuals and the protection of human rights.

Theories of *monism* conceive the relationship between international and municipal legal orders as more coherent and in fact unified, their validity deriving from one common source. The chief consequence of monism would be the direct application of international law within national legal orders, without the need for any 'transformation'. In several monist States, including many European civil law jurisdictions such as France, Spain, Germany, and the Netherlands, international law is incorporated directly into domestic law, usually by operation of the constitution, and requires no further enabling legislation. In a word, valid international law would be 'self-executing'.

The Austrian theorist Hans Kelsen saw monism as a logical necessity, claiming that international and municipal legal orders all derived their validity from the same source, a single basic norm called the *Grundnorm*.[5] For Kelsen, the *Grundnorm* entails that international law and municipal legal orders form a single system of norms, all depending on the *Grundnorm* as their source of validity.[6]

[2] The classic texts making this argument were primarily developed by German and Italian academics: see H Triepel, 'Les rapports entre le droit interne et le droit international' (1923) 1 Recueil des Cours 77; K Strupp, 'Les règles générales du droit international de la paix' (1934) 47 Recueil des Cours 258, 389; D Anzilotti, 'Teoria generale della responsabilità dello Stato nel diritto internazionale' (1902) in *Scritti di diritto internazionale pubblico* vol I (Cedam, 1956).

[3] See R Jennings and A Watts, *Oppenheim's International Law* (9th edn, Stevens & Sons, 1992), 53.

[4] See Art VI of the US Constitution (1789); and in English common law, see *JH Rayner (Mincing Lane) Ltd v Department of Trade and Industry* [1990] 2 AC 418, and the earlier *R v Keyn (Ferdinand) (The Franconia)* (1876–7) LR 2 Ex D 63, 203. See also P Capps, 'The Court as Gatekeeper: Customary International Law in English Courts' (2007) 70 MLR 458; and R O'Keefe, 'The Doctrine of Incorporation Revisited' (2008) 79 BYBIL 7.

[5] See H Kelsen, *General Theory of Law and State* (2nd edn 1967, Transaction reprint, 2005), 559.

[6] *Ibid*, 564.

The exact content of the *Grundnorm* is a complex question not entirely answered by Kelsen himself. He suggested the rather circular idea that 'states ought to behave as they have customarily behaved' as the *Grundnorm*.[7] What is relevant here is that Kelsen's monist theory of law would entail that international norms could automatically apply within municipal orders, without transformation;[8] and that any municipal rule contrary to international law would not be void but would entail the international responsibility of the State.[9]

Several distinguished international lawyers, most prominently Sir Hersch Lauterpacht, built on Kelsen's theory to argue that, in such a unified system, international law would sit at the apex, setting out the legal conditions through which States, and thus their domestic legal orders, could exist.[10] Lauterpacht argued that municipal law ought always to comply with international law, given that both legal orders share a foundation in promoting the well-being of individuals through human rights.[11] Monism, if regarded thus, rests on a view of the function of law as very much possessing a universalist, possibly humanist, character, and suggesting that international law is imbued with a moral content and purpose above and beyond merely accommodating competing interests.[12] This will be discussed later, in Section 4.2.2.2.1.

THEORY AND DEBATES Monism and Dualism: Accommodating Incompatible Obligations?

Kelsen became famous for contending that there is no middle ground between monism and dualism: *tertium non datur* ('no possible third way'). Rosalyn Higgins put it concisely: '[m]onists contend that there is but a single system of law, with international law being an element within it alongside all the various branches of domestic law . . . Dualists contend that there are two essentially different legal systems, existing side by side within different spheres of action—the international plane and the domestic plane' (R Higgins, *Problems and Process:*

[7] *Ibid*, 564, though he also suggested that it is not a norm of positive law, but a 'hypothesis of juristic thinking'. This has changed over time: see H Kelsen, *Das Problem der Souveränität und die Theorie des Völkerrechts* (2nd edn Aalen, Scientia Verlag, 1928, reprint 1960) 217, where he suggested it was *pacta sunt servanda*, discussed further in Chapter 5.

[8] See H Kelsen, *Principles of International Law* (Rinehart & Co, 1952), 293.

[9] See H Kelsen, *Introduction to the Problems of Legal Theory: A Translation of the First Edition of the Reine Rechtslehre or Pure Theory of Law* (BL Paulson and S Paulson tr, Clarendon Press, 1992), 111, *et seq.*

[10] See H Lauterpacht (ed), *Oppenheim's International Law* (8th edn, Longman, 1955), 38. Other jurists were similarly inclined: see A Verdross, 'Le fondement du droit international' (1927) 16 Recueil des Cours 247, 287; G Scelle, 'Règles générales du droit de la paix' (1933-IV) 46 Recueil des Cours 331, 353: 'Le monisme est fusion plus qu'hiérarchie' ['Monism is fusion rather than hierarchy'].

[11] H Lauterpacht, *International Law and Human Rights* (OUP, 1950), 70. For a more recent exponent of this position, see A Cassese, *International Law* (2nd edn, OUP, 2005), 215.

[12] See, e.g., Cassese, *ibid*, 216. However, this conclusion was in fact a departure from Hans Kelsen, who took a more agnostic position and even argued that the choice of the primacy of international law was dictated by ethical and political preferences, and the *Grundnorm* could easily come from domestic legal orders: see Kelsen (n 5) 587–8.

International Law and How to Use It (OUP, 1994), 209). Described thus, the two positions seem incommensurable on the conceptual plane, as they strive to describe the same thing through unity (monism) and the management of diversity (dualism).

A more pragmatic approach, favoured by Gerald Fitzmaurice and Charles Rousseau, sought to sketch out a solution that avoided grand principles (see Fitzmaurice's Hague Lectures, note 1, 68–80; and C Rousseau, *Droit international public* (Pedone, 1979), 4–16). Adopting an admittedly dualist starting point, they proposed that international and municipal legal orders operated as distinct *systems*, each supreme in its field. However, in cases of incompatibility between *obligations* of international and municipal law, international law would not repeal rules of municipal law, but would address the conflict through the rules on State responsibility (covered in Chapter 10). Such a solution could allow an international tribunal to declare a State in breach of international law, while not pronouncing on the validity of municipal law within its own legal order.

A neat illustration of this approach would be the ICJ's judgment in *Nottebohm ((Liechtenstein v Guatemala), Second Phase, ICJ Reports 1955*, p 4). Liechtenstein sought to exercise diplomatic protection over the German-born Nottebohm, which was challenged by Guatemala on the basis of purportedly tenuous links to Liechtenstein. Rather than consider the validity of Nottebohm's naturalization under Liechtensteinian law, the ICJ emphasized that it would consider only whether the grant of nationality by Liechtenstein had produced international legal effects which had to be recognized by Guatemala (p 20).

For further reading, see P-M Dupuy, 'Relations Between the International Law of Responsibility and Responsibility in Municipal Law' in J Crawford, A Pellet, and S Olleson (eds), *The Law of International Responsibility* (OUP, 2010), 173; and A Nollkaemper, 'Rethinking the Supremacy of International Law' (2010) 65 ZaöRV 65.

Monism and dualism define the relationship between international and domestic legal orders in radically divergent ways, and one particular criticism of both theories is that neither satisfactorily account for the practice of international and national courts, which discharge an important role in implementing the relation between international and municipal law.[13] It remains the prerogative of the State, through its national constitutional arrangements, to decide whether its legal order is monist or dualist. This would suggest that the controversy is not about the nature of international law, but about the possible methods of understanding its engagement with municipal legal orders. Though understanding the contours of the monism–dualism controversy certainly helps to theorize about the nature of international law, it may be wise to remain open to both positions—especially given the sheer number of municipal legal orders—and focus on how they relate to one another, and to international law, on a day-to-day basis.

[13] See J Crawford, *Brownlie's Principles of Public International Law* (8th edn, OUP, 2012), 50.

4.2 The relations between international and national law in practice

4.2.1 Municipal legal rules within international law

The interface between international and municipal law is, in the main, addressed through the daily work of officials of States, as well as through the judgments of national and international courts. This section will identify the chief principles in international law that have emerged incrementally through such practices.

4.2.1.1 The primacy of international law

Foremost is the principle that, under international law, a State may not invoke provisions of its own municipal/internal law as a justification for a breach of an international obligation. Dating from as far as the *Alabama Claims* arbitration after the US Civil War,[14] this principle has been upheld firmly by the PCIJ[15] and ICJ.[16] It is found in Article 3 of the ILC's Articles on State Responsibility: '[t]he characterization of an act of a State as internationally wrongful is governed by international law. Such characterization is not affected by the characterization of the same act as lawful under internal law.'[17] It is also restated categorically in Article 27 of the 1969 Vienna Convention on the Law of Treaties (VCLT) as follows: '[a] party may not invoke the provisions of its internal law as justification for its failure to perform a treaty'. Article 27 is, however, subject to an exception in Article 46 VCLT, under which a State may argue that its consent to be bound by a treaty has been invalidated by a violation which 'was manifest and concerned a rule of its internal law of fundamental importance'. The exception in Article 46 is construed very strictly: in *Land and Maritime Boundary between Cameroon and Nigeria*, the ICJ dismissed Nigeria's contention that a declaration signed by its head of State, but not ratified by the Nigerian parliament, constituted a manifest violation of its internal law: 'there is no general legal obligation for States to keep themselves informed of legislative and constitutional developments in other States which are or may become important for the international relations of these States'.[18]

[14] *Alabama Claims* arbitration, in JB Moore (ed), *International Arbitrations* vol 1 (US Government Publishing Office, 1898), 653.

[15] *SS Wimbledon, 1923, PCIJ, Ser A, No 1*, p 29; *Jurisdiction of the Courts of Danzig, 1928, PCIJ, Ser B, No 15*; *Free Zones of Upper Savoy and the District of Gex, 1930, PCIJ, Ser A, No 24*, p 12.

[16] *Anglo-Norwegian Fisheries (United Kingdom v Norway), Judgment, ICJ Reports 1951*, p 116, 132; *Applicability of the Obligation to Arbitrate under section 21 of the United Nations Headquarters Agreement of 26 June 1947, Advisory Opinion, ICJ Reports 1988*, p 12, 34; *Elettronica Sicula SpA (ELSI) (United States v Italy), ICJ Reports 1989*, p 15, 74; *Avena and other Mexican Nationals (Mexico v United States), Judgment, ICJ Reports 2004*, p 12, 65.

[17] Articles on the Responsibility of States for Internationally Wrongful Acts, adopted by the ILC on 20 August 2001: Report of the International Law Commission on the Work of its 53rd Session, UN Doc A/56/10 Chapter IV (2001) GAOR 56th Session Supp 10 (ARSIWA). See further Chapter 10, Section 10.1.1.

[18] *Land and Maritime Boundary between Cameroon and Nigeria, Merits, ICJ Reports 2002*, p 303, 430. Heads of State, under Art 7(2) VCLT, are able to bind the State purely by virtue of their function: see further, Chapter 7, Section 7.2.1. The statement was quoted approvingly in *Maritime Delimitation in the Indian Ocean (Somalia v Kenya), Preliminary Objections, ICJ Reports 2017*, p 3, 24, where the Court further explained that internal law could not be invoked to claim the nullity of an agreement in a situation where a minister was presenting full powers and the authorization to sign the said agreement.

4.2.1.2 Internal law must comply with valid international obligations

According to the PCIJ in *Exchange of Greek and Turkish Populations*, a State having assumed a valid international obligation is required to make adjustments to its internal law which may be necessary to fulfil the said obligations.[19] This is not to say that any legislation incompatible with international law can be challenged. For a breach to arise, generally there must be an actual, specific failure to apply an international obligation.[20] There are exceptions where the very enactment—or failure to enact legislation—itself constitutes a breach of an international obligation: certain multilateral human rights conventions such as the Genocide Convention,[21] the CERD,[22] the ICCPR,[23] and the Torture Convention[24] explicitly provide for States to enact legislation for implementing the provisions of the conventions.

In cases of a failure to conform to a valid international obligation, the internal act is not invalidated as a general rule. Instead, the State is responsible for any breach of international law committed even if in compliance with the internal act.[25] That general principle is vividly illustrated by the 2003 *LaGrand* and 2004 *Avena* judgments, claims by Germany and Mexico against the US concerning the right to consular notification and assistance of foreign nationals sentenced to death.

At issue in both cases was the principle in US constitutional law of 'procedural default', according to which a procedural failing which had not been raised at state levels (in Arizona and Texas, respectively) could not be argued before a federal court. The procedural default rule aimed to protect the long-established separation of powers in the US: under the Tenth Amendment to the US Constitution, the exercise of 'police powers'—and thus crimes such as the commission of murder—is reserved specifically to the states. Germany and Mexico both claimed that the rule constituted a breach of Article 36(1) of the 1963 Vienna Convention on Consular Relations (VCCR), under which States parties undertook to give full effect to the rights of notification and consular access contained in that convention 'without delay'.

In both judgments, the Court considered that the procedural default rule did not in itself violate Article 36(1). However, if a detained foreign individual was prevented

[19] See *Exchange of Greek and Turkish Populations, 1925, PCIJ, Ser B, No 10*, p 20.

[20] *Interpretation of the Statute of the Memel Territory, 1932, PCIJ, Ser A/B, No 49*, p 294, 336; *International Responsibility for the Promulgation of Laws in Violation of the Convention (Article 1 and 2 of the American Convention on Human Rights)* (1994) 116 ILR 320, 332 (ACtHR). See also A McNair, *The Law of Treaties* (2nd edn, OUP, 1961), 100. *Cf* Fitzmaurice (n 1) 1, 89.

[21] Convention on the Prevention and Punishment of the Crime of Genocide (adopted 9 December 1948, entered into force 12 January 1951), 78 UNTS 277, Art 5.

[22] International Convention on the Elimination of All Forms of Racial Discrimination (adopted 21 December 1965, entered into force 4 January 1969), 660 UNTS 195, Art 2.1(d).

[23] International Covenant on Civil and Political Rights (adopted 16 December 1966, entered into force 23 March 1976), 999 UNTS 171, Art 2(2).

[24] United Nations Convention Against Torture and Other Cruel, Inhuman, or Degrading Treatment or Punishment (adopted 10 December 1984, entered into force 26 June 1987), 1465 UNTS 85, Art 5.

[25] Of course, subject to the principle laid out in ARSIWA (n 17) Art 12, under which a breach is committed when an act of a State is not in conformity with what is required, 'regardless of its origin or character'. Legislation that itself violates an international law obligation—e.g., permitting slavery despite the obligation to prohibit slavery in the Slavery Convention—would itself constitute a breach.

from challenging a conviction and sentence on the basis that their national State was not notified without delay—as was the case both for brothers in *LaGrand* and some 50 Mexican nationals in *Avena*—a breach of Article 36(1) VCCR could result.

Because in *LaGrand* the executions had already taken place in Arizona, only in *Avena* did the Court recognize an obligation of the USA 'to permit review and reconsideration' of the cases of forty-nine Mexican nationals on death row in Texas.[26] However, in *Medellín v Texas* (552 US 491 (2008)), the US Supreme Court ruled in Texas's favour that the ICJ judgment in *Avena* did not constitute enforceable federal law in the USA, and that the President lacked the requisite constitutional authority to overrule the procedural default rule. Texas executed Mr Medellín in 2009, and though Mexico rapidly escalated the situation to the ICJ, the case was ultimately dismissed for lack of jurisdiction.[27] Shortly after the 2004 *Avena* judgment, the Bush Administration denounced the 'compromissory clause' (see Chapter 12, Section 12.3.2.3.3) in the VCCR conferring jurisdiction on the ICJ, meaning that no future disputes regarding the VCCR could be brought to that court against the USA.

CASE SPOTLIGHT ***Alleged Violations of Sovereign Rights and Maritime Spaces in the Caribbean Sea (Nicaragua v. Colombia), Judgment, ICJ Reports 2022,*** **p 266**

A recent judgment of the Court provides a vivid illustration of the interaction between domestic legislation and international law obligations. Nicaragua had challenged the scope of Colombian Presidential Decree 1946 (as modified in 2014), arguing that Article 2 of the Decree created an unusual 'integral contiguous zone' in which Colombia could exercise enforcement and security powers in the sea which would be in violation of customary international law. The Court, after a careful analysis of Decree 1946, concluded that Colombia's legislation as designed was such that, if implemented, exceeded its maritime rights, and would encroach on Nicaragua's sovereign rights in its exclusive economic zone (paras 170–187; on the notion of an EEZ, see Chapter 18, Section 18.3.5). The issue before the Court was thus whether Colombian internal law, even if not actually implemented, was in and of itself a breach of that State's international obligations, and the consequences arising from such a breach.

The Court first recalled that, in principle, no general rule applies to the enactment of national legislation and that each situation is specific to the circumstances of the case; however, when taken in in context, Decree 1946 had contributed to the dispute between the two States. The Court's solution was to declare that the responsible State, Colombia, was under 'the obligation, *by means of its own choosing*, to bring the provisions of . . . Decree 1946 into conformity with customary international law' in order to respect Nicaragua's sovereign rights (para 194). This case neatly illustrates the fact that domestic law may breach international obligations, and equally, how the respect in international law for internal sovereignty prevents the review or annulment of any domestic legislation by an international court.

[26] See also the '*Breard*' case filed by Paraguay on similar grounds, but later discontinued: *Vienna Convention on Consular Relations (Paraguay v United States), Order on Discontinuance, ICJ Reports 1998*, p 426.

[27] *Request for Interpretation of the Judgment of 31 March 2004 in the Case concerning Avena and Other Mexican Nationals (Mexico v United States of America), Provisional Measures, ICJ Reports 2008*, p 311; and *Judgment, ICJ Reports 2009*, p 3.

4.2.1.3 **Treatment of municipal law by international courts**

This is an area which has been studied in considerable detail.[28] When an international court examines municipal laws, it usually treats these as 'facts which express the will and constitute the activities of States'.[29] This treatment of municipal law has a few important implications. Foremost, an international court should apply national law as it would be applied in the State concerned, and not substitute its own interpretation. Thus, an international court should generally defer to the interpretation of a State's own national authorities and, in particular, its highest national court; it is not a court of appeal. In the *Serbian Loans* and *Brazilian Loans* judgments, the PCIJ was asked to construe contracts concluded under French law between French bondholders, on the one hand, and a State (the Kingdom of the Serbs, Croats, and Slovenes in one case, Brazil in the second) on the other. The PCIJ emphasized that as an international court which deals with inter-State disputes under international law, as a matter of principle it should not contradict the rulings of national courts.[30] Instead, the international court should 'take note' of the outcome of a domestic decision and deal with its international implications.[31] This is not an absolute rule. In 2010, in the *Diallo* judgment, the ICJ declared that in exceptional circumstances an international court may depart from the construction adopted by a national authority of its own law, such as where a manifestly incorrect interpretation is put forward in the context of a pending case.[32]

Besides these general rules, there are a number of fields in international law where the application of municipal law rules is referred to within international law. For example, as discussed in investment law disputes, the concept of 'nationals' of parties to a bilateral investment treaty (BIT) connotes persons who enjoy the status of nationals under a State's internal law,[33] and certain obligations such as those of 'national treatment' and the obligation of non-discrimination hinge on the application of internal law.[34] In respect of international crimes, considered later in Chapter 17, both the 1948 Genocide Convention and the 1984 Torture Convention stipulate that implementing legislation must accept a uniform definition of genocide and torture, respectively, and take various

[28] See, generally, K Marek, 'Les rapports entre le droit international et le droit interne à la lumière de la jurisprudence de la Cour permanente de Justice internationale' (1962) 66 RGDIP 260; JA Stoll, *L'application et l'interprétation du droit interne par les juridictions internationales* (Institut de sociologie de l'Université de Bruxelles, 1962); Y Shany, *Regulating Jurisdictional Relations between National and International Courts* (OUP, 2007).

[29] See *Certain German Interests in Polish Upper Silesia, 1926, PCIJ, Ser A, No 7*, p 19.

[30] See *Serbian Loans*, 1929, PCIJ, Ser A, No 20, p 46; *Brazilian Loans (France v Brazil), 1929, PCIJ, Ser A, No 21*, p 125.

[31] See *Certain Questions of Mutual Assistance in Criminal Matters (Djibouti v France), Judgment, ICJ Reports 2008*, p 177, 230; and also *Anglo-Norwegian Fisheries (United Kingdom v Norway), Judgment, ICJ Reports 1951*, p 116, Sep Op Lord McNair, 181.

[32] *Ahmadou Sadio Diallo (Guinea v Democratic Republic of the Congo), Judgment, ICJ Reports 2010*, p 639, para 70. See also *Fraport AG Frankfurt Airport Services Worldwide v the Philippines*, ICSID Case No ARB/03/25, Award of 23 December 2010, paras 236, 242.

[33] See, e.g., Convention on the Settlement of Investment Disputes between States and Nationals of other States, 575 UNTS 159, Art 25(1).

[34] Though investment cases abound, in the general international context the PCIJ has made several statements in relation to protected minorities: see *German Settlers in Poland, Advisory Opinion, 1923, PCIJ, Ser B, No 6*; and *Minority Schools in Albania, 1935, PCIJ, Ser A/B, No 64*, p 4.

legislative, administrative, judicial, and other measures to criminalize such acts within their jurisdiction.[35] Finally, as addressed in Chapter 19, there are international environmental conventions that require States to adopt a certain common definition of a polluting substance, or to implement a certain procedure, such as the obligation to conduct an environmental impact assessment conforming to international standards.[36]

4.2.2 **International law applied within municipal legal orders**

Every municipal order is potentially able to devise a different mechanism for the application of international law.[37] Consequently, there is a wide spectrum of possible options for national constitutional frameworks to address the role of international law.[38] Three overarching questions are predominant: first, whether treaties and customary international law are to be treated differently; secondly, what mechanism of implementation is required; and, thirdly, at which rank will international law sit in the hierarchy of rules of municipal law. These would seem in keeping with the monism–dualism controversy discussed in the previous section, but in fact each legal system deals with these questions differently.

4.2.2.1 **The incorporation of customary international law into municipal law**

A key distinction in municipal law relates to the incorporation (transformation) of different sources of international law, with a special emphasis placed on the distinction between treaties and customary international law. Almost invariably, national systems acknowledge and recognize customary international law as part of their municipal legal systems through judicial recognition.

This has been the case in several common law States with an otherwise dualist approach, including Australia[39] and Canada.[40] In the UK, a leading historical statement

[35] See 1948 Genocide Convention (n 21) Art V; 1984 Torture Convention (n 24) Art 2(1). It is also worth noting that the Torture Convention has established a Committee against Torture, the functions of which include monitoring national implementation of the Convention: see Chapter 16, Section 16.3.3.2, for further information.

[36] See, e.g., Convention on Environmental Impact Assessment in a Transboundary Context (signed 25 February 1991, entered into force 10 September 1997), 1989 UNTS 309.

[37] See, generally, A Nollkaemper, *National Courts and the International Rule of Law* (OUP, 2011); A Nollkaemper, 'Internationally Wrongful Acts in Domestic Courts' (2007) 101 AJIL 760; A Cassese, 'Modern Constitutions and International Law' (1985-III) 192 Recueil des Cours 335; S Fatima, *Using International Law in Domestic Courts* (OUP, 2005).

[38] See, e.g., A Peters, 'The Globalization of State Constitutions' in A Nollkaemper and JE Nijman (eds), *New Perspectives on the Divide between National and International Law* (OUP, 2007), 254–70; D Shelton (ed), *International Law and Domestic Legal Systems* (OUP, 2011), twenty-seven domestic legal orders are canvassed from a comparative perspective.

[39] *Potter v BHP Co Ltd* (1906) 3 CLR 479, 495, 506–7; *Chow Hung Ching v R* (1948) 77 CLR 449. See also S Reye, 'The Place of Customary International Law in Australian Law: Unfinished Business' (2001) 21 Australian YBIL 39.

[40] *R v Hape* [2008] 1 LRC 551, paras 34–46; *Reference re Exemption of US Forces from Canadian Criminal Law* [1943] 4 DLR 11, 41; *Reference re Ownership of Offshore Mineral Rights of British Columbia* [1967] SCR 792; *R v Munyaneza* [2009] QJ No 4913, ILDC 1339 (CA 2009). See also G La Forest, 'The Expanding Role of the Supreme Court of Canada in International Law Issues' (1996) 34 Canadian YBIL 89.

is that of Lord Denning in *Trendtex v Central Bank of Nigeria*: '[s]eeing that the rules of international law have changed—and do change—and that the courts have given effect to the changes without any Act of Parliament, it follows . . . inexorably that the rules of international law, as existing from time to time, do form part of English law'.[41] In the USA, a similar principle was set out by the Supreme Court in the *Paquete Habana* case:

> International law is part of our law, and must be ascertained and administered by the courts of justice of appropriate jurisdiction as often as questions of right depending on it are duly presented for their determination. For this purpose, where there is no treaty and no controlling executive or legislative act or judicial decision, resort must be had to the customs and usages of civilized nations.[42]

CASE SPOTLIGHT ***Keyu and others v Secretary of State for Foreign and Commonwealth Affairs*** **[2015] UKSC 69**

In recent years, the UK Supreme Court was required to consider whether the UK government was under an obligation under Article 2(1) ECHR to 'hold a public inquiry or other similar investigation' into the deaths of twenty-four unarmed civilians in Batang Kali in 1948, which was at that time part of British Malaya.

A key submission of the claimants was that by virtue of the common law, a customary international law obligation to investigate the killings also bound the UK government. The UK Supreme Court held that no such customary international law obligation to investigate the killings existed. However, in his speech, Lord Mance held that a presumption existed that customary international law 'can and could shape the common law' whenever consistent with constitutional principles, statutes, and common law rules (para 150). Lord Neuberger agreed with the substance of Lord Mance's points (see para 122).

Lord Mance's statement seems to give some nuance to the general position of UK courts in *Trendtex v Central Bank of Nigeria* and *R v Jones*. Interestingly, *Keyu* also evinces the interaction of the decisions of municipal courts in their engagement with international law. Lord Mance relied on the Federal Court of Australia's judgment in *Nulyrimma v Thompson* [1999] FCA 1992; that case concerned the possible prosecution of Australian State officials for the alleged genocide of the indigenous Australian population, and a similar question arose as to the criminalization of genocide in Australian law through the operation of customary international law. Wilcox J drew a distinction between civil and criminal law, suggesting that '[i]n the absence of enabling legislation, the offence genocide is not cognisable in the courts . . .' (para 32). The civil–criminal distinction might serve to reconcile *Trendtex* with the finding of Lord Bingham in *R v Jones* [2006] UKHL 16 that even in relation to international crimes, 'there now exists no power in the courts to create new criminal offences . . .

[41] *Trendtex Trading Corp v Central Bank of Nigeria* [1977] QB 529, 554 (Denning LJ). This position was reiterated in *R (Campaign for Nuclear Disarmament) v Prime Minister of the United Kingdom* (2002) 126 ILR 727, 738. For further reading, see O'Keefe, 'Doctrine of Incorporation' (n 4).

[42] *Paquete Habana*, 175 US 677, 700 (1900): though there is some scholarly debate, this position still obtains in the USA: see *Restatement, Third, of the Foreign Relations Law of the United States* (American Law Institute, 1987), vol 1, §111, comment (*d*); *Sosa v Alvarez-Machain*, 542 US 692, 737–8 (2004); and *Samantar v Yousuf*, 130 S Ct 2278 (2010).

when it is sought to give domestic effect to crimes established in customary international law, the practice is to legislate' (para 28).

The *Keyu* statement has been clarified in *R (Akarcay) v Chief Constable of the West Yorkshire Police, Home Secretary and National Crime Agency* [2017] EWHC 159 (Admin), in which it was explained that even if customary international law imposed an obligation of non-recognition (in that case of Northern Cyprus), it could not form part of the common law as to do so 'would contravene the unequivocal constitutional principle that questions of recognition are for the executive' (para 23).

As regards civil law systems, the German Basic Law (*Grundgesetz*) provides in Article 25 that '[t]he general rules of public international law form part of the Federal law. They take precedence over the laws and directly create rights and duties for the inhabitants of the Federal territory.'[43] Constitutional provisions on the applicability of general or customary international law also exist in the constitutions of Italy,[44] Portugal,[45] and South Africa.[46] Similarly, the 1946 Constitution of Japan mentions in Article 98(2) that both 'treaties concluded by Japan and established laws of nations shall be faithfully observed', a reference commonly understood to mean that both relevant treaty and customary international law are incorporated into Japan's legal system.[47] Using a slightly different method, the French *Conseil constitutionnel* has accepted the applicability of custom in the French legal system,[48] despite some ambiguity in the 1958 Constitution of the Fifth Republic, which includes no mention of international law but does contain a *renvoi* ('reference') to the preamble of the 1946 Constitution, which mentions that 'the French Republic, true to its traditions, conforms to the rules of public international law'.[49]

4.2.2.2 **General methods of treaty implementation**

The incorporation of treaties into municipal law, unlike with customary international law, is effected rather differently across various States, though there seem to be two predominant approaches worth reviewing.

[43] German Basic Law of 23 May 1949, amended by the Unification Treaty (31 August 1990), 30 ILM 457.

[44] See 1948 Constitution of the Italian Republic, art 10(1): '[t]he Italian legal system conforms to the generally recognized rules of public international law'.

[45] See Constitution of the Portuguese Republic, art 8(1), which provides that the rules and principles of general or customary international law are an integral part of Portuguese law.

[46] See 1996 Constitution of the Republic of South Africa, s 232: 'customary international law is law in the Republic unless it is inconsistent with the Constitution or an Act of Parliament'.

[47] See also Y Iwasawa, 'The Relationship between International Law and National Law: Japanese Experiences' (1993) 64 BYBIL 333, 345.

[48] See *Re Self-Determination of the Comoros Islands* (30 December 1975), Rec 41, 74 ILR 91; *Nationalization Law* (16 January 1982), Rec 18, 75 ILR 700; *Law on the Evolution of New Caledonia* (8 August 1985), Rec 63. See also *Treaty on European Union* (9 April 1992), Rec 55, 93 ILR 337, in which the *Conseil* accepted, in relation to the Treaty of Maastricht establishing the European Union, that the *pacta sunt servanda* rule contained in Art 26 VCLT was binding upon France as a matter of customary international law, despite the fact that France is not a party to the VCLT.

[49] 1946 Constitution of the Fourth Republic, at Preamble, §14.

4.2.2.2.1 ***Incorporation upon ratification into the municipal legal order***

Civil law jurisdictions

In theory, in some jurisdictions international treaties that are duly ratified by the appropriate authorities are automatically incorporated into the internal law of the State. By virtue of such automatic incorporation, the obligations contained in that treaty must be applied and obeyed by State officials and private individuals within the jurisdiction of that State without any further implementing legislation. Usually, this requires publication of the treaty in the official records of a State (in many States, known as the 'Official Gazette'); but that is usually nothing more than a procedural requirement, requiring no legislative intervention.

Though many States provide for automatic incorporation, in practice they often require parliamentary ratification. For example, the 1958 Constitution of the French Republic accepts valid treaties as part of French domestic law; though most ordinary treaties can be signed and ratified by the President,[50] certain categories of treaties must be ratified by the French parliament.[51] Once duly ratified, treaty provisions override domestic law,[52] though never the French Constitution.[53] The 1978 Constitution of Spain acknowledges binding treaties as part of the Spanish legal system, provided that they are compatible with the Constitution; if not, however, the Constitution itself is to be amended.[54] The German Basic Law provides that treaties which regulate its political relations or relate to subjects of federal legislation require ratification by federal statute;[55] once in force, these will apply on a similar footing to ordinary statutes, though hierarchically inferior to the Basic Law.[56] Several other civil law States' constitutions also proclaim the supremacy of treaties over ordinary legislation.[57]

An interesting further example is the Constitution of the Netherlands, which proclaims the supremacy of treaties over prior and subsequent national law,[58] provided they have been approved by the legislature, the States-General. What is more, the Dutch

[50] 1958 French Constitution, art 52.

[51] *Ibid*, art 53, which enumerates peace treaties, treaties providing for membership in international organizations, a cession, exchange, or acquisition of territory, or the modification of legislation. That said, ratification does not automatically allow obligations flowing from the treaty to be actionable.

[52] *Ibid*, art 55. This position has been confirmed by the French *Conseil d'État* in *Sarran, Levacher et al* (30 October 1998), 1081–90; and by the French *Cour de Cassation* in *Pauline Fraisse*, Decision No 450, Case No 99-60.274 (2 June 2000).

[53] *Cafés Jacques Vabre* case, commented in (1975) 16 CMLR 336; *In re Nicolo* (1990) 84 AJIL 765.

[54] See 1978 Constitution of the Kingdom of Spain, arts 95–6.

[55] German Basic Law (n 43) Art 59(2).

[56] See A Paulus, 'Germany' in D Sloss (ed), *The Role of Domestic Courts in Treaty Enforcement* (CUP, 2009), 209, 204–18.

[57] See, e.g., 1975 Constitution of the Hellenic Republic, art 28.1; Constitution of Azerbaijan, art 151; Constitution of Kazakhstan, art 4; Constitution of Bulgaria, art 5.4; and Constitution of Moldova, art 8. See, generally, VS Vereshchetin, 'New Constitutions and the Old Problem of the Relationship between International Law and National Law' (1996) 7 EJIL 29, 34–7; and GM Danilenko, 'Implementation of International Law in CIS States: Theory and Practice' (1999) 10 EJIL 51, 56–63.

[58] See Arts 91 and 94 of the Constitution of the Netherlands; see also A Nollkaemper in D Sloss (ed), *The Role of Domestic Courts in Treaty Enforcement: A Comparative Study* (CUP, 2009), 326, 332–5; and J Klabbers, 'The New Dutch Law on the Approval of Treaties' (1994) 44 ICLQ 629.

legal order is perhaps the only national legal order that implies the supremacy of self-executing international legal obligations over provisions of the Constitution.[59]

Common law jurisdictions

The formal supremacy of treaties over ordinary legislation is accompanied by a general obligation on domestic courts to construe legislation, as far as possible, in a manner which does not conflict with a State's international obligations. The canonical judgment in English courts is that of Lord Denning in *Saloman v Commissioners of Customs and Excise*: he concluded that the court could refer to an unincorporated treaty which was internationally binding on the UK, as it formed part of the background to the statutory provision in issue: 'we ought always to interpret our statutes so as to be in conformity with international law'.[60] However, in *Alcom v Republic of Colombia and others*, the UK House of Lords was called upon to decide whether a judgment could be executed against the ordinary bank account of a diplomatic mission, a question left outside the UK State Immunity Act 1978 (SIA). Lord Diplock suggested that one could not merely look at the international law in force at the time of passage of the SIA, and declared that:

> It makes it highly unlikely that Parliament intended to require United Kingdom courts to act contrary to international law unless the clear language of the statute compels such a conclusion.[61]

Reading these cases together, it would seem that a presumption exists that statutes should be construed in line with international legal obligations, even if not fully incorporated; but this would not go so far as to render an unincorporated treaty directly applicable within the UK legal order. That position is also taken in US courts. In *United States v The Palestine Liberation Organization and others*, the Southern District Court of New York held that the US Anti-Terrorism Act 1988 could not supersede the earlier 1946 Headquarters Agreement, a treaty between the United Nations and the USA. A later statute could only prevail over a treaty in cases where Congress had clearly demonstrated its intent to override the treaty through a domestic provision:

> unless this power is clearly and unequivocally exercised, this court is under a duty to interpret statutes in a manner consonant with existing treaty obligations. This is a rule of statutory construction sustained by an unbroken line of authority for over a century and a half.[62]

4.2.2.2.2 ***Specific legislative implementation to ensure execution of a treaty***

The second method is to require specific legislative incorporation of an international rule, which requires, for each and every international law rule, legislation to exist to translate the provisions of a treaty into national legislation or, at the very least, for the legislature to enjoin the automatic application of an international rule without reformulating that rule. In dualist legal systems, generally, specific incorporation is required with respect to a treaty which has been ratified in order for State officials and individuals

[59] Art 94 of the Constitution of the Netherlands; and see further J Gerards, 'The Irrelevance of the Netherlands Constitution, and the Impossibility of Changing It' (2016) 77 *Revue interdisciplinaire d'études juridiques* 207, at 217.

[60] [1967] 2 QB 116.

[61] *Alcom v Republic of Colombia and others* [1984] 2 All ER 6.

[62] F.Supp 1456 (1988); 82 ILR 282.

to be bound to comply with its provisions. This requirement can be construed as a form of democratic control as, without it, the executive would be able to create legal obligations without legislative consent. For example, in the UK, even a duly ratified treaty does not have direct effect but requires legislation in order to be fully incorporated into the UK legal order. In the *Thomas v Baptiste* case, the Privy Council acknowledged the constitutional principle that a treaty entered into by the executive could not alter national law until it had been incorporated through enabling legislation: 'the terms of a treaty cannot effect any alteration to domestic law or deprive the subject of existing legal rights unless and until enacted into domestic law or by authority of the legislature. When so enacted, the courts give effect to the domestic legislation, not to the terms of the treaty.'[63] Similarly, in *Maclaine, Watson & Co*, it was affirmed that as a matter of UK constitutional law, the royal prerogative to enter into treaties 'does not extend into altering the law or conferring rights on individuals or depriving individuals of rights which they enjoy without the intervention of Parliament. Treaties, as it is sometimes expressed, are not self-executing. Quite simply, a treaty is not part of English law unless and until it has been incorporated into the law by legislation.'[64]

CONTEMPORARY DEVELOPMENTS 'Brexit' in International Law

On 24 June 2016, the UK voted by 51.9 per cent to 48.1 per cent to withdraw from the European Union (colloquially known as 'Brexit'). The European Union is unlike most international organizations in that its decisions can be automatically binding in municipal law, and it requires an unprecedented level of supranational integration stretching across virtually every area of governance, from agricultural standards to banking to security policy. Brexit remains very relevant from an international law perspective, given that the UK's stated intention to deviate from EU law in certain sectors might have substantial international implications, in particular in matters relating to international trade.

From the perspective of the relationship between international and municipal law, Brexit raises specific issues about the continued applicability of EU law within the UK after its departure. When the UK was an EU member, section 3(1) of the European Communities Act 1972 allowed for EU law to have direct effect within the UK legal order without further incorporation. The British government has now passed the European Union (Withdrawal) Act 2018, which has repealed section 3(1), and has incorporated all valid EU law at the date of withdrawal into UK law. Through this procedure, a new category of domestic law, 'retained EU law', has been created, and now (after the end of the transition period on 31 December 2020) may be subject to amendment or repeal under standard UK legislation.

[63] *Thomas v Baptiste* [2000] 2 AC 1 (PC), 23 (Lord Millett); *ibid*, 31–3 (Lords Hoffmann and Goff, diss).

[64] *Maclaine, Watson & Co Ltd v Department of Trade and Industry* [1989] 3 All ER 523, 544–5 (Oliver LJ); see also *British Airways v Laker Airways* [1985] AC 58; and *A (FC) and Others (FC) v Secretary of State for the Home Department* [2005] UKHL 71, para 27 (Bingham LJ), in which it was noted that a lack of enabling legislation from Parliament was of particular relevance in determining that a court should not apply an unincorporated treaty.

Brexit was achieved first through the 2020 EU–UK Withdrawal Agreement, through which the UK left the EU, and now through the EU–UK Trade and Cooperation Agreement (TCA) (signed 30 December 2020, ratified 30 April 2021) that governs relations between the EU and the UK. The TCA is a much looser form of agreement, and there is no automatic direct effect of new EU law in the UK. This means that over time, as EU law and UK law evolve, there is no requirement to achieve or even to aspire to dynamic alignment.

Under the Withdrawal Agreement, the Protocol on Ireland/Northern Ireland provides that in Northern Ireland, certain EU law in relation to the free movement of goods and the EU Customs Union rules will continue to have direct effect in Northern Ireland, maintaining no hard border on the island of Ireland. In 2023, the 'Windsor Framework' adjusted the operation of the Protocol to facilitate trade moving between Northern Ireland and the island of Great Britain, which has enabled the restoration of devolved government in Northern Ireland.

For further background reading, see T Liefländer, M Kellerbauer, and E Dumitriu-Segnana (eds), *The UK–EU Withdrawal Agreement: A Commentary* (OUP, 2021); and J Santos Vara and RA Wessel (eds), *The Routledge Handbook on the International Dimension of Brexit* (Routledge, Abingdon, 2021).

The US system is somewhat different. Article VI§2 of the US Constitution proclaims that all treaties validly entered into 'shall be the supreme Law of the Land and the Judges in every state shall be bound thereby', placing treaties on the same level as federal legislation, and prevailing over state legislation. As its Supreme Court declared in the classic *Foster v Neilson* judgment of 1829:

> Our constitution declares a treaty to be the law of the land. It is, consequently, to be regarded in courts of justice as equivalent to the act of the legislature, whenever it operates of itself without the aid of any legislative provision. But when the terms of the stipulation import a contract, when either of the parties engages to perform a particular act, the treaty addresses itself to the political, not the judicial department; and the legislature must execute the contract before it can become a rule for the Court.[65]

However, because Article II§2 of the Constitution requires the 'advice and consent' of two-thirds of the Senate, a practice has developed in which the Senate identifies certain provisions as 'self-executing', and thus requiring no further implementing legislation. 'Self-executing' treaty obligations were considered in *Sei Fujii v California*,[66] where the question arose, in the context of wartime seizures of the property of Japanese citizens, as to whether the Charter of the United Nations was a self-executing treaty. The Supreme Court of California concluded that the relevant provisions of the Charter were not intended to be self-executing, as they 'do not purport to impose legal obligations on the individual member nations or to create rights in private persons'; further legislative

[65] *Foster v Neilson*, 27 US 253, 314 (1829). To illustrate, on ratifying the ICCPR in 1992, the US government attached a declaration stating that Arts 1 through 27 of the Covenant were non-self-executing and, to date, there has not yet been any implementing legislation, so they do not yet have direct effect in the USA. See also, generally, DL Sloss, 'The Domestication of International Human Rights: Non-Self-Executing Declarations and Human Rights Treaties' (1999) 24 Yale JIL 129.

[66] *Sei Fujii v California*, 38 Cal (2d) 718 (1952).

action would thus be required.[67] Once implemented, it is the implementing legislation and not the international treaty which is regarded as valid US law.[68] As the commentary on *LaGrand* and *Avena* in Section 4.2.1.2 illustrates, the point came controversially to the fore in US courts in various capital punishment cases which led to international litigation before the ICJ.[69]

4.3 Practical issues faced by domestic courts in relation to international law

It is evident that the role of international law in municipal legal orders, and especially municipal courts' engagement with international law, remains a live and highly interesting issue. The next sections follow examples of the current, practical problems faced by some municipal courts in relation to the role of international law within their respective legal orders. Though a retreat from the broader approach favoured in this book, this section will primarily refer to the decisions of courts in the UK and the USA, given both their leading historical role in relation to these specific questions and the fact that their practice is often taken up by other jurisdictions.

4.3.1 The executive and questions of international law before national courts

In most municipal legal orders, the separation of powers has meant that the authority to conduct foreign relations generally falls to the executive branch; most governmental expertise relating to international law is found within that branch as well. Moreover, national courts are often called upon to avoid, where possible, situations where national law will be in conflict with a State's international obligations.[70] As such, it may not be entirely surprising that in a number of municipal legal orders, the executive can provide guidance and direct a national court on questions of international law.[71] In France, the *Conseil d'État* may seek guidance from the Ministry of Foreign Affairs on the construction of an international agreement, though the French courts may decide that the treaty is sufficiently clear ('*acte clair*') and depart from any advice given.[72] In the USA, the

[67] *Ibid*, 721. See also *Medellín v Texas*, 552 US 491, 509 and 511 (2008).

[68] See US Third Restatement (n 42), ch 2, 'Status of International Law and Agreements in the United States', §[111]; and A Aust, *Modern Treaty Law and Practice* (2nd edn, CUP, 2013), 174–6.

[69] See also *Breard v Pruett* and *Breard v Greene* 140 L.Ed 2d 529 (1998), 118 ILR 23, which were the subject of *Vienna Convention on Consular Relations (Paraguay v United States), Provisional Measures, Order of 9 April 1998, ICJ Reports 1998*, p 248; *Sanchez-Llamas v Oregon*, 548 US 331 (2006); *Medellín v Texas* (2008) (n 67).

[70] See earlier, Section 4.2.2.2.1.

[71] International law does not go so far as to prescribe the appropriate separation of powers in municipal legal orders; however, in *Difference Relating to Immunity from Legal Process of a Special Rapporteur of the Commission on Human Rights, Advisory Opinion, ICJ Reports 1999*, p 62, paras 60–2, the ICJ gave some indications as to what form of guidance the executive branch could offer to a domestic court.

[72] See *Gisti* case (29 June 1990), 111 ILR 499 (French *Conseil d'État*); *Agyepong* case (2 December 1994), 111 ILR 531 (French *Conseil d'État*). But *cf Beaumartin v France*, Judgment of 24 November 1994, ECHR Ser A, no 296-B, 19 EHRR 485, in which the ECtHR challenged the practice as incompatible with the right of access to an independent and impartial tribunal embodied in Art 6 of the ECHR.

executive can give advice in court cases concerning sensitive questions of international law, either through *amicus curiae* briefs or through 'executive suggestions'.[73] The courts retain the power to disregard executive suggestions in cases where the State Department provides guidance on, for example, an act of State[74] or sovereign immunity.[75]

Conversely, the UK operates a stricter separation of powers to uphold judicial independence, and the practice of *amicus curiae* intervention by the government is rather less usual.[76] However, when establishing certain categories of facts, such as the status of a foreign State or government, or whether diplomatic immunity exists in respect of an individual, certain legislative acts such as the Diplomatic Privileges Act 1964[77] and the State Immunity Act 1978[78] permit the government to provide 'executive certificates' (a 'Foreign Office certificate' when issued by the Foreign and Commonwealth Office) confirming such facts, following a request from a competent judicial body. In UK courts, legislation requires that executive certificates are treated as conclusive.[79] In the *Ex parte Trawnik* case, it was held that executive certificates could be reviewable only if they constituted a nullity, in that they were not authentic certificates, or if it was manifest that they had been issued outside the scope of any relevant statutory competence to do so.[80] More recently, in the *Mohammed Gul* judgment,[81] the English Court of Appeal, appraising the status of a Foreign Office certificate declaring that the conflicts in Afghanistan (after December 2001) and Iraq (after 28 June 2004) constituted non-international armed conflicts, took the 'provisional view that the Certificate was conclusive', and that the facts in the case file required no further enquiry.

HISTORICAL BACKGROUND Executive Certificates in Relation to Protectorates

During the European colonial period, many territories were considered integral parts of Great Britain, France, or Belgium, and thus possessing no international legal personality. However, there was also a widespread practice among the European empires of proclaiming

[73] See, e.g., *Air France and British Airways v Port Authority of New York and New Jersey*, 558 F.2d 75 (1977) (US Second District Court of Appeal).

[74] See, e.g., *Bernstein v NV Nederlandsche-Amerikaansche Stoomvart-Maatschappij*, 210 F.2d 375 (1954); *First National City Bank v Banco Nacional de Cuba* 406 US 759, 768 (1972); *WS Kirkpatrick & Co v Environmental Tectonics*, 493 US 400, 404–10 (1990).

[75] Though the US Foreign Sovereign Immunities Act has transferred to the courts the determination of sensitive questions of State immunity (see Chapter 9), the State Department continues to file *amicus curiae* briefs and to expect US courts to defer to its views: see *Habyarimana v Kagame*, 821 F.Supp 2d 1244 (2011), where the Second District Court of Appeals accepted the determination that the serving head of State of Rwanda was immune from suit even for acts committed prior to assuming office.

[76] Though it occasionally occurs (see, e.g., *R v Bow Street Metropolitan Stipendiary, ex p Pinochet Ugarte (No 1)* [1999] UKHL 52; and *Alcom v Colombia* (n 61)); the executive, through the Attorney General, will nominate counsel to present the government's views, without pressure to comply.

[77] Diplomatic Privileges Act 1964, s 4.

[78] State Immunity Act 1978, s 21.

[79] See Diplomatic Privileges Act, s 7; State Immunity Act 1978, s 21; International Organisations Act 1968, s 8; *R (Alamieyeseigha) v Crown Prosecution Service* [2005] EWHC 2704 (Admin); *R (Sultan of Pahang) v Secretary of State for the Home Department* [2011] EWCA Civ 616; *Khurts Bat v Republic of Mongolia* [2011] EWHC 2029 (Admin). See generally C Warbrick, 'Executive Certificates in Foreign Affairs: Prospects for Review and Control' (1986) 35 ICLQ 138; and E Wilmshurst, 'Executive Certificates in Foreign Affairs: The United Kingdom' (1986) 35 ICLQ 157.

[80] *R v Secretary of State for Foreign and Commonwealth Affairs, ex p Trawnik* (1985) The Times, 18 April, QBD.

[81] *R v Mohammed Gul* [2012] EWCA Crim 280, paras 20 *et seq*.

'protectorates', or placing entities under their protection, without claiming sovereignty over them. These included Brunei (British protectorate 1906–84), most of Morocco (French/Spanish protectorate 1912–56), and Ruanda-Urundi (Belgian protectorate 1918–62).

The formal status of protectorates as independent legal persons is both a question of international and municipal law, and was a sensitive question politically. It was in relation to protectorates that the advice of the executive branch became determinative. In *Duff Development Co Ltd v Kelantan* ([1924] AC 727; 2 AD 124), there was a claim to immunity in the English courts asserted by the 'State of Kelantan'. Kelantan's status at that time was as one of the 'Unfederated Malay States', a nominally independent grouping of States under the British protectorate. Upon receiving from the Colonial Office a statement that Kelantan was to be regarded as an independent State, the House of Lords declared that 'where such a statement is forthcoming, no other evidence is admissible or needed . . . it was not the business of the Court to inquire whether the Colonial Office rightly concluded that the Sultan [of Kelantan] was entitled to be recognised as a sovereign by international law'. Following this decision, the use of executive certificates in relation to other areas of international law expanded in the UK.

4.3.2 **Non-justiciability: certain questions beyond the competence of municipal courts**

The notion of 'justiciability', which exists primarily in the USA and the UK, suggests that there are limits to the types of matters which cannot be tried according to law; these are *non-justiciable*, as no court can be regarded as competent to engage with such matters.[82] Usually, non-justiciable questions are understood as touching upon sensitive issues of foreign relations on which no judicial standards would seem to exist, and in which judicial interference might constitute a serious trespass on the separation of powers.[83] In a canonical statement in *Maclaine Watson v International Tin Council*, the UK House of Lords declared that it is 'axiomatic that municipal courts have not and cannot have the competence to adjudicate upon or to enforce the rights arising out of transactions entered into by independent sovereign States between themselves on the plane of international law'.[84] More recently, in *R (Bancoult) v Secretary of State for Foreign and Commonwealth Affairs*, it was held that claimed fishing rights of Mauritius within the British Indian Ocean Territory could not be adjudicated, given the absence of Mauritius as a party to the case.[85]

UK courts have recognized a number of matters as non-justiciable including, *inter alia*, the making of war and peace and the disposition of the armed forces,[86] the conduct

[82] On the general concept of justiciability, see D McGoldrick, 'The Boundaries of Justiciability' (2010) 59 ICLQ 981; P Daly, 'Justiciability and the "Political Question" Doctrine' [2010] Public Law 160; M Nicholson, 'The Political Unconscious of the English Foreign Act of State and Non-Justiciability Doctrine(s)' (2015) 64 ICLQ 743; R Masterman, *The Separation of Powers in the Contemporary Constitution* (OUP, 2011), 89–114.

[83] See *R v Lyons* [2002] UKHL 44, para 40 (Hoffmann LJ), para 105 (Millett LJ); *Korea National Insurance Corporation v Allianz Global Corporate & Speciality AG* [2008] EWCA Civ 1355, para 32.

[84] *Maclaine Watson v International Tin Council* [1989] 3 All ER 523, 544 (Oliver LJ). The judgment also emphasized the importance of keeping the two concepts of non-justiciability and immunity separate: see Chapter 9.

[85] [2013] EWHC 1502 (Admin), para 153.

[86] *R v Jones* [2006] UKHL 16, para 65 (Hoffmann LJ); see also *Keyu and others v Secretary of State for Foreign and Commonwealth Affairs* [2015] UKSC 69, para 145 (Mance LJ).

of foreign affairs,[87] and the conclusion of treaties.[88] The doctrine continues to be refined. In the 2017 *Belhaj & Rahmatullah* judgment, a case concerning the alleged involvement of the UK in the detention and maltreatment of foreign nationals in Libya and Afghanistan, the UK Supreme Court held that, though falling short of torture, such treatment could not be regarded as an act of State requiring judicial abstention 'in view of the nature and seriousness of the infringements of individual fundamental rights involved'.[89] In *Ukraine v Law Debenture Trust*, which concerned Russian acts of aggression against Ukraine, Russia had claimed that its acts were non-justiciable foreign Acts of State. Though in 2019 the English Court of Appeal held that coercive acts illegal under international law would thus constitute 'duress' under English law,[90] in 2023 the UK Supreme Court did not focus on the seriousness of the international law violations; reframing the matter purely as the domestic act of 'duress' and dismissing Russia's claims of non-justiciability on the basis of the consent of both parties to the jurisdiction of English law.[91]

In *Occidental Exploration v Ecuador*, the English Court of Appeal held that an award rendered under a US–Ecuador BIT gave rise to justiciable rights, even though the BIT was not part of English law; this was because the BIT had intended to give rise to rights in favour of private investors capable of enforcement in domestic proceedings.[92]

CONTEMPORARY DEVELOPMENTS The Justiciability of Unincorporated Treaties in the UK

There exists a strictly dualist view that if treaties are not duly incorporated (translated) into the domestic legal order through appropriate legislation, then they remain within the prerogative of the executive, and disputes regarding compliance with them ought also to be regarded as non-justiciable. However, recent developments suggest that even in cases where a binding treaty which has not been incorporated into domestic law there might be an exception to the doctrine of non-justiciability in situations where directly enforceable human rights law is engaged.

[87] *R (Al-Rawi) v Secretary of State for Foreign and Commonwealth Affairs* [2006] EWCA Civ 1279, paras 131 *et seq* (Laws LJ).

[88] *See A v Secretary of State for the Home Department* [2005] 2 AC 68, 146 (Scott LJ); *R (Wheeler) v Office of the Prime Minister* [2008] UKHL 20.

[89] *Belhaj & Rahmatullah (No 1) v Straw & Ors* [2017] UKSC 3, para 97 (Mance LJ); Neuberger LJ (para 168) and Hale LJ (para 36) suggested that a public policy exception would 'almost always' render justiciable a claim concerning a breach of *jus cogens*.

[90] *Ukraine v Law Debenture Trust* [2019] QB 1121, para 160.

[91] See *Ukraine v Law Debenture Trust* [2023] UKSC 1. See further P Capps, 'Act of State and the Limits of Adjudication' (2024) 140 Law Quarterly Review 130–56; *High Commissioner for Pakistan in the United Kingdom v Prince Muffakham Jah* [2019] EWHC 2551 (Ch); [2020] Ch 421; *Maduro Board v Guaidó Board* [2021] UKSC 57.

[92] *Occidental Exploration & Production Co v Ecuador* [2006] QB 432, 457. See also *In the Matter of AY Bank Ltd* [2006] EWHC 830 (Ch), paras 51 *et seq*.

In *R (Al-Jedda) v Secretary of State for Defence* [2008] 1 AC 332, the claimant contended that he had suffered detention at the hands of British forces which were occupying Iraq at that time, and that such detention constituted a breach of the ECHR, which is incorporated into UK law through the Human Rights Act 1998. Though the UN Charter has not been incorporated in full, the UK United Nations Act 1946 allows the executive to implement Security Resolutions without parliamentary approval. Security Council Resolution 1546 (2004), which established the parameters for US/UK occupation forces in Iraq, was the relevant resolution in that case.

Despite this, the House of Lords considered that it was competent to examine the effects of Resolution 1546, given the likelihood that obligations flowing from the ECHR (an incorporated treaty) would be considered by the ECtHR in the light of obligations under the UN Charter. It would seem that there are two possible explanations: either the courts have identified tension between an incorporated and an unincorporated treaty, and have given primacy to the incorporated treaty; or somehow the courts have given higher regard to human rights of a fundamental nature.

The effect of the United Nations Act 1946 was further considered in *Ahmed v HM Treasury* [2010] UKSC 2, in which the Supreme Court held that the Act, despite empowering the government to implement Security Council decisions, did not lawfully empower the executive to issue orders which significantly violated fundamental human rights without explicit Security Council derogation from them.

In the USA, the doctrine of non-justiciability has been known as the 'political questions' exception, which operates to prevent courts from considering sensitive political issues in the field of foreign affairs.[93] Though not consistently upheld, the exception has been invoked especially in relation to the political status of a foreign entity,[94] the conduct of foreign affairs, and the deployment of armed forces.[95] In *Greenham Women against Cruise Missiles v Reagan*, a suit by the plaintiffs to prevent the US deployment of cruise missiles at a UK air base was declared inappropriate for judicial resolution, and thus non-justiciable.[96] The political questions doctrine does not exclude cases merely because they present sensitive political issues; the question at hand must be of a political nature such that judicial resolution is not appropriate.[97] For example, in *Linder v Portocarrero*, which concerned the murder of a US citizen working for the Nicaraguan government by rebel forces (the 'Contras'), the US 11th Circuit Court of Appeals ruled that the political question doctrine was not

[93] See the *Baker v Carr* judgment, 369 US 186, 217 (1962); *Underhill v Hernández*, 168 US 250 (1897). See further the classic L Henkin, 'Is There a "Political Question" Doctrine?' (1975) 85 Yale LJ 597; and more recently, JC Harrison, 'The American Act of State Doctrine' (2016) 47 Georgetown JIL 507, at 556–61.

[94] See *Coleman v Miller*, 307 US 433, 450 (1939).

[95] *Goldwater v Carter*, 444 US 996 (1976).

[96] 591 F.Supp 1332 (1984).

[97] See, e.g., *Klinghoffer v SNC Achille Lauro*, 937 F.2d 44, 49 (1991); *Japan Whaling Association v American Cetacean Society* 478 US 221 (1986).

implicated because the complaint neither challenged the legitimacy of US policy against Nicaragua nor sought or required the court to decide on the legality of conduct in relation to the civil war in that State.[98] In *Kadić v Karaždić*, the definition of a political question was further confined:

> Not every case 'touching foreign relations' is non-justiciable ... and judges should not reflexively invoke these doctrines [political question and act of State doctrines] to avoid difficult and somewhat sensitive decisions in the context of human rights.[99]

There are a number of exceptions to the 'political questions' doctrine in the USA. In *Kirkpatrick v Environmental Tectonics*, the plaintiff had sued the defendant for securing a contract with the Nigerian Air Force through bribery. The Supreme Court held that the political questions doctrine did not apply in that case because the validity of a foreign sovereign act, that of Nigeria, was not in issue: it would arise only when a court 'must decide—that is, when the outcome of a case turns upon—the effect of official action by a foreign sovereign.'[100]

Though the notion of justiciability has been most developed in the common law jurisdictions, several prominent civil law jurisdictions have also developed cognate concepts to justify judicial intervention or intervention in affairs of States.[101] In France, the *acte de gouvernement* doctrine removes from the competence of French tribunals the review of an executive act in two situations: either the act (i) 'project[s] onto the international plane the manifestation of the wishes of the French authorities and consequently only [has] meaning in the context of the relations between the French State and an international organization and another State'; or the act (ii) 'exclusively [involves] an assessment of the appropriateness of action from the standpoint of foreign policy'.[102] The *acte de gouvernement* doctrine has been applied in relation to various matters of French foreign relations including, *inter alia*, the decision whether to publish an international agreement,[103] the suspension of an international agreement,[104] and even the deployment of French troops against Yugoslavia in relation to the situation in Kosovo.[105] In Italy, a similar doctrine (the *teoria dell'atto do governo*) prevails, as Article VIII(5) of the Italian Constitution reserves certain matters for the executive and the legislature, such as declarations of war.[106]

[98] 963 F.2d 332, 337 (1992); see also *Koohi v United States*, 976 F.2d 1328, 1331–2 (1992).

[99] See *Kadić v Karaždić*, 70 F.3d 232, 249 (1995).

[100] *Kirkpatrick v Environmental Tectonics*, 110 US 701 (1990).

[101] See E Benvenisti, 'Judicial Misgivings Regarding the Application of International Law' (1993) 4 EJIL 159; D Amoroso, 'A Fresh Look at the Issue of Non-justiciability of Defence and Foreign Affairs' (2010) 23 Leiden JIL 933.

[102] *United Kingdom and Government of Hong Kong* [1993] Rec Lebon 267, 106 ILR 233 (*Commissaire du Gouvernement Vigoroux*).

[103] *De Malglaive* [1970] Rec Lebon 635, 72 ILR 236.

[104] *Prefect of La Gironde v Mahmedi* [1992] Rec Lebon 445, 106 ILR 204.

[105] *Mégret* [2000] Rec Lebon 291. See also *Committee against the Iraq War* [2003] Rec Lebon 707.

[106] *President of the Council v Marković*, Corte di Cassazione 5 June 2002, Judgment No 8157, 128 ILR 652.

CASE SPOTLIGHT ***President of the Council v Marković*****, Corte di Cassazione (5 June 2002), Judgment No 8157 Italy, 128 ILR 652**

The *Marković* judgment was internationally significant for a number of reasons, not all relating to the relevance of international law in the Italian legal order. In this case, the claimants, Serbian civilians whose relatives were killed during an aerial bombardment in Belgrade by NATO forces in 1999, contended that the Italian government was liable for the deaths, alleging two bases of liability: joint liability for Italy as a NATO member; or the fact that bombardment was carried out from bases on Italian territory. The *Corte* declared these claims inadmissible:

> The selection of a method for conducting hostilities is amongst those acts which are performed by the Government. All such acts are expressions of a political function which, under the Constitution, is envisaged as emanating from a constitutional organ. The nature of this function is that it is impossible to protect individual interest from its effects on the basis that those acts falling within its scope are incapable of precise definition . . . With regard to acts of this type, no court has the power to review the manner in which the function is exercised.

One can see the obvious embarrassment for the Italian government had the *Corte* been prepared to rule on the legality of Italy's conduct, as it would have potentially brought into question the entire legality of the NATO armed intervention against Yugoslavia. Having said that, it is not as though the international judicial apparatus would have been competent to rule on the question: in 1999, and then 2004, the ICJ declared that it did not have jurisdiction over Yugoslavia's request for a ruling in respect of the use of force against it by NATO: see *Legality of Use of Force (Federal Republic of Yugoslavia v Belgium et al), Provisional Measures, Order of 2 June 1999, ICJ Reports 1999*, p 124; and *Legality of Use of Force (Serbia and Montenegro v Belgium et al), Preliminary Objections, Judgment, ICJ Reports 2004*, p 279.

In Germany, conversely, there is no tradition of automatic judicial deference to the executive in matters of foreign policy, and there exist provisions of the Basic Law defending the right of individual petition against any public authority,[107] as well as the principle of *Organstreit*, of resolving disputes between constitutional organs.[108] In fact, the Federal Constitutional Court in Karlsruhe even sits outside the ordinary court system to hear cases associated with enforcement of the Basic Law.[109] This means that German courts can hear disputes relating to the deployment of armed forces, as they did in relation to the *International Military Operations* case, in which the government's decision to deploy German troops alongside NATO troops to enforce Security Council resolutions was challenged, albeit unsuccessfully. Though Article 87a(2) of the Basic

[107] German Basic Law, Art 19(4): '[s]hould any person's right be violated by public authority, recourse to the court shall be open to him'.

[108] *Ibid*, Art 93(1)(1), which permits suits to be launched between different organs of the federal government on questions of competence.

[109] *Ibid*, Arts 92–4, 100.

Law only allows the deployment of German troops for the purposes of 'defence', the Constitutional Court declaring it to be a permissible operation here, provided that it remained within the framework of a 'system of mutual collective security'.[110]

Even in such a strongly constitutionalized system such as that of Germany, issues relating to the judicial review of questions of foreign policy or defence can be declared inadmissible. In the *Cruise Missile* judgment concerning the deployment of nuclear missiles on German territory, the Constitutional Court declined the case, partly on the basis that there existed no data against which the court could ascertain the alleged risk to life, and that in any event it was the responsibility of the federal government to decide upon Germany's foreign and defence policies.[111] In response to a claim on the deployment of chemical weapons on German territory, the Constitutional Court declined to hear the case, on the basis that a complaint would only be admissible provided that it challenged the manner in which specific acts or omissions of a public authority were taken (e.g., the failure to take precautionary measures) and was not only an objection to the substance of decision taken.[112]

4.3.3 **Judicial restraint in relation to acts of State**

A delicate question concerns how a municipal court is to give effect to the laws or executive acts of a foreign State which breach international law. When faced with such claims, a national court is being called upon not only to ascertain the relevant international legal rule but also to pronounce itself on whether the act of another State has breached said rule. In so doing, the court risks inflaming foreign relations between States and embarrassing the executive; serious questions also arise as to which standards ought to be applied to assess the validity of foreign legislation and acts. It is for this reason that the law of immunities, discussed in Chapter 9, has developed. But equally, a doctrine of 'judicial restraint' has been developed by courts when scrutinizing the acts of another sovereign ('act of State'). The now classic statement of the US Supreme Court in *Underhill v Hernández* neatly encapsulates the act of State doctrine:

> every sovereign State is bound to respect the independence of every other sovereign State, and the courts of one country will not sit in judgment on the acts of the government, done within its own territory.[113]

Other US courts have confirmed the applicability of the doctrine in respect of the acts of foreign States; for example, classifying a grant of a concession to exploit natural resources as an inherently sovereign act.[114] Above all, it has been asserted that such a rule relates to internal constitutional balances.[115]

[110] 90 BVerfGE 286 (1994), 106 ILR 319, 327–30.

[111] *Cruise Missiles (Danger to Life)*, 66 BVerfGE 39 (1983), 106 ILR 353, 362.

[112] See, e.g., *Chemical Weapons Deployment (Danger to Life)*, 77 BVerfGE 170 (1987), 106 ILR 389, 395. See further P Quint, 'The Most Extraordinarily Powerful Court of Law the World Has Ever Known? Judicial Review in the United States and Germany' (2006) 65 Maryland LR 152, 166.

[113] *Underhill v Hernández* (n 91) 252.

[114] See *Clayco Petroleum Corporation v Occidental Petroleum Corporation and others* 712 F.2d 404 (1983); 81 ILR 522.

[115] See *Banco Nacional de Cuba v Sabbatino* 376 US 398 (1964).

CASE SPOTLIGHT ***Republic of the Philippines v Marcos and Others* 802 F.2d 344 (1986)**

In February 1986, President Ferdinand Marcos of the Philippines fled the country after a twenty-year dictatorship. The new government actively sought the assistance of the US courts in order to recover real estate in New York illegally embezzled by Marcos while in power. The total amount of money stolen may have equalled or exceeded the $30 billion USD Philippines national debt. It is a highly unusual case because it represents an example of a State actively disavowing any protection for its previous acts, claiming that a corrupt government had misappropriated real property.

The Second District Court of Appeals (in New York) accepted the Philippine position that Marcos's acts were not its own. Moreover, the District Court declined to apply the judicial restraint doctrine, reasoning that any misappropriation by Marcos was a purely private act. Accordingly, the Philippine government's request was not tantamount to expropriation: '[t]he complaint seeks recovery of property illegally taken by a former head of State, not confiscation of property legally owned by him'. The court issued an injunction freezing the assets.

The *Philippines v Marcos* case helped to shape the outer limits of the judicial restraint doctrine, and vividly illustrates the relevance of the international–municipal law interaction with other areas of international law: in this case, the recognition of the new government of another State. The latter point is further covered in Chapter 5, Section 5.3.2.

The UK has also adopted a similar doctrine of judicial restraint in relation to the acts of foreign sovereign States. In *Buttes Gas and Oil Co v Hammer (No 3)*, Lord Wilberforce in a majority judgment held that:

> there exists in English law a general principle that courts will not adjudicate upon the transactions of foreign sovereign States ... it seems desirable to consider this principle, if existing, not as a variety of 'act of State' but one for judicial restraint or abstention ... This principle is not one of discretion, but is inherent in the very nature of the judicial process.[116]

The British practice regarding judicial restraint was examined in *Kuwait Airways Corporation v Iraqi Airways Co*, in which Iraqi forces had seized ten commercial aircraft belonging to the plaintiff during the invasion of Kuwait by Iraq in 1990. By a decree of the Revolutionary Command Council (RCC), an organ of the Iraqi State, the aircraft were transferred to the defendant. After the ouster of Iraqi forces, during which some of the aircraft were destroyed by bombing, the plaintiff claimed the return of the aircraft and payment of the value of the destroyed aircraft, as well as damages. The House of Lords was called upon to consider the validity of the RCC decree in the light of the fact that the invasion of Kuwait was a clear violation of international law, and concluded it appropriate to disregard the judicial restraint doctrine in relation to the acts of foreign States:

> like the confiscatory decree of the Nazi government of Germany in 1941, a law depriving those whose property has been plundered of the ownership of their property in favour of the aggressor's own citizens will not be enforced or recognised in proceedings in this

[116] *Buttes Gas & Oil Co v Hammer (No 3)* [1982] AC 888, 932–3 (Wilberforce LJ).

> country. Enforcement or recognition of this law would be manifestly contrary to the public policy of English law . . . International law, for its part, recognises that a national court may properly decline to give effect to legislative and other acts of foreign States which are in violation of international law.[117]

More recently, in the *Belhaj & Rahmatullah* judgment, the two plaintiffs had argued that they had suffered years of torture in Iraq and in Libya, respectively, and that UK security services had cooperated in their unlawful rendition and detention in these States. Lord Sumption drew an important distinction between a 'municipal law act of State' (the treatment of persons or property by a State acting *jure imperii*), which required English courts not to adjudicate on the legality or validity of a State's sovereign acts under its own law, but is limited territorially; and an 'international law act of State', which required English courts not to adjudicate on the lawfulness of the extraterritorial acts of foreign States in their dealings with other States or the subjects of other States.[118]

4.4 Conclusion: accommodating plural orders

Theory helps us to understand the world. In relation to the interplay between municipal and international legal orders, the monism–dualism debate helps us to clarify the logic used by the panoply of actors, and especially courts, which stand at that interface between international and municipal legal orders. Though perhaps the classic dualist and monist positions show a certain fatigue, one should resist the temptation to reduce dualism to an outdated form of legal nationalism, and to elevate monism to some sort of 'courageous committed internationalism'.[119] Though monism certainly contains the promise of universalism within it, the experience in dualist legal systems has helped to develop a rich set of tools through which to accommodate the inevitable conflicts that can arise through the engagement of legal orders with one another. What is more, in a technologically advanced world where people continually traverse boundaries, and where States are ever more likely to act beyond what have traditionally been understood as their domestic prerogatives, monist–dualist controversies seem almost quaintly archaic, in the light of more pressing issues of global collective concern.

What, then, to make of the relationship between municipal law and international law? The lawyer's temptation is often to reduce conflict and to promote harmonization, but perhaps some systematic thinking about the accommodation of plural orders has become more necessary.[120] Perhaps the reality lies somewhere in between, in the

[117] *Kuwait Airways Corporation v Iraqi Airways Co (No 2)* [2002] UKHL 19, para 29 (Nicholls LJ); see also para 114 (Steyn LJ); paras 138–40 (Hope LJ).

[118] *Belhaj & Rahmatullah* (n 89), paras 228–34 (Sumption LJ). See further E Bjorge and C Miles, 'Crown and Foreign Acts of State before British Courts: *Rahmatullah, Belhaj* and the Separation of Powers' in CA Bradley (ed), *The Oxford Handbook of Comparative Foreign Relations Law* 715.

[119] As does Cassese (n 11) 234–6.

[120] See, e.g., N Krisch, *Beyond Constitutionalism* (OUP, 2011); N Walker, 'The Idea of Constitutional Pluralism' (2002) 65 MLR 317.

continued story of many different legal systems overlapping with one another and seeking a form of accommodation. Municipal legal orders reflect the diversity of political communities around the world; and each in turn engages regularly with norms and rules of international law, at times requiring guidance from other branches of government. That diversity has in the past provided a useful laboratory from which the most effective doctrines for the avoidance of embarrassment or outright conflict between States has emerged. For its part, though the international legal order brings with it the promise of universality, harmonization, and cooperation, it comes with its own set of challenges, not least on how to apply or engage with rules of national law. Understanding and harnessing the diversity of purposes for which law exists might prove the key for the continued renewal and development of international relations.

Further reading

T Bingham, *Widening Horizons: The Influence of Comparative Law and International Law on Domestic Law* (Hamlyn Lectures, CUP, 2010).

Delivered from a judicial perspective, a lucid account of the engagement between different legal orders.

S Fatima, *Using International Law in Domestic Courts* (Hart, 2005).

A clear synthesis of the breadth of principles used by English courts when engaging with international law.

M Lando, 'Reframing the English Foreign Act of State Doctrine' (2023) 87 MLR 343.

An ambitious reframing of the foreign Act of State doctrine around 'limitations' and 'exceptions' that challenges the traditional approach to questions of justiciability, abstention, and restraint.

M Nicholson, 'The Political Unconscious of the English Foreign Act of State and Non-Justiciability Doctrine(s)' (2015) 64 ICLQ 743.

An incisive review of UK court practice with respect to questions of international law.

A Nollkaemper, *National Courts and the International Rule of Law* (OUP, 2011).

This impressive book reviews judicial control of the exercise of public powers by States, mapping domestic practice.

A Nollkaemper and J Nijman (eds), *New Perspectives on the Divide between National and International Law* (OUP, 2007).

Gathers essays reflecting on classic themes and contemporary challenges in understanding the municipal-international relationship.

A Roberts, 'Comparative International Law? The Role of National Courts in International Law' (2011) 60 ICLQ 57.

Clear, well-structured, and comparative account of how national courts engage with international law.

Y Shany, *Regulating Jurisdictional Relations between National and International Courts* (OUP, 2007).

Through a 'vertical' account, explains the relationship between national and international courts.

D Shelton, *International Law and Domestic Legal Systems: Incorporation, Transformation, and Persuasion* (OUP, 2011).

A systematic overview of twenty-seven key municipal legal systems and how they incorporate international law.

A Sloss, *The Role of Domestic Courts in Treaty Enforcement: A Comparative Approach* (CUP, 2009).

Surveying twelve domestic court systems, a practice-based illustration of the daily engagement of municipal courts with international law.

JG Starke, 'Monism and Dualism in the Theory of International Law Considered from the Standpoint of the Rule of Law' (1957) 92 Recueil des Cours 5.

A classic work engaging with the basic monism–dualism theoretical debate.

PART II
Subjects of international law

5

States as subjects of international law

5.1 Introduction: the nature of the State

International law is the product of history, of various events and choices incrementally building upon each other. As the international legal system became more established, and the question of whether it created rights and obligations became more settled, a second question emerged: to whom are these rights and obligations to apply, to an individual or some sort of entity? After all, rights and obligations must apply to some person or legal subject. It is on that very basic premise that the international legal system has devised the concept of *personality*, to describe when an entity is capable of exercising international rights and/or duties.[1]

Legal personality is not binary; one can have different categories of legal subjects. Indeed, domestic legal systems have a wide variety of legal subjects, including categories of individuals (e.g., citizens, foreigners within their territory), as well as legal persons (corporate bodies, associations, institutions of the State). Each category of legal subject, while enjoying the status of a subject under international law, may be differentiated by the capacities, powers, rights, and obligations that a legal person of that description might enjoy under domestic law.

In international law, the number of subjects is in fact quite limited, and dominated by one category above all: States. The very concept of the State has played an extraordinarily important role in defining the relations between individuals on both the domestic and international planes. For many centuries, in fact, they were the exclusive subjects of international law, save for unusual exceptions such as the Holy See and the Maltese Order.

In any event, under international law it is States that possess full, objective legal personality, endowing them with full legal capacity with respect to rights, powers, and obligations within that legal system. Within international law, these include, *inter alia*: the ability to appear before international tribunals (or national tribunals) in order to enforce rights under international law; to be subject to obligations under international law; to make binding international agreements (treaties); and to enjoy some or all immunities.

[1] C Walther, 'Subjects of International Law' in R Wolfrum (ed), *Max Planck Encyclopedia of Public International Law* (2nd edn, OUP, published online, 2007), para 21.

HISTORICAL BACKGROUND The Non-territorial International Person: the Holy See and the Sovereign Military Order of Malta

Most international law texts touch upon the situations of the Holy See and the Sovereign Order of Malta, two unusual entities that illustrate the slightly haphazard development of the international law on statehood. The Papal States were an influential player in early modern Europe: a theocracy governed by the Roman Catholic Church, the Papal States laid claim to authority over all Christians in Europe (and later, worldwide). Simultaneously, the Papal States exercised sovereign control, as well as a substantial swathe of territory, in central Italy, centred on Rome. During the Italian Wars of Unification in the 1860s, Rome and all other papal territory were conquered by the nascent Kingdom of Italy. The Pope sought refuge in St Peter's Basilica and refused to accept the temporal sovereignty of the Italian State until the Lateran Treaty of 1929, when Italy recognized its sovereignty over the tiny territory of Vatican City.

The Lateran Treaty confirmed the dual character of the papacy: at once the sovereign over Vatican City, and simultaneously the head of the 'Holy See', a non-territorial institution with its distinct international personality. This unusual situation has received international recognition: a permanent observer at the United Nations since 1964, in 2004 the Holy See was granted the status of 'observer non-member State' (see UNGA Res 58/314 (1 July 2004)). Vatican City is not a UN member State. In *JC and Ors v Belgium* App No 11625/17 (12 October 2021), the ECtHR rejected a claim that Belgian domestic courts had breached the right of access to justice when they upheld that the Holy See benefited from State immunity in proceedings concerning compensation for the systematic mishandling of child abuse and paedophilia cases, but the ECtHR did not take a position on the Holy See's international status, stating simply that the Belgian courts had not been unreasonable or arbitrary. For incisive critiques on the contemporary status of the Holy See, see N Tzouvala, 'The Holy See and Children's Rights: International Human Rights Law and Its Ghosts' (2015) 84 Nordic JIL 59; and JR Morss, 'The International Legal Status of the Vatican/Holy See Complex' (2015) 26 EJIL 927.

As for the Order of Malta, officially the 'Sovereign Military Hospitaller Order of St John of Jerusalem, of Rhodes and Malta', it was sovereign over the island of Malta from 1530 until occupation of the island by Napoleon Bonaparte in 1798, whereupon it persisted in its claims to sovereignty from a base in Rome, while performing humanitarian work for the poor and the sick. In *Nanni v Pace and the Sovereign Order of Malta* (1935–7) 8 AD 2, the Italian Court of Cassation examined the history of the Order, and declared that its international personality persisted notwithstanding the British occupation of Malta, at least in its relations with the Italian State. This finding was on the basis that international law recognized the personality of certain collective units whose scope transcended 'by virtue of their universal character the territorial confines of any single State'. To this day, the Order still issues international passports for travel and postal stamps, and was in 1994 accorded permanent observer status at the United Nations: see UNGA Resolution 48/265 (24 August 1994).

These examples are not just historically interesting: with climate change threatening low-lying island States, the notion of a sovereign State without territory may very quickly re-emerge. The ILC Study Group on Sea-Level Rise in International Law has, in a recent paper, drawn attention to whether a presumption of the continuity of statehood can apply to a State permanently deprived of its territory (see UN Doc A/CN.4/774 (19 February 2024), paras 26–28, 33–5).

See further E Allen and M Prost, 'Ceci n'est pas un État: The Order of Malta and the Holy See as Precedents for Deterritorialized Statehood?' (2022) 31 RECIEL 171.

Conversely, other entities regarded as subjects under international law, whether individuals or national liberation movements, have come to be regarded as having international personality only through conferral or recognition by States.[2] In the case of international organizations, by being created by States and thus enjoying a sort of 'delegated' personality.[3] This may mean that they do not enjoy the full capacities of States. International organizations will be further explored in Chapter 6.

5.2 The criteria for statehood

5.2.1 Conceptualizing statehood

States vary wildly with respect to territorial size, economic weight, military capacity, and political power. However, formally speaking, they are all equal and sovereign; States may therefore determine freely their internal organization and their international acts, without authority being imposed from above or from another State. Sovereignty is not so much a natural construct but one that is social, much like the age of legal adulthood in domestic law. In practice, the sovereignty required for statehood requires a centralized, organized structure capable of exercising effective control over a given territory and those individuals found within it.

Historically, a State could not delegate essential attributes of statehood. For example, Liechtenstein's 1920 application to join the League of Nations was rejected on the basis that the principality could not discharge all of the obligations contained in the League Covenant, as it had delegated certain attributes of sovereignty to Switzerland, a non-member, and had no army.[4] However, at present that view seems to have relaxed considerably, with Liechtenstein, Monaco, Andorra, and San Marino all having joined the UN in the early 1990s despite these European micro-States effectively entrusting their neighbours with central issues of State concern such as defence or foreign policy.[5]

The question thus naturally arises: how does an entity become a State in the first place? Paradoxically, given the advantages derived from statehood, there is little formal guidance in international law as to how a State emerges, leaving the question of statehood to case-by-case practice,[6] and leaving open the place of recognition by existing States. Of the few relevant textual definitions, recourse is traditionally made to Article 1 of the Montevideo Convention on the Rights and Duties of States,

[2] In relation to the individual as an international legal person, see A Klejdgaard-Pedersen, *The International Legal Personality of the Individual* (OUP, 2018). That said, individual human rights receive international protection: see Chapter 16.

[3] In this respect, see *Reparation for Injuries to the United Nations, Advisory Opinion, ICJ Reports 1949*, p 173, which confirms the capacity of States to endow international personality on the UN.

[4] League of Nations, *Reports of the First Assembly* (1920), 217.

[5] See further J Duursma, *Fragmentation and the International Relations of Micro-States* (CUP, 1996).

[6] A detailed compendium of practice is that of J Crawford, *The Creation of States in International Law* (2nd edn, OUP, 2006).

listing four criteria for statehood. It provides that a 'state as a person of international law should possess the following qualifications:

- a permanent population;
- a defined territory;
- a government; and
- the capacity to enter into relations with other states'.[7]

Although the Montevideo Convention was only signed by a few Latin American States, it is widely regarded as codifying the customary international law existing at that time. As such, even though the Montevideo criteria are arguably non-exhaustive and require re-examination,[8] taken together they remain the best starting point for a meaningful discussion of statehood.

5.2.2 **Population**

That a State requires a population of inhabitants is indisputable: one cannot rule over a territory without inhabitants over which to exercise control. There is no minimum requirement for population, as is demonstrated by a number of tiny States.[9] Nor is there any concern as to how the population comes to reside there: for example, unlike virtually all other States, Vatican City citizenship (which is required for residence) is only conferred *jus officii*, or on the grounds of a professional appointment.[10] The population need not inhabit the territory continuously: in *Western Sahara*, the ICJ recognized the nomadic Sarahawi population's link to the territory of Western Sahara despite their seasonal movements into Morocco and Mauritania.[11]

5.2.3 **Territory**

5.2.3.1 **Existence of a defined territory**

The second requirement specified in the Montevideo Convention is that a State possess territory over which it exercises control over a sustained period of time. It is true that international law tolerates a few exceptions to this: a prominent historical example was the recognition by the Allies of 'Governments in Exile' during the Second World War where the exiled governments of Poland, Norway, the Netherlands, Belgium,

[7] Montevideo Convention on the Rights and Duties of States (1934) 165 LNTS 19, 28 AJIL Supp 75.

[8] See T Grant, 'The Montevideo Convention and its Discontents' (1998) 37 Columbia JTL 403; and M Craven, *The Decolonization of International Law: State Succession and the Law of Treaties* (OUP, 2007), 220–1, who suggests that criteria must be exercised with some degree of intensity or of effectiveness.

[9] To the European micro-States described in Section 5.2.1, one can add Nauru, Vanuatu, Tuvalu, Palau, Kiribati, and the Marshall Islands, all of which have populations in the tens of thousands, but are members of the United Nations. The effects of climate change on such low-lying island States are considered in Chapter 19.

[10] The Vatican City State law on citizenship only recognizes three categories of citizenship: cardinals resident in Vatican City or Rome; diplomats of the Holy See; and persons residing in Vatican City because of their office or service.

[11] See *Western Sahara, Advisory Opinion, ICJ Reports 1975*, p 12.

Luxembourg, Yugoslavia, and Greece continued to act on behalf of their States despite occupation by Nazi Germany. However, the survival of States without territory rests on the legal fiction that they may one day recover control over territory.[12] The amount of territory can be minuscule: Vatican City today is deemed to exercise sovereignty over an enclave of Rome of just 0.5 km^2, a sufficient toehold to assert territorial sovereignty.

HISTORICAL BACKGROUND The International Personality of Palestine

An interesting illustration of the link between territory and statehood is the situation of Palestine, hotly contested since the 1947 withdrawal of the UK from the League mandate it held over the territory. Following UNGA Resolution 181(II), which recommended that Palestine be partitioned into separate Arab and Jewish States, on 14 May 1948 Israel unilaterally declared itself an independent State, and was immediately attacked by neighbouring Arab States. After that conflict, Israel held considerably more territory than under the 1947 partition plan, with the remaining territories nominally Palestinian. However, the 'Gaza Strip' fell under Egyptian occupation and administration, and the 'West Bank' and the eastern part of the city of Jerusalem under the occupation and administration of Jordan.

In 1964, the 'Palestinian Liberation Organization' (PLO) was established to achieve the 'liberation of Palestine' through armed struggle. Then, in the 'Six-Day War' of 1967, Israel claimed 'anticipatory self-defence' (see Chapter 14) and occupied the Gaza Strip, the West Bank, and East Jerusalem.

In 1988, the PLO endorsed a 'two-State solution' and issued a declaration of independence of Palestine in Algiers. In 1993 the 'Oslo Accords' provided for interim self-government by the 'Palestinian National Authority', thus detaching the government from the PLO and establishing a separate parliament and government in the Gaza Strip and the West Bank. The Palestinian Authority now exercises nominal control over two territories. The prevailing position in international law is that Israel is in belligerent occupation of all the territories that it took in the Six-Day War, including East Jerusalem, with the rights and duties that go with such an occupation: see *Construction of a Wall in the Occupied Palestinian Territory, Advisory Opinion, ICJ Reports 2004*, p 169. The question arises: if Israel is in belligerent occupation, can 'Palestine' lawfully claim control over that territory?

The situation is further complicated given that, in 2005, Israel announced that it would disengage unilaterally from the Gaza Strip, though it completely controls access to Gaza by land, sea, and air and operates a blockade. Gaza is controlled internally by Hamas, an organization which opposes the existence of Israel, while Fatah controls most of the West Bank. Israel continues to occupy the West Bank and claims to have annexed East Jerusalem.

Perhaps given this convoluted situation, Palestine's statehood remains in dispute. It has not been admitted to the United Nations, though in December 2012, it was accorded the status of 'non-member observer State' by the General Assembly (see UNGA Res 67/19 (29 November 2012)). Palestine has also joined UNESCO, the International Criminal Court, and other international organizations, in addition to acceding to more than seventy multilateral treaties.

[12] See Section 5.1.

After Palestine's latest application for membership was vetoed once again in the Security Council, the General Assembly adopted Resolution A/RES/ES-10/23 (10 May 2024), in which it 'determined' that Palestine was ready for membership, and recommended that the Council 'reconsider the matter favourably'.

As of late 2024, Palestine is recognized by 147 States, though it lacks the recognition of three permanent members of the Security Council: France, the UK, and the USA.

The criterion of defined territory does not go so far as to require fully defined or settled boundaries for the State.[13] Albania's frontiers were not set in 1920, but it was admitted to the League of Nations; Bosnia and Herzegovina and Croatia were admitted into the UN in 1992 despite violent boundary disputes with the Federal Republic of Yugoslavia. As the ICJ's docket demonstrates, several African and Latin American States have ongoing disputes over their borders; and Israel, Georgia, and Cyprus also have substantial uncertainty over their exact frontiers. As such, a consistent nucleus of territory, which is indisputably under the effective control of the entity claiming to be a State, seems to suffice.

5.2.3.2 **Modes of acquiring and disposing of territory**

In earlier periods, there was much international activity in the acquisition and loss of territory by States, and detailed rules with respect to these processes emerged.[14] States may transfer title to territory to one another peacefully, usually through cession. Examples of cession include the 1819 Florida Cession from Spain to the USA,[15] the Alaska Purchase of 1867 from Russia to the USA,[16] and the exchange of Heligoland and Zanzibar between Great Britain and Germany in 1890.[17] The formal handover of territory not accompanied by the creation of a new State has become relatively infrequent in recent years, with small cessions (formal transfers) of territory becoming the exception and not the rule. Such transfers are usually the outcome of a dispute-settlement process:[18] see, for example, the imposition of the Iraq–Kuwait boundary by the Security Council pursuant to a report from the Iraq–Kuwait Boundary Demarcation Commission.[19] Similarly, a change in legal circumstances can engender a transfer, such

[13] *Deutsche Continental Gas-Gesellschaft v Polish State* (1929) 5 ILR 11, 15.

[14] Detailed historical analyses may be found in M Shaw, 'Territory in International Law' (1982) 13 Netherlands YBIL 61; J Castellino and S Allen, *Title to Territory in International Law: A Temporal Analysis* (Ashgate, 2002); and JHW Verzijl, *International Law in Historical Perspective* (Martinus Nijhoff, 1970), vol III, 297 *et seq*.

[15] Treaty of Amity, Settlement, and Limits Between the United States of America and His Catholic Majesty ('Adams-Onís Treaty'), signed 22 February 1819.

[16] Treaty concerning the Cession of the Russian Possessions in North America by his Majesty the Emperor of all the Russias to the United States of America, signed 30 March 1867, entered into force 28 May 1867.

[17] Treaty of Heligoland–Zanzibar (Great Britain–Germany), signed 1 July 1890, entered into force 4 August 1890.

[18] See, e.g., *Land and Maritime Boundary between Cameroon and Nigeria (Cameroon v Nigeria: Equatorial Guinea Intervening), Merits, ICJ Reports 2002*, p 303; at the ICJ, or the *Ethiopia–Eritrea Boundary Commission (Ethiopia v Eritrea), Decision on Delimitation of the Border* (13 April 2002), XXV RIAA 83.

[19] MH Mendelson and SC Hulton, 'The Iraq–Kuwait Boundary' (1993) 64 BYBIL 135; and J Klabbers, 'No More Shifting Lines? The Report of the Iraq–Kuwait Boundary Demarcation Commission' (1994) 43 ICLQ 904.

as the expiration in 1997 of the UK's lease of Hong Kong and, in 1999, that of Portugal with respect to the territory of Macao. In both cases, sovereignty was regarded as having passed to the lessee for the duration of the lease, and having reverted to China, the lessor State.[20]

Given the importance of possessing territory for asserting the existence of a State, it is worth briefly recalling the historical methods through which States came to possess territory. During European voyages of discovery, first into the Americas, the Pacific, and Asia in the sixteenth century, and until the expeditions into the interior of Africa and Asia in the nineteenth century, *discovery* was said to give rise to an inchoate (incomplete) title, which could be perfected by subsequent acts, such as possession in fact and effective occupation of the territory. A vivid illustration of this point is found in the *Island of Palmas* arbitration of 1928, between the USA and the Netherlands.[21] The island in issue lay between the Philippines (then under US sovereignty) and Indonesia (then under Dutch sovereignty). The USA, which had acquired the Philippines by cession from Spain in 1898, claimed title through the Spanish 'discovery' of the islands, which according to the USA were previously *terra nullius*. The Netherlands had, however, occupied and administered the island since well before 1898. Max Huber, the sole arbitrator in that case, concluded that by 1898 (the 'critical date' for determining title in the case), discovery alone was no longer sufficient, declaring that 'effective occupation' was required: 'the actual continuous and peaceful display of state functions is in case of dispute the sound and natural criterion of territorial sovereignty'.[22]

The concept of a 'critical date' suggests that there exists a determinative moment at which the rights of the parties have crystallized so that acts after that date do not further alter the legal position.[23] This is a reflection of international law's relative fluidity, as it obliges one to assess the law by considering whether it is different to that in the past (the concept of 'inter-temporal law'[24]), and it opens space for the law to develop as later events can supersede a valid title in certain circumstances. Whether such circumstances are relevant is determined by how the 'critical date' is chosen, and no real criteria exist that might assist a court or tribunal as to how to choose such a date. In *Island of Palmas*, arbitrator Huber chose the relevant date to be the cession from Spain to the USA, as Spain could not cede to the USA greater rights than it possessed. Had another critical date been selected, possibly based on other criteria, the outcome of the case might have been different.

Because of the prohibition on the use of force in international law, addressed further in Chapter 14, it would suggest *a fortiori* there is also a prohibition on territorial

[20] This is specific to the lease agreement: Sino-British Joint Declaration on Hong Kong (19 December 1984), 1399 UNTS 33, and the Sino-Portuguese Joint Declaration on Macau (13 April 1987), 1498 UNTS 228.

[21] *Island of Palmas (United States v Netherlands)* (1928) 2 RIAA 829, 838.

[22] *Ibid*. For a more recent example, see the *Eritrea/Yemen* arbitral award (9 October 1998) XXII RIAA 209, 268: for territory to be acquired, it is necessary to demonstrate 'an intentional display of power and authority over [a] territory, by the exercise of jurisdiction and state functions, on a continuous and peaceful basis'.

[23] See further LFE Goldie, 'The Critical Date' (1963) 12 ICLQ 1251; and MN Shaw, 'Title, Control and Closure? The Experience of the Eritrea–Ethiopia Boundary Commission' (2007) ICLQ 755, 760 *et seq*.

[24] TO Elias, 'The Doctrine of Inter-Temporal Law' (1980) 74 AJIL 285.

annexation resulting from military conquest.[25] Glaring examples of failed claims in this regard are Indonesia's invasion of East Timor in 1975 and Iraq's invasion of Kuwait in 1990.[26] More recently, though, Russia's 2014 invasion of Crimea has not been reversed, and in 2022, Russia claimed to annex the Ukrainian Donetsk, Kherson, Luhansk, and Zaporizhzhia oblasts. That said, in all these cases, Russia justified its claim to these territories not on conquest, but on a specious assertion of the right to self-determination of their respective populations.[27]

5.2.4 **Effective government**

The third criterion in the Montevideo Convention, of 'a government', is somewhat more complex than its bland wording might suggest. The criteria of territory and population are relatively descriptive, and may be judged empirically. However, the requirement of 'effective government' is rather subjective and is underlain by the idea that a people must be sufficiently organized, socially and politically, to be viewed as an entity. Therefore, a State can only exist if it is in a position to uphold its international legal duties and obligations, both internally and externally.[28]

In sum, there must be some sort of minimally coherent political structure through which law and order can be guaranteed effectively, though the political structures that are required need not take a specified form (e.g., that of the modern constitutional State, with its separation of legislative, executive, and judicial powers). On this point, international law is neutral, which suggests that, for example, there is no democratic entitlement in international law;[29] a point underlined by all manner of authoritarian regimes that exist today. Such a studied neutrality derives from international law's history: as described in Chapter 1, during the colonial epoch the so-called 'standard of civilization' was applied to entities deemed unworthy of recognition as States, and 'protection' or outright incorporation into European colonial empires was justified on that ground. The Ottoman Empire, China, Japan, and Latin America were denied participation in international fora throughout the nineteenth century on that basis, despite meeting the factual criteria of defined territory and permanent population. Nevertheless, the claim occasionally resurfaces that only certain forms of State government should be recognized as proper, usually requiring respect for democratic principles and a commitment

[25] See I (Wuerth) Brunk and M Hakimi, 'The Prohibition of Annexations and the Foundations of Modern International Law' (2024) 118 AJIL 417.

[26] See also *Legal Consequences of the Construction of a Wall in the Occupied Palestinian Territory Advisory Opinion, ICJ Reports 2004*, p 136, 165, in which the ICJ emphasized the prohibition of acquisition of territory by annexation in the original British Mandate for Palestine.

[27] Russia bases its claim on referenda held throughout these territories, though it is hardly the case that these referenda satisfied any international standards: see A Peters, 'The Crimean Vote as an Abuse of the Institution of the Territorial Referendum' in C Calliess (ed), *Staat und Mensch im Kontext des Völker- und Europarechts: Liber Amicorum für Torsten Stein* (Nomos, 2015), 255; and S Masol, 'Orwellian Rulings of the Russian Constitutional Court on the Donetsk, Kherson, Luhansk and Zaporizhzhia Provinces of Ukraine' EJIL:Talk (25 October 2022).

[28] See the views of arbitrator Huber in *Island of Palmas* (n 21).

[29] J Crawford, 'Democracy in International Law' (1990) 64 BYBIL 113.

to human rights.[30] Instead of suggesting that a State is some sort of second-class subject of international law, a 'democratic governance' argument now suggests that governance is a matter concerning the rights of individuals under international law.[31] There is, however, little State practice supporting the argument.

CASE SPOTLIGHT ***The Åland Islands Dispute*, LNOJ Sp Supp No 4 (1920), p 3**

A dispute had arisen between Sweden and Finland over the Åland Islands, in which a plebiscite (direct consultation of the people) demonstrated overwhelming support from the population for reunification with Sweden. Sweden supported the independence movement in the light of the principle of self-determination. The issue was referred to the Council of the League of Nations, which appointed an International Committee of Jurists to investigate the situation and make substantive recommendations.

The key legal question concerned the secession of Finland from the Russian Empire, declared by the Finnish Diet (legislature) in 1917. Though the revolutionary Soviet government recognized the nascent Finnish State, factions within Finland itself (including sections of the army) rejected Finnish independence, leading to internal strife and the intervention of the Soviet army in 1920 on the side of the new government. As such, questions existed as to the effective independence of Finland. In its advisory report, the Committee concluded that the League was competent over the issue of the Åland Islands; though sovereignty formally belonged to Finland, it 'had not yet acquired the status of a definitely constituted State', and although the date for Finland's statehood was hard to identify with precision, it 'certainly did not take place until a stable political organization had been created, and until the public authorities had become strong enough to assert themselves throughout the territories of the state without the assistance of the foreign troops'.

Ultimately, the League Council was to determine that the sovereignty over the Åland Islands rested with Finland, though subject to the protection of certain minority and linguistic rights of the islanders, and their permanent demilitarization through a treaty. Even so, the case is an important illustration of how 'effective government' is a necessary component of independence, requiring not only a formal declaration but also the establishment of competent and effective public authorities that can act independently, without external support.

It has been suggested that, in certain cases, the criterion of effective control can be relaxed somewhat when there exists significant international recognition. Several former colonies were admitted to the UN before being able to extend their control over their territory, Zaire and Guinea-Bissau being prominent examples.[32] A more recent example was the 1992 recognition of Croatia, and Bosnia and Herzegovina, by the

[30] See, prominently, T Franck, *Fairness in International Law and Institutions* (OUP, 1995), and certain chapters in GH Fox and BR Roth (eds), *Democratic Governance and International Law* (CUP, 2000).

[31] This tendency posits that liberal democratic structures are the only legitimate form of government: see, e.g., TM Franck, 'The Emerging Right to Democratic Governance' (1992) 86 AJIL 46; A-M Slaughter, 'International Law in a World of Liberal States' (1993) 6 EJIL 503.

[32] Zaire is particularly noteworthy because from 1960 to 1964, it was governed under MONUC, an international peacekeeping force sent when it was the Belgian Congo.

members of the then-European Community,[33] despite the chaos surrounding those States' declarations of independence and the presence of non-governmental forces over substantial parts of their territory.[34] These acts of recognition paved the way for their admission to the UN shortly thereafter, an event which crystallized their statehood as Article 4 of the UN Charter only allows for 'States' to be admitted to the UN.

Once established, statehood carries with it a presumption of continuity: it will persist even if there is a partial or total collapse in governmental structures and an inability of the central government to exercise effective control over the State. Somalia and Syria, to give two examples, have been riven with civil conflict for years—in the case of Somalia, for decades—with the central government only controlling parts of the State in each case. A governmental collapse, therefore, does not impact on the existence of a State as a State under international law, even though portions of its territory might fall under the authority of another group. There are several explanations for this desire for continuity, probably due to the enormous legal consequences a removal of statehood would entail, as well as a desire to keep treaty and customary legal obligations in force, especially with respect to human rights.[35] It is for this reason that the dangerous concept of a 'failed State'—which has been used to describe Somalia since the 1990s and, more recently, the new State of South Sudan—remains controversial.[36] Though only in its early stages, a similar question is being studied by the ILC Study Group on the effects of sea-level rise in international law, which will address the possibility of an existing State being permanently deprived of its territory, and the implications for its continued statehood.[37]

5.2.5 **Capacity to enter into international relations**

The final criterion for statehood enumerated in the Montevideo Convention is the capacity to enter into relations with other States. The capacity requirement is not merely objective, referring to formal structures that might be in place; it is also substantive, in that it attaches importance to the recognition of a State, as a State, by other States.[38] In essence, such capacity derives from independence. A territory, even with a permanent population and a government as such, could not be a State if under the direct or indirect control of another State.[39] That principle took on a number of attributes, most

[33] On 15 January 1992 and 6 April 1992, respectively.

[34] These had not gone unnoticed: see the Badinter Commission's Opinions No 4 (on Bosnia & Herzegovina) and No 5 (on Croatia); and the Declaration on Yugoslavia and Guidelines on the Recognition of New States in Eastern Europe and in the Soviet Union of 16 December 1991, 92 ILR 178. See also R Müllerson, *International Law, Rights and Politics* (Routledge, 1994), 130.

[35] In fact, human rights obligations persist even if a State has become extinct and a new State takes its place: see later Section 5.4.

[36] Craven (n 8) 220 suggests that this concept reintroduces the 'civilising mission' into international law; See also Crawford, *Creation of States* (n 6) 719–22; and S Ratner, 'The Cambodia Settlement Agreements' (1993) 87 AJIL 1.

[37] ILC (P Galvão Teles and JJ Ruda Santolaria, Co-Chairs), paper of the Study Group on 'Sea-level rise in relation to international law', UN Doc A/CN.4/774 (19 February 2024).

[38] See later Section 5.3 for a fuller treatment of the place of recognition.

[39] As suggested in *Austro-German Customs Union, 1931, PCIJ, Ser A/B, No 41*; and the *French Indemnity* case (1931) in Moore, 5 International Arbitrations 4447.

prominently with respect to imperialism, where autonomous entities within broader empires were typically not considered to be capable of entering into relations with other States.

Although with respect to non-self-governing colonies the lack of capacity was rather clear, self-governing entities that were not regarded as fully independent in substance were also considered to lack the capacity to enter into relations with other States. Thus, while Canada (1867), Australia (1900), New Zealand (1907), and South Africa (1910) had in turn each been proclaimed as 'self-governing Dominions' within the British Empire, their foreign relations were still handled through the Imperial Government in London, including the declarations that led them into World War I. After 1918, the Dominions were regarded as sufficiently independent to sign the Pact of Paris and join the League of Nations in their own right; yet Dominions were only empowered to issue formal declarations of war in their own name after promulgation of the Statute of Westminster in 1931.[40]

Independence cannot merely be in name; a degree of actual independence is also required. This was vividly demonstrated by the questionable 'grant' of independence by South Africa to Transkei, Bophuthatswana, Venda, and Ciskei in the 1970s, so as to reduce the number of black citizens of South Africa. Yet the 'Bantustans', as they were called, enjoyed little actual independence: besides South Africa contributing the vast majority of their financing, they were ungovernable entities subject to South Africa's ultimate control, with Bophuthatswana in particular split into a number of non-contiguous zones scattered across South African territory.[41] Given this unsustainability, and the racial discrimination on which it was premised, the UN regarded their claims to be invalid and called upon all States not to recognize the new entities.[42]

A similar state of affairs characterizes the declaration of independence of the Turkish Republic of Northern Cyprus (TRNC) in 1983; besides Türkiye, which to this day maintains a large military force in northern Cyprus, no other State has recognized Northern Cyprus as a new State. What is more, various international bodies have denied its claim to statehood. In particular, the UN Security Council declared the TRNC declaration of independence to be invalid, and has repeatedly denounced the presence of the Turkish armed forces.[43] Moreover, the European Court of Human Rights has noted the collective refusal of States to recognize that Northern Cyprus is a new State.[44]

[40] See Statute of Westminster 1931 (UK), s 3 (conferring on Dominions the full power to make laws having extraterritorial application). The Dominions each passed domestic resolutions declaring war against Nazi Germany in World War II.

[41] The UK Minister of State issued a statement of non-recognition precisely on this basis: see FCO, 'United Kingdom Materials on International Law' (UKMIL) (1986) 57 BYBIL 507–8. The 1993 South African Constitution repealed all laws in relation to the Bantustans and reincorporated these into South Africa: see further J Dugard, 'International Law and the South African Constitution' (1997) 8 EJIL 77.

[42] See UNGA Res 31/6 (26 October 1976), GAOR 31st Sess, Supp 39, 10. The effects of such collective non-recognition are discussed later, in Section 5.3.1.3.

[43] UNSC Res 353 (20 July 1974), 357 (14 August 1974), 358 (15 August 1974), 359 (15 August 1974), 360 (16 August 1974), 365 (13 December 1974).

[44] See also the European Court of Human Rights' judgment in *Cyprus v Turkey*, App No 25781/92; 120 ILR, at 10: 'it is evident from international practice . . . that the international community does not recognize the "TRNC" as a state under international law'. Collective non-recognition is discussed later, in Section 5.3.1.3.

That said, the rule on actual independence should not be regarded as an absolute requirement, as in exceptional circumstances there may be residual control by another entity. Such was the situation in Bosnia and Herzegovina, where the Dayton Peace Agreements of 1995 stipulated that an international 'High Representative' was the 'final authority in theatre' with respect to its implementation, but it was still considered to be an independent State.[45]

HISTORICAL BACKGROUND The International Personality of Taiwan

One should take care when considering the curious situation of Taiwan, which styles itself the 'Republic of China' and is not a member of the United Nations. However, it participates in the World Trade Organization (WTO), the Organization of the Petroleum Exporting Countries (OPEC), the International Olympic Committee (IOC), and other international organizations as 'Chinese Taipei', and other variants. Usually these organizations allow for 'separate customs territories' to be members in addition to States, thus paving the way for its membership.

That curious situation is a product of history: the island of Taiwan was ceded by China to Japan in 1895, only to be surrendered by Japan to an unspecified recipient under the 1951 Peace Treaty of San Francisco between Japan and forty-eight Allied States. In the meantime, as the Chinese Civil War came to a close in 1949, the Communists proclaimed the 'People's Republic of China' on the mainland while the Nationalist regime (the 'Republic of China') took refuge on Taiwan and the Pescadores. That situation has persisted to the present.

The People's Republic of China opposes any recognition of separate statehood for any government in Taiwan, preferring instead the reunification of all of China under the 'One China, Two Systems' approach. The same goes for the government of the Republic of China in Taiwan; separate statehood is an unsought status, as it does not claim to be a separate State. Rather, its government claims to be the sole legal representative of all China, thus itself perpetuating a situation of deliberate ambiguity.

At present, the People's Republic of China (with its capital in Beijing) is recognized by the vast majority of States, with the Republic of China in Taipei only recognized by fourteen UN member States and the Holy See. Despite this, most UN member States maintain robust economic, cultural, and technical links with Taiwan through an 'Economic and Cultural Office'.

As such, rather than viewing the example of Taiwan as an example of contested statehood, the better view would be to regard the situation as a dispute between competing governments, neither of whom contests the unity of China as such, and with each putting forward a claim to represent the Chinese State on the international plane.

5.2.6 Emerging or unsettled criteria: respect for democracy, human rights, and the right to self-determination

Recent years have witnessed debates as to whether the criteria codified in the Montevideo Convention have become obsolete or insufficient. In the next section, a few of the proposed criteria for the creation of new States will be considered, and whether sufficient practice justifies their inclusion as part of the new international law on statehood.

[45] See the General Framework Agreement for Peace in Bosnia and Herzegovina ('Dayton Peace Agreement') (1995) 35 ILM 75 (14 December 1995), annex 10.

5.2.6.1 **Respect for democracy, the rule of law, and human rights**

Limited practice appears to suggest that entities aspiring to statehood must conform with additional standards demanded by the international community of States of which they seek membership. These include respect for democracy, human rights and the rights of minorities, as well as respect for existing international frontiers, as further conditions for granting recognition. A leading instrument was the 1991 set of Guidelines adopted by the European Community (EC) (as it then was) for the recognition of new States in Eastern Europe.[46] The EC declared that entities seeking recognition as States could only be recognized if they respected existing boundaries (the principle of *uti possedetis*), commitments to disarm, guaranteed the rights of national or ethnic minorities, and displayed a commitment to democracy, the rule of law, and human rights. These guidelines were applied by the 'Badinter Commission' appointed by the EC to give advice on the factual developments emerging during the dissolution of the former Yugoslavia.[47]

However, it bears noting that respect for democracy, the rule of law, or human rights have not been formally determinative factors for the admission to the UN of Timor-Leste (2002), Montenegro (2006), or South Sudan (2011). In this respect, it would seem that such standards are best regarded as possible emerging standards rather than firmly recognized additions to the criteria specified in the Montevideo Convention.

5.2.6.2 **Self-determination**

Respect for the right of peoples to 'self-determination', repeatedly recognized as an obligation *erga omnes* by the ICJ,[48] is frequently invoked as an additional criterion for an entity claiming statehood. However, the concept of self-determination is challenging to define and raises basic questions as to what constitutes a sufficiently coherent group to demand exercise of the right (e.g., a people, a nation, a colonized population, a national minority). Moreover, self-determination is intimately linked to complex theories of political organization and nationalism,[49] and causes further debates as to the extent of the right, and whether is it limited to internal self-government, or whether it might also confer the right to secede from one State and join another State, or constitute the creation of a new State. Despite these concerns, self-determination has entered the international legal lexicon, being recognized in the UN Charter in Article 1(2), as well as in the two UN Covenants on Human Rights in Article 1(1).[50]

[46] 'Guidelines on the Recognition of New States in Eastern Europe and in the Soviet Union' (16 December 1991) in UKMIL (1991) 62 BYBIL 559–60.

[47] See Opinion No 1 of 29 November 1991, 92 ILR 164–5; and Opinion No 8 of 4 July 1992, 92 ILR 201, of the Arbitration Commission of the Peace Conference on Yugoslavia (known after its Chairman, Robert Badinter of France). See later Section 5.4 for a history of the disintegration of the former Yugoslavia.

[48] Recognized by the ICJ as 'an essential principle' of contemporary international law, and having *erga omnes* character, in its 1995 judgment in *East Timor (Portugal v Australia), Jurisdiction & Admissibility, ICJ Reports 1995*, p 90, 102, and its 2004 advisory opinion in *Construction of a Wall* (n 25) 171–2. Most recently, the ICJ reconfirmed the *erga omnes* character of self-determination in *Legal Consequences of the Separation of the Chagos Archipelago from Mauritius in 1965, Advisory Opinion, ICJ Reports 2019*, p 95, paras 150–61; and in *Policies and Practices of Israel in the Occupied PalestinianTerritory, including East Jerusalem, Advisory Opinion of 19 July 2024*, para 232.

[49] For conceptual criticism on the topic, see Craven (n 8) 232–4.

[50] See International Covenant on Civil and Political Rights (signed 19 December 1966, entered into force 23 March 1976), 999 UNTS 171; International Covenant on Economic, Social and Cultural Rights (signed 16 December 1966, entered into force 3 January 1976), 993 UNTS 3.

Why, then, are some claims of self-determination given legal effect at international law and others not? Part of the confusion is terminological: though international lawyers tend to draw a line between 'internal' and 'external' types of self-determination, only the latter of which leads to a change of State boundaries, self-determination is an overarching category with at least four varieties of the concept.[51]

First is the self-determination claimed by every existing sovereign State, to recognition as a single political unit that can govern itself, freely, without external interference. One sees this embodied in the UN Charter's provisions in Article 2, which reaffirm the sovereign equality of States (para 1), the prohibition against the use of force against a State (para 4), and the right to non-interference in their internal affairs (para 7).[52] In the merits phase of *Nicaragua*, the ICJ read Article 2(4) of the Charter in the light of the recognition of self-determination in Article 1(2) to conclude that they afford a State 'the choice of a political, economic, social and cultural system, and the formulation of foreign policy'. Such political self-determination for existing States is, in the main, virtually uncontested.[53]

A second variety of self-determination that has received international legal recognition is the right of colonized people, or those under alien domination, to independence. This would be foreshadowed in the League Mandates system under which the former territories of the defeated State were placed under mandate rule instead of given outright to the victorious allies.[54] Under Article 77 of the UN Charter, the UN Trusteeship system can be used by any State to voluntarily place its colonies within the Trusteeship system. Article 73 of the Charter further stated, significantly, that:

> Members of the United Nations which have or assume responsibilities for the administration of territories whose people have not yet attained a full measure of self-government recognise the principle that the interest of the inhabitants of these territories are paramount[.]

Paragraph 1 of the General Assembly's Declaration on the Granting of Independence to Colonial Countries and Peoples[55] went further: '[t]he subjection of peoples to alien subjugation, domination and exploitation constitutes a denial of fundamental human rights, is contrary to the Charter of the United Nations and is an impediment to the promotion of world peace and co-operation'.[56] The right of colonial peoples to independence would be acknowledged by the ICJ in various opinions, including *Namibia*,[57]

[51] See G Hernández and T Sparks, 'Categorising Self-Determination: Four Forms' (2021) 63 German Year Book of International Law 223. A rich conceptual study of self-determination is found in Tom Sparks, *Self-Determination in the International Legal System: Whose Claim, to What Right?* (Hart, 2022).

[52] *Military and Paramilitary Activities in and Against Nicaragua (Nicaragua v United States), Merits, ICJ Reports 1986*, p 14, at para 205.

[53] Sparks (n 49) chs 3–4 even argues that it has acquired the status of a peremptory norm of *jus cogens*.

[54] The Mandate system would not be without its problems: for a critique of the economic and political systems put into place through the Mandate system, see N Tzouvala, *Capitalism as Civilisation* (CUP, 2020), chs 3 and 4.

[55] UNGA Res 1514 (XV) (14 December 1960).

[56] *Ibid*, at para 1. Such claims tended to homogenize, however, the identity of the colonized population. A critical account postcolonial State creation is that of M Shahabuddin, *Minorities and the Making of the Postcolonial States* (CUP, 2021).

[57] *Legal Consequences for States of the Continued Presence of South Africa in Namibia (South West Africa) notwithstanding Security Council Resolution 276 (1970), Advisory Opinion, ICJ Reports 1971*, p 16, para 53.

Western Sahara,[58] and *East Timor*.[59] The Court went further in the 2019 *Separation of the Chagos Archipelago* advisory opinion, in which it declared that a right of colonies to self-determination has existed in customary international law since at least 1965, relying in part on the 1960 Declaration as having a 'declaratory character with regard to the right of self-determination as a customary norm'.[60] State practice would seem to reconfirm this right, with the rapid decolonization of Asia and Africa from 1960 to 1975 leading to a trebling of UN membership.

Outside the colonial context, self-determination claims based in purely in the separate or distinctive identity of a people have not been recognized as leading to a right to statehood. Though the existing State may well consent or tolerate a referendum taking place (as happened in respect of Quebec in 1979 and 1995, or Scotland in 2014[61]), there seems to be no right to hold a referendum under international law, as the following commentary on Catalonia and the Kurdish region of Iraq illustrates. Moreover, the rights of indigenous peoples to self-determination do not alone seem to give rise to a secessionary right, despite the obvious overlaps with colonization.[62] That said, practice is not altogether clear, as is evidenced by the non-colonial, but successful, secessions of Slovenia, Croatia, and Bosnia and Herzegovina from the former Yugoslavia, and the self-determination claims invoked by Latvia, Lithuania, and Estonia when they claimed independence, on the basis of continuity with their statehood pre-1940, from the Soviet Union.

However, what if a defined people with a separate identity suffer from gross and systematic abuses within an existing State? Amongst municipal courts, the Canadian Supreme Court has hinted that external self-determination may arise if 'a definable group is denied meaningful access to government to pursue their political, economic, social and cultural development . . . a right to external self-determination arises because they have been denied the ability to exert internally their right to self-determination'.[63] A similar claim has been advanced by Kosovo, which has linked its claim to self-determination to a right to 'remedial secession', based on gross violations of human rights against the Kosovo Albanian population by Serbia prior to 1998.[64] Though heavily contested, these raise the possibility of a restricted exception of remedial self-determination outside the colonial context, though debate continues.

[58] *Western Sahara* (n 11) para 162. In *Commission and Council v Front Polisario*, Joined Cases C-778/21P, C-798/21P, C-779/21P and C-799/21P (4 October 2024), the CJEU upheld the annulment of provisions in EU-Morocco trade agreements that applied to Western Sahara, invoking the right to self-determination of the population and their lack of consent to the trade agreements concerned. See further S Cassella, 'L'union européenne et le Sahara occidental: Le rôle du droit européen dans les effectivités des obligations internationales *erga omnes*' (2018) LXIV Annuaire Français de Droit International 81.

[59] *East Timor* (n 46) para 29.

[60] *Chagos Archipelago* (n 46) 150–61.

[61] Recently, the UK Supreme Court held that, in the absence of approval from the Westminster Parliament, the Scottish Parliament had no right unilaterally to call a second independence referendum: see *Reference by the Lord Advocate of Devolution Issues (Scotland)* [2022] UKSC 31.

[62] See Chapter 16, Section 16.3.4; and generally N Jones, *Self-Determination as Voice: the Participation of Indigenous Peoples in International Governance* (CUP, 2024) especially chs 1–2.

[63] *Reference Re Secession of Quebec*, Canadian Supreme Court (1998) 2 SCR 217, 161 DLR (4th) 385, 115 ILR 536, para 138.

[64] The ICJ refused to pronounce itself on the question: see *Accordance with International Law of the Unilateral Declaration of Independence in respect of Kosovo, Advisory Opinion, ICJ Reports 2010*, p 403, 439, para 83. See, however, the Written Statement of Albania, ICJ Pleadings 2009, paras 86–92; and Written Statement II of the Authors of the Declaration of Independence, ICJ Pleadings 2009, paras 4.46–4.53, which brought attention to the 'terrible actions by Serbia from 1989–1999'.

THEORY AND DEBATES The Status of Independence Referenda in International Law

Though referenda and plebiscites have been held for some time, since the 2000s one can observe the increased practice of holding referenda in aspiring States, perhaps even being some form of emerging new principle. Notably, UN-supervised referenda were held in the cases of Timor-Leste (1999), Montenegro (2005), and South Sudan (2010), the three newest members of the United Nations. The referendum in Montenegro is of particular interest, given that only 55.5 per cent of the population voted for secession from Serbia and Montenegro. Though only narrowly passing the 55 per cent threshold set prior to the referendum, the result was sufficient for Montenegro's uncontroversial admission to the UN in the same year (see UNGA Res 60/264, UN Doc A/60/L.58 & Add.1, and S/RES/1961 (22 June 2006)).

Despite this practice, even when an affirmative vote for independence is given, a referendum result is not per se legally binding, especially in situations where the referendum is held without UN supervision or against the wishes of the central government. Though the most prominent is the ICJ's 2010 advisory opinion in *Kosovo*; two examples from September 2017, Catalonia and Kurdistan, also merit mention. The Catalan regional government had unilaterally convened a referendum, despite its suspension by the Spanish Constitutional Court and a boycott by voters against secession. Of the 42 per cent of registered voters who cast a ballot, some 92 per cent voted in favour of Catalonia becoming an independent republic. On 27 October, by a 70–10 vote (though fifty-five members boycotted the vote), the Catalan *Parlament* invoked the democratically expressed will of the people to declare the independence of a 'Catalan Republic', unilaterally, though it suspended the effect of the declaration to allow a negotiated secession. In response, the Spanish government dissolved the Catalan legislature, invoking Article 155 of the Spanish Constitution, and called for fresh elections on 21 December 2017. No State has recognized Catalonia as an independent State: see A Remiro Brotóns and H Torroja, 'Public International Law and the Catalan Secession Process' (2024) 16 Hague Journal on the Rule of Law 31.

The Kurdish population is concentrated in a region divided between Iraq, Syria, Iran, and Türkiye, and has long sought independent statehood despite fierce resistance from those four States. In September 2017, a referendum was held in the Kurdish Autonomous Region of Iraq; from a turnout of 72 per cent, 92 per cent voted in favour of independence from Iraq. The Kurdish regional government, though maintaining throughout that the people had the right to choose independence democratically, offered to negotiate independence with the Iraqi government; instead, Iraq launched a military campaign to retake control, forcing the resignation of the Kurdish regional president. No State has recognized an independent Kurdistan: see L Radpey, *Towards an Independent Kurdistan: Self-Determination in International Law* (Routledge, 2024).

Conversely, a violation of the right to self-determination, or a norm of a similar status, might result in a denial of recognition from other States. The example of Rhodesia is instructive: its claim to statehood was repeatedly denied by the UN,[65] on the basis that the Rhodesian government, drawn exclusively from the minority white settler

[65] UNGA Res 2024 (XX) (11 November 1965) and 2151 (XXI) (17 November 1966), UNSC Res 216 (12 November 1965) and 217 (20 November 1965).

population, sought to impose apartheid on the majority black population, and could not make any reasonable claim to represent the whole of the population of the territory. Similarly, the UN rejected the declaration of independence of the Republika Srpska, a component unit of Bosnia and Herzegovina, by 'strongly reaffirm[ing]' its call to respect the territorial integrity of that State, and affirming that 'any entities unilaterally declared . . . will not be accepted'.[66] This was due to the close connection of the Republika Srpska with the violent civil war and ethnic cleansing raging at that time in the former Yugoslavia. In the ICJ's 2010 advisory opinion on *Kosovo*, the Court distinguished the Kosovar declaration of independence from those of Rhodesia, Northern Cyprus, and the Republika Srpska, on the basis that these three 'were, or would have been, connected with the unlawful use of force or other egregious violations of norms of general international law, in particular those of a peremptory character (*jus cogens*)'.[67]

5.3 Recognition of States and governments

5.3.1 Competing theories on the recognition of States

5.3.1.1 The declaratory and constitutive theories of recognition

As can be observed from the previous sections, the existence of a State seems to rest partly on its capacity to engage in international relations with other States—a subjective and, to an extent, highly politicized factor. In this respect, it is immaterial whether or not a State meets all the factual criteria for statehood laid out in the Montevideo Convention if other States refuse it *recognition* as a State and to enter into relations with it. 'Recognition' is a formal procedure through which an existing State and a new State recognize each other as being capable of exercising all the capacities of statehood. Once recognition has occurred, the existence of the new State is deemed opposable (can be relied upon or invoked) against the recognizing State, with all the legal consequences that flow from the statehood of the new State.

This process of recognition, albeit primarily a political act, may have far-reaching legal effects. Mainstream scholarly debate[68] tends to focus on the legal effects of recognition, with two dominant theories of recognition: the *declaratory theory*, according to which recognition merely formalizes an already extant situation; and the *constitutive theory*, according to which recognition contributes to the emergence of the State as such. The legal effects of the two competing theories are radically distinct, and merit careful scrutiny.

[66] See UNSC Res 787 (16 November 1992).

[67] *Kosovo* (n 61) 437, para 81. For further detail, see later Section 5.3.1.2.

[68] See, e.g., S Talmon, 'The Constitutive versus the Declaratory Doctrine of Recognition: *Tertium Non Datur?*' (2004) 75 BYBIL 101; C Warbrick, 'Recognition of States' (1992) 41 ICLQ 473; and also C Warbrick, 'Recognition of States' (1993) 42 ICLQ 43. This 'neutralization' of the loaded ideological overtones of an act such as recognizing a State as sovereign would be achieved in the early twentieth century by Lassa Oppenheim: see M Clark, 'A Conceptual History of Recognition in British International Legal Thought' (2016) 87 BYBIL 18, 71 *et seq*.

The *declaratory theory* of recognition maintains that the legal effects of recognition are limited, and that the act of recognition only confirms the pre-existing legal capacity of the State. In other words, whether or not an entity is recognized by other States, it is still a State once it fulfils the criteria for statehood. Recognition would then be confirmation or evidence of statehood, rather than any determinative condition. The declaratory theory arose during a time of much uncertainty in international law as to how States emerge, in line with a desire to remove the politics from such claims, and to minimize the power of existing States to deny legal personality.

Conversely, the *constitutive theory* of recognition suggests that recognition by other States is a necessary condition for statehood, even if all the criteria for statehood are otherwise satisfied. In other words, the act of recognition 'constitutes' the State. Such a view derives from the concept of the community of States as a political community of sorts,[69] where membership is conditional on a sufficient degree of acceptance by existing members. The constitutive theory gives legal weight to the views of existing States, such that the lack of recognition is fatal to a claim of statehood.[70]

The declaratory theory finds support in some judicial and arbitral decisions,[71] as it is also consistent with traditional elements of State practice. However, the constitutive theory explains a number of situations where an entity aspiring to statehood was unable to exist in the long term due to collective non-recognition by other States.[72] In 1967, Biafra declared independence from Nigeria and triggered a violent civil war; without any meaningful recognition, the struggle was abandoned and within five years it was reincorporated into Nigeria.[73] The 'Bantustans' of apartheid-era South Africa, declared independent during the 1970s, met with no recognition from any other State and were reincorporated into South Africa in 1993.[74] In 1965, Rhodesia declared independence from the UK and promulgated a constitution based on principles of apartheid. Rhodesia met with no recognition save from South Africa, and was denied admission to the UN. It was only after a new constitution was drafted, abandoning the racist principles of Rhodesia, and a brief reversion to British colonial rule that Zimbabwe emerged as an independent State in 1980.[75] This collective non-recognition may be partially explained

[69] See further A Green, *Statehood as a Political Community: International Law and the Emergence of New States* (CUP, 2024).

[70] See further the intriguing normative theory of recognition of P Kilibarda, *Recognition of States in International Law* (OUP, 2024).

[71] See, e.g., *Deutsche Continental Gas-Gesellschaft v Polish State* (1929): 'the State exists *par lui-même* and the recognition is nothing else than a declaration of this existence'; and the Badinter Commission's *Opinion Nos 1, 8 & 10* (1991–2), according to which the former Yugoslav republics were already States at the time of recognition.

[72] A supporter of the constitutive theory of recognition is C Hillgruber, 'The Admission of New States to the International Community' (1998) 9 EJIL 491.

[73] Although the United Nations did not discuss the situation in Biafra, the OAU Resolution on Nigeria reaffirmed the principle of the territorial integrity of States: see OAU Doc AHG/Res.51 (IV), reprinted in (1967) 6 ILM 1243. For background, see DA Ijalaye, 'Was Biafra at Any Time a State in International Law?' (1971) 65 AJIL 551.

[74] See UNGA Res 31/6A (26 October 1976) and, more generally, J Dugard, *International Law: A South African Perspective* (Kenwyn, 1994), ch 5.

[75] According to the terms of the 'Lancaster House Agreement' of 21 December 1979: see *Southern Rhodesia: Report of the Constitutional Conference held in Lancaster House, London, September–December 1979*, Cmnd 7802 (HMSO, 1980).

in that all of these breakaway entities violated in some way a peremptory norm (*jus cogens*), thus echoing the ICJ's statement in *Kosovo* on the matter.[76]

Today, recognition seems to play an important role in the controversies surrounding the statehood of Kosovo, Russian-dominated entities South Ossetia, Abkhazia, and Transnistria, and the TRNC discussed earlier. Kosovo declared independence on 17 February 2008 despite lacking effective control over Serb-inhabited areas in the north.[77] The status of recognition is unclear, however; at present, Kosovo is recognized by just under a hundred States (and some twelve have purported to withdraw recognition), was permitted to give its views in relation to the ICJ advisory opinion on the effects of its declaration of independence,[78] and has become of member of at least ten international organizations, including the IMF and the World Bank. Despite gradually improving relations with Serbia,[79] it has not been admitted to the UN. South Ossetia and Abkhazia, two entities asserting independence from Georgia, and Transnistria (asserting independence from Moldova), are recognized only by the Russian Federation and a handful of other States.[80] Serious doubts persist as to whether any of these fulfil the criterion of an effective government, given the strong military presence of Russia. With respect to the TRNC, the Turkish army maintains a large contingent in the northern third of the island of Cyprus, and the TNRC remains militarily, politically, and economically dependent on Türkiye; the only State to extend it recognition.

5.3.1.2 **Reconciling the two dominant theories; is there a duty to recognize?**

Which theory is preferable? Rather than preferring one theory, the two theories coexist and each helps to illuminate the role that recognition plays within statehood. Although the declaratory theory suggests that politics do not themselves generate legal effects, in fact it is impossible for an entity aspiring to statehood to fulfil its capacity to enter into relations with other States if no other State will do so. In this respect, the declaratory theory seems unable to explain the effects of such a refusal by other States. The constitutive theory serves, then, to explain why entities which would apparently fulfil the criteria for statehood might nevertheless be denied that status. It also serves to explain the curious phenomenon of 'collective recognition', through which an act of mass recognition (such as admission to the UN) to an entity might serve to allay concerns about

[76] For further discussion, see later Section 5.3.1.2.

[77] This declaration was purportedly 'under international supervision' as stipulated in the 'Ahtisaari Plan': see Letter dated 26 March 2007 from the Secretary-General addressed to the President of the Security Council, Addendum, Comprehensive Proposal for the Kosovo Status Settlement, Annex IX, International Civilian Representative, United Nations Security Council, 26 March 2007, art 4.1.

[78] *Kosovo* (n 61) 407–8, para 3.

[79] The EU-sponsored 'Orhin Agreement' on the path to normalization between Kosovo and Serbia (agreed 18 March 2023) has intensified exchanges between the two. Serbia, though not required to recognize an independent Kosovo, is prohibited from objecting to Kosovar membership in international organizations. Moreover, both parties recognize their respective official documents (e.g., passports or licence plates) and agree to exchange permanent missions in each other's capital. The objective of the Ohrin Agreement in its preamble is to create 'a legally binding agreement on comprehensive normalization' between the two.

[80] Besides Russia, only Nicaragua, Venezuela, Nauru, and Syria recognize South Ossetia and Abkhazia. In 2013, Vanuatu withdrew its recognition of Abkhazia, as did Tuvalu in respect of both entities in 2014, recognizing the territorial integrity of Georgia as including the two regions.

its statehood, despite lacking in some of the Montevideo criteria.[81] In all likelihood, the act of collective recognition has 'cured' any defects that Zaire (in 1960) or Bosnia and Herzegovina (in 1993) might have had with respect to the Montevideo criterion of effective government. Yet the constitutive theory also suffers from its own flaws: it ascribes legal weight to the refusal by other States to enter into legal relations with a State, and suggests that the essentially political act of recognition carries with it a legal component. Although most commentators agree that recognition remains a discretionary act,[82] Hersch Lauterpacht has argued that there is a duty to recognize any entity which fulfils the criteria for statehood.[83] Such a duty would suggest that existing States' discretion of recognition might be limited, though in practice States have any number of reasons, political and otherwise, why they may wish to recognize—or not—an entity aspiring to statehood.

5.3.1.3 **A duty of collective non-recognition?**

In addition, there is also a claimed duty *not* to recognize a particular entity when there are strong reservations as to the legality or the morality of the actions adopted to bring about that entity's factual claim to statehood. In the 1930s, the 'Stimson doctrine'[84] made precisely such a claim with respect to the proclamation by Japan, after invading and occupying the Chinese region of Manchuria in 1931, of the puppet State of Manchukuo.

In the Charter era, that doctrine of non-recognition of entities committing serious breaches of international law has been reaffirmed in a number of documents, most prominently the 1970 General Assembly Declaration on Friendly Relations[85] and Security Council Resolution 242 (1967),[86] passed with respect to the 1967 Arab–Israeli War, both stated unequivocally that no territorial acquisition resulting from the threat or use of force would be lawful. Again, a similar sentiment certainly motivated States' refusal to recognize Rhodesia in 1965,[87] the Bantustans in South Africa,[88] the TRNC in 1983,[89] and the claimed annexation of Kuwait by Iraq in 1990. Finally, in 2010, the ICJ suggested in its advisory opinion on the *Declaration of Independence in respect of Kosovo* that a State ought not to be recognized if the events leading to its foundation were connected to egregious violations of international law or of peremptory norms

[81] See J Dugard, *Recognition and the United Nations* (Grotius, 1987), 41 *et seq*; H Lauterpacht, *Recognition in International Law* (CUP, 1947), 400.

[82] *Opinion No 10 of the Arbitration Commission at the EC Conference on Yugoslavia (Badinter Commission)* (1992) 92 ILR 206.

[83] Lauterpacht, *Recognition* (n 76) 24, 55, 76–7.

[84] Diplomatic Note of 7 January 1932 sent by US Secretary of State for Foreign Affairs Henry Stimson to the Governments of Japan and China (1932) 1 Hackworth 334. The 'Stimson Doctrine' was endorsed by a resolution of the Assembly of the League of Nations which declared that members of the League should not recognize a situation, treaty, or agreement brought about by means contrary to the Covenant of the League or the Pact of Paris: see LNOJ, Special Supp No 11, 8.

[85] Declaration on Principles of International Law concerning Friendly Relations and Co-operation among States in accordance with the Charter of the United Nations, GA RES 25/2625 (XXV) (24 October 1970).

[86] UNSC Res 242 (22 November 1967).

[87] See UNSC Res 216 (12 November 1965).

[88] See earlier discussion at Section 5.2.5.

[89] See UNSC Res 541 (18 November 1983) and UNSC Res 550 (11 May 1984), both of which declared the Turkish Cypriot declaration of independence to be 'illegal'.

(*jus cogens*).[90] It is perhaps more accurate to conclude that both theories serve to explain different facets of the effects of recognition, but that neither of them fully accommodates the complexity of the fact.

5.3.2 **Recognition of governments**

5.3.2.1 **General rules on recognition of governments**

The recognition of governments is a distinct process from the recognition of a State. When dealing with the recognition of a State, at issue is the very existence of the State as a subject of international law. With a change in government, recognition is normally only an issue when there has been a drastic or unconstitutional change in government; for example, a *coup d'état*, a revolution, or a civil war leaving different factions asserting that they represent the totality of a State. The question of recognition of governments concerns only the status of the administrative authority but not the identity of the State itself, which does not cease to be an international legal person merely because its government has been overthrown. Recognition of a government thus constitutes acceptance that it has the authority to govern or control the territory and population of a State, and the recognizing State accepts that it will deal with that government as the governing authority of the State.[91]

Recognition of governments following an unconstitutional change can take place either *de jure* or *de facto*. *De jure* recognition, a formal act, usually follows when the recognizing State is satisfied that the new government enjoys, 'with a reasonable prospect of permanence, the obedience of the mass of the population . . . effective control of much of the greater part of the territory of the state concerned'.[92] What is more, a new government should not be subordinated to a foreign power and should be able to make decisions independently. *De facto* recognition is slightly different: it suggests that while a government may be in power and effective authority, the recognizing State has doubts over the legitimacy of the government and how it came to power. A good example was how the UK recognized the Soviet Union only *de facto* in 1921 and *de jure* in 1924.[93]

CASE SPOTLIGHT ***Tinoco Arbitration (United Kingdom/Costa Rica)*** **(1923) 1 RIAA 369, reprinted in (1924) 18 AJIL 147**

A 1917 *coup d'état* in Costa Rica led by Frederico Tinoco led to a change of government in that State and the adoption of a new constitution. Following his election as President, Tinoco administered Costa Rica until 1919, when he in turn was deposed and the previous

[90] *Kosovo* (n 61) 437, para 81.

[91] A recent contribution to scholarship in the field is N Pavlopoulos, *The Identity of Governments in International Law* (OUP, 2024).

[92] See the 'Morrison statement' of the then UK Under-Secretary of State for Foreign Affairs, 799 HC Deb, col 23, 6 April 1970. See also *Tinoco Arbitration (United Kingdom/Costa Rica)* (1923) 1 RIAA 369: 'the non-recognition by other nations of a government claiming to be a national personality, is usually appropriate evidence that it has not attained the independence and control entitling it by international law to be classed as such'.

[93] The distinction between *de jure* and *de facto* recognition in the UK's recognition of the Soviet Union was determinative in the case of *Luthor v Sagor* [1921] 1 KB 456, [1921] 3 KB 532.

constitution restored. The new government repudiated contractual obligations undertaken by Tinoco's administration to British nationals. The British government contested the validity of the repudiation.

The sole arbitrator, William H Taft of the US Supreme Court and a former President, found in favour of Costa Rica and drew two important conclusions that influenced international law on the recognition of governments.

First, he found that, in conformity with 'well-settled international law', *de facto* regimes such as the Tinoco regime were able to bind subsequent governments, irrespective of the manner in which they gained power: '[t]o speak of a revolution creating a *de facto* government, which conforms to the limitations of the old constitution, is to use a contradiction in terms'. Secondly, although the UK did not recognize the Tinoco government, it was not estopped from exercising diplomatic protection (see Chapter 11) over British nationals, as the Tinoco regime constituted a *de facto* government that could create rights for British nationals that could be protected.

The principles invoked in the *Tinoco* arbitration are still relevant today in relation to the responsibility of States for the acts of insurgent governments, and the case was cited by the ILC in its Commentaries to the Articles on State Responsibility (see Chapter 9). Today that doctrine has assumed renewed relevance in a new debate on the concept of 'odious debt', according to which a government is not responsible for repaying funds raised by insurgent regimes for personal purposes or profit.

For further reading, see J King, *The Doctrine of Odious Debt in International Law* (CUP, 2016), esp ch 3; and on a cognate topic of 'crippling compensation', M Paparinskis, 'Crippling Compensation in the International Law Commission and Investor-State Arbitration' (2022) 37 ICSID Review—Foreign Investment Law Journal 289.

The consequences of mere *de facto* recognition are significant: for example, a government only recognized *de facto* cannot claim State property or invoke State immunity (see Chapter 9) in the courts of the recognizing State. But the consequences of non-recognition of a government are at their most significant in the realm of diplomatic relations. Without recognition, there can be no exchange of diplomatic envoys, and there is no formal means of communication between two States. Two examples of how non-recognition adds complexity to international relations are the USA's refusal to engage both with the post-1959 government of Cuba and the post-1979 government of Iran. Although both Cuba and Iran remain members of the UN alongside the USA, the latter State maintains a 'United States Interests Section' through the Swiss embassies in Havana and Tehran, respectively;[94] it is only through these intermediaries, or other informal channels, that communications are conducted.

5.3.2.2 **US and UK practice since 1977**

The recognition of governments by the USA has declined since 1977, when it separated recognition from the approval of the policies of a foreign government: 'US practice has been to de-emphasize and avoid the use of recognition in cases of changes of

[94] Although many diplomatic and consular services are maintained by these Sections, they are formally not accredited in the same manner as normal US diplomatic and consular officials.

governments and to concern ourselves with the question of whether we wish to have diplomatic recognition with the new governments'.[95] In 1980, precisely for that reason, the UK government announced that it would no longer recognize governments at all.[96] This emerging practice poses a problem in domestic courts, as hitherto such courts could rely on a determination by the executive—in the UK, for example, through certificates issued by the Foreign and Commonwealth Office. With the new policy of non-recognition, US and UK courts have had to arrive at their own determinations, which has resulted, as suggested by Hobhouse J in *Somalia v Woodhouse Drake*, in the development of criteria for recognizing a government:

- whether the entity is the constitutional government;
- the degree and nature of the administrative control, if any, exercised over the territory;
- whether the UK government has had any dealings with that government and the nature of those dealings;
- the extent of international recognition that it has as a government (in marginal cases only).[97]

It may be that *de jure* recognition has returned as a tool of foreign policy in the last decade. In 15 July 2011, the USA and the UK joined some thirty other States and seven international organizations in recognizing the National Transitional Council (NTC) as the sole legitimate governing authority in Libya, despite its lack of effective control over much of Libya, including the capital, Tripoli. It is at least arguable that this intensity of recognition, backed with the authorization to use force by the Security Council, was a key element that contributed to the NTC's victory over the Qaddafi government.[98] Later that year, the Syrian National Council (SNC) was recognized by nine States as the legitimate representative of the Syrian people, including Libya, Egypt, France, the UK, and the USA. Yet this did not go further: with no Security Council authorization to use force, a decade-long civil conflict led to the displacement of nearly one million Syrians.[99] In a stunning reversal, Syrian President Bashir Assad fled Damascus on 8 December 2024 after opposition forces quickly overwhelmed his regime and entered Damascus, though early State responses were cautious about bestowing recognition on a specific faction. Finally, a string of coups in northern Africa in the early 2020s have met with widespread condemnation, the severance of French military ties, and suspension from ECOWAS. In July 2024, Mali, Burkina Faso, and Niger announced their joint withdrawal from ECOWAS with immediate effect.

[95] See (1977) Digest of United States Practice in International Law 20.

[96] See UK Statement of 1980 (1980) 51 BYBIL 367.

[97] *Republic of Somalia v Woodhouse Drake & Carey Suisse SA* [1993] QB 54 (UK).

[98] A Schuit, 'Recognition of Governments in International Law and the Recent Conflict in Libya' (2012) 14 International Community LR 381.

[99] See S Talmon, 'Recognition of Opposition Groups as the Legitimate Representative of a People' (2013) 12 Chinese JIL 219.

CONTEMPORARY DEVELOPMENTS A Renaissance in Formal (*De Jure*) Recognition? Venezuela, Afghanistan, and Myanmar

Several recent crises have called further attention to *de jure* recognition as a foreign policy instrument. The 2018 Venezuelan presidential crisis was triggered when Nicolas Maduro won an election widely dismissed by opposition parties as rigged. In January 2019, Juan Guaidó, leader of the National Assembly, invoked a constitutional provision and asserted he was 'acting president'. Despite Western support for Guaidó, Maduro continued to serve. New elections held in 2024 did not change the situation with Maduro claiming a narrow victory backed by the Supreme Court. However, opposition leader Edmundo González Urrutia has himself claimed a landslide victory, with support from the United States, European Union, and ten Latin American States. At the time the book went to press, Maduro remained in power.

In August 2021, a stunned world watched as a Taliban insurgency, which coincided with the US and allied withdrawal from Afghanistan, took effective control over the provincial capitals on 6 August; by 15 August, Afghan President Ashraf Ghani had fled and the Taliban had captured the capital, Kabul, declaring itself the 'Islamic Emirate of Afghanistan'. The unprecedented collapse of the Afghan government took many by surprise; though no State has explicitly recognized the Taliban as the legitimate government of Afghanistan, in January 2024 China became the first State to accept the accreditation of an ambassador appointed by the Taliban. Certain other States, for example Iran, Qatar, and Turkmenistan, have also allowed the Taliban to take control of the Afghan embassy in their capital.

The unfolding situation in Myanmar since 2021 has also raised the question of *de jure* recognition. In 2021 President Win Myint and 'State Counsellor' Aung San Suu Kyi were arrested and detained, with civilian rule suspended and military rule imposed under a now four-year 'state of emergency' under a military junta, the 'State Administrative Council' ('SAC'). However, the military junta has received widespread condemnation and only relatively limited de facto recognition (see 'Illegal and Illegitimate', a paper of the Special Rapporteur on human rights in Myanmar presented to the UN Human Rights Council (A/HRC/52/CRP.2 (31 January 2023). It was concluded that the leaders of the deposed ruling party (the 'National Unity Government') command a 'far stronger claim to legitimacy' both through State recognition and the response of international organizations such as ASEAN and the EU.

5.3.2.3 Effects of non-recognition in municipal law

Because the act of recognizing a government remains at its root a political act, it remains a prerogative of the executive branch of government in most municipal legal systems. The judicial branch, which does not have the power to recognize a State or a government, is bound to implement any legal effects flowing from a determination made by the executive to recognize or to deny recognition to a State or a new government. In part, this explains why the US and UK governments have adopted a policy of non-recognition of governments by the executive, leaving the courts to determine these situations on the facts.

Non-recognition in international law has far-reaching effects within the legal systems of the non-recognizing State.[100] An unrecognized government will not have standing to sue in its own name in the courts of the non-recognizing State. Nor will an unrecognized government enjoy any immunities that generally accrue with statehood. The laws of an unrecognized entity claiming to be a State or government, in particular, will not be given effect in a court.[101] Finally, any property belonging to its predecessor will not be recognized as its property. These general rules are not absolute, as there exist some exceptions. For example, in UK law, the following categories of legislation would remain valid:

- acts of perfunctory administration, or of a private nature, such as private property transactions, marriages, and divorces, where the courts may 'take note' of certain acts of a foreign sovereign if it is effective in its territory;[102]
- acts of a delegated sovereign, where the court may enquire as to whether an act of a non-recognized entity is being exercised pursuant to a *delegation* of power from a recognized government;[103]
- the acts of foreign corporations, which are given legal personality so long as they are incorporated under the laws of a settled legal system.[104]

5.4 **Continuity and extinction of statehood; the emergence of new States**

Returning to the acquisition of statehood, such status creates a strong, but not indisputable, presumption that it is enduring, and will always continue. A change of circumstances will not immediately extinguish the legal personality of a State, whether such instability comes from occupation by another State (as seen in the occupation by Nazi Germany of Poland, Czechoslovakia, the Netherlands, Belgium, Denmark, Norway, and France during World War II or the occupation of Kuwait by Iraq in 1990) or a collapse in governmental authority (as in Somalia since the early 1990s or the situation in Syria from late 2011 until late 2024 Syria).

Very occasionally, a State will become extinct. A State may become extinct through *political union* with one or another State to form a new State, such as when Egypt and Syria united between 1958 and 1961 into a short-lived 'United Arab Republic',[105]

[100] A quintessential case is that of *Luthor v Sagor* (n 87) where the recognition *de facto* of the Soviet government was held to be determinative by the UK Court of Appeal in whether effect could be given to the acts and legislation of the Soviet government. On the retroactivity of recognition, see also *Haile Selassie v Cable and Wireless Ltd (No 2)* [1939] 1 Ch 182; and *Spain v Owners of the Arantzazu Mendi* [1939] AC 256.

[101] *Carl Zeiss Stiftung v Rayner and Keeler Ltd (No 2)* [1967] 1 AC 853. This can have harsh results for individuals: see *Adams v Adams* [1970] 3 All ER 572.

[102] *Hesperides Hotels v Aegean Turkish Holidays* [1978] QB 205; *Carl Zeiss Stiftung v Rayner & Keeler* (n 95).

[103] See *Carl Zeiss Stiftung v Rayner & Keeler* (n 95) where the House of Lords concluded that the Soviet government had delegated powers to the government of the German Democratic Republic.

[104] See the UK Foreign Corporations Act 1991, s 1(1).

[105] Official, a republic with two 'regions': see Provisional Constitution of the UAR, reprinted in (1959) 8 ICLQ 374.

or when North and South Yemen united to form the 'Republic of Yemen' in 1990.[106] Political union is similar, but not identical, to the *incorporation* of one State by another State, as occurred during the reunification of Germany in 1990, when the Federal Republic of Germany permitted the constitutional accession of the five *Länder* that composed the German Democratic Republic, thus extinguishing the latter State.[107] A further historical example is that of Newfoundland, an independent Dominion within the British Empire after 1907, which fell on financial difficulties and in 1934 voluntarily relinquished self-rule to the British imperial government, one of the few entities ever to do so. *De jure*, however, Newfoundland remained an independent Dominion until 1949, when Newfoundland voted to become a province of Canada.[108]

Incorporation is usually consensual, and it is to be distinguished from *annexation*, usually (but not invariably) a unilateral act of seizure of territory that is later legitimated by recognition by other States. This was the case, for example, with the annexation of then-independent Hawaii into the United States in 1898.[109] Examples of unsuccessful annexations in the twentieth century include the *Anschluss* of 1938, through which Nazi Germany annexed Austria, and the annexation of Kuwait by Iraq in 1990.

The dismemberment of a State into new States can lead to a number of outcomes. The first is *dissolution*: the existing State disappears and new States succeed to its rights and obligations but not to its personality. This is exemplified in the 1993 'Velvet Divorce' that dissolved Czechoslovakia peacefully and established Czechia and Slovakia as new States.[110] As the accompanying comment explains, a more violent dissolution characterized the breakup of the Socialist Federal Republic of Yugoslavia (SFRY).[111]

HISTORICAL BACKGROUND The Disintegration of the SFRY (1990–2000)

The SFRY was established after World War II, though it had previously existed as the Kingdom of the Serbs, Croats, and Slovenes. Comprised of six republics (Bosnia-Herzegovina, Croatia, Macedonia, Montenegro, Serbia, and Slovenia), it was a multilingual, multicultural, and multi-confessional State. Through a policy of studied neutrality pursued by President Josip Tito, the SFRY played a key role in the Non-Aligned Movement during the Cold War.

After the death of President Tito in 1980, tensions arose between the six republics, culminating in unilateral declarations of independence from Slovenia and Croatia in June 1991. Slovenia seceded with minimal violence, but conflict in Croatia raged until a 1992

[106] See (1991) 30 ILM 829 and R Goy, 'La Réunification du Yemen' (1990) Annuaire français du droit international 249.

[107] See State Treaty on German Economic, Monetary and Social Union (1990) 29 ILM 1108; and State Treaty on Unification (1991) 30 ILM 457, 498. Art 23 of the Basic Law (*Grundgesetz*) of the Federal Republic permitted the reunification of Germany.

[108] British North America Act 1949 (UK; 'the Newfoundland Act' in Canada).

[109] Effected under a joint resolution of the US Congress popularly called the 'Newlands Resolution' on 7 July 1898, No 55, 30 Stat 750 (USA), which 'resolved' that the Republic of Hawaii had 'signified its consent . . . to cede absolutely and without reserve to the United States of America, all rights of sovereignty of whatsoever kind'.

[110] J Malenovsky, 'Problèmes liés à la Partition de la Tchécoslovaquie' (1993) AFDI 305.

[111] See UNGA Res 55/12 (1 November 2000).

UN-brokered ceasefire. After a 1992 referendum in Bosnia-Herzegovina, in which Bosnian Muslims and Croats voted overwhelmingly for independence, though Bosnian Serbs did not, violent conflict erupted along ethnic lines.

In response to these rapid changes, the Badinter Commission declared in its *Opinion No 1* (92 ILR 162 (29 November 1991)) that the SFRY 'was in the process of dissolution'. In its *Opinion No 8* (92 ILR 199 (4 July 1992)), it concluded that the SFRY 'no longer existed', basing itself on the adoption of a new constitution as the Federal Republic of Yugoslavia (FRY), and numerous UN resolutions referring to the 'former SFRY' (in particular, SC Res 752 and 757). In its *Opinion No 10* (92 ILR 206 (4 July 1992)), the Commission concluded that the FRY (Serbia and Montenegro) was a 'new State', and not the continuing State to the SFRY. The FRY was only to change its view in late 2000, when it applied successfully for admission to the United Nations as a new State, 'Serbia and Montenegro' (UNGA Res 55/12 (1 November 2000)). Montenegro voted in a referendum to secede in 2005, and was admitted to the United Nations in 2006.

Why is this relevant? The continuity of personality between the SFRY and the FRY would have entailed the succession of membership in the United Nations and other organizations for the FRY, a prominent point in several ICJ cases. Instead, the FRY was to be considered a new State in some, but not all, cases.

For example, the SFRY and the FRY were deemed continuous in *Application of the Convention on the Prevention of the Crime of Genocide (Bosnia and Herzegovina v Federal Republic of Yugoslavia), Preliminary Objections, ICJ Reports 1996*, p 595, and especially in the *Application for Revision of the Judgment of 11 July 1996, in the Case concerning the Application of the Convention on the Prevention and Punishment of the Crime of Genocide (Bosnia and Herzegovina v Federal Republic of Yugoslavia), Judgment, ICJ Reports 2003*, p 7. However, in *Legality of the Use of Force (Serbia and Montenegro v Belgium), Preliminary Objections, ICJ Reports 2004*, p 279, filed by the then-FRY against seven NATO States (Belgium, Canada, France, Germany, Italy, the Netherlands, Portugal, and the UK), the FRY was determined to be a new State before it was admitted to the UN in 2000, and thus not eligible to submit a case against the NATO States in 1999.

There is a contradiction between the ICJ's decisions in 2003 and 2004 that has never quite been resolved neither in doctrine nor through practice.

The concept of 'continuing State' invoked by the FRY is important, as a continuing State retains the international personality of the original State: it is the same legal person, and need not reapply for membership in international organizations or re-accede to treaties. The continuing State would also, in principle, assume the public debts of the disintegrating State. The best contemporary example of a 'continuing State' is Russia, after the 1991 Alma-Ata Protocol, acknowledged the collapse of the USSR and proclaimed the 'Commonwealth of Independent States' but also supported 'Russia's continuance of the membership of the [USSR] in the United Nations, including permanent membership of the Security Council, and other international organizations'.[112] Consequently, Russia has long been regarded as the continuing State of the USSR, though, as a result of

[112] See (1992) 31 ILM 148–9, 151.

Russia's aggressive acts in February 2022, Ukraine suggested that the Russian continuation was in fact illegitimate.[113] A similar historical situation was faced in the partition of British India in 1947, where the Republic of India was regarded as the continuing State and did not have to reapply for UN membership, but the new Republic of Pakistan was admitted as a new member State.[114]

Succession to treaties takes on a number of forms, depending on the scope and subject matter of a treaty. A 'localized treaty', which imposes obligations with respect to a specific territory (e.g., the delimitation of boundaries, the establishment of navigational rights, or a right of transit), will continue to attach to that territory even if a new State becomes sovereign.[115] Conversely, a non-localized treaty will not automatically remain in force for a newly independent State that emerges from the process of decolonization, which may claim a so-called *tabula rasa* ('clean slate') under international law—though it can choose to succeed to those obligations it wishes to accept. However, there is an exception to the 'clean slate' principle with respect to succession to human rights treaties: as the UN Human Rights Committee stated in 1997, 'once the people are accorded the protection of the rights under the Covenant, such protection devolves with territory and continues to belong to them, notwithstanding change in government of the State party, including dismemberment in more than one State or State succession or any subsequent action of the State party designed to divest them of the rights guaranteed by the Covenant'.[116]

5.5 Conclusion: statehood and international personality

The legal personality of the State remains deeply rooted in the structure of an international legal system which was developed to govern relations between them. The very idea of the State constitutes the archetype against which all other subjects of international law are measured. To this day, States remain the only actors fully capable of respecting international legal obligations, fully liable for breaches of international law,

[113] Foreign Ministry of Ukraine, 'The Illegitimacy of the Russian Federation's Presence in the UN Security Council and in the United Nations as a Whole' (Statement of Ukraine to the UN, 20 December 2022).

[114] UNGA Res 108(II) (30 September 1947). Though further back historically, it has been argued that despite a huge loss of territory, Türkiye was the continuing State of the Ottoman Empire: see P Dumberry, 'Is Turkey the "Continuing" State of the Ottoman Empire under International Law?' (2012) 59 Netherlands ILR 236.

[115] For more recent illustrations, see *Iron Rhine (Belgium v the Netherlands),* (2005) 27 RIAA 35, 64 (right of transit); *Navigational and Related Rights (Costa Rica v Nicaragua), ICJ Reports 2009*, p 213 (navigational rights); *Obligation to Negotiate Access to the Pacific Ocean (Bolivia v Chile), Merits, ICJ Reports 2018*, p 507 (right of territorial passage). Though it only has twenty-two States parties, see also Vienna Convention on State Succession with Respect to Treaties (signed 22 August 1978, entered into force 6 November 1996), 1946 UNTS 3 (VCSSRT), Arts 16–17.

[116] Human Rights Committee, General Comment 26 (610, UN Doc A/53/40, Annex VII (8 December 1997), para 4). But *cf* VCSSRT (n 108), which makes no such exception for human rights. The question of State succession to treaties is complex and has been studied elsewhere: see, e.g., M Kamminga, 'State Succession in Respect of Human Rights Treaties' (1996) 7 EJIL 469; and B Simma, 'From Bilateralism to Community Interest in International Law' (1994-VI) 250 Recueil des Cours 354–8.

and the most important with respect to the development of new rules of international law. For all the issues with State sovereignty, and with heavy caveats, moreover, the State remains the most legitimate expression of a people seeking to govern themselves within a common political community. For that reason alone, the State will remain the paramount international actor.

That said, international law has moved beyond a system applying exclusively between States, and the chapter which follows will focus on the place of international organizations. Later chapters will address how individuals, indigenous peoples, non-governmental organizations, or multinational corporations might also bear rights and obligations under international law, wielding influence that poses a challenge to the orthodox view of international law as a State-based legal order.

Further reading

A Cassese, *Self-Determination of Peoples: A Legal Reappraisal* (CUP, 1995).

A human rights-centric approach to self-determination and the creation of States in international law.

J Crawford, *The Creation of States in International Law* (2nd edn, OUP, 2006).

A magisterial survey of decades of relevant practice, including secession, decolonization, and the succession of State obligations.

J Dugard, *Recognition and the United Nations* (CUP, 1987).

Comprehensive and lucid, with a particular focus on the principles underlying collective recognition that predates the dissolutions of the Soviet Union and the former Yugoslavia.

T Grant, 'The Montevideo Convention and its Discontents' (1998) 37 Columbia JTL 403.

Perhaps the most incisive dissection of the Montevideo criteria for statehood.

K Knop, *Diversity and Self-Determination in International Law* (CUP, 2002).

A refreshing critical analysis that shifts from describing the right to self-determination to illuminating its effects in relation to colonized peoples, ethnic communities, indigenous groups, and others.

H Lauterpacht, *Recognition in International Law* (CUP, 1947).

A classic in the field, written in the aftermath of World War II and representative of Lauterpacht's turn to universalism and human rights.

SD Murphy, 'Democratic Legitimacy and Recognition of States and Governments' (1999) 48 ICLQ 545.

A post-Cold War account of the debate surveying the claim that democratic legitimacy has become a new criterion for recognition.

JE Nijman, *The Concept of International Legal Personality* (TMC Asser Press, 2004).

A historical perspective, including a broad intellectual and sociopolitical survey of the context in which the concept of international legal personality was developed.

N Pavlopoulos, *The Identity of Governments in International Law* (OUP, 2024).

A novel argument that carefully surveys practice on the identity of governments and a typology of the practices of recognition—or denial thereof—by States.

R Portmann, *Legal Personality in International Law* (CUP, 2010).

A systematic survey of the rights, duties, and obligations that are associated with legal personality in international legal practice.

S Talmon, *Recognition of Governments in International Law* (Clarendon Press, 2000).

A focused, systematic account of the international legal practice on the recognition of governments.

J Vidmar, *Democratic Statehood in International Law: The Emergence of New States in post-Cold War Practice* (Hart, 2013).

An extremely thorough account of recent practice relating to the creation of new States.

6

International organizations

6.1 Introduction: beyond the State

As explained in Chapter 5, the primacy of the State as subject has remained a touchstone of the international legal order. Yet a number of other actors, most prominently international organizations created by States, play an increasingly important role. This chapter provides an introduction to international organizations, their differences to States, and their position within the international legal order. The chapter will conclude with an introduction to the structure of the United Nations, the world's pre-eminent international organization.

6.2 Institutionalized cooperation: the rise of international organizations

International organizations are a comparatively recent phenomenon. The very first international organizations were created either to deal with localized questions such as the management of international waterways or neutral territory. The classic examples of these are the Rhine Commission, established in 1815, and the Danube Commission, established in 1856. They were concerned with narrow, technical matters through which States would benefit from the existence of a permanent institution; for example, to gather information or to establish technical standards. Some of these, which are still in existence, include the International Telegraph Union (1865)[1] and the Universal Postal Union (1874). The Hague Conference of 1899 brought with it the creation of the Permanent Court of Arbitration (PCA), a consensual mechanism of appointing panels of arbitrators to resolve specific disputes between consenting States.

HISTORICAL BACKGROUND The Permanent Court of Arbitration

The Permanent Court of Arbitration (PCA), founded in 1899, is one of the oldest and most unusual international organizations. Headquartered in the Peace Palace in The Hague, it is essentially a standing registry maintaining a list of arbitrators from which States may compose

[1] Known since 1932 as the International Telecommunication Union (ITU).

a panel. Rather than having a permanent judiciary, each specific dispute is resolved by a special panel appointed by parties to that dispute, and they may agree to establish specific rules of procedure to suit their purposes. In part for these institutional features, the PCA and its very name were mocked by JB Scott:

> the Permanent Court [of Arbitration] is not permanent because it is not composed of permanent judges; it is not accessible because it has to be constituted for each case; it is not a court because it is not composed of judges.
>
> (JB Scott (ed), *The Proceedings of the Hague Peace Conferences: The Conference of 1907: Vol II* (OUP, 1920), 319)

Despite such criticisms, the PCA was not dissolved upon the creation of the PCIJ and later the ICJ, despite these courts being endowed with permanent judicial appointments and fixed rules of procedure.

Though for decades in the shadow of its more visible cousin, the PCA has operated quietly for near a century. Its long experience and flexibility with respect to jurisdiction, procedure, and the composition of arbitral panels have proved popular with States. In fact, the PCA docket (list of cases) surpassed that of the ICJ in 2014 for the first time; and it has even opened offices in Buenos Aires, Mauritius, and Singapore to expand its global reach.

Important recent decisions under the PCA's auspices include the *Iron Rhine (Belgium/the Netherlands)* (Case 2003-02), *Abyei arbitration (Sudan/Sudan People's Liberation Movement)* (Case 2008-07), and *South China Sea (Philippines/China)* (Case 2013-19). The PCA is further studied in Chapter 12.

The PCA's continued existence attests to the enduring desire of States for diverse institutional settings for conducting international affairs.

The functions of international organizations began to shift with the creation of the League of Nations in 1919. It was the first international organization formed with the aim of dealing with wider political questions that affected inter-State relations, including the maintenance of international peace and security. The League was plagued with institutional difficulties in the interwar era, in part due to the requirement of unanimity in the Council of the League. However, many institutional features already present in the League system (such as the existence of an organ empowered with the maintenance of international peace and security: the Security Council) survived with relatively little modification in the UN Charter. As such, the emergence of international organizations should be seen as an iterative process of evolution and consolidation.

Today, international organizations exist in virtually all fields of transnational and global collective concern. In the broadest sense, they facilitate international cooperation in all areas from the harmonization of tariffs to the management of delicate ecosystems, and range in their scope from small bilateral commissions regulating transboundary resources to regional security and economic organizations, all the way to the universalist aspirations of the UN.

6.3 What is an 'international organization'?

Despite significant diversity in the form and function of various international organizations, in Article 2(a) of the 2011 Articles on the Responsibility of International Organizations (ARIO), the ILC attempted to set out a broad definition as follows:

> 'international organization' means an organization established by a treaty or other instrument governed by international law and possessing its own international legal personality. International organizations may include as members, in addition to States, other entities.[2]

If one is to accept the ILC's statement on this point as an accurate reflection of customary international law, three key conditions should be highlighted.

(i) *Membership:* First, an international organization befitting the name needs to be established and composed predominantly of States, though non-State entities may also be members. This is important, as it limits the term 'international organizations' to (predominantly) intergovernmental organizations such as the UN, the WTO, or the ITU, clearly distinguishing them from transnational non-governmental organizations, such as the Red Cross, Amnesty International, or Greenpeace. Despite their international efforts, all of the latter entities are constituted under municipal law, and States are not their members. International organizations may have a closed membership—for example, for regional integration (ASEAN, the EU, and Mercosur)—but also with respect to their purposes (the Francophonie, for example, requires a commitment to promoting the French language, but not that French be an official language of the member).

CONTEMPORARY DEBATES The Unusual Status of the International Committee of the Red Cross

The International Committee of the Red Cross (ICRC) is often mistaken for an international organization. Formed in 1863, and highly influential in the drafting of the Geneva Conventions, the ICRC in fact describes itself as the 'largest humanitarian network in the world', a movement which exists to 'alleviate human suffering, protect life and health, and promote human dignity especially during armed conflicts and other emergencies' (see *The ICRC: Its Mission and Work* (ICRC Publications, 2016)).

The ICRC's status as a non-governmental organization is clear from its governance structure: its supreme Assembly is composed of fifteen to twenty-five Swiss nationals and not the representatives of States. As such, it has no international legal personality as would, for example, the United Nations or the European Union. It cannot claim the privileges and immunities which apply to international organizations (IOs). However, the Geneva Conventions expressly confer special status on the ICRC as a monitoring or implementation body. What is more,

[2] See ILC, 'Articles on the Responsibility of International Organizations' in Report on the Work of its 63rd Session, UN Doc A/66/10 Chap V (9 December 2011) GAOR 66th Session Supp 10, Art 2(a).

States regularly consult the ICRC, often confidentially, in relation to the interpretation of the Conventions, even though it has no formal authority. As such, despite its non-governmental status, the ICRC plays an immense indirect role in the development of the law of armed conflict, as is covered in Chapter 15.

For further reflections on the ICRC's status at international law, see E Debuf, 'Tools to do the job: The ICRC's Legal Status, Privileges and Immunities' (2016) 97 897/898 IRRC 319.

(ii) *International legal personality:* An international organization requires, at a minimum, a set of organs through which it may assert a will that is sufficiently distinct from its members that it may be regarded as autonomous. An international organization cannot be merely the aggregate of its members taking a decision. Usually, it is sufficient for at least one of its organs to be able to take decisions on certain matters on the basis of a set procedure.[3] Thus, the OECD, with a set of distinct organs and a permanent administrative apparatus, has legal personality. The G20, on the other hand, which has no such permanent organs and is administered each year by the State hosting the annual G20 meeting, does not qualify. Legal personality will be discussed later, in Section 6.4.

(iii) *Governed under international law:* An international organization must be constituted under, and be governed by, international law. As was acknowledged in Article 2(a) of the ARIO, this usually occurs by means of a treaty, though this is not the exclusive means of creating an international organization. For example, the ICTY and ICTR were established as subsidiary bodies by resolutions of the Security Council, itself a UN organ.[4] Both the OSCE and OPEC emerged slowly through a series of multilateral conferences where so-called 'final acts' and resolutions were passed that gradually gave rise to them as international legal persons.

HISTORICAL BACKGROUND The Creation of the Iran–US Claims Tribunal through Joint Unilateral Acts

Iran's Islamic Revolution in 1980 created great upheaval in Iran, eventually overthrowing its monarchical government in favour of an Islamic republic. This, in turn, created significant friction with the USA, not least due to the nationalization of US-owned oil concessions and the storming of the US embassy in Tehran in 1979. Relations between the two States became strained and in response the USA froze very substantial Iranian assets held in US bank accounts.

[3] For example, in the Marrakech Agreement establishing the World Trade Organization (1994) 1867 UNTS 3 (WTO Agreement), Art IX(1) provides that in both the Ministerial Conference (its plenary organ) and the General Council (its executive organ), decisions are to be taken by 'consensus' or, failing that, by simple majority.

[4] Statute of the International Criminal Tribunal for the former Yugoslavia, UNSC Res 808 (1993) (22 February 1993), and UNSC Res 827 (25 May 1993), (1993) 32 ILM 1159; Statute of the International Criminal Tribunal for Rwanda, UNSC Res 955 (8 November 1994), (1994) 33 ILM 1598.

The two States were at an impasse as to their respective interests, and could barely come to the same negotiating table, much less agree to a treaty between them. That friction led to a significant innovation in how international organizations could be created: after months of efforts, the Iran–United States Claims Tribunal (IUSCT) was established through a *joint unilateral act* by the two parties. Through the good offices of Algeria, the 'Claims Settlement Declaration' was made, which concerned the settlement of claims between Iran and the USA (19 January 1981). This document took note of unilateral declarations of Iran and the United States that they committed to the constitution of a tribunal for the settlement of claims between them and their nationals. The Tribunal would be constituted of three Iranian nationals, three US nationals, and three nationals of third States, and would operate from The Hague.

The IUSCT enjoyed a flurry of activity in the 1980s, and contributed significantly to the development of international law in relation to foreign investments, the treatment of foreign nationals, and the resolution of situations of multiple nationality (see Chapter 19, Section 19.4). It continues in operation in The Hague today, and is a good example of an IO governed by international law through other means than a traditional treaty.

Similarly, though States may together invest in an inter-State enterprise for the performance of commercial functions, the enterprise is not governed by international law if it is formally established under the corporate law of one of the States. This is the case for Airbus, a French company with German, Spanish, and British government investors, or SAS Scandinavian System AB, a Swedish company, where the Swedish, Danish, and Norwegian governments hold the majority of shares. These are corporations governed under domestic law, and are not international organizations.

The ILC's definition of an international organization raises a wider doctrinal concern, namely, whether it is possible to arrive at an all-encompassing set of principles of general application to international organizations. This is for two reasons: first, in light of the fact that there may be radical differences in the forms an international organization may take. Secondly, the law governing each organization derives from that organization's specific constituent instrument, and there may be specific particularities for each organization.[5] Yet for all this, certain common principles, primarily deriving from customary international law, govern basic questions such as the interpretation of the constituent instrument of an international organization, the determination of whether it possesses legal personality, and the principles through which its responsibility under international law may be established. Clearly, an international organization may not violate a peremptory norm of international law (*jus cogens*).[6]

[5] The concept of 'rules of the organization' is understood as the constituent instruments, decisions, resolutions, and other acts of the international organization adopted in accordance with those instruments, as well as the established practice of the organization: see Vienna Convention on the Law of Treaties (signed 23 May 1969, entered into force 27 January 1980), 1155 UNTS 331, Art 5; Vienna Convention on the Law of Treaties between International Organizations and States and between International Organizations (signed 21 March 1986) (1986) 25 ILM 543, Art 2(j).

[6] See Art 41 ARIO, which broadly mirrors the approach taken in the ARSIWA, Art 40.

6.4 Legal personality of international organizations

Legal personality, in essence, represents recognition by actors in a legal order (in international law, primarily States) that the legal person concerned is entitled to hold rights and bear obligations derived from law. For this reason, establishing the personality of international organizations is a significant question within international law, and must be distinguished from the question of whether an international organization may also hold legal personality under the domestic law of a State. The two will be addressed separately.

6.4.1 Legal personality under international law

6.4.1.1 The conferral of international legal personality on an international organization

For much of international law's development, the classical position was that States, and only States, could hold international legal personality. International organizations, being set up by States to discharge certain functions, hold a derivative international personality in that international personality must be bestowed by the members which have created it.

The easiest means to do so is explicitly by treaty. Several constituent instruments, such as those of the European Union,[7] the World Trade Organization,[8] and ASEAN,[9] expressly bestow international legal personality on their respective organization. However, even in the absence of a treaty provision (as is the case with the UN Charter), international personality may be deduced through other means. In the seminal *Reparation for Injuries* advisory opinion, Count Bernadotte of Sweden, acting as a mediator in Jerusalem on behalf of the UN, had been murdered in Israel. The General Assembly sought an opinion from the ICJ as to whether the UN had the capacity to bring a claim for reparation against Israel. Despite no Charter provision on legal personality, the ICJ concluded decisively that the UN possessed sufficient legal personality to be able to bring an international claim against a State for reparation for injures done to the organization and its agents.

Though Article 104 of the Charter imposes an obligation on member States to recognize the legal personality of the UN within their domestic legal systems, it is silent on the question as to whether the organization possesses legal personality under international law. And yet, the Court deduced *international* legal personality as being necessary for

[7] See the Treaty of Lisbon (signed 13 December 2007, entered into force 1 December 2009) [2007] OJ C306/1, Art 47.

[8] See Marrakesh Agreement establishing the World Trade Organization, Art VIII.

[9] See Charter of the Association of South-East Asian Nations (ASEAN), Art 3.

the UN to discharge the functions that had been assigned to it by its members in the Charter:

> the Organization was intended to exercise and enjoy, and is in fact exercising and enjoying, functions and rights which can only be explained on the basis of the possession of a large measure of international personality and the capacity to operate on the international plane.[10]

What is more, the Court was even willing to recognize the international personality of the UN as having an objective character, in that its legal personality required no recognition from non-member entities and States which had not consented to the creation of the organization in order to be opposable to them:

> fifty States, representing the vast majority of the members of the international community, had the power, in conformity with international law, to bring into being an entity possessing objective international personality, and not merely personality recognized by them alone, together with capacity to bring international claims.[11]

The underlying logic deployed by the Court was that international organizations could possess such rights, powers, privileges, and immunities distinct from their members, and as are necessary for them to exercise their functions, even if not explicitly laid out in their constituent instruments.[12] Several theories explore this question. One, broadly a 'functionalist' approach, involves ascribing implied powers to an organization which are necessary to give effect to an explicit power.[13] To illustrate, the fact that Article 57 of the Charter bestows upon the UN the power to conclude agreements with other international organizations would mean that it was also necessary for it to hold international personality. Without that power, it could not take on any binding international obligations. A second approach known as 'will theory' contends that international legal personality exists only if the members of that organization explicitly intended for it to possess such personality; intention is deduced from the capacities, powers, rights, and duties bestowed on the organization by its members.[14] Will theory's emphasis on explicit evidence of intent aligns broadly with a positivist vision of the intention of the creators of the organization. Thirdly, a more empirical, 'objective' approach could suggest that international law sets out certain objective criteria, such as possessing organs that have separate decision-making powers from their members. If an international organization meets these criteria, its legal personality follows automatically, as it is *inherent* in its nature of

[10] *Reparation for Injuries suffered in the Service of the United Nations, Advisory Opinion, ICJ Reports 1949*, p 174, 179.

[11] *Ibid*, 185. In practice, States do not routinely refuse to acknowledge the personality of an organization merely because they are not a member: see ARIO (n 2) p 76, para 9; CF Amerasinghe, *Principles of the Institutional Law of International Organizations* (2nd edn, CUP, 2005), 87.

[12] See later, Section 6.5.2, on the interpretation of constituent instruments of an international organization.

[13] J Klabbers, *An Introduction to International Organizations Law* (4th edn, CUP, 2015), 56 et seq. See also V Engström, *Constructing the Powers of International Institutions* (Martinus Nijhoff, 2012).

[14] See Klabbers (n 13) 46–7; HG Schermers and N Blokker, *International Institutional Law: Unity within Diversity* (6th edn, Martinus Nijhoff, 2018), para 1565; P Sands and P Klein (eds), *Bowett's Law of International Institutions* (6th edn, Sweet & Maxwell, 2012), para 15-006.

being an international organization.[15] All three theories could justify the view that the UN's members had ascribed certain rights, obligations, and functions on the organization for which it was necessary for it to possess international personality. Their key point of difference in whether personality is functionally implied, can be deduced from the will of the organization's members, or is a logical consequence of the bestowal of such powers.

6.4.1.2 **The consequence of possessing international legal personality for international organizations**

Though it must be emphasized that the particular rights, obligations, and duties of an international organization are highly specific to each organization and its constituent instruments, there are some general consequences that all international organizations share in common. An international organization, though a collective entity, must be capable of possessing international rights and bearing international obligations and duties as distinct from those of its members.[16] Legal personality endows an organization with the capacity to bring an international claim in order to maintain its legal rights.[17] It is important not to confuse this potential capacity with an absolute right to have standing: as will be discussed in Chapter 12, any international dispute-settlement body must also have the jurisdiction to be seized of (to hear) the claim.[18]

The power of *jus tractatuum* suggests that an international organization may enter into a valid international agreement with another legal person, usually a State or another international organization, which is then subject to the law of treaties.[19] International organizations are also responsible for the non-fulfilment of the obligations that they bear under international law.[20] The logical corollary to this rule is that if an international organization is the bearer of a certain obligation, its members are presumed not to be liable with respect to that obligation.[21] The responsibility of international organizations will be discussed later, in Section 6.6.

Under international law, an international organization may also possess certain privileges and immunities which are necessary for the independent and efficient functioning of the organization. As will be discussed later, these are usually applicable within an organization's host State, though may also extend to other member States.[22] However,

[15] ND White, 'Separate but Connected: Inter-Governmental Organizations and International Law' (2008) 5 International Organizations Law Review 175; see also F Seyersted, *Objective International Personality of International Organizations: Do Their Capacities Really Depend on the Conventions Establishing Them?* (Krohns Bogtnykker, 1963), 47.

[16] Klabbers (n 13) 50; Amerasinghe (n 11) 68–9. See also E Lauterpacht, 'The Development of the Law of International Organization by the Decisions of International Tribunals' (1976) 152 Recueil des Cours 377, 407.

[17] Schermers and Blokker (n 14) para 1856.

[18] For example, Art 34 of the ICJ Statute only confers upon it the competence to be seised of disputes between States.

[19] Vienna Convention on the Law of Treaties between States and International Organizations (1986), Preamble, para 11.

[20] ARIO (n 2) Art 3.

[21] However, the presumption is rebuttable: e.g., it does not apply if the members of the organization and the organization have schemed to circumvent their respective international obligations: see ARIO (n 2) Commentary to Art 62, 163, paras 2 *et seq*.

[22] See R Higgins, *Problems and Process: International Law and How We Use It* (OUP, 1994), 91: 'members—and *a fortiori* the headquarters State—may not one and the same time establish an organization and fail to provide it with those immunities that ensure its role as distinct from that of the host State'.

they may also extend to the right to send and receive legations, which is inextricably tied to their ability to engage in dialogue with and be heard in international fora.

6.4.2 **Legal personality in domestic law**

6.4.2.1 **General principles**

International legal personality does not automatically entail domestic legal personality, despite the fact that international organizations often require the capacity to perform legal acts in domestic law. A practical example is that an international organization will require, when establishing its headquarters in a host State, the capacity to enter into employment contracts, purchase or rent out its premises, buy and sell equipment, and institute legal proceedings. Accordingly, many international instruments follow the example of Article 104 of the UN Charter and require that members provide the organization with the requisite domestic legal personality so as to function appropriately.[23]

Each legal system is in principle free to develop its own conditions for legal personality. As a general rule, it will recognize domestic legal personality in accordance with the particular relationship between its national law and international law (see Chapter 4). Several provisions in constituent instruments, such as Article 104 of the Charter or Article 335 of the Treaty on the Functioning of the European Union, create an obligation for States parties to accord the organization with the capacity necessary for the exercise of its functions under domestic law. For a State with a monist tradition, ratification of such a treaty provision suffices for an international organization's legal personality to be given effect under domestic law.[24] States from the dualist tradition, like the UK and other common law States, will generally require appropriate legislation transposing the treaty into domestic law in order for personality to exist under domestic law.[25]

In accordance with the *pacta tertiis* maxim embodied in Article 34 VCLT, non-member States are not obliged to recognize domestic legal personality, as they are third parties not bound by the constituent instrument. However, third States sometimes do accord domestic legal personality to an international organization of which they are not a member, in application of the principle of comity between nations (an exhortation to States to behave courteously with one another). For example, in *Arab Monetary Fund v Hashim*,[26] the English High Court recognized the legal personality of the Arab Monetary Fund (AMF), of which the UK was not a member, because that organization

[23] See, e.g., Lisbon Treaty on European Union (n 7), Art 282. For more information, see A Reinisch, *International Organizations in Domestic Courts* (CUP, 2000), 44.

[24] Prominent examples include the USA and Belgium with respect to the UN, *UN v B* (1952) 19 ILR 490, *Manderlier v Organisation des Nations Unies & Etat Belge (Ministre des Affaires Etrangères)* (1972) 45 ILR 446; the Netherlands with respect to the UN Relief and Rehabilitation Administration, *UNRRA v Daan* (1949) 16 ILR 337; and Italy with respect to NATO, *Branno v Ministry of War* (1955) 22 ILR 756.

[25] With respect to the International Tin Council, see *JH Rayner (Mincing Lane) Ltd v Department of Trade and Industry* [1989] 3 WLR 969, 1012c.

[26] *Arab Monetary Fund v Hashim* [1990] 1 All ER 685 (UK). In *Westland Helicopters Ltd v Arab Organization for Industrialization* [1995] 2 All ER 387, [1994] 108 ILR 564 (UK), the English High Court nevertheless pointed out that in such cases, the legal regime governing the status and capacities of the organization remained questions of international law.

had been accorded legal personality under the law of the host State, the United Arab Emirates. Under English law, taking into account the international law consideration of 'comity', the correctness of the incorporation procedure under UAE law would determine whether the AMF would have legal personality in the UK.[27]

6.4.2.2 **Consequences of domestic legal personality: privileges and immunities**

International organizations require certain privileges and immunities in order to perform their functions effectively, and without interference from a recognizing or host State.[28] Several States have enacted domestic legislation governing these.[29] Such privileges and immunities also commonly find recognition in treaties, whether they be the constituent instrument of the organization,[30] multilateral treaties,[31] or bilateral agreements between international organizations and member States.[32] It is not fully clear whether customary international law might accord certain privileges and immunities to international organizations.[33] Such privileges and immunities may include: immunity from the judicial jurisdiction of a State; immunity from measures of execution, such as seizure of property or other assets; the inviolability of premises, property, and archives; currency and fiscal privileges; and freedom of communication. Though many of these might be specific to the arrangement relating to the international organization, they are also broadly mirrored in the international legal regime governing the immunities of States: see Chapter 9 for more details.

6.5 Powers of international organizations

6.5.1 **Express and implied powers of international organizations**

The classic position is that international organizations only possess such powers as were expressly attributed to them from the constituent instrument whence they derive their authority.[34] Member States establishing an organization for the purpose of fulfilling

[27] See also *UNRAA v Daan* (1949) 16 ILR 337.

[28] See Klabbers (n 13) ch 7.

[29] See, e.g., International Organizations Act 1968 (UK); Foreign Missions and International Organizations Act 1991 (Canada); Federal Act on the Privileges, Immunities and Powers of International Organizations 2007 (Switzerland); Privileges and Immunities Act 1970 (Kenya).

[30] See, e.g., the general statement in UN Charter, Art 105.

[31] See, e.g., the 1946 General Convention on the Privileges and Immunities of the United Nations (adopted 13 February 1946, entered into force 17 September 1946), 1 UNTS 15; 1947 Convention on the Privileges and Immunities of the Specialized Agencies of the United Nations (adopted 21 November 1947, entered into force 2 December 1948), 33 UNTS 261; Agreement on Privileges and Immunities of the OAS (signed 15 May 1949), OAS TS 22.

[32] See, e.g., Headquarters Agreement between the United Nations and the United States (signed 26 June 1947, entry into force 21 October 1947), 11 UNTS 147; Headquarters Agreement between the International Criminal Court and the Netherlands (adopted 7 June 2007, entered into force 1 March 2008), 2517 UNTS 173; Agreement between the World Trade Organization and the Swiss Confederation (signed 31 May 2005), WT/GC/1/Add.1.

[33] See, e.g., Reinisch (n 23) 145; Amerasinghe (n 11) 344–8. But *cf* Sands and Klein (n 14), para 15-039 (2009 edn); and M Wood, 'Do International Organizations Enjoy Immunity under Customary International Law?' (2014) 10 International Organizations Law Review 287.

[34] *Jurisdiction of the European Commission of the Danube between Galatz and Braila, Judgment, 1926, PCIJ, Ser B, No 14*, p 64.

certain functions, such as promoting regional economic integration[35] or to facilitate international cooperation in relation to a specific objective,[36] will generally endow that organization with the appropriate powers to give effect to those functions. These may include the creation of specified organs in order to achieve their tasks, or granting of competence over certain subjects or categories of disputes; or whatever other aspect that its member States desire.

As described in relation to international personality, however, international organizations may also possess powers that are not explicitly conferred by their constituent instrument, but that can be *implied* as they are considered necessary for the organization to fulfil its functions. In *Interpretation of the Greco-Turkish Agreement*, the PCIJ accepted that if a treaty was silent, it could examine the agreement as a whole and see whether a power was to be implied in the existence of another explicit power.[37] As discussed earlier, the ICJ held in its *Reparation for Injuries* opinion that the UN was entitled to claim on behalf of its agent, even though that power was not to be found in the Charter. In a classic statement, the Court observed that:

> Under international law, an Organization must be deemed to have those powers which, though not expressly provided . . . are conferred upon it by necessary implication as being essential to the performance of its duties.[38]

CASE SPOTLIGHT ***Certain Expenses of the United Nations (Article 17, paragraph 2, of the Charter), Advisory Opinion, ICJ Reports 1962*, p 151**

The *Certain Expenses* advisory opinion given by the ICJ was a landmark decision in respect of the implied powers of the organs of an international organization. It arose when certain United Nations members withheld the payment of financial contributions assessed to them by the General Assembly on the basis that they disagreed with a certain peacekeeping mission. The question was posed to the ICJ as to whether the General Assembly was permitted to authorize expenses with respect to peacekeeping forces in the Sinai peninsula and in the Congo.

The central issue was that, under Article 24 of the Charter, the Security Council had 'primary' responsibility for the maintenance of international peace and security, and the Council's paralysis during the Cold War put the validity of certain peacekeeping missions into question. However, the Court found that though the UN Charter did not set out the General Assembly's responsibility in relation to the maintenance of international peace and security, under its budgetary powers set out in Article 17(2) of the Charter, the Assembly could incur expenses that were appropriate in fulfilling the purposes of the United Nations as a whole (p 168).

[35] See, e.g., Charter of the Association of Southeast Asian Nations (adopted 20 November 2007, entered into force 15 December 2008), 2624 UNTS 223, Art 1; Treaty Establishing the Economic Community of West African States (adopted 28 May 1975), 1010 UNTS 7, Art 3; Lisbon Treaty on European Union (n 7) Art 2.

[36] See, e.g., Convention on the Prohibition of the Development, Production, Stockpiling and Use of Chemical Weapons and on their Destruction (adopted 3 September 1992, entered into force 29 April 1997), 1974 UNTS 45, Art VIII (1)(a)(1); WTO Agreement (n 3) Art III.

[37] *Interpretation of the Greco-Turkish Agreement of 1st December 1926, Advisory Opinion, 1928, PCIJ, Ser B, No 16*, p 20, para 47.

[38] *Reparation for Injuries suffered in the Service of the United Nations, Advisory Opinion, ICJ Reports 1949*, p 174, p 182. In Lauterpacht (n 16) 430–2, it is argued that the essential character of a power does not mean that it is 'indispensably required'.

It could even establish peacekeeping operations without these being regarded as *ultra vires* acts (p 177). UN member States had an obligation to contribute to the costs of such missions.

The *Certain Expenses* opinion is notable due to the endorsement of the doctrine of 'implied powers', which applies not only to organs of international organizations but to the organization itself. But perhaps more significant is the fact that the advisory opinion turned on whether the expenses authorized were appropriate for the stated purposes of the organization as a whole. The Court adopted a functional approach: 'when the Organization takes action which warrants the assertion that it was appropriate for the fulfilment of one of the stated purposes of the United Nations, the presumption is that such action is not *ultra vires* the Organization', in other words not beyond one's legal authority (p 168).

As the *Certain Expenses* opinion demonstrates, States creating an international organization cannot always envisage every possible outcome or situation, and in practice have often created organizations with functions that require certain implied powers necessary to discharge those functions, 'by necessary intendment' in the words of the ICJ.[39] For example, nothing in Chapter VII of the Charter expressly endows the Security Council with competence over, for example, money laundering in relation to the extraction of natural resources, drug trafficking, or the financing of terrorism; nevertheless, the Council has drawn a link to the threat to international peace and security caused by terrorist acts.[40] Moreover, in 2007 the Council for the first time held a debate on the impact of climate change on international peace and security, another topic on which the Charter is silent.[41] While including new threats to peace is necessary, there is always a risk of overreach when deducing powers from outside the four corners of a text, lest its legitimacy be challenged. This will be further explored in Section 6.5.3.2.

6.5.2 **Interpretation of constituent instruments**

As the ICJ has long stated, '[f]rom a formal standpoint, the constituent instruments of international organizations are multilateral treaties, to which the well-established rules of treaty interpretation apply'.[42] Certain characteristics of the constituent instruments of international organizations, however, shape their interpretation, as acknowledged by the Court:

> the constituent instruments are also treaties of a particular character; their object is to create new subjects of law endowed with a certain autonomy, to which the parties entrust the

[39] See *Effect of Awards of Compensation made by the United Nations Administrative Tribunal, Advisory Opinion, ICJ Reports 1954*, p 47, p 57, where the Court validated the United Nations' power to create an administrative tribunal.

[40] See, e.g., UNSC Res 2195 (2014) (19 December 2014). See also UNSC Res 1373 (2001) (28 September 2001), passed in the aftermath of the 9/11 attacks on New York City, which was the first to call upon all States to take measures to prohibit the financing of terrorist activities.

[41] See UNSC Verbatim Record (17 April 2007) UN Doc S/PV.5663. Recently, the Council rejected a resolution that would have integrated climate-related risk as a central component of UN strategies aiming to counter the risk of conflict relapse. See UNSC Verbatim Record (13 December 2021) UN Doc S/PV.14732.

[42] *Legality of the Use by a State of Nuclear Weapons in Armed Conflict, Advisory Opinion, ICJ Reports 1996*, p 66, para 19.

> task of realizing common goals. Such treaties can raise specific problems of interpretation, owing, *inter alia*, to their character which is conventional and at the same time institutional; the very nature of the organization created, the objectives which have been assigned to it by its founders, the imperatives associated with the effective performance of its functions, as well as its own practice, are all elements which may deserve special attention when the time comes to interpret these constituent treaties.[43]

Though the creators of international organizations will have set out the purposes, functions, and form of the organization, and those of its constituent organs, the practices of the organization and its organs are also important in interpreting how the organization will function. For example, the ICJ observed in *Certain Expenses* that 'each organ of the Organization must, in the first place at least, determine its own jurisdiction';[44] such a power (*la compétence de la compétence*) is essential in understanding the scope of powers set out for each organ within the constituent instrument of an organization.[45] The subsequent practice of the organization, and of its members, may also shape the interpretation of a constituent instrument, with the best-known example of this being in the *Namibia* advisory opinion, where the Court, referring to the consistent practice of the Security Council and its members, observed that an abstention by a permanent member of the Security Council was a 'concurring vote' and not a veto, within the meaning of Article 27(3) of the UN Charter.[46]

There might also be judicial interpretation of constituent instruments in some cases. For example, the ECtHR has claimed the role of authoritative interpreter of the ECHR, and ITLOS occupies a similar role in relation to UNCLOS. Though the power to interpret the UN Charter authoritatively was not attributed to the ICJ in the Charter, from the outset it has declared that a capability to interpret the Charter cannot be excluded from the normal exercise of its judicial power.[47] Moreover, the ICJ may receive requests for advisory opinions from UN principal organs and UN specialized agencies on questions falling within the scope of their competence, which includes the interpretation of their constituent instruments. These are in turn entitled to receive 'authoritative legal guidance' and 'enlightenment as to the course of action [they] should take'.[48] Usually the

[43] *Ibid.*

[44] *Certain Expenses of the United Nations, (Article 17, paragraph 2, of the Charter) Advisory Opinion, ICJ Reports 1962*, p 151, 168.

[45] Developed first as a doctrine relating to judicial jurisdiction: see Chapter 12, Section 12.3.2.3.5.

[46] *Legal Consequences for States of the Continued Presence of South Africa in Namibia (South West Africa) notwithstanding Security Council Resolution 276 (1970), Advisory Opinion, ICJ Reports 1971*, p 16, paras 20–2.

[47] *Conditions for Admission of a State to Membership in the United Nations (Article 4 of the Charter), Advisory Opinion, ICJ Reports 1947*, p 57, 61. See also *Reparation for Injuries* (n 38) 185; *International Status of South West Africa, Advisory Opinion, ICJ Reports 1950*, p 128, 131 *et seq*; *Certain Expenses* (n 44) 168. See also J Sloan and G Hernández, 'The Role of the International Court of Justice in Developing the Institutional Law of the United Nations' in CJ Tams and J Sloan (eds), *The Development of International Law by the International Court of Justice* (OUP, 2012), 197.

[48] See UNGA Res 1731 (XVI) (12 December 1961) (concerning the interpretation of Art 17(2) UN Charter). See also D Akande, 'The Competence of International Organizations and the Advisory Jurisdiction of the International Court of Justice' (1998) 9 EJIL 437, esp 452–7.

constituent instrument of the international organization will provide for competence to request such advisory opinions.[49]

6.5.3 **Decision-making in international organizations**

6.5.3.1 **Binding decisions of international organizations**

As discussed earlier, international personality relates to the idea of autonomy: it gives the international organization the capacity to take decisions relating to the functions entrusted to it. The most evident of these relate to how the international organization takes decisions. These may take the form of prescribing harmonized standards for their members to adopt, as do the International Telecommunications Union, the Food and Agriculture Organization, and the International Labour Organization.

For an international organization to be able to act effectively, it is often necessary for its member States to support and implement its functions. Accordingly, many international organizations may take certain decisions that are addressed to and binding on member States, such as the imposition of embargoes or sanctions by the UN Security Council, ECOWAS, the Commonwealth, or the European Union. Occasionally, such action may be taken against a non-member State as well: the EU has maintained arms embargos and sanctions which are binding upon all EU member States—for example, against Zimbabwe for its human rights violations and against Iran for its nuclear programme.

Many other decisions of international organizations are more mundane, and relate to the internal workings of the organization itself, such as establishing rules of procedure, staff regulations, or, occasionally, a decision to establish a subsidiary organ. These internal workings may be crucial, however, in determining how the organization will in fact discharge its functions in relation to its members, as do the rules of procedure of the ICJ, the ICC, or the WTO.

6.5.3.2 ***Ultra vires* decisions of international organizations**

The potential exists for an organization which takes a decision that exceeds the scope of its functions for that decision to later be characterized as *ultra vires* by a judicial institution, though the competence to do so remains a sensitive matter.[50] For example, the ICJ does not possess the power of judicial review over decisions of the Security Council,[51] though it may come to interpret and apply the Council's resolutions.[52]

[49] See Constitution of the World Health Organization (adopted 22 July 1946, entered into force 7 April 1948), 14 UNTS 185, Art 76; Convention on the International Maritime Organization (adopted 6 March 1948, entered into force 17 March 1958), 289 UNTS 48, Art 70; Constitution of the United Nations Educational, Scientific and Cultural Organization (adopted 16 November 1945, entered into force 4 November 1946), 4 UNTS 275, Rule 38.

[50] *See Nuclear Weapons in Armed Conflict* (n 42) para 20.

[51] *Namibia* (n 46), p 44, para 89.

[52] *Questions of Interpretation and Application of the 1971 Montreal Convention arising from the Aerial Incident at Lockerbie (Libyan Arab Jamahiriya v United States), Provisional Measures, ICJ Reports 1992*, p 115, paras 39–41; and *Accordance with International Law of the Unilateral Declaration of Independence by the Provisional Institutions of Self-Government of Kosovo, Advisory Opinion, ICJ Reports 2010*, p 403, para 85.

In addition to review by an international court, the possibility exists for national and regional courts to invalidate, or find unlawful, measures taken under domestic law in the implementation of a decision of an international organization. This may be because the measure does not comply with domestic law, but it may also be based on the failure of a challenged measure to comply with international legal standards. Because such acts reflect, or even mirror verbatim, decisions of the organization, in practice these constitute a review of the decision of the international organization.

The most prominent of these have involved decisions of the Security Council, which are binding on all UN members. For example, in the *Kadi II* judgment, the Court of Justice of the European Union (CJEU) had to consider the imposition of targeted sanctions against a person purported to have links with Al Qaeda, in implementation of the Security Council's resolutions on combatting terrorism. It concluded that the imposition of targeted sanctions was inconsistent with Mr Kadi's fundamental rights due to insufficient evidence that he was in fact involved with Al Qaeda.[53] A similar question was decided in favour of the applicant in the *Nada v Switzerland* judgment of the ECtHR.[54]

CASE SPOTLIGHT ***Legal Consequences for States of the Continued Presence of South Africa in Namibia (South West Africa) notwithstanding Security Council Resolution 276 (1970), Advisory Opinion, ICJ Reports 1971*, p 16**

The *Namibia* advisory opinion of the ICJ concerned South Africa's claim that, despite several Security Council resolutions to the contrary, it was still entitled under the Mandate conferred upon it by the League of Nations to govern Namibia (South West Africa) and impose the apartheid system within it. The Security Council referred the matter to the ICJ with a question that required the Court to provide an interpretation of Security Council Resolution 276 which had not been passed under Chapter VII, the section of the Charter under which it is stated that resolutions are binding on all member States.

The Court, though vehemently denying that it possessed a power of judicial review over Security Council resolutions, concluded that Resolution 276 was adopted in conformity with the relevant provisions of the Charter, and that, given the presence of mandatory terms within the text of the resolution itself, it created binding obligations requiring States to recognize South Africa's presence in Namibia as unlawful (para 114).

The question of whether the Court may review the resolutions of the Security Council remains live. See further J Sloan and G Hernández, 'The Role of the International Court of Justice in Developing the Institutional Law of the United Nations' in CJ Tams and J Sloan (eds), *The Development of International Law by the International Court of Justice* (OUP, 2012), 197, 224–32; D Akande, 'The International Court of Justice and the Security Council: Is there Room for Judicial Control of Decisions of the Political Organs of the United Nations?' (1997) 46 ICLQ 309; JE Álvarez, 'Judging the Security Council' (1996) 90 AJIL 28.

[53] See Joined Cases C-584/10 P, C-593/10 P and C-595/10 P, *Commission, Council, and United Kingdom v Yassin Abdullah Kadi (Kadi II)* (July 2013) (ECJ).

[54] *Nada v Switzerland* App No 10593/08 (ECtHR) [2012] ECHR 1691.

6.5.3.3 **Non-binding recommendations, determinations, and declarations**

In determining whether a given decision of an international organization may be binding on an addressee, one must first consider whether the constituent instrument of the organization bestows on it the power to take such binding decisions without the consent of that specific addressee. A few organs of international organizations possess limited powers to do so, as consented to by their member States when constituting the organization. Examples include:

- The UN Security Council, which may bind all UN members in relation to matters falling within its primary responsibility to maintain international peace and security.[55]
- The International Civil Aviation Organization, which has the power to establish rules regulating aircraft flying over the high seas.[56]
- The World Health Assembly, which may adopt regulations which are binding on all member States of the WHO, unless they opt out.[57]
- European Union institutions, which, usually when working together, may enact legislation (regulations, directives) that binds all members.[58]

Secondly, one must examine the text of a decision itself to determine whether it demonstrates an intention, on the part of the organ, for the decision to be binding. This might be through express reference to the power to do so in its constituent instrument, but may also be through the text of the decision itself and whether it evinces clearly the intention to issue a binding decision.

Many organs of international organizations lack the power to issue binding decisions on members, though may issue other types of instruments. The UN General Assembly is a prominent example of a body only permitted to issue *recommendations*, usually in the form of resolutions, to members on matters within the scope of the UN.[59] Even the Security Council, which does possess the power to pass binding resolutions under Chapter VII of the Charter, can pass resolutions which are not binding, under Chapter VI.[60] Resolutions may reflect existing international law, of course, but they are not regarded as being law-creative in themselves.[61] Even if the rather grandiose term 'Declaration' is used instead, such an appellation does not in itself change the non-binding nature of a resolution.[62] The same would go for a code of conduct, which

[55] UN Charter, Art 25.

[56] Convention on International Civil Aviation (adopted 7 December 1944, entered into force 4 April 1947), 15 UNTS 295, Art 12.

[57] See Constitution of the WHO (n 49) Arts 21–2.

[58] See Art 16 of the Lisbon Treaty (n 7), and Art 238 of the Treaty on the Functioning of the European Union (adopted 13 December 2007, entered into force 1 December 2009) [2008] OJ C115/47.

[59] See Arts 10–14 Charter.

[60] The range of the Council's resolutions is covered in Chapter 14, Section 14.5.

[61] *South West Africa (Ethiopia v South Africa; Liberia v South Africa), Second Phase, ICJ Reports 1966*, p 6, para 98. See also K Skubiszewski, 'Recommendations of the United Nations and Municipal Courts' (1972–3) 46 BYBIL 353.

[62] See UN Office of Legal Affairs, 'Chapter VI: Selected Legal Opinions of the Secretariats of the United Nations and Related Intergovernmental Organizations' (1981) UNJY 149: '[i]n the practice of the United Nations a Declaration is a formal and solemn instrument suitable for those occasions when principles considered to be of special importance are being enunciated. . . . there is legally no distinction between a declaration and a recommendation which is less formal.'

provides guidance to actors as to preferred or best practice, without prescribing such conduct as being binding;[63] or determinations, which consist of findings of fact and possible legal characterizations of these, without being regarded as legally binding.

CASE SPOTLIGHT ***East Timor (Portugal v Australia), Jurisdiction and Admissibility, ICJ Reports 1995*, p 90**

The 1995 judgment of the ICJ in *East Timor* involved Portugal, the former colonial power in East Timor, filing a claim against Australia in relation to the latter State's conclusion of treaties with Indonesia, which had been occupying East Timor since 1975. Though the case is best known in relation to the standing of Portugal to claim on the basis of the breach of an obligation *erga omnes*, the *East Timor* judgment was also invaluable in clarifying the nature of determinations of international organizations. Portugal had requested that the Court declare as binding various statements made in resolutions of the General Assembly and Security Council that East Timor was a non-self-governing territory with Portugal as the administering power. This was met by a flat rejection by the Court:

> it cannot be inferred from the sole fact that a number of resolutions refer to Portugal as the administering Power of East Timor that they intended to establish an obligation on third States to treat exclusively with Portugal. The Court is not persuaded, however, that the relevant resolutions went so far (103–4).

Though the Court took pains to state that its decision was without prejudice as to whether the resolutions under discussion could be binding, it considered that they could not be taken as 'givens' in establishing the scope of the dispute between Portugal and Australia. The judgment demonstrates the challenge in ascribing binding force to resolutions of international organizations, which must be considered on a case-by-case basis and not in a blanket manner.

Though recommendations, determinations, and declarations may not be binding as such, they cannot be regarded as devoid of legal effect: some constituent instruments oblige members to have regard, in good faith, to such non-binding decisions when deciding upon their own course of action. This is particularly the case with specialized institutions dealing with technical or scientific questions, such as the WTO Agreement on Sanitary and Phytosanitary Measures, which in its Article 3 encourages members to base their sanitary and phytosanitary (SPS) measures on standards adopted by other international organizations. A presumption exists that measures in conformity with such standards comply with the relevant WTO provisions.[64] Such non-binding decisions or resolutions may even constitute an authoritative interpretation of the constituent instrument of the organization, which cannot be ignored by its members.[65] As such, though not formally binding, the organization and its organs may provide a measure of

[63] The OECD, in particular, regularly issues codes of conduct and other guides which, without being binding, are not devoid of legal significance: for an overview, see H Ascensio and N Bonucci (eds), *Le pouvoir normatif de l'OCDE* (Pedone, 2013).

[64] A presumption that was tested in the WTO, *Beef Hormone case—Report of the Appellate Body* (16 January 1998) WT/DS26/AB/R and WT/DS48/AB/R.

[65] See GJH van Hoof, *Rethinking the Sources of International Law* (Kluwer, 1983).

normative guidance to its members as to what course of action to take in relation to the functions of that organization.

In practice, the non-binding status of a decision of an international organization is not determinative. A non-binding decision may refer to binding obligations within existing international law, or it might be embraced by States such that, in time, it is taken as reflecting customary international law.[66] As the ICJ noted in the *Nuclear Weapons* advisory opinion:

> General Assembly resolutions, even if they are not binding, may sometimes have normative value. They can, in certain circumstances, provide evidence important for establishing the existence of a rule or the emergence of an *opinio juris*. To establish whether this is true of a given General Assembly resolution, it is necessary to look at its content and the conditions of its adoption; it is also necessary to see whether an *opinio juris* exists as to its normative character. Or a series of resolutions may show the gradual evolution of the *opinio juris* required for the establishment of a new rule.[67]

In this respect, international organizations, in particular in their capacity as a forum for discussion and debate between States, may constitute an important part of the international lawmaking process, even if certain of their decisions are not formally binding.

6.6 Responsibility of international organizations

6.6.1 Background

One of the more settled principles of international law is that actors who commit a violation of international law are obliged to make reparations in one form or another to the injured party.[68] As is the focus of Chapter 10, this principle has long applied to States; and given the consequences of a distinct legal personality described earlier, it makes logical sense to extend the principle to international organizations.[69] However, as this chapter has explained, the responsibility of an international organization largely depends on the constituent instrument of that organization, which dictates the form of the organization and its ability to take decisions independently of its members. In addition to these, we must consider the questions of control which arise when an organization acts in concert with its members, when members act at the behest of the organization, or when members lend the organization assistance, whether in the form of material resources or placing an organ of a State at the disposal of the organization.

[66] The most obvious examples being the Universal Declaration of Human Rights, UNGA Res 217(III)A (10 December 1948) (adopted by 48 votes to none; 8 abstentions), and the Declaration of Principles of International Law concerning Friendly Relations Among States, GA Res 2625 (XXV) (24 October 1970) (adopted unanimously).

[67] *Legality of the Threat or Use of Nuclear Weapons, Advisory Opinion, ICJ Reports 1996*, 254–5, para 70. See also *Military and Paramilitary Activities in and against Nicaragua (Nicaragua v United States), Merits, Judgment, ICJ Reports 1986*, p 14, 99 *et seq.*

[68] *The Factory at Chorzów (Claim for Indemnity) (Germany v Poland), Jurisdiction, 1927, PCIJ, Ser A, No 8*, p 5, 21.

[69] ILC, 'Articles on the Responsibility of States for Internationally Wrongful Acts' in Report of the International Law Commission on the Work of its 53rd Session, UN Doc A/56/10 Chap IV (2001) GAOR 56th Session Supp 10, Art 2.

HISTORICAL BACKGROUND The International Tin Council (ITC)

For decades, international organizations rarely took action that could engage their international responsibility. However, the spectacular collapse in 1985 of the ITC, an international organization based in London, led to a spate of litigation in the English courts as to the nature and scope of the responsibility of the ITC.

The ITC was an international organization established to regulate the price of tin on world markets. It was empowered to borrow money in order to 'buffer stock' tin, buying the material when prices were low and selling it when prices were high. However, the emergence of aluminium as a viable substitute led to a permanent drop in the price of tin, and the ITC incurred liabilities of £900 million, thus becoming insolvent. Creditors, in particular commercial banks, faced enormous losses, and tin-producing firms around the world were faced with collapse, closing dozens of mines.

All such parties turned to the member States of the ITC for redress, all of which disclaimed any responsibility for the ITC's debts or demise. Actions were filed in the English courts (and elsewhere) seeking to establish the liability of the ITC for its debts. All these actions were dismissed by the House of Lords in *JH Rayner v Department of Trade and Industry* [1988] 3 All ER 257 (HL) (at the appeal phase, [1988] 3 All ER 257 (CA)) on the grounds that the ITC, headquartered in London and possessing domestic personality under English law, was an organization autonomous from its members, and that this fact precluded their liability. This finding shows that the relationship between an organization and its members can have significant repercussions.

For further reading, see IA Mallory, 'Conduct Unbecoming: The Collapse of the International Tin Agreement' (1990) 5 American University ILR 835.

6.6.2 The Articles on the Responsibility of International Organizations (ARIO)

The seminal ITC litigation was one of the reasons motivating the ILC to consider the issue of the responsibility of international organizations, culminating in its adoption in 2011 of the Articles on the Responsibility of International Organizations (ARIO).[70] These are modelled closely on the Commission's earlier work on the law of State responsibility.[71] However, the ARIO have come under substantial criticism on a number of grounds.[72] These include:

- for seeking unduly to apply all-encompassing rules and principles to international organizations which differ substantially in the nature and scope of their mandate and functions;

[70] See ARIO (n 2), ch V. [71] See Chapter 10, Section 10.1.

[72] See, e.g., J d'Aspremont, 'The Articles on the Responsibility of International Organizations: Magnifying the Fissures in the Law on State Responsibility' (2012) 9 International Organizations Law Review 15; M Hlavkova, 'Legal Responsibility of International Organizations in International Law: Summary of the International Law Discussion Group meeting held at Chatham House' (Chatham House, 10 February 2011). See also the tepid, and at times hostile, comments received from international organizations themselves: ILC, 'Responsibility of International Organizations: Comments and observations received from international organizations', UN Doc A/CN.4/637 (14 February 2011).

- for relying too heavily on the law of State responsibility, despite the fundamental differences between a State and an international organization; and
- for their lack of grounding in relevant practice, and thus representing less an exercise in codification but in fact one based on progressive development, mostly by analogy.

The ILC has responded to many of these criticisms in its 2011 Commentary to the ARIO.[73]

Though it is true that international organizations vary significantly in their form and functions, their entitlement to legal personality suggests that a few very basic principles ought to apply, such as the general principle of liability for one's internationally wrongful acts elucidated in *Chorzów Factory* (found in Article 3 ARIO) or the notion that internationally wrongful conduct must be attributed to an international actor (found in Article 4 ARIO).[74] In addition, the ILC took care to insert a *lex specialis* clause that preserves, to an extent, the specific regimes created by each international organization's constituent instrument. In this respect, the ILC's attempt in the ARIO to accommodate the wide range of international organizations may not fully settle the regime which applies to them, but provides an important focal point for consideration which may in turn shape future practice.

CONTEMPORARY DEBATES How Can International Responsibility be Shared between an International Organization and a State?

International legal personality assumes the capacity to have rights and obligations under international law. The classical paradigm of responsibility, as adopted by the ILC in the ARISWA and ARIO, is relatively straightforward: actors remain responsible for the acts that they themselves have committed, or at least are attributable to them.

However, with respect to concerted operations committed by multiple actors, especially when international organizations act in concert with their member States, the clarity of attribution as explained prior becomes live and convoluted. In such cases, member States are implementing the decisions of the organization, or perhaps even acting under its operational control; or one member State is leading and coordinating the acts of other members.

One is the basic question as to whether responsibility can be separated at all. Can one break down a complex operation into discrete acts and apportion responsibility accordingly? Or should all involved actors bear joint responsibility for the unlawful act? Who has the authority to decide how responsibility should be borne?

A recent key example of shared responsibility arose in *The Netherlands v Mustafić-Mujić et al* and *Nuhanović v Netherlands* HR 6 September 2013, NJ 2013 (*Hoge Raad*, Dutch Supreme Court). These are significant as the applicants were claiming against the Netherlands for the acts of its peacekeeping forces ('Dutchbat'), which were formally under UN operational control. The Dutch Supreme Court, guided by the ARIO, concluded that the wrongful

[73] See ARIO (n 2) 69–71.

[74] Jan Klabbers (n 13) 310 *et seq* has suggested that this approach presupposes not a separate *personality* as such, but the *agency* of an international organization entails its autonomy as a rational or even moral agent, capable of taking decisions on its own.

acts of Dutchbat could be subject to 'dual attribution', to both the Netherlands and United Nations, and that even if the UN had had effective control over Dutchbat, this did not automatically mean that it had exclusive responsibility for its wrongful acts. In *Urgenda v the Netherlands* (Dutch Supreme Court, Case No 19/00135, 20 December 2019), moreover, the Dutch Supreme Court held that though the obligation to prevent climate change was shared, the Netherlands' share could be treated as *divisible* and thus calculated at a 25 per cent reduction from 1990 levels.

There remains a considerable grey area around the extent and application of shared responsibility, though recently published research in the area may clarify the issues: see, for example, A Nollkaemper, J d'Aspremont, C Ahlborn, B Boutin, N Nedeski, and I Plakokefalos (coll D Jacobs), 'Guiding Principles on Shared Responsibility in International Law' (2020) 31 EJIL 15.

International organizations take decisions and operate in a distinct framework that makes them dependent on States; their practice requires that particular attention be given to the allocation of responsibility between international organizations and their member States.[75] The general rule is that the conduct of organs and agents of an organization, when acting in the performance of their functions, are regarded as those of the organization (Article 6 ARIO). However, the question is considerably more complex when faced with the fact that international organizations usually possess few enforcement organs and must often operate through their members; this is particularly so when members place their organs at the disposal of the international organization.[76] In such cases, though the organ is effectively 'lent' to the organization, it nonetheless remains an organ of the lending State as the State retains a measure of strategic control over that organ. The classic example is of UN peacekeeping organs, which are subsidiary organs of the UN and act under the control of the Security Council and General Assembly, but are invariably composed of troops contributed by States, which retain jurisdiction and some degree of residual control over their armed forces. Article 7 ARIO seeks to address this issue, concluding that the act of an organ placed at the disposal of an international organization is considered an act of that organization 'if the organization exercises effective control over that conduct'. As such, the ILC considered the effectiveness of factual control exercised by the organization as determinative.

[75] An important project was conducted at the University of Amsterdam, called 'Shared Responsibility in International Law'. The project has led to a collection of articles and three edited volumes seeking to consider relevant theory and practice in the field: see, in particular, A Nollkaemper and D Jacobs, 'Shared Responsibility in International Law: A Conceptual Framework' (2013) 32 Michigan JIL 359; A Nollkaemper and I Plakokefalos (eds), *Principles of Shared Responsibility in International Law* (CUP, 2014); A Nollkaemper and D Jacobs (eds), *Distribution of Responsibilities in International Law* (CUP, 2015); A Nollkaemper and I Plakokefalos (eds), *The Practice of Shared Responsibility in International Law* (CUP, 2017); and A Nollkaemper, J d'Aspremont, C Ahlborn, B Boutin, N Nedeski, and I Plakokefalos (coll D Jacobs), 'Guiding Principles on Shared Responsibility in International Law' (2020) 31 EJIL 15.

[76] The ILC, in the Commentary to Art 7 ARIO (n 2), p 20, para 3, uses the example of the model contribution agreement relating to military contingents placed at the disposal of the United Nations by its member States.

Returning to the peacekeeping example, it means that the organization must have actual operational control over the specific act the legality of which is impugned. In this respect, the ILC broke explicitly with the test of 'ultimate authority or control' that was applied by the ECtHR to declare inadmissible applications against troop-contributing States in *Behrami v France* and *Saramati v France, Germany and Norway*.[77] The ECtHR's position was untenable, in that it would permit States to retain control over their troops within their national chain of command, yet it would entirely exclude liability for any of their actions.[78] As such, it is to be welcomed that the ECtHR has since moved somewhat away from this finding. In *Al-Jedda v United Kingdom* the Court expressly referenced the 'effective control' standard used by the ILC in the ARIO, which suggests that it had considered the ILC's arguments against *Behrami and Saramati*. However, it should be noted that the Court made a point to distinguish, and not to overrule, its earlier decision in *Behrami and Saramati*.[79]

Given the high likelihood of international organizations working in concert with member States or other international organizations, the sections of the ARIO where joint, collective, or supportive acts are envisaged become increasingly important. As with most of the ARIO, the ILC has sought to extend much of the practice relating to State responsibility into the realm of international organizations. Thus, international organizations which provide material aid or assistance to another actor in the commission of an internationally wrongful act are themselves committing a breach (Article 14 ARIO). They are also responsible if they direct or control, and in particular if they coerce, another actor into committing a breach (Articles 15–16 ARIO), though coercion is very rare in international law. States are equally responsible for most of these breaches if they aid or assist, direct or control, or coerce an international organization (Articles 58–61 ARIO).

Finally, an international organization may not circumvent international law by passing a decision binding its members to act in a manner that would constitute a breach of international law if the organization were to commit the act itself. According to Article 17(1) ARIO, the very decision binding its members to act would constitute a breach of international law. Nor may an international organization authorize its members to act in a manner that would constitute a breach of international law if the organization were to commit the act itself. In this case, Article 17(2) ARIO requires both the authorization of an organization to its member State, and for the member States to take action pursuant to that authorization, for the organization to be found in breach of circumventing its obligations. The reverse is also true: member States may not circumvent responsibility for breaches of their own obligations simply by causing the organization to perform an act which, if performed by the member States, would have been a breach of their

[77] *Behrami v France* and *Saramati v France, Germany and Norway* App Nos 71412/01 and 78166/01 (ECtHR, 2 May 2007) (2007) 45 EHRR 85.

[78] See M Milanović and J Papić, 'As Bad as it Gets: The European Court of Human Rights' *Behrami and Saramati* Decision and General International Law' (2009) 58 ICLQ 267.

[79] *Al-Jedda v United Kingdom* App No 27021/08 (ECtHR, 7 July 2011) (2011) 53 EHRR 23, para 84.

obligations.[80] As such, member States cannot transfer functions to an international organization simply in order to shield themselves from international responsibility.[81]

6.7 The United Nations system

It is fitting to conclude this chapter with a review of the UN, the world's pre-eminent international organization.[82] The UN makes a strong claim to universality: only the Holy See and a few entities whose statehood is contested (such as Kosovo, Palestine, and Taiwan, all discussed in Chapter 5) are not members of the UN.

The UN's purposes are particularly broad, with Article 1 of the UN Charter listing:

- the maintenance of international peace and security and the taking of effective collective measures to that end;
- the development of friendly relations between nations based on the equal rights and self-determination of peoples;
- the promotion of international cooperation regarding problems of an economic, social, cultural, or humanitarian character;
- the encouragement of respect for human rights, without distinction as to race, sex, language, or religion.

The breadth of these purposes touches upon nearly all aspects of international life, and is coupled with the UN's explicit aim to be a centre for harmonizing the actions of nations in the attainment of these common ends. What is more, Article 103 of the Charter contains a so-called 'supremacy clause': obligations for member States under the Charter 'shall prevail' over any competing legal obligations. This supremacy clause elevates UN Charter obligations above other treaty obligations, and further buttresses its claim to pre-eminence among international organizations.[83]

6.7.1 Institutional structure

In addition to listing its six principal organs, the UN Charter provides for the creation of subsidiary organs and a number of semi-autonomous specialized agencies operating under the aegis of the organization. These are briefly mapped out in turn.

[80] ARIO (n 2), Art 61.

[81] *Bosphorus Hava Yollari Turizm ve Ticaret Anonim Sirketi v Ireland* App No 45036/98 (ECtHR, 30 June 2005), 157–8: in such cases, 'the State is considered to retain Convention liability in respect of treaty commitments subsequent to the entry into force of the [ECHR]'.

[82] Though this brief introduction is useful for the newcomer, thorough accounts of the United Nations abound, with a recent contribution being the magisterial R Higgins, P Webb, D Akande, S Sivakumaran, and J Sloan (eds), *Oppenheim's International Law: United Nations* (OUP, 2017). Somewhat more accessible is that of S Chesterman, I Johnstone, and DM Malone, *Law and Practice of the United Nations: Documents and Commentary* (2nd edn, OUP, 2016).

[83] R Liivoja, 'The Scope of the Supremacy Clause of the United Nations Charter' (2008) 57 ICLQ 583; H Kelsen, 'Conflicts between Obligations under the Charter of the United Nations and Obligations under other International Agreements' (1948–9) 1 U Pittsburgh LR 284; R Kolb, 'Does Article 103 of the Charter of the United Nations Apply only to Decisions or also to Authorizations adopted by the Security Council?' (2004) 64 ZaöRV 21.

6.7.1.1 **Organs of the United Nations**

There are two types of organs within the UN under Article 7 of the Charter. Foremost, there are six principal organs under Article 7(1):

(i) the General Assembly;
(ii) the Security Council;
(iii) the Economic and Social Council (ECOSOC);
(iv) the Trusteeship Council;
(v) the International Court of Justice; and
(vi) the Secretariat.

In addition to these, under Article 7(2), subsidiary organs can be created by the principal organs, many of which have been created to fulfil specific functions.[84] Prominent subsidiary organs created by the General Assembly include the Human Rights Council, the ILC, the Office of the UN High Commissioner for Refugees (UNHCR), and UNICEF. The Security Council created the ad hoc tribunals in respect of the former Yugoslavia and Rwanda, as well as the UN Compensation Commission (UNCC) in respect of Iraq. Under ECOSOC, one finds functional commissions such as the Commission on the Status of Women and the Commission on Sustainable Development, as well as a range of standing bodies and expert bodies such as the Commission on Transnational Corporations, the UN Conference on Trade and Development (UNCTAD), and the Committee on Natural Resources.

6.7.1.1.1 ***The General Assembly***

The General Assembly is the plenary organ of the UN as, under Article 9, it is the only principal organ in which all 193 UN members are represented and have an equal vote. The Assembly meets annually, in regular sessions held in the autumn, to discuss the broad range of matters falling within the scope of the Charter (Article 10; for a non-exhaustive list, see Articles 11–17). The Assembly has also convened ten emergency special sessions.[85] In practice, much of its work is located within six main committees, where the bulk of substantive discussion and decision-making takes place.[86]

The decisions of the General Assembly, called 'resolutions', are passed either by simple majority or, on 'important questions' such as the admission of a new member, by two-thirds majority (Article 18). They are not binding, save those which are in internal administrative matters such as establishing the organization's budget (Article 17).[87]

[84] See D Sarooshi, 'The Legal Framework Governing United Nations Subsidiary Organs' (1996) 67 BYBIL 413.

[85] In relation to Hungary in 1956; the DR Congo in 1960; the Middle East in 1956, 1958, 1967, 1980, 1982, and 1997, the last of which is a 'rolling' session on Palestine which is still ongoing; Afghanistan in 1980; and Namibia in 1981.

[86] These are: Disarmament and International Security; Economic and Financial; Social, Humanitarian and Cultural; Special Political and Decolonization; Administrative and Budgetary; and Legal Affairs. There are also a number of procedural committees, the most well known being the Credentials Committee (which assesses the credentials of member States' representatives to the organization).

[87] See *Certain Expenses* (n 44).

As described earlier, some the Assembly's resolutions are regarded as reflecting customary international law, or may yet be influential on future State practice which might lead to the formation of a new customary legal rule.[88]

6.7.1.1.2 ***The Security Council***

The UN Security Council, which sits continuously, is the closest equivalent to an executive organ. The Council is composed of five permanent members (China, France, Russia, the UK, and the USA) and ten members elected by the General Assembly for two-year terms (Article 23). The ten non-permanent members are elected bearing in mind geographical representation: five seats are allocated to Africa and Asia, two to Latin America, two to West European and other States, and one to Eastern Europe. Though each of its members has one vote, under Article 27 the 'concurring' vote of all five permanent members is needed in non-procedural matters. In effect, this means that the permanent members wield a veto with respect to all substantive decisions, though it bears noting that in practice abstention is not deemed to constitute a veto.[89]

The Council has primary responsibility over issues relating to the maintenance of international peace and security (Article 24); its practice in this respect is covered in Chapter 14.[90] The Council may also make recommendations to the General Assembly with respect to the admission, suspension, and expulsion of members (Articles 4–6). Judges of the ICJ are elected both by the Assembly and the Council, though with no veto (Article 4, Statute of the ICJ). Perhaps most importantly, the Charter may only be amended with the support of all the permanent members of the Council, in addition to two-thirds of the General Assembly (Article 108 Charter).

Though the Security Council has no legislative powers, it enjoys a unique power in that its decisions—but not its recommendations—are binding upon all member States (Article 25).[91] This power is not unlimited; the Council cannot adopt general measures as would a legislature, such as ordering States to protect against climate change; it is generally used in response to a specific situation, such as the ordering of military or peacekeeping action in one State. However, in recent years, the Council has adopted various binding resolutions, such as Resolutions 1373 (2001) and 1540 (2004) in relation to international terrorism, which have a 'quasi-legislative' character,[92] as they call

[88] On this point, see J Castañeda, *Legal Effects of United Nations Resolutions* (Columbia UP, 1969); K Skubiszewski, 'Resolutions on the UN General Assembly and Evidence of Custom' in *International Law at the Time of its Codification. Essays in Honour of Roberto Ago* (Giuffrè, 1987), 503; JA Barberis, 'Les resolutions des organisations internationales en tant que source du droit des gens' in U Beyerlin, *Recht zwischen Umbruch und Bewahrung—Festschrift für Rudolf Bernhardt* (Springer, 1995), 21. For examples see n 66.

[89] See *Namibia* (n 46) paras 20–2. See also A Stavropoulos, 'The Practice of Voluntary Abstentions by Permanent Members of the Security Council under Article 27(3) of the Charter' (1967) 61 AJIL 737.

[90] For some general reading, see G Arangio-Ruiz, 'On the Security Council's Law-Making' (2000) 83 Rivista di Diritto Internazionale 609; DL Bosco, *Five to Rule them All: The UN Security Council and the Making of the Modern World* (OUP, 2009); and V Lowe, A Roberts, J Welsh, and D Zaum (eds), *The United Nations Security Council and War: The Evolution of Thought and Practice since 1945* (OUP, 2008).

[91] See, on the limits of this power, A Tzanakopoulos, *Disobeying the Security Council: Countermeasures against Wrongful Sanctions* (OUP, 2011); and K Doehring, 'Unlawful Resolutions of the Security Council and their Legal Consequences' (1997) 1 Max Planck YBUNL 91.

[92] See S Talmon, 'The Security Council as World Legislature?' (2005) 99 AJIL 175; see also JE Álvarez, 'Hegemonic International Law Revisited' (2003) 97 AJIL 873.

upon States to establish general measures and are accompanied by the establishment of committees designed to monitor member State compliance.

CONTEMPORARY DEBATES The Exercise of the Veto and Security Council Reform

The veto given to the permanent members of the Security Council was a reflection of prevailing power relations in 1945. The Soviet Union, in particular, had insisted on the right to veto as a condition for its participation in the UN system, and the Soviet Union (now Russia) has exercised the veto most frequently, followed closely by the USA. Historically, the veto aimed, in part, to avoid the fate of the League of Nations, which suffered fatally from the non-participation of the USA and Soviet Union from the outset and the withdrawal of Germany, Japan, and Italy. The other three permanent members, China, the UK, and France, have exercised the veto relatively infrequently, though it should be noted that China has a preference for abstention on resolutions not directly related to its national interests.

The Council's permanent membership has attracted much criticism in recent years, leading to calls for reform. Important countries in the Global South such as Brazil and India are excluded, as well as substantial financial contributors such as Germany and Japan, the principal defeated powers after World War II. These have banded together as the 'G4', arguing for their inclusion as veto-wielding permanent members alongside two African members. A substantial group of States have opposed the G4 through the 'Uniting for Consensus' (UfC) group, proposing instead an intermediate category of permanent/semi-permanent members, without the power of the veto. No serious proposal has since been tabled which would abolish the veto or remove any current permanent members, though there have been calls to restrict the use of the veto in situations of humanitarian catastrophe (see Chapter 14, Section 14.4.2). However, in part due to public outcries over the use of the veto in relation to armed conflicts in Ukraine and Gaza, a provocative recent proposal has suggested that strategic interpretation of the Charter might spur some 'non-amendment reform' and enable the UN to limit the scope of the veto: see OA Hathaway, M Mills, and H Zimmerman, 'Crisis and Change at the United Nations: Non-Amendment Reform and Institutional Evolution' (2025) 46 Michigan Journal of International Law 1.

6.7.1.1.3 ***Other principal organs***

Economic and Social Council

ECOSOC is responsible, as its name might suggest, for economic and social matters within the organization. ECOSOC is composed of fifty-four members elected from the Assembly for three-year terms (Article 61 Charter). Encompassing a broad range of activities, ECOSOC may make non-binding recommendations to the General Assembly, relevant specialized agencies, or directly to member States (Article 62 Charter).

ECOSOC has particular responsibility for international human rights, and it was active in preparing the major human rights covenants (the ICCPR and ICESCR) and other treaties. In addition, ECOSOC also coordinates the activity of the UN, with a wide number of specialized agencies with functions falling under its range of activities, such as UNESCO.

The Secretariat

The UN Secretariat supports the work of the UN organs (save for the ICJ, with its own Registry). Secretariat staff are meant to be wholly independent of national governments and may only seek or receive instructions from the UN itself (Article 100). They are, in this regard, a sort of international civil service.[93]

The Secretariat is headed by the Secretary-General, who is appointed by the General Assembly upon the unanimous recommendation of the Security Council (Article 97). They (regrettably, no woman has yet held the post[94]) discharges various administrative functions; and, importantly, the Secretary-General may bring to the attention of the Security Council any matter which may threaten international peace and security (Article 99), and may exercise good offices to resolve or to contain international crises.[95] The influence of the Secretary-General has been somewhat dependent on the views and outlook of the particular office-holder.[96] Since 2017, the current office-holder has been António Guterres, of Portugal.

The Trusteeship Council

The Trusteeship Council was set up to supervise the 'trust territories' created under Chapter XII of the Charter. Trust territories comprised territories either under a mandate of the League of Nations or detached from enemy States after World War II.

Though the Charter envisaged the voluntary placement of a territory into the trusteeship system (Article 77), this mechanism was never used. Namibia (South West Africa), discussed earlier in Section 6.5.3.2, was never placed by South Africa into the trusteeship system. The ICJ found in an advisory opinion that while there was no legal obligation in the Charter to transfer a mandated territory into a trust territory, the obligations under the mandate agreement signed between South Africa and the League of Nations were still valid.[97] Trust territories gradually gained their independence; the last, Palau, gained UN membership in 1994, at which point the Trusteeship Council suspended its operations.

The International Court of Justice

The principal judicial organ of the UN, the judgments of the ICJ have proven highly influential on the development of international law, as the ample references to its judgments in this book demonstrate. The Court, and its practice, are addressed in more detail in Chapter 12, Section 12.3.2.

[93] See S Schwebel, 'The International Character of the Secretariat of the United Nations' in S Schwebel (ed), *Justice in International Law* (CUP, 1994), 248.

[94] It should be noted that during the 2016 campaign for a new Secretary-General, considerable effort was mounted to elect a female Secretary-General, but it was ultimately unsuccessful.

[95] TM Franck and G Nolte, 'The Good Offices Function of the UN Secretary-General' in A Roberts and B Kingsbury (eds), *United Nations, Divided World* (OUP, 1994), 143.

[96] A good collection of essays on the role of the Secretary-General is S Chesterman (ed), *Secretary or General? The UN Secretary-General in World Politics* (CUP, 2007).

[97] *International Status of South West Africa, Advisory Opinion, ICJ Reports 1950*, p 128.

6.7.1.2 Specialized agencies and the United Nations

Unlike the subsidiary organs, specialized agencies are independent international organizations in their own right, established through a separate treaty and brought into relationship with the UN by means of a specific agreement (see Articles 57 and 63 Charter). As befits their name, specialized agencies operate in defined fields but, like the UN, their responsibilities and membership are global in scope. There are currently sixteen specialized agencies, some of which predate the UN, others of which were launched more or less contemporaneously with it, and others which have emerged over time in response to the interests of States:

1. the International Telecommunications Union (1865);
2. the Universal Postal Union (1874);
3. the International Labour Organization (1919);
4. the International Bank for Reconstruction and Development (the 'World Bank Group') (1944);[98]
5. the International Monetary Fund (1945);
6. the Food and Agriculture Organization (1945);
7. the United Nations Educational, Scientific and Cultural Organization (1945);
8. the International Civil Aviation Organization (1947);
9. the World Health Organization (1948);
10. the World Meteorological Organization (1950);
11. the International Atomic Energy Agency (1957);
12. the International Maritime Organisation (1959);
13. the United Nations Industrial Development Organization (1966);
14. the World Intellectual Property Organization (1967);
15. the International Fund for Agricultural Development (1974); and
16. the World Tourism Organization.

6.8 Conclusion

International organizations are now an indispensable feature of the international landscape. Though they vary significantly in their structure, functions, and powers, they facilitate cooperation on an immense range of subjects, allowing for States to pool their expertise and resources to resolve problems of global collective concern through a more or less permanent forum. In this respect, the potential to resolve problems through international institutions retains an enduring appeal to States, and seems to suggest that they will continue, when they feel it is appropriate, to establish new multilateral organizations through which to focus their collaboration.

[98] Several agencies are affiliated to the World Bank Group: the International Finance Corporation (1956); the International Development Association (1960); and the Multilateral Investment Guarantee Agency (1988).

Further reading

JE Álvarez, *International Organizations as Law-Makers* (OUP, 2005).

A detailed study of the influence of international organizations on the development of international law.

CF Amerasinghe, *Principles of the Institutional Law of International Organizations* (2nd edn, CUP, 2005).

A classic reference work, this book seeks to capture the overarching principles which apply across international institutions.

B Conforti and C Focarelli (eds), *The Law and Practice of the United Nations* (5th edn, Brill, 2016).

A practical overview of the law and practice of the UN, from its inception to the present, with a specific focus on contemporary problems.

R Higgins, P Webb, D Akande, S Sivakumaran, and J Sloan (eds), *Oppenheim's International Law: United Nations* (OUP, 2017).

A multi-authored compendium of the UN's legal and institutional practice, with a focus on the day-to-day realities of UN practice.

J Klabbers, *An Introduction to International Organizations Law* (3rd edn, CUP, 2015).

A concise overview of the law relating to international organizations.

E Lagrange and J-M Sorel (eds), *Traité de droit des organisations internationales* (LGDJ, 2013).

A modern classic, the leading French-language study on the law of international organizations.

P Sands and P Klein (eds), *Bowett's Law of International Institutions* (6th edn, Sweet & Maxwell, 2012).

A comprehensive, detailed resource of great utility to both academic and practitioner audiences.

HG Schermers and N Blokker, *International Institutional Law: Unity within Diversity* (6th edn, Martinus Nijhoff, 2018).

This monumental compendium captures a range of practice and the immense breadth of international organizations.

B Simma, D-E Khan, G Nolte, and A Paulus (eds), *The Charter of the United Nations: A Commentary* (4th edn, OUP, 2024).

Freshly revised for 2024, systematic, article-by-article commentary on the Charter of the UN remains an acclaimed study.

R V irzo and I Ingravellow (eds), *Evolutions in the Law of International Organizations* (Martinus Nijhoff, 2015).

A recent study of the law of international organizations with a focus on issues of responsibility and accountability.

PART III
International law in operation

7

The law of treaties

7.1 Introduction: written agreements between States

As Lord McNair put it in his classic work, *The Law of Treaties*, 'the making of treaties is one of the oldest and most characteristic exercises of independence or sovereignty on the part of States'.[1] The so-called 'Eternal Treaty', which dated from *c* 1258 BC and ended a long war between the Egyptians and Hittites, is perhaps the oldest treaty for which we have copies of the text.[2] With the emergence of organized political communities, written agreements quickly emerged as a useful method of ensuring that obligations would be observed as binding. Slowly, the principle of *pacta sunt servanda* ('agreements shall be faithfully observed') crystallized into customary law. Perhaps the oldest principle of international law, it underlies every single international agreement, raising the expectation that States will fulfil the obligations to which they have consented.

'Treaties', an umbrella term used to describe these written agreements, are not the only source of rights, obligations, and duties under international law. These may also emerge from the unwritten practices of States and other actors that create customary law obligations or from general principles. In this respect, international law is no different than municipal legal orders, where, in addition to unwritten delicts/tort-based obligations, individuals may consent formally to enter into legal obligations through contracts, or follow certain procedures prescribed by law so as to acquire or dispose of property. The essential point to retain is that treaties record an agreement, between two or more international actors, in which they consent to be bound by legal obligations; they are a crucial means for the development of international law. Two basic principles of international law are thus in play: that a party is only bound by the provisions of a treaty to which it has consented; but once it is bound, a party shall abide by its obligations faithfully.[3]

[1] A McNair, *The Law of Treaties* (rev edn OUP, 1961), 35.

[2] The Egyptian version of the treaty is engraved on the walls of two temples in Thebes (the Ramesum and the Temple of Amun-Re at Karnak), and the Hittite version on clay tables discovered in Hattusa, in the 1890s. A copy of the treaty is displayed at UN Headquarters in New York.

[3] As the PCIJ memorably described it in the *SS Wimbledon, 1923, PCIJ, Ser A, No 1*, p 25, treaty-making is an 'attribute of State sovereignty'.

This chapter will survey what is known as the 'law of treaties': the basic form of treaties and how they are made; the rules according to which reservations can be made to parts of a treaty; the scope of treaty obligations, and in particular the rules for their interpretation; and, finally, the possible grounds under which a treaty can be terminated or suspended. Long considered to be customary international law, the rules governing treaties were largely codified in the 1969 Vienna Convention on the Law of Treaties (VCLT), which entered into force in 1980.[4] In an interesting interplay between treaty and custom, most, if not all of the provisions of the VCLT are now regarded as a codification of customary international law.[5] These include the rules of treaty interpretation,[6] those on material breach and its impact on suspension or termination of treaties,[7] the effect of a fundamental change of circumstances,[8] and, perhaps the most important of all, *pacta sunt servanda*: treaties are binding upon parties to them and must be performed in good faith.[9] The VCLT is the cornerstone of the law of treaties and its structure will guide the framework of this chapter.

7.2 **Basic concepts and principles**

As laid out in Article 2(1)(a) VCLT, a 'treaty' can be embodied in a single instrument or in two or more related instruments. It is:

- a written agreement;
- between international legal subjects; and
- governed by international law.

In short, then, a treaty must be *written* in order to fall under the scope of the VCLT. Though this does not mean that oral agreements have no effect in international law,[10] it does mean that the law of treaties embodied in the VCLT does not govern oral agreements.

[4] Vienna Convention on the Law of Treaties (signed 23 May 1969, entered into force 27 January 1980), 1155 UNTS 331 (VCLT).

[5] See, e.g., *Fisheries Jurisdiction (United Kingdom v Iceland), Jurisdiction and Admissibility, ICJ Reports 1974*, p 3, 18; *Sovereignty over Pulau Litigan and Pulau Sipidan (Indonesia/Malaysia), ICJ Reports 2002*, p 625, 645–6; *US—Gasoline*, WTO Doc WT/DS2/AB/R (29 April 1996), 16–17; *US—Gambling*, WTO Doc WT/DS285/AB (7 April 2005), 51; *Kadi & Al Barakaat International Foundation v Council & Commission* [2008] ECR I-06351, para 291; and *Opel Austria v Council of the European Union* (1997) 113 ILR 295, 323–4.

[6] *Kasikili/Sedudu Island (Botswana/Namibia), Judgment, ICJ Reports 1999*, p 1045, para 18; *Mutual Assistance in Criminal Matters (Djibouti v France), Judgment, ICJ Reports 2008*, p 177, at 219, para 112; *Beagle Channel arbitration (Chile/Argentina)* (1977) XXI RIAA 53.

[7] *Legal Consequences for States of the Continued Presence of South Africa in Namibia (South West Africa) notwithstanding Security Council Resolution 276 (1970), Advisory Opinion, ICJ Reports 1971*, p 16, 47; *Gabčíkovo-Nagymaros Project (Hungary/Slovakia), Judgment, ICJ Reports 1997*, p 7, para 46.

[8] *Icelandic Fisheries Jurisdiction* (n 5) 21.

[9] *Gabčíkovo-Nagymaros* (n 7) 78–9.

[10] VCLT (n 4) Art 3 provides that it is 'without prejudice' to oral agreements, and is a codification of customary international law: see *Obligation to Negotiate Access to the Pacific Ocean (Bolivia v Chile), Merits, ICJ Reports 2018*, p 1, para 97.

It does not matter exactly what an agreement is called; the term 'treaty' is non-specific, and agreements can include the 'Charter' of the United Nations, the international human rights 'Covenants', the Rome 'Statute' of the ICC, the Kyoto 'Protocol', and many other names besides.[11] This flexibility also applies to a treaty's form: so long as an agreement is in writing and complies with the very basic requirements of Article 2(1)(a), instruments such as the minutes of a meeting,[12] post-meeting joint declarations, or MOUs (memoranda of understanding),[13] or even press releases or joint communiqués[14] between States, have been upheld as falling within the scope of the law of treaties—provided, of course, that they clearly demonstrate the parties' intention to be bound to an agreement.

While States remain the most active actors entering into treaty relations, international organizations may become parties to treaties, whether between themselves or with a State.[15] Accordingly, the law of treaties is reflected in several multilateral conventions, chief among them the VCLT; the Vienna Convention on Treaties between States and International Organizations of 1986 VCLT-IO (though not yet in force, it follows the 1969 VCLT closely, and may be thought to be reflective of custom to a similar extent); and the Vienna Convention on Succession of States in respect of Treaties. In 2011, the ILC adopted Articles on the Effects of Armed Conflicts of the Law of Treaties, which purport to be a codification of international law on the matter, and which are premised on the notion that the outbreak of armed conflict ought to affect the stability of legal relations as little as possible.[16]

At times, a treaty may also provide for other specific entities such as international organizations or 'separate customs territories' to join, or be amended in order to do so. Two examples include the potential accession of the European Union to the ECHR,[17] and the fact that the Marrakech Agreement establishing the WTO has always allowed

[11] In discussions on the Draft Articles on the Law of Treaties, the ILC also listed 'pact', 'act', 'agreement', 'concordat', 'declaration', 'agreement', and '*modus vivendi*' as formal terms. Even informal agreements such as 'exchange of notes', 'exchange of letters', 'memorandum of agreement', and 'agreed minute' constitute valid international agreements: see (1966) ILC Ybk vol II, pt 2, 188.

[12] See *Maritime Delimitation and Territorial Questions between Qatar and Bahrain (Jurisdiction and Admissibility) Judgment, ICJ Reports 1994*, 112, at para 27, where it was held that, provided the requisite intent to be bound exists, agreed and signed minutes between two States may constitute a treaty: see Section 7.4.3.2. See also *Delimitation of the Maritime Boundary in the Bay of Bengal (Bangladesh/Myanmar), Judgment, ITLOS Reports 2012*, p 4, where the Tribunal for the Law of the Sea rejected signed minutes, though for lack of intent, not for their form as such.

[13] In *Land and Maritime Boundary between Cameroon and Nigeria (Cameroon v Nigeria: Equatorial Guinea intervening), Merits, ICJ Reports 2002*, p 303, para 50, the ICJ concluded that the post-meeting joint 'Thomson-Marchand Declaration' had the status of an international agreement. In *Maritime Delimitation in the Indian Ocean (Somalia v Kenya), Preliminary Objections, ICJ Reports 2017*, p 3, paras 36–50, esp paras 45–50, the ICJ took the view that an MOU constituted an internationally binding agreement upon signature, with no need for ratification (see later, Sections 7.2.1.2.1–7.2.1.2.2).

[14] See also *Aegean Sea Continental Shelf (Greece v Turkey), Preliminary Objections, ICJ Reports 1978*, p 3, 39, para 96; and *Pulp Mills on the River Uruguay (Argentina v Uruguay), ICJ Reports 2010*, p 14, paras 138–40.

[15] See *South West Africa (Ethiopia v South Africa; Liberia v South Africa), Preliminary Objections, ICJ Reports 1962*, p 319, 330.

[16] ILC, 'Articles on the Effect of Armed Conflicts on the Law of Treaties', UNGA Res A/66/99 (9 December 2011), Annex 1.

[17] Though the EU has not yet acceded, following a negative recommendation from the CJEU: see Opinion 2/13 (18 December 2014).

for non-State 'separate customs territories' such as Hong Kong, Macao, and Taiwan to be members.[18]

Because a treaty's purpose is to create binding international legal obligations, the law of treaties applies to agreements 'governed by international law'.[19] Accordingly, an agreement between States (or international organizations) concerning a matter to be governed by municipal law, such as certain commercial transactions, would not constitute a treaty under international law.[20] Similarly, international agreements between parties that are not intended to create legal obligations, such as the 2018 Global Compact for Refugees[21] or documents said to constitute 'soft law',[22] do not constitute treaties. However, a unilateral statement by a State may have binding effect under certain conditions, provided that the State's intention to be bound is sufficiently clear.[23]

CONTEMPORARY DEVELOPMENTS The Provisional Application of Treaty Provisions

The provisional application of treaties is permitted under Article 25 VCLT, and does not mean that the treaty enters into force more quickly, merely that its provisions will be applied prior to its entry into force. An interesting case study into the binding force of treaties involves Syria and the Chemical Weapons Convention (CWC). After extensive reports circulated that Syria was using chemical weapons against its own population, and in the face of international condemnation, its government decided to sign and ratify the CWC. After signature but pending its entry into force in 2013, Syria requested permission from the Organization for the Prohibition of Chemical Weapons (OPCW) to apply provisionally the terms of the CWC.

Provisional application of treaties is particularly important in economic agreements, such as the recent UK–EU Trade and Cooperation Agreement, which was provisionally applied from January to April 2021 to ensure the transition created by Brexit— but it raises important questions as to the nature of the rights and obligations flowing from treaties not yet in force. After long studies of the topic since 2013, and six reports, in 2021 the ILC adopted the Guide to Provisional Application of Treaties: see UN Doc A/76/10 (2021), para 51.

Of course, the use of chemical weapons by Syria remains controversial. On 22 April 2021, the Conference of States Parties to the CWC adopted a Decision (OPCW Doc C-25/DEC.9) to suspend voting and participatory rights for Syria, due to the conclusion by the OPCW Investigation and Identification Team that Syria has continued to use chemical weapons.

[18] See Marrakech Treaty establishing the World Trade Organization (1994) 1867 UNTS 3, at Art XII, para 1.

[19] (1965) ILC Ybk vol II, 12.

[20] E.g., the lease of a building by a State from another State to house its embassy, which would be a contract under national law even though concluded between two States.

[21] See UNGA Res 73/151 (17 December 2018).

[22] Other examples include the 1992 Rio Declaration on Environment and Development and the 1975 Helsinki Final Act of the OSCE. Despite their grandiose titles, the 2000 UN Millennium Declaration (UNGA Res 55/2 (8 September 2000)) and the 2005 World Summit Outcome (UNGA Res 60/1 (24 October 2005)) are, formally at least, simply resolutions passed by the United Nations General Assembly.

[23] See *Nuclear Tests (Australia v France; New Zealand v France), Jurisdiction and Admissibility, ICJ Reports 1974*, p 253, paras 42–3.

7.2.1 The making of treaties

7.2.1.1 Formal conditions to enter into treaty relations

There are few formalities required to enter into a treaty, though principles have been developed to ensure that a State or international organization, as an abstract entity that must act through human representatives, has duly authorized representatives to consent to it being bound. Certain high-ranking office-holders are presumed to hold such authority without further formalities. As a matter of established practice, dating back from the era when a monarch was the personification of the State, such office-holders include:[24]

- heads of State;[25]
- heads of government, such as prime ministers;
- ministers for foreign affairs;[26]
- heads of diplomatic missions, for the purpose of adopting a treaty between the accrediting State and the State to which they are accredited; and
- representatives accredited by States to an international organization for the purpose of adopting the text of a treaty.

In principle, any other representative purporting to act in the name of a State must produce appropriate 'full powers'. These are documents issued by a competent State authority, such as the foreign ministry or the head of State, that designate an individual to represent the State regarding all acts relating to a treaty, including negotiating the treaty or consenting to the State being bound.[27] It should be noted that full powers are not needed if the other parties to the agreement have acted in such a way that their intention was to regard that person as representing the State.[28]

In this regard, States are increasingly looking beyond these traditional office-holders and authorizing a specified person, occupying a defined function, to bind the State within their relevant remit. In *Maritime Delimitation in the Indian Ocean*, a Minister for National Planning and International Co-operation was authorized by the Prime Minister of the Transitional Federal Government of Somalia to negotiate and to bind the State.[29] Moreover, even a lack of full powers is not fatal: though in principle a person

[24] VCLT (n 4) Art 7(2). This list was confirmed by the ICJ in *Land and Maritime Boundary between Cameroon and Nigeria* (n 13) 303, para 265.

[25] In *Application of the Convention on the Prevention and Punishment of the Crime of Genocide (Bosnia and Herzegovina v Yugoslavia), Preliminary Objections, ICJ Reports 1996*, p 595, 661–2, the Court relied on the VCLT (n 4) to declare that 'every Head of State is presumed to be able to act on behalf of the State in its international relations'.

[26] See *Legal Status of Eastern Greenland (Denmark/Norway), 1933, PCIJ, Ser A/B, No 53*, p 71, in which a verbal statement by Norway's Foreign Minister was binding upon Norway.

[27] VCLT (n 4) Art (2)(1)(c). See also *Land and Maritime Boundary between Cameroon and Nigeria* (n 13) para 265.

[28] VCLT (n 4) Art 7(1)(a)–(b).

[29] *Maritime Delimitation in the Indian Ocean* (n 13) para 43. See also *Armed Activities in the Territory of the Congo (New Application: 2002) (Democratic Republic of the Congo v Rwanda), Jurisdiction and Admissibility, ICJ Reports 2006*, p 6, para 47. But *cf* the statement made by ITLOS in *Delimitation of the Maritime Boundary in the Bay of Bengal (Bangladesh/Myanmar), Judgment, ITLOS Reports 2012*, para 83, in which the list of 'high-ranking office holders' enumerated in VCLT (n 4) Art 7(2)(a) was deemed to be exhaustive.

lacking these (or not holding high office) may not bind the State, under Article 8 VCLT a State may subsequently confirm an act of such officials as its own. For example, in 1951 a delegate endowed with authority only from Norway, but not from Sweden, purported to sign a convention relating to cheese on behalf of both States. Under the principle codified in Article 8, the signature would have been inapplicable in relation to Sweden, but Sweden's government confirmed the unauthorized act, and consented to be bound.[30]

Of course, the reverse situation can occur, where an authorized representative of a State was expressly instructed not to give consent but nonetheless did so. In such cases, Article 47 VCLT provides that consent may only be invalidated if the State notified other negotiating States beforehand of the restriction placed on its representative.

7.2.1.2 **Expressing consent to be bound**

'Adoption' of a treaty represents the closure of negotiations, and means that the final text of a proposed treaty can be brought to the negotiating parties for them to express their consent to be bound. Though a specified threshold, for example, two-thirds of States present at an international conference may vote to 'adopt' a treaty text and end the negotiations,[31] adoption does not suffice to bind the negotiating parties. Not even a convention adopted by *consensus*, a practice where voting is put off until 'every effort is made to achieve unanimous agreement',[32] or through unanimity, would be binding.

Instead, there are a number of possible paths by which a party may consent to be bound, including signature, exchange of instruments constituting a treaty, ratification, acceptance, approval, or accession.[33]

7.2.1.2.1 ***Consent by signature***

Signature can be a solemn ritual, used to mark the end of negotiations with pomp and ceremony. However, the purpose of signature is rarely to express consent to be bound; it is usually but a first step towards ratification, acceptance, or approval under domestic law. The signature of a treaty does not even impose a promise by the signatory to ratify the treaty or to take further steps towards ratification; if ratification is necessary, in the interim, a signatory is only bound to a good faith, albeit autonomous, obligation to 'refrain from acts which would defeat the object and purpose of a treaty'.[34] For example, if State A agrees to purchase currency-minting equipment from State B, State B should not destroy the said equipment between signature and ratification. Moreover, under Article 18(a) VCLT, it may even remove itself from this interim obligation if it makes clear that it no longer intends to ratify, as was vividly exemplified by the USA's dramatic 'unsigning' of the Rome Statute in 2002.[35]

[30] The episode is recounted in (1966) ILC Ybk vol II, p 195.

[31] VCLT (n 4) Art 9. Voting by two-thirds majority is also the practice of the General Assembly: see Art 18 of the UN Charter.

[32] This definition of 'consensus' was used by the Director of the General Legal Division, Office of Legal Affairs, in 1974: see UN *Juridical Yearbook*, 1974, 163–4.

[33] VCLT (n 4) Art 11.

[34] *Ibid*, Art 18. See O Dörr, 'Article 18', in O Dörr and K Schmalenbach (eds), *Vienna Convention on the Law of Treaties: A Commentary* (Springer, Berlin 2018), at 220.

[35] See ET Swaine, 'Unsigning' (2003) 55 Stanford LR 2061. In 2016, Vladimir Putin also 'formally withdrew' Russia's signature from the Rome Statute: see Presidential Decree and Byelaw No 361—pп of the Russian Federation (16 November 2016).

As with most formalities, the law of treaties remains flexible regarding signature. Negotiating parties may agree that signature is the final stage of a treaty-making process and equals consent to be bound, as the ICJ concluded was the case in the MOU between Somalia and Kenya in *Maritime Delimitation in the Indian Ocean.*[36] A treaty may also provide expressly that full powers also allow for signature to equal consent to be bound. This happens occasionally for relatively routine and non-controversial treaties in which States wish to avoid cumbersome legislative or administrative processes,[37] or in situations of urgency where the parties have identified a need to act swiftly.

7.2.1.2.2 ***Consent by ratification***

Ratification is the process through which the competent authorities within a State, usually a legislature, express their consent to be bound to an international agreement. As the ICJ explained in relation to ratification (and accession), these are each 'a simple act of will on the part of the State manifesting an intention to undertake new obligations and to acquire new rights in terms of the treaty'.[38] Article 14 VCLT provides that ratification is necessary when provided by a treaty or otherwise established by the intention of the parties, or when the signature of a State representative (whether holding full powers or not) has been made subject to ratification in order to bind the State.

So long as a competent organ or authority is identified under domestic law that may consent for the State to be bound to an international legal obligation, international law remains neutral as to which organ it might be.

HISTORICAL BACKGROUND What Authority Acts on Behalf of the State?

At least since the time of Pufendorf and Vattel,[39] treaty-making power has been regarded as a prerogative of sovereigns. As such, the process of ratification developed as monarchs increasingly took the view that they were the personification of the State (as the French King Louis XIV memorably remarked, '*l'État, c'est moi*': 'the State is me'), and asserted the right to approve what their plenipotentiaries (literally, 'holders of full powers to negotiate') arranged. In the eighteenth century, as forms of representative or parliamentary democracy took hold in certain States, domestic approval became the realm of representative institutions. For example, the US Constitution, Article II§2, cl 2 provides that the 'advice and consent' of two-thirds of the Senate is needed.

In the UK, ratification is formally regarded as a Crown prerogative, though further parliamentary ratification is required in most cases that require changes to internal law or may impact upon the private rights of British subjects. This was established in *Parlement Belge* ((1879) 4 PD 129 (UK)), involving a cargo boat belonging to the King of the Belgians for which he claimed immunity pursuant to a treaty that had not been ratified by Parliament. The Probate, Admiralty, and Divorce Divisions of the High Court concluded that such immunity could not be extended to a cargo boat, even given the existence of a treaty covering such cargo boats, in the absence of parliamentary approval.

[36] *Maritime Delimitation in the Indian Ocean* (n 13) paras 45, 47. See VCLT (n 4) Art 12.

[37] *Maritime Delimitation in the Indian Ocean* (n 13) paras 45, 47. See VCLT (n 4) Art 12.

[38] *Application of the Convention on the Prevention and Punishment of the Crime of Genocide (Croatia v Serbia), Preliminary Objections, ICJ Reports 2008*, p 412, 450.

[39] See Chapter 1, Section 1.2.2.

The principle was reaffirmed in *A (FC) and Others (FC) v Secretary of State for the Home Department* [2005] UKHL 71, para 27 (Bingham J). A similar situation exists in other Commonwealth realms, such as Canada and Australia. Recently, in *R (Miller) v Secretary of State for Exiting the European Union* [2017] UKSC 5, the UK Supreme Court determined that the government could not exercise the royal prerogative to withdraw from the Treaty on European Union, as the Treaty contained rights enacted through primary legislation, and thus required further legislation.

Other States limit or exclude the intervention of the legislature. For example, articles 52–3 of the French Constitution allows the President of France to sign and to ratify most treaties without parliamentary consent, and only requires certain categories of treaties (such as treaties of peace, cession, or modifying internal law) to be ratified through implementing legislation. A similar clause may be found in many other States: see, for example, Section 190 of the Constitution of Thailand.

The second element of ratification is that parties formally exchange or deposit their respective instruments of ratification. With multilateral treaties, it generally falls to one party or, increasingly, the Secretariat of the United Nations, to act as a 'depositary', which gathers and maintains information relating to ratification, and also applies rules on eligibility for controversial actors such as Palestine and Kosovo, or in respect of admissible reservations.[40] Nevertheless, the exchange of instruments remains a matter of courtesy: ratification is effective as a matter of law and, unless specified in the treaty, does not depend on any notification or the exchange of instruments in order to be binding.[41]

7.2.1.2.3 ***Consent by accession***

A State may also consent, through a process called 'accession', to be bound by a treaty that has long been finalized.[42] This may be because the treaty entered into force before it became a State, as with the UN Charter and any State created after 1945; or perhaps a change of political circumstances within a State has entailed a change in policy, as occurred when Spain joined NATO and the EU after its transition to democratic government.

[40] See PTB Kohona, 'Some Notable Developments in the Practice of the UN Secretary-General as a Depositary of Multilateral Treaties: Reservations and Declarations' (2005) 99 AJIL 433.

[41] However, in principle they may not be relied upon in proceedings before UN organs. The ICJ, in *Military and Paramilitary Activities in and against Nicaragua (Nicaragua v United States), Jurisdiction and Admissibility, ICJ Reports 1984*, p 392, took a very relaxed view to the formalities of ratification when it concluded that Nicaragua's signature—but not ratification—of the PCIJ Statute was 'rectified' by Nicaragua's ratification of the ICJ Statute.

[42] VCLT (n 4) Art 15. This is subject, of course, to a State's right to enter reservations to that treaty: see Section 7.3, later.

Accession is frequently used when States join an existing international organization, such as Guyana's accession to the OAS in 1991, Cambodia's accession to ASEAN in 1999, or Albania's accession to NATO in 2009. It may also be used when a State that has participated in multilateral treaty negotiations, but did not originally sign, changes course, as did Japan in 2007 when it acceded to the ICC Rome Statute.

Accession is only possible if the treaty is open for non-parties to accede, and certain conditions may be imposed. Examples include the ICCPR, which requires that acceding parties be members of the United Nations;[43] the OECD Anti-Bribery Convention, which only allows OECD members and full participants in the OECD Working Group on Bribery in International Business Transactions[44] to accede; and the Mercosur Treaty, which only allows for members of the Latin American Integration Organization to join.[45]

7.2.2 **The entry into force of treaties**

Absent an express decision to the contrary, a treaty enters into force as soon as the consent to be bound of all negotiating States has been established.[46] Some multilateral conventions specify a minimum number of ratifications necessary for the treaty to enter into force: this was the case with the 1998 Rome Statute, which achieved its necessary sixty ratifications in 2002. Other treaties specify that they take effect from a certain date or within a specified time period following the last necessary ratification. Failing to reach a minimum does occur: the 2004 United Nations Convention on Jurisdictional Immunities of States and Their Property (see Chapter 9, Section 9.2.3.2) is still not in force, as only nineteen of the thirty necessary ratifications have been achieved. The same can be said of the VCLT-IO, mentioned at the start of Section 7.2.

7.2.3 **Amendment and modification of treaties**

Parties to a treaty may, for whatever reason they wish, decide to modify the obligations between them. The VCLT provides two such mechanisms for them to do so: amendment (Articles 39 and 40) and modification (Article 41).

Amendment, the more formal procedure, requires the consent of all the parties to an agreement, and all the formalities that would have accompanied the original conclusion of the treaty.[47] There are several procedural steps to be taken to amend a multilateral treaty. First, all proposals must be circulated to all parties, all of which have the right to decide whether to participate in negotiations to amend the treaty, or to opt out of an amending agreement and thus remain bound by the existing terms. Parties may also agree a

[43] International Covenant on Civil and Political Rights (signed 16 December 1966, entered into force 23 March 1976), 993 UNTS 3, Art 48(1).

[44] Six non-OECD members are parties: Argentina, Brazil, Bulgaria, Peru, Russia, and South Africa.

[45] Treaty of Asunción establishing a Common Market between the Argentine Republic, the Federative Republic of Brazil, the Republic of Paraguay and the Eastern Republic of Uruguay (signed 26 March 1991, entered into force 29 November 1991), 2140 UNTS 257 ('Mercosur Treaty'), Art 24.

[46] VCLT (n 4) Art 24.

[47] *Ibid*, Art 39.

different amendment procedure: for example, Article 108 of the UN Charter provides that two-thirds of member States, including all five permanent members of the Security Council, must ratify an amendment to the Charter that will bind all member States.[48]

Modification entails two or more, but not all, parties seeking to modify the treaty. In such cases, they may conclude an agreement to do so *inter se* ('between themselves'), but only if it is possible or not prohibited by the treaty, does not affect the enjoyment by other parties of their rights under the treaty, and is not incompatible with the object and purpose of the treaty.[49] Modification therefore raises interesting legal questions of how obligations binding some, but not all, parties will operate, as parties not accepting the modifications remain bound by the old version of the treaty.

Moreover, though a new party wishing to accede to an amended treaty is generally bound by the treaty in its amended form, if there are parties that are not bound by the amendments for some reason, then the new party is bound by the old treaty in relation to those parties. For this reason, certain treaties (including the UN Charter, discussed earlier) contain a specified amendment formula that binds all States, irrespective of their consent; others prohibit modifications between certain parties only. The latter prohibition makes sense, in particular, for normative standard-setting treaties such as environmental or human rights treaties. As such, modification between some, but not all, parties is relatively uncommon in practice, as it calls into question the ideal of legal certainty, or knowing the applicable law for a given situation.

7.3 Reservations to treaties

7.3.1 What is a 'reservation'?

Before moving to the actual application of treaties, a key issue relating to the conclusion of treaties needs to be covered. Reservations to treaties are unilateral acts through which States choose to exclude or to modify the legal effect of a given provision when consenting to be bound by a treaty obligation.[50] The existence of reservations was a concession to concerns over universality, especially in relation to multilateral conventions, as it allows for a negotiating party that has concerns over only a few treaty provisions to reject or exclude these yet still become a party to the treaty.

Reservations to treaties are governed in the VCLT in Articles 19 to 23. Reservations are in principle permissible; however, their use may be limited to certain parts of the treaty,[51] or are prohibited altogether by the treaty.[52] For example, the UN Convention

[48] See R Zacklin, *The Amendment of the Constitutive Instruments of the United Nations and Specialized Agencies* (1968; Brill reissue, 2005).

[49] VCLT (n 4) Art 41(1)(b).

[50] *Ibid*, Art 2(d).

[51] See, e.g., *North Sea Continental Shelf (Germany v Denmark; Germany v the Netherlands), ICJ Reports 1969*, p 3, in which Art 12 of the 1958 Convention on the Continental Shelf prohibited reservations to Arts 1–3.

[52] VCLT (n 4) Art 19.

on the Law of the Sea,[53] the Chemical Weapons Convention,[54] and the Rome Statute of the ICC[55] all expressly prohibit reservations of any kind. Reservations may also be prohibited for being incompatible with the object and purpose of the treaty.[56] Again, in principle, reservations do not require the acceptance of all parties unless required by the treaty itself, though occasionally, mathematical formulae have been adopted for determining the compatibility of a reservation with the object and purpose of a treaty.[57] Further, a reservation is prohibited if it is clear from the object and purpose of a treaty, or the fact that it has a limited number of negotiating parties (such as a regional organization), that the application of the treaty in its entirety is an essential condition for the parties to be bound.[58] Reservations must be made in writing, following a specific procedure,[59] though they may be withdrawn at any time by a reserving State.[60]

Given how they modify a State's consent to be bound, reservations are a hotly disputed area in the law of treaties. For this reason, in 2011 the ILC adopted a *Guide to Practice on Reservations to Treaties*, to provide a 'toolbox' to practitioners (such as legal advisers to States and international organizations, legal advocates and practitioners, and diplomats).[61] The non-binding Guide is not a draft convention and aims merely to gather and collect relevant practice that might illuminate how the rules are to be interpreted, and to make certain recommendations as to how the law on reservations to treaties could be developed.[62]

7.3.2 **Reservations and the object and purpose of a treaty**

The possibility of filing a reservation aims to preserve flexibility; it is an inducement to States to join a treaty regime that they may otherwise have to reject entirely. It was not always so: when the League of Nations acted as a depositary, it would only allow reservations accepted by all other parties. Failing unanimous acceptance, both the reservation and the consent to be bound were treated as null and void.

[53] United Nations Convention on the Law of the Sea (signed 10 December 1982, entered into force 16 November 1994), 1833 UNTS 3, Art 309.

[54] Convention on the Prohibition of the Development, Production, Stockpiling and Use of Chemical Weapons and on their Destruction (opened for signature 13 January 1993, entered into force 29 April 1997), 1975 UNTS 45, Art XXII.

[55] Rome Statute of the International Criminal Court (adopted 17 July 1998, entered into force 1 July 2002), 2187 UNTS 3, Art 120.

[56] See later, Section 7.3.2, regarding the compatibility of reservations with the object and purpose of a treaty.

[57] E.g., the International Convention on Elimination of All Forms of Racial Discrimination (adopted 21 December 1965, entry into force 4 January 1969), 660 UNTS 195, Art 20, which provides that a reservation is incompatible with the purpose of that treaty if two-thirds of contracting parties object to it.

[58] VCLT (n 4) Art 20, paras 1–2. [59] *Ibid*, Art 23. [60] *Ibid*, Art 22.

[61] *Guide to Practice on Reservations to Treaties*, adopted at the 3125th Meeting of the International Law Commission (63rd session), Supp 10.

[62] A useful analysis to the *Guide to Practice* is the 'Symposium: The International Law Commission's Guide to Practice on Reservations to Treaties' (2013) 24 EJIL 1055–152; see also K McCall-Smith, 'Mind the Gaps: The ILC's Guide to Practice and Reservations to Human Rights Treaties' (2014) 16 International Community Law Review 263.

The tension between universality and integrity came to a head with the opening for signature of the 1948 Genocide Convention. Several important States, led by the USSR, were extremely reluctant to ratify the Convention, in part due to their view that the right to make a reservation was a necessary attribute of State sovereignty and, by definition, a reservation which sets out the scope of a State's consent was always valid. Other States objected to the possibility of reservations to the Convention, insisting that the integrity of the treaty should take precedence, as to do otherwise would allow for differentiated obligations between the parties. In *Reservations to the Genocide Convention*, the General Assembly decided to refer the question to the ICJ, which gave an advisory opinion that was highly influential in drafting the VCLT.

CASE SPOTLIGHT ***Reservations to the Convention on the Prevention and Punishment of the Crime of Genocide, Advisory Opinion, ICJ Reports 1951*, p 15**

The *Reservations to the Genocide Convention* opinion made a number of key observations that influenced the provisions of the VCLT on reservations. Most significantly, the Court affirmed the general principle that a reservation would be valid provided that it was not objected to by all other parties, and was compatible with the object and purpose of a treaty. Moreover, only a State that objected on the basis of incompatibility with the object and purpose could consider the reserving State not to be a party to the Convention (p 29; a so-called 'hard objection').

The Court's focus on the object and purpose of a treaty was doubtless grounded in the special, non-reciprocal nature of the obligations to prevent and punish acts of genocide, now recognized as a prohibition of *jus cogens*. As the Court took pains to clarify:

> In such a Convention the contracting States do not have any interests of their own; they merely have, one and all, a common interest, namely the accomplishment of those high purposes which are the *raison d'être* of the Convention. Consequently in a convention of this type one cannot speak of the individual advantages or disadvantages to States, or of the maintenance of a perfect contractual balance between rights and duties. (p 23)

Based on this interpretation of the object and purpose of the Convention, the Court took the view that the General Assembly and signatory States intended that as many States as possible should participate. To exclude a State 'would not only restrict the scope of its application, but would detract from the authority of the moral and humanitarian principles which are its basis' (p 24).

The *Reservations to the Genocide Convention* opinion did leave some ambiguity. The object and purpose test remains problematic; as the 2011 ILC *Guide to Practice* demonstrates, the best the ILC could do was introduce a circular test whereby '[a] reservation is incompatible with the object and purpose of the treaty if it affects an essential element of the treaty that is necessary to its general tenor, in such a way that the reservation impairs the *raison d'être* of the treaty' (see ILC *Guide to Practice*, para 3.1.5). The Genocide Convention had a single purpose, the prevention and punishment of genocide; but how would such a test work in considering a complex multilateral treaty with multiple objects and purposes, such as those establishing the European Union?

Finally, the Court left open the most difficult question: who possesses the authority to make the determination whether or not a proposed reservation is incompatible? As a general rule, there is no institution which has the authority to do so; determination is left to individual parties to a treaty, thus leaving a purportedly objective criterion to subjective determination.

For further reading, see C Redgwell, 'Universality or Integrity? Some Reflections on Reservations to Multilateral Treaties' (1993) 64 BYBIL 245, 253 *et seq*; and J Klabbers, 'Some Problems Regarding the Object and Purpose of Treaties' (1997) 8 Finnish YBIL 138.

7.3.3 **Identifying a reservation**

As Article 2(1)(d) VCLT specifies, 'however phrased or named', a reservation is identified by its effect of modifying or excluding the legal effect of certain treaty provisions. It is important to focus on the legal effect of a statement, and not to fixate on the title or name ascribed. Parties can make other statements with regard to a treaty where no binding consequence is intended, such as understandings, political statements, or interpretative declarations. Interpretative declarations, for instance, are nothing more than a unilateral statement that purports to specify or clarify the meaning of a treaty provision, and in principle are not binding on other parties.[63] However, at times they may be drafted such that they modify the legal effect of a treaty and, for that reason, they are treated as a reservation. As the ILC's 2011 *Guide to Practice* explains, whatever its title, the character of such unilateral statements is determined by 'the legal effect that its author purports to produce'.[64]

Two cases serve to illustrate the point. In the *Anglo-French Continental Shelf* arbitration of 1977, the UK suggested that a reservation made by France to Article 6 of the Geneva Convention on the Continental Shelf was in reality only an interpretative declaration.[65] The tribunal in that case studied France's reservation and concluded that, although some elements of the reservation contained elements of interpretation, it made the application of Article 6 dependent on acceptance by other States of certain conditions imposed by France. As such, the tribunal concluded that France's statement served to exclude or modify the legal effect of Article 6, and thus constituted a reservation.[66] The second relevant case is the 1988 judgment of the European Court of Human Rights in *Belilos v Switzerland*, considered in more depth in the accompanying comment.[67]

[63] See, e.g., *Temeltasch v Switzerland* (1983) 5 EHRR 417; and ILC *Guide to Practice* (n 61), Guideline 1.2. See further R Sapienza, 'Les déclarations interprétatives unilatérales et l'interprétation des traités' (1999) 103 RGDIP 601; LDM Nelson, 'Declarations, Statements and "Disguised Reservations" with Respect to the Convention on the Law of the Sea' (2001) 50 ICLQ 767; D McRae, 'The Legal Effects of Interpretative Declarations' (1978) 49 BYBIL 155.

[64] ILC *Guide to Practice* (n 61), Guideline 1.3. Such unilateral statements are also to be interpreted similarly to reservations: see Guideline 1.3.1.

[65] *Delimitation of the Continental Shelf between the United Kingdom and France* (1979) XVIII RIAA 3, para 50.

[66] *Ibid*, para 51.

[67] *Belilos v Switzerland* (1988) ECHR Ser A No 132, 10 EHRR 418, 20–2.

CASE SPOTLIGHT ***Belilos v Switzerland*** **(1988) ECHR Ser A No 132, 10 EHRR 418**

The *Belilos* case at the ECtHR concerned an applicant who complained that she had not received a fair trial when convicted of a criminal offence for taking part in a protest. Switzerland objected to her complaint, on the basis that it fell within an 'interpretative declaration' it had filed when it ratified the ECHR in 1971.

The Court was called upon to consider the nature of the interpretative declaration, whereupon it decided that, irrespective of what it had been called, it needed to focus on the substantive content of the declaration, and the intention of Switzerland when it had lodged it. The Court took the view that Switzerland had intended to 'avoid the consequences which a broad view of the right of access to the courts . . . would have for the system of public administration and of justice in [its] cantons and consequently . . . put forward the declaration as qualifying [its] consent to be bound' by the ECHR (18–19). Given the fact that Switzerland's interpretative declaration had all the legal effects of a reservation, it was assessed in the light of the prohibition on reservations of a general character in Article 57 ECHR and found impermissible under that provision (20–1).

The consequences of impermissibility were significant. The ECtHR took the view that 'it is beyond doubt that Switzerland is, and regards itself as, bound by the Convention irrespective of the validity of declaration' (21–2), and that it was thus entitled to *sever* the offending reservation. The consequences of severability in relation to impermissible reservations are that the party remains bound by the treaty as a whole, but without the benefit of the offending reservation.

7.3.4 **Legal consequences of impermissible reservations**

Article 21 VCLT addresses the legal effect of reservations. As a general rule, a reservation modifies, for the reserving party in its relations with other parties, a specific provision of a treaty. If another party objects to the reservation, the reservation cannot be invoked by the reserving party in its relations between those two States. However, if another party accepts the reservation, or has been silent, the matter ends there: the reservation is valid between the parties, as the silent party is deemed to have acquiesced.

The matter becomes more complex when another party objects to the reservation, but not to the entry into force of the treaty between itself and the reserving party (a 'soft' objection). The Arbitral Tribunal in the 1977 *Anglo-French Continental Shelf* arbitration faced exactly this situation. When ratifying the 1958 Geneva Convention on the Continental Shelf, France had filed a reservation to Article 6 that excluded its application from most of its coasts, including the Channel and North Sea.[68] The UK objected to this reservation simply as one it was 'unable to accept', without giving further justification.

[68] France's reservation is reproduced in AE Boyle, 'The Law of Treaties and the *Anglo-French Continental Shelf* Arbitration' (1980) 29 ICLQ 498, 501.

Before the tribunal, France argued that the UK's reservation was intended to prevent the Geneva Convention from entering into force: a 'hard' objection. The tribunal, examining the reservation, concluded that the UK's objection could only be interpreted as preventing the entry into force of the Convention if that intention was expressly stated, for example if the UK had objected on the basis that France's reservation was contrary to the object and purpose of the treaty, and thus impermissible.[69] What, then, was the effect of France's reservation and the UK's objection to it? In the Tribunal's own words:

> the combined effect of the French reservations and their rejection by the United Kingdom is neither to render article 6 [of the 1958 Geneva Convention on the Continental Shelf] inapplicable *in toto*, as the French Republic contends, nor to render it applicable *in toto*, as the United Kingdom contends. It is to render the article inapplicable as between the two countries *to the extent of the reservations*.[70]

Thus, in cases when an objecting party does not object expressly to the entry into force of a treaty as between it and the reserving party (again, a 'soft' objection), the treaty would enter into force between the parties, but excluding the effects of reservation and objection on a specific provision or article: 'the provisions to which the reservation relates do not apply as between the two States to the extent of the reservation'.[71] Stated more plainly, most of the treaty binds both parties but excludes those provisions to which there was no consent between the reserving party and the objecting party. Such provisions fall away in respect of their treaty relations: they simply become 'inapplicable' as between the two States.

The most complex situation arises when a State formulates a reservation to which other States parties object on the basis that it is incompatible with the object and purpose of the treaty and thus impermissible, and where the objecting parties refuse to have treaty relations with the reserving State (a 'hard' objection). The uncertain consequences of a hard objection can be problematic when, for example, a multilateral convention seeks to create an integral, universally applicable treaty regime; this is often the case with human rights protection, as well as other matters of global collective concern, such as the seas or the environment. The normative, standard-setting character of such treaties is such that their provisions do not merely establish enmeshed bilateral rights and obligations between parties but, rather, a system of coherent application, which merits differentiated treatment.[72] There are two dominant schools of thought on the question. First is the 'permissibility' school, which suggests that a reservation can be

[69] *Anglo-French Continental Shelf* (n 65) para 44.

[70] *Ibid*, para 52 (emphasis added). Boyle (n 68) 505 took the view that, given the combined effect of reservation and objection, the 'void' was then filled by rules of customary law, which cannot be subject to reservation and objection (see Chapter 2, Section 2.2.2.2.3, on persistent objection to the formation of new rules of custom).

[71] VCLT (n 4) Art 21(3). This is not to say that the entire article becomes inapplicable, merely those clauses which are affected by the reservation.

[72] *Belilos v Switzerland* (n 67). On the normative character of certain multilateral treaties, see further B Simma and GI Hernández, 'Reservations to Human Rights Treaties: Where do we Stand?' in E Cannizzaro (ed), *The Law of Treaties Beyond the Vienna Convention: Essays in Honour of Giorgio Gaja* (OUP, 2011), 60; and K McCall-Smith, 'Severing Reservations' (2014) 63 ICLQ 599.

objectively assessed for compatibility with the object and purpose of a treaty; if that is the case, no amount of acceptance by other parties can cure the defect, and the reserving State cannot be a party. The second, known as the 'opposability school', endorses the view that the validity of a reservation depends entirely on whether it is accepted by other parties; this is a subjective appraisal.[73] More simply, the acceptance of all other parties would be constitutive of the permissibility of the reservation.

A debate has emerged as to whether, in situations where a reservation is found to be impermissible, an 'exception' can permit only the reservation to be invalid, and thus severed from the consent to be bound of the reserving State as a whole (the so-called 'severability doctrine'). A well-known illustration of severability arguably occurred when Maldives acceded to the Convention on the Elimination of All Forms of Discrimination against Women (CEDAW) in 1993. In doing so, Maldives entered a reservation such that it would not comply with any principles in CEDAW that: (i) it considered 'contradictory to the principles of the Islamic Sharia'; or (ii) would oblige it to change its constitution or legislation. Austria and Portugal objected to both reservations, arguing that they were incompatible with the object and purpose of CEDAW and thus 'inadmissible', though accepting Maldives could be a party to the treaty.[74] These exemplify the 'permissibility doctrine' whereby an invalid reservation does not invalidate consent as a whole. Sweden went even further and suggested that it considered the Maldives' consent to be bound to the treaty as a whole to be 'invalid',[75] a relatively rare application of the 'opposability doctrine' whereby an invalid reservation inhibits the entry into force of the treaty as a whole.

It seems that though severability is not clearly established as a general rule of international law, a specific practice seems to exist in relation to multilateral human rights treaties where the severability doctrine is applied regularly. Some human rights conventions, in particular the ECHR and the IACHR, assign the competence to decide upon the permissibility of reservations to their respective institutions and courts as established through them. Amongst these, in *Belilos* the European Court of Human Rights was first to establish the principle that, in cases where a reservation has been declared impermissible for being contrary to the object and purpose of the ECHR, it will *sever* the reservation from the ratification and hold the State party to be bound to the Convention in its entirety.[76] In the *Loizidou (Preliminary Objections)* case, the ECtHR concluded that Turkish reservations, excluding the jurisdiction of the Commission and Court to entertain applications relating to acts occurring in Northern Cyprus, were impermissible due to their being of a general character. The Court then concluded that, in the light of the nature of the human rights obligations embodied in the ECHR, the effect of impermissibility would be that the reservations were null and would be

[73] ILC, 'First Report on Reservations' UN Doc A/CN.4/470 (30 May 1995) at 49, para 102.

[74] Maldives' reservations are found at 1726 UNTS 238 (1994). Austria and Portugal's objections are at 1830 UNTS 312 (1994).

[75] 1830 UNTS 13 (1994). Since 2001, Sweden seems to have moved towards a 'permissibility' approach where offending reservations would be severed: see McCall-Smith (n 72) 621.

[76] *Belilos v Switzerland* (n 67) paras 52–5, 60.

severed. Despite Turkey's explicit intention to exclude applications against it relating to Northern Cyprus, Turkey's consent to jurisdiction remained in place, and the applications were deemed to be admissible.[77] The Inter-American Court of Human Rights also affirmed the severability principle in the 2001 *Hilaire v Trinidad and Tobago* judgment; intriguingly, it rejected Trinidad and Tobago's argument that if the reservation was invalid, its consent would be void *ab initio*.[78]

THEORY AND DEBATES **Impermissible Reservations and Human Rights Conventions: Towards a 'Reservations Dialogue'?**

In 1994, the UN Human Rights Committee (HRC) issued its controversial General Comment No 24 (UN Doc CCPR/C/21/Rev.1/Add.6). Building on the ECtHR's statements in *Belilos* and *Loizidou*, the HRC emphasized the special nature of human rights treaties—in particular, for endowing individuals with rights—and concluded that the general rules in the VCLT were 'inappropriate to address the problems of reservations to human rights treaties' (para 17). It took the view that reservations offending either *jus cogens* or customary law human rights norms were incompatible with the object and purpose of the Covenant (para 8), and that the effect of 'such a reservation will generally be severable, in the sense that the Covenant will be operative for the reserving party without benefit of the reservation'. What is more, as the HRC determined that it would be inappropriate for States parties to do so unilaterally, it also concluded that '[i]t necessarily falls to the Committee to determine whether a specific reservation was or was not compatible with the object and purpose of the Covenant' (para 18). In *Rawle Kennedy v Trinidad and Tobago* (Comm No 845/1999, Decision (2 November 1999), UN Doc A/55/40, vol II, Annex I, A), the HRC would adopt this position, even though it meant that Trinidad and Tobago subsequently denounced the First Optional Protocol to the ICCPR.

The HRC's view on severability was at first strongly opposed by the ILC, which emphasized the adequacy of Article 19(c) VCLT in relation to human rights treaties. To the ILC, it fell to States parties to determine whether a reservation was incompatible with a treaty's object and purpose (see ILC, 'Preliminary Conclusions on Reservations to Normative Multilateral Treaties Including Human Rights Treaties' (1997) ILC Ybk vol II, pt 2, 57). The ILC's views have shifted: in 2007, in a meeting between the ILC and human rights bodies, there was consensus on both the special character of human rights treaties and the competence of the relevant human rights bodies to assess the validity of reservations. Though the parties could not agree upon the severability of an offending reservation from the expression of consent, the ILC and the human bodies in attendance did emphasize the importance of the 'reservation dialogue' between the reserving State and the human rights body.

The ILC's 2011 *Guide to Practice* (see Annex), though it makes no explicit mention of severability, nevertheless concluded in Guideline 4.5.2 that a rebuttable presumption existed that if a reservation was invalid, the reserving party would be bound by the treaty without the benefit of the reservation. That presumption could be rebutted if a State clearly expressed, within twelve months, the contrary intention that, without the benefit of a reservation, it was not bound to the treaty as a whole.

[77] *Loizidou v Turkey (Preliminary Objections)* App No 15318/89 (1995) ECHR Ser A No 310, pp 22–9.

[78] *Hilaire v Trinidad and Tobago (Preliminary Objections)*, IACtHR Ser C No 80 (1 September 2001), para 49.

For further reading, see B Simma and G Hernández, 'Reservations to Human Rights Treaties: Where Do We Stand?' in E Cannizzaro (ed), *The Law of Treaties beyond the Vienna Convention: Essays in Honour of Giorgio Gaja* (OUP, 2011), 60; K McCall-Smith, 'Severing Reservations' (2014) 63 ICLQ 599; and M Wood, 'Institutional Aspects of the Guide to Practice on Reservations' (2013) 24 EJIL 1099.

7.4 The scope of treaty obligations

7.4.1 The principle *pacta sunt servanda*

Article 26 VCLT lays out the key principle of *pacta sunt servanda*, '[e]very treaty in force is binding upon the parties to it, and must be performed by them in good faith'. Without the minimum belief that States ought to perform their treaty obligations in good faith, there seems little point on insisting that international law is capable of binding States, or even in functioning as a legal system as such.[79] Good faith was notably affirmed by the ICJ in the 1997 *Gabčíkovo-Nagymaros* judgment, where Hungary raised several arguments suggesting that the bilateral treaty between it and Slovakia had been terminated. The Court rejected each and every one of Hungary's submissions, concluding that the reciprocal wrongful conduct of the parties could not bring a binding treaty to an end or justify its termination[80] and that even in cases of reciprocal breach, under the principle of *pacta sunt servanda* parties were obliged to seek a solution within the cooperative context of the binding treaty.[81]

7.4.2 Treaties and third parties

As a general rule, a treaty cannot create obligations for a third State without its consent (*pacta tertiis nec nocent nec prosunt*).[82] Under Article 35 VCLT, a third State may become bound by a provision of a treaty if the original parties envisaged that possibility, but only when the third State expressly consents to that obligation in writing. In effect, such written consent forms a sort of collateral agreement which forms the basis of that State's obligation.[83] There is but one exception to the *pacta tertiis* rule under Article 38 VCLT: if the rules set forth in a treaty provision have entered into customary international law, the rule can bind a third State. However, in such cases, there would be both sufficient State practice and *opinio juris* to mould a rule into custom, and it would not be the treaty itself that would be binding on the non-party State, but the customary legal rule.

[79] See (1966) ILC Ybk vol II, pt 2, p 211; and Sir G Fitzmaurice, 'Some Problems Regarding the Formal Sources of International Law' in FM van Asbeck et al (eds), *Symbolae Verzijl* (Martinus Nijhoff, 1958), 153.

[80] *Gabčíkovo-Nagymaros* (n 7) paras 114, 133.

[81] *Ibid*, para 142.

[82] VCLT (n 4) Art 34. See further I Sinclair, *The Vienna Convention on the Law of Treaties* (2nd edn, Manchester UP, 1984), 93–8; A Aust, *Modern Treaty Law and Practice* (3rd edn, CUP, 2013), ch 12; McNair, *Law of Treaties* (n 1).

[83] See (1966) ILC Ybk vol II, pt 2, p 227.

Conversely, with respect to the possibility of a third State enjoying rights *in favorem tertii* ('in favour of a third party'), Article 36 VCLT does not require the written consent of the third State, and in fact presumes its 'assent' unless the contrary is indicated. In the *Free Zones of Upper Savoy and Gex* judgment, the PCIJ declared that 'it cannot be lightly presumed that stipulations favourable to a third State have been adopted with the object of creating an actual right in its favour ... it must be ascertained [in each particular case] whether the States which have stipulated in favour of the third State meant to create for that State an actual right which the latter has accepted as such'.[84]

Once established, an obligation relating to a third State can only be revoked or modified with the consent of both parties to a treaty and that third State.[85] Similarly, once a right has been bestowed on a third State, it may only be revoked or modified with the consent of the third State unless it is established explicitly that such consent is not required under the treaty. For example, in the *Free Zones in Upper Savoy and Gex* case, France had argued that Article 435 of the Treaty of Versailles (to which Switzerland was not a party), had abrogated certain provisions on preferential customs regimes established in the 1815 Final Act of the Congress of Vienna, of which Switzerland was the beneficiary. The PCIJ concluded that Article 435 could not bind Switzerland, a non-party to the Treaty of Versailles, 'except to the extent to which that country accepted it'.[86]

The VCLT is silent regarding situations where a treaty goes beyond an agreement between States and creates an 'objective' regime, such as a boundary demarcation or the delimitation of maritime rights, and their continued validity *erga omnes*. Though it is well accepted that a territorial or maritime title created on the basis of a treaty is independent of the original treaty, this point is not merely theoretical. Examples of such situations include treaties providing for the freedom of navigation in international waterways such as the Suez Canal, Kiel Canal, and the Bosphorus Straits.[87]

7.4.3 **Interpretation of treaties**

7.4.3.1 **The primary means of treaty interpretation**

International lawyers constantly engage with the overarching question of treaty interpretation,[88] a key process in the implementation of international law.[89] The VCLT sought, therefore, to present certain guiding principles, in Articles 31 to 33, to assist

[84] *Free Zones of Upper Savoy and the District of Gex, Second Phase, 1932, PCIJ, Ser A/B, No 46*, p 96, 147–8.

[85] VCLT (n 4) Art 37.

[86] *Free Zones in Upper Savoy and Gex* (n 83) 141.

[87] See the *Wimbledon* case (n 3), p 22, where the PCIJ noted that 'an international waterway ... for the benefit of all the nations of the world' was established in the Kiel Canal. For further discussion, see Aust (n 81) 228–9; O Corten and P Klein (eds), *The Vienna Convention on the Law of Treaties: A Commentary* (OUP, 2012), 929 *et seq*.

[88] See GI Hernández, 'Interpretation' in J Kammerhofer and J d'Aspremont (eds), *Post-Modern Approaches to International Legal Positivism* (CUP, 2014), 317; McNair, *Law of Treaties* (n 1), 345–50.

[89] Some classic works include Sir H Lauterpacht, 'Restrictive Interpretation and the Principle of Effectiveness in the Interpretation of Treaties' (1949) 26 BYBIL 48; S Sur, *L'interprétation en droit international public* (LGDJ, 1974); and Aust (n 81) ch 13. Modern monographs on the topic abound: see R Gardiner, *Treaty Interpretation* (2nd edn, OUP, 2017); A Orakhelashvili, *The Interpretation of Acts and Rules in Public International Law* (OUP, 2008); I Venzke, *How Interpretation Makes International Law: On Semantic Change and Normative Twists* (OUP, 2012).

those who apply the law, in particular to judicial and arbitral tribunals, as the act of interpretation is often regarded as 'a judicial function, whose purpose is to determine the precise meaning of a provision, but which cannot change it'.[90]

Generally speaking, there seem to be three common aims of the process of treaty interpretation. The first approach, generally styled an 'objective' approach, aims to discern the objective meaning of the actual text of a treaty provision, and to emphasize 'textuality', or the analysis of the words used.[91] The second method would be to peek 'behind' the text itself, and look to the intention of the parties to an agreement as a means to resolve any ambiguities; this is often termed a 'subjective approach'.[92] A third approach is seen as teleological or 'purposive', and emphasizes the object and purpose of a treaty as the foundation against which the meaning of any specific provision should be understood.[93]

Though these methods of interpretation differ substantially in emphasis, all strive to identify the aim or meaning of a treaty provision, and no method excludes the others entirely. Article 31 VCLT, which lays down the general rule in its first paragraph, comprises aspects of all three methods, prescribing that '[a] treaty shall be interpreted in good faith in accordance with the ordinary meaning to be given to the terms of the treaty in their context and in light of its object and purpose'. Article 31 can certainly be taken as reflective of customary international law, having been applied frequently by several international courts and tribunals.[94]

THEORY AND DEBATES Article 31 VCLT and the Methods of Interpretation

It is true that Article 31 VCLT is considered to be customary international law. But widespread acceptance need not entail clarity: as Martti Koskenniemi has drily noted, Article 31 refers indiscriminately to 'virtually all thinkable interpretative methods' (M Koskenniemi, *From Apology to Utopia: The Structure of International Legal Argument* (CUP reissue, 2005), 334, fn 89). Whatever one's view on Article 31, it is true that the methods of interpretation laid out in it remain tightly intertwined: in its early advisory opinion in *Admission of a State to the United Nations* (*ICJ Reports 1950*, p 4), the ICJ stated that 'the first duty of a tribunal which is called upon to interpret and apply provisions of a treaty, is to endeavour to give effect to them in their natural and ordinary meaning in the context in which they occur' (p 8).

[90] *Laguna del Desierto* arbitration *(Argentina/Chile)* (1994) 113 ILR 1, 44. *Cf* J Stone, 'Fictional Elements in Treaty Interpretation' (1955) 1 Sydney LR 344.

[91] See G Fitzmaurice, 'The Law and Procedure of the International Court of Justice, 1951–54: General Principles, and Sources of Law' (1953) 30 BYBIL 1, 204–7.

[92] See H Lauterpacht, 'De l'interprétation des traités: rapport et projet de résolutions' (1950) 43 Annuaire de l'Institut de droit international 366.

[93] See Fitzmaurice, 'Law and Procedure' (n 90) 207–9.

[94] See, e.g., *Restrictions on Imports of Tuna—United States*, GATT Dispute Settlement Panel Report (1994), (1994) 33 ILM 839, 892; *Iron Rhine (Belgium/the Netherlands)*, Arbitral Award of 24 May 2005, para 45; *Application of the Convention for the Prevention and Punishment of the Crime of Genocide (Bosnia and Herzegovina v Serbia), Merits, ICJ Reports 2007*, p 43, 109–10; *Responsibility and Obligations of States Sponsoring Persons and Entities with Respect to Activities in the Area, Advisory Opinion of 1 February 2011*, ITLOS Case No 17, para 57; and *Maritime Dispute (Peru v Chile), Judgment, ICJ Reports 2014*, p 3, para 57.

Is there a hierarchy between the different methods outlined in Article 31? It would seem that formally there is none. When proposing what became Article 31, the ILC thought of the three methods as unified, using a colourful metaphor: 'all the various elements, as they were present in any given case, would be thrown into the *crucible*, and their interaction would give the legally relevant interpretation' ((1966) ILC Ybk vol II, pt 2, pp 219–20). It is true that the ICJ has now settled on an approach that seemingly starts with a search for ordinary meaning in the text (see, e.g., *Territorial Dispute (Libyan Arab Jamahiriya/Chad), Judgment, ICJ Reports 1994*, p 6, para 41; *Oil Platforms (Iran v United States), Preliminary Objections, ICJ Reports 1996*, p 806, para 23). But this is hardly mechanistic: in a 2023 academic survey of the Court's stated interpretative method across a range of cases, one observes a more pragmatic, iterative approach, drawing from all of the rules of the VCLT when the context has required it: see S Lekkas, P Merkouris, and D Peat, 'The Interpretative Practice of the International Court of Justice' (2023) 26 Max-Planck YBIL 316.

Rather than to divine a hierarchy where none exists, perhaps the equally pragmatic approach of the Eritrea–Ethiopia Boundary Commission is useful: in its *Decision on Boundary Delimitation* (130 ILR 1, p 34), it suggested that Article 31 served as a comprehensive guide to discern the 'common will' of the parties. It is perhaps in this more pragmatic understanding of Article 31 as a set of guidelines, rather than the seeking of a rigid hierarchical method, that the complex phenomenon of treaty interpretation becomes more easily understandable.

Turning now to other features of Article 31, the term 'context' mentioned therein has been understood to refer to the preamble and annexes of a treaty instrument, as well as any external agreement or instrument made by the parties in connection with it.[95] To give a classic example, in its advisory opinion on *Interpretation of the Convention of 1919 concerning Employment of Women during the Night*, the PCIJ interpreted the terms of Article 3 of that Convention in light of the object and purpose of the Convention, which it considered to be found in the preamble of the Convention and its Articles 1 and 2.[96]

A further controversial question concerns what constitutes relevant 'subsequent practice', an additional 'primary' means of interpretation.[97] Subsequent practice of the parties can represent a tacit agreement between them to depart from their original intention as embodied in the text of the treaty. Perhaps for this reason, though it acknowledges the principle, the ICJ has adopted a restrictive interpretation of what may be considered relevant subsequent practice. In the *Kasikili/Sedudu Island* judgment, it excluded the unilateral acts of one of the parties that was purely for internal purposes, as well as a subsequent agreement between Botswana and Namibia, which the Court declared had no effect on the interpretation of the relevant treaty.[98] In *Whaling in the Antarctic*, in interpreting the International Convention on the Regulation of Whaling (ICRW), the Court similarly excluded resolutions of the International Whaling Commission as possible subsequent practice within the terms of Article 31(3) VCLT, as these resolutions had

[95] *United States Nationals in Morocco (France v United States), ICJ Reports 1952*, p 176, 196.

[96] *1932, PCIJ, Ser A/B, No 50*, p 365, 373.

[97] VCLT (n 4) Art 31(3).

[98] *Kasikili/Sedudu Island* (n 6) paras 49, 52–79.

not been adopted with the support of all States parties to the Convention.[99] However, in interpreting a bilateral treaty between Costa Rica and Nicaragua, in which the parties disputed the use of a generic term, '*objetos de comercio*' ('objects of commerce'), the Court embraced a concept of 'evolutive interpretation' as subsequent practice, in which parties could ascribe a meaning or content to a term that was capable of evolving, so as to make allowance for, among other things, developments in international law.[100] The Court cautioned that, in such instances of evolutive interpretation, where subsequent practice is deemed as a relevant element it must respect the parties' common intention at the time the treaty was concluded, and not depart from it.[101]

Finally, Article 31(3)(c) VCLT provides, somewhat controversially, that other 'relevant rules' of international law may be taken into account when interpreting a treaty. This provision has been used by the ICJ in the *Oil Platforms* judgment to justify recourse to the UN Charter and its rules concerning the use of force in interpreting the Iran–United States Treaty of Amity, Economic Relations and Consular Rights.[102] In *Certain Questions of Mutual Assistance*, the Court acknowledged Article 31(3)(c) as being customary law, and thus interpreted a 1986 Convention on Mutual Assistance in Criminal Matters, between Djibouti and France, in light of the 1977 Treaty of Friendship and Co-operation between those same States.[103] More recently, in *Certain Iranian Assets*, though the Court again endorsed the principle, on the facts it rejected an Iranian claim that the customary international law on immunities was incorporated, by reference or implication, in Articles IV and X(1) of the 1955 Treaty of Amity between Iran and the USA.[104]

7.4.3.2 **Supplementary means of treaty interpretation**

Though Article 31 VCLT is expansive in its list of 'primary' means of interpretation, situations nevertheless arise where, after application of these primary means, the meaning of a treaty provision remains ambiguous or obscure, or perhaps might lead to a manifestly absurd or unreasonable result. In such cases, Article 32 VCLT allows for the use of *supplementary means of interpretation*,[105] such as the use of preparatory materials (*travaux préparatoires*), or investigation of the circumstances of a treaty's conclusion.

[99] *Whaling in the Antarctic (Australia v Japan; New Zealand intervening), Judgment, ICJ Reports 2014*, p 226, para 83. It bears noting that these resolutions were also opposed by Japan, the respondent.

[100] *Dispute regarding Navigational and Related Rights between Costa Rica and Nicaragua, Judgment, ICJ Reports 2009*, p 213, paras 64–8. See also *Pulp Mills on the River Uruguay (Argentina v Uruguay), Judgment, ICJ Reports 2010*, p 14, 83.

[101] *Ibid*, para 64. See further ILC, 'Draft Conclusions on Subsequent Agreements and Subsequent Practice in relation to the Interpretation of Treaties, with Commentaries in Report of the International Law Commission on the Work of its Seventieth Session', GAOR A/73/10 Supp No 10 (2018).

[102] *Oil Platforms (Iran v United States), Judgment, ICJ Reports 2003*, p 161, 182.

[103] *Certain Questions of Mutual Assistance in Criminal Matters (Djibouti v France), Judgment, ICJ Reports 2008*, p 177, 219.

[104] *Certain Iranian Assets (Iran v United States), Preliminary Objections, ICJ Reports 2019*, p 7, paras 55, 67–80.

[105] (1966) ILC Ybk vol II, pt 2, p 223.

CONTEMPORARY DEVELOPMENTS The Use of *Travaux Préparatoires* by the International Court of Justice

Recourse to supplementary means of interpretation can be controversial, whether one is confirming an interpretation arrived at under Article 31, or in situations where they are deployed to aid in the interpretative process. The Court used to be reluctant to engage with supplementary means: in *Maritime Delimitation and Territorial Questions between Qatar and Bahrain*, both parties relied on preparatory materials in support of their submissions in relation to whether Qatar could submit a unilateral application to the ICJ. Warning that preparatory work should be used with the utmost caution, the Court rejected the submissions of both parties as to the weight of preparatory materials, choosing instead to rely only upon the actual terms of a written agreement (the 'Minutes') as the expression of their common intention (para 41). On that basis, the Court concluded that a unilateral application by one of the parties was sufficient for its jurisdiction to be established. One could surmise that the Minutes were considered to suffice to constitute a written agreement for this reason, though the Court does not acknowledge the point.

More recently, in *Application of the International Convention on the Elimination of All Forms of Racial Discrimination (Georgia v Russian Federation), Preliminary Objections, Judgment, ICJ Reports 2011*, p 70, paras 142–7; *Jadhav (India v Pakistan), Judgment, ICJ Reports 2019*, p 418 paras 76–86; and *Application of the* International *Convention on the Elimination of All Forms of Racial Discrimination (Qatar v United Arab Emirates), Preliminary Objections, ICJ Reports 2021*, p 71, paras 89–97, the Court has considered arguments from both parties relating to *travaux préparatoires*. In all three cases, though the Court expressly concluded that it 'need not resort to supplementary means of interpretation' to arrive at an interpretation, it acknowledged that both parties had relied on them in their submissions and considered it appropriate to examine the *travaux préparatoires* in order to confirm its reading of the relevant provisions being disputed, and to ensure that no different conclusion might arise from the *travaux préparatoires*.

Finally, Article 33 VCLT addresses treaties authenticated in more than one language. This is of considerable importance given the long-standing practice, begun with Article 111 of the UN Charter, that each of the versions in which the text of a multilateral convention is 'drawn up' is considered to be equally authentic.[106] In its merits judgment in *Nicaragua*, the ICJ examined both the French and English versions of Article 53 of its Statute in order to align them and arrive at an interpretation that was consistent with both language versions.[107] The Court there was following the PCIJ's long-standing practice in *Mavrommatis Palestine Concessions*: '[w]here two versions possessing equal authority exist, one of which appears to have a wider bearing than the other, [the Court] is bound to adopt the more limited interpretation which can be made to harmonize with both versions and which . . . is . . . in accordance with the common intention of the parties'.[108]

[106] *Ibid*, pp 224–5. [107] *Nicaragua (Jurisdiction and Admissibility)* (n 41) 405–6.

[108] *Mavrommatis Palestine Concessions, Judgment No 2, 1924, PCIJ, Ser A, No 2*. For further reflections on linguistic issues, see GI Hernández, 'On Multilingualism in the International Legal Process' in H Ruiz-Fabri, R Wolfrum, and J Gogolin (eds), *Select Proceedings of the European Society of International Law* (2008) (Hart, 2010), vol 2, 441.

7.4.3.3 The 'principle of effectiveness' and treaty interpretation

A further interpretive maxim, *ut res magis valeat quam pereat*,[109] suggests that treaties are to be interpreted with reference to their declared objects and purposes, and that provisions should be interpreted to give the fullest effect consistent with the normal sense of the words and with other parts of the text.[110] The 'principle of effectiveness' has three corollaries. First, all provisions of the treaty are presumed to have been intended to have significance, or to be necessary to convey the intended meaning. Secondly, the treaty as a whole, and each of its provisions, must be taken to have been intended to secure some purpose. Thirdly, any interpretation that would make the text ineffective or meaningless would be incorrect.[111]

Though the ICJ regards the principle as having an 'important role' in the law of treaties,[112] it cannot be invoked simply to give effect to a provision where the intention of the parties was wholly contrary to the desired interpretation. For example, in *Interpretation of Peace Treaties*, the ICJ was asked to advise whether the UN Secretary-General could appoint the third member of a Treaty Commission upon the request of one side to the dispute if the other side (Bulgaria, Hungary, and Romania) refused to appoint its own representative. The natural and ordinary meaning of the relevant provisions in the peace treaties envisaged the appointment of the third member only after the other two had been nominated. As such, the Court concluded that the principle of effectiveness did not allow it to attribute a meaning to the provisions that would offend their letter and spirit.[113]

The principle of effectiveness can therefore only be invoked to give effect to provisions in accordance with the intentions of the parties,[114] and in conformity with international law.[115] There seem to be two areas of international law in which it has proven relevant. The first is where a treaty operates as the constitutuent instrument of an international organization, so as to infer certain powers which are deemed necessary in the context of the functions and purposes of that organization, in particular relating to the United Nations.[116] The second is the principle of the 'dynamic' interpretation of treaties,

[109] 'That the thing may rather have effect than to fail/to be destroyed.'

[110] This wording was used by Sir Gerald Fitzmaurice, 'Treaty Interpretation and Other Treaty Points, 1951–54' (1957) 33 BYBIL 203.

[111] It has been cautioned that the teleological aspect of the principle of effectiveness is similar to the 'object and purpose' criterion and, in the same way, must be employed with some caution: see H Thirlway, 'The Law and Practice of the International Court of Justice: Part Three (1960–1989)' (1992) 63 BYBIL 1.

[112] *Fisheries Jurisdiction (Spain v Canada), Preliminary Objections, ICJ Reports 1998*, p 432, 455.

[113] *Interpretation of Peace Treaties with Bulgaria, Hungary and Romania, Advisory Opinion, Second Phase, ICJ Reports 1950*, p 221, 226–30.

[114] *Ambatielos (Greece v United Kingdom), Judgment, ICJ Reports 1952*, p 29.

[115] *Fisheries Jurisdiction (Spain v Canada)* (n 111) 455.

[116] *Reparations for Injuries caused in the Service of the United Nations, Advisory Opinion, ICJ Reports 1949*, p 174 (on the legal personality of the organization); *Competence of the General Assembly for the Admission of a State, Advisory Opinion, ICJ Reports 1950*, p 4 (on the rules for admission of new members); *Certain Expenses of the United Nations (Article 17, paragraph 2, of the Charter), Advisory Opinion, ICJ Reports 1962*, p 151 (on the budgetary powers of an organ of an international organization); and *Namibia* (n 7) (on the survival of the mandates of the League of Nations under the Trusteeship system of the United Nations). Jan Klabbers calls this the doctrine of *functionalism*: see 'The Transformation of International Organizations Law' (2015) 26 EJIL 9.

used notably by the ECtHR. In a series of seminal cases, the Court held that the ECHR had established a specialized, 'objective' legal order, and had to be interpreted as a 'living instrument', to evolve 'in the light of present-day conditions' to secure the human rights enshrined in it.[117] The ECtHR's interpretation of the ECHR could be seen as a form of *lex specialis* in relation to human rights regimes, or could be seen as a strongly teleological interpretation based on the object and purpose of the treaty.

7.5 Grounds for invalidity, termination, and suspension

7.5.1 Possible invalidity of treaties

Despite the relative elasticity of formalities regarding a treaty, there remain circumstances in which a treaty comes to be regarded as invalid. The VCLT envisages roughly two categories of situations when invalidity may be invoked, relative grounds for invalidity (Articles 46–50) and absolute grounds for invalidity (Articles 51–3); both lead to different outcomes. Relative grounds for invalidity may be invoked by one party as against the offending party, but do not affect the validity of a treaty as a whole between the remaining parties. In short, the treaty becomes voidable between the invoking and offending parties. Conversely, absolute grounds for invalidity render the treaty void *ab initio* and devoid of legal effect between all parties: the treaty is regarded as having never existed at all, and all parties are released from their legal obligations flowing from it.

Relative grounds for nullity often relate to a lack of competence to bind the State or a procedural defect, and are enumerated in the VCLT as follows:

- the treaty was concluded through a manifest violation of a rule of the internal law of a party which was of fundamental importance;[118]
- a State representative has been placed under a restriction such that they cannot bind the State, when other negotiating States are aware of such a restriction;[119]
- a State has committed a certain type of error;[120]
- a State was induced to consent through the fraud of another negotiating State;[121] or
- a State representative has been corrupted by another negotiating State.[122]

In modern diplomatic relations, it is safe to say that such circumstances are rare,[123] and never has a State successfully availed itself of one of the relative grounds for nullity before an international court.[124]

[117] *Golder v United Kingdom* (1975) 1 EHRR 524; *Tyrer v United Kingdom* (1978) 2 EHRR 1; *Marckx v Belgium* (1979) 2 EHRR 330. See also *Loizidou v Turkey (Preliminary Objections)* App No 15318/89 (1995) ECHR Ser A No 310.

[118] VCLT (n 4) Art 46(1).

[119] *Ibid*, Art 47.

[120] *Ibid*, Art 48.

[121] *Ibid*, Art 49.

[122] *Ibid*, Art 50.

[123] Aust (n 81) 252, suggests that in his thirty years with the British Foreign and Commonwealth Office, there was no serious issue of invalidity raised.

[124] See, e.g., the unsuccessful attempts of Nigeria to invoke a defect of internal law in *Land and Maritime Boundary between Cameroon and Nigeria* (n 13) para 265; of Somalia to do likewise in *Maritime Delimitation in the Indian Ocean* (n 13) para 49; and of Thailand to invoke error in *Temple of Preah Vihear (Cambodia v Thailand), Judgment, ICJ Reports 1962*, p 6, at 26.

Absolute grounds for invalidity will lead to the nullity *ab initio* of a treaty; it will be as though the treaty never existed. Absolute invalidity will operate as a matter of law; no judicial or other declaration is needed.[125] This is the case when a treaty has been signed due to coercion of a representative,[126] or through the threat or use of force by one party against another.[127] Though situations where the consent of one party is fundamentally compromised are rare, one example is when President Hacha of Czechoslovakia was coerced by Göring and Ribbentrop to sign a treaty with Nazi Germany in 1931, allowing it to establish a protectorate over Bohemia and Moravia. A second may well be Article II of the bilateral Treaty of Basic Relations of 1965, in which South Korea and Japan 'confirmed that all treaties or agreements concluded by [the Parties] on or before August 22, 1910 [date of the annexation of Korea by Japan], are already null and void.'[128] There is ambiguity, however, regarding the basis for this nullity and whether it was due to coercion, aggression, or otherwise.

There is an exception for peace treaties that arise due to the military defeat of one party by another, such as the 1919 Treaty of Versailles in relation to Germany or the defeat of Iraq by the US-led coalition in 1990. In these two cases, a circuitous answer was devised, that no coercion could be said to exist as the aggressor had breached international law from the outset. On both occasions, was claimed that the victorious powers had acted in conformity with international law.[129]

Finally, Article 53 VCLT provides that a treaty in breach of a peremptory norm (of *jus cogens*) is void. It is unusual in that absolute invalidity may exist due to a matter not of form, but due to a defect in the substance of the treaty. Article 64 VCLT further specifies that if a new peremptory norm emerges, any existing treaty in conflict with it becomes void and terminates automatically. It is thus clear from the wording of Articles 53 and 64 that no derogation is permitted from peremptory norms, though there is controversy as to which norms are viewed as peremptory, not to mention the process through which they come to be regarded as such. In particular, the question arises as to how many States are required to compose the 'international community

[125] J Klabbers, 'The Validity and Invalidity of Treaties' in D Hollis (ed), *The Oxford Guide to Treaties* (OUP, 2012), 551, 567–8.

[126] VCLT (n 4) Art 51.

[127] *Ibid*, Art 52. See the drafting history surveyed by G Del Negro, 'The Validity of Treaties Concluded under Coercion of the State: Sketching a TWAIL Critique' (2017) 10 European Journal of Legal Studies 39.

[128] For a historical account of how Japanese advisers deployed international law arguments to purport lawfully to annex Korea, see A Dudden, *Japan's Colonization of Korea: Discourse and Power* (University of Hawaii Press, 2006). Though not effected by treaty, an analogy may well be to the text of the 'Declaration on Austria' of the British, Soviet, and American Governments (1 November 1943) that they regarded the *Anschluss* of Austria into Nazi Germany to be 'null and void' and flowing from the latter's aggression: reprinted in State Department, *A Decade of American Foreign Policy: Basic Documents, 1941–49* (Department of State Publications, Washington, 1950), at 13.

[129] In relation to the 1919 Treaty of Versailles, it bears mentioning that it was signed before the prohibition on the use of force had entered into customary international law, so it is likely that there was no legal concept of duress as a ground of invalidity at the time.

of States as a whole'.[130] As Chapter 3 explored, the concept of peremptory norms also introduces a hierarchy of norms into the international legal system that arguably changes its very nature as its legal system.[131] Yet the idea that certain types of conduct are in violation of international public policy is hardly new,[132] and if the category of peremptory norms is to have any substantive legal meaning, it surely follows that no State may simply contract out of it.

7.5.2 **Termination and suspension of treaties**

Unlike an invalid treaty, which is *devoid* of any legal effect, a terminated treaty is one which *no longer* generates legal effect. Though after termination the parties are released from any obligation further to perform the treaty,[133] termination of a treaty does not affect any rights, obligations, or the legal situation of the parties created through the treaty prior to its termination.[134] Suspension of a treaty is somewhat different, in that the treaty is not definitively put to an end; rather, the parties are released from any mutual obligations resulting from the treaty during the period of suspension.[135] The modalities for both the termination and suspension of treaties are laid out in Articles 54–9 VCLT.

7.5.2.1 **Termination or suspension by operation of the treaty**

A treaty may contain a specific provision allowing for its termination or suspension; if not, all parties may give their consent to its termination or suspension.[136] A treaty might also set out a procedure for its denunciation by only one or some parties, leading to their effective withdrawal from the treaty regime after a period of time. For example, Bolivia, Venezuela, and Ecuador have all denounced the ICSID Convention through a provision that requires a denouncing party to give six months' notice before withdrawal is effective.[137] Though controversial, during the notice period, the three States remained bound by the Convention, and investors were permitted to file new cases, the resolution of which might extend well beyond the withdrawal date. A similar legal situation prevailed with respect to Russia for cases filed during the period between its denunciation of the European Convention of Human Rights on 15 March 2022 and its effective withdrawal from the Convention only six months later.[138]

[130] Such controversy may be the reason why the ICJ only acknowledged the category of *jus cogens* in 2006: see *Armed Activities in the Territory of the Congo (New Application: 2002) (Democratic Republic of the Congo v Rwanda), Jurisdiction and Admissibility, ICJ Reports 2006*, p 6, para 64.

[131] See, e.g., P Weil, 'Towards Relative Normativity in International Law' (1983) 77 AJIL 413–42.

[132] As early as the 1930s, Alfred Verdross was advancing the argument that immoral treaties were void *ab initio*: see A von Verdross, 'Forbidden Treaties in International Law' (1937) 31 AJIL 571.

[133] VCLT (n 4) Art 70(1)(a). [134] *Ibid*, Art 70(1)(b). [135] *Ibid*, Art 72.

[136] *Ibid*, Art 54 provides the general rule for termination; Art 57 VCLT addresses the suspension of a treaty.

[137] ICSID Convention on the Settlement of Disputes between States and Nationals of Other States, (1965) 575 UNTS 159, Arts 71–2.

[138] See art 58 ECHR; *Kutayev v Russia*, Judgment of the Third Section, ECtHR App No 17912/15 (24 January 2023), paras 77–80; *Svetova and ors v Russia*, Judgment of the Third Section, ECtHR App No 54714/17 (24 January 2023), paras 26–8. See also IACtHR, *Obligations in Matters of Human Rights of a State that has Denounced the ACHR and the OAS Charter, Advisory Opinion, IACtHR Doc OC-26/20* (9 November 2020), which addressed the issue in that context.

Parties may also stipulate that a treaty will be of limited duration, or terminated automatically when its purposes or objects have been fulfilled. This might be the case, for example, when a common project such the construction of a dam on a riparian boundary has been completed. Such treaties are relatively rare, as most common projects of that nature will still require some long-term supervision, maintenance, and management, and thus the existence of continued obligations. One ought also not to presume that a treaty establishing a boundary, or to purchase equipment, has been terminated once performance has been executed: though the treaty might appear to have been fully performed, the treaty is still needed in order to address possible disputes that might arise about obligations under the treaty.

Article 58 VCLT provides that some, but not all, parties may by agreement suspend the operation of a multilateral treaty *inter se*, but only if provision is made in the treaty for *inter se* suspension; and similarly to Article 41 VCLT in relation to the modification of treaty provisions, it does not affect the rights or obligations of other parties, and it is not incompatible with the object and purpose of the treaty.

7.5.2.2 **Termination or suspension without specific provision**

In many cases, a treaty neither contains specific provisions regarding denunciation or withdrawal. In such situations, a party may only do so if the parties intended to allow such a possibility, or where the right may be implied by the nature of the treaty.[139] It does not apply, for example, with respect to the ICCPR: in General Comment No 26,[140] the HRC noted that the Covenant contained no provision for denunciation or withdrawal, and moreover, that no evidence existed that the parties intended to admit of such a possibility. The Committee further also concluded that the Covenant, a multilateral instrument codifying important human rights, was not of such a nature so as to imply a right of denunciation or withdrawal.

If all the parties to an existing treaty conclude a later agreement on the same subject matter, Article 59 VCLT provides that the earlier treaty may be then deemed to have been terminated.[141] However, this would only be the case if it is apparent that the subject matter covered by the treaty is fully governed by the later agreement, or where there is such an incompatibility between the terms of the earlier and later treaty that, in practice, it is impossible to comply with both treaties at the same time. Otherwise, Article 30 VCLT will be applicable; it seeks to accommodate the effect of successive treaties relating to the same subject matter, and in which a number of scenarios are contemplated for resolving a possible conflict between successive treaties when the earlier one has not been terminated or suspended in operation under Article 59 VCLT.

[139] VCLT (n 4) Art 56.

[140] See Human Rights Committee, General Comment No 26 (1997), A/53/40, annex VII.

[141] VCLT (n 4) Art 59.

7.5.2.3 **Further grounds for termination**

In addition to the situations earlier where a treaty is terminated through prior or subsequent agreement, the VCLT has envisaged three further grounds which may allow one party to terminate or suspend its treaty obligations: material breach, supervening impossibility of performance, and fundamental change of circumstances.

7.5.2.3.1 ***Material breach***

If a party is in material breach of a treaty obligation, the logic of reciprocity suggests that other parties to that agreement may terminate or at least suspend their obligations under that agreement in relation to that State. This is the long-standing principle of *inadimplenti non est adimplendum* ('one has no need to respect his obligation if the counter-party has not respected his own'), codified in Article 60 VCLT. The ICJ has described this as the 'fundamental principl[e] . . . that a party which disowns or does not fulfil its own obligations cannot be recognized as retaining the rights which it claims to derive from the relationship.'[142] In practice, the *exceptio inadimpleti contractus* has rarely been invoked, perhaps due to the destabilizing effect of allowing States unilaterally to invoke material breach. That said, it is not inexistent: for example, the OIC suspended Egypt in 1979, after a declaration that Egypt was 'in flagrant violation' of its Charter when it signed the Camp David Accords, which led to the conclusion of a peace treaty with Israel.[143] It is worth acknowledging that Article 60(5) VCLT does not allow a party to invoke material breach by another party to justify the suspension of obligations in 'treaties of a humanitarian character' (discussed in Chapter 15).

CASE SPOTLIGHT ***Application of the Interim Accord of 13 September 1995 (the former Yugoslav Republic of Macedonia v Greece), ICJ Reports 2011, p 644***

Greece and the former Yugoslav Republic of Macedonia (FYROM) have for decades been in a dispute with respect to the name of the latter State, as the name 'Macedonia' is understood by both States to have historical significance. In the 'Interim Accord' that was the subject of the dispute, FYROM undertook not to use the name 'Republic of Macedonia' on an interim basis, instead being seated at the UN under FYROM, and Greece agreed not to oppose FYROM's participation in certain institutions. When FYROM adopted a prohibited symbol on its flag in 2004, Greece objected to its application to join NATO. The *inadimplenti non est adimplendum* exception was invoked by Greece as a 'general principle of law', to justify its breaches of the Interim Accord between the parties.

Greece's submission raised an interesting conceptual issue which was in need of clarification, as it simultaneously justified its conduct as an *exceptio inadimpleti* contractus (or material breach) under the law of treaties, as well as a 'countermeasure' under the law of State

[142] *Namibia* (n 7) 46, para 91. See also *Gabčíkovo-Nagymaros* (n 7) 46–7, para 94.

[143] Article 2(a)(6) of the Charter of the Organization of the Islamic Conference (signed 4 March 1972, entered into force 1 February 1974), XX UNTS 113 stipulates that that all members 'are obliged to assist the Palestinian fight against Israel'. Some have called the episode an example of material breach: see K Magliveras, *Exclusion from Participation in International Organisations* (Kluwer, The Hague 1999) at 237.

responsibility. Though we will study countermeasures in Chapter 13 (see esp Section 13.4.1), a brief explanation is that countermeasures allow for limited responses by an injured State to a breach by another State, in order to induce the State to resume compliance with its treaty obligations.

The two concepts are intimately linked and, at the ILC, Special Rapporteur James Crawford had argued that both concepts could coexist on this point, with the law of treaties being concerned 'with the content of primary rules and with the validity of attempts to alter them', and the law of State responsibility concerned with 'the question whether the conduct inconsistent with [primary] rules can be excused' (see Third Report on State Responsibility, A/CN.4507/Add3.).

Returning to the *Interim Accord* judgment, the ICJ seemed to endorse Crawford's approach, when it considered Greece's submissions that its actions might be justifiable both as a response to material breach under the law of treaties, and as a countermeasure under the law of State responsibility.

The Court acknowledged that the doctrines shared certain minimum conditions, but that FYROM had breached a single provision of the Interim Accord by using a prohibited symbol on its flag in 2004. However, FYROM had discontinued its breach as soon as Greece had expressed concern, and the Court was unconvinced that FYROM's breach was material (para 163). Consequently, the Court rejected the argument by Greece that its own breaches were justified responses to FYROM's conduct (para 164), noting in particular that there was no connection between them on the facts.

The dispute has finally drawn to a close: following a referendum in FYROM, and a vote in the Greek Parliament, the newly named 'Republic of Northern Macedonia' signed an accession protocol to join NATO on 6 February 2019.

As such, Article 60 VCLT adopts a fairly restrictive approach: an injured party must meet strict requirements to invoke material breach as a ground for suspension or termination, and its freedom of action is limited.[144] Moreover, the 'synallagmatic' (mutual agreement) structure of such an exception limits its application in cases where multilateral treaties are concerned: a breach by one State does not excuse a second State in relation to third States which have not committed any breach. The scope of what constitutes 'material breach' is similarly limited. It consists of either a repudiation of a treaty not permitted by the VCLT,[145] or the violation of a provision essential to the accomplishment of the object and purpose of that treaty.[146] Moreover, termination or suspension on the basis of a material breach cannot apply to provisions relating to the 'protection of the human person contained in treaties of a humanitarian character, in particular to provisions prohibiting any form of reprisals against persons protected by such treaties'.[147] This restriction is based on the non-reciprocal nature of such obligations, which are intransgressible.[148]

[144] See, in this respect, the Separate Opinion of Judge Simma in the previous Case Spotlight on *Application of the Interim Accord*, p 695, paras 10–13, who cautioned about the risk of abuse of a wider principle without the availability of some form of external control such as the judicial control exercised by domestic courts.

[145] VCLT (n 4) Art 60(3). [146] See *Namibia* (n 7) 16, 46–7. [147] VCLT (n 4) Art 60(5).

[148] *Legality of the Threat or Use of Nuclear Weapons, Advisory Opinion, ICJ Reports 1996*, p 226, para 79; *Legal Consequences of the Construction of a Wall in the Occupied Palestinian Territory, Advisory Opinion, ICJ Reports 2004*, p 136, para 157.

Regrettably, the limitation in Article 60, paragraph 5, VCLT only applies to a specific category of treaties, and not to other multilateral, normative treaties where all parties have a stake in their realization, such as treaties on the environment, or those on biological and chemical weapons. The balance achieved within Article 60 VCLT lies between upholding the stability of treaty obligations and the protection of parties against the breach of another party.

7.5.2.3.2 ***Supervening impossibility of performance***

If, after a treaty has been concluded, certain circumstances emerge which render the performance of an obligation under that treaty permanently impossible, a party to an agreement may withdraw from or terminate it.[149] Such situations of what is essentially *force majeure* or an 'Act of God' are extremely rare: the doctrine applies only to unusual circumstances such as a boundary river drying up or the extinction of a certain species of straddling fish. To invoke supervening impossibility of performance, one cannot have caused that impossibility.

7.5.2.3.3 ***Fundamental change of circumstances (rebus sic stantibus)***

Finally, a controversial means available to a party is to invoke *rebus sic stantibus*, according to which a 'fundamental change of circumstances' provides the grounds to terminate a treaty. The dispute over *rebus sic stantibus* flows from the fact that it undermines *pacta sunt servanda*, the cornerstone of the law of treaties; it allows one party unilaterally to undermine the stability of treaty relations by identifying circumstances that allow it to terminate its contracted obligations.[150] As such, though the ICJ conceded the existence of the doctrine in the *Fisheries Jurisdiction* judgment, it is severely narrowed in its scope:

> [i]nternational law admits that a fundamental change in the circumstances which determined the parties to accept a treaty, if it has resulted in a radical transformation of the extent of obligation imposed by it, may, under certain conditions, afford the party affected a ground for invoking the termination or suspension of a treaty.[151]

As the Court stated, for a party to invoke the doctrine, it is necessary that such changes 'must have increased the burden of the obligations to be executed to the extent of rendering the performance something essentially different from that originally undertaken'.[152] As the following Case Spotlight illustrates, the Court followed a similarly strict line of reasoning in the *Gabčíkovo-Nagymaros* judgment.[153] The only international tribunal

[149] VCLT (n 4) Art 61.

[150] Sinclair, *Vienna Convention on the Law of Treaties* (n 81) 193; E Schwelb, 'Notes on Article 59 of the Draft Convention on the Law of Treaties as recommended for adoption to the United Nations Conference on the Law of Treaties by its Committee of the Whole in 1968' (1969) ZaöRV 39, esp 43–4; J Garner, 'The Doctrine of *Rebus Sic Stantibus* and the Termination of Treaties' (1927) 21 AJIL 409.

[151] *Icelandic Fisheries Jurisdiction* (n 5) 20–1, para 36. [152] *Ibid.*

[153] *Ibid.* See also ILC Articles on the Effect of Armed Conflicts on the Law of Treaties (n 16).

that has actually upheld *rebus sic stantibus* is the European Court of Justice, which concluded in the 1998 *Racke* judgment that the outbreak of civil war in Yugoslavia constituted a sufficiently fundamental change. Therefore, the EU could lawfully suspend its free trade agreement with Yugoslavia, which had been premised on the existence of stable State institutions which were now inexistent.[154]

CASE SPOTLIGHT ***Gabčíkovo-Nagymaros Project (Hungary/Slovakia), Judgment, ICJ Reports 1997*, p 7**

The 1997 *Gabčíkovo-Nagymaros* judgment made important clarifications in understanding the grounds for the termination of treaties. The case concerned a 1977 bilateral treaty to construct a dam on the River Danube, which runs through both countries. After both States replaced their Communist governments, Hungary no longer wished to construct the dam as had been agreed in the 1977 treaty. It invoked several grounds under the VCLT in support of its view that the 1977 treaty was no longer binding.

First, Hungary had claimed that Slovakia was in material breach of certain other treaties, justifying Hungary's termination of the 1977 treaty. The Court rejected that claim, concluding that 'only material breach of the treaty itself, by a State party to that treaty, . . . entitles the other party to rely on it as a ground for terminating the treaty' (para 106). The Court did explain that Hungary could take other permissible measures in response to the violation by Slovakia, such as countermeasures, but that it could not invoke the provisions of Article 60 VCLT to terminate its obligations. Moreover, the Court determined that Hungary's attempt to terminate the 1977 treaty was premature, given that the actions complained of had not yet violated that treaty, and that Hungary only provided Slovakia with nineteen days' notice of its intention to terminate the treaty (para 110).

Secondly, Hungary contended that to construct the dam system would cause irreparable environmental damage, and was thus entitled to claim supervening impossibility of performance in order to terminate the treaty. The Court did not deny the principle, but took the view that the permanent disappearance or destruction of an object was required under Article 61(1) VCLT, which was not the case. Moreover, the Court held that if the joint exploitation of the project was no longer possible, this was originally due to Hungary's failure to perform most of the works for which it was responsible under the 1977 Treaty (para 103).

Thirdly, Hungary argued that a number of events had cumulatively emerged as a fundamental change of circumstances between the signature of the 1977 treaty and its notice of termination in 1992. These were not insignificant: that the notion of 'socialist economic integration' underpinning the 1977 treaty had fallen away; the replacement of a joint and unified operational system with separate unilateral schemes; the emergence of market economies in both States parties; and increased environmental awareness that the project would lead to environmental devastation (para 95). The Court, nevertheless, concluded that the changed circumstances invoked by Hungary were 'not of such a nature, either individually

[154] Case C-162/95 *A Racke GmbH & Co v Hauptzollamt Mainz* [1998] ECR I-3655, para 57; and Aust (n 81) 241–2, who suggests that the CJEU's treatment of the question was closer to judicial review of the acts of the European Council.

or collectively, that their effect would radically transform the extent of the obligations to be performed . . .' (para 104). The Court's interpretation of Article 62 VCLT was very strict: a 'fundamental change of circumstances must have been unforeseen; the existence of the circumstances at the time of the Treaty's conclusion must have constituted an essential basis of consent of the parties to be bound'; and 'the stability of treaty relations requires that the plea of fundamental change of circumstances should be applied only in exceptional cases' (*ibid*).

7.6 **Conclusion**

Treaties have become the dominant mode for States to agree binding obligations between them, and have been used both to foster inter-State agreement and for broader purposes, such as the codification of customary international law. Thanks to the 1969 Vienna Convention and many decades of practice by States, the law of treaties has evolved into a sophisticated, detailed field in which new challenges are constantly being addressed. Important multilateral treaties continue to be negotiated in areas where global collective action has been seen as necessary, though a lag can be observed between social and technological change and the treaty apparatus (recent examples might include global pandemic management and the regulation of cyberspace). That said, if anything, attention has shifted away from new treaties towards securing the effective enforcement and implementation of existing treaties.

There remain challenges in the law of treaties, rooted in the notion that treaties are the expression of consent. Areas of scholarly and practical interest that have taken on significance in recent years include the validity of reservations to human rights treaties, the possible evolution of treaty obligations in accordance with subsequent practice and agreements, and the provisional application of treaties. Consequently, this highly dynamic area will continue to be central to one's appreciation of international law for many years to come.

Further reading

J Hill, *Aust's Modern Treaty Law and Practice* (4th edn, CUP, 2023).

A classic, this revised book remains a defining treatment of the practice of States and international organizations in respect of treaties.

A Bowman and D Kritsiotis (eds), *Conceptual and Contextual Perspectives on the Modern Law of Treaties* (CUP, 2018).

An innovative and collaborative account that engages deeply with certain key concepts in the law of treaties and gives a modern account of their nature and scope.

E Cannizzaro (ed), *The Law of Treaties Beyond the Vienna Convention: Essays in Honour of Giorgio Gaja* (OUP, 2011).

A timely edited volume gathering distinguished figures and a wide range of perspectives.

O Corten and P Klein (eds), *The Vienna Convention on the Law of Treaties: A Commentary* (OUP, 2012).

This article-by-article commentary is an indispensable resource for researchers, students, and practitioners.

O Dörr and K Schmalenbach (eds), *Vienna Convention on the Law of Treaties: A Commentary* (2nd edn, Springer, 2018).

Featuring primarily German-language academics, this commentary provides a distinct perspective in this dynamic area.

R Gardiner, *Treaty Interpretation* (2nd edn, OUP, 2017).

A systematic, pragmatic approach to the interpretation of treaties.

J Klabbers, *The Concept of Treaty in International Law* (Martinus Nijhoff, 1996).

A lucid account of the notion of a treaty that defends their distinct form as a source of binding obligation, challenging the claims of equivalence of soft law instruments.

H Lauterpacht, 'Restrictive Interpretation and the Principle of Effectiveness in the Interpretation of Treaties' (1949) 26 BYBIL 48.

A classic, salient work developing the concept of effectiveness.

AD McNair, *The Law of Treaties* (rev edn, OUP, 1961).

A classic amongst English-speaking international lawyers, though its last edition predates the 1969 VCLT.

A Orakhelashvili, *The Interpretation of Acts and Rules in Public International Law* (OUP, 2008).

Going further than merely the interpretation of treaties, this comprehensive compendium of practice and judicial decisions makes it a useful resource.

P Reuter, *Introduction au droit des traités* (3rd edn revised by P Cahier, PUF, 1995), also translated into English as P Reuter, *Introduction to the Law of Treaties* (2nd edn, Publications de l'Institut universitaire de hautes etudes internationales, Geneva, 1995).

An excellent French-language treatise that adopts a civil law approach to the law of treaties.

8

Jurisdiction

8.1 Introduction: the reach of the State

The term 'jurisdiction' is generally understood by international lawyers to describe the extent, and limits, of the legal competence of a State, entity, or regulatory authority, to make, apply, and enforce legal rules with respect to persons, property, and other matters. Jurisdiction is the necessary corollary to State sovereignty, for it represents the exercise of authority of that State in relation to conduct, or to consequences of events, that it deems itself competent to regulate.[1]

The importance of the principles governing jurisdiction cannot be overstated. If jurisdiction represents the power of a State or other entity to regulate the conduct of individuals and their relations with one another, it determines the public order of a society composing a State, and perhaps the very qualities that distinguish one State from another. The formulation of jurisdictional claims, to the exclusion of other States, is thus a classic exercise of sovereignty, and is safeguarded in Article 2(7) of the UN Charter as what is known as the *domaine réservé*, or 'reserved domain of domestic jurisdiction': '[n]othing contained in the present Charter shall authorize the United Nations to intervene in matters which are essentially within the domestic jurisdiction of any State or shall require the members to submit such matters to settlement under the present Charter'.

8.1.1 Domestic jurisdiction

Amongst the areas of regulation typically regarded as falling within the domestic jurisdiction of a State are the setting of conditions for the grant of nationality and the conditions under which aliens (non-nationals) may enter a State's territory. However, to assert domestic jurisdiction is not a shield against non-intervention; matters of

[1] Some classic English-language articles on the theme include FA Mann, 'The Doctrine of Jurisdiction in International Law' (1964) 111 Recueil des Cours 1; FA Mann, 'The Doctrine of Jurisdiction in International Law Revisited after Twenty Years' (1984) 186 Recueil des Cours 9; M Akehurst, 'Jurisdiction in International Law' (1972–3) 46 BYBIL 145; DW Bowett, 'Jurisdiction: Changing Problems of Authority over Activities and Resources' (1982) 53 BYBIL 1. See also the influential Harvard study on jurisdiction, which sought to codify the international rules of jurisdiction in the 1920s and 1930s: Harvard Research on International Law, 'Jurisdiction with Respect to Crime' (1935) 29 AJIL Supp 1 435, 445.

domestic regulation (such as human rights or environmental legislation) may well have international legal effects, and the question of whether a given subject falls within the domestic jurisdiction of States is one of international law.[2] For example, though a State is free to formulate conditions in its domestic law with respect to the acquisition of its nationality, the ICJ emphasized in *Nottebohm* that the international legal effect of the grant of nationality falls within the ambit of international law.[3]

HISTORICAL BACKGROUND Extraterritorial Jurisdiction: the Cuban Embargo

An interesting exercise of extraterritorial jurisdiction relates to the US–Cuba relationship and the enduring US embargo against Cuba for its nationalization of US assets since 1958, following Fidel Castro's revolution. An interesting twist in the relationship emerged in 1996, with the Cuban Liberty and Democratic Solidarity (Libertad) Act (Helms–Burton Act), 110 Stat 785, through which the USA purported to extend its embargo also to foreign companies trading with Cuba or 'trafficking' in assets formerly held by US nationals. Both the EU and the UK have in fact passed 'blocking statutes' to protect their operators from the extraterritorial application of US law.

The 1996 Helms–Burton Act paid no heed to the now-annual General Assembly resolutions that, since 1992, have called for an end to the economic, commercial, and financial blockade imposed by the USA against Cuba; now the oldest comprehensive embargo in history. Despite a thaw in the bilateral relationship between the two States in 2015, spearheaded by US President Obama, in 2017, US President Trump's opposition resumed anew, with the USA reinstating all business and travel restrictions which had been loosened. Though US President Joe Biden relaxed certain sanctions after 2021 (for example, relating to family reunification and internet access), the USA responded to protests in Cuba and 2021 and 2024 with the resumption of certain coercive measures.

The General Assembly's votes have in recent years been nearly unanimous—except when, in a dramatic shift, the USA and Israel (the only two States not voting in favour) abstained in 2016 for the first time (see UNGA Res 71/5 (26 October 2016)). Since 2017, the USA and Israel have resumed their opposition to the resolution, and are the only two States that vote against it consistently (see, e.g., UNGA Res A/79/L.6 (30 October 2024)). US assertions of extraterritorial jurisdiction in relation to Cuba thus remain internationally relevant well over a half-century later.

For further reading, see ND White, *The Cuban Embargo under International Law:* El Bloqueo (Routledge, 2016).

The exercise of jurisdiction also delimits the extent of a State's coercive powers, especially in relation to those of other States. Put more simply, a State seeking to enforce its law against a national who commits an act in the territory of another State would risk

[2] *Nationality Decrees in Tunis and Morocco, Advisory Opinion, 1923, PCIJ, Ser B, No 4*, p 7, 23–4.

[3] *Nottebohm (Liechtenstein v Guatemala), Second Phase, ICJ Reports 1955*, p 4, 20–1. See also *Anglo-Norwegian Fisheries (United Kingdom v Norway), Judgment, ICJ Reports 1951*, p 116, 132, where the ICJ distinguished the delimitation of territorial waters (falling within domestic jurisdiction) from the validity of the determination with regard to other States (within the purview of international law).

infringing on the jurisdiction of the other State, raising issues of international comity; and overreach by a highly assertive State may lead to resistance from other States. The question becomes acutely sensitive if the individual over which a State seeks to exercise jurisdiction is breaching international law in the territory of another State: that situation is discussed at Section 8.2.1.3.

8.1.2 **Jurisdiction and territory**

Jurisdiction is often closely linked with territory. The jurisdictional nexus is easy to establish over an act occurring in one's territory, and enforcement jurisdiction is far easier to exercise than beyond State borders. But jurisdiction is not territorially confined, as many States claim the jurisdiction to try offences that have occurred outside their territory, such as the nationality of the victim, the gravity of the act, or the protection of an essential State interest. What is more, the reality of diplomatic relations between States has led to certain persons, property, and circumstances being excluded from the exercise of territorial jurisdiction.[4] Simply put, jurisdiction cannot simply be equated with territorial sovereignty. It is, therefore, the role of international law to develop a framework to reconcile potentially overlapping claims of jurisdiction by multiple States.

8.2 Types of jurisdiction

8.2.1 **Distinguishing prescriptive, enforcement, and adjudicative jurisdiction**

8.2.1.1 **Jurisdiction to prescribe**

Under international law, a State may regulate conduct as it wishes; such regulation may be achieved through legislative, executive, or judicial means. A State's legislative jurisdiction, or 'jurisdiction to prescribe', through which its constitutionally recognized organs make binding laws regulating affairs in its territory and sometimes abroad, is perhaps the most prevalent.[5] This relates to the basic question of over whom, and in what situations, a State may extend its laws, compel conduct, or impose certain penalties. For example, a State has exclusive legislative jurisdiction to set the procedures through which it passes laws, or the rules of procedure for its courts. However, a State may not pass legislation to alter the procedures through which the organs of other States will operate.[6]

[4] State immunity, the immunity of State officials, and diplomatic privileges and immunities will be addressed in Chapter 9.

[5] See Committee of Ministers Recommendation R (97) 11: *Amended Model Plan for the Classification of Documents concerning State Practice in the Field of Public International Law* (12 June 1997) Part Eight, Sec II.A.

[6] However, within its own territory, a municipal court may refuse to recognize or to enforce the judgment of a court of another State; e.g., on the grounds of corruption or manifest bias.

Legislative jurisdiction requires a jurisdictional nexus for a State to exercise it validly. Territorial sovereignty is perhaps the most obvious, but a State may legislate with extra-territorial effect; for example, to levy taxes against persons not on its territory but with whom it enjoys a genuine link, such as nationality or domicile.[7] It may also nationalize the property of aliens located in its territory, but only in an exercise of prescriptive jurisdiction, as international law would not permit a State to enforce the expropriation of foreign-owned property located abroad. Even within its territory, a State may not exercise its legislative jurisdiction contrary to its international obligations. Such obligations may take the form of treaties to which the State has consented (e.g., regarding human rights, the protection of the environment, and diplomatic privileges and immunities), customary international law (e.g., the treatment of aliens located in the country), or *jus cogens* (e.g., the prohibition against torture or crimes against humanity).[8]

8.2.1.2 **Jurisdiction to enforce**

One must carefully distinguish between the capacity to make legal rules, known as *prescriptive jurisdiction*, from the capacity to ensure or to compel compliance with such legal rules, known as *enforcement jurisdiction*. Officials and organs of States exercise exclusive 'jurisdiction to enforce' over certain persons or conduct located in their territory.[9] Subject to very limited exceptions, such as the right to 'hot pursuit' in territorial waters (covered in Chapter 18), they only carry out their functions in the territory of another State with its express consent,[10] in particular with respect to apprehending persons or seizing property abroad.[11] As a general rule, while States claiming prescriptive jurisdiction will not *ipso facto* offend the sovereignty of another State, the exercise of enforcement jurisdiction may well do so in certain circumstances. Accordingly, enforcement jurisdiction is in principle confined to the territorial jurisdiction of a State, though States may cooperate to bring offenders to justice. In June 2021, for example, Europol announced that 'Operation Trojan Shield/Greenlight'—a coordinated effort between the law enforcement agencies of nearly 20 States, Europol, and the US Drug Enforcement Administration—had resulted in the arrest of 800 criminals in connection with encrypted criminal activities, including drug trafficking, organized crime, and money laundering.[12]

[7] Akehurst (n 1) 179–80.

[8] A State which abuses its legislative supremacy may also be found in breach of an international legal obligation: see Mann, 'Doctrine of Jurisdiction' (1984) (n 1) 36 *et seq.*

[9] See Council of Europe, *Amended Model Plan* (n 5) Part Eight, Sec II.C.

[10] That said, States routinely give permission for the exercise of enforcement jurisdiction in their territory: see, e.g., the 2005 amendments to the 1988 Convention for the Suppression of Unlawful Acts against the Safety of Maritime Navigation (adopted 10 March 1988, entered into force 1 March 1992), 1678 UNTS 221; or the 'ship rider' agreements between the USA with a number of Caribbean States, under which US navy vessels may enter the territorial seas of the other party to pursue vessels suspected of trafficking drugs.

[11] See also Section 8.2.4 for a description of the capture of Eichmann. These limitations may come under pressure with respect to enforcement jurisdiction in cyberspace, which by its nature is deterritorialized: see C Ryngaert, 'Extraterritorial Enforcement Jurisdiction in Cyberspace: Normative Shifts' (2023) 24 German Law Journal 537.

[12] See Europol, '800 Criminals Arrested in Biggest Ever Law Enforcement Operation against Encrypted Communication', Europol Press Release of 8 June 2021.

A standard example given is that it falls within the prescriptive jurisdiction of a State to criminalize a crime (such as rape) and extend the application of that prohibition to all its nationals located abroad; but it does not fall within its enforcement jurisdiction to deploy its police or armed forces to the territory of another State without first seeking that State's consent to apprehend an accused person. For example, in the 2019 *Jadhav* case between India and Pakistan before the ICJ, India claimed that Mr Jadhav, an Indian national, had been kidnapped from Iran and subsequently prosecuted for espionage and terrorism in Pakistan (and sentenced to death). Pakistan denied any violation, contending that in fact he had been arrested in Balochistan, on the Pakistani side of its border with Iran, having entered illegally.[13]

8.2.1.3 **Jurisdiction to adjudicate**

There also exists the competence of a State's courts to try cases in which a foreign element exists: its 'adjudicative jurisdiction'.[14] Such jurisdiction is usually conditioned on a number of grounds through which it may be claimed,[15] such as a material link between the State and the act. A good example is the well-known Alien Tort Statute (USA) which allows for civil lawsuits against foreign nationals for actions committed abroad. In 2013, the US Supreme Court severely curtailed the scope of the Alien Tort Statute, holding that it was subject to a 'presumption against extraterritoriality' that would not apply to violations of international law alleged to have occurred in foreign States and that usually it could not apply to claims involving alleged human rights abuses or other violations of international law alleged to have occurred in a foreign State.[16]

CASE SPOTLIGHT ***Case of the S.S. 'Lotus' (France v Turkey), Judgment No 9* (1927) PCIJ Ser A, No 10, p 5**

In an early case of the PCIJ, commonly referred to as the *Lotus* judgment, the complexities of prescriptive and enforcement jurisdiction became evident. The case concerned the collision of a French steamer (the *Lotus*) and a Turkish steamer (the *Boz-Kourt*), tragically resulting in eight deaths. When the *Lotus* entered Constantinople (only renamed Istanbul in 1930), criminal proceedings were entered under Turkish law against the French lieutenant. France objected on the grounds that no State could extend its law to foreign ships on the high seas, so the question in issue was whether a French national could be prosecuted by Turkish authorities for acts outside Turkish territory (albeit with effects on a Turkish-flagged vessel), on the high seas.

[13] *Jadhav (India v Pakistan), Judgment, ICJ Reports 2019*, p 418, para 21.

[14] See Council of Europe, *Amended Model Plan* (n 5) Part Eight, Sec II.B.

[15] The term 'jurisdiction' is also used in relation to the legal basis for an international tribunal to exercise its competence with respect to a given dispute. The jurisdiction of States and the jurisdiction of tribunals are sufficiently distinct concepts that they are, as a matter of tradition and legal logic, addressed separately. The jurisdiction of international tribunals will not be further considered in this chapter.

[16] *Kiobel v Royal Dutch Petroleum*, 133 S Ct 1659 (2013), in relation to the Alien Tort Statute, 28 USC § 1350 (USA). See also *Daimler AG v Bauman* 134 S Ct 746 (2014), more generally limiting extraterritorial jurisdiction in the USA against foreign corporations that are incorporated in the USA or with their principal place of business there; and *Jesner v Arab Bank Plc* 138 S Ct 1386 (2018).

The PCIJ rejected France's argument that Turkey was precluded from exercising its jurisdiction. At first confirming the principle that enforcement jurisdiction could not be exercised in the territory of another State, it remarked that:

> It does not, however, follow that international law prohibits a State from exercising jurisdiction in its own territory, in respect of any case which relates to acts which have taken place abroad, and in which it cannot rely on some permissive rule of international law. Such a view would only be tenable if international law contained a general prohibition to States to extend the application of their laws and the jurisdiction of their courts to persons, property and acts outside their territory, and if, as an exception to this general prohibition, it allowed States to do so in certain specific cases . . . Far from laying down a general prohibition to [that] effect . . . [international law] leaves [States] a wide measure of discretion which is only limited in certain cases by prohibitive rules. (at 19)

This passage is invariably quoted to support the principle that a State may extend its prescriptive jurisdiction as it wishes, unless a specific prohibition exists in international law. Yet this is not fully accurate. It is not that any State asserting a novel form of extraterritorial jurisdiction may only be opposed with evidence of a clear prohibition, as in such cases, objecting States have consistently taken the view that they have no obligation to prove that a prohibitive rule exists, usually by asserting that the acting State has 'no right' to exercise jurisdiction in that situation. The question of which party bears the burden of proof is especially relevant when one State claims to prescribe rules for persons in another State such that it would encroach upon the right of the second State, where those persons are based, to exercise jurisdiction itself over those persons.

As such, the better interpretation of the PCIJ's view in *Lotus* is that a jurisdictional nexus is required between the State claiming to exercise prescriptive jurisdiction and the conduct that it claims to regulate. Without such a linking point, of which only the principles of territoriality and nationality are firmly established, the State asserting jurisdiction bears the burden of establishing why it is entitled to legislate for anyone other than persons in its territory and for its nationals abroad. What matters most is the future co-existence between States; any jurisdictional principle invoked by a State must at least be tolerated by other States as not being contrary to international law.

A novel reading of the *Lotus* judgment is that of A Hertogen, 'Letting *Lotus* Bloom' (2015) 26 EJIL 901.

8.2.2 **The territorial principle**

To exercise jurisdictional authority over a given territory has for centuries been regarded as a necessary condition for a State to be sovereign over that territory.[17] Relative to other forms of jurisdiction, territoriality is the easiest basis on which to claim jurisdiction, whether prescriptive, enforcement, or adjudicative in its scope.

[17] A principle recognized as early as *The Schooner Exchange v McFaddon* (1812) 7 Cranch 116, 136 (Marshall CJ: '[t]he jurisdiction of a nation within its own territory is necessarily exclusive and absolute'). For a critique as to the social and political meaning of 'territory', which is sometimes lost, see BS Chimni, 'The International Law of Jurisdiction: A TWAIL Perspective' (2022) 35 Leiden JIL 29, 33–7.

8.2.2.1 **General principles of territoriality**

All persons found within the territory of a State are bound by its laws. When an alien enters the territory of a State, that alien is bound to—and enjoys protection from—the entirety of the body of laws of that State. A State obviously may create exceptions for foreign visitors, such as exempting them from military service or releasing them from paying social security, but these are written into its law. Without such domestic law exceptions, only those obligations required by international law, such as those required by treaties on diplomatic relations, customary law (in particular in relation to human rights), or *jus cogens* restrict what is otherwise the unlimited and exclusive sovereignty of a State over its territory.

A State's territory extends beyond its land territory and also encompasses its territorial waters (up to 12 nautical miles from its coastline), and the airspace above its land and sea territories.[18] Accordingly, ships within their territory, and aircraft flying above it, are subject to its jurisdiction. In practice, States leave the prescription of rules applicable on board ships or aircraft to the State of registry (the 'flag State'), and assert jurisdiction only in relation to specified matters, such as customs and excise laws, environmental protection, or matters of national security. This is not necessarily exclusive: after Malaysia Airlines flight MH17 exploded over Ukraine while en route from the Netherlands to Malaysia in early 2014, Ukraine did not assert jurisdiction alone, but co-operated in an international investigation, which led to domestic prosecutions in the Netherlands and to a joint inter-State case against Russia at the ECtHR.[19]

In this regard, the boundaries and limits entailed by the application of the territorial principle are appealingly simple; the principle certainly captures acts committed by a State's nationals against other nationals of that State, and those which occur wholly in the territory of a single State. As both the *Lotus* case and the Malaysian Airlines incidents demonstrate, however, some acts straddle multiple States, while other more complex acts might involve multiple components and actors, terrorist acts being a particularly good example.

8.2.2.2 **Subjective and objective territorial jurisdiction compared**

To address more complex situations, international law has developed several variants on territorial jurisdiction through which a State may claim to exercise jurisdiction. The first, *subjective territorial jurisdiction*, allows a State to exercise prescriptive jurisdiction where it claims to regulate an act or incident which is initiated within its territory but only completed ('consummated') outside it. *Objective territorial jurisdiction* describes the reverse situation; namely, the exercise of prescriptive jurisdiction by a State over an act or incident which originated outside its territory, but which is then concluded (again, 'consummated') within it. Imagine for a moment the implantation of malware

[18] See Chapter 18, for further discussion about State authority over different maritime areas, such as the contiguous zone and the EEZ; though these are not the territory of a State, a coastal State may be permitted to exercise limited jurisdiction.

[19] See *Ukraine and the Netherlands v Russia*, ECtHR App Nos 8019/16, 43800/14 and 28525/20. After being declared partly admissible in decisions on 30 November 2022 and 25 January 2023, hearings were held in June 2024.

in State A that then temporarily shuts down the cyber infrastructure of State B. State A would claim to exercise *subjective* territorial jurisdiction, as the malware was implanted in its territory. State B would claim to exercise *objective* territorial jurisdiction, as the consequences of implantation were suffered in its territory. Because ships and aircraft are treated as the 'floating territory' of the State of registration, the Turkish claim to exercise jurisdiction over the *Lotus* was an example of objective territorial jurisdiction, and one on which the PCIJ sided with Turkey.[20] In order to facilitate efficiency and reduce possible conflicts, States routinely sign cooperation agreements in which various collaborative methods are deployed. For example, the Channel Tunnel protocol accords the UK and France limited jurisdictional rights in the other State's territory,[21] and specifically empowers frontier officers of the other State to work in specified 'control zones' in each other's territory.[22] Taking a slightly different approach, a 1991 agreement between Denmark and Sweden created a multinational consortium with the authority to build, maintain, and control the Øresund Bridge, a binational organization that operates on both sides of the international boundary.[23]

Finally, in the 1994 Israel–Jordan Treaty of Peace, two residual areas under Jordanian sovereignty but settled by Israelis are identified in which Israeli private interests and land ownership rights are recognized. Jordan has undertaken to grant unimpeded entry to and exit from, land usage, and movement within the area to landowners, as well as the entry of uniformed Israeli police officers to investigate any incidents related to those landowners. Jordan has also agreed, in the two areas, not to enforce its criminal law to activities concerning only Israeli nationals; in such cases, Israeli legislation relating to the extraterritorial activities of Israelis may be applied.[24]

8.2.2.3 **The 'effects' doctrine: an extension of 'objective territorial jurisdiction'**

A controversial source of jurisdiction derives from a variant of 'objective territorial jurisdiction', known as the 'effects doctrine'. Spearheaded by the USA in the context of antitrust law, the USA has claimed jurisdiction over the conduct of non-US entities whose activities were intended to affect its internal market.

The first US case to recognize the doctrine was *US v Alcoa*, in which the USA asserted jurisdiction over the conduct of a non-US company, on the basis that it was part of a cartel, the collective action of which successfully influenced imports to and exports from the USA. The US District Court concluded that the intentional production of

[20] *Case of the SS 'Lotus' (France v Turkey), Judgment, 1927, PCIJ, Ser A, No 10*, p 5, 24.

[21] See Protocol concerning Frontier Controls and Policing, Co-operation in Criminal Justice, Public Safety and Mutual Assistance relating to the Channel Fixed Link (France–United Kingdom) (signed 25 November 1991, entered into force 2 August 1993), 1747 UNTS 109.

[22] See also *ibid*, Art 38(2): within the Channel Tunnel itself, both States have jurisdiction in situations where there exists uncertainty as to where the offence has been committed or when the offence may be related to an offence committed on the territory of one or the other State. In such cases, the State which first detains a suspected individual has priority in exercising jurisdiction.

[23] See Agreement on a Fixed Link over the Sound (Denmark–Sweden) (1991), 1739 UNTS 356.

[24] Treaty of Peace between the State of Israel and the Hashemite Kingdom of Jordan (adopted 26 October 1994, entered into force 10 November 1994), 2042 UNTS 351, Annex I(b) and (c), relating to the Naharayim/ Baqura Area and the Zofar/Al-Ghamr Area.

economic effects within the USA, even though all acts were committed outside that State, was sufficient to create a jurisdictional nexus: 'any State may impose liabilities, even upon persons not within its allegiance, for conduct outside its borders that has consequences within its borders which the State reprehends'.[25] The Helms–Burton Act mentioned earlier is similar in scope, asserting jurisdiction over non-US nationals for conduct abroad; in particular, the 'trafficking' in property expropriated by Cuba from US nationals.[26]

Though the effects doctrine as espoused by the USA has faced considerable international opposition, other jurisdictions have employed similar practices. In the 2017 ECJ judgment in *Intel v European Commission*, Intel (a US corporation) had contended that the European Commission's assertion of jurisdiction over it, to conclude that Intel had abused its dominant position in the global microprocessor market by granting exclusivity rebates to computer manufacturers located outside the EU, was contrary to international law. The ECJ rejected Intel's claim, stating unambiguously (and for the first time) that 'the *qualified effects test* allows the application of EU competition law to be justified under public international law when it is foreseeable that the conduct in question will have an immediate and substantial effect in the European Union'.[27]

In a twist, in 2006 the ECtHR was faced with a potential claim of human rights violations based, essentially, on the 'effects' doctrine. Mr Ben El Mahi and several other individuals and associations, all based in Morocco, submitted an application against Denmark, claiming that the publication of offensive cartoons and caricatures of the Prophet Muhammad in Denmark (in particular one showing him as a terrorist with a bomb in his turban) had caused them to suffer several human rights violations, *inter alia*, discrimination and a violation of their freedom of religion. The claim was unsuccessful: the ECtHR declared the claim inadmissible, on the basis that notwithstanding the claimed extraterritorial effects, 'there is no jurisdictional link between any of the applicants and . . . Denmark, [nor can they] come within the jurisdiction of Denmark on account of any extraterritorial act'.[28]

[25] *US v Aluminum Company of America (Alcoa)*, 148 F.2d 416 (1945). The *Alcoa* test has evolved over the decades. In *Timberlane Lumber Co v Bank of America*, 549 F.2d 597 (1976), 66 ILR 270; and *Mannington Mills v Congoleum Corporation*, 595 F.2d 1287 (1979), 66 ILR 487, US courts began to add a criterion of 'reasonableness' to the exercise of effects-based jurisdiction, though this was later rejected by the US Supreme Court in *Hartford Fire Insurance Co v California*, 113 S Ct 2891 (1993), which concluded that once US law was declared applicable, it could not be qualified or set aside for reasons of international comity.

[26] Cuban Liberty and Democratic Solidarity (Libertad) Act ('Helms–Burton Act'), 110 Stat 785 (USA). The claim of jurisdiction over 'trafficking in confiscated property' was condemned by the Inter-American Juridical Committee of the OAS as not in conformity with international law on the exercise of jurisdiction. See OAS Doc CJI/SO/II/doc.7/96 rev 5, para 9 (25 August 1996).

[27] Case C-413/14, *Intel v European Commission* (6 September 2017), para 49 (emphasis added). The conditions of 'foreseeable, immediate and substantial effects' had already been elucidated, in a slightly different context, in Case T-102/96, *Gencor v European Commission* [1999] ECR II-753. See further, on this point, C Ryngaert, *Jurisdiction in International Law* (2nd edn, OUP, 2015), 82–4.

[28] *Ben El Mahi and ors v Denmark* App No 5853/06 (ECtHR, 11 December 2006).

8.2.3 **The nationality principle**

International law doctrine makes it easy to overlook the basic reality that States remain composed of individual human beings organized into a political community. Since the *raison d'être* of sovereignty and jurisdiction is the organization of the conduct of those human beings, it follows logically that a State and its nationals (or citizens) remain inextricably linked, with the State having a long-established right to extend the application of its laws to its nationals, even for acts committed abroad. Occasionally, nationality-based jurisdiction is referred to as the 'active personality' principle, as opposed to the 'passive personality' principle whereby jurisdiction is founded on the nationality of the victim (see later, Section 8.2.5).

Abundant State practice exists of States asserting jurisdiction over certain acts of their nationals committed abroad under certain conditions, though this can be done in different ways. Some States, like Germany, Belgium, the Netherlands, and Egypt, enact general clauses that an offence be punishable both by the State of nationality and in the territory where it was committed (so-called 'double criminality').[29] The USA and the UK, conversely, exercise legislative jurisdiction expressly on the basis of nationality; for example, to prohibit certain crimes committed abroad,[30] the commission of corrupt practices or bribery abroad,[31] or proscribing the commission of acts relating to terrorist conspiracy.[32] Treaties routinely confirm the right of a State assert jurisdiction over its nationals for acts committed abroad, such as the Budapest Convention on Cybercrime.[33] Intriguingly, the Lanzarote Convention on crimes relating to the sexual exploitation or sexual abuse of children requires States to exercise jurisdiction over all those who have 'habitual residence' in a State's territory.[34]

Though no definition of the term 'nationality' as such exists, in the *Nottebohm* case the ICJ described nationality as 'a legal bond having as its basis a social fact of attachment,

[29] See *Strafgesetzbuch* (German Criminal Code), s 7(2)(1); *Loi du 17 avril 1878 concernant le titre préliminaire du Code de procedure pénale* (Belgian Preliminary Title to the Code of Criminal Procedure), art 11; *Wetboek van Strafrecht* (Dutch Criminal Code), Art 4(11); and Egyptian Penal Code, Art 3.

[30] E.g., the UK prohibits murder and bigamy (see, e.g., Official Secrets Acts 1911, s 10; 1970, s 8; and 1989, s 15); certain categories of sexual offences (see Sexual Offences (Conspiracy and Incitement) Act 1996; the Sex Offenders Act 1997; and the Sexual Offences Act 2003, s 72); and football hooliganism (see Football Spectators Act 1988, s 22). For further reading, see P Arnell, 'The Case for Nationality-Based Jurisdiction' (2001) 50 ICLQ 955.

[31] See the US Foreign Corrupt Practices Act of 1977, Pub L No 95-213, 91 Stat 1494, which extends to corporations a certain degree of connection to the USA. In addition, some States, such as the UK, extend the extraterritorial application of their law to non-national residents and others with a 'close connection' to the UK: see the Bribery Act 2010, s 12; and Sexual Offences Act 2003, ss 9, 72.

[32] See, e.g., the Anti-Terrorism Crime and Security Act 2001, Pt 12; and the Crime (International Co-operation) Act 2003, amending ss 63B and 63C of the Terrorism Act 2000.

[33] Council of Europe Convention on Cybercrime (signed 23 September 2001, entered into force 1 July 2004), ETS No 15, Art 22(1)(d).

[34] Council of Europe Convention on Protection of Children against Sexual Exploitation and Sexual Abuse ('Lanzarote Convention') (adopted 25 October 2007, entered into force 1 July 2010), 2680 UNTS 249, Art 25 (1)(e).

a genuine connection of existence, interests and sentiments, together with the existence of reciprocal rights and duties'.[35]

Two key points regarding the conferral of nationality are relevant for jurisdiction in international law. First, as a general rule, it falls within the *domaine reservé* of a State to decide who its nationals are, and to lay down conditions for the grant of nationality.[36] However, as set out in Article 1 of the 1930 Hague Convention on Nationality, this prerogative is not unlimited, and a State may not set conditions for the determination of its nationality that breach its treaty obligations, customary international law, or 'principles of law generally recognized with regard to nationality'.[37] With respect to natural persons, two common principles used by States to accord their nationality are by descent from a parent who is a national (*jus sanguinis*),[38] or by virtue of being born in the territory of the State (*jus soli*).[39] These are not mutually exclusive, and a few States recognize both types of links as sufficient to establish nationality.[40]

States may also grant their nationality to a citizen of another State, through a process called *naturalization*, which usually relates to that person establishing a durable bond with the State granting nationality; for example, through a period of residence or through marriage to a national of that State. There are certain specific limits which, if breached, might entail a lack of international legal effect for a grant of nationality. Examples include the mass imposition of nationality upon unwilling people with no link to the State, nationality obtained through fraud or corruption, or the grant of nationality in order to circumvent international legal obligations. However, under international law, there seems to be no requirement to prove a 'genuine link' for a person to be naturalized by a State, as was recently observed in the ongoing infringement proceedings brought by the European Commission against Malta for its 'golden passports' investor citizenship scheme, which allow the acquisition of nationality based on payment or investment despite the lack of residence or any other connection.[41]

[35] *Nottebohm* (n 3) 23. Several instruments provide that persons have a 'right to a nationality': see, e.g., the Universal Declaration of Human Rights, UNGA Res 217(III) (10 December 1948), Art 15; the International Covenant on Civil and Political Rights (signed 16 December 1966, entered into force 23 March 1976), 993 UNTS 3, Art 24; and the Convention on the Rights of the Child (signed 20 November 1989, entered into force 2 September 1990), 1577 UNTS 3, Art 7(1).

[36] See *Nationality Decrees in Tunis and Morocco, Advisory Opinion, 1923, PCIJ, Ser B, No 4*, p 8, 24.

[37] Hague Convention on the Conflict of Nationality Laws (signed 1930, entered into force 1937), 179 LNTS 89, Art 1. See further M Casas, 'Nationalities of Convenience, Personal Jurisdiction, and Access to Investor-State Dispute Settlement' (2008) 49 NYUJILP 63, 70–4.

[38] This is the dominant mode of conferring nationality: see, e.g., art 17 of the Spanish *Codigo Civil* (Civil Code); art 1 of the Swiss Nationality Law; s 25 of the Constitution of Nigeria; and art 2(1) of the Nationality Law of Vietnam.

[39] Most countries granting unconditional nationality on the basis of *jus soli* are in North and South America, including Canada, the USA, Mexico, Brazil, and Argentina.

[40] See, e.g., the UK—British Nationality Act 1981, s 1 (birth or adoption), s 2 (descent); Germany—see Art 116(1) of the German Basic Law (descent), Art 4 of the *Staatsangehörigkeitsgesetz* (Nationality Law) 2001 (birth, under certain conditions); and Canada—Canadian Citizenship Act, s 3(a) (acquisition by birth or adoption), s 3(b) (acquisition by descent).

[41] *European Commission v Malta*, CJEU Case C-181/23 (Op Ad-G Collins) (4 October 2024), paras 56–8.

THEORY AND DEBATES The Taxation of Nationals Residing Abroad

A State's claim to regulate morally objectionable behaviour, or behaviour against public order, is justifiable if one accepts the proposition that a State is a political community with a shared set of values. A different justification arises in relation to States who tax their nationals who reside permanently abroad, on their income earned abroad. Currently, two States do so systematically and comprehensively: Eritrea and the USA. The USA is particularly striking given that nearly six million of its nationals reside abroad.

The US taxation of global income through the Revenue Act of 1921 (Pub L No 98, §210, 42 Stat 227) has been challenged; however, in 1924 the US Supreme Court found that taxation on global income was constitutional (*Cook v Tait*, 265 US 47 (1924)). In practice, however, a matrix of legislation is required in order to secure enforcement extraterritorially. For instance, a Report of Foreign Bank and Financial Accounts (FBAR) imposes reporting requirements on individuals, whereas the Foreign Account Tax Compliance Act (FATCA), requires foreign financial institutions to report on the accounts of US nationals living abroad with deposits of more than $50,000.

The implementation of FATCA, in particular, has driven a rise in US citizens giving up their citizenship since its adoption in 2013. Moreover, foreign financial institutions—irrespective of whether they operate in the USA—find themselves subject to US jurisdiction merely by virtue of having permitted a US citizen to open a bank account.

As a matter of State practice, nationality is regarded as conferring upon a person a series of rights, such as the right to vote, the right to obtain a passport, or the right to demand protection from the State of nationality when travelling abroad. Some States limit the holding of certain offices, such as election to a legislature or appointment to a diplomatic post, to nationals only, or exclude dual nationals from certain positions.[42] States may also extend certain of these rights to non-nationals: to give a few examples, Irish and Commonwealth citizens may vote in the UK if resident there,[43] and all permanent residents may vote in New Zealand.[44] Under Article 20 (originally Article 17) of the Treaty on the European Union, a national of any member State is also a 'citizen of the European Union', and enjoys a number of rights across all member States, including freedom to move, work, and reside freely in any member State, as well as the right to vote in and run as a candidate in local or European elections.[45]

In addition, nationals often have certain obligations to a State, such as jury service, the payment of taxes, or conscription in times of armed conflict. Moreover, some States (such as Colombia, Greece, Israel, and Kuwait) provide for compulsory military

[42] The UK Foreign and Commonwealth Office does not prohibit dual nationality, but requires that candidates hold British nationality when they stand.

[43] See British Nationality Act 1981 and UK Representation of the People Act 1983, s 4(6).

[44] New Zealand Electoral Act 1993, s 74(1).

[45] Citizens of the European Union also enjoy legal protections under other provisions of EU law, most notably the Charter of Fundamental Rights of the European Union [2012] OJ C326.

service. Under international law, a State may not conscript the nationals of other States into their armed forces, and may only levy taxes upon them if a plausible link, such as residency or the place of activity, may be established. Subject to the claim of 'passive personality' (see Section 8.2.5), a State should also refrain, as a general matter, from prosecuting non-nationals for crimes committed outside its territory.[46]

With respect to legal persons such as corporations, States may accord nationality to them on the basis of their incorporation operating within the territory of that State, or may confer their nationality based on the seat of management of the corporation.[47] This distinction is key in a world of multinational corporations with subsidiaries incorporated around the world, especially in relation to matters of corporate taxation. Similarly, States are entitled to fix the conditions for the grant of their nationality to ships, for the registration of ships in their territory, and the right for a ship to fly a State's flag, provided that a 'genuine link' exists between a State and the ship.[48] Aircraft have the nationality of the State in which they are registered, though States remain free to set the conditions for registration.[49] With respect to both ships and aircraft, States generally require that the vessel or aircraft operates from a home port in the State or that a certain proportion of the owners or crew have the nationality of the State.

8.2.4 **The protective principle**

The concept of protective jurisdiction has long been invoked by States to assert that, when their vital interests are endangered, they may claim jurisdiction in order to protect themselves, even against activities committed by non-nationals that take place outside their territory. The protective principle is relatively well established in the abstract; most uncertainties lie in the extent to which it operates in practice, as well as the types of acts against which it may be invoked.[50]

As the category of 'vital interests' is not closed, States have asserted protective jurisdiction on a wide range of activities. Briefly, these include:

- espionage;[51]
- terrorist-related activities;[52]

[46] However, see the discussion on 'passive personality' at Section 8.2.5.

[47] This distinction is relevant in the context of diplomatic protection (Chapter 11), but see *Barcelona Traction, Light, and Power Company Ltd (Belgium v Spain), Second Phase, Judgment, ICJ Reports 1970*, p 3.

[48] See, e.g., United Nations Convention on the Law of the Sea (signed 10 December 1982, entered into force 16 November 1994), 1833 UNTS 3, Art 91; Convention on the Territorial Sea and the Contiguous Zone (adopted 29 April 1958, entered into force 10 September 1964), 516 UNTS 205, Art 5. It is true that the 'flag of convenience' practice, of registering ships with certain States with which they have no effective link, remains problematic: see Chapter 18, Section 18.3.7.2.

[49] See Chicago Convention on International Civil Aviation (adopted 7 December 1944, entered into force 4 April 1947), 15 UNTS 102, Art 17.

[50] Akehurst (n 1) 157–9.

[51] See, e.g., the *Lux* affair in France (1911) (see Clunet [1912] 140), the *Urios* case in Spain, [1923] 1 RecDal 238; and *US v Zehe*, 601 F.Supp 196 (D Mass 1985).

[52] See, e.g., Crime (International Co-operation) Act 2003, Pt 2, s 63D; *US v Yousef*, 327 F.3d 56 (2d Cir 2003); and *Italian South Tyrol Terrorism Case (No 2)* 71 ILR 242.

- the smuggling of narcotics;[53]
- the printing of counterfeit currency;[54]
- a conspiracy to commit treason or a *coup d'état*;[55]
- aircraft hijacking;[56]
- illegal immigration or the trafficking of human persons;[57] and
- attacks on diplomatic personnel located abroad.[58]

Though these cover a wide range of activities, they are all closely linked to essential State functions, unlike, for example, sexual offences committed abroad or competition/antitrust legislation.

CASE SPOTLIGHT ***Attorney-General of the Government of Israel v Eichmann* (1961) 36 ILR 5 (District Court of Jerusalem, Israel)**

The controversial *Eichmann* case is frequently oversimplified in international law as an exercise of pure universal jurisdiction, even though an important part of the court's reasoning rests on other questions. Eichmann, a German national and former head of the Jewish Office of the German Gestapo, was captured by Israeli agents in Argentina in 1960, and abducted to Israel without Argentina's consent. He was prosecuted in Israel under a 1951 law for war crimes and crimes against the Jewish people for crimes committed during World War II, before the entry into force of the legislation. His counsel suggested that the Israeli statute violated international law for a number of reasons: it was, *inter alia*, retroactive, and thus in violation of the *nulla poena sine lege* principle ('no punishment without valid law'), and on grounds that it constituted an excess of the exercise of jurisdiction as it concerned a crime against persons who were not nationals, and committed outside its territory. Defence counsel also challenged the peculiar circumstances through which Eichmann was delivered into custody.

The Israeli court gave extensive treatment to international law materials in arriving at its conclusions. Its first conclusion was that, due to the nature of the abhorrent crimes concerned, it was indeed possible for the Knesset, Israel's legislative body, to claim jurisdiction over these acts, which were *delicta juris gentium* (crimes against the law of nations itself). Secondly,

[53] In the USA, see *United States v Brown*, 549 F.2d 954 (4th Cir 1977), relying on the principle established in *Strassheim v Daily*, 221 US 280 (1911); and the 1986 Maritime Drug Law Enforcement Act.

[54] In the UK, see Crime (International Co-operation) Act 2003, Pt 2, s 63C, which confirms that ss 1–5 of the Forgery and Counterfeiting Act 1981 apply extraterritorially.

[55] In the UK, see *Joyce v Director of Public Prosecutions* [1946] AC 347, which is particularly interesting as it involved an American-born person who fraudulently acquired a British passport. Joyce had been accused of treason through the dissemination of pro-Nazi propaganda during World War II; and because he had benefited from the protection afforded to British passport-holders, the UK courts could exercise jurisdiction. He was thus deemed to have breached a duty of allegiance to the British Crown.

[56] See, e.g., the Hague Convention for the Suppression of Unlawful Seizure of Aircraft (signed 16 December 1970, entered into force 14 October 1971), 860 UNTS 105.

[57] See, e.g., *US v Pizzarusso*, 388 F.2d 8 (1968).

[58] See, e.g., Convention on the Prevention and Punishment of Crimes against Internationally Protected Persons, including Diplomatic Agents (signed 28 December 1973, entered into force 20 February 1977), 1035 UNTS 167, Art 3.

though the court suggested that universal jurisdiction, claimed on the basis of international law itself, would suffice to dismiss the defence of *nulla poena sine lege*, it should be noted that Israel's 'right to punish' was based on the protective principle, which allowed it to prosecute individuals for crimes injuring its 'vital interests'. A 'crime against the Jewish people', even prior to the existence of the State of Israel, was sufficient to constitute a 'linking point' allowing Israel to claim jurisdiction legitimately.

Finally, on the irregularity of the abduction from Argentina through which Eichmann was brought within the jurisdiction of Israel (he was drugged and dressed as a flight attendant for rendition), the Jerusalem court concluded that it was not Eichmann's rights that were violated, but those of Argentina in relation to its sovereignty. Because Argentina had waived its rights in a joint communiqué with Israel, the court concluded that any violation of international law that might have occurred had been 'cured'.

For a revisiting of the events leading to the *Eichmann* judgment, see W Schabas, 'The Contribution of the Eichmann Trial to International Law' (2013) 26 Leiden JIL 667; and, of course, the timeless Hannah Arendt book *Eichmann in Jerusalem: A Report on the Banality of Evil* (Viking Press, 1963).

8.2.5 **The 'passive personality' principle**

A controversial basis for prescriptive jurisdiction is the 'passive personality' principle, whereby a State is entitled to exercise jurisdiction over non-nationals for acts committed abroad, on condition that the victims are nationals of the State claiming jurisdiction.

Passive personality as a basis for jurisdiction seems to have been resurrected in recent years, with States claiming passive personality jurisdiction as a variant of jurisdiction based on universality, frequently in connection with grave violations of human rights (see Section 8.2.6.2). Though its status as a customary law principle remains unsettled, States have entered into treaties permitting passive personality jurisdiction with respect to the specific offences including hostage-taking, hijacking, and terrorism. Article 9 of the Hostages Convention allows the national State of a hostage to exercise passive personality jurisdiction over an offence committed abroad by a non-national 'if that State considers it appropriate'.[59] Article 4(b) of the Tokyo Hijacking Convention allows for a State to exercise jurisdiction if the offence has been committed against its nationals or permanent residents.[60] Article 7(2)(a) of the Terrorism Financing Convention allows States to exercise jurisdiction for certain offences committed either in the territory of a State or against a national of that State.[61] Finally, certain States have

[59] See International Convention against the Taking of Hostages (adopted 18 December 1979, entered into force 3 June 1983), 1316 UNTS 205, Art 9.

[60] Convention on Offences and Certain Other Acts Committed on Board Aircraft (Tokyo Convention) (adopted 14 September 1963, entered into force 4 December 1969), 704 UNTS 219, Art 4(b).

[61] International Convention for the Suppression of the Financing of Terrorism (opened for signature 10 January 2000, entered into force 10 April 2002) 2179 UNTS 197 (ICSFT), Art 7(2)(a).

passed legislation based on passive personality in relation to specific crimes, such as the Netherlands in relation to certain cybercrimes[62] or the USA in relation to terrorist acts committed abroad.[63]

HISTORICAL BACKGROUND The 'Unequal Treaties'

Extraterritorial jurisdiction based on passive personality jurisdiction has a long and unfortunate pedigree in international law, with treaties being imposed by European States and later, the USA, on the Ottoman Empire, Persia, Siam, China, and Japan in the nineteenth century. Such treaties, non-reciprocal, allowed for nationals of the Western powers to roam freely in the host States, subject to no laws but those of their national State. In fact, Western powers reserved the right to take jurisdiction over anyone who entered into a contract or committed a tortious or delictual act against their nationals, even though abroad.

Passive personality as the basis of jurisdiction is controversial because it allows a State to extend its jurisdiction to any acts afflicting its nationals and therefore suggests to other States that their legal systems are somehow insufficient or deficient, also allowing the asserting State to impose its laws on non-nationals. It is no surprise that such treaties were later denounced as 'unequal' by Japan (1899), Türkiye (1923 Treaty of Lausanne), and China (1943).

Be that as it may, even without such a treaty in place, the principle had been upheld with strong imperialist undertones, most prominently in the *Cutting* case of 1886 (see JB Moore, *Digest of International Law* (USGPO, 1906), vol II, 228). In that case, Mr Cutting, a US citizen, was imprisoned and convicted in Mexico on charges of libel against Mexican nationals; his allegedly libellous statements had been published in a US-based newspaper. Strong US resistance followed, including a statement by President Cleveland in his annual address to Congress in 1886 protesting the exercise by Mexico of a claim of jurisdiction 'whereby any offence committed anywhere by a foreigner . . . of which a Mexican is the object, may, if the offender be found in Mexico, be there tried and punished in conformity with Mexican laws'; Mexico's claim was regarded as 'invasive of the jurisdiction of [the United States] and highly dangerous to [its] citizens in foreign lands'. The USA considered that the burden lay upon Mexico to prove its entitlement to exercise passive personality jurisdiction over Mr Cutting. The resolution of that dispute was inconclusive, as charges were withdrawn by the injured party.

Unequal treaties are formally extinct, but the fact of their existence serves to illuminate how international law can be used to enforce inequality; even today, certain investment treaties have been subject to similar criticism: see Chapter 20, Section 20.4.4, for further detail. See further M Craven, 'What Happened to Unequal Treaties? The Continuities of Informal Empire' (2005) 74 Nordic JIL 335; and N Tzouvala, *Capitalism as Civilisation* (CUP, 2020), ch 2 (who examines the racialized 'logic of biology' underpinning some of these treaties).

[62] See the Dutch Criminal Code (n 29) Art 4(14), which extends jurisdiction over computer sabotage or data damage committed against a Dutch national, provided that the conduct also falls under Art 2 of the ICSFT (n 60).

[63] USA, Antiterrorism and Effective Death Penalty Act, 28 USC §2254 (1996).

8.2.6 **The universality principle**

With the notable exception of piracy, the universality principle suggests that the gravity of a particular offence is so abhorrent that each and every State has a legitimate interest in its repression,[64] irrespective of the nationality of the individuals, the nationality of the victims, or the place of commission of the crime.[65] As we shall observe, most relevant practice here has been in respect of criminal complaints, and not about civil cases.

8.2.6.1 **Piracy and crimes outside the jurisdiction of all States**

The paradigmatic crime for which universal jurisdiction was first established is that of piracy. Pirates operate on the high seas, outside the territorial jurisdiction of a State, and pirate groups are more often than not composed of the nationals of more than one State. Pirates came to be regarded as *hostis humani generis* ('enemy of all mankind') under customary international law, a principle that was confirmed in the 1982 UNCLOS. The essence of piracy is that it be committed for private ends and not, for example, for political reasons, with the latter type of acts regarded as hijacking or takeover. As defined in UNCLOS, piracy constitutes '[a]ny illegal acts of violence, detention or any act of depredation, *committed for private ends* by the crew or the passengers of a private ship or private aircraft' against any ship, aircraft, persons, or property, so long as such acts are committed on the high seas or outside the jurisdiction of any State.[66] Under that principle, each and every State may seize a pirate ship or aircraft on the high seas or on any other place outside the jurisdiction of a State, and its courts would have jurisdiction to impose penalties on convicted pirates. There have been substantial international initiatives to control piracy,[67] and the Security Council has authorized States to enter the territorial waters of Somalia in pursuit of pirates.[68]

Universal jurisdiction claims over pirates are not based in any inherently heinous nature of piracy, but due to the pragmatic reality that pirates operate on the high seas, beyond the jurisdiction of any State. In this sense, it would be no different than universal jurisdiction in outer space or in Antarctica, zones beyond the jurisdiction of all States: there exists a 'common interest and mutual convenience' to justify universal jurisdiction.[69] Such claims must be distinguished, therefore, from the more recent trend of invoking the universality principle in relation to grave violations of human rights, such as

[64] This is the classical understanding of universal jurisdiction: see *US v Yunis*, 681 F.Supp 896 (1988); and *Arrest Warrant of 11 April 2000 (Democratic Republic of the Congo v Belgium), Judgment, ICJ Reports 2002*, p 3, 19.

[65] A useful guide may be found in the *Princeton Principles on Universal Jurisdiction* (2001), purporting to codify existing practice and provide guidance in relation to the exercise of universal jurisdiction. See also R O'Keefe, 'Universal Jurisdiction: Clarifying the Basic Concept' (2004) 2 JICJ 735; and D Hovell, 'The Authority of Universal Jurisdiction' (2018) 29 EJIL 427.

[66] See UNCLOS (n 47) Art 101 (emphasis added).

[67] See, e.g., the Regional Cooperation Agreement on Combating Piracy and Armed Robbery against Ships in Asia (2005), NATO Operation 'Ocean Shield' (2009), and the European Union's Operation Atalanta (2008).

[68] UNSC Res 1816 (2 June 2008).

[69] 'Harvard Draft Convention on Piracy (with Comments)', (1932) 36 AJIL 749 (Supp), 764–5; see further Hovell (n 65) 441–3.

genocide, slavery, crimes against humanity, war crimes, and torture. Many of these have been made subject to the jurisdiction of States, and now form a distinct category of international crimes potentially subject to the universality principle, to which we now turn.

8.2.6.2 **Jurisdiction over international crimes**

8.2.6.2.1 ***Crimes against peace/war crimes***

Following the end of World War II, the International Military Tribunal in Nuremberg was the first international tribunal to be constituted with jurisdiction over individuals accused of committing crimes against peace, violations of the law and customs of war, and crimes against humanity.[70] Subsequently, universal jurisdiction was embedded in the four Geneva Conventions so that domestic courts would be competent to try individuals for grave breaches, including wilful killing, torture or inhuman treatment, unlawful deportation of protected persons, and the taking of hostages.[71] All of these were to apply in the context of international armed conflicts.

8.2.6.2.2 ***Crimes against humanity***

Crimes against humanity are a slightly different matter; they differ from war crimes in that they may be committed either within or outside the context of international armed conflicts. In practice, therefore, crimes against humanity are associated with the conditions retained in the Rome Statute of the ICC, being 'widespread, systematic and directed against a civilian population'.[72] There is limited practice of domestic courts asserting universal jurisdiction over crimes against humanity. However, in 2019 the ILC published the Draft Articles on Prevention and Punishment of Crimes Against Humanity, Article 2 of which adopts (with minor modifications) the same definition of crimes against humanity as in the Rome Statute, and Article 6 of which would oblige States parties to enact legislation to ensure that crimes against humanity are offences under domestic criminal law.[73] At the time this book went to press, the General Assembly was

[70] Charter of the International Military Tribunal (1945), Art 6; subsequently confirmed by UNGA Res 95(I) (11 December 1946). See also Arts 227–30 of the Treaty of Versailles (signed 28 June 1919, entered into force 10 January 1920), 225 CTS 188, which provided for jurisdiction over individuals for these crimes, including the deposed Kaiser Wilhelm II.

[71] See Art 49 of the Geneva Convention for the Amelioration of the Condition of the Wounded and Sick in Armed Forces in the Field (adopted 12 August 1949, entered into force 21 October 1950), 75 UNTS 31 (Geneva Convention I); Art 50 of the Geneva Convention for the Amelioration of the Condition of Wounded, Sick and Shipwrecked Members of Armed Forces at Sea (adopted 12 August 1949, entered into force 21 October 1950) 75 UNTS 85 (Geneva Convention II); Art 129 of the Geneva Convention Relative to the Treatment of Prisoners of War (adopted 12 August 1949, entered into force 21 October 1950) 75 UNTS 135 (Geneva Convention III); and Art 146 of the Convention Relative to the Protection of Civilian Persons in Time of War (adopted 12 August 1949, entered into force 21 October 1950) 75 UNTS 287 (Geneva Convention IV). In the Protocol Additional to the Geneva Conventions of 12 August 1949, and relating to the Protection of Victims of International Armed Conflicts (Protocol I) (signed 8 June 1977, entered into force 7 December 1978), 1125 UNTS 3, the list was extended to include, *inter alia*, attacking civilian populations.

[72] Art 7, Rome Statute of the International Criminal Court (adopted 17 July 1998, entered into force 1 July 2002), 2187 UNTS 3. See also Art 5, Statute of the International Criminal Tribunal for the former Yugoslavia (1993) 32 ILM 1159; and Art 3, Statute of the International Criminal Tribunal for Rwanda (1994) 33 ILM 1598.

[73] See (2019) ILC Ybk vol II, pt 2, UN Doc A/74/10 (2019).

actively discussing the Draft Articles and, in the Sixth Committee, adopted a resolution to open negotiations to transform them into a binding convention.

8.2.6.2.3 *Genocide*

Turning now to allegations of genocide, though these have invariably occurred in the context of armed conflicts (e.g., during World War II and, more recently, in Bosnia, Croatia, Rwanda, Kosovo, and the Democratic Republic of the Congo), there is no formal requirement for an armed conflict to exist. Article 1 of the Genocide Convention states plainly that contracting parties must 'confirm that genocide, whether committed in time of peace or time of war, is a crime under international law which they undertake to prevent and to punish'.

8.2.6.2.4 *Torture*

Finally, Article 5, paragraph 2, of the Convention against Torture (CAT)[74] obliges States to go beyond establishing jurisdiction over offences committed on their territory, by their nationals, or against their nationals, and to establish jurisdiction over any alleged offender who is present in their territory, unless the alleged offender is extradited.[75] Several States have enacted legislation going further than the CAT requirement, claiming that certain particularly heinous crimes are subject to universal jurisdiction, such as torture, genocide, or systematic rape, with Belgium a prominent example. It was Belgium's universal jurisdiction legislation with respect to war crimes that led to the *Arrest Warrant* case between it and the Democratic Republic of the Congo, where Belgium issued an arrest warrant against Congolese Foreign Minister Abdoulaye Yerodia Ndombasi, charging him with inciting massacres of Tutsi civilians.[76]

These four international crimes are covered in depth in Chapter 17, Section 17.3 ('Core crimes').

8.2.6.3 Recent developments

Universal jurisdiction is not uncontroversial. In Belgium, after complaints were filed against Israeli Prime Minister Sharon concerning incidents occurring in Lebanon in 1982[77] and against certain leading US figures for bombing incidents occurring in Iraq in the early 1990s,[78] Israel and the USA protested in particular, US officials even

[74] Convention against Torture and Other Cruel, Inhuman or Degrading Treatment or Punishment (adopted 10 December 1984, entered into force 26 June 1987), 1465 UNTS 85.

[75] In *Prosecutor v Furundžija* (Appeals Chamber Judgment), Case No IT-95-17/1A, Judgment of 21 July 2000 (2002) ILR 121, paras 154–6, the ICTY concluded, without mentioning the Torture Convention, that because the prohibition of torture was a norm of *jus cogens*, this would be sufficient to found domestic jurisdiction as it was rooted 'in the inherently universal character of the crime'.

[76] *Arrest Warrant* (n 63); the case is discussed in considerable detail in Chapter 9, Section 9.4.4.

[77] See 'US Reaction to Belgian Universal Jurisdiction Law' (2003) 97 AJIL 984, 985; and 'Complaint lodged by Survivors against Israeli Prime Minister Ariel Sharon, Director General of the Defence Ministry Amos Yaron, and other Israelis and Lebanese responsible for the Sabra and Shatila Massacre, filed in the Brussels Criminal Court (18 June 2001)' (2005) 12 Palestine YBIL 219.

[78] *Ibid*, 986–7. Other high-profile individuals included former and serving heads of State: Pinochet (Chile); Kabila (DR Congo); Kagame (Rwanda); Habré (Chad); Hussein (Iraq); Arafat (Palestine); and Castro (Cuba).

threatening to withhold further funding for a new NATO headquarters building if the law remained as it was.[79] Bowing to such pressure, in 2003 Belgium modified its legislation on universal jurisdiction[80] to require at least a minimal link to Belgium in respect of the crime concerned; in essence, the jurisdictional basis to something akin to passive personality (see earlier, Section 8.2.5).[81] It was passive personality jurisdiction which was at issue in the *Obligation to Prosecute or Extradite* dispute: whilst Mr Habré (former President of Chad) was located in Senegal, Belgium brought a claim against Senegal claiming that Senegal was under an obligation to extradite or to prosecute him (*aut dedere aut judicare*). Senegal asserted, and Belgium accepted, that in enacting implementing legislation, Senegal had complied with its obligations under Article 5, paragraph 2 of the Torture Convention. As such, the Court did not have jurisdiction to examine whether there had been any breach of that provision.[82]

Most other States that claim universal jurisdiction (e.g., Spain, the UK, the Netherlands, Canada) also require such a minimal link, though Argentina allows the prosecution of crimes committed outside Argentina's jurisdiction 'against public international law'.[83] The Argentine approach to 'pure' universal jurisdiction has attracted international attention in recent years, with a prominent case filed in 2019 in relation to crimes against the Rohingya Muslims.[84] In October 2021, a former Spanish interior minister was indicted on four counts of aggravated homicide committed during the Franco dictatorship in Spain that would have been inadmissible there under a 1977 amnesty law.[85] In September 2024, an Argentine federal court issued an arrest warrant against Venezuelan President Nicolas Maduro and thirty other individuals for potential crimes against humanity committed in Venezuela.[86]

[79] See, e.g., statement by then-US Secretary of Defence Rumsfeld, in I Black and E MacAskill, 'US Threatens Nato Boycott over Belgium War Crimes Law' (*The Guardian*, 13 June 2003) <http://www.guardian.co.uk/world/2003/jun/13/nato.warcrimes>; see also the US Department of Defense News Transcript, 'Secretary of Defense Rumsfeld at NATO Headquarters' (*US Department of Defense*, 12 June 2003) <http://archive.defense.gov/Transcripts/Transcript.aspx?TranscriptID=2742>.

[80] See *Loi relative aux violations graves du droit humanitaire* (amendments of 5 August 2003), *Moniteur belge* No 2003-3125, p 40506, also found as Belgium's Amendment to the Law of 15 June 1993 (as amended by the Laws of 10 February 1999 and 23 April 2003), *Moniteur belge* No 2003-1786, p 24846, (2003) 42 ILM 1258.

[81] See S Ratner, 'Belgium's War Crimes Statute. A Postmortem' (2003) 97 AJIL 888; and L Reydams, 'Belgium Reneges on Universality: The 5 August 2003 Act on Grave Breaches of International Humanitarian Law' (2003) 1 JICJ 679.

[82] *Obligation to Prosecute or Extradite (Belgium v Senegal), Judgment, ICJ Reports 2012*, p 422, 442–3.

[83] See Constitution of the Argentine Republic, art 118. Implementing legislation clarifies this provision as including crimes foreseen in the Rome Statute.

[84] For a copy of the complaint filed in Argentina, see <https://burmacampaign.org.uk/media/Complaint-File.pdf>. In July 2024, the Prosecutor filed a request for the issuance of arrest warrants in the case.

[85] More detail on the Argentine legislation on universal jurisdiction can be found (in Spanish) in W Jurado, *El principio de jurisdicción universal y la comunidad internacional* (Jurisprudencia Rosarina, 2018).

[86] These efforts are meant to be complementary to international efforts: see Argentine Ministry of Foreign Affairs, Press Release No 445/25 (6 September 2024), calling for the ICC Pre-Trial Chamber to issue arrest warrants against the same individuals. For a summary (in Spanish) of the order, see <http://www.saij.gob.ar/FA24260036>.

8.3 Treaty-based extensions of extraterritorial jurisdiction

Though extraterritorial jurisdiction on grounds other than nationality remains contested, States routinely resort to multilateral treaties to coordinate their efforts in repressing certain types of offences. In a time where transnational crime is at unprecedented levels, facilitated by developments in technology and a period of heightened global economic integration, such treaties are of particular salience for the assertion of jurisdiction.

Typically, these treaties accomplish certain objectives. First, as a general matter, such treaties will provide a harmonized definition of the offence or range of offences in question. They will then stipulate that States parties are under an obligation to enact certain penalties in their domestic law for offences committed, and to assert their jurisdiction over the said offences in certain circumstances. Crucially, as discussed earlier, such a treaty will often include a provision embedding the principle *aut dedere aut judicare*, which requires States parties either to extradite, upon the request of another State party, any alleged offender found in their territory, regardless of the person's nationality or of the place where the offence was committed, or to submit the case to their competent authorities for the purpose of prosecution.

Crucially, it needs to be said that *aut dedere aut judicare* is not by itself customary international law;[87] when applied by the ICJ in *Obligation to Prosecute or Extradite*, this was only pursuant to the treaty obligation of *aut dedere aut judicare* enshrined in Article 7 of the Torture Convention, and its scope restricted thereunder to *criminal* complaints.[88] In *Naït-Liman v Switzerland*, the ECtHR considered—and dismissed—the claim that Switzerland was under an obligation to recognize universal *civil* jurisdiction for torture claims, whether by virtue of customary law or pursuant to Article 14 of the Torture Convention.[89] In *Hussein v Belgium*, the ECtHR reaffirmed this statement, concluding that neither customary law nor the ECHR required Belgium to exercise universal civil jurisdiction in respect of Jordanian–Palestinian refugees forcibly deported from Kuwait during the 1990–1 Gulf War.[90]

As discussed in the various sections on the jurisdictional bases available, States have adopted treaties providing for extraterritorial jurisdiction in many fields, including torture (passive personality jurisdiction, or universal jurisdiction when the offender is

[87] As recognized in the provisional measures sought in the context of *Questions of Interpretation and Application of the 1971 Montreal Convention arising from the Aerial Incident at Lockerbie (Libyan Arab Jamahiriya v United Kingdom), Provisional Measures, ICJ Reports 1992*, p 3, 24 (Joint Declaration of Judges Evensen, Tarassov, Guillaume, and Aguilar Maudsley (translation)).

[88] *Obligation to Prosecute or Extradite* (n 80) 434.

[89] *Naït-Liman v Switzerland* (Grand Chamber) App No 51357/07 (ECtHR, 15 March 2018), para 198; *cf* F Mégret, 'The "Elephant in the Room" in Debates about Universal Jurisdiction' (2015) 6 Transnational Legal Theory 89, 99–100.

[90] *Hussein and ors v Belgium* App No 45187/12 (ECtHR, 16 June 2021), para 65. Though the claimants had filed their case before Belgium tightened its universal jurisdiction legislation in 2003 (n 75), the ECtHR held that Belgium was entitled to limit such universal jurisdiction to require a minimal link with that State, and to terminate ongoing investigations after 2003.

present on a State party's territory),[91] the taking of hostages (passive personality jurisdiction, or universal jurisdiction when the offender is present on a State party's territory),[92] the protection of certain United Nations personnel (universal jurisdiction when the offender is present on a State party's territory),[93] the hijacking of aircraft (passive personality jurisdiction in the case of the Tokyo Convention),[94] and universal jurisdiction when the offender is present on a State party's territory (in the case of the Montreal Convention and the Hague Convention[95]). In effect, these multilateral treaties achieve a sort of universal jurisdiction *inter partes*, a specialized regime through which States parties cooperate, through the enactment of domestic law proscribing certain offences, in exercising jurisdiction over the said offences, and in establishing mechanisms for information-sharing, extradition, or prosecution, so as to minimize the possibility of impunity for the commission of such an offence.[96] For example, the recent adoption of a new Ljubljana—The Hague Convention on International Co-operation in the Investigation and Prosecution of the Crime of Genocide, Crimes against Humanity, War Crimes, and other International Crimes aims to establish detailed obligations on mutual legal assistance and extradition; if it enters into force, its objective is to end impunity for these core international crimes.[97]

The crime of terrorism may in time emerge as a crime of international jurisdiction, as is evidenced by recurring efforts to arrive at an international definition of the crime.[98] Many treaties allow for extraterritorial jurisdiction in relation to specific acts closely connected with terrorism, such as the hijacking of aircraft or the taking of hostages. What is more, as mentioned earlier, passive personality jurisdiction may be exercised by States parties against anyone accused of financing terrorism.[99] Without a basis in a treaty, however, there seems to be insufficient customary practice to justify the assertion of jurisdiction over such acts.

[91] See Torture Convention (n 72) Arts 5, 7. Regarding its application, see *Obligation to Prosecute or Extradite* (n 80); and *Ex parte Pinochet (No 3)* [2000] AC 147; (2000) 119 ILR 135. The *Ex parte Pinochet* judgment is discussed at length in Chapter 9, Section 9.4.6 ('Immunity for serious crimes under international law').

[92] Hostages Convention (n 58) Arts 5(1)(d) and 5(2).

[93] See Convention on the Safety of United Nations and Associated Personnel (adopted 9 December 1994, entered into force 15 January 1999), 2051 UNTS 363, Art 14.

[94] See Tokyo Convention (n 59) Art 4.

[95] See Montreal Convention for the Suppression of Unlawful Acts against the Safety of Civil Aviation (adopted 23 September 1971, entered into force 26 January 1973), 974 UNTS 177, Art 5(a); 1970 Hague Convention (n 55) Art 4. See also the various phases of *Lockerbie* (n 84): *Provisional Measures, Orders of 14 April 1993, ICJ Reports 1992*, p 3, 114; and *Preliminary Objections, Judgment, ICJ Reports 1998*, p 9, 115; and *US v Yunis (No 2)* 681 F.Supp 896, 900–1 (1988); 82 ILR 344.

[96] R O'Keefe, 'Universal Jurisdiction: Clarifying the Basic Concept' (2004) 2 JICJ 735.

[97] On 14 February 2024, a ceremony was held in the Peace Palace in The Hague in which the Convention was opened for signature. The final text of the Convention is available at <https://www.gov.si/assets/ministrstva/MZEZ/projekti/MLA-pobuda/Final-Document-English.pdf>.

[98] See Chapter 17, Section 17.2.4, for a discussion of the Special Tribunal for Lebanon in 2005, which prosecutes individuals in connection with the 2005 assassination of Lebanese Prime Minister Hariri.

[99] ICSFT (n 60) at 7(2)(a).

CONTEMPORARY DEVELOPMENTS The US Claim of Extraterritorial Jurisdiction in Respect of Terrorist Offences

The crucial issue arises as to whether, in the absence of a relevant treaty, extraterritorial jurisdiction may be exercised against those accused of terrorism as such, even if they are not its nationals. There is limited case law and State practice in this regard, primarily from the USA, where domestic courts have in the post-9/11 period asserted jurisdiction over terrorist plots planned by non-nationals located overseas, and where overseas locations were affected.

The classic statement is found in *Flatow v Iran*, 999 F.Supp 1, 14 (1998), where the US District Court concluded that 'international terrorism is subject to universal jurisdiction'. Though the USA has enacted a 1986 Omnibus Diplomatic Security and Terrorist Act which asserts passive personality jurisdiction over physical attacks on US nationals outside its territory, US courts have applied a rather elastic test with respect to the required jurisdictional nexus with the USA. In *US v Yousef*, 327 F.3d 56 (2d Cir. 2003), a non-US national who attacked an aeroplane registered in the Philippines as a 'trial run' for an attack on the USA was prosecuted. In *US v Al-Kassar*, 582 F.Supp 2d 488 (2008), non-US nationals operating in Spain, Lebanon, and Colombia were convicted, *inter alia*, of arms trafficking and 'material support for terrorism'. US jurisdiction was also claimed on the basis that the weapons being brokered by the defendant could be used against US nationals in Colombia. In *US v Warsame*, 537 F.Supp 2d 1005 (2008), a Canadian national was charged with 'material support for terrorism' for medical training and the wiring of a loan, both to purported Al Qaeda operatives located in Afghanistan; the prosecution did not invoke the likelihood of causing imminent harm to US nationals or other US interests.

The key point for reflection is to consider whether this judicial practice in the USA is indicative of a new, permissive customary norm which allows for the exercise of extraterritorial jurisdiction over the nationals of other States who are suspected of terrorist activity abroad. The fact that a link to the State is not asserted at all suggests that it is closer to universal jurisdiction than to any protective principle.

8.4 Enduring challenges for the exercise of jurisdiction

The long-standing principles through which jurisdiction is exercised in international law are the product of centuries of iterative development, where States' interests have collided, at times aggressively, before gradually being balanced over time with the overriding principle of international comity. Two persistent problems stand out in this respect, and are exacerbated by technological and social advances: the challenge of identifying the location of a given act, and how to resolve conflicts between States that are claiming concurrent jurisdiction.

8.4.1 Challenges with identifying the location of acts

Territorial jurisdiction, in its essence, presumes that the location of an act can be clearly discerned; however, in practice this is far more complex. A contemporary example might be an online attack by private hackers located in one State, but on the financial cyber-infrastructure of another State. Does the State where the hackers are situated have territorial jurisdiction? Or can the affected State claim protective jurisdiction or 'effects' jurisdiction? What if the hackers first co-opted the network infrastructure or a router located in a third State? What if the hackers were located across various States, and directed by a person located in yet another State? The 'location' of a cybercrime is thus very much a live issue, and poses important international law questions as to jurisdiction.[100]

Domestic courts have sought to grapple with such issues by reference to how the offence may have been defined in domestic law. In the UK, a distinction between offences of 'conduct' and 'result' has emerged in case law.[101] However, the pertinent question remains whether an assertion of jurisdiction asserted, even over a defined offence, is in conformity with international law. Yet international law does not provide clear rules for determining where an act has occurred, which suggests that a fixation with geography is not appropriate in relation to complex acts involving a multitude of actors. In this respect, all that can be said is that the standard forces of international law formation must continue to run their course, either with a clear treaty framework being established, or customary law to emerge through State practice. The interaction between States remains key: a reasonable claim may be met with acquiescence by other States,[102] whereas an overreaching or fatuous claim may be met by protests or even blocking legislation, as occurred with some States in response to the more assertive claims of effects-based jurisdiction by the USA.[103]

8.4.2 **Resolving conflicts of jurisdiction between States**

Discerning the location of a composite or complex act is inherently difficult, and raises the possibility of *overlapping jurisdiction*, or situations in which two or more States can validly assert jurisdiction over specific conduct. There are surprisingly few treaties which provide for a solution to overlapping jurisdictional claims, though a notable exception is Article 30 of the Arab Convention on Combating Information Technology Offences, which specifies that in the case of multiple jurisdictional claims, priority is accorded to a State 'whose security or interests were disrupted by the offence'; then to

[100] See M Schmitt (ed), *Tallinn Manual 2.0 on the International Law Applicable to Cyber Operations* (CUP, 2017), 51–5.

[101] See, e.g., *DPP v Doot* [1973] AC 807; [1973] 1 All ER 940 (HL); *DPP v Stonehouse* [1978] AC 55; [1977] 2 All ER 909 (HL); *Liangsiriprasert v Government of the United States of America* [1991] 1 AC 225; [1990] 2 All ER 866 (PC).

[102] Acquiescence by other States can serve to buttress a State's claim to exercise jurisdiction: see *US v Suerte*, 291 F.3d 36 (2002).

[103] States prohibited the production of documents or information to the courts or authorities of foreign states. See: UK Protection of Trading Interests Act 1980; Limitation of Danish Shipowners' Freedom to Give Information to Authorities of Foreign Countries 1967; and the Law Prohibiting a Shipowner in Certain Cases to Produce Documents 1968 (Finland). For further reading, see AV Lowe, 'Public International Law and the Conflict of Laws' (1984) 33 ICLQ 575 and AV Lowe, 'Blocking Extraterritorial Jurisdiction: The British Protection of Trading Interests Act 1980' (1981) 75 AJIL 257.

the State in whose territory the offence was committed; and then by the State of nationality of the accused.[104]

In the absence of any prior agreement, the question is no longer whether the assertion of jurisdiction conforms with international law but, rather, as to how conflicting, concurrent claims are resolved, and whether guidance exists as to which claim ought to be given priority. For example, the USA and Russia clashed over the prosecution of high-profile cybercriminal Alexei Burkov, who was arrested in Israel in 2015 upon a US extradition request based on hacking-related charges (including fraud, identity theft, and money laundering). Russian judicial appeals to prevent extradition to the USA were rejected by the Israeli Supreme Court, which held that the choice between competing extradition requests remained a decision for the relevant government minister, albeit taking appropriate considerations into account.[105] In a surprising development, and despite the lack of any extradition treaty, in September 2021 the USA released Burkov from prison into Russian custody.

Such situations are compounded in cases where the legislation of two States might be in conflict. For example, if State A requires the performance of an act by its nationals, even extraterritorially, but that same act is proscribed under the laws of State B. The 'foreign sovereign compulsion' defence has emerged precisely for this reason, to excuse, for example, a failure to produce documents in pursuance of an order of a court when such disclosure would be prohibited under the criminal law of the State where the said documents are located.[106] Laws might also be enacted precisely to create conflicts with the laws of another State perceived as overreaching. This was the case when the European Community enacted regulations protecting against the effects of the US Helms–Burton and d'Amato Acts, which sought to assert extraterritorial jurisdiction in relation to Cuba, Iran, and Libya.[107]

Finally, multilateral treaties harmonizing obligations can serve to create parallel obligations in all States parties, but only occasionally create specific consultative mechanisms that can be used to eliminate possible conflicts. A notable exception is the EC–US antitrust cooperation procedure established in 1996, designed to eliminate extraterritorial applications of laws which cause difficulty for the other party.[108]

[104] See Arab Convention on Combating Information Technology Offences (signed 21 December 2010, entered into force February 2014), Art 30.

[105] See *Burkov v Minister of Justice* (Supreme Court of Israel), HCJ 7272/19 (10 November 2019). The Israeli court partially relied on the European Convention on Extradition (signed 13 December 1957, entered into force 18 April 1960), ETS No 24, Art 17, which requires States parties, when considering concurrent requests for extradition, to have regard to all the circumstances, including the dates of the requests, the nationality of the person claimed, and the relative seriousness and place of commission of the offences, but without priority for any particular element.

[106] See *Société Internationale v Rogers*, 357 US 197 (1958).

[107] See Council Regulation (EC) 2271/96, [1996] OJ L309, discussed in AV Lowe, 'US Extraterritorial Jurisdiction: the Helms-Burton and D'Amato Acts' (1997) 46 ICLQ 378.

[108] See EC–US Agreement on the Application of Positive Comity Principles in the Enforcement of their Competition Laws [1998] OJ L173. See also the United Nations (Palermo) Convention on Transnational Organized Crime (adopted 15 November 2000, entered into force 29 September 2003), 2237 UNTS 319, Art 15(5), where States parties are obliged to consult other parties which are investigating or prosecuting the same conduct.

8.5 Conclusion

International law contains a diverse, but unsystematized, body of principles and practices governing prescriptive and enforcement jurisdiction. Like with many fields of international law, jurisdictional claims remain characterized by the dynamism of State practice and the balancing of priorities such as effective enforcement and the sovereignty of States. Ultimately, jurisdictional claims cannot be resolved through the application of strict rules, given the likely overlap of perfectly permissible claims and the reality in today's world that most States seek to exert extraterritorial jurisdiction to preserve their essential interests. But such interests must be balanced, and ought not to supersede entirely the exercise by another State of its sovereign right to regulate social relations within its territory. Finally, let us not lose sight of the fact that jurisdictional claims and their overlap represent 'encounters' between rival jurisdictions, going beyond the mere conflicts of States on the international plane, and the very resolution of such conflicts and claims poses wider questions for the development of international law.[109]

Further reading

M Akehurst, 'Jurisdiction in International Law' (1972–3) 46 BYBIL 145.

A hugely influential reference on the topic of jurisdiction in international law.

DW Bowett, 'Jurisdiction: Changing Patterns of Authority over Activities and Resources' (1982) 53 BYBIL 1.

A thorough study of extraterritorial jurisdiction during a period of rapid change in the late twentieth century, notably in relation to the seas and outer space.

J Ellis, 'Extraterritorial Exercise of Jurisdiction for Environmental Protection' (2012) 25 Leiden JIL 397.

An imaginative study of the inevitable transboundary issues arising regarding jurisdictional claims relating to environmental protection.

D Hovell, 'The Authority of Universal Jurisdiction' (2018) 29 EJIL 427.

A provocative attempt to disrupt prevailing narratives on universal jurisdiction and to locate certain community and individual interests in the concept.

FA Mann, 'The Doctrine of Jurisdiction in International Law' (1964-I) 111 Recueil des Cours 1; and 'The Doctrine of International Jurisdiction Revisited after Twenty Years' (1984-III) 186 Recueil des Cours 9.

Separated by two decades, these thorough surveys address the various modes of jurisdiction and their evolution through the twentieth century.

[109] S Pahuja, 'Laws of Encounter: A Jurisdictional Account of International Law' (2013) 1 LRIL 63.

A Mills, 'Rethinking Jurisdiction in International Law' (2014) 84 BYBIL 187.

Inspired by private international law, a redescription of jurisdiction as a matter of duties and obligations rather than purely a matter of right.

R O'Keefe, 'Universal Jurisdiction: Clarifying the Basic Concept' (2004) 2 JICJ 735.

A concise distillation of universal jurisdiction, which situates it carefully within the international legal framework.

S Pahuja, 'Laws of Encounter: A Jurisdictional Account of International Law' (2013) 1 LRIL 63.

An imaginative, critical re-interpretation of jurisdiction as a 'law of encounter', of ethical and political significance.

L Reydams, *Universal Jurisdiction: International and Municipal Legal Perspectives* (OUP, 2003).

Published at a time of heightened controversy, this comprehensive study gathered extensive State practice and explained universal jurisdiction in relation to other exercises of jurisdiction.

C Ryngaert, *Jurisdiction in International Law* (2nd edn, OUP, 2015).

Presents a general theory of prescriptive jurisdiction extending across many emerging areas, including cyberspace, tax law, antitrust legislation, and sanction laws.

T Schulz, 'Carving up the Internet: Jurisdiction, Legal Orders, and the Private/Public International Law Interface' (2008) 19 EJIL 799.

A creative application of jurisdictional claims within the emerging field of internet regulation.

Y Shany, *Regulating Jurisdictional Relations between National and International Courts* (OUP, 2007).

An engaging review of the possible conflicts of jurisdiction which arise in practice between national and international courts.

T Treves, 'Piracy, Law of the Sea, and Use of Force: Developments off the Coast of Somalia' (2009) 20 EJIL 399.

Careful and systematic study of the interrelation of jurisdictional claims with other fields of international law, using Somalia as a case study.

9

Immunities

9.1 Introduction: the concept of 'immunities'

In the previous chapter, we examined the various jurisdictional bases a State can claim when asserting jurisdiction over a given subject matter. There is an important further dimension to jurisdiction, however, that goes to the heart of State sovereignty. Situations have often arisen where the national courts of a State have started proceedings concerning the legality of the conduct of another State. *Immunity from jurisdiction* describes the doctrines developed in domestic courts over time to avoid infringements on sovereignty whenever possible.

In this chapter, we will consider the immunities which appertain to a State as a legal person, as well as those which apply to State representatives. Generally speaking, immunities seek to prevent foreign courts from exercising jurisdiction regarding the conduct of another State, its agents, officials, or diplomatic representatives, as well as from adjudicating on inter-State disputes without their consent.[1]

Often an exemption from local jurisdiction exists in relation to mundane violations such as driving offences or administrative matters, but has important policy implications if the act in question constitutes an international crime.

THEORY AND DEBATES The Interplay of Immunities and Human Rights Considerations: a Linear Relationship?

Important recent developments in international human rights and international criminal law have called into question the *raison d'être* of immunities, in particular, whether these should be inapplicable in relation to serious violations of *jus cogens* norms, such as torture, genocide, war crimes, and crimes against humanity. As early as 1951, concerns had been raised: see H Lauterpacht, 'The Problem of Jurisdictional Immunities of Foreign States' (1951) 28 BYBIL 220.

As international criminal law has gained prominence, it might seem appealing that immunity ought not to be recognized for such crimes; to restrict immunity would seemingly subject States to the rule of law and the promotion of fundamental human rights. Though certain

[1] This chapter will only cover immunity from adjudication and will not consider immunity from enforcement, which a foreign State continues generally to enjoy. See for further discussion H Fox and P Webb, *The Law of State Immunity* (3rd rev edn, OUP, 2015), chs 16 and 17.

domestic court judgments suggest a move in that direction, recent developments also suggest that the law on immunities does not proceed in linear fashion. In 2012, the ICJ concluded that, 'under customary international law as it presently stands, a State is not deprived of immunity by reason of the fact that it is accused of serious violations of international human rights law or the international law of armed conflict' (*Jurisdictional Immunities of the State (Germany v Italy: Greece intervening), Judgment, ICJ Reports 2012*, p 99, para 91). Though the Court was careful to conclude that criminal proceedings against an official of the State might be a different matter, the immunity of the State would apply even in cases where violations of *jus cogens* are alleged. That question remains open within the ILC in its ongoing study of the immunity of State officials.

As such, throughout this chapter we should be careful not to presume that there is linear progress from sovereignty to human rights in relation to immunities. The relevant practice in how such immunities are recognized remains that of States and their organs, and in particular their courts, in how such immunities are recognized. The international law on immunities requires a balanced, careful assessment between various competing priorities, such as sovereign equality, diplomatic relations, peace, and human rights.

9.2 Immunities of the State

9.2.1 Origins and development: defining an 'act of State'

It is rather easy to confuse the immunities of the State with those of persons representing a State. In the absolute monarchies of early modern Europe, the sovereign was a definable person who embodied the State, and exempt from any form of judicial or enforcement process. Such is the meaning of Louis XIV's exclamation that '*l'État, c'est moi*'. A concept of 'international comity' arose, providing for the inviolability of foreign sovereigns (both personally and in relation to their possessions), and their immunity from the jurisdiction of local courts when visiting another State.[2] In mediaeval Europe, the prevailing practice consisted of sending diplomats to other States for very specific negotiations, though by the late thirteenth century the Italian city-States were actively opening embassies in each other's capitals, and sending permanent representatives to each other's courts.[3] Diplomatic representatives were thus accorded the same inviolability and immunities.

For many reasons, perhaps including imperial stature and the binding nature of judicial decisions in common law legal systems, the early customary principles

[2] See, e.g., *The Porto Alexandre* [1920] P 30 (UK CA); and *The Pesaro*, 271 US 562 (1926) (US); and for further reading, C Schreuer, *State Immunity: Some Recent Developments* (1988), 306, fn 14.

[3] For a history of diplomatic relations in early Renaissance Europe, see L von Ranke's *History of the Latin and Teutonic Nations from 1494 to 1514* (1824), and the more contemporary I Roberts (ed), *Satow's Diplomatic Practice* (6th edn, OUP, 2011), esp chs 1–5.

on immunity were developed in UK and US courts.[4] Questions of immunity are of a procedural nature, to be decided immediately before proceeding with a case, and must be distinguished from two substantive concepts, those of 'act of State' or to 'non-justiciability'.[5] 'Act of State' is a substantive defence, according to which a national court must not adjudicate over disputes relating to legislation or other governmental activities of a foreign State within its own territory.[6] The rule on non-justiciability is perhaps more difficult to define: generally, it bars a court from adjudicating on certain categories of questions, generally relating to sensitive political matters.[7] In 2017, the UK Supreme Court, in *Belhaj & Rahmatullah*, suggested that the rule of non-justiciability is a narrow sub-category of the act of State doctrine, whereby a domestic court will not adjudicate upon sovereign acts committed by a foreign State abroad.[8]

HISTORICAL BACKGROUND ***The Schooner Exchange v McFaddon*, 7 Cranch 116 (1812) (US Sup Ct)**

The first statements elucidating general principles of State immunity were made in the context of visits of the foreign warships of friendly States to national ports. Such a case was adjudicated early on by the US Supreme Court in the classic case of *The Schooner Exchange v McFaddon*. In this case, the 'libellants' (plaintiffs in courts of admiralty) alleged that a French naval vessel, docked in Philadelphia for repairs, was in fact an American schooner, the *Exchange*, but that it had been seized by France on the high seas in 1810 and renamed.

The US Supreme Court, concurring with the submissions of the US Attorney-General, rejected jurisdiction and ordered release of the French naval vessel. Chief Justice Marshall, writing for the majority, acknowledged that there existed exception for foreign sovereigns to

[4] See *Difference Relating to Immunity from Legal Process, Advisory Opinion, ICJ Reports 1999*, p 62, 88; *Jones v Saudi Arabia* [2004] EWCA Civ 1394, 129 ILR 653 (Mance LJ), para 10. See further LF Damrosch, 'The Sources of Immunity Law—Between International and Domestic Law' and W Shan and P Wang, 'Divergent Views on State Immunity in the International Community' in T Ruys, N Angelet, and L Ferro (eds), *The Cambridge Handbook of Immunities and International Law* (CUP, 2019), 40. It should also be noted that the various ILC Reports on immunities of State officials also refer generously to early British and US practice.

[5] See *International Association of Machinists & Aerospace Workers v OPEC* 649 F.2d 1354, 1359–60 (9th Cir 1981); 66 ILR 413, 418–19, where immunity was understood as a procedural principle derived from international law, while an act of State constituted a 'prudential' doctrine having internal constitutional roots.

[6] Though *cf Letelier v Republic of Chile*, 488 F.Supp 665 (1980); 63 ILR 378 (US Ct App), in which Chile invoked the act of State doctrine, on the basis that certain assassination orders against Mr Letelier had been issued in Chile. The US Court of Appeals rejected this plea, on the basis that to apply the act of State doctrine would in effect allow for the absolute immunity of Chile under another guise. For a discussion of 'absolute immunity', see later, Section 9.2.2. See also *Maclaine Watson v The International Tin Council* [1988] 3 WLR 1169, 1188; 80 ILR 191, 209 (Kerr CJ); and *Border Guards* case, Federal Supreme Court of Germany, Judgment No 5 StR 370/92 (3 November 1992).

[7] An attempt to formulate a distinct doctrine of non-justiciability was attempted by the UK House of Lords in *Buttes Gas and Oil Co v Hammer* [1982] AC 888, 931–2, 938 (Wilberforce LJ).

[8] *Belhaj & Rahmatullah (No 1) v Straw and Ors* [2017] UKSC 3 (UK) (Mance LJ, para 40; Neuberger LJ, para 123). See further Chapter 4, Sections 4.3.2–4.3.3; and P Okowa, 'Act of State and Diplomatic Protection in the Modern Constitution: Two Case Studies' in S Choudhry et al (eds), *Global Canons in an Age of Contestation: Debating Foundational Texts of Constitutional Democracy and Human Rights* (OUP, 2024) 553.

the exclusive and absolute jurisdiction of a State over its territory. In an oft-cited statement, he explained that the:

> perfect equality and absolute independence of sovereigns . . . have given rise to a class of cases in which every sovereign is understood to waive the exercise of a part of that complete exclusive territorial jurisdiction which has been stated to be the attribute of every nation. (at 137)

In other words, the US courts could not even consider the question of whether the French vessel had originally been an American schooner, as to raise the question would impugn the immunity of France. This important early statement was highly influential in establishing the state of international law in the early nineteenth century, and is an important starting point for understanding how the law on State immunity has evolved since the nineteenth century. Because immunity was equated with the absolute equality of sovereigns, immunity from domestic jurisdiction followed naturally from the fact that the courts of one State ought not, in principle, adjudge on the conduct of another State or its sovereign.

Though all three principles derive from the basic principle that a State's courts ought not to sit in judgment on the conduct of another State, even if committed abroad, the doctrines of act of State and non-justiciability relate to the nature of the conduct in question, and not the person of the defendant.[9] The distinction with immunity is that, if immunity is bestowed upon a State, under international law it is sovereign and independent and thus should be exempted from the jurisdiction of a foreign court that would normally be exercised if the defendant were not a State.

A State is an abstract entity, though it usually acts through its organs, agents, officials, or representatives. To illustrate the relevance of this point, the *Kuwaiti Airways v Iraqi Airways* case before the UK House of Lords concerned the appropriation of Kuwaiti aircraft by Iraqi Airways, a State-owned airline of Iraq, after its invasion and attempted annexation of Kuwait.[10] In response to Kuwaiti Airways' action for damages, Iraqi Airways unsuccessfully invoked the non-justiciability doctrine, contending that the seizure was authorized by the Iraqi government and that state immunity could be invoked in respect of it. The majority of the Lords concluded that an exception to the non-justiciability rule should be made. Given that international consensus existed on the illegality of Iraq's invasion of Kuwait, the Lords concluded that where there existed such a flagrant and grave internationally wrongful act, an exception could be justified under English public policy, dismissing both the non-justiciability principle and Iraq's claim that the seizure was a sovereign act which benefited from immunity.[11]

9.2.2 **Absolute immunity**

Early doctrines on immunity held that the sovereign—historically the reigning monarch, but today the State and its representatives—was completely immune from foreign jurisdiction in all circumstances and in relation to all activities. This is referred to as

[9] *Underhill v Hernández*, 168 US 250 (1897) (US Sup Ct); and *Luthor v Sagor* [1921] 3 KB 532 (UK CA).

[10] *Kuwaiti Airways Corp v Iraqi Airways Co* [2002] UKHL 19.

[11] *Ibid*, (Nicholls LJ), para 29.

'absolute immunity'. It bears repeating that the courts of the UK and the USA were historically influential in the early international law on immunities, and for that reason are cited disproportionately. In an extension of the *Schooner Exchange* principle adopted by the US Supreme Court,[12] the UK House of Lords in *Parlement Belge* held that absolute immunity also extended to cover all ships owned by a foreign State, regardless of their engagement in public service or trade.[13] Later cases extended absolute immunity to State organs[14] and to State agencies that were also separate legal persons under the law of a foreign State.[15] US courts tended, conversely, to distinguish between formal title and effective possession or control, twice rejecting a plea of immunity in relation to State-owned ships not in the possession or control of that State.[16]

It is not sufficient for immunity simply to be asserted; a foreign State should submit some form of evidence that its claim is not merely illusory.[17] To illustrate, in *Duff Development Company v Kelantan*,[18] the question arose as to whether Kelantan, a Malay entity under British protection, was a State. Kelantan submitted an 'executive certificate',[19] issued by the British government, confirming its status as an independent State. The House of Lords considered that the executive certificate served as recognition by the UK Crown of the sovereignty of a foreign ruler, binding upon UK courts. Kelantan was thus entitled to sovereign immunity.

9.2.3 **Restrictive immunity**

9.2.3.1 **Domestic practice**

Early cases in the USA and the UK were at odds with a more restrictive form of immunity that was practised in the courts of States with civil law traditions, notably Italy, Belgium, and the Egyptian mixed courts.[20] Since the end of the nineteenth century, they had all adopted a restrictive doctrine, recognizing absolute immunity only relating to acts committed in the exercise of sovereign authority (*acta jure imperii*) and not for trading activities or acts that a private person could perform (*acta jure gestionis*).[21] A key

[12] See earlier, Section 9.2.1 ('Origins').

[13] *The Parlement Belge* (1879–90) 5 Prob Div 197 (CA); and the earlier *Charkieh* case, LR 4 A & E 59 (1873), which had proposed a restrictive doctrine of immunity.

[14] *Krajina v Tass Agency* [1949] 2 All ER 274; 16 AD 129.

[15] *Baccus SRL v Servicio Nacional de Trigo* [1957] 1 QB 438; 23 ILR 160.

[16] See *The Navemar*, 303 US 68 (1938); 9 AD 176 (US Sup Ct) and *Mexico v Hoffman*, 324 US 30 (1945); 12 AD 124 (US Sup Ct).

[17] *Juan Ysmael v Republic of Indonesia* [1955] AC 72; 21 ILR 85; *USA and France v Dollfus Mieg et Compagnie* [1952] AC 582.

[18] *Duff Development Company v Kelantan* [1924] AC 797; 2 AD 124.

[19] It has been asserted that the executive certificate was almost certainly falsified: see P Capps, 'British Policy and the Recognition of Governments' (2014) Public Law 230. Executive certificates are further addressed in Chapter 4, Section 4.3.1.

[20] These are surveyed in Fox and Webb (n 1) 35; and the earlier H Lauterpacht, 'The Problem of Jurisdictional Immunities of Foreign States' (1951) 28 BYBIL 220.

[21] *Kuwaiti Airways Corporation v Iraqi Airways* Co [1995] 1 WLR 1147, 1160; 103 ILR 340 (Goff LJ); *United States of America v Public Service Alliance of Canada (Re Canada Labour Code)* (1992) 91 DLR (4th) 466; 94 ILR 281. See also Fox and Webb (n 1) 151; and A Orakhelashvili, 'Jurisdictional Immunity of States and General International Law—Explaining the *Jus Gestionis v Jus Imperii* Divide' and W Shan and P Wang, 'Divergent Views on State Immunity in the International Community' in T Ruys, N Angelet, and L Ferro (eds), *The Cambridge Handbook of Immunities and International Law* (CUP, 2019), 105.

development in the recognition of the restrictive form of immunity came in the *Empire of Iran* case, in which a builder sought to recover the cost of repairs carried out to the Iranian Embassy in (then-West) Germany. In that case, the German *Bundesgerichtshof* (Federal Constitutional Court) extensively surveyed bilateral and multilateral treaties, State practice, and academic writing before concluding that a restrictive doctrine of State immunity was permitted under international law, with the nature of the relevant act being determinative.[22]

In common law jurisdictions, the twentieth century brought an expansion of States' commercial activities, in particular with the creation of public corporations and the nationalization of various economic sectors. This phenomenon gave rise to a reaction against the doctrine of absolute immunity, which would arguably confer unfair advantages to State enterprises over private entrepreneurs.

In the UK, judicial consensus on the absolute nature of immunity had already begun to unravel by the late 1930s in the *SS Cristina* case, concerning a Spanish ship requisitioned during the Spanish Civil War.[23] Though the majority upheld the sovereign immunity of the Spanish Republican Government, a strong minority questioned the absolute nature of State immunity in relation to State trading vessels.[24] A more restrictive doctrine of State immunity was not adopted, however, until the 1970s through a series of cases,[25] culminating in the adoption of the UK State Immunity Act 1978 (SIA).[26] This followed closely after the US Foreign Sovereign Immunities Act 1976 (FSIA), the first statute to introduce the restrictive doctrine in a common law jurisdiction.[27] Quite a few other States, most from common law traditions but also including Argentina, enacted similar legislation.[28] They were complemented by case law in several other States.[29] A 2015 study of judicial, legislative, and executive practice suggested that

[22] *Empire of Iran Case* (1963) 45 ILR 57, 89. See also the earlier *Dralle v Czechoslovakia* (1950) 17 ILR 155 (Austrian Sup Ct).

[23] *Compania Naviera Vascongado v SS Cristina* [1938] AC 485; 9 AD 250 (UK).

[24] Lord MacMillan, Lord Thankerton, and Lord Maugham all questioned the absolute nature of immunity in relation to State trading vessels: *ibid*, 498, 260.

[25] See *The Philippine Admiral* [1977] AC 373; [1976] 1 All ER 78; 64 ILR 90 (UK PC) (in relation to goods supplied to a Philippine trading vessel); *Trendtex Trading Corporation v Central Bank of Nigeria* [1977] 1 QB 529; [1977] 1 All ER 881 (in relation to a commercial letter of credit issued by the defendant State organ); 64 ILR 111 (UK CA); *Io Congreso del Partido* [1981] 2 All ER 1064, 64 ILR 308 (in relation to a State-owned commercial vessel); *Alcom v Republic of Colombia* [1984] 2 All ER 6; 74 ILR 179 (in relation to an embassy bank account used for commercial transactions).

[26] Foreign Sovereign Immunities Act (1977) 90 Stat 2891 (US). Further detail on contemporary UK practice has been reported in Fox and Webb (n 1), ch 7.

[27] State Immunity Act 1978 (UK). As early as 1952, the US Department of State had announced that it would hew to the restrictive theory of sovereign immunity: 'Tate Letter' (1952) 26 Department of State Bulletin 984. See also *Victory Transport Inc v Comisaria General de Abastecimientos y Transportes*, 336 F.2d 354 (2d Cir 1964), and four judges in *Alfred Dunhill of London Inc v Republic of Cuba*, 425 US 682 (1976). For further discussion, see Fox and Webb (n 1) ch 8.

[28] See, e.g., Canadian State Immunity Act 1982; Immunities and Privileges Act 1984 (Malaysia); Pakistan State Immunity Ordinance 1981; Singapore State Immunity Act (1979); South African Foreign States Immunities Act 1981; Malawi Immunities and Privileges Act 1984; Israel Foreign States Immunity Law 2008; and Immunity of Foreign States from the Jurisdiction of Argentinian Courts Act 1995.

[29] See, e.g., *Ministry of Defence of Government of UK v Ndegna* (1983) 103 ILR 235 (Kenyan CA); *Fang and Others v Jiang and Others* [2007] NZAR 240 (New Zealand HC); *Kramer v Government of Belgium; Embassy of Belgium* [1989] 1 CLRQ 126; 103 ILR 299 (Nigeria).

about two-thirds of States have adopted a restrictive approach to immunity, but around one-third of States still adhere to the absolute immunity rule.[30] That said, there are some major shifts: Russia (since 2016) and China (since 2024) have shifted to the restrictive approach.[31]

9.2.3.2 **International practice**

Despite the evolution of State immunity during the twentieth century, with limited European treaties signed in the 1920s and the 1970s,[32] it was not until 2002 that the ICJ ruled directly on State immunity on the international level. In the *Arrest Warrant* judgment, the ICJ held that a serving Minister for Foreign Affairs, Abdoulaye Yerodia, was immune from criminal jurisdiction, even in respect of violations of international crimes such as torture, crimes against humanity, and war crimes.[33] In *Obligation to Prosecute or Extradite*, the Court did not challenge the exercise of universal jurisdiction against former Chadian President Hissène Habré, who was accused of torture. However, it bears noting that Mr Habré had sought refuge in a third State, Senegal, and that neither Chad nor Senegal had invoked Mr Habré's immunity.[34] It was, however, in the significant *Jurisdictional Immunities of the State* judgment in which the Court declared that proceedings in Italian courts against Germany relating to war damage caused by Nazi Germany during World War II were a violation of Germany's immunity.[35] The Court's conclusion hinged on its review of judicial decisions of national courts for evidence of State practice:

> of particular significance to be found in the judgments of national courts faced with the question whether a foreign State is immune, the legislation of those States which have enacted status dealing with immunity, the claims to immunity advanced by States before

[30] P-H Verdier and E Voeten, 'How Does Customary International Law Change? The Case of State Immunity' (2015) 50 International Studies Quarterly 209, 214. See also W Shan and P Wang, 'Divergent Views on State Immunity in the International Community' in T Ruys, N Angelet, and L Ferro (eds), *The Cambridge Handbook of Immunities and International Law* (CUP, 2019), 61.

[31] See Federal Law on Jurisdictional Immunity of a Foreign State and a Foreign State's Property in the Russian Federation, SZ RF (Russian Collection of Legislation) 2015, No 45, 6198 (entered into force 1 January 2016); and Law of the People's Republic of China on Foreign State Immunity (Standing Committee of the National People's Congress of the PRC) (1 September 2023, entered into force 1 January 2024).

[32] See 1926 Brussels Convention for the Unification of Certain Rules concerning the Immunities of Government Vessels (adopted 10 April 1926, entered into force 8 January 1937), 179 LNTS 199 and the 1972 European Convention on State Immunity (adopted 16 May 1972, entered into force 11 June 1976), 1495 UNTS 182 (ECSI).

[33] *Arrest Warrant of 11 April 2000 (Democratic Republic of the Congo v Belgium), Judgment, ICJ Reports 2002*, p 3.

[34] *Questions relating to the Obligation to Prosecute or Extradite (Belgium v Senegal), Judgment, ICJ Reports 2012*, p 422. See also *Certain Questions of Mutual Assistance in Criminal Matters (Djibouti v France), Judgment, ICJ Reports 2008*, p 177, para 196, in which the ICJ laid out the expectation that a State must notify another State that it intends to claim immunity, so the court of the forum State does not fail to respect any entitlement to immunity, and thus constitute a breach of international law by a State organ.

[35] *Jurisdictional Immunities of the State (Germany v Italy: Greece intervening), Judgment, ICJ Reports 2012*, p 99. The present author has elsewhere commented on the alternative justifications available to the Court: see GI Hernández, 'A Reluctant Guardian: The International Court of Justice and the Concept of "International Community"' (2012) 83 BYBIL 13.

foreign Courts and the statements made by States, first in the course of the extensive study of the subject by the International Law Commission and then in the context of the adoption of the UN Convention.[36]

With respect to treaty practice, in 2004 the General Assembly adopted the United Nations Convention on Jurisdictional Immunities of States and their Property,[37] the first international convention on State immunity.[38] In Articles 10–17, the UN Convention enshrines a restrictive doctrine of State immunity with regard to most civil and commercial proceedings in domestic courts. Some uncertainty nevertheless surrounds it: though it is true that some international courts have cited the UN Convention favourably,[39] only twenty-two States have ratified it, of which fourteen are European, and it requires thirty ratifications to enter into force.[40]

States may change their position over time, even in multiple directions. For example, though in 2005 Hong Kong had enacted legislation enshrining the restrictive State immunity doctrine,[41] in *FG Hemisphere Associates v Congo*[42] the Hong Kong Court of Final Appeal applied the absolute immunity doctrine as follows: '[Hong Kong] cannot, as a matter of legal and constitutional principle, adhere to a doctrine of state immunity which differs from that adopted by [China]. The doctrine of State immunity practised in [Hong Kong], as in the rest of China, is accordingly a doctrine of absolute immunity.'[43] As China has in 2024 shifted to the restrictive immunity doctrine, Hong Kong (and Macau) will follow suit.

9.3 State immunity in practice

The general move towards a restrictive doctrine of immunity requires a better understanding of the distinction between governmental acts that will, or will not, benefit from immunity. In this regard, the *acta jure imperii/acta jure gestionis* distinction described earlier is useful in distinguishing between sovereign and non-sovereign acts, though it does not fully explain how this operates in practice.

As a matter of method, governmental activities are generally presumed to benefit from immunity, barring a list of exceptions. As explained in Article 5 of the UN Convention,

[36] *Jurisdictional Immunities of the State, ibid*, para 55.

[37] UNGA Res 59/38 (2 December 2004) (UN Convention), which emphasized that the UN Convention does not cover criminal proceedings.

[38] The 1926 Brussels Convention (n 32) only removed immunity in respect of State-owned or operated ships, and the 1972 ECSI (n 32) is regional in nature, and in any event has only been ratified by eight States.

[39] The ICJ, in *Jurisdictional Immunities of the State* (n 35); the ECtHR in *Oleynikov v Russia* App no 36703/04 (ECtHR, 14 March 2013), para 66; *Cudak v Lithuania* App no 15869 (ECtHR, 23 March 2010), para 72; *Sabeh el Leil v France* App no 34869/05 (ECtHR, 29 June 2011), para 19.

[40] Moreover, as of 2022 there are only twenty-eight signatories.

[41] Law of the People's Republic of China on Judicial Immunity from Measures of Constraint for the Property of Foreign Central Banks (25 October 2005).

[42] [2010] 2 HKLRD 66.

[43] *Democratic Republic of the Congo and others v FG Hemisphere Associates LLC* [2011] HKCFA 42 (FACV 5-7/2010). The duty stems from Article 13 of Hong Kong's Basic Law, which considers immunity to fall within the remit of the Central People's Government as it constitutes an act of State or foreign affairs.

'[a] State enjoys immunity in respect of itself and its property, from the jurisdiction of the courts of another State, subject to the provisions of the present Convention.'[44] This raises two important considerations: (i) the nature of the entity performing an act, and whether an entitlement to State immunity encompasses the acts of that entity; and (ii) the nature of the governmental act itself, and whether it may be classified as an act for which a sovereign State may invoke immunity. These two points are examined in the following sections.

9.3.1 **The definition of a 'State' in the law on immunities**

For the purpose of State immunity, Article 2(1)(b) of the UN Convention lays down a definition of the State that is widely regarded as reflecting customary international law:

(i) The State and its various organs of government.[45] A defendant State may waive its immunity and submit voluntarily to the jurisdiction of the forum State. Waiver can be explicit, but may also be implied in certain circumstances, for example by consenting to jurisdiction by prior written agreement, by instituting proceedings itself, or by taking steps in pending proceedings.[46]

(ii) Constituent units (such as provinces or states) of a federal State, or political subdivisions of a State (such as municipalities) that are entitled to perform acts in the exercise of sovereign authority, and are acting in that capacity.[47]

(iii) Agencies or other instrumentalities of the State, to the extent they are entitled to perform and are actually performing acts in the exercise of sovereign authority of the State.[48] Most relevant is the degree of functional control exercised by the State, and whether it is acting on behalf of the State.[49] As such, control and autonomy are not merely a matter of formal entitlement, though these may provide evidence of a degree of autonomy.[50]

(iv) Individuals acting in the capacity of representatives of the State, the immunity of which might persist after they have left office (see later, Section 9.4.2.2).

[44] *Cf Victory Transport*, 336 F.2d 354 (1964), in which the US Second District Court denied any presumption of immunity, and required that any activity in question fall within one of the categories of acts of a strictly political or public nature.

[45] In *Jones v Ministry of Interior for the Kingdom of Saudi Arabia and Ors* [2006] UKHL 26, paras 30, 78, the UK House of Lords confirmed an earlier ruling that the term 'government' also extends to individual employees or officers of a foreign State.

[46] See UN Convention (n 37) Art 8; UK SIA (n 27) s 2; US FSIA (n 26) s 1605(a)(1). See further C Amirfar, 'Waivers of Jurisdictional Immunity' and W Shan and P Wang, 'Divergent Views on State Immunity in the International Community' in T Ruys, N Angelet, and L Ferro (eds), *The Cambridge Handbook of Immunities and International Law* (CUP, 2019), 167.

[47] *Cf* UK SIA, s 14(5), which requires an Order in Council to recognize the immunity of federal component entities see *Alamieyeseigha v CPS* [2005] EWHC 2704 (Admin), paras 38 *et seq*. Art 28 of the ECSI (n 32) establishes an 'opt-in' system whereby federal States may declare that their component entities are entitled to immunity.

[48] Natural persons may also fall under 'agents or instrumentalities': see *Samnatar v Yousuf*, 130 S Ct 2278, 2287–9 (2010) (US Sup Ct); *Propend Finance Pty v Sing* [1997] EWCA Civ 1433, 111 ILR 611; and *Jones v Saudi Arabia* (n 46) paras 30, 78.

[49] *Trendtex v Central Bank of Nigeria* (n 25) 385; *Baccus SRL v Servicio Nacional del Trigo* [1957] 1 QB 438, 467; *Czarnikow Ltd v Rolimpex* [1979] AC 351, 364 (Wilberforce LJ), 367 (Viscount Dihorne).

[50] See, e.g., *First National City Bank v Banco Para el Comercio Exterior de Cuba (Bancec)* 462 US 611 (1963); 80 ILR 566 (US Sup Ct); *Foremost-McKesson v Islamic Republic of Iran*, 905 F.2d 438 (DC Cir 1990).

An interesting point to note is that criteria (ii) and (iii) in the UN Convention are cumulative, in that they require both authorization and actual performance of an act by an entity. This is a detail on which practice is not entirely coherent. The US FSIA encompasses any 'agencies or instrumentalities' without necessarily specifying that these must be acting in the exercise of the sovereign authority of the State.[51] Conversely, the UK SIA demands that any non-executive organs of the State or its agents must actually be exercising sovereign authority for immunity to attach to those acts.[52]

9.3.2 **Applicability of immunity to the acts of a State**

9.3.2.1 **General principle: acts of a sovereign nature are immune**

Once it is determined that an act has been performed by an entity that may be encompassed within the meaning of the term 'State' for the purpose of claiming jurisdictional immunity, the question arises as to whether the act or activity in question is of a sovereign (*jure imperii*) or non-sovereign nature (*jure gestionis*). The conceptual distinction seems relatively straightforward, in that sovereign acts (*acta jure imperii*) are those which, by their nature, are in the exercise of sovereign authority, and thus a State is entitled to claim immunity in respect of them.[53] In *Empire of Iran*, the German *Bundesgerichtshof* pointed to a 'generally recognized sphere of sovereign activity' encompassing 'the activities of the authorities responsible for foreign and military affairs, legislation, the exercise of police power and the administration of justice'.[54] In *Trendtex*, the English Court of Appeal held that the conduct of the Central Bank of Nigeria, though apparently a State entity under its enabling statute, was not entitled to claim immunity due to the commercial nature of the activities in which it was engaged, which did not fall within the areas of sovereign activity to which immunity could apply.[55] In the later *Gécamines v Hemisphere Associates*, the UK Privy Council was called upon to pronounce on the legal status of a State-owned corporation of the Democratic Republic of the Congo, and concluded that:

> constitutional and factual control and the exercise of sovereign functions do not without more convert a separate entity into an organ of the state. Especially where a separate juridical entity is formed by the state for what are on the face of it commercial or industrial purposes, with its own management and budget, the strong presumption is that its separate corporate status should be respected, and that it and the state forming it should not have to bear each other's liabilities. It will . . . take quite extreme circumstances to displace this presumption.[56]

Such 'extreme circumstances' would only exist in situations where 'the affairs of the entity and the state were so closely intertwined and confused that the entity could not properly be regarded for any significant purpose as distinct from the state and vice versa'.[57]

[51] US FSIA (n 26) s 1605(a)–(b).
[52] But *cf* the UK SIA (n 27) s 14(1)(c).
[53] *Jurisdictional Immunities of the State* (n 35) para 61.
[54] *Empire of Iran* (n 22) 80–1.
[55] *Trendtex v Central Bank of Nigeria* (n 25).
[56] *La Générale des Carrières et des Mines ('Gécamines') v FG Hemisphere Associates LLC* [2012] UKPC 27.
[57] *Ibid.*

In the ICJ's 2019 judgment on preliminary objections in *Certain Iranian Assets*, Iran had sought to claim sovereign immunity for the acts of the State-owned Bank Markazi.[58] Though the Court did not have jurisdiction to proceed further on the point, it did observe that publicly owned enterprises may enjoy immunities under customary international law when they engage in activities *jure imperii*.[59]

The distinction between *jure imperii/jure gestionis* acts is far from straightforward, and it is perhaps best to examine practice to determine which exceptions to immunity exist on a case-by-base basis.

CASE SPOTLIGHT ***Trendtex Trading Corp Ltd v Central Bank of Nigeria*** **[1977] QB 529 (English Court of Appeal)**

The *Trendtex* case was a landmark judgment in which the *acta jure gestionis* doctrine was formally recognized for the first time by a domestic court. Trendtex Trading had sold cement to the Government of Nigeria and the Central Bank of Nigeria issued a letter of credit. On becoming inundated with cement, the succeeding Nigerian government ordered the Central Bank not to honour the letter of credit. The plaintiff sued the bank for payment and the Central Bank invoked immunity.

A key point in *Trendtex* was whether the Central Bank of Nigeria was an organ of the State, due to its separate legal personality under domestic law. Lord Denning, writing for the majority, found that in principle the issue was not whether the bank was formally an apparatus of the State under Nigerian law but the nature of the activities in question. The nature of the contracts, in this case relating to the letters of credit, was commercial.

The court then considered, and rejected, the doctrine of absolute immunity, on the basis that it had been developed at a time when no sovereign State engaged in commercial activities. Reviewing international practice, and in particular the views of the majority in *Alfred Dunhill v Cuba*, Lord Denning adopted the view that absolute immunity had been abandoned, and that a doctrine of restrictive immunity, according to which *acta jure gestionis* would not benefit from immunity, was now customary international law.

The *Trendtex* judgment led to the adoption of the UK SIA the following year, which codified in statute the restrictive doctrine on immunity, and has not been amended substantially since. But, more significantly, the doctrine of restrictive immunity has spread to nearly two-thirds of States.

9.3.2.2 Acts of a private or commercial nature tend not to be immune

The most significant exception to immunity relates to commercial transactions between a foreign State and a private actor. Because it is sometimes difficult precisely to ascertain the commercial character of activities, the UN Convention follows the approach in the ECSI and the legislation of several States, by enumerating certain categories of private or commercial transactions that are presumed to be non-immune. Part III of the UN

[58] *Certain Iranian Assets (Iran v United States) (Preliminary Objections), ICJ Reports 2019*, 7.
[59] *Ibid*, paras 62–5.

Convention lists the following categories of acts, which are reflected also in the UK SIA and the ECSI:

(i) *Commercial transactions* (Article 10). In section 3(3) of the UK SIA, these explicitly include the sale of goods or supply of services, loans, or other financial transactions, and apply generally to all acts in which it is engaged other than in the exercise of sovereign authority.[60] Section 1603(d) of the US FSIA defines 'commercial activity' as 'a regular course of commercial conduct or a particular commercial transaction or act', and US courts have held a substantial range of activities to be commercial in nature.[61]

(ii) *Contracts of employment* (Article 11),[62] for ordinary professional activities such as being a medical secretary[63] or a domestic worker.[64] However, these do not apply if the individual is recruited to perform governmental functions, such as diplomatic or consular officers, or on a special mission.[65] State practice does vary, with certain States (e.g., the UK, South Africa, Pakistan, and Malawi) having more restrictive legislation regarding the scope for employees to sue a State under the employment contract exception.[66]

(iii) *Personal injuries and damage to property* (Article 12);[67] these remove immunity in respect of death or personal injury, or physical infliction of damage to a person or their tangible property. In a recent UK case, *Al Masarir v Saudi Arabia*, the court invoked this exception to remove the immunity of the respondent in respect of the use of spyware to hack the claimant's devices and gain access to

[60] UK SIA (n 27) s 3(3). See *Alcom v Republic of Colombia* [1984] 2 All ER 6, 10; 74 ILR 183; *Planmount v Zaire* [1980] 2 Lloyd's Rep 393 (UK QB); *Maclaine Watson v Department of Trade and Industry* [1988] 3 WLR 1933; 80 ILR 49. In the US, see *Callejo v Bancomer*, 764 F.2d 1011 (1985); *Argentina v Weltover Inc*, 119 L Ed 2d 394 (1992); 100 ILR 509.

[61] *Gemini Shipping v Foreign Trade Organization for Chemicals and Foodstuffs* (1981) 63 ILR 569 (foodstuffs); *NAC v Federal Republic of Nigeria* (1978) 63 ILR 137 (cement); *Argentine Airways v Ross* (1974) 63 ILR 195 (activities of State airlines).

[62] UK SIA (n 27) s 4; ECSI (n 32) Art 5. See *Arab Republic of Egypt v Gamal Eldin* [1996] 2 All ER 238. For further discussion, see H Fox, 'Employment Contracts as an Exception to State Immunity: Is All Public Service Immune?' (1995) 66 BYBIL 97; R Garnett, 'State Immunity in Employment Matters' (1997) 46 ICLQ 81.

[63] In *Barrandon v USA* (2000) 116 ILR 622, the French *Cour de Cassation* held that a nurse/medical secretary was not responsible for the public service functions of the US Embassy. Therefore, to dismiss her was an ordinary administrative act to which immunity did not attach.

[64] See, e.g., *Benkharbouche v Secretary of State for Foreign and Commonwealth Affairs and Secretary of State for Foreign and Commonwealth Affairs and Libya v Janah* [2017] UKSC 62, in respect of the mistreatment of two domestic workers employed at the Libyan and Sudanese embassies in London. The UK Supreme Court found that the employment of domestic workers was not an exercise of sovereign authority, and declared that ss 4(2)(b) and 16(1)(a) of the SIA, which conferred immunity on Libya and Sudan, respectively, were incompatible with the Human Rights Act 1998.

[65] *Saudi Arabia v Ahmed* [1996] 2 All ER 248; 104 ILR 629. In *Norwegian Embassy v Quattri* (1991) 114 ILR 525, the Italian *Corte di Cazzazione* concluded that only acts carried out in exercising the public law functions of a foreign State were entitled to immunity.

[66] See P Webb, 'The Immunity of States, Diplomats and International Organizations in Employment Disputes: The New Human Rights Dilemma?' (2016) 27 EJIL 745.

[67] See also UK SIA (n 27) s 5; ECSI (n 32) Art 11.

private information; even if some of the spyware was deployed from outside the UK, the location of the infected devices meant that the injury was considered to have taken place within the UK.[68]

(iv) *Ownership, possession, and use of moveable and immoveable property* (Article 13),[69] including the administration of trust property, the estate of a bankrupt person, or the winding up of an insolvent company.

(v) *Intellectual and industrial property* (Article 14);[70] these include patents, trademarks, copyrights, industrial design.

(vi) *Participation in companies or other collective bodies* (Article 15),[71] whether unincorporated or incorporated, provided that such collective bodies have participants other than States or international organizations.

(vii) *State-owned or State-operated ships used for other than government non-commercial purposes* (Article 16);[72] this would apply primarily to shipping vessels or transport ferries, and would certainly exclude warships or other ships on government non-commercial service, such as the official transport of the head of State.[73]

State practice suggests that the decisive criterion is the nature of the conduct or transaction, and not its purpose, which is only relevant at the enforcement stage.[74] The UN Convention adopts a slightly more contextual approach. Though the nature of the transaction remains preponderant, its purpose 'should also be taken into account if the parties to the contract or transaction have so agreed, or if, in the practice of the State of the forum, that purpose is relevant to determining the non-commercial character of the contract or transaction.'[75]

The contextual approach has some support in common law judicial decisions. In *I° Congreso del Partido*, two shipping vessels, one owned by a Cuban State enterprise, were under contract to deliver sugar to a Chilean company.[76] After the overthrow of President Allende by General Pinochet, the Cuban government ordered suspension of shipments of sugar and their diversion to North Vietnam. Before the UK House of

[68] *Al Masarir v Saudi Arabia* [2022] EWHC 2199, para 132.

[69] See also UK SIA (n 27) s 6; ECSI (n 32) Arts 9 and 10; and *United States v Dolfus Mieg* [1952] AC 582 (UK House of Lords).

[70] UK SIA (n 27) s 7; ECSI (n 32) Art 8.

[71] UK SIA (n 27) s 8.

[72] *Ibid*, s 10(1)–(2). As described earlier, this represents a move away from the *Parlement Belge* vision of absolute immunity (n 13) to embody the restrictive immunity later confirmed in *Io Congreso del Partido* (n 25).

[73] Fox and Webb (n 1) 433; *Allianz Via Insurance v USA* (1999) 127 ILR 148 (French Ct of Appeal).

[74] See, e.g., US FSIA (n 26) s 1603(d), UK SIA (n 27) s 13; *Empire of Iran* (n 22) 80–1; *Trendtex v Nigeria* (n 25) 356; *Planmount v Zaire* (n 61) 1110; *Svenska Petroleum Exploration AB v Lithuania* [2006] EWCA 1529; and *Holubek v Government of the United States* (1961) 40 ILR 73 (Austrian Sup Ct). See also 1972 ECSI (n 32) Art 4, under which an exception is made for obligations flowing from a contract signed by a State.

[75] UN Convention (n 37) Art 2(2). The ILC had first recommended this 'two-step' approach: see Report of the ILC on the Work of its 43rd Session, UN Doc A/46/10 (1991), 29–30, in which it recommended underlining the non-commercial nature of certain contracts or transactions due to their public purpose, e.g., the procurement of medicines to fight a spreading epidemic or the supply of foodstuffs.

[76] *Io Congreso del Partido* (n 25).

Lords, Cuba pleaded immunity for breach of the commercial contract, on the basis that State policy considerations had underlain the breach. Lord Wilberforce, writing for the majority, emphasized the importance of examining the 'whole context' in which a 'relevant act' was undertaken so as to determine whether it was *jure gestionis*.[77] Notably, governmental motive could not transform an act essentially *jure gestionis* into one of *jure imperii* character: 'it is not just that the purpose or motive of the act is to serve the purposes of the State, but that the act is *of its own character* a governmental act, as opposed to an act which any private citizen can perform'.[78]

9.3.3 **Non-commercial tortious acts**

9.3.3.1 **Injury to persons and damage to property**

Though commercial activities are the most well-entrenched activities for which immunity has been removed, Article 12 of the UN Convention, echoed by common law State practice and the ECSI,[79] provides an exception from immunity for certain non-contractual activities that lead to delictual (in civil law) or tortious (in common law) responsibility. This exception allows for immunity to be removed in civil proceedings for pecuniary compensation for death or injury to persons, or damage to or loss of tangible property, if caused by an act or omission attributable to a State, and which occurred in the territory of the forum State.[80]

The exception in Article 12 of the UN Convention is narrow in two respects. First, it is confined to the physical infliction of damage to a person or property: non-physical injuries such as libel or defamation, or financial damage, are *a fortiori* excluded. Secondly, in line with immunity legislation in prominent common law jurisdictions, the exception is limited to acts occurring on the territory of the forum State. It thus excludes any extraterritorial applicability as regards a foreign State.[81]

9.3.3.2 **Serious violations of human rights or of a peremptory norm (*jus cogens*)**

So long as personal injury or damage results from an act in the exercise of sovereign authority, a victim may claim for damages; there is no requirement that personal injury or damage to property be caused in the course of commercial activities. This principle has raised questions as to whether a wide exception to State immunity for non-contractual claims necessarily entails the lifting of immunity in relation to claims

[77] *Ibid*, 318. Though the test laid out by Lord Wilberforce was accepted by the majority, he was actually in the minority as he concluded that the acts were of a sovereign nature and therefore immune.

[78] *Ibid*, 320. See further *Littrell v United States of America (No 2)* [1995] 1 WLR 82, 95; 100 ILR 439; *Holland v Lampen-Wolfe* [2000] 1 WLR 1573, 1577; and *Kuwaiti Airways v Iraqi Airways* (n 10).

[79] See, e.g., UK SIA (n 27) s 5; US FSIA (n 26) s 1605(a)(5); ECSI (n 32) Art 11.

[80] On the prohibition of State immunity in cases involving tortious/delictual acts, see Fox and Webb (n 1) ch 15; and Schreuer, *State Immunity* (n 2) ch 3.

[81] The ICJ, in *Jurisdictional Immunities of the State* (n 35) para 65, pointedly did not 'resolve the question whether there is in customary international law a "tort exception" to State immunity applicable to *acta jure imperii* in general'.

of serious human rights violations, in particular in relation to terrorist acts. Early cases were not promising for human rights advocates. In *Saudi Arabia v Nelson*, the US Supreme Court declared that exceptions to immunity could only be invoked if enumerated in the FSIA, and concluded that despite allegations of wrongful arrest, imprisonment, and torture of Nelson by the Saudi police, 'a foreign State's exercise of the power of its police has long been understood for the purposes of the restrictive theory as peculiarly sovereign'.[82] The same reasoning has prevailed in the Superior Court of Ontario, Canada, in *Bouzari v Iran*, in which the exceptions listed in the Canadian State Immunity Act 1982 were considered exhaustive. The Canadian court regarded the exercise of police, law enforcement, and security powers as 'inherently exercises of governmental authority and sovereignty', and concluded that customary international law provided State immunity for acts committed outside the forum State, even allegations of torture.[83] Both Canada and the USA have responded by enacting legislation to create an exception to immunity in relation to terrorist activity that is linked or otherwise attributable to a State, as has Australia; this legislation has withstood judicial review.[84]

There are also two landmark cases in the UK which take a restrictive view of the nature of legislative exceptions to immunity. In *Al-Adsani v Kuwait*, the Court of Appeal held that only the exceptions listed in the SIA provided for the lifting of immunity, and that 'implied' exceptions did not exist even where allegations were made of the violation of a *jus cogens* norm (in that case, torture).[85] The case was then taken against the UK to the ECtHR, in which Al-Adsani contended that Article 6 of the ECHR, concerning the right to due process of individuals, created an exception to State immunity with regard to civil proceedings for torture.[86] The ECtHR upheld the view of the English Court of Appeal that no such exception existed under international law, and concluded that immunity would still apply in civil proceedings where acts of torture are alleged.[87] The House of Lords, in *Jones v Saudi Arabia*, later confirmed that allegations of *jus cogens* violations were insufficient to remove immunity; and that, moreover, no implicit

[82] 123 L Ed 2d 47, 57, 61 (1993), 100 ILR 544, 553. See also *Princz v Federal Republic of Germany*, 26 F.3d 1166 (3d Cir 1994). The FSIA (n 26) was amended by the Antiterrorism and Effective Death Penalty Act 1996 to create an exception to immunity in relation to 'State sponsors of terrorism' (as designated by the State Department) which, *inter alia*, commit a terrorist act or an act which results in the death or personal injury of a US citizen. See *Simpson v Libya*, 470 F.3d 356 (3d Cir 2006).

[83] *Bouzari v Iran* (2002) 124 ILR 247, 435.

[84] In 2012, Canada enacted the Justice for Victims of Terrorism Act 2012, which amends s 6(1) of the Canada State Immunity Act to lift the immunity of a foreign State that has been listed by the Governor-General in Council as a sponsor of terrorism. *Kazemi Estate v Iran* [2014] 3 SCR 176 was an important case in respect of the 2012 amendments. For British judicial practice to the same effect, see *Propend Finance v Sing* (n 49) 667–71; and for the American, see *Simpson v Libya* (n 82) and *Bank Markazi, aka the Central Bank of Iran v Peterson* 136 S Ct 1310 (2016) (US), where the US Supreme Court has confirmed the lawfulness of US legislation to create a 'terrorism exception' to State immunity in US court.

[85] [2006] 1 LLR 104; 107 ILR 536.

[86] *Al-Adsani v United Kingdom* App No 35763/97, ECHR 2001-XI, 34 EHRR 11 (Grand Chamber) paras 54–5, 61; as confirmed in *Jones and Others v United Kingdom* [2014] ECHR 32, paras 188 *et seq.*

[87] *Al-Adsani v UK, ibid*, para 66.

exception existed beyond those already listed in legislation.[88] The House of Lords reasoned that the recognition of immunity, as a procedural bar to the exercise of jurisdiction, does not conflict with the substantive prohibition of torture.[89] That procedural/substantive distinction was also adopted by the ICJ in *Jurisdictional Immunities of the State*,[90] and illustrates a position according to which the hierarchically superior status of *jus cogens* norms does not pre-empt the procedural bar of State immunity, at least in civil proceedings.

It is true that there has been some divergent practice. In 2000, the Greek Supreme Court, in *Prefecture of Voiotia v Germany*, refused to recognize Germany's immunity and awarded $30 million in damages to Greek nationals for personal injuries and loss of property caused by acts of the German military authorities during World War II.[91] The Italian Court of Cassation, in the *Ferrini* judgment (2004), also disregarded Germany's immunity and awarded monetary damages for forcible deportation and labour of an Italian national by German military authorities during World War II.[92] The Italian proceedings led Germany to file an application before the ICJ in *Jurisdictional Immunities of the State*, claiming a violation of its immunity represented by *Ferrini* and later decisions. In 2012, the Court upheld Germany's claim fully. With respect to Germany's claim of immunity from adjudication, the ICJ rejected as unfounded the contention of any existing 'territorial tort exception' to State immunity. Regarding the forcible deportation and enforced labour of Italian nationals entitled to prisoner of war status, it concluded that:

> State practice in the form of judicial decisions supports the proposition that State immunity for *acta jure imperii* continues to extend to civil proceedings for acts occasioning death, personal injury or damage to property committed by the armed forces and other organs of a State in the conduct of armed conflict, even if the relevant acts take place on the territory of the forum State.[93]

It bears emphasizing that the Court only addressed the immunity of the State itself, and did not consider the scope of immunity which might apply in criminal proceedings against an official of a State.[94] That situation will be addressed in Section 9.4.

[88] *Jones v Saudi Arabia* (n 46) para 9 (Bingham LJ); 109 ILR 717. That said, in *Belhaj & Rahmatullah* (n 8), several judges (Mance LJ, para 102; Sumption LJ, paras 268–78; see also Neuberger LJ, para 168, which comes close to endorsing Lord Sumption's view) suggested that a violation of *jus cogens*, or a serious infringement of individual fundamental rights (in that case, arbitrary rendition, detention, and severe mistreatment) fell outside any rule of judicial abstention in relation to foreign acts of State.

[89] *Jones v Saudi Arabia, ibid.*

[90] See earlier (n 35).

[91] *Prefecture of Voiotia v Federal Republic of Germany*, 11/2000 AP (Aerios Pagos or Greek Supreme Court); 123 ILR 513. *Cf* the later *Margellos v Federal Republic of Germany*, 6/2002 AP, 129 ILR 526, in which the Greek Supreme Court seemed to retreat from that view.

[92] *Ferrini v Federal Republic of Germany*, Cass 5044/2004 (Italian *Corte di Cazzazione* or Italian Court of Cassation), 128 ILR 659.

[93] *Jurisdictional Immunities of the State* (n 35) para 77.

[94] *Ibid*, para 91.

CASE SPOTLIGHT ***Jurisdictional Immunities of the State (Germany v Italy; Greece intervening), Judgment, ICJ Reports 2012*, p 3**

A striking feature of the ICJ's *Jurisdictional Immunities* judgment was its insistence on setting out a general rule on the nature of State immunity. Italy had refuted Germany's submissions with three specific arguments on the nature of State immunity in international law:

(i) that no State immunity existed in respect of serious violations of international humanitarian law, if amounting to war crimes and crimes against humanity;

(ii) that there could be no State immunity under international law for violations of *jus cogens* norms; and

(iii) that immunity could be disregarded in the particular case because all other attempts to obtain reparations for the victims had failed.

The Court rejected the notion that the *jure imperii/jure gestionis* distinction was salient in assessing the legality of a State's conduct. For the Court, the distinction referred merely to whether a given act fell to be assessed by reference to the law governing the exercise of sovereign power, or the law concerning non-sovereign activities of a State (para 60). Rejecting several Italian arguments regarding the conflict between State immunity and violations of *jus cogens* norms, the ICJ determined that the procedural nature of a plea of immunity stood independently from the *jus cogens* character of the claimed violations (para 93).

The Court's insistence on a strict distinction between procedural and substantive rules has opened it to criticism, notably for ignoring recent developments in other judicial institutions as to the possible impact on procedural rules of the substantive nature of certain norms; and perhaps even the propriety of judicial institutions elevating judge-made procedural canons over substantive legal norms that have developed through State practice.

Another criticism that can be levelled against the Court is that, rather than elucidating a general rule, it could have chosen several other strategies. To give two examples: the Court could have given more weight to the fact that Germany had paid reparations to Italy; and in the two States' 1961 Agreement, Italy had expressly waived any further claims from it or its citizens. For further analysis of these alternative strategies, see GI Hernández, *The International Court of Justice and the Judicial Function* (OUP, 2014), 234–5.

9.4 Immunities enjoyed by state officials and representatives from foreign criminal jurisdiction

9.4.1 Basic principles

Due in part to the historical conflation of State and sovereign that defined the scope of immunity, mechanisms have also been developed that allow various categories of officials of States to invoke immunity in the courts of another State. Some of these officials receive a degree of protection due to their inseparability from the very personality of the State; in particular, heads of State and heads of government, as well as other senior government officials such as ministers of foreign affairs. Other high-ranking officials receive protection when they are exercising functions on behalf of the State abroad. These will be considered in turn.

9.4.2 Types of immunity from jurisdiction

9.4.2.1 Immunity *ratione personae*

There are two forms of immunity which are relevant for high-ranking officials of States, diplomatic and consular representatives, and representatives on special missions. The first is immunity *ratione personae*, a wide personal immunity extending to the totality of the person's acts, both official and private. The justification for such broad immunity is found with respect to the functions they exercise on behalf of the State: these are considered so central to the conduct of international relations that absolute personal immunity is necessary. *Ratione personae* immunity applies to both official and private acts of such office-holders, with the idea that the mere possibility of being subject to the jurisdiction of the receiving State would *ipso facto* interfere with the person's exercise of their official functions. Imagine a monarch, prime minister, or ambassador under arrest; whatever the gravity of the accusations, their arrest or detention would be regarded as a serious violation of the dignity and sovereignty of the sending State. As such, certain categories of officials enjoy complete personal inviolability and freedom from arrest and/or detention, and absolute immunity from criminal jurisdiction.[95] Such immunities exist solely to facilitate the discharge of particular offices of State and, as such, lapse when the office-holder has left office.

9.4.2.2 Immunity *ratione materiae*

A more restrictive form of immunity, immunity *ratione materiae*, applies not to the *officials* and representatives of a State, but to the *acts* performed in their official or representative capacity. These derive in part from the immunities of the State described in Section 9.2, and are thus determined more by the nature of the acts in question rather than to the particular office. Immunity *ratione materiae* can potentially apply to the acts of all State officials, and also subsists even after the office-holder has left office, as it relates to the act performed on behalf of the State.

In 2022, the ILC adopted, on first reading, a set of 18 Draft Articles on immunity of State officials from foreign criminal jurisdiction, with commentaries.[96] Draft Article 2 defines these as 'acts performed by a State official in the exercise of State authority.'[97] This intentionally broad-brush definition encompasses any official, organ, or agent of the State of any kind, provided that the scope of the duties of that person have been performed in an official capacity.[98]

As with State immunity, both categories of official or representative immunity operate as procedural bars to jurisdiction and, according to the ILC, must be considered swiftly, 'as soon as they are aware that a foreign official may be affected by a criminal proceeding'.[99] Moreover, they can be waived by the competent authorities of the sending

[95] See *Arrest Warrant* (n 33).

[96] ILC Report on the Work of its 73rd Session (2022), GAOR 76, Supp No 10 (A/76/10), ch VI, for the Draft Articles on the Immunity of State Officials from Foreign Criminal Jurisdiction, including Commentaries, as adopted on first reading.

[97] *Ibid*, Draft Art 2, p 203.

[98] *Ibid*, Commentary to Draft Art 2, 217–9, paras 8–9, and which thus embraces the relatively broad definition laid out in *Mutual Assistance in Criminal Matters* (n 34) para 191.

[99] *Ibid*, Draft Art 8, 243.

State, as they are immunities belonging to that State and do not belong to an official or representative. Prominent examples of waivers include the waiver by the Philippines in respect of former President Marcos and his wife, Imelda, and that of Chad in respect of former President Habré.[100]

9.4.3 **Heads of State**

Historically, the claims of monarchs to sovereignty meant that there was little to distinguish the head of State from the identity of the State itself. Any rights and competences which fell to the head of State were exercised in the name of 'their' State; for example, the conclusion of a treaty or the sending of diplomats and consuls. As such, head of State immunity is not an individual right, but an attribute of State sovereignty.[101]

The privileges and immunities enjoyed by a head of State have also moved away from absolute 'sovereign immunity' (personal immunity of the sovereign) to a rather more restrictive doctrine. However, because the head of State acts as the highest representative of the State, distinct rules in relation to sovereign immunity exist. In *Mutual Assistance in Criminal Matters*, the ICJ restated the principle of head of State immunity as follows:

> A Head of State enjoys in particular 'full immunity from criminal jurisdiction and inviolability' which protects 'against any act of authority of another State which could hinder [them] in the performance of [their] duties.' Thus the determining factor in assessing whether or not there has been an attack on the immunity of the Head of State lies in the subjection of the latter to a constraining act of authority.[102]

The Court took pains to emphasize that head of State immunity was analogous to diplomatic immunity, with all the privileges and immunities of diplomatic agents being necessarily applicable to a head of State.[103] This coincides with the view prevailing in the UK, where the State Immunity Act 1978 confers on a foreign head of State complete personal inviolability and absolute immunity from criminal jurisdiction *ratione personae*, whether on a private or official visit.[104] Judicial decisions in other States also seem to adopt that position.[105]

[100] *Ibid*, Draft Art 11, 253 *et seq*, which refer (at 258, fn 1083) to the *Ferdinand et Imelda Marcos c Office fédéral de la police* (Fed Sup Ct of Switzerland, Judgment of 2 November 1989, ATF 115 Ib 496, pp 501–2), and the letter from Ministry of Justice of Chad to investigators of the district of Brussels of 7 October 2002.

[101] See Art 7 VCLT; and *Land and Maritime Boundary between Cameroon and Nigeria (Cameroon v Nigeria: Equatorial Guinea intervening), Merits, ICJ Reports 2002*, p 303, paras 263–8.

[102] *Mutual Assistance in Criminal Matters* (n 34) para 170.

[103] *Ibid*, para 174, citing by analogy to the Vienna Convention on Diplomatic Relations 1961 (adopted 18 April 1961, entered into force 24 April 1964), 500 UNTS 95 (VCDR), Art 29, which states: '[t]he person of a diplomatic agent shall be inviolable. He shall not be liable to any form or arrest or detention. The receiving State shall treat [them] with due respect and shall take all appropriate steps to prevent any attack on [their] person, freedom or dignity.'

[104] UK SIA (n 27) s 20, which suggests that immunity is equivalent to that of diplomatic agents in the VCDR. See also the judgment of the Bow Street Magistrates' Court in *Mugabe* of 14 January 2004, reprinted in (2004) 53 ICLQ 770; and *Ex parte Pinochet (No 3)* [2000] 1 AC 147, 201–2 (Browne-Wilkinson LJ), 210 (Goff LJ), 244 (Hope LJ), 265 (Saville LJ), 269 (Millett); 119 ILR 135.

[105] In France, see *Ghaddafi*, French Court of Cassation (13 March 2001), (2004) 125 ILR 508; and in the US, see *Tachiona v USA*, 386 F.3d 205 (3d Cir 2004), concerning the immunity of Zimbabwean President Robert Mugabe.

For acts performed in their official capacity as an organ of a State, the same immunities which apply to the State itself will be applicable. For acts performed in their personal capacity, a head of State generally enjoys immunity from civil jurisdiction. Such immunity is subject to the three exceptions codified in Article 31(1) of the Vienna Convention on Diplomatic Relations (VCDR), relating to private immoveable property, wills and successions, and professional or commercial activity that is purely outside their functions.[106]

Because head of State immunity only applies to an individual due to their representative function of a State to which immunity attaches, immunity can be waived by the individual, or by an authorized representative of the sending State.[107] Moreover, upon leaving office, a head of State will enjoy only a subsisting immunity *ratione materiae* for official acts performed while in office.[108]

9.4.4 **Heads of government and ministers for foreign affairs**

In the 2002 *Arrest Warrant* judgment, the ICJ confirmed that a serving head of State's immunity *ratione personae* emanates from their capacity as a representative of the State. The ICJ further observed that because serving heads of government and serving ministers for foreign affairs perform comparable functions in representing States in international relations, immunity *ratione personae* also extends to them.[109] These three high officials—head of State, head of government, and minister of foreign affairs—are singled out by virtue of their representative function of the State, which is of a general character. Furthermore, unlike a diplomatic official who is accredited only to one or more receiving States simultaneously,[110] the three high-ranking office-holders may invoke immunity in relation to any State.

CASE SPOTLIGHT ***Arrest Warrant of 11 April 2000 (Democratic Republic of the Congo v Belgium), Judgment, ICJ Reports 2002*, p 3**

The *Arrest Warrant* judgment merits somewhat deeper scrutiny, as it concerned an arrest warrant issued by Belgium against Mr Abdoulaye Yerodia Ndombasi, who at the time of the warrant in 2000 was the incumbent foreign minister of the Democratic Republic of the

[106] See, e.g., *BCCI v Price Waterhouse* [1997] All ER 108, where the actions of the head of State of the UAE were immune despite not being performed in an official capacity; and *Harb v HM King Fahd bin Abdul Aziz* [2005] EWCA Civ 632, recognizing head of State immunity in relation to ancillary relief in matrimonial proceedings.

[107] See Fox and Webb (n 1) ch 11, who discuss the UK framework in *R v Madan* [1961] QB 1, 7; and *Aziz v Republic of Yemen* [2005] EWCA Civ 745, para 47.

[108] *Republic of the Philippines v Marcos (No 1)*, 806 F.2d 344 (2d Cir 1986), concerning the invocation of sovereign immunity by a deposed former head of State. In *HRH Prince Aziz Bin Fahd Bin Abdul Aziz v Harb* [2015] EWCA Civ 481, in which it was held that because no distinction existed between a former head of State who is still alive and one who has died in office, the estate of a late head of State (in this case, a king) cannot claim State immunity for private acts performed whilst head of State.

[109] *Arrest Warrant* (n 33) 20–1, para 51. In *Cengiz v Bin Salman,* Case No 20-300 (6 December 2022), the District Court of Washington DC upheld the immunity *ratione personae* of Mohammed bin Salman in his capacity as prime minister of Saudi Arabia, despite substantial evidence that he had conspired with Saudi agents to orchestrate the extrajudicial killing of journalist Jamal Khashoggi.

[110] As is permitted under VCDR (n 96) Art 6.

Congo (DRC). Belgium sought to exercise universal jurisdiction over Mr Yerodia for his alleged involvement in grave breaches of international humanitarian law. The Belgian legislation on universal jurisdiction in force at that time, the Act concerning the Punishment of Grave Breaches of International Humanitarian Law of 10 February 1999 ((1999) 38 ILM 921), expressly set aside any immunities which might apply. The Belgian legislation was unprecedented at the time.

The Court concluded that Belgium's legislation could not exclude the immunity an incumbent foreign minister enjoys under international law, noting the functions exercised by the office of foreign minister in relation to diplomatic activities, representation of the State, and the powers to act on behalf of and bind the State in treaty relations. As such, the ICJ declared that serving foreign ministers, and heads of government, enjoyed complete personal inviolability and absolute immunity from criminal jurisdiction *ratione personae*, even in situations where war crimes or crimes against humanity were in issue (pp 20, 24).

By the time the judgment was issued in 2002, Mr Yerodia was no longer foreign minister for the DRC. Nevertheless, the Court held that the violation by Belgium had occurred at the time the arrest warrant was issued in 2000 (pp 14–15). Perhaps also due to the ICJ's judgment, the Belgian Act has since been substantially amended, and the provision removing immunity has been repealed.

9.4.5 **Immunity of other State officials**

The immunity regime applicable to other individuals acting on behalf of a State—for example, a minister of defence or a minister of trade—is less clear-cut than for the three office-holders mentioned previously. In the *Arrest Warrant* case, the ICJ was fairly strict: only 'certain holders of high-ranking office in a State, such as the Head of State, Head of Government and Minister for Foreign Affairs, enjoy immunities from jurisdiction in other States, both civil and criminal'.[111] ILC Draft Article 3 has reprised the same short list,[112] though it acknowledges limited practice does exist that has extended immunity *ratione personae* beyond the so-called 'troika'.[113] However, immunity *ratione personae*

[111] Though in *Arrest Warrant* (n 33) 20 (and reaffirmed in *Certain Questions of Mutual Assistance* (n 34) 240), the ICJ had formally restricted its conclusions to criminal proceedings, it has been argued that 'it is difficult to see how the rationale for and resultant nature of the immunity of the relevant state offices from foreign civil proceedings could be different': R O'Keefe and C Tams, *The United Nations Convention on Jurisdictional Immunities of States and their Property: A Commentary* (OUP, 2013), 87. But *cf* the very recent judgment of the English Court of Appeal in *Re Al M (Immunities)* [2021] EWCA Civ 890, in which Dingemans LJ suggested that 'there is no exact equivalence between a Head of Government and Head of State' (para 23) and that the earlier High Court was correct to conclude, as it had, that the applicant did not establish that under customary law there is immunity from civil jurisdiction for the private acts of the head of government (para 26, referring to the judgment of the High Court, paras 47–54).

[112] ILC, Draft Articles on Immunity of State Officials from Foreign Criminal Jurisdiction (n 96), Commentary to Draft Article 3, paras 8–9.

[113] Ibid., paras 11–13, pointing to inconclusive practice, but acknowledging two judgments of UK courts in which immunity *ratione personae* was acknowledged: in *Re General Shaul Mofaz* (Bow Street Magistrates' Court, 12 February 2004) (2004) 128 ILR 709 (for a serving Minister of Defence) and *Re Bo Xilai* (Bow Street Magistrates' Court, 8 November 2005) (2005) 128 ILR 713 (immunity attaching to special victims).

is not indispensable for every State official in order to ensure the effective performance of their duties.[114] As such, to confer immunity *ratione materiae* on other State officials seems more sensible, given that a State, as a juridical entity, can only act through the individuals who are its organs and agents. The 2004 UN Convention recognizes these as immunities of the State itself,[115] as do the domestic courts of several States.[116] Moreover, the State would bear responsibility for any breaches of international law caused by the official acts of those individuals. As such, all State officials, no matter their function, enjoy immunity *ratione materiae* from civil proceedings, but only in respect of their official acts.

9.4.6 **Immunity for serious crimes under international law**

The House of Lords' *Pinochet* decision[117] is a watershed, one of the first domestic judgments where a claim to immunity *ratione materiae* was rejected. This case concerned former Chilean President Augusto Pinochet, who was in the UK when the Spanish government requested his extradition to face charges of torture for acts that occurred after 29 September 1988. That is the date from which the 1998 UK Criminal Justice Act had criminalized torture if committed by a public official. The *Pinochet* judgment raises an important question: does the definition of 'official acts' exclude acts done in clear violation of international law, including international crimes or breaches of *jus cogens*? And, if so, can *ratione personae* immunity nevertheless be invoked by officials accused of such crimes?

Institutional and legal developments to end impunity and strengthen international criminal responsibility in the last two decades have raised the question as to whether serious international crimes can truly be considered as official acts, benefiting from immunity. '[F]or international conduct which is so serious as to be tainted with criminality to be regarded as attributable only to the impersonal State and not to the individuals who ordered or perpetrated it is both unrealistic and offensive to common notions of justice.'[118]

[114] See *Saltany v Reagan and others* (1988) 80 ILR 19, affirmed (1989) ILR 680; and A Watts, 'The Legal Position in International Law of Heads of States, Heads of Government and Foreign Ministers' (1994) 247 Recueil des Cours 9, 53.

[115] UN Convention (n 37) Art 1(b)(iv). See also ILC Second Report (n 111), which also concludes that all high-ranking official visitors other than the '*troika*' would only enjoy special mission immunity.

[116] In the UK, see *Propend Finance v Sing* (n 49) 669; and *Jones v Saudi Arabia)* (n 46). In the USA, see *Samantar v Yousuf*, 130 S Ct 2278 (2010), which regarded such immunity as regulated by the common law and not subject to the FSIA (n 26). In Canada, see *Jaffe v Miller* (1993) 93 ILR 446; and *Walker v Baird* (1994) 16 OR (3d) 504.

[117] See *Pinochet (No 3)* (n 103) (Hope LJ, 881, 887; Browne-Wilkinson LJ, 848; Hutton LJ, 888). For a US example, see *Wei Ye v Jiang Zemin*, 383 F.3d 620 (3d Cir 2004).

[118] Watts (n 112) 82. See further D Akande and S Shah, 'Immunities of State Officials, International Crimes, and Foreign Domestic Courts' (2010) 21 EJIL 815; and R Pedretti, *Immunity of Heads of State and State Officials for International Crimes* (Brill, 2015).

THEORY AND DEBATES **Reading the Judgment *Ex parte Pinochet (No 3)* [2000] 1 AC 147**

The House of Lords' judgment in *Pinochet* is exceptionally complex, with eight of the Lords delivering separate opinions accompanied by different reasoning. In issue was the status of the prohibition against torture as a treaty-based and customary-based norm, and whether its *jus cogens* status was relevant in relation to the sovereign immunity of a head of State. A few of the Lords (Millett, Phillips, and Hope LJJ) held that the *jus cogens* nature of the prohibition against torture was sufficient to disregard immunity. However, the majority (including Browne-Wilkinson LJ, writing the lead judgment) concluded that the waiver of immunity was only 'fully constituted' upon the entry into force of the Torture Convention in the three States (Chile, Spain, and the UK). This last point was significant, as the Convention contained no provision which explicitly restricted foreign head of State immunity. The majority did rally around on one point: if the Convention could be interpreted in two plausible but opposite ways, the interpretation of the Convention most consistent with relevant *jus cogens* norms was to be preferred.

Reading the *Pinochet* judgment is methodologically interesting from an international law perspective. Judgments written in the common law tradition differ significantly from those of civil law jurisdictions, or the ICJ, in that there is no collective judgment of the 'court'. But for lawyers outside the common law tradition, the question arises: if all the judges based their decision on different reasons, what is the legal basis for the judgment? And how is it relevant for understanding the international law on head of State immunity?

A partial response can be found in the fact that judicial decisions do not formally make international law. Decisions of municipal courts are better viewed as evidence of State practice in certain areas, such as immunity, and they demonstrate the manner in which judicial institutions apply international law in practice. This means that one ought not to fixate on what *Pinochet* 'says' but, rather, consider how it fits in within a wider panoply of evidence, especially in relation to State practice.

Two leading analyses of the *Pinochet* judgment are those of R van Alebeek, 'The Pinochet Case: International Human Rights Law on Trial' (2000) 71 BYBIL 29, and A Bianchi, 'Immunity versus Human Rights: the *Pinochet* Case' (1999) 10 EJIL 237.

The removal of immunity for serious international crimes remains potentially explosive, given the sensitivities of a foreign court having to adjudge on the conduct of a serving head of State, head of government, or foreign minister (often known as 'the troika' in this area of international law).

In such cases, no general exception from immunity presently exists under customary international law, and the ICJ's conclusion in the 2001 *Arrest Warrant* judgment, though cautious, remains relevant: immunity *ratione personae* in respect of incumbent holders of high State office in a State represents an absolute bar to the criminal jurisdiction of national courts, even with respect to serious international crimes.[119] When the office-holder has left office, they enjoy only immunity *ratione materiae* in respect

[119] *Arrest Warrant* (n 33) 20. *Arrest Warrant* represents an unusual example of a judgment where the ICJ relied on the judicial decisions of national courts, in that case the *Ghaddafi* case in the French Court of Cassation (n 104), and the *Pinochet (No 3)* judgment of the UK House of Lords (n 103).

of official acts committed while in office.[120] In the ILC's Draft Articles on Immunity of State Officials from Foreign Criminal Jurisdiction, Draft Article 7 suggests immunity *ratione materiae* shall not apply in respect of six core international crimes (genocide, crimes against humanity, war crimes, apartheid, torture, and enforced disappearance); the ILC pointedly does not qualify this exception as extending to immunity *ratione personae* and warned in its commentary that, as presently drafted, it elicited concerns about whether this reflected the current state of State practice.[121]

At present, the Commission has not included acts potentially falling within the 'territorial exception' to which immunity would be disregarded for crimes committed by a foreign official in the territory of another State, on the basis that these are subject to the principle of territorial sovereignty under domestic criminal law.[122] The territorial exception merits some further detail, as two conditions must be met for it to apply: the forum State must not have consented either to the presence of the foreign official on its territory, or to the activity carried out by that official that gave rise to the commission of the crime.[123] Illustrative examples of acts that might engage the territorial exception include political assassination, espionage, and sabotage committed by foreign officials. For example, in *Khurts Bat and Mongolia*, the High Court of England and Wales dismissed Mongolia's assertion of immunity *ratione materiae* in a case in which an alleged abduction and serious bodily injury had been committed by the head of the Mongolia General Intelligence Agency, upon the instruction of Mongolia.[124]

That immunity *ratione materiae* from criminal jurisdiction persists for high-ranking officials of States raises the concern that serious international crimes go unpunished. For that reason, the statutes of international criminal tribunals have tended to exclude immunity with respect to heads of State or any other holder of a high office of State,[125] provided of course that the requisite basis for jurisdiction is met. Consequently, in recent years there have been high-profile trials and arrest warrants against heads of State, including Slobodan Milošević (Yugoslavia), who passed away before a judgment could be given by the ICTY.[126] Charles Taylor (Liberia) was prosecuted by the SCSL, a

[120] *Ibid*, 26, para 61; and *Pinochet (No 3)* (n 103), 847 (Browne-Wilkinson LJ), 882–7 (Hope LJ), 904 (Saville LJ).

[121] See ILC, Draft Articles on Immunity of State Officials from Foreign Criminal Jurisdiction (n 96), 230. In the Commentary to Draft Article 7, paras 9–12 illustrate how within the ILC itself, there is considerable disagreement on the status of such an exception even for jurisdiction *ratione materiae*. Draft Article 7 will proceed to second reading in 2025, but naturally remains contentious.

[122] *Ibid*, Commentary to Draft Article 7, paras 24–7.

[123] *Ibid*, Commentary to Draft Article 7, para 27.

[124] *Khurts Bat and Mongolia v Investigating Judge of the German Federal Court and Secretary of State for Foreign and Commonwealth Affairs (intervening)* [2011] EWHC 2029 (Admin), [2012] 3 WLR 180.

[125] See the Treaty of Versailles (signed 28 June 1919, entered into force 10 January 1920), 225 CTS 188, Art 227; the Agreement for the Prosecution and Punishment of the Major War Criminals, and Charter of the International Military Tribunal annexed thereto, as published in (1945) 39 AJIL Supp 259, Art 7; Charter of the International Military Tribunal for the Far East, (1946) TIAS No 1589, Art 6; the Statute of the International Criminal Tribunal for the former Yugoslavia (1993), UNSC Res 827 (25 May 1993), Art 7; Statute of the International Criminal Tribunal for Rwanda, UNSC Res 955 (8 November 1994), Art 6; the Rome Statute of the International Criminal Court (adopted 17 July 1998, entered into force 1 July 2002), 2187 UNTS 3, Art 27; and the Statute for the Special Court for Sierra Leone, UNSC Res 1315 (14 August 2000), Art 6(2).

[126] *Prosecutor v Milošević* (Prosecution Opening Statement) IT-02-54 (8 November 2001).

hybrid tribunal established through an agreement between the UN and Sierra Leone, and thus competent to disregard the customary law rule on sovereign immunity which applied between sovereign States.[127]

Furthermore, the ICC Prosecutor has issued warrants for the arrest of Sudanese President Al Bashir, on the basis of a referral by the Security Council of the Darfur situation. In 2019, the ICC Appeals Chamber concluded that there was no customary rule to justify head of State immunity before international criminal tribunals.[128] The Security Council had also referred the 2011 conflict in Libya to the ICC Prosecutor, but a warrant against former Libyan President Qaddafi was terminated upon his death in November 2011.[129] The most controversial ICC arrest warrants are directed against heads of State, such as Russian President Vladimir Putin, which is so sensitive that it has not been published.[130] Even so, during the 2023 'Brics' summit, South Africa decided to issue blanket diplomatic immunity to all leaders, in potential breach of its obligations under the Rome Statute; in the end, perhaps bowing to pressure, Putin attended via videoconference. A similar arrest warrant was issued on 21 November 2024 against Israeli Prime Minister Benjamin Netanyahu. These new developments will be considered in further depth in Chapter 17, Section 17.2.3.3.3.

CASE SPOTLIGHT The *Nezzar* Case (*A v Ministère public de la Confédération*, BStGer of 25 July 2012 (BB.2011.140))

In 2012, the Swiss Federal Criminal Court handed down a judgment of great interest in relation to immunity. In that case, Mr Khaled Nezzar, a former defence minister and former member of the collective presidency of Algeria (the *Haut Comité d'État* or 'High Council of State') faced charges of war crimes and crimes against humanity against Algerian nationals during the Algerian civil war (1992–2000). Counsel for Mr Nezzar invoked both *ratione personae* and *ratione materiae* immunity.

On the question of immunity, the Federal Criminal Court dismissed any *ratione personae* immunity as irrelevant for a former head of State, and focused exclusively on whether he had *ratione materiae* immunity. On that point, the court identified a paradox between criminalizing serious international crimes and maintaining a wide interpretation of immunity *ratione materiae*, and concluded that in such cases the latter would have to yield (para 5.4.3). Though that conclusion has potentially wide-ranging significance, it must crucially be noted that in this case, Algeria did not invoke immunity on Mr Nezzar's behalf.

The *Nezzar* judgment raises interesting questions on universal jurisdiction. In particular, it represents a significant departure from the finding in *Prosecutor-General v Desiré Bouterse*,

[127] *Prosecutor v Taylor* (Decision on Immunity from Jurisdiction) SCSL-2003-01-I (31 May 2004); (2004)128 ILR 239. See further Chapter 17, Section 17.2.4.

[128] See *Prosecutor v Al Bashir* (First Warrant of Arrest) ICC 02/05-001/09-3 (4 March 2009) and (Second Warrant of Arrest) ICC 02/05-01/09-94 (12 July 2010); and *Prosecutor v Al Bashir, Judgment in the Jordan Referral re Al Bashir Appeal*, ICC-02/05-01/09 OA2 (6 May 2019), para 113.

[129] *Prosecutor v Gaddafi* (Warrant of Arrest) ICC 01/11-13 (27 June 2011).

[130] See ICC Press Release, 'Judges issue arrest warrants against Vladmir Putin and Maria Alekseyevna Lvova-Belova' (17 March 2023).

LJN: AB1471 (Dutch *Hoge Raad*) (18 September 2001), in which the Dutch Supreme Court dismissed charges against Mr Bouterse, military leader of Suriname from 1980 to 1987, on the basis that the Netherlands had no connection whatsoever with Mr Bouterse and the acts in question.

For further reading, see I Wuerth, '*Pinochet*'s Legacy Reassessed' (2012) 106 AJIL 731.

9.5 **Diplomatic immunities between States**

As described earlier, the incorporeal nature of the State requires the intercession of individuals to act on its behalf. As such, there are centuries of long-standing practice of States exchanging permanent diplomatic representatives, usually known as an ambassador (between Commonwealth States, a 'High Commissioner'), who are specifically accredited to conduct diplomatic relations. With the expansion of international trade and commerce, the office of consul is also highly relevant. Finally, at times States require dialogue on highly specialized areas for specific purposes, requiring the sending of a special envoy.

The immunities of these three categories of representatives have been codified in three multilateral conventions. Two of these, the 1961 VCDR,[131] and the 1963 Vienna Convention on Consular Relations (VCCR),[132] are generally accepted as codifications of customary international law. A third, the 1969 Convention on Special Missions (CSM), extends certain privileges and immunities to officials and agents of the State when engaged in specific missions, but has only attracted thirty-eight ratifications.[133] As the ICJ commented in the *Tehran Hostages* judgment:

> the rules of diplomatic law . . . constitute a self-contained regime, which on the one hand, lays out the receiving State's obligations regarding the facilities, privileges and immunities to be accorded to diplomatic missions and, on the other, foresees their possible abuse by members of the mission and specifies the means at the disposal of the receiving State to counter any such abuse.[134]

Taken together, the various conventions constitute a comprehensive framework for conducting diplomatic relations, balancing the interests of both sending and receiving States.

[131] VCDR (n 102). See also the Convention on the Prevention and Punishment of Crimes against Internationally Protected Persons, including Diplomatic Agents 1973 (adopted 14 December 1973, entered into force 20 February 1977), 1035 UNTS 167.

[132] Vienna Convention on Consular Relations 1963 (adopted 24 April 1963, entered into force 19 March 1967), 596 UNTS 261.

[133] Convention on Special Missions 1969 (adopted 8 December 1969, entered into force 21 June 1985), 1400 UNTS 231.

[134] *United States Diplomatic and Consular Staff in Tehran (United States v Islamic Republic of Iran), Judgment, ICJ Reports 1980*, p 3, 40.

9.5.1 **Diplomatic immunity**

The functions of a diplomatic mission include the representation, promotion, and protection of the interests and nationals of the sending State, as well as the exchange of information and friendly relations, within the sending State (Article 3 VCDR). This last point was raised controversially before the ICJ in 2018, where Palestine contended that US President Trump's decision to relocate the US Embassy to Jerusalem, under a 'special international regime' under General Assembly Resolution 181(II), was in breach of the VCDR.[135] The case turned, of course, on the status of Palestine as a State capable of instituting proceedings, but as of late 2024, no updates of any kind have been published on the Court's website.

States are not obliged to entertain diplomatic relations; they exist by virtue of mutual consent between the sending and receiving State.[136] As such, the head of a diplomatic mission cannot be accredited unilaterally by the sending State, but requires the prior consent (*agrément*) of the receiving State to be obtained.[137] For example, the Vatican did not respond to France's request for accreditation of Laurent Stefanini for nine months, and the request was ultimately abandoned.[138] Under Article 9 VCDR, prior consent may be revoked at any time by a receiving State, without having to furnish reasons. Often a declaration of *persona non grata*, States not infrequently resort to revoking diplomatic credentials, as did the USA against Russian diplomats after allegations of Russian interference in the 2016 US elections,[139] or as did Türkiye in October 2021 against the ambassadors of ten Western States, for advocating for the release of imprisoned businessman and philanthrophist Osman Kavala.[140]

Article 2 VCDR extends to diplomatic missions between States; but through consent, full diplomatic status (and the privileges and immunities attaching to it) can also be extended to other actors. For example, EU delegations in nearly 150 States enjoy full diplomatic immunity, an issue that arose in an unseemly row in 2021 between the UK and the EU where, during the Brexit negotiations, the UK attempted unsuccessfully to limit the immunities of the EU delegation in London.

The process of designation of the premises of a diplomatic mission was recently considered by the ICJ in *Immunities and Criminal Proceedings in France*, in which the parties were in disagreement as to the degree of mutual consent required under Article 2

[135] See *Relocation of the United States Embassy to Jerusalem (Palestine v United States), Application Instituting Proceedings of 28 September 2018*, paras 5–7.

[136] VCDR (n 102) Art 2.

[137] *Ibid*, Art 4. The same rule applies to defence attachés, but not to lower ranked diplomatic agents: see VCDR, *ibid*, Art 7.

[138] The Vatican's reluctance to agree to Mr Stefanini's accreditation was purportedly due to his sexual orientation, according to news reports: see, e.g., H Sherwood and K Willsher, 'France drops bid to appoint gay Vatican ambassador' https://www.theguardian.com/world/2015/oct/12/france-drops-bid-to-appoint-gay-vatican-ambassador-laurent-stefanini-reports (*The Guardian*, 10 October 2015); S Kirchgaessner, 'Vatican suspected of rejecting gay French ambassador' http://www.theguardian.com/world/2015/apr/10/vatican-suspected-rejecting-approval-gay-french-ambassador-laurent-stefanini (*The Guardian*, 10 April 2015).

[139] US Department of State, 'Actions in Response to Russian Harassment' (Press Statement of 29 December 2016).

[140] See Al Jazeera, 'Turkey's Erdoğan Orders Expulsion of 10 Western Ambassadors' (23 October 2021).

VCDR, and the degree to which a receiving State could challenge the designation by a sending State of its premises. France had objected to Equatorial Guinea's designation of premises, as it considered that the latter State was abusing its rights to shield the premises from search and seizure. The Court held that a receiving State could only object to such designation by the sending State if the objection was timely, non-arbitrary, and non-discriminatory,[141] and concluded that France's objection met all three criteria.

Once established, a diplomatic mission benefits from certain privileges and facilities. Foremost, perhaps, is *inviolability* under Article 22 VCDR, regarded as an obligation *erga omnes* by the ICJ in *Tehran Hostages*.[142] A receiving State not only is prohibited from entering a diplomatic mission without obtaining consent but also is under a special duty to take all appropriate measures to protect the mission's premises against intrusion.[143]

Though diplomatic inviolability is wide-ranging, it may no longer be unlimited, and like with State immunity, an exception to immunity for 'commercial activity' exists in art 31(1)(c) of the 1961 VCDR. In a recent judgment, the UK Supreme Court held that the exploitation of a domestic worker in circumstances of modern slavery could not benefit from diplomatic immunity, in part due to coercion and the abusive exercise of control over the victim.[144]

CONTEMPORARY DEVELOPMENTS The Raid on the Mexican Embassy in Quito

The restraint shown by the UK during Julian Assange's long sojourn in the Ecuadorian Embassy in London was not reciprocated by Ecuador when, on 5 March 2024, Ecuadorian police engaged in a major raid of the Embassy of Mexico in Quito to arrest the former Vice President of Ecuador, Jorge Glas Espinel, who had been sentenced for corruption and had been granted political asylum by Mexico.

Ecuador sought to justify the raid as an exceptional measure to protect its national security and to take a stand against impunity for criminals convicted of major offences, suggesting that asylum in such cases was in breach of the 1961 VCDR. Mexico disagreed and decried the raid as a major violation of the 1961 VCDR and the 1954 Caracas Convention on Diplomatic Asylum. Mexico immediately severed diplomatic relations with Ecuador in response. The Permanent Council of the OAS met on 9–10 April 2024 and 'strongly condemned' Ecuador's violent intrusion into the Embassy (see OAS Doc CP/Res 1253 (10 April 2024)).

[141] *Immunities and Criminal Proceedings (Equatorial Guinea v France), Preliminary Objections, ICJ Reports 2018*, p 292, para 74.

[142] *Tehran Hostages* (n 131) 30–1.

[143] *Ibid*, in which Iran was considered to be responsible for having failed to take appropriate steps to protect the US Embassy and its staff from groups of demonstrators. See further *Armed Activities in the Congo (Democratic Republic of the Congo v Uganda), Judgment, ICJ Reports 2005*, p 168, paras 337–8, 340, in which the ICJ similarly held that attacks against the Ugandan Embassy in Kinshasa, and against persons on its premises, constituted a violation of VCDR (n 102), Art 22.

[144] *Basfar v Wong* [2022] UKSC 20, paras 43, 51.

The dispute then went to the ICJ. In March 2024, Mexico instituted proceedings against Ecuador, including a request for provisional measures to protect the integrity of its abandoned embassy. In its Order of May 2024, the Court reaffirmed the importance of diplomatic inviolability, but it declined to indicate provisional measures as Ecuador had already given credible assurances to protect the premises of the Mexican diplomatic mission (*Embassy of Mexico in Quito (Mexico v Ecuador), Order on Provisional Measures of 23 May 2024*, para 32). For its part, on 29 April 2024 Ecuador filed an application against Mexico, asserting that Mexico's conduct in relation to Mr Glas Espinel was a blatant misuse of its diplomatic premises, and that its grant of political asylum constituted an intervention into Ecuador's internal affairs. Both cases proceeded.

Members of a diplomatic mission, as well as the members of a diplomatic agent's family (their 'household'[145]) enjoy wide protections under the VCDR, including *inter alia* the inviolability of their person and their freedom from arrest or detention,[146] and the inviolability of the private residence, papers, correspondence, and property of a diplomatic agent.[147] Similar immunity applies to the archives and papers of a mission,[148] its official communications, and the 'diplomatic bag', as well as for any diplomatic couriers carrying such correspondence.[149] In *Bancoult v Foreign Secretary*, the UK Supreme Court concluded that a reporting cable from the US Embassy in London back to the US State Department, which had been widely leaked without US consent via the 'Wikileaks' website, should have been admitted into evidence, as it had lost its inviolability under Articles 24 and 27(2) VCDR as it had entered the public domain.[150] In 2020, UK Ambassador Kim Darroch resigned after diplomatic cables with an unflattering portrayal of US President Trump were leaked by a tabloid newspaper.

Members of administrative and technical staff of the diplomatic mission enjoy more limited immunities.[151] Receiving States are under a duty to take all appropriate measures to prevent an attack on the person, freedom, or dignity of a diplomatic agent.[152] However, though a State is obliged to take steps to prevent physical attacks on, or

[145] VCDR (n 102) Art 36(1).

[146] *Ibid*, Arts 26, 29. This is an ancient, and fundamental, principle of diplomatic law: see E Denza, *Diplomatic Law* (OUP, 2008), 256 *et seq*; UNSC Verbatim Record (15 September 1998) UN Doc S/PV.3926; and *Tehran Hostages* (n 131) 37.

[147] VCDR, *ibid*, Art 30(1)–(2).

[148] VCDR (n 102) Art 24. The scope of Art 24 was considered by the UK House of Lords in *Shearson Lehman v Maclaine Watson (No 2)* [1988] 1 WLR 16; 77 ILR 145, and by the English High Court in *Bancoult v Secretary of State for Foreign and Commonwealth Affairs* [2013] EWHC 1502 (Admin), para 40.

[149] VCDR (n 102) Art 27. It is worth mentioning the 2017 UK Supreme Court judgment in *Reyes v Al-Maliki* [2017] UKSC 61, on the incompatibility of diplomatic immunity with human trafficking (Hale, Clarke, and Wilson LJJ), and the need to take a broad view on the inapplicability of immunity for purely professional and commercial activity outside any official functions.

[150] *R (Bancoult) v Secretary of State for Foreign and Commonwealth Affairs* [2018] UKSC 3, paras 20–1 (Mance LJ).

[151] VCDR (n 102) Art 37(2).

[152] *Ibid*, Art 29.

physical interference with, a foreign head of State, it is not obliged to eradicate all potentially insulting or offensive conduct.[153]

Diplomatic agents enjoy complete immunity *ratione personae* from the legal system of the receiving State, such jurisdiction being historically reserved to the legal system of the sending State.[154] With respect to civil or administrative jurisdiction, the immunity *ratione personae* of diplomatic agents and their family members ('household') is subject to three exceptions in the territory of the receiving State:

(i) an action relating to immoveable property, unless held on behalf of the mission and used for the mission's purposes;

(ii) litigation relating to succession matters involving the diplomatic agent as executor, heir, administrator, or legatee as a private person; and

(iii) an action relating to any professional or commercial activity exercised by the diplomatic agent as these are in fact prohibited activities for diplomatic agents.[155]

Finally, diplomatic agents are exempt from being called as a witness,[156] from contributing to social security or taxation,[157] and from customs duties and inspection.[158]

The protection of diplomatic agents is not fully one-sided, as they also owe certain duties to the receiving State, such as to respect its laws and regulations and to avoid interfering in its internal affairs,[159] to communicate with the receiving State only through official channels authorized by it,[160] and to refrain from using the premises of the mission in a manner that is incompatible with the functions of the mission, such as commercial ventures or other for-profit activities for purely personal gain.[161]

9.5.2 **Consular immunity**

Rather than to represent the sending State in its political relations with the receiving State, the role of a consul is to act as a representative of the sending State in relation to broadly administrative and technical matters, which are often private in nature. Consequently, Article 5 VCCR mentions, as part of the consular function, the protection and assistance of the nationals of the sending State, including:

- obtaining appropriate legal assistance for them;
- the promotion of trade and cultural exchange between the sending and receiving States;
- and the issuance of passports and visas.

[153] *Harb v King Fahd* [2005] EWCA Civ 632, para 40; and *Mariam Aziz v Aziz and Sultan of Brunei* [2007] EWCA Civ 712, paras 88 *et seq.*

[154] VCDR (n 102) Art 31(1). See also *Tehran Hostages* (n 131) 37; *Dickinson v Del Solar* [1930] 1 KB 376; 5 AD 299. For further detail, see Denza, *Diplomatic Law* (n 144) 280 *et seq.*

[155] VCDR, *ibid*, Art 42. But these must be outside their functions: see *ibid*, Art 31(1)(c).

[156] *Ibid*, Art 31(2). [157] *Ibid*, Arts 33, 34. [158] *Ibid*, Art 35. [159] *Ibid*, Art 41(1).

[160] *Ibid*, Art 41(2). [161] *Ibid*, Arts 41(1)–(3).

Consular immunity thus attaches to consular premises, archives, and documents in a similar manner as to diplomatic missions,[162] as well as to consular communications and movement.[163] Notably, consent may be withdrawn without giving reasons, as came to the fore in late July 2020, when the USA ordered China to close its Houston consulate (albeit whilst claiming espionage activities), and two days later China responded in kind, ordering the USA to close its own consulate in Chengdu for the same reason.[164] Due to the different functions of consuls vis-à-vis diplomats, specific consular immunity under the VCCR is more restricted. They enjoy a more limited personal inviolability from arrest or detention, as they can be arrested for a 'grave crime'[165] and they only enjoy immunity *ratione materiae* in respect of official acts.

The system of consular protection within Article 36 VCCR establishes crucial rights both for the sending State and its nationals, including: freedom of communication of consular officials with nationals of the sending State (Article 36(1)(a)); the right of a national of the sending State to request the consular post be notified without delay of their arrest or detention (Article 36(1)(b)); and a right for consular officials to visit, to converse or correspond with, and to arrange legal representation for, any national of the sending State in prison, custody, or detention (Article 36(1)(c)). Those rights came prominently to the fore in the *LaGrand* and *Avena* cases before the ICJ. In both cases, nationals of Germany and Mexico, respectively, had been tried for capital crimes in the USA and sentenced to death, but had not been notified of their right to consular protection under Article 36(1).[166] In *LaGrand*, the ICJ found that the regime of Article 36(1) VCCR creates individual rights for any persons concerned, and that the USA had breached its obligations thereunder by not informing the LaGrand brothers of their rights under that provision 'without delay'.[167] In the *Avena* case, involving more than fifty Mexican nationals sentenced to death, the ICJ reaffirmed the finding that Article 36(1) VCCR created rights for individuals, and underlined that violations of the rights of individuals may simultaneously violate the rights of the State itself.[168] Though it is true that the US courts have declared the ICJ's judgments not to constitute directly enforceable domestic law, these cases were noteworthy in being some of the first judicial decisions to recognize an individual right to consular protection under international law.[169]

9.5.3 **Special missions immunity**

Aside from the permanent diplomatic and consular missions, at times States will deploy special or ad hoc missions to other States. These can be in relation to a specific objective which does not exist in its permanent missions; for example, specialized knowledge in

[162] VCCR (n 129), Arts 31–3. [163] *Ibid*, Arts 35–6.

[164] Similarly to the VCDR (n 102), Art 9, VCCR (n 129), Art 4 requires the consent of the host State.

[165] VCDR (n 102) Art 41.

[166] The jurisdiction of the Court in both cases rested on the fact that the applicants, as well as the USA, were all parties to the Optional Protocol on Compulsory Settlement of Disputes attached to the VCCR (n 129). Following the *Avena* judgment in 2004, the USA denounced the Optional Protocol.

[167] *LaGrand (Germany v United States), Judgment, ICJ Reports 2001*, p 466, 494.

[168] *Avena and other Mexican nationals (Mexico v United States), Judgment, ICJ Reports 2004*, p 12, 36.

[169] See, e.g., *Sánchez-Llamas v Oregon*, 548 US 331 (2006); *Gandara v Bennet*, 528 F.3d 823 (11th Cir 2008); *Mora v New York*, 524 F.3d 183 (2d Cir 2008); *Medellín v Texas*, 552 US 491 (2008); *García v Texas*, 564 US (2011).

cyber operations or climate science. Such ad hoc diplomacy allows for a certain flexibility in international relations, bypassing traditional diplomatic channels.

The Convention on Special Missions (CSM) provides a framework for members of special missions to enjoy limited privileges and immunities;[170] broadly speaking, these operate on the same principle of mutual consent as do diplomatic missions.[171] The sending State must inform the host State as to the size and composition of the mission, which may be rejected by the latter in some cases;[172] both States must agree on the physical location of the mission;[173] and the host State may declare a person *non grata*[174] or withdraw its consent to the mission at any time.[175] Under the CSM, a special mission enjoys similar inviolability as diplomatic missions in respect of its facilities, premises, archives, and documents,[176] as well as in respect of their communications and the 'bag of the special mission'.[177] Members of a special mission are divided into similar categories, enjoying differentiated immunities based on their personal role, in close analogy with the provisions of the VCDR in relation to jurisdictional immunity and personal inviolability in respect of arrest or detention.[178]

The element of mutual consent required in the CSM suggests that States can enter into agreements conferring certain privileges and immunities on special missions.[179] There is also some judicial practice affirming that customary international law protects special missions to a degree. For instance, the Federal Court of Justice in (then-West) Germany, in the *Tabatabai* judgment, affirmed that an ad hoc envoy operating with the consent of the receiving State may be granted immunity by individual agreement, and thus placed on a par with members of permanent missions of States.[180] In *Freedom and Justice Party*, the Court of Appeal for England and Wales held that customary international law required a receiving State to secure the inviolability and immunity of members of special missions.[181]

9.6 Conclusion

The international law on immunities serves as a reminder of the State-centred structure of international law. The various doctrines surveyed in this chapter relating to the applicability of immunities were originally designed to safeguard the sovereignty of

[170] As the CSM only has thirty-nine States parties, it remains unclear whether its provisions are fully reflective of customary law. See further A Sanger and M Wood, 'The Immunities of Members of Special Missions' and W Shan and P Wang, 'Divergent Views on State Immunity in the International Community' in T Ruys, N Angelet, and L Ferro (eds), *The Cambridge Handbook of Immunities and International Law* (CUP, 2019), 452.

[171] CSM, Arts 2–3. [172] *Ibid*, Art 8. [173] *Ibid*, Art 17. [174] *Ibid*, Art 12.

[175] *Ibid*, Art 20(1)(e). [176] *Ibid*, Arts 22–6. [177] *Ibid*, Art 28.

[178] *Ibid*, Arts 29–35. Administrative and technical, service, and private staff are covered in CSM, Arts 36–8.

[179] See, e.g., *US v Sissiko*, 999 F.Supp 1469 (1997); 121 ILR 600; and *Re Bo Xilai* (2005) 76 BYIL 601.

[180] *Tabatabai* case (1989) 80 ILR 388, 419. See also K Böckslaff and M Koch, 'The *Tabatabai* Case: The Immunity of Special Envoys and the Limits of Judicial Review' (1982) 25 German YBIL 539.

[181] *R (Freedom and Justice Party) v Secretary of State for the Foreign and Commonwealth Office* [2016] EWCA 2010 (Admin), para 163. See also *Khurts Bat v Investigating Judge of the Federal Court of Germany* (n 121) para 29; and on this point, A Sanger, 'Immunity of State Officials from the Criminal Jurisdiction of a Foreign State' (2013) 62 ICLQ 193. See also Letter of 26 April 2012 from the Dutch Minister of Foreign Affairs and the State Secretary for Security and Justice, on the immunity of members of foreign official missions.

States by preventing their appearance before foreign courts. Diplomatic law in particular, with its ancient roots, has undergone a process of systematization in recent decades to clarify its operation and ensure that coherent international rules apply consistently. Though at times distasteful in their shielding of certain individuals from prosecution, diplomatic and consular immunities safeguard the effectiveness of diplomatic relations.

A shift in emphasis among some States towards the protection of fundamental human rights—in particular, those of a *jus cogens* nature—has propelled many States to adopt a more restrictive approach to immunities. In relation to serious international crimes such as torture, developments suggest that immunity may no longer be invoked; in particular, in international proceedings. However, the pendulum can swing both ways in this highly dynamic area, and we must remain cautious not to take an overly linear vision of international law's development.

Further reading

D Akande and S Shah, 'Immunities of State Officials, International Crimes, and Foreign Domestic Courts' (2010) 21 EJIL 815.

A valuable contemporary analysis of the interrelation between the law of immunities and international crimes.

R van Alebeek, *The Immunities and their Officials in International Criminal Law and International Human Rights Law* (OUP, 2008).

A detailed examination of where immunities have come into collision with human rights and the fight against impunity.

A Aust, 'The Law of State Immunity' (2004) 53 ICLQ 255.

A comprehensive overview of the law at the time of the adoption of the 2004 UN Convention.

A Cassese, 'When May Senior State Officials be Tried for International Crimes? Some Comments on the *Congo v Belgium* Case' (2002) 13 EJIL 853.

A spirited challenge to traditional approaches to immunity, written by a serving ICTY judge.

H Fox and P Webb, *The Law of State Immunity* (3rd rev edn, OUP, 2015).

An encyclopaedic compendium of relevant practice covering the entirety of the field.

H Lauterpacht, 'The Problem of Jurisdictional Immunities of Foreign States' (1951) 28 BYBIL 220.

A landmark piece which significantly influenced the move by UK and US courts towards the adoption of a restrictive doctrine of State immunity.

R O'Keefe and C Tams (eds), *The United Nations Convention on Jurisdictional Immunities of States and Their Property* (OUP, 2013).

An annotated commentary that carefully assesses the customary law behind each proposed article.

I Pingel-lenuzza, *Les immunités des États en droit international* (Bruylant, 1998).

A leading French-language study of the law of State immunity.

A REINISCH, 'Recent Practice of European Courts with Regard to State Immunity from Enforcement Measures' (2006) 17 EJIL 4.

A thorough survey covering relevant activity from European courts in relation to immunity from enforcement jurisdiction.

T RUYS, N ANGELET, and L FERRO (eds), *The Cambridge Handbook of Immunities and International Law* (CUP, 2019).

A timely compendium of comprehensive, yet accessible, essays on the law of international immunities.

X YANG, *State Immunity in International Law* (CUP, 2012).

An examination of a broad range of domestic court judgments and their contribution to the customary law on State immunity.

10

State responsibility

10.1 Introduction: the concept of responsibility in international law

Within international law, the term 'responsibility' has long been understood to denote how fault or blame is attributable to a legal actor for the breach of an international legal obligation. As arbitrator, Max Huber commented in *Spanish Zone of Morocco*, '... responsibility is the necessary corollary of a right. All rights of an international character involve international responsibility. Responsibility results in the duty to make reparation if the obligation in question is not met.'[1]

Responsibility, as a term of art, cannot be used interchangeably with terms such as 'duty', 'liability', or 'accountability'.[2] Those concepts relate to broader questions which are not necessarily captured within international law, whereas the international legal understanding of responsibility has developed over many centuries, taking on a relatively settled meaning.

10.1.1 The ILC Articles on State Responsibility

HISTORICAL BACKGROUND The Development of the International Law Commission's Articles on State Responsibility (2001)

For many centuries, States were considered to be the sole international actors entitled to bear rights and obligations, and the law on international responsibility began to develop through a large body of customary law, some of which came to be recognized by arbitral and judicial tribunals, laying out a number of obligations of States regarding the treatment of aliens in their territory.

[1] *Spanish Zone of Morocco* (1923) 2 RIAA 615, 641; Huber's framing of responsibility was endorsed by the PCIJ in *Factory at Chorzów (Claim for Indemnity), Judgment, 1928, PCIJ, Ser A, No 17*, p 29, and by the ICJ in *Corfu Channel (United Kingdom v Albania), Judgment, ICJ Reports 1949*, p 4, 23.

[2] Notably, responsibility in this context must be distinguished from the so-called 'Responsibility to Protect', which refers to an entirely different notion: see Chapter 14, Section 14.4.2.

In the post-World War II period, the ILC was tasked with attempting to codify of the law on State responsibility, a Herculean effort which took nearly five decades before the Articles on the Responsibility of States for Internationally Wrongful Acts (ARSIWA) were adopted by the ILC in 2001 (see UN Doc A/RES/56/83 (10 December 2001)).

Unlike several other codification projects, the ILC suggested that the General Assembly 'take note' of the ARSIWA, but only consider convening a conference to conclude a convention after subsequent consideration. Presumably this was to allow for further reflection on its provisions and to allow for customary law to continue developing the ARSIWA. The General Assembly has repeatedly commended and taken note of the Articles and recommended them to the attention of governments (see UN Doc A/RES/59/35 (2 December 2004); UN Doc A/RES/62/61 (8 January 2008); UN Doc A/RES/68/104 (16 December 2013)). A working group was created by the General Assembly in 2016, so as further to explore the possible actions to be taken to advance the ARSIWA, and the General Assembly has asked the Secretary-General to compile relevant materials referring to the ARSIWA, including inviting governments to submit such information, with a view to revisiting the question in 2019 (see UN Doc A/RES/71/133 (13 December 2016)).

Given the General Assembly's repeated praise for the ARSIWA, but primarily due to widespread and repeated reference to them by States and international judicial institutions, many of the provisions in the Articles are considered highly authoritative by international lawyers and a reflection of customary international law. For further reading, see S Rosenne, 'State Responsibility: *Festina Lente*' (2004) 75 BYBIL 363; and J Crawford and S Olleson, 'The Continuing Debate on a UN Convention on State Responsibility' (2005) 54 ICLQ 959.

Whenever possible, the analytical structure deployed by the ILC in the ARSIWA[3] will be used in this chapter. The ILC based the Articles on a distinction between what it called primary and secondary rules of international law. 'Primary rules' are obligations, both substantive and procedural, binding States. Examples include the obligation not to use force against another State and to respect the diplomatic immunity of ambassadors. By contrast, 'secondary rules' are those rules that govern the consequences of non-performance, or breach, of primary rules. According to the ILC, the Articles were developed in line with the logic that the regime of international responsibility falls within the category of secondary rules.[4] This logic is adopted by the tribunal in the *Rainbow Warrior* arbitration[5] and the ICJ, in *Gabčíkovo-Nagymaros*,[6] both of which have illustrated how the law on State responsibility can be distinguished from other regimes of secondary rules, such as some of those found in the law of treaties.

[3] Articles on the Responsibility of States for Internationally Wrongful Acts, adopted by the ILC on 20 August 2001: 'Report of the International Law Commission on the Work of its 53rd Session', UN Doc A/56/10 Chap IV (2001) GAOR 56th Session Supp 10. The ILC Commentaries to the ARSIWA are found in (2001) ILC Ybk vol 2, pt 2, UN Doc A/CN.4/SER.A/2001/Add.1.

[4] See General Commentary to the ARSIWA, *ibid*, 31, paras 1–2; J Crawford, *State Responsibility: The General Part* (CUP, 2013), 14–16.

[5] *Rainbow Warrior (New Zealand v France)* (1990) XX RIAA 217.

[6] *Gabčíkovo-Nagymaros Project (Hungary/Slovakia), Judgment, ICJ Reports 1997*, p 7, 38.

10.1.2 **International organizations and other non-State actors**

State responsibility remains the archetypal and thus most developed form of international responsibility, and for clarity's sake will be the primary framework used in this chapter. Nevertheless, other international actors apart from States may also bear rights and obligations under international law.[7] The result of such capacity is the potential to bear responsibility for a breach of an international legal obligation.[8]

With this in mind, a decade after adopting the ARSIWA, the ILC adopted the Articles on the Responsibility of International Organizations (ARIO) in 2011.[9] Partly for reasons of coherence, the ILC chose to base the ARIO closely on the structure of the ARSIWA. This choice proved controversial, given the scarcity of relevant practice in relation to some international organizations,[10] but also because of inherent differences between international organizations and States. Moreover, as discussed in Chapter 6, international organizations vary considerably with respect to their degree of international personality, powers and functions, relations with their members, and decision-making procedures. Accordingly, many international organizations have objected to the idea that an overarching regime can accommodate these disparities between them.[11] Though the ARSIWA remain at the heart of this chapter, the ARIO will also be mentioned when relevant.

10.2 Core principles of international responsibility

Certain underlying rules on international responsibility are of a general character and application; however, by agreement, they may be modified, derogated from, or otherwise excluded, usually through *lex specialis*.[12] The first, embodied in Article 1 ARSIWA,[13] is the basic rule that every internationally wrongful act of a State entails responsibility. An 'internationally wrongful act' is defined as conduct, consisting of an action or omission, that: (i) is attributable to a State; and (ii) is a breach of an international obligation

[7] See *Reparation for Injuries Suffered in the Service of the United Nations, Advisory Opinion, ICJ Reports 1949*, p 174, 179.

[8] See *Difference relating to Immunity from Legal Process of a Special Rapporteur of the Commission on Human Rights, Advisory Opinion, ICJ Reports 1999*, p 62 ('*Cumuraswamy*'), para 66.

[9] ILC, 'Articles on the Responsibility of International Organizations' in Report on the Work of its 63rd Session, UN Doc A/66/10 Chap V (9 December 2011) GAOR 66th Session Supp 10.

[10] However, it bears noting that the ARIO have already been referred to in judicial practice: see, e.g., *Behrami & Saramati v France, Germany & Norway* App nos 78166/01 and 71412/01 (ECtHR, 2 May 2007), and *Al-Jedda v UK* App no 27021/08 (ECtHR, 7 July 2011) at the ECtHR; *Mothers of Srebrenica v Netherlands* (16 July 2014) District Court of The Hague (*Rechtbank Den Haag*); *Nuhanović v Netherlands* HR 6 September 2013, NJ 2013 (*Hoge Raad*, Dutch Supreme Court).

[11] See ILC, 'Comments and observations received from international organizations' (14 February 2011) UN Doc A/CN.4/637. In 2014 and 2017, the Secretary-General invited international organizations and States to submit any relevant practice with respect to the ARIO: see UNGA Res 69/126 (10 December 2014) and UNGA Res 72/122 (10 December 2017).

[12] ARSIWA (n 3) Art 55; and ARIO (n 9) Art 64.

[13] See also, by analogy, ARIO (n 9) Art 3.

of that State.[14] The rule has long been recognized in judicial and arbitral decisions as customary international law.[15] It should be emphasized, moreover, that a State may be liable for an omission. In *Corfu Channel*, the ICJ found Albania to be liable for the consequences of mines being laid within its territorial waters that caused damage to UK warships, despite not having laid them itself. However, the factual circumstances were such that the laying of the mines could not have been accomplished without Albania's knowledge. Albania's failure to notify the UK thus constituted a grave omission engaging its international responsibility.[16]

The overarching concepts of attribution and breach are at the very core of the law of international responsibility, and will be addressed in turn.

10.2.1 **Attribution**

A State is a legal fiction; a collective actor with no discernible psyche or 'state of mind', and must act through its organs or agents internationally: for example, when signing a treaty (Chapter 7) or in relation to government acts (see Chapter 9 on immunities).[17] For this reason, the international legal rules on attribution help to specify the categories of organs and agents whose conduct may engage the responsibility of a State, not least because it encourages States to exercise a degree of control over them.

The concept of attribution also allows one to identify the acts for which the State is not generally responsible, for example those of private parties such as its nationals or corporations incorporated under its domestic law. In limited circumstances, usually due to its direction or control, a State may be responsible for its failure to prevent certain acts by purely private actors, or a failure to take action to punish the individuals responsible.[18]

A preliminary point: attribution for the act of an official is entirely separate from the question of whether an official can, through their acts, bind a State to an international obligation. Though only certain senior officials, or those acting with express or presumed authority, may bind the State, the conduct of any State official, however low level, may be attributed to that State if it is also internationally wrongful.[19]

10.2.1.1 **The conduct of an organ of the State (*de jure* or *de facto*)**

Article 4 ARSIWA, which sets out the rule according to which the conduct of a State organ is to be considered an act of that State under international law, is one of the 'cornerstones of the law of State responsibility'.[20] Accordingly, the conduct of a State organ

[14] ARSIWA (n 3) Art 2; and ARIO (n 9) Art 4.

[15] See *Factory at Chorzów* (n 1) 21; *Rainbow Warrior* (n 5).

[16] *Corfu Channel* (n 1) 22–3. See also *Zafiro case* (1926) 6 RIAA 160.

[17] *German Settlers in Poland, Advisory Opinion, 1923, PCIJ, Ser B, No 6*, p 22.

[18] See, e.g., *Janes (United States v Mexico)* (1926) 4 RIAA 82; *cf Noyes (United States v Panama)* (1933) 6 RIAA 308.

[19] The latter question is governed by Arts 7 and 46 VCLT, and was discussed earlier in Chapter 7, Section 7.2.1.

[20] *Application of the Convention on the Prevention and the Punishment of the Crime of Genocide (Bosnia and Herzegovina v Serbia and Montenegro), Merits, ICJ Reports 2007*, p 43, 202; see also *Cumuraswamy* (n 8) para 62.

of whatever kind, and at whatever level in the hierarchy of the State—including any person or entity having that status under the legislation of that State—is considered an act of that State. This is so irrespective of the organ's position within the hierarchy of the State.[21]

The rule in Article 4 ARSIWA applies to what are usually designated, under a State's municipal law, as organs *de jure*. These are intentionally broad,[22] and encompass, for example: the acts of police officers;[23] those of soldiers and other members of a State's armed forces[24] (unless placed at the disposal of another State or entity);[25] the territorial subdivisions or component entities (e.g., provinces or states) of a federal State;[26] and those of the legislature and judicial organs.[27] As discussed in Section 10.2.1.2, it suffices that a State organ act in an apparently official capacity, or under the colour of authority, for its acts to be attributable to the State.

Though internal law is relevant, sometimes the formal status of a body and whether it is a State organ is unclear; accordingly, international law also examines how an entity operates in practice. Therefore, a State may not evade responsibility simply by asserting that under internal law a given entity is not actually its organ.[28]

Recently, in its judgment in *Application of the Genocide Convention (Bosnia)*, the ICJ suggested that, in exceptional circumstances, the acts of private actors may be equated to '*de facto* organs',

> provided that in fact the persons, groups or entities act in 'complete dependence' on the State, of which they are ultimately merely the instrument. In such a case, it is appropriate to look beyond legal status alone, in order to grasp the reality of the relationship between the person taking action, and the State to which [they are] so closely attached as to appear to be nothing more than its agent.[29]

[21] See Commentary to Art 4, esp paras 6–10; *Cumuraswamy* (n 8), para 62; and *Massey claim* (1927) 4 RIAA 155, 159. See also *Certain German Interests in Polish Upper Silesia, Judgment, 1926, PCIJ, Ser A, No 7*, p 19 (in relation to municipal law); *Heirs of the Duc de Guise case* (1951) XIII UNRIAA 150, 161 (regional administrative units) (Franco-Italian Conciliation Commission); *LaGrand (Germany v United States), Provisional Measures, Order of 3 March 1999, ICJ Reports 1999*, p 9, 16 (component units of a federal State); and *Rainbow Warrior* (n 5) (a State's intelligence officers).

[22] ARSIWA (n 3) Art 3; ARIO (n 9) Art 5.

[23] *Roper* (1927) 4 RIAA 145; *Pugh* (1933) 3 RIAA 1439.

[24] *Armed Activities in the Territory of the Congo (Democratic Republic of the Congo v Uganda), Judgment, ICJ Reports 2005*, p 168, 242.

[25] See *Behrami & Saramati* (n 10) para 140.

[26] *Request for Interpretation of the Judgment of 31 March 2004 in the Case concerning Avena and Other Mexican Nationals (Mexico v United States of America) (Mexico v United States of America), Judgment, ICJ Reports 2009*, p 3, 15; WTO, *Australia—Measures Affecting Importation of Salmon—Recourse to Article 21.5 by Canada* (18 February 2000) WT/DS18/RW, §7.12.

[27] See *LaGrand (Germany v United States), Judgment, ICJ Reports 2001*, p 466; *Avena and other Mexican Nationals (Mexico v United States), Judgment, ICJ Reports 2004*, p 12, 66; WTO, *United States—Import Prohibition of Certain Shrimp and Shrimp Products* (12 October 1998) WT/DS58/AB/R §173; *International Responsibility for the Promulgation and Enforcement of Laws in Violation of the Convention (Articles 1–2 of the ACHR)*, Advisory Opinion OC-14/94, Inter-American Court of Human Rights Series A No 14 (9 December 1994) §50.

[28] ARSIWA (n 3) Art 4(2); and Commentary, para 11. By analogy, see also VCLT, Art 27.

[29] *Application of the Genocide Convention* (n 20) para 392; the Court was elaborating on its earlier holding in *Military and Paramilitary Activities in and against Nicaragua (Nicaragua v United States), Merits, ICJ Reports 1986*, p 3, 62–4.

The 'complete dependence' test used by the ICJ is high, as was evidenced by the Court's own assessment of the threshold to two entities, the 'Republika Srpska' (a secessionary entity in Bosnia and Herzegovina) and the 'VRS armed forces' (the military wing of Republika Srpska) having committed serious breaches of international law. Neither of these was an organ of the Federal Republic of Yugoslavia (FRY). Bosnia had contended that Republika Srpska and the VRS were under the direct control and directly subordinate to FRY State organs. However, the ICJ concluded that despite significant support and ties between them and the FRY, factually they were more independent than 'mere instruments' of the FRY, and thus could not be equated with its organs.[30]

Due to the distinct form of international organizations, the general rule contained in Article 6 ARIO is somewhat 'functionalist' in nature: an international organization is responsible for the wrongful acts of its organ or agent, but only when acting in the performance of its functions. Certain problems arise where the organ or agent of a State is placed at the disposal of an international organization or another State, but where both retain elements of control over the organ or agent. In practice, this situation occurs most frequently when military contingents are placed at the disposal of an organization for peacekeeping purposes, as came to light in the controversial *Behrami & Saramati v France, Germany & Norway* judgment of the ECtHR.[31] Certain alleged human rights violations of members of the armed forces of those three States had arisen within the context of their deployment, under UN auspices, in Kosovo. The ECtHR declared the case inadmissible against the respondent States, on the basis that under the terms of the peacekeepers' deployment, 'the UNSC retained ultimate authority and control and . . . effective command of the relevant operational matters was retained by NATO'. Because NATO is not a party to the ECHR, the Court was pointedly silent as to the possible responsibility of the UN, under the auspices of which NATO had acted.[32]

CONTEMPORARY DEVELOPMENTS The Potential for 'Shared Responsibility'

International law only has some rudimentary mechanisms for recognizing responsibility for collective acts, but usually this has been done by apportioning responsibility for separate acts to different actors; for example, for aid or assistance to another, or coercing a State to commit an unlawful act: see Section 10.2.1.4.3.

The monolithic view of control espoused by the ECtHR in *Behrami and Saramati* has come under fire in a series of domestic judgments in the Netherlands. In the *Mustafić* and *Nuhanović* judgments, the Court of Appeal of The Hague suggested that 'it cannot be ruled out that the application of [the criterion of effective control] results in the possibility of attribution to more than one party' (*Mustafić & Nuhanović v Netherlands* (5 July 2011), LJN: BR 5386 & BR 5388, paras 5.9, 5.18, 5.20). In *Mothers of Srebrenića* and *Jaloud*, Dutch courts went further and extended the scope of application of Article 8 ARSIWA to encompass the organs of international organizations or of foreign States (*Netherlands v Stichting Mothers of Srebrenića*

[30] *Application of the Genocide Convention* (n 20) paras 394–5. [31] See *Behrami & Saramati* (n 10).

[32] *Ibid*, para 140. For a scathing critique, see M Milanović and T Papić, 'As Bad As It Gets: The European Court of Human Rights' *Behrami and Saramati* Decision and General International Law' (2009) 58 ICLQ 267.

(16 July 2019), ECLI:NL:HR:2019:1284 (*Hoge Raad* (Dutch Supreme Court)); *Jaloud v Netherlands* (20 November 2019), ECLI:NL:RBDHA:2019:1223 (District Court of The Hague)). These are known as the 'Dutchbat' cases as they concerned the responsibility of the Netherlands for the Dutch battalion of the Airborne Brigade during the Srebreniča massacre of the Bosnian conflict.

In a later judgment, *Al-Jedda v United Kingdom* App No 27021/08 (ECtHR, 7 July 2011), the ECtHR declared that, unlike in *Behrami and Saramati*, no UN resolution gave the UN effective control or ultimate authority in relation to Iraq, and that the UK was thus responsible for human rights violations committed there by its troops (paras 83–5). However, the ECtHR in *Al-Jedda* did not address the question of whether there could be joint or 'shared' responsibility between the UK and the UN.

More recently, States' shared obligations to prevent climate change have come to the fore. In the 2019 *Urgenda v the Netherlands* (Dutch Supreme Court, Case No 19/00135, 20 December 2019), the Dutch Supreme Court held that, though the obligation of the Netherlands to lower greenhouse emissions was collectively shared with other States, its specific obligations were divisible from those of other States and separately calculated. In December 2024, the ICJ advisory proceedings were held relating to *Obligations of States in relation to Climate Change*, in which the collective aspect of the obligations concerned figured prominently. The Court's opinion is expected in 2025.

For further reading, see B Boutin, 'Responsibility of the Netherlands for the Acts of Dutchbat in *Nuhanović* and *Mustafić*: The Continuous Quest for a Tangible Meaning for "Effective Control" in the Context of Peacekeeping' (2012) 25 LJIL 521; and N Nedeski, *Shared Obligations in International Law* (CUP, 2022). See also, generally, A Nollkaemper, J d'Aspremont, C Ahlborn, B Boutin, N Nedeski, and I Plakokefalos (coll D Jacobs), 'Guiding Principles on Shared Responsibility in International Law' (2020) 31 EJIL 15.

10.2.1.2 **A person or entity exercising governmental authority on behalf of a State**

Aside from their organs, States may implement their will through recourse to independent agencies, parastatal entities, or, in some cases, to corporations. Under Article 5 ARSIWA, the conduct of any such person or entity which is not an organ of the State, but which: (i) is empowered under a State's municipal law to exercise elements of governmental authority; and (ii) has acted in that specific capacity, may be attributed to the State. In today's context, many State functions are delegated or outsourced, such as the conduct of private security firms acting as prison guards, or of private airlines exercising certain immigration controls.[33] To these, one can add the situation of private or privatized corporations which retain certain public or regulatory functions, for example the minting of German currency by BH Mayer's Kunstprägeanstalt GmbH and Leipziger Edelmetallverarbeitung GmbH.[34]

[33] ARSIWA (n 3), Commentary to Art 5, 92.

[34] See also *US—Anti-Dumping and Countervailing Duties (China)*, WTO Doc WT/DS379/ABR, 11 March 2011, §318, in which the WTO Appellate Body drew from Art 5 ARSIWA to interpret the definition of a 'public body' in the context of the WTO Agreement on Subsidies and Countervailing Measures; and *Hyatt International Corporation v Government of the Islamic Republic of Iran* (1985) 9 Iran-USCTR 72, where a charitable organization was found to be in fact an 'agency, instrumentality or entity controlled by the Government of Iran'.

Moreover, some States assign quintessentially governmental functions to the organs of a second State. In such cases, Article 6 ARSIWA applies, according to which the conduct of an organ, placed at the disposal of a State by another State, is deemed an act of the second State, on behalf of which the person or entity was exercising governmental authority in carrying out that conduct. The classic example is the UK Privy Council acting as the highest appellate judicial body for certain Commonwealth members, such as Jamaica, Tuvalu, and Antigua and Barbuda. Other examples include the safeguarding of Monaco's defence by the French armed forces and the printing of Israeli currency by the Korea Minting and Security Printing Corporation.[35]

10.2.1.3 **Responsibility for acts *ultra vires***

Attribution to a State might also arise if State organs or agents, or persons exercising elements of governmental authority, commit an act which is *ultra vires* (exceeds the competence of) the State, or otherwise contravenes its instructions.[36] The underlying logic behind this principle is that a State cannot take refuge behind the fact that it may have given different instructions to these actors. Put differently, a State must oversee or otherwise control the organs and entities through which it operates. In *Velásquez Rodríguez*, the Inter-American Court of Human Rights declared that unlawful conduct may arise from acts of any State organs, officials, or public entities,

> independent of whether the organ or official has contravened provisions of internal law or overstepped the limits of his authority: under international law a State is responsible for the acts of its agents undertaken in their official capacity and for their omissions, even when those agents act outside the sphere of their authority or violate internal law.[37]

The substance of the rule embodied in Article 7 ARSIWA had already been laid down in a series of early arbitral awards, setting out the principle that officials purporting to be acting under the colour of apparent authority could also make the State responsible. In the now-classic *Caire* claim, a French national was murdered by two Mexican officers after they failed to extort money from him. The French–Mexican Claims Commission concluded, in an oft-cited remark, that the responsibility of Mexico was engaged 'in view of the fact that they acted in their capacity of officers and used the means placed at their disposition by virtue of that capacity'.[38] Examples of such means can include the wearing of a uniform, the brandishing of a badge or other identification, or the use of other State insignia. The point was further elaborated in the *Youmans* claim, in which Mexican soldiers sent to disperse a riot which was threatening the lives of US nationals,

[35] ARSIWA (n 3), Commentary to Art 5, 98.

[36] See ARSIWA (n 3) Art 7.

[37] *Velásquez Rodríguez v Honduras*, Judgment, IACtHR Ser C No 4 (29 July 1988), (1989) 28 ILM 378, para 170; see also *Ilaşcu v Moldova and Russia* App No 48787/99 (ECtHR, 8 July 2004), para 319; and *Blake v Guatemala*, Judgment, IACtHR Series C No 36 (24 January 1998).

[38] *Caire (France/Mexico)* (1929) 5 RIAA 516, 530. See also *Mossé* case (1953) 13 RIAA, 486, 494, where acts performed by officials 'within the apparent limits of their functions, in accordance with a line of conduct which was not entirely contrary to the instructions received', would be attributable to the State.

instead joined the rioters and shot at the house in which the US nationals were sheltering. The US–Mexico Mixed Claims Commission concluded that because at the time the soldiers were 'on duty under the immediate supervision and in the presence of a commanding officer', Mexico's responsibility had been engaged.[39] State responsibility is also engaged in situations if the official has acted in error or committed an 'honest mistake'.[40]

The 'apparent' nature of authority can often be blurred. A useful illustration can be found in the *Mallén* claim, where the claimant had been a victim of two assaults committed by a US police officer. In the first assault, the impugned officer was not on duty, whereas the second assault took place in a jail following an arrest, during which the officer was on active duty. The US–Mexico Mixed Claims Commission distinguished between the two acts, terming the first assault an act of a private person 'who happened to be an official', and thus could not engage the responsibility of the USA.[41] The second assault, though an abuse of authority, engaged US responsibility due to the showing of a badge and the incarceration of Mr Mallén: '[t]hough his act would seem to have been a private act of revenge which was disguised, . . . as an official act of arrest, the act as a whole can only be considered as the act of an official'.[42]

A more recent example is the 2018 extrajudicial killing of Jamal Khashoggi, a Saudi national, by Saudi State agents in its consulate in Istanbul. After a six-month investigation, UN Special Rapporteur Agnès Callamard concluded that, even though Saudi Arabia denied knowledge of the execution claimed, the Saudi agents involved had contravened instructions, as they had 'acted under cover of their official status and used means placed at their disposal on account of that status'.[43]

10.2.1.4 **Other circumstances where a State may be responsible**

As a general rule, a State is not responsible for the acts of other actors which neither act under its authority nor are its organs or agents. However, there do exist certain circumstances under which responsibility may be attributed for the conduct of private persons, groups of persons, or those of another State or an international organization.

10.2.1.4.1 ***Acts under the direction or control of a State***

The conduct of a person or group of persons may be attributed to a State if they are 'in fact acting on the instructions of, or under the direction or control of, that State in carrying out the conduct'.[44] A point of contention arises as to the degree of direction or control which is necessary to engage responsibility, as demonstrated in the commentary accompanying the ICJ's judgment in *Nicaragua*.

39 *Youmans (United States/Mexico)* (1926) 4 RIAA 110, 116.

40 See generally *Union Bridge Company case* (1924) 6 RIAA 138.

41 *Mallén case (United States v Mexico)* (1927) 4 UNRIAA 173, 174. 42 *Ibid.*

43 UN Doc A/HRC/41/CRP.1 (19 June 2019), 44. In October 2024, Canada accused Indian diplomats of collaborating with a criminal gang to murder Hardeep Singh Nijjar, a Canadian national, outside a Sikh temple in British Columbia. Canada claims to hold credible evidence of Indian officials' participation in the crime, but India has so far declined to co-operate in the criminal investigation.

44 ARSIWA (n 3) Art 8; see Commentary to Art 8, 47–9.

CASE SPOTLIGHT ***Military and Paramilitary Activities In and Against Nicaragua (Nicaragua v United States), Merits, ICJ Reports 1986*, p 14**

Simply referred to as the *Nicaragua* judgment, the ICJ's 1986 judgment was of great import for the law on State responsibility.

Following a 1979 *coup d'état* by the communist Sandinistas, US President Reagan terminated aid to Nicaragua on the grounds that it was aiding guerrillas in El Salvador by allowing Soviet arms through its territory. Nicaragua advanced several claims against the USA, claiming in particular that the USA was responsible for the acts of contras, irregular paramilitary units seeking to overthrow the Sandinistas.

After a highly contested jurisdictional phase, the USA refused to make submissions on the merits. The Court, however, upheld important contentions on the part of Nicaragua that are highly salient in relation to the law on State responsibility.

Foremost is the Court's determination that, for State responsibility to be engaged, it was insufficient for the USA to have taken a preponderant role in the financing, organizing, training, supplying, and equipping of the contras, or even in selecting its targets. This finding was in accordance with the principle whereby a State is responsible for the acts of private persons or groups of persons if their conduct is pursuant to the instructions or direction of a State, or where it has exercised *effective control* over the conduct which has led to the breach (pp 64–5). Simply put, the USA's conduct did not rise to the threshold of effective control.

The Court's finding in *Nicaragua* has been endorsed by the ILC in Article 8 ARSIWA as the 'effective control test', and was further confirmed by the ICJ in the 2007 *Application of the Genocide Convention (Bosnia)* judgment (209–10). Therefore, a State can theoretically be held responsible for the actions of non-State actors, but the degree of control which is necessary to engage responsibility is a threshold yet to be crossed.

Military and Paramilitary Activities in and against Nicaragua remains one of the key international judgments, having contributed to our understanding of a range of areas. See further the 2012 Leiden Journal of International Law Symposium, 'Nicaragua: 25 Years Later', including commentary on all areas of international law in which the judgment was influential.

The effective control test in *Nicaragua* is relatively high, and stipulates a fairly precise degree of control over specific acts. A doctrinal controversy arose when the ICTY Appeals Chamber, in its controversial *Tadić* judgment, challenged the 'effective control' test and suggested that the degree of control might vary according to the circumstances of each case.[45] In the specific circumstances of that case, which involved issues of individual criminal responsibility and the application of international humanitarian law, the ICTY declared an 'overall control' test to be the appropriate threshold.[46]

A decade letter, the ICJ in turn rebutted the ICTY's overall control test as 'unsuitable' in relation to the law of State responsibility:

> the 'overall control' test has the major drawback of broadening the scope of State responsibility well beyond the fundamental principle governing the law of international

[45] *Prosecutor v Tadić* (Appeals Chamber Judgment) ICTY-94-1-A (15 July 1999) (1999) 38 ILM 1518, 1541, para 117.

[46] *Ibid*, 1546, para 145. The ILC reacted coolly to the ICTY's challenge: see Commentary to Art 8, 48, para 5.

> responsibility: a State is responsible only for its own conduct, that is to say the conduct of persons acting, on whatever basis, on its behalf . . . [T]he 'overall control' test is unsuitable, for it stretches too far, almost to breaking point, the connection which must exist between the conduct of a State's organs and its international responsibility.[47]

It is true that the ICTY had hoped to challenge the effective control test, at least in matters of international criminal responsibility. The ICJ's firm rebuttal of the ICTY's position has been criticized for being unduly formalist and limiting the ambit of State responsibility.[48] However, it bears noting that the ICJ did not overturn two aspects of the overall control test. First, the Court took pains to emphasize that it 'attaches the utmost importance to the factual and legal findings made by the ICTY in ruling on the criminal liability of the accused before it',[49] leaving the overall control test untouched in relation to questions of individual criminal responsibility. Secondly, the ICJ left open the possible applicability of the overall control test in classifying an armed conflict as international or non-international in nature: 'it may well be that the [overall control] test is applicable and suitable'.[50] In 2022, the District Court of The Hague found, in relation to the downing of Flight MH17 over eastern Ukraine, that the said area was under the 'overall control' of Russia, and on that basis that the armed conflict in eastern Ukraine should be classified as international in nature.[51]

10.2.1.4.2 ***Insurrections, revolutions, and the adoption of private acts by the State***

Generally, provided that a State demonstrates a degree of due diligence in taking preventive measures or enacting appropriate legislation, it is not responsible for violence committed by private citizens in its territory.[52] There is little consensus on what due diligence actually entails, though arbitrator Huber's finding in *Spanish Zone of Morocco* seems to favour a contextual, case-by-case approach: a State is 'obliged to exercise only that degree of vigilance which corresponds to the means at its disposal . . . the vigilance which from the point of view of international law a state is required to exercise, may be characteried as *diligentia quam in suis*'.[53] That contextual approach has been applied recently by several arbitral tribunals in relation to the obligation to provide full protection and security against riots and looting.[54]

[47] *Application of the Genocide Convention* (n 20) 210, para 406.

[48] A Cassese, 'The *Nicaragua* and *Tadić* Tests Revisited in Light of the ICJ Judgment on Genocide in Bosnia' (2007) 18 EJIL 649; R Goldstone and R Hamilton, '*Bosnia v Serbia*: Lessons from the Encounter of the International Court of Justice with the International Criminal Tribunal for the Former Yugoslavia' (2008) 21 Leiden JIL 95.

[49] *Application of the Genocide Convention* (n 20) para 403.

[50] *Ibid*, para 404.

[51] See District Court of The Hague (the Netherlands), judgment of 17 November 2022, No CLI:NL:RBDHA:2022:14040. The classification of armed conflicts is further addressed in Chapter 15, Section 15.2.2.

[52] D Momtaz, G Cahin, and O de Frouville, 'Attribution of Conduct to the State' in J Crawford, A Pellet, and S Olleson (eds), *The Law of International Responsibility* (OUP, 2010), 257, 261–4.

[53] *Spanish Zone of Morocco* (n 1) 644.

[54] See *Wena Hotels v Egypt*, Award, 8 December 2000 (2000) 43 ILM 896, where Egypt was held liable for the damage caused by rioting because it had been in a position to adopt measures of vigilance, prevention, and enforcement, but did not act. See also *Pantechniki v Albania*, Award, Case No ARB/07/21 (ICSID, 30 July 2009); and GI Hernández, 'The Interaction Between Investment Law and the Law of Armed Conflict in the Interpretation of Full Protection and Security Clauses' in F Baetens (ed), *Investment Law within International Law: Integrationist Perspectives* (CUP, 2013), 21.

In addition, there are limited circumstances in which the violent acts of insurrectionist movements and revolutionaries may become attributable to a State. Under Article 10 ARSIWA, where an insurrectional movement has successfully become the new government of the State, or has established a new State on a portion of the previous State's territory, that State will be held responsible for its acts prior to the assumption of authority.[55] This finding may well be relevant in the August 2021 takeover of Afghanistan by the Taliban. Conversely, the acts of an unsuccessful insurrection against a government are not considered acts of that State. No modern example exists of a State being held responsible for negligent failure to suppress insurgents.[56]

Article 10 ARSIWA extends only to the agents of a revolutionary government, and not private persons who are supporters. As the Iran–US Claims Tribunal decided in *Short v Iran*, a successful claim requires the identification of an agent of the revolutionary movement, which was not met in that case.[57] In *Yeager v Iran*, the same tribunal held Iran liable for detentions and expulsions carried out by the 'Revolutionary Guards' organization in the immediate aftermath of the Iranian Revolution. Though the Guards were not formally recognized as part of the apparatus of the Iranian State, they were found to be exercising public functions with the knowledge and acquiescence of the revolutionary government.[58]

A State may also accrue responsibility for the acts of private persons or entities if it acknowledges and adopts their conduct as its own.[59] This principle was prominently applied by the ICJ in the *Tehran Hostages* judgment, in relation to the storming of the US Embassy in Tehran, and consulates in Tabriz and Shiraz, by 'militant students' who were in no way organs or agents of Iran. For the Court, the approval given by Ayatollah Khomeini and several organs of the revolutionary Iranian State, followed by the decision to continue the occupation of the embassy, were such that Iran was regarded as having adopted those acts. Iran was thus internationally responsible for the acts committed by the militant students.[60] The ILC Commentary suggests that 'adoption' is a higher threshold than mere 'approval' or 'endorsement', and 'carries with it the idea that the conduct is acknowledged by the State as, in effect, its own conduct'.[61]

10.2.1.4.3 ***Responsibility in connection with the act of another State***

A State's responsibility might also be engaged for the act of another actor, if it is somehow implicated in the conduct of the latter. Although 'complicity' as a concept does

[55] See *Bolivar Railway Company* (1903) 9 RIAA 445; *Pinson* (1928) 5 RIAA 327.

[56] ARSIWA (n 3) Art 55, Commentary to Art 10, para 15.

[57] *Alfred W Short v Islamic Republic of Iran* (1987) 16 Iran-USCTR 76, 85. See also *Rankin v Islamic Republic of Iran* (1987) 17 Iran-USCTR 135.

[58] *Kenneth P Yeager v Islamic Republic of Iran* (1987) 17 Iran-USCTR 92, 104.

[59] ARSIWA (n 3) Art 11.

[60] See *United States Diplomatic and Consular Staff in Tehran (United States v Islamic Republic of Iran), Judgment, ICJ Reports 1980*, p 3, 34–5. The breaches in question were of the obligation to protect diplomatic premises embodied in Art 22 of the 1961 Vienna Convention on Diplomatic Relations (adopted 18 April 1961, entered into force 24 April 1964), 500 UNTS 95.

[61] ARSIWA (n 3), Commentary to Art 11, para 6.

not exist within the law of international responsibility,[62] responsibility can arise in the following situations:

(i) if a State aids or assists another actor in breaching an obligation owed by both of them. The aid or assistance must be materially significant, and the State is only responsible for the aid and assistance, not the breach itself;[63]

(ii) if a State exercises direction or control over another actor, in which case the State will be responsible for the breach itself;[64]

(iii) if a State coerces another actor into breaching an obligation owed by both of them, in which case the State will be responsible for the breach itself;[65] or

(iv) if a member State of an international organization circumvents an international obligation by causing the organization to act such that, had the act been committed by that State, it would have constituted a breach of that obligation.[66]

In all four situations, the State must have knowledge of the circumstances of the wrongful act committed by the other actor, and the act must also have been wrongful had it been committed by the State itself. The responsibility of international organizations may be triggered under similar circumstances.[67] It bears emphasizing that a State is responsible only to the extent of its own wrongful conduct. To illustrate, in *Nicaragua (Merits)*, the USA was only responsible for its own wrongful conduct, which was the act of training and financing the contras who were seeking to overthrow the Nicaraguan government. It was not, however, responsible for the acts of the contras as a whole, as it did not instruct them how to act.[68]

CONTEMPORARY DEVELOPMENTS International Obligations of Non-State Actors, Especially Corporations

Historically, international law has been rather undeveloped in relation to the responsibility of non-State actors. No general regime has attempted to cover breaches of international law by individuals or corporations, though in the last decades there are certain civil liability regimes established in environmental treaties in relation to shipowners, nuclear operators, and producers of genetically modified organisms (see Chapter 19). Moreover, international criminal law now addresses individual responsibility for the commission of international crimes (see

[62] *Application of the Genocide Convention* (n 20) 217. But *cf.* M Jackson, *Complicity in International Law* (OUP, Oxford 2015), esp chs 6–7.

[63] ARSIWA (n 3) Art 16; ARIO (n 9) Art 58.

[64] ARSIWA (n 3) Art 17; ARIO (n 9) Art 59.

[65] ARSIWA (n 3) Art 18; ARIO (n 9) Art 60. Potentially, a State that 'instigates' another State to commit an internationally wrongful act is a form of complicity based on a general principle of law against instigation: see M Jackson, 'State Instigation in International Law: A General Principle Transposed' (2019) 30 EJIL 391.

[66] ARIO (n 9) Art 60.

[67] See *ibid*, Arts 14–17.

[68] *Nicaragua (Merits)* (n 29) paras 75–80, 238, 242, 252.

Chapter 17). In the absence of such treaty provisions, however, the non-criminal responsibility of individuals remains a matter for a State's municipal law.

The open-ended intergovernmental Working Group on human rights and transnational corporations and other business enterprises, operating under the auspices of the UN Human Rights Council, continues to work on a draft of a binding business and human rights treaty that would provide clarity on the duties of transnational corporations, oblige States to a higher degree of human rights due diligence, and lay out better remedies for victims (for the updated draft, see UN Doc A/HRC/55/59/Add.1 (13 February 2024)).

For further discussion, see M Karavias, *Corporate Obligations under International Law* (OUP, 2013); and N Bernaz, *Business and Human Rights. History, Law and Policy: Bridging the Gap* (Routledge, 2017). For more critical perspective, see G Baars, *The Corporation, Law, and Capitalism* (Brill, 2019); and the edited collection by D Brinks, J Dehm, K Engle, and K Taylor (eds), *Power, Participation and Private Regulatory Initiatives: Human Rights in Supply Chain Capitalism* (U Penn Press, 2021).

10.2.2 **The existence of a breach**

10.2.2.1 Violation of an international obligation

The second element of international responsibility is the existence of a breach of an international legal obligation. This makes logical sense: if a State's conduct causes substantial damage or harm, no responsibility can be engaged if no breach or violation of an international obligation is found, even if the conduct breaches the internal law of a State.[69] Moreover, save for exceptional circumstances where a specific obligation provides otherwise, there is no generalized system of strict liability under international law.[70]

It follows logically that an international obligation must bind a State at the time of the breach.[71] This corollary raises interesting questions in relation to customary law, as it may not be clear exactly when a new customary rule will have crystallized.[72] The archetypal situation is the emergence of the customary rule prohibiting slavery and the slave trade amid widespread slaving. Claims for reparation had arisen as early as 1817 but it was unclear whether the prohibition had fully crystallized by that point.[73]

[69] For more detail, see Chapter 4, Section 4.2.1.1.

[70] But see exceptionally *Trail Smelter* (1949) 3 RIAA 1905, 1965, where Canada was held responsible under international law for the damage caused by air pollution produced by a smelter located in its territory; and the 1972 Convention on International Liability for Damage Caused by Space Objects (adopted 29 March 1972, entered into force 1 September 1972), 961 UNTS 187, Art 2, which provides for absolute liability for damage caused by its objects in space.

[71] ARSIWA (n 3) Art 13.

[72] See *Fisheries Jurisdiction (United Kingdom v Iceland), Jurisdiction and Admissibility, ICJ Reports 1974*, p 3. For further reading on the inter-temporal rule, see R Higgins, 'Time and the Law: International Perspectives on an Old Problem' (1997) 46 ICLQ 501; and SFDI (ed), *Le droit international et le temps: Colloque de Paris* (Pedone, 2001).

[73] *Le Louis* (1817) 2 Dodson 210.

Another pertinent challenge is how to determine exactly at which point a breach will have occurred. Under Article 14 ARSIWA, a breach occurs at the moment when the act occurs, unless it is of a 'continuing character', in which case it extends over the entire period during which the wrongful act continues. Accordingly, there is no breach of an international obligation when an act has been committed prior to the entry into force of the obligation, whatever its continuing effects. A classic example remains the expropriation of property, the legality of which is assessed only at the moment of expropriation, and not when a later obligation comes into force.[74] Conversely, where a breach extends after the entry into force of the relevant international obligation, such as a seizure of property not involving formal expropriation, the State will be responsible for any breach after the entry into force of the obligation. In the *Loizidou* case, the ECtHR declared that it could not adjudge on the original expulsion of Mrs Loizidou from her home in the northern area of Cyprus in 1974, as that act had occurred before Turkey (as it was known then; now Türkiye) had accepted the right of individual petition, and was therefore inadmissible. However, as Mrs Loizidou was still being denied access to her property in those areas of Cyprus under Turkish control, the Court declared that this continuing exclusion was a separate breach, and was thus admissible.[75]

10.2.2.2 **Is there a requirement of fault?**

There is still some debate as to whether international law contains a general requirement of *culpa* (fault). Early on, arbitral awards hewed to a theory of so-called 'objective responsibility', according to which it sufficed that an internationally wrongful act which had caused injury and could be attributed to a State was sufficient to engage its responsibility, irrespective of any intention.[76] Certain judicial decisions have, however, intimated that a degree of subjective fault is required. For example, in *Corfu Channel* the ICJ determined that Albania's omission to notify transiting ships that mines had been laid in its territorial sea had engaged its responsibility.[77] As this was on the basis that Albania had constructive knowledge of the mine-laying activities, Albania's responsibility rested upon the violation of the specific legal obligation 'not to allow knowingly its territory to be used for acts contrary to the rights of other States'.[78] However, it does not go so far as to recognize a general principle of fault in international law.

In *Application of the Genocide Convention*, the ICJ excluded any element of fault within the general regime of State responsibility, reaffirming the 'well-established' customary international law rule in Article 4 ARSIWA that the conduct of a State organ gives rise to a State's responsibility if that conduct is internationally wrongful.[79] This

[74] See, e.g., *Pey Casado and Foundation President Allende v Chile* Case No ARB/98/2 (ICSID, 8 May 2008), para 608.

[75] *Loizidou v Turkey (Preliminary Objections)* App No 15318/89 (1995) ECHR Ser A No 310 and *(Merits)* App No 15318/89 (ECtHR, 18 December 1996); see also *Papamichalopoulos and others v Greece* App No 14556/89 (ECtHR, 24 June 1993).

[76] See the *Neer claim* (1926) 4 RIAA 60; *Caire* (n 38) 529–31. See also, generally, *Roberts* (1926) 6 RIAA 77; *The Jessie* (1921) 6 RIAA 57.

[77] *Corfu Channel* (n 1) 18; *Home Missionary Society claim (United States v Great Britain)* (1920) 6 RIAA 42.

[78] *Ibid*, 22. [79] *Application of the Genocide Convention* (n 20) 202.

seems broadly in line with the ILC's Commentary to Article 2 ARSIWA, which lays down the general rule that international responsibility does not require fault in order to characterize an act or omission as internationally wrongful. However, Article 2 ARSIWA leaves open the possibility that a necessary element of fault exists in relation to a specific obligation.[80] For example, in *Pulp Mills on the River Uruguay*, because Uruguay had breached certain procedural obligations of notification and cooperation which had been laid out in a 1975 treaty between the parties, the ICJ held that Uruguay had breached substantive duties relating to the protection and preservation of the marine environment.[81]

10.2.2.3 **The existence of harm or damage**

The existence of harm or damage is not a precondition for international responsibility; in principle, it suffices that an internationally wrongful act exists and is attributed to a State or international organization. This is in part because no material harm might result, even from a manifest breach of a State's rights. Examples include the violation of airspace, the mining of data from a State's governmental cyber-infrastructure, or the infringement of the inviolability of diplomatic premises. In such cases, responsibility is still engaged, but international courts and tribunals may award 'satisfaction' or other forms of declaratory relief instead of financial or other forms of reparation (see later, Section 10.5).[82]

CASE SPOTLIGHT ***Construction of a Road in Costa Rica along the San Juan River (Nicaragua v Costa Rica)*** **and** ***Certain Activities carried out by Nicaragua in the Border Area (Costa Rica v Nicaragua), Merits, ICJ Reports 2015*, p 665**

These joined cases (unusual in the Court's practice) concerned proceedings in which both States contended that the other had been causing transboundary harm to its territory through their respective projects, with Nicaragua dredging the San Juan River and Costa Rica carrying out road construction works. Though the case also concerned claims about violations of sovereignty, there is particular interest in the allegations of Costa Rica that Nicaragua had violated international environmental obligations in connection with its dredging activities. Despite not having suffered material injury, Costa Rica had claimed that Nicaragua had failed to exercise due diligence because it had not conducted any environmental impact assessment, thus creating a risk of potentially adverse impacts resulting from its activities.

The Court accepted Costa Rica's submission that, in principle, no actual transboundary harm need occur for there to be a breach of an international legal obligation. However, upon examination of the evidence, the Court rejected Costa Rica's submissions on the facts, determining that the dredging programme planned by Nicaragua did not give rise to a risk of significant transboundary harm (para 111); and that, moreover, Costa Rica had not provided any convincing evidence of significant harm (para 120).

[80] See ARSIWA (n 3), Commentary to Art 2, 36, para 10; and Crawford (n 4) 99, 113–14.

[81] *Pulp Mills on the River Uruguay (Argentina v Uruguay), Judgment, ICJ Reports 2010*, p 14, 82–3.

[82] *Corfu Channel* (n 1) 35–6; *Pulp Mills on the River Uruguay* (n 80) 102.

The Court's judgment in the joined cases helps to confirm the notion that a breach of an international obligation might be committed, irrespective of whether material harm or injury was sustained by the complaining party. Moreover, it draws significantly on the 2010 *Pulp Mills on the River Uruguay* judgment, which illustrates the complexities raised by the assessment of scientific evidence when international courts address transboundary pollution cases. Because scientific evidence cannot always support legal claims dependent on concepts like attribution and causation, these cases are perhaps illustrative of the challenges faced by lawyers in arguing responsibility for transboundary pollution.

Chapter 19, on international environmental law, further addresses the challenges inherent in legal regulation of environmental protection.

10.3 Circumstances precluding wrongfulness

International law also provides for what are termed *circumstances precluding wrongfulness*, through which an act which would normally be internationally wrongful is not deemed as such. In such situations, international responsibility is not engaged. These are akin to defences or excuses in municipal legal orders.[83] The ILC, in Chapter V of the ARSIWA, has enumerated those circumstances precluding wrongfulness which have been recognized in customary international law.

Before turning to each category, three general points are pertinent. First, a circumstance precluding wrongfulness is a justification for specific conduct in a defined situation. It does not create an exception to the relevant international obligation, which continues to apply. Second, as will be detailed later, a State or international organization cannot invoke any circumstance precluding wrongfulness to justify the violation of a peremptory norm.[84] As memorably illustrated by the ICJ, in no case can a genocide justify a counter-genocide.[85] Third, if a circumstance precluding wrongfulness comes to an end, the State invoking such a circumstance loses its justification for its own wrongful conduct. If it does not terminate such conduct, its own responsibility may be engaged.

10.3.1 **Consent**

A State may consent validly that another State act in a manner which, but for that consent, would have been internationally wrongful.[86] A State may allow another State to use its airspace or to intervene militarily on its territory; for example, to suppress an insurgency. A recent example of this is when Iraq consented to US and UK intervention

[83] A leading contribution in this area is F Paddeu, *Justification and Excuse in International Law: Concept and Theory of General Defences* (CUP, 2018).

[84] ARSIWA (n 3) Art 26; ARIO (n 9) Art 26; see also ILC, 'Peremptory Norms of General International Law (*Jus Cogens*): Text of the Draft Conclusions and Draft Annex Provisionally Adopted by the Drafting Committee on First Reading', UN Doc CN.4/727 (2019), Draft Conclusion 18.

[85] *Application of the Genocide Convention* (n 20), *Counter-claims, Order of 17 December 1997, ICJ Reports 1997*, p 243, 258, para 35.

[86] ARSIWA (n 3) Art 20; see also ARIO (n 9) Art 20.

against ISIS/*Daesh*, acting on its territory in 2014.[87] Consent is nevertheless not unlimited. For example, an act which exceeds the limits of the consent given cannot be justified through reference to that original act of consent. What is more, consent is to be construed strictly, as did the ICJ when examining the scope and extent of the consent given by the Democratic Republic of the Congo to the presence of Ugandan troops on its territory.[88] Moreover, as discussed earlier, consent cannot excuse peremptory norms: a State cannot authorize another State to conduct torture or genocide, as such consent cannot be 'valid'.[89] Finally, if the obligation is owed to more than one party, consent only precludes the wrongfulness of conduct with respect to a consenting party, and cannot justify the breach of an international obligation vis-à-vis non-consenting parties.[90]

10.3.2 **Self-defence**

Article 21 ARSIWA recognizes that the invocation of self-defence allows a State to justify conduct which would otherwise be unlawful. A State may even use force against another State in self-defence, an 'inherent' right recognized under Article 51 of the United Nations Charter. Nonetheless, it is widely understood that such force must comply with the requirements of necessity and proportionality in order to remain within the limits of self-defence.[91]

In the Commentary to Article 21 ARSIWA, the ILC pointed out that a mere assertion that an act is taken in self-defence does not suffice to preclude wrongfulness. This is true especially in relation to certain provisions of international humanitarian law and human rights obligations, which have been qualified as 'intransgressible principles of international customary law' by the ICJ.[92]

10.3.3 **Countermeasures**

Article 22 ARSIWA provides that a 'countermeasure' taken validly will preclude the wrongfulness of an act which would otherwise be unlawful. As further analysed in Chapter 13, 'countermeasures' are non-forcible acts which would ordinarily be wrongful, but which are justified as a 'valid means of self-help' in response to the internationally wrongful act of another.

[87] HC Deb 26 September 2014 (UK), vol 585, col 1255. See Chapter 14, Section 14.3.5.

[88] *Armed Activities in the Territory of the Congo* (n 24) para 53.

[89] See ARSIWA (n 3), Commentary to Art 20, 73, para 4, and Commentary to Art 26. Coercion is another ground for consent to be invalidated: the ILC Commentary refers to the infamous 1938 *Anschluss* through which Austria was absorbed into Nazi Germany.

[90] In *Customs Régime between Germany and Austria, Advisory Opinion, 1931, PCIJ, Ser A/B, No 41*, p 37.

[91] *Nicaragua (Merits)* (n 29) 103, para 194; see also Chapter 14, Section 14.3.2. See generally F Paddeu, 'Self-Defence as a Circumstance Precluding Wrongfulness: Understanding Article 21 of the Articles on State Responsibility' (2015) 85 BYBIL 90.

[92] See ARSIWA (n 3), Commentary to Art 21, 74, paras 3–4, referring to the ICJ's *Legality of the Threat or Use of Nuclear Weapons, Advisory Opinion, ICJ Reports 1996*, p 226, 257, para 79. At 242, the ICJ noted that respect for the environment is also one of the elements which is relevant in assessing whether an action is necessary and proportionate.

International law imposes a number of procedural and substantive conditions in order for an act to be categorized as a countermeasure:

- it must be taken in response to a previous wrongful act of another State directed against the injured State;
- the injured State must have called upon the wrongdoing State to cease its wrongful conduct or to make reparation;
- the countermeasure must be commensurate or proportional to the injury suffered;
- it should be reversible, as its purpose must only be to induce the wrongdoing State to comply with its obligations under international law; and
- it should be terminated as soon as the wrongdoing State resumes compliance.[93]

10.3.4 *Force majeure*

Force majeure has long referred to situations where the State is powerless to act due to the occurrence of an irresistible force or unforeseen event, wholly beyond its control, and which makes it materially impossible to fulfil its obligation.[94] Examples include physical events such as earthquakes, floods or drought, or human factors such as a State carrying out devastating military operations on another State's territory.[95] The emphasis is on the fact that the State had no choice, and could not have resisted the event or escaped the breach.[96]

As such, the threshold for *force majeure* to apply is very high. Even when acknowledging the doctrine, most international tribunals have dismissed assertions of *force majeure* in circumstances where the obligation was merely burdensome, but not materially impossible.[97] What is more, *force majeure* can neither be invoked in situations where the State has caused or induced the situation in question,[98] nor in situations where the State has, through its actions, accepted the risk of the occurrence of an event, for example by failing to take precautionary measures against a foreseeable situation.[99]

[93] *Ibid*, 55–7; these are in large part embodied in the ARSIWA (n 3) Arts 49–53.

[94] ARSIWA (n 3) Art 23. [95] See *ibid*, Commentary to Art 23, para 3.

[96] The ILC commissioned a survey of State practice, international judicial decisions, and doctrine in relation to *force majeure*: see Study prepared by the Secretariat (1978) ILC Ybk vol II, pt 1, para 61, UN Doc A/CN.4/315. A more recent contribution to understanding the concept is that of F Paddeu, 'A Genealogy of Force Majeure in International Law' (2011) 82 BYBIL 381.

[97] See, e.g., *Affaire relative à la concession des phares de l'Empire ottoman* ('*Lighthouses Arbitration*') (1956) XII UNRIAA 155, 219–20; *Russian Indemnity* (1912) XI UNRIAA 421, 443; *Serbian Loans (France v Serbia), Judgment, 1929, PCIJ, Ser A, No 20*, p 39; *Brazilian Loans (France v Brazil), Judgment, 1929, PCIJ, Ser A, No 21*, p 120; *Rainbow Warrior* (n 5) 252–3. But *cf* the earlier *Gill* case (1931) 5 RIAA 159, where Mexico successfully invoked *force majeure* in relation to the sudden and unforeseen acts of insurrectionists, which had led to the destruction of the home of a British national residing in Mexico.

[98] ARSIWA (n 3), Commentary to Art 23, para 9; see also *Libyan Arab Foreign Investment Company and the Republic of Burundi* (1994) 96 ILR 318, para 55.

[99] *Ibid*, para 10. For further reading, see F Paddeu, 'A Genealogy of *Force Majeure* in International Law' (2012) 82 BYIL 381.

10.3.5 **Distress**

Situations of 'distress' refer only to situations where the author of an act had no other way to save their own life or the lives of other persons entrusted to the author's care.[100] Examples include when US military aircraft entered Yugoslav airspace in 1946 in order to escape an extreme threat of mechanical and navigational failure to the plane and its occupants,[101] or when in 1975 British naval vessels entered the territorial waters of Iceland to seek shelter from severe weather.[102] As the *Rainbow Warrior* arbitration further illustrates, the invocation of distress is limited strictly to the protection of human life.[103]

CASE SPOTLIGHT ***Rainbow Warrior (New Zealand/France)*** **(1990) 20 RIAA 217**

The *Rainbow Warrior* case concerned the sinking of the splendidly named Greenpeace vessel *Rainbow Warrior*, which had been protesting against French nuclear testing in the South Pacific. On 10 July 1985, acting under the orders of the Directorate General of External Security, two French operatives (Major Mafart and Captain Prieur) caused the ship to explode, killing a dual Dutch–Portuguese national, Fernando Pereira. New Zealand apprehended the operatives, who were sentenced to ten years' imprisonment. The pair were later transferred to Hao, an atoll in French Polynesia, pursuant to a diplomatic settlement that neither could leave Hao except with the mutual consent of both parties.

While the dispute concerning the sinking of the vessel had been settled by the UN Secretary-General in a ruling of 6 July 1986, an arbitration arose due to the fact that both Major Mafart and Captain Prieur were evacuated from Hao without New Zealand's consent. France sought to invoke circumstances requiring the wrongfulness of its conduct, including necessity, distress, and *force majeure*. In respect of distress, it contended that there existed 'a case of extreme urgency involving elementary humanitarian considerations' to justify the removal of the two officers, referring to Major Mafart's ill health and Captain Prieur having fallen pregnant.

Though the tribunal accepted the admissibility of France's contentions, it rejected them for failing to meet three required conditions: the existence of exceptional circumstances of extreme urgency of a medical or humanitarian nature; the re-establishment of the original situation as soon as the emergency had come to an end; and all good faith efforts to obtain the consent of the other party (para 79). The tribunal also distinguished these from the grounds for suspending or terminating treaty obligations, thus clarifying a major point of doctrinal controversy.

Rainbow Warrior is also significant for addressing important points relating to reparation. It is often cited as a seminal example of how reparation can take the form of financial compensation but also 'satisfaction', either through the form of a non-pecuniary apology or expression of regret by the breaching party, or through a declaratory judgment of wrongfulness by a third party. The various forms of reparation are addressed later, in Section 10.5.

[100] ARSIWA (n 3) Art 24. [101] See *ibid*, Commentary to Art 24, para 2.

[102] Though Iceland did not contest the principle, it asserted that British vessels had entered its waters for the sole purpose of provoking an incident: see ARSIWA (n 3), Commentary to Art 24, 79, para 3; and UNSC Verbatim Record (16 December 1975), UN Doc S/PV.1866, para 24.

[103] ARSIWA (n 3), Commentary to Art 24, para 6.

10.3.6 **Necessity**

Necessity is a broader plea than distress, encompassing conduct which is 'the only means for [a] State to safeguard an essential interest against a grave and imminent peril'.[104] Given the highly subjective criterion of defining an 'essential interest', and the obvious potential for misuse, the ILC has subjected the plea of necessity to a stringent set of conditions:

- the conduct must be the *only* means available to the State;
- the plea cannot seriously impair an essential interest of other States or the international community as a whole;
- the relevant obligation cannot exclude a plea of necessity; and
- the State invoking necessity cannot have contributed to the situation.[105]

In the ARIO, the ILC was even more exacting, and prohibited an international organization from invoking necessity in relation to its own interests. Instead, an international organization may only invoke necessity in relation to a grave and imminent peril to the essential interests of its member States, or of the international community as a whole.[106]

The canonical example of a plea of necessity remains the 1837 *Caroline* incident, where British armed forces entered US territory and attacked and destroyed the *Caroline*, a naval vessel, claiming it to be a necessary attack in self-defence.[107] The British–American correspondence in *Caroline*, further discussed under the law on self-defence in Chapter 14, Section 14.3.1, has occasionally been taken as reflecting customary law,[108] but as the ILC rightly noted, it took place at a time when the law concerning the use of force 'had a quite different basis than it has at present'.[109] In response to US protests, the British government raised the necessity of self-defence and self-preservation, to which the USA replied that any such conduct had to result from 'a necessity of self-defence, instant, overwhelming, leaving no choice of means, and no moment for deliberation'.[110]

Though accepted as a rule of customary international law, the invocation of necessity has not fared well in most international courts or tribunals, being unsuccessful in the *Russian Indemnity* arbitration,[111] the *Société commerciale de Belgique* judgment,[112]

[104] *Ibid*, Art 25(1)(a).

[105] Many of these are reflected in the ICJ's judgment *Gabčíkovo-Nagymaros* (n 6) 40–1, paras 51–2, which in turn relied upon the draft of what became ARSIWA (n 3) Art 25.

[106] ARIO (n 9) Art 25(1)(a). See, e.g., an organization accessing a confidential email account of an employee when 'necessary for reasons of urgency or because of the prolonged absence of the account holder', *T.O.R.N. v CERN* Case No 2183 (ILO Administrative Tribunal, 3 February 2003).

[107] See ARSIWA (n 3), Commentary to Art 25, para 5, citing diplomatic correspondence between the two States.

[108] MN Schmitt, '"Change in Direction" 2006: Israeli Operation in Lebanon and the International Law of Self-Defense' (2008) 29 Mich JIL 127, 145–6.

[109] ARSIWA (n 3), Commentary to Art 25, para 5.

[110] See *British and Foreign State Papers, 1840–1841* (Ridgway, 1857) vol 29, 1129.

[111] *Russian Indemnity* (n 96) para 6.

[112] *Société commerciale de Belgique (Belgium v Greece), Judgment, 1939, PCIJ, Ser A/B, No 78*, p 160.

Rainbow Warrior,[113] *Gabčíkovo-Nagymaros*,[114] and *M/V Saiga (No 2)*.[115] However, the *Torrey Canyon* incident may reflect a successful invocation of necessity.[116] In that situation, a Liberian oil tanker went aground off British territorial waters, leading the UK to sink the vessel in order to prevent the further spillage of oil and the destruction of its marine environment. The UK justified its conduct by emphasizing the situation of extreme danger, and that the decision to bomb the ship took place only after all other means had been exhausted.[117]

More recently, after the 1999–2002 Argentine financial crisis, Argentina raised a plea of necessity before several investment tribunals in order to justify a series of measures. The majority of tribunals rejected the plea, usually on the basis that no essential interest was faced with a grave and imminent peril, that Argentina had other lawful means at its disposal, or that Argentina had itself contributed to the situation.[118] However, in *LG&E Energy Corp v Argentina*, the tribunal did uphold Argentina's plea, while affirming that 'necessity should be only strictly exceptional and should be applied exclusively when faced with extraordinary circumstances'.[119]

The serious, unforeseen, and extraordinary onset of the Covid-19 pandemic has disrupted global supply chains, civil aviation, and non-discrimination in travel, and even freedoms such as those of assembly, protest, and movement. Though no international State practice has yet brought a State to invoke the Covid-19 pandemic as a circumstance precluding wrongfulness—whether necessity or a cognate defence such as *force majeure*, or more plausibly, distress—there is nothing to suggest that the existing law may not be applicable, raising interesting legal questions for future reflection.[120]

THEORY AND DEBATES The Cross-cutting Nature of Necessity and Proportionality

Necessity and proportionality are cross-cutting concepts through much of international law. As can be seen in the earlier example, necessity can exist as a condition for self-defence to be validly invoked; it can also constitute a circumstance precluding wrongfulness; and there exists a cognate concept of 'military necessity' in the law of armed conflict. Though they are named similarly, they are not at all the same, as they correspond to different concepts of what

[113] *Rainbow Warrior* (n 5) 254, where the very existence of the defence of necessity was challenged.

[114] *Gabčíkovo-Nagymaros* (n 6) 40–1, paras 51–2.

[115] (1999) 120 ILR 143 (ITLOS).

[116] See ARSIWA (n 3), Commentary to Art 25, para 9.

[117] See Home Office, *The 'Torrey Canyon'* (Cmnd 3246, 1967).

[118] See, e.g., *CMS Gas Transmission Company v Argentine Republic* Case No ARB/01/8 (ICSID, 12 May 2005; see also Decision on Annulment of 25 September 2007); *Enron Corporation and Ponderosa Assets LP v Argentine Republic* Case No ARB/01/3 (ICSID, 22 May 2007); *Sempra Energy International v Argentine Republic* Case No ARB/02/16 (ICSID, 28 September 2007); *BG Group plc v Republic of Argentina (Final Award)* (UNCITRAL, 24 December 2007).

[119] *LG&E International Inc v Argentine Republic* Case No ARB/02/1 (ICSID, 3 November 2006); (2007) 46 ILM 40, 228. On the Argentine financial crisis more generally, see M Paparinskis, 'Circumstances Precluding Wrongfulness in International Investment Law' (2016) 31 ICSID Rev 484.

[120] For further reflections on this point, see M Paparinskis, 'COVID-19 Claims and the Law of International Responsibility' (2020) 11 Journal of International Humanitarian Legal Studies 311.

is 'necessary', covered further in Section 10.3.6. Proportionality is a similarly open-textured concept, applying throughout international law but requiring different assessments depending on where it is used. Within the law of armed conflict, proportionality is assessed in relation to military objectives; in WTO (trade) law, proportionality is a criterion for assessing the validity of a countermeasure; within international environmental law it imposes a balancing test in relation to obligations of precaution and prevention; and in the law of self-defence, it is assessed in relation to the force necessary to repel an attack (and not merely tit-for-tat). These are intertwined notions which require careful, case-by-case study, and not the imposition of uniform rules.

There is little extensive reading on necessity and proportionality which raises the wider cross-cutting issues, but see Y Shany, 'Towards a General Margin of Appreciation Doctrine' (2006) 16 EJIL 907; T Franck, 'On Proportionality of Countermeasures in International Law' (2008) 102 AJIL 715; and D Akande and T Liefländer, 'Clarifying Necessity, Imminence and Proportionality in the Law of Self-Defense' (2013) 107 AJIL 563.

10.4 **Invocation of international responsibility**

10.4.1 **General considerations**

International responsibility does not exist in a void; in order to be made operative, another actor must be able to invoke that responsibility. Historically, only a State which had suffered a direct injury could invoke the responsibility of the wrongdoing State.[121] In the *Reparations* advisory opinion, the ICJ broadened the principle to also encompass an international organization which had suffered direct injury.[122] These rules are set out in Article 42(a) ARSIWA and Article 43(a) ARIO. It should be noted that *lit.* b(i) of both articles also recognizes the right of a 'specially affected' party to claim in relation to collective obligations; that is, an obligation owed to a group of States or the international community as a whole.[123] For the ILC, an example of a 'specially affected' State was a coastal State which suffered particular adverse impacts from a breach of Article 194 UNCLOS, binding all States parties to take measures to preserve the marine environment. Though the obligation may be owed to all States parties to UNCLOS, those coastal States would be specially affected by any breach.[124]

International law makes no distinction between a State that has suffered direct injury and one that is specially affected: both are 'injured States' which are entitled to invoke responsibility and to demand any means of redress contemplated in international law; in particular, those covered later in Section 10.5.

[121] *Mavrommatis Palestine Concessions (Greece/United Kingdom), Judgment No 2, 1924, PCIJ, Ser A, No 2*, p 12.

[122] *Reparation for Injuries Suffered in the Service of the United Nations, Advisory Opinion, ICJ Reports 1949*, p 174, 181–2.

[123] The ILC explained, in ARSIWA (n 3), Commentary to Art 42, 119, para 12, that the term 'specially affected' is taken from Art 60(2) VCLT.

[124] *Ibid*. UNCLOS is considered in Chapter 18.

10.4.2 **Invocation of responsibility by non-injured parties**

An increasing number of multilateral agreements purport to protect wider collective interests such as fundamental human rights, the environment, outer space, and the management of the high seas. The question arises whether there are circumstances in which a party that has neither suffered direct injury nor is specially affected may nevertheless invoke international responsibility. Before turning to the relevant provision of the ARSIWA, Article 48, a brief detour into some ICJ judgments may help to understand the interest of a non-injured party. The starting point is the Court's judgment in *South West Africa (Second Phase)*, in which Ethiopia and Liberia had justified their *locus standi* by claiming an *actio popularis* (a Roman law concept through which any member of a community has the right to bring legal action in vindication of a public interest) against South Africa in relation to the imposition of apartheid in South West Africa. The Court rejected the plea of *actio popularis* as inexistent in international law.[125] It took pains to note that, though 'States may have a legal interest in vindicating a principle of international law, even though they have . . . suffered no material prejudice . . . such rights or interests, in order to exist, must be clearly vested in those who claim them, by some text or instrument, or rule of law.'[126]

A shift came scarcely four years later with the *Barcelona Traction* judgment. The Court pointedly raised a distinction between obligations of a purely bilateral nature and 'obligations of a State towards the international community as a whole', which, '[by] their very nature . . . are the concern of all States. In view of the importance of the rights involved, all States can be held to have a legal interest in their protection; they are obligations *erga omnes*.'[127] These passages became the subject of much academic debate, though in practice had little effect.[128] For example, in *Nuclear Tests*, the ICJ determined that the dispute had become moot and that, subsequently, it needed not pronounce itself on the *erga omnes* nature of Australia's claim against France with respect to the latter conducting nuclear tests in the South Pacific.[129] In *East Timor*, despite recognizing the *erga omnes* character of the right to self-determination, the Court nevertheless dismissed the application of Portugal against Australia, on the basis that to do so would be to adjudge on the lawfulness of the conduct of Indonesia, which had occupied East Timor since 1974 and which had not consented to the Court's jurisdiction. In the Court's opinion, 'the *erga omnes* character of a norm and the rule of consent to jurisdiction are two different things.'[130]

[125] *South West Africa (Ethiopia v South Africa; Liberia v South Africa), Second Phase, Judgment, ICJ Reports 1966*, p 6, 47. [126] *Ibid*, 31.

[127] *Barcelona Traction Heat, Light and Power Company (Belgium v Spain), Second Phase, Judgment, ICJ Reports 1970*, p 3, 32. Obligations *erga omnes* were considered in depth in Chapter 3, Section 3.4.

[128] P Dupuy, 'Action publique et crime international de l'Etat' (1979) 25 AFDI 539; FA Mann, 'The Doctrine of *Jus Cogens* in International Law' in H Ehmke and others (eds), *Festschrift für Ulrich Scheuner* (Duncker & Humblot, 1973); R Higgins, 'Aspects of the Case Concerning the Barcelona Traction, Light and Power Company, Ltd' (1971) 11 Va JIL 327.

[129] See *Nuclear Tests (Australia v France; New Zealand v France), Jurisdiction and Admissibility, ICJ Reports 1974*, p 253.

[130] *East Timor (Portugal v Australia), Jurisdiction, ICJ Reports 1995*, p 90, 102.

It was in light of this equivocal case law that the ILC proposed Article 48 ARSIWA, which proposed the conditions for which a State other than an injured State would be entitled to invoke responsibility for a breach.[131] First, the *locus standi* of a State which is not an injured State is limited to the breach of either: (i) an obligation owed to a group of States established for the protection of a collective interest of the group; or (ii) an obligation owed to the international community as a whole.[132] Secondly, the remedies available to a State other than an injured State are more limited. It may claim only for cessation of the wrongful act, which includes assurances and guarantees of non-repetition, or for reparation to be accorded, but only in the interest of the injured party.[133]

In 2001, the text of Article 48 ARSIWA represented a marked example of progressive development by the ILC. However, in two recent cases it has been upheld as customary international law in relation to obligations *erga omnes partes*, or those obligations arising between parties to a treaty. In the 2012 *Obligation to Prosecute or Extradite* judgment, Belgium had filed proceedings both as a specially affected State and a non-injured State in relation to the extradition or prosecution of Mr Hissène Habré, former president of Chad, who had sought refuge in Senegal. In relation to Belgium's *locus standi*, though not expressly referring to the ARSIWA, the ICJ endorsed the approach taken in Article 48(1)(b) in relation to a dispute arising under the Convention against Torture, which is an archetypal multilateral treaty establishing multilateral obligations in the collective interest:

> The States parties to the Convention have a common interest to ensure, in view of their shared values, that acts of torture are prevented and that, if they occur, their authors do not enjoy impunity . . . That common interest implies that the obligations in question are owed by any State party to all the other States parties to the Convention. All the States parties 'have a legal interest' in the protection of the rights involved . . . These obligations may be defined as 'obligations *erga omnes partes*' in the sense that each State party has an interest in compliance with them in any given case.[134]

The following year, in the *Whaling in the Antarctic* dispute, Australia filed proceedings before the ICJ against Japan, for violating provisions of the ICRW[135] in relation to the prohibition on the killing of whales for purposes not related to scientific research.[136] In order to deny the Court jurisdiction, Japan invoked Australia's reservation in relation to disputes relating to the delimitation of maritime zones. The Court noted that:

> it is significant that Australia alleges that Japan has breached certain obligations under the ICRW and [not] because the whaling activities envisaged in the programme take place in the maritime zones over which Australia asserts sovereign rights or in adjacent areas.

[131] These are transposed, *mutatis mutandis*, into ARIO (n 9) Art 49.

[132] ARSIWA (n 3) Art 48(1)(a)–(b).

[133] *Ibid*, Art 48(2)(a)–(b). See later, Section 10.5, for a discussion of available remedies.

[134] *Questions relating to the Obligation to Prosecute or Extradite (Belgium v Senegal), Judgment, ICJ Reports 2012*, p 422, para 68. At para 70, the Court pointedly declined to adjudicate on Belgium's claim that it was a 'specially affected State' falling within Art 42 ARSIWA.

[135] International Convention for the Regulation of Whaling (signed 2 December 1946, entry into force 10 November 1948), 161 UNTS 72.

[136] *Whaling in the Antarctic (Australia v Japan), Judgment, ICJ Reports 2014*, p 226.

> The nature and extent of the claimed maritime zones are therefore immaterial to the present dispute, which is about whether or not Japan's activities are compatible with its obligations under the ICRW.[137]

It merits mentioning that the ICRW preamble sets out the common interest of all parties 'to provide for the proper conservation of whale stocks and thus to make possible the orderly development of the whaling industry'. In this respect, though it is true that Japan did not object on the ground of admissibility, the standing of a non-injured State to invoke obligations *erga omnes partes*, at least, seems now to be a settled part of international law.[138]

10.5 The consequences of an internationally wrongful act

The point of legal responsibility is to help to determine the legal situation that exists between parties, and whether an aggrieved party is entitled to respond in some form. Put differently, if a party believes that another has breached an international obligation, how can it somehow restore the situation which was impaired or threatened through the breach? In Part Two of the ARSIWA (and of the ARIO), the ILC sought to enumerate the remedies available to an aggrieved party in response to a breach of an obligation by another. These are divided between measures broadly related to *cessation*, or the basic obligation to stop the unlawful situation, and those within the category of *reparation*, which refers to all measures which may be taken in order to wipe out the consequences of breach, over and above cessation.

10.5.1 Cessation

An obligation of cessation requires a wrongdoing party to cease a wrongful act and, when appropriate, to offer appropriate assurances and guarantees of non-repetition.[139] Such measures exist in order to safeguard the future relationship between parties, as well as further obligations binding between them. In the *Rainbow Warrior* arbitration, the tribunal explained that cessation only applies if the act was of a continuing character, and if the violated rule is still in force at the time of judgment.[140] In the *LaGrand* case, the USA had failed to notify Germany concerning two German nationals facing execution, and thus had breached the 1961 Vienna Convention on Consular Relations (VCCR). The Court considered that Germany's request for general assurances of non-repetition was fulfilled through a US commitment to implement a programme to ensure compliance with the VCCR,[141] and declined Germany's request for further, specific assurances as unnecessary.[142]

137 *Ibid*, para 40.

138 For a more radical argument, see S Thin, *Beyond Bilateralism: A Theory of State Responsibility for Breaches of Non-Bilateral Obligations* (Edward Elgar, 2024).

139 ARSIWA (n 3) Art 30.

140 *Rainbow Warrior* (n 5) 264; see also ARSIWA (n 3), Commentary to Art 30, 89, para 3.

141 *LaGrand* (n 27) 513.

142 *Ibid*, 514.

10.5.2 **Reparation**

The obligation of a wrongdoing party to make full reparation for any injury caused by a breach is a long-standing principle in international law. Embodied in Article 31 ARSIWA, it reflects the classic statement of the PCIJ in *Factory at Chorzów*: 'Reparation must, as far as possible, wipe out all the consequences of the illegal act and re-establish the situation which would, in all probability, have existed if the act had not been committed.'[143] The ICJ has referred to this principle repeatedly, for example in *Gabčíkovo-Nagymaros*,[144] *LaGrand*,[145] and *Application of the Genocide Convention (Bosnia)*.[146] The notion of 'injury' refers to material or moral harm or damage caused by the wrongful act, which means that non-material interests or acts affecting the honour, dignity, or prestige of a State entitle a victim State to claim reparation, even if those acts have not resulted in pecuniary or material loss.[147]

Article 34 ARSIWA sets out the recognized forms of reparation in international law: restitution, compensation, and satisfaction. Each will be discussed in turn.

10.5.2.1 ***Restitutio in integrum* (Article 35 ARSIWA)**

Restitutio in integrum ('full restoration in kind') is perhaps the most obvious method of securing reparation, as it literally involves the re-establishment of the pre-existing situation. As the PCIJ stated in *Factory at Chorzów*, only when restitution is not possible does one turn to possible financial payment.[148] In Article 35(a) ARSIWA, the ILC suggested that restitution is not necessary if it is 'materially impossible'; for example, if the property or object claimed has been permanently lost or destroyed.

Restitution seems best suited to certain types of claims, such as the return of unlawfully seized objects or territory[149] or the release of persons.[150] It can also involve so-called 'juridical restitution', where offending legislation is annulled, revoked, or amended in an attempt to restore the antecedent legal framework.[151]

10.5.2.2 **Compensation (Article 36 ARSIWA)**

Though it seems sensible first to seek to restore the *status quo ante* through restitution, there are many circumstances in which restoration would be materially impossible, politically sensitive, or otherwise impracticable.[152] In such cases, it is 'a well-established

[143] *Factory at Chorzów* (n 1) 47–8; see further FE Torres, 'Revisiting the *Chorzów Factory* Standard of Reparation – Its Relevance in Contemporary International Law and Practice' (2021) 90 Nordic Journal of International Law 190.

[144] *Gabčíkovo-Nagymaros* (n 6) 80.

[145] *LaGrand* (n 27) 485.

[146] *Application of the Genocide Convention* (n 20) 232.

[147] *Rainbow Warrior* (n 5) 266–7.

[148] *Factory at Chorzów* (n 1) 47; see also *Spanish Zone of Morocco* (n 1) 621–5, 651–742; *Enron v Argentina* (n 117) para 359; *Sempra v Argentina* (n 117) para 401.

[149] See, e.g., *Temple of Preah Vihear (Cambodia v Thailand), Judgment, ICJ Reports 1962*, p 6, 36–7.

[150] See *Tehran Hostages* (n 59) 44–5.

[151] See, e.g., *Arrest Warrant of 11 April 2000 (Democratic Republic of the Congo v Belgium), Judgment, ICJ Reports 2002*, p 3, 33, where Belgium was ordered to cancel its unlawful arrest warrant; *cf Avena* (n 27), where Mexico's request, for an order to annul the death sentences passed without consular notification or assistance, was rejected.

[152] See, e.g., *Government of Kuwait v American Independent Oil Company (Aminoil)* (1982) 66 ILR 519, 533; *Texaco arbitration* (1978) 17 ILM 1; *Liamco case* (1981) 20 ILM 1, 63–4.

rule of international law that an injured State is entitled to obtain compensation from the State which has committed an internationally wrongful act for the damage caused by it'.[153] Claims for compensation are in practice the most common; they aim to offset or reverse material losses which have been sustained as a result of the breach.[154] These losses may have been suffered by the State itself, for example to its property or its personnel, or by its nationals, on whose behalf the State is exercising diplomatic protection.[155] Under international law, it bears noting that compensation is not punitive, and the ILC Commentary pointed out that exemplary or 'moral' damages do not fall under the category of compensation but, rather, satisfaction.[156]

The quantification of financially assessable damage is often complex and is frequently addressed on a case-by-case basis,[157] with examples from judicial and arbitral practice. As a matter of valuation, compensation for seized or destroyed property may be assessed on the basis of the 'fair market value' of that property.[158] In certain situations, compensation for loss of profits (*lucrum cessans*) can also be awarded.[159] In its 2022 judgment on compensation in the *Armed Activities in the Congo* case between the DRC and Uganda, the Court adopted an avowedly broad-brush approach as it dealt with sensitive questions relating to how to calculate compensation for the value of the loss of lives sustained during a devastating armed conflict.[160]

10.5.2.3 **Satisfaction (Article 37 ARSIWA)**

Reparation sometimes has a highly symbolic or political element, beyond restitution or compensation. The concept of 'satisfaction' in Article 37(2) ARSIWA encompasses such forms of non-material vindication for injury, for example against the violation of a State's airspace, when State representatives or its symbols have been insulted, or when diplomatic inviolability has been breached.[161]

Satisfaction can take a wide range of forms, including acknowledgement that a breach was committed, which can also be effected through a declaratory judgment of a court or tribunal;[162] or an official apology or expression of regret on the part of the wrongdoing

[153] *Gabčíkovo-Nagymaros* (n 6) 81. ARSIWA (n 3) Art 36 adds that such compensation might include 'loss of future profits'.

[154] *Factory at Chorzów* (n 1) 47.

[155] See ARSIWA (n 3), Commentary to Art 36, para 5.

[156] *Ibid*, Commentary to Art 36, para 1.

[157] J Crawford, *Brownlie's Principles of Public International Law* (8th edn OUP, 2012), 572.

[158] See cases listed in ARSIWA (n 3), Commentary to Art 36, para 22; and *CMS v Argentina* Case no ARB/01/08 (ICSID, 12 May 2005) para 402.

[159] See cases listed under ARSIWA (n 3), Commentary to Art 36, para 27; and the more recent *Certain Activities Carried out in the Border Area (Costa Rica v Nicaragua), Judgment on Compensation, ICJ Reports 2018*, p 15; *Ahmadou Sadio Diallo (Republic of Guinea v Democratic Republic of the Congo), Judgment on Compensation, ICJ Reports 2012*, p 324; and *Arctic Sunrise Arbitration (the Netherlands v Russia) (Annex VII Tribunal), Award on Compensation of 10 July 2017*, PCA Case No 2014-02.

[160] *Armed Activities in the Territory of the Congo (Democratic Republic of the Congo v Uganda), Reparations, Judgment, ICJ Reports 2022*, p 13.

[161] For a recent example, see the 2015 judgment in *Certain Activities carried out in the Border Area* (n 157) para 229, where the ICJ declared Costa Rica's sovereignty to have been violated by a Nicaraguan military incursion on its territory, that had already been withdrawn.

[162] See, e.g., *Corfu Channel* (n 1) 35–6; *Application of the Genocide Convention* (n 20) 239; *Pulp Mills on the River Uruguay* (n 80) 102, 106; *Armed Activities in the Congo (Reparations)* (n 158) paras 388–9.

party.[163] In all cases, satisfaction must remain proportionate to the non-material injury suffered and should not be regarded as 'humiliating' to the responsible State.[164]

10.5.3 **Serious breaches of peremptory norms (aggravated responsibility)**

A residual question relating to international responsibility concerns whether there can be differentiated treatment of wrongdoers, which would highlight the *consequences* flowing from a 'serious breach' of an peremptory norm of *jus cogens*.

'Seriousness' is defined in Article 40(2) ARSIWA as a 'gross or systematic failure by the responsible State' to fulfil such obligations. Article 41 ARSIWA sets out a number of consequences for a serious breach of a peremptory norm. States are under a duty to cooperate, through lawful means, to bring such breaches to an end. In addition, they are under a duty not to recognize as lawful situations created by a serious breach of a peremptory norm, and under a duty to refrain from rendering aid or assistance in maintaining that situation. The ILC restated these in its 2019 Provisional Draft Conclusion 19.[165]

On such serious breaches of peremptory norms, it is useful to study carefully the recent advisory opinion on *Policies and Practices of Israel in the Occupied Palestinian Territory*.[166] There, the ICJ observed that the obligations violated by Israel, primarily those relating to self-determination, the prohibition of the use of force to acquire territory, and certain obligations of international humanitarian law as well as international human rights law, were obligations *erga omnes*.[167] The Court took the view that all UN Member States 'are under an obligation not to recognize any changes in the physical character or demographic composition' of the Occupied Palestinian Territory; and crucially, a peremptory character, it concluded that, 'in view of the character and the importance of the rights and obligations involved, . . . all States are under an obligation not to recognize as legal the situation arising from the unlawful presence of Israel in the Occupied Palestinian Territory[, and] to ensure that any impediment resulting from the illegal presence of Israel [therein] to the exercise of the Palestinian people of its right to self-determination is brought to an end.'[168]

Finally, in the *Jurisdictional Immunities of the State* judgment, the ICJ referred explicitly to Article 41 ARSIWA, and seems to have endorsed it when observing that:

> recognizing the immunity of a foreign State in accordance with customary international law does not amount to recognizing as lawful a situation created by the breach of a *jus cogens* rule, or rendering aid and assistance in maintaining that situation, and so cannot contravene the principle in Article 41.[169]

[163] *Rainbow Warrior* (n 5) 274; *Vienna Convention on Consular Relations (Paraguay v United States of America), Provisional Measures, Order of 9 April 1998, ICJ Reports 1998*, p 248; *LaGrand* (n 27) para 123.

[164] ARSIWA (n 3) Art 37(3).

[165] See ILC, Draft Conclusions on Peremptory Norms (n 83), and Commentary.

[166] *Policies and Practices of Israel in the Occupied Palestinian Territory, including East Jerusalem, Advisory Opinion of 19 July 2024.*

[167] *Ibid*, para 274. At para 233, the Court stated that 'in cases of foreign occupation such as the present case, the right to self-determination constitutes a peremptory norm of international law'.

[168] *Ibid*, para 279. See also *Legal Consequences of the Separation of the Chagos Archipelago from Mauritius in 1965, Advisory Opinion, ICJ Reports 2019*, p 95, para 182.

[169] *Jurisdictional Immunities of the State (Germany v Italy: Greece intervening), Judgment, ICJ Reports 2012*, p 99, 140, para 93.

HISTORICAL BACKGROUND State Crimes and the Famous 'Article 19' of the Draft Articles on State Responsibility (1996)

The law on State responsibility opens the fascinating question as to whether a State can also bear criminal responsibility for its acts. In 1976, efforts led by Special Rapporteur Roberto Ago culminated in the now-infamous Article 19 in the 1996 Draft Articles on State Responsibility, which defined 'the breach of an obligation so essential for the protection of fundamental interests of the international community' as constituting an international crime of State. Such crimes broadly mapped on to violations of peremptory norms such as genocide or acts of aggression.

The notion in Draft Article 19 that a State could be held criminally responsible proved highly controversial, not least within the ILC itself. This was due not only to the punitive element of criminal responsibility but also in raising the question of how to punish a State for the commission of a crime. Special Rapporteur Ago sought to justify the inclusion of Draft Article 19 on three grounds: that *jus cogens* had arisen as a non-derogable set of principles; that international individual criminal responsibility was now fully established; and that the UN Charter contained provisions for enforcement action for a State committing such breaches. Nevertheless, Draft Article 19 elicited strong objections from States given the potential implications of being indicted for a State crime.

In a pragmatic move, the Special Rapporteur James Crawford abandoned the notion of crimes of State, instead proposing a focus, endorsed by the ILC in Article 40 ARSIWA, on the consequences of a 'serious breach by a State of an obligation arising under a peremptory norm of general international law'.

The idea of 'State crimes', after having initially been mooted by the ILC, seems now to be abandoned definitively: in its 2007 judgment in *Application of the Genocide Convention*, the ICJ concluded that the responsibility of a State arising from the violation of peremptory norms is 'not of a criminal nature' (para 170).

10.6 Conclusion

Responsibility remains a crucial area in any legal system, and is of particular interest for international lawyers, not only for practical reasons (many disputes are settled on the basis of its rules) but also for wider scholarly theorizing. The international law on responsibility is an area of constant change and development, and is emblematic of the complex phenomena through which international law develops and changes. Though State responsibility has developed through centuries of gradual iteration, the responsibility of international organizations remains quite unsettled; a crucial concern when international organizations are increasingly asserting themselves as key actors in areas such as peacekeeping or through economic sanctions. What is more, there remain open complex technical questions that relate, *inter alia*, to shared or differentiated responsibility, the possibility of a continuous breach of legal obligations, and the types of remedies that arise. The degree to which law, and legal rules, can assist in resolving the complexities of establishing causation are also unsatisfactory, especially in relation to increasingly complex disputes involving technical or scientific expertise. But there are wider questions, too. What place can there be for collective responsibility, or can responsibility be shared? Should responsibility be proportionate with the gravity of an act; for example, for violating a peremptory norm? Finally, is international law moving away from a bilateralist concept towards some form of community-based framework, where the community can respond collectively to a violation?[170] These, and other wider questions, will continue to drive the development of the law of responsibility within a shifting international legal order.

Further reading

A Cassese, 'The *Nicaragua* and *Tadić* Tests Revisited in Light of the ICJ Judgment on Genocide in Bosnia' (2007) 18 EJIL 649.

Sitting on the ICTY when the *Tadić* judgment was rendered, Cassese challenges the ICJ's finding that *Tadić* did not concern matters of State responsibility.

J Crawford, *State Responsibility: The General Part* (CUP, 2013).

Written by the Special Rapporteur who finalized the ARSIWA, this magisterial guide to case law and practice is an indispensable reference work.

J Crawford, A Pellet, and S Olleson (eds), *The Law of International Responsibility* (OUP, 2010).

This comprehensive edited collection gathers a broad range of perspectives relating to responsibility.

P-M Dupuy, *Obligations multilatérales, droit impératif et responsabilité internationale des États* (Pedone, 2003).

A leading French-language collection with a specific focus on multilateral obligations and peremptory norms.

JA Frowein, 'Reactions by Not Directly Affected States to Breaches of Public International Law' (1994) 248 Recueil des Cours 345.

A key contribution on whether non-affected States may respond to breaches of international legal obligations.

V Gowlland-Debbas, 'Security Council Enforcement Action and Issues of State Responsibility' (1994) 43 ICLQ 55.

Written during the post-Cold War revival of the Security Council, this article raised critical questions about its role in enforcement.

M Koskenniemi, 'Solidarity Measures: State Responsibility as a New International Order?' (2001) 72 BYBIL 337.

Scrutinizes the public order dimensions of key provisions of the ARSIWA and their wider implications.

M Milanović, 'State Responsibility for Genocide' (2006) 17 EJIL 553.

A careful look at the control tests of the ICJ and ICTY.

[170] See B Simma, 'From Bilateralism to Community Interest in International Law' (1994) 250 Recueil des Cours 217, 331.

N NEDESKI, *Shared Obligations in International Law* (CUP, 2022).

The first book-length treatment of the complexities of collective/shared obligations, and their consequences for the law on State responsibility.

A NOLLKAEMPER and I PLAKOKEFALOS (eds), *Principles of Shared Responsibility in International Law* (CUP, 2015).

Part of the wider SHARES Project, this edited volume grapples with questions of joint, corollary, and shared responsibility.

F PADDEU, *Justification and Excuse in International Law: Concept and Theory of General Defences* (CUP, 2018).

A careful examination of the language used by States to justify and excuse their conduct, with practical consequences for the law of international responsibility.

M RAGAZZI (ed), *International Responsibility Today: Essays in Memory of Oscar Schachter* (Brill, 2005).

A noteworthy edited collection gathering several distinguished international lawyers.

PART IV
International disputes and responses to breaches

11

Diplomatic protection and issues of standing

11.1 Introduction: standing to raise international claims

The law on international responsibility covered in the preceding chapter only addresses the question of identity: who is the actor who committed a wrongful act, and is thus responsible for making reparation? Once that is answered, other questions arise: who is entitled to claim for injuries that might have arisen from the wrongful act? In which fora may such a claim be entertained? These questions serve to identify the actor—usually a State, but possibly other international legal persons—that may claim in relation to a given wrong. Broadly subsumed under the concept of *locus standi* or 'standing', this is the term for the ability of a party to demonstrate sufficient connection to assert a claim. Many of these are covered in Chapter 3, in relation to obligations *erga omnes*.

This is, to be sure, a substantial field, and will be covered in two parts. The first half of this chapter will focus on the notion of 'diplomatic protection', or the idea that a State may espouse the claims of its nationals and claim on their behalf. The second half of this chapter will focus on the rules relating to the admissibility of claims of 'diplomatic protection'. Because diplomatic protection by a State to persons necessarily extends beyond its territory, its exercise has potential ramifications for the sovereignty of other States. Certain rules have therefore emerged to avoid the uncomfortable situation where States submit legal claims as a strategic tool in international relations. Many of these are reflected in the Articles on Diplomatic Protection proposed by the ILC in 2006.[1] In such situations, even if *locus standi* can be established, the admissibility of a claim before an international tribunal is precluded.

[1] ILC, 'Draft Articles on Diplomatic Protection' adopted by the ILC on 30 May 2006: Report of the International Law Commission on the Work of its 58th Session, UN Doc A/61/10 Chap IV (2006) GAOR 61st Session Supp 10 (ADP). The ADP have been commended several times by the General Assembly, the most recent acknowledgement being in 2019: see UNGA Res 74/426 (21 November 2019).

HISTORICAL BACKGROUND The 'Vattelian Fiction' in International Law

The famous 'Vattelian fiction' in international law, named after the Swiss jurist Emer de Vattel, is well explained in his own words: '[w]hoever uses a citizen ill, indirectly offends the state, which is bound to protect this citizen' (E de Vattel, *The Law of Nations* (1797), B.II.Ch. VI., §71). Though Vattel had only contended that the link was indirect, over time the expression 'Vattelian fiction' came to be understood as the principle that, under international law, it was exclusively the right of the State that had suffered injury that had standing to claim on behalf of its nationals. As the PCIJ noted in the *Mavrommatis* case:

> It is an elementary principle of international law that a State is entitled to protect its subjects, when injured by acts contrary to international law committed by another State, from whom they have been unable to obtain satisfaction through ordinary channels. By taking up the case of one of its subjects and by resorting to diplomatic protection or international judicial proceedings on his behalf, a State is in reality asserting its own rights—its rights to ensure, in the person of its subjects, respect for the rules of international law. (*Mavrommatis Palestine Concessions, Judgment No 2, 1924, PCIJ, Ser A, No 2,* p 7, 12)

The Vattelian fiction constitutes to this day the basis for a State to espouse the claim of its nationals through diplomatic protection. In other words, anyone who causes injury to a national, whether on the territory of a State, on the high seas, or in outer space, is accountable to the State of nationality. This principle is the basis for much of the international law on diplomatic protection covered in this chapter.

11.2 Legal interest as a prerequisite to admissibility of claims

11.2.1 International law and *locus standi*

As a remnant of early twentieth-century institutional design, only States have the capacity to bring an action before an international tribunal, unless specified in the 'constituent instrument' (treaty of establishment) of the tribunal.[2] A constituent instrument can broaden standing to accommodate non-State entities, such as the WTO Agreement (which allows 'separate customs territories' such as Hong Kong or Macao, and the European Union, to be members, and thus to bring an action) or the European Convention on Human Rights (which allows individuals to bring claims). Generally, however, an individual, corporation, or other legal person does not have standing, and must rely on the State of nationality to espouse a claim on its behalf.

[2] See, e.g., Statute of the International Court of Justice, as annexed to the Charter of the United Nations (signed 26 June 1945, entered into force 24 October 1945), 1 UNTS xvi, Art 34; 1899 Hague Convention regulating the Pacific Settlement of International Disputes (1899), 91 BFSP 970, (1901) UKTS No 9 (Cd 798), Art 15; 1907 Hague Convention regulating the Pacific Settlement of International Disputes (1907), UKTS No 6 (Cmd 4575, 1971); Art 37 of 1907 Hague Convention; and Statute of the International Tribunal for the Law of the Sea, as annexed to the United Nations Convention on the Law of the Sea (signed 10 December 1982, entered into force 16 November 1994), 1833 UNTS 3, Art 20.

Most legal systems set out the basic principle that only claimants who establish a demonstrable interest may bring an action in respect of a wrong. This principle was explained well in the ICJ's advisory opinion in *Reparations for Injuries*: 'only the party to whom an international obligation is due can bring a claim in respect of its breach'.[3] It is now generally accepted that except for obligations *erga omnes*, only the specific beneficiary of an international obligation has the right to enforce that right.[4]

11.2.2 **Claims concerning obligations *erga omnes***

As the ICJ explained in *Barcelona Traction*, obligations *erga omnes* rest on values considered fundamental to the international legal order; they are obligations in which 'all States can be held to have a legal interest in their protection'.[5] Accordingly, a non-injured State may nevertheless be recognized as having a legal interest with respect to enforcement.

CASE SPOTLIGHT ***South West Africa, Second Phase (Ethiopia v South Africa; Liberia v South Africa), Second Phase, Judgment, ICJ Reports 1966*, p 6**

The *South West Africa* cases before the ICJ occurred within the context of a UN General Assembly that was expanding rapidly with newly independent States. Because South Africa's mandate over South West Africa (independent since 1990 and now known as Namibia) had been conferred by the now-defunct League of Nations, the question of standing was particularly relevant. As such, Ethiopia and Liberia, which had been the only African members of the League, filed a claim against South Africa in relation to its racially discriminatory policies of apartheid, given the seriousness of the obligations being breached by South Africa in its administration of South West Africa.

Though in 1962 the Court had determined that it had jurisdiction over the case, in 1966 it declared the claims of Ethiopia and Liberia to be inadmissible against South Africa, on the basis that neither of them possessed any legal interest in respect of the subject matter of the dispute. The Court considered their claims to be a plea of *actio popularis*, which is a claim to take legal action not in protection of direct or individual interests, but in vindication of a public interest; it denied the possibility of *actio popularis* in international law (p 47).

The 1966 judgment became notorious, due partly to the fact that it was decided by the casting vote of the president (a situation only repeated thirty years later in the *Nuclear Weapons* advisory opinion). The backlash against the Court, especially from States in the Non-Aligned Movement, led to a near-decade of inactivity in the Court in the mid- and late 1970s, despite a partial shift in direction by the Court in the 1971 *Namibia* advisory opinion. The Court's docket did not recover fully until the mid-1980s.

[3] *Reparation for Injuries suffered in the Service of the United Nations, Advisory Opinion, ICJ Reports 1949*, p 174, 181–2. See also *Military and Paramilitary Activities in and against Nicaragua (Nicaragua v United States), Merits, Judgment, ICJ Reports 1986*, p 14, para 262, where the Court rejected a US submission that it could take action on behalf of the Organization of American States (OAS).

[4] *Barcelona Traction, Light, and Power Company, Limited (Belgium v Spain), Second Phase, Judgment, ICJ Reports 1970*, p 3, para 35.

[5] *Ibid*, para 33.

The most complete treatment of this dispute is that of J Dugard, *The South West Africa/Namibia Dispute: Documents and Scholarly Writings on the Controversy between South Africa and the United Nations* (UC Press, 1973).

It is true that the broader *actio popularis* claims of Ethiopia and Liberia were rejected by the Court in *South West Africa*. However, certain multilateral instruments, especially those with a normative character such as human rights treaties, are now seen to create obligations *erga omnes partes* ('as between all the parties'), recognizing the legal interest of all States parties and thus, their right validly to bring an action in situations of breach, irrespective of any kind of individual or special link between the breach and the State invoking it. This principle was confirmed by the ICJ in two relatively recent judgments. In *Obligation to Prosecute or to Extradite*, the Court concluded that certain provisions of the Torture Convention were of common interest to all States parties. As such, all parties (including Belgium in that case) could invoke the responsibility of another State party for a failure to comply.[6] Similarly, in *Whaling in the Antarctic*, in which Japan's programme of scientific whaling was claimed to be in breach of the International Convention on the Regulation of Whaling, Japan did not even object to the *locus standi* of Australia to bring a claim that was essentially *erga omnes partes*.[7] The Court proceeded to the merits without acknowledging any concerns over Australia's *locus standi*.

Any concerns over a requirement to prove injury or legal interest seem to be resolved now by the Court's judgment in *Application of the Genocide Convention (The Gambia v Myanmar)*. Provided that a dispute between the parties exists, the *erga omnes* character of the prohibition against genocide in the Convention was successfully invoked by The Gambia to contend that, even as a non-injured State, it had standing to pursue a claim before the Court.[8]

11.2.3 **Direct and indirect interests**

Historically, international law would automatically recognize a State's legal interest in respect of an injury to its nationals. Over time, however, a distinction has emerged between the direct interests of a State related to its sovereign rights, and an injury that affects its indirect interests. Examples of direct injuries would include an injury to a State's organs or property; for example, to its head to State or diplomatic personnel, or to State-owned infrastructure, military equipment, or vessels.[9] Indirect injuries

[6] *Obligation to Prosecute or Extradite (Belgium v Senegal), Judgment, ICJ Reports 2012*, p 422, paras 68–9.

[7] *Whaling in the Antarctic (Australia v Japan: New Zealand intervening), Judgment, ICJ Reports 2014*, p 226.

[8] *Application of the Convention on the Prevention and Punishment of the Crime of Genocide (The Gambia v Myanmar), Preliminary Objections, ICJ Reports 2022*, p 477, paras 106–10. The finding on standing was relied upon by the Court in *Application of the Convention on the Prevention and Punishment of the Crime of Genocide in the Gaza Strip (South Africa v Israel), Order on Provisional Measures of 26 January 2024*, para 33.

[9] ADP (n 1) Commentary to Art 14, para 12.

include primarily injuries sustained by a State's nationals, whether they be individuals or corporations.

The direct/indirect distinction is pertinent as various procedural conditions apply in respect of a State's claim for an indirect injury to its nationals, most prominently the exhaustion of local remedies. Conversely, a State sustaining a direct injury may immediately bring an action to an international tribunal. Yet no clear rule exists in practice for distinguishing between direct and indirect claims. The complexity of assessing such claims is further compounded in situations where it is unclear whether the injury relates to direct or indirect interests, especially in so-called 'mixed claims' where elements of direct injury to a State are intertwined with injuries to its nationals (see later, Section 11.4.2).

11.3 Establishing protection

11.3.1 Diplomatic protection for indirect injuries: a State prerogative

At its essence, diplomatic protection consists of the espousal by a State of a claim against another State for an injury caused to a national, whether a natural or legal person.[10] In *Barcelona Traction*, the ICJ explained that diplomatic protection is a State prerogative, to be exercised 'by whatever means and to whatever extent it thinks fit, for it is its own right that the State is asserting. Should the natural or legal person on whose behalf it is acting consider that their rights are not adequately protected, they have no remedy in international law.'[11] It follows that if a State does pursue the claim and recovers compensation, it becomes State property, and the national has no right to such compensation under international law. What is more, once a State has taken up a claim of one of its nationals, the State is the sole claimant under international law, even if later opposed by the injured national.[12]

CONTEMPORARY DEVELOPMENTS From Diplomatic Protection to a Duty to Protect?

The ICJ expressed the orthodox position in *Barcelona Traction*: '[t]he State must be viewed as the sole judge to decide whether its protection will be granted, to what extent it is granted, and when it will cease' (paras 78–9). However, both ILC Special Rapporteurs working on diplomatic protection raised the possibility that international legal developments have transformed the exercise of diplomatic protection into a legal duty to be exercised by the State on behalf of the injured individual (see Preliminary Report (Bennouna), UN Doc A/CN.4/484 (1998), paras 34–7, 65–6; and First Report (Dugard), UN Doc A/CN.4/506, paras 17, 61).

[10] *Ibid*, Art 1.

[11] *Barcelona Traction* (n 4) para 78; see also ADP (n 1) Art 19; and *Kaunda v President of South Africa (CCT 23/04)* [2004] ZACC 5, paras 26–7.

[12] *Lonrho Exports Ltd v ECGD* [1996] 4 All ER 673, 687 (UK).

Whether the underlying principle has evolved, treaty developments in fields such as international human rights law and international investment law are extending beyond traditional mechanisms of diplomatic protection, to create mechanisms through which individuals enjoy additional rights under international law. In turn, these are shifting the place of the individual: see the *Ahmadou Sadio Diallo* case, in which in 2007 the ICJ recognized such individual rights in treaty law (*Guinea v Democratic Republic of the Congo, Preliminary Objections, ICJ Reports 2007*, p 582, 599). Furthermore, the European Court of Human Rights has observed that the duty to make representations on behalf of an individual might be legally mandatory as a consequence of the obligation laid out in Article 1 of the ECHR, to 'secure for everyone within its jurisdiction' rights guaranteed in the Convention (*Ilaşcu and Others v Moldova and Russia* App No 48787/99 (ECtHR, 8 July 2004)).

These new developments, beyond the field of diplomatic protection, may be no more than *lex specialis*; but they expand the scope of available protection for individuals under international law. However, it is far from certain that they are evolving into any State duty under customary international law. For example, the Guantánamo Bay situation remains a black spot, both legally and as a matter of policy. Nearly 800 men have been detained by the USA in its Guantánamo Bay air base, sometimes for many years, without trial. Other States have collaborated in having captured and transported them there, notably through a problematic practice of 'extraordinary rendition' (extrajudicial transfer). There have been allegations of torture and ill-treatment. However, certain States have been reticent to espouse the claims of their nationals, and in some cases their municipal courts have had to intervene, as in the UK with the *Abbasi* judgment and in Canada with the *Khadr* judgment (both discussed later). States seem, regrettably, still willing to look the other way.

Moreover, though a State might pass legislation creating an obligation upon the State to protect its nationals abroad, as several States have done in their constitutions,[13] the enforcement of such provisions is a matter for municipal law. In practice, municipal courts applying such constitutional provisions have tended to accord the executive a rather wide margin of discretion. For example, in South Africa a consistent line of case law, beginning with *Kaunda v President of South Africa*, has dismissed the claim of a constitutional right of diplomatic protection, reaffirming the discretionary nature of diplomatic protection.[14] Though a Crown prerogative in the UK, it has laid out guidance in its *Rules regarding the Taking up of International Claims*,[15] Rule VIII of which provides that the UK government may intervene if the claimant has suffered a denial of

[13] See ILC, 'First Report on Diplomatic Protection' (John Dugard, Special Rapporteur) (20 April 2000), UN Doc A/CN.4/506, para 80, which identified at least twenty-five domestic constitutions across all regions of the world.

[14] See *Kaunda* (n 10) paras 61, 67–77; *Rootman v President of the Republic of South Africa (Case 016/06)* 2006 SCA 80 (RSA); *Van Zyl v Government of the Republic of South Africa (Case 170/06)* 2007 SCA 109 (RSA); but *cf Van Abo v Government of the Republic of South Africa (Case CCT 67/08)* [2009] ZACC 15 (RSA), in which the South African Constitutional Court seems to narrow somewhat the discretion of the government, which is nevertheless under an obligation to consider a request for protection under constitutional law. See further D Tladi, 'The Right to Diplomatic Protection, the *Von Abo* Decision, and One Big Can of Worms: Eroding the Clarity of *Kaunda*' (2009) 20 Stellenbosch Law Review 14.

[15] See UKMIL (1999) 70 BYBIL 526.

justice, fundamental violations of human rights, or if it believes a third State is in violation of its international obligations.[16]

The UK Rules were considered by the Court of Appeal in the *Abbasi v Secretary of State* case,[17] in which an applicant, detained by US authorities in Guantánamo Bay, sought diplomatic protection from the UK government on the basis that a legitimate expectation existed in relation to protecting the rights of British nationals abroad. The court concluded that the applicant had a legitimate expectation to have his request 'considered', subject to the exceptional possibility of judicial review if a refusal to do so was 'irrational or contrary to the rules of natural justice'.[18] However, in general, the exercise of diplomatic protection remains the prerogative of the executive, and does not give rise to a duty under English law.[19]

Though a few municipal courts have recognized a right to diplomatic protection under municipal law, they have maintained that no customary international legal obligation exists on the State. In the *Hess Decision*, the German *Bundesverfassungsgericht* upheld a constitutional right to diplomatic protection while rejecting that such a right was required under customary international law.[20] In the *Khadr* judgment, the applicant was detained in Guantánamo Bay and the Canadian government refused to exercise diplomatic protection. The Supreme Court of Canada (SCC) stated that, though the right of protection is not generally enforceable, if irrational or contrary to a legitimate expectation, Canadian courts can intervene exceptionally if a right under the Canadian Charter of Rights and Freedoms was being infringed.[21] The SCC considered the executive's refusal in Mr Khadr's case to constitute a violation of his Charter rights to life, liberty, and security of the person.[22]

Finally, it bears mentioning that the espousal of diplomatic protection does not suffice for the hearing of a claim; a competent tribunal or court must also have the appropriate jurisdiction. A classic example is when the UK sought to espouse a claim at the ICJ on behalf of the Anglo-Iranian Oil Company, against the nationalization of its assets by Iran. Though the UK pointed to a 1933 concessionary contract between the company and Iran and suggested that it had a double character as a treaty between the UK and Iran, the Court did not agree, and arrived at the conclusion that it lacked jurisdiction.[23]

11.3.2 **Nationality of claims**

The exercise of diplomatic protection depends on a requisite link between the State seeking to assert protection and the individual who has suffered injury. Nationality has traditionally provided that link. As the PCIJ commented in *Panevezys-Saldutiskis*,

[16] *Ibid*, 528–9. See further the analysis of the *Kaunda* and *Behlaj* cases in P Okowa, 'Act of State and Diplomatic Protection in the Modern Constitution: Two Case Studies' in S Choudhry et al (eds), *Global Canons in an Age of Contestation: Debating Foundational Texts of Constitutional Democracy and Human Rights* (OUP, 2024) 553.

[17] *Abbasi v Secretary of State for Foreign and Commonwealth Affairs* [2002] EWCA Civ 1598.

[18] *Ibid*, para 104. [19] *Ibid*, paras 98–9. [20] *Hess Decision*, BVerfGE 55, 340; 90 ILR 396.

[21] *Canada (Prime Minister) v Khadr* [2010] 1 SCR 44, paras 36–7. [22] *Ibid*, para 39.

[23] *Anglo-Iranian Oil Company (United Kingdom v Iran), Preliminary Objection, Judgment, ICJ Reports 1951*, p 89.

'[a] State is in reality asserting its own right to ensure the protection of its nationals under international law. It is the bond of nationality between the State and the individual which alone confers upon the State the right of diplomatic protection.'[24] It is for this reason that Article 44 of the ILC ARSIWA stipulated that the responsibility of a State may not be invoked if the claim is not brought in accordance with any applicable rule relating to nationality of claims.[25] Nationality remains the crucial link between an individual and a State's ability to protect them; a failure to establish nationality will generally render a claim inadmissible due to the lack of a legal interest of the State.[26]

However, the requirement of nationality is not an absolute rule. Two generally accepted exceptions are the right of a State to extend protection to aliens aboard ships or aeroplanes registered with the flag of that State, and non-national members of a State's armed forces, such as the French and Spanish Foreign Legions, the Gurkhas in Singapore, and the Mahal and Garin Tzabar programmes for non-Israeli Jews in Israel[27]. States also provide consular services to nationals of other States if the receiving State is appropriately notified.[28] Exceptionally, and generally on a temporary basis, diplomatic protection may be afforded to the nationals of other States with the prior consent of the receiving State.[29]

In operation, there is the Canada–Australia Consular Services Sharing Agreement, which applies to reciprocal consular assistance where either State does not maintain a diplomatic presence.[30] Similarly, Article 20 of the Lisbon Treaty on European Union, and Article 46 of the EU Charter of Fundamental Rights, bestow on all nationals of EU States the right to receive diplomatic and consular assistance from any EU State.[31]

Finally, stateless persons may receive diplomatic protection under certain conditions. The obvious example is that of stateless Jews following the end of World War II, though today refugees from all lands may also benefit from diplomatic protection in

[24] *Panevezys-Saldutiskis Case (Estonia v Lithuania), Preliminary Objection, Order of June 30th 1938, 1938, PCIJ, Ser A/B, No 76*, p 53. For a similar analysis, see also *Mavrommatis Palestine Concessions, Judgment No 2, 1924, PCIJ, Ser A, No 2*, p 7.

[25] ILC, 'Articles on the Responsibility of States for Internationally Wrongful Acts', adopted by the ILC on 20 August 2001: Report of the International Law Commission on the Work of its 53rd Session, UN Doc A/56/10 Chap IV (2001) GAOR 56th Session Supp 10, Art 44. The ILC Commentaries to the ARSIWA are found in (2001) ILC Ybk vol II, pt 2, UN Doc A/CN.4/SER.A/2001/Add.1.

[26] See generally E Denza, 'Nationality and Diplomatic Protection' (2018) 65 NILR 463.

[27] Many States' armed forces permit the recruitment of non-nationals: J Crawford, *Brownlie's Principles of Public International Law* (9th edn, OUP, 2019), 676; A Watts, 'The Protection of Alien Seamen' (1958) 7 ICLQ 691.

[28] Vienna Convention on Consular Relations 1963 (adopted 24 April 1963, entered into force 19 March 1967), 596 UNTS 261, Art 8. Art 27 also allows for a third State to protect such premises in exceptional circumstances, such as armed conflicts.

[29] Vienna Convention on Diplomatic Relations 1961 (adopted 18 April 1961, entered into force 24 April 1964), 500 UNTS 95, Arts 45(c) and 46 (also in exceptional circumstances such as the rupture of diplomatic relations).

[30] See, e.g., Exchange of Notes Constituting an Agreement Regarding the Sharing of Consular Services Abroad (Canada–Australia) (entered into force 7 August 1986), 1459 UNTS 137.

[31] In respect of its implementation, see EU Council Directive 2015/637 [2015] OJ L106/1. In practice, prior consent has not been required, as notification to non-member States seems largely to have sufficed: see Denza (n 25) 475–6.

certain States. In 2005, the Belgian Constitutional Court held that recognized refugees in Belgium should be considered as holding Belgian nationality for the purpose of the exercise of extraterritorial jurisdiction over acts committed abroad by Total Fina Elf.[32] However, in 2006 the English Court of Appeal in *Al-Rawi v Secretary of State* denied standing to exercise diplomatic protection on behalf of resident aliens or refugees.[33]

Stateless persons are particularly vulnerable to State overreach, as they fall within the gaps of diplomatic protection, and their basic human rights are less easily enforceable than those of persons who may avail themselves of the protection of a State. Moreover, a disproportionate number of stateless persons belong to marginalized communities and other vulnerable groups, such as the children of migrant workers. For this reason, several international instruments seek to reduce statelessness in international law, though the question is not without its challenges.[34]

11.3.2.1 **International law and a grant of nationality**

As discussed in Chapter 8, Section 8.2.3, the conferment of nationality is a sovereign prerogative of a State, though with some debate as to the precise role of international law in determining nationality for the purpose of diplomatic protection.[35] This is because grants of nationality under municipal law must conform with relevant international legal rules in order to be internationally valid and recognized by other States.[36] As such, nationality conferred under laws that are discriminatory in character, inconsistent with fundamental principles of human rights, enacted *mala fides* ('in bad faith'), or based on a tenuous connection (such as aliens in transit, involuntary mass naturalizations of persons who do not wish to hold a nationality of a State), may be disregarded.[37] The ICJ's judgment in *Nottebohm* was one of the first to lay out conditions for the international validity of a domestic conferment of nationality, emphasizing the importance of a 'genuine connection' and dismissing Liechtenstein's right to assert protection vis-à-vis Guatemala.[38]

[32] Judgment of 13 April 2005, *Jurisprudence de Liège, Mons et Bruxelles* 2006, at 54; *Chronique de droit public/Publiekrechtelijke Kronieken* 2006, 125 (annotation by W Verrijdt); the case would be closed in March 2008 due to lack of jurisdiction: see Judgment of 29 October 2008 (Belgian Court of Cassation), *Pasicrisie* 2008, 2395. See further Chapter 16, Section 16.5, for an overview of the international law governing refugees and other migrants.

[33] *Al-Rawi and Others v The Secretary of State for Foreign and Commonwealth Affairs* [2006] EWCA Civ 1279.

[34] The question of statelessness and the human rights of stateless persons are addressed in Chapter 16, Section 16.5.3.

[35] See Chapter 8, Section 8.2.3, for more general discussion as to the relevance of nationality in international law.

[36] Convention on Certain Questions Relating to the Conflict of Nationality Laws (signed 12 April 1930, entered into force 1 July 1937), 179 UNTS 89. Art 1 embodies the conclusion of the PCIJ in *Nationality Decrees in Tunis and Morocco, Advisory Opinion, 1923, PCIJ, Ser B, No 4*, p 8, 24. See also *Flegenheimer Claim* (1958) 25 ILR 91, 96–112.

[37] See Dugard, First Report (n 12) para 104, pointing especially to discrimination based on race, gender, or religious affiliation.

[38] *Nottebohm (Liechtenstein v Guatemala), Second Phase, ICJ Reports 1955*, p 4. Dugard, First Report (n 12) para 108, has intimated that there was evidence before the Court that the conferral of Liechtensteinian nationality on Nottebohm was potentially made in bad faith.

In *Nottebohm*, the ICJ's 'genuine connection' test drew a curious distinction between a State's prerogatives under domestic jurisdiction and their international legal effect, which has remained controversial, even to this day. Three years after *Nottebohm*, the Italy–US Claims Commission confined the applicability of a genuine link test only to situations where dual nationals are seeking the protection of one State against the other.[39] In *Barcelona Traction*, the ICJ refused to extend the principle to corporations, and refrained from pronouncing further on its correctness as a matter of general international law.[40] More recently, Article 4 of the ILC's 2006 Articles on Diplomatic Protection (ADP) does not impose any condition of a genuine link on the holding of nationality, and in its Commentary, suggests that *Nottebohm* should be limited to its facts alone.[41] In the preliminary objections phase of *Ahmadou Sadio Diallo*, the ICJ did not acknowledge any possible lack of a 'genuine connection' in respect of the exercise of diplomatic protection by Guinea over Mr Diallo, who had been resident in the Congo for thirty-two years.[42] It should be noted, however, that Mr Diallo had been born in Guinea to Guinean-born parents, and resided there for seventeen years, which lends credence to those who suggest that the unique matrix of facts makes it difficult to distil any general principle from *Nottebohm*.[43]

CASE SPOTLIGHT ***Nottebohm (Liechtenstein v Guatemala), Second Phase, ICJ Reports 1955, p 4***

The ICJ's *Nottebohm* judgment was one of the first to lay out conditions for the validity of a conferment of nationality on the international plane. The Principality of Liechtenstein had asserted a claim for reparation against Guatemala for the mistreatment of Friedrich Nottebohm, a German-born national who from 1905 until 1943 had been permanently resident and conducting his business activities in Guatemala.

Nottebohm had naturalized as a Liechtensteiner in 1939, after a few brief visits to the principality, obtaining dispensation from a three-year residence requirement by paying 37,500 Swiss francs. According to German nationality law which was valid at that time, in doing so he forfeited German nationality, and re-entered Guatemala on a visa on his new Liechtenstein passport in 1940. At no time did Mr Nottebohm acquire Guatemalan nationality. Guatemala, however, challenged the propriety of Liechtenstein exercising diplomatic protection and espousing Nottebohm's claims.

After Guatemala entered World War II against Germany in 1941, in 1943 he was arrested as an 'enemy alien' and deported to the USA, with all his property confiscated by Guatemala by legislative decree. After 1946, Guatemala refused to admit him.

[39] *Flegenheimer* (n 35) 148–50. For questions of multiple nationality, see later, Section 11.3.2.3.

[40] *Barcelona Traction* (n 4) para 70. See further Denza (n 25) 465–6.

[41] ADP (n 1) Art 4 provides only that 'a State of nationality means a State whose nationality a person has acquired, in accordance with the law of that State, by birth, descent, naturalization, succession of States or in any other manner, not inconsistent with international law'.

[42] *Ahmadou Sadio Diallo (Republic of Guinea v DRC), Preliminary Objections, ICJ Reports 2007*, p 582, para 41.

[43] See P Okowa, 'Case concerning *Ahmadou Sadio Diallo (Republic of Guinea v DRC), Preliminary Objections*' (2008) 57 ICLQ 219.

Before the ICJ, Liechtenstein sought to exercise diplomatic protection over Mr Nottebohm. Guatemala questioned the validity of Liechtenstein's bestowal of nationality under international law. The Court determined that the naturalization of Mr Nottebohm was within the domestic jurisdiction of Liechtenstein; its prerogative to bestow nationality could thus not be challenged under international law (at 20–1). However, the Court determined that 'nationality must correspond to the factual situation' in order to apply vis-à-vis other States, and that accordingly Liechtenstein could not invoke diplomatic protection against Guatemala (at 22). The Court observed that in respect of dual nationality, earlier international arbitral decisions had given preference to 'real and effective nationality . . . based on stronger factual ties between the person concerned and one of the States whose nationality is involved', with factors such as habitual residence, centre of interests, family ties, and participation in public life all being relevant (at 22). The Court explained that nationality was a 'legal bond having as its basis a social fact of attachment, a genuine connection of existence, interests and sentiments, together with the existence of reciprocal rights and duties' (at 23). Only where this 'genuine connection' could be demonstrated would a State of nationality be entitled to exercise its diplomatic protection, and the Court considered Mr Nottebohm's links to Liechtenstein to be 'extremely tenuous' to the point where, if anything, the facts suggested the 'absence of any bond of attachment' and 'lacking in genuineness, especially when compared to the "long-standing and close connection between him and Guatemala"' (at 25–6). The latter point is significant in that the Court's decision was not to invalidate Liechtenstein's grant of nationality, but the more nuanced and specific conclusion that Liechtenstein 'is not entitled to extend its protection to Nottebohm *vis-à-vis* Guatemala' (at 26).

11.3.2.2 **The continuity of nationality**

For diplomatic protection to be exercised, the link of nationality should exist both on the date of injury and the date of the official presentation of the claim.[44] This is not an absolute presumption: diplomatic protection may still be exercised if, between the two dates, nationality was lost and reacquired 'in a manner not inconsistent with international law'.[45] This may be the case in situations of forced or involuntary change of nationality, such as when a new State emerges or territory is ceded. A change of nationality should not, however, be opportunistic: diplomatic protection is prohibited in respect of a person who, at the time of injury, was a national of the State against which a claim is filed and only subsequently acquired the nationality of the applicant State.[46]

11.3.2.3 **Multiple nationality**

In the contemporary world, many individuals possess dual or multiple nationality, which raises particular challenges in relation to the exercise of diplomatic protection. Though a person with multiple nationality is free to seek protection from any State of

[44] ADP (n 1) Art 5(1): '[c]ontinuity is presumed if . . . nationality existed at both these dates'.
[45] *Ibid*, Art 5(2); see also J Crawford, *State Responsibility: The General Part* (CUP, 2013), 577.
[46] *Ibid*, Art 5(3).

which they are a national against any other State,[47] in theory, a State cannot extend diplomatic protection to one of its nationals against a State whose nationality that person also holds.[48] This poses a challenge with respect to individuals like Nazanin Zaghari-Ratcliffe, a dual British–Iranian national who was detained in Iran on specious charges of spreading propaganda. Breaking from its ambivalence as to whether it could exercise diplomatic protection over dual nationals against their other State of nationality,[49] in 2019 the UK asserted diplomatic protection over her situation, on the basis that 'her treatment fails to meet Iran's obligations under international law'.[50] The dispute seems have been intermixed with other tensions in the Iran-UK relationship: Ms Zaghari-Ratcliffe was released on 16 March 2022, immediately after a payment of nearly £400 million was made by the UK to Iran, ostensibly to resolve outstanding debts.[51]

International law may have evolved, however, to the point where in situations where a dual/multiple national seeks the protection of one State of nationality against another State of nationality, a test of 'effective' or 'predominant' nationality is applicable. The ILC takes the view, in Article 7 of the ADP, that a State of nationality may exercise diplomatic protection against another State of nationality if the nationality of the applicant State is 'predominant' at both the time of the injury and the date the claim is presented. Though no clear criteria of 'predominance' are specified, the ILC Commentary to Article 7 suggests that the term is meant to describe the balancing exercise to be undertaken by a competent tribunal to assess the merits of various competing nationalities, enumerating a long list of relevant factors including habitual residence, time spent in each country, family ties, place of family life, taxation, military service, employment, financial interests, and more.[52]

The ILC's view is not without support. Though with many caveats, the *Nottebohm* judgment at the ICJ had already conveyed some support for a 'real and effective nationality'.[53] In a series of awards, the Iran–United States Claims Tribunal (IUSCT) considered claims against Iran by dual Iran–US nationals in order to determine the scope of its jurisdiction. Though not exactly questions of diplomatic protection, and perhaps limited to the specific situation and the existence of an agreement between the two parties to establish the tribunal (the 1981 Algiers Accords), over the years the Tribunal has developed a test of 'dominant and effective nationality' at the time of the injury which is useful: according to that test, if their dominant and effective nationality was

[47] *Ibid*, Art 6. See also *Salem Case (Egypt v USA)* (1932) 2 RIAA 1161, 1168; *Mergé Case (USA v Italy)* (1955) 14 RIAA 235; (1955) 22 ILR 143.

[48] 1930 Convention on Conflict of Nationality Laws (n 35) Art 4; and see further Denza (n 25) 468–9. But as early as the *Canevaro Claim (Italy v Peru)* (1912) 11 RIAA 397, that rule came under challenge.

[49] See Comments of the UK to Art 7 of the ADP (n 1), UN Doc A/CN.4/561/Add.1, p 7.

[50] See UK FCO, 'Foreign Secretary affords Nazanin Zaghari-Ratcliffe diplomatic protection' (Press Release 7 March 2019). Intriguingly, in the 'Notes to Editors', the FCO suggests that the general threshold conditions required under international law include, 'in the case of a dual national, *predominant nationality*', and asserts, remarkably, that: '[w]e assess that Mrs Zaghari-Ratcliffe meets these conditions'.

[51] See UK FCO, 'Foreign Secretary statement on Iran' (Statement of 16 March 2022).

[52] See ADP (n 1) 41–7; but cf Denza (n 25) 478, who suggests that Art 7 of the ADP is more favourable to the principle than traditional or even current practice.

[53] *Nottebohm* (n 39) 24.

American, they could validly claim against Iran.[54] A similar test was applied by the UN Compensation Commission, which considered claims of Iraqi dual nationals against Iraq arising out of its occupation of Kuwait in 1990–1.[55]

11.3.2.4 Nationality of corporations and shareholders

One particular problem that has bedevilled international lawyers concerns how to determine the nationality of a corporation for the purpose of diplomatic protection. After all, corporations are legal persons but their origin and functions are, of course, rather distinct from those of a natural person. Corporations are inevitably linked to shareholders, who in a globalized world emanate from any number of States and who might purchase and sell shares frequently.

CONTEMPORARY DEVELOPMENTS Multiple Nationalities and International Law

Until as late as the mid-twentieth century, dual nationality was prohibited in most States, and there even existed several treaties to reduce this phenomenon (see, e.g., the 1930 Hague Convention and the 1963 European Convention on the Reduction of Cases of Multiple Nationality). Though those laws have been loosened, and today millions of people hold multiple passports, even the test to revert to a 'predominant nationality' suggests that when stripped down, and whatever one's formal status might be, one has a primary bond with only one State.

That is a convenient legal fiction but factually inaccurate. What of persons with genuine and effective links to multiple States? There are persons born and raised in one State but with parents from another State who then go and work part-time in that second State, but maintain links and a partial residence in the first State. To what extent does a 'predominant nationality test' risk oversimplifying the complex realities of today's world?

Another problem arises with the nationals of one State who reside more or less permanently in a second State, while never becoming nationals. Though international practice permits claims of jurisdiction over permanent residents, a State may only exceptionally espouse the claims of non-nationals. Such individuals may have to seek the protection of a State with whom their substantive links are very tenuous, or even a State they have fled. This is exacerbated in situations where the State of nationality does not allow for renunciation, such as Cuba or Iran.

A final controversial debate concerns when nationality is conferred en masse to nationals of another State even in the absence of an application by the persons concerned. During the early 2010s, media reports circulated that Russia was issuing passports to individuals, without the need for an application, in the Crimea, Abkhazia, and South Ossetia; these preceded conflicts in which Russia asserted that it was intervening to protect its own nationals. Adding to the complexity is the fact that Ukraine, like many States, prohibits dual nationality. Such examples illustrate the continued challenges posed by multiple nationality for international law.

[54] See *Esphanian v Bank Tejarat* (1983) 2 Iran–USCTR 157, 166; *Islamic Republic of Iran v United States of America* (Case No A/18) (1984) 5 Iran–USCTR 251; (1984) 75 ILR 176; *Malek v Islamic Republic of Iran* (1988) 19 Iran–USCTR 48. See also *Saghi v Islamic Republic of Iran* (1993) 87 AJIL 447.

[55] UNSC, 'Decision taken by the Governing Council of the United Nations Compensation Commission: Criteria for additional Categories of Claims' (28 November 1991), UN Doc S/AC.26/1991/7/Rev.1, para 11.

11.3.2.4.1 ***Corporations***

With respect to the nationality of corporations, a number of possibilities present themselves. In principle, the simplest solution is that the State of incorporation, which is responsible for all requirements of corporate accountability such as auditing, reporting, and the holding of shareholders' meetings, be the State of nationality for the purpose of exercising diplomatic protection.

This relatively formalistic approach underlay the reasoning taken by the ICJ in the *Barcelona Traction* case, which is still considered the leading authority on the question of diplomatic protection of corporations and their shareholders. The company in issue in that case, the Barcelona Traction, Light and Power Company, had been incorporated and was headquartered under Canadian law. However, some 88 per cent of its shareholders were of Belgian nationality, leading Belgium to file a claim on behalf of its shareholders against Spain, which had taken a number of financial measures that led to the insolvency of the company in 1948 (though it remained formally in existence). The Court concluded that the fact of incorporation was determinative of the nationality of Barcelona Traction; finding that a 'close and permanent connection has been established, fortified by the passage of half a century'.[56] It held that it was not necessary in that case to 'pierce the corporate veil', or to treat the rights or duties of a corporation as the rights or liabilities of its shareholders, even though the company had a strong link to Belgium and also operated in Spain. The Court further rejected that a 'genuine connection' test such as that elucidated in *Nottebohm* had gained any general acceptance under international law.[57]

The Court's reasoning is somewhat awkward, as it emphasizes the clear, 'genuine' connection of the Company to Canada, but negates that a genuine connection test applies. Nevertheless, the Court's reasoning rested on the fact that a company is a legal person under municipal law, and thus legally distinct from its shareholders. Accordingly, if that company suffered an injury, under international law only it could claim for that injury, no matter the interests or effects to shareholders: 'although two separate entities may have suffered from the same wrong, it is only one entity whose rights have been infringed'.[58] Moreover, even though Canada had declined to exercise diplomatic protection, Belgium had no subsidiary right to claim. The Court considered that to allow otherwise might sow confusion in economic relations, as international companies' shares are 'widely scattered and frequently change hands'.[59]

The formalism exhibited by the Court in the *Barcelona Traction* judgment may be intellectually elegant, but it has met with a degree of criticism, especially as the operations of today's multinational corporations increasingly challenge its practical effectiveness. As is well known, corporations routinely incorporate in one jurisdiction purely for fiscal or tax reasons, with their operations increasingly located in another State. For example, given the Court's curt refusal to consider the question in *Barcelona Traction*,[60] a strict reading would suggest that, for foreign investors establishing a subsidiary as a

[56] *Barcelona Traction* (n 4) 42. [57] *Ibid.* [58] *Ibid*, 35. [59] *Ibid*, 49.

[60] *Ibid*, 48: 'whatever the validity of this theory may be, it is certainly not applicable to the present case, since Spain is not the national State of Barcelona Traction'.

vehicle for their activities in a host State—a common practice—the only State entitled to exercise diplomatic protection over that subsidiary is the State which is most likely to cause injury to it.[61]

What is more, there exists some practice where States have been prepared to extend diplomatic protection to shareholding interests in foreign corporations, which has led the ILC to recommend, in Article 9 of the ADP, to provide for the place of incorporation as the first criterion for the nationality of corporations, but with the State of the seat of management and the financial control of the corporation as alternative options if 'no sufficient connection' with the State of incorporation exists. Certain investment tribunals have already employed this method for the purposes of establishing jurisdiction *ratione personae*.[62]

11.3.2.4.2 ***Shareholders***

Given the ICJ's decision in *Barcelona Traction*, shareholders are reliant upon the diplomatic protection of the corporation in which they have invested. Under customary international law, shareholders may only seek protection from their State of nationality when their direct rights are affected. Article 12 of the ADP lists as examples of direct rights the rights to dividends, to attend and vote at general meetings, to share in the assets of the company after liquidation, and any that might subsist if the company ceases to exist.[63] The ICJ in *Barcelona Traction* expressly rejected the possibility that a 'practically defunct' corporation, or one that was 'completely paralysed', could be equated to a company that has actually ceased to exist. For the Court, the description 'practically defunct . . . lacks all legal precision'.[64]

However, as the *Elettronica Sicula (ELSI)* case demonstrates, a treaty may depart from the general principle of subordinating shareholders' rights to the rights of the corporation, and enshrine the protection of shareholders' rights. In that case, two US corporations, Raytheon and Machlett, held 100 per cent of the shares in ELSI, incorporated under Italian law. The ICJ Chamber in that case declared the US claim for diplomatic protection admissible, despite Italian objections. This was due to a clause in the Italy–US Treaty of Friendship, Commerce and Navigation, which granted each other's nationals, corporations, and associations certain rights in relation to their participation in corporations and associations having the nationality of the other State.[65] The possibility of rights conferred directly by treaties is of key importance in the context of bilateral investment treaties and certain human rights regimes, the *raison d'être* of which is to confer such direct treaty rights on individuals.

The ICJ made further pronouncements on the protection of corporations and shareholders in the *Diallo* case, in which Mr Diallo, a Guinean national, had established

[61] Though the majority was silent on this question, some judges in *Barcelona Traction* were prepared to recognize diplomatic protection in such situations. See notably the Separate Opinions of Judge Tanaka, p 121, 130–5; Judge Jessup, p 162, 168 *et seq*; Judge Gros, p 267, 268–79; and Judge Fitzmaurice, p 63, 72–5 (paras 14–20).

[62] See the case law of investment tribunals cited in ADP (n 1) Commentary to Art 9, 52–5.

[63] *Ibid*, 36 para 47, 40–1 paras 64–8.

[64] *Ibid*, 41.

[65] *Elettronica Sicula case (United States v Italy), Judgment, ICJ Reports 1989*, p 15, para 101.

two companies in the DRC (then known as Zaire), Africom-Zaire and Africontainers-Zaire. These companies had issued loans to the DRC, as well as several mining and oil companies operating in the DRC. When Diallo and the two companies filed actions to recover the debts, they were met with resistance from DRC authorities and their actions failed in the DRC's courts.

Guinea asserted diplomatic protection on two separate grounds. First, Diallo's 1995 expulsion from the DRC was taken to frustrate irrevocably his efforts to enforce an international judgment against Zaire Shell for $US60 billion and thus his direct rights. Secondly, in relation to the two corporations, Guinea pointed specifically to Article 11(2) of the ADP, which allows for the exceptional possibility of 'substitution' of claimants. Under Article 11(2), a corporation may assign its rights to shareholders for the purpose of litigation when two conditions are met: if the State of nationality is alleged to have committed the violation of international law, and if incorporation in that State is a precondition for doing business.[66] The DRC objected, relying on *Barcelona Traction* to contend that Guinea lacked standing in relation to the two companies, as these were incorporated under Congolese law, and with rights distinct and separate from those of Diallo, who was a shareholder. The DRC naturally also denied Guinea's claim as to substitution.

First addressing Diallo's direct rights, the ICJ first concluded that Guinea had *locus standi* on the basis that his direct rights as '*associé*' were affected by the DRC's acts, given the defined obligations of an *associé* under Congolese law.[67] The Court's position was that protection of shareholders' rights was 'not to be regarded as an exception to the general legal regime of diplomatic protection for natural or legal persons, as derived from customary international law'.[68] The Court, however, denied Guinea's claim of substitution, though it acknowledged that *Barcelona Traction* had not addressed whether substitution could be effected to protect shareholders if the breaching State was also the State of nationality. Instead, without commenting on whether Article 11(2) of the ADP reflected customary international law, it considered that the said provision did not apply as there was no requirement under Congolese law that the two corporations be incorporated.[69] As such, *Diallo* may be regarded as authority for the proposition that the direct rights of shareholders may validly be espoused by a State, but not for any wider prospect of lifting the corporate veil, or for shareholders to pursue claims for injuries sustained by a corporation.

The rights of foreign investors are often the subject of international investment claims, which are further considered in Chapter 20, Section 20.4.

11.4 The exhaustion of local remedies

11.4.1 Basic principles

An important principle of customary international law requires that before an international claim is brought by a claimant State on behalf of a national which has sustained an injury, all means of redress provided by the local State should have been fully attempted.[70] Based on mutual respect for State sovereignty, this is termed the 'exhaustion of local

[66] *Diallo* (n 42) 612–14, paras 82–5. [67] *Ibid*, 606, para 63. [68] *Ibid*, 606, para 64.
[69] *Ibid*, 615, paras 89–90. [70] *ELSI* (n 63) 42.

remedies'. Article 14 of the ADP defines local remedies as 'legal remedies which are open to the injured person before the judicial or administrative courts or bodies, whether ordinary or special, of the State alleged to be responsible for causing the injury'. According to this rule, if there is a pending suit before local courts (as was the case in the *Interhandel* case),[71] or if certain available remedies, such as the right to appeal, have not been used (as was the case in the *Ambatielos* arbitration),[72] the claim will be declared inadmissible.[73]

CASE SPOTLIGHT ***Interhandel (Switzerland v United States), ICJ Reports 1959*, p 6**

Interhandel BV was a Swiss corporation whose assets had been seized by the USA during World War II on the basis that they were enemy, and not neutral, property under the Trading with the Enemy Act. When Switzerland filed a claim at the ICJ, the USA filed four preliminary objections, three of which were rejected. The fourth US objection, that local remedies had not been exhausted, was upheld; this was partly because Interhandel had filed proceedings that were, at the time of the decision by the ICJ, still pending before the US Supreme Court. This is, in many ways, the classic understanding of how local remedies function.

The exhaustion of local remedies rule is sensible, in that municipal courts are often better placed to consider the facts, assess evidence, and calculate any compensation due. The rule promotes a degree of international comity, in that a local State is first given an opportunity to repair the injury. Moreover, the rule takes into account that a failure to provide local redress for a breach of an international obligation might constitute a denial of justice, thus engaging State responsibility separately. For these reasons, both Article 44 of the Articles on State Responsibility and Article 14 of the ADP reaffirm the principle in *Interhandel*: no claim may be presented by a State unless the injured person has exhausted all available and effective local remedies.

Interhandel is a key authority for the exhaustion of local remedies rule. However, it is equally well known in respect of a wider issue involving the jurisdiction of the Court. The USA had also objected on the basis that it had a reservation to the Court's jurisdiction concerning disputes 'with regard to matters which are essentially within the domestic jurisdiction of the United States of America as determined by the United States of America' (the 'Connally reservation'). The legality of this reservation is a controversial question due to the 'self-judging' aspects of its content (see Chapter 12, Section 12.3.2.3.4), but the Court was able to avoid making any pronouncements on the objection on the basis that, during oral proceedings, the USA had explained that the issue had lost practical significance.

The evasiveness of the Court on the point led to President Klaestad and Judge Lauterpacht publishing dissents in which they questioned the validity of the US declaration. The issue arose again in the judgment on jurisdiction in *Military and Paramilitary Activities (Nicaragua v United States)*, where the ICJ did not pronounce itself on the legality of self-judging provisions except in passing. It was only in the *Mutual Assistance in Criminal Matters (Djibouti v France)* judgment of 2008 where the Court finally suggested that though such self-judging clauses were not invalid as such, any discretion exercised pursuant to them was not unlimited, and had to be pursued in good faith.

[71] *Interhandel (Switzerland v United States), Jurisdiction and Admissibility, ICJ Reports 1959*, p 6.

[72] *Ambatielos (United Kingdom v Greece)* [1956] 12 RIAA 83; (1956) 23 ILR 306.

[73] *Interhandel* (n 69) 27; *Diallo* (n 42) 599–600, paras 42–4.

Obviously, a State need not exhaust local remedies when its direct rights are affected.[74] Established examples of direct injury include injury to State property[75] or to diplomatic and consular staff.[76] A number of further exclusions exist where local remedies need not be exhausted, and are gathered in Article 15 of the ADP, reflecting existing practice and case law:

(i) if there are no reasonably available local remedies to provide effective redress, or these provide 'no reasonable possibility' of redress, with a recent example being the effect of statutory sanctions regimes against Iranian companies to deny access to US court proceedings;[77]

(ii) if there is undue delay in the remedial process which is attributable to the State which is claimed to have committed the violation.[78] The failure of a State to investigate disappearances and killings, for example, may provide evidence that no effective remedy is available;[79]

(iii) if there is no relevant (jurisdictional) connection between the injured person and the State accused of the wrongful act. The ILC suggests that local remedies need not be exhausted in cases of transboundary environmental harm, or the shooting down of an aircraft merely passing over one's territory;[80]

(iv) if the injured person is manifestly precluded from pursuing local remedies;[81] or

(v) if the State which is claimed to have committed the violation has waived the requirement that local remedies be exhausted. Waiver clauses are common in investment treaties,[82] though any such waiver must be express and cannot be tacit.[83]

[74] See later, Section 11.4.2 (on mixed claims); and ADP (n 1) Art 14(3).

[75] *Corfu Channel case (United Kingdom v Albania), Judgment, ICJ Reports 1949*, p 4.

[76] *United States Diplomatic and Consular Staff in Tehran (United States v Islamic Republic of Iran), Judgment, ICJ Reports 1980*, p 3.

[77] See *Certain Iranian Assets (Iran v United States), Judgment, ICJ Reports 2023*, p 51, para 72. This is lower than the 'obvious futility' threshold required in *Finnish Ships Arbitration (Finland v UK)* (1934) 3 RIAA 1479, and somewhat closer to that suggested by Judge Sir Hersch Lauterpacht in *Norwegian Loans (France v Norway), Judgment, ICJ Reports 1957*, p 9, 39. See also *Loewen Group v United States* (2004) 128 ILR 334, para 168.

[78] *El Oro Mining and Railway Company (Limited) (Great Britain v Mexico)* (1931) V RIAA 191, 198; *Administration of the Prince von Pless, Preliminary Objections, 1933, PCIJ, Ser A/B, No 52*, p 4.

[79] *Aksoy v Turkey* App No 21987/93 (ECtHR, 18 December 1996); *Kaya v Turkey* App No 22729/93 (ECtHR, 19 February 1998) paras 106–8; *Tepe v Turkey* App No 27244/95 (ECtHR, 9 May 2003) para 19. Undue delay to investigate may itself be a violation: see, e.g., International Covenant on Civil and Political Rights (signed 16 December 1966, entered into force 23 March 1976), 993 UNTS 3, Art 9(3); and American Convention on Human Rights (signed 22 November 1969, entered into force 18 July 1978), 1144 UNTS 123, Art 46(2)(c).

[80] CF Amerasinghe, *Local Remedies in International Law* (2nd edn, CUP, 2004), 169; T Meron, 'The Incidence of the Rule of Exhaustion of Local Remedies' (1959) 35 BYBIL 83, 94.

[81] This paragraph is termed by the ILC as an exercise in progressive development: see ADP (n 1), Commentary to Art 15, at 83, para 11.

[82] See, e.g., Convention on the Settlement of Investment Disputes between States and Nationals of other States (signed 18 March 1965, entered into force 14 October 1966), 575 UNTS 159, Art 26.

[83] *ELSI* (n 63) 42, para 50; *American International Group v Iran* (1983) IV Iran–USCTR 96.

11.4.2 **Mixed claims**

To recall, diplomatic protection allows States to espouse the claims of their nationals on the international plane, and does not apply to a State claiming for direct injuries suffered by it. There are situations, however, where the same act has caused injury to both a State's direct interests and those of its nationals. When such a 'mixed' claim is presented, it may well be that local remedies need not be exhausted.

The mere presence of a State interest is not enough to dispense a national from the obligation to exhaust local remedies before the State may exercise diplomatic protection. If that were the case, any State could evade the exhaustion of local remedies by alleging an interest, such as seeking a guarantee of non-repetition, or by asking for an interpretation or application of a treaty obligation. In the *Interhandel* dispute, Switzerland had argued that alongside the injuries sustained by its national, the Interhandel corporation, its claim was also for direct injury caused by the failure of US authorities to apply the terms of an applicable treaty. The Court rejected Switzerland's claim:

> one interest, and one alone, that of Interhandel, . . . has induced the Swiss Government to institute proceedings. This interest is the basis for the present claim and should determine the scope of the action brought before the Court by the Swiss Government in its alternative as well as in its principal form.[84]

Similarly, in *ELSI*, the ICJ Chamber rejected the US contention that it had also suffered direct injury from the breach of a treaty obligation, observing that 'the matter which colours and pervades the United States Claim as a whole is the alleged damage to Raytheon and Machlett', both US nationals.[85]

The ICJ has clarified further aspects of the rule recently, in the *Application of the CERD* dispute between Ukraine and Russia. Russia had submitted that because the Convention aimed to protected individuals from racial discrimination, the rule was applicable; Ukraine, for its part, contended that its claims related not to the individual rights of its citizens but to a 'systematic campaign' orchestrated by Russia in breach of CERD. The Court, upholding the customary status of the rule on exhaustion of local remedies, considered that Ukraine was not adopting the cause of one or more of its nationals, but was challenging a pattern of conduct by Russia, and that the rule was thus not applicable.[86]

11.5 **The treatment of aliens under international law**

This final section will deal with the treatment of 'aliens' (non-nationals), a long-standing field of regulation dating at least from the Jay Treaty of 1794 between Great Britain and the USA.[87] In recent years, the traditional rules have been subsumed by several

[84] *Interhandel* (n 69) 29. [85] *ELSI* (n 63) para 91.

[86] *Application of the International Convention on the Elimination of All Forms of Racial Discrimination (Ukraine v Russian Federation), Preliminary Objections, ICJ Reports 2019*, p 558, paras 129–30. On the wider issue, see J Howley, *Overlapping Individual and Interstate Claims in International Law* (OUP, 2024).

[87] Treaty of Amity, Commerce, and Navigation, Between his Britannic Majesty and the United States of America (signed 19 November 1794, entered in force 28 October 1795), 8 Stat 116.

multilateral treaties protecting human rights, as well as significant changes wrought through the networks of bilateral investment treaties; in particular, those concluded under the auspices of the ICSID Convention (see Chapter 20, Section 20.4). However, given the historical influence of these rules for the development of international law, a brief survey is appropriate here.

11.5.1 **National treatment and the Calvo clause**

The nineteenth and early twentieth centuries were marked by discord between States as to the appropriate standard of treatment of foreign nationals (aliens) under international law. Many States, especially in Latin America, made recourse to the famous 'Calvo doctrine' arguing for the 'national treatment' of aliens, discussed in the accompanying commentary. European States, later joined by the USA, countered that an 'international minimum standard' of treatment existed for the protection of foreign nationals, which frequently imposed a higher standard of treatment than those owed to a State's own nationals. This was perhaps due to the sheer intensity of European activity in other States, whether in their colonies or directly in the territory of other independent States.

HISTORICAL BACKGROUND Whither the Calvo Clause?

Carlos Calvo was an eminent Argentine jurist who was deeply concerned about the extraterritorial interference by European powers, and increasingly the USA, in his home country and in the independent Latin American republics. The 'Calvo doctrine' he propounded was that the State was only under an international legal obligation to treat aliens to the same standard as its own nationals ('national treatment'), and that local remedies had to be exhausted before pursuing an international claim.

Calvo's justification for no further obligation than 'national treatment' was that it was necessary to prevent the abuse of the jurisdiction of less powerful States, which might in particular lack the resources of colonial empires and bind them to apply a higher standard to aliens than to their own nationals. Further expressions of such inequality were the extraterritorial treaties imposed on China, Japan, Siam, and the Ottoman Empire by Western States, through which Western nationals were largely exempted from the exercise of national jurisdiction.

Though the exhaustion of local remedies is now a rule of customary international law, other aspects of the Calvo doctrine have arguably been superseded by the eventual emergence of an international minimum standard, which itself is being augmented through the network of bilateral investment treaties. Nevertheless, the Calvo doctrine represented a brave assertion of sovereignty from a historically peripheral region, and its failure demonstrates the enduring role of power politics within the making of international law. Later attempts at rebalancing economic disparities between States through law would draw inspiration from the Calvo doctrine, especially in the wake of decolonization (see Chapter 20, Section 20.1).

For further reading, see DR Shea, *The Calvo Clause: A Problem of Inter-American and International Law and Diplomacy* (University of Minnesota Press, 1955).

11.5.2 The emergence of the international minimum standard

Several awards during that period applied a rule that came to be regarded as an application of the international minimum standard. A series of decisions from the US–Mexico Mixed Claims Commission concluded that Mexico's acts were to be assessed according to international minimum standards.[88] The General Commission in the *Neer* case put forward a famous statement that the treatment of aliens would fall short of international standards if it:

> should amount to an outrage, to bad faith, to wilful neglect of duty, or to an insufficiency of governmental action so far short of international standards that every reasonable and impartial man would readily recognise its insufficiency.[89]

The *Neer* standard was fairly high in practice, and applied generally to procedural shortcomings such as a denial of justice, failing to take enforcement action,[90] unreasonably long or arbitrary detention, and harsh and inhumane treatment while in prison.[91]

Considerable developments in international human rights standards have since set out a number of minimum conditions for the expulsion of aliens; these are to be enforced both by municipal courts and international tribunals. Notably, States cannot expel a foreign national without convincing reasons, a standard first laid out in the 1903 *Boffalo* arbitration between Italy and Venezuela.[92] Article 13 ICCPR takes up that standard, and requires that expulsion be pursuant to a lawful decision and with a right to appeal, except where compelling reasons of national security intervene.[93] Moreover, the standards of expropriation developed in the early case law have been further clarified through the case law of investment tribunals (see Chapter 20, Section 20.4.3).

11.6 Conclusion

The rules surrounding diplomatic protection by States and the admissibility of their claims are illustrative of the continued centrality of State sovereignty in international law. From the rules on nationality, the exhaustion of local remedies, and the obligations on the treatment of aliens, this area of the law demonstrates the complex interplay between international and municipal law on very practical questions, of interest to both the scholar and practitioner. What is more, significant complexities posed by situations of multiple nationality and the challenge of how to treat multinational enterprises both remain enduring problems with contemporary significance.

[88] *LFH Neer and Pauline Neer (USA) v Mexico* (1926) 4 RIAA 60; *García and Garza* (1926) 4 RIAA 119; *Roberts Claim* (1926) 4 RIAA 77.

[89] *Neer, ibid*, 61–2.

[90] See, e.g., *Janes Claim* (1926) 4 RIAA 82.

[91] *Roberts Claim* (n 86); see also *Quintanilla Claim* (1926) 4 RIAA 101.

[92] *Boffolo Case (Italy v Venezuela)* (1903) 10 RIAA 528.

[93] See also European Convention on Establishment (signed 13 December 1955, entered into force 23 February 1965), 529 UNTS 141, Art 3 (expulsion only being possible if an alien endangers national security or offends against public order and morality); European Convention on Human Rights (signed 4 November 1950, entered into force 3 September 1953), 213 UNTS 222, Fourth Protocol, ETS 46 (in force 1968), Art 4 (prohibiting the collective expulsion of aliens).

To date, practice and case law have remained somewhat incoherent, especially in relation to the nationality of claims. The ILC's 2006 Articles on Diplomatic Protection are a significant contribution to the field, consolidating settled practice, highlighting ambiguities, and proposing concrete solutions. If these are eventually adopted in the form of a treaty, they will codify this important area of international law. Even if, like the 2001 Articles on State Responsibility, they are not transformed into a convention, they may nevertheless provide a focal point for States, guiding them in the development of new customary international law.

Further reading

CF Amerasinghe, *Diplomatic Protection* (OUP, 2008).

Comprehensively identifies the key cases and practice, as well as highlighting the main points of controversy.

L Condorelli, 'La protection diplomatique et l'évolution de son domaine d'application' (2003) 86 Rivista di diritto internazionale 5–26.

A leading French-language piece on the scope and future direction of the rules on diplomatic protection.

JF Flauss (ed), *La Protection Diplomatique* (Bruylant, 2003).

A strong edited collection gathering leading French-language scholars on diplomatic protection.

C Forcese, 'Shelter from the Storm: Rethinking Diplomatic Protection of Dual Nationals in Modern International Law' (2005) 37 George Washington International Law Review 469–500.

A spirited call for a different approach to resolving questions of multiple nationality.

E Milano, 'Diplomatic Protection and Human Rights before the International Court of Justice: Re-Fashioning Tradition?' (2004) 35 NYIL 85–142.

A key piece linking questions of diplomatic protection with the emergence of human rights.

A Vermeer-Künzli, 'Diallo and the Draft Articles: The Application of the Draft Articles on Diplomatic Protection in the *Ahmadou Sadio Diallo* Case' (2007) 20 LJIL 941–54.

Comment on one of the most significant recent cases in the field of diplomatic protection.

C Warbrick, 'Protection of Nationals Abroad: Current Legal Problems' (1988) 37 ICLQ 1002.

An insightful, detailed account of some of the outstanding doctrinal controversies relating to the protection of nationals abroad.

A Watts, 'Nationality of Claims: Some Relevant Concepts' in V Lowe (ed), *Fifty Years of the International Court of Justice: Essays in Honour of Sir Robert Jennings* (CUP, 1996), 424–39.

A succinct survey of the rules of nationality of claims.

S Wittich, 'Direct Injury and the Incidence of the Local Remedies Rule' (2000) 5 Austrian Review of International and European Law 121–87.

A highly interesting piece on the direct/indirect distinction with respect to injuries.

12

International dispute settlement and the ICJ

12.1 Introduction: to resolve disputes through law, not war

Woven deeply into the fabric of modern international law is the belief that law will enable the peaceful resolution of international disputes.[1] Many international institutions were founded in service of that ideal, with two principal mechanisms developed. In this chapter, we will briefly review these, beginning with the various political or diplomatic methods available for dispute settlement. We will then turn to third-party dispute arbitration and adjudication, with a particular focus on the ICJ, given its particular status as the 'principal judicial organ' of the United Nations,[2] with general subject-matter jurisdiction over any questions of international law. Moreover, the ICJ's structure was frequently utilized as a model for later judicial institutions, and it has made an enormous contribution to the development of international law.[3]

Before turning to these mechanisms, it is useful briefly to define the notion of a 'dispute', which goes beyond a mere 'disagreement'. The PCIJ sought in *Mavrommatis Palestine Concessions* to define the term, in a much-reprised statement, as 'a disagreement over a point of law or fact, a conflict of legal views or of interests'.[4] An international dispute would generally involve two or more parties, typically but not exclusively States. The dispute might involve legal or political aspects, often both; and in principle, the existence of dispute is a question of substance or fact, though as the following commentary illustrates, there are some nuances to this position.

[1] See Chapter 1 for the importance of this theme in understanding the importance of international law; and see A Peters, 'International Dispute Settlement: A Network of Cooperational Duties' (2003) 14 EJIL 1.

[2] Charter of the United Nations (signed 26 June 1945, entered into force 24 October 1945), 1 UNTS xvi (UN Charter), Art 92.

[3] I have elsewhere engaged in a detailed treatment of the Court: see generally GI Hernández, *The International Court of Justice and the Judicial Function* (OUP, 2014).

[4] *Mavrommatis Palestine Concessions, Judgment No 2, 1924, PCIJ, Ser A, No 2*, p 7, 11. The Court continues to quote *Mavrommatis* approvingly: see, e.g., *Application of the International Convention on the Elimination of All Forms of Racial Discrimination (Georgia v Russian Federation), Preliminary Objections, Judgment, ICJ Reports 2011*, p 70, para 30; *Obligation to Prosecute or Extradite (Belgium v Senegal), Judgment, ICJ Reports 2012*, p 422, para 46.

CONTEMPORARY DEVELOPMENTS **Refining the Concept of the 'Existence of a Dispute' in Recent Cases**

One might expect that the notion of the 'existence of a dispute' would have long been settled in the Court's case law. Yet important clarifications have arisen in recent years, with significant statements on the existence of a dispute in recent cases.

In *Obligations concerning Negotiations relating to Cessation of the Nuclear Arms Race and to Nuclear Disarmament ((Marshall Islands v United Kingdom), Preliminary Objections, ICJ Reports 2016*, p 833), claims had been brought by Marshall Islands against all known nuclear States—knowing that the Court had no jurisdiction in respect of most—on the basis that, by failing to disarm their nuclear arsenals, they had failed to fulfil its obligations under Article VI of the Treaty on the Non-Proliferation of Nuclear Weapons (NPT). Only the claims against India, Pakistan, and the United Kingdom had some plausible jurisdictional basis, with the most striking being the proceedings against the UK. After hearings on preliminary objections, the Court issued a highly exceptional 8-8 decision (the tie was broken by the casting vote of the president) in which it found that it had no jurisdiction over the Marshall Islands' claim, concluding that it had failed to demonstrate that the UK was aware, or could not have been unaware, of a disagreement between the parties (para 38). The Marshall Islands could prove no direct communication with the UK, but only adduced evidence of statements in various UN bodies; in some of which the UK was not represented. The Court considered these were not directed with sufficient specificity to the respondent (paras 50–2).

This relatively new criterion of 'awareness' was invoked in the case brought by The Gambia asserting grave abuses against Myanmar's Rohingya minority (*Application of the Convention on the Prevention of the Crime of Genocide (The Gambia v Myanmar: Seven States intervening), Preliminary Objections, ICJ Reports 2022*, p 477). Amongst various objections, Myanmar asserted that the existence of a dispute required 'mutual awareness' between the parties of their opposing views, and that not only was sufficient 'particularity' required, but that a respondent must have opposed the original claim. Finding that between several statements by The Gambia in UN bodies and a Note Verbale (a diplomatic communication) addressed directly to Myanmar, the Court held that Myanmar could not have failed to know of the existence of a disagreement between the parties (paras 65–75). Moreover, though Myanmar had not responded to the Note Verbale, the Court determined that the existence of the dispute could be inferred from Myanmar's silence (para 76), thus discarding the need for any 'mutual awareness'. In two more recent cases involving the Genocide Convention, the Court has further clarified its understanding of 'awareness' of a disagreement, concluding that in certain cases, the public statements of both parties can be sufficient to establish a 'positive opposition of views' (see *Allegations of Genocide under the Convention on the Prevention of the Crime of Genocide (Ukraine v Russian Federation: 32 States intervening), Preliminary Objections, ICJ Reports 2024*, paras 47–50; *Application of the Convention on the Prevention of the Crime of Genocide in the Gaza Strip (South Africa v Israel), Order on Provisional Measures of 26 January 2024*, paras 26–8).

For further reading on the Court's interpretation of the 'existence of a dispute', see J McIntyre, 'Put on Notice: The Role of the Dispute Requirement in Assessing Jurisdiction and Admissibility before the International Court' (2018) 19(2) Melbourne JIL 546; and M Casas, 'Functional Justiciability and the Existence of a Dispute: A Means of Jurisdictional Avoidance?' (2019) 10 JIDS 599.

In any event, Article 2(3) of the UN Charter stipulates that all States 'shall settle their international disputes by peaceful means in such a manner that international peace and security and justice are not endangered'.[5] This obligation is buttressed by Article 33(1) of the Charter, which enumerates a choice of means to States: negotiation, inquiry, mediation, conciliation, arbitration, judicial settlement, resort to regional agencies or arrangements, or other peaceful methods of their choice. Various resolutions of the General Assembly have adopted that non-hierarchical enumeration. It provides a useful structure through which to review the various options available to States.[6]

Finally, it bears noting that regional agencies of the UN, as well as independent regional organizations such as the African Union, the OAS, the OSCE in Europe, and the Arab League, also play an important role in international dispute settlement.[7]

12.2 Diplomatic techniques of international dispute settlement

12.2.1 Negotiation

Negotiation is not a technical term, and refers to the straightforward idea of gathering the parties to a dispute with a view to its resolution. As the ICJ explained in *Application of the CERD*, the cooperation of both parties may not even be required. Negotiation requires nothing more than 'a genuine attempt by one of the disputing parties to engage in discussions with the other disputing party, with a view to resolving the dispute'.[8] Negotiation, by definition, does not involve third parties, may be conducted in secret or in public, and its scope may be entirely defined by the parties. Negotiation frequently precedes or accompanies other modes of dispute settlement, and is no bar to other proceedings such as litigation.[9] Finally, ongoing litigation can sometimes be abandoned due to a negotiated settlement.[10] As one can observe, negotiation is eminently flexible.

Successful negotiations hinge on the goodwill and mutual desire of the parties to reach some form of accommodation. What is more, negotiations cannot redress an imbalance in political, strategic, or economic power between parties, and it may well be that a weaker party will prefer third-party settlement precisely for that reason.

[5] See also UNGA, 'Manila Declaration on the Peaceful Settlement of International Disputes', UN Doc A/37/10 (15 November 1982), para 7, which lays out a duty for States to persevere in seeking a peaceful solution even when early attempts fail.

[6] This enumeration is reprised in the Manila Declaration, para 5, and the earlier UNGA, 'Declaration on Principles of International Law Concerning Friendly Relations and Co-operation among States', UNGA Res 25/2625 (XXV) (24 October 1970); UNGA, 'Declaration on the Occasion of the Twenty-fifth Anniversary of the United Nations' (24 October 1970), UN Doc A/RES/2627(XXV).

[7] See, e.g., E de Brabandere, *Merrills' International Dispute Settlement* (7th edn, CUP, 2022), ch 11; P Sands and P Klein, *Bowett's Law of International Institutions* (6th edn, Sweet & Maxwell, 2009); J Collier and V Lowe, *The Settlement of Disputes in International Law* (2nd edn, OUP, 1999 A 3rd edition with A Tzanakopoulos is forthcoming in 2026).

[8] *Application of CERD* (n 4) 132.

[9] *Aegean Sea Continental Shelf (Greece v Turkey), Preliminary Objections, ICJ Reports 1978*, p 3, para 29.

[10] *Aerial Incident of 3 July 1988 (Iran v United States), Order of 22 February 1996, ICJ Reports 1996*, p 9.

In some cases, negotiations may be required as a precondition for further avenues to be explored. In the ICJ's 2011 judgment in *Application of the CERD*, Russia objected successfully to Georgia's invocation of a compromissory clause that required six months of negotiations before the Court could be seised (could validly take jurisdiction), and in which Georgia's protests and notifications in the days preceding submission were found not to constitute such negotiations.[11] What would negotiation entail? In *North Sea Continental Shelf*, the ICJ suggested that States under an obligation to negotiate should conduct themselves so that the negotiations are 'meaningful', and meetings would not suffice when either State merely 'insists upon its own position without contemplating any modification of it'.[12] As such, an obligation to negotiate does not presuppose an obligation to arrive at an accord but, instead, should be understood as a general duty to discuss with other parties in good faith.

12.2.2 **Mediation and 'good offices'**

Though the flexibility of negotiation ensures its use within international relations, in many cases negotiation alone is insufficient to resolve a dispute. In such cases, States sometimes try to enlist the assistance of a third party in order to facilitate an agreement between contesting parties, through 'good offices' or mediation. These mechanisms were recognized in the 1899 and 1907 Hague Conventions, which laid a duty on the parties to resort to good offices or mediation whenever practicable before having recourse to arms.[13] The Hague Conventions also provided that any signatory could offer good offices or mediation in the course of a dispute,[14] and that such mechanisms were not binding.[15]

The term 'good offices' is used for the most informal third-party involvement; generally, as a willing conduit for communications between disputants. This third party has often been a high-ranking official such as a head of State (frequently the Pope), foreign minister, or ambassador, or an official from an international organization, such as the UN Secretary-General. Notable examples include the Secretary-General's good offices in situations such as the Argentina–UK dispute over the Falkland Islands in 1982, the conflict in Afghanistan in 1988, and in the enduring dispute over Northern Cyprus.[16]

[11] *Application of CERD* (n 4). A more successful example of negotiations being held unsuccessfully were the two years of negotiations and exchanges between Ukraine and Russia, in which alleged violations of CERD were made: see *Application of the International Convention on the Elimination of All Forms of Racial Discrimination (Ukraine v Russian Federation), Preliminary Objections, ICJ Reports 2019*, p 558, paras 118–20. Compromissory clauses will be discussed later, in Section 12.3.2.3.3.

[12] *North Sea Continental Shelf (Federal Republic of Germany v Denmark; Federal Republic of Germany v the Netherlands), Judgment, ICJ Reports 1969*, p 3, 47. See also *Land and Maritime Boundary between Cameroon and Nigeria (Cameroon v Nigeria: Equatorial Guinea intervening), Merits, ICJ Reports 2002*, p 303, 423; and *Legality of the Threat or Use of Nuclear Weapons, Advisory Opinion, ICJ Reports 1996*, p 226, 263–4.

[13] Hague Convention for the Pacific Settlement of International Disputes (signed 29 July 1899, entered into force 4 September 1900), 187 CTS 410; Hague Convention for the Pacific Settlement of International Disputes (signed 18 October 1907, entered into force 26 January 1910), 205 CTS 277, Art 2.

[14] *Ibid*, Art 3. [15] *Ibid*, Art 6.

[16] For further examples, see Merrills (n 7) ch 2; A O'Donoghue, 'Good Offices: Grasping the Role of Law in Conflict' (2014) 34 Legal Studies 469.

As opposed to 'good offices', a 'mediator' will take on a more active role beyond merely facilitating communication. Disputing parties need to agree on the role that the mediator will play in resolving a dispute. As such, a mediator might do no more than reconcile the parties and ensure continued communications. They might go further, seeking to accommodate the diverging claims, counselling parties, and encouraging them to continue to negotiate, or even devising their own solutions. The priority for the mediator is to find conditions that parties can accept in order to resolve the dispute; it does not matter from where these solutions may come. The USA mediated between the UK and Argentina in the Falklands crisis,[17] and it is said that Algeria played an important role in mediating between Iran and the USA pursuant to the 1979 hostages crisis.[18]

International organizations can also act as mediators under certain conditions. Article 38(1)(b) of the ECHR requires the ECtHR 'to place itself at the disposal of the parties with a view to securing a friendly settlement of the matter on the basis of respect for human rights'. If such a settlement is achieved, the Court will throw out the case.[19]

There is no standard procedure for either the exercise of good offices or the conduct of mediation, and the lines between them often become blurred, especially when discussions are kept confidential. Like negotiation, however, the flexibility of these two procedures has much to commend them, and such intercession may contribute appreciably to the resolution of a dispute.

12.2.3 **Inquiry**

An 'inquiry', in its broadest sense, is a process in which information is gathered in relation to a disputed factual issue. In international law, the value of an inquiry lies in establishing an impartial record of the facts, which help to establish fault and causation, and how to calculate loss and injury. It can serve to defuse tensions between disputants and help them arrive at a settlement. In some cases, disputing parties may agree to accept the outcome of this process and therefore resolve the dispute.

The idea of a 'commission of inquiry'—that is, a group of individuals tasked with conducting an inquiry—being used as a mechanism for peaceful dispute settlement was first found in the 1899 Hague Convention. Such commissions emerged possibly as a reaction to the unexplained explosion of the US battleship *SS Maine* in Havana (Cuba was then a Spanish overseas province), which provoked the Spanish–American War of 1898.[20] A commission of inquiry was prominently constituted in 1904 in the 'Dogger Bank' incident, where Russian naval ships fired on British fishing vessels in the

[17] See Merrills (n 7) ch 2.

[18] See G Sick, 'The Partial Negotiator: Algeria and the US Hostages in Iran' in S Touval and IW Zartman (eds), *International Mediation in Theory and in Practice* (Westview Press, 1985), 21.

[19] See, e.g., *Sünnetçi v Turkey* App No 28632/95 (after severe torture in detention, but upon an expression of regret and a payment of €25,000 by Turkey); and *Özgür Kiliç v Turkey* App No 42591/98 (after two instances of ill-treatment in custody, but upon an expression of regret and payments of €27,000 and €25,000 by Turkey). See further H Keller, M Forowicz, and L Engi, *Friendly Settlements before the European Court of Human Rights* (OUP, 2010).

[20] For a history of such commissions, see N Bar-Yaacov, *International Disputes* (OUP, 1974), ch 3, esp 33–4.

mistaken belief that they were hostile Japanese torpedo craft. The commission's final report of events was accepted by both parties in a peaceful resolution.[21]

Despite early adoption, the Hague Convention mechanism was rarely used, and it remained limited to determinations of fact.[22] However, in recent years, the United Nations and its organs have made more frequent use of commissions, which have expanded beyond pure fact-finding to include the legal evaluation of relevant facts, as well as the gathering and assessment of criminal evidence. In recent years, such fact-finding operations seem to have moved away from dispute settlement and towards bringing atrocities to light and mobilizing action from the UN or other bodies, with mixed effects.[23]

Prominent examples of commissions established under the Security Council include: the UN Compensation Commission to resolve claims against Iraq following its failed invasion of Kuwait in 1990;[24] the commission of inquiry established in respect of the occupation of East Timor;[25] and the commission of inquiry established in respect of the Yugoslavia conflicts in the early 1990s.[26] More recently, independent international commissions of inquiry (or fact-finding missions) have been established by the UN Human Rights Council in respect of situations in Libya, Yemen, and Myanmar.[27] The independent international commission of inquiry in respect of the Occupied Palestinian Territory was established in 2021.[28] Since the explosion of violence in the Gaza Strip commencing 7 October 2023, it has issued two extensive reports identifying a series of grave violations of peremptory norms (*jus cogens*) by both Hamas (war crimes) and Israel (war crimes and crimes against humanity).[29]

12.2.4 **Conciliation**

A further dispute-settlement method, the process of 'conciliation', further formalizes the role of the third party, which may investigate a dispute and propose a solution, usually through the submission of a non-binding final report to be considered by the parties. Blending elements of mediation and inquiry, conciliation has most often been employed

[21] *Ibid*, esp 70.

[22] At *ibid*, 179–95, see the 1962 *Red Crusader* inquiry between the UK and Denmark. A number of bilateral treaties between the USA and other States, known as the 'Bryan treaties', encouraged the creation of permanent commissions of inquiry: *ibid*, 113–17; however, only one was ever constituted, in the *Leteiler and Moffitt* case (1992) 88 ILR 727.

[23] See LJ van den Herik, 'An Inquiry into the Role of Commissions of Inquiry in International Law: Navigating the Tensions between Fact-Finding and Application of International Law' (2014) 13 Chinese JIL 507. A more sceptical stance is taken in the symposium introduced by MA Becker and SMH Nouwen, 'International Commissions of Inquiry: What Difference Do They Make? Taking an Empirical Approach' (2019) 30 EJIL 819.

[24] UNSC Res 687 (3 April 1991).

[25] UNSC Res 384 (22 December 1975).

[26] UNSC Res 780 (6 October 1992).

[27] See, e.g., UN Doc A/HRC/RES/43/39 (22 June 2020) (Libya); UN Doc A/HRC/RES/36/31 (29 September 2017) (Yemen); UN Doc A/HRC/RES/34/22 (3 April 2017) (Myanmar). The UN Human Rights Council maintains an updated list at <https://www.ohchr.org/en/hr-bodies/hrc/co-is>.

[28] See UN Doc A/HRC/RES/S-30/1 (28 May 2021) (Occupied Palestinian Territory).

[29] See UN Doc A/HRC/56/CRP.3 (10 June 2024); UN Doc A/79/232 (11 September 2024).

in the interwar period, often in the form of permanent commissions established by treaty.[30] The 1928 General Act on the Pacific Settlement of International Disputes[31] proposed rules for conciliation commissions with respect to their composition and procedure, but most prominently with respect to their functions; namely, 'to elucidate the questions in dispute, to collect with that object all necessary information by means of an enquiry or otherwise, and to endeavour to bring the parties to an agreement'.[32] It bears emphasizing that the recommendation of the conciliation commission is virtually never binding,[33] and most treaties referring to conciliation awards stipulate no more than that they should be considered in good faith.[34] Conciliation commissions became less common after World War II,[35] though there have been attempts at revitalization.[36] Recently, a conciliation process conducted between Australia and Timor-Leste led to the successful conclusion of a treaty concerning their oil-rich maritime boundary.[37]

Finally, though conciliation commissions have rarely been used, it bears noting that a number of multilateral environmental instruments have provided for 'non-compliance procedures' through which special committees receive submissions with respect to non-compliance by a State party, and issue non-binding recommendations with a view to securing an amicable solution of the matter.[38] Though not strictly related to inter-State disputes, these innovative mechanisms are further addressed in Chapter 19.

[30] Merrills (n 7) 60 noted that some 200 conciliation treaties were in force in 1940.

[31] 1928 General Act for the Pacific Settlement of international Disputes (adopted 26 September 1928, entered into force 16 August 1929), 93 LNTS 343, amended by the Revised General Act for the Pacific Settlement of International Disputes (adopted 28 April 1949, entered into force 20 September 1950), 71 UNTS 101.

[32] *Ibid*, Art 15(1). See also Regulations on the Procedure of International Conciliation, as adopted by the Institute of International Law (1961) 49(2) Annuaire de l'Institut de droit international 385, Art 1.

[33] Though see Treaty of Basseterre establishing the Organization of Eastern Caribbean States (adopted 18 June 1981), 20 ILM 1166, Art 14(3), which stipulates that decisions from the conciliation procedure are compulsory.

[34] See, e.g., Vienna Convention for the Protection of the Ozone Layer 1985, Art 11(5); Vienna Convention on the Representation of States in their Relations with International Organizations, Art 85(7); United Nations Convention on the Law of the Sea 1992, Art 7(2); and Convention on Biological Diversity 1992, Annex II, Part 2, Art 5.

[35] Though see, e.g., Franco-Siamese Conciliation Commission, 1947; Belgian–Danish Commission, 1952; Franco-Swiss Commission, 1955; East African Community Commission ('Umbricht Commission'), 1977. These and others are further discussed in Merrills (n 7) ch 4.

[36] See 1961 Regulations of the Institute of International Law (n 30); UNGA, 'UNCITRAL Model Rules for Conciliation in International Commercial Disputes', UN Doc A/RES/35/52 (4 December 1980); UNGA, UN Model Rules for the Conciliation of Disputes Between States, UN Doc A/RES/50/50 (29 January 1996); and Optional Conciliation Rules adopted by the Permanent Court of Arbitration (1996).

[37] See *Report and Recommendations of the Compulsory Conciliation Commission between Timor-Leste and Australia on the Timor Sea (9 May 2018)*, PCA Case No 2016-10, available at https://pca-cpa.org/en/cases/132/. The Report and Recommendations were a crucial element in the Treaty between Australia and Timor-Leste Establishing their Maritime Boundaries in the Timor Sea (signed 6 March 2018, entered into force 30 August 2019).

[38] See Montreal Protocol on Substances that Deplete the Ozone Layer (signed 16 September 1987, entered into force 1 January 1989), 1522 UNTS 3, Art 8; Kyoto Protocol to the UN Framework Convention on Climate Change (signed 11 December 1997, entered into force 16 February 2005), 2303 UNTS 148, Art 18; Convention on Access to Information, Public Participation in Decision-Making and Access to Justice in Environmental Matters (signed 25 June 1998, entered into force 30 October 2001), 2161 UNTS 447 (Aarhus Convention), Art 15; Cartagena Protocol on Biosafety to the Convention on Biological Diversity (signed 29 January 2000, entered into force 11 September 2003), 2226 UNTS 208, Art 34.

CASE SPOTLIGHT The *Jan Mayen Island* Conciliation Commission Report (1981) 20 ILM 797, 62 ILR 108

A significant conciliation commission was created in respect of Jan Mayen Island, which considered the delimitation of the continental shelf between Iceland and Jan Mayen Island, which is Norwegian territory. A not-insignificant factor exacerbating the long-standing dispute between those States was the potential for discovery of oil in many of the areas disputed between them.

A three-person Commission was appointed, received submissions from Iceland and Norway, and delivered its non-binding report in 1981. Taking into account Iceland's 'strong economic interests' and various other considerations, the Commission's report proposed both a boundary line and 'joint development zone' covering the area where oil deposits might exist. The joint development zone, in particular, had not been suggested by either disputant, demonstrating the potential for conciliation commissions to go beyond the positions of disputing parties and propose novel solutions.

The Jan Mayen Commission's report was so successful that it led to the conclusion of a bilateral Agreement on Fishery and Continental Shelf Questions (1981, 2124 UNTS 226) in which its recommendations were adopted. The outcome is demonstrative of how flexible conciliation can produce more durable compromises than a solution based purely on the legal rights of the parties, and how conciliation can be a useful and effective tool for fair dispute settlement.

For a fuller account of the process, see EL Richardson, 'Jan Mayen in Perspective' (1988) 82 AJIL 443.

12.3 Legally binding methods of dispute settlement

The array of diplomatic techniques available to parties to resolve a dispute is complemented by various means of settling disputes through the application of binding solutions based on the law. Two in particular, arbitration and adjudication, are principally developed from earlier forms of non-binding settlement. Though these are different, they are linked by two principal characteristics. Foremost, they allow for a third party to issue a decision that is binding on the parties. Secondly, resorting to these methods requires the prior consent of the parties. The chief distinction between arbitration and adjudication is the degree of control exercised by the parties over arbitral tribunals, including their composition, procedure, and applicable law, when compared with a permanent international court.

12.3.1 Arbitration

Arbitration is a long-established and highly visible mechanism for the resolution of international disputes. The 1794 Jay Treaty between Great Britain and the USA, established to settle claims arising between them after the latter's assertion of independence from British imperial control,[39] was the forerunner of modern international arbitration.[40] The Jay Treaty was distinctive in that the parties decided to establish 'mixed commissions', where each party appoints one arbitrator, and the party-appointed arbitrators appoint one or more further arbitrators, who collectively resolve outstanding claims on the basis of international law.[41]

HISTORICAL BACKGROUND The *Alabama* Arbitration and the US Civil War

One of the most significant early arbitral awards is that relating to the sinking of the Confederate ship the *CSS Alabama* during the US Civil War, a war between the Union and the 'Confederate States of America' (eleven southern states that wished to preserve slavery on their territory and secede from the union). Though Great Britain claimed neutrality, it recognized the Confederacy as a belligerent and supplied it with warships, including the building of the *Alabama*. The *Alabama* inflicted serious damage on the Union side, including the sinking of sixty-four Union vessels. After the Union defeated the Confederacy in 1864, the USA considered that Great Britain owed it compensation for its breach of obligations of neutrality.

In 1871, the Treaty of Washington provided that a mixed commission be created to resolve outstanding disputes between the parties. This would be composed of five arbitrators, of whom Her Britannic Majesty, the President of the USA, the King of Italy, the President of the Swiss Confederation, and the Emperor of Brazil were each to appoint one. The arbitral panel unanimously held Great Britain to be responsible for the direct damage caused by the *Alabama*, and awarded the USA $15,500,000 in damages. Besides the fact that both States complied, which made it a successful arbitration process, the *Alabama* award made two important contributions to international law.

First, the tribunal was required to resolve whether it had jurisdiction over several billion dollars' worth of claims for 'indirect damages' asserted by the USA, and adjudged that these did not fall within its jurisdiction. In so doing, it made a crucial contribution to the development of today's principle of *compétence de la compétence* (the power of a tribunal to determine its own jurisdiction) found in Article 36(6) of the ICJ Statute. The ICJ expressly referred to the *Alabama* case in *Nottebohm* (*ICJ Reports 1953*, p 111, 119) as the first recognition of that principle, which is discussed later in this chapter.

Secondly, the Treaty had set out certain obligations of due diligence for a neutral party between belligerents and, importantly, precluded Britain from invoking its domestic law as a defence for its acts. The principle was upheld by the Commission in determining that Britain had violated its international legal obligations, and has been recognized in Article 27 VCLT and by the ICJ (see, e.g., *Anglo-Norwegian Fisheries, ICJ Reports 1951*, p 116, 181). The principle therefore stands that a State can never invoke a provision of municipal law, or the absence of one, as a defence to a breach of international law.

For further reading, see T Bingham, 'The Alabama Claims Arbitration' (2005) 54 ICLQ 1; and A Cook, *The 'Alabama' Claims* (Cornell UP, 1975).

[39] Treaty of Amity, Commerce and Navigation 1794, named after then-US Secretary of State John Jay.

[40] Abundant literature exists: see L Simpson and H Fox, *International Arbitration* (Frederick A Praeger, 1959); Collier and Lowe (n 7) 189–279; L Caflisch, 'L'avenir de l'arbitrage interétatique' (1979) 25 AFDI 9; Merrills (n 7) ch 5.

[41] A concise summary of the legacy of the Jay Treaty arbitrations is G Schwarzenberger, 'Present-Day Relevance of the Jay Treaty Arbitrations' (1978) 53 Notre Dame Lawyer 715.

The success of the *Alabama* arbitration led to further arbitrations in the late nineteenth century—notably, those concerning the *Bering Sea*[42] and the *British Guiana and Venezuela Boundary*[43]—and propelled the development of international arbitration, culminating in the creation of the Permanent Court of Arbitration (PCA) at the first Hague Conference in 1899.[44] Under Article 15 of the 1899 Hague Convention, international arbitration was defined as 'the settlement of differences between States by judges of their own choice and on the basis of respect for law', a definition adopted in Article 37 of the 1907 Hague Convention and later endorsed by the PCIJ and the ICJ.[45]

Defined thus, arbitration is eminently suited for situations where a binding solution is required; for example, in territorial or maritime boundary disputes. Arbitration allows States, on an ad hoc basis, to agree to constitute a tribunal by special agreement (a *compromis*), setting out the consent of the parties to arbitration and the conditions through which this will proceed. Such conditions include defining the scope of the dispute, the selection of arbitrators, the procedure followed by the tribunal, and the applicable law.[46] Such control distinguishes arbitration from adjudication; the parties retain much more control over how proceedings are conducted. Arbitration has been a continuous fixture in international law, with seminal arbitral awards including *Tinoco*,[47] *Island of Palmas*,[48] and *Trail Smelter*.[49]

As for the PCA itself, it is not really a permanent court.[50] It is better understood as an international organization that provides permanent and readily available means to facilitate international arbitration. The PCA maintains a roster of approved arbitrators, with each State party nominating four persons; offers administrative support as a registry; and proposes model optional rules for parties to adapt for their purposes.[51]

Arbitration was temporarily eclipsed by the promise of international adjudication in the interwar period, during which the PCA suffered from decades of relative inactivity. However, in the last two decades, the PCA has experienced a veritable renaissance, facilitating awards to the point where, in 2014, its General List surpassed that of the ICJ for the first time. The PCA has acted as registry in some highly sensitive boundary disputes, including the *Red Sea Islands*,[52] the Eritrea–Ethiopia Boundary Commission,[53] and the

[42] (1893): see Moore's Digest of International Arbitrations, vol I, 755.

[43] (1899) 92 BFSP 970.

[44] The legacy of the PCA has been noted elsewhere: see M Fitzmaurice and CJ Tams (eds), *Legacies of the Permanent Court of International Justice* (Brill, 2013); Hernández, *Judicial Function* (n 3) 14–20; M Hudson, *The Permanent Court of International Justice 1920–1942* (Macmillan, 1943), 11.

[45] See *Interpretation of Article 3, paragraph 2, of the Treaty of Lausanne, Advisory Opinion, 1925, PCIJ, Ser B, No 12*, p 26; *Maritime Delimitation and Territorial Questions between Qatar and Bahrain, Merits, ICJ Reports 2001*, p 40, 76–7.

[46] For more detail regarding arbitral proceedings, see Merrills (n 7) ch 5; and Collier and Lowe (n 7) ch 8.

[47] *Tinoco Arbitration (United Kingdom/Costa Rica)* (1923) 1 RIAA 369, reprinted in (1924) 18 AJIL 147.

[48] *Island of Palmas (United States/the Netherlands)* (1928) 2 RIAA 829.

[49] *Trail Smelter (United States/Canada)* (1941) 3 RIAA 1905.

[50] S Rosenne (ed), *The Hague Peace Conferences of 1899 and 1907 and International Arbitration: Reports and Documents* (TMC Asser Press, 2001) commented drily that 'the Convention of 1899 gave only the phantom of a court, an impalpable specter or, to speak more precisely, it gave a secretariat and a list'.

[51] The PCA's webpages at <http://www.pca-cpa.org> list these model optional rules.

[52] *Red Sea Islands (Eritrea/Yemen)* (2001) 40 ILM 900 (territory) and 983 (maritime delimitation).

[53] *Eritrea–Ethiopia Boundary Commission* (Delimitation Decision of 13 April 2002) (2002) 129 ILR 1.

Abyei arbitration involving the secession of South Sudan from Sudan.[54] The PCA has also provided support for significant inter-State disputes, such as those involving the *Rainbow Warrior* ship,[55] the *Mox Plant* nuclear plant,[56] and the *Iron Rhine* railway.[57] In addition, the PCA is increasingly active in 'mixed arbitrations'; that is, disputes between an individual (or an investor) and a State on the other side. Often, these are under the auspices of ICSID, a centre for inter-State disputes with its own dispute-settlement mechanism.[58]

Another institution, the Iran–United States Claims Tribunal (IUSCT), has left a striking legacy with respect to mixed arbitrations. Composed of three arbitrators from Iran, three from the USA, and three from 'neutral States', the Iran–US Claims Tribunal was created in 1981 despite acrimonious circumstances between the two parties, thanks to the intercession of the Algerian government. It has resolved a large number of disputes where nationals of each State have been able to claim directly against the other State, and its decisions have made significant contributions to various areas of international law, such as diplomatic protection, State responsibility, and the rules on the treatment of aliens.[59]

12.3.2 **Adjudication and the ICJ**

12.3.2.1 **Why the ICJ?**

Adjudication involves the resolution of international disputes through a permanent judicial body, with fixed rules of procedure and the power to issue binding judgments. In recent decades, adjudication has become very popular, as evidenced by the proliferation of international, regional, and supranational courts and tribunals.[60] This section will focus on the principal judicial organ of the United Nations, the ICJ in The Hague. There are several characteristics which mark the ICJ out for special consideration. The first is the Court's wide competence, which may extend over disputes between any States. It is not limited to a specific region, and States need not even be members of the United Nations.[61] What further sets the ICJ apart from other judicial institutions open to all States is the fact that the ICJ is also a court of general jurisdiction; unlike bodies with limited subject-matter jurisdiction, such as the ITLOS or the WTO panels, it may adjudicate disputes over any question of international law brought before it. This includes many of the specialized regimes (such as the law of the sea, international trade law, or international criminal law) covered in this book.

[54] *Government of Sudan v People's Liberation Movement/Army (Abyei Arbitration)* (2009) 48 ILM 1254.

[55] *Rainbow Warrior (New Zealand/France)* (1986) 74 ILR 241, (1990) 82 ILR 499.

[56] *OSPAR Arbitration of the Mox Plant Dispute (Ireland/United Kingdom)* (2003) 42 ILM 330.

[57] *Arbitration regarding the Iron Rhine (Belgium/the Netherlands)* (2005) 140 ILR 130.

[58] Investor–State arbitration will be considered further in Chapter 20, Section 20.4.

[59] The IUSCT has published some thirty volumes of decisions involving inter-State claims, individual-State claims, and purely private claims. For further reading, see CN Brower and JD Brueschke, *The Iran–United States Claims Tribunal* (Martinus Nijhoff, 1998).

[60] Two books that help navigate the sheer volume of judicial institutions include R Mackenzie, C Romano, Y Shany, and P Sands, *Manual of International Courts and Tribunals* (2nd edn, OUP, 2010); C Romano, Y Shany, and K Alter (eds), *The Oxford Handbook of International Adjudication* (OUP, 2014).

[61] Statute of the International Court of Justice, as annexed to the Charter of the United Nations (signed 26 June 1945, entered into force 24 October 1945), 1 UNTS xvi, Art 34.

HISTORICAL BACKGROUND Institutional Continuity from the PCIJ to the ICJ

The ICJ, established in 1946, is in fact the continuator of the PCIJ founded in 1922 and linked to, but independent from, the League of Nations. The ICJ Statute, annexed to and forming part of the UN Charter, is a transposition of the PCIJ Statute, duly modified in order to integrate the ICJ as one of the principal organs of the United Nations.

The PCIJ Statute had aspired to break from the impermanent structures of the PCA and establish a permanent court with fixed rules of procedure, though its jurisdiction remained one based on the consent of States. These features, alongside others surveyed later in this chapter, were retained, such as the 'Optional Clause' mechanism, the election of judges, the place of the judge ad hoc, and its advisory function, which were first developed in the PCIJ Statute. Of particular importance, of course, were the sources listed in Article 38 of the PCIJ and ICJ Statutes, which as Chapter 2 demonstrates, continues to be regarded as the definitive enumeration of the sources of international law.

This continuity reflected a strategy to preserve the legacy of the PCIJ, and the ICJ conscientiously cites PCIJ case law even to the present day. Between them, the PCIJ and ICJ have accounted for a continuous line of judicial decisions for over a century, and have influenced the creation of all other international courts as well as the development of international law more generally.

For further reading, see GI Hernández, *The International Court of Justice and the Judicial Function* (OUP, 2014), ch II.

12.3.2.2 The organization of the Court

The ICJ is composed of fifteen individuals, elected by the General Assembly and the Security Council to nine-year staggered terms (five judges every three years).[62] No two individuals may be nationals from the same State, and they must be impartial, taking decisions independently and not as State representatives.[63] Article 9 of the Statute seeks to ensure 'in the body as a whole the representation of the main forms of civilization and of the principal legal systems of the world'. In practice, this has meant that each region represented in the United Nations has representation on the Court. There was also a long-standing convention that there would always be judges from the five permanent members of the Security Council, until 2017, when Judge Christopher Greenwood of the UK withdrew his candidacy and Judge Dalveer Bhandari, of India, was elected with stronger support in the General Assembly.[64] In 2024, Judge Kirill Gevorgian of Russia was not re-elected, giving way to Judge Bogdan Aurescu, of Romania.

Another representational issue is that gender representation on the bench was, until recently, non-existent. The first female judge, Dame Rosalyn Higgins (UK), was elected

[62] *Ibid*, Art 13. [63] *Ibid*, Art 3.

[64] For a succinct description of the context of the 2017 elections to the ICJ, see D Akande, 'ICJ Elections 2017: UN General Assembly and Security Council Elect Four Judges to the ICJ but fail to Agree on a Fifth, yet again!' *EJIL:Talk* (11 November 2017).

in 1995 and subsequently elected the Court's first female president in 2006. Judge Joan Donoghue (USA) was elected its second female president, in 2021. Of the fifteen judges on the ICJ at present, only four (Julia Sebutinde, Xue Hanqin, Hilary Charlesworth, and Sarah Cleveland) are female.

Cases, in principle, are heard by the full bench, unless the parties decide to establish a chamber of the Court composed of fewer judges.[65] A further interesting feature of the ICJ, as evidence of its arbitral heritage, is the office of judge ad hoc. Article 31(2) of the ICJ Statute provides that if no judge of the nationality of a party sits on the Court, they are entitled to choose a person to sit as judge ad hoc for the duration of the case; this person need not be one of their nationals. The presence of judges ad hoc has been questioned, on the basis that they affect external perceptions of the Court as an impartial and independent organ.[66] However, there are also those who have defended the presence of judges ad hoc as helping to persuade the parties that all their arguments will have been fully understood.[67] In any event, judges ad hoc continue to be an integral part of the Court's work and are regularly appointed by parties.

Importantly, though, a few rules are set in the Court's Statute and the Court itself enjoys the power to develop procedural rules for its functions.[68] The Rules have been modified over the decades.[69] The Court has also specified the procedure through which its judgments are drafted[70] and regularly issues 'Practice Directions' to recommend how parties should engage with it.[71] While its judgments are adopted by majority vote by 'the Court' as a collective body, all judges have the right to add an individual statement of their views, whether dissenting or concurring (or a mere 'declaration').[72] In the case of a tie, the President of the Court has a casting vote, which has been used six times, most recently in the Court's 2016 judgment on nuclear disarmament obligations between the Marshall Islands and the UK.[73]

[65] The chamber mechanism has not been successful, with few cases decided in this manner. A proposed 'Chamber for Environmental Matters' created in 1993 was never used by States, and has been defunct since 2006.

[66] See I Scobbie, '"Une hérésie en matière judiciaire"? The Role of the Judge ad hoc in the International Court' (2005) 4 JLPICT 421; A Oraison, 'Réflexions sur l'institution du juge ad hoc siégeant à la Cour internationale de Justice' (1998) Revue Belge de Droit International 272.

[67] The most eloquent defenders have in fact been judges ad hoc: see Sir Elihu Lauterpacht's Dissenting Opinion in the *Application of the Convention on the Prevention and Punishment of the Crime of Genocide (Bosnia and Herzegovina v Yugoslavia), Provisional Measures, ICJ Reports 1993*, p 325, 408–9, paras 4–6; and Dissenting Opinion of Thomas Franck in *Sovereignty over Pulau Litigan and Pulau Sipadan (Indonesia/Malaysia), Judgment, ICJ Reports 2002*, p 625, 691. For further discussion, see Hernández, *Judicial Function* (n 3) 145–54.

[68] ICJ Statute (n 59) Art 30.

[69] The Rules of Court were fully revised in 1978, and last amended in 2023. These are available online at <http://www.icj-cij.org/en/rules>.

[70] See 'Resolution concerning the Internal Judicial Practice of the Court' (1976), available online at <http://www.icj-cij.org/en/other-texts/resolution-concerning-judicial-practice>.

[71] There are thirteen Practice Directions, available online at <http://www.icj-cij.org/en/practice-directions>.

[72] The Court's deliberative process was studied in depth in Hernández, *Judicial Function* (n 3) ch 4.

[73] *Obligations concerning Negotiations relating to Cessation of the Nuclear Arms Race and to Nuclear Disarmament (Marshall Islands v United Kingdom), Preliminary Objections, ICJ Reports 2016*, p 833. The claims of the Marshall Islands against India and Pakistan were dismissed as neither of the latter two States had accepted the jurisdiction of the Court.

12.3.2.3 **The contentious function of the Court**

The Court's jurisdictional structure illustrates the distinction between international adjudication and arbitration. Both rely, of course, on State consent, with various mechanisms offered in the ICJ Statute, which itself is annexed to the UN Charter. However, in marked contrast with arbitration, the Court's existence as a permanent judicial institution requires States submitting their disputes to it to accept the Court's established rules of procedure.

The Court's jurisdiction is separated into two distinct functions. It may decide disputes between States (its contentious jurisdiction), and it may give advisory opinions to certain institutions and organs which are qualified to make a request (its advisory jurisdiction).

12.3.2.3.1 ***Contentious jurisdiction***

Under Article 34(1) of the Court's Statute, only States may be parties in contentious proceedings; non-State actors, including private persons, international organizations, and corporations, may not appear as parties before it. The Court is open to all UN members, which under Article 35 are *ipso facto* parties to the Statute. The Security Council has set conditions of access for non-member States,[74] though that is largely obsolete today given the UN's near-universal membership.

Unlike the ECJ or the WTO dispute-settlement mechanism, being a party to the ICJ Statute does not mean that a State has consented to the compulsory jurisdiction of the Court. It is well established that the Court can only adjudicate over a State with its consent,[75] and that such consent must be 'voluntary and indisputable'.[76]

Under Article 36 of the Statute, there are three principal 'heads of jurisdiction' through which parties consent to the Court's jurisdiction:

- cases referred to the Court by the parties by agreement;
- matters provided for in the UN Charter;
- questions arising in other treaties which contain 'compromissory clauses' (clauses that express the prior consent of parties to the Court's jurisdiction); and
- acceptance by a State, in advance of a dispute arising, of the jurisdiction of the Court in relation to international law disputes (the so-called 'Optional Clause').

These will each be addressed in turn.

12.3.2.3.2 ***Special agreement (compromis)***

The most straightforward method for the Court to take jurisdiction is for States to agree to submit a specific dispute to it, through a 'special agreement' or *compromis* not unlike those used in arbitral proceedings.[77] Normally, in such cases, seisin (the taking

[74] See UNSC Res 9 (15 October 1946).

[75] See *Certain Questions of Mutual Assistance in Criminal Matters (Djibouti/France), Judgment, ICJ Reports 2008*, p 177, 200; *Armed Activities in the Territory of the Congo (New Application: 2002) (Democratic Republic of the Congo v Rwanda), Jurisdiction and Admissibility, Judgment, ICJ Reports 2006*, p 6, 39.

[76] *Corfu Channel (United Kingdom v Albania), Preliminary Objection, ICJ Reports 1948*, p 13, 31.

[77] See earlier, Section 12.3.1.

of jurisdiction by the Court) is established by both States notifying the Court that they have come to such an agreement. At times, however, a party approaches the Court to claim that there exists a prior agreement regarding jurisdiction, and the other party objects to that claim; this must be addressed in a 'preliminary objections' phase on jurisdiction and/or admissibility.

Form is not important: what matters is evidence of the existence of consent. A notable illustration of this situation is the dispute between Qatar and Bahrain, in which the Court concluded that the minutes of a 1990 bilateral meeting constituted an international agreement through which the parties had consented to bring the dispute to the Court.[78] The consent by both States need not be established already by the time of the filing of an application. Through a procedure known as *forum prorogatum*, which is enshrined in Article 38(5) of the Court's Rules, one State may invite another State to accept jurisdiction in respect of a particular dispute where jurisdiction would not otherwise exist. Though quite a rare occurrence, in *Mutual Assistance in Criminal Matters* France accepted Djibouti's invitation to bring a dispute to the Court under Article 38(5) of the Rules.[79]

12.3.2.3.3 ***Compromissory clauses***

The Court may also have jurisdiction over disputes arising over international treaties in force, provided that these contain a 'compromissory clause'. Many key multilateral treaties contain precisely such a provision, which confers on the Court the jurisdiction to resolve disputes relating to their interpretation or application. Milestone cases have been decided in respect of some of these, including the 1948 Genocide Convention (Art IX),[80] the 1963 Vienna Convention on Consular Relations (VCCR) (through its Optional Protocol),[81] and the 1984 Torture Convention (Art 22).[82] The Court's website lists more than 300 bilateral and multilateral treaties which contain compromissory clauses in relation to the ICJ or the PCIJ.[83] A recent application invokes for the first time Article 66, the compromissory clause in the UN Convention against Corruption.[84]

[78] *Maritime Delimitation and Territorial Questions between Qatar and Bahrain (Qatar v Bahrain), Jurisdiction and Admissibility, Judgment, ICJ Reports 1994*, p 112, 121. See also *Maritime Delimitation in the Indian Ocean (Somalia v Kenya), Preliminary Objections, ICJ Reports 2017*, p 3, para 43, where a memorandum of understanding (MOU) between the two parties was held to constitute such an agreement; and *Arbitral Award of 3 October 1899 (Guyana v Venezuela), Preliminary Objections, Judgment of 18 December 2020*, paras 104–8, in which the parties conferred on the Secretary-General the authority to choose the means of dispute settlement in a binding treaty between them (the 'Geneva Agreement'). In interpreting the Geneva Agreement, the Court concluded that the Secretary-General was entitled to decide that the Court should have jurisdiction over the dispute.

[79] *Mutual Assistance in Criminal Matters* (n 75) paras 60–4.

[80] *Application of the Convention on the Prevention and Punishment of the Crime of Genocide (Bosnia and Herzegovina v Serbia and Montenegro), Merits, ICJ Reports 2007*, p 43; and *Application of the Convention on the Prevention and Punishment of the Crime of Genocide (Croatia v Serbia), Merits, ICJ Reports 2015*, p 3.

[81] *Avena and other Mexican Nationals (Mexico v United States), Judgment, ICJ Reports 2004*, p 12.

[82] *Obligation to Prosecute or Extradite (Belgium v Senegal), Judgment, ICJ Reports 2012*, p 422.

[83] See <http://www.icj-cij.org/en/treaties>.

[84] See *Request Relating to the Return of Property Confiscated in Criminal Proceedings (Equatorial Guinea v France), Application Instituting Proceedings of 29 September 2022*, paras 17–20.

Compromissory clauses signify the consent of all parties in relation to matters covered by the treaty, and may be invoked unilaterally by any party. However, a State may attach a reservation (see Chapter 7, Section 7.3) excepting itself in full or in part from the application of a compromissory clause, as did Rwanda successfully with respect to the Genocide Convention and other human rights instruments in 2006.[85] States may also opt out entirely from an optional protocol to a convention that confers jurisdiction on the Court, as did the USA in relation to the Optional Protocol to the VCCR, after losing a few cases under that Convention.[86]

As with cases brought through special agreement, a State may file preliminary objections to an application filed unilaterally, in which the Court must consider whether its seisin has been fully established. Memorable cases before the Court have concerned preliminary objections that the treaty's scope does not extend to the subject matter in dispute (lack of jurisdiction *ratione materiae*)[87] or that a compromissory clause cannot apply because the treaty was not in force between the parties during the relevant period (lack of jurisdiction *ratione temporis*).[88]

12.3.2.3.4 ***The 'Optional Clause'***

A crucial development in the ICJ Statute rests in Article 36(2), what is known as the 'Optional Clause'; a complex mechanism which allows States to 'opt in' to the Court's jurisdiction over disputes involving them. Originally, it was proposed by the drafters of the Statute that the Court would have 'compulsory jurisdiction'; that is, any State party to the Statute would be able to bring any international dispute against another State by unilateral application. However, in the League of Nations and later in the United Nations, States expressed strong resistance to a system of compulsory jurisdiction, and the Optional Clause system was crafted as a compromise, allowing some States to opt out, and others to opt in.[89]

The basic features of the Optional Clause system are outlined in Article 36(2) of the Statute. States are invited to file a declaration with the UN Secretary-General that they recognize the Court's jurisdiction as compulsory in relation to legal disputes on a wide number of matters, thereby removing the need for a special agreement or

[85] *Armed Activities in the Congo (Congo v Rwanda)* (n 73), 18–19, paras 19–22. See also *Norwegian Loans (France v Norway), Judgment, ICJ Reports 1957*, p 9; and *Fisheries Jurisdiction (Spain v Canada), Preliminary Objections, ICJ Reports 1998*, p 432.

[86] See *LaGrand (Germany v United States), Judgment, ICJ Reports 2001*, p 466; *Avena* (n 81) 12; *Vienna Convention on Consular Relations (Paraguay v United States), Provisional Measures, Order of 9 April 1998, ICJ Reports 1998* ('*Breard*'), p 248.

[87] Most recently, see *Application of the International Convention on the Elimination of All Forms of Racial Discrimination (Qatar v United Arab Emirates), Preliminary Objections, Judgment, ICJ Reports 2021*, p 71, paras 81–8, in which because the term 'national origin' in Art 1 of CERD was held not to encompass present nationality, the claims of indirect racial discrimination based on nationality were outside the scope of the Convention, and thus beyond the jurisdiction of the Court.

[88] See, e.g., *Military and Paramilitary Activities in and against Nicaragua (Nicaragua v United States), Jurisdiction and Admissibility, Judgment, ICJ Reports 1984*, p 392; *Legality of Use of Force (Yugoslavia v Belgium et al), Provisional Measures, Order of 2 June 1999, ICJ Reports 1999*, p 124, paras 22 *et seq*.

[89] For a brief history of the adoption of the Optional Clause regime, see Hernández, *Judicial Function* (n 3) 25–7 (regarding the League era), and 38–9 (during the 1945 San Francisco Conference).

compromissory clause. Filing such a declaration under the Optional Clause 'makes a standing offer to the other States parties to the Statute which have not yet deposited a declaration of acceptance. The day one of those States accepts that offer . . . the consensual bond is established and no further condition needs to be met.'[90] As of 2018, there were seventy-three declarations in force, or about one-third of the UN membership.[91]

As a unilateral act, a State consenting to the Court's jurisdiction via the Optional Clause may have a reservation attached to it.[92] States enter these reservations, though, at their own peril as Article 36(2) makes jurisdiction conditional on the basis of *reciprocity*. In *Norwegian Loans*, the Court memorably upheld Norway's reliance on the French declaration as follows:

> since two unilateral declarations are involved, such jurisdiction is conferred upon the Court only to the extent to which the declarations coincide in conferring it. A comparison between the two declarations shows that the French declaration accepts the Court's jurisdiction within narrower limits than the Norwegian declaration; consequently, the common will of the parties, which is the basis of the Court's jurisdiction, exists within these narrower limits indicated by the French reservation.[93]

Interestingly, this reservation before the Court was highly controversial, as it excluded from the Court's jurisdiction matters falling within the domestic jurisdiction of France, 'as understood' by France. The French reservation was similar in scope to the 'Connally amendment' contained in the US declaration, excluding all matters falling within the domestic jurisdiction of the USA, 'as understood by' the USA.[94] The 'self-judging' character of such a reservation was questioned in a separate opinion by Judge Lauterpacht, who considered it invalid on the basis that it contradicted the Court's power in Article 36(6) to determine the extent of its own jurisdiction (the principle known as *la compétence de la compétence*, see later Section 12.3.2.3.5).[95]

Another controversial type of reservation excludes disputes relating to a multilateral treaty from the jurisdiction of the Court, unless all the parties to the treaty affected by the decision are also parties to a given case. A version of this type of reservation, contained in the US declaration and known as the 'Vandenberg amendment', was upheld in

[90] *Land and Maritime Boundary between Cameroon and Nigeria (Cameroon/Nigeria: Equatorial Guinea intervening), Preliminary Objections, ICJ Reports 1998*, p 275, 291.

[91] The ICJ website keeps an up-to-date record of these at <http://www.icj-cij.org/en/declarations>.

[92] *Fisheries Jurisdiction* (n 81) 454; see Chapter 7 (Treaties).

[93] *Certain Norwegian Loans (France v Norway), Judgment, ICJ Reports 1957*, p 9, 23. See also *Right of Passage over Indian Territory (Portugal v India), Preliminary Objections, ICJ Reports 1957*, p 125, 145; and *Interhandel Case (Switzerland v United States), Preliminary Objections, ICJ Reports 1959*, p 6, 23.

[94] See L Henkin, 'The Connally Reservation Revisited and Hopefully, Contained' (1971) 65 AJIL 374; and L Preuss, 'The International Court of Justice, the Senate and Matters of Domestic Jurisdiction' (1946) 40 AJIL 720. See also M Shaw, *Rosenne's Law and Practice of the International Court 1920–2015* (Martinus Nijhoff, 2017), vol II, 761 *et seq*.

[95] See *Norwegian Loans* (n 89), Separate Opinion of Judge Lauterpacht, 43 *et seq*, where he argued that the reservation was an integral part of the French declaration and could not be severed, thus rendering the entire declaration invalid *ab initio*. However, *cf* the *Belilos v Switzerland* judgment of the ECtHR (1988) Ser A No 132; 10 EHRR 418, in which a virtually identical declaration was 'severed' from the acceptance of jurisdiction.

the *Nicaragua* judgment. It excluded from the jurisdiction of the Court matters arising under Article 2 of the UN Charter.[96] The Court decided, however, that the Vandenberg reservation did not exclude disputes arising under customary international law, and proceeded to hear the case. This was controversial even on the bench, with several strongly worded dissenting opinions.[97]

THEORY AND DEBATES What Kinds of Reservations can be Filed?

As demonstrated by the controversies around the 'self-judging' and multilateral reservations, the Optional Clause system allows for States to tailor their acceptance to their needs and often States will exclude, for purely strategic or political reasons, certain categories of disputes.

Some exclusions prevent disputes between certain groups of States. Many Commonwealth members, including Barbados, Canada, India, Kenya, Malawi, Malta, and the UK, exclude the Court's jurisdiction over matters involving other members of the Commonwealth, partly due to the historical affinity between them. Another example is the declaration of Lithuania, which excludes disputes arising from a military operation conducted by a security and defence organization of which it is a member; Lithuania is a member of NATO. These are filed for reasons of comity, or a desire that certain allies not find themselves opposed before the Court.

Other reservations exclude certain sensitive subject matter, for reasons of domestic or foreign policy. Australia, Canada, Japan, and New Zealand's declarations all contain reservations excluding the jurisdiction of the Court over certain matters relating to marine conservation and exploitation, or in respect of certain geographical areas in the high seas. These are in part due to their purported desire to act freely in protecting their interests on the high seas. In 2004, the USA entered a reservation to the compromissory clause in the VCCR to exclude from the Court's jurisdiction any disputes arising under that treaty. In 2017, the UK amended its reservation to exclude disputes concerning nuclear weapons and disarmament, after a claim by the Marshall Islands was rejected by the Court.

Reservations embody the right of a State to choose not to submit disputes for judicial settlement and, for that reason, they remain a sensitive topic. The 'self-judging' and 'multilateral treaty' reservations discussed in this chapter have already proven legally contentious, and the 2017 reservation by the UK may yet become contentious. Moreover, the ability to carve out limitations is not unlimited; for example, in respect of the fundamental object and purpose of a treaty (see, in this regard, Chapter 7, Section 7.3.2). As such, a State seeking to enter a reservation to jurisdiction may need to remain cautious, lest the reservation be struck out at the jurisdictional phase by the Court.

[96] For further discussion, see C Tomuschat, 'Article 36' in A Zimmermann and C Tams (eds), in collaboration with C Tomuschat and K Oellers-Frahm (eds), *The Statute of the International Court of Justice: A Commentary* (3rd edn, OUP, 2019), 712, 774–6; Shaw, *Rosenne's Law and Practice* (n 90) 751.

[97] See, e.g., *Nicaragua (Jurisdiction)* (n 84), Dissenting Opinion of Judges Jennings (529–38), Oda (216–19), and Schwebel (302–6). See further F Bordin, 'The *Nicaragua v United States* case: An Overview of its Epochal Judgments' in S Obregón and B Samson (eds), *Nicaragua before the International Court of Justice* (Springer, 2018), 59.

12.3.2.3.5 ***Preliminary objections: jurisdiction and admissibility***

A State may challenge the jurisdiction of the Court on the basis that it has not validly consented to it, or that the two parties do not agree on the extent of the Court's jurisdiction. These are known as *preliminary objections* and must be resolved before the Court can proceed to the merits in a case.[98] It falls to the Court to resolve such questions and challenges under the principle *compétence de la compétence* (the power for a court to determine its own jurisdiction), embodied in Article 36(6) of the Statute. In such circumstances, the Court will hold a preliminary phase of hearings to consider the arguments of the parties in respect of its jurisdiction.

During this preliminary phase, it is not uncommon for parties to also raise objections relating to the admissibility of an application, or of certain points raised within it. Admissibility is not always easy to distinguish from jurisdiction. Generally speaking, objections relating to jurisdiction relate to one of three categories:

- that the Court is not competent over the dispute for a variety of reasons, such as a lack of party consent (*ratione personae*);
- the time at which the dispute occurred falls outside the mutual consent of the parties, or the dispute arose before any international obligation existed (*ratione temporis*); or
- its subject matter falls outside the jurisdiction of the Court, perhaps due to a reservation by one State or because it does not fall within the relevant consent given, whether by special agreement or compromissory clause (*ratione materiae*).

By contrast, the admissibility of a claim has more to do with whether, for reasons of propriety or for other compelling reasons, the Court ought to decline to hear the claims of the parties. An important consideration of admissibility has been the failure of a State to demonstrate sufficient legal interest to have the standing to bring a claim. Thus, in the controversial *South West Africa* judgment, the case did not proceed to the merits because Ethiopia and Liberia did not possess the requisite legal interest regarding the imposition of apartheid in South West Africa.[99] In *Monetary Gold* and *East Timor*, the Court declared that the cases were inadmissible because to do so would pronounce on the legality of conduct of a third State without its consent: the so-called 'indispensable third party' rule.[100]

In cases where a State is espousing the claim of its nationals, one ground for inadmissibility would be the failure to exhaust local remedies in the respondent State's courts on the basis that the respondent State should have an opportunity to rectify the claim

[98] Art 79 of the Rules demands that objections be raised within three months after the delivery of the Memorial of the applicant State. See *Avena* (n 81) para 24, where the Court made clear that failure to comply with such time limits will not result in the inability to argue the objection, but that these may not be argued in a separate phase of the case.

[99] *See South West Africa (Ethiopia v South Africa; Liberia v South Africa), Second Phase, Judgment, ICJ Reports 1966*, p 6, para 99.

[100] See *Monetary Gold removed from Rome in 1943 (Italy v France, United Kingdom and United States) Preliminary Question, ICJ Reports 1954*, p 19, 32–3; and *East Timor (Portugal v Australia), Jurisdiction and Admissibility, ICJ Reports 1995*, p 90, paras 26–33.

before resort is made to international adjudication.[101] Another ground would be that the nationals are not entitled to the protection of the State[102] or, in the case of a corporation, that it does not have the nationality of the applicant State.[103]

12.3.2.4 **Incidental proceedings before the Court**

There also exist various incidental proceedings that can be filed before the Court which each merit summary mention.

Provisional measures. A party can request the Court to order provisional measures to preserve the rights of the parties; for example, if something might occur that would cause irreparable harm to one of the parties.[104] Actual requests for provisional measures have concerned the execution of a national,[105] the destruction of cultural property,[106] and the construction of factories endangering the environment.[107] The subject matter of such requests has become more overtly sensitive, including breaches of peremptory norms of *jus cogens*, such as a claim of genocide against the Rohingya population in 2020[108] or the adoption of unilateral sanctions by the USA against Iran after ex President Trump's withdrawal from the Joint Comprehensive Plan of Action in 2018.[109] Such provisional measures, which are binding,[110] may be ordered so long as the Court has prima facie jurisdiction, a lower threshold which may be overturned in the jurisdictional phase.[111]

Counterclaims. Additionally, a State party to a dispute may file a 'counterclaim', a separate legal claim which is nonetheless directly connected to the subject matter of the dispute.[112] For example, Serbia filed a counterclaim against Croatia, in which it contended that the respondent had also committed genocide; this was addressed within the

[101] See *Interhandel* (n 89) 27. The exhaustion of local remedies principle discussed here is exactly the same as that explained in Chapter 11, Section 11.4.

[102] *Nottebohm (Liechtenstein v Guatemala) (Second Phase), Judgment of April 6th, 1955, ICJ Reports 1995*, p 4. See Chapter 11, Section 11.3.2.1 for further discussion of this case.

[103] *Barcelona Traction Heat, Light and Power Co (New Application: 1962) (Belgium v Spain), Judgment, ICJ Reports 1970*, p 3, para 101; see Chapter 11, Section 11.3.2.4.1 for further discussion of this case.

[104] ICJ Statute (n 59) Art 41. Detailed studies of the Court's practice in respect of provisional measures are found in Shaw, *Rosenne's Law and Practice* (n 90) ch 24; S Rosenne, *Provisional Measures in International Law* (OUP, 2005); and K Oellers-Frahm and C Tomuschat, 'Article 41' in A Zimmermann and C Tams (eds), in collaboration with C Tomuschat and K Oellers-Frahm (eds), *The Statute of the International Court of Justice: A Commentary* (3rd edn, OUP, 2019), 1135.

[105] *Breard* (n 82); *LaGrand* (n 82).

[106] *Request for Interpretation of the Judgment of 15 June 1962 in the Case concerning the Temple of Preah Vihear (Cambodia v Thailand), Provisional Measures, Order of 18 July 2011, ICJ Reports 2011*, p 537.

[107] *Pulp Mills on the River Uruguay (Argentina v Uruguay), Provisional Measures, Order of 13 July 2006, ICJ Reports 2006*, p 113.

[108] *Application of the Convention on the Prevention of the Crime of Genocide (The Gambia v Myanmar), Provisional Measures, ICJ Reports 2020*, p 3, para 16.

[109] *Alleged Violations of the 1955 Treaty of Amity, Economic Relations, and Consular Rights (Iran v United States), Provisional Measures, ICJ Reports 2018*, p 623, para 98.

[110] See *LaGrand* (n 82) paras 98 *et seq*.

[111] See, e.g., *Request for Interpretation of the Judgment of 31 March 2004 in the Case concerning* Avena and Other Mexican Nationals *(Mexico v United States), Judgment, ICJ Reports 2009*, p 3, para 15; *Application of CERD* (n 4) paras 85–6.

[112] Art 80, Rules of Court.

main proceedings.[113] Counterclaims may be challenged at any time for being inadmissible for lack of a connection to the principal dispute.[114]

Joinder. States may bring proceedings as joint applicants, or a State may bring a claim against several States. However, where two States have brought independent proceedings against the same respondent in respect of the same subject matter, the Court can, under Article 47 of the Rules, direct that the proceedings be joined. Joinder entails the cases being heard and determined together, by a single judgment.[115]

Intervention. The Statute envisages two situations in which a third State may apply to intervene: should it consider itself to have an interest of a legal nature which may be affected by the Court's decision (Article 62), or should it seek to put forward its views in proceedings in which the construction of a multilateral convention to which it is a party is in issue (Article 63)? The threshold for permitted intervention is fairly high and may be opposed by the parties, as was seen in the few earlier cases in which intervention was permitted by the Court.[116] A successful intervention can, in theory, allow for a third State to become a party; however, in all cases thus far, intervention was limited to the filing of submissions to the Court.

CONTEMPORARY DEVELOPMENTS The Resurgence of Interventions in ICJ Proceedings since 2022

The possibility for States to intervene in ICJ proceedings was relatively quiescent until the unprecedented mass intervention by 33 States sympathetic to Ukraine in its case taken against Russia in response to false allegations of genocide which, in Ukraine's view, had given rise to Russia's armed attack against it in 2022. All 33 States intervened under Article 63 and purported to give their views on the construction of the Genocide Convention, and only

[113] *Application of the Convention on the Prevention and Punishment of the Crime of Genocide (Croatia v Serbia), Counter-claims, Order of 4 February 2010, ICJ Reports 2010*, p 3. *Application of the Convention on the Prevention and Punishment of the Crime of Genocide (Bosnia and Herzegovina v Yugoslavia), Counter-claims, Order of 17 December 1997, ICJ Reports 1997*, p 243, 256.

[114] *Ibid*; see also *Oil Platforms (Islamic Republic of Iran v United States), Judgment, ICJ Reports 2003*, p 161, 210.

[115] Joinder was ordered in the *South West Africa* cases (n 95) (Ethiopia and Liberia against South Africa), in the *North Sea Continental Shelf* cases (n 12) (Denmark and the Netherlands against Germany), and *Construction of a Road in Costa Rica along the San Juan River (Nicaragua v Costa Rica)* and *Certain Activities carried out by Nicaragua in the Border Area (Costa Rica v Nicaragua), Merits, ICJ Reports 2015*, p 665. In late 2021, Armenia and Azerbaijan both filed cases against the other, alleging violations of CERD. Hearings on provisional measures and preliminary objections were organized sequentially, and orders and judgments were published on the same day, at the time of going to press the cases have not been formally joined, despite identical titles: see *Application of the International Convention on the Elimination of Racial Discrimination (Armenia v Azerbaijan), Preliminary Objections, Judgment of 12 November 2024*; and, *Application of the International Convention on the Elimination of Racial Discrimination (Azerbaijan v Armenia), Preliminary Objections, Judgment of 12 November 2024.*

[116] Nicaragua intervened in *Land, Island and Maritime Frontier Dispute (El Salvador/Honduras), Order, ICJ Reports 1990*, p 92; Equatorial Guinea in *Land and Maritime Boundary (Cameroon/Nigeria), Application to Intervene, Order, ICJ Reports 1999*, p 1029; the Philippines in *Sovereignty over Pulau Litigan and Pulau Sipadan (Indonesia/Malaysia), Order, ICJ Reports 2001*, p 575; Greece in *Jurisdictional Immunities of the State (Germany v Italy), Order, ICJ Reports 2011*, p 494; and New Zealand in *Whaling in the Antarctic (Australia v Japan), Order, ICJ Reports 2013*, p 3.

one—the USA—was found on the basis of reciprocity to be inadmissible due to the USA's own reservation to the compromissory clause embodied in Article IX (see *Allegations of Genocide under the Convention on the Prevention of the Crime of Genocide (Ukraine v Russian Federation: 32 States intervening), Order of 9 June 2023 on the Admissibility of the Declarations of Intervention*). After the Court's judgment on preliminary objections—where it did not make extensive reference to the interventions—Poland adjusted its intervention so as also to apply to intervene as a party with a legal interest under Article 62.

Though it is unavoidable that there will be political strategy behind the choice to intervene, not least to bring public visibility to any claims, the intended purpose of intervention is not political, but for States to give their view on the interpretation of treaties that might affect them. That said, such interventions also suggest that States take seriously the interpretative authority of the Court's judgments.

Notwithstanding the Court's amendments to Article 82 of its Rules to clarify the time limits for the filing of declarations (see ICJ Press Release of 28 February 2024), States seem now emboldened in further use of this procedure, at least in cases involving obligations *erga omnes*. At the time of press, there were a range of declarations of intervention under Article 63 in *Application of the Convention on the Prevention of the Crime of Genocide (The Gambia v Myanmar), Order of 3 July 2024 on the Admissibility of the Declarations of Intervention)*; eight pending Article 63 declarations relating to *Application of the Convention on the Prevention of the Crime of Genocide in the Gaza Strip (South Africa v Israel)*, and two applications, by Nicaragua and the State of Palestine, for permission to intervene under Article 62.

Interpretation. Under Article 60 of the Statute, the Court's judgments are final and without appeal; but it provides that 'in the case of a dispute as to the meaning or scope of the judgment, the Court shall construe it upon the request of any party'.[117] Such requests must be generally directed at obtaining clarification of the operative part of the judgment (the *dispositif*), and not the Court's reasoning.[118] As such, parties also may not request answers with respect to points that were not decided by the Court.[119]

Revision. A party may apply for revision of a judgment of the Court under Article 61 of the Statute, if it is based upon the discovery of a fact decisive to the judgment of the Court. The fact must have existed at the time the judgment was given; it cannot arise after the judgment was rendered.[120] Furthermore, the fact must have been unknown to

[117] See also Art 98(1) of the Court's Rules.

[118] See *Request for Interpretation of the Judgment of 11 June 1998 in the Case concerning the Land and Maritime Boundary between Cameroon and Nigeria (Cameroon v Nigeria), Preliminary Objections, ICJ Reports 1999*, p 31, 35; *Request for Interpretation of the Judgment of 15 June 1962 in the Case concerning the Temple of Preah Vihear (Cambodia v Thailand), Judgment, ICJ Reports 2013*, p 281, para 34.

[119] *Request for Interpretation of the Judgment of 20 November 1950 in the Asylum case, ICJ Reports 1950*, p 402; *Application for Revision and Interpretation of the Judgment of 24 February 1982 in the Case concerning the Continental Shelf (Tunisia v Libyan Arab Jamahiriya), Judgment, ICJ Reports 1985*, p 192, 214–20.

[120] *Application for Revision of the Judgment of 11 September 1992 in the Case concerning the Land, Island and Maritime Frontier Dispute (El Salvador/Honduras: Nicaragua intervening) (El Salvador v Honduras), Judgment, ICJ Reports 2003*, p 392, 398–9.

the party applying for revision, though not due to negligence: if a fact could have been discovered through the application of normal diligence, then the application for revision would be inadmissible.[121] For reasons of legal certainty, applications for revision must be made within six months of discovery of the fact, and no more than ten years after the judgment has been given.

12.3.2.5 The advisory function of the Court

A significant feature from the League Covenant that carried over into the UN Charter is the Court's competence to give advisory opinions upon the request of certain international bodies, including organs of international organizations.[122] Accordingly, Article 96 of the Charter, complemented by Article 65 of the ICJ Statute, allows the General Assembly and Security Council to make a request with respect to 'any legal question'. Other UN organs and specialized agencies, as well as separate international organizations such as the IMO and the ILO, are able to request opinions on legal questions arising within the scope of their activities. This doctrine has its limits: in 1996, the Court declined to give the WHO an advisory opinion on the legality of the use of nuclear weapons in armed conflict, holding that its request was *ultra vires* (went beyond) the functions laid out in the WHO Constitution.[123]

The central feature of the advisory opinion is its non-binding character: it provides guidance to the requesting organ in respect of its own actions.[124] The requesting body may follow or dismiss the opinion freely though, in practice, it may find it difficult to reject the Court's view on the existence and content of a binding legal obligation. Since the function of the Court in advisory proceedings is not the resolution of disputes between parties, the Court has stated that the giving of advisory opinions is part of its participation in the activities of the United Nations. As such, it should not be refused,[125] unless 'compelling reasons' exist which oblige the Court to refuse on the grounds of judicial propriety.[126]

Significantly, States may not request advisory opinions; these are not vehicles for dispute settlement and should not be used to evade the consent of an unwilling respondent. However, a potential problem can arise even with respect to competent requesting organs; namely, as the Court explained in *Western Sahara*, 'circumstances disclose that to give a reply would have the effect of circumventing the principle that a State

[121] See, e.g., *Continental Shelf (Tunisia/Libya) Request for Revision and Interpretation* (n 115) 206–7.

[122] See Hernández, *Judicial Function* (n 3) 74–85; Shaw, *Rosenne's Law and Practice* (n 90) vol III, ch 30; R Kolb, *The International Court of Justice* (Hart, 2013) 1019 *et seq*; FD Berman, 'The Uses and Abuses of Advisory Opinions' in N Ando, E McWhinney, and R Wolfrum (eds), *Liber Amicorum Judge Shigeru Oda* (Kluwer, 2002), vol 2, 809.

[123] See *Legality of the Threat or Use of Nuclear Weapons in Armed Conflict (WHO), Advisory Opinion, ICJ Reports 1996*, p 66.

[124] *Reservations to the Convention on Genocide, Advisory Opinion: ICJ Reports 1951*, p 15.

[125] See *Western Sahara, Advisory Opinion, ICJ Reports 1975*, p 12, para 23.

[126] See *Legality of Nuclear Weapons (WHO)* (n 119) 235; *Construction of a Wall in Occupied Palestinian Territory, Advisory Opinion, ICJ Reports 2004*, p 136, 156; *Declaration of Independence in Respect of Kosovo, Advisory Opinion, ICJ Reports 2010*, p 403, 417; *International Fund for Agricultural Development, Advisory Opinion, ICJ Reports 2012*, p 10, 25.

is not obliged to submit its disputes to be submitted to judicial settlement without its consent'.[127] The ICJ's opinion in *Western Sahara* seemed to extrapolate from *Eastern Carelia*, in which the PCIJ declined a request from the League Assembly concerning a dispute in which both Finland (a member of the League) and the USSR (a non-member of the League) were involved. The PCIJ declined the request on the basis that the USSR was not a member, and did not address the issue of whether requests for advisory opinions concerning disputes between States can be made without the consent of those States.[128]

The Court's concern with consent is somewhat lessened in advisory cases than with contentious cases, perhaps because the basis of the Court's advisory jurisdiction is not based on the consent of disputing parties, and its advisory opinions have no binding force in any event. Though circumvention of consent could be a further 'compelling reason' for the Court to exercise its discretion under Article 65, the ICJ has generally not allowed State objections to prevent the giving of an advisory opinion to a requesting body.[129] In 2018, the UK invoked a similar objection unsuccessfully in its pleadings concerning a request by the General Assembly for an opinion on the separation of the Chagos Islands from Mauritius at the time of decolonization.[130]

In its 2004 advisory opinion on the *Construction of a Wall* in occupied Palestinian territory, the Court had to respond to Israel's written statement (Israel refused to appear before the Court) that the wall in issue was part of a wider dispute, the settlement of which was outside the Court's jurisdiction. Though the Court accepted the principle that its giving of an opinion should not circumvent the principle of consent to judicial settlement, it took the view that the Palestinian question was one of 'particularly acute concern to the United Nations, and one which is located in a much broader frame of reference than a bilateral dispute';[131] accordingly, no compelling reasons existed to preclude it from giving legal advice to the General Assembly.

12.4 **Conclusion**

From the most informal negotiations to highly proceduralized adjudication, the variety of methods available to States to resolve their disputes would seem to embody the promise of international law to safeguard international peace. One can see the overriding importance of consent in designing these mechanisms, as many States remain unwilling to cede control over their disputes in favour of more legalized methods of dispute settlement, suggesting that the importance of political considerations remains high.

[127] *Western Sahara* (n 121) para 32.

[128] *Status of Eastern Carelia, Advisory Opinion, 1923, PCIJ, Ser B, No 5*, p 7.

[129] See, e.g., *Interpretation of Peace Treaties with Bulgaria, Hungary and Romania, Advisory Opinion, First Phase, ICJ Reports 1950*, p 65, 71. It has been argued that this should be done more openly: see M Lando, 'Advisory Opinions of the International Court of Justice in Respect of Disputes' (2023) 61 Columbia JTL 67.

[130] *Legal Consequences of the Separation of the Chagos Archipelago from Mauritius in 1965, Request for Advisory Opinion*, CR 2018/21 (3 September 2018) (UK), 26–40. See also Written Statement of the United Kingdom, paras 7.5–7.19.

[131] *Construction of a Wall* (n XXX) para 159.

In such a context, it is tempting to dismiss the role of legal methods of dispute settlement—in particular, adjudication—as marginal to 'high politics'. Indeed, when one examines the body of work of a court such as the ICJ, one finds a multitude of seemingly minor disputes such as boundary adjustments, navigational rights, diplomatic immunities, or treaty interpretation. Yet, the Court and other judicial institutions have often found themselves confronted with significant political disputes, of both a bilateral and more global nature. More importantly, in an international legal order lacking centralized lawmaking organs, the Court plays an immensely influential role in the development of international law. By clarifying legal principles where ambiguity may have existed, interpreting treaties and other written forms of law in response to new and unforeseen situations, it actively contributes to the processes of international lawmaking. In this respect, the judicial settlement of disputes goes beyond merely the safeguarding of international peace, and very much forms part of the dynamic practice of international law.[132]

Further reading

L Boisson De Chazournes, M Kohen, and J Viñuales (eds), *Diplomatic and Judicial Means of Dispute Settlement* (Martinus Nijhoff, 2012).

A broad-brush collection with an array of contributions covering the entirety of the field.

J Collier and AV Lowe, *The Settlement of Disputes in International Law* (OUP, 1999).

A broad tour of the various available dispute-settlement mechanisms, this book will soon go into a revised edition.

D French, M Saul, and N White (eds), *International Law and Dispute Settlement: New Problems and Techniques* (Hart, 2010).

A comparative survey of current dispute-settlement mechanisms that are available.

GI Hernández, *The International Court of Justice and the Judicial Function* (OUP, 2014).

Written by the present author, this book situates the Court and its function within wider international lawmaking processes.

R Kolb, *The International Court of Justice* (Hart, 2014).

More concise than the multi-volume *Rosenne*, this comprehensive book addresses all features of the ICJ.

JG Merrills, *International Dispute Settlement* (6th edn, CUP, 2017).

Freshly revised, this comprehensive treatise provides an outstanding survey of the venues available in international law.

P Pazartzis, *Les engagements internationaux en matière de règlement pacifique des différends entre États* (LGDJ, 1992).

A leading French-language study on the obligation to settle disputes peacefully contained in the UN Charter.

132 See further Hernández, *Judicial Function* (n 3) 87–93.

M Shaw, *Rosenne's Law and Practice of the International Court 1920–2015* (Martinus Nijhoff, 2017), vol II.

A magisterial compendium of all aspects of the Court's procedure and practice.

Y Tanaka, *The Peaceful Settlement of International Disputes* (CUP, 2017).

A recent, accessible, and detailed account of modern developments in peaceful international dispute settlement.

H Thirlway, *The International Court of Justice* (OUP, 2016).

A concise, precise, and useful survey of the ICJ, given from the perspective of its former Principal Legal Secretary.

A Zimmermann and C Tams (eds), in collaboration with C Tomuschat and K Oellers-Frahm (eds), *The Statute of the International Court of Justice: A Commentary* (3rd edn, OUP, 2019).

A meticulous article-by-article analysis of the ICJ Statute, written by highly distinguished academics and practitioners.

13

Enforcement short of force

13.1 Introduction: self-help in international law

In its essentially decentralized form, which emphasizes the sovereign equality of States, the international legal order has developed its own specific set of remedies and enforcement strategies for States' breaches of obligation. Given the lack of a centralized authority to impose and enforce measures upon a responsible State, aggrieved States are obliged to take measures unilaterally in order to protect their interests. The lack of centralized coercive mechanisms led many legal theorists to condemn international law as altogether lacking the qualities of a legal system,[1] or to consider it a form of 'primitive' legal system.[2] Consider briefly the fact that within the modern State individuals do not have the right to enforce their rights, such as seizing a neighbour's property to make good a debt; instead it falls to the State, which claims a monopoly on force, to enforce the rights of individuals.[3]

Historically, permissible measures of 'self-help' ranged from diplomatic rebukes to military force, with the Austro-Hungarian declaration of war on Serbia in August 1914 an example of the latter. Even the 1929 Kellogg–Briand Pact outlawing the use of force in international relations permitted certain measures 'short of war', but that conceivably permitted the use of force up to a threshold below that of 'war'.[4] However, under the UN Charter, resort to force outside self-defence and collective security, through regional organizations or the Security Council, has been removed from the measures available to States.[5] Both war and armed reprisals by a State have thus been categorically forbidden.[6] Chapter VII of the Charter has sought to centralize the use of force to the UN, and in particular the Security Council, under Article 42.

[1] HLA Hart, *The Concept of Law* (3rd edn, Clarendon Press, 2012), ch 10, 'International Law'.

[2] See H Kelsen, *Law and Peace in International Relations: The Oliver Wendell Holmes Lectures* (Harvard University Press, 1942), 51–5; H Kelsen, *Pure Theory of Law* (M Knight tr, 2nd edn, UCP, 1970), 323.

[3] Though probably confined to the common law model, for a general discussion on the nature of sanctions and a critique of John Austin's command-authority model, see Hart, *The Concept of Law* (n 1) esp 35–48.

[4] The use of force in international law is addressed in depth in Chapter 14.

[5] The first structures found in the Covenant of the League of Nations purported to restrict the use of force unilaterally, followed by the Kellogg–Briand Pact of 1929, and culminating in Art 2(4) and the collective security regime in Chapter VII of the Charter of the United Nations (signed 26 June 1945, entered into force 24 October 1945), 1 UNTS xvi. See Chapter 14 for a fuller account of such available measures.

[6] See later, Section 13.2.2.

This chapter will survey the categories of redress that are available to an aggrieved State, and it is important to define each briefly as they are laid out in each chapter. First, we will address the category of reprisals, a category of responses with a punitive element that has increasingly come to be regarded as obsolete.[7] Next, we will briefly address so-called 'acts of retorsion', defined in the Articles on the Responsibility of States for Internationally Wrongful Acts (ARSIWA) as unfriendly responses to the acts of other States, but which are perfectly lawful and do not breach any international obligation.[8]

The major section in this chapter will analyse *countermeasures*, the primary measures available to States in order to induce compliance of wrongdoers with their international obligations. In the last decades, there has been the codification and attempted development by the ILC, in the ARSIWA, of an international regime regulating 'countermeasures'. To characterize an act as a 'countermeasure' is to concede its illegality in normal circumstances: by definition, countermeasures are acts which are 'intrinsically unlawful, but are justified by the alleged initial failing to which they were a response'.[9] Countermeasures may not in any case involve the use of armed force. While the Security Council also has the power to impose non-forcible measures against a State in breach of international obligations which leads to a threat to the peace,[10] this power does not exclude the power of States to resort to countermeasures unilaterally and at their own risk.[11]

Finally, the term 'sanctions' is often regarded as an umbrella term, used by legal theorists in the broad sense of any punitive or coercive measures deployed against an offending party.[12] However, the term 'sanctions' has been reserved by the ILC for enforcement action taken by international organizations[13] (as Cassese put it, these are 'sanctions properly so called');[14] and that usage will be adopted here. Sanctions will be addressed in Section 13.5.

[7] See generally LK Kunz, 'Sanctions in International Law' (1960) 54 AJIL 324.

[8] This follows the definition given in the ILC, 'Articles on the Responsibility of States for Internationally Wrongful Acts', with Commentaries, adopted by the ILC on 20 August 2001: 'Report of the International Law Commission on the Work of its 53rd Session', UN Doc A/56/10 Chap IV (2001) GAOR 56th Session Supp 10, The ILC Commentaries to the ARSIWA are found in (2001) ILC Ybk vol 2, pt2, UN Doc A/CN.4/SER.A/2001/Add.1. See Commentary to Art 54, 137, para 3.

[9] D Alland, 'Countermeasures of General Interest' (2002) 13 EJIL 1221, 1221.

[10] UN Charter (n 5) Arts 39, 41.

[11] These are mirrored in the power of certain regional security organizations, such as ECOWAS, the OAS, and the Arab League, to impose sanctions on their members. See Treaty of the Establishment of an Economic Community of West Africa (adopted 28 May 1975, entered into force 28 May 1975), 1010 UNTS 17, Art 77; Charter of the Organization of American States (signed 30 April 1948, entered into force 13 December 1951), 1952 UNTS 48, Art 9; Pact of the League of the Arab States (signed 22 March 1945, entered into force 10 May 1945), 70 UNTS 237, Art 18; H Schermers and N Blokker, *International Institutional Law: Unity within Diversity* (5th edn, Martinus Nijhoff, 2011), 916–58.

[12] See generally Kunz (n 7); JL Brierly, *The Basis of Obligation in International Law* (Clarendon Press, 1932), 68 suggests that 'centralized sanctions' are the hallmark of the modern State, but that is not the sense in which the term is used here.

[13] See ARSIWA, Commentary to Art 22 (n 8) 75, para 3.

[14] A Cassese, *International Law* (2nd edn, OUP, 2003), 311; see also V Gowlland-Debbas, 'Introduction' in V Gowlland-Debbas (ed), *United Nations Sanctions and International Law* (Kluwer, 2001), 1, 6–7.

13.2 Reprisals in international law

13.2.1 What are reprisals?

The concept of 'reprisal' has long been used to describe an act of retaliation taken by a State against another State, whether in peacetime or during an armed conflict. Armed reprisals could be taken in times of war as retaliation for the belligerent act of another, and at times States would also take forcible measures 'short of war' against one another. The overarching characteristic of reprisals is that they are acts taken in response to the act of another actor.

One of the agreed characteristics of reprisals is that the term has punitive connotations. Unlike countermeasures, a narrower category of non-forcible responses (discussed later in Section 13.4), reprisals are not limited to acts that would induce another actor to end a breach and resume compliance with international law.[15] Reprisals, by contrast, may be punitive or retaliatory in nature. Reprisals are the older concept, but given the development of the law on countermeasures, many non-punitive measures that would historically have been understood as reprisals are now considered to be countermeasures. They are also subject to a number of conditions, as illustrated by the arbitral award in *Naulilaa*.

HISTORICAL BACKGROUND The *Naulilaa* Arbitration (*Portugal v Germany*), (Case No 360) (1928) 2 RIAA 1011; (1928) 4 AD 526

The *Naulilaa* arbitration was an important case in relation to the evolving law on reprisals. At issue was the accidental murder of a German official and two officers by Portuguese soldiers in South West Africa during World War I, and whether Germany was entitled to retaliate by sending German troops to destroy Portuguese ports and kill Portuguese soldiers.

The Special Arbitral Tribunal set out its view that international law stipulated five conditions for reprisals, concluding that the first three had not been met by Germany:

(1) a reprisal is an act which is normally illegal but is rendered lawful by the fact that it is in response to a prior unlawful act;

(2) a reprisal must be preceded by a request to redress the injury;

(3) reprisals are also bound by the condition of proportionality, with an excessive reprisal being unlawful;

(4) a reprisal must be limited by 'considerations of humanity' and good faith; and

(5) a reprisal must aim only to impose on the offending State reparation for the offence, the return to legality, and the avoidance of new offences.

Though reprisals as a category have become obsolete, the criteria set out in the *Naulilaa* arbitration were influential in specifying the conditions for countermeasures, as evidenced by the reference to these conditions in the *Air Services Agreement* arbitration.

[15] *Gabčíkovo-Nagymaros Project (Hungary/Slovakia), Judgment, ICJ Reports 1997*, p 7, paras 83–5.

13.2.2 **The prohibition on armed reprisals**

Armed or 'belligerent' reprisals have become increasingly prohibited under the ban on the use of force, as laid down in Article 2(4) of the UN Charter and customary international law. Article 2(4) of the UN Charter expressly prohibits the 'threat or use of force against the territorial integrity or political independence of any state, or in any other manner inconsistent with the Purposes of the United Nations'. Moreover, Article 2(3) specifies that international disputes should be settled by peaceful means and 'in such a manner that international peace and security, and justice, are not endangered'. In its *Nuclear Weapons* advisory opinion, the ICJ found 'armed reprisals in time of peace . . . are considered to be unlawful'.[16] In a 1964 Security Council resolution relating to British military action within Yemen, the Security Council 'condemn[ed] reprisals as incompatible with the purposes and principles of the United Nations'.[17] Six years later, in the Declaration on Principles of International Law Concerning Friendly Relations and Cooperation among States, the General Assembly noted that 'states have a duty to refrain from acts of reprisal involving the use of force'.[18] The existence of the prohibition is further reinforced by States' military manuals.[19]

Today reprisals, even in situations of armed conflict, seem generally obsolete. For example, belligerent reprisals against civilian populations, cultural property, or the environment are strictly prohibited.[20] This would mean that a reprisal is only lawful if it also conforms with the law on self-defence, especially with respect to the criterion of proportionality, a principle noted by the ICJ in its *Nuclear Weapons* advisory opinion.[21] Even non-forcible reprisals in armed conflicts seem increasingly unlawful. For example, Ethiopia's suspension of prisoner of war exchanges with Eritrea was considered unlawful by the Ethiopia–Eritrea Claims Commission, due to the humanitarian character of the rights of prisoners of war.[22] However, the language of belligerent reprisals has not vanished entirely. In April 2018, France, the UK, and the USA launched strikes against targets at three sites in Syria, in retaliation for a chemical weapons attack on

[16] *Legality of the Threat or Use of Nuclear Weapons, Advisory Opinion, ICJ Reports 1996*, p 226, para 46.

[17] UNSC Res 188 (9 April 1964).

[18] UNGA Res 2625 (XXV) (24 October 1970).

[19] In addition to the military manuals of prominent NATO States, Cameroon's Disciplinary Regulations state clearly that 'it is prohibited for soldiers in combat: . . . to engage in reprisals', Cameroon, *Disciplinary Regulations* (1975), Art 32; similarly, Congo's Disciplinary Regulations state 'it is prohibited [for soldiers in combat] . . . to take hostages, to engage in reprisals or collective punishments', *Congo, Disciplinary Regulations* (1986), Art 32(2).

[20] See Geneva Convention Relative to the Protection of Civilian Persons in Time of War (adopted 12 August 1949, entered into force 21 October 1950), 75 UNTS 287 (Geneva Convention IV), Art 33(3); Protocol Additional to the Geneva Conventions of 12 August 1949, and relating to the Protection of Victims of International Armed Conflicts (Protocol I) (signed 8 June 1977, entered into force 7 December 1978), 1125 UNTS 3, Arts 51(6), 52, 53(c), 55; *Prosecutor v Kupreškić and others ('Lasva Valley')* (Judgment) IT-95-16-T (14 January 2000), para 529. For further detail on reprisals in the law of armed conflict, see J-M Henckaerts and L Doswald-Beck, *ICRC Study on Customary International Humanitarian Law* (CUP, 2005), 145–8.

[21] *Nuclear Weapons* (n 16) 246.

[22] Eritrea–Ethiopia Claims Commission, *Prisoners of War—Eritrea's Claim 17* (Partial Award) (2003) XXVI RIAA 23, para 159 (fn omitted).

civilians in Douma, an enclave of Damascus. These were justified as retaliation for the devastating humanitarian consequences of the use of chemical weapons on the Syrian population, and for being an unacceptable security threat to all States.[23]

By way of conclusion, armed reprisals have long been subject to restrictions under the law of armed conflict (see Chapter 15) and thus subject to a number of additional restrictions that mitigate their punitive character.[24] This is a further distinguishing factor between reprisals and other unilateral forms of self-help, such as acts of retorsion, to which we turn.

13.3 **Acts of Retorsion**

'Retorsion' in international law refers to any unfriendly, but perfectly lawful, act taken by a State (or other international actor) to put pressure on another party.[25] The 'retorsionary' aspect of the concept connotes the fact that it is taken in response to an injurious act taken by another party. Provided that they are not covered by a specific obligation (e.g., a treaty) binding the acting party, acts of retorsion are not unlawful. The retorsionary aspect crucially distinguishes these from countermeasures, acts that would normally be unlawful in the first instance but are exceptionally justified when they comply with a number of conditions. Countermeasures will be examined in Section 13.4.

Retorsion may encompass a broad range of acts, including:

- the recalling of an ambassador or the breaking off of diplomatic relations;
- the withholding of voluntary aid or financial assistance;
- the discontinuance or suspension of trade or other exchanges that a State is not under a treaty obligation to maintain;[26]
- the restriction of travel or the imposition of visas for nationals from the targeted State, in the absence of a treaty obligation[27];

[23] See, e.g., USA, UK, and France joint statement (21 August 2018), available at <https://www.gov.uk/government/news/us-uk-france-statement-on-the-chemical-weapons-attack-in-syria>.

[24] See DW Bowett, 'Reprisals Including Recourse to Armed Force' (1972) 66 AJIL 1; RW Tucker, 'Reprisals and Self-Defence: The Customary Law' (1972) 66 AJIL 581; K Skubiszewski, 'Use of Force by States. Collective Security. Law of War and Neutrality' in M Sørensen (ed), *Manual of Public International Law* (St Martin's Press, 1968), 753–5.

[25] See the ARSIWA (n 8), Commentary to Art 54, 137, para 3.

[26] During an impasse in negotiations concerning the status of Northern Ireland after the British withdrawal from the European Union, in 2022 the EU delayed negotiations and the signature of a treaty that would have given the UK associate membership to participate in the Horizon Europe research funding scheme. The EU never announced that it was withholding membership, but this informal retaliatory measure was regarded as a political response due to frustration over the UK's failure to implement the Northern Ireland Protocol.

[27] In June 2023, Hardeep Singh Nijjar, a Canadian national, was murdered outside a Sikh temple in Canada. After Canada paused trade negotiations due to suspicions of Indian officials' involvement and began making formal accusations, India suspended the issuance of new visas for Canadian nationals, and in October 2024, both States expelled six diplomats from the other.

- the imposition of fiscal duties on goods from the target State, provided they are not in violation of a treaty obligation;
- revocation of diplomatic status, through a declaration that diplomatic representatives are *persona non grata*, which may be done at any time and with no reasons given (see Chapter 9, Section 9.5.1, for examples);[28] or
- the restriction of imports from, and exports to, a targeted State, again if not in violation of treaty obligations.[29]

THEORY AND DEBATES Are there Additional Conditions for Acts of Retorsion to be Lawful?

Most scholars take the view that 'retorsion' only covers lawful responses to the act of another State. As such, retorsion is not a circumstance precluding wrongfulness for an act that might otherwise be unlawful; it is simply a lawful response to the act of another. It is this lawful character that distinguishes an act of retorsion from a countermeasure, which would be unlawful in the first instance, but is justified through other conditions. 'Retorsion', then, would be a descriptive term simply to connote the unfriendly nature of the act, in response to the act of another State.

If they are unfriendly but perfectly lawful, can acts of retorsion be subject to any additional conditions? Naturally, acts of retorsion must conform with *jus cogens* and general international law. But, for example, given their very nature as responses, would it make sense for acts of retorsion to be proportionate in gravity to the breach which gave rise to the wish for a response in the first place?

Though there is a scarcity of State practice and *opinio juris*, as States do not generally justify their lawful acts as being acts of retorsion, there would not seem to be any rule of proportionality in respect of unfriendly, but perfectly lawful, acts of retorsion. As an act moves from the category of being lawful to being unlawful, it makes sense to impose additional conditions, but if the very definition of retorsion is based on the legality of the act, they may be taken at any time, and for whatever reason.

In this respect, acts of retorsion remain an important category, alongside that of 'countermeasures', of available responses to a breach of international law by another State or international organization.

[28] In May 2024, after Spain recognized the State of Palestine, Israel ordered Spain to cease offering consular services from the Spanish Consulate-General in Jerusalem to Palestinians, calling these 'preliminary punitive measures' an attack on Israeli sovereignty.

[29] See, e.g., J Crawford, *The International Law Commission's Articles on State Responsibility* (CUP, 2002), 281. In response to a crackdown in France on Muslim Brotherhood groups in the aftermath of the beheading of Samuel Paty, Turkish President Erdoğan called in October 2020 for a boycott of French products by Turkish citizens, but did not, e.g., suspend any imports or impose tariffs or duties on French products. This may well be an example of an act of retorsion: an unfriendly act which is not internationally unlawful per se.

13.4 Countermeasures

13.4.1 **What are countermeasures?**

The term 'countermeasures' refers to a specific category of non-forcible measures which may lawfully be taken in response to a breach of an international obligation by another State. These measures constitute breaches of obligations on the part of the aggrieved state towards the responsible state. However, these breaches are excused, precisely because they are taken as the only category covered in response to a previous breach by the responsible state, and to the extent that they aim at inducing the compliance of that state with its international obligations. They are also subject to further procedural and substantive limitations, such as a prior call on the responsible State to comply with its obligations, and a prohibition against affecting the human rights obligations or humanitarian obligations of the responsible State. Illustrative examples include the suspension of payments under a treaty, the suspension of treaty-based landing rights for aircraft, the closure of ports to ships flagged to the offending State, and others.

Countermeasures are the only such category that was authoritatively defined by the ILC in its 2001 ARSIWA.[30] In this respect, the use of countermeasures is a particularly attractive form of 'self-help' for an aggrieved State which seeks reassurance that it remains in compliance with its international obligations. Under the ILC paradigm, countermeasures have generally superseded the old category of reprisals, with an important exclusion: countermeasures cannot be taken within the context of the law of armed conflict.

According to the ILC, which draws upon various conditions that had been outlined in the *Air Services Agreement* case,[31] a countermeasure is a limited category of acts. It can only be taken by an injured State against a State which is responsible for an internationally wrongful act, and only in order to induce the breaching State to comply with its obligations.[32] A countermeasure, therefore, is not punitive in character,[33] a key distinction between countermeasures and reprisals.

A countermeasure is also to be distinguished from the consequences of non-performance of treaty obligations described in Chapter 7, Section 7.5.2.3. Specifically, there is a principle codified in Article 60 VCLT, *inadimplenti non est adimplendum*, which provides that a party which disowns or fails to fulfil its own obligations under a treaty cannot invoke its own rights under that treaty.[34] Those are limited to the material breach of a treaty between two parties, and only deal with obligations within that treaty.

[30] See ARSIWA (n 8) Arts 22 and 49(2)–(3).

[31] In the *Air Services Agreement case (United States/France)* (1978) 54 ILR 303, the arbitral tribunal drew upon various principles first elucidated in the earlier *Naulilaa* arbitration (*Portugal v Germany*) (Case No 360) (1928) 2 RIAA 1011; (1928) 4 AD 526. These common threads in relation to reprisals demonstrate the common genealogy, but different paths taken, between reprisals and countermeasures.

[32] ARSIWA (n 8) Art 49(1), which relied on the earlier finding in *Gabčíkovo-Nagymaros* (n 15) 55, para 83.

[33] *Ibid*, para 7. See also *Gabčíkovo-Nagymaros* (n 15) paras 83–5.

[34] *Legal Consequences for States of the Continued Presence of South Africa in Namibia (South West Africa) notwithstanding Security Council Resolution 276 (1970), Advisory Opinion, ICJ Reports 1971*, p 16, 46, para 91. See also *Gabčíkovo-Nagymaros* (n 15) 46–7, para 94.

This does not mean that a given non-forcible measure cannot be classified simultaneously as a response to a material breach and a countermeasure, provided it meets the different set of requirements for both.

In practice, justifications of this nature are rarely successful. For example, in *Interim Accord of 13 September 1995*, Greece had argued that its objection to NATO membership for the former Yugoslav Republic of Macedonia constituted both a response to the respondent's material breach of the accord between the two parties, and a countermeasure. The ICJ rejected both these arguments on the facts, but did not question the fact that the same act might be classified as both.[35] In this sense, one must conclude that *inadimplenti non est adimplendum* may indeed be a type of sanction, but is presently limited in scope by the conditions set out in Article 60, and does not apply outside the framework of the law of treaties.[36]

CASE SPOTLIGHT ***Air Services Agreement (United States/France)* (1978) 54 ILR 303**

The term 'countermeasures' was first used in the context of the 1978 Air Services Agreement arbitration between the USA and France. That seminal dispute concerned a bilateral air services agreement concluded by the parties to facilitate commercial air travel by, *inter alia*, providing for certain landing and disembarking rights. France, which objected to the practice of US-based Pan American Airlines (PanAm) to stop in London and transfer passengers to a smaller aircraft before landing in Paris (so-called 'change of gauge'), began prohibiting PanAm passengers from disembarking in Paris. The USA announced retaliatory measures, which had yet to be implemented by the time of the arbitration, that would have prohibited certain French flights from landing in the USA.

The arbitral tribunal determined that PanAm's change of gauge in London was in conformity with the US–France agreement. More importantly, the tribunal was the first to declare that: '[i]f a situation arises, which in one State's view, results in the violation of an international obligation by another State, the aggrieved State is entitled, within the limits set by general rules of international law, pertaining to the use of armed force to affirm its rights through "countermeasures"' (p 337). The arbitral tribunal emphasized that countermeasures were subject to many of the same conditions set out in relation to reprisals in the *Naulilaa* arbitration.

The *Air Services Agreement* arbitration contributed substantially to the move away from reprisals to the narrower category of countermeasures, and in particular was greatly influential in the drafting of the ILC Articles on State Responsibility Relating to Countermeasures, which were applied by the ICJ in *Gabčikovo-Nagymaros*.

[35] *Application of the Interim Accord of 13 September 1995 (Former Yugoslav Republic of Macedonia v Greece), Judgment, ICJ Reports 2011*, p 644, paras 162–4. This case is further examined in Chapter 7, Section 7.5.2.3.1.

[36] For further consideration, see B Simma and C Tams, 'Article 60' in O Corten and P Klein (eds), *The Vienna Convention on the Law of Treaties: Article by Article Commentary* (OUP, 2012), 1351.

A countermeasure must be reversible or capable of suspension; it involves the suspension of one or more international obligations towards the responsible State 'for the time being'.[37] A countermeasure is thus temporary or provisional. Since its aim is to induce the responsible State to comply again with its obligations, it follows sensibly that a countermeasure ought itself not to create new situations which are irreversible, and should be discontinued immediately once the responsible State is no longer breaching an international obligation and is complying with its secondary obligations under the law of State responsibility, including the obligation to make 'full' reparation.[38] When a countermeasure amounts to the suspension of a treaty obligation, a State must act so that performance of that obligation can be resumed.[39] Moreover, once the wrongful act has ceased, or the dispute has been submitted to a tribunal with binding authority, a countermeasure must be suspended.[40]

A countermeasure is only justified if it is proportional to the injury suffered by the aggrieved State.[41] The standard of evaluation against which the proportionality of a countermeasure is assessed is difficult to ascertain. Historically, a countermeasure ought not to be manifestly disproportionate in gravity and magnitude to the original breach by the responsible State. According to the *Air Services Agreement* tribunal, proportionality is calculated not only in relation to quantifiable injury but also in relation to the positions of principle involved.[42] In *Gabčíkovo-Nagymaros*, Hungary and Slovakia had brought a dispute to the ICJ over a treaty to build a dam on the River Danube. This treaty had been signed in the 1980s, after which there was a collapse of Communist governments in both States and, in the case of Slovakia, a succession of a State due to the dissolution of Czechoslovakia. Hungary had refused to proceed with construction of the dam under the treaty, and Slovakia assumed unilateral control of part of the River Danube in response to Hungary's refusal to complete the project as agreed between the two parties. The Court, in assessing Slovakia's response, determined that it was not a lawful countermeasure because it was not a proportionate response.[43] Recalling that a countermeasure is instrumental, in that it aims to induce the other party to resume compliance, it is highly unlikely that a purely retributive countermeasure will be found to be proportionate. Because the proportionality of a countermeasure is assessed against the objective of inducing compliance, a countermeasure of a substantially similar kind (e.g., the suspension of payments under an investment treaty following a breach of that treaty), or perhaps even in a similar field as the original breach (in *Air Services Agreement*, the US countermeasures also concerned the landing rights

[37] ARSIWA (n 8) Art 49(2)–(3). [38] See *ibid*, Commentary to Art 49, 130–1, para 7.

[39] *Ibid*, Art 49(3). The ICJ confirmed the existence of this condition in *Gabčíkovo-Nagymaros* (n 15) 56–7, para 87.

[40] ASRIWA, *ibid*, Art 53; see also *Interim Accord of 13 September 1995* (n 32), p 644, para 164; and *United States—Continued Suspension of Obligations in the EC—Hormones Dispute*, Case No AB-2008-5, Report of the Appellate Body (14 November 2008), para 382. [41] ASRIWA, *ibid*, Art 51.

[42] *Air Services Agreement* (n 28) para 83. See also the difficulties of ascertaining proportionality in relation to armed reprisals in the *Naulilaa* arbitration (n 28) 1026–8.

[43] *Gabčíkovo-Nagymaros* (n 15) 56–7, paras 85–7.

of aircraft on the same routes), is perhaps a more fitting response than a countermeasure in an entirely different area of international relations. Certain other judicial and arbitral bodies, in particular the WTO Appellate Body, have expressly referred to the ILC's proportionality test in circumstances which may provide further guidance as to emerging practice.[44]

It bears emphasizing, however, that non-reciprocal countermeasures can still be proportionate, and in fact are the only option in cases where the aggrieved State is responding to a breach of an obligation that cannot be breached by way of countermeasures; for example, a violation of human rights by the breaching State. The aggrieved State could not similarly breach human rights by way of countermeasures, and would have to resort to countermeasures in another area of international law.

Finally, there are also procedural conditions for the taking of countermeasures, to ensure these are being taken in good faith and do not serve to escalate a dispute between parties. The ARSIWA provide that countermeasures may only be taken after a request to fulfil its obligations has been made to the responsible party, followed by a notification of any decision to take countermeasures, as well as an offer to negotiate.[45] Only when the breaching State does not engage in negotiations, and fails to correct the breach and resume its compliance with its international obligations, may an aggrieved State resort to countermeasures. On a related point, countermeasures cannot excuse a State from fulfilling its obligations under 'applicable' dispute-settlement procedures.[46] Such relevant dispute-settlement procedures are frequently found in the same treaty framework that imposes substantive obligations on contracting parties.[47] For example, the enforcement mechanism established in the WTO Agreement allows for countermeasures in the case of a breach of WTO obligations, subject to authorization from its internal dispute-settlement mechanisms.[48] Unilateral withdrawal of such consent would undermine the fundamental aims of such procedures, substituting unilateral action for peaceful dispute settlement. As such, no State may withdraw unilaterally its consent to an applicable dispute-settlement procedure by claiming it is a countermeasure.[49]

[44] See, e.g., WTO, *United States—Transitional Safeguard Measure on Combed Cotton Yarn from Pakistan* (8 October 2001), WT/DS192/AB/R, para 120; WTO, *United States—Definitive Safeguard Measures on Imports of Circular Welded Carbon Quality Line Pipe from Korea* (15 February 2002), WT/DS202/AB/R, para 259; ICSID, *Archer Daniels Midland Company and Tate & Lyle Ingredients Americas, Inc v United Mexican States* (21 November 2007), ARB(AF)/04/05, para 152.

[45] ARSIWA (n 8) Art 52(1). Many of these are taken from the *Naulilaa* arbitration (n 28), albeit in the context of reprisals. Note, however, recent statements that notification is not an absolute requirement in relation to cyber countermeasures, which are highly sensitive and reliant on a degree of surprise: see, e.g., UK Attorney General Jeremy Wright, 'Cyber and International Law in the 21st Century' (23 May 2018); Israel Deputy Attorney General Roy Schöndorf, 'Israel's Perspective on Key Legal and Practical Issues Concerning the Application of International Law to Cyber Operations' (speech at the US Naval War College of 8 December 2020).

[46] ARSIWA (n 8) Art 50(2)(a).

[47] See *Air Services Agreement* arbitration (n 28) para 81.

[48] The WTO system is discussed further in Chapter 20, Section 20.3.2. But the WTO system does not exclude countermeasures for non-WTO obligations: see D Azaria, 'Trade Countermeasures for Breaches of International Law outside the WTO' (2022) 71 ICLQ 389.

[49] See *United States Diplomatic and Consular Staff in Tehran (United States v Islamic Republic of Iran), Judgment, ICJ Reports 1980*, p 3, 28.

There is an exception to the procedural requirements stated in the ARSIWA: case law has accepted claims of having to take 'urgent' countermeasures in certain instances. This is not a claim of necessity but a dispensation from notification or negotiation in certain circumstances. For example, an injured State may wish to freeze or take control of the assets of a responsible State within its jurisdiction, without any relevant notification, so as to avoid their immediate withdrawal.

13.4.2 **Substantive conditions on countermeasures**

The ILC set out a number of additional limitations on the exercise of countermeasures, in effect ensuring that these cannot violate fundamental rules of the international legal order and, in particular, certain basic interests accepted by all States.

1. *Countermeasures must be non-forcible.*[50] A countermeasure cannot violate the obligation to refrain from the threat or use of force, especially as defined under Article 2(4) of the UN Charter. The concept of a 'forcible countermeasure', which would serve to cure a unilateral use of force that would ordinarily be unlawful, simply does not exist in international law, not even under the right to self-defence, which is an entirely different category of response.[51]
2. *Countermeasures may not breach obligations for the protection of fundamental human rights, or obligations of a humanitarian character concerning reprisals.*[52] In its commentary to the ARSIWA, the ILC pointed to a number of international covenants which specify that certain categories of human rights are non-derogable even in times of war or other public emergency: these include Article 4 of the ICCPR, Article 15 of the ECHR, and Article 27 of the ACHR. It follows logically that a countermeasure by an aggrieved State cannot infringe on non-derogable rights, and possibly even derogable rights such as the right of access to a court, or the freedom of expression or association. In General Comment No 8 of the Committee on Economic, Social and Cultural Rights, the effect of economic sanctions on civilian populations was discussed. It was emphasized that such sanctions had to take full account of the obligations in the ICESCR and that it was 'essential to distinguish between the basic objective of applying political and economic pressure on the governing elite of a country to persuade them to conform to international law, and the collateral infliction of suffering upon the most vulnerable groups within the targeted country'.[53] Furthermore, international humanitarian law, discussed in Chapter 15, prohibits armed reprisals against a number of

[50] ARSIWA (n 8) Art 50(1)(a). See also 'Declaration on Principles of International Law concerning Friendly Relations and Co-operation among States', UNGA Res 2625 (XXV) (24 October 1970), para 1: 'States have a duty to refrain from acts of reprisal involving the use of force.'

[51] ARSIWA, *ibid*, Commentary to Art 50, 132, para 5; see also *Arbitration between Guyana and Suriname* (2008) 47 ILM 164, para 446 (fn omitted). See earlier, Section 13.2.2, for a discussion on 'armed reprisals'; and Chapter 14, Section 14.3, on the right to self-defence.

[52] ARSIWA, *ibid*, Art 50(2)(b)–(c).

[53] UNESC, 'General Comment No 8 (1997)' (12 December 1997), UN Doc E/C.12/1997/8, para 1.

categories of individuals and, in particular, civilians and other victims of international armed conflicts.[54] Put another way, these limitations on countermeasures emphasize the non-reciprocal nature of human rights law and humanitarian law.

3. *Countermeasures may not breach peremptory norms of international law* (jus cogens).[55] The rule that countermeasures cannot be in breach of norms of *jus cogens* is only logical, given, as discussed in Chapter 3, the hierarchically superior status enjoyed by norms of *jus cogens*. Recalling that peremptory norms of international law are norms that bind all States, and from which no derogation is permitted, evidently, an aggrieved State cannot derogate from norms of *jus cogens* even for the purpose of taking countermeasures.
4. *Countermeasures cannot excuse a State from respecting diplomatic and consular inviolability.*[56] Under the VCDR and VCCR, a range of permissible responses is available to a State under diplomatic and consular law. A State has the right to declare a person *non grata* ('no longer welcome'), to suspend diplomatic relations, or to recall an ambassador. These are not countermeasures as they are not unlawful. Instead, as they are permitted responses under diplomatic and consular law, they are generally regarded as acts of retorsion. In *Hostages in Tehran*, the ICJ explained that 'the rules of diplomatic law . . . constitute a self-contained regime which, on the one hand, lays down the receiving State's obligations . . . and, on the other, foresees their possible abuse by members of the mission and specifies the means at the disposal of the receiving State to counter any such abuse'.[57] Obligations concerning the inviolability of diplomatic and consular premises and persons under international law, as specified in Chapter 9, Section 9.5, cannot be the subject of countermeasures as they are owed even to a State which is responsible for a breach of international law and cannot be suspended or breached, even by way of countermeasures.

13.4.3 **Countermeasures and third States**

Normally, a countermeasure is a unilateral response in a bilateral relationship; taken by an injured State, it must be directed exclusively against the responsible State.[58] A third State or other party cannot be the target of a countermeasure; nor can a countermeasure justify the disregard of treaty obligations granting rights to third States, especially those of an *erga omnes* nature, as these States have nothing to do with the initial

[54] These are found in Geneva Convention Relative to the Treatment of Prisoners of War (adopted 12 August 1949, entered into force 21 October 1950), 75 UNTS 135 (Geneva Convention III); Geneva Convention Relative to the Protection of Civilian Persons in Time of War (adopted 12 August 1949, entered into force 21 October 1950), 75 UNTS 287 (Geneva Convention IV); and Additional Protocol I (n 20).

[55] ASRIWA (n 8) Art 50(1)(d). Also Art 26, which specifies that no circumstance precluding wrongfulness can be invoked in relation to an act which is in breach of an obligation arising under a peremptory norm of international law.

[56] ASRIWA, *ibid*, Art 50(2)(b).

[57] *Hostages in Tehran* (n 45) 40.

[58] See ARSIWA (n 8) Commentary to Art 49, 130, paras 4–8. It is true that the positions of third parties may be affected incidentally, but to affect those States cannot be the *aim* of the countermeasure.

wrongful act.[59] As discussed in Chapter 10, Section 10.4.1, under Article 42 ARSIWA, a State (or IO) is 'injured' in three scenarios: first, when there is a breach of an obligation owed to it individually; secondly, in situations where a State (or IO) is specially affected by the breach of an obligation owed to it which is *erga omnes (partes)*; and finally, where the breach is of such character as radically to change the position of all other States to whom the obligation is owed.

One might recall that the structure of obligations *erga omnes*—in particular, in multilateral treaties of a normative character such as human rights treaties or environmental treaties—allows a State which has not been directly injured to invoke the responsibility of the breaching State.[60] However, if they are not specifically affected by the breach, for the purposes of taking a countermeasure they are (for want of a better term) 'indirectly injured' States.

In this respect, it is important to note that under Article 54 ARSIWA, the ILC took no position on the possibility of a State 'other than the injured State' taking lawful measures against the responsible State.[61] Sometimes called 'third-party countermeasures' or 'countermeasures in the general interest', they arise when a breach of an obligation *erga omnes* is invoked by an 'indirectly' injured State (or IO) to justify actions taken in support of the injured party or actor in order to ensure cessation of a breach and reparation to the injured State.[62] The question logically remains, then, as to the extent to which non-injured States 'may legitimately assert a right to act against unremedied breaches'.[63]

Countermeasures taken by a third State or in the 'general interest' raise a number of questions, not least the issue of how proportionality is to be assessed. A chief point to highlight in this regard is that countermeasures, even if taken in parallel with other States, remain a unilateral, or perhaps multilateral, but not a collective response in the institutional sense.[64] Moreover, resort to such responses opens up the potential for abuse, thus undermining the utility of centralized institutional sanctions such as those available under Chapter VII of the Charter, which are distinct.[65] Early practice seemed uncertain, though by 2001 the ILC could point to the collective measures against South Africa in protest against apartheid, or those taken against Iraq in response to its forcible

[59] See Cassese, *International Law* (n 14) 305.

[60] ASRIWA (n 8) Art 48(2); see also *Obligation to Prosecute or Extradite (Belgium v Senegal), Judgment, ICJ Reports 2012*, p 422, para 70; and *Whaling in the Antarctic (Australia v Japan: New Zealand intervening), Judgment, ICJ Reports 2014*, p 226, para 40.

[61] See ARSIWA (n 8) Commentary to Art 54, 139, para 7; and A Tzanakopoulos, 'State Reactions to Illegal Sanctions' in P Eden and M Happold (eds), *Economic Sanctions and International Law* (Hart, 2016), 67, 72–3.

[62] *Ibid*. The idea of third State responses has a long pedigree, predating the law on countermeasures: see, e.g., M Akehurst, 'Reprisals by Third States' (1970) 44 BYBIL 1; M Dawidowicz, 'Public Law Enforcement without Public Law Safeguards? An Analysis of State Practice on Third-Party Countermeasures and Their Relationship to the UN Security Council' (2006) 77 BYBIL 333; L-A Sicilianos, 'The Classification of Obligations and the Multilateral Dimension of the Relations of International Responsibility' (2002) 13 EJIL 1127.

[63] ARSIWA (n 8), Commentary to Art 54, 137.

[64] Though it has been noted that the alternative is hardly better, 'replacing one subjectivity (of states) by another (of the Security Council)': see P Klein, 'Responsibility for Serious Breaches of Obligations Deriving from Peremptory Norms of International Law and United Nations Law' (2002) 13 EJIL 1241, 1249.

[65] Alland (n 9) 1237. See also A Tzanakopoulos, *Disobeying the Security Council* (OUP, 2011), 72.

annexation of Kuwait in 1990.[66] Increasingly, scholars are taking the view that countermeasures in the general or community interest may be justified in cases of breaches of peremptory norms or of other obligations owed *erga omnes (partes)*.[67] They are increasingly supported by practice that has intensified in recent years. Recently, the USA, Japan, and certain EU member States imposed economic measures on Iran for purported breaches of Articles II and III(1) of the Non-Proliferation Treaty (NPT), these were as measures taken concertedly, in the collective interest *inter partes*, on the basis that the legal interest of each party to the NPT had been affected.[68] Another striking recent example is the characterization by Bahrain, Egypt, Saudi Arabia, and the United Arab Emirates, in the context of their dispute with Qatar in *Jurisdiction of the ICAO Council*, of their concerted adoption of aviation restrictions and other restrictive but non-forcible measures relating to territorial, maritime, and aerial lines of communication against Qatar, as 'countermeasures'.[69]

THEORY AND DEBATES **Towards 'Collaborative' Countermeasures?**

Recent years have witnessed an intensification of countermeasures taken by third States in support of an injured State, with most focus being on the classification of certain coercive measures as genuine countermeasures. Less studied, however, is the question of collaboration or concertation in the taking of countermeasures and whether there are conditions for such collaboration. Such collaboration raises important questions as to the nature of the response by each individual actor—questions of joint or shared responsibility, and important questions as to the extent of permissible concertation, consultation, and the forms of aid and assistance offered. For example, can collaboration in the taking of countermeasures be taken only by injured or specially affected States, or may all sympathetic States also do so? For genuine collaboration to occur, must the injured State also take countermeasures, or does it suffice for it to formulate a request for assistance and have other States take 'proxy countermeasures' on its behalf?

[66] See ARSIWA (n 8), Commentary to Art 54, 138–9, esp paras 3–4, 6. E Zoller, *Unilateral Peacetime Remedies: An Analysis of Countermeasures* (Transnational Publishers, 1984), 104 had earlier commented that some of these measures were not collective countermeasures but, rather, institutional countermeasures (e.g., the European Community's sanctions against Argentina in 1982), thus further adding confusion to the debate.

[67] Tzanakopoulos (n 61) 72; C Hillgruber, 'The Right of Third States to Take Countermeasures' in C Tomuschat and J-M Thouvenin (eds), *The Fundamental Rules of the International Legal Order:* Jus Cogens *and Obligations* Erga Omnes (Martinus Nijhoff, 2006), 265; C Tams, *Enforcing Obligations* Erga Omnes *in International Law* (CUP, 2005); LA Sicilianos, 'Countermeasures in Response to Grave Violations of Obligations Owed to the International Community' in J Crawford, A Pellet, and S Olleson (eds), *The Law of International Responsibility* (OUP, 2010), 1137–48; Schmitt and Watts (n 59) 198–99 (and at 207–13, pointed to emerging practice on taking collective measures in cyberspace, but it should be noted most of these were in relation to individuals, and not countermeasures against States).

[68] See PE Dupont, 'Countermeasures and Collective Security: The Case of the EU Sanctions Against Iran' (2012) 17 JCSL 301.

[69] *Appeal relating to the Jurisdiction of the ICAO Council under Article 84 of the Convention on International Civil Aviation (Bahrain, Egypt, Saudi Arabia and United Arab Emirates v Qatar), Judgment, ICJ Reports 2020*, p 81, para 43.

These collaborative aspects of countermeasures have the potential to raise serious questions going to the heart of the regime of legal responsibility. Given in particular the connection between third-State responses and certain communitarian aspects of the obligations being breached, including their peremptory status, observing the practice and responses of States in the coming years may be determinative as to the scope and extent of collaboration. Significantly, in December 2023, the EU Council adopted an 'Anti-Coercion Instrument' (See EU Regulation 2023/2675 (22 November 2023)), recognizing for the EU Council the power to decide on responses to perceived economic coercion against the Union itself or its members, and to act in concert if necessary.

For further analysis of these issues, see F Paddeu and M Jackson, 'The Countermeasures of Others: When can States Collaborate in the Taking of Countermeasures?' (2024) 118 AJIL 231; and regarding cyberspace, see MN Schmitt and S Watts, 'Collective Cyber Countermeasures' (2021) 12 Harvard National Security Journal 176.

13.4.4 **Countermeasures and international organizations**

As described in Chapter 6, there exist many international organizations that possess international legal personality. Because international organizations are the creation of States and generally operate to discharge purposes which States have assigned to them, there has been more controversy as to the extent to which international organizations may take countermeasures, or whether it falls to the member States of an international organization to take such measures. The paucity of practice has not helped. The ILC has, with Articles 51–7 of the Articles on the Responsibility of International Organizations (ARIO)[70] made certain proposals in respect of countermeasures by and against international organizations; however, these are in part an exercise in progressive development.

CONTEMPORARY DEVELOPMENTS Lawmaking Through the ILC Articles on the Responsibility of International Organizations (ARIO)

Even in draft form, the ARIO have been referred to by international and domestic courts. For example, one can look to the European Court of Human Rights (see, e.g., *Behrami and Behrami v France; Saramati v France, Germany and Norway* (2007) 45 EHRR SE 85 and *Al-Jedda v UK* App No 27021/08 (ECtHR, 7 July 2011)), as well as the courts of the Netherlands (see *Mothers of Srebrenića v State of the Netherlands* (16 July 2014) District Court of The Hague (*Rechtbank Den Haag*); *Nuhanović v Netherlands* HR 6 September 2013, NJ 2013 (*Hoge Raad*, Dutch Supreme Court)). However, this could raise concerns that the ILC is being misconstrued as a lawmaking actor. By its own admission, many of the articles in the ARIO do not reflect actual practice, and reason by analogy from the law on State responsibility. Is this problematic?

[70] ILC, 'Articles on the Responsibility of International Organisations' in Report on the Work of its 63rd Session, UN Doc A/66/10 Chap V (9 December 2011) GAOR 66th Session Supp 10.

In drafting the proposed articles on countermeasures within the ARIO, the ILC sought to strike a balance between, on the one hand, the proposition that an international legal person may wish to resort to self-help to enforce its rights and, on the other, the desire to prevent member States taking unilateral countermeasures against an international organization; for example, by withholding the payment of dues, for perceived wrongful acts, or acts *ultra vires*.

The ILC also received widespread comments from external bodies and States, further strengthening its approach. In relation to countermeasures specifically, the ILC's approach relied on submissions made by the WHO, UNESCO, and the OSCE, as well as of submissions of Denmark and the five Nordic countries, Malaysia, Japan, the Netherlands, Switzerland, and Belgium to justify this view (see Commentary to Article 51, paras 2–3).

The controversy the ARIO have elicited is perhaps illustrative of the limitations of reasoning purely by analogy. Though they will undoubtedly continue to play an important role, the practice of States and IOs will prove determinative as to whether the ILC's proposals will crystallize into customary international law, or be adopted in a treaty.

Bearing in mind that the ARIO represent more an attempt at progressive development than codification, in recognizing a general right to countermeasures by and against an international organization, the ILC has proposed a few significant restrictions on the exercise of that right. Foremost, the standard of evaluation of countermeasures taken against an international organization is higher. Though they must be proportionate in relation to inducing the responsible organization to resume compliance, any such countermeasures must, 'as far as possible, be taken in such a way as to limit their effects on the exercise by the responsible international organization of its functions'.[71] If one is to follow the ILC's proposals in the ARIO, the member States of an organization, if contemplating taking a countermeasure against that organization, cannot violate the 'rules of the organization', usually found in its constituent instrument and other related documents\. Member States must first exhaust other appropriate means which are available to induce compliance, such as dispute-settlement mechanisms. They cannot invoke the breach of that organization's rules, unless such countermeasures are also provided for in the said rules, a rather odd circumstance as virtually no international organization expressly authorizes the taking of countermeasures by member States against the organization.[72]

13.4.5 **Coercive or restrictive measures: economic coercion**

It is true that several General Assembly resolutions have declared coercive economic intervention, which is intended to undermine the territorial integrity or political independence of a State, as unlawful.[73] Economic coercion—for example, entailing the

[71] ARIO, *ibid*, Art 51(4). [72] ARIO, *ibid*, Arts 22, 52.

[73] See, *inter alia*, UNGA, 'Declaration on the Inadmissibility of Intervention in the Domestic Affairs of States' (21 December 1965), UN Doc A/RES/2131, 'Declaration on Friendly Relations between States' (n 46); UNGA, 'Declaration on Permanent Sovereignty over Natural Resources' (17 December 1973), UN Doc A/RES/3171; and UNGA, 'Charter of Economic Rights and Duties of States' (12 December 1974), UN Doc A/RES/3281.

imposition of far-reaching sanctions, the suspension of development aid, and the freezing of funds—may be as devastating to a country's population as an armed conflict. Moreover, they disproportionately are targeted towards States in the Global South, with their unilateral aspect raising questions as to their broader legitimacy.[74]

Yet for all this, States do not have a right to be free of economic coercion in any meaningful sense,[75] except if measures taken against it were of such a nature as to be internationally unlawful; for example, those that breach a norm of *jus cogens*, intransgressible norms of humanitarian law or human rights, or rise to the level of a prohibited intervention in the political affairs of another State or a threat or use of force.[76] In its 2023 judgment in *Certain Iranian Assets*, in which the legality of certain targeted sanctions taken by the USA versus Iran were in issue, the ICJ was only able to evaluate the legality of US coercive measures taken against Iran by reference to the 1955 bilateral Treaty of Amity between them; it avoided the wider questions about the permissibility of similar measures in the absence of a treaty.[77]

For some decades, there has been practice where States have imposed a range of unilateral measures,[78] sometimes with devastating effect.[79] The question that has arisen is whether such unilateral measures are lawful in certain circumstances. The issue is that this category is not legally precise, at least not in the sense that, for example, reprisals or countermeasures are. The Human Rights Council sought to describe 'unilateral coercive measures' as 'the use of economic, trade or other measures taken by a state, group of states or international organizations acting autonomously to compel a change of policy of another state or to pressure individuals, groups or entities in targeted states to influence a course of action without the authorization of the Security Council'.[80] What arises from this definition is that such unilateral responses are not necessarily countermeasures, in that they do not necessarily depend on their being a response to a prior unlawful act, and are not necessarily aimed at inducing a return to compliance by a responsible state. Put more simply: if a unilateral restrictive measure cannot be an act of retorsion or a countermeasure, are there situations where it nevertheless might be

[74] See the provocative only 'Symposium: Third World Approaches to International Law (TWAIL) and Economic Sanctions', Yale Journal of International Law (20 June 2023), https://yjil.yale.edu/posts/2023-06-20-symposium-third-world-approaches-to-international-law-twail-economic-sanctions, in which the wider stakeholders and issues at stake are problematized using a decidedly postcolonial and critical lens.

[75] See A Tzanakopoulos, 'The Right to be Free of Economic Coercion' (2015) 4 CJICL 616.

[76] Boisson de Chazournes (n 70) 1209–10.

[77] *Certain Iranian Assets (Iran v United States), Judgment, ICJ Reports 2023*, p 51.

[78] On the term 'unilateral sanctions' to refer to the measures taken by an organization against a third (non-member) State, see A Tzanakopoulos, 'Sanctions Imposed Unilaterally by the European Union: Implications for the European Union's International Responsibility' in AZ Marossi and MR Barrett (eds), *Economic Sanctions under International Law* (Springer, 2015), 145, 148 *et seq*.

[79] See, e.g., Bowett (n 24) 4; OY Elagab, *The Legality of Non-Forcible Counter-Measures in International Law* (Clarendon Press, 1988), 212–13; L Boisson de Chazournes, 'Other Non-Derogable Rights' in J Crawford, A Pellet, and S Olleson (eds), *The Law of International Responsibility* (OUP, 2010), 1205.

[80] Human Rights Council Advisory Committee, 'Progress Report: Recommendations on mechanisms to assess the negative impact of unilateral coercive measures on the enjoyment of human rights and to promote accountability', UN Doc A/HRC/28/74 (2015), para 9. It has used the term consistently: see, e.g., HRC, 'Human Rights and Unilateral Coercive Measures' UNHRC Res 54/15 (13 October 2023).

lawful? This terminological situation is only exacerbated by certain actors taking such measures calling them 'unilateral' or 'targeted' *sanctions*, which do not meet the collective character for sanctions as described in Section 13.5.

Well-known examples of such coercive measures include the US embargoes on Cuba from 1960,[81] on Iran in 1979, and on the Soviet Union in 1980. Other States and IOs have also imposed restrictive measures, notably the Arab oil-producing States in 1973–4 in support of Palestinian self-determination, and the ongoing 'smart sanctions' (including an arms embargo and the freezing of assets) imposed by the EU and its members against Zimbabwe following the expulsion of EU election observers. That said, the EU measures against Zimbabwe were ostensibly justified under conditionality clauses found in the Cotonou Agreement which committed Zimbabwe to certain fundamental human rights guarantees.[82]

The adoption of unilateral restrictive measures has intensified over the last decade, with the EU's justifications of particular interest. Prominently, the EU, the USA and their allies issued a range of restrictive measures against Russia first after the military occupation and purported annexation of Crimea in 2014, called into question by the UN General Assembly.[83] At that juncture, the EU justified its coercive measures under various security exceptions in the 1994 EU-Russia Partnership Agreement.[84] As a response to Russia's armed attack against Ukraine in 2022, which was categorically condemned by the General Assembly,[85] the EU adopted a vast range of economic, financial, and trade measures against Russia; in particular, the mass freezing and potential confiscation of €300 billion in Russian State assets.[86]

Finally, since 2017 the EU, the USA and their allies have adopted a range of restrictive measures against Venezuela, following contested elections (see Chapter 5, Section 5.3.2.2).[87] The EU's measures were the subject of a legal challenge by Venezuela in the General Court of the EU, in which, for the first time, questions concerning the nature and legality of EU restrictive measures against third States under international law arose.[88] Intriguingly, the General Court explicitly rejected Venezuela's claim that these restrictive measures were 'unlawful countermeasures', and instead proclaimed that the EU had 'independent EU measures' arising under EU law to safeguard fundamental

[81] It is true, however, that the General Assembly condemns the US embargo on Cuba on an annual basis, suggesting that the US embargo does not comply with international law. For further detail, see Chapter 8, Section 8.1.1.

[82] Partnership agreement between the Members of the African, Caribbean and Pacific Group of States of the One Part, and the European Community and its Member States, of the Other Part, Art 96, June 23, 2000, 2000 OJ (L 317) 3 (Cotonou Agreement).

[83] GA Res 68/262 (27 March 2014). The G8 also suspended Russia, reverting to its previous name: the G7.

[84] On these justifications under Article 99, see CJEU, *PJSC Rosneft Oil Company v Her Majesty's Treasury and Others* [2017] C-72/15.

[85] See, e.g., GA Res ES/11/1 (2 March 2022); GA Res ES/11/2 (24 March 2022); GA Res ES/11/5 (14 November 2022); GA Res ES/11/6 (23 February 2023).

[86] See, e.g., EU Council Regulation 2024/1745 (amending Regulation 833/2014) and EU Council Regulation and Implementing Regulation 2024/1746 amending EU Council Regulation 269/2014 (25 June 2024).

[87] See EU Council Decision (CFSP) 2017/2074 (13 November 2017).

[88] *Bolivarian Republic of Venezuela v Council of the European Union*, Case T-65/18 RENV.

principles of EU law, and that such could go further than the limits imposed by the law on countermeasures.[89]

The key issue arising in relation to these coercive measures has called into question the temporariness and reversibility conditions relating to the taking of countermeasures—a term not being invoked by the EU in any event. When mirrored by similarly restrictive measures taken by the USA, Japan, Canada, the UK, and other States, questions arise as to the extent to which these restrictive or coercive measures may be legally justifiable under international law—and perhaps more importantly, under which rubric.

13.5 Sanctions

13.5.1 What are sanctions?

The proliferation of international institutions since World War II has meant that, however fledgling, international law has developed a partial centralization of sanctions, particularly through the Security Council. It is true that in the early decades of the UN, compliance and enforcement were difficult to implement, as there was a hope that States would carry out their legal obligations without the need for institutional coercive enforcement.[90]

The end of the Cold War and the increased activity of the Security Council, however, have in recent years increased the relevance of sanctions as a collective enforcement tool. As described in the introduction, the term 'sanctions' is understood in international law in a narrower sense, to refer to measures which are:

(i) ordinarily themselves in breach of an international obligation;

(ii) a coercive response to the breach of another State;

(iii) taken in execution of a decision of an organ of an international organization which is legally competent to make a relevant decision or recommendation.[91]

The preference for collective decision-making is justified by the idea that States may, collectively rather than unilaterally, arrive at a more balanced assessment of an unlawful situation, and may act with a greater respect for law and the need to safeguard peaceful international relations.

This section will focus primarily on sanctions, properly so called, imposed by United Nations organs, though it is true that other international organizations, and, in particular, regional security organizations, have also imposed sanctions against their members.[92] Beyond the UN, of interest are the punitive measures until recently pursued by

[89] *Ibid* para 113. [90] O Schachter, 'United Nations Law' (1994) 88 AJIL 1; see also Kunz (n 7).

[91] See G Abi-Saab, 'The Concept of Sanction in International Law' in V Gowlland-Debbas (ed), *United Nations Sanctions and International Law* (Kluwer, 2001), 38.

[92] To give a few examples, the OAS suspended Cuba (1962–2009) and Nicaragua (2009–11), and imposed economic sanctions against Haiti in 1992. ECOWAS imposed sanctions against Liberia from 1989 to 1997, Sierra Leone from 1997 to 2001, Togo in 2005, and Mali from 2012; it suspended Côte d'Ivoire from 2010 to 2011. See generally A Abass, *Regional Organisations and the Development of Collective Security: Beyond Chapter VIII of the UN Charter* (Hart, 2004), ch 5.

the European Commission against Poland in respect of various legislative provisions which undermine the application of EU law and are in violation of various EU treaties.[93] Certain measures, such as the suspension of voting rights, are not possible unless a 'serious and persistent breach' is identified by unanimity (excluding the State concerned) under Article 7 of the Treaty on European Union.

13.5.2 **Sanctions in United Nations practice**

13.5.2.1 **Sanctions and the Security Council**

Once the United Nations Security Council has determined that there is breach or threat to the peace under Article 39 of the Charter, it has the power to impose on a State any type of measure which does not involve the use of armed force.[94] Under Article 41, this may include 'complete or partial interruption of economic relations and of rail, sea, air, postal and telegraphic, radio and other means of communication, and the severance of diplomatic relations'. As these are under Chapter VII of the Charter, they are binding, unlike any recommendations that the General Assembly may suggest.[95]

Though such sanctions share common features with countermeasures, they are distinct in a few key respects. Above all, sanctions are the decisions taken by international organizations against their own member States, in response to a breach of the law of that international organization. Countermeasures, by contrast, may be taken in parallel by several States, but are not 'collective' measures in the same sense as sanctions. Furthermore, the Security Council can impose sanctions as an anticipatory response to a 'threat', before an actual breach of an international obligation has occurred; and in this respect, they are also distinct from countermeasures, which are only lawful in response to the unlawful act of another actor.[96]

HISTORICAL BACKGROUND Sanctions and Apartheid in South Africa

Apartheid (in Afrikaans, 'the state of being apart', literally 'apart-hood') was a system of racial segregation in South Africa enforced through legislation by the National Party (NP), the governing party from 1948 to 1994. Though racial segregation had already existed under Dutch and then British colonial rule, an officially structured policy was introduced after the general election of 1948 classifying inhabitants into distinct racial groups. White minority rule was entrenched, public services such as education and medical care were segregated, and the

[93] On 27 October 2021, Poland was ordered by the ECJ to pay the European Commission €1,000,000 daily for failing to suspend the application of the offending legislative provisions: see Case C-204/21 R, *Commission v Poland* (27 October 2021). After the re-election of Donald Tusk's government and a new Polish action plan, in May 2024 the European Commission closed these proceedings.

[94] Schachter (n 76) 12; Gowlland-Debbas (n 14) 9; Zoller (n 63) 106–7.

[95] The General Assembly memorably recommended sanctions against Francoist Spain in 1951, as well as North Korea and China, South Africa, and Israel: see B Conforti, *The Law and Practice of the United Nations* (Kluwer Law, 2000), 214–17.

[96] However, cf Tzanakopoulos (n 61) ch 3, who argues that States are under an obligation not to be a threat to peace.

rights, associations, and movements of the majority black inhabitants and other ethnic groups were curtailed.

Crucially, apartheid was introduced into the territory of South West Africa, administered by South Africa under a mandate from the League of Nations, revoked in 1966 via United Nations Resolution 2145. This was the subject of a series of cases at the ICJ, culminating in the 1971 *Namibia* advisory opinion.

Apartheid sparked significant international and domestic outrage. Many States imposed unilateral embargoes, or acted through regional organizations. In addition, the Security Council imposed an arms embargo through Resolution 418 (1977), which progressively tightened through Resolutions 421 (1977), 473 (1980), 558 (1984), and 591 (1986). In Resolution 569 (1985), the Council imposed comprehensive sanctions against South Africa and called for the release of political prisoners, including Nelson Mandela.

Though belated, the international response to apartheid contributed to its fall. In 1990, President de Klerk began negotiations to end apartheid, and South West Africa gained independence as Namibia. These changes culminated in multiracial democratic elections in 1994, won by the African National Congress under Nelson Mandela, producing a much more integrated and representative democracy.

13.5.2.2 **Types of sanctions in practice**

Generally, sanctions imposed by the Council have been economic in nature, and have included full or partial trade, communications, financial, commercial, and arms embargoes. They have, however, also suspended scientific, technical, or cultural cooperation. Significant sanctions and arms embargoes were imposed during the Cold War, first against the white minority government in Rhodesia from 1965 to 1977, until the territory became independent as Zimbabwe,[97] and then in 1977–94, against the apartheid regime in South Africa.[98]

During the 1990s and early 2000s, the Council became increasingly active in resorting to the imposition of economic sanctions and arms embargoes, beginning with the comprehensive sanctions imposed on Iraq following its invasion of Kuwait and culminating in the 2003 invasion of Iraq.[99] Economic sanctions or arms embargoes, and sometimes both,[100] have been imposed against Libya in respect of the Lockerbie

[97] UNSC Res 216 (12 November 1965); UNSC Res 217 (20 November 1965); UNSC Res 221 (9 April 1966); UNSC Res 232 (16 December 1966); UNSC Res 253 (29 May 1968); UNSC Res 409 (27 May 1977).

[98] UNSC Res 418 (4 November 1977).

[99] UNSC Res 660 (2 August 1990); UNSC Res 661 (6 August 1990); UNSC Res 665 (25 August 1990); UNSC Res 669 (24 September 1990). These were followed by further sanctions: see UNSC Res 687 (3 April 1991); UNSC Res 707 (15 August 1991); UNSC Res 715 (11 October 1991); UNSC Res 1284 (17 December 1999). See also UNSC Res 1441 (8 November 2002), giving Iraq a 'final opportunity to comply' and threatening 'serious consequences'.

[100] A repertoire of the use of economic sanctions by the Security Council (up to 2010) can be found in E López-Jacoiste, 'The UN Collective Security System and its Relationship with Economic Sanctions and Human Rights' (2010) 14 Max Planck YBUNL 273. For a repertory of practice up to 2000, see Conforti (n 81) 185–94. The General Assembly has also recommended sanctions against certain States. See also B Kondoch, 'The Limits of Economic Sanctions under International Law: The Case of Iraq' (2001) 7 International Peacekeeping 267.

incident,[101] and in response to conflicts in Somalia,[102] Rwanda,[103] Liberia,[104] Sierra Leone,[105] the Democratic Republic of the Congo,[106] and Sudan.[107] Unusually, they were imposed on all parties during the violent dissolution of Yugoslavia,[108] and on both Ethiopia and Eritrea during their inter-State conflict.[109] More recently, the Council has imposed sanctions on Libya, North Korea, and Syria. Of recent interest have been the Security Council sanctions imposed on Iran in respect of its failure to cooperate with the International Atomic Energy Agency (IAEA), and which since 2006 had imposed an arms embargo, banned the supply of nuclear-related technology, and imposed an asset freeze on individuals and companies related to the nuclear enrichment programme.[110] When the five permanent members of the Council (plus Germany) and Iran agreed the July 2015 Joint Comprehensive Plan of Action (JCPOA) under which Iran agreed to various denuclearization measures and a comprehensive inspections regime, the Security Council began to lift the nuclear-related elements of the sanctions.[111] Former US President Trump would withdraw unilaterally in 2018 and imposed new sanctions against Iran, leading to an Iranian claim before the ICJ and the suspension by Iran of some of its commitments under the JCPOA.[112] Though in October 2021, US President Biden had indicated a commitment to return the US to full compliance with the JCPOA and to stay in full compliance, so long as Iran did the same,[113] negotiations floundered and as of late 2024, only limited sanctions against Iran had been lifted, with no US re-entry into the JCPOA.

Most sanctions are targeted against a State for breaching international law, and thus have a retributive or punitive character. But sanctions can also have an exemplary character, being imposed on a State in order to deter other States from committing the same act.[114] A striking example of exemplary sanctions is Security Council Resolution 1343, in which the Council imposed sanctions on Liberia after determining that Liberia had been providing support to the Revolutionary United Front (RUF) in Sierra Leone.[115] After the imposition of these sanctions, Liberia withdrew all support in accordance

[101] UNSC Res 731 (21 January 1992).

[102] UNSC Res 733 (23 January 1992); UNSC Res 751 (24 April 1992); UNSC Res 1356 (19 June 2001); UNSC Res 1407 (3 May 2002); UNSC Res 1425 (22 July 2002); UNSC Res 1744 (20 February 2007); and UNSC Res 1772 (20 August 2007).

[103] UNSC Res 918 (17 May 1994); UNSC Res 1005 (17 July 1995); UNSC Res 1011 (16 August 1995); UNSC Res 1013 (7 September 1995); UNSC Res 1053 (23 April 1996); UNSC Res 1161 (9 April 1998).

[104] UNSC Res 788 (19 November 1992); UNSC Res 985 (13 April 1995).

[105] UNSC Res 1132 (8 October 1997); UNSC Res 1171 (5 June 1998).

[106] UNSC Res 1493 (28 July 2003); UNSC Res 1533 (12 March 2004); UNSC Res 1596 (18 April 2005); UNSC Res 1649 (21 December 2005); UNSC Res 1698 (31 July 2006).

[107] UNSC Res 1556 (30 July 2004); UNSC Res 1591 (29 March 2005).

[108] UNSC Res 713 (25 September 1991); see also UNSC Res 724 (15 December 1991); UNSC Res 757 (30 May 1992); UNSC Res 820 (17 April 1993).

[109] UNSC Res 1298 (17 May 2000).

[110] UNSC Res 1373 (23 December 2006) and UNSC Res 1979 (9 June 2010).

[111] UNSC Res 2231 (20 July 2015).

[112] *Alleged Violations of the 1955 Treaty of Amity, Economic Relations, and Consular Rights (Iran v United States), Provisional Measures, ICJ Reports 2018*, p 623, para 98.

[113] See Joint Statement by the French President, German Chancellor, Prime Minister of the United Kingdom and President of the United States on Iran (30 October 2021).

[114] Zoller (n 63) 184.

[115] Such support was in breach of UNSC Res 1132 (8 October 1997).

with the Security Council's will. Resolution 1343 represents the first time that sanctions were imposed on a State because of its refusal to comply with sanctions imposed by the Security Council against another State.[116]

Though economic sanctions are non-forcible in character, they have a potentially devastating effect on the stability and resilience of a society, and may engender serious human and environmental suffering, especially among the most vulnerable groups in a State, such as women and children.[117] For example, when comprehensive sanctions were imposed against Saddam Hussein's regime in Iraq, there was a drastic decline in access to basic services affecting wide sectors of the civilian population.[118] During the 1990s, the Federal Republic of Yugoslavia saw a severe drop in income levels, employment, health care, and nutrition during the period where comprehensive sanctions were imposed against it by most Western States.[119] In General Comment No 8, the UN Committee on Economic, Social and Cultural Social Rights (CESCR) warned that collective sanctions 'often cause significant disruption in the distribution of food, pharmaceuticals and sanitation supplies, jeopardise the quality of food and the availability of clean drinking water, severely interfere with the functioning of basic health and education systems, and undermine the right to work'.[120]

13.5.2.3 **Limits on the imposition of sanctions**

The international reaction to the most severe sanctions regimes has raised the question of whether there are limits on Security Council action. It is true that the principle that general international law binds international organizations[121] would, at first glance, also ring true in relation to the United Nations. However, the argument has been made that the specific functions and powers conferred upon the organization under the UN Charter and, in particular, Article 103, give primacy to the Charter and obligations flowing therefrom. This is especially so for obligations created pursuant to Chapter VII, which prevail over conflicting treaty or customary law obligations.[122] This does not

[116] See further D Cortright and GA Lopez, *Sanctions and the Search for Security: Challenges to UN Action* (Lynne Rienner, 2002), esp 82 *et seq.*

[117] Some have gone so far as to call sanctions 'economic warfare': see, e.g., F Stenhammar, 'United Nations Targeted Sanctions, the International Rule of Law and the European Court of Justice's Judgment in Kadi and al-Barakaat' (2010) 79 Nordic Journal of International Law 113, 120.

[118] See, e.g., World Health Organization Regional Office for the Eastern Mediterranean, *The Work of the WHO in the Eastern Mediterranean Region, Annual Report of the Regional Director (1999)* (WHO Publications, 2000); UNICEF, *Child and Maternal Survey (1999)* (UNICEF Publications, 1999); FAO, *Evaluation of Food and Nutrition Situation in Iraq* (1997) (FAO Publications, 1997). See also SP Marks, 'Economic Sanctions as Rights and Public Health Imperatives' (1999) 89 American Journal of Public Health 1509; and R Provost, 'Starvation as a Weapon: Legal Implications of the United Nations Food Blockade against Iraq and Kuwait' (1992) 30 Columbia JTL 577.

[119] See, e.g., R Garfield, *Economic Sanctions, Health, and Welfare in the Federal Republic of Yugoslavia 1990–2000* (UNICEF Publications, 2000).

[120] General Comment No 8 (n 50) para 3.

[121] See K Daugirdas, 'How and Why International Law Binds International Organizations' (2016) 57 Harvard ILJ 325.

[122] J Álvarez, 'The Security Council's War on Terrorism: Problems and Policy Options' in E de Wet and A Nollkaemper (eds), *Review of the Security Council by Member States* (Intersentia, 2003), 119, 133. A strong disagreement is expressed in Tzanakopoulos (n 61) ch 3.

mean that the Council is unbound: at the very least, under Article 24(2) of the Charter it is bound by the purposes and principles embodied therein.[123] Moreover, the argument has been made cogently that the Council is also bound by norms of *jus cogens*, though if it were to breach such norms, the reaction remains unclear.[124] It has also been suggested that when imposing economic sanctions, the Council is also bound to conform to the principles of necessity and proportionality in relation to the objective sought, usually the restoration of peace and security or the termination of a threat to the peace.[125] Finally, it has been argued that sanctions could be reviewed on these bases by the ICJ,[126] a possibility that had been left open by the withdrawal of the *Lockerbie* cases.[127]

Finally, after serious reactions to the comprehensive regime of sanctions imposed on Iraq after 1990, the Council's imposition of sanctions has in practice nearly always included an exemption for humanitarian supplies and, more generally, has called for respect of the human rights of the target population, though as mentioned earlier, in practice this is very difficult to achieve.[128] An awareness of the potential devastation wrought by sanctions has led to the abandonment of comprehensive sanctions in favour of more targeted measures; for example, to goods fuelling the threat (such as oil or diamonds, or even timber)[129] or to governmental officials responsible for the threat instead of civilian populations.[130]

[123] See, e.g., I Brownlie, 'International Law at the Fiftieth Anniversary of the United Nations' (1995) 255 Recueil des Cours 9, 217; R Higgins, 'The Advisory Opinion on Namibia. Which UN Resolutions are Binding under Article 25 of the Charter?' (1972) 21 ICLQ 278; J Delbrück, 'Article 24' in B Simma and others (eds), *The Charter of the United Nations: A Commentary* (2nd edn, OUP, 2002), 445; K Zemanek, 'Is the Security Council the Sole Judge of Its Own Legality?' in E Yakpo and T Boumedra (eds), *Liber Amicorum Mohamed Bedjaoui* (Martinus Nijhoff, 1999), 640.

[124] The most striking statement on this point remains the Separate Opinion of Judge ad hoc Lauterpacht in *Application of the Convention on the Prevention and Punishment of Genocide (Bosnia and Herzegovina v Yugoslavia), Order on Provisional Measures, ICJ Reports 1993*, p 407, 440, para 100. See also Tzanakopoulos (n 61) 71; A Tzanakopoulos, 'The *Solange* Argument as a Justification for Disobeying the Security Council in the Kadi Judgments' in M Avbelj, F Fontanelli, and G Marinico (eds), *Kadi on Trial: A Multifaceted Analysis of the Kadi Judgment* (Routledge, 2014), 124; A Orakehlashvili, 'Security Acts: Meaning and Standards of Review' (2007) 11 Max Planck UNYB 143, 150; C Olivier, 'Human Rights Law and the International Fight against Terrorism: How do Security Council Resolutions Impact on States' Obligations under International Human Rights Law (Revisiting Security Council Resolution 1373)?' (2004) 73 Nordic JIL 399, 414.

[125] Three classic examples include UNSC Res 661 (6 August 1990), in relation to Iraq's occupation of Kuwait; UNSC Res 748 (31 March 1992), in relation to the surrender by Libya of the two suspects in the Lockerbie bombing; and UNSC Res 253 (29 May 1968), in relation to the termination of white-minority rule in Rhodesia.

[126] See J Dugard, 'Judicial Review of Sanctions' in V Gowlland-Debbas (ed), *United Nations Sanctions and International Law* (Kluwer, 2001), 83, 88–9.

[127] See generally Tzanakopoulos (n 61), ch 4; J Álvarez, 'Judging the Security Council' (1996) 90 AJIL 1; B Graefrath, 'Leave to the Court what Belongs to the Court: The Libyan Case' (1993) 4 EJIL 184; and M Bedjaoui, *The New World Order and the Security Council: Testing the Legality of its Acts* (Martinus Nijhoff, 1994).

[128] Recent examples of this include UNSC Res 1973 (2011) (17 March 2011) establishing a no-fly zone in Libya; UNSC Res 2206 (2015) (3 March 2015), in relation to South Sudan.

[129] See, e.g., UNSC Res 2270 (2 March 2016) prohibiting the sale or supply of aviation fuel to North Korea.

[130] See, e.g., UNSC Res 2206 (n 114) establishing a travel ban on designated individuals in relation to South Sudan.

CONTEMPORARY DEVELOPMENTS 'Smart Sanctions' and the *Kadi* Judgment

In the last decade, there has been a move to limit human suffering imposed by sanctions with so-called 'smart sanctions', targeting specific individuals or otherwise tailored more narrowly. Security Council Resolution 1267 was the first such resolution passed by the Security Council; it aimed at targeting individual members or supporters of the Taliban or Al Qaeda through 'smart sanctions'. A committee would maintain a list of individuals whose funds and assets would be frozen by relevant member States, and who would be subject to a travel embargo. What was key was that these individuals were unconnected with the government of any particular State.

These 'smart sanctions', however, have been criticized for violating the human rights of these individuals, most memorably by the European Court of Justice in the infamous Joined Cases C-402/05 and C-415/05, *Kadi and Al Barakaat International Foundation v Council* [2008] ECR I-6351. Known as the *Kadi* judgment, the ECJ found that obligations under Resolution 1267, as implemented by EU member States, were in violation of the fundamental rights of Mr Kadi under European law. The judgment was particularly significant because of the ECJ's conclusion that obligations created under Resolution 1267, and thus under Chapter VII, did not prevail over human rights treaty obligations, despite the application of Article 103 of the Charter.

Though the Security Council still targets individuals in this manner, the *Kadi* controversy has led to further reflection on the extent to which sanctions targeting individuals may infringe on international human rights law.

13.6 **Conclusion**

This chapter has reviewed the range of techniques available to an aggrieved actor, in most cases a State, in response to a breach of international law by another actor. Many of these are unilateral measures of self-help, and perhaps embody a resigned pragmatism that, at present, the decentralized international legal order needs to accommodate these unilateral moves for fear of wider repercussions. Perhaps encouraging is the fact that, increasingly, countermeasures remain the only legal circumstance which allows for the breach of an international obligation in response to the breach of another. Unarmed reprisals are largely obsolete, replaced by countermeasures, and armed reprisals are nearly categorically banned in the law of armed conflict. Acts of retorsion are no more than simply unfriendly, having never been unlawful to begin with. Yet the language of retaliation, and other punitive rhetoric, continues to colour unilateral measures of self-help and lends confusion to this area when the terminology is not fully clear.

Great hope is placed in the legitimacy of an international organization to deliberate collectively and take collective decisions to impose sanctions or other measures. This does not mean, however, that collective measures are *a fortiori* preferable; one need only see the inconsistent and often controversial exercise of that power by the Security Council. One should not fixate on collective sanctions as themselves the solution to non-compliance with international law but, rather, part of a wider diplomatic, political, and legal process through which the member States of the United Nations may act collectively in pursuance of a common goal. Together, the panoply of unilateral, regional, and collective measures is best seen as a combination of complementary techniques to minimize the potential for force to be exercised, though they should be exercised carefully so as to avoid catastrophic results.

Further reading

D Alland, 'Countermeasures of General Interest' (2002) 13 EJIL 1221.

A scholarly examination of the possibility of third-party countermeasures in international law, affecting more than a directly injured State.

D Alland, 'The Definition of Countermeasures' in J Crawford and S Olleson (eds), *The Law of International Responsibility* (OUP, 2010), ch 79.

A good descriptive treatment of the concept of countermeasures in the context of the law on State responsibility.

M Asada (ed), *Economic Sanctions in International Law and Practice* (Routledge, 2021).

Including chapters with contributors from various disciplines, including international law, this highly contemporary compendium also looks at various recent case studies.

J Dugard, 'Judicial Review of Sanctions' in V Gowlland-Debbas (ed), *United Nations Sanctions and International Law* (Kluwer, 2001), 83.

A novel argument favouring increased accountability of the Security Council with respect to its decisions regarding the imposition of sanctions.

OY Elagab, *The Legality of Non-Forcible Counter-Measures in International Law* (Clarendon Press, 1988).

A comprehensive history of the emergence of an autonomous concept of countermeasures in international law.

JM Farrall, *United Nations Sanctions and the Rule of Law* (CUP, 2007).

A thorough, critical review of the practice of the Security Council in relation to sanctions.

M Kanetake, *The UN Security Council and Domestic Actors: Distance in International Law* (Routledge, 2017).

A book-length review of the Security Council's exercise of authority over individuals at the domestic level, an intensifying practice in the past two decades.

ME O'Connell, 'Debating the Law of Sanctions' (2002) 13 EJIL 63.

An overview of the continued shifts in the imposition of collective sanctions during the immediate post-Cold War revitalization of Security Council practice in the area.

L-A Sicilianos, *Les réactions décentralisées à l'illicite: des contre-mesures à la légitime défense* (LGJD, 1990).

A leading French-language treatment of the law on countermeasures.

A Tzanakopoulos, *Disobeying the Security Council* (OUP, 2011).

A novel argument advocating the use of countermeasures by States in response to decisions of the Security Council that breach rules of *jus cogens*.

14

The use of force and collective security

14.1 Introduction: the role of law in constraining international violence

Historically, international law has been marked by a lack of clarity in relation to violence between different international actors. On the one hand, the desire to abolish or otherwise restrict violence forms part of the very fabric of international law and is part of its *raison d'être*.[1] Yet for most of modern international law's history, resort to war was legally permissible as an attribute of statehood, and even a form of settling disputes. In this respect, international law's role has developed incrementally to allocate the legitimate use of violence between different international actors, rather than a blanket prohibition on force.

HISTORICAL BACKGROUND The Concept of 'Just War' and its Contemporary Relevance

There was an important current in international law scholarship which, informed by a long tradition of Christian theology, sought to situate the concept of 'just war' developed by St Augustine and St Thomas Aquinas within the context of modern international law. These included not only Francisco de Vitoria and Francisco Suárez but also Hugo Grotius and Emer de Vattel. Vattel famously argued that '[l]a guerre doit être regardée comme juste d'une part et d'autre' ('war must be regarded as just by one side and the other') (E de Vattel, *Le droit des gens* (1820), vol 2, 274).

Over time, the concept of just war has given rise to a distinction between the 'law of war' and the 'law of peace', with a different paradigm applying to each: international humanitarian law (see Chapter 15) developed from the first category. Grotius suggested that the laws of war could only be applicable to a 'just war', which for him would only be 'just' in situations of self-defence, the protection of property, and the punishment for wrongs suffered by the nationals of a State. The distinction persisted for centuries, being used as late as *Oppenheim's International Law* (1992).

[1] Seminal works on the history of international law and war include S Neff, *War and the Law of Nations* (CUP, 2005); J Stone, *Aggression and World Order* (UC Press, 1958); D Kennedy, *Of War and Law* (Princeton UP, 2006); N Bobbio, 'Esquisse d'une théorie sur les rapports entre la guerre et le droit' in N Bobbio et al (eds), *La guerre et ses theories* (PUF, 1970).

Further reading on the history of just war theory includes J Von Elbe, 'The Evolution of the Concept of the Just War in International Law' (1939) 33 AJIL 669; M Walzer, *Just and Unjust Wars* (2nd edn, Basic Books, 1977); and S Neff, *War and the Law of Nations* (CUP, 2005), ch 3.

The general tolerance for war persisted well into the first decades of the twentieth century, allowing for intervention and other coercive measures, as well as the lawful conquest of territory. Early twentieth-century examples include the forced cession of Puerto Rico, the Philippines, and Guam by Spain to the USA,[2] and the southern half of the island of Sakhalin by Russia to Japan.[3] Conquest through armed force was even permitted in situations of *debellatio* (the complete defeat and destruction of a warring party), as occurred when the British Empire annexed the former South African Republic at the close of the second Boer War in 1902, and the American annexation of Hawaii. Most legal efforts during the period, such as the Hague Conventions signed in 1899 and 1907, focused instead on the methods of conducting warfare (*jus in bello*, or international humanitarian law) rather than the right to wage war (*jus ad bellum*).[4] A notable exception was the 'Drago Doctrine' embodied in the Second Hague Convention, which forbade recourse to war merely to recover contractual debts owed to a State's nationals,[5] a pernicious practice employed by European States against Latin American and Asian States in the nineteenth century.[6]

The 1919 Covenant of the League of Nations marked a shift in the relationship between law and force.[7] Henceforth, Article 10 of the Covenant bound members of the League to respect and preserve the territorial integrity and existing independence of all members. States were still permitted to resort to war. However, before doing so, members were required to seek arbitration, judicial settlement, or involvement of the League Council (Article 12), and to wait three months after an arbitral award, judgment, or Council report before declaring war. This three-month period aimed to quell political friction. Perhaps most significantly, under Articles 15–17, the Covenant empowered the Council to intervene in disputes, coordinate responses to an aggressive resort to war, conduct inquiries into the circumstances of disputes, and recommend action to League members.[8] That embryonic system of collective security, though not particularly successful, would serve as the predecessor for the later UN Charter system.

[2] 1898 Treaty of Paris (signed 10 December 1898, entry into force 11 April 1899), 11 Bevans 615.

[3] 1905 Treaty of Portsmouth (signed 5 September 1905), 199 CTS 144.

[4] The Hague Conventions are described in Chapter 15, Section 15.1.

[5] Hague Convention II of 1907 Respecting the Limitations of the Employment of Force for the Recovery of Contract Debts ('Drago–Porter Convention') (signed 18 October 1907, 26 January 1910), 205 CTS 250.

[6] See I Brownlie, *International Law and the Use of Force by States* (OUP, 1963), 28 *et seq*.

[7] Covenant of the League of Nations (signed 28 June 1919, entry into force 10 January 1920), 108 LNTS 188.

[8] For further detail, see R Kolb, 'Article 15' in R Kolb (ed), *Commentaire sur le Pacte de la Société des Nations, article par article* (Bruylant, 2014).

A further landmark in the pre-Charter period was the 1928 'Kellogg–Briand Pact', named after the US and French representatives who spearheaded its adoption.[9] Parties to the Pact agreed to renounce war as an instrument of national policy in their relations with one another.[10] Though widely ratified, the Pact did not prevent violence during the 1930s, as is evident from Japan's occupation of Manchuria, Italy's conquest of Ethiopia, the USSR's invasion of Finland, and Germany's annexation of Austria and occupation of Czechoslovakia and Poland. However, the Pact maintained its relevance after World War II, both in respect of the 'crimes against peace' prosecuted in the Nuremberg and Tokyo international military tribunals (see Chapter 17), and the fact that its prohibition on the resort to war was embedded in the UN Charter, to which we now turn.

14.2 The Charter prohibition on the use of force

Today, the United Nations Charter embodies the indispensable principles of international law on the use of force. These include the prohibition on the unilateral use of force found in Article 2(4), and the recognition of the inherent right of all States to use force in self-defence found in Article 51. Finally, under Chapter VII, a collective security system centred upon the Security Council was established for the maintenance of international peace and security.

14.2.1 Article 2(4) of the UN Charter

The prohibition on the use of force first outlined in the Kellogg–Briand Pact was taken up in a 'cornerstone'[11] provision of the United Nations Charter, Article 2(4), which has established a prohibition against a State unilaterally threatening or using force against another State.

> All Members shall refrain in their international relations from the threat or use of force against the territorial integrity or political independence of any State, or in any other manner inconsistent with the Purposes of the United Nations.

Though succinct, Article 2(4) can be interpreted by reference to the Charter's preamble, 'to save succeeding generations from the scourge of war', and in particular in Article 1, which includes *inter alia* '[the maintenance of] international peace and security, and to that end: to take effective collective measures for the prevention and removal of threats to the peace and for the suppression of acts of aggression and other breaches of the peace'.

[9] General Treaty for the Renunciation of War (signed 27 August 1928, entry into force 24 July 1929), 94 LNTS 57 (Kellogg–Briand Pact). See the engaging, somewhat optimistic, account of the pact in O Hathaway and S Shapiro, *The Internationalists: How a Radical Plan to Outlaw War Remade the World* (Simon & Schuster, 2017).

[10] Kellogg–Briand Pact, *ibid*, Art I.

[11] *Armed Activities on the Territory of the Congo (Democratic Republic of the Congo v Uganda), Judgment, ICJ Reports 2005*, p 168, 223, para 190.

Though in 1945 there was some debate as to whether Article 2(4) was a novel rule,[12] it is now unequivocally regarded as customary international law, binding on all States;[13] some even argue that it is a rule of *jus cogens*.[14] Moreover, some key General Assembly declarations have elaborated on the scope of the prohibition embodied in Article 2(4). Three declarations in particular—the Friendly Relations Declaration (1970),[15] the Definition of Aggression (1974),[16] and the Effectiveness of the Principle prohibiting the Threat or Use of Force (1987)[17]—have added important clarifications: a prohibition on wars of aggression; a prohibition on threatening or using force to change existing international frontiers; a duty to refrain from forcible reprisals; a prohibition on force to deprive peoples of their right to self-determination; and a prohibition on States from organizing, instigating, assisting, or participating in acts of civil strife or terrorism in another State.[18]

The interpretation of the prohibition on the use of force remains controversial, with certain terms within the UN Charter requiring further scrutiny.

14.2.2 **Use of force in 'international relations'**

To use 'force' is generally understood to encompass armed force used directly or indirectly (e.g., through proxy or irregular armed forces, or mercenaries) against another State. As the ICJ illustrated in *Nicaragua*, various actions of the USA were categorized as forcible—and thus unlawful—acts: the laying of mines in Nicaragua's territorial waters; attacks on its ports and installations; and its arming and training of the *Contras* that had resulted in the *Contras'* violent operations.[19] Though the provision of aid and assistance, including funding, was not sufficient to constitute the use of force, they could constitute unlawful intervention.[20] Such a characterization could be relevant for States aiding and supporting various opposition groups ranging from the situations in Syria to Venezuela, and has been invoked repeatedly by Russia against Western States that have furnished Ukraine with military and humanitarian assistance.

[12] Brownlie (n 6) 66.

[13] See *Military and Paramilitary Activities in and against Nicaragua (Nicaragua v United States), Merits, ICJ Reports 1986*, p 14, para 190; *Armed Activities in the Congo* (n 11) 223.

[14] T Kleinlein, 'Ch 1: Purposes and Principles, Article 2' in B Simma et al (eds), *Charter of the United Nations: A Commentary* (4th edn, OUP, 2024), 164; *cf.* JA Green, 'Questioning the Peremptory Status of the Prohibition of the Use of Force' (2011) 32 Michigan JIL 215.

[15] 'Declaration on Principles of International Law concerning Friendly Relations and Co-operation among States', UNGA Res 2625 (XXV) (24 October 1970).

[16] 'Definition of Aggression', UNGA Res 3314 (XXIX) (14 December 1974).

[17] 'Enhancement of the Effectiveness of the Principle of Refraining from the Threat or Use of Force', UNGA Res 42/22 (18 November 1987).

[18] See O Corten, 'The Controversies Over the Customary Prohibition on the Use of Force: A Methodological Debate' (2005) 16 EJIL 803; G Arangio-Ruiz, *The UN Declaration on Friendly Relations and the System of Sources of International Law* (Martinus Nijhoff, 1979).

[19] *Nicaragua (Merits)* (n 13) 228.

[20] *Ibid.* For a further study of the rule on non-intervention, see M Roscini, *International Law and the Principle of Non-Intervention* (OUP, 2024), esp ch 2–3.

The use of force does not encompass the imposition of sanctions, boycotts or embargoes, or other forms of non-forcible or economic coercion.[21] Having said that, as discussed in Chapter 13, Sections 13.4–13.5, the General Assembly has called into question the legality of economic coercion, proclaiming in the Friendly Relations Declaration that '[n]o State may use or encourage the use of economic, political or any other type of measures to coerce another State in order to obtain from it the subordination of the exercise of its sovereign rights and to secure from it advantages of any kind'.[22] Furthermore, there seems to be an increasing consensus that, if a cyber operation has the scale and effects of a use of force—notably, physical destruction or loss of life—the said operation is to be regarded as a use of force.[23]

The term 'international relations' in Article 2(4) suggests that it does not apply, in principle, to the use of force *within* States, for example, by a State to quell a rebellion within its territory. This has raised questions regarding the 'categorization of conflicts', in relation to whether a conflict was inter- or intra-State in nature; for example, during the Korean and Vietnam wars, and especially the violent disintegration of the former Yugoslavia.[24] Certain States have also, problematically, asserted the right to use force to enforce their claims to disputed territory. India justified its 1961 invasion of Goa on the basis that Portugal was unlawfully occupying an integral part of its territory.[25] Argentina invaded the Falkland Islands in 1982, rejecting the UK's claim to legal title.[26] Similarly, Iraq invaded Kuwait in 1990, claiming that it had pre-colonial title.[27] China has maintained that it is not prohibited from using force to recover the island of Taiwan, on the basis that it remains part of its sovereign territory.

CONTEMPORARY DEVELOPMENTS Russia and Ukraine

The ongoing armed conflict between Russia and Ukraine is longstanding, and it is helpful to understand the situation today in its historical context. Both were part of the Soviet Union until 1990; in 1954, the Crimean peninsula was transferred within that State from the Russian SFSR to the Ukrainian SFSR. Ukraine retained Crimea, which has a Russian-speaking majority, upon gaining independence in 1991, though already in 2008 began to complain that Russia had been issuing passports *en masse* in the region.

An international crisis erupted in February 2014, with Crimea and Ukrainian cities Donetsk and Luhansk openly revolting with what appeared to be Russian military support.

[21] See O Corten, *The Law against War* (2nd Hart, 2021), 61, 100. C Tams, 'Article 2(4)' in B Simma et al (eds), *Charter of the United Nations: A Commentary* (4th edn, OUP, 2024), 289.

[22] As recalled verbatim in the 'Charter of Economic Rights and Duties of States', UNGA Res 3281 (XXIX) (12 December 1974).

[23] Corten (n 21) 98–108. See further F Delerue, *Cyber Operations in International Law* (CUP, 2020), 289–90; M Roscini, *Cyber Operations and the Use of Force in International Law* (OUP, 2014), 54; and generally, M Schmitt (ed), *Tallinn Manual on the International Law Applicable to Cyber Operations* (2nd edn, CUP, 2017).

[24] See C Gray, 'Bosnia and Herzegovina: Civil War or Inter-State Conflict?' (1996) 67 BYBIL 155.

[25] See UNSC Verbatim Record (18 December 1961), UN Doc S/PV.987.

[26] UNGA, 'Status of the Falkland Islands' (1982) UNYB 1320.

[27] UNSC, 'Iraq-Kuwait Boundary' (1991) UNYB 189.

Ukraine claimed a violation of Article 2(4) of the Charter, but Russia insisted that only 'local self-defence units' had instigated the revolts. On 16 March 2014, a contested referendum was held, in which 95 per cent of voters favoured the incorporation of Crimea into Russia. On 17 March 2014, the Crimea authorities declared independence, and four days later ratified the Treaty of Accession of Crimea into the Russian Federation. Ukraine objected vehemently, and considered Crimea under 'temporary occupation', though Russian Foreign Minister Lavrov justified these acts by reference to a purported right to self-determination of Crimeans, the fact that many Crimean residents are Russian nationals, and allegations of human rights abuses. General Assembly Resolution 68/232 declared the referendum invalid and called on States not to recognize any change in Crimea's status, but the Security Council has never taken a position on the status of Crimea, perhaps unsurprisingly, given Russia's certain veto.

As for Donetsk and Luhansk, from 2014 they operated as breakaway entities without international recognition, until 21 February 2022, when they were recognized by Russia as newly independent republics. A shocking escalation of violence erupted on 24 February 2022, when Russian armed forces crossed through the north and east into Ukraine in what Russia called a 'special military operation' that Putin argued was aimed to 'protect the people' of the two breakaway republics from mass atrocities, including genocide, and to 'demilitarize and denazify' Ukraine. Since then, the two States have been locked in a violent armed conflict with major international repercussions.

After Russia vetoed a draft resolution in the Security Council, the Russian invasion was condemned as an 'act of aggression' by the General Assembly (GA Resolution ES-11/1 (2 March 2022), which would be cited by the International Court of Justice in its order on provisional measures calling for a suspension of hostilities in Ukraine (see *Allegations of Genocide under the Convention on the Prevention and Punishment of the Crime of Genocide (Ukraine v Russian Federation), Provisional Measures, Order of 16 March 2022, ICJ Reports 2022*, p 211, at para 86). Over fifty States and the EU provided military aid to support Ukraine's claim of self-defence, with a number of measures taken against Russia (see Chapter 13, Section 13.4.5).

Russia contested this interpretation and argued that it acted in accordance with the UN Charter, invoking its own self-defence (to protect its own nationals in Ukraine) and the 'collective self-defence' of Donetsk and Luhansk (see Section 14.3). Russia also initially argued that its operation was aimed to prevent the Ukrainian government from engaging in genocide against Russian-speakers, though later distanced itself from this argument (see *Allegations of Genocide*, paras 32–3).

The ongoing armed conflict has wide repercussions and engages many aspects of the use of force which will be addressed throughout this chapter.

14.2.3 **The meaning of 'threat or use of force'**

Article 2(4) of the Charter prohibits not only the actual use of force but also the threat of force.[28] The notion of 'threat' was addressed by the ICJ in its advisory opinion on the *Legality of the Threat or Use of Nuclear Weapons*,[29] finding that the mere possession

[28] For further reading, see N Stürchler, *The Threat of Force in International Law* (CUP, 2007) and N White and R Cryer, 'Unilateral Enforcement of Resolution 687: A Threat Too Far?' (1999) 29 California Western International Law Journal 243.

[29] *Legality of the Threat or Use of Nuclear Weapons, Advisory Opinion, ICJ Reports 1996*, p 226, 246–7.

of nuclear weapons was not a threat, but noting that the policy of nuclear deterrence functioned on the basis of the credible possibility of resort to nuclear weapons in exceptional circumstances. A 'signalled intent to use force if certain events occur' was understood to constitute a threat under Article 2(4), provided that the envisaged use of force would itself be unlawful; for example, by being directed against the territorial integrity or political independence of a State.[30] Naturally, a threat of a forcible act which met all the requirements of self-defence (see later, Section 14.3) would not breach Article 2(4).

Since 2022, certain Russian officials have made statements suggesting that it would deploy nuclear weapons against States supporting Ukraine. On 25 September 2024, Putin warned that if Russia were attacked with conventional weapons, it would consider nuclear retaliation in self-defence.[31] The 'first use' of nuclear weapons might, however, breach the conditions of necessity and proportionality in the law on self-defence (see later Section 14.3.2).

14.2.4 **Preserving the territorial integrity and political independence of a State**

During the Cold War, vigorous debates occurred concerning the prohibition in Article 2(4) against the use of force 'against the territorial integrity or political independence of any State'. Certain States interpreted this statement to permit limited uses of force, which to them did not violate territorial integrity or political independence. For example, in *Corfu Channel*, the UK defended a forcible minesweeping operation to recover evidence in Albanian territorial waters, on the basis that Albania's territorial integrity and political independence were not threatened. The ICJ rejected this construal of Article 2(4), on the basis that the operation was 'the manifestation of a policy of force' which would be reserved 'for the most powerful States', and thus violated Albania's territorial integrity.[32]

In the merits phase of *Nicaragua*, the ICJ decisively rejected a restrictive interpretation of Article 2(4).[33] Similarly, the Eritrea–Ethiopia Claims Commission concluded that recourse to force would violate international law even in situations where the State resorting to force had a valid claim to territory: 'border disputes between States are so frequent that any exception to the threat or use of force for territory that is allegedly occupied unlawfully would create a large and dangerous hole in a fundamental rule of international law'.[34] An expansive interpretation of the prohibition in Article 2(4) has thus prevailed at the ICJ at least, though as will be shown later, certain States have sought to broaden their right to use force, usually through a broad interpretation of the right to self-defence.

[30] *Cf* the controversial arbitral award in *Guyana/Suriname, Award of UNCLOS Annex VII Arbitral Tribunal* (2007) XXX RIAA 1–143 where a Surinamese naval vessel's order to an oil rig to leave its waters within twelve hours or 'face the consequences' was seen as constituting a threat.

[31] See Address by President Putin of 25 September 2024.

[32] *Corfu Channel (United Kingdom v Albania), Judgment, ICJ Reports 1949*, p 4, 34.

[33] *Nicaragua (Merits)* (n 13) 106–8.

[34] Eritrea–Ethiopia Claims Commission, Partial Award: *Jus Ad Bellum*—Ethiopia's Claims 1–8 (2005) XXVI RIAA 457, para 10.

14.3 The right to self-defence and Article 51 of the Charter

14.3.1 The scope of the right of unilateral self-defence

There is, of course, a significant exception in international law to Article 2(4), embodied in Article 51 of the Charter, according to which a State may use force unilaterally in order to defend itself:

> Nothing in the present Charter shall impair the inherent right of individual or collective self-defence if an armed attack occurs against a Member of the United Nations, until the Security Council has taken measures necessary to maintain international peace and security. Measures taken by Members in the exercise of this right of self-defence shall be immediately reported to the Security Council and shall not in any way affect the authority and responsibility of the Security Council under the present Charter to take at any time such action as it deems necessary in order to maintain or restore international peace and security.

One can dispense quickly with the obligation to report acts of self-defence to the Security Council; though the provision uses the mandatory 'shall', practice over the years has shown that a failure to notify the Council before taking action does not taint the act of self-defence with any illegality.[35]

Certain scholars contend that Article 51 is an exhaustive formulation of the conditions under which self-defence may be exercised, and should be narrowly construed.[36] Others take a broader interpretation of self-defence as an 'inherent' customary law right, allowing for its exercise in situations beyond those envisaged by the Charter; in particular, in responding to situations other than armed attack by a State, and with no deference to the Security Council.[37] The latter group point to the 1837 correspondence between Great Britain and the USA following the destruction of the American schooner *Caroline*, which had been supplying American nationals conducting raids in British North America (now Canada).[38] The British justified this as an act of self-defence. The US Secretary of State responded that self-defence was permitted only in cases in which the 'necessity of self-defence, instant, overwhelming, leaving no choice of means, and no moment for deliberation'.[39] If the *Caroline* view holds, it would potentially broaden the notion of self-defence to encompass, *inter alia*, acts of 'pre-emptive self-defence' which aim to prevent an imminent strike by another State or acts of terrorism by a non-State actor. This controversial doctrine will be studied later, in Section 14.3.6.

[35] *Nicaragua* (n 13) para 200. C Gray, *International Law and the Use of Force* (4th edn, OUP, 2018), 129–30 does suggest that it weakens a State's claim to be acting in self-defence.

[36] See, e.g., Brownlie (n 6) 251; Gray (n 33) 124–5. The discussion in Section 14.3.6 further develops the point, in respect of anticipatory or pre-emptive claims of self-defence.

[37] D Bowett, *Self-Defence in International Law* (Frederick Praeger, 1958), 185–6; Stone (n 1) 43, 95–6. See also the commentary to the *Nicaragua (Merits)* judgment of the ICJ (n 13), Section 14.2.4. The Council itself has qualified the right to self-defence as 'inherent' in respect of the United States' response to the 9/11 attacks by Al-Qaida: UNSC Res 1368 (12 September 2001) and UNSC Res 1373 (28 September 2001).

[38] See 29 BFSP 1137; 30 BFSP 195; all documents are reproduced in RY Jennings, 'The *Caroline* and *McLeod* Cases' (1938) 32 AJIL 82.

[39] Letter from US Secretary of State Webster to Lord Ashburton (6 August 1842) in JB Moore (ed), *A Digest of International Law* (USGPO, 1906), 409, 412.

As this chapter will show, the prevailing debates regarding the concept of self-defence tend to turn on technical, factual questions. Having said that, the legal debate occludes the moral and ethical tensions just below the surface. It is worth bearing in mind this tension; any claim to use violence or force in self-defence remains a shield, a defence invoked to justify the killing and suffering of others, and to demand sacrifices from one's own side.[40]

14.3.2 **Necessity and proportionality**

Though there are debates about the scope of the right of self-defence, there is near-universal consensus that force used in self-defence is not limitless, but must be both necessary and proportionate.[41] The *Caroline* correspondence made clear that action taken in self-defence must not be unreasonable or excessive, 'since the act, justified by the necessity of self-defence, must be limited by that necessity, and kept clearly within it'.[42] The ICJ has repeatedly confirmed these limitations as applicable to both collective and unilateral acts of self-defence, and reflective of customary international law.[43] The conditions of necessity and proportionality also reaffirm the position that the use of force in self-defence under Article 51 is an exception to the Article 2(4) prohibition on using force. Conceptually at least, it renders self-defence a response to the direct consequences of an armed attack of another actor, such as occupation, even if there are no active hostilities.[44]

In the context of self-defence, 'necessity' is understood as requiring that the defending State has no other means of repelling an armed attack other than recourse to armed force.[45] For example, in *Oil Platforms*, the USA invoked necessity to justify the fact that it had attacked certain Iranian oil platforms in the Persian Gulf, as the USA believed dangerous military activities were taking place on the platform. The ICJ rejected that argument, noting that the USA had not complained to Iran regarding any military activities before the strike, as well as the USA's own admission that one specific attack on an oil platform had been a 'target of opportunity'.[46]

'Proportionality' is somewhat harder to assess, though it must be emphasized that it is not assessed in relation to the original armed attack. Rather, proportionality is assessed in relation to what is necessary to halt or repel an armed attack and to recover territory, which 'may well have to assume dimensions disproportionate to those of the attack suffered'.[47] Looking to the practice of the ICJ, proportionality seems best assessed

[40] For a thoughtful analysis, see further F Mégret, 'To Surrender or to Fight On? A Human Rights Perspective of Self-Defense' (2023) 5 Jus Cogens 1.

[41] For further detail, see Gray (n 33) 157–65.

[42] See n 36 earlier.

[43] *Nicaragua (Merits)* (n 13) 103; *Nuclear Weapons* (n 28) 245; *Oil Platforms (Islamic Republic of Iran v United States of America), Judgment, ICJ Reports 2003*, p 161, 183; *Armed Activities in the Congo* (n 11) 223.

[44] See D Akande and A Tzanakopoulos, 'Legal: Use of Force in Self-Defence to Recover Occupied Territory' (2022) 32 EJIL 1299; but cf T Ruys and F Rodríguez Silvestre, 'Illegal: The Recourse to Force to Recover Occupied Territory and the Second Nagorno-Karabakh War' (2021) 32 EJIL 1287.

[45] See, e.g., ILC, 'Eighth Report by Special Rapporteur Roberto Ago' (1980), UN Doc A/CN.4/318/Add.5–7.

[46] *Oil Platforms* (n 40) 198.

[47] Ago's Eighth Report (n 41) 69. See also Gray (n 33) 159; and D Kretzmer, 'The Inherent Right to Self-Defence and Proportionality in *Jus Ad Bellum*' (2013) 24 EJIL 235.

on a case-by-case basis, considering: the scale of a whole operation, including in some cases a series of attacks;[48] the scale and scope of a given operation in relation to the territory of the target State;[49] and the types of weaponry employed, which might require an examination of whether such weapons are proportionate under the law applicable in armed conflict.[50] Though this provides little comfort to a State contemplating an armed response, proportionality remains a complex balancing exercise.[51]

14.3.3 **The meaning of 'armed attack'**

As set out in Article 51, self-defence can only be invoked in response to an 'armed attack'; the drafters of the Charter would have understood an 'armed attack' in the conventional sense of the armed forces of one State entering the territory of another State by land, sea, or air. Today, an armed attack does not require the invasion of territory: in *Oil Platforms*, the ICJ drew a distinction between mine and missile attacks aimed at US military vessels, which could constitute an 'armed attack', and those aimed at private ships flying the US flag, which would not amount to attacks on the USA.[52]

CASE SPOTLIGHT ***Military and Paramilitary Activities in and Against Nicaragua (Nicaragua v United States), Merits, Judgment, ICJ Reports 1986, p 14***

Frequently referred to simply as the *Nicaragua* judgment, the ICJ's 1986 decision in this case was of huge significance for international law, and particularly in respect of the law on the use of force. Following a 1979 *coup d'état* by the communist Sandinistas, US President Reagan terminated aid to Nicaragua on the ground that it was aiding guerrillas in El Salvador by allowing Soviet arms through its territory. Nicaragua advanced several claims against the USA's actions, claiming violations of Article 2(4) of the Charter as well as customary law in respect of the use of force.

After a highly contested jurisdictional phase, the USA refused to make submissions on the merits. The Court, however, upheld several important contentions made by Nicaragua that are highly salient. First, it upheld the Nicaraguan claim that direct force had been used by the USA in laying mines in its territorial waters, and by attacking and damaging Nicaraguan ports, oil installations, and a naval base. Secondly, it upheld Nicaragua's contention that self-defence is an 'inherent' right, pre-existing the Charter in customary law. For the Court, it:

> is only meaningful on the basis that there is a 'natural' or 'inherent' right of self-defence and it is hard to see how this can be other than of a customary nature, even if its present content has been confirmed and influenced by the Charter . . . It cannot, therefore, be

[48] *Oil Platforms* (n 40) 198. [49] *Armed Activities in the Congo* (n 11) 223.

[50] *Nuclear Weapons* (n 28) 245. Proportionality under the law of armed conflict is considered in Chapter 15, Section 15.4.1.1.

[51] For further guidance on these limitations, see the comprehensive book by JG Gardam, *Necessity, Proportionality and the Use of Force by States* (CUP, 2000). Necessity and proportionality are also detailed further in Chapter 10, Section 10.3.6.

[52] *Oil Platforms* (n 40) 189–90.

held that Article 51 is a provision which 'subsumes and supervenes' customary international law. (p 94)

Moreover, the Court provided important clarifications on what acts fell within the meaning of armed attack in customary law. Drawing on the 1974 GA Declaration on the *Definition of Aggression*, this would include 'the sending by or on behalf of a State of armed bands . . . which carry out acts of armed force against another State of such gravity as to amount to an actual armed attack' (p 103). The Court pointedly emphasized the degree of government control required; it clarified that acts such as the provision of weapons, or logistical or other support might constitute a threat or use of force, or unlawful intervention, but that such assistance fell short of an armed attack which would trigger the right of self-defence (p 104).

The *Nicaragua* judgment has been hugely influential across international law on the use of force, as well as on the law on State responsibility. As was discussed in Chapter 10, the Court took the view that it was insufficient for the USA to have taken a preponderant role in the financing, organizing, training, supplying, and equipping of the *Contras*, or even in selecting its targets; for the legal responsibility of the USA to be engaged, it had to have *effective control* over any operations in the course of which international law was breached (pp 64–5).

For further reading on the *Nicaragua* judgment, see for example the Symposium in volume 25, issue 1 of the Leiden JIL (2012); and FL Bordin, 'The Nicaragua v United States Case: An Overview of the Epochal Judgments' in ES Obrégon and B Samson (eds), *Nicaragua before the International Court of Justice: Impacts on International Law* (Springer, 2018), 59–83.

The scale and gravity of an operation is relevant in assessing whether it meets the threshold of an armed attack, or whether it constitutes a 'less grave form' of force. In *Nicaragua*, the Court stated that a border skirmish or 'mere frontier incident' did not rise to the level of an armed attack triggering the right of self-defence.[53] In *Oil Platforms*, the Court held that a series of missile strikes against private vessels and a Kuwaiti tanker reflagged to the USA did not, on the facts, rise to the level of an armed attack.[54] A further illustration is how, in 2018, double agent Sergei Skripal and his daughter were exposed in Salisbury (UK) to the deadly 'Novichok' nerve agent, which had been developed by the Soviet Union in the 1970s. Then-British Prime Minister Theresa May called this an 'unlawful use of force',[55] a careful choice of words as it would allow for non-forcible retorsionary acts, such as the expulsion of twenty-three Russian diplomats that followed; but she did not suggest that it arose to the level of an armed attack that would trigger a right to self-defence. This calculus may well be different in respect of a string of assassinations conducted by Israel, including of Hezbollah commander Fuad Shukr in Lebanon and Hamas leader Ismael Haniyeh in Tehran, both on 31 July 2024;

[53] *Nicaragua (Merits)* (n 13) 101.

[54] *Oil Platforms* (n 40) 187–92, para 72. However, several dissentients (Judges Higgins (225–40), Kooijmans (256–65), and Buergenthal (270–89)) pointed out the difficulty for a victim State to establish whether a minor incursion was accompanied by the specific intention to harm.

[55] See Oral Statement of Prime Minister Theresa May to the House of Commons on 14 March 2018, available at <https://www.gov.uk/government/speeches/pm-commons-statement-on-salisbury-incident-response-14-march-2018>.

and the Secretary-General of Hezbollah, Hassan Nasrallah, and Iranian brigadier-general, Abbas Nilfouroushan, in a Beirut suburb on 27 September 2024. On 1 October 2024, claiming self-defence in response to these assassinations, Iran launched 200 ballistic missiles at Israeli targets, seriously escalating the conflict between Israel and Iran. The next day, US President Biden asserted that Israel had a right to respond, but 'in proportion'.[56]

14.3.4 **Self-defence and non-State actors**

Most acts of self-defence have been in response to armed attacks committed by other States. However, the question has long been debated as to whether an attack committed by a non-State actor may also trigger the right of self-defence of the attacked State, especially as Article 51 does not require explicitly that an armed attack must be committed by another State. Most prominent was the response to the Al Qaida attacks on the World Trade Center and the Pentagon in the USA in September 2001. The Security Council passed Resolutions 1368 and 1373 condemning these as 'terrorist attacks', which it characterized as a 'threat to the peace' and not expressly as an 'armed attack'.[57] Moreover, in both resolutions the Council affirmed the USA's inherent right to self-defence, for the first time recognizing, albeit indirectly, that the notion of an armed attack might also extend to the use of force by terrorist organizations without any State involvement.[58]

Since 2001, there have been other responses to terrorist actors operating from outside the territory of the State claiming self-defence. In 2006, Hezbollah, a terrorist group operating from southern Lebanon, killed eight Israeli soldiers and abducted two others. Israel did not invoke self-defence against Lebanon, but against Hezbollah, the non-State actor, and mounted a land, sea, and air attack on Hezbollah-held areas of Lebanon. Security Council debates on the issue did not take a position on whether there could be an 'armed attack' committed by a non-State actor, or self-defence claimed in response to non-State terrorist actions. Rather, it focused on whether Israel's actions were disproportionate.[59] The Council's debates in relation to the 2008–9 and 2013–14 land, sea, and air operations by Israel in Gaza, where Israel removed its troops but retained control over movement in and out of the territory, were similarly inconclusive.[60] A UN Independent Commission of Inquiry has been established in relation to the 2014

[56] See Remarks by President Biden Before Air Force One Departure (2 October 2024), White House Briefing Room (www.whitehouse.gov).

[57] UNSC Res 1368 (12 September 2001); UNSC Res 1373 (28 September 2001).

[58] See further C Tams, 'The Use of Force Against Terrorists' (2010) 20 EJIL 359, 379–81 and R Van Steenberghe, 'Self-Defense in Response to Attacks by Non-State Actors in the Light of Recent State Practice: A Step Forward?' (2010) 26 Leiden JIL 183, 193.

[59] UNSC Res 1701 (2006) (11 August 2006). Earlier Council debates also avoided discussion of the point: see, e.g., UNSC Verbatim Record (14 July 2006), UN Doc S/PV.5489.

[60] See, e.g., UNSC Verbatim Record (6–7 January 2009), UN Doc S/PV.6061; UNSC Verbatim Record (25 March 2009), UN Doc S/PV.6100; UNSC Verbatim Record (18 July 2014), UN Doc S.PV.7220. For further information on the 2006 Gaza incidents, see UNGA, 'Report of the United Nations Fact Finding Mission in the Gaza Conflict (Goldstone Report)' (15 September 2009), UN Doc A/HRC/12/48; and Chapter 15, Section 15.3.5.2.

Gaza incidents.[61] A late 2019 offensive by Turkey into a 30-km 'safe zone' in Kurdish-majority areas in northern Syria was justified by Turkish President Recep Erdoğan as an attack not against Syria, but as necessary to expel 'terrorist organizations' with ties to the similarly designated Kurdistan Workers Party from the border regions.[62] The ICJ twice considered the question, albeit inconclusively, of whether a State can be attacked in self-defence in response to acts that are not attributable to it. In the merits phase of *Armed Activities in the Territory of the Congo*, the Court rejected claim by Uganda that its armed intervention in Congolese territory constituted self-defence against the rebel 'Allied Democratic Forces' (ADF). The Court, observing that the ADF was not sent by the Congo or otherwise under its control, felt 'no need to respond to the contentions of the Parties as to whether and under what conditions contemporary international law provides for a right of self-defence against large-scale attacks by irregular forces'.[63]

In the *Construction of a Wall* advisory opinion, the Court considered that Article 51 was of 'no relevance' in respect of Israel's actions, given that Israel exercised control of the occupied Palestinian Territory whence the threats against it originated (and had not claimed that a foreign State was responsible).[64]

Perhaps the most plausible argument for invoking self-defence against independent non-State actors is that a State which is 'unable or unwilling' to prevent its territory from being used to carry out an attack against another State is effectively 'aiding and abetting' the acts of non-State actors.[65] The 'unwilling or unable' doctrine has been accepted in other fields of international law,[66] and has been put forward by a few scholars in relation to the use of force in self-defence.[67] However, most others have taken a sceptical view of the 'unwilling or unable' doctrine,[68] even in the light of its recent invocation by the USA and some of its allies—chiefly the UK, Australia, Canada, and Turkey—in relation to

[61] UNHRC, 'Ensuring Respect for International Law in the Occupied Palestinian Territory, including East Jerusalem' (24 July 2014), UN Doc A/HRC/RES/S-21/1.

[62] As reported by Al Jazeera, 'Turkey begins Ground Offensive in Northern Syria' (10 October 2019).

[63] *Armed Activities in the Territory of the Congo (Democratic Republic of the Congo v Uganda), Judgment, ICJ Reports 2005*, p 168, pp 222–3. See further P Okowa, '*Case Concerning Armed Activities in the Territory of the Congo (Democratic Republic of the Congo v Uganda)*' (2006) 55 ICLQ 742.

[64] *Legal Consequences of the Construction of a Wall in Occupied Palestinian Territory, Advisory Opinion, ICJ Reports 2004*, p 136, 194.

[65] On the State unwilling to act, see also Dissenting Opinion of Judge Jennings in *Nicaragua (Merits)* (n 13) 543; on the State unable to act, the Separate Opinions in *Armed Activities in the Congo* (n 11) by Judges Kooijmans, 314, and Simma, 337. See further T Ruys and J Verhoeven, 'Attacks by Private Actors and the Right of Self-Defence' (2005) 10 JCSL 289.

[66] See, most prominently, with respect to the complementarity principle in Art 17 of the Rome Statute of the International Criminal Court, Chapter 17, Section 17.2.3.3.1.

[67] See, e.g., A Deeks, '"Unwilling or Unable": Toward a Normative Framework for Extraterritorial Self-Defense' (2015) 52 Virginia JIL 483; N Lubell, *Extraterritorial Use of Force against Non-State Actors* (OUP, 2010); J Pejic, 'Terrorist Acts and Groups: A Role for International Law' (2004) 75 BYBIL 71.

[68] See Gray (n 33), ch 5, esp 237 *et seq*; J Brunnée and SJ Toope, 'Self-Defence against Non-State Actors: Are Powerful States Willing but Unable to Change the Law?' (2018) 67 ICLQ 263; AA Haque, 'The Use of Force Against Non-State Actors: All Over the Map' (2021) Journal on the Use of Force and International Law 27; K Trapp, 'Self-defence in Response to Armed Attacks by Non-State Actors' in M Weller (ed), *The Oxford Handbook of the Use of Force in International Law* (OUP, 2015), ch 31; T Ruys, *Armed Attack and Article 51 of the Charter* (CUP, 2010), ch 4(2); O Corten, *The Law against War* (2nd edn, Hart, 2021), ch 3.

Syria and ISIS/*Daesh*.[69] The doctrine has met with considerable academic scepticism in relation to the use of force; even against terrorists.[70]

A right to use self-defence against non-State actors thus remains controversial. A State wishing to use force against another State would be able to determine unilaterally that the targeted State fails to meet the test and then to intervene without further international scrutiny. Though there is a degree of practice that suggests that States regard themselves as entitled to use force against non-State actors, the legal basis remains unclear.[71] One innovative argument suggests that the exceptional nature of self-defence cannot extend to non-State actors, but that self-defence against non-State actors may be a *defence*, a circumstance precluding wrongfulness.[72] This area of the law may be one where the traditional prohibition in Article 2(4) becomes increasingly blurred.[73]

CONTEMPORARY DEVELOPMENTS Israeli Operations in Gaza and Lebanon: Self-defence?

The atrocities committed by Hamas on 7 October 2023 were followed by an intense military campaign by Israel in the Gaza Strip, causing the deaths of more than 40,000 civilians; on 1 October 2024, Israel launched a ground invasion of southern Lebanon against Hezbollah. Though both operations were justified as an exercise of Israel's right to self-defence, they are factually distinct and any legal assessment depends on an understanding of the legal arguments that have been advanced.

Israel invoked a right to defend itself against Hamas to justify its military operations in Gaza (see Ministry of Foreign Affairs of Israel paper, 'Hamas-Israel Conflict 2023: Key Legal Aspects' (2 November 2023)), implying that the 7 October atrocities constitute an armed attack. Though the intensity of Hamas's operations, including massacres and hostage-taking, certainly meet the factual threshold for an armed attack, it is not clear how Article 51 can be used to allow an armed response by Israel in Gaza. The statehood of Palestine is not universally accepted, and of course contested by Israel (see Chapter 5, Section 5.2.3.1), so it stands to reason that Israel's assertion of self-defence cannot be against Palestine itself, or the attribution of Hamas' acts thereto; it at best rests on a tendentious claim that governing 'authorities' in the Gaza Strip are 'unwilling and unable' to prevent armed attacks by non-State actors.

This line of reasoning, however, rests on the idea that the 7 October attacks triggered the right to self-defence under Article 51, and in principle are not connected to a wider conflict. Moreover, it is true that after the Court's 2004 advisory opinion on the *Construction of a Wall*,

[69] See Letter from the United States to the Secretary General dated 22 September 2014, UN Doc S/2014/695; for analysis, see O Corten, 'The "Unwilling or Unable" Test: Has it Been, and Could it be, Accepted?' (2016) 29 Leiden JIL 777; and Gray (n 33) 237–48.

[70] C Tams, 'The Use of Force against Terrorists' (2009) 20 EJIL 359; V Lowe, '"Clear and Present Danger": Responses to Terrorism' (2005) 54 ICLQ 185.

[71] See, e.g., the practice surveyed in D Bethlehem, 'Self-Defense Against an Imminent or Actual Armed Attack by Nonstate Actors' (2012) 106 AJIL 770, 773.

[72] See F Paddeu, 'Use of Force against Non-State Actors and the Circumstance Precluding Wrongfulness of Self-Defence' (2017) 30 Leiden JIL 93.

[73] M Hakimi, 'Defensive Force against Non-State Actors: The State of Play' (2015) 91 International Law Studies 1.

which rejected Israel's claim to invoke self-defence against non-State actors in occupied territory, Israel withdrew from the Gaza Strip in 2005, asserting that it was no longer occupied territory. However, such an argument is not tenable in the light of Security Council Resolution 2720 (22 December 2023), which in its preamble stressed that '[t]he Gaza Strip constitutes an integral part of the territory occupied in 1967'. Moreover, in *Policies and Practices of Israel in the Occupied Palestinian Territory, including East Jerusalem, Advisory Opinion of 19 July 2024*, the ICJ concluded that Israel's military disengagement from Gaza was insufficient to release it from its obligations under the law of occupation, because even after 2005, 'Israel remained capable of exercising, and continued to exercise, certain key elements of authority over the Gaza Strip' including over its borders, security restrictions, and overall military control (para 93). In such circumstances, it is arguable that self-defence under Article 51 can even be invoked, and the doctrine might not be applicable to Israel's military operations.

The legal analysis proceeds differently in respect of Israel's attacks against Hezbollah in southern Lebanon that began on 23 September 2024 and rapidly escalated into a full-scale ground invasion. After 7 October 2023, Hezbollah had intensified a number of violent cross-border military operations in northern Israel and the Israel-occupied Golan Heights, with over 560 casualties in Lebanon and more than 50 in Israel, leading to the displacement of Israeli civilians southwards. Israel also justified its invasion on the grounds that, under Security Council Resolution 1701 (11 August 2006), Hezbollah was required to withdraw from southern Lebanon south of the Litani river, where there were no Lebanese armed forces and only peacekeepers (the United Nations Interim Force in Lebanon (UNIFIL)—whom Israel has called upon to evacuate southern Lebanon. Israel launched strikes as far north as Beirut, the capital of Lebanon; and according to the UN, the Israeli military deliberately fired at UNIFIL headquarters and peacekeepers. Whatever one's views on whether self-defence can be invoked when another State is unwilling or unable to constrain terrorist attacks by non-State actors, it bears recalling that such acts must also comply with other elements of the law on self-defence; including that they be necessary and proportionate.

In early December 2024, after the collapse of the Assad regime in Syria, Israel began a series of air and ground strikes against military targets in Syria, which Israel asserted were to safeguard its essential national security interests and to prevent certain 'strategic military capabilities left behind by the Syrian military so that they will not fall into the hands of jihadists': see statement of Prime Minister Netanyahu of 10 December 2024.

14.3.5 **Collective self-defence**

The exercise of collective self-defence was expressly adopted in the text of Article 51 in 1945, as a response to the desire of Latin American States to retain regional autonomy.[74] Collective self-defence can take the form of collective security under the auspices of the United Nations, as was invoked by the Security Council in the preamble of Resolution 661, following the invasion of Kuwait by Iraq.[75] Regional self-defence alliances can also intervene lawfully to aid member States that request it. For example, Article 5 of the NATO Treaty stipulates that an armed attack against one member is regarded as an

[74] See HP Aust, 'Article 51', in B Simma et al (eds), *Charter of the United Nations: A Commentary* (4th edn, OUP, 2024), 1769.

[75] UNSC Res 661 (6 August 1990).

armed attack against all of them; it was famously invoked in the aftermath of the 9/11 attacks against the USA by NATO's member States, and remains an obstacle for Ukraine to join NATO. There are similar collective self-defence provisions in the constituent instruments of the OAS and ECOWAS.[76]

More recently, the right to collective self-defence has been invoked in relation to airstrikes and other military operations against ISIL/*Daesh* in Iraq and, more controversially, in Syria, where in 2014 the USA was expressly invited by Iraq 'to lead international efforts to strike ISIL sites and military strongholds',[77] but with no mention that Iraq had been a victim of armed attacks emanating from Syrian territory. In 2017, US President Trump escalated these operations with strikes on pro-Assad forces directly on Syrian territory,[78] and thus going beyond the requests for assistance from Iraq.

The exercise of collective self-defence requires the explicit consent of the attacked State, to ensure that the need for assistance is genuine. In *Nicaragua*, the USA had justified its armed intervention in Nicaragua as collective self-defence on behalf of El Salvador.[79] Though the ICJ agreed that third States may come to the aid of an attacked State in collective self-defence, the victim State 'must form and declare the view that it has been so attacked', and the 'use of collective self-defence by the third State for the benefit of the attacked State . . . depends on a request addressed by that State to the third State'.[80] As El Salvador had not made any such request, the Court rejected the US contention.

14.3.6 **Pre-emptive or anticipatory self-defence**

Serious controversy remains over whether the right of self-defence also encompasses a right to 'pre-emptive' self-defence, aiming to avert a potential armed attack before it occurs. Most scholars reject the 'pre-emptive self-defence' doctrine on the basis that it is incompatible with the wording of Article 51, which refers to an actual armed attack, and the object and purpose of the Charter, to restrict the capacity of member States to use force.[81] Indeed the ICJ, in the *Armed Activities* judgment,

[76] OAS Charter (1948), Art 3(h); ECOWAS Protocol on Mutual Assistance and Defence (1981), Art 2.

[77] See Letter from Iraq to the President of the Security Council dated 20 September 2014, UN Doc S/2014/691; Letter from the US to the Secretary-General, dated 23 September 2014, UN Doc S/2014/695; Letter from the UK to the Secretary-General and the President of the Security Council, dated 25 November 2014, UN Doc S/2014/851.

[78] Gray (n 33) 118.

[79] This is hardly a singular occurrence. Other instances where 'assisted' States may not have requested armed intervention include the Soviet Union interventions in Hungary (1956), Czechoslovakia (1968), and Afghanistan (1979).

[80] *Nicaragua (Merits)* (n 13) 104; see also *Oil Platforms* (n 40) 186–7.

[81] See Brownlie (n 6) 256–7; Gray (n 33) 170–5; Bowett (n 35) 188–93, 267; Y Dinstein, *War, Aggression, and Self-Defence* (6th edn, CUP, 2017), 213–14; V Lowe, *International Law* (Clarendon Press, 2007), 277; see also Institute of International Law, 'Present Problems of the Use of Armed Force in International Law' (27 October 2007), Doc 10B Resolution EN, para 6: '[t]here is no basis in international law for the doctrine of "preventive" self-defence in the absence of an actual or manifestly imminent armed attack'. For a more cautious view, see Aust, 'Article 51'(n 74)1795–201.

seems obliquely to have ruled out pre-emptive self-defence, at least from the ambit of Article 51:

> Article 51 of the Charter may justify the use of force in self-defence only within the strict confines there laid down. It does not allow the use of force by a State to protect perceived security interests beyond those parameters. Other means are available to a concerned State, including, in particular, recourse to the Security Council.[82]

However, the customary law right to self-defence seems to allow for limited 'anticipatory' action against a manifestly imminent armed attack, especially in light of modern technology which allows for the launch of an attack with tremendous speed.[83] Supporters of this view suggest that the customary law on self-defence, dating to the *Caroline* correspondence, did not exclude self-preservation against a manifestly imminent armed attack.

According to two reports of the Secretary General, it is that element of imminence that distinguishes *anticipatory* self-defence from *pre-emptive* self-defence.[84] Both reports conclude that anticipatory self-defence against 'imminent threats are fully covered by Article 51';[85] however, where a threat is less than imminent, no pre-emptive action should be taken without resort to the Security Council.

There is a paucity of State practice that expressly invokes a right to take pre-emptive action, as most States instead justify their actions as a response to an armed attack.[86] A recent example is the January 2020 drone strike in Baghdad (Iraq) by the USA against Iranian Quds Force Commander Qasem Soleimani (one of the highest-ranked officials in the Iranian government). Though initially, US President Trump justified the strike due to Soleimani's alleged plotting of 'imminent' attacks on Americans, the USA wrote to the Security Council to claim that the Soleimani strike was in self-defence, a response to escalating Quds Force-backed militia attacks against its diplomats and service members, notably an attack against the US Embassy in Baghdad on 31 December 2019.[87]

Other commonly invoked examples of anticipatory or even pre-emptive self-defence are frequently justified as 'ordinary' self-defence in response to another attack. In 1967, Israel launched a strike against its Arab neighbours which had mobilized their troops along its borders, but did not invoke anticipatory self-defence to justify its actions. Instead, Israel asserted self-defence in response to an Egyptian blockade of its southern

[82] *Armed Activities in the Congo* (n 11) 223–4.

[83] See Bowett (n 35) 119–92; T Franck, *Fairness in International Law and Institutions* (OUP, 1992), 267; M Schmitt, 'The Law of Cyber Warfare: *Quo Vadis?*' (2014) 25 Stanford Law and Policy Review 269, 285.

[84] See UNGA, 'Report of the Secretary-General's High-level Panel on Threats, Challenges and Change' (2 December 2004), UN Doc A/59/565, paras 189 *et seq*; and UNGA, 'In Larger Freedom: towards development, security and human rights for all' (21 March 2005), UN Doc A/59/2005, para 125.

[85] See also IDI Resolution 10A (27 October 2007), art 3, which only accepted an 'actual or *manifestly imminent*' armed attack would give rise to the right to self-defence (emphasis added). This expression was meant to be highly restrictive: see O Corten, 'Les resolutions de l'Institut de droit international sur la légitime défense et sur les actions humanitaires' (2007) XXX Revue belge de droit international 599, 602–4.

[86] Gray (n 33) 170–5, 226–7; *cf* WM Reisman and A Armstrong, 'Past and Future of the Claim of Preemptive Self-Defense' (2006) 100 AJIL 525.

[87] See Letter of 8 January 2020 from US Ambassador Kelly Craft to the Security Council, which explicitly referred to Art 51 of the Charter.

port of Eilat, the conclusion of a military pact between Jordan and Egypt, and the expulsion of UN peacekeeping forces from the area by Egypt.[88]

A striking assertion of pre-emptive self-defence related to the 1981 Israeli strike on an Iraqi nuclear reactor under construction, where Israel claimed a right of pre-emption against the production of nuclear weapons destined for use against it. Though the strike was condemned unanimously by the Security Council as a 'clear violation of the Charter',[89] the USA took the view that the Council's condemnation did not reject the possibility of pre-emptive self-defence, but was limited to the particular facts at hand.[90]

Finally, US President George W Bush announced a controversial *National Security Strategy* in which the pre-emption of terrorist attacks required a reconsideration—essentially, the omission—of the requirement of imminence.[91] Though invoked rhetorically when the USA and its allies began military operations against Iraq in March 2003, they also relied primarily upon existing Security Council resolutions as the purported justification for their acts.[92]

Nevertheless, the 'Bush Doctrine' went much further than anticipatory self-defence, moving pre-emptive self-defence to a radically preventive posture, and considerably beyond the bounds of international law.[93] Unsurprisingly, most States have objected.[94]

14.3.7 **Intervention to protect one's nationals**

There is some controversy as to whether the scope of self-defence also permits a State to use force outside its territory in order to protect its nationals.[95] Historically, certain States, in particular the USA, Israel, and the UK, have invoked the protection of nationals to justify forcible acts of self-defence against another State.[96] Recently, this

[88] Gray (n 33) 171; Dinstein (n 76) 216–17. See, generally, JN Moore (ed), *The Arab–Israeli Conflict* (Princeton UP, 1974).

[89] UNSC Res 487 (1981) (19 June 1981); see also Security Council debates during the period (1981) 20 ILM 965–7. There was no such reaction in relation to the Israeli bombing of the Deir ez-Zor reactor in Syria in 2007: see Gray (n 33) 212–13.

[90] 1981 UNYB 275.

[91] *The National Security Strategy of the United States of America* (September 2002) <https://2009-2017.state.gov/documents/organization/63562.pdf>, 1, 15.

[92] See Letter by the US to the President of the Security Council, dated 21 March 2003 (21 March 2003), UN Doc S/2003/351 (a passing reference to self-defence appears in the final substantive paragraph). See also Letter by the United Kingdom to the President of the Security Council, dated 20 March 2003 (21 March 2003), UN Doc S/2003/350; Letter from Israel to the Secretary-General (5 March 2003), UN Doc S/2003/352.

[93] See C Gray, 'The Bush Doctrine Revisited: The 2006 National Security Strategy of the USA' (2006) 5 Chinese JIL 555; M Bothe, 'Terrorism and the Legality of Preemptive Force' (2003) 14 EJIL 227; H Duffy, *The 'War on Terror' and the Framework of International Law* (CUP, 2005), 209–12; Reisman and Armstrong (n 80).

[94] See the practice canvassed in Bethlehem (n 66).

[95] In favour: see Bowett (n 35) 87 *et seq*; Dinstein (n 76) 274–7. Against: see Gray (n 33) 165–9; Brownlie (n 6) 232.

[96] The USA invoked this ground when intervening in the Dominican Republic (1965), Grenada (1983) (1983 UNYB 211), Panama (1989), as well as Operation Eagle Claw, an aborted attempt to resolve the 1980 Iran hostage crisis. Israel justified Operation Thunderbolt, its rescue of nationals on a hijacked plane from Entebbe in Uganda, similarly: see 1976 UNYW 314. During the 1956 Suez crisis, the UK claimed a similar right in relation to Egypt and also to extend to the protection of nationals abroad 'where the territorial State is unable or unwilling to do so': see UK Ministry of Defence, *Manual of the Law of Armed Conflict* (MOD, 2004), 2.

ground was invoked by France in relation to several of its former African colonies, and by Russia to justify its 2008 intervention in Georgia and its 2014 annexation of Crimea.[97] Most of this practice has not been condemned by the Security Council as unlawful, perhaps unsurprisingly given that most of the States involved are permanent members with the power of veto. Nevertheless, the legality of forcible intervention to protect nationals abroad remains contentious.[98]

14.4 Humanitarian intervention and the responsibility to protect

14.4.1 Humanitarian intervention

A key debate over the scope of Article 2(4) concerns whether a distinct exception allows for the use of force motivated by humanitarian considerations. Such an exception for 'humanitarian interventions' would allow the use of force to protect people in another State from gross and systematic human rights violations, or to avert a humanitarian catastrophe, when the target State is unwilling or unable to act.[99] Clearly, the doctrine of humanitarian intervention is highly controversial because unilateral intervention of any kind is hard to reconcile with Article 2(4) of the Charter. More ominously, the doctrine is susceptible to abuse. It is routinely invoked by powerful States with the capability to intervene in order to safeguard their strategic interests, and with little risk to them, given that they favour aerial bombardments of the target State over the deployment of ground troops so as to avoid public protest.[100]

Perhaps for this reason, most interventions that could have been understood as humanitarian in nature were in fact justified as instances of self-defence. These include the Indian intervention to support self-determination in Bangladesh (1971), the Tanzanian intervention in Uganda which overthrew the dictator Idi Amin (1979), and the Vietnamese intervention in Cambodia which deposed Pol Pot (1979).[101] In 1993, in response to widespread repression of the Kurds of the north and the Shiites and Marsh Arabs of the south, the USA, the UK, and France imposed Air Exclusion Zones ('no-fly zones') in the north and the south of Iraq. Even then, only the UK defended its

[97] *Ibid*. See EU Council, 'Independent International Fact-Finding Mission on the Conflict in Georgia: 2009 Report' (30 September 2009). See also *Application of the International Convention on the Elimination of All Forms of Racial Discrimination (Georgia v Russian Federation), Preliminary Objections, Judgment, ICJ Reports 2011*, p 70 (dismissed for lack of jurisdiction); *Georgia v Russia (II)* App No 38263/08 (ECtHR, 19 December 2011).

[98] See, generally, Ruys and Verhoeven (n 60).

[99] Leading contributions in this area include S Chesterman, *Just War or Just Peace?* (OUP, 2001); B Simma, 'NATO, the UN, and the Use of Force: Legal Aspects' (1999) 10 EJIL 1; F Tesón, *Humanitarian Intervention: An Inquiry into Law and Morality* (3rd edn, Transnational Publishers, 2005). See also Gray (n 33) ch 2, 32–75, and in relation specifically to Syria, 57–8. For a more critical posture, see D Kennedy, *The Dark Sides of Virtue* (Princeton UP, 2004), 235–324.

[100] See, e.g., A Orford, *Reading Humanitarian Intervention* (CUP, 2003), 193, describing the NATO intervention in Yugoslavia, which killed an estimated 500 Yugoslav civilians.

[101] See Gray (n 33) 40.

intervention as 'justified in cases of extreme humanitarian need'.[102] Perhaps the most significant example of when States have invoked humanitarian intervention is the NATO action, discussed in the accompanying commentary, responding to Yugoslavia's repression and displacement of ethnic Albanians in Kosovo.

THEORY AND DEBATES Humanitarian Intervention and Kosovo

In March 1999, NATO declared that it would intervene in Kosovo, then a province of the Federal Republic of Yugoslavia (FRY), to forestall a humanitarian catastrophe against the Kosovar population. A seventy-eight-day aerial bombardment campaign by NATO against the FRY ensued; in particular, in Belgrade.

The legal justifications for the Kosovo operation were rather convoluted. Expressed primarily in Security Council debates, a draft resolution condemning the operation was rejected 12 to 3 by the Council, following vetoes from the UK, the USA, and France (see UNSC Verbatim Record (26 March 1999), UN Doc S/PV.3989). As the UK contended there,

> The action being taken is legal. It is justified as an exceptional measure to prevent an overwhelming humanitarian catastrophe . . . Renewed acts of repression by the authorities of the Federal Republic of Yugoslavia would cause further loss of civilian life and would lead to displacement of the civilian population on a large scale and in hostile conditions. Every means short of force has been tried to avert this situation. In these circumstances, and as an exceptional measure on grounds of overwhelming humanitarian necessity, military intervention is legally justifiable. The force now proposed is directed exclusively to averting humanitarian catastrophe, and is the minimum judged necessary for that purpose. (UNSC Verbatim Record (24 March 1999), UN Doc S/PV.3988, 12).

Moreover, because Yugoslavia instituted proceedings at the ICJ against nine NATO members, States set out their legal justifications in their written pleadings to the Court. Though most of them seemed to rely on a combination of humanitarian intervention and implied authorization by the Security Council, Belgium would join the UK to argue explicitly that humanitarian intervention was an accepted doctrine in international law (*Legality of the Use of Force (Yugoslavia v Belgium and nine other States), Provisional Measures, Order of 2 June 1999, ICJ Reports 1999*, p 124, Oral Proceedings, ICJ CR 1999/15 (10 May 1999), at 15–7 (Belgium)).

Following the end of hostilities, Security Council Resolution 1244 welcomed the withdrawal of Yugoslav forces from Kosovo and established the United Nations Mission in Kosovo, but pointedly neither endorsed nor condemned the NATO intervention. The 'Independent International Commission on Kosovo' concluded that the NATO military intervention was 'illegal but legitimate' (see *The Kosovo Report: Conflict, International Response, Lessons Learned* (OUP, 2000), 4). In this respect, the Kosovo operation is a unique example of States explicitly invoking humanitarian intervention, but one that did not receive approval from many non-participating States. If anything, the widespread negative reactions to the Kosovo

[102] See FCO (UK), Memorandum to Parliament, reproduced in (1992) 63 BYBIL 825. It has been observed in J Crawford, *Brownlie's Principles of Public International Law* (9th edn, OUP, 2019), 728 that no sources were provided to support this view, and that the UK has itself been inconsistent, equivocating between the revival of UNSC Res 668 (20 September 1990) and an argument based on humanitarian intervention.

operation seem to confirm the unlawfulness of forcible unilateral humanitarian intervention, and impelled the development of the 'Responsibility to Protect' doctrine.

For further details, see D Franchini and A Tzanakopoulos, 'The Kosovo Crisis—1999' in T Ruys and O Corten (eds) and A Hofer (ass ed), *The Use of Force in International Law—A Case-Based Approach*' (OUP, 2018), pp 594–622.

14.4.2 The 'Responsibility to Protect' doctrine

As described previously, the doctrine of humanitarian intervention did not fare well after the Kosovo intervention; if anything, State objections intensified after 1999.[103] A new initiative began in 2001 with the Canadian-sponsored, but independent, 'International Commission on Intervention and State Sovereignty' (ICISS), which proposed the 'Responsibility to Protect' doctrine (R2P) as a refocusing of the humanitarian principles underlying the rejected doctrine of humanitarian intervention.[104] The R2P doctrine was then endorsed in several United Nations instruments; in particular the 2005 World Summit Outcome by the General Assembly[105] and Security Council Resolution 1674 on the protection of civilians in armed conflict.[106]

The R2P doctrine would permit, and even require, international action in the face of certain international crimes;[107] it would allow States to intervene in situations where a State failed in its duty to protect its own citizens.[108] The R2P doctrine has been constructed according to 'three pillars'.[109] Under its first, it seeks to reconceive sovereignty so as also to impose on States a responsibility to protect individuals over which they have jurisdiction. The second pillar emphasizes capacity-building and international assistance, whenever possible. Under the third pillar, in exceptional circumstances humanitarian considerations may justify the use of force. As the World Summit Outcome laid out:

> In this context, [the international community, through the United Nations, is] prepared to take collective action, in a timely and decisive manner, through the Security Council, . . . should peaceful means be inadequate and national authorities are manifestly failing to

[103] The G77 (an informal group of 132 non-aligned States) foreign ministers denounced the doctrine: see the Declaration on the Occasion of the Twenty-Third Annual Ministerial Meeting of the Group of 77 (24 September 1999), para 69.

[104] See ICISS, *The Responsibility to Protect* (14 August 2002), UN Doc A/57/303, Annex.

[105] High-Level Panel on Threats, Challenges and Change, *A More Secure World: Our Shared Responsibility*, UN Doc A/59/565 (6 December 2004); Report of the Secretary-General (21 March 2005), A/59/2005; UNGA, World Summit Outcome (25 October 2005), UN Doc A/RES/60/1, paras 138–9.

[106] UNSC Res 1674 (28 April 2006).

[107] For further definitions of these 'core crimes', see Chapter 17, Section 17.3.

[108] For mainstream legal debates on the R2P doctrine, see A Peters, 'Humanity as the Alpha and Omega of Sovereignty' (2009) 20 EJIL 513; C Focarelli, 'The Responsibility to Protect and Humanitarian Intervention: Too Many Ambiguities for a Working Doctrine' (2008) 13 JCSL 191; and C Stahn, 'Responsibility to Protect: Political Rhetoric or Emerging Legal Norm?' (2007) 101 AJIL 99. For perhaps the leading counterpoint in the field, see A Orford, *International Authority and the Responsibility to Protect* (CUP, 2011).

[109] UNGA, 'Report of the Secretary-General' (12 January 2009), UN Doc A/63/677.

> protect their populations from genocide, war crimes, ethnic cleansing and crimes against humanity.[110]

Distilled somewhat, a sort of 'residual responsibility' arises with respect to the imprecisely defined 'international community'[111]—understood in this context to be all States, through the United Nations—to take action once all peaceful avenues have been exhausted. A key distinction between R2P and humanitarian intervention is the requirement that collective action by the international community *must* be undertaken pursuant to Security Council authorization under Chapter VII.[112] This opens up the possibility of the veto being exercised by the Council's permanent members, as there is nothing more than a polite intimation in the World Summit Outcome that the permanent members should 'refrain' from exercising their veto in cases of genocide, war crimes, ethnic cleansing, and crimes against humanity.[113]

R2P has been invoked with increasing frequency in Security Council resolutions passed under Chapter VII. This practice would suggest that, while the Council may not yet have a duty to act, it certainly can claim the right to act thereunder.[114] Nevertheless, the doctrine remains problematic. In this respect, though R2P at least represents a retreat from the unilateral use of force, the manner in which humanitarian considerations are enforced remains a matter of some controversy.

CONTEMPORARY DEVELOPMENTS Libya: From Peacekeeping to Regime Change?

When in 2011 a violent civil war erupted between the Qaddafi government and rebel forces, the Security Council authorized member States to 'protect civilians and civilian populated areas under threat of attack in [Libya], including Benghazi'. Though a foreign occupation

[110] World Summit Outcome (n 99) para 139.

[111] The present author has elsewhere challenged the term as devoid of legal meaning: see GI Hernández, 'A Reluctant Guardian: The Concept of "International Community" and the International Court of Justice' (2013) 83 BYBIL 13.

[112] Though the High-Level Panel (n 99) had suggested that no such authorization might be necessary in exceptional circumstances, the World Summit Outcome (n 99) expressly recognized the necessity of Council authorization.

[113] High-Level Panel, *ibid*, para 256.

[114] See, *inter alia*, UNSC Res 1653 (27 January 2006), in relation to the Great Lakes region; UNSC Res 1706 (31 August 2006), in relation to Sudan; UNSC Res 1970 (26 February 2011) and UNSC Res 1973 (17 March 2011), in relation to Libya; UNSC Res 1975 (30 March 2011), in relation to Côte d'Ivoire; UNSC Res 2014 (21 October 2011), in relation to Yemen; UNSC Res 2085 (20 December 2012), in relation to Mali; UNSC Res 2109 (11 July 2013), UNSC Res 2206 (3 March 2015), UNSC Res 2573 (27 April 2021), UNSC Res 2577 (28 May 2021), UNSC Res 2625 (15 March 2022), UNSC Res 2633 (25 May 2022), UNSC Res 2677 (15 March 2023), UNSC Res 2683 (30 May 2023), and UNSC Res 2731 (30 May 2024) in relation to South Sudan; UNSC Res 2121 (10 October 2013), UNSC Res 2499 (15 November 2019), UNSC Res 2605 (12 November 2021), UNSC 2659 (14 November 2022), and UNSC Res 2709 (15 November 2023) in relation to the Central African Republic; UNSC Res 2139 (22 February 2014) and UNSC Res 2449 (13 December 2018) in relation to Syria; UNSC Res 2237 (2 September 2015), in relation to Liberia; UNSC Res 2277 (30 March 2016), and UNSC Res 2556 (18 December 2020), UNSC Res 2612 (20 December 2021), UNSC Res 2666 (20 December 2022), and UNSC Res 2717 (19 December 2023) in relation to the Democratic Republic of the Congo.

force was explicitly excluded, they were authorized to establish a no-fly zone (UNSC Res 1973 (17 March 2011), paras 4 and 7).

Ostensibly, Resolution 1973 was a novel invocation of the R2P doctrine for protecting civilians; but it also evinced a marked tilt against the Qaddafi regime. What unfolded was highly controversial. A NATO-led mission immediately established no-fly zones over much of Libyan airspace, as well as a naval blockade. By May 2011, Western troops were allegedly captured on film in Libya, which would be in violation of Security Council Resolution 1973. As NATO strikes continued to target government forces throughout the summer, NATO governments began to recognize the 'National Transitional Council' rebel group as the government of Libya. Finally, on 20 October 2011, NATO intercepted a convoy of vehicles carrying Qaddafi, who was captured by rebel forces and killed.

As Resolution 1973 invoked the responsibility to protect civilians from humanitarian catastrophe, NATO member States began to insist that the overthrow of Qaddafi was the only means to protect civilians. The drift from a peacekeeping operation into a policy of forcible regime change has come under criticism: see, for example, the UK Foreign Affairs Committee, 'Libya: Examination of intervention and collapse and the UK's future policy options' (HC 119, 14 September 2016). The illegality of interventions to secure regime change has been consistently upheld, though no sanctions have been brought against NATO member States.

For further reading, see G Ulfstein and HF Christiansen, 'The Legality of NATO's Use of Force in Libya' (2013) 62 ICLQ 709; and C Henderson, 'International Measures for the Protection of Civilians in Libya and Côte d'Ivoire' (2011) 60 ICLQ 767.

14.5 **Collective security: authorizing the use of force**

The UN Charter, in aiming to prohibit the unilateral use of force, sought to create a comprehensive collective security system. Article 24 of the Charter granted the Security Council primary responsibility for the maintenance of international peace and security. The Council, it is worth recalling, is composed of fifteen members; and under Article 27, the concurring vote on non-procedural questions of all five permanent members (China, France, Russia, the UK, and the USA) is required, in what is known as the 'veto' power.[115] During the Cold War especially, the veto made enforcement action through the Council difficult.

Under Chapter VI of the Charter, the Security Council may take recommendatory measures with respect to the pacific settlement of disputes. However, under Chapter VII, the Council is the only organ that may authorize the use of force in response to threats to, or breaches of, international peace and security, as well as acts of aggression. Decisions of the Council taken under Chapter VII are binding upon all of its members under Article 25, emphasizing the importance of the preservation of peace. In the sections which follow, we will briefly outline the procedure for the exercise of enforcement action.

[115] In *Legal Consequences for States of the Continued Presence of South Africa in Namibia (South West Africa) notwithstanding SC Res 276 (1970), Advisory Opinion, ICJ Reports 1971*, p 16, 22, the ICJ interpreted the term 'concurring' in Art 27 as to require the veto to be positively exercised; as such, an abstention would not count.

14.5.1 **Determination of the situation by the Security Council**

Prior to taking any enforcement action under Chapter VII, under Article 39 the Council must first arrive at a determination that there exists a threat to the peace, a breach of the peace, or an act of aggression. In practice, the Security Council enjoys wide discretion in determining whether a situation falls under Article 39.

The three situations spelt out in Article 39 merit further examination, with a 'threat to the peace' being the broadest category. Its breadth allows for the Council to take action even if a breach of the peace or act of aggression has not yet occurred. Of course, such flexibility is not uncontroversial. In the *Tadić* judgment on jurisdiction, the ICTY noted that to determine the existence of a threat is a determination of fact, and not a legal judgment.[116]

The first threat to the peace was determined to exist during the 1948 crisis in the former mandate in Palestine, when the new State of Israel was proclaimed amidst hostilities from neighbouring Arab States.[117] For the Council, the threat to the peace was an imminent armed conflict between States.[118] In later cases, the Council has taken a wide view of what might constitute a threat to the peace, making determinations regarding a range of situations, including severe intra-State violence,[119] serious violations of human rights and humanitarian law,[120] and terrorism.[121] In 2017, the Council even declared the Ebola outbreak in West Africa to be a threat to international peace and security.[122]

The determination that there is a full-fledged breach of the peace by the Security Council is rare, though there have been four such determinations: the 1950 invasion of South Korea by North Korea;[123] the invasion of the Falkland Islands by Argentina in 1982;[124] the 1980–8 Iran–Iraq War;[125] and the 1990 Iraqi invasion of Kuwait.[126] Though there has been much discussion about defining the act of aggression, to date there has been no determination by the Council that an act of aggression has occurred.[127]

[116] *Prosecutor v Tadić* (Jurisdiction) ICTY-94-1 (10 August 1995), (1995) 105 ILR 419, 435.

[117] UNSC Res 54 (15 July 1948), UN Doc S/RES/54 (1948).

[118] See, e.g., UNSC Res 1298 (17 May 2000) in response to an escalation of fighting between Ethiopia and Eritrea.

[119] See, e.g., UNSC Res 788 (19 November 1992), in relation to Liberia; UNSC Res 1132 (8 October 1997); UNSC Res 1156 (16 March 1998), in relation to Sierra Leone.

[120] UNSC Res 794 (3 December 1992), UN Doc S/RES/794 on the collapse of Somalia; UNSC Res 929 (22 June 1994), UN Doc S/RES/929 on the genocide in Rwanda; UNSC Res 1078 (9 November 1996) on the conflict in Zaire.

[121] UNSC Res 731 (21 January 1992); UNSC Res 748 (31 March 1992), regarding Libya's failure to respond to the Lockerbie bombings; UNSC Res 1373 (28 September 2001), in relation to the financing of terrorism in response to the 2001 attacks against the USA.

[122] UNSC Res 2177 (18 September 2014), UN Doc S/RES/2177.

[123] UNSC Res 1501 (26 August 2003).

[124] UNSC Res 502 (3 April 1982).

[125] UNSC Res 598 (20 July 1987).

[126] UNSC Res 660 (2 August 1990).

[127] See, e.g., the resolution on the Definition of Aggression (n 16), Art 1, referred to in *Armed Activities in the Congo* (n 11) 223; see also the 2010 definition of the crime of aggression in the ICC's amended Rome Statute, Art 8*bis*(1), discussed further in Chapter 17, Section 17.3.4.

14.5.2 Collective responses under Chapter VII of the Charter

Following an Article 39 determination, the Security Council may also authorize a wide range of measures to maintain or restore international peace and security, provided of course that it always acts in accordance with the Purpose and Principles of the United Nations (Article 24(2) of the Charter), and presumably also without violating a peremptory norm.[128] Moreover, Article 103 of the Charter is a sort of 'supremacy clause', stipulating that obligations under the Charter, which include resolutions of the Security Council, prevail over other rules of international law.

As such, the Security Council is indeed restricted by the obligation to respect the principles of necessity and proportionality, and to abide by norms of *jus cogens*; but its decisions prevail over obligations of a non-peremptory nature.[129]

14.5.2.1 Non-forcible measures

Non-forcible measures under Article 41 have recently been imposed in an increasingly diverse range of situations, such as against the Taliban regime in Afghanistan for supporting terrorism,[130] North Korea's ballistic missile and nuclear programmes,[131] and Iran's similar nuclear programmes.[132] Specific practice relating to economic sanctions and arms embargoes imposed by the Council is addressed in Chapter 13, Section 13.5.

Though justified under its more general powers under Chapter VII, not explicitly under Article 41, the Security Council also created the ad hoc criminal tribunals for the former Yugoslavia and for Rwanda, in response to the violent conflicts in each; these tribunals are discussed later, in Chapter 17.[133]

14.5.2.2 Forcible measures

14.5.2.2.1 The inability to establish a standing UN army

If non-forcible measures prove insufficient to maintain or restore international peace and security, Article 42 of the Charter bestows on the Security Council the competence to bind UN members to a wide range of actions 'by air, sea or land forces as may be necessary'. In theory, Article 42 was a fallback mechanism. Chapter VII laid out a process through which, after concluding agreements with the Security Council under Article 43, States would place armed forces, national air-force contingents, and other military resources necessary for collective international enforcement; in short, a standing United Nations military. To date, however, no State has concluded an agreement with the Council under Article 43, and the Council has been obliged to rely on member States to volunteer, on an ad hoc basis, the use of their forces to enforce its decisions.[134]

[128] See A Tzanakopoulos, *Disobeying the Security Council* (OUP, 2011), ch 3.

[129] Crawford, *Brownlie's Principles* (n 96) 762.

[130] Among many, see UNSC Res 1267 (15 October 1999); UNSC Res 1390 (16 January 2002); UNSC Res 1455 (17 January 2003); UNSC Res 1617 (29 July 2005); and UNSC Res 1735 (22 December 2006).

[131] UNSC Res 1718 (14 October 2006).

[132] UNSC Res 1737 (23 December 2006); UNSC Res 1744 (20 February 2007); UNSC Res 1803 (3 March 2008); and UNSC Res 1929 (9 June 2010).

[133] UNSC Res 827 (25 May 1993) and UNSC Res 955 (8 November 1994).

[134] For more detail, see Gray (n 33) 262–3.

14.5.2.2.2 *The interpretation of Article 42*

Over time, the Council has gradually developed its powers under Article 42 to take collective enforcement measures.[135] Until 1990, the only example of collective use of force pursuant to Security Council authorization was its 1950 recommendation that other members come to the collective aid of South Korea in repelling an armed attack by North Korea.[136]

HISTORICAL BACKGROUND The United Nations Intervention in Korea

After World War II, the Korean peninsula, which had been under Japanese occupation since 1910, was temporarily partitioned along the 38th parallel by the Soviet Union and the USA. Efforts to reunify the peninsula peacefully were wholly unsuccessful and, following a series of border incidents, the North Korean Peoples' Army invaded South Korea in 1950. Neither State was at that time a member of the United Nations.

In Security Council Resolution 83 (27 June 1950), which did not invoke Article 42 *eo nomine* ('by name'), but referred to Chapter VII in general terms, the Council authorized member States to 'furnish such assistance to South Korea as may be necessary to repel the armed attack and to restore international peace and security in the area'. Sixteen States contributed troops to the ad hoc operation, though the Council had little effective control over the actual operation: under Security Council Resolution 84 (7 July 1950), the USA had the power to appoint the commander of the unified forces, which would be permitted to fly the United Nations flag.

Resolution 83 was highly controversial; it had been passed in the absence of the USSR, which had been boycotting the Security Council in protest at the seating of representatives of the Republic of China (based on the island of Taiwan) in the Chinese seat. After this incident, and with vehement protests against the Korea situation, the USSR resumed its seat on the Council.

The piecemeal structure used in Korea, which remains partitioned today, is emblematic of the failure to establish a permanent collective security system, but perhaps demonstrated the malleability of the Charter regime. Moreover, it has served as the blueprint for all subsequent operations under Chapter VII, including peacekeeping operations.

In August 1990, Iraq invaded Kuwait and sought to annex its entire territory. Iraq claimed that Kuwait had been artificially separated from it to serve colonial interests. The Council condemned the invasion categorically,[137] determined that the annexation had no legal validity, and called upon all States and international organizations not to recognize it.[138] In the face of Iraqi defiance, the Security Council adopted Resolution

[135] See generally Gray (n 33) ch 7, 341–86; and for more detail, D Sarooshi, *The United Nations and the Development of Collective Security* (OUP, 1999).

[136] The Council generally acts under Chapter VII instead of referring to Art 42. However, the General Assembly has eleven times invoked 'Uniting for Peace', UNGA Res 377 (V) (1950), allowing the Assembly to consider matters and make collective recommendations when it deems the Council to have failed to exercise its responsibility to maintain international peace and security.

[137] UNSC Res 660 (2 August 1990).

[138] UNSC Res 662 (9 August 1990). See also UNSC Res 664 (18 August 1990) and UNSC Res 667 (16 September 1990).

678 (1990), in which it authorized member States to take 'all necessary measures' to repel the Iraqi invasion and restore Kuwaiti sovereignty. Though not expressly invoking Article 42, that telling phrase, 'all necessary measures', has come to be understood as an authorization to use force.[139] A coalition was formed of more than thirty States to act in the collective self-defence of Kuwait, with its explicit consent, under US leadership. On 16 January 1991, the coalition launched Operation Desert Storm, which aimed to expel Iraq from Kuwait and to enforce the Council's will.[140] Operation Desert Storm, which commanded broad international and regional support,[141] therefore reconfirmed the power of the Council to authorize member States to take armed actions in the absence of a standing UN army.

14.5.2.2.3 ***So-called revived or implied authorization***

Due to the iterative process through which the powers in Chapter VII have been developed, several grey areas have remained divisive. One notable example is the claim that subsequent events can 'revive' an earlier authorization to use force. Revived authorization was first invoked by the UK and the USA in relation to Security Council Resolution 687 (1991), which had imposed a ceasefire and condemned the repression of Kurdish and Shia minorities in the north and south of Iraq, respectively. The UK and the USA claimed that Iraq's violations of the ceasefire in these areas 'revived' an authorization to use force in 1993[142] and then in 1998, when Iraq withdrew its cooperation with UN weapons inspections.[143] NATO also claimed 'revival' in respect of its air campaign against the FRY, in which there are indications that it regarded the FRY's failure to comply with certain resolutions of the Council as justification to use force,[144] even without express authorization to do so.[145]

A strikingly controversial application of the doctrine of 'implied' authorization arose in relation to Iraq in March 2003. Grandly entitled Operation Iraqi Freedom, a US–UK-led coalition[146] invaded Iraq with the stated aim of eliminating weapons of mass destruction: their legal justification was Security Council authority under a 'combined

[139] Tellingly, it was not used in UNSC Res 1441 (8 November 2002), relating to the 2003 invasion of Iraq.

[140] For further detail, see Gray (n 33) 342–3; see also O Schachter, 'United Nations Law in the Gulf Conflict' (1991) 85 AJIL 452.

[141] Participating forces came from all five continents, including Kuwait itself, four permanent members of the Council (the USA, the UK, France, and the USSR), and influential Arab and Gulf States including Egypt, Syria, Saudi Arabia, Qatar, Bahrain, Oman, the UAE, and Morocco.

[142] For the UK, see Statement of the Minister of State at the Foreign Office (27 January 1993), UKMIL (1993) 64 BYBIL 739; UKMIL (1994) 65 BYBIL 683; for the USA, see F Kirgis, *International Organizations: In their Legal Setting* (2nd edn, West, 1993), 856. The UK also relied on humanitarian intervention as a justification to act: see UKMIL (2001) 72 BYBIL 694; and earlier, Section 14.4.1.

[143] See UKMIL (1998) 69 BYBIL 589.

[144] UNSC Res 1160 (31 March 1998); UNSC Res 1199 (23 September 1998); and UNSC Res 1203 (24 October 1998).

[145] See further Gray (n 33) 364–7.

[146] The so-called 'Multi-National Force' was supported by up to forty-five States, though in terms of actual troops and resources deployed, it was overwhelmingly shouldered by the USA, the UK, and, to a lesser extent, Australia: see Gray (n 33) 371–7.

effect of Resolutions 678, 687 and 1441'.[147] The UK Foreign and Commonwealth Office also gave a more elaborate justification.[148]

It is true that Resolution 1441 had found Iraq in 'material breach' of its ceasefire and disarmament obligations under Resolution 687, had given it a 'final opportunity to comply with its disarmament obligations', and had established an enhanced inspections regime.[149] However, the Council was divided bitterly on whether Resolution 1441 authorized the further use of force, or revived an earlier authorization implicitly. Though Resolution 1441 threatened 'serious consequences' against Iraq for non-compliance,[150] several of the Council's members—especially Russia, China, and France—argued vehemently that the resolution 'excludes any automaticity in the use of force', and that it fell to the Council alone to determine whether there had been a material breach by Iraq.[151] It bears mentioning that only after the UK and USA had failed to secure a second resolution to use force did they contend that no second resolution was necessary, with UK Foreign Secretary Jack Straw asserting memorably that Iraq's weapons of mass destruction were deployable imminently, 'within 45 minutes'.[152]

Though the legal justification for the use of force against Iraq on the basis of revived or implied authorization has been defended by a few scholars,[153] the prevailing position in legal scholarship has been to reject the doctrine of revival after the passage of more than a decade.[154] Later resolutions concerning the subsequent occupation of Iraq left the legality of the initial invasion unaddressed.[155] The Iraq intervention therefore remains emblematic of the central role played by the Council in authorizing the use of force.[156]

[147] See letter from the UK addressed to the President of the Security Council dated 20 March 2003 (UN Doc S/2003/350); letter from the USA addressed to the President of the Security Council dated 20 March 2003 (UN Doc S/2003/351); and letter from Australia addressed to the President of the Security Council (20 March 2003) (UN Doc S/2003/352).

[148] FCO (UK), 'Iraq: Legal Basis for the Use of Force' (17 March 2003).

[149] UNSC Res 1441 (8 November 2002), referring back to UNSC Res 678 (29 November 1990), which had authorized the 1991 operation against Iraq, and UNSC Res 687 (3 April 1991), which required Iraq to disarm its weapons of mass destruction and to cooperate with UN weapons inspectors.

[150] UNSC Res 1441, *ibid* para 13.

[151] See UNSC Verbatim Record (8 November 2002), UN Doc S/PV.4664, 5 (France), 8 (Russia), 13 (China). In a rare Joint Statement (UN Doc S/2002/236, 8 November 2002), the three States also 'registered satisfaction' that, in their view, the USA and the UK had 'confirmed this understanding in their explanations of vote'.

[152] See J Straw, 'Reintegrating Iraq into the International Community is a Cause with Compelling Moral Force', speech delivered at Royal Institute for International Affairs (21 February 2003).

[153] See, e.g., C Greenwood, 'International Law and the Pre-Emptive Use of Force: Afghanistan, Al-Qaida and Iraq' (2003) 4 San Diego JIL 7; and the contributions of WH Taft IV, TF Buchwald, RN Gardner, and J Yoo in '*Agora*: Future Implications of the Iraq Conflict' (2003) 97 AJIL 553.

[154] See, e.g., Gray (n 33) 382–6; E Papastravdis, 'Interpretation of Security Council Resolutions under Chapter VII in the Aftermath of the Iraqi Crisis' (2007) 56 ICLQ 83; R Wolfrum, 'The Attack of September 11, 2001, the Wars Against the Taliban and Iraq' (2004) 7 MPUNYB 1; J-M Sorel, 'L'ONU et l'Irak: Le vil plomb n'est pas transformé en or pur' (2004) 108 RGDIP 845; and the contributions of Falk and Franck in the AJIL Agora on Iraq (n 147).

[155] See, e.g., UNSC Res 1472 (28 March 2003); UNSC Res 1476 (24 April 2003); UNSC Res 1483 (22 May 2003); UNSC Res 1490 (3 July 2003); UNSC Res 1500 (14 August 2003); UNSC Res 1511 (16 October 2003); UNSC Res 1518 (24 November 2003); UNSC Res 1537 (30 March 2004); UNSC Res 1546 (8 June 2004); UNSC Res 1556 (30 July 2004); UNSC Res 1619 (11 August 2005); UNSC Res 1637 (8 November 2005).

[156] For a more detailed analysis, see M Weller, *Iraq and the Use of Force in International Law* (OUP, 2010).

CONTEMPORARY DEVELOPMENTS The Chilcot Inquiry (or the *Iraq Inquiry in the UK*)

In 2009, UK Prime Minister Gordon Brown announced that an inquiry would take place as to the UK's involvement in Iraq between 2001 and 2009, with particular attention to the military intervention in 2003; it became known as the 'Chilcot Inquiry' after its Chair, Sir John Chilcot. From 2009 to 2011, the committee heard evidence from a wide range of witnesses, including former cabinet ministers, senior civil servants, diplomats, and high-ranking military officers. Former UK Prime Minister Blair was publicly questioned in January 2010 and January 2011.

The Final Report of the Inquiry, published in July 2016, confirmed that the invasion was conducted before all peaceful disarmament attempts had been exhausted and that war was thus not a last resort. Further, the Final Report concluded that the decision to go to war was based on unconfirmed, flawed intelligence and the subsequent military operations were not only underprepared but their consequences not fully considered. While broad in nature, the report did not directly address the legality of the military action in Iraq, instead noting—with some restraint—that the circumstances surrounding the decision on the legality of the UK's participation were 'far from satisfactory', and undermined the authority of the Security Council. It should, however, also be noted that the Report did not allege any instance of lying, deceit, or manipulation on the part of the relevant UK authorities.

The twelve-volume Final Report of the Iraq Inquiry, and a useful Executive Summary, are available at <http://www.iraqinquiry.org.uk>. A symposium covering a range of angles, and including contributions from senior figures and new voices, was published in volume 87 of the British Year Book of International Law (2016). Amongst those pieces is an essay on the parallel commission of inquiry held in the Netherlands about the 2003 invasion of Iraq: see NJ Schrijver, 'The Dutch Committee of Inquiry on the War in Iraq and the Basis in International Law for the Military Intervention', pp 125–48.

14.5.2.2.4 ***Authorizing force in the context of peacekeeping missions***

The Charter does not explicitly provide for peacekeeping activities; these arose over time in the absence of a standing United Nations force under Article 43 of the Charter, through general provisions governing the functions of the Security Council and the General Assembly. The majority of peacekeeping activities are in fact authorized by the Assembly and not by the Council, despite the latter having primary responsibility for the maintenance of international peace and security.

The first peacekeeping force of its kind, the United Nations Emergency Force ('UNEF I') (1956–7), was established by the General Assembly with the consent of Egypt, the host State, to defuse the crisis surrounding the nationalization of the Suez Canal. Under the terms of the mission, UNEF I was permitted to enter Egyptian territory to secure the area from the Suez Canal to the Egyptian–Israeli border; but force could only be used in self-defence. UNEF I was operational until 1967, when the Egyptian government ordered the immediate evacuation of all UN peacekeeping forces. After a ceasefire following the 1973 'Yom Kippur War' between Israel and its Arab neighbours, 'UNEF II' was deployed, again with Egyptian consent, to supervise the ceasefire and guarantee the implementation of Security Council Resolution 340.

The second major mission, in respect of the civil war in the newly independent Congo ('ONUC'), was, in fact, authorized by the Security Council, though not referring to a specific Charter provision. In the *Certain Expenses* advisory opinion,[157] the ICJ was asked to consider the role of the General Assembly in continuing the funding for peacekeeping operations such as ONUC. Though the Charter endows the Security Council with primary responsibility for the maintenance of international peace and security, the Court considered that such responsibility was not exclusive, and that it was open to the General Assembly to also continue peacekeeping action. Accordingly, the Court declared that the Assembly could require all member States to contribute to the expenses of peacekeeping missions, given the Assembly's overall responsibility for the budget of the United Nations.

Since the end of the Cold War, peacekeeping missions have increasingly been granted the ability to use force for distinct purposes. During the disintegration of Yugoslavia, the violence in the western Balkans was such that humanitarian operations were authorized exceptionally to take 'all necessary measures' to protect 'safe areas' and enforce no-fly zones in Bosnia.[158] A 1992–3 Somalia peacekeeping operation (the 'Unified Task Force') was also authorized to take 'all necessary means' to establish 'a secure environment for humanitarian relief operations', given the 'magnitude of the human tragedy caused ... further exacerbated by the obstacles being created to the distribution of humanitarian assistance, constitutes a threat to international peace and security'.[159] The Somalia operation was a failure, having 'limited impact on the peace process and limited impact on security in the face of interclan fighting and banditry'[160] and was terminated in March 1995.[161]

Haiti. After a 1994 military coup deposing democratically elected President Jean-Bertrand Aristide in Haiti, the Security Council authorized an armed intervention ('UNMIH') to restore President Aristide to power, an unusual objective.[162] In later peacekeeping operations following military coups, such as UNAMSIL in Sierra Leone, objectives have been limited to ensure the safety of the mission and the protection of civilians under imminent threat.[163]

Rwanda. When, in April 1994, the Presidents of Rwanda and Burundi were killed in an aeroplane crash, a horrifying civil conflict exploded, with Hutu opposition leaders massacred and genocidal activities directed against the Tutsi minority. After a delay of several months, the Security Council authorized the French-led peacekeeping mission ('UNAMIR') to use all necessary means to intervene to protect displaced persons

[157] *Certain Expenses of the United Nations (Article 17, paragraph 2, of the Charter), Advisory Opinion, ICJ Reports 1962*, p 151.

[158] UNSC Res 981 (31 March 1995); UNSC Res 982 (31 March 1995); UNSC Res 983 (31 March 1995).

[159] UNSC Res 794 (3 December 1992); UNSC Res 814 (26 March 1993).

[160] 'Report of the Secretary-General on the Implementation of Security Council Resolution 837' (1993) (1 July 1993), UN Doc S/26022.

[161] UNSC Res 954 (4 November 1994).

[162] UNSC Res 875 (16 October 1993). See further Gray (n 33) 343–5.

[163] UNSC Res 1270 (22 October 1998); UNSC Res 1289 (7 February 1999). See also UNSC Res 1299 (19 May 2000); UNSC Res 1346 (30 March 2001).

and civilians at risk; in particular, by establishing a protected zone in south-western Rwanda.[164]

Democratic Republic of the Congo (formerly Zaire). The 1999 Lusaka Ceasefire Agreement, purporting to end a long-standing civil war, led to the deployment of MONUC, with the power to take 'necessary action' to ensure the safety of the mission and afford protection to civilians under imminent threat of physical violence.[165] MONUC acquired further functions over the years; after a 2000 conflict between Uganda and Rwanda, the Council authorized it to monitor a ceasefire between these forces and their disengagement from Congolese territory,[166] and in 2008 it was authorized to facilitate the organization of local elections and the disarmament of armed groups and militias in the east of the Congo.[167] MONUC was transformed into a UN Stabilization Mission ('MONUSCO') in 2010, with an expanded mandate to ensure the effective protection of civilians, ensure the safety of humanitarian personnel and human rights defenders, and support the stabilization efforts of the government.[168] After yet another outburst of violence, an 'Intervention Brigade' was created in 2013 with the mandate to neutralize armed groups.[169]

Sudan. In response to a violent civil war in the south of Sudan, the Security Council established a protection force ('UNAMIS'), which had certain limited powers to facilitate contact with the warring parties and prepare for an expected UN peace support mission.[170] After a 2005 Comprehensive Peace Agreement, a new mission ('UNMIS') was established, with a mandate to take 'necessary action', again to ensure the safety of the mission and its personnel and the protection of civilians against threats of violence.[171] Despite the 2006 Darfur Peace Agreement, the deteriorating situation led to the expansion of the size and mandate of UNMIS to take 'all necessary measures' to achieve its objectives.[172] This was strengthened by the establishment of a hybrid UN–African Union operation in Darfur ('UNAMID').[173] In 2011, South Sudan became independent, with protection forces being established by the Security Council to minimize violence in the new State,[174] though violence broke out again, with a new peacekeeping mission ('UNMISS') despatched with little success.[175]

164 UNSC Res 929 (22 June 1994).

165 UNSC Res 1279 (30 November 1999).

166 UNSC Res 1304 (16 June 2000); see also UNSC Res 1316 (23 August 2000); UNSC Res 1332 (14 December 2000); UNSC Res 1341 (22 February 2001).

167 UNSC Res 1797 (30 January 2008); UNSC Res 1804 (13 March 2008).

168 UNSC Res 1925 (28 May 2010); see also UNSC Res 2053 (27 June 2012).

169 UNSC Res 2098 (28 March 2013).

170 UNSC Res 1547 (11 June 2004); UNSC Res 1564 (18 September 2004); UNSC Res 1574 (19 November 2004).

171 UNSC Res 1590 (24 March 2005).

172 UNSC Res 1705 (29 August 2006); UNSC Res 1709 (22 September 2006); UNSC Res 1714 (6 October 2006); UNSC Res 1755 (30 April 2007).

173 UNSC Res 1769 (31 July 2007).

174 UNSC Res 1990 (27 January 2011); UNSC Res 1996 (8 July 2011).

175 UNSC Res 2155 (27 May 2014); and see Report of the Secretary-General (UN Doc S/2016/951) (10 November 2016) in which UNMISS's mandate was reviewed 'with grave concern'.

14.5.3 **Regional arrangements under Chapter VIII**

In Chapter VIII, the Charter foresees the possibility of actions being taken by 'regional arrangements or agencies' to enforce international peace and security as appropriate, provided that their actions are consistent with the purposes and principles of the UN (Article 52), authorized by the Council, or with the consent of the host State (Article 53) and notified to the Council (Article 54). There are certain advantages to regional arrangements over global collective security, chief among them being the proximity to the causes of conflicts and to local norms, and the ability to deploy rapidly as compared to the deliberative procedures of the Security Council. It should also be noted that membership in such regional organizations may provide the legal justification for a regional intervention in certain cases, perhaps through a mutual defence clause or a commitment to certain obligations. In recent years, for example, there have been proposals that the EU's Common Security and Defence Policy be transformed into a combined military force.[176]

It is true that during the Cold War regional interventions were sometimes looked upon as perpetuating hegemonic politics; in particular, when these organizations were dominated by an influential regional State. That criticism was palpable with respect to US-led OAS interventions in Cuba (1962)[177] and the Dominican Republic (1965); the Soviet-led Warsaw Pact intervention in Czechoslovakia (1968);[178] and the US-supported Organization of East Caribbean States operation in Grenada (1983).[179] Since the end of the Cold War, regional and sub-regional forces have collaborated more readily with UN missions, even outside their region. These include the OAS in Haiti (1993); the Economic Community of West African States (ECOWAS) in Liberia (1990–7), Sierra Leone (1997–2000), and Côte d'Ivoire (2004); the Commonwealth of Independent States (CIS) in Tajikistan (1994); the OSCE in Georgia (1996); the European Union in the Democratic Republic of the Congo (2005);[180] the African Union in Darfur (2007);[181] and NATO in Libya (2011).[182]

[176] See, e.g., French President Macron's 'Initiative for Europe: A Sovereign, United, and Democratic Europe' (speech delivered at the Sorbonne University on 26 September 2017). The English version is available at <https://www.diplomatie.gouv.fr/IMG/pdf/english_version_transcript_-_initiative_for_europe_-_speech_by_the_president_of_the_french_republic_cle8de628.pdf>.

[177] See, e.g., VP Nanda, 'The United States' Action in the 1965 Dominican Crisis: Impact on World Order' (1966) 43 Den LJ 439 (Part I); (1967) 44 Den LJ 225 (Part II); CG Fenwick, 'Editorial Comment: The Dominican Republic: Intervention or Collective Self-Defense' (1966) 60 AJIL 64.

[178] See RM Goodman, 'The Invasion of Czechoslovakia: 1968' (1969) 4 Int Lawyer 42.

[179] Though no powerful State was a member, the USA was widely regarded as supporting that mission. See Gray (n 33) 420.

[180] See further UNSC, 'A Regional-Global Security Partnership: Challenges and Opportunities' (28 July 2006), UN Doc S/2006/590; UNSC, 'Relationship between the United Nations and Regional Organizations, in Particular the African Union, in the Maintenance of International Peace and Security' (7 April 2008), UN Doc S/2008/186; see also Gray (n 33) 414.

[181] See earlier, Section 14.5.2.2.4.

[182] It should be noted that in UNSC Res 1973 (n 108), para 5, the potential participation of the Arab League was also acknowledged.

14.6 Conclusion

In reviewing the historical evolution of the international law on the use of force, one might consider that institutional and legal developments serve to allocate the legitimate use of violence as a strategic tool. Certainly, most legal instruments surveyed in this chapter, and especially the Charter, have the constraint of war as their central objective. This might be true in relation to States, which wage war with one another with decreasing frequency, and the potential utility of peacekeeping missions; though as demonstrated in this chapter, the latter can also exacerbate conflict rather than prevent it. Nevertheless, the last decades have demonstrated that the theatre of force has moved from State-State conflicts to encompass non-State actors, liberation groups, terrorist organizations, and a wide range of further actors. It is in relation to these new developments that the Charter regime for collective security and self-defence remains inconclusive, and State practice piecemeal.

A further, final point merits reflection. International law does not seek to prohibit the use of force fully: as both this chapter and Chapter 15 demonstrate, there are highly developed legal rules that render certain violent acts perfectly permissible. Law, in this respect, functions simultaneously to constrain and to facilitate violence. One should be cautious, therefore, in presuming a linear progression towards stronger rules against using force in international law. Regrettably, the arc of history does not bend unequivocally towards peace.

Further reading

I Brownlie, *International Law and the Use of Force by States* (OUP, 1963).

Though somewhat dated, a classic English-language treatise in the field.

S Chesterman, *Just War or Just Peace? Humanitarian Intervention and International Law* (OUP, 2000).

Insightful, lucid analysis of the problematic concept of humanitarian intervention.

O Corten, *The Law against War: The Prohibition on the Use of Force in Contemporary International Law* (2nd edn, Hart, 2021).

Translated from a leading French-language monograph, this meticulous and rigorous study adopts an unflinchingly sceptical approach to the legal authority to use force

C Gray, *International Law and the Use of Force* (4th edn, OUP, 2018).

Freshly updated, this is one of the most authoritative and accessible introductions to the area.

C Henderson, *The Use of Force in International Law* (2nd edn, CUP, 2024).

A systematic and thoroughly up-to-date account of State and international organizations practice.

G Heathcote, *The Law on the Use of Force: A Feminist Analysis* (Routledge, 2011).

A distinct and unique account of the law on the use of force through a feminist lens.

AV Lowe, A Roberts, and D Zaum (eds), *The UN Security Council and War* (OUP, 2008).

A comprehensive edited collection drawing from both lawyers and international relations theorists.

N Lubell, *Extraterritorial Use of Force against Non-State Actors* (OUP, 2010).

Detailed and careful analysis of State practice relating to actions taken against non-State actors.

S Neff, *War and the Law of Nations* (CUP, 2005).

A historical analysis on how the rules on the use of force have evolved.

A Orford, *Reading Humanitarian Intervention: Human Rights and the Use of Force in International Law* (CUP, 2003).

A reinterpretation of the narratives justifying humanitarian intervention, directed at the cultural and economic effects of militarized humanitarianism.

T Ruys, *Armed Attack and Article 51 of the UN Charter* (CUP, 2010).

An incisive, detailed study of the crucial conditions that trigger the right to self-defence.

T Ruys, O Corten, and A Hofer (eds), *The Use of Force in International Law: A Case-Based Approach* (OUP, 2018).

This recent publication provides an exhaustive survey of a wide array of military interventions and international responses to these.

D Sarooshi, *The United Nations and the Development of Collective Security* (OUP, 1999).

A rigorous exposition of how the UN's collective security system developed incrementally.

PART V
Specialized regimes

15

The law of armed conflict

15.1 Introduction: defining 'the law of armed conflict'

15.1.1 Restraining or legitimizing violence?

Much faith has been placed in international law's ability to restrain and even to abolish war. One of the great achievements of the Charter era was the prohibition, in Article 2(4), against resort to armed force. The right to resort to armed force, known as '*jus ad bellum*' (literally, 'right to war'), is the regime governing the permissibility of entering into war in the first place. Despite the restrictions in the Charter covered in Chapter 14, international law does not fully forbid the use of force, and armed violence between and within States continues to erupt periodically.

Out of necessity, therefore, an older body of law co-exists alongside *jus ad bellum*, called '*jus in bello*' (literally, 'law in war'), which aims to restrain the actual conduct of hostilities. This is regardless of whether the initial resort to force was lawful or unlawful. The basic imperative of the *jus in bello* is to account for humanitarian principles by prohibiting certain types of weapons, or protecting certain categories of persons, such as wounded combatants or others who are *hors de combat* ('outside combat'), prisoners of war, or the civilian population. *Jus in bello* is the focus of this present chapter.

A note on terminology: since the adoption of the 1949 Geneva Conventions, there has been a move away from the term 'war' in favour of a more precise term; that of 'armed conflict'. States wished to ensure that the Geneva Conventions would apply to armed conflicts as a matter of fact, even if conflicting parties refused formally to recognize or to declare a state of war (see Section 15.2.1). Within scholarship, there has also been a shift away from the term 'law of war' to 'international humanitarian law' (IHL), to reflect the growing influence of the humanitarian aims of the law.[1] Though 'IHL' is a term embraced by the ICJ,[2] the ICTY, and the International Committee of the Red Cross (ICRC), certain scholars object to the term 'international humanitarian law': Jean Pictet memorably noted that to do so implies 'that the laws of war have an exclusively humanitarian purpose, when their evolution has in fact reflected

[1] ME O'Connell, 'Historical Development and Legal Basis' in D Fleck (ed), *The Handbook of International Humanitarian Law* (3rd edn, OUP, 2013), esp 11–13.

[2] See *Legality of the Threat or Use of Nuclear Weapons, Advisory Opinion, ICJ Reports 1996*, p 226, 256.

various practical concerns of states and their armed forces on grounds other than those which may be considered humanitarian'.[3] Readers might also bear in mind a countervailing argument: whatever the terminology, international humanitarian law is also a powerful legitimating force which, in rendering certain categories of violence impermissible, paradoxically ends up tolerating those forms of violence which are not prohibited.[4]

For these reasons, in this chapter the terms 'law of armed conflict' and 'international humanitarian law' are used as synonyms to describe the relevant legal regime.

15.1.2 Historical development and the 1899/1907 Hague Conventions

Though restraints on the conduct of warfare have existed in many cultures since antiquity,[5] the modern law of armed conflict arose as an attempt to contain the violence and suffering that had intensified due to military and industrial innovations in the mid-nineteenth century, violently exemplified in the Crimean War of 1853–56, the Franco-Austrian War of 1859, and the US Civil War of 1861–65. The foundation of the ICRC in 1863, the adoption of the First Geneva Convention in 1864 protecting wounded soldiers in the field,[6] and Francis Lieber's proposed 'instructions' in the 1863 'Lieber Code'[7] were all enacted against this backdrop; together, they were highly influential in establishing the modern law of armed conflict.

HISTORICAL BACKGROUND The International Committee of the Red Cross (ICRC)

Sometimes called the 'first non-governmental organization', the ICRC plays an influential role within the law of armed conflict. It was founded by the Swiss Henry Dunant, who had witnessed the suffering of wounded soldiers and the lack of medical personnel during the 1859 Battle of Solferino, a particularly violent engagement in the Franco-Austrian War leading to the unification of Italy.

After years of effort, in 1863 Dunant was able to convene an international conference with eighteen delegates from European States, which resolved to found national relief societies for

[3] J Pictet, *Humanitarian Law and the Protection of War Victims* (AW Sijthoff, 1975), 11.

[4] See C af Jochnick and R Normand, 'The Legitimation of Violence: A Critical History of the Laws of War' (1994) 35 Harvard ILJ 49; and D Kennedy, *Of Law and War* (Princeton UP, 2005).

[5] See, e.g., the focus on ancient Greece and Rome, and the mediaeval Islamic world, in the Special Issue (2008) 26(3) Law and History Review; A Roberts, 'Judaic Sources of and Views on the Laws of War' (1988) 37 Naval Law Review 21; Sun Tzu's *Art of War* (*c* fourth century BC), ch III; the Sanskrit-language *Mahabharata* (*c* 200 BC) and *Code of Manu*, both studied in WS Armour, 'Customs of Warfare in Ancient India' (1922) 8 Transactions of the Grotius Society 71; and A Al-Dawoody, 'Islamic Law and International Humanitarian Law: An Introduction to the Main Principles' (2018) 99 IRCR 995.

[6] Convention for the Amelioration of the Condition of the Wounded in Armies in the Field (signed 22 August 1864, entered into force 22 June 1865), 129 CTS 361.

[7] F Lieber, *General Orders No 100, Adjutant General's Office: Instructions for the Government of Armies of the United States in the Field, prepared by Francis Lieber* (USGPO, 1863).

wounded soldiers. All was to be coordinated by an international league which would work to develop international law in the area: the ICRC. Importantly, the ICRC was founded as a private institution, and not an international organization; it was named after the 'Red Cross', its common protective symbol for medical personnel in the field. In the following year, the 1864 Geneva Convention was signed, the first treaty guaranteeing neutrality and protection for wounded soldiers and protection for medical personnel. The ICRC's contributions to humanitarian relief were widespread in the decades to follow, and in 1949, the four Geneva Conventions established legal mandates for the ICRC with respect to visiting prisoners of war and supporting relief efforts in response to natural disasters.

Though a private organization independent from States, on 6 October 1990 the ICRC was granted observer status by the UN General Assembly and enjoys international legal personality (*cf* Chapter 6, Section 6.4.1, on the legal personality of international organizations). Its work continues to this day in more than eighty States, under the protected symbols of the 'Red Cross', the 'Red Crescent' (first used by the Ottoman Empire, and now widely used in Islamic States), and since 2005 the 'Red Crystal', an additional emblem devoid of any national, political, or religious connotations. Though a cliché, it is truly a *sui generis* organization.

These tentative first efforts were followed by the 1899 and 1907 Hague Peace Conferences, convened on the invitation of Russian Czar Nicholas II.[8] The Hague Conferences produced a body of treaties regulating the conduct of land and naval warfare, known colloquially as 'Hague Law'.[9] The Hague Conventions proscribed, *inter alia*, the use of certain types of arms or projectiles for causing unnecessary suffering, the use of poison or poisoned weapons, and the laying of submarine mines. Significantly, they were based on the famous 'Martens clause' (named after Russian (Estonian) jurist Friedrich von Martens), the principle that international humanitarian law would resolve any possible gaps in application, and which made its first appearance in the 1899 Second Hague Convention:

> in cases not included by the Regulations . . . populations and belligerents remain under the protection and the empire of the principles of international law, as they result from the usages established between civilized nations, from the laws of humanity, and the requirements of the public conscience.[10]

[8] For a history, see A Eyffinger, 'A Highly Critical Moment: Role and Record of the 1907 Hague Peace Conference' (2007) 54 NILR 197.

[9] The non-legal term 'Hague Law' was used by the ICJ in *Nuclear Weapons* (n 2) 256. There are fourteen 'Hague Conventions', all of which can be found at <https://www.icrc.org/ihl>.

[10] See Hague Convention (II) with respect to the Laws and Customs of War on Land (adopted 29 July 1899, entered into force 4 September 1900), 187 CTS 429, preamble.

15.1.3 **The 1949 Geneva Conventions**

Though the interwar period had led to modest new developments, a more comprehensive regime was established after World War II through the four 1949 Geneva Conventions,[11] popularly known as 'Geneva Law'.[12] The Geneva Conventions, unlike the more technical Hague Conventions, were focussed on the humane treatment and protection of persons not actively engaged in warfare, such as the sick, the wounded, and prisoners of war.

Together, the four Geneva Conventions proscribe practices such as torture, forced displacement of civilians unless imperatively necessary, illegal executions, and reprisals against protected persons. They also mandate certain minimum standards for the treatment of prisoners, enemy hospital staff, and other protected categories of persons. Geneva Convention IV also extended protection to civilians who, as a result of armed hostilities or occupation, found themselves under the power of a State, which was not sovereign over the occupied territory.

The Geneva Conventions are regarded as a unified regime; this is due to certain common provisions laid down in identical form across all four conventions. Common Article 2 (they are 'Common Articles' in that they share identical terms) holds that the four Geneva Conventions apply to all international armed conflicts, even if some of the States involved do not recognize that they are in a state of war. In addition, it makes clear that the Conventions do not require reciprocity, in that all parties to a conflict are not required to have ratified the Conventions. Instead, each Convention applies in the mutual relations of the ratifying States and, equally, in their relations with any other State, provided the latter 'accepts and applies' its provisions on an ad hoc basis. Common Article 3, which will be considered in further detail in Section 15.2.2.1, lays out further rules binding all States parties to certain minimum obligations, in relation to armed conflicts 'not of an international character'.

The Geneva Conventions have been ratified by 196 parties, most recently Palestine, the accession of which was accepted by the Swiss government (depositary of the Geneva Conventions) on 10 April 2014. Though, of course, numbers are not fully determinative, the universal ratification of the Geneva Conventions is compelling evidence that they have passed in their entirety into customary international law.[13] Their broadly

[11] Geneva Convention for the Amelioration of the Condition of the Wounded and Sick in Armed Forces in the Field (adopted 12 August 1949, entered into force 21 October 1950), 75 UNTS 31 (Geneva Convention I); Geneva Convention for the Amelioration of the Condition of Wounded, Sick and Shipwrecked Members of Armed Forces at Sea (adopted 12 August 1949, entered into force 21 October 1950), 75 UNTS 85 (Geneva Convention II); Geneva Convention Relative to the Treatment of Prisoners of War (adopted 12 August 1949, entered into force 21 October 1950), 75 UNTS 135 (Geneva Convention III); Geneva Convention Relative to the Protection of Civilian Persons in Time of War (adopted 12 August 1949, entered into force 21 October 1950), 75 UNTS 287 (Geneva Convention IV).

[12] The non-legal term 'Geneva Law' was used by the ICJ in *Nuclear Weapons* (n 2) 256. For further explanation of the differences between 'Hague Law' and 'Geneva Law', see Y Dinstein, *The Conduct of Hostilities under the Law of International Armed Conflict* (3rd edn, CUP, 2016), 21–3; F Bugnion, 'Droit de Genève et droit de La Haye' (2001) 83 IRRC 901; and RJ Erickson, 'Protocol I: A Merging of the Hague and Geneva Law of Armed Conflict' (1979) 19 Virginia JIL 557.

[13] See T Meron, 'The Geneva Conventions as Customary Law' (1987) 81–2 AJIL 348; ICRC, 'International Humanitarian Law and the Challenges of Contemporary Armed Conflicts' (2007) 867 IRRC (September 2007), 719–57, 742. See further the Report of the Secretary-General, UN Doc S/25704 (3 May 1993), 9; and *Nuclear Weapons* (n 2) 256.

accepted customary status allowed the Eritrea–Ethiopia Claims Commission to refer to the Geneva Conventions in various arbitral awards, despite the fact that Eritrea had not acceded to them until 14 August 2000, well after the relevant conflicts had taken place.[14]

The Geneva Conventions were strengthened in 1977 by the adoption of two Additional Protocols, which added updated rules relating to international armed conflicts (between States: IACs)[15] and non-international armed conflicts (between a State and non-State actors, or two non-State actors alone: NIACs).[16] A third Additional Protocol, concerning the protected emblems of the ICRC (the Red Cross, the Red Crescent, and the new Red Crystal), entered into force in 2007.[17] The Additional Protocols do not enjoy the same widespread ratification as the Geneva Conventions themselves, and they are not universally accepted as a codification of customary law.[18] However, it bears noting that the ICTY has long claimed that certain provisions of Additional Protocols I and II, in particular those which purport to restate pre-existing rules contained in various Hague Regulations, have entered into customary law.[19]

Besides the Hague and Geneva Convention frameworks, other relevant multilateral treaties include the 1954 Hague Convention on the Protection of Cultural Property,[20] the 1972 Biological Weapons Convention,[21] the 1977 Environmental Modification Convention,[22] the 1980 Certain Conventional Weapons Convention, the 1992 Chemical Weapons Convention,[23] and the 1997 Ottawa Landmines Convention.[24] What is more,

[14] See Eritrea–Ethiopia Claims Commission, *Partial Award on the Claims relating to Prisoners of War—Eritrea's Claim 17* (1 July 2003), 42 ILM 1056, 1083, paras 36–41; and *Partial Award on the Claims relating to Civilians—Eritrea's Claims 15, 16, 23, and 27–32* (17 December 2004), (2005) 44 ILM 630, para 28. The Commission took the view that a customary norm and treaty norm with substantively the same content could coexist, endorsing the ICJ's conclusions in *Military and Paramilitary Activities in and against Nicaragua (Nicaragua v United States of America), Merits, ICJ Reports 1986*, p 14, 94–5.

[15] Protocol Additional to the Geneva Conventions of 12 August 1949, and relating to the Protection of Victims of International Armed Conflicts (Protocol I) (signed 8 June 1977, entered into force 7 December 1978), 1125 UNTS 3. At the time of writing, AP I has been ratified by 174 parties.

[16] Protocol Additional to the Geneva Conventions of 12 August 1949, and relating to the Protection of Victims of Non-International Armed Conflicts (Protocol II) (signed 8 June 1977, entered into force 7 December 1978), 1125 UNTS 609. At the time of writing, AP II has been ratified by 169 parties.

[17] Protocol Additional to the Geneva Conventions of 12 August 1949, and relating to the Adoption of an Additional Distinctive Emblem (Protocol III) (signed 8 December 2005, entered into force 14 January 2007), (2006) 45 ILM 558. At the time of writing, AP III has been ratified by seventy-nine parties.

[18] Significant non-parties to either AP I or AP II include Eritrea, India, Indonesia, Iran, Israel, Pakistan, Somalia, Turkey, and the USA.

[19] See *Prosecutor v Kupreškić et al* (Judgment) IT-95-16-A (14 January 2000), paras 521–5. See also F Pocar, 'To What Extent is Protocol I Customary International Law' (2002) 78 International Law Studies 337, 343–6.

[20] Hague Convention for the Protection of Cultural Property in the Event of Armed Conflict (signed 14 May 1954, entered into force 7 August 1956), 249 UNTS 240.

[21] Convention on the Prohibition of the Development, Production and Stockpiling of Bacteriological (Biological) and Toxic Weapons and on their Destruction (opened for signature 10 April 1972, entered into force 26 March 1975), 1015 UNTS 163.

[22] Convention on the Prohibition of Military or Any Other Hostile Use of Environmental Modification Techniques (opened for signature 18 May 1977, entered into force on 5 October 1978), 610 UNTS 151.

[23] Convention on the Prohibition of the Development, Production, Stockpiling and Use of Chemical Weapons and on their Destruction (opened for signature 13 January 1993, entered into force 29 April 1997), 1974 UNTS 45.

[24] Convention on the Prohibition of the Use, Stockpiling, Production and Transfer of Anti-Personnel Mines and on their Destruction (opened for signature 3 December 1997, entered into force 1 March 1999), 2056 UNTS 211.

it should be noted that IHL has been designated *lex specialis* by the ICJ in its interaction with norms of international human rights law (IHRL).[25] Though there are certainly nuances, as a general proposition norms of IHL, being specifically applicable to situations of armed conflict, prevail over general international law and IHRL should a state of armed conflict exist. However, IHL must be interpreted against the backdrop of IHRL and, whenever possible, the two regimes are meant to be complementary to one another.[26]

Finally, the statutes of a number of international criminal courts and tribunals confer jurisdiction on their respective institutions to try individuals for 'grave breaches' and 'other serious violations' of the 'laws and customs of war'. Their judgments and decisions comprise a body of case law which has served to clarify and advance our understanding of IHL.[27]

15.2 Scope of application

15.2.1 Ascertaining the existence of an armed conflict

Historically, a sense of chivalry or honour impelled formal declarations of war, to give an enemy sufficient time to prepare a defence.[28] That sentiment was embodied in Article 1 of the 1907 Hague Convention (III), which required that 'hostilities between [States] must not commence without previous and explicit warning, in the form either of a reasoned declaration of war or of an ultimatum with conditional declaration of war'.[29] A declaration of war was a 'performative act', inasmuch as the declaration would *create* the legal state of war between belligerents.

Today, armed conflicts have evolved far beyond purely inter-State wars to encompass a variety of different types of actors and scenarios, ranging from localized skirmishes to nuclear warfare. After the general prohibition on recourse to war was embodied in Article 2(4) of the UN Charter, since 1945, war is rarely 'declared' formally. States instead *recognize* that 'a state of war' or 'a state of armed conflict' (the correct technical

[25] *Nuclear Weapons* (n 2) para 26; see also *Construction of a Wall in the Occupied Palestinian Territory, Advisory Opinion, ICJ Reports 2004*, p 136, para 106.

[26] See L Hill-Cawthorne, 'Just Another Case of Treaty Interpretation? Reconciling Humanitarian Law and Human Rights Law in the ICJ' in M Andenas and E Bjorge (eds), *A Farewell to Fragmentation: Reassertion and Convergence in International Law* (CUP, 2015); R Provost, *International Human Rights and Humanitarian Law* (CUP, 2002); H Krieger, 'A Conflict of Norms: The Relationship between IHL and Human Rights Law in the ICRC Customary Law Study' (2006) 11 JCSL 265; see also *Report of the International Commission of Inquiry on Darfur to the United Nations Secretary-General, Pursuant to Security Council Resolution 1564 of 18 September 2004* (2005), para 143.

[27] See R Heinsch, 'Judicial "Law-Making" in the Jurisprudence of the ICTY and ICTR in Relation to Protecting Civilians from Mass Violence' in P Ambach, F Bostedt, G Dawson, and S Kostas (eds), *The Protection of Non-Combatants During Armed Conflict and Safeguarding the Rights of Victims in Post-Conflict Society* (Brill, 2015), 297.

[28] See A Pearce Higgins, *EH Hall: A Treatise on International Law* (8th edn, OUP, 1924), 444.

[29] *Hague Convention (III) relative to the Opening of Hostilities* (signed 18 October 1907, entered into force 26 January 1910), 205 CTS 264, Art 1.

term since 1949) exists. A historical example is the 1982 Falklands War in which neither Argentina nor the UK ever acknowledged a state of armed conflict between them. Instead, the UK declared a 'Total Exclusion Zone' in the South Atlantic: '[a]ny ship and any aircraft, whether military or civil ... found within the zone [without UK authorization] will be regarded as operating in support of the illegal occupation [and accordingly] be liable to be attacked by British forces.'[30] Argentina followed by declaring its own exclusion zone in the South Atlantic.[31]

Other examples abound. Prior to the 2003 invasion of Iraq, the US Congress did not declare war but 'authorized' President George W Bush to 'defend the national security of the United States' and to 'enforce all relevant [UN Security Council] Resolutions regarding Iraq.'[32] During the 2012 Heglig Crisis, South Sudan denounced the takeover of the contested border town of Abyei as an 'act of war', deploying soldiers against Sudan in response;[33] at no point, however, did either State declare war on the other. The 2020 armed conflict between Azerbaijan and Armenia began with offensives by both States, followed by simple declarations of compliance with IHL. The conflict would end forty-four days later with a ceasefire agreement signed between Russia, Armenia, and Azerbaijan.[34] The 2022 armed aggression against Ukraine has only ever been named by Russia, including President Putin, as a 'special military operation.'[35] More recently, on 8 October 2023 the Israeli cabinet declared that a 'war [had been] forced on ... Israel in a murderous terrorist assault from the Gaza Strip' as of 7 October 2023.[36]

Given that declarations of war have fallen into disuse, Common Article 2 of the 1949 Geneva Conventions does not define 'armed conflict' but provides only that the Conventions become applicable 'in all cases of declared war or of any other armed conflict which may arise between two or more [parties], even if the state of war is not recognized by one of them.' A fact-based definition of 'armed conflict' was put forward by the ICTY Appeals Chamber in *Prosecutor v Tadić*,[37] a variant of which was adopted by the ILC in its 2011 Articles on the Effects of Armed Conflicts on Treaties: a 'situation in which there is resort to armed force between States or protracted resort to armed force between governmental authorities and organized armed groups.'[38] Generally speaking,

[30] (1982) 53 BYBIL 542 (28 April 1982).

[31] UN Doc S/15069 (11 May 1982).

[32] See *Authorization for Use of Military Force Against Iraq Resolution of 2002* HJ Res 114 (16 October 2002), PL No 107-243, Stat 1498 (USA).

[33] See BBC, 'Sudan: Abyei seizure by north "act of war", says south' (BBC News, 22 May 2011) < https://www.bbc.co.uk/news/world-africa-13491445>.

[34] See BBC, 'Armenia, Azerbaijan and Russia sign Nagorno-Karabakh Peace Deal' (BBC News, 20 November 2020) < https://www.bbc.co.uk/news/world-europe-54882564 >.

[35] See the factual account in *Allegations of Genocide under the Convention on the Prevention and Punishment of the Crime of Genocide (Ukraine v Russian Federation), Preliminary Objections, Judgment of 2 February 2024*, paras 31–2.

[36] However, *cf* Government of Israel, Resolution 941 (8 October 2023), which declared a 'special home front situation' in the Gaza border region.

[37] See *Prosecutor v Tadić* (Decision on the Defence Motion for Interlocutory Appeal on Jurisdiction) ICTY-94-1-A (2 October 1995), para 70. That definition was drawn partly from J Pictet, *Commentary on the Geneva Conventions of 12 August 1949* (ICRC, 1952), vol I, 29.

[38] See 'Report of the International Law Commission on its Sixty-third Session' (2011), UN Doc A/66/10, 173, Art 2(b). The ILC was also inspired by the Institut de droit international's resolution, 'The Effects of Armed Conflicts on Treaties' (Helsinki Session, 28 August 1985), Art 2.

an international armed conflict thus will come into effect immediately upon the resort to armed force between two States, whatever the justifications offered or any formal/informal act of recognition.[39] Conversely, the existence of a non-international armed conflict requires a degree of 'protraction', a term that is generally understood to refer to a minimum of intensity, but not of duration.[40] All civil disturbances and tensions in which the intensity of violence falls below the threshold for 'protraction' are not armed conflicts.[41] Importantly, there is no minimum duration: an intensely violent two-day period in Argentina has been held to meet the threshold for 'protraction' and thus triggered the existence of an armed conflict.[42]

15.2.2 **Classifying armed conflicts**

15.2.2.1 **Distinguishing international and non-international armed conflicts**

There has long been a distinction between the rules applicable to an IAC, between two or more States, and a NIAC, between a State and non-State actor (or between non-State actors). On the one hand, the Geneva Conventions, coupled with the later Additional Protocol I (AP I), focus primarily on international conflicts. These are not limited merely to inter-State conflicts: Article 1(4) of AP I extends the Protocol's scope of application to include armed conflicts 'in which peoples are fighting against colonial domination and alien occupation and against racist regimes in the exercise of their right to self-determination', prima facie equating colonial situations to IACs.

In Additional Protocol II (AP II), one finds situations of internal armed conflict (termed a 'non-international armed conflict' or 'NIAC' in the Geneva Conventions), involving opposing factions, which under customary international law do not need to be a State, but a conflict purely between non-State armed groups.[43] Usually, domestic law governs such conflicts, due to abiding fear of States about interference in their internal affairs, and a concern that non-State entities might receive international legitimacy. For these reasons, the Geneva Conventions only contain, in their Common Article 3, certain minimum safeguards applying to non-international armed conflicts:

(i) humane and non-discriminatory treatment of persons taking no active part in hostilities and, in particular, prohibitions against murder, cruel treatment,

[39] K Mačák, *Internationalized Armed Conflicts in International Law* (OUP, 2018), 15, citing *inter alia Prosecutor v Delalić et al (Čelebići Trial Judgment)* IT-96-21-T (16 November 1998), para 184; R Provost, *International Human Rights and Humanitarian Law* (CUP, 2002), 250; and A Clapham, 'Concept of International Armed Conflict' in A Clapham, P Gaeta, and M Sassolì (eds), *The 1949 Geneva Conventions: A Commentary* (OUP, 2015), para 38.

[40] See *Prosecutor v Boškoski & Tarčulovski (Trial Judgment)* IT-04-82-T (10 July 2008), para 177; *Prosecutor v Haradinaj, Balaj and Brahimaj (Trial Judgment)* IT-04-84-T (3 April 2008), para 49. See also ILC, 'Report on the Effects of Armed Conflicts on the Law of Treaties' (n 36) 182–3, Commentary to Art 2, para 8.

[41] See T Meron, 'Towards a Humanitarian Declaration on Internal Strife' (1984) 78 AJIL 859; T Meron and A Rosas, 'A Declaration of Minimum Humanitarian Standards' (1991) 85 AJIL 375.

[42] *Abella v Argentina*, Case 11.137, IACtHR Report No 55/97, IACHR Doc OEA/Ser.L/V/II.95 Doc 7 (18 November 1997), para 156.

[43] A leading work in the area is S Sivakumaran, *The Law of Non-International Armed Conflict* (OUP, 2012).

or torture committed against them; the taking of hostages; humiliating and degrading treatment; and sentencing and executions in the absence of due process; and

(ii) care for the sick and the wounded, even if they were previously combatants.

THEORY AND DEBATES Self-determination and the Internationalization of Conflicts

Enduring challenges remain in the classification of armed conflicts involving self-determination, where the very creation of a new State, through secession from an existing State, would by definition transform a NIAC into an IAC. A key illustration arose during the violent dissolution of Yugoslavia. Though undoubtedly Croatia and, later, Bosnia-Herzegovina emerged as States, it is difficult even now to pinpoint the moment at which the armed conflict between them and the rump Federal Republic of Yugoslavia could have been reclassified as 'international'. The ICJ struggled with this very question in the *Application of the Genocide Convention* cases and the *Legality of the Use of Force* cases in which questions regarding the parties' statehood were disputed, and resolved at times with potentially contradictory results (see, in particular, the 2003 and 2004 judgments, respectively, in those two cases).

The constitutive theory of recognition (see Chapter 5), if legitimate, would go some way to capturing the complexities of the issue, but a very real question emerges: what legal rules should be applied in respect of an entity claiming statehood, as the classification of the conflict as NIAC or IAC might change in line with evolving facts on the ground? Though not involving self-determination, the 2011 armed conflict in Libya (see 'Historical Background', Section 15.2.2.2) further illustrates the complexities in relation to internationalization.

Though Common Article 3 reflects a strong humanitarian impulse, it is but one provision in an area where textual precision is highly prized; by itself, it affords no protection to participants in hostilities. These limitations impelled the adoption of AP II in 1977, a set of rules less comprehensive than in AP I and which aimed at enshrining further legal protections in situations of NIAC. There is some debate as to whether the provisions of AP II have entered into customary international law; however, there is some evidence found in the military manuals of several non-State parties which instruct their armed forces to respect similar rules as those embodied in the Additional Protocols.[44] AP II's thresholds for intensity of violence and the existence of organized armed groups are high, requiring a clear organizational structure and effective control over territory, and thus serve to exclude many conflicts from its scope. Moreover, as a treaty, AP II only applies between its States parties; it cannot apply to conflicts between two organized

[44] T Meron, 'International Criminalization of Internal Atrocities' (1995) 89 AJIL 554, 559–65; N Quénivet, 'Applicability Test of Additional Protocol II and Common Article 3 for Crimes in Internal Armed Conflict' in S Solomon, D Jinks, and J Maogoto (eds), *Applying International Humanitarian Law in Judicial and Quasi-Judicial Bodies* (Asser Press/Springer, 2014); F Pocar, 'To What Extent is Protocol I Customary International Law?' (2003) 78 International Law Studies 337.

armed groups or to the conduct of a non-State party except to the extent that its provisions might reflect customary law.

15.2.2.2 **Blurred lines: 'internationalized' armed conflicts and the 'unification' of international humanitarian law**

The distinction between IACs and NIACs is marked by a relative fluidity between the two categories, which raises challenges for the classification of a conflict involving multiple actors. The ICTY has had to face complex questions relating to the support given by the Federal Republic of Yugoslavia (FRY) to Bosnian Serb militias against the internationally recognized Bosnia and Herzegovina, namely, whether such support could 'internationalize' an internal armed conflict. In *Tadić*, the ICTY Appeals Chamber set out two scenarios for internationalization: first, if another State were to intervene directly in a conflict or, alternatively, if a party to an internal armed conflict were acting 'on behalf of' another State, the conflict is transformed into IAC.[45] Secondly, it may also be that a 'mixed' conflict exists, in which different rules apply to different parties in parallel armed conflicts, with some zones governed under the law of IACs and others by the law on NIACs.[46] The question of party status remains crucial in determining the applicable law to an armed conflict.[47]

HISTORICAL BACKGROUND Classifying the Libyan Conflict of 2011

The Libyan situation which erupted in 2011 is illustrative of the difficulties in classification. Riots erupted in Benghazi, a major city, on 15 February 2011, quickly escalating into a conflict between Qaddafi's government and a coalition of anti-Qaddafi militias (the 'National Transitional Council'). On 10 March 2011, the President of the ICRC issued a news release taking the view that the conflict constituted a NIAC. By this point, most observers agreed that the intensity of the conflict clearly met the level of organization and territorial control required, and thus triggering the application of AP II.

Early on, the conflict captured international attention: in Security Council Resolution 1970 (26 February 2011), the Council deplored the government's 'incitement to hostility and violence against the civilian population', calling for a ceasefire and the entry of humanitarian aid convoys, and imposing an arms embargo and other sanctions. When these were ignored, Security Council Resolution 1973 (17 March 2011) authorized United Nations members to use 'all necessary means' to protect civilians in Libya. A coalition of States, including several

[45] *Prosecutor v Tadić* (Judgment of Appeals Chamber) IT-94-1-A (15 July 1999), para 84. But see the ICJ's judgment in *Application of the Convention on the Prevention and Punishment of the Crime of Genocide (Bosnia and Herzegovina v Serbia and Montenegro), Judgment, ICJ Reports 2007*, p 43, para 413, in which the ICJ required the exercise of 'effective control' over operations in order for attribution to the FRY under the law of State responsibility: see Chapter 10, Section 10.2.1.4.1.

[46] See D Willmott, 'Removing the Distinction between International and Non-International Armed Conflict in the Rome Statute of the International Criminal Court' (2004) 5 Melbourne ILR 196. HP Gasser, 'Internationalized Non-International Armed Conflicts: Case Studies of Afghanistan, Kampuchea and Lebanon' (1983) 33 American University LR 145.

[47] A Wentker, *Party Status to Armed Conflict in International Law* (OUP, 2024).

NATO members, began to intervene directly in Libya. At this point, it could be said that the conflict had become 'internationalized', and that the legal regime applicable to an IAC in the Geneva Conventions and AP I would apply to operations between the Qaddafi government and intervening States.

Internationalization is an uncertain phenomenon. Legally speaking, serious questions remain open as to whether both legal regimes apply in parallel to different actors, or whether the more robust legal rules governing IAC come to apply to all military operations. A more recent case study might be the non-international armed conflict in Syria where Russian and Iranian support for Assad have not internationalized the conflict but where, since 2016, Turkish occupation of three zones of Northern Syria, ostensibly on behalf of the Syrian opposition, would certainly entail these particular zones being subject to the law on belligerent occupation which applies in IACs; the brief strikes against Syria by France, the UK, and the USA in 2017 and 2018 may also have generated very brief IACs.

A rich literature exists considers these questions, with recent highlights including N Zamir, *Classification of Conflicts in International Humanitarian Law* (Edward Elgar, 2017); and K Mačák, *Internationalized Armed Conflicts in International Law* (OUP, 2018).

For this reason, certain scholars argue that the distinction between the two regimes has become obsolete, and have called for a 'unification' of international humanitarian law.[48] Notably, international criminal jurisdictions have suggested that the distinction between inter-State and IACs was losing relevance insofar as the protection of human dignity was concerned.[49]

From a purely humanistic stance, one can understand the desire that all victims be treated alike. However, alongside the concern that eliminating the distinction could potentially weaken the application of international human rights law,[50] there are practical reasons for its existence. Much of the law on IAC relates to concepts such as the status of 'combatant' of members of the armed forces, as the belligerent occupation of territory and enemy nationality; however, notions of combatancy and occupation are all alien to civil conflicts.[51] Finally, States hold justified concerns in relation to the implications of unification for their ability to quell internal rebellions and regarding the legitimacy of revolutionary groups and their exercise of violence.[52]

[48] See L Moir, 'Towards the Unification of International Humanitarian Law' in R Burchill, ND White, and J Morris (eds), *International Conflict and Security Law: Essays in Memory of Hilaire McCoubrey* (CUP, 2005), 108; C Bassiouni, 'The New Wars and the Crisis of Compliance with the Law of Armed Conflict by Non-State Actors' (2007) Journal of Criminal Law and Criminology 698, 731; WM Reisman and J Silk, 'Which Law Applies to the Afghan Conflict?' (1988) 82 AJIL 465.

[49] See the ICTY Appeals Chamber statements in *Tadić* (n 42) para 98; See also *Prosecutor v Furundžija*, IT-95'17/1, 121 ILR 213, p 271. The ICC was equally critical in *Prosecutor v Lubanga Dyilo* (Art 74 of the Statute) ICC-01/04'-01/06 (14 March 2012), para 539.

[50] L Hill-Cawthorne, 'Humanitarian Law, Human Rights Law and the Bifurcation of Armed Conflict' (2015) 64 ICLQ 293.

[51] JG Stewart, 'Towards a Single Definition of Armed Conflict in International Humanitarian Law: A Critique of Internationalized Armed Conflict' (2003) 85 IRRC 313, 345.

[52] See D Fleck, 'The Law of Non-International Armed Conflict' in D Fleck (ed), *The Oxford Handbook of International Humanitarian Law* (3rd edn, OUP, 2013), ch 12.

15.3 Categories of persons under international humanitarian law

15.3.1 Combatants

A defining feature of the law of armed conflict is the identification of persons who are actively engaged in hostilities, termed *combatants*. Combatants are obliged to abide by the law of armed conflict and afforded certain protections if captured; but equally, combatants may lawfully be targeted.

15.3.2 Prisoner of war status

Under Article 4 of the Third Geneva Convention, certain categories of persons are entitled, if captured, to 'Prisoner of War' (POW) status. In turn, those categories have proven useful in defining the scope of the term 'combatants' and those who are excluded from being legitimate targets.

The archetypal combatant is a member of a State's armed forces, militia, or volunteer corps. Moreover, as the methods and means of warfare have evolved, other categories of persons analogized to the classic soldier have been recognized as warranting similar protection. Thus, participants in a conflict who are not part of the regular armed forces of a State have become entitled to protection as 'combatants', if they are:

- under the command of an individual;
- under a fixed distinctive sign and bearing weapons;
- clearly distinguished from the civilian population by their uniforms;
- and, above all, obliged to comply with the international law of armed conflict.[53]

Though not customary international law, Article 43 of AP I further defines the notion of 'combatant' and their rights and obligations, in particular, being entitled to the status of prisoner of war if captured. Article 44 of AP I further enshrines the rights of a combatant to POW status when captured in situations of armed conflict.

15.3.2.1 Protected persons beyond regular State armed forces

Militias and volunteer corps: organized groups of individuals not necessarily under the control of a State, but who operate much like regular armed forces with an organized command structure, bearing arms and a fixed distinctive sign, and respecting the laws of armed conflict. The condition to bear a distinctive sign has been relaxed somewhat, so as also to protect *partisans* of organized resistance movements (GC III, Article 4(A)(2)), and *guerrillas*, irregular combatants resorting to guerrilla warfare, usually within the framework of a war of national liberation (Article 44.3 of AP I).[54]

[53] See the Hague Regulations, Annex to Hague Convention (IV) respecting the Laws and Customs of War on Land (signed 18 October 1907, entered into force 26 January 1910), 187 CTS 227, Art 1; GC I (n 11) Art 13; GC II (n 11) Art 13; GC III (n 11) Art 4.

[54] See E Crawford, *The Treatment of Combatants and Insurgents under the Law of Armed Conflict* (OUP, 2010), and H Verthy, *Guérrilla et droit humanitaire* (2nd edn, ICRC, 1983).

Authorized persons accompanying the armed forces: these include war correspondents, supply contractors, or members of military labour units (Article 4(A)(3) of GC III), and are also entitled to POW status if captured.

Participants in a levée en masse *('mass levy')*: during the Franco-Prussian War of 1870–1, French civilians spontaneously took up arms, without time for much military organization, to defend France against imminent Prussian invasion. Such individuals would also benefit from POW status, provided they carry arms openly and respect the laws and customs of war (Article 4(A)(6) of GC III). The concept has been traced as far back as the revolutionary wars in the USA and France.[55]

15.3.2.2 **Obligations owed to POWs**

The Third Geneva Convention establishes a detailed regime governing the treatment for POWs, centred chiefly on the protection of their life and person. They must be treated humanely and not subject to insults or public humiliation, thus excluding a parade of prisoners or exhibiting them publicly to a mob.[56] A detaining State may only question a POW to divulge their name, date of birth, rank, and serial number; they cannot be tortured or otherwise coerced into disclosing any information of any kind whatsoever.[57] Significantly, though POWs are neither criminals nor hostages, they remain subject to the laws and orders of the detaining State, and may be punished for offences committed during their detention and, exceptionally, for criminal offences committed before capture.[58] For example, after his capture by the USA, Panamanian General Noriega was tried for drug trafficking offences that took place during his period in office.[59]

POWs are to be removed from the zone of hostilities; they can never be used as human shields or be the subject of reprisals, and no considerations of military necessity can justify their ill-treatment.[60] Upon the cessation of active hostilities, POWs must be released and repatriated.[61] Repatriation is not absolute; for example, after the 1991 Gulf War, many Iraqi POWs asked to remain in Saudi Arabia rather than be repatriated to Iraq.

CONTEMPORARY DEVELOPMENTS The Recruitment of Child Soldiers

The practice of recruiting child soldiers has consisted of removing children from their families, invariably by force, and indoctrinating them to serve in armed forces. Particularly newsworthy examples include the Lord's Resistance Army in Uganda, the Revolutionary United Front in Sierra Leone, and the *Union des Patriotes Congolais* in the Democratic Republic of the Congo.

The recruitment of child soldiers is unambiguously unlawful, given how they are forced both to witness and to commit unspeakable violence. What is more, child soldiers are often abused, exploited, injured, or even killed. There is some ambiguity about the precise age at

[55] See E Crawford, 'The Historical and Legal Development of the *Levée en Masse* in the Law of Armed Conflict' (2017) 19 Journal of the History of International Law 329.

[56] GC III (n 11) Art 13. [57] *Ibid*, Art 17. [58] *Ibid*, Arts 82, 85.

[59] *United States v Noriega*, 808 F.Supp 791 (SD Fla 1982) (USA).

[60] GC III (n 11) Art 23. [61] *Ibid*, Art 118.

which an individual stops being a 'child'. Article 77 of AP I requires States to take 'all feasible measures in order that children who have not attained the age of *fifteen* years do not take a direct part in hostilities, and, in particular, [to] refrain from recruiting them'. The 2000 Optional Protocol to the 1989 UN Convention on the Rights of the Child sets out measures to protect children under *eighteen* from having to participate in armed conflicts. The Security Council has repeatedly called for the protection of children in armed conflict, without specifying an age (see, e.g., UNSC Res 1882 (4 August 2009), UN Doc S/RES/1882).

The ICC Trial Chamber judgment in *Prosecutor v Lubanga Dyilo (Thomas)*, Judgment of 14 March 2012, Case No ICC-01/04-01/06 was the first conviction for conscription or enlisting children in armed conflicts; it is further analysed in Chapter 17, Section 17.2.3.3.2. Early in 2021, ICC Trial Chamber IX convicted Dominic Ongwen of the conscription and enlisting of child soldiers (see *Prosecutor v Ongwen (Dominic)*, ICC-02/04-01/15-1819-RED, Decision of 4 February 2021). Crucially, in its sentencing decision, the Chamber took into consideration that Ongwen himself had been abducted and recruited when he was nine years old, and decided accordingly to reduce his sentence from the maximum life imprisonment to twenty-five years in prison (see Decision on Sentencing of 6 May 2021, esp paras 388–9).

The persistent recruitment of child soldiers is an example of how, despite robust legal safeguards, some of the most vulnerable members of society can be forced into participating in armed conflicts and the guidelines and measures of the Geneva Convention might fall short. UNICEF has been active in releasing children from armed forces and helping them to reintegrate them in their communities and their families.

For further reading, see the jointly authored book led by Shaheed Fatima KC, *Protecting Children in Armed Conflict* (Hart, 2018); MA Drumbl and JC Barrett (eds), *Research Handbook on Child Soldiers* (Edward Elgar, 2018); and M Happold, *Child Soldiers in International Law* (MUP, 2022).

15.3.2.3 **The exclusion of mercenaries from the POW status**

There have long been 'soldiers for hire', *mercenaries,* paid to engage in armed violence on behalf of a foreign State.[62] These must, of course, be distinguished from regular units of the armed forces of States composed of foreign volunteers, such as the French Foreign Legion and the British Gurkhas. The practice of recruiting mercenaries waned considerably with the professionalization of armed forces in the eighteenth and nineteenth centuries. However, in the aftermath of decolonization, large numbers of demobilized professional soldiers from Western States were employed, purely for private gain, by colonial powers and ruling elites in newly independent (and often fragile) African States. This was partly for internal security and intelligence, but also to fight against national liberation movements; their presence was found to lead to widespread violence.[63] Accordingly, in Article 47 of AP I, mercenaries are categorically denied the protections afforded by POW or combatant status.[64]

[62] S Percy, *Mercenaries: The History of a Norm in International Relations* (OUP, 2007).

[63] For an account of this phenomenon in the 1960s and 1970s, see H Tonkin, *State Control over Private Military and Security Companies in Armed Conflict* (CUP, 2011), 11–17.

[64] See also the International Convention against the Recruitment, Use, Financing and Training of Mercenaries (adopted 4 December 1989, entered into force 20 October 2001), 2163 UNTS 75.

Recently, the euphemistically known 'private military security companies' (PMSC), resembling classic mercenary groups but recruiting nationals organized into corporations, have come into fashion, especially with respect to ancillary tasks relating to armed conflict such as the detention of prisoners, the protection of military convoys, or the organization of logistics. PMSCs were used by the USA and the UK during the occupation of Iraq, eliciting significant controversy. The most infamous was the 2004 incident relating to Abu Ghraib prison, where photographs were released of several CACI International and Titan Corp employees abusing and torturing prisoners while conducting interrogations on behalf of the USA.[65] Though they have since been operating under national regulation,[66] the General Assembly has condemned PMSCs as one of the 'new modalities of mercenarism'.[67] In 2008, the ICRC and Switzerland sponsored the non-binding *Montreux Document on Private Military and Security Companies* containing some 70 recommendations on good practice in this area.[68]

15.3.3 **So-called 'unlawful combatants'**

The USA has advocated this highly problematic category since at least World War II. In the *Ex parte Quirin* judgment, the US Supreme Court declared seven German servicemen who had abandoned their uniforms and were set to carry out acts of sabotage to be 'unlawful combatants'.[69] Purportedly, persons who take part in hostilities, but who fail the tests for lawful combatancy laid down in Articles 43 and 44 of AP I, fall into this category. In 2002, US President George W Bush revitalized the category, declaring that 'captured Taliban personnel' during the US intervention in Afghanistan would not be entitled to POW treatment whilst in custody in the US base at Guantánamo Bay.[70]

Most international lawyers agree that an intermediate category of 'unlawful combatant', entitled to neither the basic protections for combatants nor civilians, is unacceptable.[71] Through three judgments, the US Supreme Court established that the

[65] P Cockburn, 'Iraqis win $5.8m from US firm in Abu Ghraib torture lawsuit' (*The Independent*, 9 January 2013) <https://www.independent.co.uk/news/world/middle-east/iraqis-win-5-8m-from-us-firm-in-abu-ghraib-torture-lawsuit-8444907.html>. See further Tonkin (n 60) ch 1; L Green, *The Contemporary Law of Armed Conflict* (3rd edn Manchester UP, 2008), 138 *et seq*.

[66] In the UK, s 370 of and Sch 15 to the Armed Forces Act 2006 make civilians accompanying the armed forces subject to military law. In the USA, under HR 5122 (US Congress), 'National Defense Authorization Act for Fiscal Year 2007', PMSCs are subject to the Uniform Code of Military Practice.

[67] UNGA Res 62/145 (4 March 2008). For further reading, see Crawford (n 50); D Richemond-Barak, 'Rethinking Private Warfare' (2011) 5 Law & Ethics of Human Rights 158.

[68] As of late 2024, some 59 States, the EU, OSCE, and NATO have formally expressed support for the Montreux document: see <https://www.eda.admin.ch/eda/en/fdfa/foreign-policy/international-law/international-humanitarian-law/private-military-security-companies/participating-states.html>.

[69] See *Ex parte Quirin* 317 US 1 (1942); see also *Barghouti* [Israeli case of 2002], para 11.2.

[70] See White House Fact Sheet: Status of detainees at Guantánamo (7 February 2002).

[71] See, e.g., T Franck, 'Criminals, Combatants, or What—An Examination of the Role of Law in Responding to the Threat of Terror' (2005) 98 AJIL 686; J Pejić, 'Conflict Classification and the Law Applicable to Detention and the Use of Force' in E Wilmshurst (ed), *International Law and the Classification of Conflicts* (OUP, 2012), 80; K Doermann, 'The Legal Situation of "Unlawful/Unprivileged Combatants"' (2003) IRRC 45; M Finaud, 'L'abus de la notion de 'combattant illegal': une atteinte au droit international humanitaire' (2006) 110 RGDIP 861.

Guantánamo Bay detainees could not be held in a legal vacuum. In *Rasul v Bush*, it held that detainees were entitled to challenge the legality of their detention in US courts.[72] In *Hamdan v Rumsfeld*, it declared that the 'Military Commissions' established to try the detainees were contrary to the Geneva Conventions.[73] Finally, in *Boumediene v Bush*, it concluded that the detainees had the right of *habeas corpus* under US constitutional law.[74]

Though in 2018 President Trump signed an executive order keeping the prison open indefinitely,[75] as of late 2024, that number had fallen to some 15 detainees. The Guantánamo Bay situation nevertheless remains problematic, as detainees remain denied the status of POW or of any protective status under IHL.[76] In this respect, the more cautious view is to regard persons who fail to meet the tests for lawful combatancy under Articles 43 and 44 of AP I as, at a minimum, entitled to the basic customary humanitarian guarantees codified in Article 75 AP I (see later, Section 15.3.5).

15.3.4 **The wounded and sick**

The 1949 First and Second Geneva Conventions (concerning the battlefield and naval warfare, respectively), require the humane treatment of wounded or sick soldiers without distinction, and specify that accompanying medical personnel, establishments, and units such as hospital ships, enjoy inviolability.[77] Torture and biological experimentation are explicitly forbidden, and parties undertake that the wounded or sick, even if from the enemy camp, are not wilfully to be left without medical assistance and treatment.[78] In every respect, enemy detainees are to be treated as POWs and receive protection and care.[79] In short, the wounded and sick are not to be treated as combatants: they are considered *hors de combat*.

What is more, the distinctive emblems of the ICRC mentioned earlier (the Red Cross, the Red Crescent, and the Red Crystal), are never to be misused, under criminal penalty or even the war crime of perfidy, defined in Article 37(1) of AP I as any act 'inviting the confidence of an adversary to believe that he is entitled to, or is obliged to accord, protection under the laws of armed conflict, with the intention of betraying that confidence'.[80]

[72] See *Rasul v Bush*, 124 SC 2686 (2004) (USA).
[73] *Hamdan v Rumsfeld*, 126 SC 2749 (2006) (USA).
[74] *Boumediene v Bush*, 553 US 723 (2008) (USA).
[75] See 'Presidential Executive Order on Protecting America Through Lawful Detention of Terrorists' (30 January 2018).
[76] F Johns, 'Guantánamo Bay and the Annihilation of the Exception' (2005) 16 EJIL 613; Lord Steyn, 'Guantánamo Bay: The Legal Black Hole' (2004) 53 ICLQ 1; T Gill and E van Sliedrecht, 'Guantánamo Bay: A Reflection on the Legal Status and Rights of "Unlawful Enemy Combatants"' (2005) 1 Utrecht Law Review 28.
[77] See GC I (n 11), Chap VII, esp Art 21; GC II (n 11), Chap III, esp Arts 12–13. Inviolability is similar to that enjoyed by diplomats and consuls: see Chapter 9, Section 9.5.
[78] *Ibid*, Art 12.
[79] *Ibid*, Arts 14–15.
[80] See the more detailed provisions in GC I (n 11) Chap VII.

15.3.5 **Civilians**

15.3.5.1 **Defining 'civilians'**

Although the 1907 Hague Regulations laid out certain obligations of an occupying State towards the civilian population,[81] before the troubled era of the 1930s and 1940s it was rare that civilians were subject to direct attack. The 1949 Fourth Geneva Convention was, accordingly, the first treaty to focus on the protection of civilian persons in times of armed conflict. The Fourth Geneva Convention lays out a comprehensive regime, including respect for the individual person, honour, convictions, and religious practices of civilians, the prohibition of torture and other cruel, inhuman, and degrading treatment, hostage-taking, and reprisals.[82] 'Civilians' constitute a residual category; they neither are combatants nor fall within another subcategory of protected persons, such as wounded and sick combatants, medical personnel, or POWs. AP I defines a civilian as any person who is not a combatant; in cases of doubt, the person is to be considered a civilian.[83]

15.3.5.2 **Civilians in situations of belligerent occupation**

The need for protection of civilians is particularly acute when the nationals of one belligerent State find themselves 'in the power' of another belligerent State, whether they are in the territory of an enemy State or in territory under 'belligerent occupation'.[84] According to the Hague Regulations, territory is considered to be occupied 'when it is actually placed under the authority of the hostile army . . . and where such authority has been established and can be exercised',[85] even if there has been no resistance.[86] In other words, the 'Occupying Power' must have displaced the ousted government and substituted its *de facto* authority. That test of actual control was applied by the ICJ in *Armed Activities in the Congo (Democratic Republic of the Congo v Uganda)*, where it required a demonstration that Ugandan forces were both stationed in the territory of the Congo and had in fact substituted their authority for that of the Congolese government.[87] According to the Eritrea–Ethiopia Claims Commission, however, the protections laid out in international humanitarian law 'should not be cast into doubt because

[81] The Hague Regulations (n 49) are recognized as customary international law: see *Construction of a Wall* (n 25) 172; and *Armed Activities in the Territory of the Congo (Democratic Republic of the Congo v Uganda), Judgment, ICJ Reports 2005*, p 168, 229.

[82] GC IV (n 11) Arts 27–34. See also the 1907 Hague Regulations (n 49), an earlier attempt at regulating such activities.

[83] See AP I (n 11) Art 50(1); and the earlier GC IV (n 11) Art 4.

[84] Relevant literature on the law of occupation abounds: see, e.g., E Benvenisti, *The International Law of Occupation* (2nd edn, OUP, 2012); Y Dinstein, *The International Law of Belligerent Occupation* (CUP, 2009); S Wills, 'Occupation Law and Multi-National Operations: Problems and Perspectives' (2006) 77 BYBIL 256; and the special edition on occupation in (2012) 94 IRRC.

[85] Hague Regulations (n 49) Art 42. This article was specifically confirmed as customary international law by the ICJ in *Construction of a Wall* (n 25) 167; and *Armed Activities in the Territory of the Congo* (n 76) 229.

[86] See Geneva Conventions I–IV (n 11) Common Art 2(2).

[87] *Armed Activities* (n 76) 230. On the relationship between occupation and control more generally, see N Kalandarishvili-Mueller, *Occupation and Control in International Humanitarian Law* (Routledge, 2020).

the belligerents dispute the status of territory . . . respecting international protections in such situations does not prejudice the status of the territory'.[88]

A robust series of obligations bind the 'Occupying Power' (the State in actual control) in occupied territory. These include:

- an obligation to respect the laws in force in the occupied territory, which include relevant human rights obligations;[89]
- a prohibition of individual or mass forcible transfers of civilians from occupied territory, including a prohibition on the transfer of its own civilian population into that territory;[90]
- the protection of private property from confiscation, pillage, or reprisals;[91]
- the humane treatment of protected persons, without discrimination, and, in particular, their family rights, religious convictions, and practices, manners, and customs;[92]
- the proper functioning of institutions devoted to the care and education of children;[93] and
- ensuring adequate food and medical supplies and services for the population.[94]

CASE SPOTLIGHT ***ICJ, Policies and Practices of Israel in the Occupied Palestinian Territory, Advisory Opinion of 19 July 2024***

Since the 1967 Six-Day War, in which Israel defeated a coalition of its Arab neighbours, Israel has exerted control over non-contiguous Palestinian territories in the West Bank, the Gaza Strip, and East Jerusalem. In 2024, the ICJ responded to a request of the General Assembly as to the legal consequences of Israel's sustained occupation of these territories.

Though contested by Israel, it is widely recognized that the status of Israel in these territories is that of an 'Occupying Power', and according to numerous UN organs, in these territories it is thus bound by the Geneva Conventions and the rules on occupation (see ICJ, *Construction of a Wall in the Occupied Palestinian Territory*, 2004, para 78; *Policies and Practices of Israel in the Occupied Palestinian Territory*, 2024, paras 86–90), the Security Council (Resolutions 242 (22 November 1967) and 2334 (23 December 2016)), and the General Assembly (Resolutions 77/208 (15 December 2022)).

[88] Eritrea–Ethiopia Claims Commission, *Partial Award: Central Front, Ethiopia's Claim 2* (28 April 2004), XXVI RIAA 155, para 28.

[89] Hague Regulations (n 49) Art 43; *Construction of a Wall* (n 25) 178 *et seq*; *Armed Activities* (n 76) 231, 242–3. See also Wills (n 79) 265 *et seq.*

[90] GC IV (n 11) Art 49. This issue came particularly to the fore in *Construction of a Wall* (n 25) 183–4, where the ICJ declared that 'the Israeli settlements established in the Occupied Palestinian Territory, including East Jerusalem, have been established in breach of international law'.

[91] Hague Regulations (n 49) Arts 46–7; GC IV (n 11) Art 33. But see Hague Regulations, Art 53(2), which allows for the requisition of private property for military purposes, subject to restitution and compensation fixed when peace is made.

[92] GC IV (n 11) Art 27.

[93] *Ibid*, Art 50.

[94] *Ibid*, Arts 55–6.

In 2004–5, Israel implemented a 'Disengagement Plan' from the Gaza Strip, dismantling Israeli settlements and withdrawing its physical military presence, though retaining control over airspace, territorial waters, land borders, the flow of goods and persons in and out of Gaza, and other functions. Israel asserted that since it had 'no permanent physical presence' in Gaza, it was thus no longer an Occupying Power bearing obligations towards Gaza's population (for a summary of this view, see Israeli Supreme Court (*A and B v State of Israel* (Appeal Decision)), Criminal Appeal Nos 6659/06, 1757/07, 8228/07, and 3261/08 (11 June 2008) (Israel SC), ILDC 1069 (IL 2008)).

In 2024, the ICJ clarified that because Israel had previously established its authority in Gaza, and that notwithstanding its physical military withdrawal, Israel still bears obligations under the law of occupation, 'to the extent that it remains capable of exercising, and continues to exercise, elements of its authority in place of the local government . . . even more so since [the atrocities committed by Hamas on] 7 October 2023'; Israel's obligations under the law of occupation 'remained commensurate with the degree of its effective control over Gaza' (*Policies and Practices of Israel*, paras 93–4).

The Court also devoted many paragraphs to examine Israel's settlement policy in the West Bank and East Jerusalem, and concluded that in the light of numerous violations of the international law on belligerent occupation, including the settlement of Israeli civilians (paras 115–9), the confiscation or requisitioning of land (paras 120–3), the forced displacement of Palestinians (paras 142–7), violence by settlers against Palestinians (paras 149–152), and unnecessary or disproportionate force against Palestinians by Israeli security forces (paras 153–154), Israel's settlement policy constituted a violation of international law (paras 155–6).

Though the Court also examined certain practices tantamount to annexation and the offending scope of discriminatory legislation, the most striking conclusion in the advisory opinion was at paragraph 261, where it concluded that the 'sustained abuse by Israel of its position as an occupying Power' violated 'fundamental principles of international law and renders Israel's presence in the Occupied Palestinian Territory unlawful'. Such a finding is highly unusual; as with many rules of IHL, belligerent occupation is generally regarded as a factual situation entailing the respect for certain obligations, and the Court did not seem to base its finding of illegal occupation on the manner in which Israel had come to control the Occupied Palestinian Territory. Moreover, the Court took pains to emphasize that despite the illegality of its occupation, Israel was not released from its obligations under the law of occupation towards the Palestinian population (para 264).

The 2024 advisory opinion has drawn unprecedented attention to the Court, and its full implications within international law may take years to be clearly observed: but already in September 2024, the General Assembly voted overwhelmingly to demand an immediate end to Israel's unlawful occupation of the Occupied Palestinian Territory, as well as Israel's compliance with other obligations stipulated by the Court in its opinion (see A/RES/ES-10/24 (18 September 2024), paras 2–3).

An Occupying Power must take measures to preserve cultural property situated in occupied territory and damaged by military operations.[95] Moreover, though an Occupying Power may utilize certain public property to meet its security needs, the essential needs of the population, and to defray the administrative costs of the occupation, it may only

[95] See, generally, the 1954 Hague Convention on the Protection of Cultural Property in Armed Conflict (n 20).

do so as 'administrator and usufructuary'.[96] This rule was acknowledged by the US–UK-led Provisional Coalition Authority in Iraq, which undertook to 'ensure that Iraq's oil is protected and used for the benefit of the Iraqi people'.[97]

15.4 Conduct of hostilities

As with the protection of victims of armed conflicts, many provisions govern the conduct of hostilities: in short, the methods and means through which warfare is carried out, and which apply across the law of armed conflict.

15.4.1 The principle of distinction

15.4.1.1 The interaction between distinction, proportionality, and precaution

According to the ICJ, a 'cardinal principle' of the law of armed conflict is the 'rule of distinction', a rule of customary international law enshrined in Article 48 of AP I.[98] The said rule embodies an obligation to protect the civilian population and civilian objects, and to distinguish these at all times from combatants and military objectives, which may be targeted in military operations.[99] A belligerent State is thus prohibited from committing any acts designed to spread terror among the civilian population,[100] or from removing objects indispensable for their survival, such as foodstuffs or water supplies.[101]

Though Article 51 of AP I prohibits the targeting of civilians and the civilian population, it may be that certain persons 'take a direct part in hostilities', in that they engage in specific, unorganized hostile acts in the context of a wider armed conflict.[102] In such cases, there is a 'temporary, activity-based loss' of the protections afforded to civilians, as they have become 'direct participants in hostilities'.[103] There must be a clear link between their participation and their loss of protection: a civilian must be actively

[96] Hague Regulations (n 49) Art 55. The concept of 'usufruct' derives from Roman law and is common in many civil law systems, but not in common law-derived legal systems: it denotes a right to enjoy the use and advantages of the property of another, but not the right to destroy or alienate the property as though it were one's own. An imperfect analogy can be made to the common law institution of the 'trust'.

[97] See Letter from the United States and United Kingdom to the President of the Security Council (8 May 2003), UN Doc S/2003/538. The occupation of Iraq (2003–5) is meticulously detailed in Benvenisti (n 79) ch 9. See also ICJ, *Policies and Practices of Israel in the Occupied Palestinian Territory, Advisory Opinion of 19 July 2024* paras 124–33, in which the Court declared that Israel's exploitation of natural resources in the Occupied Palestinian Territory had been inconsistent with such obligations.

[98] *Nuclear Weapons* (n 2) 257.

[99] *Ibid*; Dinstein (n 9) ch 4. See also AP I (n 11) Art 57(5), where no feasible precautions are sufficient to authorize attacks against the civilian population, civilians, or civilian objects.

[100] AP I (n 11) Art 51(2).

[101] *Ibid*, Art 54.

[102] See, e.g., *ibid*, Arts 43(2), 51(3), and 67(1)(e); and AP II (n 11) Art 13(3).

[103] AP I (n 11) Art 51(3). See N Melzer (ed), *Interpretative Guidance on Direct Participation in Hostilities* (ICRC, 2009), 44–5; *cf* MN Schmitt, 'The Interpretive Guidance on the Notion of Direct Participation in Hostilities: A Critical Analysis' (2010) 1 Harvard National Security Journal 5; and Dinstein (n 9) 174 *et seq*.

preparing the execution of, or in fact executing, a specific act of direct participation of hostilities at the moment of attack.[104] Under Article 45 of AP I, civilians directly participating in hostilities are not afforded the protections of combatants and, if captured, they do not acquire POW status; however, under Article 45(3), they do enjoy the minimum guarantees afforded to all persons under Article 75 AP I.

Under Article 52(2) AP I, military objectives are limited to those objects (persons, installations, targets) which 'by their nature, location, purpose, or use make an effective contribution to military action and whose total or partial destruction, capture or neutralization, in the circumstances ruling at that time, offers a definite military advantage'. Such advantages must be concrete, and an attack cannot be launched if it only offers 'potential or indeterminate advantages'.[105] Nevertheless, the definition in Article 52(2) grants the attacking States a certain degree of discretion, subject to respect for the principle of proportionality. Through this principle, 'incidental' civilian casualties or damage to civilian objects (reduced to 'collateral damage') sustained during an otherwise lawful attack on a military target are legally tolerated so long as they are not 'excessive in relation to the concrete and direct military advantage anticipated'.[106] It bears emphasizing that proportionality is not measured merely in relation to numbers, but is a rather indeterminate standard which takes into account the military advantage to be gained by the operation as a whole.[107] In this respect, considerable deference is given to the military objectives as by the attacking State, and though the law seeks to uphold some balance, the application of proportionality remains a highly contested notion in practice.[108]

As an attempt to forestall unlimited discretion, Article 57 of AP I imposes a number of obligations concerning 'precautions in attack'. These include 'passive precautions' in paragraph 1, with 'constant care' required in order to avoid or minimize loss of civilian life, injury to civilians, and damage to civilian objects. They also include 'active precautions': under paragraph 2(a), parties must take all feasible measures to distinguish civilians and civilian objects from military objectives, as well as take all feasible precautions in the choice of means and methods of attack to avoid or minimize civilian suffering. They must, in most cases, give 'effective advance warning' of any attacks which may affect the civilian population (paragraph 2(c)). Though there are few authoritative decisions that illustrate the scope of this provision, in 2005 the Eritrea–Ethiopia Claims Commission determined that the dropping of a cluster bomb by an Eritrean aircraft

[104] See Melzer (n 98) 65; UK, *Manual of Military Law* (HMSO, 1958), paras 86, 634, and somewhat obliquely, *Joint Service Manual on the Law of Armed Conflict*, JSP 393 (JDCC, 2004), para 2.5.2; Switzerland, *Basic Military Manual* (1987), art 66(1); Germany, *Military Manual* (1992), §302.

[105] See Pictet, ICRC Commentary (n 35) paras 2024, 2028.

[106] AP I (n 11) Art 57(2). The proportionality test embodied in Art 57 was regarded as customary international law in *Prosecutor v Kupreškic and others* (Judgment) IT-95-16 (14 January 2000), para 524; and by the Ethiopia–Eritrea Claims Commission, *Partial Award: Central Front* (n 83) paras 17, 110.

[107] See Green (n 61) 311; see also the position of the UK, in A Roberts and R Guelff (eds), *Documents on the Law of War* (3rd edn, OUP, 2000), 511.

[108] J Gardam, 'Proportionality and Force in International Law' (1993) 87 AJIL 391; J Klabbers, 'Off Limits? International Law and the Excessive Use of Force' (2006) 7 Theoretical Inquiries in Law 59; and E-C Gillard, 'Proportionality in the Conduct of Hostilities: The Incidental Harm Side of the Assessment' (Chatham House Research Paper, 10 December 2018).

over an Ethiopian area, causing many civilian casualties, was in breach of this provision as the pilots had not taken all feasible precautions before the conduct of the strike.[109] In 2024, a UN Commission of Inquiry found that, despite the fact that an RPG rocket had been fired at Israel forces from a house in Be'eri, the firing of tank shells by Israeli forces against that house violated the principles of distinction, precaution, and proportionality due to the knowledge that there were civilians inside.[110]

15.4.1.2 **'Dual-use' objects**

Certain installations or objects—for example, a naval base or a munitions factory—are intrinsically military; however, a challenge arises as to how to classify an installation or object that might have both military and civilian purposes, or 'dual-use'.[111] There is no mention of 'dual-use' objects in AP I, though Article 52(3) AP I stipulates that in cases of doubt as to 'whether an object which is normally dedicated to civilian purposes' is being used for military operations, 'it shall be presumed not to be so used'. If being used for military operations, even if dual-use, then it is a legitimate military objective under the principle of distinction, with the civilian impact being assessed in relation to whether the attack was proportionate and appropriate precautions have been taken. Such pragmatism arises because of the possibility of abuse by another party, for example to hide military installations within civilian-populated areas in an act of subterfuge (so-called 'human shields'). In 2023 and 2024, virtually all Israeli strikes that have killed civilians in Gaza and now in Lebanon have been justified by Israel on the basis that Hamas and Hezbollah leaders had been embedding themselves within the civilian population.[112]

A classic example of a dual-use installation was the Radio-Television Serbia (RTS) headquarters building in the centre of Belgrade, bombed by NATO in 1999. Though normally used to transmit news and entertainment to civilians, NATO emphasized the dual-use character of the building, in that it served as a back-up communications transmitter and radio relay stations for the Serbian military and special police forces. NATO's decision to bomb the building was taken after an assessment of collateral damage, after which it distributed leaflets and sent advance warning of the bombing, which was timed for the middle of the night, during which the smallest possible number of civilian employees were likely to be present. Sixteen civilians were killed, leading to an unsuccessful claim before the European Court of Human Rights in the *Banković* case,[113]

[109] See Ethiopia–Eritrea Claims Commission, *Partial Award: Central Front* (n 83) paras 110–13.

[110] Independent International Commission of Inquiry on the Occupied Palestinian Territory, including East Jerusalem, and Israel, 'Detailed findings on attacks carried out on and after 7 October 2023 in Israel', UN Doc A/HRC/56/CRP.3 (10 June 2024), esp paras 278–98.

[111] Many of these possible dual-use objects, such as bridges, roads, and power stations, were considered by the Eritrea–Ethiopia Claims Commission, *Partial Award: Western Front, Aerial Bombardment and Related Claims, Eritrea's Claims 1, 3, 5, 9–13, 14, 21, 25, and 26* (19 December 2005), XXVI RIAA 291, at para 113, which also concluded that Art 52 of AP I (n 11) is customary international law.

[112] See, e.g., IDF Press Release, 'Over 1300 Hezbollah Targets Struck Over the Last Day' (24 September 2024); IDF Press Release, 'Hidden Weapons Located in a Multi-Story Building and a Terrorist's apartment in the Gaza City Area' (20 July 2024).

[113] *Banković and others v Belgium and 16 other Contracting Parties also Parties to the North Atlantic Treaty* App No 52207/99 (ECtHR, 19 December 2001).

declared inadmissible on the basis that the territory was not under the jurisdiction of the respondent States. This proved to be a controversial judgment, limiting the extraterritorial application of human rights law.[114] Later, an ICTY fact-finding report concluded that NATO had taken all required precautions in the attack to minimize collateral damage, and complied with the principles of proportionality and distinction in targeting.[115]

15.4.2 **Regulation of permissible weapons**

15.4.2.1 **General principles**

In the context of hostilities, belligerent parties do not have the unfettered discretion to choose the means and methods of warfare.[116] It is balanced by the second 'cardinal principle' of IHL, the 'principle of humanity'. As the Court found in *Legality of the Threat or Use of Nuclear Weapons,* 'it is prohibited to cause unnecessary suffering to combatants. It is accordingly prohibited to use weapons causing them such harm or uselessly aggravating their suffering.'[117] The Court found that these fundamental rules bind all States, irrespective of whether they were parties to the relevant treaties, as they constituted 'intransgressible principles of international customary law'.[118] Despite the inherent suffering caused by armed violence, such rules are at least a palliative, aiming to limit indiscriminate or 'unnecessary suffering', in the detached language of Article 22 of the Hague Regulations.

A broad range of treaties prohibit various categories of weapons, including, *inter alia*, explosive and 'dum-dum' (expanding) bullets,[119] poisonous weapons and gases, including asphyxiating gases,[120] bacteriological (biological) weapons,[121] chemical weapons,[122] landmines,[123] weapons with a widespread, long-lasting, or severe effect on the environment,[124] blinding laser weapons,[125] and cluster munitions.[126] In early 2021, the Treaty

[114] See R Lawson, 'Life after *Banković:* On the Extraterritorial Application of the European Convention on Human Rights' in F Coomans and M Kamminga (eds), *Extraterritorial Application of Human Rights Treaties* (Intersentia, 2004), 83; see also, generally, M Milanović, *Extraterritorial Application of Human Rights Treaties* (OUP, 2011).

[115] ICTY, *Final Report to the Prosecutor by the Committee established to Review the NATO Bombing Campaign against the Federal Republic of Yugoslavia* (2000) 39 ILM 1257, paras 71–9. See also WJ Fenrick, 'Targeting and Proportionality during the NATO Bombing Campaign against Yugoslavia' (2001) 12 EJIL 489; JA Burger, 'International Humanitarian Law and the Kosovo Crisis' (2000) 82 IRRC 129; P Rowe, 'Kosovo 1999: The Air Campaign' (2000) 82 IRRC 147.

[116] See AP I (n 11) Art 53; and Hague Regulations (n 49) Art 22.

[117] *Nuclear Weapons* (n 2) 257, commenting on Hague Regulations (n 49) Art 23(3) and AP I (n 11) Art 35(2).

[118] *Ibid.* [119] 1899 Hague Declaration (3), concerning Expanding Bullets (29 July 1899).

[120] 1899 Hague Declaration (2), concerning Asphyxiating Poisonous Gases (29 July 1899); and Protocol for the Prohibition of the Use in War of Asphyxiating Poisonous or Other Gases, and of Bacteriological Methods of Warfare (signed 17 June 1925, entered into force 8 February 1928), 94 LNTS 65.

[121] 1972 Biological Weapons Convention (n 21). [122] 1993 Chemical Weapons Convention (n 23).

[123] 1997 Ottawa Landmines Convention (n 24).

[124] 1977 Environmental Modification Convention (n 22); see also AP I (n 11) Arts 35(3), 55.

[125] Protocol IV (1995) to the Convention on Prohibitions or Restrictions on the Use of Certain Conventional Weapons which may be Deemed to be Excessively Injurious or to have Indiscriminate Effects (signed 10 October 1980, entered into force 2 December 1983), 1342 UNTS 137.

[126] 2008 Convention on Cluster Munitions (adopted 30 May 2008, entered into force 1 August 2010), 2688 UNTS 39.

Prohibiting Nuclear Weapons entered into force, though without the ratification of any declared nuclear power.[127] It has been pointed out, moreover, that generally a weapon comes to be prohibited not when it is particularly deadly but, rather, at the moment it is no longer in use, perhaps replaced by newer, more devastating technologies.[128] For example, white phosphorus, used by many major military powers for its obscurant or illuminating effect, is unregulated despite its burning and asphyxiating effects, as witnessed in its use in Fallujah by occupying forces against Iraqi insurgents in 2004.[129]

15.4.2.2 **The unresolved status of nuclear weapons**

A conspicuous uncertainty clouds the legal status of nuclear weapons. From the 1960s to the 1980s, frequent condemnations were made by the General Assembly, without the support of Western States;[130] however, such resolutions are not binding, and the ICJ's analysis of these specific resolutions in 1996 found them falling short of establishing the requisite *opinio juris* to crystallize a customary prohibition on such weapons.[131] States were only able to agree on the Nuclear Non-Proliferation Treaty (NPT),[132] a compromise solution which allowed the five declared nuclear powers at the time (all veto-wielding members of the Security Council) to continue to maintain their nuclear arsenals. However, other States that have since detonated a nuclear weapon refuse to become parties: India, Pakistan, North Korea, and Israel.[133] Iran, a party to the NPT, demilitarized its nuclear programme in 2016 after a Joint Comprehensive Plan of Action (JCPOA) involving the five permanent members of the Security Council and Germany. However, in 2018 US President Trump announced the USA's unilateral withdrawal from the JCPOA, a situation that remained in effect as of late 2024. In April 2017 a major escalation occurred when North Korea (a non-party to the NPT) tested a ballistic missile and the USA threatened sanctions against it. This tension culminated in an unprecedented North Korea–US summit in Singapore on 12 June 2018, where a joint statement on security and the denuclearization of the Korean peninsula was issued.[134] Though in October 2020 North Korea unveiled nuclear ballistic missiles capable of crossing the Pacific, and in January 2021 unveiled submarine-launched ballistic missiles, the Security Council has not yet taken any action in respect of North Korea's

[127] Treaty on the Prohibition of Nuclear Weapons (signed 20 September 2017, entered into force 22 January 2021), 3379 UNTS (page number not yet determined), UN Treaty No. 56487.

[128] Jochnick and Normand (n 3) 69–70.

[129] See 'US Defends Use of White Phosphorus Munitions in Iraq' (2006) 100 AJIL 487; *cf* Israeli Ministry of Foreign Affairs, *The Operation in Gaza: Factual and Legal Aspects* (July 2009), paras 406–30; and UK Ministry of Defence, *The Manual of the Law of Armed Conflict* (OUP, 2004), para 6.1.2.

[130] UNGA Res 1653 (XVI) (24 November 1961); UNGA Res 2936 (XXVII) (29 November 1972); UNGA Res 36/92 (9 December 1981).

[131] See *Nuclear Weapons* (n 2) 254–5.

[132] Treaty on the Non-Proliferation of Nuclear Weapons (signed 1 July 1968, entered into force 5 March 1970), 729 UNTS 161.

[133] See Stockholm International Peace Research Institute (SIPRI) Yearbook 2014 (OUP, 2014). Israel remains an 'undeclared power', as it does not acknowledge that it possesses nuclear weapons.

[134] The Joint Statement can be found online at <https://www.bbc.co.uk/news/world-asia-44453330>.

nuclear programme, following a veto by Russia in 2024 that would have extended the mandate of a Panel of Experts assisting the '1718 DPRK Sanctions Committee'.[135]

The ICJ has occasionally considered the delicate question of nuclear weapons, though has provided little further clarity, and often dismissed claims due to a lack of jurisdiction or their inadmissibility. A 1974 dispute regarding French nuclear tests in the South Pacific, filed by Australia and New Zealand, did not proceed to the merits following a French unilateral declaration that it would conduct no further tests.[136] A request for an advisory opinion filed by the World Health Organization in 1994 was rejected due to the question falling outside the scope of the organization's activities (*ultra vires*).[137] Most recently, the Marshall Islands initiated proceedings against three nuclear States—India, Pakistan, and the UK—regarding a breach of the obligation to disarm contained in Article VI of the NPT. All three cases were dismissed for want of jurisdiction in late 2016.[138]

It was only in response to the General Assembly's request for an advisory opinion in *Legality of the Threat or Use of Nuclear Weapons*[139] that the Court proceeded in 1996 to give its view on the question; and made several contributions to understanding the law applicable to nuclear weapons. The Court concluded that no specific or express prohibition of nuclear weapons existed in positive international law; it rejected an analogy with the use of poisonous gases[140] and an extension of the obligation to protect the natural environment so as to prohibit the use of nuclear weapons.[141] However, the Court declared that the use of nuclear weapons was nevertheless subject to the law of armed conflict: for example, the prohibitions on unnecessary suffering,[142] the principle of distinction,[143] and the principle of proportionality of the means of warfare chosen.[144] Given the technical challenges in controlling a nuclear explosion, it is inherently difficult to use them precisely against a target. In a somewhat vague statement, the Court declared that in this light, it would 'generally be contrary' to the law of armed conflict to use nuclear weapons.[145] However, this statement must be contrasted with the very next statement, that the Court could not 'conclude definitively whether the threat or use of nuclear weapons would be lawful or unlawful in an extreme circumstance of self-defence, in which the very survival of a State would be at stake'.[146] This passage is a most notorious conclusion in the Opinion, and split the Court evenly, with the casting vote of the president being invoked only for the second time in the history of the PCIJ and ICJ. Though hardly surprising, in light of the ambiguity of the law itself, the Court's

[135] See UN Doc S/PV.9591 (28 March 2024).

[136] See *Nuclear Tests (Australia v France; New Zealand v France), Jurisdiction and Admissibility, ICJ Reports 1974*, p 253, p 457. See also I Scobbie, 'Discontinuance in the International Court: The Enigma of the *Nuclear Tests* Cases' (1992) 41 ICLQ 808.

[137] *Legality of the Use by a State of Nuclear Weapons in Armed Conflict, Advisory Opinion, ICJ Reports 1996*, p 66, para 31.

[138] These three cases all turned on slightly different facts, and specificities over the UK's conduct meant that the bench was evenly divided, with the case only dismissed by the casting vote of the president: see *Obligations concerning Negotiations relating to Cessation of the Nuclear Arms Race and to Nuclear Disarmament (Marshall Islands v United Kingdom), Preliminary Objections, ICJ Reports 2016*, p 833.

[139] *Ibid*, 833. [140] *Ibid*, 247–8. [141] *Ibid*, 241–3. [142] *Ibid*, 262. [143] *Ibid*, 257.

[144] *Ibid*, 246. [145] *Ibid*, 266, para 105(2)(E) of the *dispositif*. [146] *Ibid*, 266.

ambivalence has been widely criticized and studied in international legal scholarship, and serves to illustrate the challenges faced by the Court in addressing this politically sensitive question.[147]

15.5 Questions of implementation and enforcement

As with many other areas of international law, the enforcement and implementation of the law of armed conflict remains its Achilles' heel. The outbreak of warfare, by definition, seemed to exclude other avenues for dispute settlement, and belligerents have proven reluctant to submit to external scrutiny, preferring to take matters into their own hands. Over time, a number of implementation and enforcement measures have been developed to mitigate the lack of external oversight, though these do not fully ensure the enforcement of IHL.

THEORY AND DEBATES The Emergence of 'Drones'

In recent years, the use of unmanned aerial vehicles (UAVs), commonly known as 'drones', has both become increasingly frequent and controversial. For the last decade, the USA has been using drones in Yemen, Afghanistan, and some areas of Pakistan to effect 'targeted killings' of purported terrorists, asserting that there exists no prohibition on the use of drones in IHL. Interestingly, the USA takes the view that the 'war on terror' campaign already puts it into a situation of armed conflict (*jus in bello*), allowing the USA to dispense with criminal prosecution and to target individuals in order to pre-empt terror attacks, even though they are located on the territory of other States. In response to criticism, in 2013 then-US President Obama issued 'Presidential Policy Guidance' which sought to regulate the use of drones, in effect incorporating a very high duty to take precautionary measures to protect the civilian population, and imposing Congressional oversight *ex post facto*.

It is true that, as with nuclear weapons, no specific prohibition exists on the use of drones; at best, they are subject to the requirements of IHL (see, e.g., MS Schmitt, '"Drone Attacks" under the *Jus ad Bellum* and *Jus in Bello:* Clearing the "Fog of Law"' (2010) 13 Yearbook of International Humanitarian Law 311). Moreover, many States use operational armed drones, with striking recent examples including their extensive use by both Russia and Ukraine against one another since 2022; Iran launching drones against Israel in April 2024; and drone attacks against Israel by Houthis in Yemen and Hezbollah in Lebanon. Israel has also made extensive use of tactical drones in Gaza after 7 October 2023. That said, even with recent advances, drones are not necessarily more accurate than human-controlled weapons, with 'collateral' civilian casualties still being reported in high ratios. This raises important questions with respect to the compliance of drone attacks with the cardinal principle of distinction.

[147] D Akande, 'Nuclear Weapons, Unclear Law?' (1997) 68 BYBIL 165; L Boisson de Chazournes and P Sands (eds), *International Law, the International Court of Justice and Nuclear Weapons* (CUP, 1999). On the Court's declaration of a *non liquet* in the Opinion, see also G Hernández, *The International Court of Justice and the Judicial Function* (OUP, 2014), ch VIII.

Finally, there is of course scholarly discussion which criticizes the phenomenon of drones from a non-legal perspective, illuminating the dehumanizing effects entailed by the remote deployment of lethal force at the touch of a button, and the terror that drone strikes can instil in a civilian population: see, for example, R Mignot-Madhavi, *Drones and International Law: A Techno-Legal Theory* (CUP, 2023); G Chamayou, *Drone Theory* (J Lloyd tr, Penguin, 2015). The debate continues.

15.5.1 **The law on belligerent reprisals**

Belligerent reprisals or counter-attacks, or the ability of a State to breach the law of armed conflict in response to a prior violation by an enemy, are the most rudimentary form of redress. Such controversial practices include the starvation of civilians, the execution of POWs, or the defilement of occupied territory.

Due to their controversial and reprehensible nature, in recent years belligerent reprisals are increasingly constrained, in parallel with the development of countermeasures in general international law covered in Chapter 13. Today, 'belligerent reprisals' are only permitted if: they are a last resort; the decision to do so is taken at the highest level; their purpose is to ensure the termination of the prior unlawful act of the enemy and a return to legality; and they are proportionate to the prior unlawful act.[148] Importantly, proportionality is measured here against the prior illegal act, and is, as such, a 'tit for tat' or retaliatory measure. This is a different proportionality test than in the law on self-defence, in which it is measured against the means necessary to bring about an end to an armed attack.[149] An illustration of such retaliatory measures is the 2024 series of escalating Israeli and Iranian missile strikes against one another justified by both States as being retaliatory responses.[150]

There are certain categories of acts which are now expressly prohibited under the law of armed conflict, even if taken as reprisals. For example, belligerents in an IAC are prohibited from targeting the civilian population for the purpose of reprisal.[151] Furthermore, the Geneva Conventions and AP I have explicitly prohibited in all circumstances the targeting of: POWs;[152] the wounded, sick, or shipwrecked, medical personnel or units, or religious personnel;[153] cultural objects and places of worship;[154]

[148] See Green (n 61) 148–9; V Bílková, 'Belligerent Reprisals in Non-International Armed Conflicts' (2014) 63 ICLQ 31; J-M Henckaerts and L Doswald-Beck (eds), *Customary International Humanitarian Law* (CUP, 2005), vol 1, rule 145, 516; CJ Greenwood, 'Reprisals and Reciprocity in the New Law of Armed Conflict' in MA Meyer (ed), *Armed Conflict in the New Law: Aspects of the 1977 Geneva Protocols and the 1981 Weapons Convention* (BIICL, 1989), 227.

[149] See Chapter 14, Section 14.3.2.

[150] Both States made public representations on the retaliatory nature of their attacks. See also the statement of the Secretary-General to the Security Council, UN Doc SG/SM/22400 (2 October 2024), in which he termed these retaliatory measures as 'tit-for-tat violence'.

[151] AP I (n 11) Art 52. With respect to NIAC, this principle is somewhat more controversial, as was illustrated in *Prosecutor v Zoran Kupreškić et al* (Judgment) IT-95-16 (14 January 2000).

[152] See the entirety of GC III (n 11).

[153] AP I (n 11) Art 20.

[154] *Ibid*, Art 53.

foodstuffs, water supplies, and other objects indispensable for the survival of the civilian population;[155] and works or installations 'containing dangerous forces' (which can wreak devastating damage if destroyed), namely dams, dykes, and nuclear generating stations.[156]

15.5.2 **The assumption of international responsibility**

As Chapter 10 explained, a State in breach of an international obligation is required to provide reparation for that breach.[157] This core principle also extends to the law of armed conflict: in Article 3 of the Hague Regulations, restated in Article 91 of AP I, such reparation is to take the form of financial compensation.

An agreement on reparations has often been imposed as part of a peace settlement between States. After the 1871 Franco-Prussian War, France was required to pay a war indemnity of 5 million gold francs;[158] and Part VIII of the Treaty of Versailles (1919) required Germany to pay 132 billion gold marks to the Allied Powers in compensation, a debt that was only cleared in 2010.[159] At times, international bodies have overseen the payment of compensation, as was done by the UN Compensation Commission established by the Security Council to process claims for compensation against Iraq after its unlawful invasion and occupation of Kuwait,[160] or through the Eritrea–Ethiopia Claims Commission, established to arbitrate all claims for loss or damage, including violations of the law of armed conflict, which had occurred in the conflict between the two States.[161]

Compensation claimed by an individual against a belligerent State has been more rare, and is often dismissed on the grounds that the State enjoys sovereign immunity for acts of war.[162] What is more, the application of State responsibility in this area does not easily extend to responsibility for violations committed by non-State actors, a problem given the rise in non-international armed conflicts in recent years.

[155] *Ibid*, Art 54. [156] *Ibid*, Art 56. [157] See Chapter 10, Section 10.2,'State responsibility'.

[158] See Treaty of Peace between France and Germany, signed in Frankfurt (10 May 1871).

[159] See C Suddath, 'Why Did World War I Just End?' (*Time*, 4 October 2010).

[160] See UNSC Res 687 (3 April 1991); UNSC Res 692 (20 May 1991).

[161] See Eritrea–Ethiopia Claims Commission, *Partial Awards on Prisoners of War, Ethiopia's Claim 4* (1 July 2003), XXVI RIAA 73, reprinted in (2003) ILM 1056; Eritrea's Claim 17 (1 July 2003), XXVI RIAA 23, reprinted in (2003) ILM 1083.

[162] *Kalogeropoulou and others v Greece and Germany* App no 59021/00 (ECtHR, 12 December 2002); *Filipino ex 'comfort' women v Japanese Government* (Tokyo District Court, 1998, 390); *Sjoerd Albert Lapre and others v Government of Japan* (Tokyo District Court, 1998, 20–40); *Princz v Federal Republic of Germany*, 813 F.Supp 22, 1175 (DDC 1992). There have been exceptions in Greece (see *Prefecture of Voiotia v Germany* (Greek Constitutional Court, 2000, 198–200)) and Italy (*Ferrini v Repubblica Federale di Germania* (Italian Court of Cassation, 2004, 10–30)). However, the immunity of the State against such claims was expressly upheld by the ICJ in *Jurisdictional Immunities of the State (Germany v Italy: Greece intervening), Judgment, ICJ Reports 2012*, p 99, 152.

THEORY AND DEBATES Cyber Technology and the Law of Armed Conflict

Cyberspace, the virtual domain supported by the world's telecommunications infrastructure, is emerging as an important medium in international law. No comprehensive treaty exists to govern cyberspace and the conduct of States and private actors in it. In 2008, Estonia was the subject of widespread 'cyberattacks' against its telecommunications infrastructure, for which Russian 'hackers' were purportedly responsible. A massive cyberattack was also directed at Iranian uranium enrichment facilities in 2010, with claims that the operation was attributable to the USA and Israel. In the ongoing dispute between Ukraine and Russia, Ukraine regularly accuses Russian hackers of interfering, at the behest of the Russian government, with its power grid, financial systems, and other cyber infrastructure.

There are important unresolved challenges existing in respect of cyberspace. Foremost is the question of how to attribute the acts of individual hackers—who are non-State actors—which has implications both for responsibility as well as in the law of armed conflict. The risk of error has increased significantly, as sophisticated concealment techniques emerge: for example, in August 2021 news reports emerged that security vendor FireEye suggested that a Chinese espionage group was targeting Israeli cyber infrastructure, with deliberate efforts such as using the Farsi language, to suggest that their infiltration was the work of Iran.

Another question relates to thresholds: can the damage caused by cyberattacks be of such gravity as to trigger the start of an armed conflict; for example, through the disabling of security protocols so as to damage a building or installation such as a dam? Moreover, what duties of diligence do States owe in relation to the prevention of cyberattacks emanating from their country?

International efforts are ongoing. An International Group of Experts, convened by NATO and the Cooperative Cyber Defence Centre of Excellence (CCDCOE) to study the applicability of existing international law in relation to cyberspace, published the *Tallinn Manual 2.0 on the International Law applicable to Cyber Operations* (CUP, 2017). In 2021, a UN 'Group of Governmental Experts on Advancing Responsible State Behaviour in Cyberspace' (GGE) published a report (see UN Doc A/76/135 (14 July 2021)) focusing on possible cooperative measures to address existing and potential threats in the field of information security. In General Assembly Resolution 75/240 (31 December 2020), the General Assembly established a new five-year 'Open-Ended Working Group' on security of and in the use of information and communications technologies; work remains ongoing.

For further reading in this area, see K Mačák, 'From Cyber Norms to Cyber Rules: Re-engaging States as Law-makers' (2017) 30 Leiden JIL 877; and more generally, F Delerue, *Cyber Operations in International Law* (CUP, 2020).

15.5.3 **Individual criminal responsibility**

It may also be that a breach of IHL rises to the level of a 'serious' violation of the laws and customs of war; it is then known as a 'war crime'. These acts can under special circumstances also be punishable on the same level as crimes against humanity or genocide. Such a crime may trigger the prosecution of an individual before a national court in a number of ways. States have long asserted jurisdiction over their own armed forces under their own national or military law (a 'court martial'). An example is the 2016 investigation by the Iraq Historic Allegations Team in the UK over war crimes committed during the occupation of Iraq.[163] Moreover, the Third Geneva Convention also allows States to prosecute captured enemy combatants for war crimes.[164] As was described in Chapter 8, Sections 8.2.5 and 8.2.6, States are increasingly asserting jurisdiction over individuals who have committed war crimes, no matter their location or even the nationality of the accused. In 2024, a UN Commission of Inquiry investigated various incidents after 7 October 2023 in relation to the Israel-Hamas conflict; it concluded that there were 'reasonable grounds' to establish the existence of a range of war crimes committed during the conflict.[165]

An accused may also face prosecution by one of the increasing number of international criminal tribunals that have been established. The Rome Statute of the International Criminal Court, for example, makes express reference to 'grave breaches' of the Geneva Conventions in its Article 8(2), and enumerates a number of specific crimes, including: torture or inhuman treatment, including biological experiments; pillaging a town or place; the forced displacement of the civilian population; declaring that no quarter will be given; the use of poison, asphyxiating gases, and other weapons which might cause superfluous injury or unnecessary suffering; and the compelling of a POW to serve in the forces of a hostile State. The statutes of the ad hoc tribunals for the former Yugoslavia and Rwanda (ICTY and ICTR), the Special Court for Sierra Leone (SCSL), and the Extraordinary Chambers of the Courts of Cambodia (ECCC) use similar terms when defining war crimes. These are further covered in Chapter 17 of this book.

15.5.4 **Other measures of compliance; the role of the Red Cross**

Finally, a number of less formal measures are available to induce belligerents to comply with IHL. An old international practice, codified across the four Geneva Conventions, allows for the designation of a 'Protecting Power', a neutral State which may be designated to act on behalf of a belligerent and its nationals so as to ensure that the obligations under the Conventions are implemented. Though rarely used in practice,[166] a belligerent would be entitled to designate a Protecting Power, though the consent of all belligerents would be necessary. The Protecting Power would then have access to POW and detention camps, and attend trials of POWs and civilians.[167]

Crucially, across the Conventions, a State Party detaining enemy wounded, shipwrecked, POWs, or civilians is obliged to accept 'the offer of the services of a humanitarian organization, such as the International Committee of the Red Cross, to assume

[163] See K Rawlinson, 'Nearly 300 British veterans face investigation over alleged Iraq war crimes' (*The Guardian*, 9 January 2016).

[164] See GC III (n 11) Arts 82, 85.

[165] Independent International Commission of Inquiry on the Occupied Palestinian Territory, including East Jerusalem, and Israel, 'Detailed findings on attacks carried out on and after 7 October 2023 in Israel', UN Doc A/HRC/56/CRP.3 (10 June 2024), esp paras 278–98.

[166] R Kolb, 'Protecting Powers' in A Clapham, P Gaeta, and M Sassòli (eds), *The 1949 Geneva Conventions: A Commentary* (OUP, 2015), 556–7.

[167] GC I (n 11) Art 10, GC II (n 11), GC III (n 11) Common Arts 8–11; GC IV (n 11) Arts 9–12; AP I (n 11) Art 5.

the humanitarian functions performed by Protecting Powers'.[168] This is but one of the provisions of the Geneva Conventions which accords a special status to the ICRC, an organization that predates them by almost a century and has proved an indispensable actor in the implementation of humanitarian law.[169] The ICRC is a highly active organization that has discharged its mandates under the Geneva Conventions by providing external scrutiny; for example, by visiting POWs, all with a view to monitor respect for IHL. Much of the ICRC's work is based on confidential visits and secret communications with parties to a conflict, and its reports and legal assessments are often only communicated to the belligerents.[170] Though there have been calls for 'naming and shaming', the ICRC continues to hold to the view that a behind-the-scenes approach allows it to preserve its neutrality and to discharge its functions effectively.[171]

15.6 Conclusion: the limits of law in restraining violence

Decades of efforts have brought forward the legal regime that governs the conduct of armed conflict, and aims to alleviate the suffering that it causes. As this chapter has demonstrated, there are now overarching normative rules preserving humanitarian considerations even under the most inhumane of circumstances. Yet, as military technology develops ever more effective means of inflicting violence, the law of armed conflict struggles to keep pace, at times in a piecemeal and iterative manner.

There is, however, a wider concern. Though an absence of any legal rules in armed conflict would be unthinkable, it cannot be denied that the transformation of 'war' into a legal concept has done as much to legitimate violence as to restrain it. By declaring certain types of acts to be entirely lawful and permissible,[172] war is accepted pragmatically as an inevitable social phenomenon, to be controlled through law rather than to be resisted. As a final reflection, perhaps it is useful to think not only about how the law could be made more effective, but more on the value and place of law in the discourse on containing violence.

[168] GC I (n 11) Art 10(3); GC II (n 11) Art 10(3); GC III (n 11) Art 10(3); GC IV (n 11) Arts 10(3), 11(3).

[169] This position has been recognized judicially: see *Construction of a Wall* (n 25) 175–6, where the ICJ referred to the 'special place' of the ICRC with respect to the Fourth Geneva Convention; and the Eritrea–Ethiopia Claims Commission, *Partial Award (Prisoners of War)* (n 153) paras 58, 61–2, in which the Commission found that the ICRC's significant responsibility in respect of providing 'necessary and vital external scrutiny of the treatment of POWs' had entered into customary international law.

[170] The ICRC has broken its silence twice, in the former Yugoslavia in 1995 and in respect of Myanmar in 2007. For the latter, see ICRC, 'Myanmar: ICRC denounces major and repeated violations of international humanitarian law', ICRC News Release 82/07 (29 June 2007).

[171] See ICRC, 'Confidentiality: key to the ICRC's work but not unconditional, Interview with ICRC Deputy Director of Operations' (20 September 2010). See also SR Ratner, 'Behind the Flag of Dunant: Secrecy and the Compliance Mission of the International Committee of the Red Cross' in A Bianchi and A Peters (eds), *Transparency in International Law* (CUP, 2013), 297.

[172] See, in particular, D Kennedy, 'Lawfare and Warfare' in J Crawford and M Koskenniemi (eds), *Cambridge Companion to International Law* (CUP, 2013), 181–2; and, generally, Kennedy, *Of Law and War* (n 3).

Further reading

J d'Aspremont and J de Hemptinne, *Droit international humanitaire: thèmes choisis* (Pedone, 2012).

A clear and succinct French-language introduction to the major debates.

A Clapham and P Gaeta, *The Oxford Handbook of International Law in Armed Conflict* (OUP, 2014).

Gathering leading scholars in the area of the law of armed conflict, this is an indispensable resource covering the entirety of the field.

E Crawford and A Pert, *International Humanitarian Law* (3rd edn, CUP, 2024).

This engaging, freshly updated textbook explains the major concepts very clearly, with a particular focus on accessibility.

E David (ed), *Les principes de droit des conflits armés* (6th edn, Bruylant, 2018).

A spirited reflection on the nature and scope of the law of armed conflicts, with a highly original concluding chapter that addresses the psycho-social root causes of IHL violations.

Y Dinstein, *The Conduct of Hostilities under the Law of International Armed Conflict* (3rd edn, CUP, 2016).

Written by a leading scholar in the field, this monograph captures many of the operational realities of the law of armed conflict, and is a valuable resource for practitioners as well.

D Fleck (ed), *The Handbook of International Humanitarian Law* (4th edn, OUP, 2021).

A magisterial work of value for practitioners and academics, this edited collection is updated regularly.

D Kennedy, *Of Law and War* (Princeton UP, 2005).

An incisive critique of the role that law plays in regulating and legitimating the use of military force.

T Meron, *The Humanization of International Law* (Hague Academy, 2006).

An engaging and eloquent account of changes wrought by the 'humanization' of international law.

C Rousseau, *Le droit des conflits armés* (Pedone, 1983).

A classic, if somewhat dated, French-language work which beautifully captures the underlying tensions in the law of armed conflict.

M Sassolì, *International Humanitarian Law* (2nd edn, Elgar, 2024).

A magisterial, compelling account by a leading proponent of a humanitarian approach to armed conflicts.

S Sivakumaran, *The Law of Non-International Armed Conflict* (OUP, 2012).

This prize-winning monograph provides detailed and thoughtful coverage of the law on non-international armed conflicts.

16

International human rights and refugee law

16.1 Introduction: individuals in a State-centred system

Historically, international law focused on the peaceful coexistence of sovereign, independent States. Save for some rudimentary rules on the protection of aliens (see Chapter 11, Section 11.5), individual human beings could not bear rights or obligations under international law.[1] As with all orthodoxies, however, the view that individuals fell under domestic jurisdiction was gradually eroded by a number of exceptions. A distinct international legal regime protecting human rights emerged after World War II; and with it, the place of the individual in international law has changed significantly.[2]

Though international law has certainly experienced a proliferation of human rights instruments and institutions since 1945, the wider context in which human rights abuses and violations occur is often insufficiently considered. There is controversy about the purported universality of human rights law versus the role of culture in understanding these; issues with enforcement in a State-centric system; and concerns about the relevance of human rights in areas such as trade and environmental protection. In sum, the discourse of 'human rights' remains a contested, and by no means politically neutral, field.

One cannot provide a detailed account of the vast field of international human rights law in just one chapter; instead, the chapter will provide an overarching survey of the various human rights instruments, mechanisms, and institutions that exist at the international and regional levels.[3] Given the recent prominence of refugees, internally displaced persons, and migrants, the regimes addressing them are surveyed briefly in the final section.

[1] For a criticism of this view, see P Alston, *Non-State Actors and Human Rights* (OUP, 2005).

[2] Comprehensive accounts include K Parlett, *The Individual in the International Legal System* (CUP, 2011); A Kjeldgaard-Pedersen, *The International Legal Personality of the Individual* (OUP, 2018); and A Clapham, 'The Role of the Individual in International Law' (2010) 21 EJIL 25.

[3] See the Further Reading at the end of this chapter for literature on the substantive principles of human rights law, such as human dignity or freedom, or debates about fairness, access to justice, and equality.

16.2 The individual in international law

16.2.1 A brief history of the protection of individuals

From the late nineteenth century onwards, States began to accept basic obligations to refrain from mistreating aliens, to protect them from the acts of private citizens, or to compensate them for confiscated or destroyed property.[4] It is the prohibition of slavery and the slave trade which remain the classic illustration of individual protections entering the field of international law. Propelled by the 1807 Slave Trade Act,[5] the UK—the world's largest slave trader in the eighteenth century—exerted pressure on other States to abolish their own slave trades, claiming humanitarian concerns, but perhaps due to concern about slavery's distorting effect on global competition.[6] Though in the 1885 General Act of the Berlin Conference, parties recognized that 'trading in slaves is prohibited in conformity with the principles of international law',[7] States would only accept the prohibition of slavery within their borders with the 1926 Slavery Convention.[8]

HISTORICAL BACKGROUND The League of Nations and the Protection of Individuals

The League of Nations (discussed in Chapter 1, Section 1.4.1) has left a mixed legacy in relation to human rights protection. An infamous incident was the rejection of a Japanese proposal for racial discrimination to be prohibited in the League Covenant. During this period, rights were primarily construed as belonging to groups (ethnic, religious, or linguistic minorities; certain categories of workers; and prisoners of war), rather than individuals. Of course, that paradigm would change with the advent of the UN Charter.

Nonetheless, the League's institutions did contribute to advancing individual protection. Foremost, the League facilitated treaties in respect of the protection of ethnic, linguistic, or religious minorities, primarily in Eastern Europe, which were not given statehood in the 1919 Peace Treaties. Minority rights are addressed in Section 16.3.4.

Moreover, the International Labour Organization (ILO), an agency of the League created under Part XIII of the Treaty of Versailles, was innovative in that it included the participation of States, trade union organizations, and employers' associations. In the first years of the ILO, important conventions were signed in respect of labour standards such as the minimum age to work, night work for women and young persons, and maternity protection (see A Alcock, *A History of the International Labour Organization* (Macmillan, 1971)).

[4] See Chapter 20, Section 20.4.1.

[5] Abolition of the Slave Trade Act 1807 (UK). Slavery itself was outlawed in the British Empire with the Slavery Abolition Act 1833 (UK).

[6] See JJ Martinez, *The Slave Trade and the Origins of International Human Rights Law* (OUP, 2012); JJ Martinez, 'Antislavery Courts and the Dawn of International Human Rights Law' (2008) 117 Yale LJ 550; and V Nanda and MC Bassiouni, 'Slavery and the Slave Trade: Steps Towards Eradication' (1972) 12 Santa Clara LR 424.

[7] General Act of the Berlin Conference, 26 February 1885, C 4361 1885 (UK), Art 9. The 1884–5 Berlin Conference is discussed in Chapter 1, Section 1.3 ('Colonialism and empire').

[8] Convention to Suppress the Slave Trade and Slavery (signed 25 September 1926, entered into force 9 March 1927), 60 LNTS 254.

However, the League also operated a questionable Mandate system created under Articles 22–3 of the League Covenant, under which certain former German and Ottoman territories were administered as a 'sacred trust of civilization'. Though there were certain minimal obligations relating to the rights and welfare of local inhabitants, rights protection was often regarded as subordinated to economic or security considerations, or perhaps even in service of these (for more on the Mandate system, see N Tzouvala, *Capitalism as Civilisation: A History of International Law* (CUP, 2020), ch 2).

Though the League's record in relation to human rights remains decidedly mixed, the innovations pioneered during the League period would set the foundations for future human rights protection.

16.2.2 **International human rights law after 1945**

Though sometimes hailed as a decisive turning point, the adoption of the UN Charter after World War II is a cautious iteration on what had come before. Article 1 set out to achieve 'international co-operation in . . . promoting and encouraging respect for human rights and fundamental freedoms for all without distinction as to race, sex, language, or religion'. However, this must be tempered with the proviso, under Article 2(7), that 'nothing contained in the present Charter shall authorize the United Nations to intervene in matters which are essentially within the jurisdiction of any State'.

Under Article 55 of the Charter, it was provided that the UN 'shall promote universal respect for, and observance of human rights'. Article 56 would give this obligation more depth, binding members to 'take joint and separate action in cooperation with the organisation for the achievement of [human rights purposes]'. With the promotion of human rights being one of the purposes of the organization, a modest institutional framework was created to support it, as well as the establishment of institutions for their effective observation and enforcement.

16.3 Human rights in the UN Charter system

16.3.1 **The Universal Declaration of Human Rights, 1948**

In 1948, the General Assembly adopted the famed Universal Declaration of Human Rights (UDHR).[9] One must be cautious: the UDHR is not itself a legally enforceable treaty, but a resolution of the General Assembly. However, many of its provisions have influenced the adoption of major multilateral treaties, or have come to reflect customary international law,[10] at times through influencing the drafting of State

[9] UNGA Res 217 (III) (10 December 1948). There was no dissenting vote, but the Byelorussian SSR, Czechoslovakia, Poland, Saudi Arabia, Ukrainian SSR, USSR, and Yugoslavia abstained.

[10] Though *cf* B Simma and P Alston, 'The Sources of Human Rights Law: Custom, *Jus Cogens* and General Principles' (1988) 5 Australian YBIL 82, who contend that human rights might better be understood as general principles of law.

constitutions;[11] and frequent reference to the UDHR is made by international courts to interpret obligations contained in certain treaties. As early as 1950, the European Court of Human Rights referred to the UDHR in the *Golder* judgment as an 'aid' in the interpretation of the ECHR.[12] In the 1980 *Hostages in Tehran* judgment, the ICJ invoked the UDHR in interpreting Iran's obligations: 'to subject [hostages] to physical constraint in conditions of hardship is itself manifestly incompatible [with the UN Charter and] with the fundamental principles enunciated in the Universal Declaration of Human Rights'.[13] In this respect, the UDHR is illustrative of how 'soft law'[14] can, over time, emerge to be legally authoritative.

16.3.2 **The International Human Rights Covenants, 1966**

16.3.2.1 **Why two separate human rights covenants?**

It was envisaged from the outset that the UDHR would propel the drafting of a binding, universally applicable 'International Bill of Human Rights'. However, due in part to Cold War politics, progress was achieved only on specific offences for which the Holocaust and other tragedies had provoked universal outrage, such as the 1948 Genocide Convention.

In order to break the impasse, two overarching covenants were adopted separately in 1966: the International Covenant on Civil and Political Rights (ICCPR)[15] and the International Covenant on Economic, Social and Cultural Rights (ICESCR).[16] Taken together, the Covenants embody the aspirations for human rights protection first expressed in the UDHR in legally enforceable form but, by separating the two categories of rights, States could prioritize those rights most important to them.

THEORY AND DEBATES Civil and Political Rights Versus Economic and Social Rights

The Cold War division between States was rooted in differing ideological conceptions regarding the implementation of human rights. Western, primarily developed, States focused on *individual civil and political rights*, or 'first-generation rights', such as freedom of expression,

[11] For a detailed survey of domestic court practice, see H Hannum, 'The Status of the Universal Declaration in National and International Law' (1995) 25 Georgia JICL 287.

[12] *Golder v United Kingdom* (1975) ECHR Ser A No 18, 1 EHRR 524.

[13] *United States Diplomatic and Consular Staff in Tehran (United States v Islamic Republic of Iran), Judgment, ICJ Reports 1980*, p 3.

[14] See Chapter 2, Section 2.3.4.

[15] International Covenant on Civil and Political Rights (signed 16 December 1966, entered into force 23 March 1976), 993 UNTS 3 (174 States parties). The ICCPR is accompanied by two optional protocols: one relates to the processing of individual communications (23 March 1976, 116 States parties), 999 UNTS 171; the second relates to the abolition of the death penalty (15 December 1989, ninety-one States parties), 1642 UNTS 414.

[16] International Covenant on Economic, Social, and Cultural Rights (signed 19 December 1966, entered into force 3 January 1976), 999 UNTS 171 (172 States parties). The ICESCR is accompanied by an optional protocol relating to the processing of individual communications (10 December 2008, entered into force 5 May 2013, twenty-nine States parties).

the right to a fair trial, or the right to democratic participation. In theory, these usually require *negative action* from a State (e.g., a State must refrain from violating freedom of movement within a State). Communist States, and many newly independent States, however, emphasized the primacy of *economic, social, and cultural rights*, including rights to food, health, and education ('second-generation rights'). To accomplish these rights, concerted *positive action* is required on the part of States, but the obligation to do so is rather less concrete (e.g., a State may be encouraged to ensure an adequate supply of food, but not bound to achieve it). It was this division that required the adoption of two separate human rights covenants in 1966.

With the end of the Cold War, there has been increasing recognition of the interdependent relationship between human rights. This is to say that, rather than insisting on a division between them, there is an understanding that they operate together in a context, and that their implementation is not in fact that different. For example, civil and political rights require State action, such as establishing courts and police training, while economic and social rights do not always require the intervention of the State, but sometimes mere facilitation, such as allowing access to humanitarian assistance or the permission to build schools or hospitals.

A more holistic, integrated approach to human rights was poignantly illustrated by the onset of the Covid-19 pandemic. Article 12(2) ICESCR has returned to the fore; it provides that certain positive measures to be taken to ensure the right to health, including the 'prevention, treatment and control of epidemic . . . and other diseases' and 'the creation of conditions which would assure to all medical service and medical attention in the event of sickness'. If such positive measures in relation to health are an obligation of good diligence, for example not to cause transboundary harm (see further Chapter 19, Section 19.3.2), these could ideally be mobilized alongside 'first-generation' principles of non-discrimination that might be applicable to vulnerable populations such as the elderly or those with pre-existing health conditions.

For further insights using the lens of prisoners' rights, see N Jain, 'Pandemics as Rights-Generators' (2020) 114 AJIL 677.

In line with the perception that civil and political rights can be enforced more readily than economic and social rights, their *chapeau* ('umbrella') provision is different. Whereas Article 2 ICCPR requires States 'to respect and to ensure' the rights recognized in it, the corresponding Article 2 ICESCR pledges States 'to take steps, individually and through international assistance and cooperation . . . to the maximum of its available resources, with a view to achieving progressively the full realization of the rights recognized' in the Covenant.[17]

The obligations contained in the ICCPR are those traditionally associated with rights relating to liberty and security of the person, equality before the law, and access to a fair trial. States parties must submit regular reports to the UN Human Rights Committee

[17] See also *Government of the Republic of South Africa and Ors v Irene Grootboom and ors* (4 October 2000), [2000] ZACC 19 (Constitutional Court of South Africa), giving content to progressive realization. The court reconceptualized the 'right to housing' as a 'bundle' of concomitant procedural rights: everyone should have access to available accommodation; individuals cannot be evicted from their homes in an inhumane manner. See further, G Quinot and S Liebenberg, 'Narrowing the Band: Reasonableness Review in Administrative Justice and Socio-Economics Rights Jurisprudence in South Africa' (2011) 22 Stellenbosch LR 639, 654–6; and B Saul, D Kinley and J Mowbray, 'Article 2(1)' in B Saul, D Kinley and J Mowbray (eds), *The International Covenant on Economic, Social and Cultural Rights: Commentary, Cases and Materials* (OUP, 2014), at 133.

(UNHRC) on all measures adopted to give effect to the Covenant.[18] Significantly, a State party may complain to the UNHRC of another party's non-compliance with the Covenant, though under Article 41 ICCPR such complaints are only admissible on a reciprocal basis, when both parties have recognized the UNHRC's competence to receive complaints[19] and all local remedies have been exhausted.[20] The ICCPR's First Optional Protocol allows for individuals under the jurisdiction of an acceding party to complain directly to the UNHRC for violations of the Covenant in specific circumstances, again also subject to the exhaustion of local remedies.[21] In response to a complaint, a State will furnish written explanations and identify whether any remedial action will be taken for a violation. Though the UNHRC's 'views' will not be binding,[22] they are published, a fact that may influence States in making legislative or administrative changes.[23]

Conversely, the ICESCR encompasses a broad range of rights relating to work, social security, education, housing, health care, and other attributes relating to living standards. Both Covenants contain a strong prohibition against discrimination in relation to race, colour, sex, language, religion, nationality, and political opinion.[24] Parties must submit reports on measures adopted to the UN Economic and Social Council (ECOSOC), a principal organ of the United Nations.[25]

The Committee on Economic, Social and Cultural Rights (CESCR) assists in monitoring compliance with the Convention.[26] Unlike the UNHRC and the HRC, the CESCR was established in 1987 as a committee of independent experts.[27] Given the challenges discussed earlier in realizing many of the economic, social, and cultural rights embodied in the ICESCR, the Committee focuses primarily on examining States' reports and the preparation of general comments, in which it provides guidance as to the interpretation of the Convention. Since May 2013, the CESCR may receive individual complaints and inter-State complaints against States that have ratified the First Optional Protocol to the ICESCR.[28]

[18] See generally Y Tyagi, *The UN Human Rights Committee: Practice and Procedure* (CUP, 2011).

[19] *Ibid*, 325–85. The inter-State procedure has not yet been invoked.

[20] See further Chapter 11, Section 11.4.

[21] Tyagi (n 18) 386–630.

[22] CCPR, General Comment No 33 (2008) CCPR/C/GC/33, §§31–5. See also JS Davidson 'Intention and Effect: The Legal Status of the Final Views of the Human Rights Committee' (2001) New Zealand LR 125.

[23] Tyagi (n 18) 626–9, referring to *Lovelace v Canada* (1981) HR Comm No 27/1977; 68 ILR 17; *Toonen v Australia* (1994) 112 ILR 328.

[24] ICCPR (n 15) Arts 2(1), 26; however, ICESCR (n 16) Art 2(1) allows developing States a measure of discretion in assuring certain rights to non-nationals, though the prohibition on discrimination is of immediate effect: CESCR General Comment No 3 (UN Doc E/1991/23) (14 December 1990).

[25] See Chapter 6, Section 6.7.1.1.3 ('Economic and Social Council').

[26] See later Section 16.3.3.2.

[27] ICESCR (n 16) Arts 16–22. For a general overview, see P Alston and G Quinn, 'The Nature and Scope of States Parties' Obligations under the International Covenant on Economic, Social and Cultural Rights' (1987) 9 HRQ 156; B Simma, 'The Implementation of the International Covenant on Economic, Social and Cultural Rights' in F Matscher (ed), *The Implementation of Economic, Social and Cultural Rights* (NP Engel, 1991), 75.

[28] UN Doc A/63/435 (28 November 2008). The inter-State procedure is based on the same principle of reciprocity as that under the HRC.

Both the UNHRC and the CECSR, as well as the specialized treaty bodies which monitor the nine core human rights treaties (surveyed in Section 16.3.3.2), also publish 'General Comments'—interpretive statements that provide guidance to States on the interpretation or application of their respective treaties. Over time, general comments have come to be regarded as authoritative interpretations of the Covenants, as the outcome of long discussions between experts and in consultation with States and civil society. As the ICJ explained in *Ahmadou Sadio Diallo*, when considering issues arising in relation to human rights treaties, 'it believes that it should ascribe great weight to the interpretation adopted by this independent body that was established specifically to supervise the application of that treaty'.[29] In this respect, general comments have acquired a certain degree of authority, and cannot be easily dismissed.

16.3.3 **Subsidiary organs and specialized agencies in the UN system**

The General Assembly has overall competence to initiate studies and to investigate in respect of any issue, including human rights.[30] Under its auspices, several standing committees have been created, such as the subject-specific Special Committees on Decolonization and against Apartheid, as well as issue-driven bodies such as the UN Council for Namibia and the Special Committee to Investigate Israeli Practices in the Occupied Territories. Moreover, the General Assembly has created the Office of the UN High Commissioner for Human Rights[31] and the Office of the UN High Commissioner for Refugees.[32] ECOSOC, under Article 62 of the Charter, has more specific powers to make recommendations on human rights, draft conventions to be passed on to the General Assembly, and call international conferences on human rights matters.

16.3.3.1 **From UNCnHR (1946) to the Human Rights Council (2006)**

Historically, the most prominent human rights-focused organ was the UN Commission on Human Rights (UNCnHR), the only subsidiary organ foreseen in Article 62 of the Charter; it was established by ECOSOC in 1946.[33] UNCnHR's principal functions have included the preparation of recommendations and draft documents and conventions, with its first success being the 1948 UDHR. At first, UNCnHR lacked investigatory

[29] *Ahmadou Sadio Diallo (Guinea v Democratic Republic of the Congo), Judgment, ICJ Reports 2010*, p 639, at para 66. See T Opsahl, 'The General Comments of the Human Rights Committee' in J Jenkewicz, KH Klein, JD Kühne, H Petersmann, and R Wolfrum (eds), *Festschrift für Karl Joseph Partsch zum 75* (Duncker & Humblot, 1989), 273.

[30] Charter of the United Nations (signed 26 June 1945, entered into force 24 October 1945), 1 UNTS xvi ('UN Charter'), Arts 13–14.

[31] UNGA Res 48/141 (20 December 1993); see also A Clapham, 'Creating the High Commissioner for Human Rights: The Outside Story' (1994) 5 EJIL 556; H Steiner, P Alston, and R Goodman, *International Human Rights* (OUP, 2012), 824–35.

[32] See later, Section 16.5.1.

[33] ECOSOC Resolution 9 (II) (21 June 1946). See Steiner, Alston, and Goodman (n 31) 844 *et seq*; D McGoldrick, *The Human Rights Committee* (OUP, 1994); S Joseph, 'New Procedures Concerning the Human Rights Committee's Examination of State Reports' (1995) 13 NQHR 5.

powers in relation to individual complaints;[34] however, in 1967, both UNCnHR, and a Sub-Commission established under it, were mandated to study country-specific complaints relating to alleged consistent patterns of human rights violations, and to make recommendations to ECOSOC.[35] It would later establish ad hoc working groups of experts, and appoint special rapporteurs to deal with thematic concerns such as summary executions, mercenaries, and the trafficking of children.[36] In 1970, ECOSOC passed Resolution 1503, establishing what is known as the '1503 procedure', a confidential complaints procedure through which a Working Group would review communications received and refer to the Sub-Commission those most likely to reveal gross violations of human rights.[37]

UNCnHR was plagued with difficulties from the start, in part due to its design as a body of State representatives elected from the UN's total membership. This meant that States with dubious human rights records were often elected, thus undermining public confidence in the Commission.[38] Ultimately, the more corrosive issue was the fact that UNCnHR had discretion as to which situations it would examine, a discretion that was purportedly exercised with political considerations in mind.[39] The growing disquiet with UNCnHR led to calls for its replacement and, in 2006, the forty-seven-member Human Rights Council (HRC) was established in its stead, reporting directly to the General Assembly.[40] States are elected according to a regional distribution: thirteen seats for the African Group; thirteen for the Asian Group; six for the Eastern European Group; eight for the Latin American and Caribbean group; seven for the Western European and Other group.

The HRC inherited the UNCnHR's system of special procedures, including the ability to appoint independent experts with a mandate to report on these from a thematic or country-specific perspective, as well as a complaints mechanism modelled on the '1503 procedure'.[41] In a significant departure, however, it adopted a new universal periodic

[34] ECOSOC Resolution 75 (V) (5 August 1947) declared that UNCnHR 'has no power to take any action in regard to any complaint concerning human rights'.

[35] ECOSOC Resolution 1235 (XLII) (6 June 1967), which named it the 'Sub-Commission on the Promotion of Human Rights'.

[36] For a succinct analysis, see P Alston, 'The Commission on Human Rights' in P Alston (ed), *The United Nations and Human Rights: A Critical Appraisal* (Clarendon Press, 1992), 126.

[37] ECOSOC Resolution 1503 (XLVIII) (27 May 1970); as modified by ECOSOC Resolution 2000/3 (19 June 2000). The '1503 procedure' has attracted criticism: see N Rodley, 'Monitoring Human Rights by the UN System and Non-Governmental Organisations' in D Kommers and G Loescher (eds), *Human Rights and American Foreign Policy* (University of Notre Dame Press, 1979), 157; H Möller, 'Petitioning the United Nations' (1979) 1 Universal Human Rights 57.

[38] See, e.g., the concerns gathered by Amnesty International, 'Meeting the Challenge', AI Index, IOR 40/008/2005.

[39] In 'Follow-up to the outcome of the Millennium Summit: Note by the Secretary-General', UN Doc A/59/565 (2 December 2004), para 283, it was suggested that States potentially stood for election to UNCnHR precisely to deflect possible attention from their own human rights records.

[40] See UNGA Res 60/251 (15 March 2006).

[41] See Human Rights Council Resolution 5/1 (18 June 2007), 'Institution-Building', which also provided for the establishment of the HRC Advisory Committee, composed of eighteen experts serving in a personal capacity.

review (UPR) mechanism, under which every State would be obliged to submit reports, face questioning, and receive recommendations in relation to its human rights record.[42] The UPR mechanism was intended to create a new climate of accountability, universal respect for human rights, and for reviews to be de-politicized and conducted in a non-confrontational manner.[43] However, the HRC's continuity with the old UNCnHR system has been criticized from the start as being insufficiently distinct.[44]

THEORY AND DEBATES Political Selectivity and the Human Rights Council

Political selectivity—the ability for the Council to select which situations it will take up and which situations it will ignore—remains an issue. The HRC's 'Special Sessions' were designed to move past political selection, but in their early days focused single-mindedly on Israeli conduct in occupied Palestinian territory and incursions into Lebanon, causing loud complaints from the USA and Israel.

In the last the Council has taken up situations including the Rohingya Muslim population in Myanmar (2017), the occupied Palestinian territory (2018 and 2021), Iran (2022), Sudan (2023), and the Democratic Republic of the Congo (2025). However, as with UNCnHR, certain States with questionable human rights records have sought election to the HRC, arguably to be able to influence whether their specific situation will be taken up. In the most recent elections in 2024, for example, Bolivia, the Democratic Republic of the Congo, Ethiopia, and Qatar were elected.

That strategy might be less effective in recent years; for example, when in 2017 the eighth annual report of the OHCHR singled out twenty-nine States which actively retaliated against citizens that cooperated with the UN on human rights, nine of them were active members of the HRC (see UN Doc A/HRC/36/31 (20 September 2017)). Such a development could be taken either as a positive step, as members of the HRC are subject to scrutiny, or negatively in the hypocrisy of human rights violators being entrusted with human rights protection.

The USA's relationship with the HRC remains ambivalent. In 2018, Nikki Haley, former US Ambassador to the UN, announced the US withdrawal from the HRC, a 'cesspool of bias' that she accused of singling out Israel, yet ignoring the atrocities of the 'world's most inhumane regimes' (see BBC, 'US quits "biased" UN human rights council' (20 June 2018), available at http://www.bbc.co.uk/news/44537372). Though re-elected to the HRC in 2021, the US opted not to run for re-election, and shortly after its term ended in January 2025, President Trump began his second term announcing that the US would no longer participate nor support the HRC.

For further reading, see R Freedman, *The United Nations Human Rights Council: A Critique and Early Assessment* (Routledge, 2015); and E Tistounet (ed), *The UN Human Rights Council: A Practical Anatomy* (2nd edn, Edward Elgar, 2025).

42 See UNGA Res 60/251 (n 40) para 5*(e)*. 43 See HRC Resolution 5/1 (n 41).

44 See FJ Hampson, 'Critical Assessment ("Shot in the Foot"): An Overview of the Reform of the UN Human Rights Machinery' (2007) 7 HRLR 7; and N Ghanea, 'From UN Commission on Human Rights to UN Human Rights Council: One Step Forwards or Two Steps Sideways?' (2006) 55 ICLQ 695.

16.3.3.2 **Specialized treaty bodies**

In addition to the UNHRC and the CESCR, there exist a number of specialized treaty bodies entrusted with the implementation of the 'core' human rights treaties. Given their broad scope, they will be surveyed in passing.[45] These bodies are:

- Committee on the Elimination of Racial Discrimination;[46]
- Committee on the Elimination of Discrimination against Women;[47]
- Committee against Torture;[48]
- Committee on the Rights of the Child (CRC);[49]
- Committee on the Protection of the Rights of All Migrant Workers and Members of their Families ('Committee on Migrant Workers') (CommMW);[50]
- Committee on the Rights of Persons with Disabilities (CRPD);[51] and
- Committee on Enforced Disappearances (CED).[52]

[45] Regarding these specialized bodies, see N-H Grohmann, *Strengthening the UN Human Rights Treaty Bodies: An Analysis of the Committees' Legal Powers and the Possibilities for Reform* (Mohr Siebeck, 2024); and M O'Flaherty, *Human Rights and the UN: Practice Before the Treaty Bodies* (2nd edn, Kluwer, 2002).

[46] International Convention on the Elimination of All Forms of Racial Discrimination (adopted 21 December 1965, entered into force 4 January 1969), 600 UNTS 195 (CERD) (182 States parties). See generally P Thornberry, *The International Convention on the Elimination of All Forms of Racial Discrimination* (OUP, 2016); and R Wolfrum, 'The Committee on the Elimination of Racial Discrimination' (1999) 3 MPUNYB 489.

[47] Convention on the Elimination of All Forms of Discrimination against Women (adopted 18 December 1979, entered into force 3 September 1981), 1249 UNTS 13 (CEDAW) (189 States parties). See generally HB Schöpp-Schilling and C Flinterman (eds), *The Circle of Empowerment: Twenty-Five Years of the UN Committee on the Elimination of Discrimination against Women* (Feminist Press, 2007); A Byrnes, 'The "Other" Human Rights Body: The Work of the Committee on the Elimination of Discrimination Against Women' (1989) 14 Yale JIL 1.

[48] Convention against Torture and other Cruel, Inhuman and Degrading Punishment (signed 10 December 1984, entered into force 26 June 1987), 1465 UNTS 85 (CAT) (175 States parties). See M Nowak and E McArthur, *The UN Convention against Torture: A Commentary* (2nd edn OUP, 2019), esp 475–495; M Evans, 'Getting to Grips with Torture' (2002) 51 ICLQ 365.

[49] Convention on the Rights of the Child (signed 20 November 1989, entered into force 2 September 1990), 1577 UNTS 3 (CRC) (196 States parties). See OC Jančič (ed), *The Rights of the Child in a Changing World: 25 Years after the UN Convention on the Rights of the Child* (Springer, 2015); T Liefarrd and JE Doek (eds), *Litigating the Rights of the Child: The UN Convention on the Rights of the Child in Domestic and International Jurisprudence* (Springer, 2014).

[50] International Convention on the Protection of the Rights of All Migrant Workers and Members of Their Families (signed 18 December 1990, entered into force 1 July 2003), 2220 UNTS 3 (CMW) (60 States parties). See P de Guchteneire, A Pecoud, and R Cholewinksi (eds), *Migration and Human Rights: The United Nations Convention on Migrant Workers' Rights* (CUP, 2009); S Hune and J Niessen, 'The First UN Convention on Migrant Workers' (1991) NQHR 133.

[51] Convention on the Rights of Persons with Disabilities (signed 13 December 2006, entered into force 3 May 2008), 2515 UNTS 3 (CRPD) (191 States parties). E Flynn, *From Rhetoric to Action: Implementing the UN Convention on the Rights of Persons with Disabilities* (CUP, 2013); R Kayess and P French, 'Out of Darkness into Light? Introducing the Convention on the Rights of Persons with Disabilities' (2008) 8 HRLR 1.

[52] International Convention on the Protection of All Persons from Enforced Disappearance (signed 20 December 2006, entered into force 23 December 2010), 2716 UNTS 3 (CPPED) (seventy-seven States parties). See generally ML Vermeulen, *Enforced Disappearance: Determining State Responsibility under the International Convention for the Protection of All Persons from Enforced Disappearance* (Intersentia, 2012); S McCrory, 'The International Convention for the Protection of All Persons from Enforced Disappearance' (2007) 7 HRLR 545.

The specialized treaty bodies are not subsidiary organs of the UN, as they are established under their respective treaties; however, they receive support from the UN Secretariat through the UN Centre for Human Rights in Geneva. They are also structured similarly: each body is composed of between ten and twenty-five individuals serving not as State representatives but as independent experts.

As with the UNHRC and the CESCR, the treaty bodies discharge a number of functions. These include the scrutiny of reports submitted by States parties, usually over intervals of two to five years. Upon identifying possible issues from the initial reports, and making recommendations, many of the committees enter into a process of dialogue with States parties with a view to addressing concerns.[53] Most of the Committees also regularly issue general comments, building on the model pioneered by UNHRC, consisting of interpretive guidance regarding obligations under their respective treaties. Under an enabling Optional Protocol, all the specialized treaty bodies may entertain complaints from individual nationals of States that have ratified the Protocol. Committee deliberations are confidential and reports are not binding, but are considered in a 'judicial spirit'.[54] A few bodies also provide for inter-State complaints on a reciprocal basis, but these procedures have as yet not been invoked.

Given the sheer number of specialized treaty bodies and their similar, overlapping functions, there are challenges relating to access to resources and funding, as well as the consistency of their practice. In 2014, the General Assembly introduced substantial reforms, increasing resources and funding to reduce backlogs, and streamlining procedures to improve efficiency, effectiveness, and harmonization of the interpretation and application of the various human rights conventions.[55] Moreover, since 2016, the UN Secretary-General is to submit biennial reports to the General Assembly on the status of the human rights treaty body system.[56]

16.3.4 **Collective or group rights**

The term 'collective rights' goes beyond the notion that human rights are based on an individual's right to human dignity, but are partially defined by the communities to which they belong. These are often called 'third-generation rights' or the 'second wave of second-generation rights' involving collective and international solidarity.[57] Though some rights are purely collective, certain legal rights appertaining to groups often bestow rights upon individual group members to claim on behalf of the group. Three particular themes—the right to self-determination; ethnic, linguistic, or other minorities within a State; and indigenous groups—merit brief attention here.

[53] Useful recommendations were made by N Pillay, *Strengthening the United Nations Human Rights Treaty Body System: A Report by the United Nations High Commissioner for Human Rights*, UN Doc A/66/860 (22 June 2012), esp section 3.1.1.

[54] A term used in General Comment No 33, 'The Obligations of State Parties under the Optional Protocol to the [ICCPR]' (5 November 2008), UN Doc CCPR/C/GC/33, para 11.

[55] UNGA Res 68/268 (9 April 2014). [56] UNGA Res 71/118 (18 July 2016).

[57] See R Freedman, '"Third Generation" Rights: Is there Room for Hybrid Constructs within International Human Rights Law?' (2013) 2 CJICL 935.

Self-determination. Self-determination is most prominent in the context of decolonization, where a people subject to alien subjugation, domination, and exploitation can declare independence and form their own government, leading to the creation of a new independent State.[58] Within the human rights context, there has been substantial recognition of the collective right to self-determination as exercised internally within an existing State:[59] self-determination is entrenched as a collective right in Common Article 1(1) of the ICCPR and ICESCR, by virtue of which peoples 'freely determine their political status and freely pursue their economic, social and cultural development'.[60]

As discussed in Chapter 5, there is no consensus either as to the definition of self-determination in this context or regarding the 'peoples' meant to exercise the right.[61] In the 1975 *Western Sahara* advisory opinion, the ICJ described self-determination as a 'need to pay regard to the freely expressed will of peoples',[62] saying little more about the definition as such. The Human Rights Committee published General Comment 12, suggesting that self-determination formed part of a wider framework in which specific rights guaranteed in the ICCPR could be implemented.[63] In *Policies and Practices of Israel* and the earlier *Construction of a Wall*, the ICJ concluded successively that the conduct of Israel had the effect of severely impeding the exercise of self-determination—a right *erga omnes*—by the Palestinian people in relation to the occupied Palestinian territory.[64]

Minority rights. The first expression of collective rights protection was in relation to the minorities regime adopted under the League of Nations, through which certain States in Central and Eastern Europe accepted international obligations relating to minorities within their borders.[65] Many of the cases heard by the PCIJ, the ICJ's predecessor, concerned the interpretation of the so-called 'minorities treaties'.[66]

[58] See *Accordance with International Law of the Unilateral Declaration of Independence in Respect of Kosovo, Advisory Opinion, ICJ Reports 2010*, p 403, 436, para 70. See further Chapter 5, Section 5.2.3.2.

[59] See *Reference v Secession of Quebec* (1998) 161 DLR (4th) 385, 437–8; 115 ILR 536 (Supreme Court of Canada). In *Katangese Peoples' Congress v Zaire*, Case No 75/92, reprinted in (1995) 13 NQHR 478, the right to self-determination of Katanga was interpreted as requiring respect for the sovereignty and territorial integrity of Zaire.

[60] Similar wording can be found in the African Charter of Human and Peoples' Rights (signed 17 June 1981, entered into force 21 October 1986), 1520 UNTS 323 ('Banjul Charter'), Art 20; and the non-binding Final Act of the Helsinki Conference on Security and Co-operation in Europe (1 August 1975), 14 ILM 1292.

[61] F Kirgis, 'Degrees of Self-Determination in the United Nations Era' (1994) 88 AJIL 304.

[62] *Western Sahara, Advisory Opinion, ICJ Reports 1975*, p 12, 33.

[63] UN Doc HRI/GEN/1/Rev.9 (Vol I) (13 March 1984). See also the CERD Committee's General Recommendation 21, UN Doc A/51/18 (1996).

[64] *Policies and Practices of Israel in the Occupied Palestinian Territory, including East Jerusalem, Advisory Opinion of 19 July 2024*, paras 232–233, 274; *Construction of a Wall in the Occupied Palestinian Territory, Advisory Opinion, ICJ Reports 2004*, p 136, 171–2.

[65] There were minorities treaties binding certain States (e.g., Poland and Czechoslovakia), minorities clauses in general peace treaties (e.g., Hungary and Türkiye), and special treaties relating to Danzig, Upper Silesia, and Memel. See generally P Thornberry, *International Law and Minorities* (Clarendon Press, 1993), 38 *et seq* and 434 *et seq*.

[66] See, e.g., *Treatment of Polish Nationals and Other Persons of Polish Origin or Speech in the Danzig Territory, Advisory Opinion, 1932, PCIJ, Ser A/B, No 44*, p 4; or *Minority Schools in Albania, 1935, PCIJ, Ser A/B, No 64*, p 17. For more on the foundation of the PCIJ, see Chapter 1, Section 1.4.1.

Though the Council of Europe has a regional treaty on minorities,[67] on a global scale there is only the non-binding Declaration on the Rights of Persons Belonging to National or Ethnic, Religious or Linguistic Minorities,[68] which identifies existing human rights that are also relevant to the protection of minorities. Cast in the language of individual and not collective rights, Article 27 ICCPR protects the rights of individual members of ethnic, religious, and linguistic minorities to enjoy their own culture, profess and practise their own religion, and use their own language.[69] International law's ambivalence towards minority rights has been subject to heavy criticism.[70]

Indigenous persons. An early definition of indigenous populations is that they are 'composed of the existing descendants of the peoples who inhabited the present territory of a country wholly or partially at the time when persons from a different culture or ethnic origin arrived there from other parts of the world'.[71] Construed thus, indigenous persons therefore form a special category who, broadly speaking, enjoy a particular relationship to their traditional territory and are deserving of enhanced status.[72] Members of indigenous groups can complain of individual violations of collective rights under Article 27 ICCPR.[73]

A prominent instrument is the 2007 UN Declaration on the Rights of Indigenous Peoples, though 'indigenous peoples'—a departure from the earlier use of 'indigenous populations'—are not defined therein.[74] The Declaration is noteworthy in that indigenous peoples and their NGOs were prominently represented during the drafting process. It was a novel, more inclusive approach rather unlike the earlier ILO conventions on indigenous peoples, which were essentially State-led.[75] Besides certain collective

[67] European Framework Convention for the Protection of Minorities (signed 10 November 1994, entered into force 1 February 1998), ETS 157.

[68] UNGA Res 47/135 (8 December 1992). See A Eide, 'Commentary to the Declaration on the Rights of Persons Belonging to National or Ethnic, Religious or Linguistic Minorities' (1998), UN Doc E/CN.4/Sub.2/AC.5/1998/WP.1.

[69] For further reading, see M Weller (ed), *Universal Minority Rights: A Commentary on the Jurisprudence of International Courts and Treaty Bodies* (OUP, 2007).

[70] See in particular M Shahabuddin, *Ethnicity in International Law: Histories, Politics and Practices* (CUP, 2016); and M Shahabuddin, *Minorities and the Making of the Postcolonial States* (CUP, 2021).

[71] UNCnHR, 'Preliminary Report on the Study of the Problem of Discrimination Against Indigenous Populations' (1972), UN Doc E/CN.4/Sub. 2/L.566, ch II, para 34. See also the Final Report of Special Rapporteur Martínez Cobo, *Study of the Problem of Discrimination Against Indigenous Populations* (UN Doc 1983E/CN.4/Sub.2/1983/21).

[72] See generally M Åhrén, *Indigenous Peoples' Status in the International Legal System* (OUP, 2016); P Thornberry, *Indigenous Peoples and Human Rights* (Manchester UP, 2002); and J Anaya, *Indigenous Peoples in International Law* (2nd edn, OUP, 2004).

[73] See *Lovelace* (n 23); *Kitok v Sweden* (UNHRC Comm No 197/1985, (1988) 96 ILR 637); *Ominayak and the Lubicon Lake Band v Canada* (UNHRC Comm No 167/1984, (1990) 96 ILR 667); and *Länsmann v Finland* (UNHRC Comm 511/1992, (1996) 115 ILR 300). See also HRC General Comment No 23 (1994), UN Doc HRI/GEN/1/Rev.1, 38.

[74] UNGA Res 61/295 (13 September 2007). See also the Outcome document of the 1st World Conference of Indigenous Peoples, UNGA Res 69/2 (25 September 2014); and UNGA Res 70/232 (23 December 2015), entitled 'Rights of Indigenous Peoples'.

[75] See ILO Convention No 107 Concerning the Protection and Integration of Indigenous and Tribal and Semi-Tribal Populations in Independent Countries (adopted 26 June 1957, entered into force 2 June 1959), 328 UNTS 247, replaced by ILO Convention No 169 Concerning Indigenous and Tribunal Peoples in Independent Countries (adopted 27 June 1989, entered into force 5 September 1991), 28 ILM 1832.

rights tailored to the circumstances of indigenous peoples (including rights to practise cultural traditions and recognition of their distinctive relationship to their land), Article 3 of the Declaration recognizes their right to self-determination, a departure from earlier treaties.[76] Though not binding on States, the 2007 Declaration embodies an important step forward in the international recognition of indigenous peoples, and has already been referred to by international and municipal courts.[77]

CASE SPOTLIGHT ***Kaliña and Lokono Peoples v Suriname*, IACtHR Ser C No 309 (25 November 2015)**

The Kaliña and Lokono peoples, indigenous groups in Suriname, complained to the IACtHR that Suriname had not established a legal and regulatory framework recognizing their rights to collective ownership of their traditional lands and natural resources. Instead, Suriname issued restrictions on hunting and fishing, opened up mining operations, and even authorized the building of vacation homes and casinos, displacing the local indigenous peoples from the Marowijne River, with which they had a strong spiritual relationship.

The IACtHR was strongly critical of this failure by Suriname, and found a violation of Article 3 ACHR given the impact of this failure on other rights. The Court also found that Suriname had violated Article 21 ACHR, which safeguards in broad terms the rights of indigenous and tribal peoples to their own social, cultural, and economic development, and in particular their spiritual relationship with the territory they have traditionally used. The Court emphasized the sociocultural facets of environmental protection (para 173), and how the lack of participation of the Kaliña and Lokono peoples in decision-making relating to conservation (paras 197–8) and mining concessions (para 212) were also violations.

This judgment marks a significant shift in the IACtHR's case law on indigenous rights. Foremost, the Court asserted categorically that, under the ACHR, indigenous peoples are entitled, *as collective entities*, to recognition of their *collective legal personality* (para 279(i)(a)). This represents a welcome advance from traditional human rights proceedings, centred on the individual, and a concrete move to the judicial enforcement of collective rights. However, the IACtHR was cautious in limiting the Kaliña and Lokono peoples' right to *consultation* to the encroachments by private parties onto their territory. There is lively debate as to whether international law now requires the *consent*, rather than mere consultation, of indigenous peoples with respect to the use or exploitation of their lands.

Finally, in addressing the relationship between international environmental law and human rights obligations, the IACtHR suggested that these are compatible on the problematic assumption that indigenous practices help environmental conservation. Unproductively, this assumption essentializes indigenous identity and reinforces the myth of the 'Noble Savage', implying that 'indigenous people in their wisdom harmoniously engage with nature'. While

[76] See further A Xanthaki, 'Indigenous Rights in International Law over the Last 10 Years and Future Developments' (2009) 10 Melbourne JIL 27; and MC Lâm, *At the Edge of the State: Indigenous Peoples and Self-Determination* (Transnational, 2000).

[77] E.g., see *Case of the Saramanka People v Suriname* (28 November 2007), IACtHR Ser C No 173; *Cal v Attorney-General* (Claim 121/2007) (18 October 2007) (Supreme Court of Belize); and, N Jones, *Self-Determination as Voice: the Participation of Indigenous Peoples in International Governance* (CUP, 2024), ch 4.

this connection has been exploited successfully by indigenous peoples, 'it also brings unintended consequences to indigenous peoples, who now can only use their land in sustainable ways and are excluded from certain forms of development that should otherwise accrue as a matter of human rights': L Lixinski, *Case of the Kaliña and Lokono Peoples v Suriname*, IACtHR Ser C No 309 (25 November 2015) (2015) 111 AJIL 147.

16.4 Regional systems of human rights protection

In parallel with the emergence of human rights protection at the international level, several regional frameworks exist.[78] In this section, the European, American, and African human rights conventions and accompanying institutions will be briefly surveyed.[79]

16.4.1 The European Convention system

The most comprehensive and long-standing regional human rights system is that centred upon the European Convention on Human Rights (ECHR).[80] All 46 members of the Council of Europe are parties, with Russia having been expelled/withdrawn after its invasion of Ukraine in February 2022.[81] It should not be confused with the European Union's Charter of Fundamental Rights, which has been binding on EU member States since 2009.[82]

The ECHR covers the classic civil and political rights, including the freedoms of expression and assembly (Articles 10 and 11); prohibitions of torture, slavery, and forced labour (Articles 3 and 4); and the right to a fair trial (Article 6).[83] All forty-seven member States of the Council of Europe—not to be confused with the Council of the European Union—are parties to the ECHR, which requires accepting the jurisdiction of the European Court of Human Rights (the ECtHR). The ECtHR itself is divided into

[78] A useful survey is that in D Shelton and P Carozza (eds), *Regional Protection of Human Rights* (2nd edn, OUP, 2008).

[79] Since 2009, the Arab Human Rights Committee reviews State reports on compliance with the Arab Charter of Human Rights; and in the same year, an ASEAN Intergovernmental Commission on Human Rights was established. See M Rishmawi, 'The Arab Charter on Human Rights and the League of Arab States: An Update' (2010) 10 HRLR 169; and N Doyle, 'The ASEAN Human Rights Declaration' (2014) 63 ICLQ 67. The Asia–Pacific region has no comprehensive system.

[80] European Convention on Human Rights and Fundamental Freedoms (signed 4 November 1950, entered into force 3 September 1953), ETS 5 (ECHR). Out of an abundant literature see: DJ Harris, M O'Boyle, EP Bates, and CM Buckley (eds), *Harris, O'Boyle and Warbrick: Law of the European Convention on Human Rights* (5th edn, OUP, 2023); B Rainey, E Wicks, and C Ovey, *Jacobs, White, and Ovey: The European Convention on Human Rights* (8th edn, OUP, 2020); and F Sudre, *Droit européen et international des droits de l'homme* (16th edn, LGDJ, 2023).

[81] A clear account of the incident is found in K Dzehsiarou and K Donal, 'Suspension and Expulsion of Members of the Council of Europe: Difficult Decisions in Troubled Times' (2019) 68 ICLQ 443.

[82] Treaty on European Union [2012] OJ C326/01, Art 24.

[83] There are, additionally, fourteen Protocols to the ECHR (n 80) addressing certain additional rights, establishing new procedures, and generally refining the European human rights system over time. See generally P Webb and A Clooney, *The Right to a Fair Trial in International Law* (OUP, 2021).

chambers of judges, which hear cases in the first instance; the Grand Chamber, consisting of all seventeen judges, is its highest body.[84]

When the ECHR was adopted in 1950, individuals did not have an automatic right to make claims. The now defunct 'European Commission on Human Rights' (ECnHR) could hear inter-State complaints as of right, but could only address individual complaints in respect of States that had made the requisite declaration.[85] With respect to the ECtHR, individual complaints were first heard by the ECnHR for a report, and only then either referred to the ECtHR, either by the ECnHR or by the State party concerned.[86]

However, in 1990, Protocol 9 enabled the ECtHR to permit individuals directly to file a case against a State party exercising jurisdiction over them; and since 1994, Protocol 11, which has been accepted by all States parties, has made this jurisdiction compulsory.[87] Individuals may thus petition the ECtHR for specific violations of any of the rights under the Convention or one of its protocols, provided that they have sought to exhaust all local remedies, the claim is filed within a reasonable time, they have not made an anonymous claim, and that it is not 'manifestly ill-founded'.[88] Individual claims must assert a concrete violation and not an abstract human rights issue.[89]

The ECtHR has rendered tens of thousands of judgments that have made an important contribution to general international human rights law. Several such contributions merit brief attention.

The first is how the ECtHR developed the principle of interpreting the European Convention as a 'living instrument' in the *Tyrer* case,[90] which meant that its meaning could shift and evolve over time, in light of present conditions. This 'living instrument' doctrine is more akin to certain domestic constitutions (e.g., Canada, South Africa) than the canons of treaty interpretation.

A second important interpretive principle developed is the 'margin of appreciation', according to which States parties benefit from a degree of discretion in respect of their application of the Convention.[91] The 'margin of appreciation' doctrine has seen some take-up in other regional human rights courts, though not yet in other international courts such as the ICJ.[92]

[84] On the specificities of the procedure of the ECtHR, see P Leach, *Taking a Case to the European Court of Human Rights* (4th edn, OUP, 2017); and K Reid, *A Practitioner's Guide to the European Convention on Human Rights* (5th edn, Sweet & Maxwell, 2015).

[85] ECHR (n 80) Art 25. [86] *Ibid*, Art 48.

[87] In addition to the abolition of the European Commission (ECnHR), Protocol 11 has enabled the ECtHR to issue advisory opinions upon the request of the Committee of Ministers of the Council of Europe: see *ibid*, Art 47.

[88] See *ibid*, Art 35, *Boyle and Rice v UK* (1988) ECHR Ser A vol 131; *Cyprus v Turkey*, Judgment of 10 May 2001, paras 82 *et seq*.

[89] See, e.g., *Marckx v Belgium* (1979) ECHR Ser A vol 31; *Pine Valley v Ireland* (1991) ECHR Ser A vol 222.

[90] *Tyrer v UK*, ECHR Ser A No 26 (1979–80) 2 EHRR 1; see also *Golder* (n 12) in which the ECtHR interpreted the right to a fair trial in Art 6 of the ECHR also to encompass a right of access to court. See generally G Letsas, 'Strasbourg's Interpretive Ethic: Lessons for the International Lawyer' (2010) 21 EJIL 509.

[91] See, e.g., *Brannigan and McBride v UK* (1994) ECHR Ser A No 258-B, para 43; *Handyside v UK* (1981) ECHR Ser A vol 24. See further A Legg, *The Margin of Appreciation in International Human Rights Law: Deference and Proportionality* (OUP, 2013).

[92] On this point, *cf* Y Shany, 'Toward a General Margin of Appreciation Doctrine in International Law?' (2006) 16 EJIL 907.

Significantly, the ECtHR seems to be moving towards an expansive interpretation of 'jurisdiction' in Article 1 of the ECHR. Though jurisdiction is 'essentially territorial',[93] violations can occur 'extraterritorially',[94] or outside the territory of a State party, in certain circumstances, such as:

1. the extradition or expulsion of an individual to a non-party;[95]
2. acts occurring in a territory under the 'effective overall control' of a State party, such as Türkiye's control over the northern third of the island of Cyprus, or Russia's effective control over the separatist entities of Abkhazia and South Ossetia;[96] and
3. acts of State agents exercising sufficient 'authority and control' over individuals, such as those of British soldiers during the occupation of Iraq.[97] In September 2021, the ECtHR held that the 2006 assassination of Alexander Litvinenko in UK territory constituted an 'exercise of physical power and control' by Russia, and was thus attributable to that State.[98]

CASE SPOTLIGHT ***Al-Jedda v United Kingdom*** **App No 27021/08 (ECtHR, Grand Chamber)**

The *Al-Jedda v UK* case involved the indefinite detention without charge of Mr Al-Jedda, a dual British–Iraqi national, in a facility in southern Iraq run by British military forces. In a 2007 judgment, the UK House of Lords had concluded that the detention was not unlawful, as the UK had been authorized so to act under Security Council Resolution 1546 (8 June 2004). Al-Jedda then complained to the European Court of Human Rights.

The Grand Chamber rejected the UK's argument that merely due to Security Council authorization all conduct became attributable to the UN and 'more importantly, for the purposes of this case—ceased to be attributable to the troop-contributing nations' (para 80). Though the Grand Chamber sought to distinguish the two, this finding represented a

[93] See the infamous *Banković v Belgium et al* App No 52207/99, ECHR 2001-XII, paras 63–7, where human rights violations caused by NATO member States' bombing of Belgrade were declared inadmissible. But *cf Ilaşcu v Moldova and Russia*, App No 48787/99, ECHR 2004-VII, paras 312–13, where it was held that a State would not be responsible for violations of the ECHR occurring on territory under military occupation by another State, or under the control of a rebel group. In *Georgia v Russia No II* App No 38263/08 (ECtHR, 25 January 2021), the Grand Chamber adhered to a restrictive jurisdictional approach, invoking *Banković*, to conclude that during the 'active' phase of armed conflict between the parties (8–12 August 2008), there was a 'context of chaos' that precluded the attribution of any acts: see para 138.

[94] See generally M Milanović, *Extraterritorial Application of Human Rights Treaties* (OUP, 2013).

[95] *Soering v UK* (1989) ECHR Ser A vol 161, 35–6.

[96] *Loizidou v Turkey* (*Preliminary Objections*) App No 15318/89 (1995) ECHR Ser A No 310, 24–7; see also *Ilaşcu* (n 92) paras 314–19; and *Georgia v Russia No II* (n 92), but only in respect of events after 8–12 August 2008, the so-called 'active' phase of armed conflict.

[97] *Al-Skeini v UK*, App No 55721/07 (2011) 53 EHRR 18, paras 13–17; *Al-Jedda v UK* App No 27021/08 (2011) 53 EHRR 23. See also *Jaloud v the Netherlands* App No 47708/08 (2015) 60 EHRR 29, para 139, where the Netherlands had argued unsuccessfully that the troops were effectively subordinate to the UK and the USA as 'lead nations' in Iraq.

[98] *Carter v Russia* App No 20914/07 (ECtHR, 21 September 2021).

significant departure from its earlier approach in the joined cases *Behrami and Behrami v France* (App No 71412/01) and *Saramati v France, Germany and Norway* (App No 78116/01 (2007) 45 EHRR 85). Those applications had been declared inadmissible, precisely on the basis that the respondent States were engaged in concerted military operations as part of KFOR (the 'Kosovo Force'), a NATO-led presence in Kosovo authorized under Security Council Resolution 1244 (1998).

Perhaps more significantly, the Grand Chamber addressed how to resolve conflicts between human rights obligations under the ECHR and resolutions of the Security Council. This is a sensitive issue as, in principle, obligations under Article 103 of the UN Charter override other international obligations (see Chapter 3, Section 3.2). The Grand Chamber found that, in the absence of 'clear and explicit language' in Resolution 1546 to depart from international human rights obligations, any ambiguity required the Court to 'choose the interpretation which is most in harmony with the . . . Convention and which avoids any conflict of obligations' (para 102). Such a statement created an important new interpretative presumption, that the Security Council cannot implicitly set aside human rights obligations, and can only do so explicitly; and was further confirmed in *Nada v Switzerland* (App No 10593/08 (ECtHR, 12 September 2012)).

For further reading, see M Milanović, '*Al-Skeini* and *Al-Jedda* in Strasbourg' (2012) 23 EJIL 121.

16.4.2 **The Inter-American Convention system**

The inter-American system of human rights protection developed somewhat differently from its European counterpart.[99] From the outset, rights protection fell under the scope of the seven-member Inter-American Commission on Human Rights (IACnHR), an organ of the Organization of American States (OAS) established in 1960.[100] At first, its functions were limited to promoting the awareness and study of human rights across the Americas, though it could, upon receiving complaints from individuals, publish recommendations with respect to alleged violations of the non-binding American Declaration of the Rights and Duties of Man.[101] Thus, when the American Convention on Human Rights (ACHR) came into force in 1978, it strengthened the position of the Inter-American Commission, which could henceforth apply and interpret binding treaty obligations.[102] Substantively, the ACHR protects similar rights to the ECHR, though with some variations; for example, under Article 4, the right to life is deemed to start 'in general, as from conception'.[103]

[99] For a history, see C Medina, *The Inter-American Convention on Human Rights* (Intersentia, 2014); T Buergenthal and D Shelton, *Protecting Human Rights in the Americas* (4th edn, NP Engel, 1995); Steiner, Alston, and Goodman (n 31) 1020 *et seq*.

[100] Bogotá Charter of the Organization of American States (OAS) (adopted 30 April 1948, entered into force 13 December 1951), 119 UNTS 1609.

[101] See *Basic Documents Pertaining to Human Rights in the Inter-American System* (OAS Publications, 1992).

[102] American Convention on Human Rights (signed 22 November 1969, entered into force 18 July 1978), 1144 UNTS 123. The ACHR (known also as the Pact of San José) has twenty-three parties after Venezuela denounced the Convention in 2013.

[103] See JA Frowein, 'The European and the American Conventions on Human Rights—A Comparison' (1980) 1 HRLJ 44.

Significantly, the ACHR established the Inter-American Court of Human Rights (IACtHR).[104] The IACtHR's jurisdiction is optional, with twenty States having recognized its jurisdiction. Under the new framework—and unlike with the ECtHR—individuals or groups of persons, including NGOs, may lodge a petition with the Inter-American Commission,[105] and either the Commission or a State may further refer a case to the Court. Inter-State complaints may also be made, but both States must have recognized the competence of the Commission.[106]

The ACHR also allows the Court to issue advisory opinions, upon the request of either a State party or certain bodies established under the OAS Charter.[107] There have been more than twenty-five advisory opinions rendered, with the most famous addressing the effect to be given to reservations to the Convention. Drawing from the ECtHR, the IACtHR found that human rights treaties were distinct from traditional multilateral treaties, in that they were non-reciprocal in nature, and focused on the achievement of the basic rights of individuals.[108]

One distinctive aspect is the role of the IACnHR in bringing attention to human rights issues through non-judicial means. The IACnHR has published reports on situations in certain States and on themes such as enforced disappearance, torture, refugees, or LGTBQIA2S+ rights; and it has appointed special rapporteurs in relation to the rights of indigenous peoples, women, and children.[109] This investigatory function is perhaps tailored for a region where liberal democratic regimes have only become entrenched since the 1980s, and which has in addition been plagued by substantial external interference.[110]

The IACtHR's most prominent cases are intimately related to the contemporary politics and history of Latin America and the Caribbean. These include the *Velásquez Rodríguez* case, in which the Court found forced disappearances caused by Honduras to violate the ACHR;[111] and the *Barrios Altos* cases, in which the IACtHR declared that Peruvian amnesty legislation was in breach with the ACHR and thus null *ab initio* (void of all legal effect).[112] In *Sawhoyamaxa Indigenous Community*, the IACtHR concluded that traditional possession of land by indigenous peoples has equivalent effects to the

[104] See generally JM Pasqualucci, *The Practice and Procedure of the Inter-American Court of Human Rights* (2nd edn, CUP, 2013); L Bourgorgue-Larsen and AU de Torres, *The Inter-American Court of Human Rights* (OUP, 2011). For a more critical perspective, see N Torres Zuñíga, *The Inter-American Court of Human Rights: The Legitimacy of International Courts and Tribunals* (Routledge, 2023).

[105] ACHR (n 101) Art 44. [106] *Ibid*, Art 45. [107] *Ibid*, Art 64.

[108] *The Effect of Reservations on the Entry into Force of the American Convention on Human Rights*, Advisory Opinion OC-2/92, IACtHR Ser A No 2 (1983) 22 ILM 33; 67 ILR 559. See further Chapter 7, Section 7.3.4 ('Legal consequences of impermissible reservations').

[109] These reports are available at <http://www.oas.org/en/iachr/reports/country.asp>.

[110] An accessible history is found in S Cardenas, *Human Rights in Latin America: A Politics of Terror and Hope* (U Penn Press, 2011).

[111] *Velásquez Rodríguez v Honduras*, IACtHR Ser C No 4 (29 July 1988) (1989) 28 ILM 378. See also *Godínez Cruz v Honduras*, IACtHR Ser C No 5 (20 January 1989), 95 ILR 320.

[112] *Barrios Altos (Chumbipuma Aguirre and ors v Peru)*, IACtHR Ser C No 87 (30 November 2001) (2002) 41 ILM 91. See C Binder, 'The Prohibition of Amnesties by the Inter-American Court of Human Rights' (2012) 12 German LJ 1203.

formal issue of property title, and may entitle such peoples to demand official recognition and registration, even when they have been obliged to leave those lands.[113]

16.4.3 **The African Charter system**

All fifty-four members of the African Union have signed the 1981 Banjul Charter of Human and Peoples' Rights.[114] The Banjul Charter differs substantially from its European[115] and inter-American counterparts, enshrining economic, social, and cultural rights, such as a right to health or a right to education; and various 'peoples' rights' beyond collective rights, including the right to development and to a 'satisfactory' environment. It is also the only human rights convention that details the duties of an individual to the State, society, and family.[116]

Under Article 30 of the Banjul Charter, the African Commission on Human and Peoples' Rights (ACnHPR) was established in 1986.[117] Composed of eleven members, the Commission can deal with complaints from individuals and NGOs, examines periodic reports submitted by member States, and can adopt resolutions and declarations. It may also appoint special rapporteurs to investigate human rights violations in specific areas, as well as working groups that monitor and investigate specific questions.

A significant complaint brought by two NGOs concerned the Ogoni people in Nigeria and violations caused to their economic, social, and cultural rights by Nigeria's collaboration with the Shell Petroleum Development Company in oil exploration.[118] In an important communication, the ACnHPR concluded that their acts were in breach of the right to health (Banjul Charter, Article 16), the right to a satisfactory environment (Article 24), and the right of peoples to dispose freely of their wealth and natural resources (Article 21(1)).[119]

The ACnHPR may also hear inter-State complaints, with the most well known being submitted by the Democratic Republic of the Congo against Burundi, Rwanda, and Uganda. The Commission determined that, in their occupation of parts of the Congo, the three respondent States had violated the 'right to peace' contained in Article 23 of

[113] *Sawhoyamaxa Indigenous Community v Paraguay*, IACtHR Ser C No 146 (29 March 2006). See earlier, Section 16.3.4 on indigenous peoples.

[114] See earlier, n 60.

[115] Though it is worth mentioning that the European Social Charter (revised) (adopted 3 May 1996, entered into force 1 July 1999), CETS No 163, does protect economic and social rights in Europe alongside the ECHR.

[116] On these distinctive features of the Banjul Charter (n 60), see UO Umozurike, *The African Charter on Human and Peoples' Rights* (2nd edn, Nijhoff, 2012); A Bello, 'The African Charter on Human and Peoples' Rights' (1985) 194 Recueil des Cours 5.

[117] For an evaluation of the system, see, e.g., M Evans and R Murray, *The African Charter on Human and Peoples' Rights: The System in Practice, 1986–2006* (2nd edn, CUP, 2008); R Murray, *The African Commission on Human and Peoples' Rights* (Hart, 2000); F Ouguergouz, 'La Commission africaine des droits de l'homme et des peuples' (1989) AFDI 557.

[118] *Social and Economic Rights Action Center (SERAC) and Center for Economic and Social Rights (CESR)/ Nigeria*, ACnHPR Comm 155/96 (27 October 2001). See further F Coomans, 'The *Ogoni* Case before the African Commission on Human and Peoples' Rights' (2003) 52 ICLQ 749.

[119] The ACnHPR has also recognized rights to shelter, housing, and food, which are not expressly recognized in the Banjul Charter (n 60) as being made necessary by the combination of expressly recognized rights: see paras 60–2, 64–6.

the Banjul Charter; moreover, they had committed a series of human rights violations during the occupation.[120]

The African Court of Human and Peoples' Rights (ACtHPR) was established after a Protocol adopted in 1998 under the Organization for African Unity (OAU, since 2000 the African Union (AU)) entered into force.[121] States parties,[122] the Commission, and African inter-governmental organizations have automatic access to the Court, and may also request advisory opinions.[123] Moreover, a few States also allow NGOs or individuals to bring cases directly to the Court.[124]

Pursuant to a 2008 Protocol, the ACtHPR will be merged into a proposed African Court of Justice and Human Rights (ACJHR), also including jurisdiction for inter-State disputes as well as over international crimes (under an amendment introduced in the 2014 Malabo Protocol). The new ACJHR will come into being when fifteen African Union member States have ratified the 2008 Protocol;[125] as of early 2025, only seven States parties are parties to the Protocol.[126]

16.5 Refugees, migrants, and other displaced persons

The underlying logic of international human rights law rests on the protection of individuals under the municipal law of a State. But what of individuals who have fled the jurisdiction of a State and are either unwilling or unable to seek protection from their original country? Do the reasons why people flee their country of nationality matter? What rights might such individuals possess? The centrality of borders and the restrictions on personal movement inherent in this area go far beyond human rights law, calling into question basic notions of society and human dignity.[127]

Under international law, only certain defined categories of persons receive protection from their home State, depending on their reasons for having left their home and whether they have crossed an international border. The following sections will consider

[120] See Communication 227/99, African Commission, *Twentieth Activity Report*, EX.CL/279 (IX), Annex IV, 11 *et seq*. Disputes between these States were also submitted to the ICJ, with the dispute between Congo and Uganda now awaiting a decision on reparations. See Chapter 14, Section 14.3.4, for further discussion of this case.

[121] Protocol on the Establishment of an African Court of Human Rights (10 June 1998, entered into force 25 January 2004), Art 12. See also D Padilla, 'An African Human Rights Court: Reflections from the Perspective of the Inter-American System' (2002) 2 African HRLJ 185; RW Eno, 'The Jurisdiction of the African Court of Human and People's Rights' (2002) 2 African HRLJ 223.

[122] As of the time of press, thirty-four States parties have ratified the Protocol (see <http://en.african-court.org>).

[123] 1998 Protocol (n 120) Art 4. At the time of press, fifteen advisory opinions have been published, and only one request is pending.

[124] Under a declaration made under Article 34(6): Burkina Faso, Gambia, Ghana, Guinea-Bissau, Mali, Malawi, and Niger. Côte d'Ivoire, Benin, Tanzania, and Tunisia have withdrawn their declarations.

[125] Protocol on the Statute of the African Court of Justice and Human Rights (adopted 1 July 2008, not yet in force) (2009) 48 ILM 334.

[126] At the time of press, Angola, Benin, Burkina Faso, Congo, Gambia, Libya, Liberia, and Mali.

[127] For an ambitious and incisive critique, see T Achiume, 'Racial Borders' (2022) 110 Georgetown LJ 445; and see the argument in S Dehm, 'Framing International Migration' (2015) 3 London Review of International Law 133.

the following categories: refugees and asylum seekers; internally displaced persons (IDPs); stateless persons; and migrant workers.

16.5.1 **The 1951 Refugee Convention**

The 1951 Convention Relating to the Status of Refugees[128] was drafted in response to mass European migration following Nazi mass extermination—in particular, the Holocaust—and Stalinist expansion into Central and Eastern Europe.[129] The refugee protection system is overseen by the Office of the UN High Commissioner for Refugees, which supervises the application of the Convention, publishes guidelines as to its interpretation, and calls attention to the problems of internally displaced and stateless persons.[130]

16.5.1.1 **Determining refugee status**

The Refugee Convention sets out a detailed definition for who qualifies as a 'refugee' in Article 1: a refugee is someone with a 'well-founded fear of persecution' and who is 'unable or unwilling' to avail themselves of the protection of their country of nationality.[131] Under Article 1A.2, a person must cross an international boundary to claim refugee status in the country of asylum.[132] However, under an exclusion clause, persons having committed certain serious crimes are excluded from refugee status even if they would otherwise qualify.[133]

There is no agreed procedure for States to follow when determining whether a person fulfils the criteria of a refugee, though a 'Handbook of Guidelines' for determining refugee status is updated regularly with indications to States on how to interpret the Refugee Convention.[134] Moreover, though there is no international body to which an individual can complain, there are some domestic judicial decisions that may shed light on how the various criteria for refugee status operate in practice. These will be briefly surveyed in this section.

[128] Convention Relating to the Status of Refugees (signed 28 July 1951, entered into force 22 April, 1954), 189 UNTS 150. See A Zimmermann (ed), *The 1951 Convention Relating to the Status of Refugees and its 1967 Protocol: A Commentary* (OUP, 2011).

[129] For comprehensive overviews, see JC Hathaway, *The Rights of Refugees under International Law* (OUP, 2005); H Lambert (ed), *International Refugee Law* (Routledge, 2010); and G Goodwin-Gill and J McAdam, *The Refugee in International Law* (3rd edn, OUP, 2007).

[130] Statute of the OUNHCR, UNGA Res 428(V) (14 December 1950), Annex, Art 8(a). For further reading on UNHCR, see C Lewis, *UNHCR and International Refugee Law* (Routledge, 2014); and V Türk, 'The Role of UNHCR in the Development of International Refugee Law' in F Nicholson (ed), *Refugee Rights and Realities: Evolving International Concepts and Regimes* (CUP, 1999), 153.

[131] If stateless, the country of 'habitual residence': see Art 1A.2, and later, Section 16.5.3. In cases of multiple nationality, an individual must naturally have a well-founded fear of persecution in all countries of nationality.

[132] A detailed commentary is found in A Zimmermann and C Mahler, 'Article 1A, para. 2' in A Zimmermann (ed), *The 1951 Convention Relating to the Status of Refugees and its 1967 Protocol: A Commentary* (OUP, 2011), 281.

[133] Refugee Convention (n 126) Art 1F lists crimes against peace, war crimes, crimes against humanity, a 'serious non-political crime' outside the country of refuge, or acts 'contrary to the purposes and principles of the United Nations'. Exclusion is a broad topic, on which much has been written: see A Zimmermann and P Wennholz, 'Article 1F' in A Zimmermann (ed), *The 1951 Convention Relating to the Status of Refugees and its 1967 Protocol: A Commentary* (OUP, 2011), 579.

[134] UNHCR, *Handbook and Guidelines on Procedures and Criteria for Determining Refugee Status under the 1951 Convention and the 1967 Protocol relating to the Status of Refugees* (reissued December 2011), UN Doc HCR/1P/4/ENG/Rev.3.

Persecution under the Convention must fall under one (or more) of five grounds enumerated in Article 1:[135]

Race. The understanding of the social construct of 'race'[136] in the Refugee Convention has been interpreted in line with Article 1 of the CERD and encompasses both ethnic and national origin, as well as social groups of common descent.[137]

Religion. Persecution on religious grounds targets an individual or group based on their faith; or lack of faith, in the case of atheists. Persecution can be directed against adherents of the same faith, perhaps based on divisions within a faith group or a person's refusal to conform with certain tenets; or those of a different conviction altogether.[138]

Nationality. Nationality refers to the civil status of citizenship and how one is treated within a territory; it can be directed against the nationals of another State or a stateless person—in particular, those being deprived arbitrarily of access to a nationality to which they would be legally entitled. Persecution may also arise if, for example, an invading State occupied another State and targeted the existing population.

Membership of a particular social group. Potentially the broadest category, 'membership of a particular social group' has sometimes been used to include groups not otherwise covered who suffer persecution, such groups being defined either by voluntary association or by certain inherent shared characteristics. Both domestic courts and UNHCR guidelines have broadened refugee status under this category to include persons fleeing persecution in relation to:

- gender (against women and girls), when fleeing persecution either by the State or by private actors—for example, their own relatives;[139]
- victims of human trafficking;[140] and
- sexual orientation and gender identity, even when authorities have contended that these can be 'concealed', on the basis of their immutability.[141]

135 A full analysis of practice and interpretation of the five grounds can be found in Zimmermann and Mahler (n 130).

136 Art 1*(c)* of the UNESCO Declaration on Race and Racial Prejudice (27 November 1978) stated that all human beings belong to a single species, descended from a 'common stock'.

137 In *Sejdić and Finci v Bosnia and Herzegovina*, App Nos 27996/06 and 34836/06 (ECtHR, Grand Chamber, 22 December 2009), the applicants were denied from standing for election to the House of Representatives on the basis of their ethnicity (Sejdić was Roma and Finci was Jewish), despite being citizens. The Grand Chamber declared this discrimination to be in breach of ECHR (n 79) Art 14.

138 For some interpretive guidance, see UNHCR, Guidelines on International Protection No 6: 'Religion-Based Refugee Claims under Article 1A.2 of the 1951 Convention and/or the 1967 Protocol' (28 April 2004), UN Doc HCR/GIP/04/06.

139 See *González et al ('Cotton Field') v Mexico*, IACtHR Ser C, No 205 (16 November 2009); and *Islam v Secretary of State for the Home Department, R v Immigration Appeal Tribunal and Another, ex p Shah* [1999] 2 AC 629 (UK), where the House of Lords accorded two Pakistani women refugee status, as they feared being killed after being accused of adultery.

140 UNHCR, *Guidelines on International Protection No 7: The Application of Article 1A.2 of the 1951 Convention and/or 1967 Protocol to Victims of Trafficking and Persons at Risk of Being Trafficked* (7 April 2006), HCR/GIP/06/07. See also *Canada (Attorney General) v Ward* [1993] 2 SCR 689, 739 (Canada).

141 UNHCR, *Guidelines on International Protection No 9: Claims to Refugee Status based on Sexual Orientation and/or Gender Identity within the context of Article 1A.2 of the 1951 Convention and/or its 1967 Protocol* (23 October 2012), HCR/GIP/12/01. See also Joined Cases C-199–201/12, *X, Y, Z v Minister voor Immigratie en Asiel*, CJEU (7 November 2013); *OM v Hungary* App No 9912/15 (ECtHR, 5 July 2016); *RT (Zimbabwe) et al v Secretary of State for the Home Office* [2012] UKSC 38 (UK).

CASE SPOTLIGHT ***Canada (Attorney General) v Ward*** **[1993] 2 SCR 689 (Supreme Court of Canada)**

Patrick Ward had fled Northern Ireland to escape being murdered by the 'Irish National Liberation Army' (INLA), from which he had defected. He had been assigned by the INLA to guard some hostages; when he learned they were to be executed, he permitted their escape. After being tortured by the INLA and imprisoned by Ireland for his role in the hostage-taking, he fled to Canada and claimed refugee status.

In deciding on Ward's claims, the Supreme Court made a number of important statements in relation to the determination of refugee status. First, the Court declared that acts by private citizens, combined with the State's inability to protect, would be sufficient to constitute persecution (713–14). More importantly, the *Ward* judgment laid out a broader interpretation of 'membership in a particular social group' to take into account the 'defence of human rights and anti-discrimination that form the basis for the international refugee protection initiative'. These groups are defined by:

- an 'innate or unchangeable characteristic', such as gender, linguistic background, and sexual orientation;
- members who are associated 'for reasons so fundamental to their human dignity' that they should not be forced to forsake the association, such as human rights activists; and
- a former voluntary status, 'unalterable due to its historical permanence'. The Supreme Court suggested that 'one's past is an immutable part of the person' (739).

Though the Court found that Ward's prior membership of the INLA did not fall within these social groups, it did consider that Ward was persecuted by the INLA because of his political opinion, specifically his belief that the killing of innocent hostages is an unacceptable means of achieving political change (750).

The *Ward* judgment has become very influential in interpreting the criteria for persecution under the Refugee Convention, and its teleological approach to interpretation has been taken up by UNHCR and other domestic courts.

Originally, forcibly displaced persons fleeing 'armed conflict and generalized violence' were excluded from the scope of the Convention, on the basis that they were not fleeing persecution as such.[142] However, prompted by the increase in recent decades of mass displacement by fleeing armed conflicts, in 2016 UNHCR published guidelines suggesting that events occurring in situations of armed conflict and generalized violence could, in certain cases, amount to persecution.[143]

Political opinion. Persecution based on political opinion extends beyond political affiliation or membership of a political party and can be attributed, for example, to

[142] In the 1979 version of the Handbook and Guidelines for Determining Refugee Status (n 132) paras 164–6, such persons were not deemed by UNCnHR to be suffering persecution under the five enumerated grounds.

[143] UNHCR, *Guidelines on International Protection No 12: Claims for refugee status related to situations of armed conflict and violence under Article 1A.2 of the 1951 Convention and/or 1967 Protocol and the regional refugee definitions* (2 December 2016), HCR/GIP/16/12.

journalists whose work attracts an imputed political opinion,[144] or even on taking a position on upholding freedom of expression.[145]

Earlier, the five grounds for persecution were discussed; what follows is a swift overview of the other components of the definition.

Well-founded fear. Domestic courts have interpreted 'well-founded fear' as a primarily, but not exclusively, subjective standard in relation to the individual applicant. This means that the fear must be prima facie[146] reasonable to the actual applicant, with tribunals taking into account factors such as age (a child will have a different level of rational fear than an adult) or previous experiences in assessing how well founded or justified their fear of persecution may be.[147]

Persecution. 'Persecution' entails a fairly high threshold for a violation; it is related, but not limited, to the possible violation of fundamental human rights such as torture, slavery, inhuman or degrading treatment, or losing one's life.[148] By itself, so-called 'mere' discrimination does not arise to the level of persecution, though a single act may be sufficiently serious to satisfy the threshold.[149] Persecution need not be committed by a State or State actors; a failure by the State to ensure adequate protection to an individual can also create a need for surrogate international protection.[150]

Inability or unwillingness. An applicant must be 'unable' (e.g., because there is no protection under municipal law) or 'unwilling' (e.g., because the State itself is complicit in their persecution) to avail themselves of the protection of their country of nationality. In cases of persecution involving a rebel group controlling parts of a State's territory, certain courts in developed States have denied refugee claims, suggesting that a refugee can be deported safely to another part of the State where the government is still in control and can offer protection (the so-called 'internal protection alternative').[151]

[144] *Secretary of State for the Home Department v MSM (Somalia)* [2016] EWCA Civ 715 (UK).

[145] *Klinko v Canada (Minister of Citizenship and Immigration)* [2000] 3 FC 327 (Canada).

[146] UNHCR, *Guidelines on International Protection No 11: Prima Facie Recognition of Refugee Status* (24 June 2015), HCR/GIP/15/11, para 5.

[147] *Attorney-General of Canada v Ward* (n 138); *HJ (Iran) and HT (Cameroon) v Secretary of State for the Home Office* [2010] UKSC 31, paras 17 *et seq* (UK).

[148] *Urim Gashi, Astrit Nikshiqi v Secretary of State for the Home Department* HX-75677–95, HX/75478/95, 1996 UKIAT No 13695, 14, where, drawing on language from *Soering v UK* (n 94), a 'flagrant denial' of freedom of religion can also constitute persecution.

[149] See, e.g., *Minister of Immigration and Multicultural Affairs v Ibrahim* [2000] HCA 55 (High Court of Australia). Cumulative discriminatory acts can together rise to the level of persecution: see R Dowd, 'Dissecting Discrimination in Refugee Law: An Analysis of its Meaning and its Cumulative Effect' (2011) 23 IJRL 28.

[150] *Islam v Secretary of State for the Home Department, R v Immigration Appeal Tribunal and Another, ex p Shah* [1999] 2 AC 629 (UK); see also 2 BvR 260/98 and 2 BvR 1353/98 (German Federal Constitutional Court), 10 August 2000, reprinted in (2002) 14 IJRL 158.

[151] *Dyli v Secretary of State for the Home Department* [2000] UKIAT 00001. See also Directive 2011/95/EU of the European Parliament and of the Council of 13 December 2011 on Standards for the Qualification of Third-Country Nationals or Stateless Persons as Beneficiaries of International Protection, for a Uniform Status for Refugees or for Persons Eligible for Subsidiary Protection, and for the Content of the Protection Granted (Recast) [2011] OJ L337/9 (EUQD), Arts 6 and 7.

16.5.1.2 Non-refoulement

Article 33(1) of the Refugee Convention contains the most important guarantee for refugees, that of *non-refoulement*: individuals will not be expelled or returned to their country of nationality if their 'life or freedom would be threatened' on account of one of the five protected grounds in Article 1.[152] This guarantee of *non-refoulement* binds all States parties and is also found in Article 3(1) of the Convention against Torture and, in a lesser but similar form, in the ICCPR and the ECHR.[153]

The guarantee of *non-refoulement* in the Refugee Convention is not absolute; Article 33(2) rejects it for persons 'whom there are reasonable grounds for regarding as a danger to the security of the country in which [they are], or who, having been convicted by a final judgment of a particularly serious crime, constitutes a danger to the community of that country'. The standard of proof for *non-refoulement* is 'would be threatened', which is somewhat higher than 'well-founded fear'.[154] Though US courts have interpreted the two thresholds as being separate,[155] some domestic courts, like that of the UK, merge the two tests such that there is a 'reasonable degree of likelihood that the prosecution will occur'.[156]

Practical implementation of the *non-refoulement* rule remains inconsistent, with significant grey zones. Though States parties must comply with Article 33 of the Refugee Convention, they remain entitled to introduce systems of immigration control and visa requirements. Article 33(1) prohibits a return to the border of the State from which they are fleeing, but not to any other State. These have led to distasteful restrictions such as the 'first country of arrival rule' or 'safe third country rule', which have created 'chains of deportation' at the end of which a refugee has found themselves in the first State where they arrived after having fled their home State. Certain Western States, moreover, practise 'extraterritorial *refoulement*', intercepting refugees on the high seas and keeping them outside territorial waters.[157]

[152] E Lauterpacht and D Bethlehem, 'The Scope and Content of the Principle of *Non-Refoulement*: Opinion' in E Feller, V Türk, and F Nicholson (eds), *Refugee Protection in International Law* (CUP, 2003), para 216.

[153] Though no guarantee against *refoulement*, ICCPR (n 15) Art 13 provides that an alien lawfully present in a territory can only be expelled pursuant to a lawful decision and be allowed to have that decision reviewed. In *Soering v UK* (n 94), *Chahal v UK* App No 22414/93 (ECtHR, 1996) and *Saadi v Italy* App No 37201/06 (ECtHR, 2008), the ECtHR 'read in' a guarantee against *refoulement* if there was a risk of a violation to rights protected under the ECHR.

[154] As described earlier in Section 16.5.1.1.

[155] *INS v Cardoza-Fonseca*, 480 US 401 (1987) (US); *INS v Stević*, 467 US 407 (1984).

[156] *R v Secretary of State for the Home Office, ex p Sivakumaran and Conjoined Appeals (UNHCR Intervening)* [1988] AC 958 at 993 (UK).

[157] In *Sale v Haitian Centers Council*, 509 US 155 (1993), the US Supreme Court upheld as lawful the practice of intercepting Haitians in international waters and returning them to Haiti, but the IACHR found it to breach Art 33 of the Refugee Convention: see *Haitian Interdiction Case* 10.675 IACommHR No 51/96 OEA/Ser.L/V/II.95 doc.7 Rev [1997] 550, paras 156–8. A similar 2012 Italy–Libya agreement has already been declared unlawful by the ECtHR's Grand Chamber: see *Hirsi Jamaa and Ors v Italy* App No 27765/09 (ECtHR, 23 February 2012).

CONTEMPORARY DEVELOPMENTS The Dubious Legality of 'Offshore Processing Centres'

For a number of years, Australia has engaged in a practice similar to the USA of extraterritorial *refoulement*, by turning back boats with asylum seekers so they cannot reach its territory. So as to circumvent accusations of *non-refoulement*, Australia has adopted an even stricter policy of transferring asylum seekers on board to 'offshore processing centres', to assess their asylum claims; however, even if they are found to be refugees, they are not allowed to be settled in Australia. One processing centre is in Nauru; a second, on Manus Island (Papua New Guinea), will be finally shut down at the end of 2021 after the Papuan Supreme Court ruled in 2016 that restricting the movement of asylum seekers is unconstitutional.

Several human rights groups have complained that Australia's policy amounts to the indefinite detention of asylum seekers, and that detainees in the Nauru and Manus camps suffer from appalling living conditions and physical and sexual assaults. Making matters worse, at times the administration of asylum claims has reprehensively been delegated by Australia to private companies, without right to appeal (see, on this point, T Gammeltoft-Hansen, *Access to Asylum: International Refugee Law and the Globalisation of Migration Control* (CUP, 2011)). UNHCR has long urged action by Australia, citing the grim living conditions in both camps (reports are compiled at https://www.unhcr.org/en-au/united-nations-observations.html).

Despite these shortcomings, others are following Australia's dubious example. Denmark passed legislation in June 2021 allowing for relocation of asylum seekers outside the EU, though in 2024 the UK abandoned plans to offshore asylum seekers to Rwanda after the UK Supreme Court ruled it unlawful (see *R (on the application of AAA and ors) v Home Secretary* [2023] UKSC 42). The European Union and its members have considered similar practices, proposing offshore processing camps in Albania Ukraine, Morocco, or even further afield in Mali, Niger, or Chad. Certain of member State Greece's islands are also being used as *de facto* processing centres, with asylum seekers barred from leaving for the mainland without completing specific tests, and often waiting for months or years. Moreover, pursuant to a 2016 agreement with the EU, Türkiye accepts the return of certain Turkish asylum seekers from Greece before their claims are processed; for every individual returned, in addition to billions of euros in aid, the EU resettles one Syrian refugee processed by UNHCR in Türkiye.

Despite scathing criticism of this policy, which may well violate the principle of *non-refoulement*, offshore processing will remain a key feature of EU efforts: see, in particular, the 2024 EU Pact on Migration and Asylum. In 2025 the European Commission was to table further proposals on this problematic initiative.

16.5.1.3 The Global Compact on Refugees

The legal framework for protection of refugees has been severely criticized. For this reason, in 2016 the General Assembly unanimously adopted the 'New York Declaration for Refugees and Migrants',[158] pledging to enhance the protection of both refugees and migrants through a 'Comprehensive Refugee Response Framework' (CRRF) (annexed to the New York Declaration) and a programme of action to support refugees, host

[158] See UNGA Res 71/1 (3 October 2016).

States, and other stakeholders. The Global Compact on Refugees (GCR) was proposed by the UNHCR in its 2018 annual report to the General Assembly,[159] and was endorsed by the General Assembly on 17 December 2018.[160] Though non-binding, the GCR sets out several guiding principles, a focus on the prevention and addressing root causes, and commits States to the implementation of the CRRF through an extensive programme of action. The GCR also lays out discussions for biannual high-level meetings and, every four years, a 'Global Refugee Forum' to take stock of current developments. The first such Forum was convened in 2019; it next met in 2023 and will meet again in 2027.

16.5.2 **Internally displaced persons (IDPs)**

Earlier, it was explained that the 1951 Refugee Convention requires that applicants claiming refugee status be outside their State of nationality. What, then, of persons fleeing their homes involuntarily within a State? Under international law, these are termed 'internally displaced persons' (IDPs), and though in theory they benefit from the protection of international human rights law, it is clear that internal displacement brings its own specific challenges. The International Organization of Migration (IOM) estimates that there are nearly seventy-two million internally displaced persons in fifty-six countries as a result of conflict, violence, or natural disasters,[161] none of which meet the criteria laid out in Article 1A(2) of the Refugee Convention.

Though there is no binding convention with respect to internally displaced persons, in 1998 States agreed a set of 'Guiding Principles on Internal Displacement', a restatement of existing human rights and humanitarian norms that are relevant to internally displaced persons.[162] Though not binding, many of its principles have been incorporated by States into their municipal legal orders,[163] and they have in addition been referred to by the Security Council, the General Assembly, and other UN bodies. The Guiding Principles describe IDPs as persons or groups fleeing their homes in situations of armed conflict or generalized violence, human rights violations, and national or human-made disaster, but crucially—and unlike refugees—who have not crossed an international boundary. This looser definition does not require a fear of persecution, and thus includes many persons who would otherwise be unable to claim any protective status under the 1951 Convention.

UNHCR has a long history of involvement with internally displaced persons;[164] since 1992, the Secretary-General has appointed a UN Representative on Internally

[159] UNGA Res 73/12 Pt II (13 September 2018).

[160] See UNGA Res 73/151 (17 December 2018). This is a distinct document from the Global Compact on Safe, Orderly, and Regular Migration adopted on 10 December 2018: see later, n 186.

[161] See IOM World Migration Report 2024 (IOM Publications, 2024). This represents a trebling of IDPs since records began in 1998.

[162] UNHCR, Guiding Principles on Internal Displacement (11 February 1998), UN Doc E/CN.4/1998/53/Add.2.

[163] A number of these are cited in Report of W Kälin, Representative of the Secretary-General on the Human Rights of Internally Displaced Persons (11 February 2009), UN Doc A/HRC/10/13/Add.3; and are referenced online at <http://www.refworld.org/idps.html>.

[164] The formal basis for UNHCR's mandate with IDPs is found in UNGA Res 48/116 (20 December 1993), which *inter alia* enables requests to be made to UNHCR by the Secretary-General or other principal organs of the UN. See also UNGA Res 53/125 (9 December 1998).

Displaced Persons and the UN Human Rights Council appointed a Special Rapporteur on the human rights of displaced persons in 2016. On a regional level, the 2009 Kampala Convention[165] protects IDPs in Africa, and seeks to establish a detailed legal framework of the rights and remedies of IDPs.

Though the protection of IDPs remains manifestly inadequate, they benefit from the protection of international human rights law, such as freedom of movement within a territory (Article 12 ICCPR), non-discrimination (Article 26 ICCPR, Article 5 CERD), or the right to adequate housing (Article 11 ICESCR). The Guiding Principles gather these, and other principles relating to rights during displacement, return, resettlement and reintegration, and humanitarian assistance. For example, Principle 15, an important rule akin to the guarantee against *non-refoulement*, protects IDPs from forcible return or resettlement to their home, if it is unsafe. The principles of the GCR also acknowledge the challenges for IDPs.[166]

16.5.3 **Stateless persons**

Citizenship is often regarded as a form of participation in a political community; but as history has shown us, it is also a form of protection that entitles its holder to certain fundamental rights.[167] By stripping an individual or group of citizenship, that person may no longer participate in the political process, may not be able to work or live legally in the territory of a State, and may lose access to housing, health care, and education. Though citizenship is not formally necessary to enjoy these rights, its removal paves the way for their denial. During World War II, Jews and the Roma were famously denationalized and deprived of rights in Nazi Germany.[168]

Historically, it has been the exclusive prerogative of a State to settle rules on the acquisition or conferral of their nationality;[169] an individual's statelessness was not their concern. With mass migration, battles for gender equality, and the rise of nationalism throughout the nineteenth and early twentieth centuries, the first efforts began to be made for international law to address statelessness. In the 1920s, States agreed to regulate issues of dual nationality and statelessness; for example, regarding women marrying foreign men, and their children, and signed a treaty providing modest protection to these two groups.[170] Following the mass movements of peoples during and after World

[165] African Union Convention for the Protection and Assistance of Internally Displaced Persons in Africa (Kampala Convention) (signed 22 October 2009, entered into force 6 September 2012, thirty-four States parties).

[166] See GCR (n 158) paras 12, 53, and 89.

[167] H Arendt, *The Origins of Totalitarianism* (Harcourt, 1951), 299, argued that citizenship was the only practicable way to enjoy human rights. Malcolm X, *By Any Means Necessary: Speeches, Interviews, and a Letter by Malcolm X* (G Breitman ed, Pathfinder Press, 1970), 56, took the opposite view, that citizenship status prevented Afro-Americans from enjoying their rights, and that a transnational 'right to be a human being' was more important. See further A Çubukçu, 'Thinking against Humanity' (2017) 5 LRIL 251.

[168] For further reading on scope of the 'Nuremberg Laws', RGB I No 100 (16 September 1935), see, e.g., S Friedlander, *Nazi Germany and the Jews, 1933–45* (Harper Collins, 2009).

[169] See *Nationality Decrees in Tunis and Morocco, Advisory Opinion, 1923, PCIJ, Ser B, No 4*, para 38; *Nottebohm (Liechtenstein v Guatemala), Second Phase, ICJ Reports 1955*, p 4, 20.

[170] See, e.g., Hague Convention on Certain Questions relating to the Conflict of Nationality Laws and the Protocol relating to a Certain Case of Statelessness (signed 13 April 1930, entered into force 1 July 1937), 179 LNTS 89 (No 4137).

War II, States began to recognize the value of nationality for individuals. Article 15 of the UDHR proclaimed the 'right to a nationality' and that it not be arbitrarily deprived from individuals; and in 1954, the first convention giving certain rights to stateless persons would be signed.[171] In 1961, the more ambitious Convention on the Reduction of Statelessness was adopted, obliging parties to grant nationality to those born on their territory who would otherwise be born stateless (Article 1) and, significantly, prohibiting denationalization on racial, ethnic, religious, or political grounds (Article 9).[172]

For all this, the practice of deprivation of citizenship exists still today, with recent legislative developments in Europe being of concern. Belgium and France have enacted legislation that allows the government to deprive a national of citizenship if convicted of serious terrorist offences;[173] Germany, the Netherlands, and the UK have gone a step further: there is no legal requirement for a criminal conviction before depriving a national of citizenship.[174] Normally, an order of deprivation ought not to result in statelessness, and thus in practice most legislation is only applicable against dual nationals.[175]

Statelessness and orders to deprive nationality are exceptionally complex and are not mere accidental phenomena, but often produced by explicit State policy.[176] The ongoing saga of Shamima Begum is a vivid demonstration. In 2015, British-born Begum (aged 15 at the time) had travelled to Syria to align herself with ISIL. The Home Secretary deprived her of British citizenship in 2019 on national security grounds, claiming she was also a Bangladeshi national.[177] In 2021, Begum's appeal for leave to return to the UK to fight the deprivation order was rejected by the UK Supreme Court on the grounds that she had no effective right of appeal against deprivation; her potential statelessness was not in issue.[178]

[171] Convention relating to the Status of Stateless Persons (signed 28 September 1954, entered into force 6 June 1960), 360 UNTS 117 (ninety-nine parties).

[172] Convention on the Reduction of Statelessness (signed 30 August 1961, entered into force 13 December 1975), 989 UNTS 175 (eighty-two parties). The text of Art 9 is echoed in CERD (n 46) Art 5(d)(iii).

[173] See Belgian Code of Nationality 1984, arts 23§1, 23/1 and 23/2 (since 2012, if convicted in relation to specific terrorist offences); and French Civil Code, art 25 (since 2003, if convicted in relation to specific terrorist offences). See further MP Bolhuis and J van Wijk, 'Citizenship Deprivation as a Counterterrorism Measure in Europe: Possible Follow-up Scenarios, Human Rights Infringements and the Effect on Counterterrorism' (2020) 22 European Journal of Migration and Law 338, ss 2.1, 2.2, and 2.6.

[174] See German Nationality Act, Art 28(1), where since 2019, evidence of participation in combat operations with a terrorist organization abroad suffices; Dutch Nationality Act, arts 14(2) and 14(4) (removing the requirement of criminal conviction in 2016); and British Nationality Act 1981, s 40(2) (if deprivation is 'conducive' to the public good). See further Bolhuis and van Wijk, *ibid*, ss 2.3–2.6.

[175] French Code Civil, art 25; Belgian Code of Nationality 1984, arts 23, 23/1, and 23/2; German *Grundesgetz* 1949 (Basic Law), s 16; Dutch Nationality Act, art 14(8); and British Nationality Act 1981, s 40(4) (see also, to this effect, *Home Secretary v Al-Jedda* [2013] UKSC 62 (9 October 2013)). Uniquely, in 2014 the British Nationality Act was amended by s 40(4A), which also tolerates a deprivation order leading to statelessness if, *inter alia*, there are 'reasonable grounds' for believing that the person can become the national of another State.

[176] See N Jain, 'Manufacturing Statelessness' (2022) 116 *AJIL* 237.

[177] In *Begum v Home Secretary*, SIAC Appeal No 163/2019 (7 February 2020), the Special Immigration Appeals Commission (SIAC) decided that Ms Begum had not been left stateless, and that she is a Bangladeshi national, despite the Bangladeshi government denying that claim.

[178] *Begum v Home Secretary* [2021] UKSC 7 (26 February 2021).

Finally, several multilateral human rights conventions also seek to protect certain rights appertaining to nationality,[179] though in 2021, the ICJ held (by a single vote) that the term 'national origin' in the CERD did not extend to 'nationality' in the sense of citizenship and thus could be a valid ground of discrimination, outside the scope of that Convention.[180] Moreover, UNHCR has been tasked by the General Assembly to monitor issues relating to statelessness, as well as to provide assistance to stateless persons, whether *de jure* (formally deprived of nationality) or *de facto* (effectively deprived of a nationality).[181] UNHCR provides substantial guidance to States, in the form of handbooks and guidelines, in relation to questions raised of statelessness.[182] However, UNHCR cannot review the decisions of States to deprive or to change the legal status of an individual; nor can it restore citizenship. Much remains to be done to protect stateless persons, though perhaps a way forward is found in the GCR, which acknowledges that statelessness may be both a cause and consequence of refugee movements, and commits UNHCR and States to contribute resources to reduce the phenomenon of statelessness.[183]

THEORY AND DEBATES Climate Migrations: What Rights for Fleeing Citizens of Low-lying Island States?

Disasters linked to natural hazards are prolific: between 2008 and 2015, more than 200 million people were displaced by disasters, giving rise to the term 'climate refugees'. A rather new at-risk group are the citizens of small low-lying island States such as Kiribati, Vanuatu, the Marshall Islands, and Tuvalu. Due to climate change and the rise in sea level, the territory of these States is in danger of vanishing completely during the twenty-first century, rendering these persons stateless. Along with the disappearance of their island territories, all the institutions of a modern State, such as legislatures, police, courts, education, or health care would disappear as well. The potential of a 'de-territorialized State' is discussed in Chapter 5, Section 5.2.3. The issue in this legal regime is that climate refugees of this kind would not meet the criteria laid out in the 1951 Refugee Convention, which was designed to address situations of persecution. Should 'climate change migrants' be given the status of refugees? What rights to

[179] See UDHR (n 9) Art 15; CEDAW (n 47) Art 9 (gender equality in relation to the acquisition or loss of nationality); ICCPR (n 15) Art 24; CERD (n 46) Art 5 (a right to a nationality without racial or ethnic discrimination); and CRC (n 49) Art 7(1) (on children's right to a nationality); Migrant Workers Convention (n 50) Art 29 (on the right to a nationality of the children of migrant workers).

[180] *Application of the International Convention on the Elimination of All Forms of Racial Discrimination (Qatar v United Arab Emirates), Preliminary Objections, Judgment ICJ Reports 2021*, p 71, paras 81–8.

[181] See UNGA Res 3274 (XXIX) (10 December 1974); extended most recently in GA Res 61/137 (25 January 2007).

[182] See, e.g., UNCHR, *Handbook on Statelessness* (UNHCR Publications, 2014), superseding three 2012 Guidelines concerned, respectively, with the definition of a stateless person, procedures for determination of statelessness, and the status of stateless persons in national law. See further Guidelines on Statelessness No 4, UN Doc HCR/GS/12/04 (21 December 2012) (on children's right to a nationality); and Guidelines on Statelessness No 5, UN Doc HCR/GS/20/05 (20 May 2020) (on loss and deprivation of nationality), Section C of which (pp 14–24) covers the deprivation of nationality.

[183] GCR (n 158) para 83; see also paras 5, 60.

a nationality would they have if their State becomes defunct? Perhaps most importantly, could climate migrants invoke a right to settle in a new State?

This unique situation has implications across international law, touching upon refugee and migration law, environmental protection, and human rights. In a 2024 ILC Study Group report on sea-level rise on international law (UN Doc A/CN.4/774 (19 February 2024), it was acknowledged that, beyond the refugee law framework, the principle of *non-refoulement* has grown as a concept and is reflected in a range of multilateral human rights treaties (paras 234–6). In particular, the Study Group addressed *Teitiota v New Zealand*, in which HRC recognized that in some cases, like sea-level rise in Kiribati, the severe adverse effects of climate change might expose individuals to violations of key ICCPR provisions on the right to life (Article 6) and not to be subjected to torture or cruel, inhuman, or degrading treatment (Article 7), thus triggering the *non-refoulement* obligations of the potential sending State (HRC Doc CCPR/C127/D/2728/2016 (23 September 2020), para 9.11). Though the *Teitiota* reasoning has not as yet been followed in other cases, it is clear that sustained reflection is needed as to the protection and support offered to the most vulnerable to extreme climate harms.

For further reading, see J MacAdam, *Climate Change, Forced Migration, and International Law* (OUP, 2012), ch 5, '"Disappearing States", Statelessness, and Relocation'.

16.5.4 **Migrant workers**

Finally, there are so-called 'migrant workers', working people employed in a country other than their own. Minimal international labour standards are enshrined in conventions supervised by the International Labour Organization (ILO),[184] and only two focus specifically on the more vulnerable situation of migrant workers.[185] As such, in 1990 the Convention on Migrant Workers (CMW)[186] was adopted to clarify and strengthen certain basic protections for migrant workers. Besides recalling that more general human rights instruments apply equally to migrant workers, it specifies certain additional rights for 'regular' migrant workers (those who have entered into a country lawfully), such as the right to family reunification (Article 44(2) CMW), and calls upon States to impose sanctions on traffickers, smugglers, and employers who exploit irregular migrants (Article 68(1) CMW). However, the CMW has only been ratified by fifty-two States, none of which are among the major destinations for migrant workers.

Finally, there are also several non-binding instruments, such as the ILO Multilateral Framework on Labour Migration[187] and the annual reports and other activities of the UN

[184] A list of the eight 'fundamental' ILO conventions is available on the ILO's website: < https://www.ilo.org/international-labour-standards#standards>.

[185] See esp Convention concerning Migration for Employment (Revised), ILO Convention No 97 (signed 1 July 1949, entered into force 22 January 1952), 120 UNTS 71; Convention concerning Migrations in Abusive Conditions and the Promotion of Equality of Opportunity and Treatment of Migrant Workers, ILO Convention No 143 (signed 24 June 1975, entered into force 9 December 1978), 1120 UNTS 323.

[186] See earlier, n 50.

[187] As the ILO itself describes them on the cover, they are 'non-binding principles and guidelines for a rights-based approach to labour migration': see ILO, *Multilateral Framework on Labour Migration* (ILO Publications, 2006).

Special Rapporteur on the Human Rights of Migrants.[188] As with the Global Compact for Refugees, there are separate discussions on a Global Compact on Migration, a set of guiding principles that aim for a holistic and integrated legal framework to manage international migration, as well as address its root causes and the vulnerabilities created thereby.[189] The General Assembly hosted an intergovernmental conference on international migration in Marrakech on 10–11 December 2018 and adopted the Global Compact for Safe, Regular, and Orderly Migration.[190] Though hardly sufficient in themselves,[191] the Global Compacts remain the most recent restatement in the area.

16.6 **Conclusion**

The plethora of human rights institutions and instruments surveyed in this chapter show that human rights protection is at the forefront of international lawyers' minds. There are those who argue passionately that individual human rights protection has transformed the international legal order from the inside.[192] However, international human rights law continues to face certain challenges. For example, while it enshrines a degree of recognition for individuals, this has generally been done through the consent of States. This should not be underestimated, as this tactic reinforces the authority of the State as the source of human rights,[193] and not some extra-legal moral or ethical standard.[194]

Perhaps that is a necessary compromise in order to achieve certain protections, but a challenging one nonetheless. It is certainly true that international human rights law aspires to a world without injustice, without suffering, where law can be a tool to hold States and other powerful actors to account. The question remains open as to whether international human rights law can meet these lofty aspirations.

188 These reports can be found at <https://www.ohchr.org/EN/Issues/Migration/SRMigrants/Pages/AnnualReports.aspx>.

189 For the final draft of the 'Global Compact for Safe, Orderly and Regular Migration' (11 July 2018), see <https://refugeesmigrants.un.org/sites/default/files/180711_final_draft_0.pdf>.

190 On 10 December 2018, and without a vote, States adopted the 'Draft Outcome Document of the Intergovernmental Conference to Adopt the Global Compact for Safe, Orderly, and Regular Migration', UN Doc A/CONF.231/3 (30 July 2018). See UN, 'World Leaders Adopt First-Ever Global Compact on Migration, Outlining Framework to Protect Millions of Migrants, Support Countries Accommodating Them', UN Doc DEV/3375 (10 December 2018).

191 See BS Chimni, 'The Global Compact on Refugees: One Step Forward, Two Steps Back' (2018) 30 International Journal of Refugee Law 630; SB Woldermariam, A Maguire, and J von Meding, 'Forced Human Displacement, the Third World and International Law: A TWAIL Perspective' (2019) 20 Melbourne JIL 248.

192 A Peters, *Beyond Human Rights: The Legal Status of the Individual in International Law* (CUP, 2016), 8; the older G Scelle, *Précis du droit des gens* (Sirey, 1932), 32; and H Lauterpacht, *International Law and Human Rights* (FA Praeger, 1950), 72. See, generally, P Alston, *Non-State Actors and Human Rights* (OUP, 2005); and R McCorquodale, 'An Inclusive International Legal System' (2004) 17 Leiden JIL 477.

193 M Koskenniemi, 'The Future of Statehood' (1991) 32 Harvard ILJ 397, 406.

194 See, e.g., JJ Shestack, 'The Philosophic Foundations of Human Rights' (1998) 20 HRQ 201; and the materials collected in M Ishay (ed), *The Human Rights Reader: Major Political Essays, Speeches and Documents from Ancient Times to the Present* (2nd edn, Routledge, 2007).

There are, moreover, continued debates on how to measure the implementation of human rights, and the challenges associated with measuring effectiveness.[195] It is true that protection remains piecemeal, and at times decidedly lacking, as is the case with indigenous peoples, economic migrants, children, and other vulnerable groups. Human rights law has also been invoked as a language of accountability and one justifying ill-treatment, illustrated for example in the continued debate about 'extra-legal migrants' and the harshness with which States continue to treat people they deem to fall in this category.[196] Some more radical criticisms even suggest that human rights law discourses are counterproductive for human rights protection.[197]

The redemptive potential of human rights law, therefore, remains an issue for continued debate, and the importance of context in this area is particularly heightened. If the protection and promotion of individual rights are truly to become the heart of public international law, further attention needs to be paid not merely to problems of enforcement or compliance, but also to the structural causes of human rights abuses.

Further reading

I Bantekas and L Oette, *International Human Rights Law and Practice* (3rd edn, CUP, 2020).

A freshly updated, practice-centred guide to the field that is highly accessible to students.

C Costello, M Foster, and J McAdam, *The Oxford Handbook of International Refugee Law* (CUP, 2011).

An exhaustive, in-depth analysis of international refugee law and practice, drawing from various standpoints and with a critical edge.

T Gammeltoft-Hansen, *Access to Asylum: International Refugee Law and the Globalisation of Migration Control* (CUP, 2011).

An incisive analysis of the impact of new practices, particularly outsourcing to non-State actors, on international refugee law.

GS Goodwin-Gill and J McAdam, *The Refugee in International Law* (3rd edn, OUP, 2007).

A classic reference that captures the international legal regime relating to refugees.

J Hathaway and M Foster, *The Law of Refugee Status* (2nd edn, CUP, 2014).

The first edition was an instant classic; this complete revision incorporates contemporary developments.

[195] See, e.g., M Green, 'What We Talk About When We Talk About Indicators: Current Approaches to Human Rights Measurement' (2001) 23 HRQ 1062.

[196] See I Mann, *Humanity at Sea: Maritime Migration and the Foundations of International Law* (CUP, 2017); and C Dauvergne, *Making People Illegal* (CUP, 2008).

[197] See D Kennedy, 'International Human Rights Movement: Part of the Problem?' (2002) 15 Harvard HRJ 101; and the notion of human rights law being an instrument of 'planned misery' in S Marks, 'Human Rights and Root Causes' (2011) 74 MLR 57.

S MARKS, *A False Tree of Liberty: Human Rights in Radical Thought* (OUP, 2019).

An ambitious history of the 'idea' of human rights, tracing connections with other social forces and ideologies such as capitalism, industrialization, and empire.

D MOECKLI, S SHAH, and S SIVAKUMARAN, *International Human Rights Law* (3rd edn, OUP, 2017).

An accessible yet thorough textbook that distils the essential materials for students.

S MOYN, *The Last Utopia: Human Rights in History* (Harvard UP, 2010).

A critical history of the history of human rights that challenges orthodox narratives.

K PARLETT, *The Individual in the International Legal System* (CUP, 2011).

A leading compendium of practice relating to the place of individuals across various fields of international law.

O DE SCHUTTER, *International Human Rights Law: Cases, Materials, Commentary* (3rd edn, CUP, 2019).

A up-to-date compendium of significant human rights materials accompanied by lucid commentary.

D SHELTON (ed), *The Oxford Handbook of International Human Rights Law* (OUP, 2013).

A broad collection of essays that guide the reader into the great debates that colour the field.

H STEINER, P ALSTON, and R GOODMAN, *International Human Rights* (3rd edn, OUP, 2012).

A wide-ranging, comprehensive account focused on core concepts rather than an institutional survey.

C TOMUSCHAT, *Human Rights* (3rd edn, OUP, 2014).

An account of 'human rights in action' blending conceptual analysis with a reformist agenda.

17

International criminal law

17.1 Introduction: what is international criminal law?

Historically, international law regarded accountability and responsibility almost purely through the lens of the State, and contained neither substantive rules nor the requisite institutions to prosecute an individual. The lonely exception was the crime of piracy, where pirates were regarded as *hostes humanis generis*: 'the enemies of all humankind'.[1] However, piracy as an international crime primarily entailed permitting universal jurisdiction for all States to prosecute domestically for piratical acts on the high seas, where no State was sovereign.[2] Efforts began in the nineteenth century to criminalize the slave trade, a move coloured by a sense of reproach over the heinous nature of slavery, but these tended to be unilateral claims made by powerful maritime States to suppress and prosecute slavers.[3]

Today, that situation has changed dramatically. There exist several institutions, most prominently the International Criminal Court (ICC), which have given shape both to the substance of the crimes themselves and to the method for their effective prosecution. Through international criminal law, the criminal responsibility and liability of individuals, even if acting in groups, are now addressed internationally.

International criminal law is a broad area within public international law, and this introductory chapter is but a thematic introduction to the field. The chapter will first survey the emergence of international criminal courts and tribunals, culminating with the ICC, before turning to the international crimes themselves. Finally, international criminal law struggles in resolving the tension between modes of collective and individual liability, which will briefly be surveyed in the last section.

[1] Discussed in Chapter 18, 'The law of the sea', Section 18.3.7.2.

[2] See Chapter 8, 'Jurisdiction', Section 8.2.6, 'The universality principle'. For a historical review of the pre-1990 international law on piracy, see DH Johnson, 'Piracy in Modern International Law' (1957) 43 Transactions of the Grotius Society 63; GE White, 'The Marshall Court and International Law: The Piracy Cases' (1989) 83 AJIL 727.

[3] Slavery Abolition Act 1833, (UK); Act Prohibiting Importation of Slaves 1807, 2 Stat 426 (1807) (USA).

17.2 The emergence of international criminal law

17.2.1 Versailles, Nuremberg, and Tokyo

In the aftermath of World War I, the 1919 Treaty of Versailles contained clauses condemning German Kaiser Wilhelm II for 'the supreme offence against international morality and the sanctity of treaties',[4] and authorizing the military tribunals of the Allies to try individuals accused of 'acts in violation of the laws and customs of war'.[5] Wilhelm II had fled to exile in the Netherlands, which refused to extradite him on the basis that the crimes he was accused of were not contemplated in the Dutch Constitution.[6]

After World War II, the victorious Allied Powers set up international military tribunals in Nuremberg[7] and Tokyo.[8] These two tribunals were given jurisdiction over crimes against peace (aggression), crimes against humanity, and war crimes.[9] Both tribunals declared that 'international law imposes duties and liabilities upon individuals as well as upon States', and that 'crimes against international law are committed by men, not by abstract entities, and only by punishing individuals who commit such crimes can the provisions of international law be enforced'.[10]

The Nuremberg and Tokyo trials have been criticized as a form of 'victors' justice',[11] given that only Axis Powers nationals or collaborators were prosecuted, the relative elasticity of the rules of evidence applied, and the inability of defendants to appeal or challenge the selection of judges. By far the largest objection, however, was that they had created law *ex post facto* 'to suit the passion and clamor at the time'.[12] Nevertheless, their contribution to international criminal law has been significant,[13] especially as their constitutive charters and decisions subsequently received endorsement from the General

[4] Treaty of Versailles (signed 28 June 1919, entered into force 10 January 1920), 225 CTS 188, Art 227.

[5] *Ibid*, Art 228.

[6] A few minor officials were tried before German courts in Leipzig: see C Mullins, *The Leipzig Trials: An Account of the War Criminals' Trials and a Study of German Mentality* (HG & G Witherby, 1921). There are few other examples of unsuccessful proposals for international criminal trials. For a succinct list, see D Guilfoyle, *International Criminal Law* (OUP, 2016), 59–60.

[7] See Agreement for the Prosecution and Punishment of the Major War Criminals, and Charter of the International Military Tribunal annexed thereto (hereinafter 'Nuremberg Charter'), as published in (1945) 39 AJIL Supp 259.

[8] For the Charter of the International Military Tribunal for the Far East (hereinafter 'Tokyo Charter'), established by a proclamation by General McArthur on 19 January 1946, see (1946) TIAS No 1589, 3.

[9] See Nuremberg Charter (n 7) Art 6; Tokyo Charter (n 8) Art 5.

[10] See *Trial of the Major War Criminals before the International Military Tribunal, Nuremberg: 14 November 1945–1 October 1946* (Nuremberg, 1947), 41.

[11] For a polemical view, see D Zolo, *Victor's Justice: From Nuremberg to Baghdad* (Verso Books, 2009). See more generally, on the place of international criminal tribunals in establishing historical narratives, B Sander, *Doing Justice to History: Confronting the Past in International Criminal Courts* (OUP, 2021).

[12] See statement of WO Douglas, Associate Justice of the United States Supreme Court, in HK Thompson and H Strutz, *Dönitz at Nuremberg: A Reappraisal* (Institute for Historical Review, Torrance, 1983).

[13] See, e.g., T Taylor, *An Anatomy of the Nuremberg Trial* (Back Bay Books, 1993); BVA Röling and A Cassese, *The Tokyo Trial and Beyond* (CUP, 1992); KJ Heller, *The Nuremberg Military Tribunal and the Origins of International Criminal Law* (OUP, 2011); R Minear, *Victor's Justice: The Tokyo War Crimes Trial* (Princeton UP, 1971); Y Tanaka, T McCormack, and G Simpson (eds), *Beyond Victor's Justice? The Tokyo War Crimes Trial Revisited* (Brill, 2012).

Assembly and the ILC.[14] Both the 1948 Genocide Convention[15] and the 'grave breaches' provisions in the 1949 Geneva Conventions,[16] negotiated right after Nuremberg and Tokyo, envisaged prosecution for international crimes, albeit in national courts. In 1954, the ILC drew up a Draft Code of Offences against the Peace and Security of Mankind, reaffirming that individuals could be punished for crimes under international law.[17] The Draft Code would form the foundation for the ILC's 1996 'Code of Crimes against the Peace and Security of Mankind'.[18] Despite these efforts, the notion of international criminal proceedings remained controversial, and four decades would pass before the next international criminal proceedings would take place.

17.2.2 **The *ad hoc* International Criminal Tribunals for the former Yugoslavia and Rwanda**

The end of the Cold War ushered in a new period of activity by the Security Council. In response to mass atrocities committed during the violent disintegration of the former Yugoslavia, the Security Council decided to create the International Criminal Tribunal for the former Yugoslavia (ICTY) in 1993.[19] Shortly after the shocking genocide in Rwanda in 1994, in which 800,000 persons were killed, the Council created the International Criminal Tribunal for Rwanda (ICTR), the statute of which was closely modelled on that of the ICTY.[20] Though both Tribunals are no longer in active operation, their legacy for international criminal justice was significant.

THEORY AND DEBATES The Multilayered Approach to Justice in Rwanda

Running alongside the ICTR and the work of Rwandan national courts in prosecuting offenders, from 2001, Rwanda also featured the 'Gacaca' courts, a large-scale system adapted from a traditional, communal form of justice. The Gacaca courts were deemed necessary to address

[14] See UNGA Res 95 (I) (11 December 1946); and ILC, 'Report of the International Law Commission on Principles of the Nuremberg Tribunal' (1950) ILC Ybk vol II, 195.

[15] Convention on the Prevention and Punishment of the Crime of Genocide (signed 9 December 1948, entered into force 12 January 1951), 78 UNTS 277, Art VI.

[16] Geneva Convention for the Amelioration of the Condition of the Wounded and Sick in Armed Forces in the Field (adopted 12 August 1949, entered into force 21 October 1950), 75 UNTS 31 (Geneva Convention I); Geneva Convention for the Amelioration of the Condition of Wounded, Sick and Shipwrecked Members of Armed Forces at Sea (adopted 12 August 1949, entered into force 21 October 1950), 75 UNTS 85 (Geneva Convention II); Geneva Convention Relative to the Treatment of Prisoners of War (adopted 12 August 1949, entered into force 21 October 1950), 75 UNTS 135 (Geneva Convention III); Geneva Convention Relative to the Protection of Civilian Persons in Time of War (adopted 12 August 1949, entered into force 21 October 1950), 75 UNTS 287 (Geneva Convention IV).

[17] See ILC, 'Report of the International Law Commission covering the work of its sixth session', UN Doc A/2693 (1954) 45 AJIL Supp 123.

[18] ILC, 'Code of Crimes against the Peace and Security of Mankind' (1996) ILC Ybk vol II, 15; see also UNGA Res 51/160 (16 December 1996).

[19] UNSC Res 827 (25 May 1993), to which the ICTY Statute is annexed.

[20] UNSC Res 955 (8 November 1994), to which the ICTR Statute is annexed.

the challenge of more than 130,000 alleged genocide perpetrators in Rwandan prisons, awaiting trial. Such a huge proportion of Rwanda's population being detained created huge structural and logistical challenges in relation to their trials, especially given Rwanda's decimated infrastructure.

The Gacaca courts were designed to fulfil two purposes: to address every individual genocide suspect regardless of seniority or social standing, and to begin the reconstruction and rehabilitation of Rwandan society. In this regard, they are a form of transitional justice. The process was intended to involve the people who experienced the genocide first-hand at every stage. The local population elected respected individuals to assume the responsibility of prosecution, thus ensuring the participation of the victims from the outset; professional lawyers were excluded from any official role.

It must be cautioned that the Gacaca courts fall short of international legal standards relating to fair trials; for example, France has long rejected the extradition of Rwandans for this very reason. But their emphasis on truth and reconciliation has elicited widespread political debate in Rwanda, and they have addressed more than one million cases (*cf* the ICTR's completion of some eighty-five trials before its closure). The Rwandan government has cited the Gacaca process as an important component in the reconstruction of Rwanda.

For further reading, see N Palmer, *Courts in Conflict: Interpreting the Layers of Justice in Post-Genocide Rwanda* (OUP, 2015); P Clark, *The Gacaca Courts and Post-Genocide Justice and Reconciliation in Rwanda: Justice without Lawyers* (CUP, 2010).

The ICTY and ICTR (the 'ad hoc Tribunals') were institutionally similar: both ad hoc Tribunals were structured into a trial chamber and an appeals chamber, the latter of which was shared in The Hague to ensure consistency in their jurisprudence.[21] They are both international tribunals with jurisdiction to prosecute 'persons responsible for serious violations of international humanitarian law' within the respective territories of the former Yugoslavia and Rwanda. These include grave breaches of the Geneva Conventions,[22] other war crimes,[23] crimes against humanity,[24] and genocide.[25] Both had an independent Prosecutor. Significantly, for crimes falling under their jurisdiction, the ad hoc Tribunals enjoyed primacy over national courts[26] and could compel any State to cooperate with the Tribunal, as they had been established by the Security Council under its powers under Chapter VII.[27] The Tribunals even shared a Prosecutor until

[21] ICTR Statute (n 20) Art 12(2). The ICTY Trial Chamber sat in The Hague, the Netherlands; the ICTR Trial Chamber sat in Arusha, Tanzania.

[22] ICTY Statute (n 19) Art 2. On account of the non-international character of the armed conflict in Rwanda, the ICTR has jurisdiction over violations of Art 3 common to the four 1949 Geneva Conventions (n 16), including the Protocol Additional to the Geneva Conventions of 12 August 1949, and relating to the Protection of Victims of Non-International Armed Conflicts (Protocol II) (signed 8 June 1977, entered into force 7 December 1978), 1125 UNTS 609.

[23] ICTY Statute (n 19) Art 3; ICTR Statute (n 20) Art 5.

[24] ICTY Statute (n 19) Art 4; ICTR Statute (n 20) Art 3.

[25] ICTY Statute (n 19) Art 5; ICTR Statute (n 20) Art 2 adopts a slightly different definition.

[26] ICTY Statute (n 19) Art 9(1); ICTR Statute (n 20) Art 8(2).

[27] ICTY Statute (n 19) Art 29; ICTR Statute (n 20) Art 28. See Chapter 14, Section 14.5.2 for further discussion as to the powers of the Council under Chapter VII.

2003,[28] when the Security Council decided that the ICTR would require its own prosecutor in order to expedite the winding-up of the Tribunal.[29] However, it bears noting that the ICTY's temporal jurisdiction (*ratione temporis*) was open-ended, beginning after 1 January 1991, which allowed the ICTY to exercise jurisdiction over incidents relating to Kosovo.[30] Conversely, that of the ICTR was limited from 1 January 1994 to 31 December 1994.[31]

The creation of the ad hoc Tribunals was not uncontroversial. With respect to the ICTY, there have been allegations of selective justice or bias against certain persons, and in its early days, all ex-Yugoslav States except for the Bosnian central government refused to cooperate with the Tribunal. It was also suggested that the Security Council had acted *ultra vires* (exceeded its powers) to constitute the Tribunals, though in this regard, the ICTY upheld the legality of its own creation in its first case, *Prosecutor v Tadić*.[32] Over the 1990s, political developments led to increased cooperation, culminating with the 2001 transfer of former Yugoslav President Milošević to the Tribunal, to face multiple charges with respect to the Kosovo conflict as well as the earlier conflicts in Croatia and Bosnia.[33] Milošević's highly publicized trial was discontinued abruptly with his death in 2005, though the Tribunal later gained custody over two particularly high-profile accused, Mr Karadžić, former President of Republika Srpska (an entity within Bosnia and Herzegovina) who, at trial, was sentenced to forty years' imprisonment in 2016;[34] its final trial judgment was regarding Mr Mladić, Commander of the Main Staff of the Bosnian Serb Army, who was given a life sentence in 2017).[35] The *Karadžić* judgment is particularly noteworthy as an emphatic rejection of a claim to immunity by a governmental official.[36] His extensive control over the key political and governmental structures of Republika Srpska was a key element in the finding that he was culpable of having committed genocide in Srebreniča, war crimes, and crimes against humanity across Bosnia and Herzegovina.

The ICTR's first judgment concerned former Kigali Mayor Jean-Paul Akayesu and was notable as the first international judgment in which systematic rape was adjudged to be a part of the *actus reus* of the crime of genocide, if accompanied by the requisite special intent to destroy, in whole or in part, a protected group.[37] In *Kambada*, a former

[28] ICTR Statute (n 20) Art 15(4), as amended.

[29] UNSC Res 1503 (28 August 2003), para 8, and Annex I.

[30] ICTY Statute (n 19) Art 8. [31] ICTR Statute (n 20) Art 7.

[32] *Prosecutor v Tadić* (Interlocutory Appeal) IT-94-1-AR-72 (2 October 1995) 70, paras 30 *et seq*.

[33] *Prosecutor v Milošević* (Second Amended Indictment 'Kosovo') IT-99-37-PT (16 October 2001); *Prosecutor v Milošević* (Second Amended Indictment 'Croatia') IT-02-54-TT (23 October 2002); *Prosecutor v Milošević* (Second Amended Indictment 'Bosnia') IT-02-54-PT (22 November 2002). See ICTY Annual Report 2006 (21 August 2006), UN Doc A/61/271, para 55.

[34] See *Prosecutor v Karadžić*, IT-95-5/18, Public Redacted Version of Judgement (24 March 2016). His appeal was denied in 2019.

[35] See *Prosecutor v Mladić* (Judgment) IT-09-92 (22 November 2017).

[36] Mr Karadžić had even contended that he had stepped down from his post and ordered off troops on the basis of a promised amnesty by the USA in the 1995 Dayton Peace Accords, but the ICTY Appeals Chamber held that 'no legitimate expectation of immunity from prosecution could arise': *Decision on Appeal of the Trial Chamber Decision of 12 October 2009*, para 52.

[37] *Prosecutor v Akayesu* (Judgment) ICTR-96-4-T (2 September 1998), esp paras 731 *et seq*.

head of government was found, for the first time, guilty of committing genocide.[38] Another notable decision (the '*Media*' judgment) concerned three radio and newspaper executives who were convicted for public incitement to genocide.[39] However, the ICTR faced its own challenges when Rwanda briefly suspended cooperation in 1999, following a decision in the Appeals Chamber in *Barayagwiza*, one of the media advocates of the genocide who was released due to human rights violations during his pre-trial detention in Cameroon.[40] Rwanda resumed cooperation when the Appeals Chamber revisited its decision and reversed it in 2000.[41]

Though at times tendentious, the case law of the ad hoc Tribunals has deeply influenced the development of international criminal law,[42] and their practice has deeply influenced the structure of the ICC; for example, on the protection of victims' and witnesses' rights. At the time of its winding-up in November 2017, the ICTY had issued 161 indictments, and concluded proceedings against 152 people, including 83 sentenced and 19 acquitted. The ICTR has issued indictments for 110 accused, though as of its closure on 31 December 2015 it had concluded proceedings in respect of eighty-five accused, including sixty-one sentenced, and fourteen acquitted, with eight fugitive cases transferred to other jurisdictions upon its closure.[43]

The ad hoc Tribunals proved costly and time-consuming, and as early as 2000 the Security Council began to press both Tribunals to develop 'completion strategies'.[44] Accordingly, proceedings began to be deferred from the ICTY and ICTR back to national courts.[45] The International Residual Mechanism for Criminal Tribunals (MICT) has been tasked with continuing the jurisdiction, rights and obligations, and essential functions of the two institutions; in essence, preserving their legacy.[46] The MICT commenced its work before the two Tribunals were wound up, though it is meant to be temporary in nature, reviewed biennially after an initial four-year term.[47] The MICT commenced operations in relation to the ICTR on 1 July 2012, and in respect of the ICTY on

[38] *Prosecutor v Kambada* (Judgment) ICTR-97-23-S (4 September 1998).

[39] *Prosecutor v Nahimana* (Judgment) ICTR-99-52-T (3 December 2003); (Appeals Chamber Judgment) ICTR-00-52-A (28 November 2007).

[40] *Prosecutor v Barayagwiza* (Appeals Chamber Judgment) ICTR-97-19-AR72 (3 November 1999).

[41] *Prosecutor v Barayagwiza* (Prosecutor's Request for Review or Reconsideration) ICTR-97-19-AR72 (31 March 2000).

[42] E.g., the ICJ has relied on ICTY case law as an authoritative statement of fact, though it has challenged certain of its legal conclusions in relation to the threshold for control: see *Application of the Convention on the Prevention and Punishment of the Crime of Genocide (Bosnia and Herzegovina v Serbia and Montenegro), Merits, Judgment, ICJ Reports 2007*, p 43; and *Application of the Convention on the Prevention and Punishment of the Crime of Genocide (Croatia v Serbia), Merits, ICJ Reports 2015*, p 3.

[43] ICTR, 'Key Figures of Cases' (*UN Mechanism for International Criminal Tribunals*) <http://unictr.unmict.org/en/cases/key-figures-cases>.

[44] UNSC Res 1329 (5 December 2000); UNSC Res 1503 (n 29). For further discussion, see R Cryer, D Robinson, and S Vasiliev, *An Introduction to International Criminal Law and Procedure* (4th edn, CUP, 2019), 133 *et seq*.

[45] See ICTY Rules of Procedure, Rule 11*bis*; ICTR Rules of Procedure, Rule 11*bis*.

[46] UNSC Res 1966 (22 December 2010).

[47] For further information, consult <http://www.unmict.org>.

1 July 2013. The MICT has competence over appeals commencing after a certain date, such as that of Mr Šešelj, former Deputy Prime Minister of Serbia, filed in April 2016;[48] and in respect of sentencing questions. Only a few proceedings are currently pending, most notably, the trial of Félicien Kabuga for genocide and crimes against humanity.

17.2.3 **The International Criminal Court**

17.2.3.1 **Foundation of the ICC**

Though the Rome Statute establishing the International Criminal Court was only concluded in 1998, there had been unsuccessful efforts to establish a permanent international criminal jurisdiction in the immediate aftermath of World War II.[49] In fact, Article VI of the Genocide Convention envisaged the possibility for an international tribunal to be established which would be competent over acts within that convention. The Cold War hindered further efforts, until in 1989 Trinidad and Tobago suggested that the General Assembly consider international prosecution for drug-related offences.[50] The General Assembly referred the matter to the ILC which, impelled in part through the creation of the ad hoc Tribunals, proposed in 1994 a Draft Statute for an International Criminal Court.[51]

The 1994 Draft Statute, building on earlier efforts, proposed an international criminal court with jurisdiction not only over the four 'core crimes' of genocide, war crimes, crimes against humanity, and aggression (known in the Nuremberg/Tokyo period as 'crimes against peace') but also over certain 'treaty crimes' found in other multilateral conventions such as terrorism, drug-related offences, and organized crime.[52] Encouraged by the Draft Statute, the General Assembly convened a Preparatory Committee (PrepCom) in late 1995 to take forward the creation of an international criminal court.[53] The work of PrepCom led to a five-week-long conference in Rome, which on 17 July 1998 concluded the Rome Statute of the International Criminal Court (Rome Statute), the jurisdiction of which would be limited to the 'core crimes' detailed later in Section 17.3.[54] Sixty States were needed to ratify the Rome Statute in order to

[48] See *Prosecutor v Šešelj* (Judgment) IT-03-67 (31 March 2016). The appeal judgment, under case number MICT-16-99, was delivered on 11 April 2018. The ICTY's final appeals judgment conducted as such was *Prosecutor v Prlić and others* (Appeals Judgment) IT-04-74-A (29 November 2017).

[49] See earlier, Section 17.2.1; as well as UNGA, 'Revised Draft Statute for an International Criminal Court', UN GAOR 9th Session Supp No 12 UN Doc A/2645 (1954) 23; UNGA Res 898 (IX) (14 December 1954).

[50] Letter dated 21 August 1989 from the Permanent Representative of Trinidad and Tobago to the Secretary-General (21 August 1989); UNGA Res 44/39 (4 December 1989).

[51] ILC, 'Report of the ILC on the Work of its 46th Session' (1994), UN Doc A/49/10, 43 *et seq*. For commentary from that time, see J Crawford, 'The ILC's Draft Statute for an International Criminal Court' (1994) 88 AJIL 140.

[52] See, e.g., Convention for the Suppression of Unlawful Seizure of Aircraft (adopted 16 December 1970, entered into force 14 October 1971), 860 UNTS 105; UN Convention against Illicit Traffic in Narcotic Drugs and Psychotropic Substances (adopted 20 December 1988, entered into force 11 November 1990), 1582 UNTS 95; UN Convention against Transnational Organized Crime (adopted 15 November 2000, entered into force 29 September 2003), 2225 UNTS 209.

[53] UNGA Res 50/46 (11 December 1995).

[54] Rome Statute of the International Criminal Court (adopted 17 July 1998, entered into force 1 July 2002) 2187 UNTS 3 ('Rome Statute').

create the ICC, a milestone achieved very rapidly; the Court thus came into being in The Hague on 1 July 2002.

As of early 2025, the Rome Statute has 125 signatories, with the most recent State party being Ukraine.[55] After preliminary examinations had been launched by the Prosecutor, both Burundi (as of 27 October 2017) and the Philippines (as of 17 March 2019) became the first States to withdraw from the Rome Statute, but their withdrawal took effect only from those dates and does not affect the jurisdiction of the Court with respect to crimes committed during the period in which these States were parties.[56]

17.2.3.2 **The structure of the ICC**

The Court is composed of four principal organs.[57] First is the *Presidency*, which consists of three judges (the President and the Vice-Presidents), elected by the Members of the Court for a maximum of two, three-year terms. The Presidency is responsible for the administration of the Court, except for the *Office of the Prosecutor* (OTP). The OTP is itself an independent organ which receives and analyses alleged crimes within the jurisdiction of the Court, and determines whether investigations are to be initiated. Together, they are supported by the *Registry*, which provides operational support to the Court.[58] The Registrar also works to support defence counsel, victims, and witnesses to safeguard their rights, in particular through a sub-organ, the Office of Public Counsel for the victims.

The fourth organ is the *Chambers*; the judges of the Court are organized into a series of chambers.[59] First comes the *Pre-Trial Division*, which oversees the work of the OTP, protects the rights of suspects, victims, and witnesses, and ensures the integrity of the OTP's investigation and the Pre-Trial proceedings. At present, three Pre-Trial Chambers within the Division (either one or three judges) decide whether or not to issue warrants of arrest, summonses to appear at the OTP, or the confirmation of charges. Once a warrant is issued, the *Trial Division* is activated; a Trial Chamber of three judges is constituted by the Presidency to try a case. A Trial Chamber will determine whether an accused is innocent or guilty of any charges. Finally, the *Appeals Division*, composed of the President and four other judges, has the competence to uphold, reverse, or amend decisions on appeal from the Pre-Trial and Trial Chambers.

The ICC is not a subsidiary organ of the United Nations. It is an independent international organization, which means that unlike, for example, the ICJ, judges and the Prosecutor are elected by the *Assembly of States Parties* (ASP). All parties to the Rome Statute are members of the ASP, which has oversight over management of the ICC, and may adopt amendments to the Rome Statute or its Rules of Procedure and Evidence.[60]

[55] The ICC maintains a chronological list of States Parties at <https://asp.icc-cpi.int/states-parties/states-parties-chronological-list>.

[56] In respect of Burundi, see Decision of Pre-Trial Chamber III, ICC-01/17-9-Red (9 November 2017) para 24; in respect of the Philippines, see Judgment of the Appeals Chamber, ICC-01/21(OA) (18 July 2023), para 111. On 12 March 2025, former President Rodrigo Duterte was surrendered to the ICC following an arrest warrant issued by Pre-Trial Chamber I.

[57] Rome Statute (n 53) Art 34. [58] *Ibid*, Art 42. [59] *Ibid*, Art 39. [60] *Ibid*, Art 112; Art 51(1).

17.2.3.3 **Jurisdiction of the ICC**

Under the Rome Statute, the ICC enjoys jurisdiction over 'the most serious crimes of concern to the international community as a whole', these reprising the long-recognized crimes of genocide, crimes against humanity, and war crimes.[61] A fourth offence, the crime of aggression, was enumerated, but not defined, in 1998, but was part of an important amendment at the 2010 Kampala Review Conference. Aggression will be addressed later, in Section 17.3.4. The ICC's jurisdiction over crimes does not extend to offences committed prior to the Statute's entry into force on 1 July 2002.[62]

Finally, there are ongoing efforts for the ICC to also assume jurisdiction over 'environmental crimes', such as environmental destruction, the over-exploitation of natural resources, and illegal dispossession.[63] Such efforts have recently gained momentum with the 2021 call for the legal implementation of a new international crime, 'ecocide', defined as 'unlawful or wanton acts committed with knowledge that there is a substantial likelihood of severe and either widespread or long-term damage to the environment being caused by those acts'.[64]

17.2.3.3.1 ***Complementarity and other preconditions to jurisdiction or admissibility***

There are essential preconditions for the exercise of jurisdiction by the ICC. In respect of situations referred by States parties or initiated by the Prosecutor *proprio motu*, either the alleged crime must have been committed on the territory of a State party or the person accused of the crime must be a national of a State party.[65] These are non-cumulative: jurisdiction is satisfied if either of the criteria on territoriality or nationality is met. A non-State party may, as did Côte d'Ivoire in 2012, lodge a declaration that it accepts the ICC's jurisdiction, but only in respect of a specific situation.[66]

Unlike the ICTY and ICTR, the ICC's jurisdiction is 'complementary' to the jurisdiction of national courts.[67] Simply put, the principle of complementarity means that national criminal justice systems enjoy primacy over the ICC, which is a court of last resort. This means that a case is inadmissible if it is being, or has been, investigated or prosecuted by national authorities. In the event of proceedings at the domestic level, the ICC must first determine that a competent national court is 'unwilling or unable genuinely' to prosecute the offences itself.[68] However, neither amnesties nor immunities conferred during peace negotiations constitute judicial proceedings before national courts.[69]

[61] *Ibid*, Art 5; Arts 6–8 further define these crimes.

[62] *Ibid*, Art 11(1).

[63] See OTP, 'Policy Paper on Case Selection and Prioritization' (16 September 2016).

[64] See *Report of the Independent Expert Panel for the Legal Definition of Ecocide: Commentary and Core Text* (June 2021), available at <https://www.stopecocide.earth/expert-drafting-panel>. In June 2021, the European Parliament passed a resolution regarding the EU's Biodiversity Strategy 2030, in which it encourages member States to promote the recognition of ecocide as a crime under the Rome Statute: EP Decision T9-0277/2021 (8 June 2021), para 157.

[65] Rome Statute (n 53) Art 12(2).

[66] *Ibid*, Art 12(3).

[67] *Ibid*, Arts 1, 17.

[68] *Ibid*, Art 17.

[69] See C Stahn, 'Complementarity, Amnesties and Alternative Forms of Justice: Some Interpretative Guidelines for the International Criminal Court' (2005) 3 JICJ 695; and D Robinson, 'Serving the Interests of Justice: Amnesties, Truth Commissions, and the International Criminal Court' (2003) 14 EJIL 481.

THEORY AND DEBATES Can Complementarity Really Aid Long-term Rehabilitation?

The complementarity principle raises fascinating questions about the interplay between international and national criminal justice. If a State is unable (or unwilling) to prosecute, will removing the individual to the ICC really help the State grow to be able to prosecute its own criminals in future? Or does it delay the development of an effective judicial system, in whatever form that is to take within the State? The ad hoc Tribunals enjoyed primary jurisdiction, privileging the international solution; but the ICC must first satisfy itself that the national authorities are genuinely unable and unwilling to prosecute an accused.

The complementarity principle is designed to encourage full and genuine domestic prosecutions of crimes, and there are encouraging signs that States have taken the principle seriously. The ICC's role is wider as a result, beyond an international criminal jurisdiction into a facilitator to assist national authorities in the prosecution of crimes. That facilitative role would require capacity-building in cooperating States, a highly contextualized understanding of specific situations, and a careful eye on the implications for State sovereignty that undue interference in national judicial processes might entail.

For further reading, see WA Schabas, 'Complementarity in Practice: Creative Solutions or a Trap for the Court?' in M Politi and F Gioia (eds), *The International Criminal Court and National Jurisdictions* (Ashgate, 2008), 25; JK Kleffner, 'The Impact of Complementarity on National Implementation of Substantive International Criminal Law' (2003) 1 JICJ 86; and J Stigen, *The Relationship between the International Criminal Court and National Jurisdictions: The Principle of Complementarity* (Nijhoff, 2008).

17.2.3.3.2 ***Who may trigger the jurisdiction of the Court?***

During the 1998 Rome Conference, there was considerable debate over the relationship between the ICC and the Security Council, and whether the latter's approval would be required for the Prosecutor to launch an investigation. The USA, in particular, stressed that the ICC 'must operate in co-ordination—not in conflict—with the Security Council'.[70] However, most other States objected, wishing that the Court and its Prosecutor enjoy independence from any form of political control.

By way of compromise, the Rome Statute implemented a range of mechanisms to activate the Court's jurisdiction. The first is *referral*: under Article 13(a), a State party can refer a situation to the Court. Unexpectedly, the bulk of such referrals have been so-called 'self-referrals', due to the realization that investigation is much easier with the consent of the territorial State. In fact, four of its earliest investigations have been 'self-referred' by a State party: Uganda's 2003 referral with respect to the Lord's Resistance

[70] Statement by the United States Ambassador to the United Nations on 17 June 1998 (17 June 1998), Press Release L/ROM/11.

Army operating within its territory;[71] the Democratic Republic of the Congo in 2004;[72] also in 2004, the Central African Republic's referral in respect of the 2002–3 internal armed conflict in its territory, with a second self-referral in 2012 in relation to renewed violence;[73] and, in 2012, Mali's referral of an ongoing internal armed conflict. Within the context of Mali's referral, the trial of Al Hassan Ag Abdoul Aziz is significant. Al Hassan, *de facto* head of police for two Islamist extremist groups, Asnar Dine and Al Qaeda in the Islamic Maghreb (AQIM), faces charges of crimes against humanity and war crimes committed by these groups, and sexual and gender-based violence.[74]

CASE SPOTLIGHT ***Prosecutor v Lubanga Dyilo (Thomas)*, Judgment of 14 March 2012, Case No ICC-01/04-01/06**

Thomas Lubanga Dyilo, a Congolese national who became the president of the 'Union des patriotes congolais' (UPC) and Commander-in-Chief of its military wing, the 'Force patriotique pour la libération du Congo' (FPLC), was indicted on three distinct offences—charges of enlisting, conscripting, and using children under the age of fifteen—to participate actively in the hostilities raging throughout the eastern part of the Democratic Republic of the Congo. The recruitment and use of child soldiers under the age of fifteen is considered a war crime under Article 8(2)(e)(vii) of the Rome Statute, and is in addition prohibited under Article 77(2) of Additional Protocol I.

Trial Chamber I of the ICC determined that there was abundant evidence that child soldiers were being conscripted, enlisted, and used by the UPC/FPLC as active participants in the conflict (Judgment, paras 609–759). Moreover, it was satisfied beyond reasonable doubt that Mr Lubanga had been informed continuously of these actions, and was involved in the planning of military operations, the provision of weapons, and in recruitment policy and initiatives. There was even evidence that he had given speeches to children under the age of fifteen to join the army. The Chamber concluded that Mr Lubanga's contributions were essential to the resulting conscription of girls and boys below the age of fifteen into the UPC/FPLC (para 1351). He was sentenced to fourteen years' imprisonment.

Though of great interest because of its clarification of war crimes in relation to child soldiers, the *Lubanga* case is also noteworthy with respect to certain findings in relation to victims. Trial Chamber I, in its August 2012 decision on reparations, went beyond merely allowing for direct victim participation in proceedings, and established that reparations should be awarded on non-discriminatory and gender-sensitive bases. Moreover, on 21 October 2016, Trial Chamber II approved the creation of a plan for symbolic collective reparations

[71] See the Situation in Uganda ICC-02/04, in which arrest warrants for crimes against humanity and war crimes in respect of five senior commanders were issued on 21 June 2005. Though four of the commanders remain at large, Ongwen surrendered voluntarily to the Court in January 2015, and his trial opened on 6 December 2016.

[72] Situation in the Democratic Republic of the Congo ICC-01/04. This referral led to the first conviction by the ICC in *Prosecutor v Lubanga Dyilo* (Judgment) ICC-01/04-01/06-2842 (14 March 2012).

[73] Situation in the Central African Republic II ICC-01/05; Situation in the Central African Republic II ICC-01/14. See later, Section 17.4.1, for a discussion of *Prosecutor v Bemba Gombo (Jean-Pierre)* (Judgment) ICC-01/05-01/08 (21 March 2016) and the decision on appeal (8 June 2018).

[74] Situation in the Republic of Mali ICC-01/12. The most recent decision in *Prosecutor v Al Hassan Ag Abdoul Aziz*, ICC/12-01/18 was on confirmation of charges (9 July 2021). The trial will open in April 2022.

for victims in affected communities. Finally, on 15 December 2017, its decision on non-symbolic collective reparations was rendered, in which it set Lubanga's liability in this respect at $US10,000,000. In this respect, the judgment in the *Lubanga* case has made an important contribution to understanding victims' participation in proceedings.

More controversially, the Prosecutor may launch a preliminary examination into a situation under Article 13(c) of the Rome Statute. If she concludes that there is a reasonable basis to proceed to further investigation, she may seek authorization from a Pre-Trial Chamber, which may authorize the commencement of a full investigation if the case appears to fall within the Court's jurisdiction.[75] Recent situations being investigated by the Prosecutor include: from 2010, into post-election violations in Kenya in 2007–8;[76] in 2011, in respect of Côte d'Ivoire;[77] in 2014, in respect of UK nationals' conduct during the 2003–8 occupation of Iraq;[78] in 2016, in respect of the situation in Georgia;[79] and, in 2017, in relation to Burundi.[80] In 2020, the Appeals Chamber reversed a decision of Pre-Trial Chamber III, and decided unanimously to authorize the Prosecutor to open an investigation in relation to Afghanistan, which would cover all acts on its territory since 1 May 2003, including those of occupying forces.[81] Recently, and not without controversy, there have been referrals in respect of situations in Bangladesh/ Myanmar (see below, Section 17.3.2) and Venezuela. In the latter situation, the launch of an investigation by the Prosecutor has not yet been authorized, given uncertainty about the credibility of ongoing investigations by national authorities.

Finally, as a partial concession to the USA, under Article 13(b) of the Rome Statute, the Security Council may refer a situation to the Prosecutor under its Chapter VII powers, even if it relates to a non-party State. The Council has twice done so, in respect of the situation in Darfur, Sudan, in 2005,[82] and in respect of Libya in 2011.[83] The support of the Security Council has perhaps emboldened the Pre-Trial Chambers to issue arrest warrants against high-ranking officials such as Sudanese President Omar Hassan

[75] Rome Statute (n 53) Art 15.

[76] See Situation in the Republic of Kenya ICC-01/09; on 31 March 2010 an investigation was opened into alleged crimes against humanity.

[77] See Situation in the Republic of Côte d'Ivoire ICC-02/11; on 3 October 2011 an investigation was opened into alleged crimes against humanity. It should be recalled that in 2012, Côte d'Ivoire, a non-State party, made a declaration under Art 12(3) of the Rome Statute to accept the jurisdiction of the Court.

[78] See Statement of the Prosecutor, Mrs Fatou Bensouda, on the reopening of the preliminary examination of the situation in Iraq, made to the United Nations Security Council (13 May 2014).

[79] See Situation in the Republic of Georgia ICC-01/15; on 27 January 2016 an investigation was opened into alleged crimes against humanity and war crimes.

[80] See Situation in the Republic of Burundi ICC-01/17; on 9 November 2017 an investigation was opened into alleged crimes against humanity.

[81] *Judgment on the appeal against the decision on the authorization of an investigation into the situation in the Islamic Republic of Afghanistan*, Decision of the Appeals Chamber (5 March 2020), ICC-02/17 OA 4. Though investigations were suspended following the Taliban's taking of power, Prosecutor Karim Khan was, at the time of going to press, calling for investigations to resume.

[82] UNSC Res 1593 (31 March 2005). *Prosecutor v Ahmad Harun and Ali Kushayb* (Warrant for Arrest for Ahmad Harun) ICC-02/05-01/07 (27 April 2007) and *Prosecutor v Ahmad Harun and Ali Kushayb* (Warrant of Arrest for Ali Kushayb) ICC-02/05-01/07-3 (27 April 2007).

[83] UNSC Res 1970 (26 February 2011).

Ahmad Al Bashir[84] and Libyan President Muammar Qaddafi, his son Saif Al-Islam Qaddafi, and brother-in-law Abudualla Al-Senussi, all of whom held high office in Libya.[85] The ICC is increasingly emboldened to issue warrants against high officials in two prominent new investigations: in March 2023, Pre-Trial Chamber II announced an arrest warrant against Russian President Vladimir Putin and others for the abduction of children from Ukraine.[86] What is more, on 21 November 2024 Pre-Trial Chamber I rejected Israel's challenges to jurisdiction and issued arrest warrants against Israeli Prime Minister Benjamin Netanyahu and former Minister of Defence, Yoav Gallant.[87] Both arrest warrants remain secret, and thus unpublished, to safeguard the conduct of the investigations.

17.2.3.3.3 ***The impact of the International Criminal Court***

Though it is rather premature to arrive at sweeping conclusions, in a rare moment of candour, the Trial Chamber in *Lubanga* pointed to former ICTY President Antonio Cassese's vivid criticism of the ICC system as a 'giant without arms and legs' due to its reliance on State cooperation.[88] This is due to the fact that evidence-gathering and the extradition of suspects to The Hague remains the duty of States parties, and not the Court itself, raising substantial challenges in the fulfilment of the Court's mandate and completion of its cases. For example, the investigation into Kenya about the OTP has since been abandoned, due to its lack of cooperation in the gathering of evidence, not least due to the fact that prominent accused include President Kenyatta of Kenya.

The controversy over potential prosecution of State officials looms large. Until recently, proceedings against Sudanese President Al Bashir in relation to the situation in Darfur, though referred by the Security Council, had not progressed due to a lack of cooperation by other States. In particular, Pre-Trial Chamber II censured South Africa in July 2017 for having failed to arrest Mr Al Bashir during a 2015 visit to an African Union summit in Johannesburg.[89] In 2017, the South African Supreme Court of Appeal concluded, with barely veiled criticism of the South African government, that Security Council

[84] *Prosecutor v Al Bashir* (First Warrant of Arrest) ICC 02/05-001/09-3 (4 March 2009) and (Second Warrant of Arrest) ICC 02/05-01/09-94 (12 July 2010).

[85] Situation in Libya ICC-01/11. See arrest warrants of 27 June 2011 (terminated upon the death of Qaddafi on 22 November 2011), 18 July 2013, and 19 August 2013. Proceedings against Al-Senussi came to an end on 24 July 2014, but Al-Islam Qaddafi remains at large.

[86] See ICC Press Release, 'Judges issue arrest warrants against Vladmir Putin and Maria Alekseyevna Lvova-Belova' (17 March 2023). See further Situation in Ukraine, ICC-01/22, referred jointly in March 2022 by 43 States Parties; on 2 March 2022, the Prosecutor proceeded to open an investigation into events since 13 June 2014.

[87] See ICC Pre-Trial Chamber I, Situation in the State of Palestine, ICC-01/18, *Decision on Israel's challenge to the jurisdiction of the Court pursuant to article 19(2) of the Rome Statute* (21 November 2024); ICC Press Release, 'ICC Pre-Trial Chamber I rejects the State of Israel's challenges to jurisdiction and issues warrants of arrest for Benjamin Netanyahu and Yoav Gallant' (21 November 2024). Though Palestine has been a party to the Rome Statute since 1 April 2015, some years passed before the ICC was satisfied that the criteria for opening an investigation were met. On 3 March 2021 the Prosecutor opened an investigation into events since 2014; on 17 November 2023 a further referral was made regarding events since 7 October 2023. See further Situation in the State of Palestine, ICC-01/18.

[88] *Prosecutor v Lubanga* (n 71) para 45.

[89] It must be said, however, that the Chamber did not refer South Africa's non-cooperation to the ASP or to the Security Council: see *Prosecutor v Al Bashir, Decision under Article 87(7) of the Rome Statute*, ICC-02/05-01/09-302 (6 July 2017).

Resolution 1593 had 'activated' the ICC's jurisdiction under Article 13(b) in relation to Al Bashir, who did not enjoy immunity at the time of his visit to Johannesburg.[90]

In May 2019, the ICC Appeals Chamber similarly censured Jordan for having failed to arrest Al Bashir during a 2015 Arab League summit. First reiterating its position that heads of State did not benefit from immunity before international criminal tribunals,[91] it declared that were a State party to arrest a head of State for extradition to the Court, it is 'only lending assistance to the Court in the exercise of the Court's jurisdiction'.[92] Crucially, the Appeals Chamber concluded that the referral by the Security Council had placed Sudan in the situation of a State party.[93] In its ongoing work on the immunity of State officials from foreign criminal jurisdiction, the ILC has pointedly avoided scrutiny of the 2019 judgment as being beyond the scope of its mandate, excluding especially those findings relating to the obligations of cooperation assumed by States parties to the Rome Statute.[94] With arrest warrants now filed against Putin, Netanyahu, and Duterte, the debate will remain very timely.

CONTEMPORARY DEVELOPMENTS The International Criminal Court and Africa

The Rome Statute has been widely ratified by African States, which constitute nearly one-third of the Assembly of States Parties. However, only four of the eighteen current judges are drawn from Africa, with heavy representation from other continents, Europe in particular. What is more, until a few years ago, virtually all of its investigations focused on sub-Saharan States, which had given rise to complaints of selective bias against Africa. Though many African States support the ICC emphatically, certain African States have begun to resist its work. In 2014, the African Union suggested a 'Merged Court' that would deal with State-to-State disputes, human rights claims, and international criminal trials, though it is not yet in effect (see Draft Protocol of amendment of the Statute of the African Court of Justice and Human Rights, AIU Doc EX.CL/846 (XXV)).

More dramatically, in late 2016 South Africa, the Gambia, and Burundi announced that they would withdraw from the ICC, though the first two later revoked their withdrawal, and only Burundi has formally withdrawn, in October 2017. Nevertheless, a non-binding resolution passed at an African Union summit in February 2017 called for 'mass withdrawal' of African States from the jurisdiction of the ICC. Then, in July 2017, the ICC ruled that South Africa had flouted duties under the Rome Statute when it failed to arrest President Al Bashir. In July 2018, Kenya wrote on behalf of the African members of the UN to ask that the General Assembly request an advisory opinion from the ICJ on the question of whether serving heads of State could benefit from immunity before the ICC (see UN Doc A/73/144 (8 July 2018)), though the African Union summit in February 2020 urged its members to withdraw the request.

[90] *Minister of Justice and Constitutional Development and Others v Southern African Litigation Centre and Others* [2016] ZASCA 17; 2016 (3) SA 317 (SCA).

[91] *Prosecutor v Al Bashir, Judgment in the Jordan Referral re Al Bashir Appeal*, ICC-02/05-01/09 OA2 (6 May 2019), paras 101–2, 110–11, and 113. As with South Africa, the Appeals Chamber overturned the decision of the Pre-Trial Chamber to refer Jordan to the Security Council for its lack of cooperation. See further the case comment on the 2019 *Al Bashir* decision by A Mudukuti (2020) 114 AJIL 103.

[92] *Ibid*, para 4, which refers to Art 27(2) Rome Statute (n 53), 'Irrelevance of Official Capacity'.

[93] *Ibid*, paras 125–35.

[94] See ILC, Eighth Report on Immunity of State Officials from Foreign Criminal Jurisdiction (Concepción Escobar Hernández, Special Rapporteur), UN Doc A/CN.4/739 (29 February 2020), paras 20–7.

It is true that the incorporation of strategic and resource-rich areas of Africa into the world economy has given rise to a disproportionate number of conflicts in sub-Saharan Africa, especially given the legacy of colonial exploitation. However, one should not draw hasty conclusions from this cross-section of reactions. All but two of the African situations currently under investigation have been referred by the affected State itself; the two exceptions, Libya and Darfur (Sudan), were referred by the Security Council. Moreover, since 2016 the ICC Prosecutor is investigating beyond Africa, including Georgia after its 2008 conflict with Russia; and in relation to the conduct of UK armed forces during the 2003–8 occupation of Iraq. A wave of recent investigations have also been opened into the situations in Afghanistan (2020), the Philippines and Venezuela (2021), Ukraine (2022), and in relation to the occupied Palestinian territory ('Gaza and the West Bank, including East Jerusalem', according to the Statement of the ICC Prosecutor in respect of an investigation in Palestine of 5 March 2021). On 17 November 2023, a group of 'like-minded States' (South Africa, Bangladesh, Bolivia, Comoros, and Djibouti) referred the situation in the 'State of Palestine' to ICC Prosecutor Karim Khan (see ICC, Statement of the Prosecutor of 17 November 2023). Nevertheless, as recently as 2023, South Africa had been making equivocal public statements about its relationship with the ICC.

For further reading, see A Abass, 'Prosecuting International Crimes in Africa: Rationale, Prospects and Challenges' (2013) 24 EJIL 933; D Tladi, 'The Immunity Provision in the AU Amendment Protocol: Separating the (Doctrinal) Wheat from the (Normative) Chaff' (2015) 13 JICJ 3; and EY Omorogbe, 'The Crisis of International Criminal Law in Africa: A Regional Regime in Response?' (2019) 66 NILR 287.

There are also concerns about the persistent refusal of the USA to collaborate. The USA not only declined to ratify the Rome Statute[95] but persuaded the Security Council to invoke Article 16, which required the Prosecutor to defer investigation or prosecution for one year.[96] Moreover, the USA has controversially signed a number of agreements with ICC States parties to shield its nationals from being surrendered or transferred to the ICC.[97] Finally, there remain powerful criticisms of the international criminal justice system as having the wrong priorities, privileging the elimination of impunity over other forms of restoration in fragile political situations, and altogether ignoring the root causes that led to atrocities being committed in the first place.[98]

[95] Though President Clinton signed it on 31 December 2000, President George W Bush dramatically 'unsigned' the Statute upon taking office: see Letter from US Under-Secretary of State for Arms Control to the Secretary-General (2002) 41 ILM 1014.

[96] UNSC Res 1422 (12 July 2002) and UNSC Res 1487 (12 June 2003). See further N Jain, 'A Separate Law for Peacekeepers; the Clash between the Security Council and the International Criminal Court' (2005) 16 EJIL 239.

[97] See M Benzing, 'US Bilateral Non-Surrender Agreements and Article 98 of the Statute of the International Criminal Court' (2004) 8 MPYUNL 182; Cryer, Robinson, and Vasiliev (n 43) 167; W Schabas, 'Article 98' in *The Rome Statute of the International Criminal Court* (2nd edn, OUP, 2016), 1342 *et seq.*

[98] See, e.g., C Schwöbel, 'The Comfort of International Criminal Law' (2013) 24 Law and Critique 23; F Mégret, 'The Politics of International Criminal Justice' (2002) 13 EJIL 1261; F Mégret, 'Justice pénale internationale et colonialisme: au-delà des évidences' (2014) XLV Revue d'études internationales; G Simpson, 'Linear Law: the History of International Criminal Law' in C Schwöbel (ed), *Critical Approaches to International Criminal Law: An Introduction* (Routledge, 2014); Sander (n 11).

17.2.4 'Internationalized' and 'hybrid' courts

Finally, one must briefly mention a series of 'hybrid' or 'mixed' criminal courts, which blend international and national elements in varying combinations. As we will explore, several derive their origin from Security Council resolutions, and many of them apply some international law or count international representation on their bench. They were designed to offer a bespoke solution bypassing the ICC (or predating its existence) and avoiding the high costs of a fully international solution like the ad hoc Tribunals. Hybrid tribunals are closer to the ground in post-conflict States where sensitive political situations or recent historical events might limit the ability of the judiciary to administer justice independently.[99]

Three hybrid courts merit further scrutiny.[100] The first is the Special Court for Sierra Leone (SCSL), established by an agreement between the government of Sierra Leone and the United Nations. The SCSL has jurisdiction over most recognized international crimes,[101] but also domestic crimes such as arson.[102] A majority of judges in all of its chambers, and its Prosecutor, are appointed by the UN Secretary-General.[103] The SCSL Statute requires that it be guided by the decision of the ICTY/ICTR Appeals Chamber on matters of international law, and by the Supreme Court of Sierra Leone in relation to questions of Sierra Leonean law.[104] The SCSL is best known for the trial of former Liberian President Charles Taylor in The Hague in 2004, where his plea of immunity was denied on the basis 'that the sovereign equality of States does not prevent a Head of State from being prosecuted before an international tribunal or court'.[105] In 2012, Taylor was convicted on all counts and sentenced to fifty years' imprisonment.[106]

The Extraordinary Chambers in the Courts of Cambodia (ECCC), created under Cambodian legislation that has been confirmed in a 2004 Agreement between the UN General Assembly and Cambodia, established a process to prosecute senior leaders of the Khmer Rouge, a paramilitary organization which had committed atrocities during the dictatorship of Pol Pot (1975–9).[107] Despite its negotiated status between the

[99] For further reading on hybrid courts, see S Williams, *Hybrid and Internationalized Criminal Tribunals* (OUP, 2013); CPR Romano, A Nollkaemper, and JK Kleffner (eds), *Internationalized Criminal Courts* (OUP, 2004); Cryer, Robinson, and Vasiliev (n 43) ch 9; LA Dickinson, 'The Promise of Hybrid Courts' (2003) 97 AJIL 295.

[100] Others include: the War Crimes Chamber within the State Court of Bosnia and Herzegovina, supported by the Security Council (UNSC Res 1503 (n 29)); the Special Panels for Serious Crimes created by the UN Transitional Administration in East Timor (UNTAET Regulation 2000/15); the Iraqi Special Tribunal authorized by the Coalition Provisional Authority after the invasion of Iraq (CPA Order No 48), renamed 'Iraqi High Tribunal' since 2005; and the Serbian War Crimes Chamber, to which certain cases have been referred by the ICTY.

[101] SCSL Statute, annexed to UNSC Res 1315 (14 August 2000), Arts 2–4.

[102] *Ibid*, Art 5.

[103] *Ibid*, Arts 12(1), 15.

[104] *Ibid*, Arts 19, 20(3).

[105] See *Prosecutor v Taylor*, Decision on Immunity from Jurisdiction, SCSL-03-01-I-059 (31 May 2004), paras 50–2. This passage was cited by the ICC Appeals Chamber with approval: see *Prosecutor v Al Bashir, Jordan Referral* (n 88) para 113.

[106] See *Prosecutor v Taylor*, Judgment of Trial Chamber II, SCSL-03-01-T (26 April 2012).

[107] The ECCC Agreement is annexed in turn to UNGA Res 57/228A (18 December 2002); UNGA Res 57/228B (13 May 2003); and UNGA, 'Human Rights Questions' (6 May 2003), UN Doc A/57/806.

UN and Cambodia, it is regarded as part of Cambodia's judicial system, albeit with significant international involvement. The ECCC has subject-matter jurisdiction over Cambodian law,[108] though jurisdiction also extends to international treaty crimes[109] and its procedural rules must conform to international standards of justice and fairness.[110] In each of its Chambers, there is a small majority of Cambodian judges, but appointees of the Secretary-General ensure international representation. A 'supermajority' is required for decision-making, which in effect requires that at least one international judge concur.[111] The ECCC's most significant decision departed from the ICTY's *Tadić* judgment in relation to JCE (see Section 17.4.2), determining that 'extended joint criminal enterprise (the third form of JCE) did not exist in customary international law from 1975 to 1979, the period in which the acts in question had occurred'.[112]

After the assassination of Prime Minister Hariri on 14 February 2005, Lebanon asked for a 'tribunal of an international character' to be established to try those responsible. The Special Tribunal for Lebanon (STL) was duly constituted by the Security Council, with a relatively narrow jurisdiction only over acts 'connected in accordance with the principles of criminal justice and . . . of a nature and gravity similar' to the Hariri assassination.[113] As with the SCSL, in all chambers there is a small majority of international judges.[114] The STL's distinctive feature is that it applies exclusively Lebanese criminal law: international criminal law may apply only if it is incorporated into Lebanese law.[115] However, the Appeals Chamber has signalled that as domestic Lebanese law must be interpreted in accordance with international law, and it was prepared to develop the crime of terrorism under customary international law, applicable to individuals in peacetime.[116] A controversial feature of the STL is its preparedness to hold trials *in absentia* (where the accused is not present) in certain circumstances.[117] This is virtually

[108] ECCC Agreement, *ibid*, Art 2.

[109] *Ibid*, Art 5, refers to the Genocide Convention (in relation to the crime of genocide), the Rome Statute (n 53) (in relation to crimes against humanity), and the 1949 Geneva Conventions (in relation to 'grave breaches' or war crimes).

[110] *Ibid*, Art 12, referring to International Covenant on Civil and Political Rights (signed 16 December 1966, entered into force 23 March 1976), 993 UNTS 3 (ICCPR), Arts 14–15.

[111] *Ibid*, Art 3.

[112] *Nuon Chea and Others* (Decision on the Appeals against the Co-Investigative Judges Order on Joint Criminal Enterprise, PTC) Case No 002-19-09-2007-ECCC/OCIJ (20 May 2010). See further M Karnavas, 'Joint Criminal Enterprise at the ECCC: A Critical Analysis of the Pre-Trial Chamber's Decision against the Application of JCE III and Two Divergent Commentaries on the Same' (2010) 21 Criminal Law Forum 445. On 16 November 2018, Nuon Chea was convicted of genocide by the Trial Chamber; he died in February 2019.

[113] STL Statute, as annexed to UNSC Res 1757 (2007), Art 1. Its temporal jurisdiction is limited to such 'connected' attacks between 1 October 2004 and 12 December 2005.

[114] *Ibid*, Arts 7–8.

[115] *Ibid*, Art 4. On this point, see NN Jurdi, 'The Subject-Matter Jurisdiction of the Special Tribunal for Lebanon' (2007) 5 JICJ 1125.

[116] See *Prosecutor v Ayyash et al* (Interlocutory Decision on the Applicable Law: Terrorism, Conspiracy, Homicide, Perpetration, Cumulative Charging in the Appeals Chamber) STL-11-01/I (16 February 2011), paras 42–148.

[117] STL Statute, Art 22, which has already been triggered: *Prosecutor v Ayyash* (n 113); and *Prosecutor v Hassan Habib Mehri* (Decision to Hold Trial *in Absentia*) STL-13-04/1/TC (20 December 2013).

unprecedented in international criminal proceedings, and though accused persons have the right to be retried, has raised serious concerns over the administration of justice.[118]

Finally, we turn to two newer hybrid courts. First is the Extraordinary African Chambers (EAC), established by an agreement between Senegal and the African Union (AU) to try international crimes in Chad during the regime of former Chadian President Hissène Habré. The judges of the EAC were appointed by the AU and its Statute provided with jurisdiction for genocide, crimes against humanity, war crimes, and torture. In May 2016, the EAC convicted Habré on counts of rape, sexual slavery, and mass murder. It was the first exercise of universal jurisdiction in Africa, and it was the first time the courts of one State have successfully prosecuted the former head of State of another State for crimes against humanity.[119] Secondly, one finds the Kosovo Specialist Chambers (KSC) established in 2015 in The Hague, a court constituted pursuant to an EU–Kosovo agreement but under Kosovan legislation. The costs of the KSC are borne by the EU and other Council of Europe States and the Chamber is staffed by EU personnel and international judges, with jurisdiction over war crimes, crimes against humanity, and 'other crimes under Kosovo law'.[120] On 15 September 2021, the Chamber opened its first trial, against Salih Mustafa.[121]

CONTEMPORARY DEVELOPMENTS Towards a Special Tribunal for Aggression Against Ukraine?

Jurisdictional and substantive issues often overlap. Despite ICC arrest warrants against Putin and other Russian officials for certain core crimes, it has been clear from the outbreak of violence that the ICC lacked jurisdiction in respect of a number of aspects of the conflict. Though Ukraine had filed formal referrals with the ICC to investigate potential war crimes and crimes against humanity relating to the 2014 Euromaidan protests, the 2014 annexation of Crimea by Russia, and the armed conflict in Donbas, these were limited referrals. In August 2024, the parliament of Ukraine voted to ratify the Rome Statute and, on 1 January 2025, Ukraine became the newest State party.

However, accession to the Rome Statute does not resolve the issue of jurisdiction by the ICC over crimes of aggression as Russia remains a non-party but the Court's jurisdiction over this specific crime extends only over officials of States parties; and Russia in fact purported to 'withdraw' its signature from the Rome Statute in 2016. For this reason, a proposed ad hoc 'special international tribunal for the crime of aggression' has been called for by a range of States—including Ukraine itself—as well as by organs of the United Nations, Council of Europe, NATO, and the European Union, to complement the ICC's investigation in respect of other core crimes.

[118] See P Gaeta, 'To Be (Present) or Not To Be (Present)' (2007) 5 JICJ 116; W Jordash and T Parker, 'Trial *in Absentia* at the Special Tribunal for Lebanon' (2010) 8 JICJ 487; R Riachy, 'Trials *in Absentia* in the Lebanese Judicial System and at the Special Tribunal for Lebanon: Challenge or Evolution?' (2010) 8 JICL 1295; N Pons, 'Some Remarks on *In Absentia* Proceedings before the Special Tribunal for Lebanon in Case of a State's Failure or Refusal to Hand over the Accused' (2010) 8 JICJ 1307.

[119] See further S Williams, 'The Extraordinary African Chambers in the Senegalese Courts: An African Solution to an African Problem?' (2013) 11 JICJ 1139.

[120] See Law No 05/L-053 of 3 August 2015 (Kosovo Assembly).

[121] See *Prosecutor v Salih Mustafa*, KSC-BC-2020-05.

The issue to be resolved is the question of how to circumvent Russia's lack of consent. Though the ICTY and ICTR were created by resolutions of the Security Council, Russia's veto makes such a mechanism unfathomable. The hybrid tribunals in relation to Sierra Leone, Lebanon, Cambodia, and Kosovo did not depend on a Security Council resolution, but rather, some treaty or agreement to which the State concerned was a party.

The jurisdiction of any such special tribunal could be modelled on earlier practice such as an agreement between Ukraine and a UN organ, such as the General Assembly (as was done for the ECCC), or with the Secretary-General (the basis for the SCSL). Potentially, Ukraine could also create a special criminal chamber under its domestic law, as was done with the KSC (albeit under an EU-Kosovo agreement), though Articles 124–5 of its Constitution impose certain limits on so-called 'extraordinary chambers'. But the salient question remains whether any such arrangement that excludes Russia can bestow jurisdiction over the prosecution of acts of Russian officials, even if acting abroad. Such an assertion of jurisdiction raises serious questions relating to the scope of immunity of State officials and the extent to which a State, or group of States, is competent to do so under customary international law. This area remains ambiguous, as the legal basis for the ICC's arrest warrant for President Putin for crimes against humanity was, as of late 2024, unpublished. Similarly, no formal mechanism has yet been formally proposed by a State or an international organization to constitute an *ad hoc* tribunal with jurisdiction over the crime of aggression.

For further reading, see O Corten and V Koutroulis, 'Tribunal for the Crime of Aggression against Ukraine – A Legal Assessment' (European Parliament Publications, December 2022); and R van Alebeek, L van den Herik and C Ryngaert, 'Prosecuting Russian Officials for the Crime of Aggression: What About Immunities?' (2023) 4 European Convention on Human Rights Law Review 115. In early 2025, a proposal was announced for a Special Tribunal to be created through a bilateral agreement between Ukraine and the Council of Europe.

17.3 'Core crimes' under international law

Though specific treaties exist in respect of the trafficking of drugs, money laundering, the unlawful arms trade, and the smuggling of nuclear and other ultra-hazardous materials, these 'treaty crimes' have not entered into customary international law, and also do not fall under the subject-matter jurisdiction of any international tribunal at present. There is, however, a category of indisputable 'core crimes' under customary international law: genocide, crimes against humanity, war crimes, and aggression (formerly crimes against peace). These are helpfully defined in an ICC document, adopted by the ASP, called the 'Elements of Crimes', which is intended to guide the Court in the interpretation and application of these crimes.[122]

There is a strange paradox inherent in adjudicating these core crimes. International criminal justice relies on a concept of prosecuting individual offenders for their criminal acts. Practically speaking, however, some of these crimes cannot be committed

[122] See Rome Statute (n 53) Art 9; and 'Elements of Crimes', as revised in ICC, 'Official Records of the Review Conference of the Rome Statute of the International Criminal Court, Kampala' (31 May–11 June 2010), ICC RC/11.

without the support of other individuals and the apparatus of the State, or at the very least, that of an organized armed group. Though co-perpetration and JCE doctrines were elaborated to take this fact into account, the core crimes in the following sections should be read with that caveat in mind.

17.3.1 **Genocide**

The prohibition against genocide is defined in Article II of the Genocide Convention, and reprised in the Rome Statute and those of the ad hoc Tribunals. It has been repeatedly upheld as a norm of *jus cogens*.[123] Genocide consists of acts involving the killing, destruction, or extermination of groups or of members of groups with the intent to destroy that national, ethnical, racial, or religious group; such acts include the prevention of births within a group and the forced transfer of children to another group.[124]

HISTORICAL BACKGROUND The emergence of the term 'genocide'

The term 'genocide', combining the Greek *genos* ('people' or 'race') with the Latin root *cide* (from *occidere*, meaning 'to kill'), was coined by Raphaël Lemkin to describe the Holocaust. The neologism entered the international legal vocabulary rapidly. Though it was not used by the Nuremberg and Tokyo Tribunals, as it was not mentioned *eo nomine* ('by name') in their respective charters, they did consider the act of persecution as a crime against humanity. It was first deployed as a term of art by the General Assembly in Resolution 96(I), and became a legal term in 1948 when the Genocide Convention was opened for signature.

The importance of the prohibition against genocide is clear: as early as 1951, the ICJ mentioned in the *Reservations to the Convention on the Prevention and Punishment of the Crime of Genocide* advisory opinion that 'the principles underlying the Convention are principles which are recognized by civilized nations as binding on States, even without any conventional obligation' (p 23). Genocide, in this respect, became the archetype of a peremptory norm of international law (see Chapter 3).

To date, no State, not even Nazi Germany, has been found culpable of having committed genocide; this is in part due to the decision after World War II to hold individuals, and not States, responsible. In its 2007 judgment in *Application of the Genocide Convention (Bosnia and Herzegovina v Serbia)*, the ICJ held that Serbia had failed in its obligation to prevent genocide in Srebreniča. Serbia was not, however, held responsible for having committed genocide itself, as the genocide was not committed by its organs *de jure* or *de facto* (see Chapter 10, Section 10.2.1.1 for further discussion). In late 2019, The Gambia invoked the Convention

[123] Canonical cases abound, as is explained in Chapter 3: see *Armed Activities on the Territory of the Congo (New Application 2002) (Democratic Republic of the Congo v Rwanda), Jurisdiction and Admissibility, ICJ Reports 2006*, p 3, para 64; *Application of the Genocide Convention (Bosnia)* (n 41) 111, para 161; *Application of the Genocide Convention (Croatia)* (n 41), 47, para 87; *Stichting Mothers of Srebreniča and others v the Netherlands* App No 65542/12 (ECtHR, 11 June 2013), para 157; *Prosecutor v Akayesu* (n 36) paras 204–8; *Prosecutor v Zoran Kupreškić et al* (Judgment) IT-95-16 (14 January 2000), para 520.

[124] See *Akayesu* (n 36) 507–8; and by the ICJ in *Application of the Genocide Convention (Croatia)* (n 41) para 166.

against Myanmar in respect of its treatment of the Rohingya That dispute is pending before the Court, and the Court's docket has burgeoned with genocide-related cases in the last few years.

For further reading on the origins of the term, see R Lemkin, *Axis Rule in Occupied Europe* (Carnegie Endowment, 1944); J Cooper, *Raphael Lemkin and the Struggle for the Genocide Convention* (Palgrave Macmillan, 2008); and P Sands, *East West Street: On the Origins of Genocide and Crimes against Humanity* (W&N, 2016), for a narrative account of Lemkin's life as being intertwined with that of international lawyer Sir Hersch Lauterpacht.

The persecution of a group on political grounds is not covered; neither is, without the physical or biological destruction of all or part of the group, the destruction of a language and a culture (so-called 'cultural genocide').[125] Rape and sexual violence, if accompanied by the requisite intent, can also constitute an act of genocide.[126]

The definition of a protected group is far from clear-cut, and international criminal tribunals have rejected any claims to an objective or 'scientific' basis for defining a protected group. Instead, it is sufficient if the perpetrator of a genocidal act perceived a victim to be part of a group which exists in a relevant cultural context, which combines both objective and subjective elements.[127]

Whatever act is committed, the *mens rea* ('mental intention') in committing an act of genocide must be the 'specific intent' (called *dolus specialis*) to destroy or exterminate a targeted group in whole or in part.[128] Indirect intention is insufficient, and for this reason, the burden of proof for genocidal intent is high, though the ICC Elements of Crimes suggest that contextual elements can be an objective point of reference for a determination of genocidal intent, such as the existence 'of a manifest pattern of similar conduct'.[129] The ICTR has held that the commission of similar acts in scale and scope, and frequency of destructive and discriminatory acts, can all help to establish genocidal intent.[130] Similarly, the deliberate withholding of key resources such as food or medical services, or the systematic expulsion of members of a targeted group from their homes,

[125] See *Application of the Genocide Convention (Bosnia)* (n 41) para 344; *Application of the Genocide Convention (Croatia)* (n 41) para 136; *Prosecutor v Krstić* (Appeals Judgment) IT-98-33-A (19 April 2004), para 25; A Cassese and P Gaeta, with L Baig, M Fan, C Gosnell, and A Whiting, *Cassese's International Criminal Law* (3rd edn, OUP, 2013), 443.

[126] *Akayesu* (n 36) para 731; *Prosecutor v Stakić* (Judgment) IT-97-24-T (31 July 2003), para 516; *Application of the Genocide Convention (Bosnia)* (n 41) para 300; *Application of the Genocide Convention (Croatia)* (n 41) para 158.

[127] *Prosecutor v Krstić* (Judgment) IT-98-33-T (2 August 2001), para 556; *Prosecutor v Semanza* (Judgment) ICTR-97-20-T (15 May 2003), para 317.

[128] See *Application of the Genocide Convention (Bosnia)* (n 41) para 187; *Application of the Genocide Convention (Croatia)* (n 41) para 132.

[129] See C Kreß, 'The Crime of Genocide and Contextual Elements: A Comment on the ICC Pre-Trial Chamber's Decision in the Al Bashir Case' (2009) 7 JICJ 297; and R Cryer, 'The Definitions of International Crimes in the Al Bashir Arrest Warrant Decision' (2009) 7 JICJ 289. In *Application of the Genocide Convention (Bosnia)* (n 41) para 189, the ICJ could only establish genocidal intent in relation to the massacre in Srebrenica.

[130] *Prosecutor v Ncamihigo* (Judgment) ICTR-01-63-T (12 November 2008), para 331.

could fulfil the conduct element, but only if accompanied by the requisite specific intent to destroy a group in whole or in part.[131]

Finally, though a genocidal act need not be widespread and systematic, the ICC's Elements of Crimes depart from customary international law and the case law of the ICTY and the ICTR, in that they require that the conduct take place 'in the context of a manifest pattern of similar conduct directed against that group or ... conduct that could itself effect such destruction', as it is difficult to establish the intention to destroy or exterminate a group on the basis of isolated acts.[132]

17.3.2 **Crimes against humanity**

The development of 'crimes against humanity' took place against the backdrop of the heinous atrocities committed by the Nazis across Europe. Outrage that the law of war did not cover many barbarous and inhumane acts committed against civilian populations impelled the inclusion of Article 6(c) of the Nuremberg Charter, which criminalized the 'murder, extermination, enslavement, deportation, and other inhumane acts committed against any civilian population'.[133] Though controversial due to its retroactive nature,[134] the concept has proven influential over the various statutes of later international criminal tribunals. However, no overarching definition of 'crimes against humanity' exists, as the constitutive instrument of each institution contains a slightly different definition of crimes against humanity. In 2019, the ILC adopted a set of Draft Articles on the Prohibition and Punishment of Crimes against Humanity which embraced roughly the same definition as Article 7 of the Rome Statute.[135]

Set against this context, Article 7 of the Rome Statute contains the most widely ratified treaty-based definition of crimes against humanity, requiring as an overarching condition that, in order to be qualified as such, an act must be 'part of a widespread or systematic attack directed against any civilian population'. Though present in Article 3 of the ICTR Statute, that condition was not present in Article 5 of the ICTY Statute, but was developed over time in its case law.[136] Article 7 enumerates, *inter alia*, enslavement,

[131] ICC Elements of Crimes (n 119) Art 6, fn 4. However, *cf Prosecutor v Blagojević* (Judgment) IT-02-60-A (9 May 2007), paras 119 *et seq*, forced migration or 'ethnic cleansing' did not by itself constitute genocide, though it might constitute a pattern of conduct demonstrating genocidal intent. See also *Application of the Genocide Convention (Bosnia)* (n 41) para 190; *Application of the Genocide Convention (Croatia)* (n 41) paras 162–3.

[132] *Krstić* (Appeals Chamber Judgment) (n 122) para 12; *Application of the Genocide Convention (Bosnia)* (n 41) para 198; and *Application of the Genocide Convention (Croatia)* (n 41) para 139.

[133] The Tokyo Charter was broadly similar, though it also added rape, imprisonment, and torture to the list.

[134] See Motion adopted by all Defence Counsel on 19 November 1945, in Judgment of the Nuremberg International Military Tribunal (n 10) 168–9.

[135] UN Doc A/74/10 (2019), Draft Art 2 (definition). For a detailed analysis, see CC Jalloh, 'The International Law Commission's First Draft Convention on Crimes against Humanity' (2020) 52 Case Western Reserve Journal of International Law 331; and LN Sadat, 'A Contextual and Historical Analysis of the International Law Commission's 2017 Draft Articles for a New Global Treaty on Crimes against Humanity' (2018) 16 JICJ 683.

[136] See *Prosecutor v Tadić* (Trial Chamber Judgment) IT-94-1-T (7 May 1997), para 644; and (Appeals Chamber Judgment) IT-94-1-A (15 July 1999), para 248.

deportation or forcible transfer of population, sexual violence such as rape, enforced prostitution, forced pregnancy, or sterilization, and the enforced disappearance of persons. To these, one can add the catch-all under subsection (k), 'other inhumane acts of a similar character intentionally causing great suffering, or serious injury to body or to mental or physical health'.

CONTEMPORARY DEVELOPMENTS Forced Displacement, Ethnic Cleansing, and the Rohingya People

The Rohingya population, estimated at *c* 1 million, are a primarily Muslim minority in the Rakhine state in the west of Myanmar (formerly Burma), which has a predominantly Buddhist population. Since Myanmar's independence in 1948, they had suffered from discrimination and repression; in particular, they have been denied citizenship under a 1982 nationality law which mandates that individuals must prove their Burmese ancestry dating back to 1823 to enjoy freedom of movement and access to other basic rights, such as health care and education. The Myanmar government asserts that they are illegal migrants from Bangladesh; the Rohingya consider themselves indigenous peoples of western Myanmar.

In a 2016 report, UN High Commissioner for Human Rights Zeid Ra'ad Al Hussein cautioned that there existed 'a pattern of gross violations against the Rohingya . . . [which] suggest a widespread or systematic attack . . . in turn giving rise to the possible commission of crimes against humanity' (UN Doc A/HRC/32/18, p 13, para 55). Nevertheless, on 25 August 2017, in retaliation for an attack by an insurgent group against Myanmar police, a systematic process of driving hundreds of thousands of Rohingya from Myanmar was triggered and, by mid-October, it was estimated that more than 500,000 Rohingya had fled, most to Bangladesh. On 13 September 2017, UN Secretary-General António Guterres warned that such a forced displacement could only be described as 'ethnic cleansing' (see UN Doc SG/SM/18676).

In late August 2018, the Office of the UN High Commissioner for Human Rights issued the Report of the Independent International Fact-Finding Mission on the events of 2016 and 2017 (see UN Doc A/HRC/39/64). The OHCHR declared that these events constitute cause for the Myanmar government, and particularly the 'Tatmadaw'—the Myanmar military and its commanding officers—to be brought before the ICC for crimes against humanity, including ethnic cleansing and genocide. At the time this book went to press, the UN Security Council remained actively seised of the issue but had not taken any specific action; nor had it referred the matter to the ICC, though in 2019 the ICC Prosecutor opened an investigation into Bangladesh/Myanmar (see ICC-01/19), on the basis of of the fact that some of the alleged acts occurred 'at least in part' on the territory of Bangladesh, a State party since 2010.

What distinguishes a 'mere' murder, rape, or enslavement—if there is such a thing—from a crime against humanity is that the latter are committed against the background of a widespread or systematic attack against the civilian population. It is important to note that these are not cumulative conditions.[137] Case law suggests that 'widespread' refers to scale, being massive, frequent, large scale, carried out collectively with considerable

[137] R Dixon and CK Hall (rev), 'Article 7 Crimes against Humanity: Para 1' in K Ambos (ed), *Rome Statute of the International Criminal Court: A Commentary* (4th edn, Beck/Hart, 2020).

seriousness, and directed against a multiplicity of victims, whereas 'systematic' refers to being thoroughly organized and following a regular pattern on the basis of a common policy.[138] The standard to establish intent to commit a crime against humanity is less stringent than for genocide, provided that there is specific intent to commit the underlying crime (murder, rape, torture), and knowledge of the broader context in which the crime is committed.[139]

To recall, crimes against humanity must be directed against a civilian population; but this may be either within the context of an armed conflict or committed during peacetime. As such, it is important to recall the distinction between civilians and non-civilians, which is not airtight.[140] For example, the mere presence of individual combatants within a preponderantly civilian population does not change their civilian character.[141] Similarly, persons *hors de combat* (inactive or injured combatants) can also be victims of crimes against humanity.[142]

If the attack fulfils all the elements for a crime against humanity, but is not directed against a civilian population, it may still fall within the category of war crimes if committed in the context of an armed conflict, to which we now turn.

17.3.3 **War crimes**

The notion of 'war crimes' exists at the intersection between international humanitarian law (IHL) and international criminal law, though the relationship between these two specialized regimes is not always clear. On one hand, the view taken in Article 6(b) of the Nuremberg Charter is that all certain violations of IHL are war crimes. On the other side lies the view of the ICTY Appeals Chamber in *Tadić*, which requires not only a 'serious' infringement of a rule of IHL but also that each rule of IHL be criminalized: 'the violation must entail, either under customary or conventional law, the individual criminal responsibility of the person breaching that rule'.[143] The first and third lists, relating to IACs and NIACs respectively, encompass 'acts against persons or property protected under the provisions' in the form of 'grave breaches' of the 1949 Geneva Conventions (IAC) or of Common Article 3 (see Chapter 15, Section 15.2.2.1), enumerating acts including torture or inhuman treatment, including biological experiments, wilfully causing serious bodily injury, forced conscription of prisoners of war, unlawful deportation, and the taking of hostages.[144] The second and fourth categories, also relating to IACs and NIACs, enumerate 'serious violations' of the laws and customs

[138] *Akayesu* (n 36) para 580; *Prosecutor v Kunarac, Kovać and Vuković* (Judgment) IT-96-23/1-A (12 June 2002), para 94; *Prosecutor v Blaskić* (Appeals Chamber Judgment) IT-95-14-A (29 July 2004), paras 203–4; and *Al Bashir* (First Warrant of Arrest) (n 88) para 81.

[139] *Kunarac, Kovać and Vuković, ibid*, para 103.

[140] See earlier, Chapter 15, 'The law of armed conflict', Section 15.4.1, 'The principle of distinction'.

[141] *Blaskić* (n 135) paras 103–16, esp para 113; *Tadić* (Trial Judgment) (n 133) para 638.

[142] *Prosecutor v Martić* (Appeals Chamber Judgment) IT-95-11-A (8 October 1998), para 313.

[143] *Tadić* (Appeals Chamber Judgment) (n 133) para 94.

[144] Substantially similar enumerations of 'grave breaches' are found in ICTY Statute (n 19) Art 2; ICTR Statute (n 20) Art 4; and SCSL Statute (n 98) Art 3.

of IHL, which in respect of IACs are contained in the 1907 Hague Regulations and the First Additional Protocol to the Geneva Conventions (there is no such list relating to NIACs). These include prohibitions against deliberate attacks on a civilian population,[145] the killing of a combatant having laid down [their] arms,[146] the use of poison or poisoned weapons,[147] committing acts of sexual violence such as rape or enforced prostitution,[148] and the use of 'human shields'.[149]

A war crime can only be committed in the context of an armed conflict, the definition of which is key. A modern definition was provided by the ILC in Article 2(b) of the 2011 Draft Articles on the Effects of Armed Conflicts on the Law of Treaties. Drawing inspiration from the ICTY in an early decision in *Tadić*,[150] the ILC suggested that '"armed conflict" means a situation in which there is resort to armed force between States or protracted resort to armed force between governmental authorities and organized armed groups'.[151] Accordingly, war crimes can be committed in both internal (non-international) armed conflicts, as well as in armed conflicts between States.[152] As the ICTY commented in *Kunarac* that though the armed conflict need not have caused the commission of the crime, it must have played a substantial role in the accused's decision and ability to commit it.[153]

17.3.4 **Aggression**

The fourth 'core crime', aggression, was originally called 'crimes against peace' in Nuremberg and Tokyo: the 'planning, preparation, initiation or waging of a war of aggression, or a war in violation of international treaties, agreements or assurances', or conspiracy to commit such acts.[154] However, there was no explicit definition of aggression proffered at the time, and only one other of the many international criminal tribunals is endowed with jurisdiction over the crime of aggression: the Iraqi Special Tribunal. Though operating under Iraqi municipal law, it has jurisdiction in relation to '[t]he abuse of position and the pursuit of policies that may lead to the threat of war or the use of force of the armed forces of Iraq against an Arab country'.[155]

The criminalization of aggression remains an extremely sensitive topic, even in light of the Charter prohibition on the use of force in its Article 2(4). It is one thing to prohibit an act, and quite another to criminalize its commission. One need only point to the fallout of the 2016 Report of the Iraq Inquiry (the 'Chilcot Report') in the UK, which

145 Rome Statute (n 53) Art 8(2)(b)(i). 146 *Ibid*, Art 8(2)(b)(vi). 147 *Ibid*, Art 8(2)(b)(xvii).
148 *Ibid*, Art 8(2)(b)(xxii). 149 *Ibid*, Art 8(2)(b)(xxiii).
150 *Prosecutor v Tadić* (Interlocutory Appeal) (n 32) para 70.
151 ILC Draft Articles on the Effects of Armed Conflicts on the Law of Treaties, in 'Report of the International Law Commission on the Work of its 63rd Session' (26 April–12 August 2011), UN Doc A/66/10, Art 2(b).
152 Rome Statute (n 53) Art 8(2)(c) and (e); *Tadić* (Appeals Chamber Judgment) IT-94-1-A (15 July 1999), paras 97, 129. 153 *Kunarac, Kovać and Vuković* (n 135) para 58.
154 Nuremberg Charter (n 7) Art 6(a); Tokyo Charter (n 8) Art 5(a).
155 Art 14(c) of its Statute: See C Kreß, 'The Iraqi Special Tribunal and the Crime of Aggression' (2004) 2 JICJ 347.

raised serious issues relating to the UK government's decision to proceed with the 2003 invasion of Iraq.[156] Even with the persuasive definition of the concept (not crime) of aggression by the General Assembly in *Definition of Aggression*, there was no consensus as to how it could constitute an international crime.[157] One obvious reason is that the decision to use aggressive force against another State is invariably conducted by the highest officials of a State, and one can only imagine their discomfort at the idea that their conduct might retrospectively be deemed to be a criminal act.

That sensitivity permeated the negotiations during the 1998 Rome Conference. While there was clear consensus that the crime of aggression ought to fall within the scope of the ICC's jurisdiction, States could simply not agree on a definition.[158] Thus, Article 5 of the Rome Statute set out that at a future review conference an amendment would add a provision defining aggression and setting out the conditions under which the Court could exercise jurisdiction. This bore fruit when at the 2010 Kampala Review Conference, involving all members of the ASP, a definition for the crime of aggression was agreed. As required, thirty States have now ratified an amendment introducing Article 8*bis*; from 31 December 2017 this provision has now been considered 'activated', and the ICC may exercise jurisdiction over acts of aggression occurring after 17 July 2018.[159]

Article 8*bis* defines aggression as 'the planning, preparation, initiation or execution, by a person in a position effectively to exercise control over or to direct the political or military action of a State, of an act of aggression which, by its character, gravity and scale, constitutes a manifest violation of the Charter of the United Nations'.[160] In effect, aggression may only be committed by those in a position to control or direct the apparatus of a State; the leaders of organized armed groups cannot be prosecuted for aggression before the ICC. Additional features of Article 8*bis* require further elaboration, notably, on how the threshold of 'manifest' will be determined, as well as the exact interrelation between the criteria of gravity, character, and scale of a violation.[161]

The newly activated Articles 15*bis–ter* of the Rome Statute set out the ways in which the ICC can exercise jurisdiction over the crime of aggression, bearing in mind the competence of the Security Council, under Article 39 of the UN Charter, to make a determination that an act of aggression has occurred.[162] Importantly, the scope of the ICC's jurisdiction *ratione personae* is narrower than for the other three core crimes, and

[156] See earlier Chapter 14, Section 14.5.2.2.3, for further information on the Chilcot Report. The UK government has published both the full Report and a 150-page Executive Summary: <http://www.iraqinquiry.org.uk>.

[157] UNGA Res 3314 (14 December 1974).

[158] A detailed history of the unsuccessful negotiations on defining the crime of aggression can be found in A Zimmerman, 'Article 5' in K Ambos (ed), *Commentary on the Rome Statute of the International Criminal Court* (4th edn, Hart, 2008), 129.

[159] See ICC Doc ASP/16/Res 5 (14 December 2017); and Rome Statute (n 53) art 15*bis*(3).

[160] See Resolution on the Crime of Aggression (12 June 2010), ICC Doc RC/Res 6, Art 8*bis*. For further reading, see N Blokker and C Kreß, 'A Consensus Agreement on the Crime of Aggression' (2010) 23 LJIL 889; D Scheffer, 'The Complex Crime of Aggression under the Rome Statute' (2010) 23 LJIL 897.

[161] See RW Heinsch, 'The Crime of Aggression After Kampala: Success or Burden for the Future' (2010) 2 Göttingen JIL 713.

[162] See Chapter 14, Section 14.5.1, on determinations under Art 39 by the Security Council.

the crime must have been committed by officials of a State party to the Rome Statute that has not opted out under Article 15(4)*bis*, even if the impugned acts have occurred on the territory of a State party. This jurisdictional condition is relevant in respect of the ongoing investigation with respect to Ukraine, and is the reason for the proposed Special Tribunal for Agression against Ukraine discussed above, in Section 17.2.4.

17.4 Selected issues relating to liability

17.4.1 Command responsibility

Because international criminal law rests on a paradigm of individual criminal responsibility, one of its challenges remains how to grapple with the hierarchically organized context in which many of these crimes take place. For this reason, the Rome Statute assigns culpability for 'command responsibility' or 'superior responsibility'; that is, the responsibility of those in effective control of subordinates who have committed offences, and where the offences have occurred as a result of a failure to exercise control.[163]

The notion of command responsibility first arose in connection with the situation concerning Japanese General Yamashita, found guilty by a US military commission.[164] This finding was upheld by the US Supreme Court, which sentenced him for having commanded troops engaged in war crimes in the Philippines on the basis that he 'must have known' of atrocities being committed, despite having been isolated from his troops at the relevant times.[165] The ICTY has interpreted command responsibility more strictly, and does not criminalize a negligent failure to obtain information, instead requiring actual knowledge or an objective 'should have known' test; namely, the possession of information of a nature which should have put the commander on notice that further investigation would be needed to prevent or repress such crimes.[166] Article 28(a) of the Rome Statute attributes command responsibility for crimes committed by forces under the command and control of military as well as civilian superiors under the following conditions: because they knew or should have known of such acts; negligence (i.e., a failure to take measures to prevent or repress such acts); or a failure to punish the acts upon knowledge of their commission. The ICC has interpreted the failure to exercise control over subordinates as requiring no causation: 'it is only necessary to prove that the commander's omission increased the risk of the commission of the crimes charged in order to hold him criminally responsible'.[167]

[163] But see *Bemba Gombo*, Judgment of Trial Chamber I (n 72) paras 424–5, according to which 'no direct causal link' needs to be established between the superior's omission and the crime committed by his subordinates. The ICTY would concur: see ICTY Appeals Chamber, *Prosecutor v Hadžihasanović and Kubura*, Judgment, Case No IT-01-47-A, 22 April 2008, para 39.

[164] *In re Yamashita* (US Military Commission) (1945) 13 Annual Digest 255.

[165] *In re Yamashita* (US Supreme Court) (1946) 13 Annual Digest 269.

[166] *Prosecutor v Delalić, Mučić, Delić and Landžo* (Judgment) IT-96-23-A (20 February 2001), paras 223, 241. This is broadly in line with the requirements of Additional Protocol I, Art 86, para 2.

[167] *Bemba Gombo* (Judgment of Trial Chamber I) (n 72) paras 424–5. For a sceptical perspective on command responsibility, see D Robinson, 'How Command Responsibility Got So Complicated: A Culpability Contradiction, Its Obfuscation, and a Simple Solution' (2012) 12 Melbourne JIL 1.

Article 28(b) of the Rome Statute, in a departure from the practices of the ICTY and ICTR, also attributes command responsibility on non-military or civilian superiors who 'knew, or consciously disregarded information that clearly indicated' that subordinates under their effective authority or control were involved in committing crimes, or because they failed to take measures to prevent or repress their commission. This is a higher standard than for civilian superiors who might also find themselves criminally responsible for their negligence, but a lower standard than that for military commanders.

CASE SPOTLIGHT ***Prosecutor v Jean-Pierre Bemba Gombo*, ICC-01/05-01/08**

The *Prosecutor v Bemba* decision of Trial Chamber III, only the second to be issued by the ICC, was rendered on 21 March 2016. Mr Bemba, former President and Commander-in-Chief of the Movement for the Liberation of the Congo (MLC), was charged for crimes against humanity and war crimes committed by an MLC contingent deployed in the Central African Republic in 2002–3. The charges faced by Mr Bemba included the organization of pillaging, rape, and murder against civilians. He was sentenced on 21 June 2016 to eighteen years' imprisonment.

The Trial Chamber's decision is notable for two important developments. The first is in relation to developing the definition of rape as a war crime and as a crime against humanity. Trial Chamber III found that aggravating circumstances could exist in this case, given that the victims were 'particularly defenceless' and their rape was committed with 'particular cruelty', as permitted under ICC Rule 145(2)(b) (see Judgment on Sentencing, paras 41–7). What is more, the case is significant given that Bemba's culpability was based on his command responsibility: acting as effective military commander (under Article 28(a) of the Rome Statute), he was found by Trial Chamber III to have had full knowledge that the MLC forces under his effective authority and control were committing or about to commit the crimes in question. The Chamber concluded that there was evidence of a consistent *modus operandi* ('method of working') apparent from the early days of the MLC's operations in the CAR. Mr Bemba was also found to have failed to take all necessary and reasonable measures to prevent or repress the commission of crimes by his subordinates (Judgment of Trial Chamber III, paras 191–209).

On 22 July 2016, counsel for Mr Bemba announced their intention to appeal the judgment. On 8 June 2018, the appeal was published, in which his convictions for war crimes were overturned. The Appeal Chamber (by a 3–2 vote) concluded that the conviction did not fairly account for Bemba's efforts to stop his troops' crimes once he became aware of them, and that his power to control them was limited since he was acting as a remote commander. For these reasons, he could not be held criminally liable for the crimes committed by MLC troops during the CAR operation (Decision of the Appeals Chamber, para 194).

In March 2021, drawing from the principles first articulated in *Bemba*, the 2019 conviction of Bosco Ntagnada for rape and sexual slavery (as well as for the recruitment of child soldiers) was upheld by the ICC Appeals Chamber (*Prosecutor v Mr Bosco Ntagnada*, ICC-01/04-02/06-2666-Red, Appeals Chamber Decision of 30 March 2021). With this decision, Mr Ntaganda has become the first person convicted for gender-based violence at the ICC.

Insightful studies of the topic of gender justice at the ICC include Rosemary Gray, *Prosecuting Sexual and Gender-Based Crimes at the International Criminal Court* (CUP, 2019); and Louise Chappell, *The Politics of Gender Justice at the International Criminal Court: Legacies and Legitimacy* (OUP, 2018).

17.4.2 **Joint liability**

There has been one major departure from the legacy of the ad hoc Tribunals, and it is on issues of joint liability. The ICTY Appeals Chamber in *Tadić* controversially devised a concept of 'joint criminal enterprise' (JCE) in its reading of Article 7(1) of the ICTY Statute.[168] The JCE doctrine allowed individuals to be held liable for crimes committed as part of a common plan carried out either jointly or by some members of a group. The Appeals Chamber explained that JCE itself constituted a form of commission, putting forward three broad forms under which individuals could be convicted. Its third form, 'extended joint enterprise', was particularly controversial. It allowed for the attribution of liability for acts falling outside any common planning, using a foreseeability test, such that JCE has been derided in scholarship as 'just convict everyone'.[169]

As a concept, JCE was rejected in Article 25(3) of the Rome Statute in favour of a more civil law oriented doctrine of 'co-perpetration'. Co-perpetration separates direct perpetration from secondary participation more systematically, and requires a greater degree of functional control over a criminal act.[170] Co-perpetration requires a higher degree of common planning between the co-perpetrators and a coordinated essential contribution by the accused in the commission of a crime, as well as the awareness that such a common plan will result in that crime.[171] Nevertheless, co-perpetration has its own doctrinal problems, which are perhaps inherent in the difficulty of attributing individual responsibility for collective acts.[172]

17.4.3 **The defence of superior orders**

It is long established in municipal legal orders that certain circumstances allow one to raise a defence for having committed a crime. In the Rome Statute, such grounds are defined and include mental incapacity or insanity due to disease or defect, intoxication, self-defence or defence of another person, and duress.[173]

[168] *Tadić* (Appeals Chamber Judgment) (n 149) paras 196, 202, 204. The doctrine was expanded considerably in *Prosecutor v Milutinović* (Motion Challenging Jurisdiction—Joint Criminal Enterprise) IT-99-37-AR72 (21 May 2003).

[169] A leading exponent of JCE was A Cassese, 'The Proper Limits of Individual Responsibility under the Doctrine of Joint Criminal Enterprise' (2007) 5 JCIJ 109. See also JD Ohlin, 'Three Conceptual Problems with the Doctrine of Joint Criminal Enterprise' (2007) 5 JICJ 109; ME Badar, '"Just Convict Everyone!"—Joint Perpetration: From *Tadić* to *Stakić* and Back Again' (2006) ICLR 293.

[170] Rome Statute (n 53) Art 25(3); applied in *Prosecutor v Lubanga* (n 71) paras 326–39. See also K Ambos, *Treatise on International Criminal Law* (OUP, 2013), vol 1, 173–6; T Weigend, 'Intent, Mistake of Law, and Co-Perpetration in the *Lubanga* Decision on Confirmation of Charges' (2008) 6 JICJ 417; and C Roxin, *Täterschaft und Tatherrschaft* (8th edn, De Gruyter Recht, 2006), 275–305.

[171] See *Prosecutor v Bemba Gombo* (Decision of the Confirmation of Charges) ICC-01/05-01/09 (15 June 2009), paras 352–9; *Prosecutor v Lubanga* (Decision of the Confirmation of Charges) ICC-01/04-01/06 (29 January 2007), paras 349–67.

[172] See generally N Jain, *Perpetrators and Accessories in International Criminal Law: Individual Modes of Liability for Collective Crimes* (Hart, 2014).

[173] Rome Statute (n 53) Art 31. It bears noting that before the ICTY and ICTR, these were relevant for sentencing, but not for determining criminal responsibility.

However, the defence of obedience to superior orders has proven highly controversial. Many founding statutes of international criminal tribunals have expressly excluded reliance on a defence of superior orders.[174] However, Article 33 of the Rome Statute permits the defence in relation to war crimes, as well as in situations where an order was backed by a legal obligation to obey, where the person had no knowledge that the order was unlawful, and that the order was not manifestly unlawful, such as orders to commit genocide or crimes against humanity nevertheless. The defence of superior orders under Article 33 was considered for the first time by the ICC in 2024, but was declared inapplicable on the basis that orders to commit conduct tantamount to war crimes are 'equally manifestly unlawful and therefore cannot be subject to the defence of superior orders'.[175]

17.5 **Conclusion**

International criminal law seems to be at a turning point: it is no longer lacking in institutional structures which exercise jurisdiction over accused, and it has become popular as a rallying cry against impunity in all its forms. Perhaps that enthusiasm misses the wider question as to whether international criminal justice is the best answer in relation to the rebuilding of societies ravaged by atrocities. There are certain markers of success: the building of institutions, the adoption of binding legal rules, and the siren song of eliminating the scourge of impunity. And yet, somehow, these conceal the fact that other alternatives have been set aside in the privileging of this particular form of justice. Moreover, the 'legitimating quality' of international criminal judgments can serve to reinforce or establish certain narratives of the past, marginalizing and excluding the voices of certain participants.[176] A trial can threaten a fragile peace settlement in which amnesties, however problematic they are in principle, might have constituted the basis of a comprehensive settlement. Judicial processes often displace the possibility of other processes known under the umbrella term 'transitional justice'. For example, the Truth and Reconciliation Commission in South Africa might never have been able to operate effectively had post-apartheid South Africa been obliged to press forward with judicial proceedings against all accused. Moreover, though ending impunity remains an important aspiration, the paradox inherent in sentencing individuals for essentially collective crimes threatens the integrity of international criminal trials, with tricky compromises in relation to procedure and evidence.

[174] See Tokyo Charter (n 8) Art 7; ICTY Statute (n 19) Art 7(4); ICTR Statute (n 20) Art 6(4); SCSL Statute (n 98) Art 6(4).

[175] Prosecutor v Al Hassan (ICC-01/12-01/18), Judgment of Trial Chamber X (26 June 2024), paras 1782–1783. See further P Gaeta, 'The Defence of Superior Orders: The Statute of the International Criminal Court Versus Customary International Law' (1999) 10 EJIL 172.

[176] See Sander (n 11), who engages in an analysis of international criminal courts and of their influence in the framing of historical narratives.

Further reading

A Alamuddin and P Webb, 'Expanding Jurisdiction over War Crimes under Article 8 of the ICC Statute' (2010) 8 JICJ 1219.

An important contribution to the shifting understanding of war crimes at the time when the definition of aggression was being drafted by States, at the Kampala Conference.

A Cassese and P Gaeta, with L Baig, M Fan, C Gosnell, and A Whiting, *Cassese's International Criminal Law* (3rd edn, OUP, 2013).

Originally written by a leading international criminal judge and academic, this treatise embodies the optimism and desire to eliminate impunity that culminated in the signing of the Rome Statute in 1998.

R Cryer, D Robinson, and S Vasiliev, *An Introduction to International Criminal Law and Procedure* (4th edn, CUP, 2019).

A detailed and considered study of the field, this is one of the better treatises available in the field.

D Guilfoyle, *International Criminal Law* (OUP, 2016).

A newer entry into the field, this treatise is a lucid, succinct account of the field.

KJ Heller, F Mégret, SH Nouwen, J Ohlin, and D Robinson (eds), *The Oxford Handbook of International Criminal Law* (OUP, 2020).

Departing from the traditional *Oxford Handbooks* format, this compendium is structured around actors, purposes, and origins of the international criminal justice system, and includes inter-disciplinary accounts as well.

N Jain, *Perpetrators and Accessories in International Criminal Law* (Hart, 2014).

A thoughtful juxtaposition of the collective and individual paradigms of liability in the emergence of international criminal justice.

S Kendall and S Nouwen, 'Representational Practices at the International Criminal Court: The Gap Between Juridified and Abstract Victimhood' (2013) 6 Law and Contemporary Problems 235.

Incisive and deeply critical challenge of the instrumentalization of victims in international criminal proceedings.

W Schabas, *An Introduction to the International Criminal Court* (6th edn, CUP, 2020).

An accessible and readable survey of the ICC, the centrepiece of the international criminal justice system.

C Schwöbel (ed), *Critical Approaches to International Criminal Law: An Introduction* (Routledge, 2014).

A timely collection of essays that take a decidedly sceptical view as to the positive contributions of this specialized regime of international law.

E Stahn, *A Critical Introduction to International Criminal Law* (CUP, 2019).

Analytically, though perhaps not methodologically critical, this clear and insightful contribution is accessible to students but conceptually rich.

E van Sliedrecht, *Individual Criminal Responsibility in International Law* (OUP, 2014).

Exceptionally clear and readable, this monograph considers the modes of participation and defences available in international criminal law.

G Werle and F Jessberger, *Principles of International Criminal Law* (3rd edn, OUP, 2014).

A structured and highly comprehensive account both of international and domestic practice and institutions relating to the field.

18

The law of the sea

18.1 Introduction: the sea as global commons

An enduring concern for international lawyers remains how to accommodate human— and State—engagement in areas not covered by land-based claims of sovereignty. Historically, this frequently related to the concept of unclaimed territory ('*res nullius*'), which at first extended to the oceans and left them open to exploitation by any and all States, subject to few legal restrictions. From that point, however, the oceans became one of the first areas in which States set limitations on what they could do; for example, through navigation and commerce treaties. It was from these first agreements that the law of the sea developed as a distinct regime of international law.[1]

The 'law of the sea' is a blanket term, describing the law relating to all bodies of water, irrespective of whether they are subject to the jurisdiction of a State. Naturally, the seas are tremendously important globally; the seas are a crucial means of communication and trade, allowing for the transport of persons and goods around the world. The seas and their subsoil are also a valuable economic resource, rich with minerals and energy reserves, not to mention fish stocks. What is more, the protection of the marine environment is an issue of pressing concern and, given the very nature of the seas and their interconnectedness, cannot succeed without substantial global collective collaboration.

Given its rich history, the law of the sea presents a fascinating case study of how customary and treaty law can develop in tandem, and also provides an interesting forum where the traditional doctrines of sovereignty and jurisdiction interact differently than in other fields of international law. The emergence of the 1982 UN Convention on the Law of the Sea (UNCLOS), in particular, drew heavily on the dynamism of customary international law in relation to the oceans during the 1960s and 1970s, and the whole UNCLOS process was a real testing ground for newly independent States to agitate for, and in fact secure, a new regime for the oceans that would be less focused on the interests of the long-established States of the Global North.[2]

1 See RP Anand, *Origin and Development of the Law of the Sea* (Brill, 1983).

2 Overseas Development Institute, 'The Third World and the Law of the Sea', ODI Briefing Paper (May 1981).

Moreover, many international legal regimes have borrowed concepts from the law of the sea and applied them in other contexts. For example, the 1944 Chicago Convention on International Civil Aviation proclaims important freedoms of navigation and communication in the air and atmosphere patterned on freedoms in the seas. The Roman law idea of *res communis* ('things common to all') was used in the 1967 Outer Space Treaty and the 1959 Antarctic Treaty, declaring that outer space and celestial bodies, and Antarctica, respectively, could not be subject to national appropriation.[3] The concept of 'global commons'[4] has also influenced international environmental law, being found not only in Part XIII of the 1982 UNCLOS[5] but also in the 1993 Convention on Biological Diversity and the 1992 United Nations Framework Convention on Climate Change.[6] More recently, the 'global commons' concept has been further deployed in other areas, for example to regulate 'cyberspace' and the internet.

18.2 The maritime regime: from *Mare Liberum* to UNCLOS

The law of the sea governs a series of overlapping sovereign interests and projections of jurisdiction, through two overarching categories. There exists a *territorial sea*, over which a coastal State can exercise jurisdiction and control virtually as an integral part of its territory. This territorial sea exists alongside the *high seas*, the area of the open seas incapable of such appropriation. Delineating between these two has been at the heart of more than four centuries of legal developments and disputes.

HISTORICAL BACKGROUND Grotius' *Mare Liberum* and the Politics of the Age of Exploration

The law of the sea originated in the doctrinal controversy as to whether the seas could be subject to the exclusive sovereignty of one State. According to this claim, advanced vigorously by Portugal and especially Spain during the early sixteenth century, the seas should be delineated and placed under the jurisdiction of a single coastal State, in part for reasons of security, but also to safeguard their own preferential trading regimes. Hugo Grotius' response in his classic treatise *Mare Liberum* ('The Free Sea') (1609) was to deny strongly this possibility, elaborating a doctrine of the seas as *res communis*, accessible to all nations but incapable of appropriation.

There was perhaps an element of strategic interest: Grotius, a Dutchman in the employ of the Dutch East Indies Company, was heavily involved in the Dutch struggle with Portugal and

[3] The 1959 Antarctic Treaty in effect 'froze' existing claims of States.

[4] See J Brunnée, 'Common Areas, Common Heritage, and Common Concern' in D Bodansky, J Brunnée, and E Hey (eds), *The Oxford Handbook of International Environmental Law* (OUP, 2007), 552. For a critical account of the origins of the concept, see S Ranganathan, 'Global Commons' (2016) 27 EJIL 693.

[5] United Nations Convention on the Law of the Sea (signed 10 December 1982, entered into force 16 November 1994), 1833 UNTS 3.

[6] See generally Chapter 19, 'The protection of the environment', but on the more general question of regime interaction as regards the law of the sea, see S Trevisanut, N Giannopoulos, and RR Holst (eds), *Regime Interaction in Ocean Governance: Problems, Theories and Methods* (Brill, 2020).

Spain over exploring and controlling commercial seafaring; in particular, trade. France and England, two other emerging maritime powers, also saw common cause with the Dutch position. A compromise emerged in Grotius' own work, *De Jure Belli et Pacis* (1625, vol II, ch 3) to safeguard both sets of interests: States were to enjoy sovereignty over their coastal waters, but the waters beyond these were to be subject to the principle of the 'freedom of the seas'. It was in this division that the distinction between the territorial sea and the high seas would emerge, with different legal regimes governing both; a division that underpins the law of the sea to this day.

For further reading, see MCW Pinto, 'Hugo Grotius and the Law of the Sea' in L Castillo (ed), *Law of the Sea, From Grotius to the International Tribunal for the Law of the Sea. Liber Amicorum Judge Hugo Caminos* (Brill, 2015), 18–47; and AG Oude Elferink, 'De Groot—A Founding Father of the Law of the Sea, Not the Law of the Sea Convention' (2009) 30 Grotiana 153.

Much of the early law of the sea had developed through traditional channels of customary law. After some initial codification attempts in 1930, four multilateral conventions on the law of the sea were agreed in 1958 in Geneva[7] that aimed to both capture existing legal rules and codify new rules. Unfortunately, the 1958 Conventions left several issues open, such as delineating the extent of the territorial sea. Dissatisfaction among newly independent States with the 1958 Conventions led to the Law of the Sea Conferences held from 1974 to 1982, a decade-long negotiation between States and international organizations which purported to codify the entirety of the law of the sea in one instrument, balancing a number of competing interests. The outcome of this process was the 1982 UN Convention on the Law of the Sea, which came into force in 1994. UNCLOS was highly significant in accommodating new economic and technological developments, as well as in creating a greater degree of State jurisdictional control over the seas, the soil, and subsoil beneath them (collectively, the 'seabed'). As such, in UNCLOS one can identify a variety of concepts including the contiguous zone, the continental shelf, and the more recent exclusive economic zone (EEZ); these will all be addressed in turn at a later point.

An important innovation in the 1982 UNCLOS is the acknowledgement that the high seas had previously been exploited in an unsustainable manner. Those from more technologically advanced States, in particular, were able to extract minerals and other resources from the deep seabed and the high seas without any legal constraints. However, to give control over these resources to coastal States would disrupt well-established navigation routes and change the character of the open seas. Other strategic interests also needed to be accommodated in UNCLOS, including environmental protection and the security interests of landlocked States and archipelagic States, oftentimes with new legal rules that did not have a basis in the existing law.

Because so many interests were finely balanced, the final draft of UNCLOS was regarded as an interlocked 'package approach'; no reservations whatsoever were permitted.[8]

[7] Convention on the Territorial Sea and the Contiguous Zone (signed 29 April 1958, entered into force 10 September 1964), 516 UNTS 205 (CTS); Convention on the High Seas (signed 29 April 1958, entered into force 30 September 1962), 450 UNTS 11 (HSC); Convention on Fishing and Conservation of Living Resources of the High Seas (signed 29 April 1958, entered into force 20 March 1966), 559 UNTS 285; Convention on the Continental Shelf (signed 29 April 1958, entered into force 10 June 1964), 499 UNTS 311 (CCS).

[8] See Chapter 7, Section 7.3, for further discussion on reservations to treaties.

This was to foreclose States from selectively embracing only those obligations that benefited them, and thus undermining the coherence of the regime.[9] However, the USA, Japan, and West European States resisted certain innovations, especially the new regime relating to the international seabed, and refused to ratify the Convention. For this reason, a 1994 'Implementation Agreement'[10] was proposed, in which provisions of Part XI of UNCLOS relating to common heritage and seabed mining were amended so as to secure more widespread acceptance of the Convention by those States.[11] UNCLOS also provided in Part XV for the establishment of the International Tribunal for the Law of the Sea (ITLOS), which has added to the methods of international dispute settlement in this area, and what are called 'Annex VII' arbitral tribunals. For reasons of space, the functioning of ITLOS and the Annex VII tribunals will not be further addressed here, though abundant resources are available to guide the inquisitive reader.[12]

At the time of writing, the amended UNCLOS has 170 parties, which include the State of Palestine and the European Union. One should note the continued non-ratification of the USA, which accepts that much of UNCLOS reflects customary international law, but rejects the applicability of certain provisions, particularly those relating to dispute settlement. Given the USA's unparalleled economic, political, and military strength, its lengthy coastline, and extensive continental shelf, one thus cannot assert unhesitatingly that the entirety of UNCLOS reflects customary law. For these reasons, the law of the sea remains an intriguing regime, with the 1982 UNCLOS, 1958 Geneva Conventions, and other treaties, and earlier customary international law, all coexisting to some extent. This interaction has come prominently to the fore in several cases,[13] and remains an interesting area for scholarship.[14]

18.3 The various maritime zones in international law

18.3.1 **The 'baseline'**

International law recognizes several defined maritime areas in which States can exercise different jurisdictional competences. Those divisions show the importance of the governing principle, 'the land dominates the sea' (the closer a certain zone is to the land,

[9] A description of the competing interests of States is succinctly captured in RR Churchill, V Lowe, and A Sander, *The Law of the Sea* (4th edn, Manchester UP, 1999), ch 1; Y Tanaka, *The International Law of the Sea* (3rd edn, CUP, 2019), ch 1; and J Harrison, *Making the Law of the Sea* (CUP, 2011), ch 2.

[10] Agreement Relating to the Implementation of Part XI of the United Nations Convention on the Law of the Sea of 10 December 1982 (signed 28 July 1994, entered into force 28 July 1996), 1836 UNTS 3.

[11] See later, Section 18.4.

[12] See, e.g., N Klein, *Dispute Settlement in the UN Convention on the Law of the Sea* (CUP, 2005); Churchill, Lowe, and Sander (n 9) ch 20; AE Boyle, 'Dispute Settlement and the Law of the Sea Convention: Problems of Fragmentation and Jurisdiction' (1997) 46 ICLQ 37; JP Quéneudec, 'Le choix des procedures de règlement des différends selon la Convention des NU sur le droit de la mer' in *Mélanges en homage à Michel Virally* (Pedone, 1991), 383.

[13] *North Sea Continental Shelf (Federal Republic of Germany v Denmark; Federal Republic of Germany v the Netherlands), Judgment, ICJ Reports 1969*, p 3; *Delimitation of the Continental Shelf: Interpretive Decision of 5 March 1978 (France/United Kingdom)* (1978) 54 ILR 6.

[14] See, e.g., Harrison (n 9); Trevisanut, Giannopoulos, and Holst (n 6); N Klein, *Maritime Security and the Law of the Sea* (OUP, 2011).

the greater the jurisdictional competence exercised by the territorial State). This principle is the starting point for the determination of the maritime rights of a coastal State.[15]

A key preliminary concept is the 'baseline', from which all maritime zones are measured. Article 5 UNCLOS sets out the general principle that a baseline is measured from the low-water mark, paralleling the coasts of the State (the '*trace parallèle*').[16] An island, defined as a 'naturally-formed area of land, surrounded by water, which is above water at the high tide', will also generate a baseline;[17] however, a 'low-tide elevation' (land which vanishes under high tide) may only extend a baseline when it is within a State's territorial sea.[18] Though the identification of baselines is generally straightforward, there are situations where the irregular geography of a State's coast has merited special attention, as with the *Anglo-Norwegian Fisheries* dispute.

CASE SPOTLIGHT ***Anglo-Norwegian Fisheries (United Kingdom v Norway), Judgment, ICJ Reports 1951*, p 116**

Numerous islands run parallel to the Norwegian coastline. These are called the *skjaergaard* and are highly irregular due to the famous fjords which characterize Norway's unique coast. As a result of its unusual geography Norway has for centuries felt entitled to construct a series of straight baselines linking the outermost points on the *skjaergaard* and enclosing waters which would normally have been part of the high seas.

The UK challenged the legality of the Norwegian method of constructing baselines, given the interests of British fishing ships. The Court held in favour of Norway as the unique geographical features of the Norwegian coast would make the *trace parallèle* approach impracticable, and require highly complex geometrical constructions (Judgment, 129).

The Court also pointed out how the UK had only recently protested against Norway's straight baseline claims; in the Court's view, these 'had been consolidated by a constant and sufficiently long practice, in the face of which the attitude of governments bears witness to the fact that they did not consider it to be contrary to international law' (Judgment, 139).

For those interested in the development of customary law, Norwegian rights had been established through its long-standing practice over a century, coupled with acquiescence; these are now codified in treaty law as well: see Article 4 of the CTS, and Article 7(1) UNCLOS.

The customary law principles developed in *Anglo-Norwegian Fisheries* have also allowed for States successfully to claim a straight baseline to enclose a bay in view of certain historic rights supported by acquiescence: examples include Canada with

[15] *Maritime Delimitation and Territorial Questions between Qatar and Bahrain (Qatar v Bahrain), Merits, ICJ Reports 2001*, p 40, 97; *North Sea Continental Shelf* (n 13) 51; *Territorial and Maritime Dispute (Nicaragua v Honduras), Judgment, ICJ Reports 2007*, p 659, 695–6, 699.

[16] See also CTS (n 7) Art 3. [17] See *ibid*, Art 10(1).

[18] UNCLOS (n 5) Art 13(2); see also *Maritime and Territorial Dispute between Qatar and Bahrain* (n 15) 102; *Territorial and Maritime Dispute between Nicaragua and Honduras in the Caribbean Sea (Nicaragua v Honduras), Judgment, ICJ Reports 2007*, p 659, 703; *Territorial and Maritime Dispute (Nicaragua v Colombia), Judgment, ICJ Reports 2012*, p 624, 641; and *Maritime Delimitation in the Indian Ocean (Somalia v Kenya), Judgment of 12 October 2021*, para 114.

respect to Hudson Bay,[19] and certain Central American States in relation to the Gulf of Fonseca.[20] A similar claim by Libya over the Gulf of Sidra as a historic bay, which would allow it to assert a closing line of some 300 miles, has faced substantial opposition from States.[21]

Finally, wholly archipelagic States such as Indonesia, Fiji, and the Philippines have claimed straight baselines around the outer limits of their islands, though these have not been uncontroversial.[22] UNCLOS has sought to accommodate various interests in relation to archipelagic States, so as to preserve existing traditional fishing rights,[23] existing submarine cables,[24] and the right of innocent passage across established archipelagic sea lanes.[25]

The baseline divides a State's various maritime zones from its internal waters, to which we now turn. For a diagram depicting these maritime zones, see Figure 18.1.

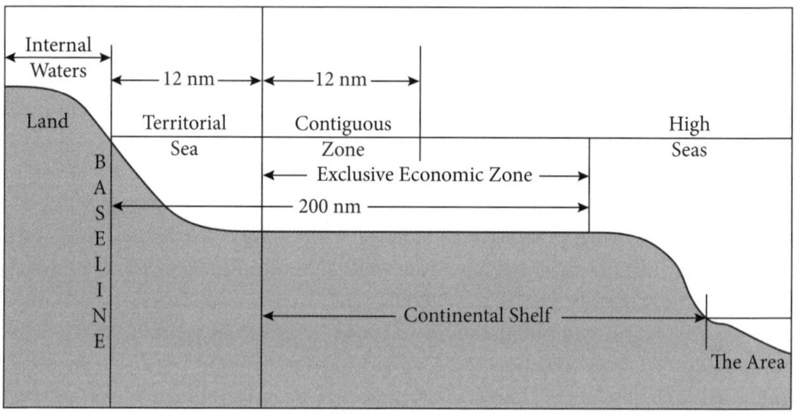

Figure 18.1 Legal boundaries of the oceans

Source: Graphic courtesy Law of the Sea: A Policy Primer project, The Fletcher School of Law and Diplomacy, Tufts University. Copyright 2017 by Trustees of Tufts College, all rights reserved.

[19] Though the United States opposes this: see 4 Whiteman Digest Int L 250–7.

[20] The Gulf of Fonseca was considered a 'pluri-State' historic bay by the ICJ in *Land, Island and Maritime Frontier Dispute (El Salvador/Honduras; Nicaragua intervening), Judgment, ICJ Reports 1992*, p 351, 609.

[21] See F Francioni, 'The Gulf of Sidra Incident (*United States v Libya*) and International Law' (1980–1) 5 Italian YBIL 85; see further Churchill, Lowe, and Sander (n 9) ch 2 and Tanaka (n 9) ch 2, 67–71.

[22] See UNCLOS (n 5) Art 46(a), which defines archipelagic States, and Art 46(b), which defines archipelagoes in technical terms. Art 47 CTS (n 7) allows an archipelagic State to draw straight baselines joining the outermost points of the outermost islands, under certain conditions. 'Offshore' archipelagoes belonging to a non-archipelagic State (e.g., the Canary Islands of Spain, the Paracel Islands of China, the Faroe Islands of Denmark, or the Galapagos Islands of Ecuador) are not subject to the same regime: see C Redgwell and A Tzanakopoulos, 'The Interaction of Treaty and Custom in the Concept of Offshore Archipelagoes' (2023) 72 ICLQ 573.

[23] UNCLOS (n 5) Art 49. [24] *Ibid*, Art 51.

[25] *Ibid*, Art 52. See also Art 53, which provides for a right of 'archipelagic sea lane passage' in 'corridors' designated by the archipelagic State, where its jurisdiction is substantially reduced in favour of international navigation.

18.3.2 **Internal waters**

Once the baseline has been drawn, all bodies of water on its landward side, such as rivers, bays, lakes, and canals, are considered 'internal waters'. A State's internal waters are essentially part of its sovereign territory: they are subject to its fullest jurisdiction, including its criminal jurisdiction, and unlike all other areas of the seas (which include the territorial seas) there is no right to 'innocent passage' for foreign ships.[26] What is more, foreign ships have no customary law right to enter another State's ports or harbours, even when they are purely merchant ships, though in practice many treaties permit this.[27] The one excuse is distress, when human life is at risk; but it does not extend to saving a ship's cargo.[28]

An interesting question arises in relation to the exercise of jurisdiction over the activities of foreign vessels in internal waters. Foreign military vessels ('warships') are considered a direct emanation (extension) of the flag State (see Section 18.3.7.2). Without the authorization of the flag State or the ship's captain, it is unlawful to enforce coastal State jurisdiction over a warship.[29] In practice, coastal States generally exercise restraint in enforcing their local law over incidents occurring on board a foreign merchant vessel, given its temporary presence in foreign waters, and perhaps in deference to the flag State.[30] However, this is a courtesy, and not a legal obligation. In their internal waters, coastal States are perfectly entitled to exercise jurisdiction over a foreign merchant vessel, and they often do so over matters such as the infringement of customary international law, incidents involving non-crew members, or the disruption of peace in a port, where they possess special enforcement powers.[31] Occasionally, a coastal State asserts enforcement jurisdiction in relation to activities of intrinsic severity, such as murder[32] or manslaughter.[33]

18.3.3 **The territorial sea and contiguous zone**

18.3.3.1 **The limits of the territorial sea**

The territorial sea encompasses those waters immediately on the seaward side of the baseline and exists as a matter of right; it need not be claimed. The extent of the

[26] Innocent passage is discussed later, in Section 18.3.4.1.

[27] The International Regime of Maritime Ports (adopted 9 December 1923), 25 LNTS 202, for example, grants access on a reciprocal basis to contracting parties. See further DC Piper, 'Navigation Provisions in United States Commercial Treaties' (1962) 11 AJCL 184.

[28] See AV Lowe, 'The Right of Entry into Maritime Ports in International Law' (1977) 14 San Diego LR 597. On distress as a circumstance precluding wrongfulness, see Chapter 10, Section 10.3.5.

[29] *The Schooner Exchange v McFaddon* (1812) 7 Cranch 116. See also Chapter 9, Section 9.2.1.

[30] See JL Lenoir, 'Criminal Jurisdiction over Foreign Merchant Ships' (1935) 10 Tulane LR 13.

[31] See *NNB and Other Members of the Crew of MS Saudi Independence and International Transport Workers' Federation v Ocean Trade Company Saudi Europe Line Ltd* and *Saudi International Shipping (Greece) Ltd* (1982) 87 ILR 96, where the Court of Appeal of The Hague held that a coastal State had jurisdiction over a foreign vessel in its internal waters in relation to strike activity affecting the legal order of that coastal State.

[32] See *United States v Wildenhaus*, 120 US 1 (1997), where the US courts asserted jurisdiction over a murder on board a Belgian vessel in New York harbour.

[33] See *R v Anderson* (1868) 1 Cox's Criminal Cases 198, where an English court exercised jurisdiction over a case of manslaughter of an American national on board a British vessel in French internal waters, claiming that all three States would have concurrent jurisdiction.

territorial sea is an interesting case study in respect of the formation of customary international law. Historically, influential maritime States, in particular the UK and the USA, only regarded claims of 3 nautical miles as appropriate. That distance was based on the so-called 'cannon-shot' rule, marking the range of a cannon shot from the beach.[34] Failure to agree a specified limit had dated back to the 1930 Hague Conference for the Codification of International Law. The 1958 CTS Convention, accordingly, did not specify any maximum limit,[35] but during the 1960s many States began to claim a territorial sea of 12 nautical miles. With eighty-five States already claiming a 12-mile territorial sea by the early 1980s, the more extensive limit was recognized in Article 3 UNCLOS.

Within the territorial sea, a coastal State is sovereign and exercises its full jurisdiction, and under Article 21 UNCLOS, it is expressly empowered to legislate with respect to vessels in its territorial sea on a number of important issues, including: the safety of navigation; the conservation of living resources and fish stocks; the preservation of the marine environment; and the prevention of infringements of its customs, fiscal, immigration, and sanitary laws.

18.3.3.1.1 *The contiguous zone*

Historically, the relatively narrow territorial sea led States to claim certain rights in areas beyond that zone; the concept of a 'contiguous zone' emerged as a compromise. Under Article 33 UNCLOS, and the earlier Article 24 CTS, the contiguous zone is a maritime area running alongside the territorial sea of a State, in which a coastal State is not sovereign, but may take certain enforcement measures to prevent and punish infringements in the territorial sea of some—but not all—of its laws, primarily those relating to 'customs, fiscal, immigration or sanitary laws and regulations'. The contiguous zone must be declared explicitly by a coastal State, and may extend up to 24 nautical miles from the coastal State's baselines, excluding the territorial sea. This means that a State claiming a 3-mile territorial sea may claim up to 21 nautical miles, and a State claiming a 12-mile territorial sea may claim a contiguous zone of 12 additional miles.[36]

18.3.4 Limitations on coastal State jurisdiction in territorial waters

18.3.4.1 Innocent passage

Though broad, the jurisdiction of a coastal State in its territorial waters is subject to several restrictions. The most important of these is found in Article 17 UNCLOS and Article 14(1) CTS, according to which a transiting foreign vessel enjoys the *right of innocent passage* in the territorial sea, which may not be impeded by the coastal State.[37]

[34] JES Fawcett, *The Law of Nations* (Basic Books, 1968), 71.

[35] In 1958, a US–Canada proposal to set the territorial sea to 6 miles, with an exclusive fisheries zone of a further 6 miles, failed by one vote: see DP O'Connell, *International Law of the Sea* (OUP, 1984), vol I, 163–4.

[36] As of late 2011, eighty-nine States had declared a contiguous zone, with the overwhelming majority claiming the maximum 24 nautical miles: see JA Roach and RW Smith, *Excessive Maritime Claims* (Martinus Nijhoff, 2012), 151.

[37] See also *Maritime and Territorial Dispute between Qatar and Bahrain* (n 15) para 223, in which the right of innocent passage was recognized as a rule of customary international law.

Innocent passage is understood as the right to cross the territorial waters of a coastal State unhindered, so long as such passage is purely for the purposes of transit, and 'so long as it is not prejudicial to the peace, good order or security of the coastal State' (Article 14(4) CTS).

UNCLOS lists a series of activities that are not innocent and might cause prejudice to the coastal State in Article 19(2). They include, *inter alia*, the threat or use of force, espionage, propaganda, breaches of customs and other regulations, wilful and serious pollution, and fishing. In this respect, UNCLOS endorses the objective approach to the innocent nature of passage, as did the ICJ in *Corfu Channel*, where it declared that the mere violation of internal law would not in itself constitute prejudice to the interests of the coastal State.[38] Though influential States have argued that these conditions are exhaustive, the text of Article 19 includes a rather open final provision in sub-paragraph (j), 'any other activity not having a direct bearing on passage'.[39] Article 24(1) UNCLOS mandates that the exercise of a coastal State's legislative competences must not impose onerous and/or discriminatory requirements to hamper innocent passage.

There is debate about the types of vessels permitted to engage in innocent passage. UNCLOS only refers to 'ships', and in *Passage through the Great Belt*, the ICJ found that structures such as oil rigs cannot claim innocent passage.[40] Certain military powers contend that warships may engage in innocent passage without prior notification or authorization, so long as such warships do not engage in any of the activities laid out under Article 19(2).[41] That interpretation remains opposed by many smaller States, especially in strategically sensitive locations, and the debate is likely to continue, especially given the increased reach of coastal States into offshore waters.

18.3.4.2 **Enforcement of coastal State jurisdiction**

Under Article 27(1) UNCLOS and Article 19(1) CTS, coastal States are exhorted generally to refrain from investigating or arresting suspects of offences committed on board foreign vessels, unless there are direct consequences for the coastal State; for example, involving the trafficking of drugs. Article 28(1) UNCLOS contains a similar provision with respect to the enforcement of jurisdiction in relation to civil proceedings. These provisions aim to uphold the primary jurisdiction and responsibility of the flag State over matters occurring on board. Finally, a foreign warship or government vessel cannot be arrested in the territorial sea, as they enjoy immunity given their status as an organ of the flag State. However, under Article 30 UNCLOS, such a vessel may be 'required' to depart immediately upon a demand of the coastal State.

[38] See *Corfu Channel (United Kingdom v Albania), Judgment, ICJ Reports 1949*, p 4, 30–1. For further detail on what constitutes 'innocent passage', see Churchill and Lowe (n 9) 82 *et seq*; O'Connell (n 35) vol 1, ch 7; Tanaka (n 9) 104 *et seq*.

[39] Churchill and Lowe (n 9) 85.

[40] *Passage through the Great Belt (Finland v Denmark), Provisional Measures, Order of 29 July 1991, ICJ Reports 1991*, p 12.

[41] See, e.g., USA and USSR, 'Uniform Interpretation of the Rules of International Law Governing Innocent Passage' (1990) 84 AJIL 239; C Gray, 'After the Ceasefire: Iraq, the Security Council and the Use of Force' (1994) 65 BYBIL 642–7; O'Connell (n 35) vol 1, 290–2; Churchill and Lowe (n 9) 54–6, 89.

Many States control, either alone or with another State, strategically important maritime passages, or *straits*, such as the Bosphorus, Gibraltar, Hormuz, and Malacca. Here, geographical and practical considerations have led to States claiming a right of international navigation. In *Corfu Channel*, though finding that the United Kingdom had conducted minesweeping operations which were a violation of Albania's sovereignty, the ICJ nevertheless took pains to emphasize that in peacetime, States 'have a right to send their warships through straits of international navigation between two parts of the high seas without the previous authorization of a coastal State, provided that the passage is innocent'.[42] Such a right became embodied in UNCLOS as the right of 'transit passage', which affirms that 'straits used for international navigation' are subject to a right of navigation or overflight solely for the purpose of transit.[43] Significantly, unlike with innocent passage, transit passage also applies to aircraft and to submerged submarines.

It bears noting that the customary legal status of transit passage is not fully settled.[44] This status is crucial for certain key non-signatories to UNCLOS, in particular the USA, which regularly asserts the right of transit passage for its warships and overflight of its aircraft through or over strategically important international straits.

Article 44 UNCLOS mandates that transit passage shall not be suspended in any circumstances, though in practice a State may invoke circumstances such as self-defence, which preclude the wrongfulness of a breach.[45]

Transit passage does not apply to straits in four situations:

- if there exists a pre-existing treaty regime governing passage through a strait;[46]
- when an alternative route exists through the high seas or economic zone of similar navigational convenience;[47]
- concerning a strait located between an island of a State and its mainland, where there exists, seaward of the island, a route of similar navigational convenience;[48] and
- if a strait connects an area of the high seas or the economic zone of a State only to the territorial sea of a third State, and thus does not facilitate international navigation.[49]

THEORY AND DEBATES Implications in Certain Straits of Extending the Territorial Sea to 12 Nautical Miles

In many straits, the extension of the territorial sea to 12 nautical miles might have meant that they would have become entirely territorial waters. This was the case in the Strait of Dover, between the UK and France, when the UK extended its territorial sea to 12 miles; it would effectively have 'de-internationalized' the Strait, with severe consequences for trade and other activities of third States. Moreover, other States might have followed suit and caused even

[42] *Corfu Channel* (n 38) 28. [43] UNCLOS (n 5) Arts 37–45. [44] Churchill and Lowe (n 9) 113.

[45] *Ibid*, 107; see also RP Anand, 'Transit Passage and Overflight in International Straits' (1986) 26 IJIL 72. See also UNCLOS (n 5) Art 45(2), which provides that when transit passage does not apply, a regime of non-suspendable innocent passage will apply.

[46] UNCLOS (n 5) Art 35(c).

[47] *Ibid*, Art 36. [48] *Ibid*, Art 38(1). [49] *Ibid*, Art 45.

further disruption to maritime shipping and trade; for example, in the Øresund (Denmark and Sweden) or the Straits of Florida (Cuba and the USA).

In order to avoid this, the UK and France issued a declaration in which they recognized the 'rights of unimpeded transit passage for merchant vessels, State vessels and, in particular, warships . . . as well as the right of overflight for aircraft' in the Strait (Home Office, UK White Paper, published in (1989) 38 ICLQ 416). The joint recognition by the two coastal States was welcomed, though it remains unclear whether it was an exceptional derogation from the general principle or marks out the development of a new customary exception to the general rule.

On balance, transit passage favours international navigation over the rights of the coastal State, particularly as transit passage is not subject to the stricter conditions of innocent passage. However, Article 39 UNCLOS lays out several restrictions on vessels engaged in transit passage, such as refraining from the threat or use of force, 'any activities other than those incident to their normal modes of continuous and expeditious transit', and compliance with international regulations concerning maritime safety and the prevention of pollution.

18.3.5 **Exclusive economic zone (EEZ)**

After World War II, less economically developed States began to assert claims of further control over natural resources within the seabed and the 'water column' (a conceptual 'column' of water from the surface of a sea to its seabed). In 1947, Chile and Peru were the first to claim 'maritime zones' of 200 nautical miles, in which they would enjoy 'sovereign rights' (exclusive rights in relation to specific activities) over all natural living and non-living resources, but in which other freedoms of the high seas—in particular, navigation—would be preserved.[50]

The decolonization of much of the Global South during the 1960s and 1970s led to further demands for sovereign rights over natural resources. Such claims also came from European States, such as Iceland, which unilaterally asserted a 50-nautical mile exclusive fishing zone, and led to the UK and Germany filing a case against it.[51] The ICJ was reluctant to take a position on the customary law at the time given the Law of the Sea Conferences simultaneously taking place;[52] it instead emphasized the notion of 'preferential rights' for a coastal State which was in a situation of special dependence on its coastal fisheries.[53]

These overlapping claims were subsumed and consolidated into what emerged as the exclusive economic zone (EEZ), embodied in Part V of UNCLOS in 1982, and quickly recognized as customary international law.[54] The EEZ allows a coastal State to

[50] See Presidential Declaration Concerning the Continental Shelf of 23 June 1947 (*El Mercurio*, 29 June 1947); Presidential Decree No 781 of 1 August 1947 (*El Peruano: Diario Oficial*, 11 August 1947).

[51] *Fisheries Jurisdiction (United Kingdom v Iceland), Jurisdiction and Admissibility, ICJ Reports 1974*, p 3.

[52] *Ibid*, 23–4. [53] *Ibid*, 25–9.

[54] *Continental Shelf (Libyan Arab Jamahiriya/Malta), Judgment, ICJ Reports 1985*, p 13, para 34.

claim a set of rights and duties in an area beyond and adjacent to the territorial sea, and may extend up to 200 nautical miles.[55] A coastal State claiming an EEZ enjoys sovereign rights for the purposes of exploration, exploitation, conservation, and management of living and non-living natural resources found within the zone, whether superjacent (above) the seabed, in the seabed itself, or in its subsoil.[56] Within the EEZ, a coastal State may also establish artificial islands or installations, conduct marine scientific research, and take measures to preserve the marine environment. Pursuant to Article 60(2) UNCLOS, a coastal State may apply customs laws and regulations in relation to these artificial islands and installations. However, these do not extend to other parts of the EEZ.[57]

In return, other States enjoy most, but not all, traditional freedoms of the high seas in relation to navigation, overflight, and the laying of cables and pipelines.[58] Part V of UNCLOS lays out detailed rules in relation to all of these rights and freedoms. Key among such rights is the broad legislative jurisdiction of coastal States in relation to the exercise of their rights in the EEZ,[59] as well as the right to take enforcement measures including 'boarding, inspection, arrest and judicial proceedings' to safeguard their rights therein.[60] For the first time in 2022, the Court concluded that a coastal State, Colombia, had violated the freedoms of a foreign State (Nicaragua) in its own EEZ by the assertion to exercise enforcement jurisdiction on fisheries management and marine environment conservation in that maritime zone.[61]

The EEZ, which has been claimed by a large number of States, is best regarded as a compromise in which certain rights and duties of the coastal State are expanded in relation to the use and conservation of natural resources, but where most of the freedoms of the high seas in relation to passage and communications have been preserved.[62] Not everything is settled: for example, only the 40-odd States parties to the Nairobi Wreck Removal Convention accept that a foreign State can remove hazardous wrecks from the EEZ of another State.[63] Another example of an unsettled manner regards the rights of landlocked States, which UNCLOS vaguely suggests may participate on an 'equitable basis' in the apportionment of the surplus of the natural resources in an EEZ in its region;[64] also the claims of States to special additional

[55] UNCLOS (n 5) Arts 55, 57. [56] *Ibid*, Arts 56(1)(a), 61–2.

[57] *Ibid*, Art 56(1)(b)–(c). See the ITLOS judgment in *M/V Saiga (St Vincent and the Grenadines v Guinea) (No 2), Admissibility and Merits* (1997) 120 ILR 143, 190–2.

[58] UNCLOS, *ibid*, Art 58. [59] *Ibid*, Art 63(4).

[60] *Ibid*, Art 72. Notably, however, Art 73 provides that any arrested vessels or crews must be promptly released upon payment of a reasonable bond; under Art 292, ITLOS enjoys an automatic jurisdiction over such claims for 'prompt release', which in fact constitute the majority of cases which have been submitted to ITLOS.

[61] *Alleged Violations of Sovereign Rights and Maritime Spaces in the Caribbean Sea (Nicaragua v. Colombia), Judgment, ICJ Reports 2022*, p 266, paras 91–101.

[62] Roach and Smith (n 36) 112.

[63] Nairobi International Convention on the Removal of Wrecks (signed 18 May 2007, entered into force 14 April 2015), 3283 UNTS 34, art 2(1). In art 3(2), States may opt to extend the right to remove wrecks into their own territorial sea, by way of a notification to the IMO Secretary-General.

[64] See UNCLOS (n 5) Arts 69, 70.

zones for purposes such as 'pollution control' or 'security'.[65] An example of where such ambiguity has led to tensions is in the Eastern Mediterranean, perhaps exacerbated by the discovery of hydrocarbons, but where overlapping Greek and Turkish claims—as well as questions relating to contested entities such as Northern Cyprus or Palestine, have risen to the fore.[66] Perhaps this is indicative of the continued fluidity of the development of the international law of the sea as a microcosm of international law as a whole, with the constant interplay of codified treaty rules and practice-based customary law.

CASE SPOTLIGHT ***Delimitation of the Maritime Boundary between Mauritius and Maldives in the Indian Ocean (Mauritius/Maldives), ITLOS Case No 28, Preliminary Objections, Judgment of 28 January 2021, ITLOS Reports 2020–2021, p 14***

The Chagos Islands are currently a British overseas territory. They were 'detached' from Mauritius in 1966, so that the UK could lease Diego Garcia, the largest island in the Chagos archipelago, to the USA. Between 1968 and 1973, the local inhabitants (the 'Chagossians') were expelled by the UK. However, the detachment took effect pursuant to several undertakings by the UK (called the 'Lancaster House Undertakings') aimed to protect existing Mauritian fishing, mining, and oil exploration rights in the waters surrounding Chagos. Significantly, the UK had undertaken to return the Chagos Islands to Mauritius when no longer needed for defence purposes.

In the last decade, British sovereignty over the Chagos Islands came under sustained legal challenge. In *Chagos Marine Protected Area Arbitration ((Mauritius v United Kingdom)*, PCA Case No 2011-03, Award of 18 March 2015), an ITLOS arbitral tribunal concluded that the UK's 2010 unilateral declaration of the world's largest 'marine protected area' (MPA) around the Chagos Islands breached Mauritian fishing rights (para 453), and showed a lack of 'due regard' for several of Mauritius's rights under the Lancaster House Undertakings; in particular, given the potential return of the Chagos Islands (para 521). In its 2019 advisory opinion on the *Chagos Islands*,[67] the ICJ concluded that the UK's conduct was in violation of the principle of self-determination (p 177), and called on the UK to withdraw from Chagos 'and complete the decolonization of Mauritius' as soon as possible (pp 178–9; the ICJ's opinion is further studied in Chapter 5, Section 5.2.6.2).

The ICJ's 2019 opinion has in particular figured prominently in a 2021 ITLOS Special Chamber judgment in a delimitation dispute between Mauritius and the Maldives. The Maldives had filed a preliminary objection, claiming that as the Chagos Islands are under UK authority, the UK was an indispensable third party to the dispute and the case should

[65] For more detail, see O'Connell (n 35) 1022–5, who outlines Canada's claim of a 100-mile-wide 'pollution-free' zone in the Arctic, in the Canadian Arctic Water Pollution Prevention Act 1970, North Korea's claim of a 50-mile 'security zone' in 1977, and the UK's establishment of an 'exclusion zone' around the Falkland Islands in 1982.

[66] See further NA Ioannides, *Maritime Claims and Boundary Delimitation: Tensions and Trends in the Eastern Mediterranean Sea* (Routledge, 2020).

[67] *Legal Consequences of the Separation of the Chagos Archipelago from Mauritius in 1965, Advisory Opinion, ICJ Reports 2019*, p 95.

be declared inadmissible. But the Chamber rejected this argument, endorsing Mauritius's argument that the ICJ's determinations with respect to the decolonization of Mauritius, though not formally binding, 'have legal effect and clear implications for the legal status of the Chagos Archipelago' such that the UK's continued claim is nothing more than 'a mere assertion' (paras 243–6). Accordingly, the ITLOS Chamber seemed to treat the ICJ's opinion as having extinguished the dispute between Mauritius and the UK: a far-reaching legal effect. As a result, in its judgment on the merits on 28 April 2023, the Chamber proceeded with a maritime delimitation using the established three-step test.

In October 2024, the UK announced that it would return sovereignty of the Chagos Islands to Mauritius, subject to the finalization of a treaty. The Diego Garcia base would remain under US–UK control under the proposal; as of early 2025, negotiations were still in progress.

18.3.6 **Continental shelf**

Thus far, we have focused primarily on maritime zones established in relation to the baselines off a State's coast. However, 'continental shelves' are also used to establish zones; the term refers to the ledges that project from the continental landmass into the seas, and are frequently covered with only relatively shallow waters when compared to the deep seas. Continental shelves are rich in oil, gas, and mineral resources considerably more accessible than those of the deep seabed (see Section 18.4). They are also attractive habitats for sedentary (and commercially exploitable) species of fish. During the twentieth century, technological developments made it possible for States to exploit these extensive resources, so it became strategically feasible and desirable for coastal States to formulate claims over the continental shelf, with US President Truman's Proclamation of 1945 being the first such claim.[68] The 1958 Geneva Convention on the Continental Shelf (CCS)[69] sought to resolve claims to the continental shelf, with most of its features retained by UNCLOS and quickly crystallized into customary international law.[70]

Within the outer limits of the continental shelf, the coastal State has sovereign rights of exploration or exploitation of its natural resources.[71] According to Article 76(1) UNCLOS, the outer limit of the continental shelf is usually defined in relation to the actual geographical formations involved, or to a distance of 200 nautical miles. Where the continental shelf in fact extends beyond 200 miles, geographical factors are taken into account but no claim can exceed 350 miles from the coast or 100 miles from the '2500-metre isobath'.[72] This is decidedly convoluted, so a Commission on the Limits

[68] 4 Whiteman Digest of Int L 756: 'the natural resources of the subsoil and seabed of the continental shelf beneath the high seas but contiguous to the coasts of the United States as appertaining to the United States, subject to its jurisdiction and control'.

[69] See n 7.

[70] See *North Sea Continental Shelf* (n 13) 31; and more generally S Friedman, *Global Governance and the International Law of the Sea* (Routledge, 2024).

[71] UNCLOS (n 5) Art 77.

[72] An 'isobath' is a line traced of all points at the same depth under the surface: see *ibid*, Art 76(5).

on the Continental Shelf (CLCS) has been established that gives recommendations to States based on scientific and technical data on where to establish the outer limit of their continental shelf.[73]

Two special features distinguish the regime governing the continental shelf from that which governs the EEZ, and though in practice there can be some confusion given that the two regimes often cover the same area, the two concepts are 'linked together in modern law'.[74] First, the definition of the continental shelf in Article 1 of the CCS only refers to the seabed and subsoil; it does not encompass the overlying waters. Secondly, unlike with the EEZ or even the contiguous zone, the continental shelf is presumed to belong to coastal States as an inherent right: a State does not need to claim it.[75] As the ICJ confirmed in *North Sea Continental Shelf*:

> the rights of the coastal State in respect of the area of continental shelf that constitutes a natural prolongation of its land territory and under the sea exist *ipso facto and ab initio*, by virtue of its sovereignty over the land, and an extension of it in an exercise of sovereign rights for the purpose of exploring the seabed and exploiting its natural resources. In short there is an inherent right.[76]

18.3.7 **High seas**

18.3.7.1 **The high seas regime in UNCLOS**

The 'high seas', as understood in Article 86 UNCLOS, encompass all areas of the sea not included in the territorial sea, internal waters, or EEZ. Reminiscent of Grotius' *Mare Liberum*, the high seas remain free and open to vessels of all States, which enjoy the long-established freedoms of navigation, fishing, overflight, and the laying of cables or pipelines,[77] the construction of artificial islands, and conducting marine scientific research.[78] These freedoms are not unlimited: UNCLOS suggests that they must be conducted with 'due regard' to the rights of other States (Article 87) and only for peaceful purposes (Article 88). The latter is particularly contentious: though naval military exercises are generally understood as peaceful, there are questions surrounding the legality of weapons testing in the high seas. In the Treaty Banning Nuclear Weapons Tests in the Atmosphere, in Outer Space and Under Water,[79] nuclear testing on the high seas is

[73] States that establish their continental shelf 'on the basis' of CLCS recommendations are final and binding: see *ibid*, Art 76(8). See Tanaka (n 9) 161 *et seq*; J Mossop, *The Continental Shelf Beyond 200 Nautical Miles: Rights and Responsibilities* (OUP, 2016); and B Magnussón, *The Continental Shelf Beyond 200 Nautical Miles: Delineation, Delimitation and Dispute Settlement* (Brill, 2015).

[74] *Libya/Malta Continental Shelf* (n 54) 33.

[75] CCS (n 7) Art 2(4); UNCLOS (n 5) 77(4).

[76] *North Sea Continental Shelf* (n 13) 22.

[77] HSC (n 7) Art 2; UNCLOS (n 5) Art 82. These predate the conventions: with respect to the freedom of navigation, see *Corfu Channel* (n 37) 22; *Military and Paramilitary Activities in and against Nicaragua (Nicaragua v United States), Merits, ICJ Reports 1986*, p 6, 111–12; with respect to fishing, see *Anglo-Norwegian Fisheries (United Kingdom v Norway), Judgment, ICJ Reports 1951*, p 116, 183.

[78] UNCLOS (n 5) Art 82.

[79] (Signed 5 September 1963, entered into force 10 October 1963), 480 UNTS 43.

expressly prohibited in Article 1, but not all nuclear States are parties. As France is not a party to this treaty, Australia and New Zealand suggested that the prohibition was a rule of customary law in their submissions in *Nuclear Tests*. However, after France declared unilaterally that it would cease testing nuclear weapons in the South Pacific, the ICJ declared the case 'moot' and did not proceed to the merits despite the fact that both applicants had requested a declaratory judgment regarding the unlawfulness of earlier tests.[80]

18.3.7.2 **Exceptions to the freedoms on the high seas in UNCLOS**

Despite the existence of these long-established freedoms, the high seas are hardly a legal vacuum. All vessels must be duly registered under the laws of one or another State with which they have a genuine link, and thus effectively possess its nationality.[81] 'Flag State jurisdiction' entails that the State of registration has, with some exceptions, the obligation to exercise its jurisdiction and control over all the activities of its vessels, including those of individuals on board.[82] If a ship is stateless, or flies more than one flag so that its true State of registry is unclear, any State may exercise jurisdiction upon it.[83]

Flag State jurisdiction is, in principle, exclusive, and its consent is necessary for another State to intervene, though UNCLOS recognizes certain exceptions:

(i) *The right of visit*, according to which the warships of a non-flag State may approach and board a vessel on the high seas when they have reasonable grounds for suspecting that a ship is engaged in piracy, the slave trade, or unauthorized radio broadcasting—though not the trafficking of drugs.[84]

(ii) *Acts of piracy*, decidedly not those of the swashbuckling rogues of old, are defined narrowly in UNCLOS as 'illegal acts of violence or detention, or any act of depredation, committed for private ends by the crew or passengers of a private ship or private aircraft' against another vessel or aircraft, either on the high seas or otherwise outside the jurisdiction of any State.[85] As illustrated by the ongoing situation in Somalia,[86] an essential characteristic of piracy is the absence of any governmental authority. In other words, 'pirates' must be acting as private parties.[87]

(iii) *'Hot pursuit'*, a situation where a foreign vessel, suspected of a breach of the laws of the coastal State and committed within one of its maritime zones, at-

[80] *Nuclear Tests (Australia v France; New Zealand v France), Jurisdiction and Admissibility, ICJ Reports 1974*, p 253. In 1995, New Zealand sought unsuccessfully to have its claim re-examined: see the Order of the Court in *ICJ Reports 1995*, p 288.

[81] UNCLOS (n 5) Art 91; HSC (n 7) Art 5. [82] UNCLOS (n 5) Art 94(1).

[83] *Molvan v Attorney General for Palestine* [1948] AC 351 (UK).

[84] UNCLOS (n 5) Art 110(1)(a)–(c). It should be noted that if suspicions are unfounded, the warship's flag State may need to pay compensation. Other exceptions are by agreement, e.g., drug trafficking.

[85] UNCLOS, *ibid*, Art 101(1). See further Tanaka (n 9) 452–6.

[86] See D Guilfoyle, 'Piracy off Somalia: UN Security Council Resolution 1816 and IMO Regional Counter-Piracy Efforts' (2008) 57 ICLQ 690.

[87] D Guilfoyle, *Shipping Interdiction and the Law of the Sea* (CUP, 2009), 36 *et seq.*

tempts to evade arrest by moving beyond these zones and into the high seas. In such situations, Article 111 UNCLOS permits a coastal State exceptionally to continue its pursuit into the high seas.[88]

(iv) *The transport of slaves*, which tragically continues to the present day, but which in UNCLOS is categorically prohibited.[89] As further explained in the accompanying comment, the suppression of forced migration and human trafficking has gained attention recently.

(v) *Collisions at sea* between foreign vessels; in such cases, Article 97 UNCLOS stipulates that penal proceedings may only be taken by the flag State or the State of nationality of the individual concerned.[90] This is a departure from the PCIJ's judgment in *Lotus*, allowing the other flag State also to exercise jurisdiction.[91]

(vi) *Suppression of the trafficking of drugs*, covered in Article 108 UNCLOS, according to which States parties agree to cooperate in respect of vessels on the high seas.[92] It bears noting that this is not a true exception, as Article 108 still requires flag State authorization: there is no automatic right of visit.[93]

(vii) *Unauthorized broadcasting* from the high seas is restricted under Article 109 UNCLOS, which allows a State which is receiving transmissions to enter the high seas to arrest the transmitting vessel.[94]

CONTEMPORARY DEVELOPMENTS Human Migration Across the Seas

For as long as humans have existed, they have moved around; and until the creation of political communities and the notion of 'nation', such movement was relatively unproblematic. In today's State-based global order, however, migrant smuggling and human trafficking have emerged as two pressing human problems; yet as Chapter 17, Section 17.5 further explores, international law still lacks a coherent framework to deal with such issues of collective concern.

'International migration law' is not a coherent, specialist regime; it touches upon vast and disparate fields from human rights law to refugee law to the law of the sea. Much forced

[88] The conditions in Art 111 UNCLOS (n 5) are cumulative: see *M/V Saiga* (n 57) 194. In *Arctic Sunrise* (*the Netherlands v Russia)* (2015) 171 ILR 1, 95–6, the Arbitral Tribunal emphasized the importance of any such pursuit being continuous—and not interrupted—to qualify as 'hot' pursuit; though it should be noted that Russia did not participate in proceedings.

[89] UNCLOS (n 5) Art 99 binds flag States to take effective measures to prevent and punish the transport of slaves; Art 110(b) allows a right of visit.

[90] See also HSC (n 7) Art 11.

[91] *Case of the SS 'Lotus' (France v Turkey), Judgment, 1927, PCIJ, Ser A, No 10*, p 25.

[92] See also the United Nations Convention against Illicit Traffic in Narcotic Drugs and Psychotropic Substances (signed 20 December 1988, entered into force 11 November 1990), 1582 UNTS 95, which has developed a detailed regulatory framework in this respect.

[93] See *R v Charrington* [1997] QCA 215 (UK), in which domestic prosecution became impossible in light of irregularities through which Malta's consent was obtained to board a vessel carrying £15m of cannabis. See W Gilmore, 'Drugs Trafficking at Sea: The Case of *R v Charrington* and Others' (2000) 49 ICLQ 477.

[94] See DH Anderson, 'Freedoms of the High Seas in the Modern Law of the Sea' in D Freestone, R Barns, and D Ong (eds), *The Law of the Sea: Progress and Prospects* (OUP, 2006), 327, esp 340–1.

migration and human trafficking takes place through the sea, given the relative ease of smuggling persons on the high seas rather than through a State's territory. In recent years, attention has been drawn to the migrant crises in 2013 in South Sudan, 2015 in Syria, and since 2018 in Venezuela, in which people have drowned while fleeing.

Though there are few solutions, there is now a Protocol against the Smuggling of Migrants by Land, Sea and Air to the UN Convention against Transnational Organized Crime (signed 15 November 2000, entered into force 29 September 2003), 2225 UNTS 209, in which flag States give consent to board ships registered with them and agree to aid the prevention of migrant smuggling. The Protocol entered into force in 2004 and currently has 151 States parties. It is a small, but vital, contribution to protecting human beings from being trafficked or smuggled forcibly across the seas.

For further reading, see AT Gallagher and F David (eds), *The International Law of Migrant Smuggling* (CUP, 2014); and V Chetail, *International Migration Law* (OUP, 2018).

In practice, flag State jurisdiction can be difficult to enforce, as some States do not have the capacity or desire to enforce their laws over all vessels flying their flag, and many States have permitted registration of ships under their flag with only a tenuous link, under so-called 'flags of convenience'. The requirement of a 'genuine link' in UNCLOS aimed to check such concerns; but as with the nationality of persons, it is controversial. In *M/V Saiga (No 2)*, ITLOS stated that the nationality of a ship was a point of fact, and explained that the genuine link requirement had been developed to secure effective implementation of the flag State's duties, and not to establish criteria for use by other States in challenging the validity of a ship's registration.[95] However, the notion of a genuine link in this context remains somewhat vague.

18.3.7.3 Other limitations or exceptions to high seas freedoms

18.3.7.3.1 Terrorism and weapons of mass destruction

Beyond UNCLOS, in 1988 the Convention for the Suppression of Unlawful Acts against the Safety of Maritime Navigation (SUA) was concluded.[96] In accordance with SUA, flag States accepted broader rights of boarding and search on the high seas with respect to their registered vessels, and fixed platforms, suspected of unlawful violent and depredatory acts.[97] In 2005, a Protocol broadened the offences under the SUA also to include activities intended to 'intimidate a population, or to compel a Government or an international organization to do or to abstain from any act', or knowingly to transport persons who have committed such unlawful acts.[98] SUA operates on a presumption, especially in cases of non-response, in favour of boarding by those States with reasonable grounds for suspicion of unlawful acts relating to terrorism, and a heavy onus on flag States not to deny such requests.[99]

[95] *M/V Saiga (No 2)* (n 57) 179.

[96] (Adopted 10 March 1988, entered into force 1 March 1992), 1678 UNTS 221.

[97] *Ibid*, Art 3.

[98] 2005 Protocol (adopted 14 October 2005, entered into force 28 July 2010), 1678 UNTS 304, inserting Art 3*bis* into SUA.

[99] See Guilfoyle (n 85) ch 9.

18.3.7.3.2 **Pollution of the marine environment**

One of the most innovative sections of UNCLOS, Part XII, devotes nearly fifty articles to protection of the maritime environment, including the high seas.[100] These cover global and regional cooperation, as well as monitoring, environmental impact assessments, and the implementation and enforcement of international and domestic law preventing pollution. Flag States must adhere to certain minimum standards with respect to activities under their jurisdiction and control, to ensure that they do not cause damage by pollution to other States.[101]

UNCLOS is complemented by a dense mesh of further treaties which, ideally, would serve to restrict State conduct so as to require that they protect against and prevent marine pollution.[102] What is more, as the 2024 ITLOS advisory opinion on climate change has demonstrated, even external rules such as climate change agreements are relevant, and together these are to be interpreted consistently and harmoniously, in keeping with the principle of systemic integration.[103] Nevertheless, the international protection of the environment remains dependent on effective and necessary cooperation between States (see Chapter 19), which is often lacking.

CONTEMPORARY DEVELOPMENTS Agreement on Marine Biodiversity of Areas Beyond National Jurisdiction (BBNJ)

The conservation of marine biodiversity beyond national jurisdiction (BBNJ) raises important debates relating to the law of the sea. What is the best means to ensure the protection of biodiversity across the oceans? How can benefits be shared and States be able to exploit and make use of marine biodiversity? After a multi-year intergovernmental conference that had been slowed by the effects of the COVID-19 pandemic, on 19 June 2023 the BBNJ Agreement was finally adopted by consensus and became the third implementing agreement under UNCLOS (UN Doc A/CONF.232/2023/4).

As befits its name, the BBNJ Agreement brings together scientific, legal, and economic expertise to conserve and ensure the sustainable use of marine biological diversity in areas beyond national jurisdiction. It regulates four inter-related issues: ensuring access for scientific research on marine genetic resources, including the fair and equitable sharing of benefits; area-based management tools such as marine protected areas; environmental impact assessments; and capacity-building and the transfer of marine technology. The Agreement establishes certain institutional structures redolent of multilateral environmental agreements, such as a Conference of the Parties and a secretariat (see Chapter 19, section 19.3.1). Opened for signature on 20 September 2023, the Agreement will enter into force

[100] UNCLOS (n 5) Arts 192–237. See also Churchill and Lowe (n 9) ch 15; Tanaka (n 9) ch 8; O'Connell (n 35) vol II, ch 25.

[101] UNCLOS, *ibid*, Art 194.

[102] Treaties regulating marine pollution in the oceans and territorial seas are covered in Chapter 19, Section 19.7.2.1, and regulate oil pollution, dumping from ships and aircrafts of wastes, and land-based sources.

[103] *Request for an Advisory Opinion submitted by the Commission of Small Island States on Climate Change and International Law, Advisory Opinion of 21 May 2024*, ITLOS Case No 31, paras 128–37.

120 days after the ratification of a sixtieth State party. On 24 April 2024, General Assembly Resolution 78/272 decided to establish a 'preparatory commission' to lay the groundwork for its imminent entry into force, including budgetary and logistical support, and setting the rules for the participation of States and other observer entities.

The UN maintains a website containing information on the new BBNJ Agreement (see https://www.un.org/bbnjagreement/en).

18.3.7.3.3 ***Straddling fish stocks***

Given their practical significance, UNCLOS contains surprisingly few provisions with respect to the management of fish stocks. The sovereign rights of coastal States are recognized for the purpose of exploring and exploiting, but also the duties for conserving and managing the fish stocks concerned, so as to ensure fish stocks are not endangered by over-exploitation.[104] Similarly, Article 116(b) UNCLOS recognizes the freedom to fish on the high seas, subject to similar rights and duties with respect to conservation and management of these fish stocks. However, with respect to the high seas, no State is given primary responsibility; there exists only a general obligation of cooperation.[105]

A serious issue arises with stocks of fish which 'straddle' the maritime zones of a State, particularly its EEZ, and the high seas. Obviously, fish will not respect lines drawn in the sea, so there is a risk that the stocks will be highly depleted by virtue of overfishing in the high seas. What is more, certain highly migratory species, such as tuna, billfish, or marlin, travel great distances, traversing through the high seas as well as coastal maritime areas of States, making them particularly vulnerable to opportunistic fishing. UNCLOS addresses both of these issues, calling on the concerned States to agree on appropriate measures such as the creation of appropriate regional organizations (Article 63) and, with respect to highly migratory species, the creation of a list of such species (Article 64). To these measures, one can add the 1995 Agreement on Straddling Stocks and Highly Migratory Species,[106] which sought to build cooperation in the conservation and management of these resources, in particular, through the adoption of a precautionary approach drawn from the 1992 Rio Declaration on the Environment.[107] Article 8(3) of the Agreement obliges States to participate in regional fisheries management organizations, though enforcement and implementation will rest primarily upon the flag State. This is significant because under Article 17, States parties may not fish for such stocks outside a framework established by the relevant regional organization. A major regional organization is the North Atlantic Fisheries Organization (NAFO),[108]

[104] UNCLOS (n 5) Arts 56(1), 61–3. [105] *Ibid*, Arts 117–20.

[106] Agreement relating to the Conservation and Management of Straddling Fish Stocks and Highly Migratory Fish Stocks (signed 4 August 1995, entered into force 11 December 2001), 2167 UNTS 3. At the time of writing, ninety States and the European Union are parties to the Agreement.

[107] See Chapter 19, Section 19.2.2.

[108] Established following the Convention on Future Multilateral Cooperation in the Northwest Atlantic Fisheries (adopted 24 October 1978, entered into force 1 January 1979), 1135 UNTS 369. The European Community is a party to the Convention.

which has operated relatively successfully, though not without some controversies, such as the incident in which Canadian officers boarded the *Estai*, a Spanish fishing vessel, 245 miles from the Canadian coast.[109] Other regional organizations also operate, including the Indian Ocean Tuna Commission (IOTC),[110] Inter-American Tropical Tuna Commission (IATTC),[111] and Western and Central Pacific Fisheries Commission (WCPFC).[112]

18.4 The deep seabed

In recent decades, even the 'deep seabed'—the ocean floor—has attracted human interest; in particular, during the 1960s when substantial mineral resources (primarily manganese, iron, nickel, and cobalt) were discovered. If the freedoms of the high seas also extended to the resources of the deep seabed, mining consortia from a few technologically advanced States would have enjoyed privileged access to the resources of the ocean floor. This could have devastated the economies of certain developing States which are highly dependent on a few minerals. Accordingly, during the Law of the Sea Conferences, a concerted effort was made by developing States to manage the mining of minerals in the deep seabed.[113] These efforts culminated in Part XI of UNCLOS, which declares the deep seabed, ocean floor, and its subsoil (euphemistically termed 'The Area')[114] as the 'common heritage of mankind': in line with the earlier Declaration of Principles Governing the Seabed and Ocean Floor, no State can claim sovereign rights there.[115] However, due to considerable resistance from Western States, which regarded the UNCLOS arrangements as tilted in favour of developing States, in 1994 an Agreement on Implementation of the Seabed Provisions was agreed so as to allay their concerns, and secure further acceptance of UNCLOS.[116]

Part IX of UNCLOS also established the International Seabed Authority (ISA), an international organization that now counts 167 members, to organize and control

[109] See *Fisheries Jurisdiction (Spain v Canada), Preliminary Objections, ICJ Reports 1998*, p 432. The *Estai* incident represented the culmination of a long-standing dispute relating to certain NAFO quotas, and Canadian concerns over overfishing.

[110] See Agreement for the Establishment of the Indian Ocean Tuna Commission (signed 25 November 1993, entered into force 27 March 1996), 1927 UNTS 329.

[111] See IATTC following the Convention for the Establishment of an Inter-American Tropical Tuna Commission (signed 31 May 1949, entered into force 3 March 1950), 126 UNTS 3.

[112] See Convention for the Conservation and Management of Highly Migratory Fish Stocks in the Western and Central Pacific Ocean (adopted 5 September 2000, entered into force 19 June 2004), 2275 UNTS 43.

[113] Many of these concerns are captured in UN Department of International Economic and Social Affairs, *Seabed Mineral Resource Development: Recent Activities of the International Consortia* (1980), UN Doc ST/ESA/107.

[114] See UNCLOS (n 5) Art 1(1).

[115] UNGA Res 2749 (XXV) (12 December 1970) also called for a moratorium on deep seabed activities.

[116] 1994 Agreement on Implementation (n 10). See BH Oxman, 'The 1994 Agreement and the Convention' (1994) 88 AJIL 687; LB Sohn, 'International Law Implications of the 1994 Agreement' (1994) 88 AJIL 696; and DH Anderson, 'Further Efforts to Ensure Universal Participation in the United Nations Convention on the Law of the Sea' (1994) 43 ICLQ 886.

activities in the area.[117] In 2011, pursuant to a request from the ISA, the Seabed Dispute Chamber of ITLOS rendered its first advisory opinion, in which it clarified numerous legal questions relating to the rights and duties of States in relation to the deep seabed.[118]

The complexity of the deep seabed regime defies easy description, though it includes many innovative cooperative elements, such as the compulsory transfer of technology.[119] One of these was the creation of the 'Enterprise', an independent commercial mining arm of the Authority which would have undertaken the mining of reserved sites on behalf of 'the international community as a whole'.[120] As of the date of writing, and perhaps due to the fact that commercial mining is not yet viable, the Enterprise does not exist as an entity. However, the Authority can also authorize a private consortium to engage in exploration and exploitation, with the proceeds being redistributed to the benefit of less-developed States.[121] The Authority may also issue binding regulations in relation to the deep seabed; in particular, in relation to the preservation of the environment and in relation to technical standards.[122] Several consortia have been authorized by the Authority since 2001, primarily focused on exploration and research in the Clarion-Clipperton Zone in the Pacific Ocean and the Central Indian Ocean Basin.

18.5 Maritime delimitation

The final aspect of the law of the sea to be considered relates to delimitation, or in other words the marking of maritime boundaries between States. Given the rich natural resources, both living and non-living, that may exist in the territorial sea or the EEZ, the delimitation of maritime boundaries can be a matter of some sensitivity for concerned States.

CONTEMPORARY DEVELOPMENTS Disputed Claims in the South China Sea

The South China Sea, in which six States have asserted overlapping maritime claims, has long been an area of legal contention. The area carries tremendous strategic importance; one-third of the world's shipping passes through it carrying goods in trade each year, it contains lucrative fisheries that are crucial for the food security of millions of people in South East Asia, and huge oil and gas reserves are believed to lie beneath its seabed.

China, Vietnam, and the Philippines have been highly active in asserting their claims in the area. At issue is the disputed status of certain island groups—in particular, the Spratlys—which are important in establishing maritime claims in the area. There is also dispute over the legal effects of the large-scale construction of artificial islands and other installations—in particular, by China—and how these affect claims to extended maritime areas.

[117] UNCLOS (n 5) Art 160.

[118] *Responsibilities and Obligations of States with respect to Activities in the Area, Advisory Opinion, ITLOS Reports 2011*, p 10.

[119] 1994 Agreement on Implementation (n 10) Annex, s 5.

[120] *Ibid*, Annex, s 2.

[121] *Ibid*, Annex, s 1.

[122] See *Responsibilities and Obligations of States Sponsoring Persons and Entities with respect to Activities in the Area (No 17)* (Advisory Opinion of 1 February 2011), ITLOS Reports 2011, p 10, 28.

Among diplomatic and political strategies, in 2013 the Philippines submitted a dispute against China to the Permanent Court of Arbitration relating to their claims in the South China Sea (PCA Case No 2013-19). China refused to participate in proceedings, pointing to treaties that required bilateral negotiations instead of arbitral settlement of border disputes. In December 2015, the tribunal decided it would hear the case. On 12 July 2016, the PCA gave a long and detailed arbitral award addressing many of these claims, focusing on several key issues in the law of the sea, including the weight given to 'historic rights'; the status of so-called 'low-tide elevations', or land which is submerged at high tide; the legality of enforcement activities in contested areas, though excluding those of a military nature; and how to use scientific expertise to assess whether the marine environment has been damaged. China immediately issued a statement rejecting the judgment as null, and has repeatedly declared that it will not recognize or abide by the award. For its part, the Philippines considers that the award is now part of international law (see President Duterte's speech to the opening of the 75th General Assembly, 27 September 2020).

Since 2017, China and the members of ASEAN (including the Philippines) have been negotiating fitfully towards a binding 'Code of Conduct for the South China Sea'. In some respects, the proposed Code would represent a departure from the PCA award, but in other respects the award may have spurred and influenced further negotiations. Recent incidents in 2023 and 2024 have demonstrated continued high tensions. Given the wealth of oil and natural resources in the South China Sea, as well as its fragile marine environment, this is a case study for the importance of an integrated approach to maritime issues.

Delimitation is also an area in which the case law of the ICJ has proven tremendously influential. This is due to both the volume of cases (maritime delimitation constitutes the bulk of the Court's judgments), and the delineation of permanent maritime frontiers between States, a 'matter of grave importance' as 'agreement is not easily to be presumed' between the parties.[123]

Maritime delimitation usually occurs from the baseline, but there is potential for dispute between States located opposite each other, or adjacent (next to) to one another. The general principle embodied in Article 15 UNCLOS (and Article 6 CTS) is that of 'equidistance': without further agreement, and unless there are special or historic circumstances, the boundary drawn follows the median line between the baseline of both States, and is equally distant at every point between them.[124] As a matter of logic, case law has established that a provisional equidistance line is drawn before it is adjusted in light of special circumstances or historic title.[125] Such special circumstances are judged

[123] *Territorial and Maritime Dispute* (n 18) 735.

[124] This principle has repeatedly been confirmed as customary international law: see *Maritime and Territorial Dispute between Qatar and Bahrain* (n 15) 94; *Territorial and Maritime Dispute* (n 18) 740–1; and the *Boundary Dispute between Dubai and Sharjah* (1981) 91 ILR 543, 663.

[125] *Maritime Delimitation in the Area between Greenland and Jan Mayen (Denmark v Norway), Judgment, ICJ Reports 1993*, p 38, 71; *Land and Maritime Boundary between Cameroon and Nigeria (Cameroon v Nigeria: Equatorial Guinea intervening), Merits, ICJ Reports 2002*, p 303, para 288; *Delimitation of the Maritime Boundary between Guyana and Suriname* (17 September 2007), XXX RIAA 1; 139 ILR 566, para 296; and *Delimitation of the Exclusive Economic Zone and Continental Shelf between Barbados and Trinidad and Tobago* (11 April 2006), XXVII RIAA 207, paras 242–4, 306.

on a case-by-case basis and may include, for example, historic navigational interests,[126] an irregular geographical configuration,[127] considerable disparity in the relative length of coasts,[128] or the presence of islands.[129]

The leading judgment in the development of the equidistance/special circumstances rule was the ICJ's 1969 decision in *North Sea Continental Shelf*. Denmark and the Netherlands maintained that the equidistance rule contained in Article 6 CTS, which had not been ratified by West Germany, was customary international law. West Germany in turn contended that a straightforward application of the equidistance rule would mean, in light of the relatively concave coastline it shared with Denmark and the Netherlands, that it would receive an inequitably small share of the continental shelf. The Court, holding that Article 6 did not reflect custom, agreed with West Germany, and concluded that customary law in fact required continental shelf delimitations to be conducted on the basis of equitable principles *infra legem* ('within the law') and taking into account relevant circumstances, such as:

> the general configuration of the coasts of the Parties, as well as the presence of any special or unusual features . . . the physical and geological structure, and natural resources, of the continental shelf areas involved, [and] the element of a reasonable degree of proportionality.[130]

The ICJ's interpretation of the equidistance rule also to encompass special circumstances, on a case-by-case basis, has resonated in later disputes involving maritime delimitation, both by the Court[131] and other judicial and arbitral bodies.[132] That approach would seem to obtain with respect to delimitations of the territorial sea, the EEZ, or both, in what is known as the 'single delimitation line'.[133]

After three decades, in its 2009 judgment on the *Maritime Delimitation in the Black Sea*, the Court confirmed the process of equidistance/special circumstances as customary law, and instated a third stage. The third stage consists of examining the length and geography of the relevant coasts to assess whether any disproportionality exists between them that would justify an adjustment of the line.[134] The ITLOS endorsed the 'three-stage test' in the *Bay of Bengal* arbitration, which is also noteworthy as the ITLOS

[126] *Maritime Boundary between Guyana and Suriname* (n 122) paras 306, 323–5.

[127] *Territorial and Maritime Dispute* (n 18) paras 268–81.

[128] *Libya/Malta Continental Shelf* (n 54) para 73.

[129] *Delimitation of the Continental Shelf (United Kingdom/France), Decision of 30 June 1977* (1977) 54 ILR 6, para 251, where the Court gave 'partial effect' to the presence of the Scilly Isles; *Continental Shelf (Tunisia/Libyan Arab Jamahiriya), Judgment, ICJ Reports 1982*, p 18, para 129, giving partial effect to the Kerkennah Islands; but *cf Maritime Delimitation in the Black Sea (Romania/Ukraine), Judgment, ICJ Reports 2009*, p 61, 123, para 188, where Serpent's Island was accorded no effect.

[130] *North Sea Continental Shelf* (n 13) 53.

[131] See, e.g., *Tunisia/Libya Continental Shelf* (n 126) 47; *Delimitation of the Maritime Boundary in the Gulf of Maine Area (Canada/United States), Judgment, ICJ Reports 1984*, p 246; *Libya/Malta Continental Shelf* (n 54) 13.

[132] See, e.g., *Anglo-French Continental Shelf* (n 126) 55, where both States were parties to the CTS (n 7).

[133] Cf. *Guinea/Guinea-Bissau Maritime Delimitation* (1985) 77 ILR 635; *St Pierre and Miquelon (Canada/France)* (1992) 31 ILM 1145; but *cf Jan Mayen Maritime Delimitation* (n 121) 37, in which the separate effects of the various conventions and customary rules were such that no single rule could be applied. UNCLOS was not yet in force between the parties.

[134] *Maritime Delimitation in the Black Sea* (n 126) 89, para 116.

declared itself competent to decide not only competing claims to maritime zones but also the continental shelf beyond 200 nautical miles.[135] On the extension of the continental shelf beyond 200 miles, the ICJ has clarified that under customary international law, no claims to an outer continental shelf can intrude within 200 nautical miles of the baselines of another State.[136]

In subsequent delimitations, such as those between Peru/Chile and Somalia/Kenya, the ICJ has persuasively reaffirmed the applicability of the three-stage test.[137] If that line of case law is authoritative, the three-stage test proceeds as follows. First, a provisional equidistance line is constructed, barring compelling reasons to the contrary. Secondly, relevant circumstances are considered which may call for an adjustment of the line in order to achieve an equitable result. Thirdly, one assesses whether the effect of the line, as adjusted in the second stage, is disproportionate in the parties' respective shares of the dispute area, in relation to the respective lengths of their relevant coasts.

A final point concerns the legal effect of a maritime delimitation on the disputing States. In the recent dispute between Ghana and Côte d'Ivoire, a special chamber of ITLOS drew a number of conclusions in respect of Article 83(3) UNCLOS, in particular, that the obligation on States in situations of ongoing or pending delimitation to make efforts to enter into provisional agreements was only one of conduct, and not of result.[138] The Special Chamber further held that the obligation to refrain from conduct that might 'jeopardize or hamper' the reaching of the final agreement in Article 83 was also one of conduct, and not of result.[139]

THEORY AND DEBATES **Intervention in Judicial Proceedings, and the *Erga Omnes* Nature of Maritime Delimitation**

As discussed in Chapter 12, under Article 59 of the ICJ Statute, the Court's decisions are binding only between the Parties. However, in relation to maritime delimitation, the boundaries which are drawn by the Court also have effect on third parties: they are *erga omnes*, creating objective facts on the ground that apply against all States. For this reason, third States have exhibited great interest in intervening in the disputes of other States, though the ICJ has been rather strict in acceding to such requests. For example, when Malta sought to intervene in the Tunisia/Libya proceedings, the Court declined its request (see *Tunisia/Libya Continental*

[135] *Delimitation of the Maritime Boundary in the Bay of Bengal (Bangladesh/Myanmar), Case No 16, Judgment, ITLOS Reports 2012*, para 240; ITLOS applied a similar test in *Delimitation of the Maritime Boundary between Mauritius and Maldives in the Indian Ocean (Mauritius/Maldives), ITLOS Case No 28, Merits, Judgment of 28 April 2023*, paras 95–8.

[136] *Question of the Delimitation of the Continental Shelf between Nicaragua and Colombia beyond 200 nautical miles from the Nicaraguan Coast (Nicaragua v Colombia), Judgment of 13 July 2023*, paras 76–9.

[137] *Maritime Dispute (Peru v Chile), Judgment, ICJ Reports 2014*, p 3, 66, paras 179–80; *Maritime Delimitation in the Indian Ocean* (n 18), paras 122–125. See also *Territorial and Maritime Dispute (Nicaragua v Colombia)* (n 18) 695–6; *Barbados/Trinidad and Tobago* (n 121) paras 242, 317; *Delimitation of the Maritime Boundary in the Atlantic Ocean (Ghana/Côte d'Ivoire), Judgment, ITLOS Reports 2017*, p 4, 144.

[138] *Ghana/Côte d'Ivoire, ibid*, 166–7.

[139] *Ibid.*

Shelf, 18–19), as it did with Italy's later request to intervene in the Libya/Malta proceedings (see *Libya/Malta Continental Shelf*, 38–46).

The Court's caution is possibly due to concerns that the process of intervention does not give the parties a chance to contest the intervening State's claims. Nor does it allow for the Court to protect the interests of the intervening State without passing judgment on the merits of that State's claims. That said, in the dispute between Cameroon and Nigeria, the Court unanimously allowed for the intervention of Equatorial Guinea, partly given that Cameroon was sandwiched with a concave coastline between the other two States, and perhaps due to the fact that neither party presented any objections (*Land and Maritime Boundary between Cameroon and Nigeria (Cameroon v Nigeria), Application to Intervene, ICJ Reports 1999*, p 1029). In this respect, one can see that intervention can still be a legitimate device for a State to present its views on a boundary that may affect it.

18.6 Conclusion

This chapter can only be an introduction to the vast and significant body of laws which govern the Earth's seas. The law of the sea remains an enduring area of common concern where the traditional distribution of sovereignty and control simply cannot, for material reasons, operate effectively. It is an area in which new and innovative models for State interaction have been developed to address scientific and technological developments; partly for the continued exploitation of the Earth's natural resources, but also in respect of increasing concern for the conservation and preservation of our natural habitat.[140] This mixed legacy will continue into the future, as technology and human consumption will continue to leverage the immense resources of the seas.

Further reading

J Barrett and R Barnes, *Law of the Sea: UNCLOS as a Living Treaty* (BIICL, 2016).

A coherent edited volume addressing how the interpretation of UNCLOS evolves over time through a selection of cross-cutting issues.

RR Churchill, V Lowe, and A Sander, *The Law of the Sea* (4th edn, Manchester UP, 2022).

A definitive introduction to the topic, this book has received a thorough update.

J Harrison, *Making the Law of the Sea: A Study in the Development of International Law* (CUP, 2011).

A detailed historical overview of the regime's development, in particular since the adoption of the 1982 UNCLOS.

N Klein, *Maritime Security and the Law of the Sea* (OUP, 2011).

Maritime security is emerging as an important contemporary issue in the law of the sea.

[140] The marine environment is further addressed in Chapter 19, Section 19.7.2.

TM Ndiaye and R Wolfrum (eds), *Law of the Sea, Environmental Law and Settlement of Disputes* (Martinus Nijhoff, 2007).

Focused on dispute-settlement mechanisms, this edited collection links the law of the sea with environmental protection.

DR Rothwell and T Stephens, *International Law of the Sea* (3rd edn, Hart, 2023).

An insightful, comprehensive analysis of the law of the sea, UNCLOS and associated agreements.

DR Rothwell, AE Elferink, K Scott, and Tim Stephens (eds), *The Oxford Handbook on the Law of the Sea* (OUP, 2015).

A broad grouping of contributors who address classic and contemporary issues.

Y Tanaka, *The International Law of the Sea* (3rd edn, CUP, 2019).

A contemporary, student-focused introduction to the law of the sea.

S Trevisanut, N Giannopoulos, and RR Holst (eds), *Regime Interaction in Global Governance: Problems, Theories and Methods* (Brill, 2020).

Ocean governance is effected through a variety of international law regimes beyond the law of the sea, such as refugee law, energy law, and environmental law; these interactions are studied rigorously and an overarching integrative account is offered.

P Vincent, *Droit de la mer* (2nd edn, Larcier, 2020).

A leading French-language monograph introducing the topic to students and scholars.

19

The protection of the environment

19.1 Introduction: the challenge of global environmental action

19.1.1 States and environmental protection: a brief history

Early international law did not place great importance on the stewardship and protection of nature, perhaps given that until the Industrial Revolution in the West, human activity was not so intense as to pose visible threats to the environment. In the 1960s, however, the human impact on the natural and physical environment became an increasing matter of public debate. Activists and NGOs began calling attention to the delocalized nature of pollution, overfishing, and toxic wastes, which respect no borders. Nobel Prize winner Elinor Ostrom would challenge the pessimism that common spaces would be exploited to the point of collapse, arguing that regulation through institutions and changes in social behaviour could prevent this.[1] The local imperative for collective action quickly took on a global dimension.

Newly prominent environmental concerns stoked uncertainty from newly decolonized States, which found themselves at a far earlier stage of economic development than Western States, which had fully reaped the fruits of industrialization. Such less-developed States claimed permanent sovereignty over natural resources,[2] suggesting that those who have most benefited from despoiling the environment should bear most of the burden for its preservation.[3]

It is not States that cause the most harm to the environment, though they often do so in dramatic fashion with large-scale projects such as the building of a dam or canal. The bulk of damage is caused by the everyday activities of a number of non-State actors, including private citizens in cars and aeroplanes, corporations operating factories which emit air pollution or toxic wastes into water, and the harvesting or hunting of animals to the point of extinction.

[1] See, e.g., E Ostrom, *Governing the Commons: The Evolution of Institutions for Collective Action* (CUP, 1990), effectively refuting the earlier G Hardin, 'The Tragedy of the Commons' (1968) 162(3859) Science 1243.

[2] See 'Declaration on Permanent Sovereignty over Natural Resources', UNGA Res 1803 (XVII) (14 December 1962).

[3] See, e.g., Venezuela and Bolivia: PDVSA, 'True Nationalization' (*Gobierno Bolivariano de Venezuela*, 26 January 2006) (Venezuela); N Schrijver, *Sovereignty over Natural Resources: Balancing Rights and Duties* (CUP, 1997), 43 (Bolivia).

Nevertheless, certain disasters have, however, captured public attention and impelled the adoption of regulation at both the international and domestic levels. These include:

- the 1967 sinking of the *Torrey Canyon* oil tanker, which led to 117,000 tonnes of crude oil spilling into the English Channel;
- the 1984 explosion of a chemical factory in Bhopal, India, causing more than 2,500 deaths due to the release of toxic chemicals into the air and the soil;
- the 1986 explosion of a nuclear reactor in Chernobyl, causing a radioactive cloud to form across most of Europe and long-term damage to the ecosystem, not to mention the death of some 4,000 persons;
- the 1998 grounding of the *Exxon Valdez* oil tanker off the Alaskan shoreline, which caused the death of thousands of birds and marine mammals; and
- the 2010 incident concerning the *Deepwater Horizon* drilling rig, the largest accidental marine oil spill in history, which caused lasting and extensive toxic damage to the ecosystem of the Gulf of Mexico, including to the adjacent land.

It is within the tensions over sovereignty and international cooperation, and the regulation of public and private spheres, that modern international environmental law has emerged as a distinct regime. Though the General Assembly has taken up environmental protection—in particular, through the UN Environment Programme (UNEP), in existence since 1972—there is no dedicated international organization which has competence over environmental matters.[4] This relatively unstructured approach to the environment, though at times piecemeal and ineffective, has also made an important contribution to the development of alternative compliance mechanisms, methods of collaboration between States and non-State actors, and the interaction between regional, international, and national bodies all in pursuit of a common goal.

19.1.2 **Defining 'the environment'**

International lawyers have struggled to arrive at a comprehensive legal definition of the environment, though a frequently quoted definition is found in the 1993 Council of Europe Convention on Civil Liability:[5] the 'environment' can include 'natural resources both abiotic and biotic, such as the air, water, soil, fauna, and flora and the interaction between the same factors; property which forms part of the cultural heritage; and the characteristic aspects of the landscape'.[6] It is a broad (and somewhat anthropocentric) formulation, in some respects raising more questions than it answers.[7] However, it encapsulates a wide range of issues, including the prevention of pollution, the

[4] On the WTO, see Chapter 20, Section 20.3.2.

[5] See Council of Europe Convention on Civil Liability for Damage Resulting from Activities Dangerous to the Environment (signed 21 June 1993), ETS 150.

[6] *Ibid*, Art 2(10).

[7] With respect to the challenges of defining the environment as including the 'characteristics of the landscape': see ILC, 'Report on the Work of its 56th Session', UN Doc A/59/10 (2004) GAOR 59th Session Supp 10, 148.

protection of species and their habitats, and protection of natural and cultural heritage, which are covered by an array of sector-specific or regional treaties. Examples of these include the 1972 World Cultural and Natural Heritage Convention,[8] the 1985 Ozone Layer Convention,[9] and the Inter-American Convention on Sea Turtles.[10]

19.2 The development of international environmental law

The story of international environmental law is one of unsystematic, but sustained, iteration. Through a series of legal developments, ranging from diplomatic conferences, judicial decisions, unilateral State practice, and, of course, through treaty-making, a series of 'core concepts' of international norms have emerged over the last forty years, coalescing into an increasingly dense, yet fragmented, regime of international environmental protection.

19.2.1 Early developments (1890–1960)

A series of early cases are seminal for understanding the traditional framework of international environmental law before the 1970s.

HISTORICAL BACKGROUND ***Bering Fur Seals Arbitration (Great Britain/United States)*** **(1893) Moore's Digest of International Arbitrations 755**

After the 1867 purchase of Alaska by the USA from the Russian Empire, the USA asserted jurisdiction beyond the Alaskan territorial sea. The US assertion was a response to the decimation of seal breeding stocks by foreign, mainly Canadian, seal hunters just outside US territorial waters. It was one of the earliest instances of a State asserting extra-territorial jurisdiction for the purpose of conservation.

In implementation of this policy, in 1886 the US Coast Guard seized three Canadian sealing vessels, despite being on the high seas. Great Britain, which at that time represented Canada in its foreign relations, complained and the matter was brought to arbitration. In defence of its arrest on the high seas, the USA purported to be legislating to protect 'the common interests of mankind', and claiming to be the only State capable of discharging that duty.

The tribunal dismissed the purported US 'right of protection or property in the fur seals' as unfounded in customary international law, which was legally correct given that the USA could not even point to any legal entitlement to do so. The case, however, is legally significant as it is perhaps the first instance of a State invoking conservation as a legal justification.

[8] UNESCO Convention on the Protection of the World Cultural and Natural Heritage (signed 16 November 1972, entered into force 17 December 1975), 1037 UNTS 151.

[9] Vienna Convention for the Protection of the Ozone Layer (signed 22 March 1985, entered into force 22 September 1988), 1513 UNTS 324.

[10] Inter-American Convention for the Protection and Conservation of Sea Turtles (signed 1 December 1996, entered into force 2 May 2001), 2164 UNTS 29.

The *Bering Fur Seals* arbitration would have a forward impact: in 1911, the Washington Fur Seals Convention between Great Britain, Japan, Russia, and the USA (signed 7 July 1911, entered into force 15 December 1911) (1911) 214 CTS 80 would come to ban pelagic sealing (in the 'open sea') and establish some of the first international legal rules on conservation.

The conception of 'common good' would further be recognized in one of the first cases decided by the PCIJ, concerning the *International Commission of the River Oder.*[11] The multi-State Commission had been set up after the 1919 Treaty of Versailles declared the Oder river system to be an 'international watercourse' and thus freely navigable.[12] Poland, concerned over its access to the Baltic Sea, disputed the territorial remit of the Commission, claimed that certain tributaries of the Oder fell outside its jurisdiction. The PCIJ ruled against Poland, concluding that the 'community of interest of riparian States' required a common right for all States to navigate freely over the whole course of the river. This was an important development in the law of international watercourses, which has since evolved to take into account the interests of all riparian States.

The next key case is the 1935 *Trail Smelter* arbitration between the USA and Canada, which concerned a long-running dispute over the emission of sulphur dioxide and other noxious materials from a privately owned zinc and lead smelter located in Trail, British Columbia, which was causing damage to trees, crops, and land located in neighbouring Washington state.[13] The tribunal found that Canada had breached an international obligation to prevent transboundary harm:

> no State has the right to use or permit the use of its territory in such a manner as to cause injury by fumes in or to the territory of another or the properties or persons therein, where the case is of serious consequence and the injury is established by clear and convincing evidence.[14]

That unprecedented finding of liability represents the first occasion of an international tribunal upholding the principle that a State is under an obligation not knowingly to allow its territory to be used in such a manner as to cause injury to another State. What is more, the tribunal required Canada to implement future monitoring of the effects of the factory's activities on the environment.[15] These two principles were to figure prominently in future environmental initiatives.

Another landmark decision is the arbitral award between France and Spain in *Lac Lanoux.*[16] The dispute had arisen when France announced plans to divert the waters

[11] *Territorial Jurisdiction of the International Commission of the River Oder (United Kingdom et al v Poland), Judgment No 16, 1929, PCIJ, Ser A, No 23.*

[12] Treaty of Peace between the Allied and Associated Powers and Germany ('Treaty of Versailles') (signed 28 June 1919, entered into force 10 January 1920) (1919) 225 CTS 188, Arts 331, 338, 341.

[13] *Trail Smelter (United States/Canada)* (1941) III RIAA 1905; in particular, Second Decision of 11 March 1941, at 1938.

[14] *Ibid*, 1965.

[15] *Ibid*, 1963, though it should be noted that Canada had voluntarily assumed liability for any pollution caused by the private smelter.

[16] *Lac Lanoux (France/Spain)* (Award of 16 November 1957), XII RIAA 281, 308.

of the Pyrenean Lake Lanoux, wholly in French territory, which would have affected the flow of certain tributary rivers into Spain. Spain invoked the existence of a principle prohibiting an upstream State from altering the waters of a river in such a manner as to cause injury to a downstream State. Because France had proposed to compensate for the flow of water into Spain and, implicitly, avoid causing substantial damage to Spain, such a principle was not applicable,[17] but France was under an international law obligation to notify Spain and to enter into consultations with it to consider its interests and prevent, so far as possible, unnecessary damage.[18] The *Lac Lanoux* award is also significant in that it was one of the first that foresaw the principle of 'equitable utilization of shared natural resources'.[19]

19.2.2 **The era of the Stockholm and Rio conferences**

Two pivotal conferences, held in Stockholm in 1972 and in Rio de Janeiro in 1992, heralded the coming of age of international environmental law.

The 1972 Stockholm Declaration on the Human Environment embodied a number of non-binding, but highly influential, 'soft law' (see later, Section 19.4) principles:[20]

- recognition that human rights and environmental protection were linked (Principle 1);
- the need for 'inter-generational equity', or to conserve the environment for future generations (Principle 2); and
- though enjoying a sovereign right to exploit their natural resources, States have a 'responsibility to ensure that activities within their jurisdiction or control do not cause damage to the environment of other States or areas beyond the limits of national jurisdiction' (Principle 21).

The Stockholm Conference was notable for its Programme of Action, which helped to establish the United Nations Environment Programme (UNEP) as a specialized subsidiary body of the General Assembly, based in Nairobi.[21] Today, UNEP remains the only international body dedicated solely to environmental matters, and it collaborates with other specialized bodies and organizations to manage environmental health risks (caused by natural or man-made disasters such as chemical or radiological incidents).

Following the work of the 'Brundtland Commission', created by the General Assembly to focus on environmental and development issues during the 1980s,[22] the 1992 Rio

[17] *Ibid.* [18] *Ibid*, 314–15.

[19] *Gabčíkovo-Nagymaros Project (Hungary/Slovakia), Judgment, ICJ Reports 1997*, p 7.

[20] 1972 Stockholm Declaration on the Human Environment (1972) 11 ILM 874. See also the comprehensive analysis in LB Sohn, 'The Stockholm Declaration on the Human Environment' (1973) 14 Harvard ILJ 423; AC Kiss, 'The Destiny of the Principles of the Stockholm Declaration' in MH Nordquist, JN Moore, and S Mahmoudi (eds), *The Stockholm Declaration and Law of the Marine Environment* (Nijhoff, 2003), 53.

[21] See UNGA, 'Institutional and Financial Arrangements for International Environmental Cooperation', UNGA Res 27/2997 (15 December 1972).

[22] The 'Brundtland Commission' is formally known as the World Commission on Environment and Development: 'Process of Preparation of the Environmental Perspective to the Year 2000 and Beyond', UNGA Res 38/161 (19 December 1983).

Conference on Environment and Development heralded a more integrative approach to environmental protection. The Rio Conference and resulting Rio Declaration on Environment and Development[23] focused on developing the central concept of *sustainable development*, or the idea that environmental protection constituted an integral part of economic and social development, and that policies should be adopted to further both goals with a view to the needs of future generations. 'Sustainable development' is a somewhat paradoxical concept, typical of the compromises emerging from complex negotiations. Though seemingly acknowledged as customary international law,[24] it means little in the abstract, and can be read as a commitment to sustainability as much as to economic progress, all without many concrete commitments.[25]

CASE SPOTLIGHT ***Gabčíkovo-Nagymaros Project (Hungary/Slovakia), Judgment, ICJ Reports 1997, p 7***

The *Gabčíkovo-Nagymaros* dispute between Hungary and Slovakia is of key importance in consolidating many of the concepts outlined in earlier case law.

The dispute concerned a major dam project which had been agreed by treaty when both States were under Communist rule. After a change of government, in 1992 Hungary concluded that the environmental ramifications of the project were so fundamental that it could withdraw unilaterally from the treaty under Article 61 VCLT. Slovakia proceeded alone with a variant of the dam project. The two States agreed to submit the dispute to the ICJ, each alleging the wrongful conduct of the other. Hungary claimed that Slovakia's unilateral activity was in breach of the treaty, and justified its termination; Slovakia rejected Hungary's claim and suggested that Hungary's refusal to participate was itself a breach.

The Court concluded that both States had acted unlawfully, and rejected Hungary's argument that environmental concerns could constitute a fundamental change of circumstances under Article 61. Though the Court called upon both States to arrive at a negotiated settlement, it did not consider that the sacrosanct principle of *pacta sunt servanda* (agreements shall be binding) could be compromised in such circumstances, and that in any event Hungary's own conduct had contributed to the situation at hand (para 103).

Though the Court declined to pronounce on the status of the precautionary principle, the *Gabčíkovo-Nagymaros* judgment has been influential in recognizing the 'importance' of the principle of sustainable development (para 143). Furthermore, it endorsed and clarified in some depth the principle of 'equitable utilization of shared natural resources' from *Lac Lanoux*, describing it as a principle of customary international law in relation to non-navigable uses of international watercourses. The Court also clarified that the shared use of resources had to be both equitable and reasonable, and respect a degree of proportionality as required by international law (para 85).

[23] 'Rio Declaration on Environment and Development', Annex I of the Report of the United Nations Conference on Environment and Development, UN Doc A/CONF.151/26 (Vol I) (12 August 1992).

[24] *Gabčíkovo-Nagymaros Project (Hungary/Slovakia), Judgment, ICJ Reports 1997*, p 7, 78.

[25] See P Birnie, A Boyle, and C Redgwell, *International Law and the Environment* (3rd edn, OUP, 2009), 53–8, 115 *et seq*; N Schrijver, *The Evolution of Sustainable Development in International Law: Inception, Meaning and Status* (Nijhoff, 2008).

As befits its name, the 1992 Rio Declaration on Environment and Development sought to link environmental protection with sustainable development, restating certain principles from the Stockholm Declaration, but also adding several new principles. Foremost is the *precautionary approach*, which would require States to use precaution in relation to possible threats of serious or irreversible damage, even when there is a lack of full scientific certainty (Principle 15). Another is the '*polluter pays*' principle, which provides that national authorities should endeavour to promote the internationalization of environmental costs, such that the polluter should in principle bear the cost of pollution (Principle 16).[26] However sensible they might seem, neither the precautionary approach nor the 'polluter pays' principle have had much success in legal disputes. The precautionary approach has been invoked unsuccessfully by States in a number of instances; for example, most prominently before the WTO Appellate Body[27] and the ICJ.[28] The 'polluter pays' principle has met with similar scepticism.[29]

Other principles have fared better. Principle 17 of the Rio Declaration requires the undertaking of an *environmental impact assessment* for proposed activities that are likely to have a significant adverse impact on the environment; this obligation was recognized as one of customary international law by the ICJ, and is discussed later at Section 19.3.1.[30] Similarly, the idea of 'common but differentiated responsibility', through which States bear responsibility for sustainable development in accordance with their own capacity, has been taken up in several treaties.[31]

The Rio Declaration was accompanied by an ambitious programme of action: *Agenda 21*. It included a set of more than 35,000 recommendations which purported to establish a cooperative framework for international environmental governance.[32] It identified programme areas and objectives in a number of sectors including: cross-cutting means of implementation, such as the transfer of technology from developed to developing

[26] See A Boyle, 'Making the Polluter Pay? Alternatives to State Responsibility in the Allocation of Transboundary Environmental Costs' in F Francioni and T Scovazzi (eds), *International Responsibility for Environmental Harm* (Graham & Trotman, 1991), 363.

[27] See WTO, *European Communities: Measures Concerning Meat and Meat Products (Hormones)—Report of the Appellate Body* (16 January 1998), WT/DS26/AB/R and WT/DS48/AB/R; ITLOS in the *Southern Bluefin Tuna Cases (Nos 3 & 4) (New Zealand v Japan; Australia v Japan)* (Provisional Measures, Order of 27 August 1999), ITLOS Reports 1999, 280.

[28] See *Gabčíkovo-Nagymaros* (n 24) and *Pulp Mills on the River Uruguay (Argentina v Uruguay), Judgment, ICJ Reports 2010*, p 14. That said, a 'precautionary approach' in respect of environmental risks is embodied in art 191(2) of the TFEU and is considered a 'general principle of EU law': see the judgment of the EU's Court of First Instance in *Artegodan v Commission*, Joined Cases T-74/00 T-76/00, T-83/00 to T-85/00, T-132/00, T-137/00 and T-141/00 [2022] ECR II-4948, para 184.

[29] In the *Rhine Arbitration (Netherlands/France)* (Award 12 March 2004) in *Permanent Court of Arbitration Award Series* (TMC Asser Press, 2008), the arbitral tribunal held conclusively that the 'polluter pays' principle is not part of international law.

[30] See *Pulp Mills on the River Uruguay* (n 28) 83. Further reading on the Rio Summit can be found in AE Boyle, *International Law and Sustainable Development: Past Achievements and Future Challenges* (OUP, 1999); HF French, *After the Earth Summit: The Future of Environmental Governance* (Worldwatch Institute, 1992).

[31] Among those discussed later, see UNFCCC (n 33) Art 3; Kyoto Protocol to the FCCC (n 39) Art 3; Montreal Protocol on Substances that Deplete the Ozone Layer (n 41) Art 5(1); CBD (n 34) Art 20(4); Paris Agreement (n 40) preamble, Arts 2(2), 4(3), 4(19). See generally D French, 'Developing States and International Environmental Law: The Importance of Differentiated Responsibilities' (2000) 49 ICLQ 38; P Cullet, *Differential Treatment in International Environmental Law* (Ashgate, 2003).

[32] UNGA, 'Report of the United Nations Conference on Environment and Development' (1992) UN Doc A/CONF.151/26/Rev.1, vol 1, 9.

States; the eradication of poverty through sustainable development; and support for national strategies, plans, and policies to achieve these. Two major framework treaties, the 1992 Framework Convention on Climate Change (UNFCCC)[33] and the 1992 Convention on the Conservation of Biological Diversity (CBD), were also negotiated.[34]

There have been two follow-up conferences to Rio 1992: the 2002 Johannesburg World Summit on Sustainable Development[35] and the 2012 UN Conference on Sustainable Development, also held in Rio (known as 'Rio+20').[36] Rather than institution-building or lawmaking, both conferences primarily focused on further progressing the goals set out in Rio 1992.

19.3 Traditional sources of international environmental law

19.3.1 Treaties and other environmental agreements

A significant proportion of international environmental law obligations are contained in treaties, which are characterized by a particularly dynamic form:[37] they often adopt a 'framework approach', with general principles and perhaps institutional mechanisms for implementation laid out in a treaty. Framework treaties are accompanied by protocols or annexes, which can be amended more flexibly than treaties, prescribing more specific, legally enforceable standards and targets. Among such framework conventions is the 1992 UNFCCC, accompanied by the 1997 Kyoto Protocol[38] and 2015 Paris Agreement.[39] The Paris Agreement did not require unanimity, but only the ratification of fifty-five States, which account for 55 per cent of global emissions, to come into force for all parties to the UNFCCC.

Framework conventions, allowing for rapid amendment of protocols and annexes, are highly useful when rapidly evolving scientific, technical, or other data are concerned.[40] This is frequently achieved through regular conferences of all parties

[33] United Nations Framework Convention on Climate Change (signed 4 June 1992, entered into force 21 March 1994), 1771 UNTS 107 (UNFCCC).

[34] Convention on Biological Diversity (signed 5 June 1992, entered into force 29 December 1993), 1760 UNTS 79 (CBD).

[35] See UNGA, 'Johannesburg Declaration on Sustainable Development' (4 September 2002), UN Doc A/CONF.199/20; UNGA, 'Draft Plan of Implementation of the World Summit on Sustainable Development' (26 June 2002), UN Doc A/CONF.199/L.1.

[36] See outcome of the Rio+20 Summit at UNGA, 'The Future We Want—Outcome Document', UNGA Res 66/288 (11 September 2012); and 2030 Agenda for Sustainable Development, which adds seventeen sustainable development goals: UNGA Res 70/1 (21 October 2015).

[37] See C Redgwell, 'Multilateral Environmental Treaty-Making' in V Gowlland-Debbas (ed), *Multilateral Treaty-Making: The Current Status of Challenges to and Reforms Needed in the International Legislative Process* (Nijhoff, 2000); RR Churchill and G Ulfstein, 'Autonomous Institutional Arrangements in Multilateral Environmental Agreements: A Little-Noticed Phenomenon in International Law' (2000) 94 AJIL 623.

[38] Kyoto Protocol to the UN Framework Convention on Climate Change (signed 11 December 1997, entered into force 16 February 2005), 2303 UNTS 148.

[39] Paris Agreement under the UN Framework Convention on Climate Change (adopted 12 December 2015, entered into force 4 November 2016), UN Doc FCCC/CP/C2015/L.9.

[40] See, e.g., Convention for the Protection of the Ozone Layer (signed 22 March 1985, entered into force 22 September 1988), 1513 UNTS 293, accompanied by the Montreal Protocol on Substances that Deplete the Ozone Layer (signed 16 September 1987, entered into force 1 January 1989), 1522 UNTS 3, and its four Amendments (London Amendment 1990; Copenhagen Amendment 1992; Montreal Amendment 1997; and Beijing Amendment 1999).

(often abbreviated to COPs). Framework treaties can also allow for differentiation of parties' obligations in line with their capabilities. For example, Article 3(1) of the UNFCCC allows for common but differentiated responsibilities of States in relation to climate change. In the Kyoto Protocol, only certain developed States listed in Annex I to the Protocol (called 'Annex I States') had the obligation to reduce greenhouse gas emissions.[41] In the 1992 Convention on Biological Diversity, many provisions impose differentiated funding and implementation obligations on States parties.[42]

As substantive obligations are difficult to specify and enforce in the international environmental law context, many conventions impose *procedural obligations* on States in order to ensure that they exercise vigilance or take preventive measures to avoid causing irreparable environmental harm.[43] Chief among these is the *duty of prior notification* of possibly affected parties, in order for appropriate consultations to take place. That duty was embodied in the ILC's Draft Article 8 on the Prevention of Transboundary Harm, and finds abundant support in practice and case law.[44]

Many of the procedural obligations of notification and consultation in situations where transboundary harm might exist have also been held to constitute a customary law obligation.[45] In particular, the requirement to conduct a transboundary 'environmental impact assessment' (EIA: see accompanying comment), which applies in Europe by treaty,[46] is considered to be customary international law. Though it is perhaps too early to say definitively, procedural obligations may be leading towards a more general duty of cooperation to protect the environment.[47]

[41] A geopolitical artefact, Annex I excludes highly developed States such as South Korea and Singapore, but includes middle-income States, such as Belarus and Ukraine, as 'Economies in Transition'. States without binding targets are called 'non-Annex I States'. See L Rajamani, 'The Principle of Common but Differentiated Responsibility and the Balance of Commitments under the Climate Regime' (2000) 9 RECIEL 120.

[42] See CBD (n 34) preamble, Arts 6, 17, 20, and 21.

[43] *Gabčíkovo-Nagymaros* (n 24) 78. See also P Okowa, 'Procedural Obligations in International Environmental Agreements' (1997) 67 BYBIL 275.

[44] ILC, 'Draft Articles on Prevention of Transboundary Harm for Hazardous Activities', in UN Doc A/56/10 (2001) GAOR 56th Session Supp 10, Art 8; See *Lac Lanoux* (n 16) 24 ILR 101, 119; *Pulp Mills on the River Uruguay* (n 28) 58–9 (albeit in the context of a bilateral treaty); *Trail Smelter* (n 13) 1966–7, 1981; Rio Declaration (n 23) Principles 18, 24; Ramsar Convention on Wetlands of International Importance (signed 2 February 1971, entered into force 21 December 1975), 999 UNTS 245, Art 3(2); ECE Convention on Long-Range Transboundary Air Pollution (signed 13 November 1979, entered into force 16 March 1983), 1302 UNTS 217, Art 5; United Nations Convention on the Law of the Sea (signed 10 December 1982, entered into force 16 November 1994), 1833 UNTS 3, Arts 204–6.

[45] *Pulp Mills on the River Uruguay* (n 28) 83; see also *Certain Activities Carried out by Nicaragua in the Border Area (Costa Rica v Nicaragua) and Construction of a Road in Costa Rica along the San Juan River (Nicaragua v Costa Rica) (Joined Cases), Merits, ICJ Reports 2015*, p 665, para 108.

[46] Espoo Convention on Environmental Impact Assessment in a Transboundary Context (signed 25 February 1991, entered into force 10 September 1997), 1989 UNTS 309.

[47] See, e.g., Principle 24 of the 1972 Stockholm Declaration (n 20); Principle 7 of the 1992 Rio Declaration (n 23); and Art 4 of the ILC Draft Articles on the Prevention of Transboundary Harm (n 45).

THEORY AND DEBATES The Legal Relevance of 'Environmental Impact Assessments' (EIAs)

An EIA has been defined as 'the process of identifying, predicting, evaluating and mitigating the biophysical, social, and other relevant effects of development proposals prior to major decisions being taken and commitments made' (International Association of Impact Assessment, 1999). In the 2010 *Pulp Mills on the River Uruguay* judgment, the ICJ recognized that the obligation to conduct an EIA is one of customary international law (para 204). Though customary international law does not fully define the scope and content of an EIA, and there is no global treaty regulating how they proceed, the EIA must be conducted prior to the implementation of a project, and should have regard to the nature and magnitude of a proposed project and its likely adverse impact on the environment (para 205).

In the more recent joined cases involving Costa Rica and Nicaragua, the ICJ considered Costa Rica's dredging of the San Juan River (which divides both States) and Nicaragua's construction of a road along the San Juan River. The Court, building on *Pulp Mills on the River Uruguay*, explained that the conduct of an EIA was interlinked with obligations of due diligence, notification, and consultation, as well as the place of scientific evidence in disputes concerning environmental matters (see joined cases *Certain Activities in the Border Area/Construction of a Road along the San Juan River*, para 104). More recently, ITLOS' 2024 advisory opinion makes clear that the obligation to conduct an EIA is not required, and in fact added specificity to the content and scope of the EIA, that it was required to consider both simple but 'cumulative impacts' on the marine environment, on the basis of the certain planned activities (paras 365–75). The obligation to conduct an EIA requires decision-makers to adhere to environmental values in arriving at their decisions, with many States' domestic legislation having enshrined procedures for the conduct of environmental assessments, such as Canada, China, India, Malaysia, Sri Lanka, and the USA.

See further N Craik, *The International Law on Environmental Impact Assessment* (CUP, 2010); and Y Tanaka, '*Costa Rica v Nicaragua* and *Nicaragua v Costa Rica*: Some Reflections on the Obligations to Conduct an Environmental Impact Assessment' (2017) 26 RECIEL 91.

19.3.2 **Customary international law and general principles**

Though there exists no general legal obligation in customary international law to protect and preserve the environment, certain customary rules nevertheless have been found in specific treaties, case law, and occasionally even soft law instruments. The most significant is the *principle of prevention*, often taking the form of the 'good neighbour' principle: accordingly, States are required to exercise due diligence in preventing their territory from being used in such a way as to cause significant damage to the environment of another State.[48]

[48] See *Dispute over the Status and Use of the Waters of the Silala (Chile v Bolivia), Merits, ICJ Reports 2022*, p 614, para 99; *Pulp Mills on the River Uruguay* (n 28), 55–6; *Legality of the Threat or Use of Nuclear Weapons, Advisory Opinion, ICJ Reports 1996*, p 226, 242; *Trail Smelter* (n 13) 1965; and Stockholm Declaration (n 20), Principle 21. See further the ILC Draft Articles on Prevention of Transboundary Harm (n 45), Commentary to Art 3, para 7, and more generally, L-A Duvic-Paoli, *The Prevention Principle in International Environmental Law* (CUP, 2018).

In earlier decades, it had been argued that the appropriate standard for prevention should be one of *strict liability*, in the sense that States are under an absolute obligation to prevent pollution and are liable for its effects, irrespective of any fault.[49] One key advantage of strict liability is that it mandates the lowest thresholds to engage responsibility, and avoids the challenges of establishing a causal link between conduct and harm, a particularly effective approach when multiple actors are involved. However laudable, there is insufficient practice, and the more orthodox view is that the standard is one of due diligence,[50] unless a treaty system does in fact provide for absolute or strict liability.

An acceleration in domestic and regional decision-making has begun to consolidate and substantiate these obligations in different forms.[51] In February 2018, the Inter-American Court of Human Rights emphasized that the right to a healthy environment under the ACHR was self-standing, and that, 'unlike other rights, protects the components of the environment . . . as legal interests in themselves, even in the absence of the certainty or evidence of a risk to individuals'.[52] In recent judgments, Dutch and Belgian courts have held that under the European Convention on Human Rights, their respective States are under an obligation to take positive measures to reduce further—by an additional 25 per cent and a 55 per cent respectively—greenhouse gas emissions in the fight against climate change.[53] Similar rulings affirming the existence of a due diligence obligation (or duty of care) of States to prevent change have been handed down by courts in Colombia[54] (in which the self-standing legal rights of the Rio Atrato and Amazon river ecosystems were recognized) and Belgium.[55] Regional human rights courts have also been active: in 2024, the Grand Chamber of the European Court of Human Rights dismissed two climate change cases on procedural grounds of jurisdiction and admissibility,[56] but it drew a number of important conclusions on the interplay between human rights law and environmental obligations in a third judgment on the

[49] See J Barboza, *The Environment, Risk and Liability in International Law* (Brill, 2010); G Handl, 'State Liability for Accidental Transnational Environmental Damage by Private Persons' (1980) 74 AJIL 525.

[50] See ILC Commentary on the Draft Articles on Prevention of Transboundary Harm (n 45) 392; *Responsibilities and Obligations of States Sponsoring Persons and Entities with Respect to Activities in the Area, Advisory Opinion, ITLOS Reports 2011*, p 10, para 117; and Birnie, Boyle, and Redgwell (n 25) 147 *et seq*.

[51] See J Setzer and C Higham, 'Global Trends in Climate Change Litigation: 2024 snapshot' (Grantham Research Institute on Climate Change and the Environment report, June 2024) and Sabin Centre for Climate Change Law (Columbia Law School), 'Climate Change Litigation Databases' (<https://climatecasechart.com>).

[52] *The Environment and Human Rights, Advisory Opinion of 15 November 2017*, IACtHR No OC-23, para 62; and *Indigenous Communities of the Lhaka Honhat Association (Our Land) v Argentina, Judgment of 6 February 2020* (IACtHR), para 203.

[53] *The Netherlands v Urgenda* (Supreme Court of the Netherlands), Case No 19/00135 (20 December 2019); *VZW Klimaatzaak v Belgium*, Court of Appeal of Brussels (30 November 2023). In January 2024, a group of residents of Bonaire, supported by Greenpeace, sued the Netherlands for the specific vulnerabilities suffered by inhabitants of low-lying areas in the Netherlands Antilles: see *Bonaire* climate case (District Court of the Hague), application of 11 January 2024. The case remains pending.

[54] Constitutional Court of Colombia, Judgment Nos T-622-16 (10 November 2016) and STC-4360-2018 (5 April 2018).

[55] *Klimaatzaak v Belgium* (Brussels Court of First Instance), Case No 2015/4585/A (17 June 2021).

[56] *Carême v France*, ECtHR Case no 7189/21 (11 April 2024); *Duarte Agostinho and Ors v Portugal and 32 other States*, ECtHR Case No 39371/20 (11 April 2024).

merits, *Verein KlimaSeniorinnen v Switzerland*.[57] In addition to a pending request for an advisory opinion on the question of climate change, in late 2023, the Inter-American Court of Human Rights released its judgment in *La Oroya v Peru*, in which victims of airborne pollution caused by metallurgical activities claimed successfully against Peru for the violation of the right to a healthy environment, which it regarded as a bundle of procedural and substantive elements.[58] There are further points in the latter judgment worth highlighting. First, there was a departure from a human rights-centred approach, instead seeing environmental conditions in themselves; potentially even as 'rights of nature', a method that might surmount potential obstacles regarding the admissibility of claims (for example, on behalf of future generations).[59] Secondly, the Court arrived at the intriguing conclusion that the right to a healthy environment 'should have the status of a peremptory norm', or *jus cogens*.[60] Finally, in early December 2024, oral proceedings were held in the ICJ in the request for an advisory opinion on *Obligations of States to Prevent Climate Change*, where a number of key questions will be addressed.

To this one might add the work of multilateral treaty monitoring bodies: in 2022, the UN Human Rights Committee found that Australia's failure to protect indigenous Torres Islanders against adverse impacts of climate change violated the human rights to enjoy their culture and to be free from arbitrary interference with their private life, family, and home.[61] In 2023, the Children's Rights Committee published its 'General Comment No 26', detailing the urgent need to address the harmful cross-border impacts of climate change and their impact on children's rights under the CRC.[62]

That there can be State responsibility for extraterritorial environmental harm is 'part of the corpus of international law relating to the environment'.[63] Moreover, there exists a general obligation to protect and preserve the marine environment laid down in Article 192 UNCLOS, a widely ratified convention; and Article 194 UNCLOS lays out an obligation of due diligence 'to take all measures . . . that are necessary to prevent, reduce and control pollution of the marine environment'. Similar obligations exist in the Outer Space Treaty[64] and the Environmental Protocol to the Antarctic Treaty,[65] as well as in soft law instruments.[66]

[57] *Verein KlimaSeniorinnen Schweiz and Ors v Switzerland*, ECtHR Case No 53600/20 (11 April 2024).

[58] *Habitantes de La Oroya v Peru (Preliminary Objections, Merits, Reparations & Costs)*, IACtHR Series C No 511 (27 November 2023). See further J Dehm, 'The Rights of Nature as a legal Response to the Global Environmental Crisis?' (2021) Netherlands YBIL 47.

[59] See, e.g., *ibid*, paras 124, 179.

[60] *Ibid* para 129.

[61] *Daniel Billy and Ors v Australia (Torres Strait Islanders Petition)*, UN Doc CCPR/C/135/D/3624/2019 (23 September 2022).

[62] CRC, 'General comment No. 26 (2023) on children's rights and the environment with a special focus on climate change', UN Doc CRC/C/GC/26 (22 August 2023).

[63] *Nuclear Weapons* (n 49) 241–2.

[64] Treaty on Principles Governing the Activities of States in the Exploration and Use of Outer Space, including the Moon and Other Celestial Bodies (signed 27 January 1967, entered into force 10 October 1967), 610 UNTS 205, Art IX.

[65] 2005 Annex to the 1991 Environmental Protocol to the 1959 Antarctic Treaty (signed 4 October 1991, entered into force 14 January 1998), (1991) 30 ILM 1455.

[66] See, e.g., UNEP Principles of Conduct in the Field of the Environment concerning Resources Shared by Two or More States (1978), Principle 3; Charter of Economic Rights and Duties of States, UNGA Res 29/3281 (17 December 1974).

Finally, a principle of *preventive action and equitable utilization of shared resources* has emerged.[67] For example, upstream users of an international river are obliged to take reasonable account of the interests of other users in downstream areas. All of these are covered in more depth in Section 19.7.2.

Historically, the precautionary approach or the 'polluter pays' principle were seen as aspirational and not binding, but they do find some take-up in treaties. For example, the 1995 Straddling Fish Stocks Agreement specifies that a precautionary approach is to be employed in the management of fish stocks straddling a State's waters and the high seas, or the waters between two States.[68] The 1992 Convention on the Protection and Use of Transboundary Watercourses and International Lakes[69] makes reference to the precautionary principle in Article 2(5)(a); and the preambles of various conventions also make reference to the principle.[70] More recently, the Seabed Disputes Chamber of ITLOS affirmed the obligation of sponsoring States to apply a precautionary approach in respect of the Nodules and Sulphides Regulations enacted under UNCLOS.[71]

19.4 'Soft law'

As explained earlier, few of the influential sources of international environmental law, such as the 1972 Stockholm Declaration, 1992 Rio Declaration, 1982 World Charter for Nature,[72] and the Rio+20 Declaration, create legal obligations in the traditional sense of compliance and responsibility.[73] However, in describing principles that can be applicable to environmental challenges, these have wielded considerable influence on the evolution of international environmental law.[74] They are in fact the quintessential embodiment of *soft law*, or certain standards of action that are recommended or represent an ideal, rather than binding as of themselves.[75] Soft law instruments are particularly popular in the environmental context, given the difficulties in establishing conclusive scientific evidence or

[67] *Gabčíkovo-Nagymaros* (n 24) 54, 56; *Rhine Arbitration* (n 29) para 222; *Lac Lanoux* (n 16) 304.

[68] Agreement relating to the Conservation and Management of Straddling Fish Stocks and Highly Migratory Fish Stocks (signed 04 August 1995, entered into force 11 December 2001), 2167 UNTS 3, Arts 5(c) and 6.

[69] Convention on the Protection and Use of Transboundary Watercourses and International Lakes (signed 17 March 1992, entered into force 6 October 1996), 1936 UNTS 269.

[70] See, e.g., UNFCCC (n 33); Vienna Convention for the Protection of the Ozone Layer (n 9); Montreal Protocol (n 41).

[71] See *Advisory Opinion on Responsibilities and Obligations in the Area* (n 51) paras 121–2, 125–7. See A Trouwborst, *Evolution and Status of the Precautionary Principle in International Law* (Kluwer, 2002); and Birnie, Boyle, and Redgwell (n 25) Ch 3.4, 137.

[72] UNGA Res 37/7 (28 October 1982), UN Doc A/37/7.

[73] See UNGA, 'The Future We Want': Rio+20 Outcome Document (n 36).

[74] See UNGA, 'Report of the 1972 United Nations Conference on Human Environment' (16 June 1972), UN Doc A/CONF.48/14/Rev.1, 3; UNGA, 'Report of the Preparatory Committee for the United Nations Conference on the Human Environment' (6 April 1970), UN Doc A/CONF.48/PC/6, preamble, para 5. Both were adopted in UNGA Res 2994 (XXVII) (15 December 1972).

[75] See A Boyle, 'Some Reflections on the Relationship of Treaties and Soft Law' (1999) 48 ICLQ 901; and D Shelton (ed), *Commitment and Compliance: The Role of Non-Binding Norms in the International Legal System* (OUP, 2000).

calculating the costs of a collective response. They may allow for a consensus to be built pending a clearer course of action, and often lead to the development of 'harder', binding norms. Classic examples of 'soft' law progressing into 'hard' rules include Principle 2 of the Rio Declaration[76] (which builds on Principle 21 of the Stockholm Declaration), the UNEP Technical Guidelines which preceded the Basel Convention on Hazardous Wastes,[77] and the UNEP and FAO Guidelines and Code which preceded the Rotterdam Convention on Prior Informed Consent.[78] Momentum is also gathering in respect of the legal implementation of a new international crime, 'ecocide', which might further contribute to the enforcement of environmental norms against individuals, State officials, and corporate directors.[79] In a tragic escalation of the Russian armed attacks against Ukraine, it was alleged in October 2024 that Russia dumped vast quantities of chemical waste into the transboundary Seym River flowing towards Ukraine, including ammonia, magnesium, and other poisonous nitrates. Since 2022, Ukraine has begun to accuse Russia of having committed such acts, with legal scholars beginning to refer to this deliberate and widespread environmental destruction as an 'eco-tragedy' or even as an 'ecocide'.[80]

19.5 States and other actors

Naturally, States remain the key actors in the making of new environmental rules, especially in relation to treaty-making and the development of customary international law. International organizations are also key fora for the creation of regional frameworks of implementation and enforcement, and may even accede to treaties provided they fulfil the requisite institutional competence to do so and the treaty provides for this.[81]

Specific administrative or regulatory bodies may also address environmental issues. These include the defunct Commission on Sustainable Development, replaced in 2013 by the United Nations High-Level Political Forum on Sustainable Development, a subsidiary organ tasked with the strengthening of sustainable development governance.[82] A key body is the Intergovernmental Panel on Climate Change (IPCC), a scientific and regulatory body established under the auspices of the United Nations for the purpose of gathering scientific data concerning climate change.

[76] The legacy of the Rio Declaration is assessed in J Viñuales (ed), *The Rio Declaration on Environment and Development: A Commentary* (OUP, 2015).

[77] Basel Convention on the Control of Transboundary Movements of Hazardous Wastes and their Disposal (signed 22 March 1989, entered into force 5 May 1992), 1673 UNTS 57.

[78] Rotterdam Convention on the Prior Informed Consent Procedure for Certain Hazardous Chemicals and Pesticides in International Trade (signed 10 September 1998, entered into force 24 February 2004), 2244 UNTS 337.

[79] See *Report of the Independent Expert Panel for the Legal Definition of Ecocide: Commentary and Core Text* (June 2021), available at <https://www.stopecocide.earth/expert-drafting-panel>.

[80] See, e.g., US Commission on Security & Co-operation in Europe, 'Russia's Ecocide in Ukraine: Environmental Destruction and the Need for Accountability' (16 July 2024). On the potential emergence of ecocide, see above, Section 2.3.4.

[81] The European Community (predecessor to the EU) is thus a party to the UNFCCC (n 33) and the Kyoto Protocol (n 39), which provide for the accession of 'regional economic integration organizations'. It is not, however, a party to CITES (n 156), which does not so provide.

[82] The United Nations helpfully gathers new developments at <http://sustainabledevelopment.un.org>.

Finally, non-governmental organizations and activist groups are unusually prominent in the making of international environmental law, participating in large conferences such as the 1992 and 2012 Rio and 2002 Johannesburg summits. NGOs serve to marshal support in States, mount transnational litigation before domestic courts (see Section 19.3.2), and even counsel States in adopting policies and mobilizing public opinion (as did Greenpeace with the *Rainbow Warrior* vessel; see Chapter 10). Certain NGOs such as the International Council of Scientific Unions (ICSU) and the International Union for the Conservation of Nature (IUCN) conduct independent research and gather data that help to focus attention on certain environmental issues.

NGOs may even influence multilateral treaty negotiations: they lobby States and can even occasionally be represented within State delegations, as happens during UNFCCC COPs and occurred during the 1992 Rio Conference when fourteen industrialized States included NGO representatives. Though State consent remains determinative, NGOs can participate at all stages of negotiation, and even seek to induce States to join international institutions.

Finally, NGOs are often accorded a role in the implementation of a treaty regime. For example, the Convention on International Trade in Endangered Species (CITES) and the CBD allow the relevant secretariats to consult with NGOs to monitor treaty implementation, and under the Aarhus Convention NGO observers may nominate candidates for the convention's Compliance Committee. Generally, however, they are not permitted to bring claims before international courts and tribunals, and have almost never been permitted to act as *amicus curiae*, providing information or expertise to 'assist' a court in a dispute.

19.6 **Enforcement of international environmental law**

The complexity of environmental governance has deterred States from traditional mechanisms for international dispute settlement. There are issues regarding standing, as it is often difficult to establish injury, not to mention the inadequacy of the law on State responsibility in establishing causation between the breach of an international law norm and its attribution to a State.[83]

Other questions include how to remedy a breach. The tragedy of international environmental law is that it has often been developed in response to irreversible harm. In such cases, reparation is impossible, and financial compensation would hardly constitute an appropriate remedy. In *Certain Activities Carried Out by Nicaragua in the Border*

[83] See C Redgwell, 'The Wrong Trousers: State Responsibility and International Environmental Law' in M Evans and P Koutrakos (eds), *The International Responsibility of the European Union: European and International Perspectives* (Hart, 2013), 257.

Area, the ICJ was faced for the first time with calculating compensation for environmental damage. Though concluding that environmental damage may be compensable under international law, it struggled with calculation: 'international law does not prescribe any specific method for the purposes of compensation for environmental damage', thus requiring a case-by-case analysis.[84]

Hence, rather than attribute responsibility for environmental damage when it occurs, the international response is often merely to develop a new mechanism to prevent future disasters.[85] However, harm may be incremental and caused over time by the conduct of many actors, raising tremendous problems regarding causation, evidence, and proof. These were in full view in *Pulp Mills on the River Uruguay*, in which Argentina was required to prove, unsuccessfully, that specific harm to their shared river was caused by the pulp mill operating in Uruguay.[86] The need for scientific expertise has compounded concerns over evidence.[87] What is more, the difficulties associated with multiple actors are compounded by the fact that so many of these actors will be private persons or corporations, to whom it is exceptionally difficult to attach international responsibility.[88]

Finally, international environmental obligations are *non-reciprocal*: their breach may cause varying degrees of damage to a multiplicity of States, or to the international community of States as a whole. An illustration is the acknowledgement of 'the common concern of mankind' in the CBD. There are recent developments in this area. In *Whaling in the Atlantic*, Australia had challenged Japan's whaling practices in the Antarctic on the basis of obligations *erga omnes* without having sustained any direct damage. Such cases demonstrate the potential of conventions such as the Whaling Convention, UNCLOS, and the 1992 OSPAR Convention for grounding environmental claims even by States which have not been directly injured. There are even a few environmental treaties that address access to justice for non-State actors,[89] an important innovation.

[84] *Certain Activities Carried out by Nicaragua in the Border Area (Costa Rica v Nicaragua), Judgment on Compensation, ICJ Reports 2018*, p 15, para 52.

[85] In December 2024, the Sixth Committee of the UN General Assembly adopted by consensus a resolution to 'elaborate and conclude a legally binding instrument on the protection of persons in the event of disasters': see UN Doc A/C.6/79/L.16 (6 December 2024).

[86] *Pulp Mills on the River Uruguay* (n 28) 71.

[87] See C Foster, *Science and the Precautionary Principle in International Law* (CUP, 2011). For reflections on the problematic relation between science and law, see also S Jasanoff, 'Serviceable Truths: Science for Action in Law and Policy' (2015) 93 Texas LR 1723.

[88] M Karavias, *Corporate Obligations in International Law* (OUP, 2013), ch 1; see also G Baars, *The Corporation, Law and Capitalism* (Brill, 2019), who argues that if anything, international law has facilitated the reach of the global corporation as 'capitalism's main engine'.

[89] See 1974 Nordic Environmental Protection Convention (signed 19 February 1974, entered into force 5 October 1976), 1092 UNTS 279, Art 3; and the Convention on Access to Information, Public Participation in Decision-making and Access to Justice in Environmental Matters (signed 25 June 1998, entered into force 30 October 2001), 2161 UNTS 447, Art 9.

CASE SPOTLIGHT ***Whaling in the Antarctic (Australia v Japan; New Zealand intervening), Judgment, ICJ Reports 2014*, p 226**

The ICJ's judgment in *Whaling in the Antarctic* has been considered a significant advance in the development of international environmental law. Australia had filed a claim against Japan, alleging that Japan's whaling programmes, ostensibly designed purely for scientific research, were in violation of obligations under the Whaling Convention providing for a near-total ban on commercial whaling. Australia's standing was not founded on any jurisdiction over the maritime zones in which Japan was conducting its whaling activities. Though not acknowledged by the Court, it was a pure *erga omnes partes* claim (see Chapter 3, Section 3.4), or one in which all States parties have a legal interest. Japan did not contest Australia's right to claim.

The Court found in favour of Australia, concluding that, while Japan's whaling programme involved 'scientific research,' it was still not conducted for the purposes of scientific research and thus violated Article VIII, paragraph 1, of the ICRW. The determination in the Court's view required an objective standard of review, rather than a deferential one, which would take the State's professed objectives at face value. The Court set out a number of relevant factors, such as the methodology, scale, and potential scientific outputs of a programme.

The Court also concluded that the design of Japan's programme and its negligible scientific output did not seem to support the purposes of scientific research. Consequently, the Court ordered Japan to revoke existing whaling permits and refrain from authorizing new ones under the current whaling programme.

The *Whaling* judgment is noteworthy for being one of the first cases in which the Court engaged with a State's assessment of complex scientific evidence, and found it wanting.

19.7 **Substantive international environmental law**

The thicket of conventions, protocols, annexes, and other international instruments covering international environmental protection can sometimes be bewildering, so it is helpful to offer an overarching view of the various legal frameworks within international environmental law.

19.7.1 **Protection of the atmosphere, the ozone layer, and climate change**

As the *Trail Smelter* arbitration (see Section 19.2.1) demonstrated, one of the earliest environmental concerns was the protection of the atmosphere from pollution, such as the burning of fossil fuels or emissions from factories and other industrial activities. The borderless nature of the atmosphere requires a concerted global response. Unlike with marine pollution (see Section 19.7.2), there is no single regime for regulating atmospheric pollution. In 2021, the ILC adopted the 'Draft Guidelines on the Protection of the Atmosphere', though these will not impose new legal principles on existing treaty regimes.[90] There are, nevertheless, three areas of international regulation: transboundary air pollution, ozone depletion, and climate change.

[90] UN Doc A/76/10 (2021), pp 13–50, with Commentaries.

19.7.1.1 **Transboundary air pollution**

In the 1979 ECE Convention on Long-Range Transboundary Air Pollution, the only major regional agreement which covers the atmosphere,[91] air pollution is defined as 'the introduction by man, directly or indirectly, of substances or energy into the air resulting in deleterious effects of such a nature as to endanger human health, harm living resources and ecosystems, and impair or interfere with amenities and other legitimate uses of the environment'.[92] That definition of pollution is restrictive, requiring actual harm, of a certain threshold or intensity, to be caused. Questions arise as to how to address situations where the sources of pollution are diffused, or if the pollution has caused low level, but widespread, damage. Given such challenges, no regional agreements beyond the Global North have been adopted.[93]

The ECE Convention is decidedly modest; it only covers 'long-range transboundary air pollution', which necessarily must originate within one State and then cause adverse effects in another State. No reduction targets are found in the framework treaty itself, which exhorts States parties in its Article 2 only to 'endeavour to limit and, as far as possible, gradually reduce and prevent air pollution'. No specific liability regimes are established in the Convention, though it is accompanied by a 1984 Protocol which creates an environmental monitoring programme to gather data, as well as further protocols with specific reduction targets for certain air pollutants.[94] Much like with many treaty regimes in the sector, the ECE Convention does make provision for the exchange of information, consultations between parties, and other monitoring activities.[95]

19.7.1.2 **Ozone depletion**

The importance of the stratospheric ozone layer cannot be overstated: it shields the Earth's surface from deadly ultraviolet radiation. In the 1980s, a global crisis emerged regarding the depletion of the ozone layer due to the use of chlorofluorocarbons (CFCs) and halons. The development of 'holes' in the ozone layer over the polar regions, especially Antarctica, was potentially deadly. Efforts culminated with the 1985 Vienna Convention for the Protection of the Ozone Layer, a framework convention that established an institutional structure (a Secretariat based in Nairobi) and the development of monitoring and data-gathering mechanisms.[96] The Convention is largely devoid of substantive obligations, exhorting parties to adopt measures that will control, limit, reduce, or prevent activities that may adversely modify the ozone layer.[97] However, its

[91] ECE Convention on Long-Range Transboundary Air Pollution (n 45).

[92] See the earlier 1974 OECD Recommendation on Transfrontier Pollution (adopted on 14 November 1974), OECD Doc OECD/LEGAL/0133, Title A, which referred more broadly to the 'environment' and not merely the 'air'.

[93] See further P Okowa, *State Responsibility for Transboundary Air Pollution in International Law* (OUP, 2000).

[94] Eight protocols setting monitoring programmes and specific targets for sulphur emissions, nitrogen oxides (and their transboundary fluxes), volatile organic compounds, persistent organic pollutants, heavy metals, and the abatement of acidification, eutrophication, and ground-level ozone have been agreed: see <https://unece.org/protocols>.

[95] ECE Convention (n 45) Arts 3–5.

[96] Vienna Convention for the Protection of the Ozone Layer (n 9) Arts 7, 11.

[97] *Ibid*, Art 2.

1987 Montreal Protocol contains precise targets for a phased reduction of CFCs and a freeze on the use of halons, with the eventual aim of halving emissions of these chemicals by 1998.[98]

Through a series of adjustments to the Convention and the addition of further protocols (such as the commitment in the 1989 Helsinki Declaration to eliminate CFCs by the year 2000), the ozone protection regime acknowledges the differentiated needs of developing and developed States; in particular, in relation to technology transfer and the provision of financial and technical incentives to encourage compliance.[99] The Montreal Protocol's innovative compliance mechanism is central in ensuring its success, setting ever more stringent targets and the constant revision of the list of controlled substances. In a rare triumph for international legal cooperation, it is even foreseen that the ozone layer may fully recover by the mid-twenty-first century,[100] though one unfortunate side effect of ozone protection has been the resort to substances, such as hydrofluorocarbons (HFCs), which contribute to irreversible climate change.

19.7.1.3 **Climate change and the regulation of greenhouse gases**

Climate change has long been at the forefront of public debates over threats to the environment.[101] The General Assembly had resolved as early as 1988 that climate change was a 'common concern of mankind', requiring global collective action.[102] It also established the IPCC (see Section 19.5), to analyse available scientific data and control the emission of 'greenhouse gases', which are progressively warming the Earth's atmosphere. The UNFCCC was the outcome of the 1992 Rio Summit, with its Article 2 outlining its purpose as the stabilization of greenhouse gases to minimize anthropogenic (caused by human activity) interference with the atmosphere. All States parties must:

- provide inventories of greenhouse gas sources and 'sinks' (a natural environment to absorb such gases);
- develop national or regional programmes to combat climate change;
- promote and cooperate the development and transfer of useful and relevant technologies for control;
- account for climate change considerations when formulating relevant social, economic, or environmental policies; and
- promote scientific research and education.[103]

[98] Montreal Protocol (n 41) Arts 2, 3.

[99] See, in particular, the 1992 Copenhagen Amendment, reprinted in (1993) 32 ILM 874. Further amendments (Montreal, 1997; Beijing, 1999; Montreal, 2007; Kigali, 2016) have strengthened the scope and specificity of the ozone protection regime: see <http://ozone.unep.org/new_site/en/montreal_protocol.php>.

[100] See O Yoshida, *The International Legal Regime for the Protection of the Stratospheric Ozone Layer* (Kluwer, 2001).

[101] See generally L Godden, 'Death, Desire, Modernity and Redemption: Climate Change and Public International Law' (2009) 10 Melbourne JIL 543; and B Mayer, *International Law Obligations on Climate Change Mitigation* (OUP, 2022).

[102] See UNGA Res 43/53 (6 December 1988); see also UNGA Res 44/207 (22 December 1989); and the 1989 Hague Declaration on the Environment (signed 11 March 1989), (1989) 28 ILM 1308.

[103] UNFCCC (n 33) Art 4(1).

There is a measure of differentiated responsibility, with developed States bound to be 'taking the lead' in modifying long-term trends of anthropogenic emissions.[104] Annex I States (see Section 19.3.1) are to provide new and additional financial resources necessary to enable developing States to meet their obligations under the Convention.[105] Such financial resources are administered by the Global Environmental Facility (GEF), a financial mechanism under the joint administration of the World Bank, UNEP, and the United Nations Development Programme.[106]

Specific emissions targets were agreed as part of the 1997 Kyoto Protocol, in which Annex I States committed themselves to legally binding and specific emissions targets and timetables for the reduction of chief greenhouse gases to 5 per cent below their emissions in 1990.[107] If a State can develop schemes, such as the regeneration of forests, which have the effect of removing greenhouse gases (in other words, 'carbon sinks'), such schemes may be used to offset its emissions targets.[108] When Russia ratified the Protocol in 2004, the threshold of fifty-five Annex I States, representing 55 per cent of overall carbon dioxide emissions within that group of States, was reached.

The Kyoto Protocol failed to meet its original goals, though it has prompted a flurry of policy, legal, scientific, technical, and infrastructure activity aimed at reducing greenhouse gas emissions. Nevertheless, very few States have met their emissions targets; Canada withdrew from the Protocol in 2014,[109] and the USA and China, the world's two biggest emitters of greenhouse gases, never became parties. A non-binding accord signed in Copenhagen in 2009, reaffirming States' commitment to the targets in the Protocol, achieved little.[110]

CONTEMPORARY DEVELOPMENTS The Climate Change Emergency and the Paris Agreement

At the twenty-first COP in late 2015, the Paris Agreement was announced, an ambitious further agreement under the UNFCCC which binds parties to a series of 'nationally determined contributions' which will intensify over time. These contributions have the purpose of limiting the increase of the global average temperature to 'well below 2°C' above pre-industrial levels. It has 195 signatories, including the European Union.

The Paris Agreement came into force on 4 November 2016, when fifty-five parties accounting for an estimated 55 per cent of the total emissions had ratified. As of late 2021, it has 192 ratifications (and 195 signatories), despite the June 2017 Declaration by then-US President Trump that the USA would withdraw. Under Article 28 of the Paris Agreement, a party cannot give notice of withdrawal within the first three years of its start date in that country (for the USA: 4 November 2016), so a four-year notice was effectively required. Consequently, the

[104] *Ibid*, Art 4(2). [105] *Ibid*, Art 4(3).

[106] The GEF is also the financial mechanism under the Convention on Biological Diversity (n 34).

[107] See Kyoto Protocol (n 39) Art 3(1). [108] See *ibid*, Art 12.

[109] When Canada invoked Art 27 and withdrew from the Kyoto Protocol in 2014, it did not nullify the Protocol; see Note by the Secretariat of the Compliance Committee (20 August 2014), UN Doc CC/EB/25/2014/2.

[110] See Copenhagen Accord, UNFCCC Decision 2/CP.15 (18 December 2009), 4–9.

USA withdrawal only took effect on 4 November 2020, the day after the US presidential election where Joe Biden was elected. One of Biden's first acts was the signing of a letter formally rejoining the Paris Agreement, which took effect after a thirty-day wait.

The Paris Agreement represents a shift from differential treatment of developing States in favour of a more symmetrical approach, where States determine their own nationally determined contributions (NDCs), which are not legally binding. However, the Parties are legally bound under Article 13 to have their progress tracked by technical expert review to assess achievement towards the NDC, and to determine ways to strengthen ambition (e.g., through a 'ratcheting mechanism' that commits States to ever-stricter targets through periodic five-year reviews). There is, therefore, a degree of 'naming and shaming' involved.

The climate emergency is intensifying: though the 2021 Glasgow Pact agreed by the UNFCCC Conference of the Parties ('COP') reaffirmed a commitment to limiting global temperature increase to 1.5°C, alongside new commitments to fight climate change, various 'global stocktakes' published by the UN continue to project that global temperature increases to between 1.8°C and 2.4°C; far exceeding the 1.5°C threshold for catastrophic climate change. International courts are also beginning to frame the international law in the field, including an advisory opinion delivered by ITLOS in 2024 on the interaction between climate change and the obligation to protect the marine environment in UNCLOS (see Section 19.7.2).

19.7.2 **Protection of the marine environment**

Rather than being covered in a separate sector-specific convention, the marine environment is encompassed in Part XII of the 1982 UNCLOS, a comprehensive multilateral convention covering most matters relating to the law of the sea.[111] Within UNCLOS, there are general obligations to protect the marine environment (Article 194) and to reduce pollution from land-based sources (Article 207), as well as more specific obligations. UNCLOS is complemented by a range of more specific treaties relating to marine pollution, such as the 1972 London Dumping Convention,[112] the MARPOL Convention, as well as various regional treaties protecting defined maritime areas.[113] Finally, UNEP has adopted a 'Regional Seas Programme' covering sectors of the oceans and important seas such as the Red Sea and the Baltic Sea. These have developed 'action plans' as well as legally binding conventions.[114]

[111] The general regime concerning the law of the sea was addressed in Chapter 18.

[112] London Convention on the Prevention of Marine Pollution by the Dumping of Wastes and Other Matter (signed 29 December 1972, entered into force 30 August 1975), 1046 UNTS 138 ('London Dumping Convention').

[113] To give three examples, see 1992 'OSPAR' Convention for the Protection of the Marine Environment of the North-East Atlantic (signed 22 September 1992, entered into force 25 March 1998), 2345 UNTS 67 (OSPAR Convention); Convention for the Protection of the Mediterranean Sea against Pollution (signed 16 February 1976, entered into force 12 February 1978), 1102 UNTS 44, and accompanying Protocols of 1980 and 1982; and the Kuwait Regional Convention for Co-operation on the Protection of the Marine Environment from Pollution (signed 24 April 1978, entered into force 1 July 1979), 1140 UNTS 154 (Persian Gulf).

[114] See further J van Dyke, 'Whither the Regional Seas Programmes' in HN Scheiber and J-H Paik (eds), *Regions, Institutions, and the Law of the Sea* (Brill, 2013), 87.

19.7.2.1 The marine environment of the oceans and territorial seas

Under Article 211(2) UNCLOS, States have a general duty to legislate for the prevention, reduction, and control of pollution caused by vessels flying their flag. The MARPOL Convention sets out more specific international rules and standards relating to pollution by ships.[115] What is more, the jurisdiction of coastal States over pollution in their territorial waters allows them to inspect ships in their territorial waters, or even commence proceedings against their owners, provided clear grounds exist for believing that the ship concerned has violated domestic or international pollution regulations.[116] Article 218 UNCLOS is innovative: if a vessel is stationed in a State's port, legal proceedings may be initiated for pollution caused by that ship within that State's jurisdiction, but also for violations of international standards committed in the high seas.[117]

The prohibition on the dumping of polluting substances is based on a precautionary approach, evolved from maintaining a 'list' of specific prohibited substances. This evolution can be traced from a 1996 Protocol to the 1972 London Dumping Convention and new regional conventions such as the 1992 OSPAR Convention (covering the north-east Atlantic). Today dumping is generally banned, with only certain permitted exceptions such as dredged materials, sewage sludge, and fish-processing wastes.[118]

The 1969 Intervention Convention[119] extended the rights of coastal States in the high seas, in part because during the 1967 *Torrey Canyon* incident, the UK Royal Air Force bombed the tanker to set the remaining oil alight and prevent further environmental catastrophe. Similarly, after the 1989 *Exxon Valdez* incident demonstrated woeful lack of preparation in dealing with such emergencies, a 1990 Preparedness Convention was signed requiring the preparation of emergency response plans for oil spill incidents.[120] The 1969 Intervention Convention was extended in 1973 to apply to hazardous substances other than oil, and in 2000 a Protocol was added to the OPRC to cover hazardous and noxious substances.

Liability has also become an issue, with a 1969 Convention on Civil Liability imposing strict liability on shipowners up to a certain ceiling, and requiring them to maintain insurance.[121] Beyond that ceiling, an International Fund may pay additional

[115] MARPOL and its six technical annexes are amended frequently: see <http://www.imo.org> for the most up-to-date version of the text of the Convention.

[116] UNCLOS (n 45) Art 220 (2).

[117] RR Churchill and AV Lowe, *The Law of the Sea* (4th edn, Manchester UP, 2022), 350.

[118] See, in this respect, P Sands and J Peel, *Principles of International Environmental Law* (4th edn, CUP, 2018), 479–85.

[119] International Convention relating to Intervention on the High Seas in Cases of Oil Pollution Casualties (signed 29 November 1969, entered into force 6 May 1975), 970 UNTS 211.

[120] International Convention on Oil Pollution Preparedness, Response and Cooperation (signed 30 November 1990, entered into force 13 May 1995), 1891 UNTS 77.

[121] International Convention on Civil Liability for Oil Pollution Damage (signed 29 November 1969, entered into force 19 June 1975), 973 UNTS 3; and 1992 Protocol (signed 27 November 1992, entered into force 30 May 1996), 1956 UNTS 255.

compensation for oil pollution damage.[122] The Fund is underwritten by levies from oil-importing States, thus suggesting that they also assume a proportion of the risks in relation to the importing of petroleum. In 2003, a Supplementary Fund was created through a further protocol.[123]

CASE SPOTLIGHT The ITLOS Advisory Opinion on Climate Change and the Marine Environment, 2024

In 2024, ITLOS delivered its much-anticipated opinion (*Commission of Small Island States on Climate Change and International Law, Advisory Opinion of 21 May 2024,* ITLOS Case No 31) covering State obligations to protect and preserve the global oceans from climate change harms, including sea-level rise, ocean warming, and acidification. ITLOS's opinion may be the first of a wave, as advisory proceedings unfolding at the ICJ and the IACtHR will also address States' obligations to combat climate change.

The jurisdiction of ITLOS is based primarily in the 1982 UNCLOS, Part XII of which establishes a regime of obligations to protect and preserve the marine environment. The ITLOS opinion broadly interpreted marine pollution to include harmful greenhouse gas emissions (GHGs) as a specific pollutant (para 75), a significant clarification for the field. In so doing, ITLOS discarded the idea that the 2015 Paris Agreement might have superseded more general obligations to cut harmful GHG emissions, and instead situated UNCLOS as a separate treaty, but one that should be interpreted and clarified by reference to the external rules of the global climate regime (paras 277, 285).

ITLOS' integrative approach brought with it some key contributions: the conclusion that States' obligations to 'take all necessary measures' had been constrained by a range of objective factors, such as an obligation to refer to the 'best available science' to assess the necessary precautions to be taken (paras 208, 213). However, its most significant finding was that States had 'stringent' due diligence obligations in relation to climate change going well beyond 'best efforts' to regulate and reduce GHG-emitting activities (paras 238–43). Through these due diligence obligations, States were under a range of further positive obligations, including the obligation to adopt an EIA looking both at specified and cumulative impacts of GHG emissions. It is a landmark ruling that draws together a range of previously open questions, and though by reason of its limited jurisdiction and the scope of the question, ITLOS could not address more the entirety of international law with respect to climate change, it sets an important precedent that may well be followed in other international courts and tribunals, and was cited abundantly by States in their written and oral statements at the ICJ in the 2024 advisory proceedings on climate change.

[122] International Convention on the Establishment of an International Fund for Compensation for Oil Pollution Damage (signed 18 December 1971, entered into force 16 October 1978), 1110 UNTS 58 'Compensation Convention'; and 1992 Protocol (signed 27 November 1992, entered into force 30 May 1996), 1953 UNTS 330. See further Churchill and Lowe (n 109) 361–3.

[123] See the 2003 Protocol to amend the Compensation Convention (signed 16 May 2003, entered into force 3 March 2005), IMO Doc LEG/CONF.14/20.

19.7.2.2 **International watercourses**

Brief mention must also be made of 'international watercourses', or those systems of surface waters and ground waters, usually composed of lakes, streams, and rivers, which are situated in more than one State. As illustrated in the *Lac Lanoux, Gabčíkovo-Nagymaros*, and *Pulp Mills* cases, the key question is how to determine the extent of a system as a unified whole, and of how certain segments can be excluded from the system and thus escape international regulation. The primary global instrument is the 1997 Convention on the Law of the Non-Navigational Uses of International Watercourses, in which the principle of equitable and reasonable utilization of such watercourses was embodied, and extended also to the 'conservation, protection, development and economy of use of the water resources of the watercourse'.[124] States are to take all appropriate measures to prevent the causing of significant harm to other watercourse States, and before taking any such measures, must consult one another, exchange relevant data, and provide timely notification.[125] What is more, Article 20 contains a general obligation to protect and preserve the ecosystems of international watercourses, a prominent point in the *Gabčíkovo-Nagymaros* dispute, illustrating the environmental risks of major infrastructure projects on international watercourses.[126]

19.7.2.3 **Conservation of marine living resources**

The regulation of marine living resources is one of the older areas of international cooperation, primarily due to economic concerns about sustainable fishing and whaling which predated the protection of the environment. The early *Bering Fur Seals Arbitration* and the 1911 Washington Fur Seals Convention established the first rules on sustainable sealing.[127] The regulation of whaling came next, with the first agreement signed in 1937. The 1946 International Convention on the Regulation of Whaling (ICRW) followed, creating the International Whaling Commission (IWC), which is entrusted with controlling the conduct of whaling, the protection of endangered species, the designation of areas as sanctuaries, and the setting of quotas on permissible catches.[128] The ICRW creates a distinction between whaling for scientific purposes and commercial whaling. As the latter has been subject to a moratorium since 1985, the distinction between the two forms of whaling remains a matter of marked controversy.[129]

[124] United Nations Convention on the Law of the Non-Navigational Uses of International Watercourses (adopted 21 May 1997, entered into force 17 August 2014), 1936 UNTS 269, Art 5. See also *Gabčíkovo-Nagymaros* (n 24) 80. See also ILC, 'Draft Articles on the Law of Transboundary Aquifers', UN Doc A/63/10 (2008) GAOR 63rd Session Supp 10, which would cover the layers (rock, sand, gravel, or silt) from which groundwater can be extracted.

[125] Watercourses Convention, *ibid*, Arts 7–12.

[126] *Gabčíkovo-Nagymaros* (n 24) 68.

[127] See earlier, Section 19.2.1. See also the Convention on the Conservation of Antarctic Seals (signed 1 June 1972, entered into force 11 March 1978), 1080 UNTS 175.

[128] International Convention for the Regulation of Whaling (signed 2 December 1946, entered into force 10 November 1948), 161 UNTS 72.

[129] The most noteworthy example is Australia's success against Japan in *Whaling in the Antarctic (Australia v Japan; New Zealand intervening), Judgment, ICJ Reports 2014*, p 226. But note that Norway has objected to the moratorium and is not bound by it, and Iceland even left the IWC between 1992 and 2002: see U Beyerlin and T Marauhm, *International Environmental Law* (Hart, 2011), 139.

In relation to fisheries, the 1995 Straddling Fish Stocks Agreement (SSA) addresses fish stocks which are highly migratory or which straddle the zones of coastal States and the high seas. Article 5 enumerates a series of general principles such as the maintenance of the sustainability of fish stocks, respect for the precautionary approach in relation to scientific evidence, and the adoption of conservation and management measures by parties to minimize pollution, protect biodiversity, and prevent overfishing.

The 1995 SSA also encourages States to participate in regional fisheries convention regimes, such as the North Atlantic Fisheries Convention[130] and the Convention on the Regulation of Antarctic Marine Resources.[131] The approach in these fisheries conventions is usually to establish fixed quotas of total allowable catches for particular stocks, to regulate fishing methods (e.g., the use of a specific mesh size for trawl nets), and to require monitoring and reporting obligations to be observed. Certain species of fish that are particularly lucrative or endangered are also the subject of species-specific conventions: see, for example, the regime governing highly migratory tuna stocks.[132] Finally, of course, the recently adopted Agreement on Biodiversity beyond National Jurisdiction ('BBNJ') will be highly relevant when it enters into force: see above, Section 18.3.7.3.2.

19.7.3 **Ultra-hazardous substances**

A recent focus has been on 'ultra-hazardous substances' that present a significant or exceptional risk of severe environmental damage.[133] Treaties that regulate ultra-hazardous substances are striking in that, rather than adopting the more common principle of due diligence, they create a regime of *strict liability*, where responsibility is engaged irrespective of fault. In so doing, the burden of proof has been shifted from the victim to the State on whose territory or jurisdiction the activity has taken place. Strict liability regimes are an unusual feature in multilateral conventions: outside the realm of ultra-hazardous substances, only the 1972 Space Liability Convention also adopts that type of regime.[134]

19.7.3.1 **Nuclear materials and activities**

The long-term and total environmental devastation wrought by a nuclear accident is a prime example of the need to regulate ultra-hazardous substances. As early as 1963, the Nuclear Weapons Test Ban Treaty[135] sought to prohibit atmospheric nuclear testing,

[130] International Convention for the Northwest Atlantic Fisheries (signed 8 February 1949, entered into force 3 July 1950), 157 UNTS 157.

[131] Convention on the Conservation of Antarctic Marine Living Resources (signed 20 May 1980, entered into force 7 April 1982), 1329 UNTS 47.

[132] Washington Convention for the Establishment of an Inter-American Tropical Tuna Commission (signed 30 May 1949, entered into force 3 March 1950), 80 UNTS 3.

[133] See G Handl, 'State Liability for Accidental Transnational Environmental Damage by Private Persons' (1980) 74 AJIL 525, 554; LF Goldie, 'Concepts of Strict and Absolute Liability and the Ranking of Liability in Terms of Relative Exposure to Risk' (1985) 16 Netherlands YIL 247; RJ Dupuy, *La responsabilité des États pour les dommages d'origine technologique et industrielle* (Pedone, 1976), esp 206–9.

[134] See Convention on International Liability for Damage Caused by Space Objects (signed 29 March 1972, entered into force 1 September 1972), 961 UNTS 187.

[135] Treaty Banning Nuclear Weapons Tests in the Atmosphere, Outer Space and Under Water (signed 5 August 1963, entered into force 10 October 1963), 480 UNTS 43.

leading to memorable cases filed in the ICJ by Australia and New Zealand against France, which had not become a party to the Treaty.[136] Moreover, the dumping of nuclear waste in the oceans is almost certainly a violation of the obligation to protect the marine environment from pollution.[137] Finally, there are treaties prohibiting either nuclear weapons or nuclear waste regionally, in Latin America,[138] the South Pacific,[139] and the Antarctic.[140]

On the civilian side, the principal UN agency concerned with nuclear safety is the International Atomic Energy Agency (IAEA), established in 1957 to facilitate the peaceful development of nuclear energy and adherence to non-proliferation safeguards. Under the auspices of the IAEA, a strict (or absolute) liability regime emerged under what is now the 1963 Vienna Convention on Civil Liability for Nuclear Damage, which was later amended in 1997.[141]

Following the Chernobyl incident in 1986, the IAEA facilitated the adoption conventions on early notification[142] and assistance,[143] to enhance international cooperation and the taking of preventive measures. These were followed by the 1994 Convention on Nuclear Safety,[144] which sets certain safety standards in relation to the safe operation of land-based nuclear power plants and other nuclear installations.[145]

CONTEMPORARY DEVELOPMENTS The 2015 Vienna Declaration on Nuclear Safety (UN Doc CNS/DC/2015/2/Rev.1)

The most recent development in respect of nuclear safety was the adoption of the 2015 Vienna Declaration on Nuclear Safety; it is a good illustration of how international environmental law develops as a response to specific incidents, and how it is in some respects constrained by a wide range of further considerations.

[136] *Nuclear Tests (Australia v France; New Zealand v France), Jurisdiction and Admissibility, Judgment, ICJ Reports 1974*, p 253.

[137] See the London Dumping Convention (n 104) Art IV (1), OSPAR Convention (n 105) Art 3, Annex II, and UNCLOS (n 45) Art 192. See also Treaty on the Prohibition of the Emplacement of Nuclear Weapons and other Weapons of Mass Destruction on the Sea-Bed and the Ocean Floor and in the Subsoil Thereof (signed 11 February 1971, entered into force 18 May 1972), 955 UNTS 115.

[138] Treaty for the Prohibition of Nuclear Weapons in Latin America (signed 14 February 1967, entered into force 22 April 1968), 634 UNTS 325.

[139] South Pacific Nuclear Free Zone Treaty (signed 6 August 1985, entered into force 11 December 1986), 1445 UNTS 177.

[140] Art 5 of the Antarctic Treaty (signed 1 December 1959, entry into force 23 June 1961), 402 UNTS 71, also designates Antarctica as the first 'nuclear waste free zone'.

[141] Vienna Convention on Civil Liability for Nuclear Damage (signed 21 May 1963, entered into force 12 November 1977), 1063 UNTS 265; and 1997 Protocol (signed 12 September 1997, entered into force 4 October 2003), 2241 UNTS 270. See also the strict liability regime on nuclear installation operations in the OECD Paris Convention on Nuclear Third Party Liability (signed 29 July 1960, entered into force 1 April 1968), 1519 UNTS 329. A 2004 Protocol amending the Convention entered into force on 1 January 2022.

[142] Convention on Early Notification of a Nuclear Accident (signed 26 September 1986, entered into force 27 October 1986), 1439 UNTS 275.

[143] Convention on Assistance in the Case of a Nuclear Accident or Radiological Emergency (signed 26 September 1986, entered into force 26 February 1987), 1457 UNTS 133.

[144] Convention on Nuclear Safety (signed 20 September 1994, entered into force 24 October 1996), 1963 UNTS 293.

[145] *Ibid*, Arts 10–19; see also the Joint Convention on the Safety of Spent Fuel Management and on the safety of Radioactive Waste Management (signed 5 September 1997, entered into force 18 June 2001), 2153 UNTS 303.

The Vienna Declaration, the outcome of a major diplomatic conference held in February 2015, was a response to a near-meltdown in Fukushima-Daiichi in Japan in 2014. The Declaration seeks to entrench principles of good practice and reporting so as to avoid future incidents, calling upon States to implement their obligations under the 1994 Convention.

A key point to retain is that the Declaration did not amend the 1994 Convention, despite a Swiss proposal which would have amended Article 18 to: (i) require that nuclear power plants be designed and constructed with the objectives of preventing accidents; and (ii) should an accident occur, mitigating its effects and avoiding releases of radionuclides causing long-term off-site contamination. Despite a degree of support, the amendment was not supported by several key States parties, led by the USA, which objected on the basis that existing nuclear power plants would have to be shut down because equipping them with the requisite features would be prohibitively expensive.

As the Convention requires that two-thirds of States parties must ratify an amendment for it to enter into force, the non-binding Vienna Declaration was adopted instead.

19.7.3.2 **Other hazardous substances and activities**

Outside the nuclear sector, several instruments regulate the management of other highly toxic and hazardous wastes, especially in relation to the hugely problematic practice of dumping such substances in the developing world. Both the London Dumping Convention and the OSPAR Convention prohibit dumping in the seas, but it was the 1989 Basel Convention[146] which first addressed the problem of dumping on land. The Basel Convention operates through a number of principles. First, a State has the right to prohibit the importation of certain hazardous wastes, and such a prohibition must be respected by other States parties.[147] Secondly, the prior written consent of a State is required before the transboundary movement of hazardous wastes into its territory.[148] Thirdly, trade with non-parties is prohibited.[149] The Basel Convention includes financial mechanisms for encouraging compliance by developing States, in the form of a Trust Fund and a Technical Cooperation Fund, and a focus on introducing better environmental practices and sound management to eliminate waste generation at its source.[150] In Africa, the regional Bamako Convention bans the import of all hazardous wastes into Africa, for any reason, by non-parties.[151]

In 1992, the Convention on the Transboundary Effects of Industrial Accidents imposed obligations of notification and consultation in case of an accident which might

[146] Basel Convention on the Control of Transboundary Movements of Hazardous Wastes and their Disposal (signed 22 March 1989, entered into force 5 May 1992), 1673 UNTS 57.

[147] *Ibid*, Art 4. [148] *Ibid*, Art 6.

[149] *Ibid*, Art 4, under which OECD members are prohibited from exporting hazardous wastes to non-OECD members.

[150] For a comprehensive analysis of the Basel Convention, see K Kummer, *International Management of Hazardous Wastes* (OUP, 2000).

[151] Bamako Convention on the Ban of the Import into Africa and the Control of Transboundary Movement and Management of Hazardous Wastes within Africa (signed 30 January 1991, entered into force 22 April 1998), 2101 UNTS 177.

have transboundary effects, and binds States to take a number of preventive measures and policies.[152] There also exist conventions in relation to 'Persistent Organic Pollutants' (POP), organic in nature but highly resistant to biodegradation. The 2001 Stockholm Convention[153] imposes strict obligations in relation to a growing list of POPs (having started with a dozen, other substances are regularly added at COPs), requiring States to eliminate and reduce the release of POPs into the environment, to manage and reduce stockpiles, and to minimize and eliminate unintentionally produced POPs. At Article 1, the Stockholm Convention explicitly adopts a precautionary approach.

Genetically modified organisms are regulated in the 2000 Cartagena Protocol on Biosafety.[154] The Cartagena Protocol applies to 'living modified organisms' (LMOs) which possess a 'novel combination of genetic material obtained through the use of modern biotechnology' and seeks to limit the unwanted release into the environment of LMOs through an 'advanced informed agreement' procedure, through which contracting parties are entitled to receive all relevant information necessary to make informed decisions on the import of LMOs into their territory. The Cartagena Protocol takes an explicitly precautionary approach in Article 1. To facilitate information exchange and to encourage national implementation, several additional institutions have been created, including a Compliance Committee, a 'Biosafety Clearing-House', and financing available through the GEF (see Section 19.7.1.3). The Cartagena Protocol has been strengthened by the Nagoya–Kuala Lumpur Supplementary Protocol, which imposes certain obligations on States to adopt or maintain legislation on civil liability and redress in municipal courts.[155]

19.7.4 **Conservation of nature**

The preservation of the environment involves not merely minimizing the human impact thereupon, but also conserving the natural ecosystems and, in particular, specific species. Thus, in addition to the many treaties and conventions which regulate the various forms in which the environment can be polluted, several treaty regimes exist which are also concerned with species and habitat protection. Though many of these are species-specific[156] or region-specific,[157] there are nevertheless five broad, multilateral species and habitat regimes meriting brief attention.

[152] Convention on the Transboundary Effects of Industrial Accidents (signed 17 March 1992, entered into force 19 April 2000), 2105 UNTS 457, Art 4.

[153] Stockholm Convention on Persistent Organic Pollutants (signed 22 May 2001, entered into force 17 May 2004), 2256 UNTS 119.

[154] Cartagena Protocol on Biosafety to the Convention on Biological Diversity (signed 29 January 2000, entered into force 11 September 2003), 2226 UNTS 208.

[155] Nagoya–Kuala Lumpur Supplementary Protocol on Liability and Redress to the Cartagena Protocol on Biosafety (signed 15 October 2010, entered into force 5 March 2018), UN Reg A-30619.

[156] See, e.g., Agreement on the Conservation of Polar Bears (signed 15 November 1973, entered into force 26 May 1976), (1974) 13 ILM 13.

[157] See the Convention on the Conservation of European Wildlife and Natural Habitats (signed 19 September 1979, entered into force 1 June 1982), 1284 UNTS 209; Protocol on Environmental Protection to the Antarctic Treaty (n 57). See also C Redgwell, 'Environmental Protection in Antarctica: The 1991 Protocol' (1994) 43 ICLQ 599; and DR Rothwell, 'International Law and the Protection of the Arctic Environment' (1995) 44 ICLQ 280.

19.7.4.1 **Wetlands of international importance**

The earliest multilateral convention dedicated to the conservation and use of a particular ecosystem was the 1971 Ramsar Convention,[158] which seeks to ensure the preservation of wetlands as a habitat for bird and fish species. The Ramsar Convention operates through the designation of a 'List of Wetlands of International Importance' (there are about 1,900) by States parties and then afforded protection under local law.[159] If a designated wetland is regarded as threatened, it can be listed on the 'Montreux Record of Ramsar sites requiring priority attention' with the consent of the State concerned.[160] As with many other environmental treaties, the Ramsar Convention provides for the dissemination of technical knowledge and technology transfer, including the Ramsar Advisory Mission which can advise States as to why a wetland may be under threat. Further, a 'Small Grants Fund for Wetland Conservation and Wise Use' has also been established for States that may lack the necessary resources for effective conservation.

19.7.4.2 **World cultural and natural heritage**

The principal objectives of the 1972 UNESCO World Heritage Convention (WHC) are the identification, protection, conservation, presentation, and transmission to future generations of the cultural and natural heritage on Earth.[161] Unusually, the WHC encompasses both the natural environment as well as cultural heritage, drawing explicit links between them. Similar to the Ramsar Convention, the WHC maintains a World Heritage List. States parties may nominate sites on their territory which they consider to possess special natural and cultural heritage, which are then inspected by the International Council for Monuments and Sites (for cultural properties) and the World Conservation Union (for natural properties). If they are deemed to meet the criteria for inscription, such sites are then designated as World Heritage Sites,[162] and become subject to regular national implementation reports, as it is the State of designation which is responsible for taking the measures necessary to ensure preservation and conservation of the site.

Though there are few coercive mechanisms, a threatened site can be placed on the 'List of World Heritage in Danger', drawing attention to the fact that major operations or assistance are necessary to conserve the site. Funding is available through the World Heritage Fund, a trust fund constituted by compulsory and voluntary contributions of

[158] Ramsar Convention on Wetlands of International Importance (n 45).

[159] For further detail, see M Bowman, P Davies, and C Redgwell, *Lyster's International Wildlife Law* (2nd edn, CUP, 2010), ch 13.

[160] Though the ultimate sanction is deletion of a wetland site from the list, this has never occurred.

[161] Convention for the Protection of the World Cultural and Natural Heritage (signed 16 November 1972, entered into force 17 December 1975), 1037 UNTS 151.

[162] UNESCO maintains a series of Operational Guidelines for Implementation which set out the criteria for designation, and was last updated in 2019: see <http://whc.unesco.org/en/guidelines/>. At the time of going press, there were some 897 cultural, 218 natural, and 39 mixed sites in 167 States parties. There are fifty-two sites listed as being in danger; for the most up-to-date figures, see: <http://whc.unesco.org/en/list>.

States parties, to facilitate compliance for developing States. The ultimate sanction is deletion from the World Heritage List, which has thrice occurred.[163]

19.7.4.3 **International trade in endangered species**

Rather than focusing purely on conservation or preservation efforts, the Convention on International Trade in Endangered Species is unusual in that it targets the very trading activity that often causes the exploitation and, eventually, extinction of endangered species.[164]

Parties designate a national 'Management Authority' and 'Scientific Authority' to implement obligations under CITES, which may seek assistance from the CITES Secretariat. When trade is not prohibited, CITES creates a licensing system of import and export permits of listed species, or products derived from them, issued by national authorities.

There are more than 5,000 animal species and 25,000 plant species classified in various appendices. Most endangered species are listed under Appendix I, and there is an outright prohibition on trade in such species, save a few limited exceptions. Threatened species are found under Appendix II: trade in such species is restricted but not prohibited; instead, States parties must impose export and re-export (but not import) permits on their trade. Finally, a State may seek international cooperation and place species under Appendix III, which requires export permits, and encourages importing States to give assistance to the concerned State.

Though the listing of a species is meant to be based on biological evidence, it can be politically controversial. For example, the African elephant first appeared in Appendix I, but as elephant populations in Botswana, Namibia, South Africa, and Zimbabwe grew, in part due to local community development efforts to engage in conservation efforts, these were placed on Appendix II, thus relaxing restrictions and permitting one-off sales of existing ivory stocks in 1997 and again in 2007.[165]

19.7.4.4 **Migratory species**

The Bonn Convention[166] aims, literally, at a moving target: the migratory species which often cross borders, and for which protection necessarily requires international cooperation. It is a framework convention in that it sets out two primary mechanisms of protection. First, both land-based and marine migratory species are covered through a series of obligations on 'Range States' (the States falling within the migratory range of a particular species) to restore and preserve the habitats of such species and to prohibit their exploitation under national law.[167] Secondly, Range States are encouraged to

[163] The Arabian Oryx Sanctuary in Oman was deleted in 2007, as was the Dresden Elbe Valley in Germany in 2009. In September 2021, Liverpool's waterfront and docklands lost World Heritage status not due to environmental concerns, but rather due to large-scale infrastructure projects that led to a 'serious deterioration' of the historic site.

[164] Convention on International Trade in Endangered Species of Wild Fauna and Flora (signed 3 March 1973, entered into force 1 July 1975), 993 UNTS 243 (CITES).

[165] See further Bowman, Davies, and Redgwell (n 151) ch 15.

[166] Bonn Convention on the Conservation of Migratory Species of Wild Animals (signed 23 June 1979, entered into force 1 November 1983), 1651 UNTS 115.

[167] *Ibid*, Art III.

conclude conservation agreements with each other for species with unfavourable prospects, for which a list is maintained in Appendix II to the Bonn Convention. Though the implementation of the Bonn Convention has not been as successful as other conservation conventions, partly due to underfunding, it has achieved some modest successes, and work is underway to harmonize the Bonn Convention with CITES and the CBD so as to improve the effectiveness of all three regimes.[168]

19.7.4.5 **Biological diversity**

By far the best-known multilateral convention on conservation, the CBD,[169] is a global framework convention which seeks to address the issue of 'biodiversity', defined in Article 2 as 'the variability among living organisms from all sources including, *inter alia*, terrestrial, marine and other aquatic ecosystems and the ecological complexes of which they are part; this includes diversity within species, between species, and of ecosystems'. Signed immediately after the 1992 Rio Conference, the CBD sought to create a holistic framework which was not species- or habitat-specific. It embedded a balance between its aims, which are the:

- conservation of biodiversity;
- sustainable use of biological resources;
- fair and equitable sharing of the benefits arising out of the use of genetic resources; and
- transfer of relevant technologies between States.[170]

The CBD has universal support, with 196 parties including the European Union, although this may be in part because its framework nature means that there are relatively few substantive obligations required of parties. Only the USA remains outside the CBD regime, allegedly due to concerns that it would have to amend domestic legislation regarding intellectual property, and engage in technology transfer regimes with other parties.[171]

A framework convention, the CBD exemplifies many of the features associated with environmental agreements; in particular, aiming at encouraging compliance by developing States through the use of the GEF funding mechanism available to other environmental agreements (see Section 19.7.1.3); the differentiation of implementation obligations according to national capabilities; and a framework for national regulation of access to biological resources (called 'bioprospecting'). National authorities can themselves develop the required measures for implementing their obligations, subject again to regular reporting to the COP. Interestingly, the CBD Secretariat cooperates closely with the Ramsar and WHC Secretariats through a series of memoranda of understanding, though it does not employ their practice of maintaining lists of protected sites. As discussed earlier, the 2000 Cartagena Protocol to the CBD addressed the transboundary movement of genetically modified organisms. The BBNJ, although concluded as an implementing agreement under UNCLOS, will also have important synergies with provisions under the CBD.

[168] See Bowman, Davies, and Redgwell (n 151) ch 16 for further discussion of the Bonn Convention.
[169] See CBD (n 34). [170] *Ibid*, Art 1. [171] See Bowman, Davies, and Redgwell (n 151) ch 17.

Ultimately, though the CBD remains relatively hortatory in nature, it constitutes an important recognition of the value and importance of biodiversity for the survival of humankind, and also links the responsibility of States to their duties for conserving and utilizing their biological resources in a sustainable manner.

19.8 Conclusion

The abundance of environmental instruments canvassed in this chapter might seem to indicate deep international cooperation on the international plane but, in reality, it is perhaps more illustrative of a reactive, relatively ineffective approach. If the scientific consensus is anything to rely upon, the global environment faces existential threats from the intensity of human and industrial activity: concerted, effective action is becoming increasingly urgent. Yet, so much of the paradigm relating to international environmental protection remains based on an archetype of claiming natural resources as part of one's sovereignty, the 'global commons'—already a loaded concept[172]—being reduced to that which is not already claimed by a State, and a tension between economic development and conservation, with the latter often being overlooked in favour of capital and growth. If the conservation of nature is regarded as being of no further value than to preserve resources for use by human beings, this trend will continue.

Not all is bleak: through the wide range of regulatory mechanisms available, certain norms and guiding principles such as the precautionary approach may yet assume far greater relevance as humankind begins to assume its responsibilities for stewarding the planet. Perhaps the redeeming feature of international environmental law is that, despite the cacophony of different treaties and institutions, a laboratory for experimentation exists to test different legal regimes, and there has been a surprising amount of legal innovation.

Further reading

E Benvenisti, *Sharing Transboundary Resources* (CUP, 2002).

A refreshing, multidisciplinary approach to the management of transboundary resources, exploring the root causes for present difficulties.

U Beyerlin and T Marauhn, *International Environmental Law* (Hart, 2011).

This concise volume takes a problem-solving perspective, with a comprehensive review of relevant topics, as well as options for improved cooperation.

[172] On the concept of 'global commons', see J Brunnée, 'Common Areas, Common Heritage, and Common Concern' in D Bodansky, J Brunnée, and E Hey (eds), *The Oxford Handbook of International Environmental Law* (OUP, 2007), 552. For a critical history of the 'tragedy of the commons' and the 'common heritage of mankind' as concepts, addressing the political and epistemological motivations of the 'integrative' approach that gave rise to them, see S Ranganathan, 'Global Commons' (2016) 27 EJIL 693.

P Birnie, A Boyle, and C Redgwell, *International Law and the Environment* (3rd edn, OUP, 2009).

Though in need of an update, a classic resource on international environmental law, with comprehensive coverage encompassing a wide range of topics.

D Bodansky, J Brunnée, and L Rajamani, *International Climate Change Law* (OUP, 2017).

An accessible but overarching survey of international climate change law across various specialized regimes of international law.

J Brunnée, 'Coping with Consent: Law-Making under Multilateral Environmental Agreements' (2002) 15 Leiden JIL 1.

An important conceptual article on the multilateral treaty's influence on customary law.

C Carlane, KR Gray, and RG Tarasofsky (eds), *The Oxford Handbook on International Climate Change Law* (OUP, 2016).

An impressive compendium covering the major themes of this pressing international concern.

M Fitzmaurice, 'International Protection of the Environment' (2001) 293 Recueil des Cours 13.

A concise survey of the topic, with case studies covering the ozone layer and international watercourses.

B Mayer, *International Law Obligations on Climate Change Mitigation* (OUP, 2022).

Measured, carefully doctrinal, and clear, this book lays out a very useful framework to understand the foundations of the current legal regime.

U Natarajan and J Dehm (eds), *Locating Nature: Making and Unmaking International Law* (CUP, 2022).

An inter-disciplinary, critical intervention that seeks to reconstruct the interaction between international law and the concept of nature.

P Okowa, *State Responsibility for Transboundary Air Pollution in International Law* (OUP, 2000).

The definitive study on the difficulties in applying international law to transboundary phenomena.

L Rajamani, *Differential Treatment in International Environmental Law* (OUP, 2006).

An inspired and highly original work on the difficulties of imposing differential obligations.

L Rajamani and J Peel, *The Oxford Handbook of International Environmental Law* (2nd edn, OUP, 2021).

Tremendously informative, this updated compendium gathers a range of distinguished experts and new voices in the field.

R Romi, *Droit international et européen de l'environnement* (3rd edn, Pedone, 2017).

A leading French-language textbook on international and European environmental law.

P Sands and J Peel, *Principles of International Environmental Law* (4th edn, CUP, 2018).

Newly updated, this very readable textbook provides a comprehensive treatment of the governing principles and a wide coverage of specific treaty regimes.

20

International economic law

20.1 Introduction: the modern global economy

Though there are economic implications in virtually every aspect of public international law, when discussing 'international economic law' one is addressing the international regimes that regulate international trade, investment, and economic development. The multilateral and bilateral treaties in these areas have become the focal point for the global economy today. International economic law developed rapidly since the end of World War II, when the 1944 Bretton Woods Accords established the International Monetary Fund (IMF) and the International Bank for Reconstruction and Development (the World Bank), placing financial institutions at the heart of the post-war settlement.[1] The law on international trade grew around the General Agreement on Trade and Tariffs (GATT), but today centres around the World Trade Organization (WTO) in Geneva. International investment law has no equivalent overarching institution, but rather exists as a dense web of bilateral investment treaties (BITs) which have emerged in the last three decades.

One should not view international economic law as a neutral framework, merely promoting economic interdependence and globalization. The international economic system that exists today is an outgrowth of the colonial exploitation by Europe of the non-European world, an enduring phenomenon which only came to a definitive end in the 1960s. Even today, if one excludes the European settler colonies established in North America and Oceania, and the occasional non-European State which has achieved development (e.g., Japan, South Korea, Singapore), the effects of colonialism are lasting.[2] There is a strong distinction between States that were able to industrialize and compete for global capital, and States reduced to a source of raw materials for extraction and export, with a low level of capital accumulation.[3] Though defenders of

[1] For the history of these institutions, see R Gardner, *Sterling-Dollar Diplomacy in Current Perspective: The Origins and the Prospects of our International Economic Order* (Columbia UP, 1980).

[2] See the United Nations Human Development Index: <http://hdr.undp.org/en/composite/HDI>. In the latest 2025 statistical update, only Hong Kong and Singapore joined eight Western States; in the top thirty, they are joined only by South Korea, the United Arab Emirates, Japan, and Israel.

[3] See, in particular, A Anghie, *Imperialism, Sovereignty and the Making of International Law* (CUP, 2005); S Beckert, *Empires of Cotton: A New History of Global Capitalism* (Penguin, 2014); and K Pomeranz, *The Great Divergence: China, Europe, and the Making of the Modern World Economy* (Princeton UP, 2000).

the colonial project might point towards improved health systems, railroads, and even the form of government of these decolonized States as evidence of the beneficial effects of colonialism, most compelling evidence suggests that Western economic domination did not promote a self-standing development process involving all sectors of the economy.[4]

As decolonization proceeded and more new States began to enter the international system from the 1950s onwards, at first they insisted on financial and technical assistance in order to achieve greater economic development. By the late 1960s, when two-thirds of the General Assembly was composed of newly independent States, they began to make further demands to rebalance the international economic system to mitigate the disadvantages under which they operated. Though they could not impose new legal rules through the General Assembly, developing States took advantage of their majority there to adopt general declarations, upon which hope was pinned that these might later crystallize into customary rules or into new treaties.

These were centred upon the General Assembly's 1974 Declaration on the New International Economic Order (NIEO),[5] discussed in the accompanying commentary. It would be followed by the 1986 Declaration on the Right to Development, which proclaimed the inalienable nature of the human right to development, and the need for national and international cooperation in order to bring about its full realization.[6]

HISTORICAL BACKGROUND The 'New International Economic Order' (NIEO)

For developing States, NIEO was seen as a means of rebalancing past economic disparities by reclaiming economic sovereignty and development. What was then called the 'Third World' of developing States used NIEO to challenge the hierarchy between states as it had arisen from colonialism, calling for the restructuring of the global legal and economic order. As Algerian jurist Mohammed Bedjaoui—who would later be elected President of the ICJ—wrote at the time, international law could be redeemed by moving away from a fixation on legal rules and engaging more closely with correcting the social injustices caused by law (see M Bedjaoui, *Towards a New International Economic Order* (UNESCO/Holmes & Meier, 1979)).

Alongside this restructuring, NIEO contained demands for full and effective participation in international economic lawmaking for developing States, (operative clause 4.c.), permanent sovereignty over natural resources (operative clause 4.e.), the regulation and supervision of transnational corporations operating in developing States (operative clause 4.g.), a more just and equitable relationship between the prices of raw materials and commodities and finished products (operative clause 4.j.), and the transfer of technology, intellectual property, and other fruits of science to aid in development (operative clause 4.p.).

[4] See S Pahuja, *Decolonising International Law: Development, Economic Growth and the Politics of Universality* (CUP, 2011). For a slightly more optimistic perspective, see the contributions in S McInerney-Lankford and R McCorquodale (eds), *The Roles of International Law in Development* (OUP, 2024).

[5] UNGA Res 3201 (S-VI) (1 May 1974), accompanied by a Programme of Action for its implementation: see UNGA Res 3202 (S-VI) (1 May 1974); and the Charter of Economic Rights and Duties of States, UNGA Res 3281 (XXIX) (12 December 1974).

[6] UNGA Res 41/128 (4 December 1986).

NIEO and associated efforts were striking in that it was not a radical restructuring project for international law. By and large, developing States were using the language of sovereignty, consent, and 'States' rights' to assert their claims for international economic justice; they were not asking for a restructuring of the capitalist basis of the international economic system, unlike, for example, efforts led by the Soviet Union for a 'socialist international law'. During the 1990s, with the emergence of the WTO, NIEO seems to have faded away as developing States have sought greater access to the existing international economic order. Leading developing States such as Brazil, Indonesia, Mexico, and especially China were co-opted into the global economic system; and it must be said that the relationship between developing States has often been competitive or exploitative rather than mutually supportive.

For further reading, see M Fakhri, *Sugar and the Making of International Trade Law* (CUP, 2014); A Anghie, 'Legacies of the New International Economic Order' (2015) 6 *Humanity: An International Journal* 145; and ME Salomon, 'From NIEO to Now and the Unfinishable Story of Economic Justice' (2013) 62 ICLQ 31.

For a number of reasons, these attempts at international economic reform ended in relative failure. Most of the post-war institutions have survived and even been strengthened, and there is still a notable gap in prosperity between developed and less-developed States. Recent economic history is key to understanding the tensions in the current international economic system, as well as the inner logic behind today's initiatives to foster development.

20.2 **International financial institutions**

The most enduring institutions in today's international economic system were established during the 1944 conference held in Bretton Woods (USA). The ensuing 'Bretton Woods Accords' aimed chiefly to avoid the monetary disruptions of the interwar period and to encourage international trade, but also enabled the USA and its principal allies to exert their overwhelming influence in the immediate post-war period and impose their free trade and free market philosophy.[7] These initiatives led to the creation of the IMF, to provide international monetary cooperation and exchange rate stability, and the World Bank, and which aimed to mobilize and collect money on the international capital market and lend it to States in need of foreign investment (at first, primarily European States devastated by the war). One aspect of the Bretton Woods Accords that never materialized was the proposed 'International Trade Organization'. Instead, the GATT system (see Section 20.3) prevailed until the 1994 Agreement to establish the WTO.

[7] See further, P Kugler, 'The Bretton Woods System: Design and Operation' in P Kugler, *Money in the Western Legal Tradition: Middle Ages to Bretton Woods* (OUP, 2016), 611; B Steil, *The Battle of Bretton Woods: John Maynard Keynes, Harry Dexter White, and the Making of a New World Order* (Princeton UP, 2013); and DD Bradlow, *The Law of International Financial Institutions* (OUP, 2023).

20.2.1 **The International Monetary Fund**

The IMF (or 'the Fund') was established by Articles of Agreement. Its purposes, laid out in Article I, include, *inter alia*:

- to ensure monetary and financial stability in international relations;
- to facilitate the development of international trade by ensuring the stability of foreign exchange and the establishment of a multilateral system of payments; and
- the alleviation of crises in the balance of payments between States.[8]

The Fund is structured differently from most international organizations covered in Chapter 6, and bears some resemblance to a private bank in terms of its shareholding structure. States that join the IMF are allocated a quota, calculated according to a complex formula based on their relative economic standing, and pay a 'capital subscription' in 'Special Drawing Rights' (SDRs), a sort of 'basket' of reserve currencies as determined by the IMF.[9] The SDR came into force to counterbalance the strength of the US dollar. At present, it is composed of the US dollar, the Japanese yen, the Euro, the British pound sterling, and (from 1 December 2015) the Chinese renmimbi.

The IMF's principal organs include the Board of Governors, a twenty-five-member Executive Board elected by States, and a managing director.[10] A system of weighted voting in the Board of Governors, as well as determining the composition of the Executive Board, ensures that the States holding the largest SDR quotas wield the greatest influence in decision-making matters. At present the USA, Japan, China, Germany, France, and the UK may appoint their own executive director to the Executive Board. Saudi Arabia is also permitted to appoint its own executive director. At present, Russia shares its Executive Director with Syria.

The IMF is endowed with a large fund that can be drawn upon to provide loans to States in difficulty and which are repaid in instalments. There are different kinds of loans, which have emerged over time in order to meet the needs of (primarily developing) States which have requested them. These include:

- Stand-By Arrangements, for purely short-term balance of payments issues;
- an Extended Fund Facility, for structural balance of payments issues which particularly afflict low-income States and 'heavily indebted poor countries' (HIPCs);
- a Supplemental Reserve Facility for very short-term financing caused by a sudden loss in market confidence; and
- the Extended Credit Facility (until 2010, known as the Poverty Reduction and Growth Facility), to provide 'concessional' lending (lending with very low interest and very long repayment terms) to low-income countries and HIPCs.[11]

[8] Articles of Agreement of the International Monetary Fund [IMF] (as amended), 2 UNTS 39, Art I.
[9] *Ibid*, Art XVIII 2(a). [10] *Ibid*, Art XII (1).
[11] For more detail on the IMF's structure, see S Schlemmer-Schulte, 'International Monetary Fund' in R Wolfrum et al (eds), *Max Planck Encyclopedia of Public International Law* (OUP, 2012), available online at <http://www.mpepil.com>.

IMF loans are conditional on a series of structural adjustments to their economies which States are obliged to undertake. At first, they were conditional on States adopting more restrictive fiscal and monetary policies. However, such loans have become conditional on far-reaching structural reforms, requiring changes such as tax reform, debt restructuring, banking reform, the privatization of utilities, and even the reduction of food subsidies. This far-reaching conditionality was infamously illustrated by IMF lending to Argentina from 1991 to 2001,[12] the 2010 bailout of Greece (in tandem with the European Commission and European Central Bank),[13] and the 1991 adjustment programme agreed by Zimbabwe.[14] These programmes have been criticized for removing important decisions from national democratic processes and for their ineffectiveness.[15]

For all this, the IMF has persisted in this approach, with only modest attempts to re-engage local actors (e.g., with Iceland in 2009, Barbados in 2018, and more recently, with Argentina),[16] even after the 2008 global financial crisis.

20.2.2 **The World Bank Group**

The International Bank for Reconstruction and Development (IBRD) was created at the same time as the IMF, in 1944: its purpose was the 'encouragement of the development of productive facilities and resources in less developed countries'.[17] While it initially focused on post-war reconstruction, for some decades its main remit has related to the financing of projects in developing countries. Over time, the IBRD would become one of five connected institutions in the 'World Bank Group', including the International Finance Corporation (IFC), the International Development Association (IDA), the Multilateral Investment Guarantee Agency (MIGA), and the International Centre for the Settlement of Investment Disputes (ICSID). Usually, the IBRD and IDA together are known as the 'World Bank'.

20.2.2.1 **The IBRD and the IDA**

Economic development is the express purpose of the IBRD, which has a range of tools available to achieve its purposes. For example, it may:

- facilitate the investment of capital for productive purposes;
- promote private foreign investment by means of guarantees or participation in loans or other investments made by private investors;

[12] See IMF Evaluation Report, 'The IMF and Argentina 1991–2001' (IMF Publications, 2004).

[13] See IMF Survey, 'Europe and IMF Agree €110 Billion Financing Plan With Greece' <http://www.imf.org/external/pubs/ft/survey/so/2010/car050210a.htm>.

[14] See C Marquette, 'Current Poverty, Structural Adjustment, and Drought in Zimbabwe' (1997) 25 World Development 1141.

[15] See JE Stiglitz, *Globalization and its Discontents* (Penguin, 2002), former chief economist of the World Bank, for a memorable criticism of IMF conditionality. See also S Pahuja, 'Technologies of Empire: IMF Conditionality and the Reinscription of the North/South Divide' (2000) 13 Leiden JIL 749; JR Vreeland, *The International Monetary Fund: The Politics of Conditionality* (Routledge, 2007); and D Rodrik, *The Globalization Paradox* (WW Norton, 2011).

[16] Ironically, though part of the troika that governed the 2009–18 bailout of Greece under similar structural adjustment programme, the IMF called for a less strict approach than the European Commission and European Central Bank.

[17] Articles of Agreement of the International Bank for Reconstruction and Development (IBRD) (1944) 2 UNTS 134, Art I.

- supplement private investors by providing finance for productive purposes; or
- promote equilibrium in the balances of payments by encouraging international investment.

Conversely, the IDA, established in 1960, provides concessional financing on very generous terms to low-income States. Its aim, above all, is to promote the economic development and raised standards of living in these parts of the world through such flexible lending.[18] At the time of going to press, seventy-eight States are eligible to borrow from the IDA.[19] The IDA's financial resources are provided by subscriptions and contributions by richer States, and the occasional loan from the World Bank itself.

The governance of the World Bank (IBRD and IBA) is shared. They are structured similarly to that of the IMF, including a Board of Governors, an Executive Board composed of twenty-five members elected by States, and a president elected by the Board. Decisions of the Board of Governors are taken by weighted voting, with votes allocated on the basis of a quota based in turn on the shares held in the Bank itself.[20] As with the IMF, the largest shareholders also appoint their own executive director under Article V (4)(b)(i). Though the Articles of Agreement stipulate only five, six States each appoint one: the USA, Japan, China, and Germany the UK, and France each appoint an executive director, as the last two States have equal shareholdings.

Under Article III 4(iii), the IBRD can provide loans and guarantees in support of reconstruction or development. From 1980, it started to provide structural adjustment loans and, in 1984, sectorial adjustment loans, which have a similarly far-reaching character as those provided by the IMF. They call for legal, regulatory, judicial, and civil service reforms, as well as loans for the privatization of public enterprises. Arguably, these also reflect the imposition on borrowing States of a prevailing neo-liberal paradigm regarding domestic governance and the place of the State.[21] Under Article III 4(i), any such loan requires 'sovereign involvement', or the guarantee by the member in whose territory the project is located. More recently, the World Bank has begun to structure its loans so as to protect the environment, collaborating with the UNDP and the UNEP in order to establish the Global Environment Facility (GEF), a trust fund that contributes to projects aiming to achieve global environmental benefits in six focal areas: climate change, biological diversity, international waters, ozone layer depletion, desertification, and persistent organic pollutants.[22] Faced with criticisms about accountability, in 1994 the World Bank established an 'Inspection Panel', a mechanism of independent experts that allows for local communities to complain if they believe they have been

[18] See Art I of the IDA Articles of Agreement, available at <http://ida.worldbank.org/sites/default/files/IDA-articles-of-agreement.pdf>.

[19] The most up-to-date list is at <https://ida.worldbank.org/about/borrowing-countries>.

[20] IBRD Articles of Agreement (n 17) Art V (2)–(5). The USA holds just under 16 per cent of shareholdings and may block any loan disbursement and/or institutional reform.

[21] For a defence of these practices, see S Schlemmer-Schulte, 'The World Bank's Role in the Promotion of the Rule of Law in Developing Countries' in S Schlemmer-Schulte and Ko-Yung Tung (eds), *Liber Amicorum Ibrahim FI Shihata: International Finance and Development Law* (Kluwer, 2001), 677; a more critical posture can be found in N Woods, *The Globalizers: the IMF, the World Bank, and their Borrowers* (Cornell UP, 2006).

[22] The GEF also operates as the financial mechanism for a number of environmental regimes: see Chapter 19, Section 19.7.2.1.

(or may be) adversely affected by a project financed by the Bank.[23] The Inspection Panel can hold the Bank to account for compliance with its policies and procedures, especially in relation to social and environmental benefits and harm.

THEORY AND DEBATES The Conditionality of Loans and Alternative Financial Institutions

One of the features of World Bank and IMF funding that is criticized for imposing the neo-liberal idea of governance relates to the *conditionality of loans*. Loans are made contingent on 'structural adjustment policies' set by the Bank, which demands that borrowing States undertake far-reaching reforms to transform their economies in order to satisfy the World Bank and IMF's views on good economic governance, market liberalization, and, in particular, the privatization of State-owned assets. Such reforms are monitored by the World Bank and the IMF and can be enforced through the suspension of funding or binding judicial proceedings (see Section 20.4). Ironically, this model of development involves the elimination of many State subsidies and State-provided services that exist in the most developed States, such as Norway, Canada, and the Netherlands.

For this reason, alternative sources of development finance have been popping up. In late 2015, a Chinese-dominated initiative called the Asian Infrastructure Investment Bank (AIIB) was launched, and now counts 110 members. Also in 2015, the BRICS established what is now known as the 'New Development Bank', aimed to pool shared resources between the BRICS members and other emerging market economies. The purpose of these initiatives is to promote infrastructure-driven, sustainable economic development in their respective areas but without the conditions relating to governance, environmental standards, and social requirements laid down by the World Bank.

Both of these initiatives remain relatively fledgling, with less than a decade of lending experience. Nevertheless, they are illustrative of the increasing desire to provide access to alternative sources of development finance. Such alternative models evince a shift in economic power towards the Global South and away from the dominance of developed States in the World Bank; but equally, they herald a challenge to the broadly 'neo-liberal' models of governance favoured by the World Bank and the Bretton Woods system towards a more regionalized, sovereigntist approach.

For further reading, see M Wan, *The Asian Infrastructure Investment Bank: The Construction of Power and the Struggle for the East Asian International Order* (Macmillan, 2016); and P Nogueira Batista, *The BRICS and the Financing Mechanisms they Created: Progress and Shortcomings* (Anthem Press, 2021).

20.2.2.2 The IFC, MIGA, and ICSID

The IFC was created in 1956 to provide funding for private sector projects in developing countries without government guarantees, and may provide loans, guarantees, or even equity participation.[24] Its focus on private enterprises makes it far more sensitive to the

[23] The Inspection Panel mechanism is described in I Shihata, *World Bank Inspection Panel* (2nd edn, OUP, 2000).

[24] See Art III (2) of the IFC Articles of Agreement, available at < https://www.ifc.org/content/dam/ifc/doc/2023/ifc-articles-of-agreement-en.pdf>.

decisions of private investors rather than the priorities of States, and the IFC expects to achieve an adequate financial return. As for MIGA, started in 1988, it aims to promote the flow of foreign direct investment to developing countries by providing political risk insurance and credit enhancement guarantees to investors. In so doing, it aims to promote investor confidence and encourage investment in less developed States.[25] Finally, the system of investment tribunals established under ICSID will be analysed in detail in Section 20.4.

20.3 International trade law

In today's global society, there exists a vast network of bilateral 'free trade agreements' (FTAs) such as the new EU–Chile Free Trade Agreement, in addition to many regional trade agreements (RTAs), including, *inter alia*, the United States, Mexico and Canada Agreement (USMCA),[26] the Mercado Común del Sur (Mercosur), the Eurasian Economic Community (EEC), and, since 2022, the ASEAN-sponsored Regional Comprehensive Economic Partnership (RCEP). There are also ongoing developments with respect to 'mega-regional' FTAs, such as the new Comprehensive and Progressive Agreement for a Trans-Pacific Partnership (CPTPP) the African Continental Free Trade Area, and the stalled discussions on the US–EU Trans-Atlantic Trade and Investment Partnership (TTIP). These are too numerous to explore in this chapter, but they all share the common backdrop of operating within a global trading system that has developed since World War II into what we now regard as the present regime of international trade law.[27] This section will focus on the multilateral trade institution, the WTO, and its less institutionalized precursor, the GATT.

20.3.1 The legacy of the GATT

20.3.1.1 The GATT as a '*de facto*' international organization

The Bretton Woods conference was not unqualifiedly successful. Though the IMF and World Bank came into existence with relative ease, the Havana Charter for an International Trade Organization (ITO), part of the USA's design for a post-war global trading order based on free enterprise, free markets, and free competition, did not enter into force. Ironically, this was because the US Senate refused to approve it, and it made little sense to initiate a global trading system without the participation of the world's largest trading nation. A provisional regime, the General Agreement on Trade and Tariffs (GATT)[28] was approved in 1947, and operated for over four decades under a

[25] See Convention Establishing the Multilateral Investment Guarantee Agency (MIGA), available at <https://www.miga.org/who-we-are/miga-convention/>.

[26] The USMCA, a revision of the earlier North America Free Trade Agreement (NAFTA), entered into force on 1 July 2020.

[27] For an analysis of the prevailing discourse, see N Tzouvala, 'The academic debate about mega-regionals and international lawyers: legalism as critique?' (2018) 6 London Review of International Law 189.

[28] General Agreement on Tariffs and Trade (adopted 30 October 1947, entered into force 1 January 1948), 55 UNTS 187. The GATT was incorporated into the WTO.

novel organizational structure. This structure formed through a series of 'sessions' held twice-yearly and was refined through six important negotiation rounds where tariffs were progressively reduced and new multilateral agreements were signed.[29] Unlike the IMF and the World Bank, which operate on weighted voting, the GATT operated under a principle of sovereign equality, with each State having one vote.

20.3.1.2 Core principles under the GATT

The operating logic behind the GATT was based in an Anglo-American post-war mindset of economic liberalism: States should negotiate bilaterally on progressive tariff reductions under its auspices.[30] Over its lifetime, six rounds of negotiations were conducted, in Annecy (1949), Torquay (1951), Geneva (1956), the 'Dillon Round' (1960–2), the 'Kennedy Round' (1964–7), and the 'Tokyo Round' (1973–9). The later three rounds moved beyond tariff reductions and also included areas such as anti-dumping and non-tariff measures, and took longer to agree multilaterally. The final round, the 'Uruguay Round' (1986–94), led to the establishment of the WTO, which is described in Section 20.3.2.

Beyond the crucial maximum tariff percentages or 'bindings' in Article II GATT, two overarching obligations were agreed in 1948. The first obligation was that of *national treatment* (NT): imported goods should be treated no worse than domestic goods under internal taxation or regulation measures.[31] In other words, by prohibiting discrimination against foreign goods and placing them on the same plane as domestic goods, domestic protectionism became untenable. The second key obligation was that each member should grant all other parties *most-favoured-nation treatment* (MFN) in relation to imports or exports.[32] In essence, what this entailed was that any preferences granted to one GATT member would automatically be extended to all other GATT members. The MFN clause, which has a long pedigree,[33] was based on the idea that if States trading between one another diligently extend MFN treatment to one another, discriminatory trade barriers will gradually disappear and a regime of equality in trade will prevail. One important exception to the MFN rule is made for regional integration agreements such as customs unions or free trade areas, most prominently the EU.

Despite these obligations, over time States proved inventive at devising other methods to protect their domestic markets. As such, a series of initiatives were undertaken to strengthen the national treatment and MFN clauses and the free trading agenda embodied in the GATT. These included prohibitions on quotas ('quantitative restrictions') on imports and exports designed to protect domestic products from foreign competition,[34] the practice of 'dumping', or the flooding of the markets of another

[29] The definitive study of GATT remains that of JH Jackson, *World Trade and the Law of GATT* (Bobbs-Merrill Co, 1969). See also DA Irwin, *Genesis of the GATT* (CUP, 2011).

[30] GATT (n 27) Art XXVIII*bis*. For a recent historical account, see A Lang, 'Global Disordering: Practices of Reflexivity in Global Economic Governance' (2024) 35 EJIL 1.

[31] *Ibid*, Art III. See further H Horn and PC Mavroidis, 'Still Hazy after All These Years: The Interpretation of National Treatment in the GATT/WTO Case-law on Tax Discrimination' (2004) 15 EJIL 39.

[32] GATT, *ibid*, Art I.

[33] An early version of the MFN clause was contained in the 1794 Treaty of Amity, Commerce and Navigation 1794, named after then-US Secretary of State John Jay as the 'Jay Treaty'.

[34] GATT (n 27) Art XI.

country with products at less than their normal value,[35] and the freedom of States to grant subsidies, particularly export subsidies.[36] There were a number of exceptions to these rules set out in the GATT, allowing a member temporarily to restrain imports in cases of serious injury to domestic industry, a balance of payments crisis, national health and safety, and concerns over national security.[37]

CASE SPOTLIGHT ***United States—Restrictions on Import of Tuna,*** **GATT DS21R-39S155 (1991)**

One of the features of the GATT is that it allowed for dispute settlement through a system of consultations and improvised panels that could settle disputes. A key Panel report (usually known as '*Tuna/Dolphin*'), sought to settle a dispute between the USA and Mexico, stemming from the decision of the USA in 1988 to protect dolphins from being killed accidentally during tuna harvesting. Specifically, it targeted the practice of using sweeping 'driftnets', particularly harmful to dolphins, and prohibited the sale of driftnet tuna in the USA.

Mexican fishermen were particularly affected by this decision and it was argued before the GATT Panel that in so doing, the USA had violated its GATT commitments. In particular, Mexico pointed to the extraterritorial nature of the US measure, which applied to tuna caught in the Pacific, well outside US waters. The USA argued that it was acting in the interests of protecting dolphins, and could thus justify its actions under Article XX of the GATT, which permitted exceptions to protect animal life or the conservation of natural resources. The Panel made clear that the US conduct had not been 'necessary' under the GATT. However, other, less intrusive measures were possible instead of the far-reaching ban on the import of tuna merely because of the way that it was 'made'.

The USA refused to endorse the Panel's report, leading to a stand-off. Moreover, the Panel's decision resulted in widespread condemnation by environmental groups who felt that the GATT Panel ignored environmental concerns in applying the provisions of the GATT, and impelled further negotiations on the WTO. This case demonstrates the limitations of the GATT. A useful comparison would be with the later '*Shrimp/Turtle*' decision: see *United States—Import Prohibition of Shrimp and Certain Shrimp Products*, WT/DS58/AB/R (1998).

20.3.1.3 Accommodating developing States

The liberalism embodied in GATT came with its drawbacks; not least with respect to less-developed States, which suffered due to their lack of infrastructure and capacity, and the scant competitiveness of their industrial products. A rigid application of rules on national treatment and MFN treatment would have entailed less-developed States being relegated to agricultural production, textiles, and clothing, and would have undermined their aspirations for further development and industrialization. Crucially for developing States, all three of these categories were excluded under the GATT, and industrialized States routinely permitted levies, quotas, and subsidies to protect them. Developing States thus pressed for preferential treatment under the GATT, and

[35] *Ibid*, Art VI. [36] *Ibid*, Art XVI. [37] *Ibid*, Arts XII–XIV, XX–XXI.

achieved a few key milestones which are still relevant today. In 1965, a Protocol added Part IV of the GATT, 'Trade and Development', codifying a principle of non-reciprocity in trade negotiations between developed and developing States, granting the latter two important concessions:

(i) the right to modify or withdraw tariff concessions on manufactured products from industrialized States, if for the promotion of particular industries;

(ii) the right to impose quotas on foreign imports to safeguard their finances and ensure the stability of monetary reserves.[38]

For their part, developed States agreed:

(i) to prioritize the lowering of import tariffs for products of particular interest to developing States;

(ii) to refrain from introducing customs duties or non-tariff import barriers on such products; and

(iii) to avoid imposing new fiscal measures that might significantly hamper the growth in consumption of primary products exported by developing States.[39]

In 1979, these were supplemented by what is known as the 'Enabling Clause',[40] which consolidated the principle of non-reciprocity and a concept of 'differential and more favourable treatment' in relation to developing States. In essence, this amounted to an optional dilution of the MFN clause, authorizing—but not obliging—GATT parties to accord more favourable treatment to developing States.[41] These adjustments in favour of developing States, though hardly sufficient, paved the way for the establishment of the WTO, to which we now turn.

20.3.2 **The World Trade Organization**

20.3.2.1 **Understanding the structure of the WTO Agreement**

By the time of the Uruguay Round in the 1980s and early 1990s, it had become clear that the GATT required a substantial overhaul. This was, not least, because of emerging concerns over the environment and continued acrimony between developed and developing States, but also due to important exclusions on trade in services, such as banking and finance, which increasingly dominated the economies of developed States. A reconstruction of global trade was achieved in 1994 with the Marrakech Agreement establishing the WTO,[42] which absorbed all the GATT agreements and legal instruments as updated through the Uruguay Round (now known as the GATT 1994), as well as newer instruments, chief among them being the General Agreement on Trade

[38] *Ibid*, Art XXXVI. [39] *Ibid*, Art XXXVII.

[40] See GATT Decision of 28 November 1979 (L/4903).

[41] See AA Yusuf, 'Differential and More Favourable Treatment: The GATT Enabling Clause' (1980) 14 Journal of World Trade Law 488.

[42] Marrakech Agreement establishing the World Trade Organization (1994) 1867 UNTS 3.

in Services (GATS),[43] the Agreement on Trade-Related Aspects of Intellectual Property (TRIPS),[44] and the Agreement on Trade-Related Investment Measures (TRIMs).[45] Perhaps the crowning achievement of the WTO Agreement was that it achieved a compulsory Understanding on Dispute Settlement (DSU),[46] though its present difficulties are examined later in Section 20.3.2.3.

It is important to note that the WTO is a wholly new institution and not merely a replacement of the GATT, though the substantive law it applies builds on the achievements from 1947 to 1994.[47] The WTO is composed of three primary organs: a Ministerial Conference that meets biennially; a General Council on which all States are represented; and the Secretariat, headed by the Director-General.[48] The General Council also operates as the Dispute Settlement Body (DSB) and the Trade Review Policy Body. Under its auspices, three councils operate for trade in goods, services, and intellectual property rights, respectively, as well as a whole sub-structure of more specific councils. In principle, consensus is required for decision-making, though some matters may be decided by majority vote,[49] and more important decisions (such as interpretation of the WTO Agreement) require a three-quarters majority.[50]

At the time of going to press, the WTO has 166 members, with Russia being the last major economy gaining admission in 2012. The largest economies still negotiating accession are those of Iran, Libya, and Algeria, in part due to their chosen economic model and political opposition from existing WTO members. Interestingly, Article XXXIII of the WTO Agreement allows a 'customs territory having full autonomy in the conduct of its trade policies' to join the WTO, thus paving the way for the European Community (now European Union), 'Chinese Taipei' (principally the island of Taiwan), and the Hong Kong and Macau special administrative regions of China to join. The EU, as a 'regional customs union', is a member of the WTO alongside the member States, and acts in matters involving its competence under EU treaties.

20.3.2.2 **Matters covered under the WTO structures**

The overarching principles of national treatment and MFN treatment have carried over into the WTO, taking into account the concessions won by developing States in relation to some preferential treatment, as well as the exceptions in the GATT described earlier, which allow a member temporarily to restrain imports in cases of serious injury to domestic industry, a balance of payments crisis, national health and safety, and

[43] General Agreement on Trade in Services, Annex 1b to the WTO Agreement (1994) 1869 UNTS 183.

[44] Agreement on Trade-Related Aspects of Intellectual Property Rights, Annex 1c to the WTO Agreement (1994) 1869 UNTS 299.

[45] Agreement on Trade-Related Investment Measures, Annex 1a to the WTO Agreement (1994) 1868 UNTS 186.

[46] Understanding on Rules and Procedures Governing the Settlement of Disputes (1994) 1869 UNTS 401, Annex 2 of the WTO Agreement ('DSU').

[47] See G Messenger, *The Development of World Trade Organization Law: Examining Change in International Law* (OUP, 2016); and M Matushita, T Schoenbaum, P Mavroidis, and M Han (eds), *The World Trade Organization: Law, Practice and Policy* (3rd edn, OUP, 2015).

[48] See WTO Agreement (n 41) Arts IV–VI. [49] *Ibid*, Art IX(1). [50] *Ibid*, Art IX(2).

concerns over national security.[51] These overarching principles apply to goods, services, intellectual property rights, and all other matters covered under the WTO Agreement and subsidiary agreements. Moreover, in June 1999, it was agreed that the General Council could grant waivers allowing preferential treatment to products of least-developed States.[52] There is a bewildering array of trade categories covered by the overlapping agreements and instruments under the WTO. The following briefly outlines what is encompassed.

Goods. There are several types of goods covered under multilateral agreements under the auspices of the WTO.[53] Presently, the main agreements in force regulate trade in goods in categories such as agriculture (including sanitary and phytosanitary standards and rules of origin), textiles, and clothing. They also include broader agreements relating to customs valuation, trade-related investment measures, anti-dumping, pre-shipment inspection, rules of origin, and import licensing procedures. Finally, there are agreements relating to subsidies and countervailing measures and safeguard actions to protect domestic industries.

Services. The trade or supply of services between WTO members was built on the design of the GATT, and is now known as the General Agreement on Trade in Services (GATS)[54] which, in principle, extends the overarching principles of trade liberalization into services.[55] There are country-specific schedules that allow for certain limitations to be attached in respect of certain categories of services, such as the number of employees in a sector, or the legal form of the service supplier (e.g., requiring incorporation or professional licensing). There are four sectoral protocols negotiated after the Uruguay Round, two of which cover financial services, one on the movement in natural persons, and one on basic telecommunications.

Intellectual property rights. The TRIPS Agreement[56] also extends the overarching principles on liberalizing world trade to intellectual property, linking it to the rules laid out in two international conventions administered by the World Intellectual Property Rights Organization (WIPO), those of Paris and Berne.[57] Intellectual property rights covered under TRIPS include copyright and related rights, trademarks, geographical indications, industrial designs, patents, and the protection of undisclosed information.[58] Pertinently, as pointed out by the World Health Assembly in March 2020 in relation to the Covid-19 outbreak, under the 2001 Doha Declaration, TRIPS 'can and

[51] GATT (n 27) Arts XII–XIV, XX–XXI.

[52] See 1999 General Council Decision on Waiver regarding Preferential Tariff Treatment for Least-Developed Countries, WT/L/304. See further I Feichtner, *The Law and Politics of WTO Waivers: Stability and Flexibility in Public International Law* (CUP, 2012).

[53] The text of the various agreements can be found on the WTO's website at <https://www.wto.org/english/docs_e/legal_e/legal_e.htm>. Those relating to goods are found under Annex A. See further Matsushita et al (n 46) chs 9 (agriculture), 10 (subsidies and countervailing measures), 11 (anti-dumping).

[54] Annex 1B to the WTO Agreement: n 41.

[55] See further Matsushita et al (n 46) ch 16.

[56] Annex 1C to the WTO Agreement: n 41.

[57] Paris Convention for the Protection of Industrial Property (as amended), 828 UNTS 107, 828 UNTS 305; Berne Convention for the Protection of Literary and Artistic Works 1972 UNTS 222 (No 11850).

[58] See further Matsushita et al (n 46) ch 17.

should be interpreted and implemented' to support WTO members in the protection of public health and the promotion of access to medicines.[59]

20.3.2.3 **Understanding on Dispute Settlement (DSU)**

The WTO's dispute-settlement mechanism (DSU) remains, to date, the most significant compulsory dispute-settlement mechanism in the international legal order; it is, for example, the only such mechanism to which both the USA and China have agreed. Though it builds on the ad hoc experience of the GATT Panels such as that in *Tuna-Dolphin*, it streamlines much of the procedure concerned, provides for tight time-frames, and allows for a series of predetermined remedies within the WTO framework. The object of this dispute-settlement system is to enforce the withdrawal of measures that are found incompatible with the WTO Agreement, especially in relation to the liberalization of free trade. For proponents of binding dispute settlement it has been hailed as a model, especially in relation to compliance and enforcement.[60]

Any dispute arising between WTO members which is not resolved after sixty days of consultations may be referred to the Dispute Settlement Body (the DSB, on which representatives of all members are present), which will establish a panel of three individuals to hear the dispute.[61] The Panel will take submissions from the parties of the dispute, as well as from third-party members of the WTO that have a 'substantial interest' in it.[62] Importantly, the Panel has the right to seek information, especially of a scientific or technical nature, from experts.[63] This last point is significant as the WTO has developed an extensive practice of using *amicus curiae* briefs which have been submitted to it.[64]

The Panel reports back to the DSB within six months, which may adopt the report unless one of the parties to the dispute appeals a question of law to the Appellate Body (AB), a standing body of seven international trade lawyers that functions much like an appellate court. An AB panel composed of three members will hear the appeal and draft a report, which is ordinarily adopted by the DSB unless there is a consensus vote not to adopt it.[65] AB reports were originally brief, touching only on a few points of law; however, due to the increased number of panel findings and legal interpretations touched

[59] World Health Assembly, 'Covid-19 Response' (19 May 2020), WHA Doc 73.1, referring to Doha Declaration on the TRIPS Agreement and Public Health, adopted by WTO Ministerial Conference (14 November 2001).

[60] See, e.g., E Petersmann, *The GATT/WTO Dispute Settlement System* (Kluwer, 1997); JG Merrills and E De Brabandere *International Dispute Settlement* (7th edn, CUP, 2022), 310–45.

[61] DSU (n 45) Art 8(5). [62] *Ibid*, Art 10(2). [63] *Ibid*, Art 13.

[64] The Appellate Body interpreted Art 13 as permitting this practice in *United States—Import Prohibition of Certain Shrimp and Shrimp Products (US—Shrimp)*, WT/DS58/AB/R (12 October 1998), paras 108–10. For a critical perspective on this practice, see D Wirth, 'Case Report. European Communities—Measures Affecting Asbestos and Asbestos-Containing Products' (2002) 96 AJIL 435, 437–9.

[65] The procedure used by the Appellate Body is found in DSU (n 45) Art 17. For a comment on the AB's development of WTO law, see Messenger (n 46) esp ch 3. That said, since 2016, the USA has blocked any further appointments to the Body, and with the expiry of the terms of two members, the AB cannot function as it is below quorum. Since 30 April 2020, the EU and 22 WTO member States have been bringing appeals within a 'multi-party interim appeal arrangement' that, under Art 25 of the DSU, can be constituted provided the WTO is notified. See further, C-F Lo, J Nakagawa and T Chen (eds), *The Appellate Body of the WTO and its Reform* (Springer, 2020).

upon by them, and the increased complexity of the appeals, the AB's reports are much longer: for example, the *Large Civil Aircraft* (2011) report is 645 pages long.[66]

Once a final decision is reached, the reports have to be implemented by the parties within fifteen months, though the timeframe is negotiable. Usually, remedies take the form of compensation and the withdrawal of offending practices. A key innovation of the WTO DSU is that if a party fails to implement a report, the aggrieved party may seek authorization from the DSB to impose countermeasures, which are coyly referred to in the DSU as 'retaliatory action' or 'suspension of concessions'.[67] This is a fascinating, unusual mode of dispute resolution, which allows for targeted, temporary measures to be taken by an aggrieved party to induce another party into withdrawing its unlawful measures, but only after a legal decision has been taken. The DSU integrates countermeasures into its enforcement regime, and States thus subject rights to invoke countermeasures under general international law (covered in Chapter 13, Section 13.4) to additional conditions. Article 22(3) of the DSU provides that countermeasures should normally be taken within the same sector in which the offending party's measure has been found, but if that is not practicable or effective, the complaining party may seek them in respect of another agreement covered under the WTO. Such countermeasures must usually be proportionate to the original wrongdoing or trade impairment, in that they should not cause more significant economic harm than the original measures.

CASE SPOTLIGHT ***European Communities–Measures Concerning Meat and Meat Products*, WT/DS26/AB/R; WT/DS48/AB/R (1998) ('EC–*Beef Hormones*')**

In 1998, the Appellate Body report known as *EC—Beef Hormones* was adopted, a seminal decision which has generated widespread interest as an illustration of the operation of the WTO dispute-settlement system. The USA had complained concerning a European Community (EC) import ban on meat and meat products treated with hormones, and was later joined by Canada, Australia, and New Zealand. Pursuant to a request by the USA to constitute a panel, later joined by Canada, two panels composed of the same members were created, taking extensive advice from scientific and technical experts. The EC maintained that its ban on meat and meat products treated with hormones was justified.

The original panels ruled that the import ban on such meat products was inconsistent with the Sanitary and Phytosanitary Standards (SPS) Agreement, which covers food safety and animal and plant health regulation. In 1998, the Appellate Body upheld the unlawfulness of the EC's import ban, as it was not based on proper risk assessment (article 5 SPS) or existing international standards, scientific justification, or necessity (article 3 SPS), and that the level of protection demanded by the EC was unjustified and arbitrary.

In 1999, the USA notified the DSB that it considered that the EC had failed to implement its rulings in due time. The USA requested authorization to suspend the application of tariff concessions and related obligations towards the EC for a sum equal to the loss suffered of US exports. After a further arbitration performed by the original panel, the USA was permitted

[66] *European Communities and certain member States—Measures Affecting Trade in Large Civil Aircraft (AB)*, WTDS/316/AB/R (2011).

[67] DSU (n 45) Arts 21–2.

to take certain 'suspensive measures' under DSU Article 22.7, illustrating the WTO countermeasures system.

Even today, the EU has still not fully complied, but the dispute has been settled by 'mutually agreed solution'. The EU has now granted preferential aspects for meat and meat products not treated with hormones.

20.3.2.4 **Final thoughts on the WTO**

The WTO embodied the aspiration for a comprehensive framework for international trade. Although it has no independent policy-making powers, it is the guardian of decades' worth of multilateral trade agreements, the forum for the negotiation of new standards, and is accompanied by a robust dispute-settlement mechanism. Despite operating through consensus, there have long been concerns that the most economically powerful States, coupled with larger developing States such as Brazil, South Africa, India, and China, can impose their will on smaller developing States, even dominating participation in the dispute-settlement processes.[68] Even the stalled 'Doha Round' (2001–present)o, which is ostensibly committed to issues of development, such as the social dimensions of globalization, higher labour standards, and other concerns, has come to a standstill.[69]

A more existential danger to the WTO system is that its dispute-settlement mechanisms remains gridlocked, with the USA blocking new appointments to its Appellate Body, and a turn towards 'mega-regional' trading areas may yet spell the end of a multilateral trading system. And there is little optimism: most recent biennial Ministerial Conference in 2024 ended with a sombre sense of stalemate. But perhaps reform must go beyond short-term power imbalances; it cannot be denied that global trading relations through the GATT/WTO have for decades been embedded in an essentially liberal trade paradigm,[70] one that may not prove sustainable in the longer run.[71]

20.4 **International investment law**

20.4.1 **The origins of investment protection**

The protection of foreign nationals, and in particular of their property when abroad, has preoccupied international lawyers for centuries.[72] Many of the seminal cases now regarded as developing the early rules on State responsibility or diplomatic

[68] See, e.g., CL Davis and S Blodgett Bermeo, 'Who Files? Developing Country Participation in GATT/WTO Adjudication' (2009) 71 Journal of Politics 1033; F Jawara and A Kwa, *Behind the Scenes at the WTO* (Zed Books, 2004).

[69] There have been some minor developments, notably a 2003 interim waiver to the obligation under TRIPS to obtain licences for the export of medical and pharmaceutical products to less-developed States, and a 2004 Framework Agreement on trade facilitation.

[70] See the classic JG Ruggie, 'International Regimes, Transactions and Change: Embedded Liberalism in the Postwar Economic Order' (1982) 36 International Organization 379.

[71] See the argument in A Lang, *World Trade Law after Neoliberalism: Reimagining the Global Economic Order* (OUP, 2011).

[72] The emergence of the modern investment system is well chronicled in M Sornarajah, *The International Law on Foreign Investment* (5th edn, CUP, 2021), chs 1 and 2; and CL Lim, J Ho, and M Paparinskis, *International Investment Law and Arbitration* (2nd edn, CUP, 2021), ch 1.

protection (see Chapters 10 and 11, respectively) were developed in the context of protecting foreign nationals and their property (or 'injury to aliens'). The nineteenth and early twentieth centuries were characterized by a strong capital outflow into Latin America, Africa, and Asia, many of which were colonies during that period. Of course, behind claims for protecting the rights and property of foreign nationals lay a sense that the responsible State was perhaps insufficiently civilized in order to guarantee effective protection. However, the decolonization of Africa and much of Asia in the 1960s led to the *nationalization* of many Western-owned enterprises. Nationalization, the compulsory taking over (expropriation) by a State of an asset held by a private investor in the furtherance of a public interest, became a particularly important issue.

Today, the debate lies between what are referred to as 'capital exporting' and 'capital importing' countries. The former have insisted on maintaining an adequate degree of control or security for the investments made by their nationals, and in particular have stressed the need for legal recourse outside the courts of the host country. Conversely, capital-importing or 'host' States are caught between a desire to attract foreign capital and investment and the need to retain control over key sectors of their economy. This tension was most acute in the decades immediately following decolonization, often leading to acrimonious disputes between investors (and their national State) and host States. Vivid historical examples include the nationalization of the Suez Canal by Egypt in 1956 and nationalization of oil-related investments by Iran and Libya in the 1970s.

Whilst nationalization (expropriation of private property) as such is clearly not unlawful under international law, it constitutes the deprivation by a State of a right of property of a foreign investor.[73] Accordingly, there is much practice to suggest that lawful expropriation must comply with certain conditions. These are detailed in the next section.

20.4.2 **The taking of foreign investors' property**

20.4.2.1 **Defining expropriation**

Originally, a 1961 Harvard draft convention defined property as encompassing 'all movable and immovable property, whether tangible or intangible, including industrial, literary and artistic property as well as rights and interests in property'.[74] However, expropriation need not only concern the taking of property. As the Iran–US Claims Tribunal established in *Starrett Housing v Iran*, expropriation may be indirect, and may also encompass any unreasonable interference with the use, enjoyment, or disposal

[73] See *De Sanchez v Banco Central de Nicaragua and Others* 770 F.2d 1385, 1397 (5th Cir 1985); *AMCO v Indonesia (Merits)* (1985) 24 ILM 1022, 1023; (1985) 89 ILR 405, 406.

[74] See 1961 Harvard Draft Convention on the International Responsibility of States for Injuries to Aliens, Art 10(7), in (1961) 55 AJIL 548. 'Property' has also been understood to include concession rights: see *Libyan American Oil Company v Libya* (1981) 20 ILM 1, 53.

of property that 'renders the rights so useless that they must be deemed to have been expropriated in substance, even if legal title remains with the original owner'.[75] Later disputes settled under BITs have clarified the scope of, and conditions for, expropriation.[76]

20.4.2.2 **An expropriation must be for public purposes**

As recognized by the PCIJ in *Certain German Interests in Polish Upper Silesia*, expropriation must be for 'reasons of public utility, judicial liquidation and similar measures'.[77] Further, an expropriation cannot be arbitrary, discriminatory, or vindictive; otherwise it will be unlawful.[78] Though not unlimited, the notion of 'public utility' is broad, and includes such purposes as the exercise of police power or defence measures in wartime. In the last decades, 'public purpose' has been interpreted as encompassing general programmes of social and economic reform, such as the nationalization of concessions relating to natural resources, in particular to oil,[79] as well as environmental concerns.[80]

20.4.2.3 **A State conducting an expropriation must pay compensation**

No matter how laudable the public purpose, in principle a State is under a duty to pay compensation unless circumstances precluding wrongfulness exist (see Chapter 10, Section 10.3). Again two positions have emerged, with capital-exporting States adhering to the US-proposed 'Hull formula' that '[n]o government is entitled to expropriate . . . without provision for *prompt, adequate and effective payment* therefor'.[81] This is a high standard, where even *lucrum cessans* ('loss of future profits') may be subject to compensation.[82] Capital-importing States, which saw most of their natural resources persisting under foreign ownership, regarded the Hull formula as excessive. Through the General Assembly, they put forward a somewhat lower standard of 'appropriate

[75] *Starrett Housing Corporation v Islamic Republic of Iran* (Interlocutory Award) (1983) 4 IUSCTR 122; See also Harvard Draft Convention, *ibid*, Art 10(3)(a); and the UK government position in relation to Indonesian decrees affecting British enterprises, (1965) 4 ILM 440, 440–7.

[76] See, e.g., *Biloune v Ghana Investment Centre* (1993) 95 ILR 183, 207–10; *Metalclad Corporation v United Mexican States* (2002) 119 ILR 615, 639–40; *Biwater Gauff v Tanzania*, Case No ARB/05/22 (ICSID, 24 July 2008), paras 455–6; *Pope and Talbot v Canada* (2000) 122 ILR 293, 335–7.

[77] *Certain German Interests in Polish Upper Silesia, Judgment, 1926, PCIJ, Ser A, No 7*, p 5; see also *Norwegian Shipowners' Claims (Norway v United States)* (1922) 1 RIAA 307; *Papamichalopoulos v Greece* (1993) Ser A No 260 (ECtHR). But *cf Libyan-American Oil Co ('Liamco') v Libyan Arab Republic* (1978) 17 ILM 3, 58–9, in which public utility was held not to be a prerequisite for the legality of a nationalization.

[78] *Liamco, ibid*, 58–9; World Bank Guidelines on the Treatment of Foreign Direct Investment (1992) 31 ILM 1363, s IV (1), and Energy Charter Treaty (signed 17 December 1994, entered into force 16 April 1998), 2080 UNTS 95, Art 13.

[79] *BP v Libyan Arab Republic (United Kingdom v Libya)* (1973) 53 ILR 297; *Agip SpA v The Government of the Popular Republic of the Congo* (1979) 67 ILR 319, 336–9.

[80] *Santa Elena v Costa Rica* (2000) 39 ILM 1317, 1329; *Too v Greater Modesto Insurance Associates* (1989) 23 Iran–USCTR 378; *Methanex v United States* (2005) 44 ILM 1345; *Saluka Investments BV v Czech Republic* (2006) 15 ICSID Rep 274.

[81] The Hull formula was named after a Note from US Secretary of State Hull to the Government of Mexico on 22 August 1938: 3 Hackworth 658–9. See (1938) 32 AJIL Supp 192. For further discussion, see ILC, 'International Responsibility: Fourth Report' (García Amador, Special Rapporteur) (26 February 1959), UN Doc A/CN.4/119 in (1959) ILC Ybk vol II, 1, 16–24.

[82] The loss of future profits is frequently the subject of investment claims: see, e.g., *AMCO v Indonesia* (n 72) 1037 (ILM) or 504 (ILR); *Metalclad v Mexico* (n 75) 641–2. See further J Bonnitcha, L Poulsen and M Waibel (eds), *The Political Economy of the Investment Treaty Regime* (OUP, 2017), 199 et seq.

compensation',[83] which has met with some approval as a codification of customary international law in the *Texaco* and *Aminoil* arbitral awards, though in these cases the 'appropriate compensation' standard has been interpreted akin to the Hull formula.[84] In an exercise in constructive ambiguity, the 1992 World Bank Guidelines on the topic state that a State may not expropriate foreign direct investment except, *inter alia*, against the payment of 'appropriate compensation' (section IV(1)), yet deem compensation to be appropriate where it is 'adequate, prompt and effective' (section IV(2)).[85] There is thus a degree of uncertainty as to how the standard is applied in practice.[86]

Certain tribunals have, furthermore, suggested that the standard for compensation should differ according to whether the expropriation by a State was lawful or unlawful.[87] In the case of an unlawful taking, *restitutio in integrum* ('to re-establish the situation which would have existed had not the act occurred') would be required, including compensation for future profits (*lucrum cessans*). Conversely, in the case of lawful taking, the standard would not include compensation for future profits, but only a lower payment, for the full value of the investment at the moment of dispossession.[88]

20.4.3 **Bilateral investment treaties**

Aside from the standard rules on the protection of foreign nationals addressed earlier, States have entered into some 3,000 bilateral investment treaties (BITs),[89] a dense mesh of bilateral obligations in which the rights of investors and of host States have been laid out. A striking feature of BITs is that they often lay out provisions for compulsory investor–State dispute settlement (ISDS) in relation to any foreign investments, often bypassing the local courts of a host State. This will be analysed in Section 20.4.4.

Given the sheer number of BITs, it is perhaps surprising that they share a number of commonalities.[90] A starting point is the definition of 'investors' who may avail

[83] See UNGA Declaration on Permanent Sovereignty over Natural Resources, UNGA Res 1803 (XVII) (14 December 1962); Charter of Economic Rights and Duties of States (n 5) Art 2.2(c); and G Abi-Saab, 'Permanent Sovereignty over Natural Resources and Economic Activities' in M Bedjaoui (ed), *International Law: Achievements and Prospects* (Nijhoff, 1991), 597.

[84] See *Texaco Overseas Petroleum Co v Libya* (1978) 17 ILM 3, 29; (1979) 53 ILR 389, 489; *Kuwait v The American Independent Oil Company (Aminoil)* (1982) 21 ILM 976, 1032; (1982) 66 ILR 519, 601; *Amoco International Finance Corporation v Islamic Republic of Iran*, Partial Award (1988) 15 Iran–USCTR 189; *INA Corporation v Islamic Republic of Iran*, Final Award (1985) 8 Iran–USCTR 373.

[85] See World Bank, 1992 Guidelines on the Treatment of Foreign Direct Investment, Section II (1992) 31 ILM 1376, the Energy Charter Treaty (n 77) Art 13 also embodies the 'prompt, adequate and effective compensation' formula.

[86] For further reading, see Sornarajah (n 71) 239–245; C McLachlan, L Shore, and M Weiniger, *International Investment Arbitration: Substantive Principles* (OUP, 2007); and NJ Calamita, 'The British Bank Nationalizations: An International Law Perspective' (2009) 58 ICLQ 119, esp 134–5.

[87] See *Amoco International Finance Corporation v Islamic Republic of Iran*, Partial Award (1987) 15 Iran–USCTR 189, 246–52.

[88] *Ibid*. But *cf* the earlier *AIG v Islamic Republic of Iran* (1983) 4 Iran–USCTR 96, 109–10, where lost profits were awarded despite the expropriation being deemed lawful.

[89] The first was between the Federal Republic of Germany and Pakistan, in 1959.

[90] Many investor States maintain a 'model BIT' which they use as a starting point for negotiation; these are in turn originally based on an OECD model BIT which was developed in the 1960s.

themselves of the protection under a BIT. Generally speaking, an investor must be a national from one State, whether natural or legal person (e.g., corporations or partnerships), who has made an investment within the second State. Indirect investments are usually also protected, which means that a corporation operating through a local subsidiary would still benefit from protection under a BIT. This is because there may be substantial tax advantages or legal requirements which are best met through local incorporation.[91] The notion of 'investment' is also broadly defined and can encompass any manner of assets, rights, and claims. These may include immoveable and moveable property, shares, intellectual property rights, or business concessions to search for, extract, or cultivate natural resources: provided they are contributed for a limited time period, that there is acceptance of an element of risk on the part of the investor, and that the contribution should enhance the economic development of the host State.[92]

Generally speaking, an investment is only protected under a BIT if it has been established in accordance with the legislation of the host State; but if falling within the scope of a BIT, the following core standards of treatment are prevalent across them:

- First, host States must accord *fair and equitable treatment* to investors, which generally must conform with an international minimum standard of protection.[93]
- Second, host States must provide *full protection and security* to investments, which places them under a duty to prevent harm to investments.[94] This is a robust obligation and applies even during armed conflicts.[95]
- Third, host States must not *discriminate* against foreign investors vis-à-vis other investors; any discriminatory treatment will usually breach a BIT.[96]
- Fourth, host States commit to *national treatment* of foreign investors, subjecting them to the same legal and regulatory regime as local investors, without discrimination.[97]

[91] See J Collier and AV Lowe, *The Settlement of Disputes in International Law* (OUP, 2000), 65–8.

[92] See, e.g., *Salini et al v Mexico*, ICSID Case No ARB/00/4, Decision on Jurisdiction of 23 July 2001, para 52; *Quiborax v Bolivia*, ICSID Case No ARB/06/2, Decision on Jurisdiction of 27 September 2012, para 220. Investment tribunals have long grappled with the lack of a definition in the ICSID Convention: see A Grabowski, 'Definition of Investment under the ICSID Convention: A Defense of *Salini*' (2014) 15 Chicago JIL 287.

[93] See, e.g., *Técnicas Medioambientales Tecmed SA v Mexico*, Award, ICSID Case No ARB(AF)/00/2; *Loewen Group Incorporated and Loewen v United States*, Award, ICSID Case No ARB(AF)/98/3. See further M Paparinskis, *The International Minimum Standard and Fair and Equitable Treatment* (OUP, 2013).

[94] See, e.g., *Azurix Corp v Argentina*, ICSID Case No ARB/01/12, Award of 14 July 2006; *American Manufacturing & Trading, Inc (AMT) v Republic of Zaire*, ICISD Case No ARB/93/1, Award of 21 February 1997. See further C Schreuer, 'Full Protection and Security' (2010) 1 JIDS 353.

[95] See generally J Zrilič, *The Protection of Foreign Investment in Times of Armed Conflict* (OUP, 2019). More recently, it has been noted that the obligation of host States to protect investments seems more stringent than the obligation to protect civilians under IHL: see K Greenman, 'Of War and International Investment Law' (2024) 73 ICLQ 579; and G Hernández, 'The Interaction between Investment Law and the Law of Armed Conflict in the Interpretation of Full Protection and Security Clauses' in F Baetens (ed), *Investment Law within International Law: An Integrationist Perspective* (CUP, 2013), 21.

[96] Most BITs contain a clause prohibiting discriminatory treatment, but these are generally regarded as reinforcing a rule of existing customary international law: see, e.g., R Bishop, J Crawford, and MW Reisman (eds), *Foreign Investment Disputes—Cases, Materials and Commentary* (Kluwer Law International, 2005), 949.

[97] See, e.g., *ADF v United States*, ICSID Case No ARB(AF)/00/1, Award of 9 January 2003; *Mondev v United States* (2003) 42 ILM 81.

- Fifth, as in international trade law, most BITs contain provisions requiring MFN treatment, according to which any subsequent BIT with another State which contains more favourable treatment for that State's investors will automatically benefit all investors covered under a BIT.[98]
- Finally, most BITs specify the avenues available for dispute settlement between a host State and a foreign investor, to which we will now turn.

20.4.4 **Investor–State dispute settlement**

Under the traditional doctrines of diplomatic protection,[99] an investor in a dispute with a host State would normally be required to exhaust all local remedies. In other words, they must rely on local law and pursue their claim through local courts until the final court of appeal had dismissed the claim. Investor–State arbitration allows a private, foreign investor to bypass the local courts and appeal immediately for international protection against a State.[100]

There is an important exception to this: the Permanent Court of Arbitration, which predates the ICJ, can act as 'appointment authority' and secretariat for investor–State disputes, provided that a BIT or other treaty so provides.[101] Occasionally, there have been institutions created in response to specific situations, such as the Iran–United States Claims Tribunal, which has jurisdiction over disputes between both States and their nationals for injuries suffered by them during the 1979 Iranian Revolution.[102]

CONTEMPORARY DEVELOPMENTS The Eclipse of the Energy Charter?

In 1998, the Energy Charter Treaty (1998) 2080 UNTS 100 (No 36116) entered into force between fifty-two States in Europe and Central Asia, as well as Japan. The Energy Charter applies to economic activity in the energy sector, such as exploitation, extraction, refining, production, distribution, and sale of energy materials and products. It has most frequently been invoked by fossil fuel investors to challenge climate-related regulations.

The Energy Charter's binding provisions, in relation to the promotion and protection of investments relating to energy, are striking. In essence, the Energy Charter imposes the equivalent of a 'network' of BITs; it is the only multilateral framework of its kind. Under Article 26, any investor who is a national of one party may invoke dispute-settlement provisions against any other party to the Energy Charter, whether it be under ICSID Rules, UNCITRAL *ad hoc* Rules, or those of the Stockholm Chamber of Commerce. Article 16 of the Charter contains an MFN clause: if a previous or future BIT gives better investment protection than the Charter, that higher level of protection will apply.

[98] See earlier, Section 20.3.1.2. [99] See Chapter 11, Section 11.4.

[100] Though most BITs do provide an opportunity for State-to-State arbitration, they are rarely invoked. A rare exception of an investment dispute being brought to the ICJ is *Elettronica Sicula SpA (ESLI) (United States v Italy), Judgment, ICJ Reports 1989*, p 15, regarding a direct claim involving the exercise of diplomatic protection on behalf of two US corporations.

[101] The PCA often facilitates disputes under the UNCITRAL Arbitration Rules: see <https://uncitral.un.org/en/texts/arbitration/contractualtexts/arbitration>.

[102] A succinct history of IUSCT arbitral practice can be found in Collier and Lowe (n 90) ch 4, 73–82.

In recent years, the ECT has faced sharp criticism. An infamous case settled under the Energy Charter was *Yukos Universal (Isle of Man) v Russian Federation*, Final Award of 18 July 2014, PCA Case No AA 227. Originally for nearly $US50 billion (some 20 per cent of Russia's annual government budget), it was overturned by The Hague District Courton the basis that Russia has not ratified the Energy Charter: see Case No C/09/477160/HA ZA 15-1 (Judgment of 20 April 2016). Moreover, the ECT has come under fire for being a significant obstacle against national policies combatting climate change, and for actively disincentivizing parties from compliance with international climate change treaties and the Paris Agreement in particular. In June 2024, the European Union and Euratom gave formal notification of their exit from the ECT to take effect in 2025. Alongside the EU, ten EU member States and the UK have announced their withdrawal and talks of a 'co-ordinated withdrawal' of all EU member States, which would severely weaken the ECT regime.

For further reading, see A Daszko, 'The Energy Charter Treaty at a Critical Juncture: of Knowns, Unknowns, and Lasting Significance' (2024) 26 JIEL 720; S Shadikhodjaev, *Energy and the Environment: Exploring the Nexus under International Economic Law* (CUP, 2024), and K Hobér, *The Energy Charter Treaty: A Commentary* (OUP, 2020).

There are several fora for investment arbitration, including the Arbitration Institute of the Stockholm Chamber of Commerce, ad hoc tribunals under the UN Commission on International Trade Law (UNCITRAL), and the International Chamber of Commerce. The dominant mechanism by far, however, is that of the International Centre for the Settlement of Investment Disputes (ICSID) which, as mentioned earlier, operates under the auspices of the World Bank.[103] ICSID is not a tribunal; instead, it creates a framework within which conciliation and arbitration may occur. As an organ of an international organization, the ICSID Secretariat, is active in providing facilities for the conduct of investment arbitrations. These include acting as a registry for a particular arbitration, helping to appoint the arbitrators, the provision of procedural rules, and more.[104] ICSID also publishes repertories of investment legislation and treaties around the world,[105] and the *ICSID Review—Foreign Investment Law Journal*, in which ICSID investment awards are published.[106]

As of late 2024, there are 165 States parties to the ICSID Convention, which provides in Article 25(2) that the jurisdiction of ICSID may be extended to disputes between a member State and an investor who is a national of another member State, provided that

[103] See Washington Convention on the Settlement of Investment Disputes between States and Nationals of Other States (1965) 575 UNTS 159 ('ICSID Convention').

[104] A detailed analysis of the ICSID facilities, including several sets of procedural rules, can be found in Collier and Lowe (n 90) ch 4, esp 59–73; and C Schreuer, *The ICSID Convention: A Commentary* (CUP, 2001).

[105] See the ten-volume loose-leaf *Investment Laws of the World* (OUP, updated periodically), <https://icsid.worldbank.org/resources/publications/Investment-Laws-of-the-World>; and the thirteen-volume loose-leaf *Investment Treaties* (OUP, updated periodically), <https://icsid.worldbank.org/resources/publications/investment-treaty-series>.

[106] The awards are also compiled in the *ICSID Reports*, published by Cambridge University Press.

both States have expressly consented to submit investment disputes to ICSID arbitration through a BIT or other relevant treaty.[107] Once such consent has been given, the State of nationality of the investor is prohibited from giving diplomatic protection to, or claiming on behalf of, the investor.[108]

An ICSID arbitration, unlike with more formal modes of international dispute settlement, can be flexible. The hearings may be held anywhere the parties agree, though often tend to be held in Washington, London, The Hague, or Paris. The dispute is usually heard by three arbitrators, appointed from a list of designated persons maintained by ICSID.[109] In theory, there is no appeal against an award rendered by an ICSID panel, but Article 52 of the ICSID Convention provides that an application to 'annul' an award on the ground of procedural irregularities may be filed. In such situations, a panel of three new persons will hear the application.[110] All ICSID members are required to recognize and enforce an ICSID award as if it were a final judgment of their own courts.[111]

The ICSID process has been highly active. As of late 2024, it has registered over 1,000 cases, with a notable increase in its pace over the last decade.[112] In theory, this would suggest that ICSID has been highly successful in helping to defuse political tensions caused by investment disputes, and avoiding the escalation of economic disputes into other avenues. However, arbitration is not an unequivocal success, as several developing States have denounced the ICSID Convention, claiming that the ICSID system has been skewed towards the interests of investors both in terms of applicable law and its interpretation by ICSID tribunals; these include Bolivia (2007), Ecuador (2009—though it rejoined in 2021), Venezuela (2012), and Honduras (2024).[113] What is more, it has not gone unnoticed in scholarship that investment arbitration remains decidedly advantageous for investors, who may evade the jurisdiction of the local courts of the host State and even have a say in the selection of arbitrators.[114] Whatever the future holds, it is clear that the protection of foreign investors under international law will remain a lively and controversial field of international legal activity.

[107] ICSID even provides 'Model Clauses' to assist States negotiating BITs: see <https://icsid.worldbank.org/resources/content/model-clauses>.

[108] ICSID Convention (n 104) Art 27.

[109] See *ibid*, Arts 37–40. The database of available persons is available at: <https://icsid.worldbank.org/about/arbitrators-conciliators/database-of-icsid-panels>.

[110] See, e.g., *Fraport AG Frankfurt Airport Services Worldwide v the Philippines*, ICSID Case No ARB/03/25, Decision on Annulment of 23 December 2010; *Victor Pey Casado v Republic of Chile*, ICSID Case No ARB/98/2, Decision on Annulment of 18 December 2012. Under Arts 50–1 of the Convention, a tribunal may also be asked to interpret or revise its own award.

[111] ICSID Convention (n 104) Art 54.

[112] See *ICSID Caseload—Statistics* (ICSID Publications, 2024–2).

[113] See A Tzanakopoulos, 'Denunciation of the ICSID Convention under the General International Law of Treaties' in R Hofmann and C Tams (eds), *International Investment Law and General International Law: from Clinical Isolation to Systemic Integration?* (Nomos, 2011), 75.

[114] See D Scheniderman, *Resisting Economic Globalization: Critical Theory and International Investment Law* (Palgrave Macmillan, 2013); HHA van Harten, *Investment Treaty Arbitration and Public Law* (OUP, 2007).

20.5 Other international initiatives on economic cooperation and development

This chapter has taken a broadly institutional, process-driven approach to international economic law. However, States and other actors on the international plane contribute to international economic cooperation on several other fronts. Though the far-reaching ambitions of developing States to proclaim a New International Economic Order were frustrated, the General Assembly remains highly active in promoting economic development within the existing system. The 2000 Millennium Development Goals, a General Assembly resolution, aimed to eradicate extreme poverty and hunger, reduce child mortality, promote gender equality, and achieve universal primary schooling.[115] In 2015, the 2030 Agenda for Sustainable Development updated these with a stronger environmentalist slant.[116]

THEORY AND DEBATES Normativity Through Standard-setting: The OECD

An influential international organization in the field of economic law, which is not part of the United Nations system, is the Organization for Economic Co-operation and Development (OECD). The criteria for membership in the OECD are stricter than UN membership, though it has expanded beyond industrial European and North American States. Recent new members include Lithuania (2018), Colombia (2020), and Costa Rica (2021).

The OECD sponsors the conclusion of treaties between its members (such as the *Convention on Combatting Bribery of Foreign Public Officials in International Business Transactions* (1997) 37 ILM 1). All OECD members are parties, as well as Argentina, Brazil, Bulgaria, Peru, Russia, and South Africa. Equally, the OECD drafts a wide number of non-binding instruments, ranging from model bilateral tax conventions to regularly revised codes of conduct, for example the Guidelines for Multinational Enterprises (last revised in 2011). Much of the OECD's influence stems precisely from these non-binding instruments, which seek to guide the behaviour both of States and non-State actors, such as corporations, in order of the global economic conditions that its members have designed the OECD to promote.

Another area in which the OECD has sought to influence policy is in the maintenance of a 'List of Unco-operative Tax Havens', jurisdictions in which its standards on transparency and the sharing of tax information are not being met. However, the OECD 'blacklist' proved highly controversial in its methodology for deciding whether a jurisdiction would be included, and no enforcement measures were ever agreed (see further, JC Sharman, *Havens in a Storm: The Struggle for Global Tax Regulation* (Cornell University Press, 2006)).

The General Assembly has also established the United Nations Development Programme (UNDP). Since 1965, UNDP has overseen and coordinated the work of the various UN specialized agencies in relation to development; in particular, the provision of technical

[115] See United Nations Millennium Declaration, UNGA Res 55/2 (18 September 2000), operative clauses 11–20.

[116] 2030 Agenda for Sustainable Development, which adds seventeen 'Sustainable Development Goals': UNGA Res 70/1 (21 October 2015).

assistance and knowledge.[117] A subsidiary organ of ECOSOC, the UNDP's mandate is the eradication of poverty through 'sustainable human development' and the building of capacity for 'good governance' in developing States; for example, through the strengthening of judicial, electoral, and parliamentary systems and the rule of law, and support for civil society organizations. UNDP is accompanied by two subsidiary bodies: the UN Conference on Trade and Development (UNCTAD), which aims to facilitate trade and investment in developing countries and provides funding for technical cooperation activities;[118] and the UN Industrial Development Organization (UNIDO), which conducts studies and surveys relating to industrialization and provides information, analysis, and advice on industrial policies and institutions.[119] The various UN agencies cannot impose binding legal norms, though they have proved instrumental in drafting and disseminating policies and codes of conduct which, through their normative potential, have proven influential. A notable example is the 2011 Guiding Principles on Business and Human Rights, adopted by the Human Rights Council.[120] Since 2014, an intergovernmental working group has been working 'to establish an open-ended intergovernmental working group on transnational corporations and other business enterprises with respect to human rights, whose mandate shall be to elaborate an international legally binding instrument to regulate, in international human rights law, the activities of transnational corporations and other business enterprises.'[121] These form part of the ongoing discussion on how to induce multinational corporations to respect human rights norms, where many recent developments seem to be taking place in domestic courts.[122] In February 2020, the Canadian Supreme Court suggested that there might be a move away from the traditional 'blanket exclusion from direct liability [for corporations] for violations of obligatory, definable, and universal norms of international law'.[123] There was also the famous 'Ogoni Nine' case brought in the Netherlands against Royal Dutch Shell for colluding with Nigerian armed forces in the unlawful arrest, detention, and execution of nine environmental and human rights activists in Nigeria. Though in 2019, the District Court of The Hague held that it had extraterritorial jurisdiction over the acts in question,[124] the claim was eventually dismissed on the merits due to insufficient evidence. Finally, in *Vedanta Resources* and *Okpabi*, the UK Supreme Court opened the door to parent corporations to be held liability for the acts of their overseas subsidiaries, based on the duty of care under tort law.[125]

[117] See UNGA Res 2029 (XX) (22 November 1965).

[118] UNCTAD, which operates as a 'conference', was first held in 1964 in Geneva; it receives funding for its technical cooperation activities from donor States in Europe, North America, and Asia, as well as major beneficiary States in the developing world.

[119] UNGA Res 2152 (XXI) (17 November 1966).

[120] See A/HRC/17/4 (16 June 2011), available at <http://www.ohchr.org/Documents/Publications/GuidingPrinciplesBusinessHR_EN.pdf>.

[121] The working group was constituted under A/HRC/RES/26/9 (14 July 2014). From 25–29 October 2021, a third revised draft treaty was debated by States during the seventh session of the conference, available at <https://www.ohchr.org/Documents/HRBodies/HRCouncil/WGTransCorp/Session6/LBI3rdDRAFT.pdf>.

[122] See N Bernaz, *Business and Human Rights: History, Law and Policy—Bridging the Accountability Gap* (Routledge, 2016).

[123] *Nevsun Resources Ltd v Araya* (Canadian Supreme Court) 2020 SCC 5 (CanLII) (28 February 2020).

[124] *v Royal Dutch Petroleum (Shell) and ors*, Judgment of 1 May 2019, Case No ECLI:NL:RBDHA:2019:6670. But *cf Kiobel v Royal Dutch Petroleum Co*, 133 S Ct 1659 (2013), and *Jesner v Arab Bank Plc* 138 S Ct 1386 (2018), in which the US Supreme Court dismisses the possibility of foreign corporate liability, even for human rights violations, before US courts.

[125] See *Vedanta Resources PLC v Lungowe* [2021] UKSC 3; *Okpabi and Ors v Royal Dutch Shell* [2021] UKSC 3.

There are several highly visible normative fora on the international level. Foremost is the 'World Economic Forum', at which representatives of States, corporate interests, civil society (NGOs), and other influential actors, including academics, converge annually in Davos, Switzerland. In turn, this feeds into the work of the G7, an annual summit of the largest industrialized States, which from 1997 to 2014 was known as the G8 as it included Russia, which was suspended indefinitely following its annexation of the Crimea from Ukraine.[126] Finally, there exists the G20 grouping of developed and larger developing States which has met annually since 2000, but which achieved particular strategic prominence after the 2008 financial crisis.

CONTEMPORARY DEVELOPMENTS Unstructured But Influential: The G20

The 'G20' is an unusual grouping which is not an international organization but an annual gathering at which the most influential States set global economic policy. Collectively, the G20 economies account for around 85 per cent of the gross world product (GWP), 80 per cent of world trade (or, if excluding EU intra-trade, 75 per cent), and two-thirds of the world population. However, as a mere gathering the G20 has no decision-making or administrative organs and no permanent Secretariat. It is the host State that organizes the annual meetings.

There are nineteen States members of the G20, representing all continents and regions: Argentina, Australia, Brazil, Canada, China, France, Germany, Italy, Japan, Mexico, India, Indonesia, Russia, Saudi Arabia, South Africa, South Korea, Türkiye, the UK, and the USA. They are joined by the European Union, which represents all of its members. Spain remains a 'permanent invited guest' alongside various international bodies, a compromise achieved partly due to concerns about the over-representation of Western Europe. There have been other invitees at past G20 summits, including the Netherlands, Singapore, and

The G20's lack of institutional structure has led to a number of criticisms relating to participation. Given its influence and the inclusion of economically powerful States, it remains opaque: there are no criteria or mechanisms for joining the G20. Though States from the Global South now participate in its deliberations, they are amongst its largest and most economically influential; there are no small, least-developed States among its ranks. What is more, there is little accountability: though not formally binding, decisions taken by the G20 and implemented by its members will undoubtedly affect many non-participating States, which have little say over these decisions. In time, as the G20 widens its reach and begins to develop set procedures for its work, it may emerge as an international organization in its own right, but at present it remains unstructured yet enormously influential.

20.6 Conclusion

International law contributes a crucial element of the framework that facilitates the financial, trade, and investment interactions through which the global economic order is constituted. However, it would be inaccurate to suggest that that frame is value-neutral. The strongly neo-liberal consensus that has underpinned the international economic

[126] The original G7 members were the USA, Japan, then-West Germany, France, and the UK. Canada and Italy were invited in 1975.

order since Bretton Woods has survived almost wholly intact since World War II, and has arguably privileged the free movement of capital and goods above other domestic and international concerns, in turn favouring a specific model of human development in which the industrialized, capitalist State remains the desired ideal.

It should be evident to the reader, moreover, that today's existing institutional structures are patently dominated by powerful States and actors, without much accountability or democratic oversight. Partly for these reasons, free trade, foreign investment, and international financing for development projects have not proved to be a magic bullet for the 'Global South', which continues to lag behind in today's global economy. There remains, nevertheless, a need for serious reflection on the structure and purpose of the global economic order, with an understanding of which actors are privileged and which are marginalized. Perhaps this might help finally to shatter some of the enduring structures which have hindered the possibilities of human development.[127]

Further reading

P Van den Bossche and D Prévost, *Essentials of WTO Law* (CUP, 2016).
Succinct, accessible, and clear introduction to the structures and institutions of the WTO.

DD Bradlow and DB Hunter (eds), *International Financial Institutions and International Law* (Kluwer, 2010).
An in-depth collection of essays addressing both the relevant international law and the impact of international financial institutions on relevant stakeholders.

P Dann, *The Law of Development Cooperation. A Comparative Analysis of the World Bank, the EU and Germany* (CUP, 2013).
A core reading in law and development that seeks to systematize the law on development cooperation.

R Dolzer and C Schreuer, *Principles of International Investment Law* (2nd edn, OUP, 2012).
Concise yet comprehensive, this book captures both institutional developments and arbitral practice.

J Faundez and C Tan (eds), *International Economic Law, Globalization and Developing Countries* (Edward Elgar, 2012).
This coherent edited collection features contributors from both international law and international political economy.

A Lang, *World Trade Law after Neoliberalism: Reimagining the Global Economic Order* (OUP, 2011).
Innovative social and legal history of the emergence of the contemporary world trade system.

[127] For incisive challenges to the orthodox narratives on international economic development, see B Rajagopal, *International Law from Below: Development, Social Movements and Resistance* (CUP, 2003); Pahuja (n 4); JL Beard, *The Political Economy of Desire: Law, Development and the Nation* (Routledge, 2003); HJ Chang, *Kicking Away the Ladder: Development Strategy in Historical Perspective* (Anthem, 2002).

CL Lim, J Ho, and M Paparinskis, *International Investment Law and Arbitration* (2nd edn, CUP, 2021).

An innovative hybrid textbook-casebook format which entwines commentary with relevant extracts across a range of topics in international investment law.

K Miles, *The Origins of International Investment Law: Empire, Environment and the Safeguarding of Capital* (CUP, 2013).

A historical account that traces the link between European colonialism and the modern regime of foreign investment protection.

S Pahuja, *Decolonising International Law: Development, Economic Growth and the Politics of Universality* (CUP, 2011).

An incisive and critical account of decolonization that challenges the received view that development is a solution to global injustice.

S Schill, *The Multilateralization of International Investment Law* (CUP, 2009).

A systematic argument that the piecemeal decisions of investment tribunals are a coherent body of case law, reinforcing a specialized regime of international law.

M Sornarajah, *The International Law on Foreign Investment* (5th edn, CUP, 2021).

This updated textbook traces both procedural and substantive developments in a comprehensive, accessible manner.

S Subedi, *International Investment Law: Reconciling Policy and Principle* (4th edn, Hart, 2020).

Going beyond mere descriptive legalism, this book traces the geopolitical struggles behind many of the institutions of the investment law landscape.

M Trebilcock, *Advanced Introduction to International Trade Law* (Edward Elgar, 2015).

Concise and accessible, this book presents the basic structure and principles in the field.

Index